# *About Pearson*

Pearson is the world's learning company, with presence across 70 countries worldwide. Our unique insights and world-class expertise comes from a long history of working closely with renowned teachers, authors and thought leaders, as a result of which, we have emerged as the preferred choice for millions of teachers and learners across the world.

We believe learning opens up opportunities, creates fulfilling careers and hence better lives. We hence collaborate with the best of minds to deliver you class-leading products, spread across the Higher Education and K12 spectrum.

Superior learning experience and improved outcomes are at the heart of everything we do. This product is the result of one such effort.

Your feedback plays a critical role in the evolution of our products and you can contact us at reachus@pearson.com. We look forward to it.

# Child Development
## Eighth Edition

# Contents

# Preface

Child development is a unique field of study. Unlike other academic disciplines, each of us has experience with its subject matter in very personal ways. It is not simply a discipline that deals with ideas and concepts and theories, but one that above all has at its heart the forces that have made each of us who we are.

This text, *Child Development*, Eighth Edition, seeks to capture the discipline in a way that sparks, nurtures, and shapes readers' interest. It is meant to excite students about the field, to draw them into its way of looking at the world, and to mold their understanding of developmental issues. By exposing readers to both the current content and the promise inherent in child and adolescent development, the text is designed to keep interest in the discipline alive long after students' formal study of the field has ended.

## Overview

*Child Development*, Eighth Edition, provides a broad overview of the field of development. It covers the full range of childhood and adolescence, from the moment of conception through the end of adolescence. The text furnishes a broad, comprehensive introduction to the field, covering basic theories and research findings, as well as highlighting current applications outside the laboratory. It covers childhood and adolescence chronologically, encompassing the prenatal period, infancy and toddlerhood, the preschool years, middle childhood, and adolescence. Within these periods, it focuses on physical, cognitive, and social and personality development.

The book seeks to accomplish the following four major goals:

- First and foremost, the book is designed to provide a broad, balanced overview of the field of child development. It introduces readers to the theories, research, and applications that constitute the discipline, examining both the traditional areas of the field as well as more recent innovations. The book pays particular attention to the applications developed by child and adolescent development specialists. Without slighting theoretical material, the text emphasizes what we know about development across childhood and adolescence, rather than focusing on unanswered questions. It demonstrates how this knowledge may be applied to real-world problems. In sum, the book highlights the interrelationships among theory, research, and application, accentuating the scope and diversity of the field. It also illustrates how child developmentalists use theory, research, and applications to help solve significant social problems.

- The second major goal of the text is to explicitly tie development to students' lives. Findings from the study of child and adolescent development have a significant degree of relevance to students, and this text illustrates how these findings can be applied in a meaningful, practical sense. Applications are presented in a contemporaneous framework, including current news items, timely world events, and contemporary uses of child development that draw readers into the field. Numerous descriptive scenarios and vignettes reflect everyday situations in people's lives, explaining how they relate to the field.

  For example, each chapter begins with an opening prologue that provides a real-life situation relating to the chapter subject area. All chapters also have a "Becoming an Informed Consumer of Child Development" section, which explicitly suggests ways to apply developmental findings to students' experience. These sections portray how these findings can be applied in a practical, hands-on way. Each chapter also includes a feature called "From Research to Practice" that discusses ways developmental research is used to answer the problems that society faces. Finally, numerous questions in figure and photo captions ask readers to take the perspective of people in a variety of professions that make use of child development, including health care professionals, educators, and social workers.

- The third goal of this book is to highlight both the commonalties and diversity of today's multicultural society. Consequently, every chapter has at least one "Developmental Diversity and Your Life" section. These features explicitly consider how cultural factors relevant to development both unite and diversify our contemporary global society. In addition, the book incorporates material relevant to diversity throughout every chapter.

- Finally, the fourth goal of the text is one that underlies the other three: making the field of child development engaging, accessible, and interesting to students. Child development is a joy both to study and to teach because so much of it has direct, immediate meaning to our lives. Because all of us are involved in our own developmental paths, we are tied in very personal ways to the content areas covered by the book. *Child Development*, Eighth Edition, then, is meant to engage and nurture this interest, planting a seed that will develop and flourish throughout readers' lifetimes.

- To accomplish this fourth goal, the book is "user-friendly." Written in a direct, conversational voice, it replicates as much as possible a dialogue between author and student. The text is meant to be understood and mastered on its own, without the intervention of an instructor. To that end, it includes a variety of pedagogical features. Each chapter contains a "Looking Ahead" overview that sets the stage for the chapter, a running glossary, a numbered summary, a list of key terms and concepts, and an epilogue containing critical thinking questions.

**The Philosophy Behind *Child Development*, Eighth Edition.** *Child Development*, Eighth Edition, blends and integrates theory, research, and applications. It is *not* an applied development book, focused solely on techniques for translating the knowledge base of development into answers to societal problems. Nor is it a theory-oriented volume, concentrating primarily on the field's abstract theories. Instead, the focus of the text is on the scope and breadth of human development during childhood and adolescence. The strategy of concentrating on the scope of the field permits the text to examine both the traditional core areas of the field and the evolving nontraditional areas of development.

Furthermore, the book focuses on the here and now, rather than attempting to provide a detailed historical record of the field. Although it draws on the past where appropriate, it does so with a view toward delineating the field as it now stands and the directions toward which it

is evolving. Similarly, while the text provides descriptions of classic studies, the emphasis is on current research findings and trends.

The book provides a broad overview of child and adolescent development, integrating the theory, research, and applications of the discipline. It is meant to be a book that readers will want to keep in their own personal libraries, one they will take off the shelf when considering problems related to that most intriguing of questions: How do people get to be the way they are?

## Specific Features

- *Chapter-opening prologues.* Each chapter begins with a short vignette describing an individual or situation relevant to the basic developmental issues addressed in the chapter. For instance, the chapter on cognitive development in infancy describes a 9-month-old infant actively discovering her surroundings, and the chapter on the physical development in adolescence provides an account of teenagers dealing with body image and appearance.

- *Looking Ahead.* These opening sections orient readers to the topics to be covered, bridging the opening prologue with the remainder of the chapter and providing orienting questions.

- *Learning Objectives.* Every chapter includes sequentially numbered learning objectives, based on Bloom's taxonomy. They allow students to clearly understand what they are expected to learn. The learning objectives are tied to the Looking Back summary at the end of each chapter and are also keyed to test bank items.

- *From Research to Practice.* Each chapter includes a feature that focuses on the ways in which research in child development can be used both in terms of everyday childrearing issues and for setting public policy. These features include discussions on research examining whether food preferences are learned in the womb, the potential long-term benefits of ADHD drugs, and whether video games can improve cognitive ability.

- *Developmental Diversity and Your Life.* Every chapter has at least one "Developmental Diversity and Your Life" section incorporated into the text. These sections highlight issues relevant to the multicultural society in which we live. Examples of these sections include discussions of the cultural dimensions of motor development, the adjustment of children from immigrant families, multicultural education, and overcoming gender and racial barriers to achievement.

- *Becoming an Informed Consumer of Child Development.* Every chapter includes information on specific uses that can be derived from research conducted by developmental investigators. For instance, the text provides concrete information on exercising an infant's body and senses, keeping preschoolers healthy, increasing children's competence, and choosing a career.
- *From the Perspective of…* These questions, interspersed throughout each chapter, ask students to take the perspective of someone working in an occupation that relies on findings of child development, including the fields of health care, education, and social work.
- *The Case of…* Every chapter includes a case study. Case studies describe an intriguing situation related to the topics discussed in the chapter, and they end by asking questions designed to evoke critical thinking about the case and the chapter content.
- *End-of-chapter material.* Each chapter ends with a summary (keyed to chapter learning objectives) and a list of key terms and concepts. This material is designed to help students study and retain the information in the chapter. Finally, a short epilogue includes critical thinking questions relating to the prologue at the opening of the chapter. Because the opening prologues serve as case studies that foreshadow the topics the chapter will address, these end-of-chapter thought-provoking questions provide a way of tying the chapter together. They also illustrate how the concepts addressed in the chapter can be applied to the real-world situation described in the opening prologue.
- *End-of-part material.* Every part of the book concludes with material that integrates different developmental domains during a particular age range. A vignette that captures a developmental issue or theme is considered jointly from a physical, cognitive, and social and personality point of view, helping students to understand how the various perspectives work together to explain development.

## What's New in This Edition?

*Child Development*, Eighth Edition, includes a set of extraordinary online interactivities designed to engage students and promote their learning. All newly created, these interactivities provide an exciting means for students to explore and more deeply understand the core concepts of child development.

Furthermore, chapter openers and epilogues have been replaced or updated, introducing students to the real-world implications of the chapter topic. Moreover, all *From Research to Practice* features—which describe a contemporary developmental research topic and its applied implications—are new to this edition.

Finally, the Eighth Edition incorporates a significant amount of new and updated information. For instance, the revision addresses important issues such as the concept of race as a social construct, malnutrition, the effects of poverty on development, and the impact of media and technology on child development. The new edition also incorporates changes relating to psychological disorders reflecting the publication of *Diagnostic and Statistical Manual of Mental Health Disorders, Fifth Edition (DSM-5)*.

New topics appear in every chapter. A sampling of specific topics that have been either newly included or expanded illustrates the scope of the revision:

### Chapter 1

Clarified race and ethnicity
Introduced concept of race as a social construct
Clarified age-graded influences
Clarified non-normative life events
Added material on Maria Montessori
New screen-time rules for children under age 2 from American Academy of Pediatrics
Relationship between childhood trauma and violence
Bullying as a form of violence
Cyberbullying
First American baby born using in vitro fertilization

### Chapter 2

Cyberbullying
Evidence on lack of a link between immunizations and autism
Clarified random assignment
New public policy material

### Chapter 3

Updated figure on rising multiple births
Update on procedure of amniocentesis
New information on prenatal screenings
Updated statistics on world hunger

New term: *fetal alcohol syndrome disorder*
Update on incidence of Down Syndrome
Replacement of term *mental retardation* with *intellectual disability*
Removed example of Dutch Hunger Winter
Added examples of polygenic inheritance
New statistics on abortion
Aftermath of miscarriage
Updated information on genetic basis of disorders and traits

## Chapter 4

New information on "kangaroo care" for premature infants
New figure on infant mortality
Added material on postpartum depression
More on skin-to-skin contact between mother and child
New *From Research to Practice* on development of food preferences

## Chapter 5

Updated photo of shaken baby brain
Incidence of shaken baby syndrome
New information on benefits of breastfeeding
Updated figure on declining rates of SIDS
New key term: *sudden unexpected infant death (SUID)*
Use of baby boxes rather than cribs
Updated informçation on malnutrition
New figure on undernutrition worldwide
New poverty figures
New prologue on sleeping through the night
SIDS and hippocampus abnormality
Brain plasticity in infancy

## Chapter 6

New material on brain growth and infantile amnesia
Changed key term from *scheme* to *schema*
New material on memory and hippocampus
Supplemented description of learning theory approach to language development

## Chapter 7

Infant understanding of morality
New data on child care delivery modalities
Still-face technique
Infant emotions
Mirror-and-rouge technique
Clarified and expanded explanation of mirror neurons

## Chapter 8

Just-right phenomenon in nutrition
Additional information on childhood depression
New figures on child abuse and neglect
Replacement figure on child abuse and neglect in the United States
Additional signs of child abuse
Distinction between overweight and obese
BMI
Reducing media exposure prior to bedtime to help sleep
Lead poisoning
Change blindness
Clarified figure on physicians, visits

## Chapter 9

How writing by hand stimulates cognitive development
Clarified difference between syntax and grammar
Updated information on the effectiveness of *Sesame Street*
New information on children and television viewing
New material on screen use
American Academy of Pediatrics 2016 policy statement on screen use
New figure on children viewing media

## Chapter 10

New learning objectives
New material on lying and preschoolers
Autism spectrum disorder and false belief
Role of rough-and-tumble play in brain development and other benefits
Warmth of authoritative and permissive parents
Parental values in Hispanic families
Racial factors in friendships
Foreshadowing Kohlberg and Gilligan

## Chapter 11

Revised learning objectives
New prologue
Long-term treatment effects for ADHD
New figure showing prevalence of obesity
Updated definition of obesity
Clarified definition of specific learning disorders
Relationship between obesity and recess
Increase over time of prevalence in psychological disorders
Updated statistics on incidence of psychological disorders in children

## Chapter 12

Updated figure on languages spoken in India
Updated material on illiteracy around the world
Revised learning objectives
Cultural factors in intelligence and Lev Vygotsky
Value of learning cursive for cognitive development
New statistics on worldwide illiteracy
New figure on rates of illiteracy by geographic area
Homeschooling material updated
Charter school efficacy data
Clarified definition of bilingualism

## Chapter 13

Dangers of inflated praise
Deleted figure on time use
Categories of bullying
Bullying reduction practices that are ineffective
Upward social comparison
Self-care drawbacks

## Chapter 14

Updated section on marijuana use
Updated statistics on sexually transmitted infections among adolescents
New prologue on body image
Updated statistics on incidence of AIDS
HPG axis
Role of hormones in activation of behavior and brain organization
Binge-eating disorder
E-cigarette use
Brain development and alcohol use
Benefits of adolescent brain immaturity

## Chapter 15

New key term: *pseudostupidity*
Invincibility fable
High school graduation rates
Statistics on reading proficiency of eighth graders
Update of statistics on women's participation in the workforce
Cognitive benefits from playing video games
Tribal Colleges and Universities (TCUs)

## Chapter 16

New section on transsexuals
Updated info on Supreme Court legalizing gay marriage

Clarified description of James Marcia's theory
Differential rates of suicide in gays, lesbians, and transsexuals
Native American suicide rates

In addition, a wealth of contemporary research is cited in this new edition. Hundreds of new research citations have been added, most from the past few years.

# New to the Indian Edition

*Child Development, 8e,* by Robert Feldman is designed to engage students and help them learn the core concepts of child development. In the adaptation version of this book, an attempt has been made to make the content culturally more appropriate for the readers. Almost all chapters have a box on developmental diversity and incorporate relevant information from the students' socio-cultural environment. Each chapter starts with a *Prologue* which allows for critical thinking in the students about the chapter and relating it to the real-world application of the concepts, and ends with *A Case of…* discussion and an *Epilogue* to summarize and highlight the concepts discussed.

A significant contribution of the book is the sections on *From Research to Practice* and *Becoming an Informed Consumer of Child Development,* which would help the reader to apply the basic knowledge of child development to practice. Apart from this, throughout the book, an explicit attempt has been made to bridge the gap between theoretical concepts and its application by referring to case studies, survey data, policy matters of the government along with research studies in the context of India.

It is important to state here that while adapting the book for readers in India, the cross-cultural essence and versatility of the original book is retained. The book would be valuable for students of child development and family studies, psychology, social work, nursing and readers who are interested in enlightening themselves with *how a child develops in its eco-cultural context.*

*Nandita Babu,*
*Professor, Department of Psychology,*
*University of Delhi*

# Acknowledgments

I am grateful to the following reviewers who provided a wealth of comments, criticism, and encouragement:

Beth Bigler, Pellissippi State Community College
Heidemarie Blumenthal, University of North Texas
Jamie Borchardt, Tarleton State University
Johnny Castro, Brookhaven College
Nate Cottle, University of Central Oklahoma
Christie Cunningham, Pellissippi State Community College
Lisa Fozio-Thielk, Waubonsee Community College
Sara Goldstein, Montclair State University
Christina Gotowka, Tunxis Community College
Joel Hagaman, University of the Ozarks
Nicole Hansen-Rayes, City Colleges of Chicago/ Daley College
Myra Harville, Holmes Community College
Mary Hughes Stone, San Francisco State University
Suzanne Hughes, Southwestern Community College
Earleen Huff, Amarillo College
Jo Jackson, Lenoir Community College
Jennifer Kampmann, South Dakota State University
Dr. William Kimberlin, Lorain County Community College
Francesca Longo, Boston College
Mark Lyerly, Burlington County College
Rebecca Marcon, University of North Florida
Kathleen Miller Green, North Idaho College
Suzanne Mira-Knippel, Southwestern Community College
Ron Mulson, Hudson Valley Community College
Tara Newman, Stephen F. Austin State University
Laura Pirazzi, San Jose State University
Katherine K. Rose, Texas Woman's University
Jeffrey Vallon, SUNY Rockland Community College
Amy Van Hecke, Marquette University
Traci Van Prooyen, University of Illinois at Springfield
Angela Williamson, Tarrant County College
Melanie Yeschenko, Community College of Allegheny County

Many others deserve a great deal of thanks. I am indebted to the many people who provided me with a superb education, first at Wesleyan University and later at the University of Wisconsin. Specifically, Karl Scheibe played a pivotal role in my undergraduate education, and the late Vernon Allen acted as mentor and guide through my graduate years. It was in graduate school that I learned about development, being exposed to such experts as Ross Parke, Joel Levin, Herb Klausmeier, and many others.

My education continued when I became a professor. I am especially grateful to my colleagues at the University of Massachusetts, who make the university such a wonderful place in which to teach and do research.

Several people played central roles in the development of this book. Stephen Hupp and Jeremy Jewell provided extraordinary work on the digital interactivities, and I am thankful for their help. I'm also grateful to John Bickford, who provided significant editorial support. John Graiff was essential in juggling and coordinating the multiple aspects of writing this book, and I am very thankful for the important role he played.

I am also grateful to the superb Pearson team, which was instrumental in the development of this book. Amber Chow, acquisitions editor, always provided good ideas, support, and direction. I am grateful for her enthusiasm and creativity. Developmental editor Stephanie Ventura, master of all details, went way beyond the call of duty to provide direction and support in every respect. I am also grateful to Program Manager Cecilia Turner, who stayed on top of every aspect of the project. Finally, I'd like to thank Marketing Manager Christopher Brown, whose skills I'm counting on. It's a privilege to be part of this world-class team.

I also wish to acknowledge the members of my family, who play such a central role in my life. My brother, Michael, my sisters-in-law and brother-in-law, and my nieces and nephews all make up an important part of my life. In addition, I am always indebted to the older generation of my family, who led the way in a manner I can only hope to emulate. I will always be obligated to Harry Brochstein, Mary Vorwerk, and Ethel Radler for their wisdom and support. Most of all, the list is headed by my father, the late Saul Feldman, and my mother, Leah Brochstein.

In the end, my immediate family deserves the greatest thanks. My son Jon, his wife, Leigh, and my grandsons Alex and Miles; my son Josh and his wife, Julie, and my granddaughter Naomi; and my daughter Sarah and her husband, Jeff, and my granddaughter Lilia, not only are nice, smart, and good-looking, but my pride and joy. And ultimately my wife, Katherine Vorwerk, provides the love and grounding that make everything worthwhile. I thank them all, with love.

*Robert S. Feldman,*
*University of Massachusetts Amherst*

# About the Author

**Robert S. Feldman** is a Professor of Psychological and Brain Sciences and the Senior Advisor to the Chancellor at the University of Massachusetts Amherst. A recipient of the College Distinguished Teacher Award, he has taught classes ranging in size from 10 to nearly 500 students. During the course of his career as a college instructor, he has taught both undergraduate and graduate courses at Mount Holyoke College, Wesleyan University, and Virginia Commonwealth University, in addition to the University of Massachusetts Amherst.

A Fellow of the American Psychological Association, the Association for Psychological Science, and the American Association for the Advancement of Science, Professor Feldman received a BA with High Honors from Wesleyan University (from which he received the Distinguished Alumni Award). He has an MS and a PhD from the University of Wisconsin–Madison. He is a winner of a Fulbright Senior Research Scholar and Lecturer award, and he has written more than 200 books, book chapters, and scientific articles. He has edited *Development of Nonverbal Behavior in Children, Applications of Nonverbal Behavioral Theory and Research*, and *The First Year of College*. He is also author of *Development Across the Life Span, Understanding Psychology*, and *P.O.W.E.R. Learning: Strategies for Success in College and Life*. His books have been translated into many languages, including Spanish, French, Portuguese, Dutch, Chinese, Korean, German, Arabic, Tagalog, Italian, and Japanese, and more than 2.5 million students have used his textbooks.

Professor Feldman's research interests include honesty and deception in everyday life, work that he described in *The Liar in Your Life*. His research has been supported by grants from the National Institute of Mental Health and the National Institute on Disabilities and Rehabilitation Research. He is also Past President of the Federation of Associations in the Behavioral and Brain Sciences Foundation, an organization that promotes the social sciences, and he is a member of the board of New England Public Radio.

Professor Feldman loves music, is an enthusiastic pianist, and enjoys cooking and traveling. He has three children and four grandchildren. He and his wife, a psychologist, live in western Massachusetts in a home overlooking the Holyoke Mountain Range.

# Chapter 1
# An Introduction to Child Development

## ∨ Learning Objectives

**LO 1.1** Define the field of child development.

**LO 1.2** Describe the scope of the field of child development.

**LO 1.3** Explain the major societal influences that determine development.

**LO 1.4** Explain the earliest views of childhood and children.

**LO 1.5** Describe the ways that childhood has been viewed since the 20th century.

**LO 1.6** Explain the key issues and questions in the field of child development.

**LO 1.7** Predict future developments in the field of child development.

# Prologue: New Conceptions

In many ways, the first meeting of Louise Brown and Elizabeth Carr was unremarkable: just two women, one in her 30s, the other in her 40s, chatting about their lives and their own children.

But in another sense, the meeting was extraordinary, for Louise Brown was the world's first "test-tube baby," born by *in vitro fertilization (IVF)*, a procedure in which fertilization of a mother's egg by a father's sperm takes place outside of the mother's body. And Elizabeth Carr was the first baby born by IVF in the United States.

Louise was a preschooler when her parents told her how she was conceived, and throughout her childhood she was bombarded with questions. It became routine to explain to her classmates that she, in fact, was not born in a laboratory. At times, she felt completely alone. For Elizabeth, too, growing up was not easy, as she experienced bouts of insecurity.

Today, however, Louise and Elizabeth are hardly unique. They are among the more than 5 million babies that have been born using the procedure, one that has almost become routine. And both became mothers themselves, giving birth to babies who were conceived, incidentally, the old-fashioned way (Falco, 2012; Gagneux, 2016; Simpson, 2017).

Louise Brown (left) and Elizabeth Carr (right)

# Looking Ahead

Louise Brown's and Elizabeth Carr's conceptions may have been novel, but their development, from infancy onward, has followed predictable patterns. While the specifics of our own development vary—some of us encounter economic deprivation or live in war-torn territories; others contend with family issues like divorce and stepparents—the broad strokes of the development that is set in motion the moment we are conceived are remarkably similar for all of us. Like LeBron James, Bill Gates, and, yes, Louise Brown and Elizabeth Carr, each and every one of us has traversed the territory known as child development.

In vitro fertilization (IVF) is just one of the brave new worlds of the 21st century. Issues ranging from cloning and the consequences of poverty on development to the effects of culture and race raise significant developmental concerns. Underlying these concerns are even more fundamental issues: How do children develop physically? How does their understanding of the world grow and change over time? And how do our personalities and our social world develop as we move from birth through adolescence?

These questions, and many others we'll encounter throughout this book, are central to the field of child development. Consider, for example, the range of approaches that different specialists in child development

might take when considering the story of Louise Brown and Elizabeth Carr:

- Child development researchers who investigate behavior at the level of biological processes might determine whether Louise's and Elizabeth's physical functioning before birth was affected by their conception outside the womb.

- Specialists in child development who study genetics might examine how the biological endowment from Louise's and Elizabeth's parents affects their later behavior.

- Child development specialists who investigate the ways thinking changes over the course of childhood might examine how Louise's and Elizabeth's understanding of the nature of their conception changed as they grew older.

- Researchers in child development who focus on physical growth might consider whether Louise's and Elizabeth's growth rate differed from children conceived more traditionally.

- Child development experts who specialize in the social world of children might look at the ways that Louise and Elizabeth interacted with other children and the kinds of friendships they developed.

Although their interests and approaches take many forms, all of these specialists share one concern: understanding the growth and change that occur during the course of childhood and adolescence. Developmentalists study how both our biological inheritance from our parents and the environment in which we live jointly affect our behavior.

More specifically, some researchers in child development focus on explaining how our genetic background can determine not only how we look but also how we behave and how we relate to others—that is, matters of personality. These professionals explore ways to identify how much of our potential as human beings is provided—or limited—by heredity. Other child development specialists look to the environment in which we are raised, exploring ways in which our lives are shaped by the world that we encounter. They investigate the extent to which we are shaped by our early environments and how our current circumstances influence our behavior in both subtle and obvious ways.

Whether they focus on heredity or environment, all child development specialists hope that their work will ultimately inform and support the efforts of professionals whose careers are devoted to improving the lives of children. Practitioners in fields ranging from education to health care and social work draw on the findings of child development researchers, using their research findings to advance children's welfare.

In this chapter, we orient ourselves to the field of child development. We begin with a discussion of the scope of the discipline, illustrating the wide array of topics it covers and the range of ages it examines, from the moment of conception through the end of adolescence. We also survey the foundations of the field and examine the key issues and questions that underlie child development. Finally, we consider where the child development field is likely to go in the future.

# An Orientation to Child Development

Have you ever wondered how it is possible that an infant tightly grips your finger with tiny, perfectly formed hands? Or marveled at how a preschooler methodically draws a picture? Or considered the way an adolescent can make involved decisions about whom to invite to a party or the ethics of downloading music files? If you've ever pondered such things, you are asking the kinds of questions that scientists in the field of child development pose.

## Defining the Field of Child Development

### LO 1.1  Define the field of child development.

**Child development** is the scientific study of the patterns of growth, change, and stability that occur from conception through adolescence. Although the definition of the field seems straightforward, this simplicity is somewhat misleading. In order to understand what child development is actually about, we need to look underneath the various parts of the definition.

In its study of growth, change, and stability, child development takes a scientific approach. Like members of other scientific disciplines, researchers in child development test their assumptions about the nature and course of human development by applying scientific methods. As we'll see in the next chapter, researchers formulate theories about development, and they use methodical, scientific techniques to systematically validate the accuracy of their assumptions.

Child development focuses on *human* development. Although there are some developmentalists who study the course of development in nonhuman species, the vast majority examine growth and change in people. Some seek to understand universal principles of development, whereas others focus on how cultural, racial, and ethnic differences affect the course of development. Still others aim to understand the unique aspects of individuals, looking at the traits and characteristics that differentiate one person from another. Regardless of approach, however, all child developmentalists view development as a continuing process throughout childhood and adolescence.

As developmental specialists focus on the ways people change and grow during their lives, they also consider stability in children's and adolescents' lives. They ask in which areas and in what periods people

**child development** The field that involves the scientific study of the patterns of growth, change, and stability that occur from conception through adolescence

show change and growth and when and how their behavior reveals consistency and continuity with prior behavior.

Finally, although child development focuses on childhood and adolescence, the process of development persists throughout *every* part of people's lives, beginning with the moment of conception and continuing until death. Developmental specialists assume that in some ways people continue to grow and change right up to the end of their lives, while in other respects their behavior remains stable. At the same time, developmentalists believe that no particular, single period of life governs all development. Instead, they believe that every period of life contains the potential for both growth and decline in abilities and that individuals maintain the capacity for substantial growth and change throughout their lives.

## Characterizing Child Development: The Scope of the Field

**LO 1.2  Describe the scope of the field of child development.**

Clearly, the definition of child development is broad, and the scope of the field is extensive. Consequently, professionals in child development cover several quite diverse areas, and a typical developmentalist will specialize in both a topical area and an age range.

**TOPICAL AREAS IN CHILD DEVELOPMENT.**  The field of child development includes three major topics or approaches:

- Physical development
- Cognitive development
- Social and personality development

A child developmentalist might specialize in one of these topical areas. As an example, some developmentalists focus on **physical development**, examining the ways in which the body's makeup—the brain, nervous system, muscles, and senses, as well as the need for food, drink, and sleep—helps determine behavior. For instance, one specialist in physical development might study the effects of malnutrition on the pace of growth in children, while another might look at how an athlete's physical performance changes during adolescence.

Other developmental specialists examine **cognitive development**, seeking to understand how growth and change in intellectual capabilities influence a person's behavior. Cognitive developmentalists study learning, memory, problem solving, and intelligence. For example, specialists in cognitive development might want to see how problem solving changes over the course of childhood or whether cultural differences exist in the way people explain the reasons for their academic successes and failures. They would also be interested in how a person who experiences significant or traumatic events early in life would remember them later in life (Alibali, Phillips, & Fischer, 2009; Dumka et al., 2009; Penido et al., 2012; Coates, 2016).

Finally, some developmental specialists focus on personality and social development. **Personality development** is the study of stability and change in the enduring characteristics that differentiate one person from another. **Social development** is the way in which individuals' interactions with others and their social relationships grow, change, and remain stable over the course of life. A developmentalist interested in personality development might ask whether there are stable, enduring personality traits throughout the life span, while a specialist in social development might examine the effects of racism, poverty, or divorce on development (Lansford, 2009; Vélez et al., 2011; Manning et al., 2017). These four major topic areas—physical, cognitive, social, and personality development—are summarized in Table 1.1.

**AGE RANGES AND INDIVIDUAL DIFFERENCES.** Child developmentalists not only specialize in chosen topical areas, but at the same time they specialize in particular age ranges. They usually divide childhood and adolescence into broad stages: the prenatal period (the period from conception to birth), infancy

**physical development** Development involving the body's physical makeup, including the brain, nervous system, muscles, and senses, as well as the need for food, drink, and sleep

**cognitive development** Development involving the ways that growth and change in intellectual capabilities influence a person's behavior

**personality development** Development involving the ways that the enduring characteristics that differentiate one person from another change over the life span

**social development** The way in which individuals' interactions with others and their social relationships grow, change, and remain stable over the course of life

**Table 1.1** Approaches to Child Development

| Orientation | Defining Characteristics | Examples of Questions Asked[a] |
|---|---|---|
| Physical development | Examines how brain, nervous system, muscles, sensory capabilities, and needs for food, drink, and sleep affect behavior | What determines the sex of a child? (3) What are the long-term consequences of premature birth? (4) What are the benefits of breast-feeding? (5) What are the consequences of early or late sexual maturation? (14) |
| Cognitive development | Emphasizes intellectual abilities, including learning, memory, language development, problem solving, and intelligence | What are the earliest memories that can be recalled? (6) What are the consequences of watching television? (9) Are there benefits to bilingualism? (12) Are there ethnic and racial differences in intelligence? (12) How does an adolescent's egocentrism affect his or her view of the world? (15) |
| Personality and social development | Examines enduring characteristics that differentiate one person from another and how interactions with others and social relationships grow and change over the life span | Do newborns respond differently to their mothers than to others? (4) What is the best procedure for disciplining children? (10) When does a sense of gender develop? (10) How can we promote cross-race friendships? (13) What are the causes of adolescent suicide? (16) |

[a] Numbers in parentheses indicate in which chapter the question is addressed.

and toddlerhood (birth to age 3), the preschool period (ages 3 to 6), middle childhood (ages 6 to 12), and adolescence (ages 12 to 20).

It's important to keep in mind that these broad periods—which are largely accepted by child developmentalists—are social constructions. A *social construction* is a shared notion of reality, one that is widely accepted but is a function of society and culture at a given time.

Although most child developmentalists accept these broad periods, the age ranges themselves are in many ways arbitrary. Some periods have one clear-cut boundary (infancy begins with birth, the preschool period ends with entry into public school, and adolescence starts with sexual maturity), while others don't.

For instance, consider the separation between middle childhood and adolescence, which usually occurs around the age of 12. Because the boundary is based on a biological change, the onset of sexual maturation, which varies greatly from one individual to another, the specific age of entry into adolescence varies from one person to the next.

Furthermore, some developmentalists have proposed entirely new developmental periods. For example, psychologist Jeffrey Arnett argues that adolescence extends into *emerging adulthood*, a period beginning in the late teenage years and continuing into the mid-20s. During emerging adulthood, people are no longer adolescents, but they haven't fully taken on the responsibilities of adulthood. Instead, they are still trying out different identities and engaging in self-focused exploration (de Dios, 2012; Nelson, 2013; Arnett, 2011, 2016).

In short, there are substantial *individual differences* in the timing of events in people's lives—a biological fact of life. People mature at different rates and

reach developmental milestones at different points. Environmental factors also play a significant role in determining the age at which a particular event is likely to occur. For example, the typical age at which people develop romantic attachments varies substantially from one culture to another, depending in part on the way that relationships are viewed in a given culture.

It is important to keep in mind, then, that when developmental specialists discuss age ranges, they are

This wedding of two children in India is an example of how cultural factors play a significant role in determining the age when a particular event is likely to occur.

talking about averages—the times when people, on average, reach particular milestones. Some children will reach the milestone earlier, some later, and many—in fact, most—will reach it around the time of the average. Such variation becomes noteworthy only when children show substantial deviation from the average. For instance, parents whose child begins to speak at a much later age than average might decide to have their son or daughter evaluated by a speech therapist.

Furthermore, as children grow older, they become more likely to deviate from the average and exhibit individual differences. In very young children, a good part of developmental change is genetically determined and unfolds automatically, making development fairly similar in different children. But as children age, environmental factors become more potent, leading to greater variability and individual differences as time passes.

**THE LINKS BETWEEN TOPICS AND AGES.** Each of the broad topical areas of child development—physical, cognitive, and social and personality development—plays a role throughout childhood and adolescence. Consequently, some developmental experts focus on physical development during the prenatal period and others on what occurs during adolescence. Some might specialize in social development during the preschool years, while others may look at social relationships in middle childhood. And still others might take a broader approach, looking at cognitive development through every period of childhood and adolescence (and beyond).

The variety of topical areas and age ranges studied within the field of child development means that specialists from many diverse backgrounds and areas of expertise consider themselves child developmentalists. Psychologists who study behavior and mental processes, educational researchers, geneticists, and physicians are only some of the people who specialize and conduct research in child development. Furthermore, developmentalists work in a variety of settings, including university departments of psychology, education, human development, and medicine, as well as nonacademic settings as varied as human service agencies and child care centers.

The diversity of specialists working under the broad umbrella of child development brings a variety of perspectives and intellectual richness to the field. In addition, it permits the research findings of the field to be used by practitioners in a wide array of applied professions. Teachers, nurses, social workers, child care providers, and social policy experts all rely on the findings of child developmentalists to make decisions about how to improve children's welfare.

# DEVELOPMENTAL DIVERSITY AND YOUR LIFE
## Taking Culture, Ethnicity, and Race into Account

*In the United States, parents praise young children who ask a lot of questions for being "intelligent" and "inquisitive." The Dutch consider such children "too dependent on others." Italian parents judge inquisitiveness as a sign of social and emotional competence, not intelligence. Spanish parents praise character far more than intelligence, and Swedes value security and happiness above all.*

What are we to make of the diverse parental expectations cited above? Is one way of looking at children's inquisitiveness right and the others wrong? Probably not, if we take into consideration the cultural contexts in which parents operate. In fact, different cultures and subcultures have their own views of appropriate and inappropriate methods and interpretations of childrearing, just as they have different developmental goals for children (Feldman & Masalha, 2007; Huijbregts et al., 2009; Chen, Chen, & Zheng, 2012).

Specialists in child development must take into consideration broad cultural factors. For example, as we'll discuss further in Chapter 10, children growing up in Asian societies tend to have a *collectivistic orientation*, focusing on the interdependence among members of society. In contrast, children in Western societies are more likely to have an *individualistic orientation*, in which they concentrate on the uniqueness of the individual.

Similarly, child developmentalists must also consider ethnic, racial, socioeconomic, and gender differences if they are to achieve an understanding of how people change and grow throughout the life span. If these specialists succeed in doing so, not only can they attain a better understanding of human development, but they may also be able to derive more precise applications for improving the human social condition.

Efforts to understand how diversity affects development have been hindered by difficulties in finding an appropriate vocabulary. For example, members of the research community—as well as society at large—have sometimes used terms such as *race* and *ethnic group* in inappropriate ways. *Race* originated as a biological concept, and initially referred to classifications based on physical and structural characteristics of species. But such a definition has little validity in terms of humans, and research shows that it is not a meaningful way to differentiate people.

For example, depending on how race is defined, there are between 3 and 300 races, and no race is genetically distinct. The fact that 99.9 percent of humans' genetic makeup is identical in all humans makes the question of race seem insignificant. Thus, race today is generally thought of as a *social construction*, something defined by people and their beliefs (Helms, Jernigan, & Mascher, 2005; Smedley & Smedley, 2005; Alfred & Chlup, 2010).

In contrast, *ethnic group* and *ethnicity* are broader terms for which there is greater agreement. They relate to cultural background, nationality, religion, and language. Members of ethnic groups share a common cultural background and group history.

In addition, there is little agreement about which names best reflect different races and ethnic groups. Should the term *African American*—which has geographical and cultural implications—be preferred over *black*, which focuses primarily on race and skin color? Is *Native American* preferable to *Indian*? Is *Hispanic* more appropriate than *Latino*? And how can researchers accurately categorize people with multiracial backgrounds (Perlmann & Waters, 2002; Saulny, 2011; Jobling, Rasteiro, & Wetton, 2016)?

The face of the United States is changing as the proportion of children from different backgrounds is increasing.

In order to fully understand development, then, we need to take the complex issues associated with human diversity into account. In fact, only by looking for similarities and differences among various ethnic, cultural, and racial groups can developmental researchers distinguish principles of development that are universal from ones that are culturally determined. In the years ahead, then, it is likely that life span development will move from a discipline that primarily focuses on North American and European development to one that encompasses development around the globe (Wardle, 2007; Kloep et al., 2009; Bornstein & Lansford, 2013).

## Cohort Influences on Development: Developing With Others in a Social World

**LO 1.3** **Explain the major societal influences that determine development.**

*In 2001, a major earthquake in Gujarat shattered the life of infants, woman, and men alike. A 2-year-old baby boy was found alive under the debris. In another rescue effort, a woman with her 3-year-old son was rescued from an apartment. These infants are now approximately 19 to 20 years old and have vivid and traumatic memories of the incident.*

*The super cyclone in Odisha on 29 October 1999 is still felt by the generation that was too young then to remember much, if anything, about that day. A boy who was six years old at that time, still remembers how the waves had swept away his father, mother, and younger brother.*

These people are in part products of the social times in which they live. Each belongs to a particular **cohort**, a group of people born at around the same time in the same place. Such major social events as wars, economic upturns and depressions, famines, natural calamities (like earthquake and cyclone), and epidemics (like the one caused by the AIDS virus) have similar influences on members of a particular cohort (Mitchell, 2002; Dittmann, 2005; Twenge, Gentile, & Campbell, 2015).

*Cohort effects* provide an example of *history-graded influences*, which are biological and environmental influences associated with a particular historical moment. For instance, children who lived in New York City during the 9/11 terrorist attack on the World Trade Center (2001) experienced shared biological and environmental challenges due to the attack. Their development is going to be affected by this normative history-graded event (Park, Riley, & Snyder, 2012; Kim, Bushway, & Tsao, 2016).

In contrast, *age-graded influences* are biological and environmental influences that are similar for individuals in a particular age group, regardless of when or where they are raised. For example, biological events such as puberty and menopause are universal events that occur at relatively the same time throughout all societies. Similarly, a sociocultural event such as entry into formal education can be considered an age-graded influence because it occurs in most cultures around age 6.

> **From an educator's perspective:** How would a student's cohort membership affect his or her readiness for school? For example, what would be the benefits and drawbacks of coming from a cohort in which use of the Web was routine, compared with earlier cohorts prior to the appearance of the Web?

Development is also affected by *sociocultural-graded influences*, which include ethnicity, social class, subcultural membership, and other factors. Sociocultural-graded influences will be considerably different for immigrant children who speak English

Society's view of childhood and what is appropriate to ask of children has changed through the ages. These children worked full time in mines in the early 1900s.

as a second language than for children born in the United States who speak English as their first language (Rose et al., 2003).

Finally, *non-normative life events* are specific, atypical events that occur in a person's life at a time when such events do not happen to most people. For example, a child whose parents die in an automobile accident when she is 6 years old has experienced a significant non-normative life event.

# Children: Past, Present, and Future

Children have been the object of study from the time that humans have walked the planet. Parents are endlessly fascinated by their children, and the growth displayed throughout childhood and adolescence is a source of both curiosity and wonderment.

But it is relatively recently in the course of history that children have been studied from a scientific vantage point. Even a brief look at how the field of child development has progressed shows that there has been considerable growth in the way that children are viewed.

## Early Views of Children

**LO 1.4  Explain the earliest views of childhood and children.**

It is hard to imagine, but some scholars believe that there was a time when childhood didn't even exist, at least in the minds of adults. According to Philippe Ariès, who studied paintings and other forms of art, children in medieval Europe were not given any special status before 1600. Instead, they were viewed as miniature, somewhat imperfect adults. They were dressed in adult clothing and not treated specially in any significant way. Childhood was not seen as a stage qualitatively different from adulthood (Ariès, 1962; Acocella, 2003; Hutton, 2004).

Although the view that children during the Middle Ages were seen simply as miniature adults may be somewhat exaggerated—Ariès's arguments were based primarily on art depicting the European aristocracy, a very limited sample of Western culture—it is clear that childhood had a considerably different meaning than it does now. Moreover, the idea that childhood could be studied systematically did not take hold until later.

During medieval times in Europe, children were thought of as miniature—although imperfect—adults. This view of childhood was reflected in how children were dressed identically to adults.

**PHILOSOPHERS' PERSPECTIVES ON CHILDREN.** During the 16th and 17th centuries, philosophers took the lead in thinking about the nature of childhood. For example, English philosopher John Locke considered a child to be a *tabula rasa*—Latin for "blank slate." In this view, children entered the world with no specific characteristics or personalities. Instead, they were entirely shaped by their experiences as they grew up. As we'll see in the next chapter, this view was the precursor of the modern perspective known as behaviorism.

Sixteenth-century French philosopher Jean-Jacques Rousseau had an entirely different view of the nature of children. He argued that children were *noble savages*, meaning that they were born with an innate sense of right and wrong and morality. Seeing humans as basically good, Rousseau argued that infants developed into admirable and worthy children and adults unless they were corrupted by negative circumstances in their lives. Rousseau also was one of the first observers of childhood to suggest that growth occurred in distinct, discontinuous stages that unfolded automatically—a concept that is reflected in some contemporary theories of child development that we'll discuss in the next chapter.

**BABY BIOGRAPHIES.** Among the first instances in which children were methodically studied came in the form of *baby biographies*, which were popular in the late 1700s in Germany. Observers—typically parents—tried to trace the growth of a single child, recording the physical and linguistic milestones achieved by their child.

But it was not until Charles Darwin, who developed the theory of evolution, that observation of children took a more systematic turn. Darwin was convinced that understanding the development of individuals within a species could help identify how the species itself had developed. He made baby biographies more scientifically respectable by producing one of his own, recording his son's development during his first year. A wave of baby biographies followed the publication of Darwin's book.

Other historical trends helped propel the development of a new scientific discipline focusing on children. Scientists discovered the mechanisms behind conception, and geneticists were beginning to unlock the mysteries of heredity. Philosophers argued about the relative influences of nature (heredity) and nurture (influences in the environment).

**FOCUS ON CHILDHOOD.** As the adult labor pool increased, children were no longer needed as a source of inexpensive labor, paving the way for laws that protected children from exploitation. The advent of more universal education meant that children were separated from adults for more of the day, and educators sought to identify better ways of teaching children.

Advances in psychology led people to focus on the ways that childhood events influenced them during their adult lives. As a consequence of these significant social changes, child development became recognized as a field of its own.

## The 20th Century: Child Development as a Discipline

**LO 1.5 Describe the ways that childhood has been viewed since the 20th century.**

Several figures became central to the emerging field of child development. For example, Alfred Binet, a French psychologist, not only pioneered work on children's intelligence but also investigated memory and mental calculation. G. Stanley Hall initiated the use of questionnaires to illuminate children's thinking and behavior. He also wrote the first book that targeted adolescence as a distinct period of development—aptly titled *Adolescence* (Hall, 1904/1916).

Even though prejudice hindered women in their pursuit of academic careers, they made significant contributions to the discipline of child development during the early part of the 1900s. For example, Leta Stetter Hollingworth was one of the first psychologists

**Table 1.2** Major Issues in Child Development

| Continuous Change | Discontinuous Change |
|---|---|
| • Change is gradual.<br>• Achievements at one level build on previous levels.<br>• Underlying developmental processes remain the same over the life span. | • Change occurs in distinct steps or stages.<br>• Behavior and processes are qualitatively different at different stages. |
| **Critical Periods** | **Sensitive Periods** |
| • Certain environmental stimuli are necessary for normal development.<br>• Emphasized by early developmentalists. | • People are susceptible to certain environmental stimuli, but consequences of absent stimuli are reversible.<br>• Current emphasis in life span development. |
| **Life Span Approach** | **Focus on Particular Periods** |
| • Current theories emphasize growth and change throughout life, relatedness of different periods. | • Infancy and adolescence emphasized by early developmentalists as most important periods. |
| **Nature (Genetic Factors)** | **Nurture (Environmental Factors)** |
| • Emphasis is on discovering inherited genetic traits and abilities. | • Emphasis is on environmental influences that affect a person's development. |

to focus on child development. Similarly, Maria Montessori, an Italian physician and educator, opened the first Montessori preschool in 1907 based on her theories of how children naturally learn (Hollingworth, 1943/1990; Denmark & Fernandez, 1993; Lillard, 2008).

During the first decades of the 1900s, one emerging trend that had enormous impact on our understanding of children's development was the rise of large-scale, systematic, and ongoing investigations of children and their development throughout the life span. For example, the Stanford Studies of Gifted Children began in the early 1920s and continue today. Similarly, the Fels Research Institute Study and the Berkeley Growth and Guidance Studies helped identify the nature of change in children's lives as they became older. Using a normative approach, they studied large numbers of children in order to determine the nature of normal growth (Dixon & Lerner, 1999).

The women and men who built the foundations of child development shared a common goal: to scientifically study the nature of growth, change, and stability throughout childhood and adolescence. They brought the field to where it is today.

## Today's Key Issues and Questions: Child Development's Underlying Themes

**LO 1.6 Explain the key issues and questions in the field of child development.**

Today, several key issues and questions dominate the field of child development. Among the major issues

(summarized in Table 1.2) are the nature of developmental change, the importance of critical and sensitive periods, life span approaches versus more focused approaches, and the nature–nurture issue.

**CONTINUOUS CHANGE VERSUS DISCONTINUOUS CHANGE.** One of the primary issues challenging child developmentalists is whether development proceeds in a continuous or discontinuous fashion (illustrated in Figure 1.1). In **continuous change**, development is gradual, with achievements at one level building on those of previous levels. Continuous change is quantitative; the basic underlying developmental processes that drive change remain the same over the course of the life span. Continuous change, then, produces changes that are a matter of degree, not of kind. Changes in height prior to adulthood, for example, are continuous. Similarly, as we'll see later in the chapter, some theorists suggest that changes in people's thinking capabilities are also continuous, showing gradual quantitative improvements rather than developing entirely new cognitive processing capabilities.

In contrast, **discontinuous change** occurs in distinct steps or stages. Each stage brings about behavior that is assumed to be qualitatively different from behavior at earlier stages. Consider the example of

---

**continuous change** Gradual development in which achievements at one level build on those of previous levels

**discontinuous change** Development that occurs in distinct steps or stages, with each stage bringing about behavior that is assumed to be qualitatively different from behavior at earlier stages

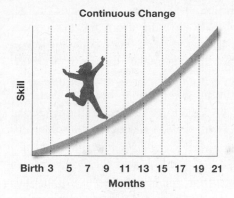

**Figure 1.1** Two Approaches to Developmental Change

The two approaches to development are continuous change, which is gradual, with achievements at one level building on those of previous levels, and discontinuous change, which occurs in distinct steps or stages.

cognitive development. We'll see in Chapter 2 that some cognitive developmentalists suggest that as we develop, our thinking changes in fundamental ways, and that such development is not just a matter of quantitative change but also one of qualitative change.

Most developmentalists agree that taking an either/or position on the continuous–discontinuous issue is inappropriate. While many types of developmental change are continuous, others are clearly discontinuous.

**CRITICAL AND SENSITIVE PERIODS: GAUGING THE IMPACT OF ENVIRONMENTAL EVENTS.** If a woman comes down with a case of rubella (German measles) in the 11th week of pregnancy, the consequences for the fetus she is carrying are likely to be devastating. They include the potential for blindness, deafness, and heart defects; however, if she comes down with the same strain of rubella in the 30th week of pregnancy, damage to the fetus is unlikely.

The differing outcomes of the disease in the two periods demonstrate the concept of critical periods. A **critical period** is a specific time during development when a particular event has its greatest consequences. Critical periods occur when the presence of certain kinds of environmental stimuli enable development to proceed normally, or when exposure to certain stimuli results in abnormal development. For example, mothers who take drugs at particular times during pregnancy may cause permanent harm to their developing fetus (Mølgaard-Nielsen, Pasternak, & Hviid, 2013; Nygaard et al., 2017).

Although early specialists in child development placed great emphasis on the importance of critical periods, more recent thinking suggests that in many realms, individuals may be more flexible than was

first thought, particularly in the domains of cognitive, personality, and social development. In these areas, there is a significant degree of **plasticity**, the degree to which a developing behavior or physical structure is modifiable. For instance, rather than suffering permanent damage from a lack of certain kinds of early social experiences, there is increasing evidence that children can use later experiences to help overcome earlier deficits.

Consequently, developmentalists are now more likely to speak of *sensitive periods* rather than *critical periods*. In a **sensitive period**, organisms are particularly susceptible to certain kinds of stimuli in their environment. A sensitive period represents the optimal period for particular capacities to emerge, and children are particularly sensitive to environmental influences. For example, a lack of exposure to language during sensitive periods may result in delayed language production in infants and toddlers.

It is important to understand the difference between the concepts of critical periods and sensitive periods. In critical periods, it is assumed that certain kinds of environmental influences produce permanent, irreversible consequences for the developing individual. In contrast, although the absence of particular environmental influences during a sensitive period may hinder development, it is possible for later

---

**critical period** A specific time during development when a particular event has its greatest consequences

**plasticity** The degree to which a developing behavior or physical structure is modifiable

**sensitive period** A specific time when organisms are particularly susceptible to certain kinds of stimuli in their environment

experiences to overcome the earlier deficits. In other words, the concept of sensitive periods recognizes the plasticity of developing humans (Hooks & Chen, 2008; Curley et al., 2011; Piekarski et al., 2017).

> **From a child care worker's perspective:** What might you do to take advantage of a sensitive period?

**LIFE SPAN APPROACHES VERSUS A FOCUS ON PARTICULAR PERIODS.** On what part of the life span should child developmentalists focus their attention? For early developmentalists, the answers tended to be infancy and adolescence. Most attention was clearly concentrated on those two periods, largely to the exclusion of other parts of childhood.

Today the story is different. The entire period encompassing conception through adolescence is now regarded as important, for several reasons. One is the discovery that developmental growth and change continue during every stage of life.

Furthermore, an important part of every person's environment is the presence of other people around him or her—the person's social environment. To understand the social influences on children of a given age, we need to understand the people who are in large measure providing those influences. For instance, to understand development in infants, we need to unravel the effects of their parents' age on their social environment. It is likely that a 15-year-old mother will provide parental influences of a very different sort from those provided by a 37-year-old mother. Consequently, infant development is in part a consequence of adult development.

**THE RELATIVE INFLUENCE OF NATURE AND NURTURE ON DEVELOPMENT.** One of the enduring questions of child development involves how much of people's behavior is due to their genetically determined nature and how much is due to nurture—the influences of the physical and social environment in which a child is raised. This issue, which has deep philosophical and historical roots, has dominated much work in child development (Wexler, 2006; Keating, 2011).

In this context, *nature* refers to traits, abilities, and capacities that are inherited from one's parents. It encompasses any factor that is produced by the predetermined unfolding of genetic information—a process known as **maturation**. These genetic, inherited influences are at work as we move from the one-celled organism that is created at the moment of conception to the billions of cells that make up a fully formed human.

Nature influences whether our eyes are blue or brown, whether we have thick hair throughout life or eventually go bald, and how good we are at athletics. Nature allows our brains to develop in such a way that we can read the words on this page.

In contrast, *nurture* refers to the environmental influences that shape behavior. Some of these influences may be biological, such as the impact of a pregnant mother's use of cocaine on her unborn child or the amounts and kinds of food available to children. Other environmental influences are more social, such as the ways that parents discipline their children and the effects of peer pressure on an adolescent. Finally, some influences are a result of larger, societal-level factors, such as the socioeconomic circumstances in which people find themselves.

If our traits and behavior were determined solely by either nature or nurture, there would probably be little debate regarding the issue. For most critical behaviors, this is hardly the case. Take, for instance, one of the most controversial arenas: intelligence. As we'll consider in detail in Chapter 12, the question of whether intelligence is determined primarily by inherited, genetic factors—nature—or is shaped by environmental factors—nurture—has caused lively and often bitter arguments. Largely because of its social implications, the issue has spilled out of the scientific arena and into the realm of politics and social policy.

**IMPLICATIONS FOR CHILDREARING AND SOCIAL POLICY.** Consider the implications of the nature-versus-nurture issue: If the extent of one's intelligence is primarily determined by heredity and consequently is largely fixed at birth, then efforts to improve intellectual performance later in life may be doomed to failure. In contrast, if intelligence is primarily a result of environmental factors, such as the amount and quality of schooling and stimulation to which one is exposed, then we would expect that an improvement in social conditions could bring about an increase in intelligence.

---

**maturation** The process of the predetermined unfolding of genetic information

The extent of social policy affected by ideas about the origins of intelligence illustrates the significance of issues that involve the nature–nurture question. As we address it in relation to several topical areas throughout this book, we should keep in mind that specialists in child development reject the notion that behavior is the result solely of either nature or nurture. Instead, the question is one of degree—and the specifics of that, too, are hotly debated.

Furthermore, the interaction of genetic and environmental factors is complex, in part because certain genetically determined traits have not only a direct influence on children's behavior but an indirect influence in shaping children's environments as well. For example, a child who is consistently cranky and who cries a great deal—a trait that may be produced by genetic factors—may influence her environment by making her parents so highly responsive to her insistent crying that they rush to comfort her whenever she cries. Their responsivity to the child's genetically determined behavior consequently becomes an environmental influence on his or her subsequent development (Stright, Gallagher, & Kelley, 2008; Barnes & Boutwell, 2012).

Similarly, although our genetic background orients us toward particular behaviors, those behaviors will not necessarily occur in the absence of an appropriate environment. People with similar genetic backgrounds (such as identical twins) may behave in very different ways, and people with highly dissimilar genetic backgrounds can behave quite similarly to one another in certain areas (Kato & Pedersen, 2005; Conley & Rauscher, 2013; Sudharsanan, Behrman, & Kohler, 2016).

In sum, the question of how much of a given behavior is due to nature and how much to nurture is a challenging one. Ultimately, we should consider the two sides of the nature–nurture issue as opposite ends of a continuum, with particular behaviors falling somewhere between the two ends. We can say something similar about the other controversies that we have considered. For instance, continuous versus discontinuous development is not an either-or proposition; some forms of development fall toward the continuous end of the continuum, while others lie closer to the discontinuous end. Few statements about development involve either-or absolutes (Rutter, 2006; Deater-Deckard & Cahill, 2007).

# The Future of Child Development

**LO 1.7  Predict future developments in the field of child development.**

We've examined the foundations of the field of child development, along with the key issues and questions that underlie the discipline. But what lies ahead? Several trends appear likely to emerge:

- As research in development continues to be amassed, the field will become increasingly specialized. New areas of study and perspectives will emerge.

- The explosion of information about genes and the genetic foundations of behavior will influence all spheres of child development. Increasingly, developmentalists will link work across biological, cognitive, and social domains, and the boundaries between different subdisciplines will be blurred.

- The increasing diversity of the population of the United States in terms of race, ethnicity, language, and culture will lead the field to focus greater attention on issues of diversity.

- A growing number of professionals in a variety of fields will make use of child developmentalists' research and findings. Educators, social workers, nurses and other health care providers, genetic counselors, toy designers, child care providers, cereal manufacturers, social ethicists, and members of dozens of other professions will all draw on the field of child development. The job outlook for workers in many of these areas is promising. For example, employment of child care workers is expected to grow 5 percent over the next 10 years (Bureau of Labor Statistics, 2017).

- Work on child development will increasingly influence public interest issues. Discussion of many of the major social concerns of our time, including violence, prejudice and discrimination, poverty, changes in family life, child care, schooling, and even terrorism, can be informed by research in child development. Consequently, child developmentalists are likely to make important contributions to 21st-century society (Block, Weinstein, & Seitz, 2005; McKinney et al., 2017). (For one example of the current contributions of work in child development, see the *From Research to Practice* box.)

# FROM RESEARCH TO PRACTICE
## Preventing Violence Toward Children

- A seven-year-old boy was found with his throat slit in the toilet of a private school in Gurugram, Haryana.
- A five-year-old was raped in the washroom of her school in Gandhinagar, Gujarat.
- A 14-year-old girl student committed suicide after being bullied by a boy from her class.
- The boy murdered a man just to get his i-Phone.
- Ritesh, a Class III student, who was a very happy and jovial boy while studying in Class II started acting more and more withdrawn and sad. He had problem in concentrating in the class. He also resisted to go out and play during the games period. Noticing the change in his behavior, his class teacher referred him to the school counsellor. Then, it was revealed that the boy was bullied and abused by a boy studying in Class IX.
- Four-year-old Sunita speaks very less and remains quiet and had no desire to play or interact with other children in the class. The counsellor didn't find any specific cognitive and language problem in the child, as when individually interviewed she could talk to the counsellor. During an interview with the mother, it was found that Sunita's father is an alcoholic and would beat her mother every night and sometimes even threaten to kill her. The child is a witness to the violence in her family.

Violence is part of the lives of many children. Over 50 percent of children around the world were the victims of violence in the past year (DocuTicker, 2010; UNICEF, 2013; Hillis et al., 2016).

How can we explain the level of violence? How do people learn to be violent? How can we control and remedy aggression? And how can we discourage violence from occurring in the first place?

Child development has sought to answer such questions from several different perspectives. Consider these examples:

- **Explaining the roots of violence.** Some child developmentalists have looked at how early behavioral and physical problems may be associated with later difficulties in controlling aggression as adults. For instance, researchers have found links between early maltreatment, physical and psychological abuse, and neglect of children and subsequent aggressive behavior. Others have looked at childhood trauma and its effects on violent behavior (Widom & Czaja, 2012; Gowin et al., 2013; Wright & Fagen, 2013).

- **Considering how bullying and other forms of violence affect school children.** Kshirsagar, Agarwal, and Bavdekar (2006) found that among children aged 8 to 12 years, bullying was reported by 157 (31.4 percent) of the 500 children interviewed. There was no significant difference in the prevalence of bullying amongst boys and girls in co-education schools. However, it was significantly low in schools enrolling girls alone. Teasing and keeping names were the commonest forms noticed in girls-alone schools. Causing physical hurt was reported by 25 students (16 percent). Furthermore, it was found that only 24 parents (24 percent) were aware that their children were being bullied. In their study on cyber bullying in Asia, Bhatt et al. (2013) observed that 53 percent of the participants (who were in the age group of 8 to 12 years) in India reported cyber bulling.

  In another study on cyber bullying among 640 high-school students (in the between classes 7 and 12) from southern India, approximately half of the participants experienced online bullying (Bhat et al., 2017).

- **Examining how exposure to aggression may lead to further violence.** Other developmentalists have examined how exposure to violence in the media and in video games may lead to aggression. For example, psychologist Craig Anderson has found that people who play violent video games have an altered view of the world, seeing it as more violent than those who do not play such games. In addition, those who play violent video games are more easily triggered into aggressive behavior, and they have decreased empathy for others. There is even evidence that use of violent video games is related to juvenile delinquency (DeWall, Anderson, & Bushman, 2013; Anderson et al., 2015).

- **Developing programs to reduce aggression.** Some child developmentalists have focused on devising programs to lower the likelihood of children behaving violently. For example, psychologists Ervin Staub and Darren Spielman devised a program to help children develop constructive ways of fulfilling their basic needs. After involvement in an intervention that included role-playing and structured discussions, participants' aggressive behavior declined (Spielman & Staub, 2003; Staub, 2011, 2013; Miller et al., 2014).

As these examples illustrate, developmental researchers are making progress in understanding and dealing with the violence that is increasingly part of modern society. Violence is just one example of the areas in which experts in child development are contributing their skills for the betterment of human society.

As we'll see throughout this book, the field has much to offer.

- **Why does violence remain such a problem not only in the United States but around the world?**
- **Because research shows that exposure to violent video games raises the level of aggression in players, do you think there should be legal limitations on the sale and distribution of such games? Why or why not?**

# BECOMING AN INFORMED CONSUMER OF CHILD DEVELOPMENT

## Assessing Information on Child Development

*If you immediately comfort crying babies, you'll spoil them.*

*If you let babies cry without comforting them, they'll be untrusting and clingy as adults.*

*Spanking is one of the best ways to discipline your child.*

*Never hit your child.*

*If a marriage is unhappy, children are better off if their parents divorce than if they stay together.*

*No matter how difficult a marriage is, parents should avoid divorce for the sake of their children.*

There is no lack of advice on the best way to raise a child or, more generally, to lead one's life. From best-sellers with titles such as *The No-Cry Sleep Solution* to magazine and newspaper columns that provide advice on every imaginable topic, each of us is exposed to tremendous amounts of information.

Yet not all advice is equally valid. The mere fact that something is in print, on television, or on a Web site does not automatically make it legitimate or accurate. Fortunately, some guidelines can help distinguish when recommendations and suggestions are reasonable and when they are not. Here are a few:

- *Consider the source and currency of the advice.* Information from established, respected organizations such as the American Medical Association, the American Psychological Association, and the American Academy of Pediatrics is likely to be the result of years of study, and its accuracy is probably high. But keep in mind that even advice from such sources changes over time. For instance, the American Academy of Pediatrics' prior "zero screen time" rule for children under the age of 2 has been replaced by the advice

that a limited amount of screen time is not harmful (American Academy of Pediatrics, 2016).

- *Evaluate the credentials of the person providing advice.* Information coming from established, acknowledged researchers and experts in a field is likely to be more accurate than that coming from a person whose credentials are obscure.

- *Understand the difference between anecdotal evidence and scientific evidence.* Anecdotal evidence is based on one or two instances of a phenomenon, haphazardly discovered or encountered; scientific evidence is based on careful, systematic procedures.

- *Keep cultural context in mind.* Although an assertion may be valid in some contexts, it may not be true in all. For example, it is typically thought that providing infants the freedom to move about and exercise their limbs facilitates their muscular development and mobility. Yet in some cultures, infants spend most of their time closely bound to their mothers with no apparent long-term damage (Kaplan & Dove, 1987; Tronick, Thomas, & Daltabuit, 1994; Manaseki-Holland et al., 2010).

- *Don't assume that because many people believe something, it is necessarily true.* For instance, consider D.A.R.E., the Drug Abuse Resistance Education antidrug program that at one time was used in about half the school systems in the United States. D.A.R.E. was designed to prevent the spread of drugs through lectures and question-and-answer sessions run by police officers. Careful evaluation, however, has found no evidence that the program is effective in reducing drug use (Rhule, 2005; University of Akron, 2006; Lilienfeld & Arkowitz, 2014).

> The key to evaluating information relating to child development is to maintain a healthy dose of skepticism. No source of information is invariably, unfailingly accurate. By keeping a critical eye on the statements you encounter, you'll be in a better position to determine the very real contributions made by child developmentalists in understanding how we change and grow over the course of childhood and adolescence.

# The Case of ...
## Too Many Choices

Jenny Claymore, midway through her third year of college, is desperate to pick a career but hasn't a clue. The problem isn't that nothing interests her; it's that too many things do. From her reading, radio listening, and TV watching, her head is full of ideas for great-sounding careers.

Jenny loves children, having always enjoyed baby-sitting and her summer work as a camp counselor—so maybe she should be a teacher. She is fascinated by all she hears about DNA and genetic research—so maybe she should be a biologist or a doctor. She is concerned when she hears about school violence—from bullying to shootings—so maybe she should go into school administration or law enforcement. She is curious about how children learn language—so maybe she should go into speech pathology or, again, teaching. She is fascinated by court cases that rely on the testimony of young children, and how experts on both sides contradict each other—so maybe she should become a lawyer.

Her college counselor once said, "Begin your search for a career by thinking about the classes you've taken in high school and college." Jenny recalls a high school course in early childhood that she loved, and she knows that her favorite class in college is her child development course. Would considering a career in child development make sense?

1. How well might a career in the field of child development address Jenny's love of children and her interest in genetic research?
2. What sort of career might focus on the prevention of school violence?
3. How might child development relate to her interest in eyewitness testimony and memory?
4. Overall, how many careers could you think of that would fit Jenny's interests?

# Epilogue

We have covered a lot of ground in our introduction to child development. We reviewed the broad scope of the field, touching on the wide range of topics that child developmentalists may address, and discussed the key issues and questions that have shaped the field since its inception.

Before proceeding to the next chapter, take a few minutes to reconsider the prologue of this chapter—about the case of Louise Brown and Elizabeth Carr, among the first children to be born through in vitro fertilization. Based on what you now know about child development, answer the following questions:

1. What are some of the potential benefits, and the costs, of the type of conception—in vitro fertilization—that was carried out for Louise's and Elizabeth's parents?
2. What are some questions that developmentalists who study either physical, cognitive, or personality and social development might ask about the effects on Louise and Elizabeth of being conceived via in vitro fertilization?
3. The creation of complete human clones—exact genetic replicas of an individual—is still in the realm of science fiction, but the theoretical possibility does raise some important questions. For example, what would be the psychological consequences of being a clone?
4. If clones could actually be produced, how might they help scientists understand the relative impact of heredity and environment on development?

# Looking Back

**LO 1.1 Define the field of child development.**

- Child development is a scientific approach to answering questions about the growth, change, and stability that occur in individuals from conception to adolescence.

**LO 1.2 Describe the scope of the field of child development.**

- The scope of the field encompasses physical, cognitive, and social and personality development at all ages from conception through adolescence.

**LO 1.3 Explain the major societal influences that determine development.**

- Culture—both broad and narrow—is an important issue in child development. Many aspects of development are influenced not only by broad cultural differences but also by ethnic, racial, and socioeconomic differences within a particular culture.

- Every person is subject to history-graded influences, age-graded influences, sociocultural-graded influences, and non-normative life events.

**LO 1.4 Explain the earliest views of childhood and children.**

- Early views of childhood considered children as miniature adults.

- While Locke viewed a child as a *tabula rasa* or "blank slate," Rousseau argued that children had an inborn sense of morality.

**LO 1.5 Describe the ways that childhood has been viewed since the 20th century.**

- Later views of childhood saw it as a distinct period in the life span and led to the emergence of the field of child development.

**LO 1.6 Explain the key issues and questions in the field of child development.**

- Four key issues in child development are: (1) whether developmental change is continuous or discontinuous, (2) whether development is largely governed by critical or sensitive periods during which certain influences or experiences must occur for development to be normal, (3) whether to focus on certain particularly important periods in human development or on the entire life span, and (4) the nature–nurture question, which focuses on the relative importance of genetic versus environmental influences.

**LO 1.7 Predict future developments in the field of child development.**

- Future trends in the field are likely to include increasing specialization, the blurring of boundaries between different areas, increasing attention to issues involving diversity, and an increasing influence on public interest issues.

# Key Terms and Concepts

child development (p. 3)
physical development (p. 4)
cognitive development (p. 4)
personality development (p. 4)

social development (p. 4)
cohort (p. 7)
continuous change (p. 10)
discontinuous change (p. 10)

critical period (p. 11)
plasticity (p. 11)
sensitive period (p. 11)
maturation (p. 12)

# Chapter 2
# Theoretical Perspectives and Research

## Learning Objectives

**LO 2.1** Describe the basic concepts of the psychodynamic perspective.

**LO 2.2** Describe the basic concepts of the behavioral perspective.

**LO 2.3** Describe the basic concepts of the cognitive perspective.

**LO 2.4** Describe the basic concepts of the contextual perspective.

**LO 2.5** Describe the basic concepts of the evolutionary perspective.

**LO 2.6** Explain the value of applying multiple perspectives to child development.

**LO 2.7** Identify the principles of the scientific method and how they help answer questions about child development.

**LO 2.8**   Summarize the major characteristics of correlational studies.

**LO 2.9**   Summarize the major characteristics of experiments and how they differ from correlational studies.

**LO 2.10**   Distinguish between theoretical and applied research.

**LO 2.11**   Explain the major research strategies.

**LO 2.12**   Identify the primary ethical principles used to guide research.

# Prologue: The First Word Spoken

It was a hot summer night, and Kajal, a 12-month-old girl, sat in a chair as her father was preparing dinner. As Kajal watched her father chop vegetables, she pointed at him and said "Papa." "What did you say?" Kajal's father asked incredulously. As he rushed to the closet to retrieve the video camera, Kajal remained silent. Then, as he returned with the camera recording, she looked at him and yelled, "Papa!"

# Looking Ahead

*Maa. No. Toffee. Dad. Jo.* Most parents can remember their baby's first word, and no wonder. It's an exciting moment, this emergence of a skill that is seemingly unique to human beings.

But is language really unique to humans? Just how does language develop over the course of infancy and childhood? Is it a built-in human capability that emerges naturally, or are there certain experiences necessary for language to develop? Are there parts of the brain that are specific to the development of language capabilities? And what is the role of learning in the rapid increase in language skills that occurs as children begin to understand and speak their native language?

To answer questions like these, we need to turn to the accumulated findings from literally thousands of developmental research studies. These studies have looked at questions ranging from brain development and the nature of social relationships to the way in which cognitive abilities grow throughout childhood and adolescence. The common challenge of these studies is to pose and answer questions of interest in development.

Like all of us, child developmentalists ask questions about people's bodies, minds, and social interactions—and about how these aspects of human life change as people age. But to the natural curiosity that we all share, developmental scientists add one important ingredient that makes a difference in how they ask—and try to answer—questions. This ingredient is the scientific method. This structured but straightforward way of looking at phenomena elevates questioning from mere curiosity to purposeful learning. With this powerful tool, developmentalists are able not only to ask good questions but also to begin to answer them systematically.

In this chapter, we consider the way in which child developmentalists ask and answer questions about the world. We begin with a discussion of the broad perspectives used in understanding children and their behavior. These perspectives provide general approaches from which to view the development along multiple dimensions. We then turn to the basic building block of the science of child development: research. We describe the major types of research that developmentalists perform to pursue their research and get answers to their questions. Finally, we focus on two important issues in developmental research: One is how to choose research participants so that results can be applied beyond the study setting, and the other is the central issue of ethics.

# Perspectives on Children

*When Roddy McDougall took his first step, his parents were elated—and relieved. They had anticipated the moment for what seemed a long time; most children his age had begun to walk months earlier. In addition, his grandparents had weighed in with their concerns, with his grandmother going so far as to suggest that he might be suffering from some sort of developmental delay, although that was based solely on a "feeling" she had. But the moment Roddy took his first step, his parents' and grandparents' anxieties fell away, and they all experienced great pride in Roddy's accomplishment.*

The concerns Roddy's relatives felt derived from their vague conceptions of how a normal child's development proceeds. Each of us has established ideas about the course of development, and we use them to make judgments and develop hunches about the meaning of children's behavior. Our experience orients us to certain types of behavior that we see as particularly important. For some people, it may be when a child says his or her first word; for others, it may be the way a child interacts with others.

Like anybody else, child developmentalists approach the field from a number of different perspectives. Each perspective encompasses one or more **theories**, broad, organized explanations and predictions concerning phenomena of interest. A theory provides a framework for understanding the relationships among a seemingly unorganized set of facts or principles.

We all develop theories about development, based on our experience, folklore, and information found in articles in magazines and newspapers. However, theories in child development are different. Whereas our own personal theories are built on unverified observations that are developed haphazardly, child developmentalists' theories are more formal, based on a systematic integration of prior findings and theorizing. These theories allow developmentalists to summarize and organize prior observations, and they also permit them to move beyond existing observations to draw deductions that may not be immediately apparent. In addition, these theories are then subject to rigorous testing in the form of research. By contrast, the developmental theories of individuals are not subject to such testing and may never be questioned at all (Thomas, 2001).

We'll consider five major perspectives used in child development: the psychodynamic, behavioral, cognitive, contextual, and evolutionary perspectives. These diverse outlooks emphasize somewhat different aspects of development that steer inquiry in particular directions. Just as we can use multiple maps to find our way around a region—for example, one map might show the roadways and another might focus on key landmarks—the various developmental perspectives provide us with different views of child and adolescent behavior. And just as maps must continually be revised, each perspective continues to evolve and change, as befits a growing and dynamic discipline.

## The Psychodynamic Perspective: Focusing on Internal Forces

**LO 2.1  Describe the basic concepts of the psychodynamic perspective.**

*When Marisol was 6 months old, she was involved in a bloody automobile accident—or so her parents told her, since she has no conscious recollection of it. Now, at age 21, she is having difficulty maintaining relationships, and her therapist is trying to determine whether her current problems are a result of the early accident.*

Looking for such a link might seem a bit far-fetched, but to proponents of the **psychodynamic perspective**, it is not so improbable. Advocates of the psychodynamic perspective believe that behavior is motivated by inner forces, memories, and conflicts of which a person has little awareness or control. The inner forces, which may stem from one's childhood, continually influence behavior throughout the life span.

**FREUD'S PSYCHOANALYTIC THEORY.**  The psychodynamic perspective is most closely associated with Sigmund Freud and his psychoanalytic theory. Freud, who lived from 1856 to 1939, was a Viennese physician whose revolutionary ideas ultimately had a profound effect not just on the fields of psychology and psychiatry but on Western thought in general (Masling & Bornstein, 1996; Wolitzky, 2011; Greenberg, 2012; Roth, 2016).

---

**theories** Explanations and predictions concerning phenomena of interest, providing a framework for understanding the relationships among an organized set of facts or principles

**psychodynamic perspective** The approach to the study of development that states behavior is motivated by inner forces, memories, and conflicts of which a person has little awareness or control

Sigmund Freud

Erik Erikson

Freud's **psychoanalytic theory** suggests that unconscious forces act to determine personality and behavior. To Freud, the *unconscious* is a part of the personality about which a person is unaware. It contains infantile wishes, desires, demands, and needs that, because of their disturbing nature, are hidden from conscious awareness. Freud suggested that the unconscious is responsible for a good part of our everyday behavior.

According to Freud, everyone's personality has three aspects: id, ego, and superego. The *id* is the raw, unorganized, inborn part of personality that is present at birth. It represents primitive drives related to hunger, sex, aggression, and irrational impulses. The id operates according to the *pleasure principle*, in which the goal is to maximize satisfaction and reduce tension.

The *ego* is the part of personality that is rational and reasonable. The ego acts as a buffer between the real world outside of us and the primitive id. The ego operates on the *reality principle*, in which instinctual energy is restrained to maintain the safety of the individual and help integrate the person into society.

Finally, Freud proposed that the *superego* represents a person's conscience, incorporating distinctions between right and wrong. It develops around age 5 or 6 and is learned from an individual's parents, teachers, and other significant figures.

In addition to providing an account of the various parts of the personality, Freud suggested the ways in which personality develops during childhood. He argued that **psychosexual development** occurs as children pass through a series of stages, in which pleasure, or gratification, is focused on a particular biological function and body part. As illustrated in Table 2.1, he

suggested that pleasure shifted from the mouth (the *oral stage*) to the anus (the *anal stage*) and eventually to the genitals (the *phallic stage* and the *genital stage*).

According to Freud, if children are unable to gratify themselves sufficiently during a particular stage—or conversely, if they receive too much gratification—fixation may occur. *Fixation* is behavior reflecting an earlier stage of development due to an unresolved conflict. For instance, fixation at the oral stage might produce an adult who is unusually absorbed in oral activities—eating, talking, or chewing gum. Freud also argued that fixation is represented through symbolic sorts of oral activities, such as the use of "biting" sarcasm.

**ERIKSON'S PSYCHOSOCIAL THEORY.** Psychoanalyst Erik Erikson, who lived from 1902 to 1994, provided an alternative psychodynamic view in his theory of psychosocial development, which emphasizes our social interaction with other people. In Erikson's view, both society and culture challenge and shape us. **Psychosocial development** encompasses changes in our interactions with and understandings of one

---

**psychoanalytic theory** The theory proposed by Sigmund Freud that suggests that unconscious forces act to determine personality and behavior

**psychosexual development** According to Sigmund Freud, a series of stages that children pass through in which pleasure, or gratification, is focused on a particular biological function and body part

**psychosocial development** The approach to the study of development that encompasses changes in the understanding individuals have of their interactions with others, of others' behavior, and of themselves as members of society

**Table 2.1** Freud's and Erikson's Theories

| Approximate Age | Freud's Stages of Psychosexual Development | Major Characteristics of Freud's Stages | Erikson's Stages of Psychosocial Development | Positive and Negative Outcomes of Erikson's Stages |
|---|---|---|---|---|
| **Birth to 12–18 months** | Oral | Interest in oral gratification from sucking, eating, mouthing, biting | Trust vs. mistrust | *Positive*: Feelings of trust from environmental support<br>*Negative*: Fear and concern regarding others |
| **12–18 months to 3 years** | Anal | Gratification from expelling and withholding feces; coming to terms with society's controls relating to toilet training | Autonomy vs. shame and doubt | *Positive*: Self-sufficiency if exploration is encouraged<br>*Negative*: Doubts about self, lack of independence |
| **3 to 5–6 years** | Phallic | Interest in the genitals; coming to terms with Oedipal conflict, leading to identification with same-sex parent | Initiative vs. guilt | *Positive*: Discovery of ways to initiate actions<br>*Negative*: Guilt from actions and thoughts |
| **5–6 years to adolescence** | Latency | Sexual concerns largely unimportant | Industry vs. inferiority | *Positive*: Development of sense of competence<br>*Negative*: Feelings of inferiority, no sense of mastery |
| **Adolescence to adulthood (Freud) Adolescence (Erikson)** | Genital | Reemergence of sexual interests and establishment of mature sexual relationships | Identity vs. role diffusion | *Positive*: Awareness of uniqueness of self, knowledge of role to be followed<br>*Negative*: Inability to identify appropriate roles in life |
| **Early adulthood (Erikson)** | | | Intimacy vs. isolation | *Positive*: Development of loving, sexual relationships and close friendships<br>*Negative*: Fear of relationships with others |
| **Middle adulthood (Erikson)** | | | Generativity vs. stagnation | *Positive*: Sense of contribution to continuity of life<br>*Negative*: Trivialization of one's activities |
| **Late adulthood (Erikson)** | | | Ego–integrity vs. despair | *Positive*: Sense of unity in life's accomplishments<br>*Negative*: Regret over lost opportunities of life |

another, as well as in our knowledge and understanding of ourselves as members of society (Dunkel, Kim, & Papini, 2012; Wilson et al., 2013; Knight, 2017).

Erikson's theory suggests that developmental change occurs throughout our lives in eight distinct stages (see Table 2.1). The stages emerge in a fixed pattern and are similar for all people.

Erikson argued that each stage presents a crisis or conflict that the individual must resolve. Although no crisis is ever fully resolved, making life increasingly complicated, the individual must at least address the crisis of each stage sufficiently to deal with demands made during the next stage of development.

Unlike Freud, who regarded development as relatively complete by adolescence, Erikson suggested that growth and change continue throughout the life span. For instance, Erikson proposed that during middle adulthood, people pass through the *generativity-versus-stagnation stage*, in which their contributions to family, community, and society can produce either positive feelings about the continuity of life or a sense of stagnation and disappointment about what they are passing on to future generations (De St. Aubin, McAdams, & Kim, 2004).

**ASSESSING THE PSYCHODYNAMIC PERSPECTIVE.** It is hard for us to grasp the full significance of psychodynamic theories, represented by Freud's psychoanalytic theory and Erikson's theory of psychosocial development. Freud's introduction of the notion that unconscious influences affect behavior was a monumental accomplishment, and that it seems at all reasonable to us shows how extensively the idea of the unconscious has pervaded thinking in Western cultures. In fact, work by contemporary researchers studying memory and learning suggests that we carry with us memories—of which we are not consciously aware—that have a significant impact on our behavior. The example of Marisol, who was in a car accident when she was a baby, shows one application of psychodynamically based thinking and research.

Some of the most basic principles of Freud's psychoanalytic theory have been called into question, however, because they have not been validated by subsequent research. In particular, the notion that people pass through stages in childhood that determine their adult personalities has little definitive research support. In addition, because much of Freud's theory was based on a limited population of upper-middle-class Austrians living during a strict, puritanical era, its application to broad, multicultural populations is questionable. Finally, because Freud's theory focuses primarily on male development, it has been criticized as sexist and may be interpreted as devaluing women. For such reasons, many developmentalists question Freud's theory (Schachter, 2005; Balsam, 2013; O'Neil & Denke, 2016).

Erikson's view that development continues throughout the life span is an important one, and it influenced a good deal of thinking about how developmental change unfolds throughout life. However, the theory is vague and hard to test in a rigorous manner. Furthermore, like Freud's theory, it focuses more on men's than women's development. In sum, although the psychodynamic perspective provides reasonably good descriptions of past behavior, its predictions of future behavior are imprecise (Zauszniewski & Martin, 1999; De St. Aubin, McAdams, & Kim, 2004).

## The Behavioral Perspective: Focusing on Observable Behavior

**LO 2.2  Describe the basic concepts of the behavioral perspective.**

*When Elissa Sheehan was 3, a large dog bit her, and she needed dozens of stitches and several operations. After the event, she broke into a sweat whenever she saw a dog and in fact never enjoyed being around any pet.*

To a child development specialist using the behavioral perspective, the explanation for Elissa's behavior is straightforward: She has a learned fear of dogs. Rather than looking inside the organism at unconscious processes, the **behavioral perspective** suggests that the keys to understanding development are observable behavior and outside stimuli in the environment. If we know the stimuli, we can predict the behavior. In this respect, the behavioral perspective reflects the view that nurture is more important to development than nature.

Behavioral theories reject the notion that people universally pass through a series of stages. Instead, people are assumed to be affected by the environmental stimuli to which they happen to be exposed. Developmental patterns, then, are personal, reflecting a particular set of environmental stimuli, and behavior is the result of continuing exposure to specific factors in the environment. Furthermore, developmental change is viewed in quantitative, rather than qualitative, terms. For instance, behavioral theories hold that advances in problem-solving capabilities as children age are largely a result of greater mental *capacities* rather than changes in the *kind* of thinking that children are able to bring to bear on a problem.

### CLASSICAL CONDITIONING: STIMULUS SUBSTITUTION.

*"Give me a dozen healthy infants, well-formed, and my own specified world to bring them up in and I'll guarantee to take any one at random and train him to become any type of specialist I might select—doctor, lawyer, artist, merchant-chief, and yes, even beggar-man and thief, regardless of his talents, penchants, tendencies, abilities ..."* (J. B. Watson, 1925, p. 14).

With these words, John B. Watson, one of the first American psychologists to advocate a behavioral approach, summed up the behavioral perspective. Watson, who lived from 1878 to 1958, believed strongly that we could gain a full understanding of development by carefully studying the stimuli that make up the environment. In fact, he argued that by effectively controlling a person's environment, it was possible to produce virtually any behavior.

**behavioral perspective** The approach to the study of development that suggests that the keys to understanding development are observable behavior and outside stimuli in the environment

John B. Watson

B. F. Skinner

As we will consider further in Chapter 4, **classical conditioning** occurs when an organism learns to respond in a particular way to a neutral stimulus that normally does not evoke that type of response. For instance, if a dog is repeatedly exposed to the pairing of the sound of a bell and the presentation of meat, it may learn to react to the bell alone in the same way it reacts to the meat—by salivating and wagging its tail with excitement. Dogs don't typically respond to bells in this way; the behavior is a result of conditioning, a form of learning in which the response associated with one stimulus (food) comes to be connected to another—in this case, the bell.

The same process of classical conditioning explains how we learn emotional responses. In the case of dog-bite victim Elissa Sheehan, for instance, Watson would say that one stimulus has been substituted for another: Elissa's unpleasant experience with a particular dog (the initial stimulus) has been transferred to other dogs and to pets in general.

OPERANT CONDITIONING. In addition to classical conditioning, other types of learning are found within the behavioral perspective. For example, **operant conditioning** is a form of learning in which a voluntary response is strengthened or weakened by its association with positive or negative consequences. It differs from classical conditioning in that the response being conditioned is voluntary and purposeful rather than automatic (such as salivating).

In operant conditioning, formulated and championed by psychologist B. F. Skinner (1904–1990), individuals learn to act deliberately on their environments

in order to bring about desired consequences (Skinner, 1957). In a sense, then, children *operate* on their environments to bring about a desired state of affairs.

Whether children will seek to repeat a behavior depends on whether it is followed by reinforcement. *Reinforcement* is the process by which a stimulus is provided that increases the probability that a preceding behavior will be repeated. Hence, a student is apt to work harder in school if he or she receives good grades, workers are likely to labor harder at their jobs if their efforts are tied to pay increases, and people are more apt to buy lottery tickets if they are reinforced by winning at least occasionally. In addition, *punishment*, the introduction of an unpleasant or painful stimulus or the removal of a desirable stimulus, will decrease the probability that a preceding behavior will occur in the future.

Behavior that is reinforced is more likely to be repeated in the future, while behavior that receives no reinforcement or is punished is likely to be discontinued, or in the language of operant conditioning, *extinguished*. Principles of operant conditioning are

---

**classical conditioning** A type of learning in which an organism responds in a particular way to a neutral stimulus that normally does not bring about that type of response

**operant conditioning** A form of learning in which a voluntary response is strengthened or weakened, depending on its association with positive or negative consequences used in **behavior modification**, a formal technique for promoting the frequency of desirable behaviors and decreasing the incidence of unwanted ones. Behavior modification has been used in a variety of situations, ranging from teaching severely intellectually disabled people the rudiments of language to helping people stick to diets (Wupperman et al., 2012; Jensen, Ward, & Balsam, 2013; Miltenberger, 2016).

**SOCIAL-COGNITIVE LEARNING THEORY: LEARNING THROUGH IMITATION.** A 5-year-old boy seriously injures his 22-month-old cousin while imitating a violent wrestling move he had seen on television. Although the infant sustained spinal cord injuries, he improved and was discharged 5 weeks after his hospital admission. (Reuters Health eLine, 2002; Ray & Heyes, 2011).

Cause and effect? We can't know for sure, but it certainly seems possible, especially looking at the situation from the perspective of **social-cognitive learning theory**, an approach that emphasizes learning by observing the behavior of another person, called a *model* (Bandura, 1994, 2002). According to developmental psychologist Albert Bandura and colleagues, a significant amount of learning is explained this way.

This approach purports that behavior is learned through observation. We don't need to experience the consequences of a behavior ourselves to learn it. Social-cognitive learning theory holds that when we see the behavior of a model being rewarded, we are likely to imitate that behavior. For instance, in one classic experiment, children who were afraid of dogs were exposed to a model, nicknamed the "Fearless Peer," who was seen playing happily with a dog (Bandura, Grusec, & Menlove, 1967). After exposure, the children who previously had been afraid were more likely to approach a strange dog than children who had not seen the model.

**ASSESSING THE BEHAVIORAL PERSPECTIVE.** Research based on the behavioral perspective has made significant contributions, ranging from techniques for educating children with severe intellectual disabilities to identifying procedures for curbing aggression. At the same time, some controversies surround the behavioral perspective. For example, although they are part of the same general behavioral perspective, classical and operant conditioning, on the one hand, and social learning theory, on the other, disagree in some basic ways. Both classical and operant conditioning consider learning in terms of external stimuli and responses, in which the only important factors are the observable features of the environment. In such an analysis, people and other organisms are like inanimate "black boxes"; nothing that occurs inside the box is understood—nor is much cared about, for that matter.

> **From an educator's perspective:** How might the kind of social learning that comes from viewing television influence children's behavior?

To social learning theorists, such an analysis is an oversimplification. They argue that what makes people different from rats and pigeons is mental activity, in the form of thoughts and expectations. A full understanding of people's development, they maintain, cannot occur without moving beyond external stimuli and responses.

In many ways, social learning theory has come to predominate in recent decades over classical and operant conditioning theories. In fact, another perspective that focuses explicitly on internal mental activity has become enormously influential: the cognitive approach, which we consider next.

# The Cognitive Perspective: Examining the Roots of Understanding

**LO 2.3 Describe the basic concepts of the cognitive perspective.**

> *When 3-year-old Jake is asked why it sometimes rains, he answers, "So the flowers can grow." When his 11-year-old sister Lila is asked the same question, she responds, "Because of evaporation from the surface of the earth." And when their cousin Ajima, who is studying meteorology in her high school science class, considers the same question, her extended answer includes a discussion of cumulonimbus clouds, the Coriolis effect, and synoptic charts.*

To a developmental theorist using the cognitive perspective, the difference in the sophistication of the

---

**behavior modification** A formal technique for promoting the frequency of desirable behaviors and decreasing the incidence of unwanted ones

**social-cognitive learning theory** An approach to the study of development that emphasizes learning by observing the behavior of another person, called a model

answers is evidence of a different degree of knowledge and understanding, or cognition. The **cognitive perspective** focuses on the processes that allow people to know, understand, and think about the world.

The cognitive perspective emphasizes how people internally represent the environment around them. By using this perspective, developmental researchers hope to understand how children and adults process information and how their ways of thinking and understanding affect their behavior. They also seek to learn how cognitive abilities change as people develop, the degree to which cognitive development represents quantitative and qualitative growth in intellectual abilities, and how different cognitive abilities are related to one another.

**PIAGET'S THEORY OF COGNITIVE DEVELOPMENT.** No single person has had a greater impact on the study of cognitive development than Jean Piaget. A Swiss psychologist who lived from 1896 to 1980, Piaget proposed that all people passed in a fixed sequence through a series of universal stages of cognitive development (summarized in Table 2.2). He suggested that not only did the quantity of information increase in each stage, but the quality of knowledge and understanding changed as well. His focus was on the change in cognition that occurred as children moved from one stage to the next (Piaget, 1962, 1983).

We'll consider Piaget's theory in detail beginning in Chapter 6, but we can get a broad sense of it now by looking at some of its main features. Piaget suggested that human thinking is arranged into *schemas*, organized mental patterns that represent behaviors and actions. In infants, such schemas represent concrete behavior—a schema for sucking, for reaching, and for each separate behavior. In older children, the schemas become more sophisticated and abstract. Schemas are like intellectual computer software that

directs and determines how data from the world are looked at and handled (Parker, 2005).

Piaget suggested that children's *adaptation*—his term for the way in which children respond and adjust to new information—can be explained by two basic principles. *Assimilation* is the process by which people understand an experience in terms of their current stage of cognitive development and way of thinking. In contrast, *accommodation* refers to changes in existing ways of thinking in response to encounters with new stimuli or events.

Assimilation occurs when people use their current ways of thinking about and understanding the world to perceive and understand a new experience. For example, a young child who has not yet learned to count will look at two rows of buttons, each containing the same number of buttons, and say that a row in which the buttons are closely spaced together has fewer buttons in it than a row in which the buttons are more spread out. The experience of counting buttons, then, is assimilated to already existing schemas that contain the principle "bigger is more."

Later, however, when the child is older and has had sufficient exposure to new experiences, the content of the schema will undergo change. In understanding that the quantity of buttons is identical whether they are spread out or closely spaced, the child has *accommodated* to the experience. Assimilation and accommodation work in tandem to bring about cognitive development.

**ASSESSING PIAGET'S THEORY.** Piaget has profoundly influenced our understanding of cognitive development and is one of the towering figures in child development. He provided masterful descriptions of

**cognitive perspective** The approach to the study of development that focuses on the processes that allow people to know, understand, and think about the world

**Table 2.2** Piaget's Stages of Cognitive Development

| Cognitive Stage | Approximate Age Range | Major Characteristics |
| --- | --- | --- |
| Sensorimotor | Birth–2 years | Development of object permanence (idea that people/objects exist even when they can't be seen); development of motor skills; little or no capacity for symbolic representation |
| Preoperational | 2–7 years | Development of language and symbolic thinking; egocentric thinking |
| Concrete operational | 7–12 years | Development of conservation (idea that quantity is unrelated to physical appearance); mastery of concept of reversibility |
| Formal operational | 12 years–adulthood | Development of logical and abstract thinking |

how intellectual growth proceeds during childhood—descriptions that have stood the test of literally thousands of investigations. By and large, Piaget's broad view of the sequence of cognitive development is accurate; however, the specifics of the theory, particularly in terms of change in cognitive capabilities over time, have been called into question. For instance, some cognitive skills clearly emerge earlier than Piaget suggested. Furthermore, the universality of Piaget's stages has been disputed. A growing amount of evidence suggests that the emergence of particular cognitive skills occurs according to a different timetable in non-Western cultures. And in every culture, some people never seem to reach Piaget's highest level of cognitive sophistication: formal, logical thought (Genovese, 2006; De Jesus-Zayas, Buigas, & Denney, 2012; Siegler, 2016).

Ultimately, the greatest criticism leveled at the Piagetian perspective is that cognitive development is not necessarily as discontinuous as Piaget's stage theory suggests. Remember that Piaget argued that growth proceeds in four distinct stages in which the quality of cognition differs from one stage to the next; however, many developmental researchers argue that growth is considerably more continuous. These critics have suggested an alternative perspective, known as the information-processing approach, which focuses on the processes that underlie learning, memory, and thinking throughout the life span.

**INFORMATION-PROCESSING APPROACHES.** Information-processing approaches have become an important alternative to Piagetian approaches. **Information-processing approaches** to cognitive development seek to identify the ways individuals take in, use, and store information.

Information-processing approaches grew out of developments in the electronic processing of information, particularly as carried out by computers. They assume that even complex behavior such as learning, remembering, categorizing, and thinking can be broken down into a series of individual, specific steps.

Like computers, children are assumed by information-processing approaches to have limited capacity for processing information. As they develop, however, they employ increasingly sophisticated strategies that allow them to process information more efficiently.

In stark contrast to Piaget's view that thinking undergoes qualitative advances as children age, information-processing approaches assume that development is marked more by quantitative advances. Our capacity to handle information changes with age, as does our processing speed and efficiency. Furthermore, information-processing approaches suggest that as we age, we are better able to control the nature of processing, and that we can change the strategies we choose to process information.

An information-processing approach that builds on Piaget's research is known as neo-Piagetian theory. In contrast to Piaget's original work, which viewed cognition as a single system of increasingly sophisticated general cognitive abilities, *neo-Piagetian theory* considers cognition as being made up of different types of individual skills. Using the terminology of information-processing approaches, neo-Piagetian theory suggests that cognitive development proceeds quickly in certain areas and more slowly in others. For example, reading ability and the skills needed to recall stories may progress sooner than the sorts of abstract computational abilities used in algebra or trigonometry. Furthermore, neo-Piagetian theorists believe that experience plays a greater role than traditional Piagetian approaches in advancing cognitive development (Case, Demetriou, & Platsidou, 2001; Yan & Fischer, 2002; Loewen, 2006).

**ASSESSING INFORMATION-PROCESSING APPROACHES.** As we'll see in future chapters, information-processing approaches have become a central part of our understanding of development. At the same time, they do not offer a complete explanation for behavior. For example, information-processing approaches have paid little attention to behavior such as creativity, in which the most profound ideas often are developed in a seemingly illogical, nonlinear manner. In addition, they do not take into account the social context in which development takes place. That's one of the reasons why theories emphasizing the social and cultural aspects of development have become increasingly popular—as we discuss next.

**COGNITIVE NEUROSCIENCE APPROACHES.** One of the most recent additions to the array of approaches taken by child developmentalists, **cognitive neuroscience approaches** look at cognitive development through

---

**information-processing approaches** Approaches to the study of cognitive development that seek to identify the ways individuals take in, use, and store information

**cognitive neuroscience approaches** Approaches to the study of cognitive development that focus on how brain processes are related to cognitive activity

Neuroscientists have found evidence that the brains of children with autism spectrum disorder are somewhat larger than those of children without the disorder. This finding might help identify cases of autism spectrum disorder early, allowing for more effective intervention and treatment.

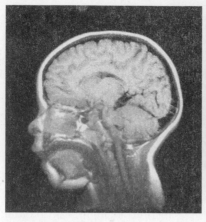
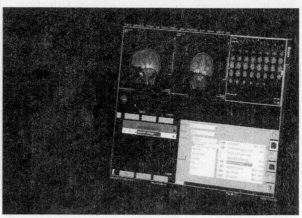

the lens of brain processes. Like other cognitive perspectives, cognitive neuroscience approaches consider internal mental processes, but they focus specifically on the neurological activity that underlies thinking, problem solving, and other cognitive behavior.

Cognitive neuroscientists seek to identify actual locations and functions within the brain that are related to different types of cognitive activity, rather than simply assuming that there are hypothetical or theoretical cognitive structures related to thinking. For example, using sophisticated brain scanning techniques, cognitive neuroscientists have demonstrated that thinking about the meaning of a word activates different areas of the brain than thinking about how the word sounds when spoken.

The work of cognitive neuroscientists is also providing clues to the cause of *autism spectrum disorder*, a major developmental disability that can produce profound language deficits and self-injurious behavior in young children. For example, neuroscientists have found that the brains of children with the disorder show explosive, dramatic growth in the first year of life, making their heads significantly larger than those of children without the disorder. By identifying children with the disorder very early in their lives, health care practitioners can provide crucial early intervention (Lewis & Elman, 2008; Guthrie et al., 2013; Grant, 2017).

Cognitive neuroscience approaches are also on the forefront of cutting-edge research that has identified specific genes that are associated with disorders ranging from physical problems such as breast cancer to psychological disorders such as schizophrenia (Ranganath, Minzenberg, & Ragland, 2008; Christoff et al., 2011; Rodnitzky, 2012). Identifying the genes that make one vulnerable to such disorders is the first step in genetic engineering, in which gene therapy can reduce or even prevent the disorder from occurring.

**ASSESSING COGNITIVE NEUROSCIENCE APPROACHES.** Cognitive neuroscience approaches represent a new frontier in child and adolescent development. Using sophisticated measurement techniques, many of them developed only in the past few years, cognitive neuroscientists are able to peer into the inner functioning of the brain. Advances in our understanding of genetics also have opened a new window into both normal and abnormal development and have suggested a variety of treatments for abnormalities.

Critics of the cognitive neuroscience approach have suggested that it sometimes provides a better *description* than *explanation* of developmental phenomena. For instance, finding that children with autism spectrum disorder have larger brains than those without the disorder does not explain why their brains became larger—that's a question that remains to be answered. Still, such work offers important clues to appropriate treatments and can ultimately lead to a full understanding of a range of developmental phenomena.

# The Contextual Perspective: Taking a Broad Approach to Development

**LO 2.4  Describe the basic concepts of the contextual perspective.**

Although child developmentalists often consider the course of development separately in terms of physical, cognitive, and personality and social factors, such

## Figure 2.1 Bronfenbrenner's Approach to Development

Urie Bronfenbrenner's bioecological approach to development offers five levels of the environment that simultaneously influence individuals: microsystem, mesosystem, exosystem, macrosystem, and chronosystem.

**SOURCE:** Adapted from Bronfenbrenner & Morris, "The Ecology of Developmental Processes," in W. Damon, ed., Handbook of Child Psychology, Vol I, TTL, 5th ed. Copyright © 1998 John Wiley & Sons, Inc.

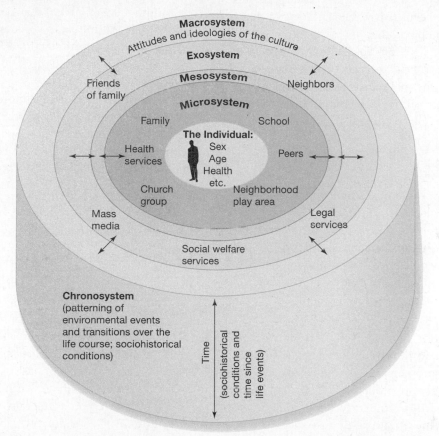

a categorization has one serious drawback: In the real world, none of these broad influences occurs in isolation from any other. Instead, there is a constant, ongoing interaction between the different types of influence.

The **contextual perspective** considers the relationship between individuals and their physical, cognitive, personality, and social worlds. It suggests that a child's unique development cannot be properly viewed without seeing the child enmeshed within a complex social and cultural context. We'll consider two major theories that fall into this category: Bronfenbrenner's bioecological approach and Vygotsky's sociocultural theory.

**THE BIOECOLOGICAL APPROACH TO DEVELOPMENT.** In acknowledging the problem with traditional approaches to life span development, psychologist Urie Bronfenbrenner (1989, 2000, 2002) has proposed an alternative perspective, called the **bioecological approach**, which suggests that five levels

of the environment simultaneously influence individuals. Bronfenbrenner notes that we cannot fully understand development without considering how a person is influenced by each of these levels (illustrated in Figure 2.1).

- The *microsystem* is the everyday, immediate environment in which children lead their daily lives. Homes, caregivers, friends, and teachers all are influences that are part of the microsystem. But the child is not just a passive recipient of these influences. Instead, children actively help construct

**contextual perspective** The perspective that considers the relationship between individuals and their physical, cognitive, personality, social, and physical worlds

**bioecological approach** The perspective that suggests that different levels of the environment simultaneously influence every biological organism

the microsystem, shaping the immediate world in which they live. The microsystem is the level at which most traditional work in child development has been directed.

- The *mesosystem* provides connections among the various aspects of the microsystem. Like links in a chain, the mesosystem binds children to parents, students to teachers, employees to bosses, friends to friends. It acknowledges the direct and indirect influences that bind us to one another, such as those that affect a mother or father who has a bad day at the office and then is short-tempered with her or his son or daughter at home.

- The *exosystem* represents broader influences, encompassing societal institutions such as local government, the community, schools, places of worship, and the local media. Each of these larger institutions of society can have an immediate, and major, impact on personal development, and each affects how the microsystem and mesosystem operate. For example, the quality of a school will affect a child's cognitive development and potentially can have long-term consequences.

- The *macrosystem* represents the larger cultural influences on an individual. Society in general, types of governments, religious and political value systems, and other broad, encompassing factors are parts of the macrosystem. For example, the value a culture or society places on education or the family will affect the values of the people who live in that society. Children are part of a broader culture (such as Western culture) and are influenced by their membership in a particular subculture (for instance, being part of the Mexican American subculture).

- Finally, the *chronosystem* underlies each of the previous systems. It involves the way the passage of time, including historical events (such as the terrorist attacks in September 2001) and more gradual historical changes (such as changes in the number of women who work outside of the home), affects children's development.

The bioecological approach emphasizes the *interconnectedness of the influences on development*. Because the various levels are related to one another, a change in one part of the system affects other parts of the system. For instance, a parent's loss of a job (involving the mesosystem) has an impact on a child's microsystem.

Conversely, changes on one environmental level may make little difference if other levels are not also changed. For example, improving the school environment may have a negligible effect on academic performance if children receive little support for academic success at home. Similarly, the bioecological approach illustrates that the influences among different family members are multidirectional. Parents don't just affect their child's behavior—the child also influences the parents' behavior.

Finally, the bioecological approach stresses the importance of broad cultural factors that affect development. Researchers in child development increasingly look at how membership in cultural and subcultural groups influences behavior.

**THE INFLUENCE OF CULTURE.** Consider, for instance, whether you agree that children should be taught that their classmates' assistance is indispensable to getting good grades in school or that they should definitely plan to continue their fathers' businesses or that children should follow their parents' advice in determining their career plans. If you have been raised in the most widespread North American culture, you would likely disagree with all three statements because they violate the premises of *individualism*, the dominant Western philosophy that emphasizes personal identity, uniqueness, freedom, and the worth of the individual.

By contrast, if you were raised in a traditional Asian culture, it is considerably more likely that you will agree with the three statements. Why? The statements reflect the value orientation known as collectivism, the notion that the well-being of the group is more important than that of the individual. People raised in collectivistic cultures tend to emphasize the welfare of the groups to which they belong, sometimes even at the expense of their own personal well-being.

The individualism–collectivism spectrum is one of several dimensions along which cultures differ, and it illustrates differences in the cultural contexts in which people operate. Such broad cultural values play an important role in shaping the ways people view the world and behave (Shavitt, Torelli, & Riemer, 2011; Marcus & Le, 2013; Cheung et al., 2016).

**ASSESSING THE BIOECOLOGICAL APPROACH.** Although Bronfenbrenner considers biological influences an important component of the bioecological approach, ecological influences are central to the theory. Some critics argue that the perspective pays insufficient attention to biological factors. Still, the bioecological approach is of considerable importance to child development, suggesting as it does the multiple levels at which the environment affects children's development.

**VYGOTSKY'S SOCIOCULTURAL THEORY.** To Russian developmentalist Lev Semenovich Vygotsky, a full understanding of development was impossible without taking into account the culture in which children develop. Vygotsky's **sociocultural theory** emphasizes how cognitive development proceeds as a result of social interactions between members of a culture (Vygotsky, 1979, 1926/1997; Winsler, 2003; Edwards, 2005; Göncü, 2012).

Vygotsky argued that children's understanding of the world is acquired through their problem-solving interactions with adults and other children. As children play and cooperate with others, they learn what is important in their society and, at the same time, advance cognitively in their understanding of the world. Consequently, to understand the course of development, we must consider what is meaningful to members of a given culture.

More than most other theories, sociocultural theory emphasizes that development is a *reciprocal transaction* between a child and the people in his or her environment. Vygotsky believed that people and settings influence the child, who in turn influences the people and settings. This pattern continues in an endless loop, with children being both recipients of socialization influences and sources of influence. For example, a child raised with his or her extended family nearby will grow up with a different sense of family life than a child whose relatives live a considerable distance away. Those relatives, too, are affected by that situation and that child, depending upon how close and frequent their contact is with the child.

Theorists who built on Vygotsky's work have used the example of *scaffolds*, the temporary platforms used by construction workers when building a structure, to describe how children learn. Scaffolding is the temporary support that teachers, parents, and others provide children as they are learning a task. As children become increasingly competent and master a task, the scaffolding can be withdrawn, allowing children to carry out the task on their own (Lowe et al., 2013; Peralta et al., 2013; Dahl et al., 2017).

**ASSESSING VYGOTSKY'S THEORY.** Sociocultural theory has become increasingly influential, despite

According to Vygotsky, through play and cooperation with others, children can develop cognitively in their understanding of the world and learn what is important in society.

Vygotsky's death more than eight decades ago. The reason is the growing acknowledgment of the central importance of cultural factors in development. Children do not develop in a cultural vacuum. Instead, their attention is directed by society to certain areas, and, as a consequence, they develop particular skills that are an outcome of their cultural environment. Vygotsky was one of the first developmentalists to recognize and acknowledge the importance of culture, and—as today's society becomes increasingly multicultural—sociocultural theory is helping us to understand the rich and varied influences that shape development (Koshmanova, 2007; Rogan, 2007; van der Veer & Yasnitsky, 2016).

# Evolutionary Perspectives: Our Ancestors' Contributions to Behavior

**LO 2.5  Describe the basic concepts of the evolutionary perspective.**

One increasingly influential approach is the evolutionary perspective, the final developmental perspective that we will consider. The **evolutionary perspective** seeks to identify behavior that is the result of our

---

**sociocultural theory** An approach that emphasizes how cognitive development proceeds as a result of social interactions between members of a culture

**evolutionary perspective** The theory that seeks to identify behavior that is the result of our genetic inheritance from our ancestors

Konrad Lorenz, seen here with geese who from their birth have followed him, considered the ways in which behavior reflects inborn genetic patterns.

genetic inheritance from our ancestors. It focuses on how genetics and environmental factors combine to influence behavior (Bjorklund and Ellis, 2005; Goetz & Shackelford, 2006; Tomasello, 2011).

Evolutionary approaches have grown out of the groundbreaking work of Charles Darwin. In 1859, Darwin argued in his book *On the Origin of Species* that a process of natural selection creates traits in a species that are adaptive to its environment. Using Darwin's arguments, evolutionary approaches contend that our genetic inheritance determines not only such physical traits as skin and eye color, but certain personality traits and social behaviors as well. For instance, some evolutionary developmentalists suggest that behaviors such as shyness and jealousy are produced in part by genetic causes, presumably because they helped in increasing survival rates of humans' ancient relatives (Easton, Schipper, & Shackelford, 2007; Buss, 2012; Geary & Berch, 2016).

The evolutionary perspective draws heavily on the field of *ethology*, which examines the ways in which our biological makeup influences our behavior. A primary proponent of ethology was Konrad Lorenz (1903–1989), who discovered that newborn geese are genetically preprogrammed to become attached to the first moving object they see after birth. His work, which demonstrated the importance of biological determinants in influencing behavior patterns, ultimately led developmentalists to consider the ways in which human behavior might reflect inborn genetic patterns.

As we'll consider later in the chapter, the evolutionary perspective encompasses one of the fastest-growing areas within the field of life span development: behavioral genetics. *Behavioral genetics* studies the effects of heredity on behavior. Behavioral geneticists seek to understand how we might inherit certain behavioral traits and how the environment influences whether we actually display such traits. It also considers how genetic factors may produce psychological disorders such as schizophrenia (Li, 2003; Bjorklund & Ellis, 2005; Rembis, 2009; Maxson, 2013).

There is little argument among child developmentalists that Darwin's evolutionary theory provides an accurate description of basic genetic processes, and the evolutionary perspective is increasingly visible in the field of life span development. However, applications of the evolutionary perspective have been subjected to considerable criticism.

Some developmentalists are concerned that because of its focus on genetic and biological aspects of behavior, the evolutionary perspective pays insufficient attention to the environmental and social factors involved in producing children's and adults' behavior. Other critics argue that there is no good way to experimentally test theories derived from the evolutionary approach because they all happened so long ago. For example, it is one thing to say that jealousy helped individuals to survive more effectively—and quite another thing to prove it. Still, the evolutionary approach has stimulated a significant amount of research on how our biological inheritance at least partially influences our traits and behaviors (Bjorklund, 2006; Baptista et al., 2008; Barbaro et al., 2017).

**Table 2.3** Major Perspectives on Child Development

| Perspective | Key Ideas About Human Behavior and Development | Major Proponents | Example |
|---|---|---|---|
| Psychodynamic | Behavior throughout life is motivated by inner, unconscious forces, stemming from childhood, over which we have little control. | Sigmund Freud, Erik Erikson | This view might suggest that an adolescent who is overweight has a fixation in the oral stage of development. |
| Behavioral | Development can be understood through studying observable behavior and environmental stimuli. | John B. Watson, B. F. Skinner, Albert Bandura | In this perspective, an adolescent who is overweight might be seen as not being rewarded for good nutritional and exercise habits. |
| Cognitive | Emphasis is on how changes or growth in the ways people know, understand, and think about the world affect behavior. | Jean Piaget | This view might suggest that an adolescent who is overweight hasn't learned effective ways to stay at a healthy weight and doesn't value good nutrition. |
| Contextual | Behavior is determined by the relationship between individuals and their physical, cognitive, personality, social, and physical worlds. | Lev Vygotsky, Urie Bronfenbrenner | In this perspective, an adolescent may become overweight because of a family environment in which food and meals are unusually important and intertwined with family rituals. |
| Evolutionary | Behavior is the result of genetic inheritance from our ancestors; traits and behavior that are adaptive for promoting the survival of our species have been inherited through natural selection. | Konrad Lorenz; influenced by early work of Charles Darwin | This view might suggest that an adolescent might have a genetic tendency toward obesity because extra fat helped his or her ancestors to survive in times of famine. |

# Why "Which Perspective Is Right?" Is the Wrong Question

**LO 2.6** **Explain the value of applying multiple perspectives to child development.**

We have considered five major perspectives on development: psychodynamic, behavioral, cognitive, contextual, and evolutionary (summarized in Table 2.3). It would be natural to wonder which of them provides the most accurate account of child development.

For several reasons, this question is not entirely appropriate. For one thing, each perspective emphasizes somewhat different aspects of development. For instance, the psychodynamic approach emphasizes emotions, motivational conflicts, and unconscious determinants of behavior. In contrast, behavioral perspectives emphasize overt behavior, paying far more attention to what people *do* than to what goes on inside their heads, which is deemed largely irrelevant. The cognitive perspective takes quite the opposite tack, looking more at what people *think* than at what they do. Finally, while the contextual perspective focuses on the interaction of environmental influences, the evolutionary perspective concentrates on how inherited biological factors underlie development.

For example, a developmentalist using the psychodynamic approach might consider how the 9/11 terrorist attacks on the World Trade Center and Pentagon might affect children, unconsciously, for their entire life span. A cognitive approach might focus on how children perceived and came to interpret and understand the terrorism, while a contextual approach might consider what personality and social factors led the perpetrators to adopt terrorist tactics.

Clearly, each perspective is based on its own premises and focuses on different aspects of development. Furthermore, the same developmental phenomenon can be looked at from a number of perspectives simultaneously. In fact, some life span developmentalists use an *eclectic* approach, drawing on several perspectives at the same time.

As noted earlier, we can think of the different perspectives as analogous to a set of maps of the same general geographical area. One map may contain detailed depictions of roads; another map may show geographical features; another may show political subdivisions, such as cities, towns, and counties; and still another may highlight particular points of interest, such as scenic areas and historical landmarks. Each of the maps is accurate, but each provides a different point of view and way of thinking. Although no one map is "complete," by considering them together, we can come to a fuller understanding of the area.

In the same way, the various theoretical perspectives provide different ways of looking at development. Considering them together paints a fuller portrait of the myriad ways human beings change and grow over the course of their lives; however, not all theories and claims derived from the various perspectives are accurate. How do we choose among competing explanations? The answer is *research*, which we consider in the final part of this chapter.

# The Scientific Method and Research

*The Greek historian Herodotus wrote of an experiment conducted by Psamtik, the King of Egypt in the 7th century B.C. Psamtik was eager to prove a cherished Egyptian belief, that his people were the oldest race on Earth. To test this notion, he developed a hypothesis: If a child was never exposed to the language of his elders, he would instinctively adopt the primal language of humanity—the original language of the first people. Psamtik was certain this would be Egyptian.*

*For his experiment, Psamtik entrusted two Egyptian infants to the care of a herdsman in an isolated area. They were to be well looked after, but not allowed to leave their cottage. And they were never to hear anyone speak a single word.*

*When Herodotus investigated the story, the priests of Hephaestus in Memphis told him that Psamtik's quest "was to know, after the indistinct babblings of infancy were over, what word the children would first articulate." Herodotus claims the experiment worked, but not as Psamtik had hoped. One day, when the children were 2 years old, they greeted the herdsman with the word "Becos!" The herdsman didn't know this word but when the children continued to use it, he contacted Psamtik. The king sent for the children who repeated the strange word to him. Psamtik did some research. Becos, it turned out, was "bread" in Phrygian. Psamtik had to conclude the Phrygians had preceded the Egyptians.*

With the perspective of several thousand years, we can easily see the shortcomings—both scientific and ethical—in Psamtik's approach. Yet his procedure represents an improvement over mere speculation and as such is sometimes regarded as the first developmental experiment in recorded history (Hunt, 1993).

**Figure 2.2** The Scientific Method

A cornerstone of research, the scientific method is used by psychologists as well as researchers from all other scientific disciplines.

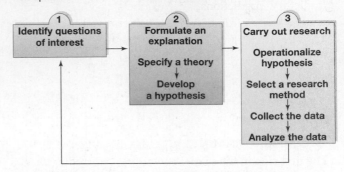

## Theories and Hypotheses: Posing Developmental Questions and Choosing a Research Strategy

**LO 2.7   Identify the principles of the scientific method and how they help answer questions about child development.**

Questions such as those raised by Psamtik lie at the heart of the study of child development. Is language innate? What are the effects of malnutrition on later intellectual performance? How do infants form relationships with their parents, and does participation in day care disrupt such relationships? Why are adolescents susceptible to peer pressure?

To answer such questions, specialists in child development rely on the scientific method. The **scientific method** is the process of posing and answering questions using careful, controlled techniques that include systematic, orderly observation and the collection of data. As shown in Figure 2.2, the scientific method involves three major steps: (1) identifying questions of interest, (2) formulating an explanation, and (3) carrying out research that either lends support to the explanation or refutes it.

Why use the scientific method, when our own experiences and common sense might seem to provide reasonable answers to questions? One important reason is that our own experience is limited; most of us encounter only a relatively small number of people

**scientific method** The process of posing and answering questions using careful, controlled techniques that include systematic, orderly observation and the collection of data

and situations, and drawing suppositions from that restricted sample may lead us to the wrong conclusion.

Similarly, although common sense may seem helpful, it turns out that common sense often makes contradictory predictions. For example, common sense tells us that "birds of a feather flock together." But it also says that "opposites attract." You see the problem: Because common sense is often contradictory, we can't rely on it to provide objective answers to questions. That's why developmental psychologists insist on using the controlled practices of the scientific method.

**THEORIES: FRAMING BROAD EXPLANATIONS.** The first step in the scientific method, the identification of questions of interest, begins when an observer puzzles over some aspect of behavior. Perhaps it is an infant who cries when she is picked up by a stranger, or a child who is doing poorly in school, or an adolescent who engages in risky behavior. Developmentalists, like all of us, start with questions about such everyday aspects of behavior, and—also like all of us—they seek to determine answers to these questions.

However, the way that developmental researchers try to find answers differentiates them from more casual observers. Developmental researchers formulate *theories*, broad explanations and predictions about phenomena of interest. Using one of the major perspectives that we discussed earlier, researchers develop more specific theories.

In fact, all of us formulate theories about development, based on our experience, folklore, and information from articles in magazines and newspapers. For instance, many people theorize that there is a crucial bonding period between parent and child immediately after birth, which is a necessary ingredient in forming a lasting parent–child relationship. Without such a bonding period, they assume, the parent–child relationship will be forever compromised.

Whenever we employ such explanations, we are developing our own theories, but the theories in child development are different. Whereas our own personal theories are built on unverified observations that are developed haphazardly, developmentalists' theories are more formal, based on a systematic integration of prior findings and theorizing. These theories allow developmental researchers to summarize and organize prior observations and to move beyond existing observations to draw deductions that may not be immediately apparent.

**HYPOTHESES: SPECIFYING TESTABLE PREDICTIONS.** Although the development of theories provides a general approach to a problem, it is only the first step. In order to determine the validity of a theory, developmental researchers must test it scientifically. To do that, they develop hypotheses based on their theories. A **hypothesis** is a prediction stated in a way that permits it to be tested.

For instance, someone who subscribes to the general theory that bonding is a crucial ingredient in the parent–child relationship might derive the more specific hypothesis that adopted children whose adoptive parents never had the chance to bond with them immediately after birth may ultimately have less secure relationships with their adoptive parents.

Others might derive other hypotheses, such as that effective bonding occurs only if it lasts for a certain length of time or that bonding affects the mother–child relationship but not the father–child relationship. (In case you're wondering, as we'll discuss in Chapter 4, these particular hypotheses have *not* been upheld; there are no long-term reactions to the separation of parent and child immediately after birth, even if the separation lasts several days, and there is no difference in the strength of bonds with mothers and bonds with fathers.)

**CHOOSING A RESEARCH STRATEGY: ANSWERING QUESTIONS.** Once researchers have formed a hypothesis, they must develop a strategy for testing its validity. The first step is to state the hypothesis in a way that will allow it to be tested. *Operationalization* is the process of translating a hypothesis into specific, testable procedures that can be measured and observed.

For example, a researcher interested in testing the hypothesis that "being evaluated leads to anxiety" might operationalize "being evaluated" as a teacher's giving a grade to a student or in terms of a child's commenting on a friend's athletic skills. Similarly, "anxiety" could be operationalized in terms of responses on a questionnaire or as measurements of biological reactions by an electronic instrument.

The choice of how to operationalize a variable often reflects the kind of research that is to be conducted. There are two major categories of research:

---

**hypothesis** A prediction stated in a way that permits it to be tested; researchers use a wide range of procedures to study human development

correlational research and experimental research. **Correlational research** seeks to identify whether an association or relationship between two factors exists. As we'll see, correlational research cannot be used to determine whether one factor causes changes in the other. For instance, correlational research could tell us if there is an association between the number of minutes a mother and her newborn child are together immediately after birth and the quality of the mother–child relationship when the child reaches 2 years of age. Such correlational research indicates whether the two factors are *associated* or *related* to one another but not whether the initial contact caused the relationship to develop in a particular way (Schutt, 2001).

In contrast, **experimental research** is designed to discover *causal* relationships among various factors. In experimental research, researchers deliberately introduce a change in a carefully structured situation in order to see the consequences of that change. For instance, a researcher performing an experiment might vary the number of minutes that mothers and children interact immediately following birth in an attempt to see whether the amount of bonding time affects the mother–child relationship.

Because experimental research is able to answer questions of causality, it represents the heart of developmental research. Unfortunately, some research questions cannot be answered through experiments, for either technical or ethical reasons (for example, it would be unethical to design an experiment in which a group of infants was offered no chance to bond with a caregiver). In fact, a great deal of pioneering developmental research—such as that conducted by Piaget

Researchers use a wide range of procedures to study human development.

and Vygotsky—employed correlational techniques. Consequently, correlational research remains an important tool in the developmental researcher's toolbox.

## Correlational Studies

**LO 2.8** Summarize the major characteristics of correlational studies.

As we've noted, correlational research examines the relationship between two variables to determine whether they are associated, or *correlated*. For instance, researchers interested in the relationship between televised aggression and subsequent behavior have found that children who watch a substantial amount of aggression on television—murders, crime, shootings, and the like—tend to be more aggressive than those who watch only a little. In other words, as we'll discuss in greater detail in Chapter 10, viewing of aggression and actual aggression are strongly associated, or correlated, with each other (Feshbach & Tangney, 2008; Qian, Zhang, & Wang, 2013; Coyne, 2016).

But does this mean we can conclude that the viewing of televised aggression *causes* the more aggressive behavior of the viewers? Not at all. Consider some of the other possibilities: It might be that being aggressive in the first place makes children more likely to choose to watch violent programs. In such a case, it is the aggressive tendency that causes the viewing behavior, not the other way around.

Or consider another possibility. Suppose that children who are raised in poverty are more likely than those raised in more affluent settings to behave aggressively *and* to watch higher levels of aggressive television. In this case, socioeconomic status causes *both* the aggressive behavior and the television viewing. (The various possibilities are illustrated in Figure 2.3.)

In short, finding that two variables are correlated proves nothing about causality. Although the variables *may* be linked causally, it may also be the case that changes in one variable do *not* cause the other variable to change.

Nevertheless, correlational studies can provide important information. For instance, as we'll see in

**correlational research** Research that seeks to identify whether an association or relationship between two factors exists

**experimental research** Research designed to discover causal relationships between various factors

## Figure 2.3 Finding a Correlation

Finding a correlation between two factors does not imply that one factor causes the other factor to vary. For instance, suppose that a study found that viewing television programs with high levels of aggression is correlated with actual aggression in children. The correlation might reflect at least three possibilities: (a) watching television programs containing high levels of aggression causes aggression in viewers; (b) children who behave aggressively choose to watch television programs with high levels of aggression; or (c) some third factor, such as a child's socioeconomic status, leads to both high viewer aggression and choosing to watch television programs with high levels of aggression.

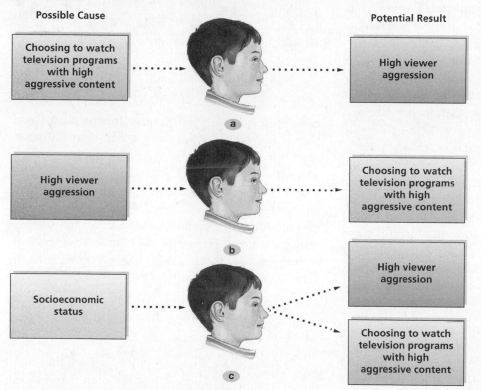

later chapters, we know from correlational studies that the closer the genetic link between two people, the more highly associated their intelligence. We have learned that the more parents speak to their young children, the more extensive the children's vocabularies. And we know from correlational studies that the better the nutrition that infants receive, the fewer cognitive and social problems they experience later (Hart, 2004; Colom, Lluis-Font, & Andrès-Pueyo, 2005; Robb, Richert, & Wartella, 2009).

**THE CORRELATION COEFFICIENT.** The strength and direction of a relationship between two factors is represented by a mathematical score, called a *correlation coefficient*, that ranges from +1.0 to –1.0. A positive correlation indicates that, as the value of one factor increases, it can be predicted that the value of the other will also increase. For instance, if we find that the more

calories children eat, the better their school performance becomes, and the fewer calories children eat, the worse their school performance becomes, then we have found a positive correlation. (Higher values of the factor "calories" are associated with higher values of the factor "school performance," and lower values of the factor "calories" are associated with lower values of the factor "school performance.") The correlation coefficient, then, would be indicated by a positive number, and the stronger the association between calories and school performance, the closer the number would be to +1.0.

In contrast, a correlation coefficient with a negative value informs us that, as the value of one factor increases, the value of the other factor declines. For example, suppose we found that the greater the number of hours adolescents spend texting, the worse their academic performance is. Such a finding would result in a negative correlation, ranging between 0 and –1.0. More texting is associated with lower performance, and less texting is associated with better performance. The stronger the association between texting and school performance, the closer the correlation coefficient will be to –1.0.

Finally, it is possible that two factors are unrelated to one another. For example, it is unlikely that we would find a correlation between school performance and shoe size. In this case, the lack of a relationship would be indicated by a correlation coefficient close to 0.

It is important to reiterate what we noted earlier: Even if the correlation coefficient involving two variables is very strong, there is no way we can know whether one factor causes another factor to vary. It simply means that the two factors are associated with one another in a predictable way.

**TYPES OF CORRELATIONAL STUDIES.** There are several types of correlational studies.

*Naturalistic observation.* **Naturalistic observation** is the observation of a naturally occurring behavior without intervention in the situation. For instance, an investigator who wishes to learn how often preschool children share toys with one another might observe a classroom over a 3-week period, recording how often the preschoolers spontaneously share with one another. The key point about naturalistic observation is that the investigator simply observes the children without interfering in any way (e.g., Fanger, Frankel, & Hazen, 2012; Snowden & Burghardt, 2017).

Naturalistic observation has the advantage of identifying what children do in their "natural habitat," and it offers an excellent way for researchers to develop questions of interest. But natural observation has a considerable drawback: Researchers are unable to exert control over factors of interest. For instance, in some cases, researchers might find so few naturally occurring instances of the behavior of interest that they are unable to draw any conclusions at all. In addition, children who know they are being watched may modify their behavior as a result of the observation. Consequently, their behavior may not be representative of how they would behave if they were not being watched.

*Ethnography and qualitative research.* Increasingly, naturalistic observation employs *ethnography*, a method borrowed from the field of anthropology and used to investigate cultural questions. In ethnography, a researcher's goal is to understand a culture's values and attitudes through careful, extended examination. Typically, researchers using ethnography act as participant observers, living for a period of weeks, months, or even years in another culture. By carefully observing everyday life and conducting in-depth interviews, researchers are able to obtain a deep understanding of the nature of life within another culture (Dyson, 2003; Blomberg & Karasti, 2013).

Ethnographic studies are an example of a broader category of research known as qualitative research. In *qualitative research*, researchers choose particular settings of interest and seek to carefully describe, in narrative fashion, what is occurring and why. Qualitative research can be used to generate hypotheses that can later be tested using more objective, quantitative methods.

Although ethnographic and qualitative studies provide a fine-grained view of behavior in particular

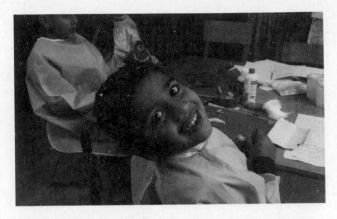

Naturalistic observation is used to examine a situation in its natural habitat without interference of any sort. What are some disadvantages of naturalistic observation?

settings, they suffer from several drawbacks. As mentioned earlier, the presence of a participant observer may influence the behavior of the individuals being studied. Furthermore, because only a small number of individuals are studied, it may be hard to generalize the findings to other settings. Finally, ethnographers carrying out cross-cultural research may misinterpret and misconceive what they are observing, particularly in cultures that are very different from their own (Polkinghorne, 2005).

*Case studies.* **Case studies** involve extensive, in-depth interviews with a particular individual or small group of individuals. They often are used not just to learn about the individual being interviewed but also to derive broader principles or draw tentative conclusions that might apply to others. For example, case studies have been conducted on children who display unusual genius and on children who have spent their early years in the wild without human contact. These case studies have provided important information to researchers and have suggested hypotheses for future investigation (Goldsmith, 2000; Cohen & Cashon, 2003; Wilson et al., 2003).

Using *diaries*, participants are asked to keep a record of their behavior on a regular basis. For example, a group of adolescents may be asked to record each time they interact with friends for more than five minutes, thereby providing a way to track their social behavior.

---

**naturalistic observation** Studies in which researchers observe some naturally occurring behavior without intervening or making changes in the situation

**case studies** Extensive, in-depth interviews with a particular individual or small group of individuals

*Survey research.* You're probably familiar with an additional research strategy: survey research. In **survey research**, a group of individuals chosen to represent some larger population is asked questions about attitudes, behavior, or thinking on a given topic. For instance, surveys have been conducted about parents' use of punishment on their children and on attitudes toward breast-feeding. From the responses, inferences are drawn regarding the larger population represented by the individuals being surveyed.

Although there's no more straightforward way of determining what people think and do than asking them directly about their behavior, it's not always an effective technique. For instance, adolescents asked about their sex lives may be unwilling to admit to various sexual practices out of embarrassment or fear that confidentiality will be breached. In addition, if the sample of people surveyed is not representative of the broader population of interest, the results of the survey have little meaning.

*Psychophysiological methods.* Some developmental researchers, particularly those using a cognitive neuroscience approach, make use of psychophysiological methods. **Psychophysiological methods** focus on the relationship between physiological processes and behavior. For instance, a researcher might examine the relationship between blood flow within the brain and problem-solving capabilities. Similarly, some studies use infants' heart rate as a measure of their interest in stimuli to which they are exposed.

Among the most frequently used psychophysiological measures are the following

- *Electroencephalogram (EEG).* The EEG records electrical activity within the brain, recorded by electrodes placed on the outside of the skull. That brain activity is transformed into a pictorial representation of the brain, permitting the representation of brain-wave patterns and diagnoses of disorders such as epilepsy and learning disabilities.

- *Computerized Axial Tomography (CAT) Scan.* In a CAT scan, a computer constructs an image of the brain by combining thousands of individual X-rays taken at slightly different angles. Although it does not show brain activity, it does illuminate the structure of the brain.

- *Functional Magnetic Resonance Imaging (fMRI) Scan.* An fMRI provides a detailed, three-dimensional,

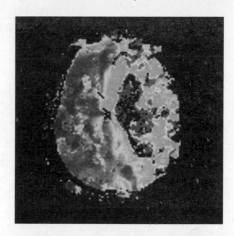

A functional magnetic resonance image (fMRI) of the brain shows brain activity at a given moment.

computer-generated image of brain activity by aiming a powerful magnetic field at the brain. It offers one of the best ways of learning about the operation of the brain, down to the level of individual nerves.

## Experiments: Determining Cause and Effect

**LO 2.9 Summarize the major characteristics of experiments and how they differ from correlational studies.**

In an **experiment**, an investigator, called an *experimenter*, typically devises two different experiences for *participants*, or *subjects*. These two different experiences are called treatments. A **treatment** is a procedure applied by an investigator. One group of participants receives one of the treatments, whereas another group of participants receives either no treatment or an alternative

---

**survey research** Research in which a group of people chosen to represent some larger population are asked questions about their attitudes, behavior, or thinking on a given topic

**psychophysiological methods** A research approach that focuses on the relationship between physiological processes and behavior

**experiment** A process in which an investigator, called an experimenter, devises two different experiences for subjects or participants

**treatment** A procedure applied by an experimental investigator based on two different experiences devised for subjects or participants

treatment. The group receiving the treatment is known as the **treatment group** (sometimes called the *experimental group*), whereas the no-treatment or alternative-treatment group is called the **control group**.

Although the terminology may seem daunting at first, there is an underlying logic to it that helps sort it out. Think in terms of a medical experiment in which the aim is to test the effectiveness of a new drug. In testing the drug, we wish to see if it successfully *treats* the disease. Consequently, the group that receives the drug would be called the *treatment group*. In comparison, another group of participants would not receive the drug treatment. Instead, they would be part of the no-treatment *control group*.

Similarly, suppose we wish to explore the consequences of exposure to movie violence on viewers' subsequent aggression. We might take a group of adolescents and show them a series of movies that contain a great deal of violent imagery. We would then measure their subsequent aggression. This group would constitute the treatment group. But we would also need another group—a control group. To fulfill this need, we might take a second group of adolescents, show them movies that contain no aggressive imagery, and then measure their subsequent aggression. This would be the control group.

By comparing the amount of aggression displayed by members of the treatment and control groups, we would be able to determine whether exposure to violent imagery produces aggression in viewers. This finding is precisely what a group of researchers determined. Running an experiment of this very sort, psychologist Jacques-Philippe Leyens and colleagues at the University of Louvain in Belgium found that the level of aggression rose significantly for the adolescents who had seen the movies containing violence (Leyens et al., 1975).

**DESIGNING AN EXPERIMENT.** The central feature of this experiment—and all other experiments—is the comparison of the consequences of different treatments. The use of both treatment and control groups allows researchers to rule out the possibility that something other than the experimental manipulation produced the results found in the experiment. For instance, if a control group was not used, experimenters could not be certain that some other factor, such as the time of day the movies were shown, the need to sit still during the movie, or even the mere passage of time, produced the changes that were observed. By employing a control group, experimenters can draw accurate conclusions about causes and effects.

The formation of treatment and control groups represents the independent variable in an experiment. The **independent variable** is the variable that researchers manipulate in the experiment. In contrast, the **dependent variable** is the variable that researchers measure in an experiment and expect to change as a result of the experimental manipulation. (One way to remember the difference is that a hypothesis predicts how a dependent variable *depends* on the manipulation of the independent variable.) In an experiment studying the effects of taking a drug, for instance, manipulating whether participants receive or don't receive a drug is the independent variable. Measurement of the effectiveness of the drug or no-drug treatment is the dependent variable.

To consider another example, let's take the Belgian study of the consequences of observing filmed aggression on future aggression. In this experiment, the independent variable is the *level of aggressive imagery* viewed by participants—determined by whether they viewed films containing aggressive imagery (the treatment group) or devoid of aggressive imagery (the control group). The dependent variable in the study? It was the activity the experimenters expected to vary as a consequence of viewing a film: the *aggressive behavior* shown by participants after they had viewed the films and measured by the experimenters. Every experiment has an independent and dependent variable.

**RANDOM ASSIGNMENT.** One critical step in the design of experiments is to assign participants to different treatment groups. The procedure that is used is known as random assignment. In *random assignment*, participants are assigned to different experimental groups, or "conditions," on the basis of chance and chance alone. For example, an experimenter might flip a coin for each participant and assign a participant to one group when

---

**treatment group** The group in an experiment that receives the treatment

**control group** The group in an experiment that receives either no treatment or an alternative treatment

**independent variable** The variable in an experiment that is manipulated by researchers

**dependent variable** The variable in an experiment that is measured and is expected to change as a result of the experimental manipulation

**Figure 2.4** Elements of an Experiment

In this experiment, researchers randomly assigned a group of adolescents to one of two conditions: viewing a film that contained violent imagery, or viewing a film that lacked violent imagery (manipulation of the independent variable). Then participants were observed later to determine how much aggression they showed (the dependent variable). Analysis of the findings showed that adolescents exposed to aggressive imagery showed more aggression later. (Based on an experiment by Leyens et al., 1975.)

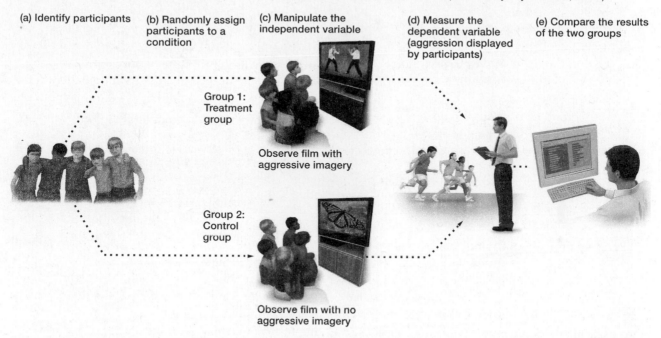

(a) Identify participants

(b) Randomly assign participants to a condition

(c) Manipulate the independent variable

(d) Measure the dependent variable (aggression displayed by participants)

(e) Compare the results of the two groups

Group 1: Treatment group

Observe film with aggressive imagery

Group 2: Control group

Observe film with no aggressive imagery

"heads" came up and to the other group when "tails" came up. By using this technique, the laws of statistics ensure that personal characteristics that might affect the outcome of the experiment are divided proportionally among the participants in the different groups. In other words, the groups are equivalent to one another in terms of the personal characteristics of the participants. Equivalent groups achieved by random assignment allow an experimenter to draw conclusions with confidence.

Figure 2.4 illustrates the Belgian experiment on adolescents exposed to films containing violent or nonviolent imagery and its effects on subsequent aggressive behavior. As you can see, it contains each of the elements of an experiment:

- An independent variable (the assignment to a film condition)
- A dependent variable (measurement of the adolescents' aggressive behavior)
- Random assignment to condition (viewing a film with aggressive imagery versus a film with nonaggressive imagery)

- A hypothesis that predicts the effect the independent variable will have on the dependent variable (that viewing a film with aggressive imagery will produce subsequent aggression)

Given the advantage of experimental research—that it provides a means of determining causality—why aren't experiments always used? The answer is that there are some situations that a researcher, no matter how ingenious, simply cannot control. And there are some situations that it would be unethical to control, even if it were possible. For instance, no researcher would be able to assign different groups of infants to parents of high and low socioeconomic status in order to learn the effects of such status on subsequent development. Similarly, we cannot control what a group of children watch on television throughout their childhood years in order to learn if childhood exposure to televised aggression leads to aggressive behavior later in life. Consequently, in situations in which experiments are logistically or ethically impossible, developmentalists employ correlational research. (See Table 2.4 for a summary of the major research strategies.)

**Table 2.4** Types of Research

| Research Method | Description | Example |
|---|---|---|
| Naturalistic observation | An investigator systematically observes naturally occurring behavior and does not make a change in the situation. | A researcher investigating bullying carefully observes and records instances of bullying on elementary school playgrounds. |
| Archival research | Existing data such as census documents, college records, and newspaper clippings are examined to test a hypothesis. | College records are used to determine whether gender differences exist in math grades. |
| Ethnography | Careful study of a culture's values and attitudes through careful, extended examination. | A researcher lives for 6 months among families in a remote African village in order to study child-rearing practices. |
| Survey research | Individuals chosen to represent a larger population are asked a series of questions about their behavior, thoughts, or attitudes. | A researcher conducts a comprehensive poll asking a large group of adolescents about their attitudes toward exercise. |
| Case study | An in-depth, intensive investigation of an individual or small group of people. | An intensive study of a child involved in a school shooting is carried out by an investigator. |
| Psychophysiological research | A study of the relationship between physiological processes and behavior. | A researcher examines brain scans of children who are unusually violent to see whether there are abnormalities in brain structures and functioning. |

Furthermore, keep in mind that a single experiment is insufficient to answer a research question definitively. Before complete confidence can be placed in a conclusion, research must be *replicated*, or repeated, sometimes using other procedures and techniques with other participants. Sometimes developmentalists use a procedure called *meta-analysis*, which permits them to combine results of many studies into one overall conclusion (Peterson & Brown, 2005).

**CHOOSING A RESEARCH SETTING.** Deciding *where* to conduct a study may be as important as determining *what* to do. In the Belgian experiment on the influence of exposure to media aggression, the researchers used a real-world setting—a group home for boys who had been convicted of juvenile delinquency. They chose this **sample**, the group of participants selected for the experiment, because it was useful to have adolescents whose normal level of aggression was relatively high, and because they could incorporate showing the films into the everyday life of the home with minimal disruption.

Using a real-world setting like the one in the aggression experiment is the hallmark of a field study. A **field study** is a research investigation carried out in a naturally occurring setting. Field studies may be carried out in preschool classrooms, at community playgrounds, on school buses, or on street corners. Field studies capture behavior in real-life settings, where research participants may behave more naturally than they would if they were brought into a laboratory.

Field studies may be used in both correlational studies and experiments. Field studies typically employ naturalistic observation, the technique we discussed previously in which researchers observe some naturally occurring behavior without intervening or making changes in the situation. For instance, a researcher might examine behavior in a child care center, view the groupings of adolescents in high school corridors, or observe elderly adults in a senior center.

However, it often is difficult to run an experiment in real-world settings, where it is hard to exert control over the situation and environment. Consequently, field studies are more typical of correlational designs than experimental designs, and most developmental research experiments are conducted in laboratory settings. A **laboratory study** is a research investigation conducted in a controlled setting explicitly designed to hold events constant. The laboratory may be a room or building designed for research, as in a university's psychology department. The ability to control the settings in laboratory studies enables researchers to learn more clearly how their treatments affect participants.

**sample** A group of participants chosen for an experiment

**field study** A research investigation carried out in a naturally occurring setting

**laboratory study** A research investigation conducted in a controlled setting explicitly designed to hold events constant

Developmentalists work in such diverse settings as a laboratory preschool, a college campus, or a human service agency.

# DEVELOPMENTAL DIVERSITY AND YOUR LIFE

## Choosing Research Participants Who Represent the Diversity of Children

In order for child development to represent the full range of humanity, its research must incorporate children of different races, ethnicities, cultures, genders, and other categories. The field of child development is increasingly concerned with issues of human diversity, but its actual progress in this domain has been slow. For instance, although our understanding of the development of non-white children has grown substantially over the past three decades, it is still as not as complete as for nonminority children (McLoyd, 2006; Cabera, 2013).

Furthermore, demographic changes have increased the need for research on minority children. According to estimates from the U.S. Census Bureau (2014), in 2014 half of all American children under the age of 5 were members of a racial or ethnic minority group (Cabera, 2013).

Even when minority groups are included in research, the particular participants may not represent the full range of variation that actually exists within the group. For example, African American infants used in a research study might well be disproportionally upper- and middle-class, because parents in higher socioeconomic groups may be more likely to have the time and transportation capabilities to bring their infants into a research center. In contrast, African Americans (as well as members of other groups) who are relatively poor will face more hurdles when it comes to participating in research.

Something is amiss when a science that seeks to explain children's behavior—as is the case with child

In order to understand development in all children, researchers must include participants in their studies who represent the diversity of humanity.

development—disregards significant groups of individuals. Child developmentalists are aware of this issue, and they have become increasingly sensitive to the importance of using participants who are fully representative of the general population (Fitzgerald, 2006).

From an educator's perspective: Why might you criticize theories that are supported only by data collected from laboratory studies, rather than from field studies? Would such criticism be valid?

# Research Strategies and Challenges

Developmental researchers typically focus on one of two approaches to research: theoretical research or applied research. The two approaches are, in fact, complementary.

## Theoretical and Applied Research: Complementary Approaches

### LO 2.10 Distinguish between theoretical and applied research.

**Theoretical research** is designed specifically to test some developmental explanation and expand scientific knowledge, whereas **applied research** is meant to provide practical solutions to immediate problems. For instance, if we were interested in the processes of cognitive change during childhood, we might carry out a study of how many digits children of various ages can remember after one exposure to multi-digit numbers—a theoretical approach. Alternatively, we might focus on how children learn by examining ways in which elementary school instructors can teach children to remember information more easily. Such a study would represent applied research, because the findings are applied to a particular setting and problem.

Often the distinctions between theoretical and applied research are blurred. For instance, is a study that examines the consequences of ear infections in infancy on later hearing loss theoretical or applied research? Because such a study may help illuminate the basic processes involved in hearing, it can be considered theoretical. But to the extent that the study helps us understand how to prevent hearing loss in children and how various medicines may ease the consequences of the infection, it may be considered applied research (Lerner, Fisher, & Weinberg, 2000).

In short, applied research can help advance our theoretical understanding of a particular topical area, and theoretical research can provide concrete solutions

to a range of practical problems. In fact, as discussed in the accompanying *From Research to Practice* box, research of both a theoretical and an applied nature has played a significant role in shaping and resolving a variety of public policy questions.

## Measuring Developmental Change

### LO 2.11 Explain the major research strategies.

For developmental researchers, the question of how people grow and change throughout the life span is central to their discipline. Consequently, one of the thorniest research issues they face concerns the measurement of change and differences over age and time. To solve this problem, researchers have developed three major strategies: longitudinal research, cross-sectional research, and sequential research.

**LONGITUDINAL STUDIES: MEASURING INDIVIDUAL CHANGE.** If you were interested in learning how a child's moral development changes between the ages of 3 and 5, the most direct approach would be to take a group of 3-year-olds and follow them until they were age 5, testing them periodically.

Such a strategy illustrates longitudinal research. In **longitudinal research**, the behavior of one or more study participants is measured as they age. Longitudinal research measures change in individuals over time, enabling researchers to understand the general course of change across some period of life.

The granddaddy of longitudinal studies, which became a classic, is a study of gifted children begun by Lewis Terman in 1921. In the study, a group of 1,500 children with high IQs were tested about every 5 years throughout their lives. The participants—who called themselves "Termites"— provided information on everything from intellectual accomplishment to personality and longevity, many until their deaths (McCullough, Tsang, & Brion, 2003; Subotnik, 2006; Warne & Liu, 2017).

**theoretical research** Research designed specifically to test some developmental explanation and expand scientific knowledge

**applied research** Research meant to provide practical solutions to immediate problems

**longitudinal research** Research in which the behavior of one or more individuals is measured as the subjects age

# FROM RESEARCH TO PRACTICE
## Using Developmental Research to Improve Public Policy

- Is the Anganwadi program effective in improving school readiness in children?
- How can we decrease female feticide?
- Are boys better suited for some jobs than girls?
- How to increase enrolment in government-funded schools in the country?
- How can we reduce bullying in schools?

Each of these questions represents a national policy issue that can be answered only by considering the results of relevant research findings (Planning Commission, 2014). By conducting controlled studies, developmental researchers have made a number of important contributions affecting education, family life, and health on a national scale. Consider, for instance, the variety of ways that public policy issues have been informed by various types of research findings (Nelson & Mann, 2011; Ewing, 2014; Langford, Albanese, & Prentice, 2017):

- *Research findings can provide policy makers a means of determining what questions to ask in the first place.* For example, studies on examination stress have led policy makers to question the Class X board examination, and the Central Board of Secondary Education (CBSE) went for an alternate model.
- *Research findings and the testimony of researchers are often part of the process by which laws are drafted.* A good deal of legislation has been passed based on findings from developmental researchers. For example, research revealed that children with developmental disabilities benefit from exposure to children without special needs, ultimately leading to passage of national legislation mandating that children with disabilities be placed in regular school classes as much as possible.
- *Policy makers and other professionals use research findings to determine how best to implement programs.* In India, evaluative research done by the NIPCID and the NCERT led to changes in the training program of Anganwadi workers for pre-schooling in their centers. Similarly, research has led to the implementation of programs for reducing maternal mortality and targeting adolescent health in Anganwadi centers. The common thread among such programs is that many of the details of the program are built on basic research (Kulkarni & Pattabhi ,1988; NIPCID, 2009).
- *Research techniques are used to evaluate the effectiveness of existing programs and policies.* Once a public policy has been implemented, it is necessary to determine whether it has been effective and successful in accomplishing its goals. To do this, researchers employ formal evaluation techniques, developed from basic research procedures.

By building on research findings, development a lists have worked hand-in-hand with policy makers, and research has had a substantial impact on public policies that can benefit us all.

- **What are some policy issues affecting children and adolescents that are currently being debated nationally?**
- **Despite the existence of research data that might inform policy about development, politicians rarely discuss such data in their speeches. Why do you think that is the case?**

Longitudinal research has also provided great insight into language development. For instance, by tracing how children's vocabularies increase on a day-by-day basis, researchers have been able to understand the processes that underlie the human ability to become competent in using language (Oliver & Plomin, 2007; Fagan, 2009; Kelloway & Francis, 2013).

Although longitudinal studies can provide a wealth of information about change over time, they have several drawbacks. For one thing, they require a tremendous investment of time because researchers must wait for participants to become older. Furthermore, participants often drop out over the course of the research, move away, become ill, or even die as the research proceeds.

Finally, participants who are observed or tested repeatedly may become "test-wise" and perform better each time they are assessed as they become more familiar with the procedure. Even if the observations of participants in a study are not terribly intrusive (such as simply recording, over a lengthy period of time, vocabulary increases in infants and preschoolers), experimental participants may be affected by the repeated presence of an experimenter or observer.

Consequently, despite the benefits of longitudinal research, particularly its ability to look at change within individuals, developmental researchers often turn to other methods in conducting research. The alternative they choose most often is the cross-sectional study.

**CROSS-SECTIONAL STUDIES.** Suppose again that you want to consider how children's moral development, their sense of right and wrong, changes from ages 3 to 5. Instead of using a longitudinal approach and following the same children over several years, you might conduct the study by simultaneously looking at three groups of children: 3-year-olds, 4-year-olds, and 5-year-olds, perhaps presenting each group with the same problem, and then seeing how they respond to it and explain their choices.

Such an approach typifies cross-sectional research. In **cross-sectional research**, people of different ages are compared at the same point in time. Cross-sectional studies provide information about differences in development among different age groups.

Cross-sectional research is considerably more economical than longitudinal research in terms of time because participants are tested at just one point in time. For instance, Terman's study conceivably might have been completed decades ago if he had simply looked at a group of gifted 15-year-olds, 20-year-olds, 25-year-olds, and so forth, all the way through a group of 80-year-olds. Because the participants would not be periodically tested, there would be no chance that they would become test-wise, and problems of participant attrition would not occur. Why, then, would anyone choose to use a procedure other than cross-sectional research?

The answer is that cross-sectional research brings its own set of difficulties. Recall that every person belongs to a particular *cohort*, the group of people born at around the same time in the same place. If we find that people of different ages vary along some dimension, it may be due to differences in cohort membership, not age *per se*.

Consider a concrete example. If we find in a correlational study that people who are 25 years old perform better on a test of intelligence than those who are 75 years old, there are several explanations. Although the finding may be due to decreased intelligence in older

people, it may also be attributable to cohort differences. The group of 75-year-olds may have had less formal education than the 25-year-olds, because members of the older cohort were less likely to finish high school and attend college than members of the younger one. Or perhaps the older group performed less well because as infants they received less adequate nutrition than members of the younger group. In short, we cannot fully rule out the possibility that differences we find among people of different age groups in cross-sectional studies are due to cohort differences.

Cross-sectional studies also may suffer from *selective dropout*, in which participants in some age groups are more likely than others to quit participating in a study. For example, suppose a study of cognitive development in preschoolers includes a lengthy assessment of cognitive abilities. It is possible that young preschoolers would find the task more difficult and demanding than older preschoolers. As a result, the younger children would be more likely than the older preschoolers to discontinue participation in the study. If the least competent young preschoolers are the ones who drop out, then the remaining sample of participants in the study will consist of the more competent young preschoolers—together with a broader and more representative sample of older preschoolers. The results of such a study would be questionable (Miller, 1998).

Finally, cross-sectional studies have an additional, and more basic, disadvantage: They are unable to inform us about changes in individuals or groups. If longitudinal studies are like videos taken of a person at various ages, cross-sectional studies are like snapshots of entirely different groups. Although we can establish differences related to age, we cannot fully determine if such differences are related to change over time.

**SEQUENTIAL STUDIES.** Because both longitudinal and cross-sectional studies have drawbacks, researchers have turned to some compromise techniques. Among the most frequently employed are sequential studies, which are essentially a combination of longitudinal and cross-sectional studies.

In **sequential studies**, researchers examine a number of different age groups at several points in time.

---

**cross-sectional research** Research in which people of different ages are compared at the same point in time
**sequential studies** Studies in which researchers examine members of a number of different age groups at several points in time

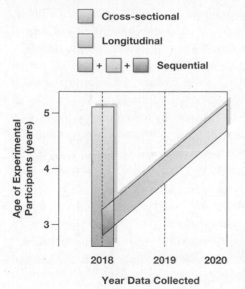

☐ **Cross-sectional**

☐ **Longitudinal**

☐ + ☐ + ☐ **Sequential**

**Figure 2.5** Research Techniques for Studying Development

In a cross-sectional study, 3-, 4- and 5-year-olds are compared at a similar point in time (in the year 2018). In longitudinal research, participants who are 3 years old in the year 2018 are studied when they are 4 years old (in 2019) and when they are 5 years old (in 2020). Finally, a sequential study combines cross-sectional and longitudinal techniques; here, a group of 3-year-olds would be compared initially in 2018 with 4- and 5-year-olds but would also be studied 1 and 2 years later, when they themselves were 4 and 5 years old. Although the graph does not illustrate this, researchers carrying out this sequential study might also choose to retest the children who were 4 and 5 in 2018 for the next 2 years. What advantages do the three kinds of studies offer?

For instance, an investigator interested in children's moral behavior might begin a sequential study by examining the behavior of three groups of children, who are 3, 4, or 5 years old at the time the study begins. (This is no different from the way a cross-sectional study would be done.)

However, the study wouldn't stop there, but would continue for the next several years. During this period, each of the research participants would be tested annually. Thus, the 3-year-olds would be tested at ages 3, 4, and 5; the 4-year-olds at ages 4, 5, and 6; and the 5-year-olds at ages 5, 6, and 7. Such an approach combines the advantages of longitudinal and cross-sectional research, and it permits developmental researchers to tease out the consequences of age *change* versus age *difference*.

Cross-sectional research allows researchers to compare representatives of different age groups at the same time.

(The major research techniques for studying development are summarized in Figure 2.5.)

## Ethics and Research

**LO 2.12  Identify the primary ethical principles used to guide research.**

In the "research study" conducted by Egyptian King Psamtik, two children were removed from their mothers and held in isolation in an effort to learn about the roots of language. If you found yourself thinking this was extraordinarily cruel, you are in good company. Clearly, such an experiment raises blatant ethical concerns, and nothing like it would ever be done today.

To help researchers deal with ethical problems, the major organizations of developmentalists, including the Society for Research in Child Development and the American Psychological Association, have developed comprehensive ethical guidelines for researchers. Among the basic principles that must be followed are those involving freedom from harm, informed consent, the use of deception, and maintenance of participants' privacy (American Psychological Association [APA], 2002; Fisher, 2004, 2005; Nagy, 2011; Toporek, Kwan, & Williams, 2012):

- *Researchers must protect participants from physical and psychological harm.* Participants' welfare, interests, and rights come before those of researchers. In research, participants' rights always come first (Fisher, 2004; Nagy, 2011; McBride & Cutting, 2016).

- *Researchers must obtain informed consent from participants before their involvement in a study.* If they are over the age of 7, participants must voluntarily agree to be in a study. For those under 18, their parents or guardians must also provide consent.

  The requirement for informed consent raises some difficult issues. Suppose, for instance, researchers want to study the psychological effects of abortion on adolescents. Although they may be able to obtain the consent of an adolescent who has had an abortion, the researchers may need to get her parents' permission as well, because she is a minor. But if the adolescent hasn't told her parents about the abortion, the mere request for permission from the parents would violate her privacy—leading to a breach of ethics.

> From a health care provider's perspective: Are there some special circumstances involving adolescents, who are not legally adults, that would justify allowing them to participate in a study without obtaining their parents' permission?

- *The use of deception in research must be justified and cause no harm.* Although deception to disguise the true purpose of an experiment is permissible, any experiment that uses deception must undergo careful scrutiny by an independent panel before it is conducted. Suppose, for example, we want to know the reaction of participants to success and failure. It is ethical to tell participants that they will be playing a game when the true purpose is actually to observe how they respond to doing well or poorly on the task. However, such a procedure is ethical only if it causes no harm to participants, has been approved by a review panel, and ultimately includes a full debriefing, or explanation, for participants when the study is over (Underwood, 2005).

- *Participants' privacy must be maintained.* If participants are videotaped—during the course of a study, for example—they must give their permission for the videotapes to be viewed. Furthermore, access to the tapes must be carefully restricted.

# BECOMING AN INFORMED CONSUMER OF CHILD DEVELOPMENT

## Critically Evaluating Developmental Research

**"Study Shows Adolescent Suicide Reaches New Peaks"**
**"Genetic Basis Found for Children's Obesity"**
**"New Research Points to Cure for Sudden Infant Death Syndrome"**

We've all seen headlines like these, which at first glance seem to herald important, meaningful discoveries. But before we accept the findings, it is important to think critically about the research on which the headlines are based. Among the most important questions that we should consider are the following:

- *Is the study grounded in theory, and what are the underlying hypotheses about the research?* Research should flow from theoretical foundations, and hypotheses should be logical and based on some underlying theory. Only by considering the results in terms of theory and hypotheses can we determine how successful the research has been.

- *Is this an isolated research study, or does it fit into a series of investigations addressing the same general problem?* A onetime study is far less meaningful than a series of studies that build upon one another. By placing research in the context of other studies, we can be much more confident regarding the validity of the findings of a new study.

- *Who took part in the study, and how far can we generalize the results beyond the participants?* As we discussed earlier in the chapter, conclusions about the meaning of research can only be generalized to people who are similar to the participants in a study.

- *Was the study carried out appropriately?* Although it is often difficult to know the details of a study from media summaries, it is important to learn as much as possible about who did the study and how it was done. For instance, did it include appropriate control groups, and are the researchers who conducted it reputable? One clue that a study meets these criteria and is well done is whether the findings reported in the media are based on a study published in a major journal such as *Developmental Psychology*, *Adolescence*, *Child Development*, or *Science*. Each of these journals is carefully edited, and only the best, most rigorous research is reported in them.

- *Were the participants studied long enough to draw reasonable developmental implications?* A study that purports to study long-term development should encompass a reasonably long time frame. Furthermore, developmental implications beyond the age span studied should not be drawn.

# The Case of…
## A Study in Violence

Lisa Manzini teaches social studies in a suburban middle school just outside New York City. She is designing a course called "Society and the Individual." Lisa has a theory she would like to test with her students in this course: that repeated exposure to violent images desensitizes people to the suffering of others. Her hypothesis is that there is an inverse relationship between the number of violent images a student is exposed to and the degree of empathy that student demonstrates.

To test her hypothesis, Lisa plans to begin by showing her students a series of images of people who are obviously suffering: war refugees, starving children, homeless adults. Students will record their reactions to these images, answering a series of questions Lisa has prepared to measure empathy on a five-point scale. Over the next 3 weeks, Lisa will present many violent images to the class, including videos of the planes hitting the Twin Towers on 9/11, beheadings of hostages by terrorists, and car bombings. At the end of each week, Lisa will show the original images of suffering. Students will again record their emotional reactions, and she will compare these to their earlier responses, and note any changes.

Lisa is certain that her findings will show a growing indifference to the suffering of others.

1. Do you think this is a good example of a theory? Is Lisa's hypothesis sound?
2. Is her study an experiment or a correlational study? Why?
3. Do you think Lisa's middle school students would be able to understand and participate in the study and provide informed consent for their participation?
4. Do you think Lisa's method will yield reliable results? Why or why not?
5. What do you suppose the students' parents would think of the study? What do you think of it?

# Epilogue

This chapter examined the way developmentalists use theory and research to understand child development. We reviewed the broad approaches to children's development, examining the theories that each has produced. In addition, we looked at the ways in which research is conducted.

In the prologue, we encountered Kajal, whose first word was "Papa." In light of what you now know about theories and research, consider the following questions about her:

1. How might child developmentalists from the behavioral and evolutionary perspectives explain Kajal's emerging use of language?
2. What differences might there be in the questions that would interest them?
3. What research methods might a child developmentalist use to study the development of language in a particular child?
4. What if the researcher wanted to study development across a group of children? What research methods might he or she use instead?

# Looking Back

**LO 2.1 Describe the basic concepts of the psychodynamic perspective.**

- The psychodynamic perspective is exemplified by the psychoanalytic theory of Sigmund Freud and the psychosocial theory of Erik Erikson.
- Freud focused attention on the unconscious and on the stages through which children must pass successfully to avoid harmful fixations.
- Erikson identified eight distinct stages of development, each characterized by a conflict, or crisis, to work out.

**LO 2.2 Describe the basic concepts of the behavioral perspective.**

- The behavioral perspective typically concerns stimulus–response learning, exemplified by classical conditioning, the operant conditioning of B. F. Skinner, and Albert Bandura's social-cognitive learning theory.

**LO 2.3 Describe the basic concepts of the cognitive perspective.**

- The cognitive perspective focuses on the processes that allow people to know, understand, and think about the world.
- Jean Piaget identified developmental stages through which all children are assumed to pass. Each stage involves qualitative differences in thinking. In contrast, information-processing approaches attribute cognitive growth to quantitative changes in mental processes and capacities.
- Cognitive neuroscientists seek to identify locations and functions within the brain that are related to different types of cognitive activity.

**LO 2.4 Describe the basic concepts of the contextual perspective.**

- The contextual perspective stresses the interrelatedness of developmental areas and the importance of broad cultural factors in human development. Urie Bronfenbrenner's bioecological approach focuses on the microsystem, mesosystem, exosystem, macrosystem, and chronosystem.
- Lev Vygotsky's sociocultural theory emphasizes the central influence on cognitive development exerted by social interactions between members of a culture.

**LO 2.5 Describe the basic concepts of the evolutionary perspective.**

- The evolutionary perspective attributes behavior to genetic inheritance from our ancestors, contending that genes determine not only traits such as skin color and eye color but also certain personality traits and social behaviors.

**LO 2.6 Explain the value of applying multiple perspectives to child development.**

- Each perspective is based on its own premises and focuses on different aspects of development.

**LO 2.7 Identify the principles of the scientific method and how they help answer questions about child development.**

- The scientific method is the process of posing and answering questions using careful, controlled techniques that include systematic, orderly observation and the collection of data.
- Theories are broad explanations of facts or phenomena of interest, based on a systematic integration of prior findings and theories.
- Hypotheses are theory-based predictions that can be tested.
- Operationalization is the process of translating a hypothesis into specific, testable procedures that can be measured and observed.
- Researchers test hypotheses by using correlational research (to determine if two factors are associated) and experimental research (to discover cause-and-effect relationships).

**LO 2.8 Summarize the major characteristics of correlational studies.**

- Correlational studies use naturalistic observation, case studies, diaries, survey research, and psychophysiological methods to investigate whether certain characteristics of interest are associated with other characteristics.
- Correlational studies lead to no direct conclusions about cause and effect.

**LO 2.9** **Summarize the major characteristics of experiments and how they differ from correlational studies.**

- Typically, experimental research studies are conducted on participants in a treatment group, who receive the experimental treatment, and participants in a control group, who do not.
- Following the treatment, differences between the two groups can help the experimenter determine the effects of the treatment.
- Experiments may be conducted in a laboratory or in a real-world setting.
- Experiments allow the experimenter to draw conclusions about cause and effect.

**LO 2.10** **Distinguish between theoretical and applied research.**

- Theoretical research tests a hypothesis with the purpose of expanding scientific knowledge, whereas applied research seeks to provide practical solutions to real-world problems.
- The two types of research are complementary because the knowledge gained in theoretical research may suggest practical solutions to real-world problems, and the discoveries made in trying to solve real-world problems may advance scientific knowledge.

**LO 2.11** **Explain the major research strategies.**

- Theoretical research is designed specifically to test some developmental explanation and expand scientific knowledge, whereas applied research is meant to provide practical solutions to immediate problems.
- To measure change at different ages, researchers use longitudinal studies of the same participants over time, cross-sectional studies of different-age participants conducted at one time, and sequential studies of different-age participants at several points in time.

**LO 2.12** **Identify the primary ethical principles used to guide research.**

- Ethical guidelines for research include the protection of participants from harm, informed consent of participants, limits on the use of deception, and the maintenance of privacy.

## Key Terms and Concepts

theories (p. 20)
psychodynamic perspective (p. 20)
psychoanalytic theory (p. 21)
psychosexual development (p. 21)
psychosocial development (p. 21)
behavioral perspective (p. 23)
classical conditioning (p. 24)
operant conditioning (p. 24)
behavior modification (p. 24)
social-cognitive learning theory (p. 25)
cognitive perspective (p. 26)
information-processing approaches (p. 27)

cognitive neuroscience approaches (p. 27)
contextual perspective (p. 29)
bioecological approach (p. 29)
sociocultural theory (p. 31)
evolutionary perspective (p. 31)
scientific method (p. 34)
hypothesis (p. 35)
correlational research (p. 36)
experimental research (p. 36)
naturalistic observation (p. 38)
case studies (p. 38)
survey research (p. 39)
psychophysiological methods (p. 39)

experiment (p. 39)
treatment (p. 39)
treatment group (p. 40)
control group (p. 40)
independent variable (p. 40)
dependent variable (p. 40)
sample (p. 42)
field study (p. 42)
laboratory study (p. 42)
theoretical research (p. 44)
applied research (p. 44)
longitudinal research (p. 44)
cross-sectional research (p. 46)
sequential studies (p. 46)

# Chapter 3
# The Start of Life: Genetics and Prenatal Development

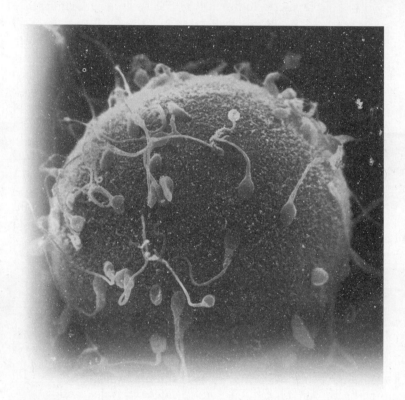

## Learning Objectives

**LO 3.1** Explain the role of genes and chromosomes in creating human life.

**LO 3.2** Summarize the basics of genetics.

**LO 3.3** Explain how genetic information is transmitted.

**LO 3.4** Identify what we learned from the mapping of the human genome.

**LO 3.5** Explain genetic counseling and its uses.

**LO 3.6** Describe how environmental factors interact in the development of individual traits.

**LO 3.7** Explain how researchers study the interaction of genetic and environmental factors in development.

**LO 3.8** Describe the influence of genetics and the environment on physical traits, intelligence, and personality.

**LO 3.9** Explain the role nature and nurture play in the development of psychological disorders.

**LO 3.10** Discuss the ways genes can influence the environment.

**LO 3.11** Explain what happens during the prenatal stages of development.

**LO 3.12** Discuss the issues that individuals face with respect to pregnancy.

**LO 3.13** Describe some threats to the fetal environment and what can be done about them.

# Prologue: Going With the Odds

When a prenatal ultrasound at 20 weeks revealed that Tim and Laura Chen's unborn son had a severe form of spina bifida (a birth defect in which an area of the spine is malformed, leaving a section of the spinal cord exposed through an opening in the back), their first question was: *Can this be fixed?* Laura's doctor outlined their choices. They could wait to enclose the spinal cord until after the baby's birth, but this might endanger the spine and brain, which can be damaged in late pregnancy. In addition, their child could still experience paralysis, cognitive impairments, and bladder and bowel issues.

The Chens' other choice was to have doctors perform surgery before birth. Doctors would tip Laura's uterus outside her body, make an incision, and sew up the hole exposing the spinal cord. There would be a greater risk of preterm labor, but a better chance of minimizing lifelong damage.

The Chens chose fetal surgery. Three years later, their son has minor bladder issues, but he walks independently and his preschool cognitive assessment placed him in the 85th percentile. "We're so lucky to be living in a time when such surgery is possible," Laura says.

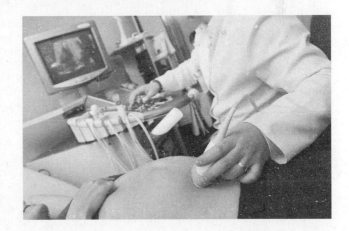

# Looking Ahead

The Chens' story illustrates the powerful benefits—and the often difficult decisions—that advances in our understanding of the prenatal period and our ability to detect physical problems prenatally have brought us.

In this chapter, we'll examine what developmental researchers and other scientists have learned about ways that heredity and the environment work in tandem to create and shape human beings. We begin with the basics of heredity, the genetic transmission of characteristics from biological parents to their children, by examining how we receive our genetic endowment. We consider behavioral genetics, an area of study that specializes in the consequences of heredity on behavior. We also discuss what happens when genetic factors cause development to go awry, and how such problems

are dealt with through genetic counseling and gene therapy.

But genes are only one part of the story of prenatal development. We also consider the ways in which a child's genetic heritage interacts with the environment in which he or she grows up—how one's family, socioeconomic status, and life events can affect a variety of characteristics, including physical traits, intelligence, and even personality.

Finally, we focus on the very first stage of development, tracing prenatal growth and change. We review some of the alternatives available to couples who find it difficult to conceive. We also talk about the stages of the prenatal period and how the prenatal environment offers both threats to—and the promise of—future growth.

# Earliest Development

We humans begin the course of our lives simply. Like individuals from tens of thousands of other species, we start as a single cell, a tiny speck probably weighing no more than 1/20-millionth of an ounce. But from this humble beginning—in a matter of just several months, if all goes well—a living, breathing, individual infant is born. This first cell is created when a male reproductive cell, a *sperm*, pushes through the membrane of the *ovum*, the female reproductive cell. These **gametes**, as the male and female reproductive cells are also known, each contain huge amounts of genetic information. About an hour or so after the sperm enters the ovum, the two gametes suddenly fuse, becoming one cell, a **zygote**. The resulting combination of their genetic instructions—more than 2 billion chemically coded messages—is sufficient to begin creating a whole person.

## Genes and Chromosomes: The Code of Life

**LO 3.1   Explain the role of genes and chromosomes in creating human life.**

The blueprints for creating a person are stored and communicated in our **genes**, the basic units of genetic information. The roughly 25,000 human genes are the biological equivalent of "software" that programs the future development of all parts of the body's "hardware."

All genes are composed of specific sequences of **DNA (deoxyribonucleic acid) molecules**. The genes are arranged in specific locations and in a specific order along 46 **chromosomes**, rod-shaped portions of DNA that are organized in 23 pairs. Only sex cells—the ova and the sperm—contain half this number, so that a child's mother and father each provide one of the two chromosomes in each of the 23 pairs. The 46 chromosomes (in 23 pairs) in the new zygote contain the genetic blueprint that will guide cell activity for the rest of the individual's life (Pennisi, 2000; International Human Genome Sequencing Consortium, 2001; see Figure 3.1). Through a process called *mitosis*, which accounts for the replication of most types of cells, nearly all the cells of the body will contain the same 46 chromosomes as the zygote.

Specific genes in precise locations on the chain of chromosomes determine the nature and function of

**Figure 3.1** The Contents of a Single Human Cell

At the moment of conception, humans receive roughly 25,000 genes, contained on 46 chromosomes in 23 pairs.

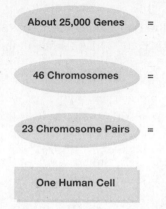

every cell in the body. For instance, genes determine which cells will ultimately become part of the heart and which will become part of the muscles of the leg. Genes also establish how different parts of the body will function: how rapidly the heart will beat, or how much strength a muscle will have.

If each parent provides just 23 chromosomes, where does the potential for the vast diversity of human beings come from? The answer resides primarily in the nature of the processes that underlie the cell division of the gametes. When gametes—sperm and ova—are formed in the adult human body in a process called *meiosis*, each gamete receives one of the two chromosomes that make up each of the 23 pairs. For each of the 23 pairs, it is largely a matter of chance which member of the pair is contributed. Consequently, there are some 8 million different combinations possible. Furthermore, other processes, such as random transformations of particular genes, add to the variability of the genetic brew. The ultimate outcome: tens of *trillions* of possible genetic combinations.

---

**gametes** The sex cells from the mother and father that form a new cell at conception

**zygote** The new cell formed by the process of fertilization

**genes** The basic units of genetic information

**DNA (deoxyribonucleic acid) molecules** The substance that genes are composed of that determines the nature of every cell in the body and how it will function

**chromosomes** Rod-shaped portions of DNA that are organized in 23 pairs

With so many possible genetic mixtures provided by heredity, there is no likelihood that someday you'll bump into a genetic duplicate of yourself—with one exception: an identical twin.

**MULTIPLE BIRTHS: TWO—OR MORE—FOR THE GENETIC PRICE OF ONE.** Although it doesn't seem surprising when dogs and cats give birth to several offspring at one time, in humans, multiple births are cause for comment. They should be: Less than 3 percent of all pregnancies produce twins, and the odds are even slimmer for three or more children.

Why do multiple births occur? Some happen when a cluster of cells in the ovum split off within the first 2 weeks after fertilization. The result is two genetically identical zygotes, which, because they come from the same original zygote, are called monozygotic. **Monozygotic twins** are twins who are genetically identical. Any differences in their future development can be attributed only to environmental factors, because genetically they are exactly the same.

There is a second, and actually more common, mechanism that produces multiple births. In these cases, two separate ova are fertilized by two separate sperm at roughly the same time. Twins produced in this fashion are known as **dizygotic twins**. Because they are the result of two separate ovum–sperm combinations, they are no more genetically similar than two siblings born at different times.

Of course, not all multiple births produce only two babies. Triplets, quadruplets, and even more births are produced by either (or both) of the mechanisms that yield twins. Thus, triplets may be some combination of monozygotic, dizygotic, or trizygotic.

Although the chances of having a multiple birth are typically slim, the odds rise considerably when couples use fertility drugs to improve the probability they will conceive a child. For example, 1 in 10 couples using fertility drugs have dizygotic twins, compared to an overall figure of 1 in 86 for Caucasian couples in the United States. Older women, too, are more likely to have multiple births, and multiple births are also more common in some families than they are in others. The increased use of fertility drugs and rising average age of mothers giving birth have meant that multiple births have increased in the past 30 years; Martin et al., 2005; Parazzini et al., 2016).

There are also racial, ethnic, and national differences in the rate of multiple births, probably due to

Monozygotic and dizygotic twins present opportunities to learn about the relative contributions of heredity and situational factors. What kinds of things can psychologists learn from studying twins?

inherited differences in the likelihood that more than one ovum will be released at a time. One out of 70 African American couples has dizygotic births, compared with the 1 out of 86 figure for White American couples (Vaughn, McKay, & Behrman, 1979; Wood, 1997).

Mothers carrying multiple children run a higher than average risk of premature delivery and birth complications. Consequently, these mothers must be particularly concerned about their prenatal care.

**BOY OR GIRL? ESTABLISHING THE SEX OF THE CHILD.** Recall that there are 23 matched pairs of chromosomes. In 22 of these pairs, each chromosome is similar to the other member of its pair. The one exception is the 23rd pair, which is the one that determines the sex of the child. In females, the 23rd pair consists of two matching, relatively large X-shaped chromosomes, appropriately identified as XX. In males, however, the members of the pair are dissimilar. One consists of an X-shaped chromosome, but the other is a shorter, smaller, Y-shaped chromosome. This pair is identified as XY.

As we discussed earlier, each gamete carries one chromosome from each of the parents' 23 pairs of chromosomes. Because a female's 23rd pair of chromosomes

**monozygotic twins** Twins who are genetically identical

**dizygotic twins** Twins who are produced when two separate ova are fertilized by two separate sperm at roughly the same time

are both Xs, an ovum will always carry an X chromosome, no matter which chromosome of the 23rd pair it gets. A male's 23rd pair is XY, so each sperm could carry either an X or a Y chromosome.

If the sperm contributes an X chromosome when it meets an ovum (which, remember, will always contribute an X chromosome), the child will have an XX pairing on the 23rd chromosome—and will be a female. If the sperm contributes a Y chromosome, the result will be an XY pairing—a male (see Figure 3.2).

It is clear from this process that the father's sperm determines the gender of the child. This fact is leading to the development of techniques that will allow parents to increase the chances of specifying the gender of their child, a topic we discuss in more detail later in the chapter.

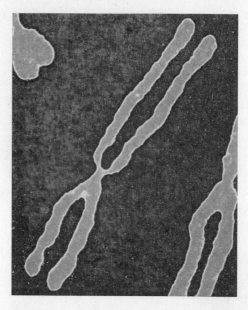

Not only is the Y chromosome important in determining gender, but it is also the site of genes controlling other aspects of development.

### Figure 3.2 Determining Sex

When an ovum and sperm meet at the moment of fertilization, the ovum is certain to provide an X chromosome, whereas the sperm will provide either an X or a Y chromosome. If the sperm contributes its X chromosome, the child will have an XX pairing on the 23rd chromosome and will be a girl. If the sperm contributes a Y chromosome, the result will be an XY pairing and the child will be a boy. Does this mean that girls are more likely to be conceived than boys?

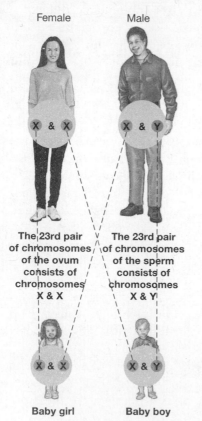

## The Basics of Genetics: The Mixing and Matching of Traits

**LO 3.2 Summarize the basics of genetics.**

What determined the color of your hair? Why are you tall or short? What made you susceptible to hay fever? And why do you have so many freckles? To answer these questions, we need to consider the basic mechanisms involved in the way that the genes we inherit from our parents transmit information.

We can start by examining the discoveries of an Austrian monk, Gregor Mendel, in the mid-1800s. In a series of simple yet convincing experiments, Mendel cross-pollinated pea plants that always produced yellow seeds with pea plants that always produced green seeds. The result was not, as one might guess, a plant with a combination of yellow and green seeds. Instead, all of the resulting plants had yellow seeds. At first, it appeared that the green-seeded plants had had no influence.

However, Mendel's additional research proved this initial impression was not true. He bred together plants from the new, yellow-seeded generation that had resulted from his original cross-breeding of the green-seeded and yellow-seeded plants. The consistent result was a ratio of three-fourths yellow seeds to one-fourth green seeds.

Gregor Mendel's pioneering experiments on pea plants provided the foundation for the study of genetics.

Why did this 3:1 ratio of yellow to green seeds appear so consistently? It took Mendel's genius to provide an answer. Based on his experiments with pea plants, he argued that when two competing traits, such as a green or yellow coloring of seeds, were both present, only one could be expressed. The one that was expressed was called a **dominant trait**. Meanwhile, the other trait remained present in the organism, although it was not expressed (displayed). This was called a **recessive trait**. In the case of Mendel's original pea plants, the offspring plants received genetic information from both the green-seeded and the yellow-seeded parents. However, the yellow trait was dominant, and consequently the recessive green trait did not assert itself.

Keep in mind, however, that genetic material relating to both parent plants is present in the offspring, even though it cannot be seen. The genetic information is known as the organism's genotype. A **genotype** is the underlying combination of genetic material present (but outwardly invisible) in an organism. In contrast, a **phenotype** is the observable trait, the trait that actually is seen.

Although the offspring of the yellow-seeded and green-seeded pea plants all have yellow seeds (i.e., they have a yellow-seeded phenotype), the genotype consists of genetic information relating to both parents.

And what is the nature of the information in the genotype? To answer that question, let's turn from peas to people. In fact, the principles are the same not only for plants and humans but also for the majority of species.

## Transmission of Genetic Information

**LO 3.3  Explain how genetic information is transmitted.**

As we have seen, parents transmit genetic information to their offspring via the chromosomes they contribute through the gamete they provide during fertilization. Some of the genes form pairs called *alleles*, genes governing traits that may take alternate forms, such as hair or eye color. For example, brown eye color is a dominant trait (B); blue eyes are recessive (b). A child's allele may contain similar or dissimilar genes from each parent. If, on the one hand, the child receives similar genes, he or she is said to be **homozygous** for the trait. On the other hand, if the child receives different forms of the gene from its parents, he or she is said to be **heterozygous**. In the case of heterozygous alleles (Bb), the dominant characteristic, brown eyes, is expressed. If the child happens to receive a recessive allele from each of its parents, and therefore lacks a dominant characteristic (bb), he or she will display the recessive characteristic, such as blue eyes.

We can see this process at work in humans by considering the transmission of *phenylketonuria (PKU)*, an inherited disorder in which a child is unable to make use of phenylalanine, an essential amino acid present in proteins found in milk and other foods. If left untreated, PKU allows phenylalanine to build up to toxic levels, causing brain damage and intellectual disability (Moyle et al., 2007; Widaman, 2009; Palermo et al., 2017).

PKU is produced by a single allele, or pair of genes. As shown in Figure 3.3, we can label each gene of the pair with a *P* if it carries a dominant gene, which causes

---

**dominant trait** The one trait that is expressed when two competing traits are present

**recessive trait** A trait within an organism that is present but not expressed

**genotype** The underlying combination of genetic material present (but not outwardly visible) in an organism

**phenotype** An observable trait; the trait that actually is seen

**homozygous** Inheriting from parents similar genes for a given trait

**heterozygous** Inheriting from parents different forms of a gene for a given trait

## Figure 3.3 PKU Probabilities

PKU, a disease that causes brain damage and intellectual disability, is produced by a single pair of genes inherited from one's mother and father. If neither parent carries a gene for the disease (a), a child cannot develop PKU. Even if one parent carries the recessive gene, but the other doesn't (b), the child cannot inherit the disease. If both parents carry the recessive gene (c), there is a one in four chance that the child will have PKU.

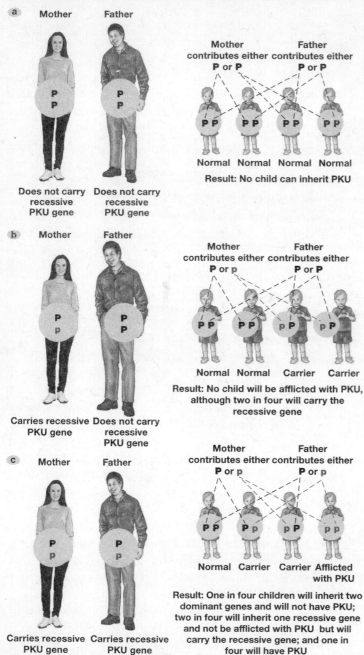

symbolized as *PP*. Consequently, no matter which member of the pair is contributed by the mother and father, the resulting pair of genes in the child will be *PP*, and the child will not have PKU.

Consider, however, what happens if one of the parents has a recessive *p* gene. In this case, which we can symbolize as *Pp*, the parent will not have PKU because the normal *P* gene is dominant. But the recessive gene can be passed down to the child. This is not so bad; if the child has only one recessive gene, it will not suffer from PKU. But what if both parents carry a recessive *p* gene? In this case, although neither parent has the disorder, it is possible for the child to receive a recessive gene from both parents. The child's genotype for PKU then will be *pp*, and he or she will have the disorder.

Remember, though, that even children whose parents both have the recessive gene for PKU have only a 25 percent chance of inheriting the disorder. Due to the laws of probability, 25 percent of children with *Pp* parents will receive the dominant gene from each parent (these children's genotype would be *PP*), and 50 percent will receive the dominant gene from one parent and the recessive gene from the other (their genotypes would be either *Pp* or *pP*). Only the unlucky 25 percent who receive the recessive gene from each parent and end up with the genotype *pp* will suffer from PKU.

The transmission of PKU is a good way of illustrating the basic principles of how genetic information passes from parent to child, although the case of PKU is simpler than most cases of genetic transmission. Relatively few traits are governed by a single pair of genes. Instead, most traits are the result of polygenic inheritance. In **polygenic inheritance**, a combination of multiple gene pairs is responsible for the production of a particular trait. Examples of polygenic inheritance include height and skin color.

Furthermore, some genes come in several alternate forms, and still others act to modify the way that particular genetic traits (produced by other alleles) are displayed. Genes also vary

the normal production of phenylalanine, or a *p* if it carries the recessive gene that produces PKU. In cases in which neither parent is a PKU carrier, both the mother's and the father's pairs of genes are the dominant form,

---

**polygenic inheritance** Inheritance in which a combination of multiple gene pairs is responsible for the production of a particular trait

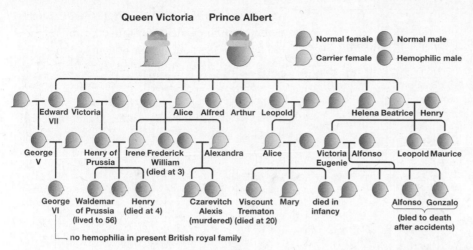

**Figure 3.4** Inheriting Hemophilia

Hemophilia, a blood-clotting disorder, has been an inherited problem throughout the royal families of Europe, as illustrated by the descendants of Queen Victoria of Britain.

**SOURCE:** Kimball, John W. (1983). Biology, 5th ed. Reprinted and Electronically reproduced by permission Education, Inc., Upper Saddle River, New Jersey.

in terms of their *reaction range*, the potential degree of variability in the actual expression of a trait due to environmental conditions. And some traits, such as blood type, are produced by genes in which neither member of a pair of genes can be classified as purely dominant or recessive. Instead, the trait is expressed in terms of a combination of the two genes—such as type AB blood.

A number of recessive genes, called **X-linked genes**, are located only on the X chromosome. Recall that in females the 23rd pair of chromosomes is an XX pair, whereas in males it is an XY pair. One result is that males have a higher risk for a variety of X-linked disorders, because males lack a second X chromosome that can counteract the genetic information that produces the disorder. For example, males are significantly more apt to have red-green color blindness, a disorder produced by a set of genes on the X chromosome.

Similarly, *hemophilia*, a blood disorder, is produced by X-linked genes. Hemophilia has been a recurrent problem in the royal families of Europe, as illustrated in Figure 3.4, which shows the inheritance of hemophilia in the descendants of Queen Victoria of Great Britain.

## The Human Genome and Behavioral Genetics: Cracking the Genetic Code

**LO 3.4** **Identify what we learned from the mapping of the human genome.**

Mendel's achievements in recognizing the basics of genetic transmission of traits were trailblazing; however, they mark only the beginning of our understanding of how those particular characteristics are passed

on from one generation to the next. The most recent milestone in understanding genetics was reached in early 2001, when molecular geneticists succeeded in mapping the specific sequence of genes on each chromosome. This accomplishment stands as one of the most important moments in the history of genetics, and, for that matter, all of biology (International Human Genome Sequencing Consortium, 2001).

For instance, the number of human genes, long thought to be 100,000, has been revised downward to 25,000—not many more than for organisms that are far less complex than the human (see Figure 3.5). Furthermore, scientists have discovered that all humans share 99.9 percent of the gene sequence. What this means is that we humans are far more similar to one another than we are different. It also indicates that many of the differences that seemingly separate people—such as race—are, literally, only skin deep. The mapping of the human genome will also help identify particular disorders to which a given individual is susceptible (Hyman, 2011; Levenson, 2012; Biesecker & Peay, 2013).

The mapping of the human gene sequence supports the field of behavioral genetics. As the name implies, **behavioral genetics** is the study of the effects of heredity on psychological characteristics. Rather than simply examining stable, unchanging characteristics such as hair or eye color, behavioral geneticists takes a broader approach, considering

---

**X-linked genes** Genes that are considered recessive and are located only on the X chromosome

**behavioral genetics** The study of the effects of heredity on behavior

## Figure 3.5 Uniquely Human?

Humans have about 25,000 genes, making them not much more genetically complex than some primitive species.

SOURCE: From Macmillan Publishers Ltd.: "International Human Genome Sequencing Consortium, Initial Sequencing and Analysis of the Human Genome," Nature. Copyright © 2001.

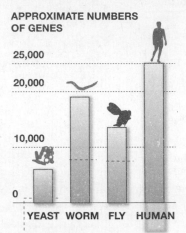

APPROXIMATE NUMBERS OF GENES

Estimated percentage of each creature's total genes found in humans are indicated by the dotted line.

## Table 3.1 The Genetic Basis of Selected Behavioral Disorders and Traits

| Behavioral Trait | Current Ideas of Genetic Basis |
| --- | --- |
| Huntington's disease | Mutations in the HTT gene. |
| Early onset (familial) Alzheimer's disease | Three distinct genes identified: APP, PSEN1, or PSEN2, which produce toxic protein fragments called *amyloid beta peptide*. |
| Fragile X syndrome | Mutations in the *FMR1* gene. |
| Attention-deficit/ hyperactivity disorder | Evidence in some studies has linked ADHD with the dopamine D4 and D5 genes, but the complexity of the disease makes it difficult to identify a specific gene beyond reasonable doubt. |
| Alcoholism | Research suggests that genes that affect the activity of neurotransmitters serotonin and GABA likely are involved in the risk for alcoholism. |
| Schizophrenia | There are more than 100 genes that have been associated with schizophrenia, but DRD2 appears to be of particular importance. |

SOURCE: Based on McGuffin, Riley, & Plomin, 2001; Schizophrenia Working Group of the Psychiatric Genomics Consortium, 2014; U.S. National Library of Medicine, 2016.

how our personality and behavioral habits are affected by genetic factors. Personality traits such as shyness or sociability, moodiness and assertiveness are among the areas being studied. Other behavioral geneticists examine psychological disorders, such as depression, attention-deficit/hyperactivity disorder, and schizophrenia spectrum disorder, looking for possible genetic links (Wang et al., 2012; Trace et al., 2013; Plomin et al., 2016; see Table 3.1).

Behavioral genetics holds substantial promise. For one thing, researchers working within the field have gained a better understanding of the specifics of the genetic code that underlie human behavior and development. Even more important, researchers are seeking to identify how genetic defects may be remedied (Plomin & Rutter, 1998; Peltonen & McKusick, 2001). To understand how a remedial possibility might come about, we need to consider the ways in which genetic factors, which normally cause development to proceed so smoothly, may falter.

**INHERITED AND GENETIC DISORDERS: WHEN DEVELOPMENT GOES AWRY.** PKU is just one of several disorders that may be inherited. Like a bomb that is harmless until its fuse is lit, a recessive gene responsible

for a disorder may be passed on unknowingly from one generation to the next, revealing itself only when, by chance, it is paired with another recessive gene. Then the gene will express itself, and a child will inherit the genetic disorder.

But there is another way that genes are a source of concern: In some cases, genes become physically damaged. For instance, genes may break down due to wear and tear or chance events occurring during the cell division processes of meiosis and mitosis. Sometimes genes, for no known reason, spontaneously change their form, a process called *spontaneous mutation*.

Alternatively, certain environmental factors, such as exposure to X-rays or even highly polluted air, may produce a malformation of genetic material. When such damaged genes are passed on to a child, the results can be disastrous in terms of future physical and cognitive development (Samet, DeMarini, & Malling, 2004; Acheva et al., 2014).

In addition to PKU, which occurs once in 10,000 to 20,000 births, other inherited and genetic disorders include:

- **Down syndrome**. As noted earlier, most people have 46 chromosomes, arranged in 23 pairs. One exception is individuals with **Down syndrome**, a disorder produced by the presence of an extra chromosome on the 21st pair. Once referred to as mongolism, Down syndrome is the most frequent cause of intellectual disability. It occurs in about 1 out of 700 births, although the risk is much greater in mothers who are unusually young or old (Davis, 2008; Adorno et al., 2013; Glasson et al., 2016).

- **Fragile X syndrome. Fragile X syndrome** occurs when a particular gene is injured on the X chromosome. The result is mild to moderate intellectual disability (Hagerman, 2011; Hocking, Kogan, & Cornish, 2012; Shelton et al., 2017).

- **Sickle-cell anemia.** Around one-tenth of the African American population carries genes that produce sickle-cell anemia, and 1 African American in 400 actually has the disease. **Sickle-cell anemia** is a blood disorder that gets its name from the shape of the red blood cells in those who have it. Symptoms include poor appetite, stunted growth, swollen stomach, and yellowish eyes. People afflicted with the most severe form of the disease rarely live beyond childhood; however, for those with less severe cases, medical advances have produced significant increases in life expectancy.

- **Tay-Sachs disease.** Occurring mainly in Jews of eastern European ancestry and in French-Canadians, **Tay-Sachs disease** usually causes death before its victims reach school age. There is no treatment for the disorder, which produces blindness and muscle degeneration prior to death.

- **Klinefelter's syndrome.** One male out of every 500 is born with **Klinefelter's syndrome**, the presence of an extra X chromosome. The resulting XXY complement produces underdeveloped genitals, extreme height, and enlarged breasts. Klinefelter's syndrome is one of a number of genetic abnormalities that result from receiving the improper number of sex chromosomes. For instance, there are disorders produced by an extra Y chromosome (XYY), a missing second chromosome (called Turner syndrome; X0), and three X chromosomes (XXX). Such disorders are typically characterized by problems relating to sexual characteristics and by intellectual deficits (Murphy & Mazzocco, 2008; Murphy, 2009; Turriff et al., 2016).

**ENVIRONMENTAL FACTORS.**  It is important to keep in mind that the mere fact that a disorder has genetic roots does not mean that environmental factors do not also play a role (Moldin & Gottesman, 1997). Consider, for instance, sickle-cell anemia, which primarily afflicts people of African descent. Because the disease can be fatal in childhood, we'd expect that those who suffer from it would be unlikely to live long enough to pass it on. This does seem to be true, at least in the United States: Compared with parts of West Africa, the incidence in the United States is much lower.

But why shouldn't the incidence of sickle-cell anemia also be gradually reduced for people in West Africa? This question proved puzzling for many years, until scientists determined that carrying the sickle-cell gene raises immunity to malaria, which is a common disease in West Africa (Allison, 1954). This heightened immunity meant that people with the sickle-cell gene had a genetic advantage (in terms of resistance to malaria) that offset, to some degree, the disadvantage of being a carrier of the sickle-cell gene.

The lesson of sickle-cell anemia is that genetic factors are intertwined with environmental considerations and can't be looked at in isolation. Furthermore, we need to remember that although we've been focusing on inherited factors that can go awry, in the vast majority of cases the genetic mechanisms with which we are endowed work quite well. Overall, 95 percent of children born in the United States are healthy and normal. For the some 250,000 who are born with some sort of physical or mental disorder, appropriate intervention often can help treat—and, in some cases, cure—the problem.

Moreover, due to advances in behavioral genetics, genetic difficulties increasingly can be forecast, anticipated, and planned for before a child's birth, enabling parents to take steps before the child is born to reduce

---

**Down syndrome** A disorder produced by the presence of an extra chromosome on the 21st pair; once referred to as mongolism

**fragile X syndrome** A disorder produced by injury to a gene on the X chromosome, producing mild to moderate intellectual disability

**sickle-cell anemia** A blood disorder that gets its name from the shape of the red blood cells in those who have it

**Tay-Sachs disease** A disorder that produces blindness and muscle degeneration prior to death; there is no treatment

**Klinefelter's syndrome** A disorder resulting from the presence of an extra X chromosome that produces underdeveloped genitals, extreme height, and enlarged breasts

the severity of certain genetic conditions. In fact, as scientists' knowledge regarding the specific location of particular genes expands, predictions of what the genetic future may hold are becoming increasingly exact, as we discuss next (Plomin & Rutter, 1998).

## Genetic Counseling: Predicting the Future From the Genes of the Present

**LO 3.5  Explain genetic counseling and its uses.**

If you knew that your mother and grandmother had died of Huntington's disease—a devastating, always fatal inherited disorder marked by tremors and intellectual deterioration—to whom could you turn to learn your own chances of coming down with the disease? The best person to consult would be a member of a field that, just a few decades ago, was nonexistent: genetic counseling. **Genetic counseling** focuses on helping people deal with issues relating to inherited disorders.

Genetic counselors use a variety of data in their work. For instance, couples contemplating having a child may seek to determine the risks involved in a future pregnancy. In such a case, a counselor will take a thorough family history, seeking any familial incidence of birth defects that might indicate a pattern of recessive or X-linked genes. In addition, the counselor will take into account factors such as the age of the mother and father and any previous abnormalities in other children they may have already had (Harris, Kelly, & Wyatt, 2013; O'Doherty, 2014; Austin, 2016).

Typically, genetic counselors suggest a thorough physical examination. Such an exam may identify physical abnormalities that potential parents may have and not be aware of. In addition, samples of blood, skin, and urine may be used to isolate and examine specific chromosomes. Possible genetic defects, such as the presence of an extra sex chromosome, can be identified by assembling a *karyotype*, a chart containing enlarged photos of each of the chromosomes.

**PRENATAL TESTING.**  A variety of techniques can be used to assess the health of an unborn child if a woman is already pregnant (see Table 3.2 for a list of currently available tests). The earliest test is a *first-trimester screen*, which combines a blood test and ultrasound sonography in the 11th to 13th week of pregnancy. In **ultrasound**

**Table 3.2** Fetal Development Monitoring Techniques

| Technique | Description |
|---|---|
| **Amniocentesis** | Done between the 15th and 20th week of pregnancy, this procedure examines a sample of the amniotic fluid, which contains fetal cells. Recommended if either parent carries Tay-Sachs, spina bifida, sickle-cell, Down syndrome, muscular dystrophy, or Rh disease. |
| **Chorionic villus sampling (CVS)** | Done at 8 to 10 weeks, either transabdominally or transcervically, depending on where the placenta is located. Involves inserting a needle (abdominally) or a catheter (cervically) into the substance of the placenta but staying outside the amniotic sac and removing 10 to 15 milligrams of tissue. This tissue is manually cleaned of maternal uterine tissue and then grown in culture, and a karyotype is made. |
| **Embryoscopy** | Examines the embryo or fetus during the first 12 weeks of pregnancy by means of a fiber-optic endoscope inserted through the cervix. Can be performed as early as week 5. Access to the fetal circulation may be obtained through the instrument, and direct visualization of the embryo permits the diagnosis of malformations. |
| **Fetal blood sampling (FBS)** | Performed after 18 weeks of pregnancy by collecting a small amount of blood from the umbilical cord for testing. Used to detect Down syndrome and most other chromosome abnormalities in the fetuses of couples who are at increased risk of having an affected child. Many other diseases can be diagnosed using this technique. |
| **Sonoembryology** | Used to detect abnormalities in the first trimester of pregnancy. Involves high-frequency transvaginal probes and digital image processing. In combination with ultrasound, can detect more than 80 percent of all malformations during the second trimester. |
| **Sonogram** | Uses ultrasound to produce a visual image of the uterus, fetus, and placenta. |
| **Ultrasound sonography** | Uses very high-frequency sound waves to detect structural abnormalities or multiple pregnancies, measure fetal growth, judge gestational age, and evaluate uterine abnormalities. Also used as an adjunct to other procedures such as amniocentesis. |

sonography, high-frequency sound waves bombard the mother's womb. These waves produce a rather indistinct, but useful, image of the unborn baby, whose size and shape can then be assessed. Repeated use of ultrasound sonography can reveal developmental patterns.

**genetic counseling** The discipline that focuses on helping people deal with issues relating to inherited disorders

**ultrasound sonography** A process in which high-frequency sound waves scan the mother's womb to produce an image of the unborn baby, whose size and shape can then be assessed

Although the accuracy of blood tests and ultrasound in identifying abnormalities is not high early in pregnancy, it becomes more accurate later on.

A more invasive test, **chorionic villus sampling (CVS)**, can be employed in the 8th to 10th week if blood tests and ultrasound have identified a potential problem. CVS involves inserting a thin needle into the amniotic fluid and taking small samples of hair-like material that surrounds the embryo. The test can be done between the 8th and 11th week of pregnancy. However, it produces a risk of miscarriage estimated to be as high as 1 in 100. Because of the risk, its use is relatively infrequent.

In **amniocentesis**, a small sample of fetal cells is drawn by a tiny needle inserted into the amniotic fluid surrounding the unborn fetus. Carried out 15 to 20 weeks into the pregnancy, amniocentesis allows the analysis of the fetal cells that can identify a variety of genetic defects with nearly 100 percent accuracy. In addition, it can determine the sex of the child. Although there is always a danger to the fetus in an invasive procedure such as amniocentesis, it is generally safe, with the risk of miscarriage 1 in 200 to 1 in 400.

After the various tests are complete and all possible information is available, the couple will meet with the genetic counselor again. Typically, counselors avoid giving specific recommendations. Instead, they lay out the facts and present various options, ranging from doing nothing to taking more drastic steps, such as terminating the pregnancy through abortion. Ultimately, the parents must decide what course of action to follow.

**SCREENING FOR FUTURE PROBLEMS.** The newest role of genetic counselors involves testing people to identify whether they themselves, rather than their children, are susceptible to future disorders because of genetic abnormalities. For instance, Huntington's disease typically does not manifest until people reach their 40s. However, genetic testing can identify much earlier whether a person carries the flawed gene that produces it. Presumably, people's knowledge that they carry the gene can help them prepare for the future (Cina & Fellmann, 2006; Tibben, 2007; Andersson et al., 2013).

In addition to Huntington's disease, more than 1,000 disorders can be predicted on the basis of genetic testing (see Table 3.3). Although such testing may bring welcome relief from future worries—if the results are negative—positive results may produce just the opposite effect. In fact, genetic testing raises difficult practical and ethical questions (Human Genome Project, 2006; Twomey, 2006; Wilfond & Ross, 2009; Klitzman, 2012).

Suppose, for instance, a woman who thought she was susceptible to Huntington's disease was tested in her 20s and found that she did not carry the defective gene. Obviously, she would experience tremendous relief. But suppose she found that she did carry the flawed gene and was therefore going to get the disease. In this case, she might well experience depression or anger. In fact, some studies show that 10 percent of people who find they have the flawed gene that leads to Huntington's disease never recover fully on an emotional level (Groopman, 1998; Hamilton, 1998; Myers, 2004; Wahlin, 2007).

Genetic testing clearly is a complicated issue. It rarely provides a simple yes or no answer as to whether an individual will be susceptible to a disorder. Instead, it typically presents a range of probabilities. In some cases, the

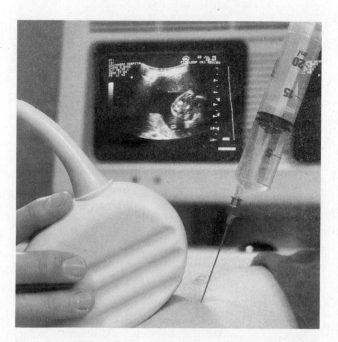

In amniocentesis, a sample of fetal cells is withdrawn from the amniotic sac and used to identify a number of genetic defects.

**chorionic villus sampling (CVS)** A test used to find genetic defects; involves taking samples of hair-like material that surrounds the embryo

**amniocentesis** The process of identifying genetic defects by examining a small sample of fetal cells drawn by a needle inserted into the amniotic fluid surrounding the unborn fetus

## Table 3.3 Some Currently Available DNA-Based Genetic Tests

| Disease | Description |
|---|---|
| Adult polycystic kidney disease | Kidney failure and liver disease |
| Alpha-1-antitrypsin deficiency | Emphysema and liver disease |
| Alzheimer's disease | Late-onset variety of senile dementia |
| Amyotrophic lateral sclerosis (Lou Gehrig's disease) | Progressive motor function loss leading to paralysis and death |
| Ataxia telangiectasia | Progressive brain disorder resulting in loss of muscle control and cancers |
| Breast and ovarian cancer (inherited) | Early onset tumors of breasts and ovaries |
| Charcot-Marie-Tooth | Loss of feeling in ends of limbs |
| Congenital adrenal hyperplasia | Hormone deficiency; ambiguous genitalia and male pseudohermaphroditism |
| Cystic fibrosis | Thick mucus accumulations in lungs and chronic infections in lungs and pancreas |
| Duchenne muscular dystrophy (Becker muscular dystrophy) | Severe to mild muscle wasting, deterioration, weakness |
| Dystonia | Muscle rigidity, repetitive twisting movements |
| Factor V-Leiden | Blood-clotting disorder |
| Fanconi anemia, group | Anemia, leukemia, skeletal deformities |
| Fragile X syndrome | Intellectual disability |
| Gaucher disease | Enlarged liver and spleen, bone degeneration |
| Hemophilia A and B | Bleeding disorders |
| Hereditary nonpolyposis colon cancer[a] | Early onset tumors of colon and sometimes other organs |
| Huntington's disease | Progressive neurological degeneration, usually beginning in midlife |
| Myotonic dystrophy | Progressive muscle weakness |
| Neurofibromatosis, type 1 | Multiple benign nervous system tumors that can be disfiguring; cancers |
| Phenylketonuria | Progressive intellectual disability due to missing enzyme; correctable by diet |
| Prader Willi/Angelman syndromes | Decreased motor skills, cognitive impairment, early death |
| Sickle-cell disease | Blood cell disorder; chronic pain and infections |
| Spinal muscular atrophy | Severe, usually lethal progressive muscle-wasting disorder in children |
| Tay-Sachs disease | Seizures, paralysis; fatal neurological disease of early childhood |
| Thalassemias | Anemias |

[a] These are susceptibility tests that provide only an estimated risk for developing the disorder.

**SOURCE:** Human Genome Project, 2006, http://www.oml.gov/scl/techresources/Human_Genome/medicine/genetest.shtml.

likelihood of actually becoming ill depends on the type of environmental stressors to which a person is exposed. Personal differences also affect a given person's susceptibility to a disorder (Bonke et al., 2005; Bloss, Schork, & Topol, 2011; Lucassen, 2012).

From an educator's perspective: What are some ethical and philosophical questions that surround the issue of genetic counseling? Might it sometimes be unwise to know ahead of time about possible genetically linked disorders that might afflict your child or yourself?

As our understanding of genetics continues to grow, researchers and medical practitioners have moved beyond testing and counseling to actively working to change flawed genes. The possibilities for genetic intervention and manipulation increasingly border on what once was science fiction. (Also see the *From Research to Practice* box.)

# The Interaction of Heredity and Environment

*Like many other parents, Jared's mother, Leesha, and his father, Jamal, tried to figure out which one of them their new baby resembled the most. He seemed to have Leesha's big, wide eyes*

# FROM RESEARCH TO PRACTICE
## Prenatal Screenings Are Not Diagnoses

When Arunima Mehera's obstetrician recommended a routine genetic screening for her unborn child, she really didn't give it much thought. She was three months into her pregnancy, and she knew that her age put her at greater risk of having a child with genetic abnormality. Testing made sense and didn't seem to have any downside.

But when the results came back positive for Edwards syndrome, a very serious and usually fatal genetic disorder caused by an extra 18th chromosome, Arunima and her husband decided to terminate the pregnancy.

However, what the couple didn't understand was that the genetic counseling, based on a simple blood test, could not definitively diagnose this condition in their unborn child. It was not meant to do that. Their confusion was understandable, given that their obstetrician explained that the test had a 99 percent detection rate. But this degree of accuracy referred only to its ability to detect the potential for a problem if one was in fact there; left unclear was that the test also often detected potential problems that turned out not to be there. In fact, for older pregnant women, screenings for Edwards syndrome return a false positive about 36 percent of the time (and they're even worse for younger women,

returning a false positive about 60 percent of the time). More invasive procedures are required to actually diagnose the prenatal condition (Lau et al., 2012; Allison, 2013; Daley, 2014).

These unregulated screenings, which were originally intended for use with high-risk patients, are increasingly being marketed to all pregnant women. Many believe that not enough is being done to ensure that women (and their doctors) understand what a positive result truly signifies and the probability that it is false. Industry research shows that some women are terminating their pregnancies based solely on a positive screening result without confirmation—and at least some of those cases turn out to have been healthy fetuses.

No one questions that prenatal screening for genetic abnormalities is beneficial, but it's clear that physicians and patients must understand how to interpret the results and should consult with a genetic specialist before making any important decisions based on a test result (Weaver, 2013; Guggenmos et al., 2015).

- **What would you tell a friend who just received a positive test result for the genetic disorder Tay-Sachs?**

---

*and Jamal's generous smile. As he grew, Jared looked like his mother and father even more. His hairline was just like Leesha's, and his teeth, when they came, made his smile resemble Jamal's even more. He also seemed to act like his parents. For example, he was a charming little baby, always ready to smile at people who visited the house—just like his friendly, jovial dad. He seemed to sleep like his mom, which was lucky because Jamal was an extremely light sleeper who could do with as little as four hours a night, whereas Leesha liked a regular seven or eight hours.*

Were Jared's ready smile and regular sleeping habits something he just luckily inherited from his parents? Or did Jamal and Leesha provide a happy and stable home that encouraged these welcome traits? What causes our behavior? Nature or nurture? Is behavior produced by inherited, genetic influences, or is it triggered by factors in the environment?

The simple answer is: there is no simple answer.

## The Role of the Environment in Determining the Expression of Genes: From Genotypes to Phenotypes

**LO 3.6**  **Describe how environmental factors interact in the development of individual traits.**

As developmental research accumulates, it is becoming increasingly clear that to view behavior as due to *either* genetic *or* environmental factors is inappropriate. A given behavior is not caused just by genetic factors, nor is it caused solely by environmental forces. Instead, as we first discussed in Chapter 1, the behavior is the product of some combination of the two.

For instance, consider **temperament**, patterns of arousal and emotionality that represent consistent

---

**temperament** Patterns of arousal and emotionality that represent consistent and enduring characteristics in an individual and enduring characteristics in an individual. Suppose we found—as increasing evidence suggests is the case—that a small percentage of children are born with temperaments that produce an unusual degree of physiological reactivity. Having a tendency to shrink from anything unusual, such infants react to novel stimuli with a rapid increase in heart rate and unusual excitability of the limbic system of the brain. Such heightened reactivity to stimuli at the start of life, which seems to be linked to inherited factors, is also likely to cause children, by the time they are 4 or 5 years old, to be considered shy by their parents and teachers. But not always: some of them behave indistinguishably from their peers at the same age (De Pauw & Mervielde, 2011; Pickles et al., 2013; Smiley et al., 2016).

What makes the difference? The answer seems to be the environment in which the children are raised. Children whose parents encourage them to be outgoing by arranging new opportunities for them may overcome their shyness. In contrast, children raised in a stressful environment marked by marital discord or a prolonged illness may be more likely to retain their shyness later in life. Jared, described earlier, may have been born with an easy temperament, which was reinforced by his caring parents (Kagan, Arcus, & Snidman, 1993; Propper & Moore, 2006; Bridgett et al., 2009; Casalin et al., 2012).

Such findings illustrate that many traits reflect **multifactorial transmission**, meaning that they are determined by a combination of both genetic and environmental factors. In multifactorial transmission, a genotype provides a particular range within which a phenotype may achieve expression. For instance, people with a genotype that permits them to gain weight easily may never be slim, no matter how much they diet. They may be *relatively* slim, given their genetic heritage, but they may never be able to get beyond a certain degree of thinness (Faith, Johnson, & Allison, 1997). In many cases, then, it is the environment that determines the way in which a particular genotype will be expressed as a phenotype (Wachs, 1992, 1993, 1996; Plomin, 1994b).

On the other hand, certain genotypes are relatively unaffected by environmental factors. In such cases, development follows its typical pattern, relatively independent of the specific environment in which a person is raised. Similarly, no matter how much health food people eat, they are not going to grow beyond certain genetically imposed limitations in height. And little Jared's hairline was probably affected very little by any actions on the part of his parents. Ultimately, of course, the unique interaction of inherited and environmental factors determines people's patterns of development.

The more appropriate question, then, is: *How much* of the behavior is caused by genetic factors, and *how much* by environmental factors? At one extreme is the idea that opportunities in the environment are solely responsible for intelligence; on the other, that intelligence is purely genetic—you either have it or you don't. The usefulness of such extremes seems to be that they point us toward the middle ground—that intelligence is the result of some combination of natural mental ability and environmental opportunity.

## Studying Development: How Much Is Nature? How Much Is Nurture?

**LO 3.7**  Explain how researchers study the interaction of genetic and environmental factors in development.

Developmental researchers use several strategies to try to resolve the question of the degree to which traits, characteristics, and behavior are produced by genetic or environmental factors. Their studies involve both nonhuman species and humans.

**NONHUMAN ANIMAL STUDIES: CONTROLLING BOTH GENETICS AND ENVIRONMENT.** It is relatively simple to develop breeds of animals that are genetically similar to one another in terms of specific traits. The people who raise Butterball turkeys for Thanksgiving do it all the time, producing turkeys that grow especially rapidly so that they can be brought to market inexpensively. Likewise, strains of laboratory animals can be bred to share similar genetic backgrounds.

By observing animals with similar genetic backgrounds in different environments, scientists can determine, with reasonable precision, the effects of specific kinds of environmental stimulation. For

---

**multifactorial transmission** The determination of traits by a combination of both genetic and environmental factors in which a genotype provides a range within which a phenotype may be expressed

example, animals can be raised in unusually stimulating environments, with lots of items to climb over or through, or they can be raised in relatively barren environments, to determine the results of living in such different settings. Conversely, researchers can examine groups of animals that have been bred to have significantly *different* genetic backgrounds on particular traits. Then, by exposing such animals to identical environments, they can determine the role of genetic background.

Of course, the drawback to using nonhumans as research subjects is that we can't be sure how well the findings we obtain can be generalized to people. Still, animal research offers substantial opportunities.

**CONTRASTING RELATEDNESS AND BEHAVIOR: ADOPTION, TWIN, AND FAMILY STUDIES.**   Clearly, researchers can't control either the genetic backgrounds or the environments of humans in the way they can with nonhumans. But nature conveniently has provided the potential to carry out various kinds of "natural experiments"—in the form of twins.

Recall that monozygotic twins are identical genetically. Because their inherited backgrounds are precisely the same, any variations in their behavior must be due entirely to environmental factors.

It would be rather simple for researchers to make use of identical twins to draw unequivocal conclusions about the roles of nature and nurture. For instance, by separating identical twins at birth and placing them in totally different environments, researchers could assess the impact of environment unambiguously. Of course, ethical considerations make this impossible. What researchers can—and do—study, however, are cases in which identical twins have been put up for adoption at birth and are raised in substantially different environments. Such instances allow us to draw fairly confident conclusions about the relative contributions of genetics and environment (Nikolas, Klump, & Burt, 2012; Suzuki, K., & Ando, J., 2014; Strachan et al., 2017).

The data from such studies are not always without bias. Adoption agencies typically take the characteristics (and wishes) of birth mothers into account when they place babies in adoptive homes. For instance, children tend to be placed with families of the same race and religion. Consequently, even when monozygotic twins are placed in different adoptive homes, there are often similarities between the two home environments. As a result, researchers can't

always be certain that differences in behavior are due to differences in the environment.

Studies of dizygotic twins also present opportunities to learn about the relative contributions of nature and nurture. Recall that dizygotic twins are genetically no more similar than siblings in a family born at different times. By comparing behavior within pairs of dizygotic twins with that of pairs of monozygotic twins (who are genetically identical), researchers can determine whether monozygotic twins are more similar on a particular trait, on average, than dizygotic twins. If so, they can assume that genetics plays an important role in determining the expression of that trait.

Still another approach is to study people who are totally unrelated to one another and who therefore have dissimilar genetic backgrounds, but who share an environmental background. For instance, a family that adopts, at the same time, two very young unrelated children probably will provide them with quite similar environments throughout their childhood. In this case, similarities in the children's characteristics and behavior can be attributed with some confidence to environmental influences (Segal, 1993, 2000).

Finally, developmental researchers have examined groups of people in light of their degree of genetic similarity. For instance, on the one hand, if we find a high association on a particular trait between biological parents and their children, but a weaker association between adoptive parents and their children, we have evidence for the importance of genetics in determining the expression of that trait. On the other hand, if there is a stronger association on a trait between adoptive parents and their children than between biological parents and their children, we have evidence for the importance of the environment in determining that trait. If a particular trait tends to occur at similar levels among genetically similar individuals, but occurs at different levels among genetically more distant individuals, signs point to the fact that genetics plays an important role in the development of that trait (Rowe, 1994).

Developmental researchers have used all these approaches, and more, to study the relative impact of genetic and environmental factors. What have they found?

Before turning to specific findings, here's the general conclusion resulting from decades of research: Virtually all traits, characteristics, and behaviors are the joint result of the combination and interaction of nature and nurture. Genetic and environmental factors work in tandem, each affecting and being affected by the other, creating the unique individual that each of us is and will become (Robinson, 2004; Waterland & Jirtle, 2004).

## The Role of Genetics on Physical Traits, Intelligence, and Personality

**LO 3.8 Describe the influence of genetics and the environment on physical traits, intelligence, and personality.**

Given that it's clear that genetic and environmental factors work together to determine our individuality, what conclusions have developmentalists reached regarding the *relative* influence of one set of factors versus the other? That is, what have researchers learned about the strength of genetic versus environmental factors with respect to particular traits, characteristics, and behaviors?

As we will see next, considerable research has been devoted to this question. We will take a look at research findings relating to the development of individuals' physical traits, intelligence, personality—and even philosophical outlook.

**PHYSICAL TRAITS: FAMILY RESEMBLANCES.** When patients entered the examining room of Dr. Cyril Marcus, they didn't realize that sometimes they were actually being treated by his identical twin brother, Dr. Stewart Marcus. So similar in appearance and manner were the twins that even longtime patients were fooled by this admittedly unethical behavior, which occurred in a bizarre case made famous in the film *Dead Ringers*.

Monozygotic twins are merely the most extreme example of the fact that the more genetically similar two people are, the more likely they are to share physical characteristics. Tall parents tend to have tall children, and short ones tend to have short children. *Obesity*, which is defined as being more than 20 percent above the average weight for a given height, also has a strong genetic component. For example, in one study, pairs of identical twins were put on diets that contained an extra 1,000 calories a day—and ordered not to exercise. Over a 3-month period, the twins gained almost identical amounts of weight. Moreover, different pairs of twins varied substantially in how much weight they gained, with some pairs gaining almost three times as much weight as other pairs (Bouchard et al., 1990).

Some traits—like curly hair—have a clear genetic component.

Other, less obvious physical characteristics also show strong genetic influences. For instance, blood pressure, respiration rates, and even the age at which life ends are more similar in closely related individuals than in those who are less genetically alike (Gottesman, 1991; Melzer, Hurst, & Frayling, 2007; Wu, Treiber, & Snieder, 2013).

**INTELLIGENCE: MORE RESEARCH, MORE CONTROVERSY.** No other issue involving the relative influence of heredity and environment has generated more research than the topic of intelligence. Why? The main reason is that intelligence, generally measured in terms of an IQ score, is a central human characteristic that differentiates humans from other species. In addition, intelligence is strongly related to success in scholastic endeavors and, somewhat less strongly, to other types of achievement.

Genetics plays a significant role in intelligence. In studies of both overall or general intelligence and of specific subcomponents of intelligence (such as spatial skills, verbal skills, and memory), the closer the genetic link between two individuals, the greater the correspondence of their overall IQ scores.

The impact of genetics on intelligence also increases with age. For instance, as fraternal (i.e., dizygotic) twins move from infancy to adolescence, their IQ scores become less similar. In contrast, the IQ scores of identical (monozygotic) twins become increasingly similar over the course of time. These opposite patterns suggest the intensifying influence of inherited factors with increasing age (Silventoinen et al., 2012; Segal et al., 2014; Madison et al., 2016).

Although it is clear that heredity plays an important role in intelligence, investigators are much more divided on the question of the degree to which it is inherited. Perhaps the most extreme view is held by psychologist Arthur Jensen (2003), who argued that as much as 80 percent of intelligence is a result of heredity. Others have suggested more modest figures, ranging from 50 percent to 70 percent. It is critical to keep in mind that such figures are averages across large groups of people, and any particular individual's degree of inheritance cannot be predicted from these averages (e.g., Devlin, Daniels, & Roeder, 1997).

In addition, environmental factors such as exposure to books, good educational experiences, and intelligent peers are profoundly influential on intelligence. Even those like Jensen who make the most extreme estimates of the role of genetics still allow for environmental factors to play a significant role. In fact, in terms of public policy, environmental influences are the focus of efforts geared toward maximizing people's intellectual success. We should be asking what can be done to maximize the intellectual development of each individual (Storfer, 1990; Bouchard, 1997; Anderson, 2007).

From an educator's perspective: Some people have used the proven genetic basis of intelligence to argue against strenuous educational efforts on behalf of individuals with below-average IQs. Does this viewpoint make sense based on what you have learned about heredity and environment? Why or why not?

**PERSONALITY: BORN TO BE OUTGOING?** Do we inherit personality? At least in part. There's increasing research evidence suggesting that some of our most basic personality traits have genetic roots. For

# DEVELOPMENTAL DIVERSITY AND YOUR LIFE

## Cultural Differences in Physical Arousal: Might a Culture's Philosophical Outlook Be Determined by Genetics?

Buddhism, a nontheistic religion that is an integral part of many Asian cultures, emphasizes harmony and peacefulness. In contrast, some traditional Western religions, such as those of Martin Luther and John Calvin, accentuate the importance of controlling the anxiety, fear, and guilt that they assume to be basic parts of the human condition.

Could such approaches to life reflect, in part, genetic factors? That is the controversial suggestion made by developmental psychologist Jerome Kagan and his colleagues. They speculate that the underlying temperament of a given society, determined genetically, may predispose people in that society toward a particular philosophy (Kagan, Arcus, & Snidman, 1993; Kagan, 2013).

Kagan bases his admittedly speculative suggestion on well-confirmed findings that show clear differences in temperament between Caucasian and Asian children. For instance, one study that compared 4-month-old infants in China, Ireland, and the United States found several relevant differences. In comparison to the Caucasian American babies and the Irish babies, the Chinese babies had significantly lower motor activity, irritability, and vocalization.

Kagan suggests that the Chinese infants, who enter the world temperamentally calmer, may find Buddhist philosophy stressing the importance of serenity more in tune with their natural inclinations. In contrast, Westerners, who are emotionally more volatile and tense, and who report higher levels of guilt, are more likely to be attracted to philosophies that articulate the necessity of controlling the unpleasant feelings that they are more apt to encounter in their everyday experience (Kagan et al., 1994; Kagan, 2003a; Zhang et al., 2013).

It is important to note that this does not mean that one philosophical approach is necessarily better or worse than the other. Nor does it mean that either of the temperaments from which the philosophies are thought to spring is superior or inferior to the other. Similarly, we must remember that any single individual within a culture can be more or less temperamentally volatile and that the range of temperaments found even within a particular culture is vast. Finally, as we noted in our initial discussion of temperament, environmental conditions can have a significant effect on the portion of a person's temperament that is not genetically determined. But what Kagan and his colleagues' speculation does attempt to address is the back-and-forth between culture and temperament. As religion may help mold temperament, so may temperament make certain religious ideals more attractive.

The notion that the very basis of culture—its philosophical traditions—may be affected by genetic factors is intriguing. More research is necessary to determine just how the unique interaction of heredity and environment within a given culture may produce a framework for viewing and understanding the world.

**Figure 3.6** Inheriting Traits

These traits are among the personality factors that are related most closely to genetic factors. The higher the percentage, the greater the degree to which the trait reflects the influence of heredity. Do these figures mean that "leaders are born, not made"? Why or why not?

**SOURCE:** Adapted from Tellegen, Auke; Lykken, David T.; Bouchard, Thomas J.; Wilcox, Kimerly J.; Segal, Nancy L.; and Rich, Stephen, "Personality similarity in twins reared apart and together," Journal of Personality and Social Psychology, Vol 54, No. 6, 1031–1039 (Jun 1988).

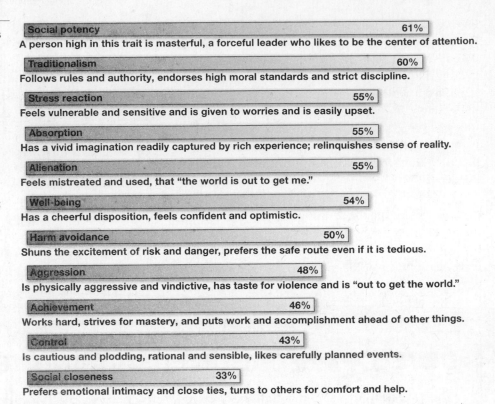

Social potency 61%
A person high in this trait is masterful, a forceful leader who likes to be the center of attention.

Traditionalism 60%
Follows rules and authority, endorses high moral standards and strict discipline.

Stress reaction 55%
Feels vulnerable and sensitive and is given to worries and is easily upset.

Absorption 55%
Has a vivid imagination readily captured by rich experience; relinquishes sense of reality.

Alienation 55%
Feels mistreated and used, that "the world is out to get me."

Well-being 54%
Has a cheerful disposition, feels confident and optimistic.

Harm avoidance 50%
Shuns the excitement of risk and danger, prefers the safe route even if it is tedious.

Aggression 48%
Is physically aggressive and vindictive, has taste for violence and is "out to get the world."

Achievement 46%
Works hard, strives for mastery, and puts work and accomplishment ahead of other things.

Control 43%
Is cautious and plodding, rational and sensible, likes carefully planned events.

Social closeness 33%
Prefers emotional intimacy and close ties, turns to others for comfort and help.

example, two of the key "Big Five" personality traits, neuroticism and extroversion, have been linked to genetic factors. *Neuroticism*, as used by personality researchers, is the degree of emotional stability an individual characteristically displays. *Extroversion* is the degree to which a person seeks to be with others, to behave in an outgoing manner, and generally to be sociable. For instance, Jared, the baby described earlier in this chapter, may have inherited a tendency to be outgoing from his extroverted father, Jamal (Horwitz, Luong, & Charles, 2008; Zyphur et al., 2013; Briley & Tucker-Drob, 2017).

How do we know which personality traits reflect genetics? Some evidence comes from direct examination of genes themselves. For instance, it appears that a specific gene is very influential in determining risk-taking behavior. This novelty-seeking gene affects the production of the brain chemical dopamine, making some people more prone than others to seek out new situations and to take risks (Serretti et al., 2007; Ray et al., 2009; Veselka et al., 2012).

Other evidence for the role of genetics in determining personality traits comes from examining twins. For instance, in one major study, researchers looked at the personality traits of hundreds of pairs of twins. Because

a good number of them were genetically identical but had been raised apart, it was possible to determine with some confidence the influence of genetic factors (Tellegen et al., 1988). The researchers found that certain traits reflected the contribution of genetics considerably more than others. As you can see in Figure 3.6, social potency (the tendency to be a masterful, forceful leader who enjoys being the center of attention) and traditionalism (strict endorsement of rules and authority) are strongly associated with genetic factors (Harris, Vernon, & Jang, 2007).

Even less basic personality traits are linked to genetics, too. For example, political attitudes, religious interests and values, and even attitudes toward human sexuality have genetic components (Bouchard, 2004; Koenig et al., 2005; Bradshaw & Ellison, 2008; Kandler, Bleidorn, & Riemann, 2012).

Clearly, genetic factors play a role in determining personality. At the same time, the environment in which a child is raised also affects personality development. For example, some parents encourage high activity levels, seeing them as a manifestation of independence and intelligence. Other parents may encourage lower levels of activity in their children, feeling that more passive children will get along better in society. Part of these parental attitudes is culturally determined; parents in the United States may encourage higher activity levels, whereas parents in Asian cultures may encourage greater passivity. In both cases, children's personalities will be shaped in part by their parents' attitudes (Cauce, 2008).

Because both genetic and environmental factors have consequences for a child's personality, personality development is a perfect example of a central fact of child development: the interplay between nature and nurture. Furthermore, the way in which nature and nurture interact can be reflected not only in the behavior of individuals but also in the very foundations of a culture, as we see in the *Developmental Diversity and Your Life* box.

## Psychological Disorders: The Role of Genetics and Environment

**LO 3.9** **Explain the role nature and nurture play in the development of psychological disorders.**

*When Elani Dimitrios turned 13, her cat, Mefisto, began to give her orders. At first, the orders were harmless: "Wear mismatched socks to school" or "Eat out of a bowl on the floor." Her parents dismissed these events as signs of a vivid imagination,* *but when Elani approached her little brother with a hammer, her mother intervened forcibly. Elani later recalled, "I heard the order very clearly: Kill him, kill him. It was as if I was possessed."*

In a sense, she *was* possessed: possessed with *schizophrenia spectrum disorder*, one of the most severe types of psychological disorders (typically referred to more simply as *schizophrenia*). Normal and happy through childhood, Elani increasingly lost her hold on reality as she entered adolescence. For the next two decades, she would be in and out of institutions, struggling to ward off the ravages of the disorder.

What was the cause of Elani's mental disorder? Increasing evidence suggests that schizophrenia is brought about by genetic factors. The disorder runs in families, with some families showing an unusually high incidence. Moreover, the closer the genetic links between someone with schizophrenia and another family member, the more likely it is that the other person will also develop schizophrenia. For instance, a monozygotic twin has close to a 50 percent risk of developing schizophrenia when the other twin develops the disorder (see Figure 3.7). By contrast, a niece or nephew of a person with schizophrenia has less than a 5 percent chance of developing the disorder (Hanson & Gottesman, 2005; Mitchell & Porteous, 2011; van Haren et al., 2012).

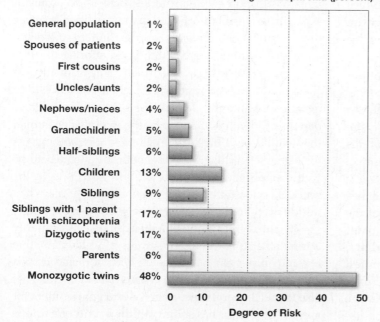

**Lifetime Risk of Developing Schizophrenia (percent)**

| Category | Risk |
|---|---|
| General population | 1% |
| Spouses of patients | 2% |
| First cousins | 2% |
| Uncles/aunts | 2% |
| Nephews/nieces | 4% |
| Grandchildren | 5% |
| Half-siblings | 6% |
| Children | 13% |
| Siblings | 9% |
| Siblings with 1 parent with schizophrenia | 17% |
| Dizygotic twins | 17% |
| Parents | 6% |
| Monozygotic twins | 48% |

Degree of Risk (0, 10, 20, 30, 40, 50)

**Figure 3.7** The Genetics of Schizophrenia

The psychological disorder schizophrenia has clear genetic components. The closer the genetic links between someone with schizophrenia and another family member, the more likely it is that the other person will also develop schizophrenia.

**SOURCE:** Gottesman, Irving I. (1991). Schizophrenia Genesis: The Origins of Madness. New York: Henry Holt and Company.

These data also illustrate that genetics alone does not influence the development of the disorder. If genetics were the sole cause, the risk for an identical twin would be 100 percent. Consequently, other factors account for the disorder, ranging from structural abnormalities in the brain to a biochemical imbalance (e.g., Hietala, Cannon, & van Erp, 2003; Howes & Kapur, 2009; Wada et al., 2012).

It also seems that even if individuals harbor a genetic predisposition toward schizophrenia, they are not destined to develop the disorder. Instead, they may inherit an unusual sensitivity to stress in the environment. If stress is low, schizophrenia will not occur. But if stress is sufficiently strong, it will lead to schizophrenia. At the same time, for someone with a strong genetic predisposition toward the disorder, even relatively weak environmental stressors may lead to schizophrenia (Mittal, Ellman, & Cannon, 2008; Stefanis et al., 2013).

Several other psychological disorders have been shown to be related, at least in part, to genetic factors. For instance, major depressive disorders, alcoholism, autism spectrum disorder, and attention-deficit/hyperactivity disorder have significant inherited components (Dick, Rose, & Kaprio, 2006; Monastra, 2008; Burbach & van der Zwaag, 2009).

The example of schizophrenia spectrum disorder and other genetically related psychological disorders also illustrates a fundamental principle regarding the relationship between heredity and environment, a principle that underlies much of our previous discussion. Specifically, the role of genetics is often to produce a tendency toward a future course of development. When and whether a certain behavioral characteristic will actually be displayed depends on the nature of the environment. Thus, although a predisposition for schizophrenia may be present at birth, typically people do not show the disorder until adolescence—if at all.

Similarly, certain other kinds of traits are more likely to be displayed as the influence of parents and other socializing factors declines. For example, adopted children may, early in their lives, display traits that are relatively similar to their adoptive parents' traits, given the overwhelming influence of the environment on young children. As they get older and their parents' day-to-day influence declines, genetically influenced traits may begin to manifest themselves as unseen genetic factors begin to play a greater role (Arseneault et al., 2003; Poulton & Caspi, 2005).

# Can Genes Influence the Environment?

**LO 3.10  Discuss the ways genes can influence the environment.**

The genetic endowment provided to children by their parents not only determines their genetic characteristics, but also actively influences their environment. There are at least three ways a child's genetic predisposition might influence his or her environment (Scarr, 1998; Vinkhuyzen et al., 2010; Sherlock et al., 2017).

First, children tend to actively focus on those aspects of their environment that are most connected with their genetically determined abilities. For example, an active, more aggressive child will gravitate toward sports, while a more reserved child will be more engaged by academics or solitary pursuits like computer games or drawing. Children also pay less attention to those aspects of the environment that are less compatible with their genetic endowment. For instance, two girls may be reading the same school bulletin board. One may notice the sign advertising tryouts for Little League baseball, whereas her less coordinated but more musically endowed friend might be more apt to spot the notice recruiting students for an after-school chorus. In each case, the child is attending to those aspects of the environment in which her genetically determined abilities can flourish.

In addition, in some cases, the gene-environment influence is more passive and less direct. For example, a particularly sports-oriented parent, who has genes that promote good physical coordination, may provide many opportunities for a child to play sports.

Finally, the genetically driven temperament of a child may *evoke* certain environmental influences. For instance, an infant's demanding behavior may cause parents to be more attentive to the infant's needs than they would be if the infant were less demanding. Or, for example, a child who is genetically inclined to be well coordinated may play ball with anything in the house so often that her parents notice. They may then decide that she should have some sports equipment.

In sum, determining whether behavior is primarily attributable to nature or nurture is a bit like shooting at a moving target. Not only are behaviors and traits a joint outcome of genetic and environmental factors, but also the relative influence of genes and environment for specific characteristics shifts over the course of people's lives. Although the pool of genes we inherit at birth sets the stage for our future development, the constantly shifting scenery and the other characters in our lives determine just how our development eventually plays out. The environment both influences our experiences and is molded by the choices we are temperamentally inclined to make.

# Prenatal Growth and Change

*Robert accompanied Lisa to her first appointment with the midwife. The midwife checked the results of tests done to confirm the couple's own positive home pregnancy test. "Yep, you're going to have a baby," she confirmed, speaking to Lisa. "You'll need to set up monthly visits for the next 6 months, then more frequently as your due date approaches. You can get this prescription for prenatal vitamins filled at any pharmacy, and here are some guidelines about diet and exercise. You don't smoke, do you? That's good." Then she turned to Robert. "How about you? Do you smoke?" After giving lots of instructions and advice, she left the couple feeling slightly dazed, but ready to do whatever they could to have a healthy baby.*

From the moment of conception, development proceeds relentlessly. As we've seen, many aspects are guided by the complex set of genetic guidelines inherited from the parents. Of course, prenatal growth, like all development, is also influenced from the start by environmental factors (Leavitt & Goldson, 1996). As we see later, both parents, like Lisa and Robert, can take part in providing a good prenatal environment.

## The Stages of the Prenatal Period: The Onset of Development

**LO 3.11  Explain what happens during the prenatal stages of development.**

When most of us think about the facts of life, we tend to focus on the events that cause a male's sperm cells to begin their journey toward a female's ovum. Yet the act of sex that brings about the potential for conception is both the consequence and the start of a long string of events that precede and follow **fertilization**, or conception: the joining of sperm and ovum to create the single-celled zygote from which life begins.

Both the male's sperm and the female's ovum come with a history of their own. Females are born with around 400,000 ova located in the two ovaries. The ova, however, do not mature until the female reaches puberty. From that point until she reaches menopause, the female will ovulate about every 28 days. During ovulation, an egg is released from one of the ovaries and pushed by minute hair cells through the fallopian tube toward the uterus. If the ovum meets a sperm in the fallopian tube, fertilization takes place (Aitken, 1995).

Sperm, which look a little like microscopic tadpoles, have a shorter life span. They are created by the testicles at a rapid rate: An adult male typically produces several hundred million sperm a day. Consequently, the sperm ejaculated during sexual intercourse are of considerably more recent origin than the ovum to which they are heading.

When sperm enter the vagina, they begin a winding journey that takes them through the cervix, the opening into the uterus, and into the fallopian tube, where fertilization may take place. Only a tiny fraction of the 300 million cells that are typically ejaculated during sexual intercourse ultimately survive the arduous journey. That's usually okay, though: It takes only one sperm to fertilize an ovum, and each sperm and ovum contains all the genetic data necessary to produce a new human.

The prenatal period consists of three phases: the germinal, embryonic, and fetal stages as discussed below.

**THE GERMINAL STAGE: FERTILIZATION TO 2 WEEKS.** In the **germinal stage**, the first—and shortest—stage of the prenatal period, the zygote begins to divide and grow in complexity during the first 2 weeks following conception. During the germinal stage, the fertilized egg (now called a *blastocyst*) travels toward the *uterus*, where it becomes implanted in the uterine wall, which is rich in nutrients. The germinal stage is characterized by methodical cell division, which gets off to a quick start: Three days after fertilization, the

---

**fertilization** The process by which a sperm and an ovum—the male and female gametes, respectively—join to form a single new cell

**germinal stage** The first—and shortest—stage of the prenatal period, which takes place during the first 2 weeks following conception

organism consists of some 32 cells, and by the next day the number doubles. Within a week, it is made up of 100 to 150 cells, and the number rises with increasing rapidity.

In addition to increasing in number, the cells of the organism become increasingly specialized. For instance, some cells form a protective layer around the mass of cells, whereas others begin to establish the rudiments of a placenta and umbilical cord. When fully developed, the **placenta** serves as a conduit between the mother and fetus, providing nourishment and oxygen via the *umbilical cord*, which also removes waste materials from the developing child. The placenta also plays a role in fetal brain development (Kalb, 2012).

**THE EMBRYONIC STAGE: 2 WEEKS TO 8 WEEKS.** By the end of the germinal period—just 2 weeks after conception—the organism is firmly secured to the wall of the mother's uterus. At this point, the child is called an *embryo*. The **embryonic stage** is the period from 2 to 8 weeks following fertilization. One of the highlights of this stage is the development of the major organs and basic anatomy.

At the beginning of the embryonic stage, the developing child has three distinct layers, each of which will ultimately form a different set of structures as development proceeds. The outer layer of the embryo, the *ectoderm*, will form skin, hair, teeth, sense organs, and the brain and spinal cord. The *endoderm*, the inner layer, produces the digestive system, liver, pancreas, and respiratory system. Sandwiched between the ectoderm and endoderm is the *mesoderm*, from which the muscles, bones, blood, and circulatory system are forged. Every part of the body is formed from these three layers.

If you were looking at an embryo at the end of the embryonic stage, you might be hard-pressed to identify it as human. Only an inch long, an 8-week-old embryo has what appear to be gills and a tail-like structure. However, a closer look reveals several familiar features. Rudimentary eyes, nose, lips, and even teeth can be recognized, and the embryo has stubby bulges that will form arms and legs.

The head and brain undergo rapid growth during the embryonic period. The head begins to represent a significant proportion of the embryo's size, encompassing about 50 percent of its total length. The growth of nerve cells, called *neurons*, is astonishing: As many as 100,000 neurons are produced every minute during the second month of life! The nervous system begins to function around the fifth week, and weak brain waves begin to be produced as the nervous system starts to function (Nelson & Bosquet, 2000).

**THE FETAL STAGE: 8 WEEKS TO BIRTH.** It is not until the final period of prenatal development, the fetal stage, that the developing child becomes easily recognizable. The **fetal stage** starts at about 8 weeks after conception and continues until birth. The fetal stage formally starts when the differentiation of the major organs has occurred.

Now called a **fetus**, the developing child undergoes astoundingly rapid change during the fetal stage. For instance, it increases in length approximately 20 times, and its proportions change dramatically. At 2 months, approximately one-half of the fetus is what will ultimately be its head; at 5 months, the head accounts for just over one-fourth of its total size (see Figure 3.8). The fetus also substantially increases in

**Figure 3.8** Body Proportions

During the fetal period, the proportions of the body change dramatically. At 2 months, the head represents approximately half the fetus, but by the time of birth, it is one-fourth of its total size.

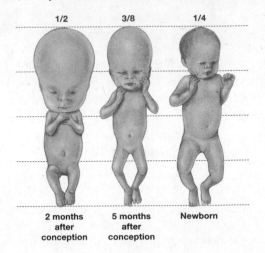

| 1/2 | 3/8 | 1/4 |

| 2 months after conception | 5 months after conception | Newborn |

**placenta** A conduit between the mother and fetus, providing nourishment and oxygen via the umbilical cord

**embryonic stage** The period from 2 to 8 weeks following fertilization, during which significant growth occurs in the major organs and body systems.

**fetal stage** The stage that begins at about 8 weeks after conception and continues until birth

**fetus** A developing child, from 8 weeks after conception until birth

weight. At 4 months, the fetus weighs an average of about 4 ounces; at 7 months, it weighs about 3 pounds; and at the time of birth, the average child weighs just over 7 pounds.

At the same time, the developing child is rapidly becoming more complex. Organs become more differentiated and start to work. By 3 months, for example, the fetus swallows and urinates. In addition, the interconnections between the different parts of the body become more complex and integrated. For example, arms develop hands; hands develop fingers; fingers develop nails.

As this is happening, the fetus makes itself known to the outside world. In the earliest stages of pregnancy, mothers may be unaware that they are, in fact, pregnant. As the fetus becomes increasingly active, however, most mothers certainly take notice. By 4 months, a mother can feel the movement of her child, and several months later, others can feel the baby's kicks through the mother's skin. In addition to the kicks that alert its mother to its presence, the fetus can turn, do somersaults, cry, hiccup, clench its fist, open and close its eyes, and suck its thumb.

The brain becomes increasingly sophisticated during the fetal stage. The two symmetrical left and right halves of the brain, known as *hemispheres*, grow rapidly, and the interconnections between neurons become more complex. The neurons become coated with an insulating material called *myelin*, which helps speed the transmission of messages from the brain to the rest of the body.

By the end of the fetal period, brain waves are produced that indicate the fetus passes through different stages of sleep and wakefulness. The fetus is also able to hear (and feel the vibrations of) sounds to which it is exposed. For instance, researchers Anthony DeCasper and Melanie Spence (1986) asked a group of pregnant mothers to read aloud the Dr. Seuss story *The Cut in the Hat* two times a day during the latter months of pregnancy. Three days after the babies were born, they appeared to recognize the story they had heard, responding more to it than to another story that had a different rhythm.

In weeks 8 to 24 following conception, hormones are released that lead to the increasing differentiation of male and female fetuses. For example, high levels of androgen are produced in males that affect the size of brain cells and the growth of neural connections, which, some scientists speculate, ultimately may lead to differences in male and female brain structure and even later variations in gender-related behavior (Reiner & Gearhart, 2004; Knickmeyer & Baron-Cohen, 2006; Burton et al., 2009; Jordan-Young, 2012).

Just as no two adults are alike, no two fetuses are the same. Although development during the prenatal period follows the broad patterns outlined here, there are significant differences in the specific nature of individual fetuses' behavior. Some fetuses are exceedingly active, whereas others are more sedentary. (The more active fetuses will probably be more active after birth.) Some have relatively quick heart rates, whereas others' heart rates are slower, with the typical range varying between 120 and 160 beats per minute (DiPietro et al., 2002; Niederhofer, 2004; Tongsong et al., 2005).

Such differences in fetal behavior are due in part to genetic characteristics inherited at the moment of fertilization. Other kinds of differences, though, are brought about by the nature of the environment in which the child spends its first 9 months of life. As we will see, there are numerous ways in which the prenatal environment of infants affects their development—in good ways and bad.

## Pregnancy Problems

**LO 3.12 Discuss the issues that individuals face with respect to pregnancy.**

For some couples, conception presents a major challenge. Let's consider some of the challenges—both physical and ethical—that relate to pregnancy.

**INFERTILITY.**  Some 15 percent of couples suffer from **infertility**, the inability to conceive after 12 to 18 months of trying to become pregnant. Infertility is negatively correlated with age. The older the parents, the more likely infertility will occur; see Figure 3.9.

In men, infertility is typically a result of producing too few sperm. Use of illicit drugs or cigarettes and previous bouts of sexually transmitted diseases also increase infertility. For women, the most common cause of infertility is failure to release an egg through ovulation. This may occur because of a hormone imbalance, a damaged fallopian tube or uterus, stress, or abuse of alcohol or drugs (Kelly-Weeder & Cox, 2007; Wilkes et al., 2009; Geller, Nelson, & Bonacquisti, 2013).

---

**infertility** The inability to conceive after 12 to 18 months of trying to become pregnant

**Figure 3.9** Older Women and Risks of Pregnancy

Not only does the rate of infertility increase as women get older, but the risk of chromosomal abnormality also increases.

**SOURCE:** Reproductive Medicine Associates of New Jersey (2002) Older women and risks of pregnancy. Princeton, NJ: American Society for Reproductive Medicine.

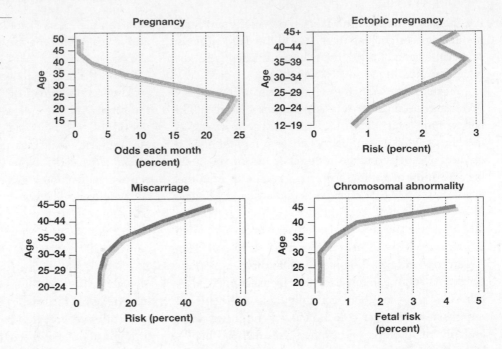

Several treatments for infertility exist. Some difficulties can be corrected through the use of drugs or surgery. Another option may be **artificial insemination**, a procedure in which a man's sperm is placed directly into a woman's vagina by a physician. In some situations, the woman's husband provides the sperm, whereas in others, it is an anonymous donor from a sperm bank.

In other cases, fertilization takes place outside of the mother's body. **In vitro fertilization (IVF)** is a procedure in which a woman's ova are removed from her ovaries, and a man's sperm are used to fertilize the ova in a laboratory. The fertilized egg is then implanted in a woman's uterus. Similarly, *gamete intrafallopian transfer (GIFT)* and *zygote intrafallopian transfer (ZIFT)* are procedures in which an egg and sperm or fertilized egg are implanted in a woman's fallopian tubes. In IVF, GIFT, and ZIFT, implantation is done either in the woman who provided the donor eggs or, in rarer instances, in a *surrogate mother*, a woman who agrees to carry the child to term. Surrogate mothers may also be used in cases in which the mother is unable to conceive; the surrogate mother is artificially inseminated by the biological father, and she agrees to give up rights to the infant (Frazier et al., 2004; Kolata, 2004).

IVF is increasingly successful, with pregnancy rates as high as 48 percent for women under 35 (but with lower rates for older women). (Actual live birth rates are lower, since not all pregnancies ultimately result in birth.) It is also becoming more commonplace, with the procedure being used and publicized by women such as actresses Marcia Cross and Nicole Kidman. Worldwide, more than 3 million babies have been created through IVF (SART, 2012).

Furthermore, reproductive technologies are increasingly sophisticated, permitting parents to choose the sex of their baby. One technique is to separate sperm carrying the X and Y chromosomes and later implant the desired type into a woman's uterus. In another procedure, lasers are used to measure the DNA in sperm to choose the sex of the child. And in still another technique, eggs are removed from a woman and fertilized with sperm using in vitro fertilization. Three days after fertilization, the embryos are tested to determine their sex. If they are the desired gender, they are then implanted into the mother (Duenwald, 2003, 2004; Kalb, 2004).

**ETHICAL ISSUES.** The use of surrogate mothers, IVF, and sex selection techniques presents a web of ethical and legal issues, as well as many emotional concerns. In some cases, surrogate mothers have refused to give up

**artificial insemination** A process of fertilization in which a man's sperm is placed directly into a woman's vagina by a physician

**in vitro fertilization (IVF)** A procedure in which a woman's ova are removed from her ovaries, and a man's sperm are used to fertilize the ova in a laboratory

the child after its birth, whereas in others the surrogate mother has sought to have a role in the child's life. In such cases, the rights of the mother, the father, the surrogate mother, and ultimately the baby are in conflict.

Even more troubling are concerns raised by sex selection techniques. Is it ethical to terminate the life of an embryo based on its sex? Do cultural pressures that may favor boys over girls make it permissible to seek medical intervention to produce male offspring, resulting in a kind of gender discrimination prior to birth? Furthermore, might a shortage of children of the less preferred sex ultimately emerge (Sharma, 2008; Bhagat, Laskar & Sharma, 2012; Kalfoglou et al., 2013)?

Going further, if it is permissible to intervene in the reproductive process to obtain a favored sex, what about other characteristics determined by genetics that it may be possible in the future to preselect for? For instance, assuming the technology advances, would it be ethical to select for a favored eye or hair color, a certain level of intelligence, or a particular kind of personality? That's not feasible now, but it is not outside the realm of possibility in the future (Bonnicksen, 2007; Mameli, 2007; Roberts, 2007).

For the moment, many of these ethical issues remain unresolved. But we can answer one question: How do children who are conceived using emerging reproductive technologies such as IVF end up faring?

Research shows that they do quite well. In fact, some studies find that the quality of family life for those who have used such techniques may be superior to that in families with naturally conceived children. Furthermore, the later psychological adjustment of children conceived using IVF and artificial insemination is no different from that of children conceived using natural techniques (DiPietro, Costigan, & Gurewitsch, 2005; Hjelmstedt, Widström, & Collins, 2006; Siegel, Dittrich, & Vollmann, 2008).

However, the increasing use of IVF techniques by older individuals (who might be quite elderly when their children reach adolescence) may change these positive findings. Because widespread use of IVF is still a recent development, we just don't know yet what will happen with aging parents (Colpin & Soenen, 2004).

**MISCARRIAGE AND ABORTION.** A *miscarriage*— medically known as a spontaneous abortion—occurs when pregnancy ends before the developing child is able to survive outside the mother's womb. The embryo detaches from the wall of the uterus and is expelled.

Some 15 percent to 20 percent of all pregnancies end in miscarriage, usually in the first several months of pregnancy. (The term *stillbirth* is used to describe the death of a developing child 20 weeks or more after conception.) Many miscarriages occur so early that the mother is not even aware she was pregnant and may not even know she has suffered a miscarriage. However, as women are able to learn they are pregnant earlier than ever before due to the advent of home pregnancy tests, the number of women who know they have suffered a miscarriage has increased.

Typically, miscarriages are attributable to some sort of genetic abnormality in the fetus. In addition, hormonal problems, infections, or maternal health problems can lead to miscarriage. Whatever the cause, women who suffer miscarriage frequently experience anxiety, depression, and grief. Because a woman's body may continue to look pregnant for a period of several weeks before it goes back to its pre-pregnant state, grief over the loss may be intensified and prolonged (Zucker & Alexander-Tanner, 2017).

Even after subsequently having a healthy child, women who have had a miscarriage in the past still have a higher risk for depression. In addition, the aftereffects may linger, sometimes for years, and these women may have difficulty caring for their healthy children (Leis-Newman, 2012; Murphy, Lipp, & Powles, 2012; Sawicka, 2016).

Each year, one in four pregnancies worldwide ends in *abortion*, in which a mother voluntarily or involuntarily (e.g., female feticide for some mothers in India) chooses to terminate pregnancy. Involving a complex set of physical, psychological, ethical, and legal issues, abortion is a difficult choice for every woman. Abortion following a prenatal screening is a major concern in India. The process has led to an inappropriate gender ratio as most families practice female feticide after prenatal screening. Therefore, prenatal screening is prohibited by law in India, unless it is prescribed by a medical practitioner for a health concern of the mother and the fetus.

By contrast, other research finds that abortion may be associated with an increased risk of future psychological problems. However, the findings are mixed, and there are significant individual differences in how women respond to the experience of abortion. The clear message is that in all cases, abortion is a complicated and difficult decision (Fergusson, Horwood, & Ridder, 2006; Cockrill & Gould, 2012; van Ditzhuijzen et al., 2013).

# The Prenatal Environment: Threats to Development

### LO 3.13 Describe some threats to the fetal environment and what can be done about them.

According to the Siriono people of South America, if a pregnant woman eats the meat of certain kinds of animals, she runs the risk of having a child who may act and look like those animals. According to opinions offered on daytime television talk shows, a pregnant mother should avoid getting angry in order to spare her child from entering the world with anger (Cole, 1992).

Such views are largely the stuff of folklore, although there is some evidence that a mother's anxiety during pregnancy may affect the sleeping patterns of the fetus prior to birth. However, there are certain aspects of a mother's and father's behavior, both before and after conception, that can produce lifelong consequences for the child. Some consequences show up immediately, but half the possible problems aren't apparent before birth. Other problems—more insidious ones—may not manifest until years after birth (Groome et al., 1995; Couzin, 2002).

Some of the most profound consequences are brought about by teratogenic agents. A **teratogen** is an environmental agent such as a drug, chemical, virus, or other factor that produces a birth defect. Although it is the job of the placenta to keep teratogens from reaching the fetus, the placenta is not entirely successful at this, and probably every fetus is exposed to some teratogens.

The timing and quantity of exposure to a teratogen are crucial. At some phases of prenatal development, a certain teratogen may have only a minimal impact. At other periods, however, the same teratogen may have significant consequences. Generally, teratogens have their largest effects during periods of especially rapid prenatal development. Sensitivity to specific teratogens is also related to racial and cultural background. For example, Native American fetuses are more susceptible to the effects of alcohol than those of European American descent (Kinney et al., 2003; Winger & Woods, 2004; Rentner, Dixon, & Lengel, 2012).

Furthermore, different organ systems are vulnerable to teratogens at different times during development. For example, the brain is most susceptible 15 to 25 days after conception, whereas the heart is most vulnerable 20 to 40 days following conception (see Figure 3.10; Bookstein et al., 1996; Pajkrt et al., 2004).

When considering the findings relating to specific teratogens, as we do next, we need to keep in mind the broader social and cultural context in which teratogen exposure occurs. For example, living in poverty increases the chances of exposure to teratogens. Mothers who are poor may not be able to afford adequate nutrition, and they may not be able to afford adequate medical care, making them more susceptible to illness that can damage a developing fetus. They are also more likely to be exposed to pollution. Consequently, it is important to consider the social factors that permit exposure to teratogens.

**MOTHER'S DIET.** Most of our knowledge of the environmental factors that affect the developing fetus comes from study of the mother. For instance, as the midwife pointed out in the example of Lisa and Robert, a mother's diet clearly plays an important role in bolstering the development of the fetus. A mother who eats a varied diet high in nutrients is apt to have fewer complications during pregnancy, an easier labor, and a generally healthier baby than a mother whose diet is restricted in nutrients (Kaiser & Allen, 2002; Guerrini, Thomson, & Gurling, 2007).

With 800 million hungry people in the world, the problem of diet is of immense global concern. Even worse, the number of people vulnerable to hunger is close to 1 *billion*. Clearly, restrictions in diet that bring about hunger on such a massive scale affect millions of children born to women living in those conditions (World Food Programme, 2016).

Fortunately, there are ways to counteract the types of maternal malnourishment that affect prenatal development. Dietary supplements given to mothers can reverse some of the problems produced by a poor diet. Furthermore, research shows that babies who were malnourished as fetuses, but who are subsequently raised in enriched environments, can overcome some of the effects of their early malnourishment. Unfortunately, the reality is that few of the world's children whose mothers were malnourished *before* their birth are apt to find themselves in enriched environments after birth (Grantham-McGregor et al., 1994; Kramer, 2003; Olness, 2003).

**MOTHER'S AGE.** More women are giving birth later in life than they were just two or three decades ago. The cause for this change is largely transformations

---

teratogen A factor that produces a birth defect

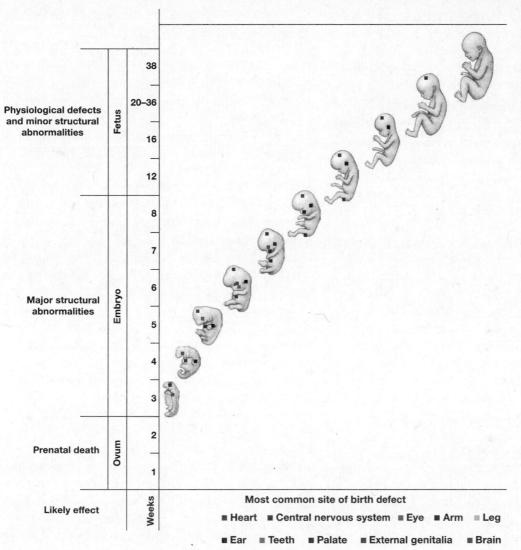

**Figure 3.10**
Teratogen Sensitivity

Depending on their state of development, some parts of the body vary in their sensitivity to teratogens.

**SOURCE:** Moore, K.L. (1974). Before we are born: Basic embrology and birth defects. Philadelphia: Saunders.

Physiological defects and minor structural abnormalities

Major structural abnormalities

Prenatal death

Likely effect

Fetus

Embryo

Ovum

Weeks

38
20–36
16
12
8
7
6
5
4
3
2
1

Most common site of birth defect
■ Heart   ■ Central nervous system   ■ Eye   ■ Arm   ■ Leg
■ Ear   ■ Teeth   ■ Palate   ■ External genitalia   ■ Brain

in society, as more women choose to continue their education with advanced degrees and to start careers prior to giving birth to their first child (Gibbs, 2002; Wildberger, 2003; Bornstein et al., 2006).

Consequently, the number of women who give birth in their 30s and 40s has grown considerably. However, this delay in childbirth has potential consequences for both mothers' and children's health. Women who give birth when over the age of 30 are at greater risk than younger women for a variety of pregnancy and birth complications. For instance, they are more apt to give birth prematurely, and their children are more likely to have low birth weights. This occurs in part because of a decline in the condition of a woman's eggs. For example, by the time a woman is 42

years old, 90 percent of her eggs contain defects of one sort or another (Gibbs, 2002; Moore & deCosta, 2006).

Older mothers are also considerably more likely to give birth to children with Down syndrome, a form of intellectual disability. About 1 out of 100 babies born to mothers over 40 years of age has Down syndrome; for mothers over 50, the incidence increases to 25 percent, or one in four. However, some research shows that older mothers are not automatically at risk for more pregnancy problems. For instance, one study found that when women in their 40s who had not experienced health difficulties were considered, they were no more likely than women in their 20s to have prenatal problems (Dildy et al., 1996; Hodapp, Burke, & Urbano, 2012).

The risks involved in pregnancy are greater not only for older mothers but also for atypically young women. Women who become pregnant during adolescence—and such pregnancies actually encompass 20 percent of all pregnancies—are more likely to have premature deliveries. Furthermore, the mortality rate of infants born to adolescent mothers is double that for mothers in their 20s (Kirchengast & Hartmann, 2003; Carson et al., 2016).

**MOTHER'S PRENATAL SUPPORT.** Keep in mind, though, that the higher mortality rate for babies of adolescent mothers reflects more than just physiological problems related to the mothers' young age. Young mothers often face adverse social and economic factors that can affect infant health. Many teen mothers do not have enough money or social support, a situation that prevents them from getting good prenatal care and parenting support after the baby is born. Poverty or social circumstances, such as a lack of parental involvement or supervision, may even have set the stage for the adolescent to become pregnant in the first place (Huizink, Mulder, & Buitelaar, 2004; Langille, 2007; Meade, Kershaw, & Ickovics, 2008).

**MOTHER'S HEALTH.** Mothers who eat the right foods, maintain an appropriate weight, and exercise appropriately maximize the chances of having a healthy baby. Furthermore, they can reduce the lifetime risk of obesity, high blood pressure, and heart disease in their children by maintaining a healthy lifestyle (Walker & Humphries, 2005, 2007).

In contrast, illness in a pregnant woman can have devastating consequences. For instance, the onset of *rubella* (German measles) in the mother prior to the 11th week of pregnancy is likely to cause serious consequences in the baby, including blindness, deafness, heart defects, or brain damage. In later stages of a pregnancy, however, adverse consequences of rubella become increasingly less likely.

Several other diseases may affect a developing fetus, again depending on when the illness is contracted. For instance, *chicken pox* may produce birth defects, whereas *mumps* may increase the risk of miscarriage.

Some sexually transmitted diseases such as *syphilis* can be transmitted directly to the fetus, who will be born suffering from the disease. In some cases, sexually transmitted diseases such as *gonorrhea* are transmitted to the child as it passes through the birth canal to be born.

*Acquired immune deficiency syndrome* (*AIDS*) can also affect a newborn. Mothers who have the disease or who merely are carriers of the virus may pass it on to their fetuses through the blood that reaches the placenta. If mothers with AIDS are treated with antiviral drugs such as AZT during pregnancy, however, less than 5 percent of their infants are born with the disease. Those infants who are born with AIDS must remain on antiviral drugs their entire lives (Nesheim et al., 2004).

**MOTHERS' DRUG USE.** Mothers' use of many kinds of drugs—both legal and illegal—poses serious risks to the unborn child. Even over-the-counter remedies for common ailments can have surprisingly injurious consequences. For instance, aspirin taken for a headache can lead to fetal bleeding and growth impairments (Griffith, Azuma, & Chasnoff, 1994).

Even drugs prescribed by medical professionals have sometimes had disastrous consequences. In the 1950s, many women who were told to take *thalidomide* for morning sickness during their pregnancies gave birth to children with stumps instead of arms and legs. Although the physicians who prescribed the drug did not know it, thalidomide inhibited the growth of limbs that normally would have occurred during the first 3 months of pregnancy.

Some drugs taken by mothers cause difficulties in their children literally decades after they are taken. As recently as the 1970s, the artificial hormone *diethylstilbestrol* (*DES*) was frequently prescribed to prevent miscarriage. Only later was it found that the daughters of mothers who took DES stood a much higher than normal chance of developing a rare form of vaginal or cervical cancer and had more difficulties during their pregnancies. Sons of the mothers who had taken DES had their own problems, including a higher rate than average of reproductive difficulties (Schecter, Finkelstein, & Koren, 2005).

Birth control or fertility pills taken by pregnant women before they are aware of their pregnancy can also cause fetal damage. Such medicines contain sex hormones that affect developing brain structures in the fetus and can cause significant damage (Miller, 1998; Brown, Hines, & Fane, 2002).

Illicit drugs may pose equally great, and sometimes even greater, risks for the environments of prenatal children. For one thing, the purity of drugs purchased illegally varies significantly, so drug users can never be quite sure what they are ingesting. Furthermore, the effects of some commonly used illicit drugs can be particularly devastating (H. E. Jones, 2006; Mayes et al., 2007; Richardson et al., 2013).

Consider, for instance, the use of *marijuana*. Certainly one of the most commonly used illegal drugs—millions of people in the United States have admitted trying it—marijuana used during pregnancy can restrict the oxygen that reaches the fetus. Its use can lead to infants who are irritable, nervous, and easily disturbed. Children exposed to marijuana prenatally show learning and memory deficits at the age of 10 (Goldschmidt et al., 2008; Willford, Richardson, & Day, 2012; Richardson, Hester, & McLemore, 2016).

During the early 1990s, *cocaine* use by pregnant women led to an epidemic of thousands of so-called "crack babies." Cocaine produces an intense restriction of the arteries leading to the fetus, causing a significant reduction in the flow of blood and oxygen, increasing the risks of fetal death and a number of birth defects and disabilities (Schuetze, Eiden, & Coles, 2007).

Children whose mothers were addicted to cocaine may themselves be born addicted to the drug and may have to suffer through the pain of withdrawal. Even if not addicted, they may be born with significant problems. They are often shorter, and their weight is less than average, and they may have serious respiratory problems, visible birth defects, or seizures. They behave quite differently from other infants: Their reactions to stimulation are muted, but once they start to cry, it may be hard to soothe them (Singer et al., 2000; Eiden, Foote, & Schuetze, 2007; Richardson, Goldschmidt, & Willford, 2009).

It is difficult to determine the long-term effects of mothers' cocaine use in isolation, because such drug use is often accompanied by poor prenatal care and impaired nurturing following birth. In fact, in many cases it is the poor caregiving by mothers who use cocaine that causes children's problems, and not exposure to the drug. Treatment of children exposed to cocaine consequently requires not only that the child's mother stop using the drug, but also an improvement in the level of care the mother or other caregivers provide to the infant (Brown et al., 2004; Jones, 2006; Schempf, 2007).

**MOTHERS' USE OF ALCOHOL AND TOBACCO.** A pregnant woman who reasons that having a drink every once in a while or smoking an occasional cigarette has no appreciable effect on her unborn child is, in all likelihood, kidding herself: Increasing evidence suggests that even small amounts of alcohol and nicotine can disrupt the development of the fetus.

Mothers' use of alcohol can have profound consequences for the unborn child. The children of alcoholics, who consume substantial quantities of alcohol during pregnancy, are at the greatest risk. Approximately 1 out of every 750 infants is born with **fetal alcohol spectrum disorder (FASD)**, a disorder that may include below-average intelligence and sometimes intellectual disability, delayed growth, and facial deformities. FASD is now the primary preventable cause of intellectual disability (Burd et al., 2003; Calhoun & Warren, 2007; Landgraf et al., 2013).

Even mothers who use smaller amounts of alcohol during pregnancy place their child at risk. **Fetal alcohol effects (FAE)** is a condition in which children display some, although not all, of the problems of FASD due to their mother's consumption of alcohol during pregnancy (Streissguth, 1997; Baer, Sampson, & Barr, 2003; Molina et al., 2007).

Children who do not have FAE may still be affected by their mothers' use of alcohol. Studies have found that maternal consumption of an average of just two alcoholic drinks a day during pregnancy is associated with lower intelligence in their offspring at age 7. Other research concurs, suggesting that relatively small quantities of alcohol taken during pregnancy can have future adverse effects on children's behavior and psychological functioning. Furthermore, the consequences of alcohol ingestion during pregnancy are long-lasting. For example, one study found that 14-year-olds' success on a test involving spatial and visual reasoning was related to their mothers' alcohol consumption during pregnancy. The more the mothers reported drinking, the less accurately their children responded (Mattson, Calarco, & Lang, 2006; Streissguth, 2007; Chiodo et al., 2012).

Because of the risks associated with alcohol, physicians today counsel pregnant women (and even those who are trying to become pregnant) to avoid drinking any alcoholic beverages. In addition, they caution

---

**fetal alcohol spectrum disorder (FASD)** Cognitive disorder caused by the pregnant mother consuming substantial quantities of alcohol during pregnancy, potentially resulting in intellectual disability and delayed growth in the child

**fetal alcohol effects (FAE)** A condition in which children display some, although not all, of the problems of fetal alcohol spectrum disorder due to the mother's consumption of alcohol during pregnancy against another practice proven to have an adverse effect on an unborn child: smoking.

Smoking produces several consequences, none of which are good. For starters, smoking reduces the oxygen content and increases the carbon monoxide of the mother's blood, which quickly reduces the oxygen available to the fetus. In addition, the nicotine and other toxins in cigarettes slow the respiration rate of the fetus and speed up its heart.

The ultimate result is an increased possibility of miscarriage and a higher likelihood of death during infancy. In fact, estimates suggest that smoking by pregnant women leads to more than 100,000 miscarriages and the deaths of 5,600 babies in the United States alone each year (Haslam & Lawrence, 2004; Triche & Hossain, 2007; Chertok et al., 2011).

Smokers are two times as likely as nonsmokers to have babies with an abnormally low birth weight, and smokers' babies are shorter, on average, than those of nonsmokers. Furthermore, women who smoke during pregnancy are 50 percent more likely to have children who are intellectually disabled. Finally, mothers who smoke are more likely to have children who exhibit disruptive behavior during childhood (Wakschlag et al., 2006; McCowan et al., 2009).

The consequences of smoking are so profound that they may affect not only a mother's children, but her grandchildren. For example, children whose grandmothers smoked during pregnancy are more than twice as likely to develop childhood asthma than children of grandmothers who did not smoke (Li et al., 2005).

**DO FATHERS AFFECT THE PRENATAL ENVIRONMENT?** It would be easy to reason that once the father has done his part in the sequence of events leading to conception, he would have no role in the *prenatal* environment of the fetus. Developmental researchers have in the past generally shared this view, and there is relatively little research investigating fathers' influence on the prenatal environment.

It is becoming increasingly clear, however, that fathers' behavior may well influence the prenatal environment. Consequently, as the example of Lisa and Robert's visit to the midwife showed, health practitioners are applying the research to suggest ways fathers can support healthy prenatal development (Martin et al., 2007; Vreeswijk et al., 2013).

For instance, fathers-to-be should avoid smoking. Secondhand smoke from a father's cigarettes may affect the mother's health, which in turn influences her unborn child. The greater the level of a father's smoking, the lower the birth weight of his children (Hyssaelae, Rautava, & Helenius, 1995; Tomblin, Hammer, & Zhang, 1998).

Similarly, a father's use of alcohol and illegal drugs can have significant effects on the fetus. Alcohol and drug use impairs sperm and may lead to chromosomal damage that may affect the fetus at conception. In addition, alcohol and drug use during pregnancy may also affect the prenatal environment by creating stress in the mother and generally producing an unhealthy environment. A father's exposure to environmental toxins in the workplace, such as lead or mercury, may bind themselves to sperm and cause birth defects (Dare et al., 2002; Choy et al., 2002; Guttmannova et al., 2016).

Finally, fathers who are physically or emotionally abusive to their pregnant partners can damage their unborn children. By increasing the level of maternal stress, or actually causing physical damage, abusive fathers increase the risk of harm to their unborn children. In fact, approximately 5 percent of women face physical abuse during pregnancy (Gazmararian et al., 2000; Bacchus, Mezey, & Bewley, 2006; Martin et al., 2006).

---

**From a health care provider's perspective:** In addition to avoiding smoking, what other sorts of things might fathers-to-be do to help their unborn children develop normally in the womb?

---

# The Case of …
## The Genetic Roll of the Dice

Randy Barnard was worried. Ever since his wife, Samantha, announced that she was pregnant with their first child, he had been having silent bouts of anxiety. He knew how heredity worked. You could unwillingly saddle your children with genetic burdens that they hadn't earned and didn't deserve. And Randy was a realist about himself. He was uncommonly shy. He was far from athletic. He wasn't outgoing. He lacked ambition. He could only pray that his child would inherit Samantha's bold personality, her drive, ambition, openness, and friendliness. If he could rig heredity to favor Samantha, the kid would surely have a better future.

# BECOMING AN INFORMED CONSUMER OF CHILD DEVELOPMENT

## Optimizing the Prenatal Environment

If you are contemplating ever having a child, you may be overwhelmed, at this point in the chapter, by the number of things that can go wrong. Don't be. Although both genetics and the environment pose their share of risks, in the vast majority of cases, pregnancy and birth proceed without mishap. Moreover, there are several things that women can do—both before and during pregnancy—to optimize the probability that pregnancy will progress smoothly (Massaro, Rothbaum, & Aly, 2006). Among them:

- *For women who are planning to become pregnant, several precautions are in order.* First, women should have nonemergency X-rays only during the first 2 weeks after their menstrual periods. Second, women should be vaccinated against rubella (German measles) at least three and preferably 6 months before getting pregnant. Finally, women who are planning to become pregnant should avoid the use of birth control pills for at least 3 months before trying to conceive, because of disruptions to hormonal production caused by the pills.

- *Eat well, both before and during (and after, for that matter) pregnancy.* It is more essential than ever to eat regular, well-balanced meals. In addition, physicians typically recommend taking prenatal vitamins, which include folic acids, which can decrease the likelihood of birth defects (Amitai et al., 2004).

- *Don't use alcohol and other drugs.* The evidence is clear that many drugs pass directly to the fetus and may cause birth defects. It is also clear that the more one drinks, the greater the risk to the fetus (O'Connor & Whaley, 2006).

- *Monitor caffeine intake.* Although it is still unclear whether caffeine produces birth defects, it is known that the caffeine found in coffee, tea, and chocolate can pass to the fetus, acting as a stimulant. Because of this, you probably shouldn't drink more than a few cups of coffee a day (Wisborg et al., 2003; Diego et al., 2007).

- *Whether pregnant or not, don't smoke.* This holds true for mothers, fathers, and anyone else in the vicinity of the pregnant mother, because research suggests that smoke in the fetal environment can affect birth weight.

- *Exercise regularly.* In most cases, women can continue to exercise, particularly following low-impact routines. However, extreme exercise should be avoided, especially on very hot or very cold days. (Paisley, Joy, & Price, 2003; Schmidt et al., 2006; Evenson, 2011; DiNallo, Downs, & Le Masurier, 2012).

---

In a moment of weakness, Randy shared his concerns with his wife. To his surprise, she laughed. She admitted that she too had been praying—praying that their baby would have kindness, intelligence, a relaxed nature, and a contemplative strain, and that he would not inherit her constant need to excel and please. She had been praying, in other words, for another Randy.

Laughing and hugging, they agreed to wait and see what mix of their traits their child would display—as well as what new, totally different traits would appear. Then they would love the child unconditionally and do their best to help him or her become a caring, loving person.

1. How would you begin to reassure Randy and Samantha about their worries that their child will be too similar to either one of them?

2. Which characteristics that they discussed are largely genetic, and which are more environmentally influenced? Are the genetic traits equivalent to fate, or can their expression be modified? Why or why not?

3. How much should Randy worry that the child will inherit his lack of ambition and athleticism? What would you tell him?

4. How much should Samantha worry about her child being overly driven to succeed and to please others?

5. Could a genetic counselor advise Randy and Samantha about which characteristics their child is likely to display? Is there any way they can be advised on how best to help their child inherit a desirable blend of their characteristics?

# Epilogue

In this chapter, we have discussed the basics of heredity and genetics, including the way in which the code of life is transmitted across generations through DNA. We have also seen how genetic transmission can go wrong, and we have discussed ways in which genetic disorders can be treated—and perhaps prevented—through new interventions such as genetic counseling.

One important theme in this chapter has been the interaction between hereditary and environmental factors in determining a number of human traits. While we have encountered many surprising instances in which heredity plays a part—including in the development of personality traits and even personal preferences and tastes—we have also seen that heredity is virtually never the sole factor in any complex trait. Environment nearly always plays an important role.

Finally, we reviewed the main stages of prenatal growth—germinal, embryonic, and fetal—and examined threats to the prenatal environment and ways to optimize that environment for the fetus.

Before moving on, return to the prologue of this chapter and the case of the Chens' son, who was treated for spina bifida before he was even born. Answer the following questions based on your understanding of genetics and prenatal development.

1. Do you believe that the Chens made the correct decision in permitting their son to be operated on *in utero* rather than waiting until after his birth? Why?
2. Research suggests that insufficient folic acid in the mother's diet contributes to incidents of spina bifida in offspring. Do you see this as a genetic or an environmental factor? Explain your thinking.
3. What kind of evidence would suggest whether or not spina bifida is an X-linked recessive disorder?
4. If it had not been possible to perform fetal surgery on the Chens' son, what do you think the best course of action would have been for his parents?

# Looking Back

**LO 3.1 Explain the role of genes and chromosomes in creating human life.**

- Genes, the basic units of genetic information, are composed of sequences of DNA molecules arranged in a specific order and location along 46 chromosomes.
- A child receives 23 chromosomes from each parent. These 46 chromosomes provide the genetic blueprint that will guide cell activity for the rest of the individual's life.
- Multiple births occur in two ways. Monozygotic (or identical) twins result when cells in the ovum split into two zygotes, while dizygotic (or fraternal) twins, which are more common, result when two separate ovum-sperm combinations produce two zygotes.
- The 23rd pair of chromosomes from the male and female determine the sex of a child. The male pair is an XY combination, while the female pair is an XX. If the union of male and female produces an XX pairing in the embryo, the child will be female; if it produces an XY, the child will be male.

**LO 3.2 Summarize the basics of genetics.**

- Gregor Mendel discovered an important genetic mechanism that governs the interactions of dominant and recessive genes and their expression in alleles.
- The underlying combination of genetic material present in an organism is its genotype; its phenotype is the observable trait that is the expression of the genotype.

**LO 3.3 Explain how genetic information is transmitted.**

- Some pairs of genes contributed by parents are alleles, genes that govern traits that may take alternate forms. If a pair contains dissimilar genes, the dominant trait will be expressed. A recessive trait will be expressed only if the pair contains similar genes.
- Traits such as hair and eye color and the presence of phenylketonuria (PKU) are alleles and follow this pattern.

- Most traits are governed not by a single pair of genes, but by multiple pairs acting in a variety of ways. This is called polygenic inheritance.

**LO 3.4  Identify what we learned from the mapping of the human genome.**

- The mapping of the human genome has provided a wealth of information about human similarity and difference. Moreover, this capability has led to the development of the field of behavioral genetics.

- Behavioral genetics focuses on personality characteristics and behaviors, and on psychological disorders such as schizophrenia. Researchers are now discovering how to remedy certain genetic defects through gene therapy.

- Examples of genetic disorders are PKU, Down syndrome, fragile X syndrome, sickle-cell anemia, Tay-Sachs disease, and Kleinfelter's syndrome.

**LO 3.5  Explain genetic counseling and its uses.**

- Genetic counselors use data from tests and other sources to identify potential genetic abnormalities in women and men who plan to have children. Recently, they have begun testing individuals for genetically based disorders, such as Huntington's disease, that may eventually appear in the individuals themselves.

**LO 3.6  Describe how environmental factors interact in the development of individual traits.**

- Behavioral characteristics are often determined by a combination of genetics and environment. Genetically based traits represent a potential, called the genotype, which may be affected by the environment and is ultimately expressed in the phenotype.

**LO 3.7  Explain how researchers study the interaction of genetic and environmental factors in development.**

- To work out the different influences of heredity and environment, researchers use nonhuman studies and human studies, particularly of twins.

**LO 3.8  Describe the influence of genetics and the environment on physical traits, intelligence, and personality.**

- Virtually all human traits, characteristics, and behaviors are the result of the combination and interaction of nature and nurture. Many physical characteristics show strong genetic influences.

- Although heredity clearly plays an important role in intelligence, environmental factors such as exposure to books, good educational experiences, and intelligent peers also are profoundly influential.

- Some basic personality traits, including neuroticism and extroversion, appear to have genetic roots, and even some less basic traits, such as political and religious values, are linked to genetics.

- However, environment affects personality, and cultural and other environmental influences interact with genetic traits to affect the way they are expressed.

**LO 3.9  Explain the role nature and nurture play in the development of psychological disorders.**

- Psychological disorders such as schizophrenia have a genetic basis, explaining why some psychological disorders seem to run in families.

- Genetics alone does not account for the development of psychological disorders, which may be affected by environmental factors.

**LO 3.10  Discuss the ways genes can influence the environment.**

- Genes may influence a person's environment in three main ways. The environment may directly reflect the person's genetic tendencies; the environment may be affected by the genetic tendencies of one or both parents; or the person's genetic tendencies may be noticed and catered to by parents.

**LO 3.11  Explain what happens during the prenatal stages of development.**

- Fertilization, the event that begins the development of life, may occur when an ovum meets and is joined by a sperm in the fallopian tube.

- The prenatal period consists of three stages: the germinal stage, the embryonic stage, and the fetal stage.

- The germinal stage (fertilization–2 weeks) is marked by rapid cell division and specialization, and the attachment of the zygote to the wall of the uterus. During the embryonic stage (2–8 weeks), the ectoderm, the mesoderm, and the endoderm begin to grow and specialize. The fetal stage (8 weeks–birth) is characterized by a rapid increase in complexity and differentiation of the organs. The fetus becomes active, and most of its systems become operational.

## LO3.12 Discuss the issues that individuals face with respect to pregnancy.

- Fertilization can be difficult for some couples. Infertility, which occurs in some 15 percent of couples, can be treated by drugs, surgery, artificial insemination, and in vitro fertilization.

- The use of surrogate mothers, in vitro fertilization, and sex selection raise ethical and legal issues for parents and advisors to consider.

## LO 3.13 Describe some threats to the fetal environment and what can be done about them.

- The fetus is susceptible to birth defects brought about by teratogens that may be introduced by the environment. The timing and amount of exposure to a teratogen can cause variations in its consequences.

- The diet, age, and health of the mother can positively or negatively affect the health of the fetus.

- Both legal and illegal drugs can have unintended negative effects on the fetus.

- The use of alcohol and tobacco during pregnancy, even in small amounts, including exposure to a father's secondhand smoke, can disrupt the development of the fetus.

- Fathers who are physically or emotionally abusive to their pregnant partners can damage their unborn children.

---

# Key Terms and Concepts

gametes (p. 54)
zygote (p. 54)
genes (p. 54)
DNA (deoxyribonucleic acid)
   molecules (p. 54)
chromosomes (p. 54)
monozygotic twins (p. 55)
dizygotic twins (p. 55)
dominant trait (p. 57)
recessive trait (p. 57)
genotype (p. 57)
phenotype (p. 57)
homozygous (p. 57)
heterozygous (p. 57)

polygenic inheritance (p. 58)
X-linked genes (p. 59)
behavioral genetics (p. 59)
Down syndrome (p. 61)
fragile X syndrome (p. 61)
sickle-cell anemia (p. 61)
Tay-Sachs disease (p. 61)
Klinefelter's syndrome (p. 61)
genetic counseling (p. 62)
ultrasound sonography (p. 62)
chorionic villus sampling
   (CVS) (p. 63)
amniocentesis (p. 63)
temperament (p. 65)

multifactorial transmission (p. 66)
fertilization (p. 73)
germinal stage (p. 73)
placenta (p. 74)
embryonic stage (p. 74)
fetal stage (p. 74)
fetus (p. 74)
infertility (p. 75)
artificial insemination (p. 76)
in vitro fertilization (IVF) (p. 76)
teratogen (p. 78)
fetal alcohol spectrum disorder
   (FASD) (p. 81)
fetal alcohol effects (FAE) (p. 81)

# Chapter 4
# Birth and the Newborn Infant

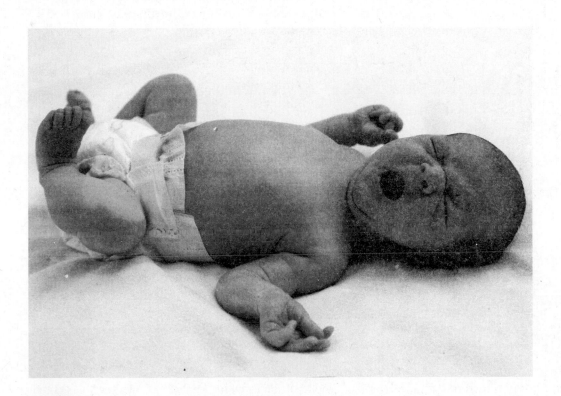

## Learning Objectives

**LO 4.1** Explain the normal process of labor.

**LO 4.2** Describe what typically happens to the neonate in the moments immediately following birth.

**LO 4.3** Compare the different birthing procedures, and explain what choices relating to the birth are available to parents.

**LO 4.4** Identify complications that can occur at birth, and explain their causes, effects, and treatments.

**LO 4.5** Describe situations for which cesarean deliveries are necessary.

**LO 4.6** List the factors that contribute to infant mortality.

**LO 4.7** Describe postpartum depression.

**LO 4.8** Identify the physical and sensory capabilities of the newborn.

**LO 4.9** Explain the early learning capabilities of the newborn.

**LO 4.10** Describe the ways newborns respond to others.

# Prologue: Expecting the Unexpected

Aarti was all set for the birth of her baby. She was constantly checking with her doctor, and had followed all the medical advices. But Aarti's labor didn't go quite the way she'd planned. Her water broke before her contractions started. In fact, her contractions didn't start for another 12 hours, and they never became regular. After 24 hours of labor, she was given an epidural procedure to relax her, but the drug and the exhaustion made it difficult to push effectively. When the baby's heartbeat began to drop, the doctor used forceps. Aarti's daughter was born within minutes. She was healthy and beautiful, but then the doctors noticed a slight elevation in her temperature, and as a result, they kept the baby in the neonatal unit for another week. Today, her daughter is a lively, curious toddler. "All's well that ends well," Aarti says, "but I learned that when it comes to childbirth, maybe it's best to expect the unexpected."

## Looking Ahead

While labor and childbirth are generally less difficult than they were for Aarti , all births are tinged with a combination of excitement and some degree of anxiety. In the vast majority of cases, delivery goes smoothly, and it is an amazing and joyous moment when a new being enters the world. The excitement of birth is soon replaced by wonder at the extraordinary nature of newborns themselves. Babies enter the world with a surprising array of capabilities, ready from the first moments of life outside the womb to respond to the world and the people in it.

In this chapter, we examine the events that lead to the delivery and birth of a child and take an initial look at the newborn. We first consider labor and delivery, exploring how the process usually proceeds, as well as several alternative approaches.

We next examine some of the possible complications of birth, ranging from premature births to infant mortality. Finally, we consider the extraordinary range of capabilities of newborns. We look not only at their

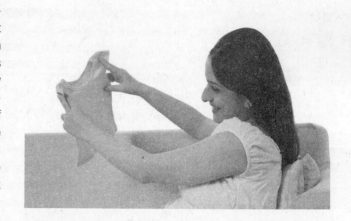

physical and perceptual abilities but also at the way they enter the world with the ability to learn and with skills that help form the foundations of their future relationships with others.

# Birth

*I wasn't completely naïve. I mean, I knew that it was only in movies that babies come out of the womb all pink, dry, and beautiful. But still, I was initially taken aback by my son's appearance. Because of his passage through the birth canal, his head was cone-shaped, a bit like a wet, partly deflated football. The nurse must have noticed my reaction because she hastened to assure me that all this would change in a matter of days. She then moved quickly to wipe off the whitish sticky substance all over his body, informing me as she did that the fuzzy hair on his ears was only temporary. I interrupted the nurse's* assurances. *"Don't worry," I stammered, tears suddenly filling my eyes. "He's absolutely the most beautiful thing I've ever seen."*

For those of us accustomed to thinking of newborns the way they are portrayed in baby food commercials, the aforementioned portrait may be surprising. Yet most **neonates**—the term used for newborns—are born resembling this one. Make no mistake, however, despite their temporary blemishes, babies are a welcome sight to their parents from the moment of their birth.

**neonate** The term used for newborns

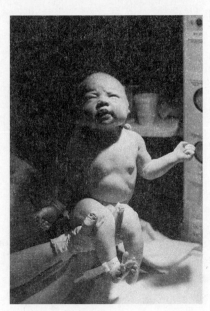

The image of newborns portrayed in commercials differs dramatically from reality.

The neonate's outward appearance is caused by a variety of factors in its journey from the mother's uterus, down the birth canal, and out into the world. We can trace its passage, beginning with the release of the chemicals that initiate the process of labor.

## Labor: The Process of Birth Begins

**LO 4.1    Explain the normal process of labor.**

About 266 days after conception, a protein called *corticotropin-releasing hormone* (CRH) triggers the release of various hormones, and the process that leads to birth begins. One critical hormone is *oxytocin*, which is produced by the mother's pituitary gland. When the concentration of oxytocin becomes high enough, the mother's uterus begins periodic contractions (Heterelendy & Zakar, 2004; Terzidou, 2007; Tattersall et al., 2012).

During the prenatal period, the uterus, which is composed of muscle tissue, slowly expands as the fetus grows. Although for most of the pregnancy it is inactive, after the fourth month, the uterus occasionally contracts in order to ready itself for the eventual delivery. These contractions, called *Braxton-Hicks contractions*, are sometimes called "false labor," because while they can fool eager and anxious expectant parents, they do not signify that the baby will be born soon.

When birth is actually imminent, the uterus begins to contract intermittently. Its increasingly intense contractions act as if it were a vise, opening and closing to force the head of the fetus against the *cervix*, the neck of the uterus that separates it from the vagina. Eventually, the force of the contractions becomes strong enough to propel the fetus slowly down the birth canal until it enters the world as a newborn. It is this exertion and the narrow birth passage that often give newborns the battered "cone head" appearance described earlier.

Labor proceeds in three stages, although there are significant individual differences in how women move through the stages. In the *first stage of labor*, the uterine contractions initially occur around every 8 to 10 minutes and last about 30 seconds. As labor proceeds, the contractions occur more frequently and last longer. Toward the end of labor, the contractions may occur every 2 minutes and last almost 2 minutes. During the final part of the first stage of labor, the contractions increase to their greatest intensity, a period known as *transition*. The mother's cervix fully opens, eventually expanding enough (usually to around 10 cm) to allow the baby's head (the widest part of the body) to pass through.

This first stage of labor is the longest. Its duration varies significantly, depending on the mother's age, race, ethnicity, number of prior pregnancies, and a variety of other factors involving both the fetus and the mother. Typically, labor takes 16 to 24 hours for first-born children, but there are wide variations. Births of subsequent children usually involve shorter periods of labor. The *second stage of labor* typically lasts around 90 minutes, although there are significant individual differences. In the second stage, the baby's head emerges further from the mother with each contraction, increasing the size of the vaginal opening. Because the area between the vagina and rectum must stretch a good deal, an incision called an **episiotomy** is sometimes made to increase the size of the opening of the vagina. In recent years, this practice has been increasingly criticized as potentially causing more harm than good, and the number of episiotomies has fallen drastically (Graham et al., 2005; Dudding, Vaizey, & Kamm, 2008; Manzanares et al., 2013).

The second stage of labor ends when the baby has completely left the mother's body. Finally, the *third stage of labor* occurs, during which the child's umbilical cord (still attached to the neonate) and the placenta are expelled from the mother. This stage is (relatively speaking) the quickest and easiest, usually taking only a few minutes.

The nature of a woman's reactions to labor reflect, in part, cultural factors. Although there is no evidence that the physiological aspects of labor differ among women of different cultures, expectations about labor and interpretations of its pain do vary significantly from one culture to another (Callister et al., 2003; Fisher, Hauck, & Fenwick, 2006; Xirasagar et al., 2011; Steel et al., 2014).

For instance, there is a kernel of truth to popular stories of pregnant women in certain societies putting down the tools with which they are tilling their fields, stepping aside and giving birth, and immediately returning to work with their neonates wrapped and bundled on their backs. Accounts of the !Kung people in Africa describe the woman in labor sitting calmly beside a tree and without much ado—or assistance—successfully giving birth to a child and quickly recovering. By contrast, many societies regard childbirth as dangerous, and some even view it in terms befitting an illness. Such cultural perspectives color the way that people in a given society view the experience of childbirth.

## Birth: From Fetus to Neonate

**LO 4.2  Describe what typically happens to the neonate in the moments immediately following birth.**

The exact moment of birth occurs when the fetus, having left the uterus through the cervix, passes through the vagina to emerge fully from its mother's body. In most cases, babies automatically make the transition from taking in oxygen via the placenta to using their lungs to breathe air. Consequently, as soon as they are outside the mother's body, most newborns spontaneously cry. This helps them clear their lungs and breathe on their own.

What happens next varies from situation to situation and from culture to culture. In Western cultures, health care workers are almost always on hand to assist with the birth. In the United States, 99 percent of births are attended by professional health care workers, but in many less-developed countries, less than half of births have professional health care workers in attendance (United Nations Statistics Division, 2012).

**THE APGAR SCALE.**   In most cases, the newborn infant first undergoes a quick visual inspection. Parents may be counting fingers and toes, but trained health care workers look for something more. Typically, they employ the **Apgar scale**, a standard measurement system that looks for a variety of indications of good health (see Table 4.1). Developed by physician Virginia Apgar, the scale directs attention to five basic qualities, recalled most easily by using Apgar's name as a guide: *a*ppearance (color), *p*ulse (heart rate), *g*rimace (reflex irritability), *a*ctivity (muscle tone), and *r*espiration (respiratory effort).

Using the Apgar scale, health care workers assign the newborn a score ranging from 0 to 2 on each of the five qualities, producing an overall score that can range from 0 to 10. The vast majority of children score 7 or above. The 10 percent of neonates who score under 7 require help to start breathing. Newborns who score under 4 need immediate lifesaving intervention.

Low Apgar scores (or low scores on other neonatal assessments, such as the *Brazelton Neonatal Behavioral Assessment Scale*, which we discuss later in the book) may indicate problems or birth defects that were already present in the fetus. Sometimes, the process of birth itself may cause difficulties. Among the most profound are those relating to a temporary deprivation of oxygen.

At various junctures during labor, the fetus may not get sufficient oxygen. This can happen for any of a number of reasons. For instance, the umbilical cord may get wrapped around the neck of the fetus. The cord can also be pinched during a prolonged contraction, thereby cutting off the supply of oxygen that flows through it.

---

**episiotomy** An incision sometimes made to increase the size of the opening of the vagina to allow the baby to pass

**Apgar scale** A standard measurement system that looks for a variety of indications of good health in newborns

## Table 4.1 Apgar Scale

A score is given for each sign at 1 minute and 5 minutes after the birth. If there are problems with the baby, an additional score is given at 10 minutes. A score of 7–10 is considered normal, whereas a baby with a score of 4–7 might require some resuscitative measures, and a baby with an Apgar score under 4 requires immediate resuscitation.

| Sign | 0 Points | 1 Point | 2 Points |
| --- | --- | --- | --- |
| Appearance (skin color) | Blue-gray, pale all over | Normal, except for extremities | Normal over entire body |
| Pulse | Absent | Below 100 bpm | Above 100 bpm |
| Grimace (reflex irritability) | No response | Grimace | Sneezes, coughs, pulls away |
| Activity (muscle tone) | Absent | Arms and legs flexed | Active movement |
| Respiration | Absent | Slow, irregular | Good, crying |

SOURCE: "A Proposal for a New Method of Evaluation in the Newborn Infant," V. Apgar, Current Research in Anesthesia and Analgesia, 32, 1953, p. 260.

Lack of oxygen for a few seconds is not harmful to the fetus, but deprivation for any longer time may cause serious harm. A restriction of oxygen, or **anoxia**, lasting a few minutes can produce cognitive deficits such as language delays and even intellectual disability due to brain-cell death (Rossetti, Carrera, & Oddo, 2012; Stecker, Wolfe, & Stevenson, 2013; Tazopoulou et al., 2016).

**NEWBORN MEDICAL SCREENING.** Just after birth, newborns typically are tested for a variety of diseases and genetic conditions. The American College of Medical Genetics recommends that all newborns be screened for 29 disorders, ranging from hearing difficulties and sickle-cell anemia to extremely rare conditions such as isovaleric acidemia, a disorder involving metabolism. These disorders can be detected from a tiny quantity of blood drawn from an infant's heel (American College of Medical Genetics, 2006).

The advantage of newborn screening is that it permits early treatment of problems that might otherwise go undetected for years. In some cases, devastating conditions can be prevented through early treatment of the disorder, such as the implementation of a particular kind of diet (Goldfarb, 2005; Kayton, 2007; Timmermans & Buchbinder, 2012).

The exact number of tests that a newborn experiences varies drastically from state to state. In some states, only three tests are mandated, while in others, more than 30 are required. In jurisdictions with only a few tests, many disorders go undiagnosed. In fact, each year, around 1,000 infants in the United States suffer from disorders that could have been detected at birth if appropriate screening had been conducted. By contrast, however, the use of early screening of infants has been called into question (American Academy of Pediatrics, 2005; Sudia-Robinson, 2011; McClain et al., 2017).

**PHYSICAL APPEARANCE AND INITIAL ENCOUNTERS.** After assessing the newborn's health, health care workers next deal with the remnants of the child's passage through the birth canal. You'll recall the description of the thick, greasy substance (like cottage cheese) that covers the newborn. This material, called *vernix*, smoothes the passage through the birth canal; it is no longer needed once the child is born and is quickly cleaned away. Newborns' bodies are sometimes covered with a fine, dark fuzz known as *lanugo*, which soon disappears. The newborn's eyelids may be puffy due to an accumulation of fluids during labor, and the baby may have blood or other fluids on parts of its body.

After being cleansed, the newborn is usually returned to the mother and, if he is present, the father. The everyday and universal occurrence of childbirth makes it no less miraculous to parents, and most cherish this time to make their first acquaintance with their child. Many hospitals in the United States acknowledge the importance of this period by providing infants and mothers as much time as possible with the infant resting on the mother's bare skin.

The significance of this initial encounter between parent and child has become a matter of considerable controversy. Some psychologists and physicians argued that **bonding**, the close physical and emotional contact between parent and child during the period immediately following birth, is a crucial ingredient for forming a lasting relationship between parent and child (Lorenz,

**anoxia** A restriction of oxygen to the baby, lasting a few minutes during the birth process, which can produce brain damage

**bonding** Close physical and emotional contact between parent and child during the period immediately following birth, argued by some to affect later relationship strength

1957). Their arguments were based in part on research conducted on nonhuman species such as ducklings. This work showed that there was a critical period just after birth when organisms showed a particular readiness to learn, or imprint, from other members of their species who happened to be present.

According to the concept of bonding applied to humans, a critical period begins just after birth and lasts only a few hours. During this period, actual skin-to-skin contact between mother and child supposedly leads to deep, emotional bonding. The corollary to this assumption is that if circumstances prevent such contact, the bond between mother and child will forever be lacking in some way. Because so many babies were taken from their mothers and placed in incubators or in the hospital nursery, the fear was that medical practices prevalent at the time often left little opportunity for sustained mother-and-child physical contact immediately after birth.

When developmental researchers carefully reviewed the research literature, however, they found little support for the existence of a critical period for bonding at birth. Although it does appear that mothers who have early physical contact with their babies are more responsive to them than those who don't have such contact, the difference lasts only a few days. Such news is reassuring to parents whose children must receive immediate, intensive medical attention just after birth. It is also comforting to parents who adopt children and are not present at their births (Miles et al., 2006; Bigelow & Power, 2012; Schmidt et al., 2016).

Although mother–child bonding does not seem critical, it is important for newborns to be gently touched and massaged soon after birth by *someone*. The physical stimulation infants receive leads to the production of chemicals in the brain that instigate growth. Consequently, infant massage is related to weight gain, better sleep-waking patterns, better neuromotor development, and reduced rates of infant mortality (Field, 2001; Kulkarni et al., 2011; van Reenen & van Rensburg, 2013).

## Approaches to Childbirth: Where Medicine and Attitudes Meet

**LO 4.3 Compare the different birthing procedures, and explain what choices relating to the birth are available to parents.**

Parents in the Western world have developed a variety of strategies—and some very strong opinions—to help them deal with something as natural as giving birth, which occurs apparently without much thought throughout the nonhuman animal world. Today parents need to decide: should the birth take place in a hospital or in the home? Should a physician, a nurse, or a midwife assist? Is the father's presence desirable? Should siblings and other family members be on hand to participate in the birth?

On the contrary, it is a completely different scenario in India. The Government of India is encouraging hospital care during childbirth for reducing maternal and infant mortality rate. In large part of suburban, rural, and tribal areas in the country, one of the major causes of maternal and infant mortality rate is the cultural beliefs and practices around home-based childbirth. Therefore, alternate approaches to childbirth are generally not encouraged in India.

In the United States, the abundance of choices is largely due to a reaction to traditional medical practices that had been common in the country until the early 1970s. Before that time, the typical birth went something like this: a woman in labor was placed in a room with many other women, all of whom were in various stages of childbirth, and some of whom were screaming in pain. Fathers and other family members were not allowed to be present. Just before delivery, the woman was rolled into a delivery room, where the birth took place. Often she was so drugged that she was not aware of the birth at all.

At the time, physicians argued that such procedures were necessary to ensure the health of the newborn and the mother. Critics, however, charged that alternatives were available that not only would maximize the medical well-being of the participants in the birth but also would represent an emotional and psychological improvement (Curl et al., 2004; Hotelling & Humenick, 2005). Some of the alternative birthing practices followed in the West are given in the box (on page 93).

**PAIN AND CHILDBIRTH.** Any woman who has delivered a baby will agree that childbirth is painful. But exactly how painful is it?

Such a question is largely unanswerable. One reason is that pain is a subjective psychological phenomenon, one that cannot be easily measured. No one is able to answer the question of whether their pain is "greater" or "worse" than someone else's pain, although some studies have tried to quantify it. For instance, in one survey women were asked to rate the pain they

# ALTERNATIVE BIRTHING PROCEDURES

Not all mothers give birth in hospitals, and not all births follow a traditional course. Among the major alternatives to traditional birthing practices are the following:

- *Lamaze birthing techniques.* The Lamaze method has achieved widespread popularity in the United States. Based on the writings of Dr. Fernand Lamaze, the method makes use of breathing techniques and relaxation training (Lamaze, 1979). Typically, mothers-to-be participate in a series of weekly training sessions in which they learn exercises that help them relax various parts of the body on command. A "coach," most typically the father or the mother's partner, is trained along with the future mother. The training allows women to cope with painful contractions by concentrating on their breathing and producing a relaxation response, rather than by tensing up, which can make the pain more acute. Women learn to focus on a relaxing stimulus, such as a tranquil scene in a picture. The goal is to learn how to deal positively with pain and to relax at the onset of a contraction (Lothian, 2005).

   Does the procedure work? Most mothers, as well as fathers, report that a Lamaze birth is a very positive experience. They enjoy the sense of mastery that they gain over the process of labor, a feeling of being able to exert some control over what can be a formidable experience. Given that, we can't be sure that parents who choose the Lamaze method aren't already more highly motivated about the experience of childbirth than are parents who do not choose the technique. It is therefore possible that the accolades they express after Lamaze births are due to their initial enthusiasm, and not to the Lamaze procedures themselves (Larsen et al., 2001; Zwelling, 2006).

   Participation in Lamaze procedures—as well as other natural childbirth techniques in which the emphasis is on educating the parents about the process of birth and minimizing the use of drugs—is relatively rare among members of lower income groups, including many members of ethnic minorities. Parents in these groups may not have the transportation, time, or financial resources to attend childbirth preparation classes. The result is that women in lower income groups tend to be less prepared for the events of labor and consequently may suffer more pain during childbirth (Lu et al., 2003).

- *Bradley Method.* The Bradley Method, which is sometimes known as "husband-coached childbirth," is based on the principle that childbirth should be as natural as possible and involve no medication or medical interventions. Women are taught to "tune into" their bodies in order to deal with the pain of childbirth.

   To prepare for childbirth, mothers-to-be are taught muscle relaxation techniques, similar to Lamaze procedures, and good nutrition and exercise during pregnancy are seen as important to prepare for delivery. Parents are urged to take responsibility for childbirth, and the use of physicians is viewed as unnecessary and sometimes even dangerous. As you might expect, the discouragement of traditional medical interventions is quite controversial (Reed, 2005).

- *Hypnobirthing.* Hypnobirthing is a new, but increasingly popular, technique. It involves a form of self-hypnosis during delivery that creates a sense of peace and calm, thereby reducing pain. The basic concept is to produce a state of focused concentration in which a mother relaxes her body while focusing inward. Increasing research evidence shows the technique can be effective in reducing pain (Olson, 2006; White, 2007; Alexander, Turnbull, & Cyna, 2009).

- *Water birthing.* Still relatively uncommon in the United States, water birthing is a practice in which a woman enters a pool of warm water to give birth. The theory is that the warmth and buoyancy of the water is soothing, easing the length and pain of labor and childbirth, and the entry into the world is soothed for the infant, who moves from the watery environment of the womb to the birthing pool. Although there is some evidence that water birthing reduces pain and the length of labor, there is a risk of infection from the unsterile water (Thöni, Mussner, & Ploner, 2010; Jones et al., 2012).

experienced during labor on a 1 to 5 scale, with 5 being the most painful (Yarrow, 1992). Nearly half (44 percent) said "5," and an additional one-quarter said "4."

Because pain is usually a sign that something is wrong in one's body, we have learned to react to pain with fear and concern. Yet during childbirth, pain is actually a signal that the body is working appropriately— that the contractions meant to propel the baby through the birth canal are doing their job. Consequently, the experience of pain is difficult for women in labor to interpret, thereby potentially increasing their anxiety and making the contractions seem even more painful.

Ultimately, every woman's delivery depends on such variables as how much preparation and support she has before and during delivery, her culture's view of pregnancy and delivery, and the specific nature of the delivery itself (Ip, Tang, & Goggins, 2009; de C. Williams et al., 2013; Wilsona & Simpson, 2016).

**USE OF ANESTHESIA AND PAIN-REDUCING DRUGS.** Among the greatest advances of modern medicine is the ongoing discovery of drugs that reduce pain; however, the use of medication during childbirth is a practice that holds both benefits and pitfalls.

About a third of women who receive anesthesia do so in the form of *epidural anesthesia*, which produces numbness from the waist down. Traditional epidurals produce an inability to walk and in some cases prevent women from helping to push the baby out during delivery. A newer form of epidural, known as a *walking epidural* or *dual spinal-epidural*, uses smaller needles and a system for administering continuous doses of anesthetic. It permits women to move about more freely during labor and has fewer side effects than traditional epidural anesthesia (Simmons et al., 2007).

It is clear that drugs hold the promise of greatly reducing, and even eliminating, pain associated with labor, which can be extreme and exhausting. But pain reduction comes at a cost: drugs administered during labor reach not just the mother but the fetus as well. The stronger the drug, the greater its effects on the fetus and neonate. Because of the small size of the fetus relative to the mother, drug doses that might have only a minimal effect on the mother can have a magnified effect on the fetus.

Anesthetics may temporarily depress the flow of oxygen to the fetus and slow labor. In addition, newborns whose mothers have been anesthetized are less physiologically responsive, show poorer motor control during the first days after birth, cry more, and may have more difficulty initiating breastfeeding (Ransjö-Arvidson et al., 2001; Torvaldsen et al., 2006).

Most research suggests that drugs, as they are currently employed during labor, produce only minimal risks to the fetus and neonate. Guidelines issued by the American College of Obstetricians and Gynecologists suggest that a woman's request for pain relief at any stage of labor should be honored and that the proper

# BECOMING AN INFORMED CONSUMER OF CHILD DEVELOPMENT

## Dealing With Labor

Every woman who is soon to give birth has some fear of labor. Most have heard gripping tales of extended, 48-hour labors or vivid descriptions of the pain that accompanies labor. Still, few mothers would dispute the notion that the rewards of giving birth are worth the effort.

There is no single right or wrong way to deal with labor; however, several strategies can help make the process as positive as possible:

- *Be flexible.* Although you may have carefully worked out what to do during labor, don't feel an obligation to follow through exactly. If a strategy is ineffective, turn to another one.
- *Communicate with your health care providers.* Let them know what you are experiencing. They may be able to suggest ways to deal with what you are encountering. As your labor progresses, they may also be able to give you a fairly clear idea of how

much longer you will be in labor. Knowing the worst of the pain is going to last only another 20 minutes or so, you may feel you can handle it.

- *Remember that labor is ... laborious.* Expect that you may become fatigued, but realize that as the final stages of labor occur, you may well get a second wind.
- *Accept your partner's support.* If a spouse or other partner is present, allow that person to make you comfortable and provide support. Research has shown that women who are supported by a spouse or partner have a more comfortable birth experience (Bader, 1995; Kennell, 2002).
- *Be realistic and honest about your reactions to pain.* Even if you had planned an unmedicated delivery, realize that you may find the pain difficult to tolerate. At that point, consider the use of drugs. Above all, don't feel that asking for pain medication is a sign of failure. It isn't.
- *Focus on the big picture.* Keep in mind that labor is part of a process that ultimately leads to an event unmatched in the joy it can bring.

use of minimal amounts of drugs for pain relief is reasonable and has no significant effect on a child's later well-being (ACOG, 2002; Alberts et al., 2007).

In accordance with these views, the American Academy of Pediatrics states that except in unusual cases, women should stay in the hospital no less than 48 hours after giving birth. Furthermore, the U.S. Congress passed legislation mandating a minimum insurance coverage of 48 hours for childbirth (American Academy of Pediatrics Committee on Fetus and Newborn, 2004).

# Birth Complications

*When Ivy Brown's son was born dead, a nurse told her that sad as it was, she was not alone: a surprisingly high number of births in her city, Washington, D.C., ended with the death of the child. That fact spurred Brown to become a grief counselor, specializing in infant mortality. She formed a committee of physicians and city officials to study the capital's high infant mortality rate and find solutions to lower it. "If I can spare one mother this terrible grief, my loss will not be in vain," Brown says.*

The infant mortality rate in Washington, D.C., capital of the richest country in the world, is 13.7 deaths per 1,000 births, exceeding the rate of countries such as Hungary, Cuba, Kuwait, and Costa Rica. Overall, 44 countries have better birth rates than the United States, which has 6.26 deaths for every 1,000 live births (U.S. Department of Health and Human Services, 2009; Sun, 2012; Central Intelligence Agency (2016). The World Factbook; see Figure 4.1).

Why is infant survival less likely in the United States than in other, less developed countries? To answer this question, we need to consider the nature of the problems that can occur during labor and delivery.

## Preterm and Postmature Babies

**LO 4.4 Identify complications that can occur at birth, and explain their causes, effects, and treatments.**

Around one out of 10 infants are born earlier than normal. **Preterm infants**, or premature infants, are born prior to 38 weeks after conception. Because they have not had time to develop fully as fetuses, preterm infants are at high risk for illness and death. In contrast, one might imagine that a baby who spends extra time in the womb might have some advantages, given

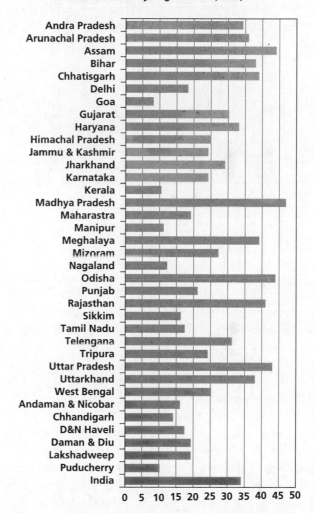

**Figure 4.1** International Infant Mortality

Infant mortality rates in selected countries. Although the United States has greatly reduced its infant mortality rate in the past 25 years, it still ranks behind numerous other industrialized countries. What are some of the reasons for this?

**SOURCE:** Accessed from NITI Aayog (http://niti.gov.in) on 6 October 2018.

the opportunity to continue growth undisturbed by the outside world. Yet **postmature infants**—those still unborn 2 weeks after the mother's due date—also face several risks.

**PRETERM INFANTS: TOO SOON, TOO SMALL.** The extent of danger faced by preterm babies largely depends

**preterm infants** Infants who are born prior to 38 weeks after conception (also known as premature infants)

**postmature infants** Infants still unborn 2 weeks after the mother's due date

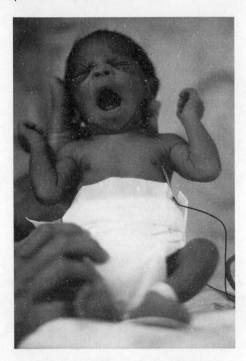

Preterm infants stand a much greater chance of survival today than they did even a decade ago.

on the child's weight at birth, which has great significance as an indicator of the extent of the baby's development. Although the average newborn weighs around 3,400 grams (about 7 1/2 pounds), **low-birthweight infants** weigh less than 2,500 grams (around 5 1/2 pounds). Only 7 percent of all newborns in the United States fall into the low-birthweight category, but they account for the majority of newborn deaths (Gross, Spiker, & Haynes, 1997; DeVader et al., 2007).

Even though most low-birthweight infants are preterm, some are small-for-gestational-age babies. **Small-for-gestational-age infants** are infants who, because of delayed fetal growth, weigh 90 percent (or less) of the average weight of infants of the same gestational age. Small-for-gestational-age infants are sometimes also preterm, but they may not be. The syndrome may be caused by inadequate nutrition during pregnancy (Bergmann, Bergmann, & Dudenhausen, 2008; Salihu et al., 2013).

If the degree of prematurity is not too great and weight at birth is not extremely low, the threat to the child's well-being is relatively minor. In such cases, the main treatment may be to keep the baby in the hospital to gain weight. Additional weight is critical because fat layers help prevent chilling in neonates, who are not particularly efficient at regulating body temperature.

Research also shows that preterm infants who receive more responsive, stimulating, and organized care are apt to show more positive outcomes than those children whose care is not as good. Some of these interventions are quite simple. For example, "kangaroo care," in which infants are held skin-to-skin against their parents' chests, appears to be effective in helping preterm infants develop. As discussed earlier, massaging preterm infants several times a day triggers the release of hormones that promote weight gain, muscle development, and abilities to cope with stress (Field et al., 2008; Athanasopoulou & Fox, 2014).

Newborns who are born more prematurely and who have birthweights significantly below average face a tougher road. For them, simply staying alive is a major task. For instance, low-birthweight infants are highly vulnerable to infection, and because their lungs have not had sufficient time to develop completely, they have problems taking in sufficient oxygen. As a consequence, they may experience *respiratory distress syndrome (RDS)*, which has potentially fatal consequences.

To deal with RDS, low-birthweight infants are often placed in incubators, enclosures in which temperature and oxygen content are controlled. The exact amount of oxygen is carefully monitored. Too low a concentration of oxygen will not provide relief, and too high a concentration can damage the delicate retinas of the eyes, leading to permanent blindness.

The immature development of preterm neonates makes them unusually sensitive to stimuli in their environment. They can easily be overwhelmed by the sights, sounds, and sensations they experience, and their breathing may be interrupted or their heart rates may slow. They are often unable to move smoothly; their arm and leg movements are uncoordinated, causing them to jerk about and appear startled. Such behavior is quite disconcerting to parents (Doussard-Roosevelt et al., 1997; Miles et al., 2006).

Despite the difficulties they experience at birth, the majority of preterm infants eventually develop normally. But the tempo of development often proceeds more slowly for preterm children compared to children born at full term, and more subtle problems sometimes

---

**low-birthweight infants** Infants who weigh less than 2,500 grams (around 5 1/2 pounds) at birth

**small-for-gestational-age infants** Infants who, because of delayed fetal growth, weigh 90 percent (or less) of the average weight of infants of the same gestational age

emerge later. For example, by the end of their first year, only 10 percent of prematurely born infants display significant problems, and only 5 percent are seriously disabled. By age 6, however, approximately 38 percent have mild problems that call for special educational interventions. For instance, some preterm children show learning disabilities, behavior disorders, or lower-than-average IQ scores. They also may be at greater risk for mental illness. Others have difficulties with physical coordination. Still, around 60 percent of preterm infants are free of even minor problems (Hall et al., 2008; Nosarti et al., 2012; El Ayoubi et al., 2016).

**VERY-LOW-BIRTHWEIGHT INFANTS: THE SMALLEST OF THE SMALL.**   The story is less positive for the most extreme cases of prematurity—very-low-birthweight infants. **Very-low-birthweight infants** weigh less than 1,250 grams (around 2 1/4 pounds) or, regardless of weight, have been in the womb less than 30 weeks.

Very-low-birthweight infants not only are tiny—some fit easily in the palm of the hand at birth—they hardly seem to belong to the same species as full-term newborns. Their eyes may be fused shut, and their earlobes may look like flaps of skin on the sides of their heads. Their skin is a darkened red color, whatever their race.

Very-low-birthweight babies are in grave danger from the moment they are born, due to the immaturity of their organ systems. Before the mid-1980s, these babies would not have survived outside their mothers' wombs. Medical advances have led to a higher chance of survival, pushing the *age of viability*, the point at which an infant can survive prematurely, to about 22 weeks—some 4 months earlier than the term of a normal delivery. Of course, the longer the period of development beyond conception, the higher are a newborn's chances of survival. A baby born earlier than 25 weeks has less than a 50–50 chance of survival (Seaton et al., 2012).

The physical and cognitive problems experienced by low-birthweight and preterm babies are even more pronounced in very-low-birthweight infants, with astonishing financial consequences. A 4-month stay in an incubator in an intensive care unit can run hundreds of thousands of dollars, and about half of these newborns ultimately die, despite massive medical intervention (Taylor et al., 2000).

Even if a very-low-birthweight preterm infant survives, the medical costs can continue to mount. For instance, one estimate suggests that the average monthly cost of medical care for such infants during the first 3 years of life may be between 3 and 50 times higher than the medical costs for a full-term child. Such astronomical costs have raised ethical debates about the expenditure of substantial financial and human resources in cases in which a positive outcome may be unlikely (Prince, 2000; Doyle, 2004; Petrou, 2006).

As medical capabilities progress and developmental researchers come up with new strategies for dealing with preterm infants and improving their lives, the age of viability is likely to be pushed even earlier. Emerging evidence suggests that high-quality care can provide protection from some of the risks associated with prematurity, and that in fact by the time they reach adulthood, premature babies may be little different from other adults. Still, the costs of caring for preterm infants are enormous: the U.S. government estimates that caring for premature infants is $26 billion a year (Hack et al., 2002; Saul, 2009).

**WHAT CAUSES PRETERM AND LOW-BIRTHWEIGHT DELIVERIES?**   About half of preterm and low-birthweight births are unexplained, but several known causes account for the remainder. In some cases, premature labor results from difficulties relating to the mother's reproductive system. For instance, mothers carrying twins have unusual stress placed on them, which can lead to early labor. In fact, most multiple births are preterm to some degree (Tan et al., 2004; Luke & Brown, 2008).

In other cases, preterm and low-birthweight babies are a result of the immaturity of the mother's reproductive system. Young mothers—under age 15—are more prone to deliver prematurely than older ones. In addition, a woman who becomes pregnant within 6 months of a previous delivery is more likely to deliver a preterm or low-birthweight infant than a woman whose reproductive system has had a chance to recover from a prior delivery. The father's age matters, too: pregnant women with older male partners are more likely to have preterm deliveries (Branum, 2006; Blumenshine et al., 2011; Teoli, Zullig, & Hendryx, 2015).

Finally, factors that affect the general health of the mother, such as nutrition, level of medical care, amount of stress in the environment, and economic support, all are related to prematurity and low birthweight. Rates of

---

**very-low-birthweight infants** Infants who weigh less than 1,250 grams (around 2 1/4 pounds) or, regardless of weight, have been in the womb fewer than 30 weeks

preterm births differ among racial groups, not because of race per se, but because members of racial minorities have disproportionately lower incomes and higher stress as a result. For instance, the percentage of low-birthweight infants born to African American mothers is double that for Caucasian American mothers. (A summary of the factors associated with increased risk of low birthweight is shown in Table 4.2; Field, Diego, & Hernandez-Reif, 2008; Bergmann, Bergmann, & Dudenhausen, 2008; Butler, Wilson, & Johnson, 2012.)

**POSTMATURE BABIES: TOO LATE, TOO LARGE.** As noted, postmature babies face risks as well. For example, the blood supply from the placenta may become insufficient to nourish the still-growing fetus adequately. Consequently, the blood supply to the brain may be decreased, leading to the potential of brain damage. Similarly, labor becomes riskier (for both the child and the mother) as a fetus who may be equivalent in size to a 1-month-old infant has to make its way through the birth canal (Shea, Wilcox, & Little, 1998; Fok and Tsang, 2006).

**Table 4.2** Factors Associated With Increased Risk of Low Birthweight

**I. Demographic Risks**
   **a.** Age (less than 17; over 34)
   **b.** Race (minority)
   **c.** Low socioeconomic status
   **d.** Unmarried
   **e.** Low level of education

**II. Medical Risks Predating Pregnancy**
   **a.** Number of previous pregnancies (0 or more than 4)
   **b.** Low weight for height
   **c.** Genitourinary anomalies/surgery
   **d.** Selected diseases, such as diabetes or chronic hypertension
   **e.** Nonimmune status for selected infections, such as rubella
   **f.** Poor obstetric history, including previous low-birthweight infant or multiple spontaneous abortions
   **g.** Maternal genetic factors (such as low weight at own birth)

**III. Medical Risks in Current Pregnancy**
   **a.** Multiple pregnancy
   **b.** Poor weight gain
   **c.** Short interpregnancy interval
   **d.** Low blood pressure
   **e.** Hypertension/preeclampsia/toxemia
   **f.** Selected infections, such as asymptomatic bacteriuria, rubella, and cytomegalovirus
   **g.** First- or second-trimester bleeding
   **h.** Placental problems, such as placenta previa or abruptio placentae
   **i.** Severe morning sickness
   **j.** Anemia/abnormal hemoglobin
   **k.** Severe anemia in a developing baby
   **l.** Fetal anomalies
   **m.** Incompetent cervix
   **n.** Spontaneous premature rupture of membrane

**IV. Behavioral and Environmental Risks**
   **a.** Smoking
   **b.** Poor nutritional status
   **c.** Alcohol and other substance abuse
   **d.** Diethylstilbestrol (DES) exposure and other toxic exposure, including occupational hazards
   **e.** High altitude

**V. Health Care Risks**
   **a.** Absent or inadequate prenatal care
   **b.** Iatrogenic prematurity

**VI. Evolving Concepts of Risks**
   **a.** Stress, physical and psychosocial
   **b.** Uterine irritability
   **c.** Events triggering uterine contractions
   **d.** Cervical changes detected before onset of labor
   **e.** Selected infections, such as mycoplasma and *Chlamydia trachomatis*
   **f.** Inadequate plasma volume expansion
   **g.** Progesterone deficiency

**SOURCE:** Adapted from "Committee to Study the Prevention of Low Birthweight," Preventing Low Birthweight, 1985, National Academy Press from Preventing Low Birthweight by the National Academy Press..

Difficulties involving postmature infants are more easily prevented than those involving preterm babies, since medical practitioners can induce labor artificially if the pregnancy continues too long. Not only can certain drugs bring on labor, but physicians also have the option of performing cesarean deliveries, a form of delivery we consider next.

## Cesarean Delivery: Intervening in the Birth Process

**LO 4.5** **Describe situations for which cesarean deliveries are necessary.**

*As Elena entered her 18th hour of labor, the obstetrician who was monitoring her progress began to look concerned. She told Elena and her husband, Pablo, that the fetal monitor revealed that the fetus's heart rate had begun to repeatedly fall after each contraction. After trying some simple remedies, such as repositioning Elena on her side, the obstetrician came to the conclusion that the fetus was in distress. She told them that the baby should be delivered immediately, and to accomplish that, she would have to carry out a cesarean delivery.*

Elena became 1 of the more than 1 million mothers in the United States who have a cesarean delivery each year. In a **cesarean delivery** (sometimes known as a *c-section*), the baby is surgically removed from the uterus, rather than traveling through the birth canal.

Cesarean deliveries occur most frequently when the fetus shows distress of some sort. For instance, if the fetus appears to be in danger, as indicated by a sudden rise in its heart rate, or if blood is seen coming from the mother's vagina during labor, a cesarean may be performed. In addition, older mothers, over age 40, are more likely to have cesarean deliveries than younger ones. Overall, cesarean deliveries in the United States now make up 32 percent of all deliveries (Tang et al., 2006; Menacker & Hamilton, 2010; Romero, Coulson, & Galvin, 2012).

Cesarean deliveries are also used in some cases of breech position, in which the baby is positioned feet first in the birth canal. Breech position births, which occur in about 1 out of 25 births, place the baby at risk because the umbilical cord is more likely to be compressed, depriving the baby of oxygen. Cesarean deliveries are also more likely in transverse position births, in which the baby lies crosswise in the uterus, or when the baby's head is so large it has trouble moving through the birth canal.

The routine use of a **fetal monitor**, a device that measures the baby's heartbeat during labor, has contributed to a soaring rate of cesarean deliveries. The rate of cesarean births is up some 500 percent from the early 1970s, when the rate stood at 5 percent (Hamilton, Martin, & Ventura, 2011; Paterno et al., 2016).

Are cesareans an effective medical intervention? Other countries have substantially lower rates of cesarean deliveries, and there is no association between successful birth outcomes and the rate of cesarean deliveries. In addition, cesarean deliveries carry dangers. Cesarean delivery represents major surgery, and the mother's recovery can be relatively lengthy, particularly compared to a normal delivery. In addition, the risk of maternal infection is higher with cesarean deliveries (Miesnik & Reale, 2007; Hutcheon et al., 2013; Ryding et al., 2015).

Finally, a cesarean delivery presents some risks for the baby. Because cesarean babies are spared the stresses of passing through the birth canal, their relatively easy passage into the world may deter the normal release of certain stress-related hormones, such as catecholamines, into the newborn's bloodstream. These hormones help prepare the neonate to deal with the stress of the world outside the womb, and their absence may be detrimental to the newborn child.

In fact, research indicates that babies born by cesarean delivery, who have not experienced labor, are more likely to have breathing problems upon birth than those who have at least progressed through some labor prior to being born via a cesarean delivery. In addition, mothers who deliver by cesarean are less satisfied with the birth experience, but their dissatisfaction does not influence the quality of mother–child interactions (Lobel & DeLuca, 2007; Porter et al., 2007; MacDorman et al., 2008).

Because the increase in cesarean deliveries is, as we have said, connected to the use of fetal monitors, medical authorities now currently recommend that they not be used routinely. There is evidence that outcomes are no better for newborns who have been monitored than for those who have not been monitored. In addition, monitors tend to indicate fetal distress when there is none—false alarms—with disquieting regularity. Monitors do, however, play a critical role in high-risk pregnancies and in cases of preterm and postmature babies (Freeman, 2007; Sepehri & Guliani, 2017).

---

**cesarean delivery** A birth in which the baby is surgically removed from the uterus, rather than traveling through the birth canal

**fetal monitor** A device that measures the baby's heartbeat during labor

# DEVELOPMENTAL DIVERSITY AND YOUR LIFE

## Cultural Beliefs and Practices around Childbirth

In India, the infant mortality rate or IMR (per 1000 live births) has decreased from 55 in 2007 to 34 in 2016 (NITI Aayog, 2018). Despite all the efforts toward improving neonatal care to reduce infant mortality rate, poor progress still remains a major concern for policy makers in India.

While childbirth is a biological event, pregnancy and birth experiences surrounding it are mostly social constructs shaped by cultural perceptions and practices. The role of such beliefs and practices around childbirth cannot be ignored by researchers and practitioners and policy makers. It is a general belief that formal healthcare services should be sought only in case of complication. For example, in rural Rajasthan, women prefer home-based childbirth (Iyengar & Iyengar et al., 2008).

Over the last decade, public health approaches to maternal health have emphasized the need for access to services such as skilled care and emergency obstetrics, but less attention was given to improving family and community practices. By recognizing and appreciating prevailing local beliefs, maternal healthcare providers can be better positioned to provide culturally-competent care to women and their families.

Withers, Kharazmi, and Lim (2018) did an extensive analysis of the research reporting the most common traditional practices relating to pregnancy and childbirth in Asia. Many women in Asia including India follow a range of practices that are influenced by their traditional beliefs. Some of the practices are: giving birth in a sitting position or lying supine on the floor; avoiding hospital due to the fear of medical intervention like cesarean section; and feeling dehumanized in a hospital setting. Taboos pertaining to food are widely prevalent in suburban, rural, and tribal areas. In one study, women in labor were fed clarified butter, ginger, lentils, milk, or teas which are believed to facilitate labor by promoting warmth (Mirzabagi et al., 2013). Various rituals are also conducted to ease and smoothen the delivery process as well as to offer blessings to the expecting mother. In India, the ritual of *God Bharai* (baby shower) is one such example wherein the expecting mothers are blessed and offered delicious food.

Women are secluded in a room during childbirth and postpartum. They are not allowed to prepare food or do other household chores due to the belief that vaginal blood is inauspicious and can cause sickness and lead to poor health of others.

Indian women are encouraged to perform normal activities as per their schedule and to be more active to remain physically healthy for a normal childbirth. They are also advised not to sleep on their back, always sit up to turn over, and never sit in a cross-legged position (Corbett & Callister, 2012).

Based on their review of research, Withers, Kharazmi, and Lim (2018) have concluded that it is important to raise awareness about the benefits of formal healthcare, while dispelling the myths and misconceptions surrounding the more dangerous practices that are followed outside the hospital.

---

Studies examining what appear, in retrospect, to be unnecessary cesareans have found racial and socioeconomic differences. Specifically, Black mothers are more likely to have a potentially unnecessary cesarean delivery than White mothers are. In addition, Medicare patients—who tend to be relatively poor—are more likely to have unnecessary cesarean deliveries than non-Medicare patients (Kabir et al., 2005).

## Infant Mortality and Stillbirth: The Tragedy of Premature Death

**LO 4.6  List the factors that contribute to infant mortality.**

The joy that accompanies the birth of a child is completely reversed when a newborn dies. The relative rarity of their occurrence makes infant deaths even harder for parents to bear.

Sometimes a child does not even live beyond its passage through the birth canal. **Stillbirth**, the delivery of a child who is not alive, occurs in fewer than 1 delivery out of 100. Sometimes the death is detected before labor begins. In this case, labor is typically induced, or physicians may carry out a cesarean delivery in order to remove the body from the mother as soon as possible. In other cases of stillbirth, the baby dies during its travel through the birth canal.

The overall rate of **infant mortality** (defined as death within the first year of life) is 6.17 deaths per

---

**stillbirth** The delivery of a child who is not alive, occurring in fewer than 1 delivery in 100

**infant mortality** Death within the first year of life

1,000 live births. Infant mortality generally has been declining since the 1960s, and declined 12 percent from 2005 to 2011 (MacDorman, Hoyert, & Matthews, 2013; Loggins & Andrade, 2014; Prince et al., 2016).

Whether the death is a stillbirth or occurs after the child is born, the loss of a baby is tragic, and the impact on parents is enormous. The loss and grief parents feel, and their passage through it, is similar to that experienced when an older loved one dies.

The juxtaposition of the first dawning of life and an unusually early death may make the death particularly difficult to accept and handle. Depression is common, and it is often intensified owing to a lack of support. Some parents even experience post-traumatic stress disorder (Badenhorst et al., 2006; Cacciatore & Bushfield, 2007; Turton, Evans, & Hughes, 2009).

# Postpartum Depression: Moving From the Heights of Joy to the Depths of Despair

**LO 4.7   Describe postpartum depression.**

*Renuka was overjoyed when she found out that she was pregnant. She had spent the months of her pregnancy happily preparing for her baby's arrival. The birth was routine, the baby a healthy, pink-cheeked boy. But a few days after her son's birth, she sank into the depths of depression. Constantly crying, confused, feeling incapable of caring for her child, she was experiencing unshakable despair.*

The diagnosis: a classic case of postpartum depression. *Postpartum depression*, a period of deep depression following the birth of a child, affects some 10 percent of all new mothers. Although it takes several forms, its main symptom is an enduring, deep feeling of sadness and unhappiness, lasting in some cases for months or even years. Mothers experiencing postpartum depression may withdraw from their family and friends, experience overwhelming fatigue or loss of energy, or feel intense irritability and anger. Furthermore, mothers may feel stigmatized by others (Mickelson et al., 2017).

In about 1 in 500 cases, the symptoms are even worse, evolving into a total break with reality. In extremely rare instances, postpartum depression may turn deadly. For example, in one notorious case, Andrea Yates, a mother in Texas, drowned all five of her children in a bathtub as a result of postpartum depression (Yardley, 2001; Oretti et al., 2003; Misri, 2007).

For mothers who suffer from postpartum depression, the symptoms are often bewildering. The onset of depression usually comes as a complete surprise. Certain mothers do seem more likely to become depressed, such as those who have been clinically depressed at some point in the past or those who have depressed family members. Furthermore, women who are unprepared for the range of emotions that follow the birth of a child—some positive, some negative—may be more prone to depression (Kim, Sherman, & Taylor, 2008; Iles, Slade, & Spiby, 2011; LaCoursiere, Hirst, & Barrett-Connor, 2012; Pawluski, Lonstein, & Fleming, 2017).

Finally, postpartum depression may be triggered by the pronounced swings in hormone production that occur after birth. During pregnancy, production of the female hormones estrogen and progesterone increases significantly; however, within the first 24 hours following birth, they plunge to normal levels. This rapid change may result in depression (Klier et al., 2007; Yim et al., 2009; Engineer et al., 2013; Glynn & Sandman, 2014).

Whatever the cause, maternal depression leaves its marks on the infant. As we'll see later in the chapter, babies are born with impressive social capacities, and they are highly attuned to the moods of their mothers. When depressed mothers interact with their infants, they are likely to display little emotion and to act detached and withdrawn. This lack of responsiveness leads infants to display fewer positive emotions and to withdraw from contact not only with their mothers but with other adults as well. In addition, children of depressed mothers are more prone to antisocial activities, including violence (Hay, Pawlby & Angold, 2003; Nylen et al., 2006; Goodman et al., 2008).

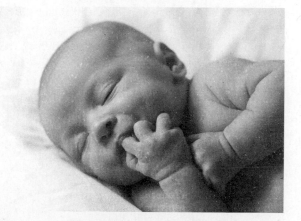

Newborns enter the world preprogrammed—through the rooting, sucking, and swallowing reflexes—to find, take in, and digest food.

# The Competent Newborn

*Relatives gathered around the infant car seat and its occupant, Kaita Castro. Kaita was born just 2 days ago, and this is her first day home from the hospital with her mother. Kaita's nearest cousin, 4-year-old Tabor, seems uninterested in the new arrival. "Babies can't do anything fun. They can't even do anything at all," he says.*

Kaita's cousin Tabor is partly right. There are many things babies cannot do. Neonates arrive in the world quite incapable of successfully caring for themselves, for example. Why are human infants born so dependent, whereas members of other species seem to arrive much better equipped for their lives?

One reason is that, in one sense, humans are born too soon. The brain of the average newborn is just one-fourth of what it will be at adulthood. In comparison, the brain of the macaque monkey, which is born after just 24 weeks of gestation, is 65 percent of its adult size. Because of the relative puniness of the infant human brain, some observers have suggested that we are propelled out of the womb some 6 to 12 months sooner than we ought to be.

In reality, evolution probably knew what it was doing: if we stayed inside our mothers' bodies an additional half-year to a year, our heads would be so large that we'd never manage to get through the birth canal (Schultz, 1969; Gould, 1977; Kotre & Hall, 1990).

The relatively underdeveloped brain of the human newborn helps explain the infant's apparent helplessness. Because of this vulnerability, the earliest views of newborns focused on the things that they could not do, comparing them rather unfavorably to older members of the human species.

Today, however, such beliefs have taken a backseat to more favorable views of the neonate. As developmental researchers have begun to understand more about the nature of newborns, they have come to realize that infants enter this world with an astounding array of capabilities in all domains of development: physical, cognitive, and social.

## Meeting the Demands of a New Environment

**LO 4.8  Identify the physical and sensory capabilities of the newborn.**

The world faced by a neonate is remarkably different from the one it experienced in the womb. He or she is met with new physical challenges and sensory experiences immediately. Consider, for instance, the significant changes in functioning that Kaita Castro encountered as she began the first moments of life in her new environment.

**PHYSICAL COMPETENCE.**  Kaita's most immediate task was to bring sufficient air into her body. Inside her mother, air was delivered through the umbilical cord, which also provided a means for taking away carbon dioxide. The realities of the outside world are different: once the umbilical cord was cut, Kaita's respiratory system needed to begin its lifetime's work.

For Kaita, the task was automatic. As we noted earlier, most newborn babies begin to breathe on their own as soon as they are exposed to air. The ability to breathe immediately is a good indication that the respiratory system of the normal neonate is reasonably well developed, despite its lack of rehearsal in the womb.

Neonates emerge from the uterus more practiced in other types of physical activities. For example, newborns such as Kaita show several **reflexes**—unlearned, organized, involuntary responses that occur automatically in the presence of certain stimuli. Some of these reflexes are well rehearsed, having been present for several months before birth. The *sucking reflex* and the *swallowing reflex* permit Kaita to begin to ingest food right away. The *rooting reflex*, which involves turning in the direction of a source of stimulation (such as a light touch) near the mouth, is also related to eating. It guides the infant toward potential sources of food that are near its mouth, such as a mother's nipple.

Not all of the reflexes that are present at birth lead the newborn to seek out desired stimuli such as food. For instance, Kaita can cough, sneeze, and blink—reflexes that help her avoid stimuli that are potentially bothersome or hazardous. (We discuss more reflexes in Chapter 5.)

Kaita's sucking and swallowing reflexes, which help her to consume her mother's milk, are coupled with the newfound ability to digest nutriments. The newborn's digestive system initially produces feces in the form of *meconium*, a greenish-black material that is a remnant of the neonate's days as a fetus.

Because the liver, a critical component of the digestive system, does not always work effectively at first, almost half of all newborns develop a distinctly

---

**reflexes** Unlearned, organized, involuntary responses that occur automatically in the presence of certain stimuli

yellowish tinge to their bodies and eyes. This change in color is a symptom of *neonatal jaundice*. It is most likely to occur in preterm and low-birthweight neonates, and it is typically not dangerous. Treatment most often consists of placing the baby under fluorescent lights or administering medicine.

**SENSORY CAPABILITIES.** Just after Kaita was born, her father was certain that she looked directly at him. Did she, in fact, see him?

This is a hard question to answer for several reasons. For one thing, when sensory experts talk of "seeing," they mean both a sensory reaction to the stimulation of the visual sensory organs and an interpretation of that stimulation (the distinction, as you might recall from an introductory psychology class, between sensation and perception). Furthermore, it is tricky, to say the least, to pinpoint the specific sensory skills of newborns who lack the ability to explain what they are experiencing.

Still, we do have some answers to the question of what newborns are capable of seeing and, for that matter, to questions about their other sensory capabilities. As an example, it is clear that neonates such as Kaita can see to some extent; although their visual acuity is not fully developed, newborns actively pay attention to certain types of information in their environment.

For instance, neonates pay closest attention to portions of scenes in their field of vision that are highest in information, such as objects that contrast sharply with the rest of their environment. Furthermore, infants can discriminate different levels of brightness. There is even evidence suggesting that newborns have a sense of size constancy. They seem aware that objects stay the same size even though the size of the image on the retina varies with distance (Chien et al., 2006; Frankenhuis, Barrett, & Johnson, 2013; Wood & Wood, 2016).

In addition, not only can newborn babies distinguish different colors, but they also seem to prefer particular ones. For example, they are able to distinguish among red, green, yellow, and blue, and they take more time staring at blue and green objects—suggesting a partiality for those colors (Dobson, 2000; Alexander & Hines, 2002; Zemach, Chang, & Teller, 2007).

Newborns are also clearly capable of hearing. They react to certain kinds of sounds, showing startle reactions to loud, sudden noises, for instance. They also exhibit familiarity with certain sounds. For example,

Starting at birth, infants are able to distinguish colors and even show preferences for particular ones.

a crying newborn will continue to cry when he or she hears other newborns crying. If, however, the baby hears a recording of his or her own crying, he or she is more likely to stop crying, as if recognizing the familiar sound (Dondi, Simion, & Caltran, 1999; Fernald, 2001).

As with vision, however, the newborn's degree of auditory acuity is not as great as it will be later. The auditory system is not completely developed. Moreover, amniotic fluid, which is initially trapped in the middle ear, must drain out before the newborn can fully hear. In addition to sight and hearing, the other senses also function quite adequately in the newborn. It is obvious that newborns are sensitive to touch. For instance, they respond to stimuli such as the hairs of a brush, and they are aware of puffs of air so weak that adults cannot notice them.

The senses of smell and taste are also well developed. Newborns suck and increase other physical activity when the odor of peppermint is placed near the nose. They also pucker their lips when a sour taste is placed on them, and they respond with suitable facial expressions to other tastes. Such findings clearly indicate that the senses of touch, smell, and taste not only are present at birth but also are reasonably sophisticated (Cohen & Cashon, 2003; Armstrong et al., 2007).

In one sense, the sophistication of the sensory systems of newborns such as Kaita is not surprising. After all, the typical neonate has had 9 months to prepare for his or her encounter with the outside world. As we discussed in Chapter 2, human sensory systems begin their development well before birth. Furthermore, the passage through the birth canal may place babies in a state of heightened sensory awareness, preparing them for the world that they are about to encounter (also see the *From Research to Practice* box).

# FROM RESEARCH TO PRACTICE
## Are Food Preferences Learned in the Womb?

Do you have friends who have a taste for certain kinds of pungent or spicy foods that you think are just awful? And perhaps you have an affinity for garlic or curry that some of your friends don't share? Where do our seemingly quirky tastes for foods come from? Research suggests that at least some of our preferences were shaped in the womb.

When researchers gave women either unflavored capsules or garlic-flavored capsules to consume during the last weeks of their pregnancy, adult volunteers who were then asked to sniff samples of the women's amniotic fluid or breast milk could easily discern who had been eating the garlic. Because fetuses at this stage of development have the ability to taste and smell, it's a reasonable conclusion that if adults could detect the garlic, so too could the fetus. And when the newborns were offered garlic-flavored milk, those whose mothers were consuming garlic during pregnancy drank it happily, while those whose mothers consumed no garlic rejected it. Experiments with other kinds of flavors showed similar results (Mennella & Beauchamp, 1996; Underwood, 2014).

Research with mice confirms a neurological basis for the link between exposure to flavors in utero and later taste preferences. When fetal mice were exposed to a mint flavor, the neural pathways were strengthened between the scent receptors for mint and the amygdala—a brain region involved in emotion (Todrank, Heth, & Restrepo, 2011).

Is it therefore likely that your food preferences today are lasting imprints of what your mother ate while carrying you? Probably not—tastes change over time as we become exposed to new foods and new flavor experiences. But where this very early influence on taste matters most is food preferences and aversions during infancy; this can be helpful to know, for example, in cases where an infant's condition requires a very specific kind of diet. And indeed, the foods that mothers preferred while pregnant likely continued on as the foods that she would feed her family. Thus it stands to reason that those of us who were exposed to garlic or curry in the womb—and then continued to eat it throughout our childhood—would still have a taste for it today (Trabulsi & Mennella, 2012).

- **What might be an evolutionary advantage to infants liking the kinds of foods their mothers eat?**

## Early Learning Capabilities

**LO 4.9  Explain the early learning capabilities of the newborn.**

*One-month-old Michael Samedi was on a car ride with his family when a thunderstorm suddenly began. The storm rapidly became violent, and flashes of lightning were quickly followed by loud thunderclaps. Michael was clearly disturbed and began to sob. With each new thunderclap, the pitch and fervor of his crying increased. Unfortunately, before very long it wasn't just the sound of the thunder that would raise Michael's anxiety; the sight of the lightning alone was enough to make him cry out in fear. Even as an adult, Michael feels his chest tighten and his stomach churn at the mere sight of lightning.*

**CLASSICAL CONDITIONING.** The source of Michael's fear is classical conditioning, a basic type of learning first identified by Ivan Pavlov (and first discussed in Chapter 2). In **classical conditioning**, an organism learns to respond in a particular way to a neutral stimulus that normally does not bring about that type of response. Pavlov discovered that by repeatedly pairing two stimuli, such as the sound of a bell and the arrival of meat, he could make hungry dogs learn to respond (in this case by salivating) not only when the meat was presented but also even when the bell was sounded without the presence of meat (Pavlov, 1927).

The key feature of classical conditioning is stimulus substitution, in which a stimulus that doesn't naturally bring about a particular response is paired with a stimulus that does evoke that response. Repeatedly presenting the two stimuli together results in the second stimulus taking on the properties of the first. In effect, the second stimulus is substituted for the first.

One of the earliest examples of the power of classical conditioning in shaping human emotions was demonstrated in the case of an 11-month-old infant known by researchers as "Little Albert" (Watson & Rayner, 1920; Fridlund et al., 2012). Although he initially adored furry animals and showed no fear of rats, Little Albert learned to fear them when, during a laboratory demonstration,

---

**classical conditioning** A type of learning in which an organism responds in a particular way to a neutral stimulus that normally does not bring about that type of response

a loud noise was sounded every time he played with a cute and harmless white rat. In fact, the fear generalized to other furry objects, including rabbits and even a Santa Claus mask. (By the way, such a demonstration would be considered unethical today, and it would never be conducted.)

Infants are capable of learning very early through classical conditioning. For instance, 1- and 2-day-old newborns who are stroked on the head just before being given a drop of a sweet-tasting liquid soon learn to turn their heads and suck at the head-stroking alone. Clearly, classical conditioning is in operation from the time of birth (Dominguez, Lopez, & Molina, 1999; Herbert et al., 2004; Welch, 2016).

**OPERANT CONDITIONING.** But classical conditioning is not the only mechanism through which infants learn; they also respond to **operant conditioning**. As noted in Chapter 2, operant conditioning is a form of learning in which a voluntary response is strengthened or weakened, depending on its association with positive or negative consequences. In operant conditioning, infants learn to act deliberately on their environments in order to bring about some desired consequence. An infant who learns that crying in a certain way is apt to bring her parents' immediate attention is displaying operant conditioning.

Like classical conditioning, operant conditioning functions from the earliest days of life. For instance, researchers have found that even newborns readily learn through operant conditioning to keep sucking on a nipple when it permits them to continue hearing their mothers read a story or to listen to music (DeCasper & Fifer, 1980; Lipsitt, 1986).

**HABITUATION.** Probably the most primitive form of learning is demonstrated by the phenomenon of habituation. **Habituation** is the decrease in the response to a stimulus that occurs after repeated presentations of the same stimulus.

Habituation in infants relies on the fact that when newborns are presented with a new stimulus, they produce an *orienting response*, in which they become quiet, attentive, and experience a slowed heart rate as they take in the novel stimulus. When the novelty wears off due to repeated exposure to the stimulus, the infant no longer reacts with this orienting response. If a new and different stimulus is presented, the infant once again reacts with an orienting response. When this happens, we can say that the infant has learned to recognize the original stimulus and to distinguish it from others.

Habituation occurs in every sensory system, and researchers have studied it in several ways. One way is to examine changes in sucking, which stops temporarily when a new stimulus is presented. This reaction is not unlike that of an adult who temporarily puts down her knife and fork when a dinner companion makes an interesting statement to which she wishes to pay particular attention. Other measures of habituation include changes in heart rate, respiration rate, and the length of time an infant looks at a particular stimulus (Brune & Woodward, 2007; Farroni et al., 2007; Colombo & Mitchell, 2009; Macchi et al., 2012).

The development of habituation is linked to physical and cognitive maturation. It is present at birth and becomes more pronounced over the first 12 weeks of infancy. Difficulties involving habituation represent a signal of developmental problems, such as intellectual disability (Moon, 2002). (The three basic processes of learning that we've considered—classical conditioning, operant conditioning, and habituation—are summarized in Table 4.3.)

**operant conditioning** A form of learning in which a voluntary response is strengthened or weakened, depending on its association with positive or negative consequences

**habituation** The decrease in the response to a stimulus that occurs after repeated presentations of the same stimulus

**Table 4.3** Learning in Infancy: Some Basic Processes

| Type | Description | Example |
|---|---|---|
| Classical conditioning | A situation in which an organism learns to respond in a particular way to a neutral stimulus that normally does not bring about that type of response. | A hungry baby stops crying when her mother picks her up because she has learned to associate being picked up with subsequent feeding. |
| Operant conditioning | A form of learning in which a voluntary response is strengthened or weakened, depending on its positive or negative consequences. | An infant who learns that smiling at his or her parents brings positive attention, and thus smiles more often. |
| Habituation | The decrease in the response to a stimulus that occurs after repeated presentations of the same stimulus. | A baby who showed interest and surprise at first seeing a novel toy may show no interest after seeing the same toy several times. |

# Social Competence: Responding to Others

### LO 4.10 Describe the ways newborns respond to others.

*Soon after Lucia was born, her older brother looked down at her in her crib and opened his mouth wide, pretending to be surprised. Lucia's mother, looking on, was amazed when it appeared that Lucia imitated his expression, opening her mouth as if she were surprised.*

Researchers registered surprise of their own when they first found that newborns did indeed have the capability to imitate others' behavior. Although infants were known to have all the muscles in place to produce facial expressions related to basic emotions, the actual appearance of such expressions was assumed to be largely random.

Beginning in the late 1970s, however, research began to suggest a different conclusion. For instance, developmental researchers found that, when exposed to an adult modeling a behavior that the infant already performed spontaneously, such as opening the mouth or sticking out the tongue, the newborn appeared to imitate the behavior (Meltzoff & Moore, 1977, 2002; Nagy, 2006).

Even more exciting were findings from a series of studies conducted by developmental psychologist Tiffany Field and her colleagues (Field, 1982; Field & Walden, 1982; Field et al., 1984). They initially showed that infants could discriminate among such basic facial expressions as those indicating happiness, sadness, and surprise. They then exposed newborns to an adult model with a happy, sad, or surprised facial expression. The results suggested that newborns produced a reasonably accurate imitation of the adult's expression.

Subsequent research, however, seemed to point to a different conclusion, as other investigators found consistent evidence only for a single imitative movement: sticking out the tongue. And even that response seemed to disappear around the age of 2 months. Because it seems unlikely that imitation would be limited to a single gesture and only appear for a few months, researchers began to question the earlier findings. Some researchers suggested that even sticking out the tongue was not imitation, but merely an exploratory behavior (Anisfeld, 1996; Bjorklund, 1997; Jones, 2006, 2007; Tissaw, 2007; Huang, 2012).

Developmental psychologist Tiffany Field carried out pioneering work on infants' facial expressions.

The jury is still out on exactly when true imitation begins, although it seems clear that some forms of imitation begin very early in life. Such imitative skills are important, because effective social interaction with others relies in part on the ability to react to other people in an appropriate manner and to understand the meaning of others' emotional states. Consequently, newborns' ability to imitate provides them with an important foundation for social interaction later in life (Meltzoff, 2002; Rogers & Williams, 2006; Zeedyk & Heimann, 2006; Legerstee & Markova, 2008).

Several other aspects of newborns' behavior also act as forerunners for more formal types of social interaction that they will develop as they grow. As shown in Table 4.4, neonates mesh with parental behavior to help produce a social relationship between child and parent, as well as social relationships with others. For example, newborns cycle through various **states of arousal**, different degrees of sleep and wakefulness, ranging from deep sleep to great agitation. Although these cycles are disrupted immediately after birth, they quickly become more regularized. Caregivers become involved when they seek to aid the infant in transitions from one state to another. For instance, a father may rhythmically rock his crying daughter in an effort to calm her. Similarly, newborns tend to pay particular attention to their mothers' voices. In turn, parents and others modify their speech when talking to infants, using a different pitch and tempo than they use with older children and adults (Smith & Trainor, 2008; Barr, 2011; Huotilainen, 2013).

**States of arousal** Different degrees of sleep and wakefulness, ranging from deep sleep to great agitation

**Table 4.4** Factors That Encourage Social Interaction Between Full-Term Newborns and Their Parents

| Full-Term Newborn | Parent |
|---|---|
| Attends selectively to certain stimuli | Provides these stimuli |
| Behaves in ways interpretable as specific communicative intent | Searches for communicative intent |
| Responds systematically to parent's acts | Wants to influence newborn, feel effective |
| Acts in temporally predictable ways | Adjusts actions to newborn's temporal rhythms |
| Learns from, adapts to parent's behavior | Acts repetitively and predictably |

**SOURCE:** C.O. Eckerman, J.M. Oehler, "Very Low Birthweight Newborns and Parents as Early Social Partners," in S.L. Friedman & M.B. Sigman eds., The Psychological Development of Low-Birthweight Children, NL: Ablex,1992.

**From a child care worker's perspective:** Developmental researchers no longer view the neonate as a helpless, incompetent creature, but rather as a remarkably competent, developing human being. What do you think are some implications of this change in viewpoint for methods of child rearing and child care?

The ultimate outcome of the social interactive capabilities of the newborn infant, and the responses such behavior brings about from parents, is to pave the way for future social interactions. Just as the neonate shows remarkable skills on a physical and perceptual level, its social capabilities are no less sophisticated.

# The Case of …
## No Place Like Home?

To have a safe childbirth, Rohit and Anjali agreed that having their child in the maternity care center of a hospital under the supervision of a doctor is the best way. Some of their friends and relatives have suggested that in case of a normal childbirth, there is no need to go to the hospital and the child can be born in a natural home environment with the help of a midwife; however, the couple disagreed. This is their first child and they do not want to take any risk. Both Rohit and Anjali are quite concerned as they have heard of many emergency situations at the end moment like unplanned cesarean due to inappropriate position of the baby, lack of oxygen to the baby, etc.

1. What ideas might Rohit suggest to help Anjali overcome his distaste for hospital deliveries? Can the hospital experience be made more personal and natural?
2. Conversely, what ideas might Rohit propose to address Anjali's fears about at-home delivery? Are there ways to make a home birth as safe as a hospital birth?
3. If you were asked to make a recommendation for Anjali and Rohit, what questions would you ask them?
4. Anjali and Rohit seem stuck on the question of at-home versus in-hospital birth. Are there other options that might address both parents' concerns? What are they, and how would they address those concerns?
5. Would your recommendation change if you found out that Anjali's mother and sisters all experienced long and painful labor and ultimately had to have cesareans? Why or why not?

# Epilogue

This chapter has covered the amazing and intense processes of labor and birth. A number of birthing options are available to parents, and these options need to be weighed in light of possible complications that can arise during the birthing process. In addition to considering the remarkable progress that has been made regarding the various treatments and interventions available for babies that are too early or too late, we examined the grim topics of stillbirth and infant mortality. We concluded with a discussion of the surprising capabilities of newborns and their early development of social competence.

Before we move on to a more detailed examination of infants' physical development, let's return for a moment to the case of Aarti's difficult labor, discussed in the prologue. Using your understanding of the issues covered in this chapter, answer the following questions.

1. Exhaustion, and the epidural she was given to help her relax, made it impossible for Aarti to push her baby out when the time came. What complications could have arisen had her daughter's birth been delayed much further?

2. If Aarti's obstetrician had determined that her daughter could not be delivered with forceps, what else could have been done? What additional complications might have arisen?

3. Do you think giving Aarti an epidural to relieve her pain and exhaustion, though it impeded her ability to push, was a good decision? What else might her doctor have done to help her relax without resorting to medication?

4. Describe what Aarti's daughter's experiences immediately following birth would have been like.

# Looking Back

## LO 4.1 Explain the normal process of labor.

- In the first stage of labor, contractions occur about every 8 to 10 minutes, increasing in frequency, duration, and intensity until the mother's cervix expands. In the second stage of labor, which lasts about 90 minutes, the baby begins to move through the cervix and birth canal and ultimately leaves the mother's body. In the third stage of labor, which lasts only a few minutes, the umbilical cord and placenta are expelled from the mother.

## LO 4.2 Describe what typically happens to the neonate in the moments immediately following birth.

- In most cases, after it emerges, the newborn, or neonate, automatically makes the transition to taking in oxygen by using its lungs.

- The health of the newborn may be assessed using the Apgar scale, a standard measurement system that indicates whether immediate life-saving intervention is needed. The infant may also undergo medical screening for a variety of diseases and genetic conditions.

- The newborn is covered in a greasy substance called vernix, which eases the passage through the birth canal. After birth, vernix is wiped away. The body of a newborn is also covered with lanugo, a fine, dark fuzz that soon disappears.

- Although it was once thought that bonding, the close physical and emotional contact between mother and child, must occur immediately after birth to form a lasting relationship, developmental researchers have found little evidence for the existence of such a critical period. However, it is important that someone massage the newborn soon after birth to release chemicals in the infant's brain that stimulate growth.

## LO 4.3 Compare the different birthing procedures, and explain what choices relating to the birth are available to parents.

- Among the major alternatives to traditional birthing practices are Lamaze, which makes use of breathing techniques and relaxation training; the Bradley Method, also known as "husband-coached childbirth," which is based on the principle that childbirth should be as natural as possible; hypnobirthing, a technique that involves a form of self-hypnosis during delivery; and water birthing, a practice in which a woman enters a pool of warm water to give birth.

- Parents-to-be have a variety of choices regarding the setting for the birth, medical attendants, and whether to include the father and other family members in the delivery room. Sometimes, medical intervention, such as cesarean birth, becomes necessary.

- Labor can be painful and exhausting. Medication can relieve both the pain and its accompanying anxiety. A new form of epidural has fewer side effects and allows a woman to move about freely during labor.

- Drugs administered during labor have a much more powerful impact on the fetus due to the difference in body weight between mother and child. Although most research suggests that pain-reducing drugs, as they are currently administered, carry minimal risk, anesthetics may depress the flow of oxygen to the fetus.

## LO 4.4 Identify complications that can occur at birth, and explain their causes, effects, and treatments.

- Preterm, or premature, infants, born fewer than 38 weeks following conception, generally have low birthweight, which can cause vulnerability to infection, respiratory distress syndrome, and hypersensitivity to environmental stimuli. These infants may even show adverse effects later in life, including slowed development, learning disabilities, behavior disorders, below-average IQ scores, and problems with physical coordination.

- Very-low-birthweight infants are in special danger because of the immaturity of their organ systems; however, medical advances have pushed the age of viability of the infant back to about 22 weeks following conception.

- Postmature babies, who spend extra time in their mothers' wombs, are also at risk. Physicians can artificially induce labor or perform a cesarean delivery to address this situation. Cesarean deliveries are performed when the fetus is in distress, in the wrong position, or unable to progress through the birth canal.

**LO 4.5 Describe situations for which cesarean deliveries are necessary.**

- In a cesarean delivery (sometimes known as a *c-section*), the baby is surgically removed from the uterus rather than traveling through the birth canal.

- Cesarean deliveries occur most frequently when the fetus shows distress of some sort.

**LO 4.6 List the factors that contribute to infant mortality.**

- Infant mortality, defined as death within the first year of life, is largely the result of socioeconomic factors. Women living in poverty tend to receive less prenatal care, a situation that results in their having a higher percentage of low-birthweight babies. Low birthweight is closely linked to infant mortality. In addition, lack of paid maternity leave makes it impossible for many low-income mothers to stay home with their infants after the birth.

**LO 4.7 Describe postpartum depression.**

- Postpartum depression, an enduring, deep feeling of sadness, affects about 10 percent of new mothers. In severe cases, its effects can be harmful to the mother and the child, and aggressive treatment may be employed.

- For some mothers the onset of depression comes as a complete surprise, while for others depression may be triggered by the pronounced swings in hormone production that follow delivery.

**LO 4.8 Identify the physical and sensory capabilities of the newborn.**

- Newborns quickly master breathing through the lungs, and they are equipped with reflexes to help them eat, swallow, find food, and avoid unpleasant stimuli.

- Although their visual acuity is not fully developed, newborns pay attention to objects that feature high contrast, and they can discriminate different levels of brightness.

**LO 4.9 Explain the early learning capabilities of the newborn.**

- From birth, infants learn through classical conditioning, operant conditioning, and habituation. For example, an infant may learn that crying in a certain way brings her parents' prompt attention. The infant in this case would be learning by operant conditioning, in which a voluntary response is strengthened or weakened by its association with a positive or negative outcome.

**LO 4.10 Describe the ways newborns respond to others.**

- Researchers have found that newborns have the capability to imitate others' behavior through facial expressions, and that the newborns can discriminate among such facial expressions as those indicating happiness, sadness, and surprise.

- Certain characteristics of neonates interact with parental behavior to help produce a social relationship between child and parent, as well as social relationships with others.

# Key Terms and Concepts

neonate (p. 88)
episiotomy (p. 90)
Apgar scale (p. 90)
anoxia (p. 91)
bonding (p. 91)
preterm infants (p. 95)
postmature infants (p. 95)

low-birthweight infants (p. 96)
small-for-gestational-age
  infants (p. 96)
very-low-birthweight
  infants (p. 97)
cesarean delivery (p. 99)
fetal monitor (p. 99)

stillbirth (p. 100)
infant mortality (p. 100)
reflexes (p. 102)
classical conditioning (p. 104)
operant conditioning (p. 105)
habituation (p. 105)
states of arousal (p. 106)

# Putting It All Together

## Beginnings

*Parents-to-be typically look forward to the birth of their child. They may speculate—just as developmentalists do—about the role of genetics and environment in their child's development, considering issues like intelligence, resemblance, personality, schooling, and neighborhood. For the birth itself, they have many options available. Some may choose to use a midwife rather than an obstetrician, and/or to give birth at a traditional hospital, but in a nontraditional way. And when the baby is born, the baby will react to the sound of the mother's voice, which he or she first heard from inside the womb. This, in turn, will foster the bond between parents and infant.*

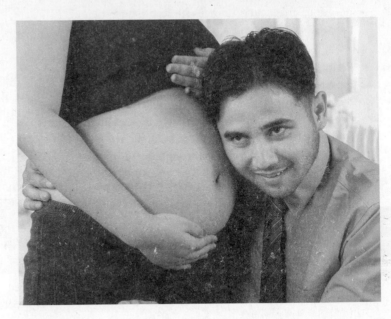

### Introduction to Development

- New parents may consider the role of genetics (nature) versus environment (nurture) in thinking about what their child will be like (p. 63).

- They also may consider how their child will develop physically, intellectually (or cognitively), and socially (p. 66).

### Prenatal Development

- Each parent contributes 23 chromosomes at conception. Their baby's sex is determined from the particular mix of one pair of chromosomes (p. 52).

- Many of an infant's characteristics will have a strong genetic component, but virtually all will represent some combination of genetics and environment (p. 62).

- An infant's prenatal development started when it was a fetus and progressed through a number of stages (p. 73).

### Birth and the Newborn

- Some women's labor is intense and painful, although others experience labor in different ways due to individual and cultural differences (p. 87).

- Some choose to use a midwife, one of several alternative birthing methods (p. 88).

- The vast majority of births are completely normal and successful (p. 83).

- Although a newborn seems helpless and dependent, he or she actually possesses from birth an array of useful capabilities and skills (p. 100).

## From a PARENT'S perspective:

- What strategies would you use to prepare yourself for the upcoming birth of your child? How would you evaluate the different options for prenatal care and delivery? How would you prepare your older child for the birth of a new baby?

  HINT: **Review pages 88–90.**

## From a HEALTH CARE PROVIDER'S perspective:

- How would you prepare new parents for the upcoming birth of their baby? How would you respond to their concerns and anxieties? What would you tell them about the different options they have for giving birth?

  HINT: **Review pages 90–93.**

## From an EDUCATOR'S perspective:

- What strategies might you use to teach parents-to-be about the stages of pregnancy and the process of birth? What might you tell them about infancy to prepare them for caring for their child?

  HINT: **Review pages 91–100.**

## From YOUR perspective:

- What would you say to new parents about the impending birth of their child? What advice would you give them about prenatal care and their decision about the use of a midwife?

  HINT: **Review pages 70–72.**

# Chapter 5
# Physical Development in Infancy

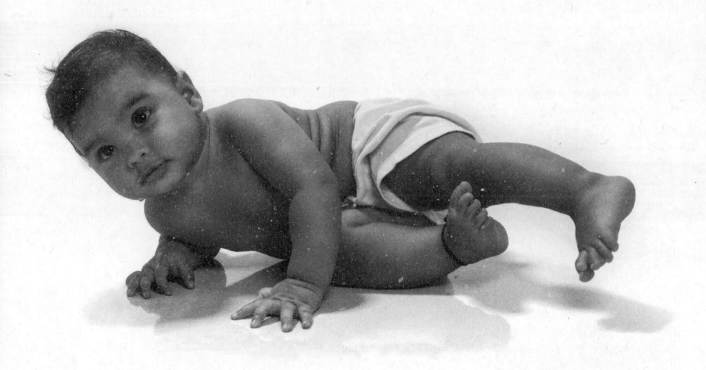

## ⌄ Learning Objectives

**LO 5.1** Describe how the human body develops.

**LO 5.2** Explain how the nervous system and brain develop.

**LO 5.3** Describe the processes by which a baby's bodily systems are integrated.

**LO 5.4** Discuss SIDS and SUID and how they can be prevented.

**LO 5.5** Describe reflexes and how they contribute to motor development.

**LO 5.6** Discuss the development and coordination of infants' motor skills.

**LO 5.7** Explain how developmental norms are used and interpreted.

**LO 5.8** Explain the relationship between nutrition and physical development.

**LO 5.9** List the visual perception skills infants have.

**LO 5.10** List the auditory perception skills infants have.

**LO 5.11** Describe infants' ability to smell, taste, and feel.

**LO 5.12** Explain multimodal perception.

# Prologue: Dreaming of Sleep

Liz and Seth Kaufman are so exhausted they have a hard time staying awake through dinner. The problem? Their 3-month-old son, Evan, who shows no signs of adopting normal patterns of eating and sleeping anytime soon. "I thought babies were these big sleep fanatics, but Evan takes little cat naps of an hour throughout the night, and then stays awake all day," Liz says. "I'm running out of ways to entertain him because all I want to do is sleep."

Evan's feeding schedule is hard on Liz, too. "He wants to nurse every hour for 5 hours in a row, which makes it hard to keep up my milk supply. Then he goes another 5 hours *not* wanting to nurse, and I'm positively, painfully engorged." Seth tries to help out, walking at night with Evan when he won't sleep, offering him a bottle of Liz's expressed milk at 3 a.m. "But sometimes he just refuses the bottle," Seth says. "Only mommy will do."

The pediatrician has assured the Kaufmans that their son is healthy and blossoming. "We're pretty sure Evan will come out of this just fine," Liz says. "It's us we're wondering about."

# Looking Ahead

Evan's parents can relax. Their son will settle down. Sleeping through the night is just one in a succession of milestones that characterize the dramatic physical attainments of infancy. In this chapter, we consider the nature of physical development during infancy, a period that starts at birth and continues until the second birthday. We begin by discussing the pace of growth during infancy, noting obvious changes in height and weight, as well as less apparent changes in the nervous system. We also consider how infants quickly develop increasingly stable patterns in such basic activities as sleeping, eating, and attending to the world.

Our discussion then turns to infants' thrilling gains in motor development as skills emerge that eventually will allow them to roll over, take the first step, and pick up a cookie crumb from the floor—skills that ultimately form the basis of later, even more complex behaviors. We start with basic, genetically determined reflexes and consider how even these may be modified through experience. We also discuss the nature and timing of the development of particular physical skills, look at whether their emergence can be speeded up, and consider the importance of early nutrition to their development.

Finally, we explore how infants' senses develop. We investigate how sensory systems such as hearing and vision operate, and how infants sort through the raw data from their sense organs and transform it into meaningful information.

# Growth and Stability

The average newborn weighs just over 7 pounds, which is less than the weight of the average Thanksgiving turkey. Its length is about 20 inches, shorter than a loaf of French bread. It is helpless; if left to fend for itself, it could not survive.

Yet after just a few years, the story is very different. Babies grow much larger, they are mobile, and they become increasingly independent. How does this growth happen? We can answer this question first by describing the changes in weight and height that occur over the first 2 years of life, and then by examining some of the principles that underlie and direct that growth.

## Physical Growth: The Rapid Advances of Infancy

**LO 5.1 Describe how the human body develops.**

Infants grow at a rapid pace over the first 2 years of their lives (see Figure 5.1). By the age of 5 months, the average infant's birth weight has doubled to around 15 pounds. By the first birthday, the baby's weight has tripled to about 22 pounds. Although the pace of weight gain slows during the second year, it still continues to increase. By the end of his or her second year, the average child weighs around four times as much as he or she did at birth. Of course, there is a good deal of variation among infants.

---

**Figure 5.1** Height and Weight Growth

Although the greatest increase in height and weight occurs during the first year of life, children continue to grow throughout infancy and toddlerhood.

**SOURCE:** Cratty, Bryant J. (1979), Perceptual and Motor Development in Infants and Children. Second Edition. New Jersey: Prentice Hall.

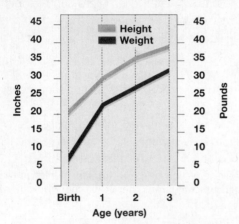

Height and weight measurements, which are taken regularly during physician visits during a baby's first year, provide a way to spot problems in development.

The weight gains of infancy are matched by increased length. By the end of the first year, the typical baby grows almost a foot and is about 30 inches tall. By their second birthdays, children average a height of 3 feet.

Not all parts of an infant's body grow at the same rate. For instance, as we saw first in Chapter 2, at birth the head accounts for one-quarter of the newborn's entire body size. During the first 2 years of life, the rest of the body begins to catch up. By age 2 the baby's head is only one-fifth of body length, and by adulthood it is only one-eighth.

There also are gender and ethnic differences in weight and length. Girls generally are slightly shorter and weigh slightly less than boys, and these differences remain throughout childhood (and, as we will see later in the book, these disparities become considerably greater during adolescence). Furthermore, Asian infants tend to be slightly smaller than North American Caucasian infants, and African American infants tend to be slightly bigger than North American Caucasian infants.

Following are four major principles (summarized in Table 5.1) that govern growth.

- The **cephalocaudal principle** states that growth follows a direction and pattern that begins with the head and upper body parts and then proceeds to the rest of the body. According to this principle, we develop visual abilities (located in the head) well before we master the ability to walk (closer to the end of the body).

- The **proximodistal principle** states that development proceeds from the center of the body outward. According to this principle, the trunk of the body grows before the extremities of the arms and legs. Development of the ability to use various parts of the body also follows the proximodistal principle. For instance, effective use of the arms precedes the ability to use the hands.

---

**cephalocaudal principle** The principle that growth follows a pattern that begins with the head and upper body parts and then proceeds down to the rest of the body

**proximodistal principle** The principle that development proceeds from the center of the body outward

**Table 5.1** The Major Principles Governing Growth

| Cephalocaudal Principle | Proximodistal Principle | Principle of Hierarchical Integration | Principle of the Independence of Systems |
|---|---|---|---|
| Growth follows a pattern that begins with the head and upper body parts and then proceeds to the rest of the body. Based on Greek and Latin roots meaning "head-to-tail." | Development proceeds from the center of the body outward. Based on the Latin words for "near" and "far." | Simple skills typically develop separately and independently. Later, they are integrated into more complex skills. | Different body systems grow at different rates. |

- The **principle of hierarchical integration** states that simple skills typically develop separately and independently, but that these simple skills are integrated into more complex ones. Thus, the relatively complex skill of grasping something in the hand cannot be mastered until the developing infant learns how to control—and integrate—the movements of the individual fingers.

- Finally, the **principle of the independence of systems** suggests that different body systems grow at different rates. For instance, the patterns of growth for body size, the nervous system, and sexual maturation are quite different.

## The Nervous System and Brain: The Foundations of Development

**LO 5.2   Explain how the nervous system and brain develop.**

*When Rina was born, she was the first baby among her parents' circle of friends. The young adults marveled at the infant, oohing and aahing at every sneeze and smile and whimper, trying to guess at their meaning. Whatever feelings, movements, and thoughts Rina was experiencing, they were all brought about by the same complex network: the infant's nervous system. The nervous system is composed of the brain and the nerves that extend throughout the body.*

**Neurons** are the basic cells of the nervous system. Like all cells in the body, neurons have a cell body containing a nucleus. But unlike other cells, neurons have a distinctive ability: they can communicate with other cells, using a cluster of fibers called *dendrites* at one end. Dendrites receive messages from other cells. At their opposite end, neurons have a long extension called an *axon*, the part of the neuron that carries messages destined for other neurons. Neurons do not actually touch one another. Rather, they communicate with

other neurons by means of chemical messengers, *neurotransmitters*, that travel across the small gaps, known as **synapses**, between neurons.

Although estimates vary, infants are born with between 100 billion and 200 billion neurons. In order to reach this number, neurons multiply at an amazing rate prior to birth. At some points in prenatal development, cell division creates some 250,000 additional neurons every minute.

At birth, most neurons in an infant's brain have relatively few connections to other neurons. During the first 2 years of life, however, a baby's brain will establish billions of new connections between neurons. Furthermore, the network of neurons becomes more complex, as illustrated in Figure 5.2. The intricacy of neural connections continues to increase throughout life. In adulthood, a single neuron is likely to have a minimum of 5,000 connections to other neurons or other body parts.

**SYNAPTIC PRUNING.**   Babies are actually born with many more neurons than they need. In addition, synapses are formed throughout life, based on our changing experiences. What happens to the extra neurons and synaptic connections?

Like a farmer who, in order to strengthen the vitality of a fruit tree, prunes away unnecessary branches, brain development enhances certain capabilities in part

---

**principle of hierarchical integration** The principle that simple skills typically develop separately and independently but are later integrated into more complex skills

**principle of the independence of systems** The principle that different body systems grow at different rates

**neuron** The basic nerve cell of the nervous system

**synapse** The gap at the connection between neurons, through which neurons chemically communicate with one another

**Figure 5.2** Neuron Networks

Over the first 2 years of life, networks of neurons become increasingly complex and interconnected. Why are these connections important?

**SOURCE:** Colonel, J. LeRoy. 1939. The Postnatal Development of The Human Cerebral Cortex, Vols. I-VIII. Cambridge, MA: Harvard University Press.

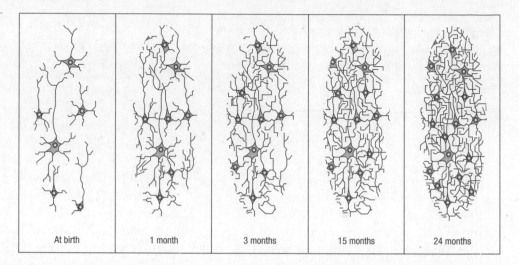

| At birth | 1 month | 3 months | 15 months | 24 months |

through a "pruning down" of unnecessary neurons. As an infant begins to experience the world, neurons that do not become interconnected with other neurons become unnecessary. They eventually die out, increasing the efficiency of the nervous system.

As unnecessary neurons are being reduced, connections between remaining neurons are expanded or eliminated. If a baby's experiences do not stimulate certain nerve connections, these, like unused neurons, are eliminated—a process called *synaptic pruning*. The result of synaptic pruning is to allow established neurons to build more elaborate communication networks with other neurons. Unlike most other aspects of growth, then, the development of the nervous system proceeds most effectively through the loss of cells (Iglesias et al., 2005; Schafer & Stevens, 2013; Athanasiu et al., 2017).

After birth, neurons continue to increase in size. In addition to growth in dendrites, the axons of neurons become coated with **myelin**, a fatty substance that, like the insulation on an electric wire, provides protection and speeds the transmission of nerve impulses. So, even though many neurons are lost, the increasing size and complexity of the remaining ones contribute to impressive brain growth. A baby's brain triples in weight during his or her first 2 years of life, and it reaches more than three-fourths of its adult weight and size by age 2.

As they grow, the neurons also reposition themselves, becoming arranged by function. Some move into the **cerebral cortex**, the upper layer of the brain, while others move to *subcortical levels*, which are below the cerebral cortex. The subcortical levels, which regulate such fundamental activities as breathing and heart rate, are the most fully developed at birth. As time passes, however, the cells in the cerebral cortex, which are responsible for higher-order processes such as thinking and reasoning, become more developed and interconnected.

For example, synapses and myelinization experience a growth spurt at around 3 to 4 months in the area of the cortex involving auditory and visual skills (areas called the *auditory cortex* and the *visual cortex*). This growth corresponds to the rapid increase in auditory and visual skills. Similarly, areas of the cortex related to body movement grow rapidly, allowing for improvement in motor skills.

Using sophisticated measurement techniques, scientists are able to determine the nature of neuronal development in infants.

**myelin** A fatty substance that helps insulate neurons and speeds the transmission of nerve impulses

**cerebral cortex** The upper layer of the brain

**Figure 5.3** Shaken Baby

This computed tomography (CT) scan shows severe brain injury in an infant suspected of being abused by caretaker shaking.

**SOURCE:** Matlung et al. (2011).

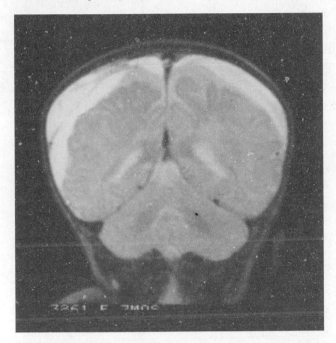

Although the brain is protected by the bones of the skull, it is highly sensitive to some forms of injury. One particularly devastating injury comes from a form of child abuse called *shaken baby syndrome*, in which an infant is shaken by a caretaker, usually out of frustration or anger because of a baby's crying. Shaking can lead the brain to rotate within the skull, causing blood vessels to tear and destroying the intricate connections between neurons. The blood vessels of the retina may bleed (see Figure 5.3).

The results can be devastating, leading to severe medical problems and long-term physical disabilities such as blindness, hearing impairment, and speech disabilities. Some children experience learning disabilities and behavior disorders. In the most severe cases, the shaking leads to death. Estimates of the incidence of shaken baby syndrome range from 1,000 to 1,500 cases a year in the United States, and 25 percent of babies who are shaken die as a result of their injuries (Hitchcock, 2012; Narang & Clarke, 2014; Grinkevičiūtė et al., 2016).

**ENVIRONMENTAL INFLUENCES ON BRAIN DEVELOPMENT.** Brain development, much of which unfolds automatically because of genetically predetermined patterns, is also strongly susceptible to environmental influences. In fact, **plasticity**, the degree to which a developing structure or behavior is modifiable as a result of experience, is a significant attribute of the brain.

The brain's plasticity is greatest during the first several years of life. Because many areas of the brain are not yet devoted to specific tasks, if one area is injured, other areas can take over for the injured area. For example, preterm infants who suffer damage due to bleeding in the brain can recover almost entirely by age 2. In addition, even when particular parts of infants' brains are injured in accidents, other parts of the brain can compensate, aiding in recovery (Guzzetta et al., 2013; Rocha-Ferreira & Hristova, 2016).

Similarly, because of the high degree of plasticity in the brain, infants who suffer brain injuries typically are less affected and recover more fully than adults who experience similar types of brain injuries, showing a high degree of plasticity. Of course, not even the brain's inherent plasticity can fully protect against severe injuries, such as those resulting from the violent shaking typical of shaken baby syndrome (Vanlierde, Renier, & DeVolder, 2008; Mercado, 2009; Stiles, 2012).

Infants' sensory experiences affect both the size of individual neurons and the structure of their interconnections. Consequently, compared with those brought up in more enriched environments, infants raised in severely restricted settings are likely to show differences in brain structure and weight (Cirulli, Berry, & Alleva, 2003; Couperus & Nelson, 2006; Glaser, 2012).

Work with nonhumans has helped reveal the nature of the brain's plasticity. Studies have compared rats raised in an unusually visually stimulating environment to those raised in more typical, and less interesting, cages. Results of such research show that areas of the brain associated with vision are both thicker and heavier for the rats reared in enriched settings (Degroot, Wolff, & Nomikos, 2005; Axelson et al., 2013; Stephany, Frantz, & McGee, 2016).

In contrast, environments that are unusually barren or in some way restricted may impede the brain's development. Again, work with nonhumans provides some intriguing data. In one study, kittens were fitted with goggles that restricted their vision so that they could view only vertical lines (Hirsch & Spinelli, 1970).

**plasticity** The degree to which a developing structure or behavior is modifiable as a result of experience

When the cats grew up and had their goggles removed, they were unable to see horizontal lines, although they saw vertical lines perfectly well. Analogously, kittens whose goggles restricted their vision of vertical lines early in life were effectively blind to vertical lines during their adulthood—although their vision of horizontal lines was accurate.

By contrast, when goggles are placed on older cats who have lived relatively normal lives as kittens, such results are not seen after the goggles are removed. The conclusion is that there is a sensitive period for the development of vision. As we noted in Chapter 1, a **sensitive period** is a specific, but limited, time, usually early in an organism's life, during which the organism is particularly susceptible to environmental influences relating to some particular facet of development. A sensitive period may be associated with a behavior—such as the development of full vision—or with the development of a structure of the body, such as the configuration of the brain (Uylings, 2006; Hartley & Lee, 2015).

The existence of sensitive periods raises several important issues. For one thing, it suggests that unless an infant receives a certain level of early environmental stimulation during a sensitive period, the infant may suffer damage or fail to develop capabilities, an effect that can never be fully remedied. If this is true, providing successful later intervention for such children may prove to be particularly challenging (Gottlieb & Blair, 2004; Zeanah, 2009).

The opposite question also arises: Does an unusually high level of stimulation during sensitive periods produce developmental gains beyond what a more commonplace level of stimulation would provide?

Such questions have no simple answers. Determining how unusually impoverished or enriched environments affect later development is one of the major questions addressed by developmental researchers as they try to find ways to maximize opportunities for developing children.

In the meantime, many developmentalists suggest that there are many simple ways parents and caregivers can provide a stimulating environment that will encourage healthy brain growth. Cuddling, talking and singing to, and playing with babies all help enrich their environment. In addition, holding children and reading to them is important, as it simultaneously engages multiple senses, including vision, hearing, and touch (Lafuente et al., 1997; Garlick, 2003).

## Integrating the Bodily Systems: The Life Cycles of Infancy

**LO 5.3 Describe the processes by which a baby's bodily systems are integrated.**

If you happen to overhear new parents discuss their newborns, chances are one or several bodily functions will be the subject of their conversation. In the first days of life, infants' body rhythms—waking, eating, sleeping, and going to the bathroom—govern the infant's behavior, often at seemingly random times.

**sensitive period** A specific, but limited time, usually early in an organism's life, during which the organism is particularly susceptible to environmental influences relating to some particular facet of development

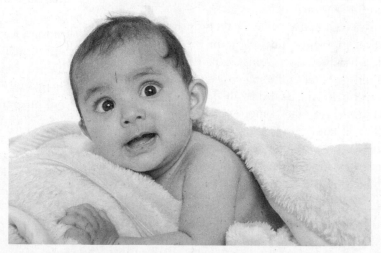

Infants cycle through various states, including crying and alertness. These states are integrated through bodily rhythms.

These most basic activities are controlled by a variety of bodily systems. Although each of these individual behavioral patterns probably is functioning quite effectively, it takes some time and effort for infants to integrate the separate behaviors. One of the neonate's major missions is to make its individual behaviors work in harmony, helping the neonate, for example, to sleep through the night (Ingersoll & Thoman, 1999; Waterhouse & DeCoursey, 2004).

**RHYTHMS AND STATES.**   A very important way that behavior becomes integrated is through the development of various **rhythms**, which are repetitive, cyclical patterns of behavior. Some rhythms are immediately obvious, such as the change from wakefulness to sleep. Others are more subtle, but still easily noticeable, such as breathing and sucking patterns. Still other rhythms may require careful observation to be noticed.

For instance, newborns may go through periods in which they jerk their legs in a regular pattern every minute or so. Although some of these rhythms are apparent just after birth, others emerge slowly over the first year as the neurons of the nervous system become increasingly integrated (Thelen & Bates, 2003; Xiao et al., 2017).

One of the major body rhythms is that of infants' **state**, the degree of awareness an infant displays to both internal and external stimulation. Such states include various levels of wakeful behaviors, such as alertness, fussing, and crying, as well as different levels of sleep. Each change in state brings about an alteration in the amount of stimulation required to get the infant's attention (Balaban, Snidman, & Kagan, 1997; Diambra & Menna-Barretio, 2004; Anzman-Frasca et al., 2013).

Some of the different states that infants experience produce changes in electrical activity in the brain. These changes are reflected in different patterns of electrical *brain waves*, which can be measured by a device called an *electroencephalogram (EEG)*. Starting at 3 months before birth, these brain wave patterns are relatively irregular. However, by the time an infant reaches the age of 3 months, a more mature pattern emerges, and the brain waves become more regular (Burdjalov, Baumgart, & Spitzer, 2003; Thordstein et al., 2006).

**PERCHANCE TO DREAM?**   At the beginning of infancy, the major state that occupies a baby's time is sleep—much to the relief of exhausted parents, who often regard sleep as a welcome respite from caregiving responsibilities. On average, newborn infants sleep some 16 to 17 hours a day; however, there are wide

Infants sleep in spurts, often making them out of sync with the rest of the world.

variations. Some sleep more than 20 hours, while others sleep as little as 10 hours a day (Murray, 2011; de Graag et al., 2012; Korotchikova et al., 2016).

Infants sleep a lot, but you probably shouldn't ever wish to "sleep like a baby." The sleep of infants comes in fits and starts. Rather than covering one long stretch, sleep initially occurs in spurts of around 2 hours, followed by periods of wakefulness. Because of this, infants—and their sleep-deprived parents—are "out of sync" with the rest of the world, for whom sleep comes at night and wakefulness during the day (Groome et al., 1997; Burnham et al., 2002). Most babies do not sleep through the night for several months. Parents' sleep is interrupted, sometimes several times a night, by the infant's cries for food and physical contact.

Luckily for their parents, infants gradually settle into a more adult-like pattern. After a week, babies sleep a bit more at night and are awake for slightly longer periods during the day. Typically, by the age of 16 weeks, infants begin to sleep as much as 6 continuous hours at night, and daytime sleep falls into regular

---

**rhythms**  Repetitive, cyclical patterns of behavior

**state**  The degree of awareness an infant displays to both internal and external stimulation

**Figure 5.4** REM Sleep Through the Life Span

As we age, the proportion of REM sleep increases as the proportion of non-REM sleep declines. In addition, the total amount of sleep falls as we get older.

**SOURCE:** Based on Roffwarg, Howard P., Muzio, Joseph N., and Dement, William C. "Ontogenetic development of the human sleep-dream cycle," Science, vol. 152, no. 3722, pp. 604-619. (1966).

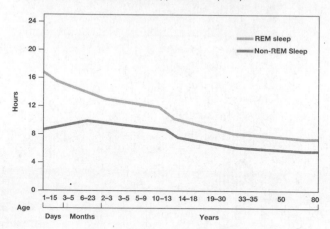

Furthermore, the brain waves of sleeping infants appear to be qualitatively different from those of adults who are dreaming. It is not until the baby reaches 3 or 4 months of age that the wave patterns become similar to those of dreaming adults, suggesting that young infants are not dreaming during active sleep—or at least are not doing so in the same way as adults do (Zampi, Fagioli, & Salzarulo, 2002).

Then what is the function of REM sleep in infants? Although we don't know for certain, some researchers think it provides a means for the brain to stimulate itself—a process called *autostimulation* (Roffwarg, Muzio, & Dement, 1966). Stimulation of the nervous system would be particularly important in infants, who spend so much time sleeping and relatively little time in alert states.

Infants' sleep cycles seem largely preprogrammed by genetic factors, but environmental influences also play a part. For instance, both long- and short-term stressors in infants' environments (such as a heat wave) can affect their sleep patterns. When environmental circumstances keep babies awake, sleep, when at last it comes, is apt to be less active (and quieter) than usual (Halpern, MacLean, & Baumeister, 1995; Goodlin-Jones, Burnham, & Anders, 2000; Galland et al., 2012).

Cultural practices also affect infants' sleep patterns. For example, among the Kipsigis of Africa, infants sleep with their mothers at night and are allowed to nurse whenever they wake. In the daytime, they accompany their mothers during daily chores, often napping while strapped to their mothers' backs. Because they are often out and on the go, Kipsigis infants do not sleep through the night until much later than babies in Western societies, and for the first 8 months of life, they seldom sleep longer than 3 hours at a stretch. In comparison, 8-month-old infants in the United States may sleep as long as 8 hours at a time (Super & Harkness, 1982; Anders & Taylor, 1994; Gerard, Harris, & Thach, 2002).

napping patterns. Most infants sleep through the night by the end of the first year, and the total amount of sleep they need each day goes down to about 15 hours (Mao et al., 2004; Sankupellay et al., 2011).

Hidden beneath the supposedly tranquil sleep of infants is another cyclic pattern. During periods of sleep, infants' heart rates increase and become irregular, their blood pressure rises, and they begin to breathe more rapidly. Sometimes, though not always, their closed eyes begin to move in a back-and-forth pattern, as if they were viewing an action-packed scene. This period of active sleep is similar, although not identical, to the **rapid eye movement (REM) sleep** that is found in older children and adults and is associated with dreaming.

At first, this active, REM-like sleep takes up around one-half of an infant's sleep, compared with just 20 percent of an adult's sleep (see Figure 5.4). The quantity of active sleep quickly declines, however, and by the age of 6 months, amounts to just one-third of total sleep time (Burnham et al., 2002; Staunton, 2005; Ferri, Novelli, & Bruni, 2017).

The appearance of active sleep periods that are similar to REM sleep in adults raises the intriguing question of whether infants dream during those periods. No one knows the answer, although it seems unlikely. First of all, young infants do not have much to dream about, given their relatively limited experiences.

> **From a social worker's perspective:**   What are some cultural or subcultural influences that might affect parents' willingness to accept recommendations from physicians and other experts?

**rapid eye movement (REM) sleep** The period of sleep that is found in older children and adults and is associated with dreaming

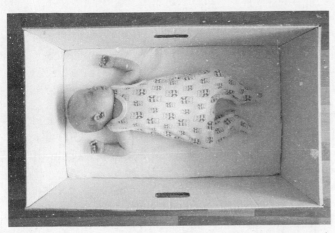

Cardboard baby boxes may be preferable to cribs for young infants.

## SIDS and SUID: The Unanticipated Killers

**LO 5.4  Discuss SIDS and SUID and how they can be prevented.**

For a tiny percentage of infants, the rhythm of sleep is interrupted by a deadly affliction: sudden infant death syndrome. **Sudden infant death syndrome (SIDS)** is a disorder in which seemingly healthy infants die in their sleep. Put to bed for a nap or for the night, an infant simply never wakes up.

SIDS strikes about 1 in 2,500 infants in the United States each year. Although it seems to occur when the normal patterns of breathing during sleep are interrupted, scientists have been unable to discover why that might happen. It is clear that infants don't smother or choke; they die a peaceful death, simply ceasing to breathe.

While no reliable means for preventing the syndrome has been found, the American Academy of Pediatrics now suggests that babies sleep on their backs rather than on their sides or stomachs—called the *back-to-sleep* guideline. In addition, they suggest that parents consider giving their babies a pacifier during naps and bedtime. Mattresses should be firm and covered by a fitted sheet, and soft objects, such as pillows and loose bedding (including crib bumpers) should be kept out of the sleep area. In fact, a simple cardboard baby box may be preferable to a crib for young infants (Senter et al., 2011; Ball & Volpe, 2013; Catalini, 2017).

The number of deaths from SIDS has decreased significantly since these guidelines were developed. Specifically, SIDS rates fell from 130 deaths per 100,000 live births in 1990 to 39 deaths per 100,000 live births in 2015. Still, SIDS is the leading cause of death in children under the age of 1 year (Eastman, 2003; Daley, 2004; Blair et al., 2006).

Some infants are more at risk for SIDS than others. For instance, boys and African Americans are at greater risk. In addition, low birth weight and low Apgar scores at birth are associated with SIDS, as is having a mother who smokes during pregnancy. Some evidence also suggests that a brain abnormality in the hippocampus, the area of the brain that affects breathing, may produce SIDS. In a small number of cases, child abuse may be the actual cause. Other hypotheses have suggested infants who die from SIDS may have had undiagnosed sleep disorders, nutritional deficiencies, problems with reflexes, or undiagnosed illnesses. Still, there is no clear-cut factor that explains why some infants die from the syndrome. SIDS is found in children of every race and socioeconomic group and in children who have had no apparent health problems (Howard, Kirkwood, & Latinovic, 2007; Richardson, Walker, & Horne, 2009; Behm et al., 2012; Horne, 2017).

SIDS is part of a broader category known as **sudden unexpected infant death, or SUID**. The most common SUID is SIDS, accounting for 43 percent of infant deaths. A quarter of SUID is caused by accidental suffocation and strangulation in bed. The remainder of SUID has no known cause identified.

Because parents are unprepared for the death of an infant in a case of SUID, the event is particularly devastating. Parents often feel guilt, fearing that they were neglectful or somehow contributed to their child's death (Krueger, 2006).

## Motor Development

Suppose a genetic engineering firm hired you to redesign newborns and charged you with replacing the current version with a new, more mobile one. The first change you'd probably consider in carrying out this (luckily fictitious) job would be in the conformation and composition of the baby's body.

---

**sudden infant death syndrome (SIDS)** The unexplained death of a seemingly healthy baby
**sudden unexpected infant death (SUID)** The death of an infant less than 1 year old and that has no immediately obvious cause

The shape and proportions of newborn babies are simply not conducive to easy mobility. Their heads are so large and heavy that young infants lack the strength to raise them. Because their limbs are short in relation to the rest of the body, their movements are further impeded. Furthermore, their bodies are mainly fat, with a limited amount of muscle; the result is that they lack strength.

Fortunately, it doesn't take too long before infants begin to develop a remarkable amount of mobility. Actually, even at birth, they have an extensive repertoire of behavioral possibilities brought about by innate reflexes, and their range of motor skills grows rapidly during the first 2 years of life.

## Reflexes: Our Inborn Physical Skills

**LO 5.5  Describe reflexes and how they contribute to motor development.**

*When her father pressed 3-day-old Christina's palm with his finger, she responded by tightly winding her small fist around his finger and grasping it. When he moved his finger upward, she held on so tightly that he suspected he could have lifted her completely off the crib floor.*

**THE BASIC REFLEXES.**  Her father was right: Christina probably could have been lifted in this way. The reason for her resolute grip was activation of one of the dozens of reflexes with which infants are born. **Reflexes** are unlearned, organized, involuntary responses that occur automatically in the presence of certain stimuli. Newborns enter the world with a repertoire of reflexive behavioral patterns that help them adapt to their new surroundings and serve to protect them.

As we can see from the list of reflexes in Table 5.2, many reflexes clearly represent behavior that has survival value, helping to ensure the well-being of the infant. For instance, the *swimming reflex* makes a baby who is lying facedown in a body of water paddle and kick in a sort of swimming motion. The obvious consequence of such behavior is to help the baby move from danger and survive until a caregiver can come to its rescue. Similarly, the *eye blink reflex* seems designed to protect the eye from too much direct light, which might damage the retina.

Given the protective value of many reflexes, it might seem beneficial for them to remain with us for our entire lives. In fact, some do: the eye blink reflex remains functional throughout the full life span. But quite a few reflexes, such as the swimming reflex, disappear after a few months. Why should this be the case?

Researchers who focus on evolutionary explanations of development attribute the gradual disappearance of reflexes to the increase in voluntary control

---

**reflexes** Unlearned, organized, involuntary responses that occur automatically in the presence of certain stimuli

---

**Table 5.2**  Some Basic Reflexes in Infants

| Reflex | Approximate Age of Disappearance | Description | Possible Function |
|---|---|---|---|
| Rooting reflex | 3 weeks | Neonate's tendency to turn its head toward things that touch its cheek. | Food intake |
| Stepping reflex | 2 months | Movement of legs when held upright with feet touching the floor. | Prepares infants for independent locomotion |
| Swimming reflex | 4–6 months | Infant's tendency to paddle and kick in a sort of swimming motion when lying facedown in a body of water. | Avoidance of danger |
| Moro reflex | 6 months | Activated when support for the neck and head is suddenly removed. The arms of the infant are thrust outward and then appear to grasp onto something. | Similar to primates' protection from falling |
| Babinski reflex | 8–12 months | An infant fans out its toes in response to a stroke on the outside of its foot. | Unknown |
| Startle reflex | Remains in different form | An infant, in response to a sudden noise, flings out its arms, arches its back, and spreads its fingers. | Protection |
| Eye-blink reflex | Remains | Rapid shutting and opening of eye on exposure to direct light. | Protection of eye from direct light |
| Sucking reflex | Remains | Infant's tendency to suck at things that touch its lips. | Food intake |
| Gag reflex | Remains | An infant's reflex to clear its throat. | Prevents choking |

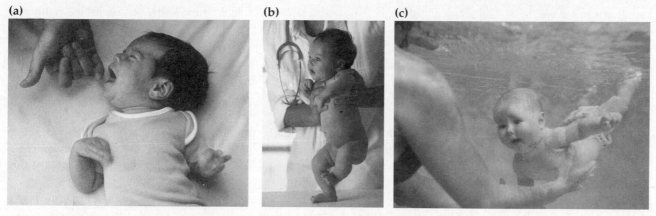

Infants show (a) the rooting reflex, (b) the stepping reflex, and (c) the swimming reflex.

over behavior that occurs as infants become more able to control their muscles. In addition, it may be that reflexes form the foundation for future, more complex behaviors. As these more intricate behaviors become well learned, they encompass the earlier reflexes (Myklebust & Gottlieb, 1993; Lipsitt, 2003).

For example, some researchers argue that the stepping reflex helps the brain's cortex develop the ability to walk. As evidence, developmental psychologist Philip R. Zelazo and his colleagues conducted a study in which they provided 2-week-old infants practice in walking for four sessions of 3 minutes each over a 6-week-period. The results showed that the children who had the walking practice actually began to walk unaided several months earlier than those who had had no such practice. Zelazo suggests that the training produced stimulation of the stepping reflex, which in turn led to stimulation of the brain's cortex, readying the infant earlier for independent locomotion (Zelazo et al., 1993; Zelazo, 1998).

Do these findings suggest that parents should make out-of-the-ordinary efforts to stimulate their infant's reflexes? Probably not. Although the evidence shows that intensive practice may produce an earlier appearance of certain motor activities, there is no proof that the activities are performed qualitatively any better in practiced infants than in unpracticed infants. Furthermore, even when early gains are found, they do not seem to produce an adult who is more proficient in motor skills.

In fact, structured exercise may do more harm than good. According to the American Academy of Pediatrics, structured exercise for infants may lead to muscle strain, fractured bones, and dislocated limbs—consequences that far outweigh the unproven benefits

that may come from the practice (National Association for Sport and Physical Education, 2006).

**ETHNIC AND CULTURAL DIFFERENCES AND SIMILARITIES IN REFLEXES.** Although reflexes are, by definition, genetically determined and universal throughout all infants, there are actually some variations in the ways they are displayed. For instance, consider the *Moro reflex*, which is activated when support for the neck and head is suddenly removed. The Moro reflex consists of the infant's arms thrusting outward and then appearing to seek to grasp onto something. Most scientists feel that the Moro reflex represents a leftover response that we humans have inherited from our nonhuman ancestors. The Moro reflex is an extremely useful behavior for monkey babies, who travel about by clinging to their mothers' backs. If they lose their grip, they fall down unless they are able to grasp quickly onto their mother's fur—using a Moro-like reflex (Zafeiriou, 2004).

The Moro reflex is found in all humans, but it appears with significantly different vigor in different children. Some differences reflect cultural and ethnic variations (Freedman, 1979). For instance, Caucasian infants show a pronounced response to situations that produce the Moro reflex. Not only do they fling out their arms, but also they cry and respond in a generally agitated manner. In contrast, Navajo babies react to the same situation much more calmly. Their arms do not flail out as much, and they cry only rarely.

In some cases, reflexes can serve as helpful diagnostic tools for pediatricians. Because reflexes emerge and disappear on a regular timetable, their absence—or presence—at a given point of infancy can provide a clue that something may be amiss in an infant's development. (Even for adults, physicians include reflexes in their diagnostic bag of tricks, as anyone knows who has had his or her knee tapped with a rubber mallet to see if the lower leg jerks forward.)

Reflexes evolved because at one point in humankind's history, they had survival value. For example, the sucking reflex automatically helps infants obtain nourishment, and the rooting reflex helps them search for the presence of a nipple. In addition, some reflexes serve a social function, promoting caregiving and nurturance. For instance, Christina's father, who found his daughter gripping his finger tightly when he pressed her palm, probably cares little that she is simply responding with an innate reflex. Instead, he will more likely view his daughter's action as responsiveness to him, a signal perhaps of increasing interest and affection on her part. As we will see in Chapter 6, when we discuss the social and personality development of infants, such apparent responsiveness can help cement the growing social relationship between an infant and its caregivers.

# Motor Development in Infancy: Landmarks of Physical Achievement

**LO 5.6  Discuss the development and coordination of infants' motor skills.**

Probably no physical changes are more obvious—and more eagerly anticipated—than the increasing array of motor skills that babies acquire during infancy. Most parents can remember their child's first steps with a sense of pride and awe at how quickly she or he changed from a helpless infant, unable even to roll over, into a person who could navigate quite effectively in the world.

**GROSS MOTOR SKILLS.**  Even though the motor skills of newborns are not terribly sophisticated, at least compared with attainments that will soon appear, young infants still are able to accomplish some kinds of movement. For instance, when placed on their stomachs, they wiggle their arms and legs and may try to lift their heavy heads. As their strength increases, they are able to push hard enough against the surface on which they are resting to propel their bodies in different directions. They often end up moving backward rather than forward, but by the age

of 6 months they become rather accomplished at moving themselves in particular directions. These initial efforts are the forerunners of crawling, in which babies coordinate the motions of their arms and legs and propel themselves forward. Crawling appears typically between 8 and 10 months. Figure 5.5 provides a summary of some of the milestones of normal motor development.

Walking comes later. At around the age of 9 months, most infants are able to walk by supporting themselves on furniture, and half of all infants can walk well by the end of their first year of life.

At the same time infants are learning to move around, they are perfecting the ability to remain in a stationary sitting position. At first, babies cannot remain seated upright without support. But they quickly master this ability, and most are able to sit without support by the age of 6 months.

**FINE MOTOR SKILLS.**  As infants are perfecting their gross motor skills, such as sitting upright and walking, they are also making advances in their fine motor skills. For instance, by the age of 3 months, infants show some ability to coordinate the movements of their limbs.

Furthermore, although infants are born with a rudimentary ability to reach toward an object, this ability is neither very sophisticated nor very accurate, and it disappears around the age of 4 weeks. A different, more precise, form of reaching reappears at 4 months. It takes some time for infants to coordinate successful grasping after they reach out, but in fairly short order they are able to reach out and hold onto an object of interest (Daum, Prinz, & Aschersleben, 2011; Foroud & Whishaw, 2012; Libertus, Joh, & Needham, 2016).

The sophistication of fine motor skills continues to grow. By the age of 11 months, infants are able to pick up off the ground objects as small as marbles—something caregivers need to be concerned about, because the next place such objects often go is the mouth. By the time they are 2 years old, children can carefully hold a cup, bring it to their lips, and take a drink without spilling a drop.

Grasping, like other motor advances, follows a sequential developmental pattern in which simple skills are combined with more sophisticated ones. For example, infants first begin picking things up with their whole hand. As they get older, they use a *pincer grasp*, where thumb and index finger meet to form a circle. The pincer grasp allows for considerably more precise motor control (Barrett & Needham, 2008; Thoermer et al., 2013).

**Figure 5.5** Milestones of Motor Development

Fifty percent of children are able to perform each skill at the month indicated in the figure; however, the specific timing at which each skill appears varies widely. For example, one-quarter of children are able to walk well at 11.1 months; by 14.9 months, 90 percent of children are walking well. Is knowledge of such average benchmarks helpful or harmful to parents?

**SOURCE:** Data from Frankenburg, W. K., Dodds, J., Archer, P., Shapiro, H., & Bresnick, B. (1992). The Denver II: A major revision and restandardization of the Denver Developmental Screening Test. Pediatrics, Vol. 89, 91–97.

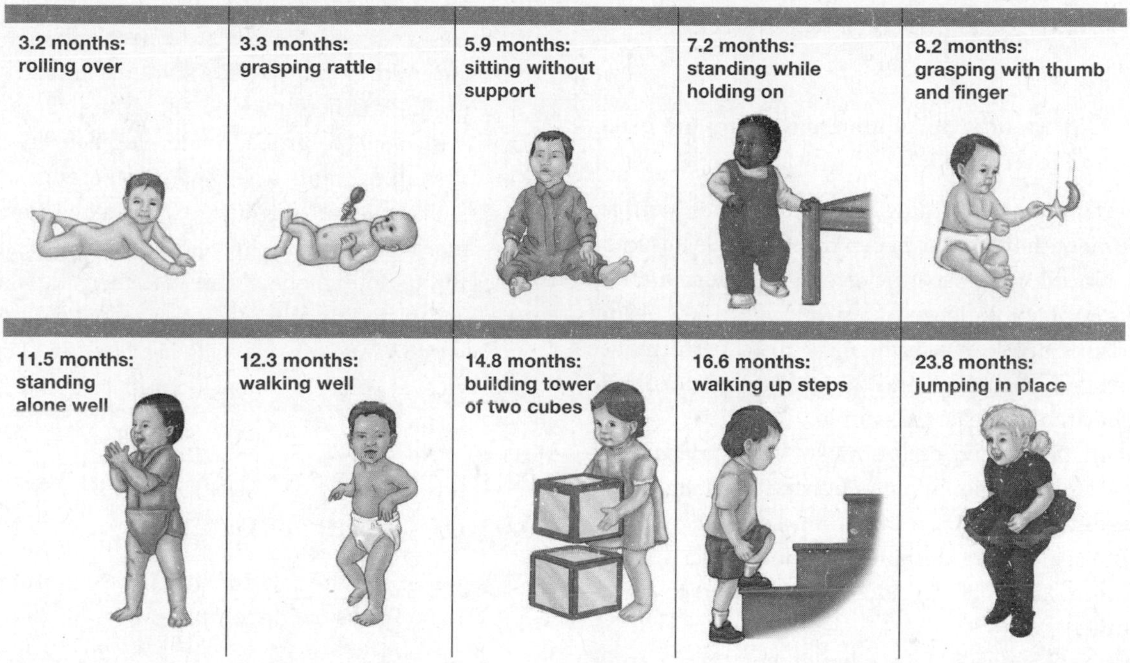

3.2 months: rolling over

3.3 months: grasping rattle

5.9 months: sitting without support

7.2 months: standing while holding on

8.2 months: grasping with thumb and finger

11.5 months: standing alone well

12.3 months: walking well

14.8 months: building tower of two cubes

16.6 months: walking up steps

23.8 months: jumping in place

**DYNAMIC SYSTEMS THEORY: HOW MOTOR DEVELOPMENT IS COORDINATED.** Although it is easy to think about motor development in terms of a series of individual motoric achievements, the reality is that each of these skills does not develop in a vacuum. Each skill (such as a baby's ability to pick up a spoon and guide it to her lips) advances in the context of other motor abilities (such as the ability to reach out and lift the spoon in the first place). Furthermore, as motor skills are developing, so are nonmotoric skills such as visual capabilities.

Developmentalist Esther Thelen created an innovative theory to explain how motor skills develop and are coordinated. **Dynamic systems theory** describes how motor behaviors are assembled. By "assembled," Thelen means the coordination of a variety of skills that develop in a child, ranging from the growth of an infant's muscles, its perceptual abilities and nervous system, to its motivation to carry out particular motor activities and its instinct to find support from the environment for them, such as by holding onto tables

and chairs (Thelen & Bates, 2003; Gershkoff-Stowe & Thelen, 2004; Thelen & Smith, 2006).

According to dynamic systems theory, motor development in a particular sphere, such as when an infant begins to crawl, is not just dependent on the brain initiating a "crawling program" that permits the muscles to propel the baby forward. Instead, crawling requires the coordination of muscles, perception, cognition, and motivation. The theory emphasizes how children's exploratory activities, which produce new challenges as they interact with their environment, lead them to advancements in motor skills (Corbetta & Snapp-Childs, 2009).

Dynamic systems theory is noteworthy for its emphasis on a child's own motivation (a cognitive state) in advancing important aspects of motor development. For example, infants need to be motivated to touch

---

**dynamic systems theory** A theory of how motor skills develop and are coordinated

something out of their reach in order to develop the skills they need to crawl to it. The theory also may help explain individual differences in the emergence of motor abilities in different children, which we consider next.

# Developmental Norms: Comparing the Individual to the Group

**LO 5.7 Explain how developmental norms are used and interpreted.**

Keep in mind that the timing of the milestones in motor development that we have been discussing is based on norms. **Norms** represent the average performance of a large sample of children of a given age. They permit comparisons between a particular child's performance on a particular behavior and the average performance of the children in the norm sample.

For instance, one of the most widely used techniques to determine infants' normative standing is the **Brazelton Neonatal Behavioral Assessment Scale (NBAS)**, a measure designed to determine infants' neurological and behavioral responses to their environment.

The NBAS provides a supplement to the traditional Apgar test (discussed in Chapter 4) that is given immediately following birth. Taking about 30 minutes to administer, the NBAS includes 27 separate categories of responses that constitute four general aspects of infants' behavior: interactions with others (such as alertness and cuddliness), motor behavior, physiological control (such as the ability to be soothed after being upset), and responses to stress (Brazelton, 1990; Davis & Emory, 1995; Canals, Fernandez-Ballart, & Esparo, 2003; Ohta & Ohgi, 2013).

Although the norms provided by scales such as the NBAS are useful in making broad generalizations about the timing of various behaviors and skills, they must be interpreted with caution. Because norms are averages, they mask substantial individual differences in the times when children attain various achievements. For example, some children may be ahead of the norm. Other perfectly normal children, such as Evan, the child described in the prologue, may be a bit behind. Norms also may hide the fact that the sequence in which various behaviors are achieved may differ somewhat from one child to another (Boatella-Costa et al., 2007; Noble & Boyd, 2012).

Norms are useful only to the extent that they are based on data from a large, heterogeneous, culturally diverse sample of children. Unfortunately, many of the norms on which developmental researchers have traditionally relied have been based on groups of infants who are predominantly Caucasian and from the middle and upper socioeconomic strata. The reason: much of the research was conducted on college campuses, using the children of graduate students and faculty.

This limitation would not be critical if no differences existed in the timing of development in children from different cultural, racial, and social groups. But they do. For example, as a group, African American babies show more rapid motor development than Caucasian babies throughout infancy. Moreover, there are significant variations related to cultural factors, as we discuss in the *Developmental Diversity and Your Life* box (de Onis et al., 2007; Wu et al., 2008; Mendonça, Sargent, & Fetters, 2016).

# Nutrition in Infancy: Fueling Motor Development

**LO 5.8 Explain the relationship between nutrition and physical development.**

*Rosa sighed as she sat down to nurse the baby—again. She had fed 5-week-old Juan about every hour today, and he still seemed hungry. Some days, it seemed like all she did was breastfeed her baby. "Well, he must be going through a growth spurt," she decided, as she settled into her favorite rocking chair and put the baby to her nipple.*

The rapid physical growth that occurs during infancy is fueled by the nutrients that infants receive. Without proper nutrition, infants cannot reach their physical potential, and they may suffer cognitive and social consequences as well (Tanner & Finn-Stevenson, 2002; Costello, Compton, & Keeler, 2003; Gregory, 2005).

Although there are vast individual differences in what constitutes appropriate nutrition—infants differ in terms of growth rates, body composition, metabolism, and activity levels—some broad guidelines do hold. In general, infants should consume about 50 calories per day for each pound they weigh—an allotment that is twice the suggested caloric intake for adults (Dietz & Stern, 1999; Skinner et al., 2004).

---

**norms** The average performance of a large sample of children of a given age

Typically, though, it's not necessary to count calories for infants. Most infants regulate their caloric intake quite effectively on their own. If they are allowed to consume as much they seem to want, and not pressured to eat more, they will do fine.

**BREAST OR BOTTLE?**  Fifty years ago, if a mother asked her pediatrician whether breastfeeding or bottle-feeding was better, she would have received a simple and clear-cut answer: bottle-feeding was the preferred method. Starting around the 1940s, the general belief among child care experts was that breastfeeding was an obsolete method that put children unnecessarily at risk.

With bottle-feeding, the argument went, parents could keep track of the amount of milk their baby was receiving and could thereby ensure that the child was taking in sufficient nutrients. In contrast, mothers who breastfed their babies could never be certain just how much milk their infants were getting. Use of the bottle was also supposed to help mothers keep their feedings to a rigid schedule of one bottle every 4 hours, the recommended procedure at that time.

Today, however, a mother would get a very different answer to the same question. Child care authorities agree: For the first 12 months of life, there is no better food for an infant than breast milk. Breast milk not only contains all the nutrients necessary for growth, but it also seems to offer immunity to a variety of childhood diseases, such as respiratory illnesses, ear infections, diarrhea, and allergies. Breastfeeding for as little as 4 months reduces infections by an average of 45 percent, and the reduction in infection is 65 percent lower for 6 months of breastfeeding compared to formula-fed babies. Breast milk is more easily digested than cow's milk or formula, and it is sterile, warm, and convenient for the mother to dispense. There is even some evidence that breast milk may enhance cognitive growth, leading to high adult intelligence (Tanaka et al., 2009; Duijts et al., 2010; Rogers & Blissett, 2017).

Breastfeeding also offers significant emotional advantages for both mother and child. Most mothers report that the experience of breastfeeding brings about feelings of well-being and intimacy with their infants, perhaps because of the production of endorphins in mothers' brains. Breastfed infants are also more responsive to their mothers' touch and their mother's gaze during feeding, and they are calmed and soothed by the experience. As we see in Chapter 6, this mutual responsiveness may lead to healthy social development (Gerrish & Mennella, 2000; Zanardo et al., 2001).

Breastfeeding may even be advantageous to mothers' health. For instance, research suggests that women who breastfeed may have lower rates of ovarian cancer and breast cancer prior to menopause. Furthermore, the hormones produced during breastfeeding help shrink the uteruses of women following birth, enabling their bodies to return more quickly to a prepregnancy state. These hormones also may inhibit ovulation, reducing (but not eliminating!) the chance of becoming pregnant, and thereby help space the birth of additional children (Kim et al., 2007; Pearson, Lightman, & Evans, 2011; Kornides & Kitsantas, 2013).

Breastfeeding is not a cure-all for infant nutrition and health, and the millions of individuals who have been raised on formula should not be concerned that they have suffered irreparable harm. (Recent research suggests that infants fed enriched formula show better cognitive development than those who were fed traditional formula.) But it does continue to be clear that the popular slogan used by groups advocating the use of breastfeeding is right on target: "Breast is best" (Birch et al., 2000; Auestad et al., 2003; Rabin, 2006; Ludlow et al., 2012; also see the *From Research to Practice* box).

**INTRODUCING SOLID FOODS: WHEN AND WHAT?**  Although pediatricians agree that breast milk is the ideal initial food, at some point infants require more nutrients than breast milk alone can provide. The American Academy of Pediatrics suggests that babies can start taking 1 to 2 tablespoons of solids at around 6 months, and two to three healthy and nutritious snacks per day after 9 months (Clayton et al., 2013).

Solid foods are introduced into an infant's diet gradually, one at a time, to allow awareness of the child's preferences and allergies. Most often cereal comes first, followed by strained fruits. Vegetables and other foods typically are introduced next, although the order varies significantly from one infant to another.

The timing of *weaning*, the gradual cessation of breast- or bottle-feeding, varies greatly. In developed countries such as the United States, weaning frequently

---

**Brazelton Neonatal Behavioral Assessment Scale (NBAS)** A measure designed to determine infants' neurological and behavioral responses to their environment

# DEVELOPMENTAL DIVERSITY AND YOUR LIFE

## The Cultural Dimensions of Motor Development

*Among the Ache people, who live in the rain forest of South America, infants face an early life of physical restriction. Because the Ache lead a nomadic existence, living in a series of tiny camps in the rain forest, open space is at a premium. Consequently, for the first few years of life, infants spend nearly all their time in direct physical contact with their mothers. Even when they are not physically touching their mothers, they are permitted to venture no more than a few feet away.*

*\*\*\**

*Infants among the Kipsigis people, who live in a more open environment in rural Kenya, Africa, lead quite a different existence. Their lives are filled with activity and exercise. Parents seek to teach their children to sit up, stand, and walk from the earliest days of infancy. For example, very young infants are placed in shallow holes in the ground designed to keep them in an upright position. Parents begin to teach their children to walk starting at the eighth week of life. The infants are held with their feet touching the ground, and they are pushed forward.*

Clearly, the infants in these two societies lead very different lives (Super, 1976; Kaplan & Dove, 1987). But do the relative lack of early motor stimulation for Ache infants and the efforts of the Kipsigis to encourage motor development really make a difference?

The answer is both yes and no. It's yes, in that Ache infants tend to show delayed motor development, relative both to Kipsigis infants and to children raised in Western societies. Although their social abilities are no different, Ache children tend to begin walking at around 23 months, about a year later than the typical child in the United States. In contrast, Kipsigis children, who are encouraged in their motor development, learn to sit up and walk several weeks earlier, on average, than American children.

In the long run, however, the differences among Ache, Kipsigis, and Western children disappear. By about age 6, there is no evidence of differences in general, overall motor skills among Ache, Kipsigis, and Western children.

As we see with the Ache and Kipsigis babies, variations in the timing of motor skills seem to depend in part on parental expectations of what is the "appropriate" schedule for the emergence of specific skills. For instance, one study examined the motor skills of infants who lived in a single city in England, but whose mothers had varied ethnic origins. In the research, English, Jamaican, and Indian mothers' expectations were first assessed regarding several markers of their infants' motor skills. The Jamaican mothers expected their infants to sit and walk significantly earlier than the English and Indian mothers did, and the actual emergence of these activities was in line with their expectations. The source of the Jamaican infants' earlier mastery seemed to lie in the treatment of the children by their parents. For instance, Jamaican mothers gave their children practice in stepping quite early in infancy (Hopkins & Westra, 1989, 1990).

In sum, cultural factors help determine the time at which specific motor skills appear. Activities that are an intrinsic part of a culture are more apt to be purposely taught to infants in that culture, leading to the potential of their earlier emergence (Nugent, Lester, & Brazelton, 1989).

It is not all that surprising that children in a given culture who are expected by their parents to master a particular skill, and who are taught components of that skill from an early age, are more likely to be proficient in that skill earlier than are children from other cultures with no such expectations and no such training. The larger question, however, is whether the earlier emergence of a basic motor behavior in a given culture has lasting consequences for specific motor skills and for achievements in other domains. On this issue, the jury is still out.

One thing that is clear, however, is that there are certain limitations on how early a skill can emerge. It is physically impossible for 1-month-old infants to stand and walk, regardless of the encouragement and practice they may get within their culture. Parents who are eager to accelerate their infants' motor development, then, should be cautioned not to hold overly ambitious goals. They might well ask themselves whether it matters if an infant acquires a motor skill a few weeks earlier than his or her peers.

The most reasonable answer is "no." Although some parents may take pride in a child who walks earlier than other babies (just as some parents may be concerned over a delay of a few weeks), in the long run, the timing of this activity will probably make no difference.

occurs as early as 3 or 4 months. However, some mothers continue breastfeeding for 2 or 3 years. The American Academy of Pediatrics recommends that infants be fed breast milk for the first 12 months (American Academy of Pediatrics, 1997; Sloan et al., 2008).

**MALNUTRITION.** *Malnutrition*, the condition of having an improper amount and balance of nutrients, produces several results, none good. For instance, malnutrition is more common among children living in many developing countries than it is among children who live in more industrialized, affluent countries. Malnourished children in these countries begin to show a slower growth rate by the age of 6 months. By the time they reach age 2, their height and weight are only 95 percent the height and weight of children in more industrialized countries.

Children who have been chronically malnourished during infancy later score lower on IQ tests and tend to do less well in school. These effects may linger even after the children's diet has improved

Infants generally start eating solid foods at around 4 to 6 months, gradually working their way up to a variety of foods.

substantially (Grantham-McGregor, Ani, & Fernald, 2001; Ratanachu-Ek, 2003; Peter et al., 2016).

The problem of malnutrition is greatest in underdeveloped countries, where overall 10 percent of

# FROM RESEARCH TO PRACTICE
## The Science of Breast Milk

Given its importance as the primary source of nutrition for breastfed infants, you might think that science has long been scrutinizing the components of breast milk and how it is digested and utilized by infants; however, that has not been the case. It's only relatively recently that researchers have been taking a close look at breast milk, and they are finding it to be surprisingly complex.

It is readily apparent to scientists that breast milk isn't just food. Its role in immunity has been recognized, if not well understood, since breastfed infants were observed to have lower mortality rates than bottle-fed infants years ago. Breast milk contains complex carbohydrates called oligosaccharides. Humans can't digest these, but bacteria can, pointing to the role of breast milk in nurturing the bacteria that normally thrive in the human gut and providing important protective functions. It turns out that these oligosaccharides are very specific—only one species of bacterium called *B. longum bv. Infantis* has all the enzymes necessary to digest them, enabling that species to dominate by far any others inhabiting the infant gut.

What makes *B. longum bv. Infantis* so special? For one thing, it crowds out other bacteria, including potentially harmful pathogens that have a hard time taking hold because they can't digest the oligosaccharides. It also produces substances that selectively encourage other beneficial bacteria to grow (Ward et al., 2007; Gura, 2014).

Even more recently, researchers discovered that infants' stomachs are less acidic and less flush with enzymes than previously thought. Instead, their ability to digest proteins is limited to only a very few specific types—and these are all the types that are found in breast milk. In fact, the milk itself provides an inactive form of some of the enzymes that the infant needs to digest it, which then become activated in the stomach environment. In a way, then, breast milk ensures its own easy digestibility. The adage that breast milk is best applies in more ways than anyone suspected, and further research may uncover even more (Dallas et al., 2014).

- **One major health risk to premature infants is infection of the gut by harmful bacteria, yet the introduction of B. longum bv. Infantis hasn't had much success preventing this. Why do you think this might be the case?**

**Figure 5.6** Underweight Children

The percentage of children under 5 years who are moderately or severely underweight.

**SOURCE:** UNICEF, WHO, World Bank Joint Child Malnutrition dataset, September 2016 update.

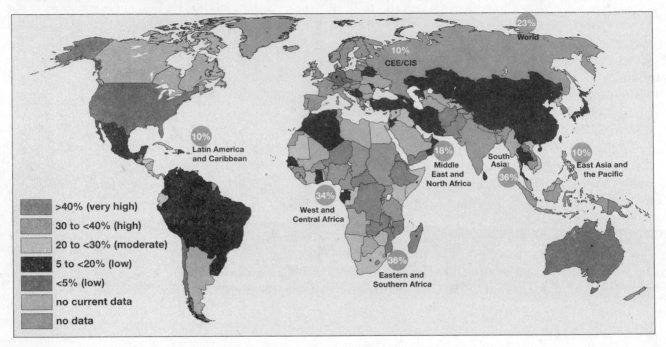

infants are severely malnourished. In some countries, the problem is especially severe. For example, 25 percent of North Korean children are stunted from chronic malnutrition, and 4 percent are acutely malnourished (Chaudhary & Sharma, 2012; United Nations World Food Programme, 2013; also see Figure 5.6).

Problems of malnourishment are not restricted to developing countries, however. In the United States, around 20 percent of children live in poverty, which puts them at risk for malnutrition. Overall, some 26 percent of families who have children 3 years old and younger live in poverty, and 6 percent of Americans live in extreme poverty, meaning their income is $10,000/year or less. And, the poverty rates are even higher for Hispanic and African American families (Addy, Engelhardt, & Skinner, 2013).

A variety of social service programs, such as the federal Supplemental Nutrition Assistance Program (SNAP), have been created to combat this issue. These programs mean that children rarely become severely malnourished, but such children remain susceptible to *undernutrition*, in which there is some deficiency in diet. Some surveys find that as many as a quarter of 1- to 5-year-old children in the United States have diets that fall below the minimum caloric intake recommended

by nutritional experts. Although the consequences are not as severe as those of malnutrition, undernutrition also has long-term costs. For instance, cognitive development later in childhood is affected by even mild to moderate undernutrition (Tanner & Finn-Stevenson, 2002; Lian et al., 2012).

Severe malnutrition during infancy may lead to several disorders. Malnutrition during the first year can produce *marasmus*, a disease in which infants stop growing. Marasmus, attributable to a severe deficiency in proteins and calories, causes the body to waste away and ultimately results in death. Older children are susceptible to *kwashiorkor*, a disease in which a child's stomach, limbs, and face swell with water. To a casual observer, it appears that a child with kwashiorkor is actually chubby. However, this is an illusion: the child's body is in fact struggling to make use of the few nutrients that are available (Douglass & McGadney-Douglass, 2008).

> **From an educator's perspective:** What might be some of the reasons that malnourishment, which slows physical growth, also harms IQ scores and school performance? How might malnourishment affect education in third-world countries?

In some cases, infants who receive sufficient nutrition act as though they have been deprived of food. Looking as though they suffer from marasmus, they are underdeveloped, listless, and apathetic. The real cause, however, is emotional: they lack sufficient love and emotional support. In such cases, known as **nonorganic failure to thrive**, children stop growing not for biological reasons but due to a lack of stimulation and attention from their parents. Usually occurring by the age of 18 months, nonorganic failure to thrive can be reversed through intensive parent training or by placing children in a foster home where they can receive emotional support.

**OBESITY.**   It is clear that malnourishment has potentially disastrous consequences for an infant. Less clear, however, are the effects of *obesity*, defined as weight greater than 20 percent above the average for a given height. Although there is no definitive association between obesity during infancy and obesity during adolescence, some research suggests that overfeeding during infancy may lead to the creation of an excess of fat cells, which remain in the body throughout life and may predispose a person to be overweight. Weight during infancy is associated with weight at age 6. Other research shows an association between obesity after age 6 and adult obesity, suggesting that obesity in babies ultimately may be found to be associated with adult weight problems. A clear link between overweight babies and overweight adults, however, has not yet been found (Taveras et al., 2009; Carnell et al., 2013; Mallan et al., 2016).

Although the evidence linking infant obesity to adult obesity is inconclusive, it is plain that the societal view that "a fat baby is a healthy baby" is not necessarily correct. Indeed, cultural myths about food clearly lead to overfeeding. But other factors are related to obesity in infants. For example, infants delivered via cesarean section are twice as likely to become obese as infants than those born vaginally (Huh et al., 2012).

Given the lack of clarity regarding infant obesity, parents should concentrate less on their baby's weight and more on providing appropriate nutrition.

# The Development of the Senses

William James, one of the founding fathers of psychology, believed that the world of the infant is a "blooming, buzzing confusion" (James, 1890/1950). Was he right?

In this case, James's wisdom failed him. The newborn's sensory world does lack the clarity and stability that we can distinguish as adults, but day by day, the world grows increasingly comprehensible as the infant's ability to sense and perceive the environment develops. In fact, babies appear to thrive in an environment enriched by pleasing sensations.

The processes that underlie infants' understanding of the world around them are sensation and perception. **Sensation** is the physical stimulation of the sense organs, and **perception** is the mental process of sorting out, interpreting, analyzing, and integrating stimuli from the sense organs and the brain.

The study of infants' capabilities in the realm of sensation and perception challenges the ingenuity of investigators. As we'll see, researchers have developed a number of procedures for understanding sensation and perception in different realms.

## Visual Perception: Seeing the World

**LO 5.9   List the visual perception skills infants have.**

*From the time of Lee Eng's birth, everyone who met him felt that he gazed at them intently. His eyes seemed to meet those of visitors. They appeared to bore deeply and knowingly into the faces of people who looked at him.*

How good in fact was Lee's vision, and what, precisely, could he make out of his environment? Quite a bit, at least up close. According to some estimates, a newborn's distance vision ranges from 20/200 to 20/600, which means that an infant can only see with accuracy visual material up to 20 feet that an adult with normal vision is able to see with similar accuracy from a distance of between 200 and 600 feet (Haight, 1991; Jones et al., 2015).

---

**nonorganic failure to thrive**  A disorder in which infants stop growing due to a lack of stimulation and attention as the result of inadequate parenting

**sensation**  The physical stimulation of the sense organs

**perception**  The sorting out, interpretation, analysis, and integration of stimuli involving the sense organs and the brain

  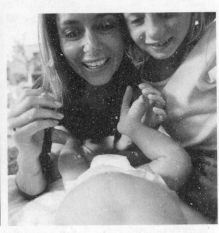

A neonate's view of the world is limited to 8 to 14 inches. Objects beyond that distance are fuzzy.

A month after birth, newborns' vision has improved, but still lacks clarifying detail.

By 3 months, infants see objects with clarity.

These figures indicate that infants' distance vision is one-tenth to one-third that of the average adult's. This isn't so bad, actually: the vision of newborns provides the same degree of distance acuity as the uncorrected vision of many adults who wear eyeglasses or contact lenses. (If you wear glasses or contact lenses, remove them to get a sense of what an infant can see of the world; see the accompanying set of photos on the next page.) Furthermore, infants' distance vision grows increasingly acute. By 6 months of age, the average infant's vision is already 20/20—in other words, identical to that of adults (Cavallini et al., 2002; Corrow et al., 2012).

Other visual abilities grow rapidly. For instance, *binocular vision*, the ability to combine the images coming to each eye to see depth and motion, is achieved at around 14 weeks. Before then, infants do not integrate the information from each eye.

Depth perception is a particularly useful ability, helping babies acknowledge heights and avoid falls. In a classic study by developmental psychologists Eleanor Gibson and Richard Walk (Gibson & Walk, 1960), infants were placed on a sheet of heavy glass. A checkered pattern appeared under one-half of the glass sheet, making it seem that the infant was on a stable floor. However, in the middle of the glass sheet, the pattern dropped down several feet, forming an apparent "visual cliff." The question Gibson and Walk asked was whether infants would willingly crawl across the cliff when called by their mothers (see Figure 5.7).

The results were unambiguous. Most of the infants in the study, who ranged in age from 6 to 14

months, could not be coaxed over the apparent cliff. Clearly the ability to perceive depth had already developed in most of them by that age. On the other hand, the experiment did not pinpoint when depth perception emerged, because only infants who had already learned to crawl could be tested. But other experiments, in which infants of 2 and 3 months were placed on their stomachs above the apparent floor and above the visual cliff, revealed differences in heart rate between the two positions (Campos, Langer, & Krowitz, 1970; Kretch & Adolph, 2013).

Still, it is important to keep in mind that such findings do not permit us to know whether infants are

---

**Figure 5.7** Visual Cliff

The "visual cliff" experiment examines the depth perception of infants. Most infants in the age range of 6 to 14 months cannot be coaxed to cross the cliff, apparently responding to the fact that the patterned area drops several feet.

**Figure 5.8** Preferring Complexity

In a classic experiment, researcher Robert Fantz found that 2- and 3-month-old infants preferred to look at more complex stimuli than simple ones.

**SOURCE:** Based on Robert L. Fantz, "Pattern Vision in Newborn Infants," Science, New Series, vol. 140, no. 3564, pp. 296-297 (1963).

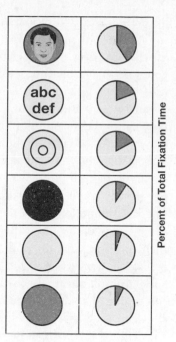

Percent of Total Fixation Time

**Figure 5.9** Distinguishing Faces

Examples of faces used in a study that found that 6-month-old infants distinguished human or monkey faces equally well, whereas 9-month-olds were less adept at distinguishing monkey faces than human faces.

**SOURCE:** Science, Vol. 296 (17 May 2002), p.1321-1322, "Is Face Processing Species-Specific During the First Year of Life?" by Olivier Pascalis, Michelle de Haan, Charles A. Nelson. Reprinted with permission from AAAS.

responding to depth itself or merely to the *change* in visual stimuli that occurs when they are moved from a lack of depth to depth.

Infants also show clear visual preferences, starting at the time of birth. Given a choice, infants reliably prefer to look at stimuli that include patterns than to look at simpler stimuli (see Figure 5.8). How do we know? Developmental psychologist Robert Fantz (1963) created a classic test. He built a chamber in which babies could lie on their backs and see pairs of visual stimuli above them. Fantz could determine which of the stimuli the infants were looking at by observing the reflections of the stimuli in their eyes.

Fantz's work was the impetus for a great deal of research on the preferences of infants, most of which points to a critical conclusion: infants are genetically preprogrammed to prefer particular kinds of stimuli. For instance, just minutes after birth, they show preferences for certain colors, shapes, and configurations of various stimuli. They prefer curved over straight lines, three-dimensional figures to two-dimensional ones, and human faces to nonhuman faces. Such capabilities may be a reflection of the existence of highly specialized cells in the brain that react to stimuli of a particular pattern, orientation, shape, and direction of movement (Hubel & Wiesel, 1979, 2004; Kellman & Arterberry, 2006; Gliga et al., 2009).

Genetics is not the sole determinant of infant visual preferences. Just a few hours after birth, infants

have already learned to prefer their own mother's face to other faces. Similarly, between the ages of 6 and 9 months, infants become more adept at distinguishing among the faces of humans, whereas they become less able to distinguish faces of members of other species (see Figure 5.9). They also distinguish between male and female faces. Such findings provide another clear piece of evidence of how heredity and environmental experiences are woven together to determine an infant's capabilities (Otsuka et al., 2012; Bahrick et al., 2016).

## Auditory Perception: The World of Sound

**LO 5.10 List the auditory perception skills infants have.**

What is it about a mother's lullaby that helps soothe a crying, fussy baby? Some clues emerge when we look at the capabilities of infants in the realm of auditory sensation and perception.

Infants hear from the time of birth—and even before. As we noted in Chapter 2, the ability to hear begins prenatally. Even in the womb, the fetus responds to sounds outside of its mother. Furthermore, infants are born with preferences for particular sound combinations (Trehub, 2003; Fujioka, Mourad, & Trainor, 2011; Pundir et al., 2012).

Because they have had some practice in hearing before birth, it is not surprising that infants have reasonably good auditory perception after they are born. Infants actually are more sensitive to certain very high and very low frequencies than adults—a sensitivity that seems to increase during the first 2 years of life. By contrast, infants are initially less sensitive than adults are to middle-range frequencies. Eventually, however, their capabilities within the middle range improve (Werner & Marean, 1996; Fernald, 2001).

It is not fully clear what, during infancy, leads to the improvement in sensitivity to mid-frequency sounds, although it may be related to the maturation of the nervous system. More puzzling is why, after infancy, children's ability to hear very high and low frequencies gradually declines. One explanation may be that exposure to high levels of noise may diminish capacities at the extreme ranges (Trehub et al., 1989; Stewart, Scherer, & Lehman, 2003).

In addition to the ability to detect sound, infants need several other abilities in order to hear effectively. For instance, *sound localization* permits us to pinpoint the direction from which a sound is emanating. Compared to adults, infants have a slight handicap in this task because effective sound localization requires the use of the slight difference in the times at which a sound reaches our two ears. Sound that we hear first in the right ear tells us that the source of the sound is to our right. Because infants' heads are smaller than those of adults, the difference in timing of the arrival of sound at the two ears is less than it is in adults, so they have difficulty determining from which direction sound is coming.

Despite the potential limitation caused by their smaller heads, infants' sound localization abilities are fairly good even at birth, and they reach adult levels of success by the age of 1 year. Interestingly, their improvement is not steady: although we don't know why, studies show that the accuracy of sound localization declines between birth and 2 months of age, but then begins to increase (Clifton, 1992; Litovsky & Ashmead, 1997; Fenwick & Morrongiello, 1998).

Infants can discriminate groups of different sounds, in terms of their patterns and other acoustical characteristics, quite well. For instance, infants as young as 6 months can detect the change of a single note in a six-tone melody. They also react to changes in musical key and rhythm. In sum, they listen with a keen ear to the melodies of lullabies their mothers and fathers sing to them (Phillips-Silver & Trainor, 2005; Masataka, 2006; Trehub & Hannon, 2009).

Even more important to their ultimate success in the world, young infants are capable of making the fine discriminations that their future understanding of language will require (Bijeljac-Babic, Bertoncini, & Mehler, 1993; Gervain et al., 2008). For instance, in one classic study, a group of 1- to 5-month-old infants sucked on nipples that activated a recording of a person saying "ba" every time they sucked (Eimas et al., 1971). At first, their interest in the sound made them suck vigorously. Soon, though, they became acclimated to the sound (through a process called *habituation*, discussed in Chapter 4) and sucked with less energy. However, when the experimenters changed the sound to "pa," the infants immediately showed new interest and sucked with greater vigor once again. The clear conclusion: infants as young as 1 month could make the distinction between the two similar sounds (Miller & Eimas, 1995).

Even more intriguingly, young infants are able to discriminate one language from another. By the age of 4 1/2 months, infants are able to discriminate their own names from other, similar-sounding words. By the age of 5 months, they can distinguish the difference between English and Spanish passages, even when the two are similar in meter, number of syllables, and speed of recitation. Some evidence suggests that even 2-day-olds show preferences for the language spoken by those around them over other languages (Palmer et al., 2012; Chonchaiya et al., 2013; Pejovic & Molnar, 2017).

Given their ability to discriminate a difference in speech as slight as the difference between two consonants, it is not surprising that infants can distinguish different people on the basis of voice. From an early age, they show clear preferences for some voices over others. For instance, in one experiment newborns were allowed to suck a nipple that turned on a recording of a human voice reading a story. The infants sucked significantly longer when the voice was that of their mother than when the voice was that of a stranger (DeCasper & Fifer, 1980; Fifer, 1987).

By the age of 4 months, infants are able to discriminate their own names from other, similar-sounding words.

Infants' sense of smell is so well developed that they can distinguish their mothers on the basis of smell alone.

How do such preferences arise? One hypothesis is that prenatal exposure to the mother's voice is the key. As support for this conjecture, researchers point to the fact that newborns do not show a preference for their fathers' voices over other male voices. Furthermore, newborns prefer listening to melodies sung by their mothers before they were born to melodies that were not sung before birth. It seems, then, that the prenatal exposure to their mothers' voices—although muffled by the liquid environment of the womb—helps shape infants' listening preferences (DeCasper & Prescott, 1984; Jardri et al., 2012; Swingley & Humphrey, 2017).

## Smell, Taste, and Feel

**LO 5.11  Describe infants' ability to smell, taste, and feel.**

What do infants do when they smell a rotten egg? Pretty much what adults do—crinkle their noses and generally look unhappy. By contrast, the scent of bananas and butter produces a pleasant reaction on the part of infants (Steiner, 1979; Pomares, Schirrer, & Abadie, 2002). What about how they respond to something sweet, or how they react to pain or touch?

**SMELL AND TASTE.**   The sense of smell is so well developed, even among very young infants, that at least some 12- to 18-day-old babies can distinguish their mothers on the basis of smell alone. For instance, in one experiment, infants sniffed gauze pads worn under the arms of adults the previous evening. Infants who were being breastfed were able to distinguish their mothers' scent from that of other adults. In contrast, those who

were being bottle-fed were unable to make the distinction. Moreover, both breastfed and bottle-fed infants were unable to distinguish their fathers on the basis of odor (Mizuno & Ueda, 2004; Allam, Marlier, & Schaal, 2006; Lipsitt & Rovee-Collier, 2012).

Infants seem to have an innate sweet tooth (even before they have teeth!), and they show facial expressions of disgust when they taste something bitter. Very young infants smile when a sweet-tasting liquid is placed on their tongues. They also suck harder at a bottle if it is sweetened. Because breast milk has a sweet taste, it is possible that this preference may be part of our evolutionary heritage, retained because it offered a survival advantage. Infants who preferred sweet tastes may have been more likely to ingest sufficient nutrients and to survive than those who did not (Blass & Camp, 2001; Porges, Lipsitt, & Lewis, 1993).

Infants also develop taste preferences based on what their mothers drank while they were in the womb. For example, one study found that women who drank carrot juice while pregnant had children who had a preference for the taste of carrots during infancy.

**SENSITIVITY TO PAIN.**   When Eli Rosenblatt was 8 days old, he participated in the ancient Jewish ritual of circumcision. As he lay nestled in his father's arms, the foreskin of his penis was removed. Although Eli shrieked in what seemed to his anxious parents as pain, he soon settled down and went back to sleep. Others who had watched the ceremony assured his parents that at Eli's age babies don't really experience pain, at least not in the same way that adults do.

Were Eli's relatives accurate in saying that young infants don't experience pain? In the past, many medical practitioners would have agreed. Because they assumed that infants didn't experience pain in truly bothersome ways, many physicians routinely carried out medical procedures, and even some forms of surgery, without the use of painkillers or anesthesia. Their argument was that the risks from the use of anesthesia outweighed the potential pain that the young infants experienced.

Today, however, it is widely acknowledged that infants are born with the capacity to experience pain. Obviously, no one can be sure whether the experience of pain in children is identical to that in adults, any more than we can tell whether an adult friend who complains of a headache is experiencing pain that is more or less severe than our own pain when we have a headache.

What we do know is that pain produces distress in infants. Their heartbeat increases, they sweat, show facial expressions of discomfort, and change the intensity and tone of crying when they are hurt (Kohut & Pillai, 2008; Rodkey & Riddell, 2013; Pölkki et al., 2015).

There appears to be a developmental progression in reactions to pain. For example, a newborn infant who has her heel pricked for a blood test responds with distress, but it takes her several seconds to show the response. In contrast, only a few months later, the same procedure brings a much more immediate response. It is possible that the delayed reaction in infants is produced by the relatively slower transmission of information within the newborn's less-developed nervous system (Anand & Hickey, 1992; Axia, Bonichini, & Benini, 1995; Puchalski & Hummel, 2002).

Research with rats suggests that exposure to pain in infancy may lead to a permanent rewiring of the nervous system resulting in greater sensitivity to pain during adulthood. Such findings indicate that infants who must undergo extensive, painful medical treatments and tests may be unusually sensitive to pain when they are older (Ruda et al., 2000; Taddio, Shah, & Gilbert-MacLeod, 2002; Ozawa et al., 2011).

In response to increasing support for the notion that infants experience pain and that its effects may be long-lasting, medical experts now endorse the use of anesthesia and painkillers during surgery for even the youngest infants. According to the American Academy of Pediatrics, painkilling drugs are appropriate in most types of surgery—including circumcision (Sato et al., 2007; Urso, 2007; Yamada et al., 2008).

**RESPONDING TO TOUCH.** It clearly does not take the sting of pain to get an infant's attention. Even the youngest infants respond to gentle touches, such as a soothing caress, which can calm a crying, fussy baby (Hertenstein, 2002; Gitto et al., 2012; Aznar & Tenenbaum, 2016).

Touch is one of the most highly developed sensory systems in a newborn, and it is also one of the first to develop; there is evidence that by 32 weeks after conception, the entire body is sensitive to touch. Furthermore, several of the basic reflexes present at birth, such as the rooting reflex, require touch sensitivity to operate: an infant must sense a touch near the mouth in order to automatically seek a nipple to suck (Haith, 1986).

Infants' abilities in the realm of touch are particularly helpful in their efforts to explore the world. Several theorists have suggested that one of the ways children gain information about the world is through touching. As mentioned earlier, at the age of 6 months, infants are apt to place almost any object in their mouths, apparently taking in data about its configuration from their sensory responses to the feel of it in their mouths (Ruff, 1989).

In addition, touch plays an important role in an organism's future development, for it triggers a complex chemical reaction that assists infants in their efforts to survive. For example, gentle massage stimulates the production of certain chemicals in an infant's brain that instigate growth. Touch is also associated with social development. In fact, the brain seems primed to respond positively to slow, gentle touch (Diego, Field, & Hernandez-Reif, 2009; Gordon et al., 2013; Ludwig & Field, 2014).

# Multimodal Perception: Combining Individual Sensory Inputs

## LO 5.12 Explain multimodal perception.

> *When Eric Pettigrew was 7 months old, his grandparents presented him with a squeaky rubber doll. As soon as he saw it, he reached out for it, grasped it in his hand, and listened as it squeaked. He seemed delighted with the gift.*

One way of considering Eric's sensory reaction to the doll is to focus on each of the senses individually: what the doll looked like to Eric, how it felt in his hand, and what it sounded like. This approach has dominated the study of sensation and perception in infancy. Let's consider another approach, however: We might examine how the various sensory responses are integrated with one another. Instead of looking at each individual sensory response, we could think about how the responses work together and are combined to produce Eric's ultimate reaction. The **multimodal approach to perception** considers how information that is collected by various individual sensory systems is integrated and coordinated.

> **From a health care worker's perspective** Persons who are born without the use of one sense sometimes develop unusual abilities in one or more other senses. What can health care professionals do to help infants who are lacking in a particular sense?

Although the multimodal approach is a relatively recent innovation in the study of how infants understand their sensory world, it raises some fundamental issues about the development of sensation and perception. For instance, some researchers argue that sensations are at first integrated with one another in the infant, while others maintain that the infant's sensory systems are initially separate and that brain development leads to increasing integration (De Gelder, 2000; Lewkowicz, 2002; Flom & Bahrick, 2007).

We do not know yet which view is correct; however, it does appear that by an early age, infants are able to relate what they have learned about an object through one sensory channel to what they have learned about it through another. For instance, even 1-month-old infants are able to recognize by sight objects that they have previously held in their mouths but have never seen (Steri & Spelke, 1988). Clearly, some cross-talk between various sensory channels is already possible a month after birth.

Infants' multimodal perception abilities showcase their sophisticated perceptual abilities, which continue to grow throughout the period of infancy. Such perceptual growth is aided by infants' discovery of **affordances**, the options that a given situation or stimulus provides. For example, infants learn that they might potentially fall when walking down a steep ramp—that is, the ramp *affords* the possibility of falling. Such knowledge is crucial as infants make the transition from crawling to walking. Similarly, infants learn that an object shaped in a certain way can slip out of their hands if not grasped correctly. For example, Eric is learning that his toy has several affordances: he can grab it and squeeze it, listen to it squeak, and even chew comfortably on it if he is teething (Flom & Bahrick, 2007; Wilcox et al., 2007; Huang, 2012; Rocha et al., 2013).

---

**multimodal approach to perception** The approach that considers how information that is collected by various individual sensory systems is integrated and coordinated

**affordances** The action possibilities that a given situation or stimulus provides

---

# BECOMING AN INFORMED CONSUMER OF CHILD DEVELOPMENT

## Exercising Your Infant's Body and Senses

Recall how cultural expectations and environments affect the age at which various physical milestones, such as the first step, occur. Although most experts feel attempts to accelerate physical and sensory-perceptual development yield little advantage, parents should ensure that their infants receive sufficient physical and sensory stimulation. There are several specific ways to accomplish this goal:

- *Carry a baby in different positions*—in a backpack, in a front pack, or in a football hold with the infant's head in the palm of your hand and its feet lying on your arm. This lets the infant view the world from several perspectives.
- *Let infants explore their environment.* Don't contain them too long in a barren environment. Let them crawl or wander around—after first making the environment "childproof" by removing dangerous objects.
- *Engage in "rough-and-tumble" play.* Wrestling, dancing, and rolling around on the floor—if not violent—are activities that are fun and that stimulate older infants' motor and sensory systems.
- *Let babies touch their food and even play with it.* Infancy is too early to start teaching table manners.
- *Provide toys that stimulate the senses,* particularly toys that can stimulate more than one sense at a time. For example, brightly colored, textured toys with movable parts are enjoyable and help sharpen infants' senses.

# The Case of …
## One Step at a Time

Lily has a son, Dikun, who is 10 months old. She found from her Facebook group that her friends also have children in the age group of 6–10 months. She was troubled by the undercurrent of competition among several of the mothers. One woman in particular trumpeted her daughter's latest triumph by narrating her development over the past few months with photographs: "Pinku began crawling at the age of 6 months. By 8 months, she was cruising the room, using furniture for support. At 10 months, she took her first independent steps."

Lily began to despair. Dikun, at 10 months, had only recently started crawling. He struggled to pull up to a standing position, but then he plopped down. Lily wondered if he'd ever walk, and she worried that the seemingly huge gap between his development and that of Pinku's meant that something was seriously wrong. Then Lilly read a study claiming that children who were given regular practice stepping in early infancy walked sooner than other children.

Although Dikun was well past the age cited in the study, Lily began a rigorous program of practice walking. Holding his hands, she marched Dikun around the house three times a day for a total of 45 minutes, righting him each time he sagged. After a week of this routine, Dikun broke down sobbing when Lily reached for his hand. He lay on the floor and refused to stand up. Frightened, Lily stopped the practice.

1. Do you think Lily's concern about Dikun's development is justified? Why or why not?
2. What could you tell Lily about the range of normal physical development in infancy that might dispel her fears?
3. Why do you think Lily's program of regular practice walking did not work the way she had hoped?
4. What might Lily do to support Dikun's gross motor development without causing him distress?
5. What are the disadvantages of comparing a child's development to that of his or her peers? What might Lily say to herself the next time her friends' comments start to worry her?

# Epilogue

In this chapter, we discussed the nature and pace of infants' physical growth and the pace of less obvious growth in the brain and nervous system and in the regularity of infants' patterns and states.

We next looked at motor development, the development and uses of reflexes, the role of environmental influences on the pace and shape of motor development, and the importance of nutrition.

We closed the chapter with a look at the senses and the infant's ability to combine data from multiple sensory sources.

Turn back for a moment to the prologue of this chapter, which describes Evan Kaufman's unsettled sleeping and eating patterns, and answer these questions.

1. Evan's parents are wondering if he will ever sleep through the night. What could you tell them about the development of rhythms in infancy to reassure them their son will eventually adopt more conventional behavior?
2. Evan's mother mentions that she's running out of ways to entertain her son because he's awake all day long. Do you think that Evan's wakefulness could be caused, in part, by too much stimulation in his environment? What advice could you give his mother that might help both her and Evan to relax?
3. Evan's father often feeds him from a bottle at night so that his wife can rest. Why is it advantageous for Evan that the bottle contains his mother's expressed milk rather than formula?
4. Based on the information in the prologue, if Evan were shown a series of photographs of women and men, do you think he would show a preference for one over the other? Explain your thinking.

# Looking Back

### LO 5.1  Describe how the human body develops.

- Human babies grow rapidly in height and weight, especially during the first 2 years of life.

- Major principles that govern human growth include the cephalocaudal principle, the proximodistal principle, the principle of hierarchical integration, and the principle of the independence of systems.

### LO 5.2  Explain how the nervous system and brain develop.

- The nervous system contains a huge number of neurons, more than will be needed as an adult. Synaptic pruning is the process by which unnecessary neurons are allowed to die.

- For neurons to survive and become useful, they must form interconnections with other neurons based on the infant's experience of the world.

- The brain can be damaged by the form of child abuse called shaken baby syndrome, which can cause terrible problems and even lead to death.

- Brain development, largely predetermined genetically, also contains a strong element of plasticity—a susceptibility to environmental influences.

- Many aspects of development occur during sensitive periods when the organism is particularly susceptible to environmental influences.

### LO 5.3  Describe the processes by which a baby's bodily systems are integrated.

- One of the primary ways that behavior becomes integrated is through the development of rhythms—cyclical patterns of behavior.

- An important rhythm pertains to the infant's state—the degree of awareness it displays to stimulation. At the beginning of infancy, the baby's major state is sleep.

### LO 5.4  Discuss SIDS and SUID and how they can be prevented.

- Sudden infant death syndrome (SIDS) is a puzzling disorder in which apparently healthy babies die in their sleep.

- Although no definitive explanation or remedy for SIDS has been found, parents are recommended to have their babies sleep on their backs rather than on their sides or stomachs.

- SIDS falls under a broader category known as sudden unexpected infant death (SUID).

### LO 5.5  Describe reflexes and how they contribute to motor development.

- Reflexes are unlearned, automatic responses to stimuli that help newborns survive and protect themselves.

- Some reflexes also have value as the foundation for future, more conscious behaviors.

### LO 5.6  Discuss the development and coordination of infants' motor skills.

- The development of gross and fine motor skills generally proceeds on a regular schedule. Babies practice and expand their inborn repertoire of motor skills along a generally consistent timetable.

- Dynamic systems theory describes how motor skills are assembled through the coordination of a wide variety of skills that a child develops, combined with the child's motivation and the support of his or her environment.

### LO 5.7  Explain how developmental norms are used and interpreted.

- Developmental norms represent the average performance of a large sample of children at a given age. Norms permit comparisons between the schedules of development across individuals.

- While the timetable for the development of motor skills is fairly regular, there are substantial individual and cultural variations. It would be incorrect to automatically interpret individual variations as deficits.

### LO 5.8  Explain the relationship between nutrition and physical development.

- Adequate nutrition is essential for physical development.

- Breastfeeding has distinct advantages over bottle-feeding, including the nutritional completeness of breast milk, its provision of a degree of immunity to certain childhood diseases, and its easy digestibility.

In addition, breastfeeding offers significant physical and emotional benefits to both child and mother.

- Solid foods are introduced into an infant's diet gradually, one at a time, to allow awareness of the child's preferences and allergies. The American Academy of Pediatrics suggests that babies can start solids at around 6 months.

- Malnutrition and undernutrition affect physical aspects of growth and also may affect IQ and school performance.

- Obesity in infancy may also be a problem, although no clear link between infant obesity and later obesity has been established.

**LO 5.9  List the visual perception skills infants have.**

- Sensation, the stimulation of the sense organs, differs from perception, the interpretation and integration of sensed stimuli.

- Even very young infants can see fairly well up close, and a baby's visual abilities grow rapidly during infancy.

- Mere hours after birth, infants learn to prefer their mother's face to other faces, and by around 9 months, babies are better at distinguishing between human faces than between those of other species.

**LO 5.10  List the auditory perception skills infants have.**

- The ability to hear begins before birth, and infants have reasonably good auditory perception after they are born, including the ability to localize sound.

- Within months, infants can discriminate tones and make the fine distinctions essential to their future ability to understand and produce speech.

**LO 5.11  Describe infants' ability to smell, taste, and feel.**

- The sense of smell is well developed at birth, as is the ability to distinguish sweet tastes from bitter ones. Infants appear to have an innate preference for sweet tastes.

- It is widely acknowledged that infants are born with the capacity to experience pain. Touch is one of the most highly developed sensory systems in a newborn, and it is also one of the first to develop.

- Infants use their highly developed sense of touch to explore and experience the world. In addition, touch plays an important role in the individual's future development, which is only now being understood.

**LO 5.12  Explain multimodal perception.**

- Multimodal perception refers to the ability to integrate and coordinate the information collected from various sensory systems.

- Infants appear to have some ability to integrate information across the senses, but the extent of their multimodal perception has not been conclusively determined.

# Key Terms and Concepts

cephalocaudal principle (p. 114)
proximodistal principle (p. 114)
principle of hierarchical integration (p. 115)
principle of the independence of systems (p. 115)
neuron (p. 115)
synapse (p. 115)
myelin (p. 116)
cerebral cortex (p. 116)
plasticity (p. 117)

sensitive period (p. 118)
rhythms (p. 119)
state (p. 119)
rapid eye movement (REM) sleep (p. 120)
Sudden Infant Death Syndrome (SIDS) (p. 121)
Sudden Unexpected Infant Death (SUID) (p. 121)
reflexes (p. 122)
dynamic systems theory (p. 125)

norms (p. 126)
Brazelton Neonatal Behavioral Assessment Scale (NBAS) (p. 127)
nonorganic failure to thrive (p. 131)
sensation (p. 131)
perception (p. 131)
multimodal approach to perception (p. 137)
affordances (p. 137)

# Chapter 6
# Cognitive Development in Infancy

 **Learning Objectives**

**LO 6.1** Describe the fundamental features of Piaget's theory of cognitive development.

**LO 6.2** Summarize the advances in cognitive development that occur during the sensorimotor stage.

**LO 6.3** Compare Piaget's theory with later research.

**LO 6.4** Explain how infants process information.

**LO 6.5** Describe infants' memory capabilities and the duration of memories.

**LO 6.6** Summarize what is known about the neurological basis of memory in children.

**LO 6.7** Explain intelligence among infants and how it is measured.

**LO 6.8** Explain the processes that underlie children's growth in language development.

**LO 6.9** Differentiate the various theories of language development.

**LO 6.10** Describe how children influence adults' language.

# Prologue: Making Things Happen

Nine-month-old Raisa Novak has just begun to crawl. "I've had to baby-proof everything," her mother, Bela, says. One of the first things Raisa discovered as she began moving about the living room was the radio. At first, she pushed all the buttons in random order. But after just a week, she knows the red button makes the radio come on. "She has always loved music," Bela says. "She is clearly thrilled that she can make it happen whenever she wants." Raisa now crawls around the house looking for buttons to push and cries when she gets to the dishwasher or the DVD player because she can't reach their buttons—yet. "I will really have my hands full when she begins to walk," Bela says.

# Looking Ahead

How much of the world do infants understand? How do they begin to make meaning of it all? Does intellectual stimulation accelerate an infant's cognitive development?

We address these and related questions in this chapter as we consider cognitive development during the first years of life. Our examination focuses on the work of developmental researchers who seek to understand how infants develop their knowledge and understanding of the world. We first discuss the work of Swiss psychologist Jean Piaget, whose theory of developmental stages served as a highly influential impetus for a considerable amount of work on cognitive development. We look at both the limitations and the contributions of this important developmental specialist.

We then cover more contemporary views of cognitive development, examining information-processing approaches that seek to explain how cognitive growth occurs. After considering how learning takes place, we examine memory in infants and the ways in which infants process, store, and retrieve information. We discuss the controversial issue of the recollection of events that occurred during infancy. We also address individual differences in intelligence.

Finally, we consider language, the cognitive skill that permits infants to communicate with others. We look at the roots of language in prelinguistic speech and trace the milestones indicating the development of language skills in the progression from baby's first words to phrases and sentences. We also look at the characteristics of adults' communication addressed to infants—characteristics that are surprisingly similar across different cultures.

# Piaget's Approach to Cognitive Development

Swiss psychologist
Jean Piaget

*Olivia's dad is wiping up the mess around the base of her high chair—for the third time today! It seems to him that 14-month-old Olivia takes great delight in dropping food from the high chair. She also drops toys, spoons—anything, it seems—just to watch how it hits the floor. She almost appears to be experimenting to see what kind of noise or what size of splatter is created by each item.*

Swiss psychologist Jean Piaget (1896–1980) probably would have said that Olivia's dad is right in theorizing that Olivia is conducting her own series of experiments to learn more about the workings of her world. Piaget's views of the ways infants learn could be summed in a simple equation: *Action = Knowledge.*

Piaget argued that infants do not acquire knowledge from facts communicated by others, nor through sensation and perception. Instead, Piaget suggested that knowledge is the product of direct motor behavior. Although many of his basic explanations and propositions have been challenged by subsequent research, as we discuss later, the view that in significant ways infants learn by doing remains unquestioned (Piaget, 1962, 1983; Bullinger, 1997; Zuccarini et al., 2016).

## Key Elements of Piaget's Theory

**LO 6.1   Describe the fundamental features of Piaget's theory of cognitive development.**

As we first noted in Chapter 2, Piaget's theory is based on a stage approach to development. He assumed that all children pass through a series of four universal stages in a fixed order from birth through adolescence: sensorimotor, preoperational, concrete operational, and formal operational. He also suggested that movement from one stage to the next occurred when a child reached an appropriate level of physical maturation *and* was exposed to relevant experiences. Without such experiences, children are assumed to be incapable of reaching their cognitive potential. Some approaches to cognition focus on changes in the *content* of children's knowledge about the world, but Piaget argued that it was critical to also consider the changes in the *quality* of children's knowledge and understanding as they move from one stage to another.

For instance, as they develop cognitively, infants experience changes in their understanding about what can and cannot occur in the world. Consider a baby who participates in an experiment during which she is exposed to three identical versions of her mother all at the same time, thanks to some well-placed mirrors.

A 3-month-old infant will interact happily with each of these images of her mother; however, by 5 months, the child becomes quite agitated at the sight of multiple mothers. Apparently, by this time, the child has figured out that she has but one mother, and viewing three at a time is thoroughly alarming (Bower, 1977). To Piaget, such reactions indicate that the baby is beginning to master principles regarding the way the world operates, meaning that she has begun to construct a mental sense of the world that she didn't have 2 months earlier.

Piaget believed that the basic building blocks of the way we understand the world are mental structures called **schemas**, organized patterns of functioning, that adapt and change with mental development. At first, schemas are related to physical, or sensorimotor, activity, such as picking up or reaching for toys. As children develop, their schemas move to a mental level, reflecting thought. Schemas are similar to computer software: they direct and determine how data

**schema** Organized mental structure and pattern

from the world, such as new events or objects, are considered and dealt with (Achenbach, 1992; Rakison & Oakes, 2003; Rakison & Krogh, 2012).

If you give a baby a new cloth book, for example, he or she will touch it, mouth it, perhaps try to tear it, or bang it on the floor. To Piaget, each of these actions may represent a schema, and they are the infant's way of gaining knowledge and understanding of this new object. Adults, however, would use a different schema upon encountering the book. Rather than picking it up and putting it in their mouths or banging it on the floor, they would probably be drawn to the letters on the page, seeking to understand the book through the meaning of the printed words—a very different approach.

Piaget suggested that two principles underlie the growth in children's schemas: assimilation and accommodation. **Assimilation** is the process by which people understand an experience in terms of their current stage of cognitive development and way of thinking. Assimilation occurs, then, when a stimulus or an event is acted upon, perceived, and understood in accordance with existing patterns of thought. For example, an infant who tries to suck on any toy in the same way is assimilating the objects to her existing sucking schema. Similarly, a child who encounters a flying squirrel at a zoo and calls it a "bird" is assimilating the squirrel to his existing schema of bird.

In contrast, when we change our existing ways of thinking, understanding, or behaving in response to encounters with new stimuli or events, **accommodation** takes place. For instance, when a child sees a flying squirrel and calls it "a bird with a tail," he is beginning to *accommodate* new knowledge, modifying his schema of bird.

Piaget believed that the earliest schemas are primarily limited to the reflexes with which we are all born, such as sucking and rooting. Infants start to modify these simple early schemas almost immediately, through the processes of assimilation and accommodation, in response to their exploration of the environment. Schemas quickly become more sophisticated as infants become more advanced in their motor capabilities—to Piaget, this is a signal of the potential for more advanced cognitive development. Because Piaget's sensorimotor stage of development begins at birth and continues until the child is about 2 years old, we consider it here in detail. (In future chapters, we'll discuss development during the later stages.)

# The Sensorimotor Period: Six Substages of Cognitive Development

**LO 6.2** Summarize the advances in cognitive development that occur during the sensorimotor stage.

Piaget suggests that the **sensorimotor stage**, the initial major stage of cognitive development, can be broken down into six substages. These are summarized in Table 6.1. It is important to keep in mind that although the specific substages of the sensorimotor period may at first appear to unfold with great regularity, as though infants reach a particular age and smoothly proceed into the next substage, the reality of cognitive development is somewhat different. First, the ages at which infants actually reach a particular stage vary a good deal among different children. The exact timing of a stage reflects an interaction between the infant's level of physical maturation and the nature of the social environment in which the child is being raised. Consequently, although Piaget contended that the order of the substages does not change from one child to the next, he admitted that the timing can and does vary to some degree.

Piaget viewed development as a more gradual process than the notion of different stages might seem to imply. Infants do not go to sleep one night in one substage and wake up the next morning in the next one. Instead, there is a rather gradual and steady shifting of behavior as a child moves toward the next stage of cognitive development. Infants also pass through periods of transition, in which some aspects of their behavior reflect the next higher stage while other aspects indicate their current stage (see Figure 6.1).

**SUBSTAGE 1: SIMPLE REFLEXES.**   The first substage of the sensorimotor period is *Substage 1: Simple reflexes*, encompassing the first month of life. During

---

**assimilation** The process in which people understand an experience in terms of their current stage of cognitive development and way of thinking

**accommodation** Changes in existing ways of thinking that occur in response to encounters with new stimuli or events

**sensorimotor stage (of cognitive development)** Piaget's initial major stage of cognitive development, which can be broken down into six substages

**Table 6.1** Piaget's Six Substages of the Sensorimotor Stage

| Substage | Age | Description | Example |
|---|---|---|---|
| **Substage 1:** Simple reflexes | First month of life | During this period, the various reflexes that determine the infant's interactions with the world are at the center of its cognitive life. | The sucking reflex causes the infant to suck at anything placed at its lips. |
| **Substage 2:** First habits and primary circular reactions | From 1 to 4 months | At this age, infants begin to coordinate what were separate actions into single, integrated activities. | An infant might combine grasping an object with sucking on it, or staring at something with touching it. |
| **Substage 3:** Secondary circular reactions | From 4 to 8 months | During this period, infants take major strides in shifting their cognitive horizons beyond themselves and begin to act on the outside world. | A child who repeatedly picks up a rattle in her crib and shakes it in different ways to see how the sound changes is demonstrating her ability to modify her cognitive schema about shaking rattles. |
| **Substage 4:** Coordination of secondary circular reactions | From 8 to 12 months | In this stage, infants begin to use more calculated approaches to producing events, coordinating several schemas to generate a single act. They achieve object permanence during this stage. | An infant will push one toy out of the way to reach another toy that is lying, partially exposed, under it. |
| **Substage 5:** Tertiary circular reactions | From 12 to 18 months | At this age, infants develop what Piaget regards as the deliberate variation of actions that bring desirable consequences. Rather than just repeat enjoyable activities, infants appear to carry out miniature experiments to observe the consequences. | A child will drop a toy repeatedly, varying the position from which he drops it, carefully observing each time to see where it falls. |
| **Substage 6:** Beginnings of thought | From 18 months to 2 years | The major achievement of Substage 6 is the capacity for mental representation or symbolic thought. Piaget argued that only at this stage can infants imagine where objects that they cannot see might be. | Children can even plot in their heads unseen trajectories of objects, so that if a ball rolls under a piece of furniture, they can figure out where it is likely to emerge on the other side. |

this time, the various inborn reflexes, described in Chapters 4 and 5, are at the center of a baby's physical and cognitive life, determining the nature of his or her interactions with the world. For example, the sucking reflex causes the infant to suck at anything placed at his or her lips. This sucking behavior,

according to Piaget, provides the newborn with information about objects—information that paves the way to the next substage of the sensorimotor period.

At the same time, some of the reflexes begin to accommodate the infant's experience with the nature of the world. For instance, an infant who is being breastfed, but who also receives supplemental bottles, may start to change the way he or she sucks, depending on whether a nipple is on a breast or on a bottle.

**SUBSTAGE 2: FIRST HABITS AND PRIMARY CIRCULAR REACTIONS.** *Substage 2: First habits and primary circular reactions*, the second substage of the sensorimotor period, occurs from 1 to 4 months of age. In this period, infants begin to coordinate what were separate actions into single, integrated activities. For instance, an infant might combine grasping an object with sucking on it or staring at something while touching it.

If an activity engages a baby's interests, he or she may repeat it over and over, simply for the sake of continuing to experience it. Olivia's "experiments" with gravity while in her high chair are an example of this. This repetition of a chance motor event helps the baby start building cognitive schemas through a process known as a *circular reaction. Primary circular reactions* are

**Figure 6.1** Transitions

Infants do not suddenly shift from one stage of cognitive development to the next. Instead, Piaget argues that there is a period of transition in which some behavior reflects one stage, while other behavior reflects the more advanced stage. Does this gradualism argue against Piaget's interpretation of stages?

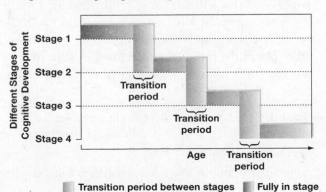

Different Stages of Cognitive Development

Stage 1
Stage 2
Stage 3
Stage 4

Transition period
Transition period
Age
Transition period

■ Transition period between stages　■ Fully in stage

schemas reflecting an infant's repetition of interesting or enjoyable actions, just for the purpose of doing them. Piaget referred to these schemas as *primary* because the activities they involve focus on the infant's own body. Thus, when an infant first puts his thumb in his mouth and begins to suck, it is a mere chance event. When he repeatedly sucks his thumb in the future, however, it represents a primary circular reaction, which he is repeating because the sensation of sucking is pleasurable.

**SUBSTAGE 3: SECONDARY CIRCULAR REACTIONS.** *Substage 3: Secondary circular reactions* involves more purposeful actions. According to Piaget, this third stage of cognitive development in infancy occurs from 4 to 8 months of age. During this period, infants begin to act upon the outside world. For instance, infants now seek to repeat enjoyable events in their environments if they happen to produce them through chance activities. A child who repeatedly picks up a rattle in her crib and shakes it in different ways to see how the sound changes is demonstrating her ability to modify her cognitive schema about shaking rattles. She is engaging in what Piaget calls secondary circular reactions.

*Secondary circular reactions* are schemas regarding repeated actions that bring about a desirable consequence. The major difference between primary circular reactions and secondary circular reactions is whether the infant's activity is focused on the infant and his or her own body (primary circular reactions), or involves actions relating to the world outside (secondary circular reactions).

During the third substage, babies' vocalization increases substantially as infants come to notice that if they make noises, other people around them will respond with noises of their own. Similarly, infants begin to imitate the sounds made by others. Vocalization becomes a secondary circular reaction that ultimately helps lead to the development of language and the formation of social relationships.

**SUBSTAGE 4: COORDINATION OF SECONDARY CIRCULAR REACTIONS.** One of the major leaps forward is *Substage 4: Coordination of secondary circular reactions*, which lasts from around 8 months to 12 months. Before this stage, behavior involved direct action on objects. When something happened by chance that caught an infant's interest, she attempted to repeat the event using a single schema. In Substage 4, however, infants begin to employ **goal-directed behavior**, in which several schemas are combined and

Piaget suggests that infants increasingly seek to repeat enjoyable events by acting on their environment.

coordinated to generate a single act to solve a problem. For instance, they will push one toy out of the way to reach another toy that is lying, partially exposed, under it. They also begin to anticipate upcoming events. For example, Piaget tells of his son Laurent, who at 8 months "recognizes by a certain noise caused by air that he is nearing the end of his feeding and, instead of insisting on drinking to the last drop, he rejects his bottle …" (Piaget, 1952, pp. 248–249).

Infants' newfound purposefulness, their ability to use means to attain particular ends, and their skill in anticipating future circumstances owe their appearance in part to the developmental achievement of object permanence that emerges in Substage 4. **Object permanence** is the realization that people and objects exist even when they cannot be seen. It is a simple principle, but its mastery has profound consequences.

Consider, for instance, 7-month-old Chu, who has yet to learn the idea of object permanence. Chu's father shakes a rattle in front of him, then takes the rattle and places it under a blanket. To Chu, who has not mastered the concept of object permanence, the rattle no longer exists. He will make no effort to look for it.

Several months later, when he is in Substage 4, the story is quite different. This time, as soon as his father places the rattle under the blanket, Chu tries to toss the cover aside, eagerly searching for the rattle.

---

**goal-directed behavior** Behavior in which several schemas are combined and coordinated to generate a single act to solve a problem

**object permanence** The concept that people and objects exist even when they cannot be seen

Chu clearly has learned that the object continues to exist even when it cannot be seen. For the infant who achieves an understanding of object permanence, then, out of sight is decidedly not out of mind.

The attainment of object permanence extends not only to inanimate objects but to people too. It gives Chu the security that his father and mother still exist even when they have left the room. This awareness is likely a key element in the development of social attachments, which we consider in Chapter 7. The recognition of object permanence also feeds infants' growing assertiveness: As they realize that an object taken away from them doesn't just cease to exist but is merely somewhere else, their only-too-human reaction may be to want it back—and quickly.

Although the understanding of object permanence emerges in Substage 4, it is only a rudimentary understanding. It takes time for the concept to be fully comprehended, and infants continue for several months to make certain kinds of errors relating to object permanence. For instance, they often are fooled when a toy is hidden first under one blanket and then under a second blanket. In seeking out the toy, Substage 4 infants most often turn to the first hiding place, ignoring the second blanket under which the toy is currently located—even if the hiding was done in plain view.

**SUBSTAGE 5: TERTIARY CIRCULAR REACTIONS.** *Substage 5: Tertiary circular reactions* is reached at around the age of 12 months and extends to 18 months. As the name of the stage indicates, during this period infants develop what Piaget labeled *tertiary circular reactions*, schemas regarding the deliberate variation of actions that bring desirable consequences. Rather than just repeating enjoyable activities, as they do with secondary circular reactions, infants appear to carry out miniature experiments to observe the consequences.

For example, Piaget observed his son Laurent dropping a toy swan repeatedly, varying the position from which he dropped it, carefully observing each time to see where it fell. Instead of just repeating the action each time (as in a secondary circular reaction), Laurent made modifications in the situation to learn about their consequences. As you may recall from our discussion of research methods in Chapter 2, this behavior represents the essence of the scientific method: An experimenter varies a situation in a laboratory to learn the effects of the variation. To infants in Substage 5, the world is their laboratory, and they

spend their days leisurely carrying out one miniature experiment after another. Olivia, the baby described earlier who enjoyed dropping things from her high chair, is another little scientist in action.

What is most striking about infants' behavior during Substage 5 is their interest in the unexpected. Unanticipated events are treated not only as interesting but also as something to be explained and understood. Infants' discoveries can lead to newfound skills, some of which may cause a certain amount of chaos, as Olivia's dad realized while cleaning up around her high chair.

**SUBSTAGE 6: BEGINNINGS OF THOUGHT.** The final stage of the sensorimotor period is *Substage 6: Beginnings of thought*, which lasts from around 18 months to 2 years. The major achievement of Substage 6 is the capacity for mental representation, or symbolic thought. A **mental representation** is an internal image of a past event or object. Piaget argued that by this stage, infants can imagine where objects might be that they cannot see. They can even plot in their heads unseen pathways of objects, so if a ball rolls under a piece of furniture, they can figure out where it is likely to emerge on the other side.

Because of children's new ability to create internal representations of objects, their understanding of causality also becomes more sophisticated. For example, consider Piaget's description of his son Laurent's efforts to open a garden gate:

> *Laurent tries to open a garden gate but cannot push it forward because it is held back by a piece of furniture. He cannot account either visually or by any sound for the cause that prevents the gate from opening, but after having tried to force it he suddenly seems to understand; he goes around the wall, arrives at the other side of the gate, moves the armchair which holds it firm, and opens it with a triumphant expression.* (PIAGET, 1954, p. 296)

The attainment of mental representation also permits another important development: the ability to pretend. Using the skill that Piaget refers to as **deferred imitation**, in which a person who is no longer present

---

**mental representation** An internal image of a past event or object

**deferred imitation** An act in which a person who is no longer present is imitated by children who have witnessed a similar act

is imitated later, children are able to pretend that they are driving a car, feeding a doll, or cooking dinner long after they have witnessed such scenes played out in reality. To Piaget, deferred imitation provided clear evidence that children form internal mental representations.

## Appraising Piaget: Support and Challenges

### LO 6.3 Compare Piaget's theory with later research.

Most developmental researchers would probably agree that in many significant ways, Piaget's descriptions of how cognitive development proceeds during infancy are quite accurate (Harris, 1987; Marcovitch, Zelazo, & Schmuckler, 2003). Yet there is substantial disagreement over the validity of the theory and many of its specific predictions.

Let's start with what is clearly correct about the Piagetian approach. Piaget was a masterful reporter of children's behavior, and his descriptions of growth during infancy remain a monument to his powers of observation. Furthermore, literally thousands of studies have supported Piaget's view that children learn much about the world by acting on objects in their environment. Finally, the broad outlines sketched out by Piaget of the sequence of cognitive development and the increasing cognitive accomplishments that occur during infancy are generally accurate (Kail, 2004; Schlottmann & Wilkening, 2012; Bibace, 2013; Müller, Ten Eycke, & Baker, 2015).

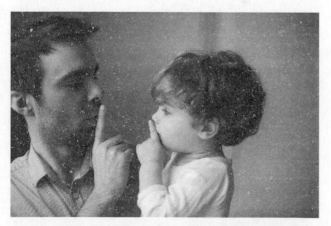

With the attainment of the cognitive skill of deferred imitation, children are able to imitate people and scenes they have witnessed in the past.

However, specific aspects of the theory have come under increasing scrutiny—and criticism—in the decades since Piaget carried out his pioneering work. For example, some researchers question the stage conception that forms the basis of Piaget's theory. Although, as we noted earlier, even Piaget acknowledged that children's transitions between stages are gradual, critics contend development proceeds in a much more continuous fashion. Rather than showing major leaps of competence at the end of one stage and the beginning of the next, improvement comes in smaller increments, growing step-by-step in a skill-by-skill manner.

For instance, developmental researcher Robert Siegler suggests that cognitive development proceeds not in stages but in "waves." According to him, children don't one day drop a mode of thinking and the next take up a new form. Instead, there is an ebb and flow of cognitive approaches that children use to understand the world. One day children may use one form of cognitive strategy, while another day they may choose a less advanced strategy—moving back and forth over a period of time. Although one strategy may be used most frequently at a given age, children still may have access to alternative ways of thinking. Siegler thus sees cognitive development as in constant flux (Opfer & Siegler, 2007; Siegler, 2007, 2012, 2016).

Other critics dispute Piaget's notion that cognitive development is grounded in motor activities. They charge that Piaget overlooked the importance of the sensory and perceptual systems that are present from a very early age in infancy—systems about which Piaget knew little, because so much of the research illustrating how sophisticated they are even in infancy was done relatively recently. Studies of children born without arms and legs (due to their mothers' unwitting use of teratogenic drugs during pregnancy, as described in Chapter 3) show that such children display normal cognitive development, despite their lack of practice with motor activities. This constitutes further evidence that the connection Piaget made between motor development and cognitive development was exaggerated (Decarrie, 1969; Butterworth, 1994).

To bolster their perspectives, Piaget's critics also point to more recent studies that cast doubt on Piaget's view that infants are incapable of mastering the concept of object permanence until they are close to a year old. For instance, some work suggests that younger infants did not appear to understand object permanence because the techniques used to test their abilities were not sensitive enough to their true capabilities (Baillargeon, 2004, 2008; Vallotton, 2011; Bremner, Slater, & Johnson, 2015).

According to researcher Renée Baillargeon, infants as young as 3 1/2 months have at least some understanding of object permanence. Baillargeon argues that it may be that younger infants don't search for a rattle hidden under a blanket because they don't have the motor skills necessary to do the searching—not because they don't understand that the rattle still exists. Similarly, the apparent inability of young infants to comprehend object permanence may reflect more about infants' memory deficits than their lack of understanding of the concept: The memories of young infants may be so poor that they simply do not recall the earlier concealment of the toy (Hespos & Baillargeon, 2008).

Baillargeon has conducted ingenious experiments that demonstrate the earlier capabilities of infants in understanding object permanence. For example, in her *violation-of-expectation* studies, she repeatedly exposes infants to a physical event and then observes how they react to a variation of that event that is physically impossible. It turns out that infants as young as 3 1/2 months show strong physiological reactions to impossible events, suggesting that they have some sense of object permanence far earlier than Piaget was able to discern (Luo, Kaufman, & Baillargeon, 2009; Scott & Baillargeon, 2013; Baillargeon et al., 2015).

Other types of behavior also seem to emerge earlier than Piaget suggested. For instance, recall the ability of neonates to imitate the basic facial expressions of adults just hours after birth, as we discussed in Chapter 4. The presence of this skill at such an early age contradicts Piaget's view that initially infants are able to imitate only behavior that they see in others, using parts of their own body that they can plainly view—such as their hands and feet. In fact, facial imitation suggests that humans may be born with a basic, innate capability for imitating others' actions, a capability that depends on certain kinds of environmental experiences, but one that Piaget believed develops later in infancy (Vanvuchelen, Roeyers, & De Weerdt, 2011; Gredebäck et al., 2012; Parsons et al., 2017).

Piaget's work also seems to describe children from developed Western countries better than those in non-Western cultures. For instance, some evidence suggests cognitive skills emerge on a different timetable for children in non-Western cultures than for children living in Europe and the United States. Infants raised in the Ivory Coast of Africa, for example, reach the various substages of the sensorimotor period at an earlier age than infants reared in France (Dasen et al., 1978; Mistry & Saraswathi, 2003; Tamis-LeMonda et al., 2012).

Despite these problems regarding Piaget's view of the sensorimotor period, even his most passionate critics concede that he has provided us with a masterful description of the broad outlines of cognitive development during infancy. His failings seem to be in underestimating the capabilities of younger infants and in his claims that sensorimotor skills develop in a consistent, fixed pattern. Still, his influence has been enormous, and although the focus of many contemporary developmental researchers has shifted to the newer information-processing approaches that we discuss next, Piaget remains a towering and pioneering figure in the field of development (Kail, 2004; Maynard, 2008; Fowler, 2017).

> **From a child caregiver's perspective:** In general, what are some implications for childrearing practices according to Piaget's observations about the ways children gain an understanding of the world? Would you use the same childrearing approaches for a child growing up in a non-Western culture? Why or why not?

# Information-Processing Approaches to Cognitive Development

*Amber Nordstrom, 3 months old, breaks into a smile as her brother Marcus stands over her crib, picks up a doll, and makes a whistling noise through his teeth. In fact, Amber never seems to tire of Marcus's efforts at entertaining her, and soon, whenever he appears and simply picks up the doll, her lips begin to curl into a smile.*

Clearly, Amber remembers Marcus and his humorous ways. But how does she remember him? And how much else can Amber remember?

To answer questions such as these, we need to diverge from the road that Piaget laid out for us. Rather than seeking to identify the universal, broad milestones in cognitive development through which all infants pass, as Piaget tried to do, we must consider the specific processes by which individual babies acquire and use the information to which they are exposed. We need, then, to focus less on the qualitative changes in infants' mental lives and consider more closely their quantitative capabilities.

**Information-processing approaches** to cognitive development seek to identify the way that individuals take in, use, and store information. According to this approach, the quantitative changes in infants' abilities to organize and manipulate information represent the hallmarks of cognitive development.

Taking this perspective, cognitive growth is characterized by increasing sophistication, speed, and capacity in processing information. Earlier, we compared Piaget's idea of schemas to computer software, which directs the computer in how to deal with data from the world. We might compare the information-processing perspective on cognitive growth to the improvements that come from use of more efficient programs that lead to increased speed and sophistication in the processing of information. Information-processing approaches, then, focus on the types of "mental programs" that people use when they seek to solve problems (Siegler, 1998; Cohen & Cashon, 2003; Fagan & Ployhart, 2015).

## Encoding, Storage, and Retrieval: The Foundations of Information Processing

**LO 6.4  Explain how infants process information.**

Information processing has three basic aspects: encoding, storage, and retrieval (see Figure 6.2). *Encoding* is the process by which information is initially recorded in a form usable to memory. Infants and children—indeed, all people—are exposed to a massive amount of information; if they tried to process it all, they would be overwhelmed. Consequently, they encode selectively, picking and choosing the information to which they will pay attention.

Even if someone has been exposed to the information initially and has encoded it in an appropriate way, there is still no guarantee that he or she will be able to use it in the future. Information must also have been stored in memory adequately. *Storage* refers to the placement of material into memory. Finally, success in using the material in the future depends on retrieval processes. *Retrieval* is the process by which material in memory storage is located, brought into awareness, and used.

We can use our comparison to computers again here. Information-processing approaches suggest that the processes of encoding, storage, and retrieval are analogous to different parts of a computer. Encoding can be thought of as a computer's keyboard, through which one inputs information; storage is the computer's hard drive, where information is stored; and retrieval is analogous to software that accesses the information for display on the screen. Only when all three processes are operating—encoding, storage, and retrieval—can information be processed.

In some cases, encoding, storage, and retrieval are relatively automatic, whereas in other cases they are deliberate. *Automatization* is the degree to which an activity requires attention. Processes that require relatively little attention are automatic; processes that require relatively large amounts of attention are controlled. For example, some activities, such as walking, eating with a fork, or reading, may be automatic for you, but at first they required your full attention.

Automatic mental processes help children in their initial encounters with the world by enabling them to easily and "automatically" process information in particular ways. For instance, by the age of 5, children automatically encode information in terms of

---

**information-processing approaches** Approaches to the study of cognitive development that seek to identify the way individuals take in, use, and store information

---

**Figure 6.2** Information Processing

Information processing is the process by which information is encoded, stored, and retrieved.

frequency. Without a lot of attention to counting or tallying, they become aware, for example, of how often they have encountered various people, permitting them to differentiate familiar from unfamiliar people (Homae et al., 2012).

Furthermore, without intending to and without being aware of it, infants and children develop a sense of how often different stimuli are found together simultaneously. This permits them to develop an understanding of *concepts*, categorizations of objects, events, or people that share common properties. For example, by encoding the information that four legs, a wagging tail, and barking are often found together, we learn very early in life to understand the concept of "dog." Children—as well as adults—are rarely aware of how they learn such concepts, and they are often unable to articulate the features that distinguish one concept (such as a dog) from another (such as cat). Instead, learning tends to occur automatically.

Some of the things we learn automatically are unexpectedly complex. For example, infants have the ability to learn subtle statistical patterns and relationships; these results are consistent with a growing body of research showing that the mathematical skills of infants are surprisingly good. Infants as young as 5 months are able to calculate the outcome of simple addition and subtraction problems. In a study by developmental psychologist Karen Wynn, infants first were shown an object—a 4-inch-high Mickey Mouse statuette. A screen was then raised, hiding the statuette. Next, the experimenter showed the infants a second, identical Mickey Mouse, and then placed it behind the same screen (Wynn, 1995, 2000).

Finally, depending on the experimental condition, one of two outcomes occurred. In the "correct addition" condition, the screen dropped, revealing the two statuettes (analogous to $1 + 1 = 2$). But in the "incorrect addition" condition, the screen dropped to reveal just one statuette (analogous to the incorrect $1 + 1 = 1$).

Because infants look longer at unexpected occurrences than at expected ones, the researchers examined the pattern of infants' gazes under the different conditions. In support of the notion that infants can distinguish between correct and incorrect addition, the infants in the experiment gazed longer at the incorrect result than at the correct one, indicating they expected a different number of statuettes. In a similar procedure, infants also looked longer at incorrect subtraction problems than at correct ones. The

conclusion: Infants have rudimentary mathematical skills that enable them to understand whether or not a quantity is accurate.

The existence of basic mathematical skills in infants has been supported by findings that nonhumans are born with some basic numeric proficiency. Even newly hatched chicks show some counting abilities. And it is not too long into infancy that children demonstrate an understanding of such basic physics as movement trajectories and gravity (Gopnik, 2010; Hespos & van-Marle, 2012; Edwards et al., 2016).

The results of this growing body of research suggest that infants have an innate grasp of certain basic mathematical functions and statistical patterns. This inborn proficiency is likely to form the basis for learning more complex mathematics and statistical relationships later in life (McCrink & Wynn, 2007, 2009; vanMarle & Wynn, 2009; Starr, Libertus & Brannon, 2013).

We turn now to several aspects of information processing, focusing on memory and individual differences in intelligence.

## Memory During Infancy: They Must Remember This …

**LO 6.5  Describe infants' memory capabilities and the duration of memories.**

*Elena Kurjak spent her infancy in an underground bunker in Bosnia in the middle of a war zone. Her mother was killed while foraging for food when Elena was just 6 months old. After that, various neighbors watched over her, but she was often alone for hours in a small playpen, with little light and no toys. No one knows how Elena interpreted her experience, but when she was adopted by an American couple at 18 months, she showed almost no emotion and did not talk or even babble. Indeed, she could barely manage to sit up and hold a bottle.*

*Elena's story, however, has a happy ending. Her adoptive parents took her to a variety of child development specialists and devoted hours to working and playing with her. Elena has a loving family and all the usual surroundings of childhood, like friends, regular schooling, and classmates. Now 6, Elena has lost almost all unhappy memories of Bosnia. Her early life seems to be a complete blank.*

How likely is it that Elena truly remembers nothing of her infancy? And if she ever does recall her first 2 years of life, how accurate will her memories be? To answer these questions, we need to consider the qualities of memory that exist during infancy.

**MEMORY CAPABILITIES IN INFANCY.** Certainly, infants have **memory** capabilities, defined as the process by which information is initially recorded, stored, and retrieved. As we've seen, infants can distinguish new stimuli from old stimuli, and this implies that some memory of the old must be present. Unless the infants had a memory of an original stimulus, it would be impossible for them to recognize that a new stimulus differed from the earlier one.

Infants' capability to recognize new stimuli from old stimuli, however, tells us little about how age brings about changes in the capacities of memory and in its fundamental nature. Do infants' memory capabilities increase as they get older? The answer is clearly affirmative. In one study, infants were taught that they could move a mobile hanging over the crib by kicking their legs (see Figure 6.3). It took only a few days for 2-month-old infants to forget their training, but 6-month-old infants still remembered for as long as 3 weeks (Rovee-Collier, 1999; Rose et al., 2011; Oakes & Kovack-Lesh, 2013).

Furthermore, infants who were later prompted to recall the association between kicking and moving the mobile showed evidence that the memory continued to exist even longer. Infants who had received just two training sessions lasting 9 minutes each still recalled about a week later, as illustrated by the fact that they began to kick when placed in the crib with the mobile. Two weeks later, however, they made no effort to kick, suggesting that they had forgotten entirely.

But they hadn't forgotten: When the babies saw a reminder—a moving mobile—their memories were apparently reactivated. The infants could remember the association, following prompting, for as long as an additional month. Other evidence confirms these results, suggesting that hints can reactivate memories that at first seem lost, and that the older the infant, the more effective such prompting is (DeFrancisco & Rovee-Collier, 2008; Moher, Tuerk, & Feigenson, 2012; Fisher-Thompson, 2017).

Is infant memory qualitatively different from that in older children and adults? Researchers generally believe that information is processed similarly throughout the life span, even though the kind of information being processed changes, and different parts of the brain may be used. According to memory expert Carolyn Rovee-Collier, people, regardless of their age, gradually lose memories, although, just like babies, they may regain them if reminders are provided. Moreover, the more times a memory is retrieved, the more enduring the memory becomes (Turati, 2008; Zosh, Halberda, & Feigenson, 2011; Bell, 2012).

**THE DURATION OF MEMORIES.** Although the processes that underlie memory retention and recall seem similar throughout the life span, the quantity of information stored and recalled does differ markedly as infants develop. Older infants can retrieve information more rapidly, and they can remember it longer. But just how long? Can memories from infancy be recalled, for example, after babies grow up?

Researchers disagree on the age from which memories can be retrieved. Although early research supported the notion of **infantile amnesia**, the lack of memory for experiences occurring before 3 years of age, more recent research shows that infants do retain memories of these years. For example, in one study, 6-month-olds were shown a series of unusual

**Figure 6.3** Early Signs of Memory

Infants who had learned the association between a moving mobile and kicking showed surprising recall ability if they were exposed to a reminder of the early memory.

---

**memory** The process by which information is initially recorded, stored, and retrieved

**infantile amnesia** The lack of memory for experiences that occurred prior to 3 years of age

events, such as intermittent periods of light and dark and strange sounds. When the children were later tested at the age of 1½ years or 2½ years, they had recalled the experience. Other research indicates that infants show memory for behavior and situations that they have seen only once (Neisser, 2004; Callaghan, Li, & Richardson, 2014).

Such findings are consistent with evidence that the physical trace of a memory in the brain appears to be relatively permanent; this suggests that memories, even from infancy, may be enduring. Memories may not be easily, or accurately, retrieved, however. For example, memories are susceptible to interference from other, newer information, which may displace or block out the older information, thereby preventing its recall.

One reason infants appear to remember less may be because language plays a key role in determining the way in which memories from early in life can be recalled. Older children and adults may only be able to report memories using the vocabulary that they had available at the time of the initial event, when the memories were stored. Because their vocabulary at the time of initial storage may have been quite limited, they are unable to describe the event later in life, even though it is actually in their memories (Bauer et al., 2000; Simcock & Hayne, 2002; Heimann et al., 2006).

The question of how well memories formed during infancy are retained in adulthood remains not fully answered. Although infants' memories may be highly detailed and can be enduring if the infants experience repeated reminders, it is still not clear how accurate those memories remain over the course of the life span. Early memories are susceptible to misrecollection if people are exposed to related but contradictory information following the initial formation of the memory. Not only does such new information potentially impair recall of the original material, but also the new material may be inadvertently incorporated into the original memory, thereby corrupting its accuracy (DuBreuil, Garry, & Loftus, 1998; Cordón et al., 2004).

In sum, the data suggest that although it is at least theoretically possible for memories to remain intact from a very young age—if subsequent experiences do not interfere with their recollection—in most cases memories of personal experiences in infancy do not last into adulthood. Current findings suggest that memories of personal experience seem not to become

accurate before age 18 to 24 months (Howe et al., 2004; Bauer, 2007; Taylor, Liu, & Herbert, 2016).

## The Neurological Basis of Memory

**LO 6.6  Summarize what is known about the neurological basis of memory in children.**

Some of the most exciting research on the development of memory comes from studies of the neurological basis of memory. Advances in brain scan technology, as well as studies of adults with brain damage, suggest that there are two separate systems involved with long-term memory. These two systems, called explicit memory and implicit memory, retain different sorts of information.

*Explicit memory* is memory that is conscious and that can be recalled intentionally. When we try to recall a name or phone number, we're using explicit memory. In comparison, *implicit memory* consists of memories of which we are not consciously aware but that affect performance and behavior. Implicit memory includes motor skills, habits, and activities that can be remembered without conscious cognitive effort, such as how to ride a bike or climb a stairway.

Explicit and implicit memory emerge at different rates and involve different parts of the brain. The earliest memories seem to be implicit, and they involve the cerebellum and brain stem. The forerunner of explicit memory involves the hippocampus, but true explicit memory doesn't emerge until the second half of the first year. When explicit memory does emerge, it involves an increasing number of areas of the cortex of the brain (Bauer, 2007; Low & Perner, 2012).

Research conducted on nonhumans reinforces the importance of the hippocampus in supporting memory development. For example, infant monkeys who have previously shown a preference for novel, previously unencountered stimuli lose their preference for novel stimuli when their hippocampus is removed. (Preference for novel stimuli is an indication of memory, since one can't prefer novel stimuli unless one recognizes that they haven't seen the stimulus before.) Similarly, brain scans show that glucose activity in the brain is related to memory in infant monkeys and is also related to their preference for novel stimuli. In short, the neuroscience behind memory is increasingly being understood (Blue et al., 2013; Thompson et al., 2014; Bachevalier, Nemanic, & Alvarado, 2015; also see the *From Research to Practice* box).

# FROM RESEARCH TO PRACTICE
## Is Brain Growth Responsible for Infantile Amnesia?

What are your earliest memories? Perhaps you recall playing with a childhood friend, or your kindergarten teacher, or bits and pieces of your fifth birthday party. But try as you might, you almost certainly can't remember anything from your infancy.

Nobody can. Psychologists have long considered the possible cause of this phenomenon, known as *infantile amnesia*, and attributed it to a lack of some function during this period of life—usually self-awareness or language—that impedes the proper encoding of memories. Now researchers are considering a different cause: the continuing growth of new brain cells.

The brain's ability to grow, change, and create new connections between cells is a good thing. This phenomenon, known as *neuroplasticity*, allows the brain to assimilate new information, and, in extreme cases, even gives it some ability to overcome damage. But as you might imagine, there comes a point where new pathways developing in the brain can interfere with or replace existing pathways, thereby "crowding out" old information. Researchers hypothesized that the rapid growth of new brain cells in the developing infant brain thereby interferes with later recall of this period of life.

To test their hypothesis, neuroscientists Sheena Josselyn and Paul Frankland and colleagues conditioned adult mice to fear a specific stimulus. They then induced increased cell growth in the hippocampal region of the mice's brains—the area responsible for recording new memories. As predicted, these mice showed less of a fear response to the conditioned stimulus than a control group of mice; the mice that experienced intervening brain cell growth in the hippocampus had forgotten their

earlier conditioning. Josselyn and Frankland and their team showed the reverse pattern with infant mice, who naturally undergo rapid brain cell development (and also experience infantile amnesia). When this natural growth was hindered, the infant mice retained information better than unhindered controls (Akers et al., 2014).

After infancy the rapid growth of brain cells slows, arriving at a balance between plasticity and stability that allows the recording of new memories while mostly retaining the old ones. Some forgetting still occurs, of course, but this is also a good thing. Most things we do are pretty mundane, Frankland says. "For healthy adult memory function, you need not only to be able to remember things but also to clear out the inconsequential memories" (Sneed, 2014, p. 28).

- **Might there be some benefit to forgetting the events of infancy?**

# Individual Differences in Intelligence: Is One Infant Smarter Than Another?

**LO 6.7** **Explain intelligence among infants and how it is measured.**

*Maddy Rodriguez is a bundle of curiosity and energy. At 6 months of age, she cries heartily if she can't reach a toy, and when she sees a reflection of herself in a mirror, she gurgles and seems, in general, to find the situation quite amusing.*

\*\*\*

*Jared Lynch, at 6 months, is a good deal more inhibited than Maddy. He doesn't seem to care much when a ball rolls out of his reach, losing interest in it rapidly. And unlike Maddy, when he sees himself in a mirror, he pretty much ignores the reflection.*

As anyone who has spent any time at all observing more than one baby can tell you, not all infants are alike. Some are full of energy and life, apparently displaying a natural-born curiosity, while others seem, by comparison, somewhat less interested in the world around them. Does this mean that such infants differ in intelligence?

Answering questions about how and to what degree infants vary in their underlying intelligence is not easy. Although it is clear that different infants show significant variations in their behavior, the issue of just what types of behavior may be related to cognitive ability is complicated. Interestingly, the examination of individual differences among infants was the initial approach taken by developmental specialists to understand cognitive development, and such issues still represent an important focus within the field.

**WHAT IS INFANT INTELLIGENCE?** Before we can address whether and how infants may differ in intelligence, we need to consider what is meant by the term "intelligence." Educators, psychologists, and other experts on development have yet to agree upon a general definition of intelligent behavior, even among adults. Is it the ability to do well in scholastic endeavors? Proficiency in business negotiations? Competence in navigating across treacherous seas, such as that shown by peoples of the South Pacific, who have no knowledge of Western navigational techniques?

It is even more difficult to define and measure intelligence in infants than it is in adults. Do we base it on the speed with which a new task is learned through classical or operant conditioning? How fast a baby becomes habituated to a new stimulus? The age at which an infant learns to crawl or walk? Even if we are able to identify particular behaviors that seem to differentiate one infant from another in terms of intelligence during infancy, we need to address a further, and probably more important, issue: How well do measures of infant intelligence relate to eventual adult intelligence?

Such questions are not simple, and no simple answers have been found. Developmental specialists, however, have devised several approaches (summarized in Table 6.2) to illuminate the nature of individual differences in intelligence during infancy.

Determining what is meant by intelligence in infants represents a major challenge for developmentalists.

**DEVELOPMENTAL SCALES.** Developmental psychologist Arnold Gesell formulated the earliest measure of infant development, which was designed to distinguish between normally developing and atypically developing babies (Gesell, 1946). Gesell based his scale on examinations of hundreds of babies. He compared their performance at different ages to learn what behaviors were most common at a particular age. If an infant varied significantly from the norms of a given age, he or she was considered to be developmentally delayed or advanced.

Following the lead of researchers who sought to quantify intelligence through a specific score (known as an intelligence quotient, or IQ, score), Gesell (1946) developed a developmental quotient, or DQ. The **developmental quotient** is an overall developmental

**developmental quotient** An overall developmental score that relates to performance in four domains: motor skills, language use, adaptive behavior, and personal-social

---

**Table 6.2** Approaches Used to Detect Differences in Intelligence During Infancy

| | |
|---|---|
| Developmental quotient | Formulated by Arnold Gesell, the developmental quotient is an overall developmental score that relates to performance in four domains: motor skills (balance and sitting), language use, adaptive behavior (alertness and exploration), and personal-social behavior. |
| Bayley Scales of Infant Development | Developed by Nancy Bayley, the Bayley Scales of Infant Development evaluate an infant's development from 2 to 42 months. The Bayley Scales focus on two areas: mental (senses, perception, memory, learning, problem solving, and language) and motor abilities (fine and gross motor skills). |
| Visual-recognition memory measurement | Measures of visual-recognition memory (the memory of and recognition of a stimulus that has been previously seen) also relate to intelligence. The more quickly an infant can retrieve a representation of a stimulus from memory, the more efficient, presumably, is that infant's information processing. |

score that relates to performance in four domains: motor skills (e.g., balance and sitting), language use, adaptive behavior (e.g., alertness and exploration), and personal-social (e.g., adequately feeding and dressing oneself).

Later researchers have created other developmental scales. For instance, Nancy Bayley developed one of the most widely used measures for infants. The **Bayley Scales of Infant Development** (also known as the *BSID-III*) evaluate an infant's development from 2 to 42 months. The Bayley Scales focus on two areas: mental and motor abilities. The mental scale focuses on the senses, perception, memory, learning, problem solving, and language, while the motor scale evaluates fine and gross motor skills (see Table 6.3). Like Gesell's approach, the Bayley Scale yields a DQ. A child who scores at an average level—meaning average performance for other children at the same age—receives a score of 100 (Lynn, 2009; Bos, 2013; Greene et al., 2013).

The virtue of approaches such as those taken by Gesell and Bayley is that they provide a good snapshot of an infant's current developmental level. Using these scales, we can tell in an objective manner whether a particular infant is ahead of or falling behind his or her same-age peers.

The scales are particularly useful in identifying the latter. In these cases, infants need immediate special attention. Tests might be administered if a parent or physician believes that an infant is suffering from developmental delays and to assess the significance of such delays. Based on their scores, early intervention programs can be put in place (Aylward & Verhulst, 2000; Sonne, 2012).

What such scales are not useful for is predicting a child's future course of development. A child whose development is identified by these measures as

relatively slow at the age of 1 year will not necessarily display slow development at age 5, or 12, or 25. The association between most measures of behavior during infancy and adult intelligence, then, is minimal (Murray et al., 2007; Burakevych et al., 2017).

> **From a nurse's perspective:** In what ways is the use of such developmental scales as Gesell's or Bayley's helpful? In what ways is it dangerous? How would you maximize the helpfulness and minimize the danger if you were advising a parent?

**INFORMATION-PROCESSING APPROACHES TO INDIVIDUAL DIFFERENCES IN INTELLIGENCE.** When we speak of intelligence in everyday parlance, we often differentiate between "quick" and "slow" individuals. According to research on the speed of information processing, such terms hold some truth. Contemporary approaches to infant intelligence suggest that the speed with which infants process information may correlate most strongly with later intelligence, as measured by IQ tests administered during adulthood (Rose & Feldman, 1997; Sigman, Cohen, & Beckwith, 1997).

How can we tell whether or not a baby is processing information quickly? To answer this question, most researchers use habituation tests. Infants who process information efficiently ought to be able to learn about stimuli more quickly. Consequently, we would expect them to turn their attention away from a given stimulus more rapidly than those who are less efficient at information processing, leading to the phenomenon of habituation. Similarly, measures of *visual-recognition memory*, the memory

**Bayley Scales of Infant Development** A measure that evaluates an infant's development from 2 to 42 months

---

**Table 6.3** Sample Items From the Bayley Scales of Infant Development

| Age | 2 months | 6 months | 12 months | 17–19 months | 23–25 months | 38–42 months |
|---|---|---|---|---|---|---|
| Mental Scale | Turns head to locate origin of sound; visibly responds to disappearance of face | Picks up cup by handle; notices illustrations in a book | Constructs tower of two cubes; can turn pages in a book | Mimics crayon stroke; labels objects in photo | Pairs up pictures; repeats a two-word sentence | Can identify four colors; past tense evident in speech; distinguishes gender |
| Motor Scale | Can hold head steady and erect for 15 seconds; sits with assistance | Sits up without aid for 30 seconds; grasps foot with hands | Walks when holding onto someone's hand or furniture; holds pencil in fist | Stands on right foot without help; remains upright climbing stairs with assistance | Strings three beads; Jumps length of four inches | Can reproduce drawing of a circle; hops two times on one foot; descends stairs, alternating feet |

**SOURCE:** Based on *Bayley, N. 7 1993. Bayley Scales of Infant Development* [BSID-II], 2nd ed., San Antonio, TX: The Psychological Corporation.

and recognition of a stimulus that has been previously seen, also relate to IQ. The more quickly an infant can retrieve a representation of a stimulus from memory, the more efficient, presumably, is that infant's information processing (Rose, Jankowski, & Feldman, 2002; Robinson & Pascalis, 2004; Trainor, 2012; Otsuka et al., 2014).

Research using an information-processing framework clearly suggests a relationship between information-processing efficiency and cognitive abilities. Measures of how quickly infants lose interest in stimuli that they have previously seen, as well as their responsiveness to new stimuli, correlate moderately well with later measures of intelligence. Infants who are more efficient information processors during the 6 months following birth tend to have higher intelligence scores between 2 and 12 years of age, as well as higher scores on other measures of cognitive competence (Domsch, Lohaus, & Thomas, 2009; Rose, Feldman, & Jankowski, 2009).

Other research suggests that abilities related to the *multimodal approach to perception*, which we considered in Chapter 5, may offer clues about later intelligence. For instance, the ability to identify a stimulus that previously has been experienced through only one sense by using another sense (called *cross-modal transference*) is associated with intelligence. A baby who is able to recognize by sight a screwdriver that she has previously only touched, but not seen, is displaying cross-modal transference. Research has found that the degree of cross-modal transference displayed by an infant at age 1 year—which requires a high level of abstract thinking—is associated with intelligence scores several years later (Rose, Feldman, & Jankowski, 1999, 2004; Nakato et al., 2011).

Although information-processing efficiency and cross-modal transference abilities during infancy relate moderately well to later IQ scores, we need to keep in mind two qualifications. First, even though there is an association between early information-processing capabilities and later measures of IQ, the correlation is only moderately strong. Other factors, such as the degree of environmental stimulation, also play a crucial role in helping to determine adult intelligence. Consequently, we should not assume that intelligence is somehow permanently fixed in infancy.

Second, and perhaps even more important, intelligence measured by traditional IQ tests relates to a particular type of intelligence, one that emphasizes abilities that lead to academic, and certainly not artistic

or professional, success. Consequently, predicting that a child may do well on IQ tests later in life is not the same as predicting that the child will be successful later in life.

Despite these qualifications, the relatively recent finding that an association exists between efficiency of information processing and later IQ scores does suggest some consistency of cognitive development across the life span. Whereas the earlier reliance on scales such as the Bayley led to the misconception that little continuity existed, the more recent information-processing approaches suggest that cognitive development unfolds in a more orderly, continuous manner from infancy to the later stages of life.

**ASSESSING INFORMATION-PROCESSING APPROACHES.** The information-processing perspective on cognitive development during infancy is very different from that of Piaget's approach. Rather than focus on broad explanations of the *qualitative* changes that occur in infants' capabilities, as Piaget does, information processing looks at *quantitative* change. Piaget sees cognitive growth occurring in fairly sudden spurts; information processing sees more gradual, step-by-step growth. (Think of the difference between a track-and-field runner leaping hurdles versus a slow but steady marathon racer.)

Because information-processing researchers consider cognitive development in terms of a collection of individual skills, they are often able to use more precise measures of cognitive ability, such as processing speed and memory recall, than proponents of Piaget's approach. Still, the very precision of these individual measures makes it harder to get an overall sense of the nature of cognitive development, something at which Piaget was a master. It's as if information-processing approaches focus more on the individual pieces of the puzzle of cognitive development, while Piagetian approaches focus more on the whole puzzle (Kagan, 2008; Quinn, 2008; Minagawa-Kawai et al., 2011).

Ultimately, both Piagetian and information-processing approaches are critical in providing an account of cognitive development in infancy. Coupled with advances in the biochemistry of the brain and theories that consider the effects of social factors on learning and cognition (which we'll discuss in the next chapter), we can begin to paint a full picture of cognitive development.

# The Roots of Language

*Vicki and Dominic were engaged in a friendly competition over whose name would be the first word their baby, Maura, said. "Say 'Mama,'" Vicki would coo, before handing Maura over to Dominic for a diaper change. Grinning, he would take her and coax, "No, say 'Daddy.'" Both parents ended up losing—and winning—when Maura's first word sounded more like "baba," and seemed to refer to her bottle.*

Maura's initial words are just the first and most obvious manifestations of language. Many months earlier, infants begin to understand the language used by others to make sense of the world around them. How does this linguistic ability develop? What is the pattern and sequence of language development? And how does the use of language transform the cognitive world of infants and their parents? We consider these questions, and others, as we address the development of language during the first years of life.

## The Fundamentals of Language: From Sounds to Symbols

**LO 6.8**  **Explain the processes that underlie children's growth in language development.**

**Language**, the systematic, meaningful arrangement of symbols, provides the basis for communication. But it does more than this: It is closely tied to the way we think about and understand the world. It enables us to reflect on people and objects and to convey our thoughts to others.

Language has several formal characteristics that must be mastered as linguistic competence is developed. They include:

- *Phonology.* Phonology refers to the basic sounds of language, called phonemes, that can be combined to produce words and sentences. For instance, the "a" in "mat" and the "a" in "mate" represent two different phonemes in English. Although English employs just 40 phonemes to create every word in the language, other languages have as many as 85 phonemes—and some as few as 15 (Akmajian, Demers, & Harnish, 1984).

- *Morphemes.* A morpheme is the smallest language unit that has meaning. Some morphemes are complete words, while others add information

necessary for interpreting a word, such as the endings -*s* for plural and -*ed* for past tense.

- *Semantics.* Semantics are the rules that govern the meaning of words and sentences. As their knowledge of semantics develops, children are able to understand the subtle distinction between "Ellie was hit by a ball" (an answer to the question of why Ellie doesn't want to play catch) and "A ball hit Ellie" (used to announce the current situation).

In considering the development of language, we need to distinguish between linguistic *comprehension*, the understanding of speech, and linguistic *production*, the use of language to communicate. One principle underlies the relationship between the two: Comprehension precedes production. An 18-month-old may be able to understand a complex series of directions ("Pick up your coat from the floor, and put it on the chair by the fireplace") but may not yet have strung more than two words together when speaking for herself. Throughout infancy, comprehension also outpaces production. For instance, during infancy, comprehension of words expands at a rate of 22 new words a month, whereas production of words increases at a rate of about nine new words a month, once talking begins (Tincoff & Jusczyk, 1999; Shafto et al., 2012; Swingley et al., 2017; see Figure 6.4).

**EARLY SOUNDS AND COMMUNICATION.**  Spend 24 hours with even a very young infant, and you will hear a variety of sounds: cooing, crying, gurgling, murmuring, and assorted types of other noises. These sounds, although not meaningful in themselves, play an important role in linguistic development, paving the way for true language (O'Grady & Aitchison, 2005; Martin, Onishi, & Vouloumanos, 2012).

*Prelinguistic communication* is communication through sounds, facial expressions, gestures, imitation, and other nonlinguistic means. When a father responds to his daughter's "ah" with an "ah" of his own, and then the daughter repeats the sound, and the father responds once again, they are engaged in prelinguistic communication. Clearly, the "ah" sound has no particular meaning. Its repetition, however, which mimics the give-and-take of conversation, teaches the infant something about turn taking and the back-and-forth of communication (Reddy, 1999).

---

**language** The systematic, meaningful arrangement of symbols, which provides the basis for communication

**Figure 6.4** Comprehension Precedes Production

Throughout infancy, the comprehension of speech precedes the production of speech.

**SOURCE:** Adapted from Bornstein & Lamb. (1992). Development in Infancy: An Introduction, McGraw-Hill.

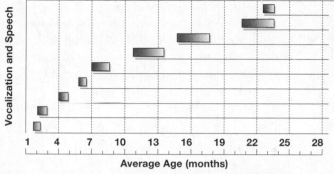

Uses first pronoun, phrase, sentence
Uses two words in combination
Says five words or more
Says first word
Two syllables with repetition of first: "ma-ma," "da-da"
Clear vocalization of several syllables
Babbling
Cooing
One syllable

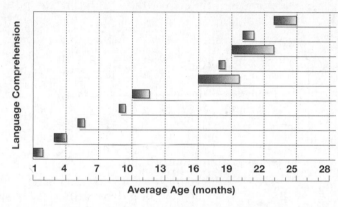

Understands two prepositions: "in," "under"
Repeats things said
Names a picture in a book: "dog"
Understands a simple question
Understands a prohibition
Responds to simple commands
Understands gestures and responds to "bye-bye"
Discriminates between friendly and angry talking
Vocalizes to social stimulation
Responds and attends to speaking voice

The most obvious manifestation of prelinguistic communication is babbling. **Babbling**, making speech-like but meaningless sounds, starts at the age of 2 or 3 months and continues until around the age of 1 year. When they babble, infants repeat the same vowel sound over and over, changing the pitch from high to low (as in "ee-ee-ee," repeated at different pitches).

Although we tend to think of language in terms of the production of words and then groups of words, infants can begin to communicate linguistically well before they say their first word.

After the age of 5 months, the sounds of babbling begin to expand, reflecting the addition of consonants (such as "bee-bee-bee-bee").

Babbling is a universal phenomenon, accomplished in the same way throughout all cultures. While they are babbling, infants spontaneously produce all of the sounds found in every language, not just the language they hear people around them speaking.

Even deaf children display their own form of babbling. Infants who cannot hear and who are exposed to sign language babble with their hands instead of their voices, and their gestural babbling is analogous to the verbal babbling of children who can speak. Furthermore, as shown in Figure 6.5, the areas of the brain activated during the production of hand gestures are similar to the areas activated during speech production, suggesting that spoken language may have evolved from gestural language (Senghas et al., 2004; Gentilucci & Corballis, 2006; Caselli et al., 2012).

**babbling** Making speechlike but meaningless sounds

**Figure 6.5** Broca's Area

Areas of the brain known as Broca's area that are activated during speech, left, are similar to the same areas activated during the production of hand gestures, right.

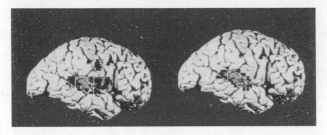

Babbling typically follows a progression from simple to more complex sounds. Although exposure to the sounds of a particular language does not seem to influence babbling initially, eventually experience does make a difference. By the age of 6 months, babbling reflects the sounds of the language to which infants are exposed (Blake & de Boysson-Bardies, 1992). The difference is so noticeable that even untrained listeners can distinguish among babbling infants raised in cultures in which French, Arabic, or Cantonese languages are spoken. Furthermore, the speed at which infants begin homing in on their own language is related to the speed of later language development (Whalen, Levitt, & Goldstein, 2007; DePaolis, Vihman, & Nakai, 2013; Masapollo, Polka, & Ménard, 2015).

There are other indications of prelinguistic speech. For instance, consider 5-month-old Marta, who spies her red ball just beyond her reach. After reaching for it and finding that she is unable to get to it, she makes a cry of anger that alerts her parents that something is amiss, and her mother hands it to her. Communication has occurred.

Four months later, when Marta faces the same situation, she no longer bothers to reach for the ball and doesn't respond in anger. Instead, she holds out her arm in the direction of the ball. With great purpose, she seeks to catch her mother's eye. When her mother sees this behavior, she knows just what Marta wants. Clearly, Marta's communicative skills—though still prelinguistic—have taken a leap forward.

Even these prelinguistic skills are supplanted in just a few months, when the gesture gives way to a new communicative skill: producing an actual word. Marta's parents clearly hear her say "ball."

**FIRST WORDS.** When a mother and father first hear their child say "Mama" or "Dada," or even "baba," (the first word of Maura, the baby described earlier in this section), it is hard not to be delighted. But their initial enthusiasm may be dampened a bit when they find that the same sound is used to ask for a cookie, a doll, and a ratty old blanket.

First words generally are spoken somewhere around the age of 10 to 14 months, but may occur as early as 9 months. Linguists differ on just how to recognize that a first word has actually been uttered. Some say it is when an infant clearly understands words and can produce a sound that is close to a word spoken by adults, such as a child who uses "mama" for any request she may have. Other linguists use a stricter criterion for the first word; they restrict "first word" to cases in which children give a clear, consistent name to a person, event, or object. In this view, "mama" counts as a first word only if it is consistently applied to the same person, seen in a variety of situations and doing a variety of things, and is not used to label other people (Hollich et al., 2000; Masataka, 2003; Koenig & Cole, 2013).

Although there is disagreement over when we can say a first word has been uttered, no one disputes that once an infant starts to produce words, vocabulary increases at a rapid rate. By the age of 15 months, the average child has a vocabulary of 10 words and methodically expands until the one-word stage of language development ends at around 18 months of age. Once that happens, a sudden spurt in vocabulary occurs. In just a short period—a few weeks somewhere between 16 and 24 months of age—there is an explosion of language, in which a child's vocabulary typically increases from 50 to 400 words (Nazzi & Bertoncini, 2003; McMurray, Aslin, & Toscano, 2009; Dehaene-Lambertz, 2017).

The first words in children's early vocabularies typically regard objects and things, both animate and inanimate. Most often they refer to people or objects who constantly appear and disappear ("Mama"), to animals ("kitty"), or to temporary states ("wet"). These first words are often **holophrases**, one-word utterances that stand for a whole phrase, whose meaning depends on the particular context in which they are used. For instance, a youngster may use the phrase "ma" to mean, depending on the context, "I want to be picked up by Mom" or "I want something to eat, Mom" or "Where's Mom?" (Dromi, 1987; O'Grady & Aitchison, 2005).

---

**holophrases** One-word utterances that stand for a whole phrase, whose meaning depends on the particular context in which they are used

Culture has an effect on the type of first words spoken. For example, unlike North American English-speaking infants, who are more apt to use nouns initially, Chinese Mandarin-speaking infants use more verbs than nouns. However, by the age of 20 months, there are remarkable cross-cultural similarities in the types of words spoken. For instance, a comparison of 20-month-olds in Argentina, Belgium, France, Israel, Italy, and the Republic of Korea found that children's vocabularies in every culture contained greater proportions of nouns than other classes of words (Tardif, 1996; Bornstein, Cote, & Maital, 2004).

**FIRST SENTENCES.**   When Aaron was 19 months old, he heard his mother coming up the back steps, as she did every day just before dinner. Aaron turned to his father and distinctly said, "Ma come." In stringing those two words together, Aaron took a giant step in his language development.

The explosive increase in vocabulary that comes at around 18 months is accompanied by another accomplishment: the linking together of individual words into sentences that convey a single thought. Although there is a good deal of variability in the time at which children first create two-word phrases, it is generally around 8 to 12 months after they say their first word.

The linguistic advance represented by two-word combinations is important because the linkage not only provides labels for things in the world but also indicates the relations between them. For instance, the combination may declare something about possession ("Mama key") or recurrent events ("Dog bark"). Interestingly, most early sentences don't represent demands or even necessarily require a response. Instead, they are often merely comments and observations about events occurring in the child's world (O'Grady & Aichison, 2005; Rossi et al., 2012).

Two-year-olds using two-word combinations tend to employ particular sequences that are similar to the ways in which adult sentences are constructed. For example, sentences in English typically follow a pattern in which the subject of the sentence comes first, followed by the verb, and then the object ("Josh threw the ball"). Children's speech most often uses a similar order, although not all the words are initially included. Consequently, a child might say "Josh threw" or "Josh ball" to indicate the same thought. What is significant is that the order is typically not "threw Josh" or "ball Josh," but rather the usual order of English, which

By age 2, most children use two-word phrases, such as "ball play."

makes the utterance much easier for an English speaker to comprehend (Hirsh-Pasek & Michnick-Golinkoff, 1995; Masataka, 2003).

Although the creation of two-word sentences represents an advance, the language used by children still is by no means adultlike. As we've just seen, 2-year-olds tend to leave out words that aren't critical to the message, similar to the way we might write a telegram for which we were paying by the word. For that reason, their talk is often called **telegraphic speech**. Rather than saying, "I showed you the book," a child using telegraphic speech might say, "I show book." "I am drawing a dog" might become "drawing dog".

Early language has other characteristics that differentiate it from the language used by adults. For instance, consider Sarah, who refers to the blanket she sleeps with as "blankie." When her Aunt Ethel gives her a new blanket, Sarah refuses to call the new one a "blankie," restricting the word to her original blanket.

Sarah's inability to generalize the label of "blankie" to blankets in general is an example of **underextension**, using words too restrictively, which is common among children just mastering spoken language. Underextension occurs when language novices think that a word refers to a specific instance of a concept, instead of to all examples of the concept (Caplan & Barr, 1989; Masataka, 2003).

---

**telegraphic speech**  Speech in which words not critical to the message are left out

**underextension**  The overly restrictive use of words, common among children just mastering spoken language

As infants like Sarah grow more adept with language, the opposite phenomenon sometimes occurs. In **overextension**, words are used too broadly, overgeneralizing their meaning. For example, when Sarah refers to buses, trucks, and tractors as "cars," she is guilty of overextension, making the assumption that any object with wheels must be a car. Although overextension reflects speech errors, it also shows that advances are occurring in the child's thought processes: The child is beginning to develop general mental categories and concepts (McDonough, 2002).

Infants also show individual differences in the style of language they use. For example, some use a **referential style**, in which language is used primarily to label objects. Others tend to use an **expressive style**, in which language is used mainly to express feelings and needs about oneself and others (Bates et al., 1994; Nelson, 1996; Bornstein, 2000).

Language styles reflect, in part, cultural factors. For example, mothers in the United States label objects more frequently than Japanese mothers, encouraging a more referential style of speech. In contrast, mothers in Japan are more apt to speak about social interactions, encouraging a more expressive style of speech (Fernald & Morikawa, 1993).

# The Origins of Language Development

**LO 6.9   Differentiate the various theories of language development.**

The immense strides in language development during the preschool years raise a fundamental question: How does proficiency in language first come about? Linguists are deeply divided on how to answer this question.

**LEARNING THEORY APPROACHES: LANGUAGE AS A LEARNED SKILL.**   One view of language development emphasizes the basic principles of learning. According to the **learning theory approach**, language acquisition follows the basic laws of reinforcement and conditioning discussed in Chapter 1 (Skinner, 1957). For instance, a child who articulates the sound "da" may be hugged and praised by her father, who jumps to the conclusion that she is referring to him. This reaction reinforces the child, who is more likely to repeat the sound, and eventually she will come to utter the word "Daddy," and be reinforced for that. Ultimately,

more and more words are uttered and reinforced, building up her vocabulary.

In sum, the learning theory perspective on language acquisition suggests that children learn to speak by being rewarded for making sounds that approximate speech. Through the process of *shaping*, language becomes more and more similar to adult speech.

There's a problem, though, with the learning theory approach. It doesn't seem to adequately explain how children acquire the rules of language as readily as they do. For instance, young children are reinforced when they make errors. Parents are apt to be just as responsive if their child says, "Why the dog won't eat?" as they are if the child phrases the question more correctly ("Why won't the dog eat?"). Both forms of the question are understood correctly, and both elicit the same response; reinforcement is provided for both correct and incorrect language usage. Under such circumstances, learning theory is hard put to explain how children learn to speak properly.

Children are also able to move beyond specific utterances they have heard, and produce novel phrases, sentences, and constructions, an ability that also cannot be explained by learning theory. Furthermore, children can apply linguistic rules to nonsense words. In one study, 4-year-old children heard the nonsense verb "to pilk" in the sentence "the bear is pilking the horse." Later, when asked what was happening to the horse, they responded by placing the nonsense verb in the correct tense and voice: "He's getting pilked by the bear."

**NATIVIST APPROACHES: LANGUAGE AS AN INNATE SKILL.**   Such conceptual difficulties with the learning theory approach have led to the development of an alternative, championed by the linguist Noam Chomsky (1999, 2005) and known as the nativist

---

**overextension**   The overly broad use of words, overgeneralizing their meaning

**referential style**   A style of language use in which language is used primarily to label objects

**expressive style**   A style of language use in which language is used primarily to express feelings and needs about oneself and others

**learning theory approach**   The theory that language acquisition follows the basic laws of reinforcement and conditioning

approach. The **nativist approach** argues that there is a genetically determined, innate mechanism that directs the development of language. According to Chomsky, people are born with an innate capacity to use language, which emerges, more or less automatically, due to maturation.

Chomsky's analysis of different languages suggests that all the world's languages share a similar underlying structure, which he calls **universal grammar**. In this view, the human brain is wired with a neural system called the **language-acquisition device (LAD)** that both permits the understanding of language structure and provides a set of strategies and techniques for learning the particular characteristics of the language to which a child is exposed. In this view, language is uniquely human, made possible by a genetic predisposition to both comprehend and produce words and sentences (Stromswold, 2006; Wonnacott, 2013; Yang et al., 2017).

Support for Chomsky's nativist approach comes from identification of a specific gene related to speech production. Further support comes from research showing that language processing in infants involves brain structures similar to those in adult speech processing, suggesting an evolutionary basis to language (Wade, 2001; Dehaene-Lambertz, Hertz-Pannier, & Dubois, 2006).

The view that language is an innate ability unique to humans also has its critics. For instance, some researchers argue that certain primates are able to learn at least the basics of language, an ability that calls into question the uniqueness of the human linguistic capacity. Others point out that although humans may be genetically primed to use language, they still require significant social experience in order for it to be used effectively (Savage-Rumbaugh et al., 1993; Goldberg, 2004).

**THE INTERACTIONIST APPROACHES.** Neither the learning theory nor the nativist perspective fully explains language acquisition. As a result, some theorists have turned to a theory that combines both schools of thought. The *interactionist perspective* suggests that language development is produced through a combination of genetically determined predispositions and environmental circumstances that help teach language.

The interactionist perspective accepts that innate factors shape the broad outlines of language development. Interactionists also argue that the specific course of language development is determined by the language to which children are exposed and the reinforcement they receive for using language in particular ways. Social factors are considered to be key to development, because the motivation provided by one's membership in a society and culture and one's interactions with others leads to the use of language and the growth of language skills (Dixon, 2004; Yang, 2006).

Just as there is support for some aspects of learning theory and nativist positions, the interactionist perspective has also received some support. We don't know, at the moment, which of these positions will ultimately provide the best explanation. More likely, different factors play different roles at different times during childhood. The full explanation for language acquisition remains to be found.

## Speaking to Children: The Language of Infant-Directed Speech

**LO 6.10  Describe how children influence adults' language.**

Say the following words aloud: Do you like the applesauce?

Now pretend that you are going to ask the same question to an infant, and speak it as you would for a young child's ears.

Chances are, several things happened when you translated the phrase for the infant. First of all, the wording probably changed, and you may have said something like, "Does baby like the applesauce?" At the same time, the pitch of your voice probably rose, your general intonation most likely had a singsong quality, and you probably separated your words carefully.

The shift in your language was due to your use of **infant-directed speech**, a style of speech that

---

**nativist approach** The theory that a genetically determined, innate mechanism directs language development

**universal grammar** Noam Chomsky's theory that all the world's languages share a similar underlying structure

**language-acquisition device (LAD)** A neural system of the brain hypothesized to permit understanding of language

**infant-directed speech** A type of speech directed toward infants, characterized by short, simple sentences

characterizes much of the verbal communication directed toward infants. This type of speech pattern used to be called *motherese*, because it was assumed that it applied only to mothers. That assumption was wrong, however, and the gender-neutral term *infant-directed speech* is now used more frequently.

Infant-directed speech is characterized by short, simple sentences. Pitch becomes higher, the range of frequencies increases, and intonation is more varied. There is also repetition of words, and topics are restricted to items that are assumed to be comprehensible to infants, such as concrete objects in the baby's environment. Infants are not the only ones who are the recipients of a specific form of speech: We change our style of speech when speaking to foreigners, as well (Soderstrom, 2007; Schachner & Hannon, 2011; Scott & Henderson, 2013).

Sometimes infant-directed speech includes amusing sounds that are not even words, imitating the prelinguistic speech of infants. In other cases, it has little formal structure, but is similar to the kind of telegraphic speech that infants use as they develop their own language skills.

Infant-directed speech changes as children become older. Around the end of the first year, infant-directed speech takes on more adultlike qualities. Sentences become longer and more complex, although individual words are still spoken slowly and deliberately. Pitch is also used to focus attention on particularly important words (Soderstrom et al., 2008; Kitamura & Lam, 2009).

Infant-directed speech plays an important role in infants' acquisition of language. As discussed next,

Infant-directed speech, also known as *motherese*, includes the use of short, simple sentences and is spoken using a pitch higher than that used with older children and adults.

infant-directed speech occurs all over the world, though there are cultural variations. Newborns prefer such speech to regular language, a fact that suggests that they may be particularly receptive to it. Furthermore, some research suggests that babies who are exposed to a great deal of infant-directed speech early in life seem to begin to use words and exhibit other forms of linguistic competence earlier (Matsuda et al., 2011; Bergelson & Swingley, 2012; Eaves et al., 2016).

> **From an educator's perspective:** What are some implications of differences in the ways adults speak to boys and girls? How might such speech differences contribute to later differences not only in speech, but also in attitudes?

# DEVELOPMENTAL DIVERSITY AND YOUR LIFE

## Is Infant-Directed Speech Similar in All Cultures?

Do mothers in the United States, Sweden, and Russia speak the same way to their infants?

In some respects, they clearly do. Although the words themselves differ across languages, the way the words are spoken to infants is quite similar. According to a growing body of research, there are basic similarities across cultures in the nature of infant-directed speech (Rabain-Jamin & Sabeau-Jouannet, 1997; Werker et al., 2007; Schachner & Hannon, 2011; Broesch & Bryant, 2015).

Consider, for instance, the comparison in Table 6.4 of the major characteristics of speech directed at infants used by native speakers of English and Spanish. Of the 10 most frequent features, six are common to both: exaggerated intonation, high pitch, lengthened vowels, repetition, lower volume, and instructional emphasis (i.e., heavy stress on certain key words such as emphasizing the word "ball" in the sentence, "No, that's a *ball*") (Blount, 1982). Similarly, mothers in the United States, Sweden, and Russia all exaggerate

## Table 6.4 The Most Common Features of Infant-Directed Speech

| English | Spanish |
|---|---|
| 1. Exaggerated intonation | 1. Exaggerated intonation |
| 2. Breathiness | 2. Repetition |
| 3. High pitch | 3. High pitch |
| 4. Repetition | 4. Instructional |
| 5. Lowered volume | 5. Attentionals |
| 6. Lengthened vowel | 6. Lowered volume |
| 7. Creaky voice | 7. Raised volume |
| 8. Instructional | 8. Lengthened vowel |
| 9. Tenseness | 9. Fast tempo |
| 10. Falsetto | 10. Personal pronoun substitution |

**SOURCE:** B.G. Blount, "Culture and the Language of Socialization: Parental Speech" in D.A. Wagner & W. W. Stevenson eds., Cultural Perspectives on Child Development. San Francisco: Freeman and Co.

and elongate the pronunciation of the three vowel sounds "ee," "ah," and "oh" when speaking to infants in similar ways, despite differences in the languages in which the sounds are used (Kuhl et al., 1997).

Even deaf mothers use a form of infant-directed speech. When communicating with their infants, deaf mothers use sign language at a significantly slower tempo than when communicating with adults, and they frequently repeat the signs (Swanson, Leonard, & Gandour, 1992; Masataka, 1996, 1998, 2000).

The cross-cultural similarities in infant-directed speech are so great, in fact, that they appear in some facets of language specific to particular types of interactions. For instance, evidence comparing American English, German, and Mandarin Chinese speakers shows that in each of the languages, pitch rises when a mother is attempting to get an infant's attention or produce a response, while pitch falls when she is trying to calm an infant (Papousek & Papousek, 1991).

Why do we find such similarities across very different languages? One hypothesis is that the characteristics of infant-directed speech activate innate responses in infants. As we have noted, infants seem to prefer infant-directed speech over adult-directed speech, suggesting that their perceptual systems may be more responsive to such characteristics. Another explanation is that infant-directed speech facilitates language development, providing cues as to the meaning of speech before infants have developed the capacity to understand the meaning of words (Trainor & Desjardins, 2002; Falk, 2004; Hayashi & Mazuka, 2017).

While talking about objects, a synchrony is observed in naming the object while pointing at the object. Mothers abundantly used verbal labels simultaneously with gestures to show novel objects or to demonstrate novel actions. The research by Gogate, Maganti, and Bharick (2015) evidenced cross cultural similarities in the use of multimodal motherese. Indian mothers, just like American mothers (in Gogate et al., 2000), spontaneously used synchrony between naming and 'showing' an object or action to their child more often when they named target referents (using words they were asked to teach, 56 percent) than non-target ones (using other words, 37 percent). Similarly, mothers used trimodally (auditory, visual, and tactile) synchronous naming more often for target referents (14 percent) than for non-target referents (5 percent).

Despite the similarities in the style of infant-directed speech across diverse cultures, evidences suggest significant differences in caregivers' communication in prosody: their gestures, vocal emotion, and speech (Bornstein, Thal, Rahn, Galperin, et al., 1992; Tamis-LeMonda, et al., 2012; Masataka, 1992). As reported by Scheiffelin (1979) and Watson-Gegeo & Gegeo (1986), mothers from the tribal communities of Kaluli of New Guinea and the Kwara'ae of the Solomon Islands do not directly speak or engage in face-to-face play with their infant. Instead, they use a high-pitched voice to address a third person on behalf of their infant, with the infant turned toward and facing the third person.

There are some important cultural differences in the *quantity* of speech that infants hear from their parents. For example, although the Gusii tribe of Kenya care for their infants in an extremely close, physical way, they speak to them less than American parents do (LeVine, 1994).

There are also some stylistic differences related to cultural factors in the United States. A major factor, it seems, might be gender. To a girl, a bird is a "birdie," a blanket a "blankie," and a dog a "doggy." To a boy, a bird is a "bird," a blanket a "blanket," and a dog a "dog."

At least that's what parents of boys and girls appear to think, as illustrated by the language they use toward their sons and daughters. Virtually from the time of birth, the language parents employ with their children differ depending on the child's sex, according to research conducted by developmental psychologist Jean Berko Gleason (Gleason et al., 1994; Gleason & Ely, 2002; Arnon & Ramscar, 2012).

Research has also shown how cross-cultural variations in caregivers' communication resulted in corresponding variations in infants' language comprehension. For example, Indian mothers used directives predominantly containing verbs such as 'give' or 'take' more often than British mothers to their 6.5- to 12.5-month-olds, suggesting verb dominance. Reciprocally, Indian infants complied with their mothers' directives more often than British infants did and, at an earlier age, showed greater verb comprehension (Reddy, Liebal, Hicks, & Jonnalgadda, et al., 2013).

It was interesting to note in the research by Gogate, Maganti, and Bharick (2015) that monolingual and bilingual mothers in India spoke differently to their infants. It was found that the monolingual mothers spoke a verb-dominant Indian language, whereas bilingual mothers spoke a noun-dominant English. Monolingual mothers named objects and actions in synchrony with an object's motion far more often than bilingual mothers. Thus, mothers tailored their use of multimodal motherese to the language(s)-specific lexical-dominance hierarchy and the degree of difficulty a lexical category might pose to their child. The authors concluded a dynamic and interactive mother-infant communicative system.

Infant-directed speech plays an important role in infants' acquisition of language. As discussed later in the text, infant-directed speech occurs all over the world, though there are cultural variations. Newborns prefer such speech to regular language, which might be indicative of the fact that they may be particularly receptive to it. Furthermore, some research suggests that babies who are exposed to a great deal of infant-directed speech early in life seem to begin to use words and exhibit other forms of linguistic competence earlier (Matsuda et al., 2011; Bergelson & Swingley, 2012; and Eaves et al., 2016).

# BECOMING AN INFORMED CONSUMER OF CHILD DEVELOPMENT

## What Can You Do to Promote Infants' Cognitive Development?

All parents want their children to reach their full cognitive potential, but sometimes efforts to reach this goal take a bizarre path. For instance, some parents spend hundreds of dollars enrolling in workshops with titles such as "How to Multiply Your Baby's Intelligence" and buying books with titles such as *How to Teach Your Baby to Read* (Doman & Doman, 2002).

Do such efforts ever succeed? Although some parents swear they do, there is no scientific support for the effectiveness of such programs. For example, despite the many cognitive skills of infants, no infant can actually read. Furthermore, "multiplying" a baby's intelligence is impossible, and such organizations as the American Academy of Pediatrics and the American Academy of Neurology have denounced programs that claim to do so.

However, certain things can be done to promote cognitive development in infants. The following suggestions, based upon findings of developmental researchers, offer a starting point (Gopnik, Meltzoff, & Kuhl, 2002; Cabrera, Shannon, & Tamis-LeMonda, 2007):

- *Provide infants the opportunity to explore the world.* As Piaget suggests, children learn by doing, and they need the opportunity to explore and probe their environment.
- *Be responsive to infants on both a verbal and a nonverbal level.* Try to speak *with* babies, as opposed

One important way to encourage cognitive development in infants is to read to them.

to them. Ask questions, listen to their responses, and provide further communication (Merlo, Bowman, & Barnett, 2007; Weisleder & Fernald, 2013).
- *Read to your infants.* Although they may not understand the meaning of your words, they will respond to your tone of voice and the intimacy provided by the activity. Reading together also is associated with later literacy skills and begins to create a lifelong reading habit. The American Academy of Pediatrics recommends daily reading to children starting at birth (American Academy of Pediatrics, 1999; Holland, 2008; Robb, Richert, & Wartella, 2009).

- *Keep in mind that you don't have to be with an infant 24 hours a day.* Just as infants need time to explore their world on their own, parents and other caregivers need time off from child care activities.

- *Don't push infants, and don't expect too much too soon.* Your goal should not be to create a genius; it should be to provide a warm, nurturing environment that will allow an infant to reach his or her potential.

# The Case of …
## The Unidentified "Miku"

Lata still remembers the day when her son, Jay, touched her arm and said, "Maa." Jay was 10 months old, and "Maa" was his first word. In the next few months, his vocabulary expanded to include doggy, dada, truck, and biku. Lata knew that "biku" meant biscuits, Jay's favorite snack. What stumped her was her son's latest word: Miku. Lata looked around every time her son said the word but she could find nothing in the kitchen or bedroom or the backyard that suggested what a "miku" might be. Jay persisted in using the word, however. When Lata repeated the word, her son smiled. "Miku," he would respond, as if confirming their mutual understanding. Lata remained baffled. It wasn't until 6 weeks later that the mystery was solved. Lata took her son to the shopping mall and her son suddenly pointed out at the pet shop. "Miku!," he cried. Lata took Jay inside the store and he was happily repeating "Miku, Miku." Lata was able to see what had caught Jay's attention: the pet shop. It was a place she had often taken her son, and the boy loved to watch the animals and birds there.

Jay continued to refer to the petshop as "Miku" until he was nearly 2 years old. In fact, Lata recalls, his first two-word sentence was "Go Miku." Lata understood that her son was asking for a trip to their favorite place.

1. How is the list of Jay's first words, including "Miku," typical of children's early vocabularies?
2. Do you consider Jay's initial use of Miku to be a holophrase? Why or why not? What distinguishes a holophrase from telegraphic speech?
3. How does Jay's first two-word sentence, "Go Miku," demonstrate an understanding of the basic conventions of his native language? How does the nativist approach to language development explain such an understanding?
4. Do you think infants ever utter nonsense words, or does each word have a concrete meaning to the baby? Explain your response in terms of what we know about infant language acquisition.
5. How can a parent influence an infant's language development? In what ways is the parent's influence limited?

# Epilogue

In this chapter, we studied infants' cognitive development from perspectives ranging from Piaget to information-processing theory. We examined infant learning, memory, and intelligence, and we concluded the chapter with a look at language.

Before we proceed to social and personality development in the next chapter, turn back to the prologue about Raisa Novak, the infant who has just learned to crawl, and answer the following questions.

1. Is Raisa's experience with the radio an example of assimilation or accommodation, according to Piaget? Explain your reasoning.
2. Piaget believed that advances in motor capability signal the potential for cognitive advances. How does the story of Raisa support his theory?
3. If Raisa and her family left home for a month, do you think Raisa would still remember how to turn on the radio? What prompts might reactivate her memory?
4. How would you expect walking independently to further enhance Raisa's cognitive development?

# Looking Back

**LO 6.1  Describe the fundamental features of Piaget's theory of cognitive development.**

- Piaget's theory asserts that children pass through stages of cognitive development in a fixed order, representing changes not only in quantity of infants' knowledge but also in the quality of that knowledge.

- According to Piaget, all children pass gradually through the four major stages of cognitive development (sensorimotor, preoperational, concrete operational, and formal operational) and their various substages when they are at an appropriate level of maturation and are exposed to relevant types of experiences.

**LO 6.2  Summarize the advances in cognitive development that occur during the sensorimotor stage.**

- Piaget divided the sensorimotor period (birth to about 2 years) into six substages. In the first three substages, infants progress from the use of simple reflexes to being able to act upon the outside world, repeating actions to bring about a desirable response or outcome.

- In the later substages, infants begin to use more calculated approaches to acting on the outside world, coordinating multiple schemas to generate a single act. They become capable of carrying out miniature experiments to see what happens.

- By the end of the fourth substage of the sensorimotor period, infants achieve object permanence; by the end of the sixth substage, they are beginning to engage in symbolic thought.

**LO 6.3  Compare Piaget's theory with later research.**

- Piaget was a masterful reporter of children's behavior, and his descriptions of growth during infancy remain a monument to his powers of observation.

- Subsequent research, however, has challenged the stage conception that forms the basis of Piaget's theory, because it appears that development proceeds in a much more continuous fashion.

**LO 6.4  Explain how infants process information.**

- Information-processing approaches to the study of cognitive development seek to learn how individuals receive, organize, store, and retrieve information.

- Information-processing approaches differ from Piaget's approach by considering quantitative changes in children's abilities to process information.

**LO 6.5  Describe infants' memory capabilities and the duration of memories.**

- Infants have memory capabilities from their earliest days, although the accuracy of infant memories is a matter of debate.

- Although it is at least theoretically possible for memories to remain intact from a very young age—if subsequent experiences do not interfere with their recollection—in most cases memories of personal experiences in infancy do not last into adulthood.

- Current findings suggest that memories of personal experience seem not to become accurate before age 18 to 24 months.

**LO 6.6  Summarize what is known about the neurological basis of memory in children.**

- *Explicit memory* is memory that is conscious and that can be recalled intentionally.

- In comparison, *implicit memory* consists of memories of which we are not consciously aware but that affect performance and behavior.

**LO 6.7  Explain intelligence among infants and how it is measured.**

- Traditional measures of infant intelligence, such as Gesell's developmental quotient and the Bayley Scales of Infant Development, focus on average behavior observed at particular ages in large numbers of children.

- Although traditional measures of infant intelligence are useful in comparing the developmental progress of an infant in relation to her peers, they have little or no ability to predict future development.

- Information-processing approaches to assessing intelligence rely on variations in the speed and quality with which infants process information.

- The information-processing approach suggests that there is continuity in cognitive development from infancy to the later stages of life. But other factors, such as environmental stimulation, are also critical in determining adult intelligence.

**LO 6.8** **Explain the processes that underlie children's growth in language development.**

- Prelinguistic communication involves the use of sounds, gestures, facial expressions, imitation, and other nonlinguistic means to express thoughts and states.

- Infants typically produce their first words between the ages of 10 and 14 months. At around 18 months, children typically begin to link words together into primitive sentences that express single thoughts.

- Beginning speech is characterized by the use of holophrases, telegraphic speech, underextension, and overextension.

**LO 6.9** **Differentiate the various theories of language development.**

- The learning theory approach to language acquisition assumes that adults and children use basic behavioral processes—such as conditioning, reinforcement, and shaping—in language learning.

- In contrast, the nativist approach proposed by Noam Chomsky holds that humans are genetically endowed with a language-acquisition device that permits them to detect and use the principles of universal grammar that underlie all languages.

- The interactionist perspective suggests that language develops through a combination of genetically determined and environmental factors.

**LO 6.10** **Describe how children influence adults' language.**

- Adult language is influenced by the children to whom it is addressed. Infant-directed speech takes on characteristics, surprisingly invariant across cultures, that make it appealing to infants and probably encourages language development.

- Adult language also exhibits differences based on the gender of the child to whom it is directed, which may have effects that emerge later in life.

# Key Terms and Concepts

schema (p. 143)
assimilation (p. 144)
accommodation (p. 144)
sensorimotor stage (p. 144)
goal-directed behavior (p. 146)
object permanence (p. 146)
mental representation (p. 147)
deferred imitation (p. 147)
information-processing
    approaches (p. 150)

memory (p. 152)
infantile amnesia (p. 152)
developmental quotient
    (p. 155)
Bayley Scales of Infant
    Development (p. 156)
language (p. 158)
babbling (p. 159)
holophrases (p. 160)
telegraphic speech (p. 161)

underextension (p. 161)
overextension (p. 162)
referential style (p. 162)
expressive style (p. 162)
learning theory approach (p. 162)
nativist approach (p. 163)
universal grammar (p. 163)
language-acquisition device
    (LAD) (p. 163)
infant-directed speech (p. 163)

# Chapter 7
# Social and Personality Development in Infancy

 ## Learning Objectives

**LO 7.1** Describe the way infants experience and decode emotions.

**LO 7.2** Explain how infants develop a sense of who they are.

**LO 7.3** Provide examples of how infants use others' emotions to interpret social situations.

**LO 7.4** Describe the mental lives of infants.

**LO 7.5** Explain the causes of stranger and separation anxiety in infants.

**LO 7.6** Define attachment in infancy.

**LO 7.7** Summarize how attachment affects an individual's future social competence.

**LO 7.8** Explain the roles of mothers and fathers in an infant's development of attachment.

**LO 7.9** Compare the roles other people play in infants' social development.

**LO 7.10** Explain how infants develop unique personalities.

**LO 7.11** Define temperament in infants and explain its origins.

**LO 7.12** Explain the causes and consequences of gender differentiation.

**LO 7.13** Describe how the definition of "family" has changed in recent years.

**LO 7.14** Describe the impact of nonparental child care on infants.

## Prologue: Emotional Rollercoaster

Chantelle Evans has always been a happy baby. That's why her mother, Michelle, was so surprised to find her 10-month-old daughter in tears when she returned to pick her up from a neighbor after having lunch with friends. "Chantelle knows Janine," Michelle says. "She sees her regularly out in the yard. I don't understand why she was so unhappy. I was only away for 2 hours." Janine told Michelle she had tried everything—rocking Chantelle, singing to her—but nothing helped. It wasn't until Chantelle, red-faced, tears streaming, saw her mother again that the baby smiled.

## Looking Ahead

Michelle Evans will someday be able to have lunch with friends without worrying that her daughter is miserable, but Chantelle's reaction is perfectly normal for a 10-month-old baby. In this chapter, we consider social and personality development in infancy. We begin by examining the emotional lives of infants, considering which emotions they feel and how well they can read others' emotions. We also look at how others' responses shape infants' reactions, and how babies view their own and others' mental lives.

We then turn to infants' social relationships. We look at how they forge bonds of attachment and the ways they interact with family members and peers.

Finally, we cover the characteristics that set apart one infant from another and discuss differences in the way children are treated depending on their gender. We'll consider the nature of family life and discuss how it differs from earlier eras. The chapter closes with a look at the advantages and disadvantages of infant child care outside the home, a child care option that today's families increasingly employ.

# Developing the Roots of Sociability

*Germaine smiles when he catches a glimpse of his mother. Tawanda looks unhappy when her mother takes away the spoon that she is playing with. Sydney grimaces when a loud plane flies overhead.*

A smile. A look of unhappiness. A grimace. The emotions of infancy are written all over a baby's face. Yet do infants experience emotions in the same way that adults do? When do they become capable of understanding what others are experiencing emotionally? And how do they use others' emotional states to make sense of their environment? We consider some of these questions as we seek to understand how infants develop emotionally and socially.

# Emotions in Infancy

### LO 7.1 Describe the way infants experience and decode emotions.

Anyone who spends any time at all around infants knows they display facial expressions that seem indicative of their emotional states. In situations in which we expect them to be happy, they seem to smile; when we might assume they are frustrated, they show anger; and when we might expect them to be unhappy, they look sad.

These basic facial expressions are remarkably similar across the most diverse cultures. Whether we look at babies in India, the United States, or the jungles of New Guinea, the expression of basic emotions is the same (see Figure 7.1). Furthermore, the nonverbal expression of emotion, called *nonverbal encoding*, is fairly consistent among people of all ages. These consistencies have led researchers to conclude that we are born with the capacity to display basic emotions (Ackerman & Izard, 2004; Bornstein, Suwalsky, & Breakstone, 2012; Rajhans et al., 2016).

Infants demonstrate a fairly wide range of emotional expressions. According to research on what mothers see in their children's nonverbal behavior, almost all think that by the age of 1 month, their babies have expressed interest and joy. In addition, 84 percent of mothers think their infants have expressed anger, 75 percent surprise, 58 percent fear, and 34 percent sadness. Interest, distress, and disgust also are present at birth, and other emotions emerge over the next few months (see Figure 7.2; Sroufe, 1996; Benson, 2003; Graham et al., 2014).

Although infants display similar *kinds* of emotions, the *degree* of emotional expressivity varies among them in different cultures. For example, by the age of 11 months, Chinese infants are generally less expressive than European, American, and Japanese infants (Camras et al., 2007; Nakato et al., 2011; Easterbrooks et al., 2013).

Does the capability of infants to express emotions nonverbally in a consistent, reliable manner mean that they actually *experience* emotions, and—if they do—is the experience similar to that of adults?

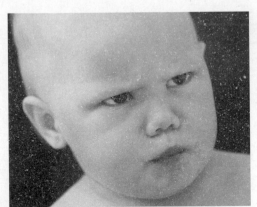

**Figure 7.1** Universals in Facial Expression

Across every culture, infants show similar facial expressions relating to basic emotions. Do you think such expressions are similar in nonhuman animals?

**Figure 7.2** Emergence of Emotional Expressions

Emotional expressions emerge at roughly these times. Keep in mind that expressions in the first few weeks after birth do not necessarily reflect particular inner feelings.

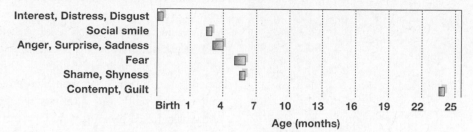

The fact that children display nonverbal expressions in a manner similar to that of adults does not necessarily mean that their actual experience is identical. In fact, if the nature of such displays is innate, or inborn, it is possible that facial expressions can occur without any accompanying awareness of an emotional experience. Nonverbal expressions, then, might be emotionless in young infants, in much the same way that your knee reflexively jerks forward when a physician taps it, without the involvement of emotions (Cole & Moore, 2015).

Most developmental researchers, however, do not think this is the case: They argue that the nonverbal expressions of infants represent actual emotional experiences. Emotional expressions may not only reflect emotional experiences, but may also help regulate the emotion itself.

It now seems clear that infants are born with an innate repertoire of emotional expressions, reflecting basic emotional states such as happiness and sadness. As infants and children grow older, they expand and modify these basic expressions and become more adept at controlling their nonverbal behavioral expressions. For example, they eventually may learn that by smiling at the right time, they can increase the chances of getting their own way. Furthermore, in addition to *expressing* a wider variety of emotions, as children develop, they also *experience* a wider array of emotions (Izard et al., 2003; Buss & Kiel, 2004; Hunnius et al., 2011).

In sum, infants do appear to experience emotions, although the range of emotions at birth is fairly restricted. As they get older, infants both display and experience a wider range of increasingly complex emotions (Buss & Kiel, 2004; Killeen & Teti, 2012; Soderstrom et al., 2017).

The advances in infants' emotional lives are made possible by the increasing sophistication of their brain. Initially, the differentiation of emotions occurs as the cerebral cortex becomes operative in the first 3 months of life. By the age of 9 or 10 months, the structures that make up the limbic system (the site of emotional reactions) begin to grow. The limbic system starts to work in tandem with the frontal lobes, allowing for an increased range of emotions (Davidson, 2003; Schore, 2003; Swain et al., 2007).

**SMILING.**    As Luz lay sleeping in her crib, her mother and father caught a glimpse of the most beautiful smile crossing her face. Her parents were sure that Luz was having a pleasant dream. Were they right?

Probably not. The earliest smiles expressed during sleep likely have little meaning, although no one can be absolutely sure. By 6 to 9 weeks, babies begin to smile reliably at the sight of stimuli that please them, including toys, mobiles, and—to the delight of parents—people. The first smiles tend to be relatively indiscriminate, as infants first begin to smile at the sight of almost anything they find amusing; however, as they get older, they become more selective in their smiles.

A baby's smile in response to another person, rather than to nonhuman stimuli, is considered a **social smile**. As babies get older, their social smiles become directed toward particular individuals, not just anyone. By the age of 18 months, social smiling, directed more toward mothers and other caregivers, becomes more frequent than smiling directed toward nonhuman objects. Moreover, if an adult is unresponsive to a child, the amount of smiling decreases. In short, by the end of the second year, children are quite purposefully using smiling to communicate their positive emotions, and they are sensitive to the emotional expressions of others (Reissland & Cohen, 2012; Wörmann et al., 2014; Planalp et al., 2016).

**social smile** Smiling in response to other individuals

When infants smile at a person rather than a nonhuman stimulus, they are displaying a social smile.

**DECODING OTHERS' FACIAL AND VOCAL EXPRESSIONS.** In Chapter 4, we discussed the possibility that neonates can imitate adults' facial expressions even minutes after birth. Although their imitative abilities certainly do not imply that they can understand the meaning of others' facial expressions, such imitation does pave the way for *nonverbal decoding* abilities, which begin to emerge fairly soon. Using these abilities, infants can interpret others' facial and vocal expressions that carry emotional meaning. For example, they can tell when a caregiver is happy to see them and pick up on worry or fear in the faces of others (Hernandez-Reif et al., 2006; Striano & Vaish, 2006; Flom & Johnson, 2011).

Infants seem to be able to discriminate vocal expressions of emotion at a slightly earlier age than they discriminate facial expressions. Although relatively little attention has been given to infants' perception of vocal expressions, it does appear that they are able to discriminate happy and sad vocal expressions at the age of 5 months (Montague & Walker-Andrews, 2002; Dahl et al., 2014).

Scientists know more about the *sequence* in which nonverbal facial decoding ability progresses. In the first 6 to 8 weeks, infants' visual precision is sufficiently limited that they cannot pay much attention to others' facial expressions. But they soon begin to discriminate among different facial expressions of emotion and even seem to be able to respond to differences in emotional intensity conveyed by facial expressions. They also respond to unusual facial expressions. For instance, they show distress when their mothers present bland, unresponsive, neutral facial expressions (Adamson & Frick, 2003; Bertin & Striano, 2006; Farroni et al., 2007).

By the time they reach the age of 4 months, infants already have begun to understand the emotions that lie behind the facial and vocal expressions of others. How do we know this? One important clue comes from a study in which 7-month-old infants were shown a pair of facial expressions relating to joy and sadness and simultaneously heard a vocalization representing either joy (a rising tone of voice) or sadness (a falling tone of voice). When the facial expression matched the tone, infants paid more attention, suggesting that they had at least a rudimentary understanding of the emotional meaning of facial expressions and voice tones (Kochanska & Aksan, 2004; Grossmann, Striano, & Friederici, 2006; Kim & Johnson, 2013).

In sum, infants learn early both to produce and to decode emotions, and they begin to learn the effect of their own emotions on others. Such abilities play an important role not only in helping them experience their own emotions, but in using others' emotions to understand the meaning of ambiguous social situations (Buss & Kiel, 2004; Messinger et al., 2012).

## The Development of Self: Do Infants Know Who They Are?

**LO 7.2 Explain how infants develop a sense of who they are.**

*Elysa, 8 months old, crawls past the full-length mirror that hangs on a door in her parents' bedroom. She barely pays any attention to her reflection as she moves by. By contrast, her cousin Brianna, who is almost 2 years old, stares at herself in the mirror as she passes and laughs as she notices, and then rubs off, a smear of jelly on her forehead.*

Perhaps you have had the experience of catching a glimpse of yourself in a mirror and noticing a hair out of place. You probably reacted by pushing the unruly hair back into place. Your response shows more than that you care about how you look. It implies that you have a sense of yourself, the awareness and knowledge that you are an independent social entity to which others react, and which you attempt to present to the world in ways that reflect favorably upon you.

We are not born with the knowledge that we exist independently from others and the larger world. Very young infants do not have a sense of themselves as individuals; they do not recognize themselves in

Research suggests that this 18-month-old is exhibiting a clearly developed sense of self.

photos or mirrors. The roots of **self-awareness**, knowledge of oneself, begin to grow at around the age of 12 months. We know this from a simple but ingenious experimental technique known as the *mirror-and-rouge technique*. An infant's nose is secretly colored with a dab of red rouge, and the infant is seated in front of a mirror. If infants touch their nose or attempt to wipe off the powder, we have evidence that the baby has at least some knowledge of its physical characteristics. For the infant, this awareness is one step in developing an understanding of itself as an independent object. For instance, Brianna, in the example at the beginning of this section, showed her awareness of her independence when she tried to rub the jelly off her forehead (Asendorpf, Warkentin, & Baudonniere, 1996; Bard et al., 2006; Rochat, Broesch, & Jayne, 2012).

Although some infants as young as 12 months seem startled on seeing the powder spot, for most, a reaction does not occur until between 17 and 24 months of age. It is also around this age that children begin to show awareness of their own capabilities. For instance, infants who participate in experiments when they are between the ages of 23 and 25 months sometimes begin to cry if the experimenter asks them to imitate a complicated sequence of behaviors involving toys, although they readily accomplish simpler sequences. Their reaction suggests that they are conscious that they lack the ability to carry out difficult tasks and are unhappy about it—a reaction that provides a clear indication of self-awareness (Legerstee, Anderson, & Schaffer, 1998; Asendorpf, 2002).

Children's cultural upbringing also impacts the development of self-recognition. For example, Greek children—who experience parenting practices that emphasize autonomy and separation—show self-recognition at an earlier age than do children from Cameroon in Africa. In the Cameroonian culture, parenting practices emphasize body contact and warmth, leading to more interdependence between infants and parents and, ultimately, later development of self-recognition (Keller et al., 2004; Keller, Voelker, & Yovsi, 2005).

In general, by the age of 18 to 24 months, infants in Western cultures have developed at least an awareness of their own physical characteristics and capabilities, and they understand that their appearance is stable over time. Although it is not clear how far this awareness extends, it is becoming increasingly evident that infants have not only a basic understanding of themselves, but also the beginnings of an understanding of how the mind operates—what is called a "theory of mind" (Lewis & Ramsay, 2004; Lewis & Carmody, 2008; Langfur, 2013).

# Social Referencing: Feeling What Others Feel

**LO 7.3 Provide examples of how infants use others' emotions to interpret social situations.**

*Twenty-three-month-old Stephania watches as her older brother Eric and his friend Chen argue loudly and begin to wrestle. Uncertain of what is happening, Stephania glances at her mother. Her mother, though, wears a smile, knowing that Eric and Chen are just playing. On seeing her mother's reaction, Stephania smiles too, mimicking her mother's facial expression.*

Like Stephania, most of us have been in situations in which we feel uncertain. In such cases, we sometimes turn to others to see how they are reacting. This reliance on others, known as social referencing, helps us decide what an appropriate response ought to be.

**self-awareness** Knowledge of oneself

**Social referencing** is the intentional search for information about others' feelings to help explain the meaning of uncertain circumstances and events. Like Stephania, we use social referencing to clarify the meaning of a situation and to reduce our uncertainty about what is occurring.

Social referencing first occurs around the age of 8 or 9 months. It is a fairly sophisticated social ability: Infants need to understand not only the significance of others' behavior, by using such cues as their facial expressions, but also the meaning of those behaviors within the context of a specific situation (Stenberg, 2009; Hepach & Westermann, 2013; Mireault, et al., 2014).

Infants make particular use of facial expressions in their social referencing, the way Stephania did when she noticed her mother's smile. For instance, in one study infants were given an unusual toy to play with. The amount of time they played with it depended on their mothers' facial expressions. When their mothers displayed disgust, they played with it significantly less than when their mothers appeared pleased. Furthermore, when given the opportunity to play with the same toy later, the infants remained reluctant to play with it, despite the mothers' now neutral-appearing facial reactions, suggesting that parental attitudes may have lasting consequences (Hertenstein & Campos, 2004; Pelaez, Virues-Ortega, & Gewirtz, 2012).

We know about the emergence of social referencing from the *still face technique* used in experiments. In the procedure, a mother faces her baby but holds a blank, neutral expression, betraying no emotion. When babies begin to use social referencing, they become increasingly agitated as the mother holds the still face. In fact, they often become more upset when their mother holds a still face than if the mother physically leaves the room (Montirosso et al., 2010; DiCorcia et al., 2016)

> **From a child care provider's perspective:** In what situations do adults rely on social referencing to work out appropriate responses? How might social referencing be used to influence parents' behavior toward their children?

Social referencing is most likely to occur when a situation is uncertain or ambiguous. Furthermore, infants who reach the age when they are able to use social referencing become quite upset if they receive conflicting nonverbal messages from their mothers and fathers. For example, if a mother shows with her facial expressions that she is annoyed with her son for knocking over a carton of milk, while his grandmother sees it as cute and smiles, the child receives two contradictory messages. Such mixed messages can be a real source of stress for an infant (Stenberg, 2003; Vaish & Striano, 2004; Schmitow & Stenberg, 2013).

## Theory of Mind: Infants' Perspectives on the Mental Lives of Others—and Themselves

### LO 7.4  Describe the mental lives of infants.

What are infants' thoughts about thinking? According to a growing body of research, infants begin to understand certain things about their own and others' mental processes at quite an early age. Investigators have examined children's **theory of mind**, their knowledge and beliefs about how the mind works and how it influences behavior. Theories of mind are the explanations that children use to explain how others think.

For instance, cognitive advances during infancy that we discussed in Chapter 5 permit older infants to come to see people in very different ways from other objects. They learn to see other people as *compliant agents*, beings similar to themselves who behave under their own power and who have the capacity to respond to infants' requests. Eighteen-month-old Chris, for example, has come to realize that he can ask his father to get him more juice (Rochat, 1999, 2004; Luyten, 2011; Slaughter & Peterson, 2012).

In addition, children's capacity to understand intentionality and causality grows during infancy. For example, 10- and 13-month-olds are able to mentally represent social dominance, believing that larger size is related to the ability to dominate other, smaller individuals and objects. Moreover, infants have a kind of innate morality, in which they show a preference for helpfulness (Thomsen et al., 2011; Sloane, Baillargeon, & Premack, 2012; Yott & Poulin-Dubois, 2016).

Furthermore, as early as 18 months, children begin to understand that others' behaviors have some meaning and that the behaviors they see people enacting are designed to accomplish particular goals, in contrast to

---

**social referencing** The intentional search for information about others' feelings to help explain the meaning of uncertain circumstances and events

**theory of mind** Knowledge and beliefs about how the mind works and how it affects behavior

the "behaviors" of inanimate objects. For example, a child comes to understand that his father has a specific goal when he is in the kitchen making sandwiches. In contrast, his father's car is simply parked in the driveway, having no mental life or goal (Ahn, Gelman, & Amsterlaw, 2000; Wellman et al., 2008; Senju et al., 2011).

Another piece of evidence for infants' growing sense of mental activity is that by the age of 2, infants begin to demonstrate the rudiments of empathy. **Empathy** is an emotional response that corresponds to the feelings of another person. At 24 months of age, infants sometimes comfort others or show concern for them. In order to do this, they need to be aware of the emotional states of others. For example, 1-year-olds are able to pick up emotional cues by observing the behavior of an actress on television (Liew et al., 2011; Legerstee, Haley & Bornstein, 2013; Xu, Saether, & Sommerville, 2016).

Furthermore, during their second year, infants begin to use deception, both in games of "pretend" and in outright attempts to fool others. A child who plays "pretend" and who uses falsehoods must be aware that others hold beliefs about the world—beliefs that can be manipulated. In short, by the end of infancy, children have developed the rudiments of their own personal theory of mind. It helps them understand the actions of others, and it affects their own behavior (van der Mark et al., 2002; Caron, 2009; also see the *From Research to Practice* box).

## Stranger Anxiety and Separation Anxiety

**LO 7.5** Explain the causes of stranger and separation anxiety in infants.

*"She used to be such a friendly baby," thought Erika's mother. "No matter who she encountered, she had a big smile. But almost the day she turned 7 months old, she began to react to strangers as if she were seeing a ghost. Her face crinkles up with a frown, and she either turns away or stares at them with suspicion. And she doesn't want to be left with anyone she doesn't already know. It's as if she has undergone a personality transplant."*

**empathy** An emotional response that corresponds to the feelings of another person

# FROM RESEARCH TO PRACTICE
## Do Infants Understand Morality?

You might think that infants don't have much of a social life beyond crying and smiling and sometimes laughing. But research shows that they understand far more than was commonly thought about social interaction, and that they even possess a rudimentary sense of morality—right or wrong, fair or unfair—that was once thought to develop years later.

In one study, infants at 3 months watched a puppet climb a hill. In some cases, another puppet helped the climbing one up the hill, while in other cases, another puppet knocked the climbing one back down to the bottom. The infants later showed a preference for the helpful puppet over the mean puppet—and the social interaction is what made the difference, because the infants showed no such preference when the puppets moved inanimate objects up or down the hill (Hamlin, et al., 2011).

In another study, 21-month-olds observed an adult in the same room who either teased them with a toy that they ultimately refused to give them or tried to give them a toy but were unable to do so because their path was blocked.

When the children had a later opportunity to be helpful, they were more likely to help the adult who tried to be nice to them than the one who teased them. It seems that even infants recognize who does and does not deserve their kindness. Other research shows that they also understand who does and does not deserve to be treated equally. Infants were unsurprised when they watched two adults perform a task and get equal rewards. But they did show surprise when they watched two adults get equal rewards after one had played while the other worked. Whether these principles of fairness are inborn or learned is still an open question, but either way, infants understand more about fairness than they might seem to (Dunfield & Kuhlmeier, 2010; Sloane, Baillargeon, & Premack, 2012).

- **Where might infants be learning these principles of fairness?**
- **What might be an advantage to helping only those who help you?**

What happened to Erika is, in fact, quite typical. By the end of the first year, infants often develop both stranger anxiety and separation anxiety. **Stranger anxiety** is the caution and wariness displayed by infants when encountering an unfamiliar person. Such anxiety typically appears in the second half of the first year.

What brings on stranger anxiety? Here, too, brain development and the increased cognitive abilities of infants play a role. As infants' memory develops, they are able to separate the people they know from the people they don't. The same cognitive advances that allow them to respond so positively to those people with whom they are familiar also give them the ability to recognize people who are unfamiliar. Furthermore, between 6 and 9 months, infants begin trying to make sense of their world, endeavoring to anticipate and predict events. When something happens that they don't expect—such as when an unknown person appears—they experience fear. It's as if an infant has a question but is unable to answer it (Volker, 2007; Mash, Bornstein, & Arterberry, 2013).

Although stranger anxiety is common after the age of 6 months, significant differences exist between children. Some infants, particularly those who have a lot of experience with strangers, tend to show less anxiety than those whose experience with strangers is limited. Furthermore, not all strangers evoke the same reaction. For instance, infants tend to show less anxiety with female strangers than with male strangers. In addition, they react more positively to strangers who are children than to strangers who are adults, perhaps because their size is less intimidating (Swingler, Sweet, & Carver, 2007; Murray et al., 2007, 2008).

**Separation anxiety** is the distress displayed by infants when a customary care provider departs. Separation anxiety, which is also universal across cultures, usually begins at about 7 or 8 months. It peaks around 14 months and then decreases. Separation anxiety is largely attributable to the same reasons as stranger anxiety. Infants' growing cognitive skills allow them to ask reasonable questions, but they may be questions whose answers they are too young to understand, such as: "Why is my mother leaving? Where is she going? Will she come back?"

Stranger anxiety and separation anxiety represent important social progress. They reflect both cognitive advances and the growing emotional and social bonds between infants and their caregivers—bonds that we'll consider later in the chapter when we discuss infants' social relationships.

The bonds that children forge with others during their earliest years play a crucial role throughout their lives.

# Forming Relationships

*Luis Camacho, now 38, clearly remembers the feelings that haunted him on the way to the hospital to meet his new sister Katy. Though he was only 4 at the time, that day of infamy is still vivid in his mind. Luis would no longer be the only kid in the house; he would have to share his life with a baby sister. She would play with his toys, read his books, sit with him in the back seat of the car.*

*What really bothered him, of course, was that he would have to share his parents' love and attention with a new person. And not just any new person—a girl. Remembering something that his cousin Tommy said about younger sisters, Luis feared that his parents would think Katy cuter and more fun than he was. He worried that he would just be in the way.*

*Luis also knew that he was expected to be cheerful and welcoming. So he put on a brave face at the hospital and walked without hesitation to the room where his mother and Katy were waiting.*

The arrival of a newborn brings a dramatic change to a family's dynamics. No matter how welcome a baby's birth, it causes a fundamental shift in the roles that people play within the family. Mothers and fathers must start to build a relationship with their infant, and older children must adjust to the presence of a new member of the family and build their own alliance with their infant brother or sister.

**stranger anxiety** The caution and wariness displayed by infants when encountering an unfamiliar person

**separation anxiety** The distress displayed by infants when a customary care provider departs

Although the process of social development during infancy is neither simple nor automatic, it is crucial: The bonds that grow between infants and their parents, siblings, family, and others provide the foundation for a lifetime's worth of social relationships.

## Attachment: Forming Social Bonds

### LO 7.6 Define attachment in infancy.

The most important aspect of social development that takes place during infancy is the formation of attachment. **Attachment** is the positive emotional bond that develops between a child and a particular special individual. When children experience attachment to a given person, they feel pleasure when they are with them and feel comforted by their presence at times of distress. The nature of our attachment during infancy affects how we relate to others throughout the rest of our lives (Fischer, 2012; Bergman et al., 2015; Kim et al., 2017).

To understand attachment, the earliest researchers turned to the bonds that form between parents and children in the nonhuman animal kingdom. For instance, ethologist Konrad Lorenz (1965) observed newborn goslings, which have an innate tendency to follow their mother—the first moving object to which they typically are exposed after birth. Lorenz found that goslings whose eggs were raised in an incubator and who viewed him just after hatching would follow his every movement, as if he were their mother. As we discussed in Chapter 4, he labeled this process *imprinting*: behavior that takes place during a critical period and involves attachment to the first moving object that is observed.

Lorenz's findings suggested that attachment was based on biologically determined factors, and other theorists agreed. For instance, Freud suggested that attachment grew out of a mother's ability to satisfy a child's oral needs.

It turns out, however, that the ability to provide food and other physiological needs may not be as crucial as Freud and other theorists first thought. In a classic study, psychologist Harry Harlow gave infant monkeys the choice of cuddling a wire "monkey" that provided food or a soft terry cloth monkey that was warm but did not provide food (see Figure 7.3). Their preference was clear: Baby monkeys spent most of their time clinging to the cloth monkey, although they made occasional expeditions to the wire monkey to nurse. Harlow suggested that the preference for the

**Figure 7.3** Monkey Mothers Matter

Harlow's research showed that monkeys preferred the warm, soft "mother" over the wire "monkey" that provided food.

warm cloth monkey provided contact comfort (Harlow & Zimmerman, 1959; Blum, 2002).

Harlow's work illustrates that food alone is not the basis for attachment. Given that the monkeys' preference for the soft cloth "mothers" developed some time after birth, these findings are consistent with the research we discussed in Chapter 3, showing little support for the existence of a critical period for bonding between human mothers and infants immediately following birth.

The earliest work on human attachment, which is still highly influential, was carried out by British psychiatrist John Bowlby (1951, 2007). In Bowlby's view, attachment is based primarily on infants' needs for safety and security—their genetically determined motivation to avoid predators. As they develop, infants come to learn that their safety is best provided by a particular individual. This realization ultimately leads to the development of a special relationship with that individual, who is typically the mother. Bowlby suggested that this single relationship with the primary caregiver is qualitatively different from the bonds formed with others, including the father—a suggestion that, as we'll see later, has been a source of some disagreement.

---

**attachment** The positive emotional bond that develops between a child and a particular individual

According to Bowlby, attachment provides a home base. As children become more independent, they can progressively roam further away from their secure base.

## The Ainsworth Strange Situation and Patterns of Attachment

**LO 7.7  Summarize how attachment affects an individual's future social competence.**

Developmental psychologist Mary Ainsworth built on Bowlby's theorizing to develop a widely used experimental technique to measure attachment (Ainsworth et al., 1978). The **Ainsworth Strange Situation** consists of a sequence of staged episodes that illustrate the strength of attachment between a child and (typically) his or her mother. The "strange situation" follows this general eight-step pattern: (1) The mother and baby enter an unfamiliar room; (2) the mother sits down, leaving the baby free to explore; (3) an adult stranger enters the room and converses first with the mother and then with the baby; (4) the mother exits the room, leaving the baby alone with the stranger; (5) the mother returns, greeting and comforting the baby, and the stranger leaves; (6) the mother departs again, leaving the baby alone; (7) the stranger returns; and (8) the mother returns and the stranger leaves (Ainsworth et al., 1978; Pederson et al., 2014).

Infants' reactions to the various aspects of the Strange Situation vary considerably, depending on the nature of their attachment to their mothers. One-year-olds typically show one of four major patterns—securely attached, avoidant, ambivalent, and disorganized-disoriented (summarized in Table 7.1).

Mary Ainsworth, who devised the Strange Situation to measure attachment.

Children who have a **secure attachment pattern** use the mother as the home base that Bowlby described. These children seem at ease in the Strange Situation as long as their mothers are present. They explore independently, returning to her occasionally. Although they may or may not appear upset when she leaves, securely attached children immediately go to her when she returns and seek contact. Most North American children—about two-thirds—fall into the securely attached category.

---

**Ainsworth Strange Situation** A sequence of staged episodes that illustrates the strength of attachment between a child and (typically) his or her mother

**secure attachment pattern** A style of attachment in which children use the mother as a kind of home base and are at ease when she is present; when she leaves, they become upset and go to her as soon as she returns

---

**Table 7.1** Classifications of Infant Attachment

| Label | Classification Criteria | | | |
|---|---|---|---|---|
| | **Seeking Proximity With Caregiver** | **Maintaining Contact With Caregiver** | **Avoiding Proximity With Caregiver** | **Resisting Contact With Caregiver** |
| **Avoidant** | Low | Low | High | Low |
| **Secure** | High | High (if distressed) | Low | Low |
| **Ambivalent** | High | High (often preseparation) | Low | High |
| **Disorganized-disoriented** | Inconsistent | Inconsistent | Inconsistent | Inconsistent |

**SOURCE:** From E. Waters, "The Reliability and Stability of Individual Differences in Infant-Mother Attachment," Child Development, vol. 49, 1978. The Society for Research in Child Development, Inc. pp. 480–494; p. 188.

In this illustration of the Strange Situation, the infant first explores the playroom on his own, as long as his mother is present. But when she leaves, he begins to cry. On her return, however, he is immediately comforted and stops crying. The conclusion: He is securely attached.

In contrast, children with an **avoidant attachment pattern** do not seek proximity to the mother and, after she has left, they typically do not seem distressed. Furthermore, they seem to avoid her when she returns. It is as if they are indifferent to her behavior. Some 20 percent of 1-year-old children are in the avoidant category.

Children with an **ambivalent attachment pattern** display a combination of positive and negative reactions to their mothers. Initially, ambivalent children are in such close contact with the mother that they hardly explore their environment. They appear anxious even before the mother leaves, and when she does leave, they show great distress. But upon her return, they show ambivalent reactions, seeking to be close to her but also hitting and kicking, apparently in anger. About 10 to 15 percent of 1-year-olds fall into the ambivalent classification (Cassidy & Berlin, 1994).

Although Ainsworth identified only three categories, a more recent expansion of her work finds that there is a fourth category: disorganized-disoriented. Children who have a **disorganized-disoriented attachment pattern** show inconsistent, contradictory, and confused behavior. They may run to the mother when she returns but not look at her, or seem initially calm and then suddenly break into angry weeping. Their confusion suggests that they may be the least securely attached children of all. About 5 to 10 percent of children fall into this category (Mayseless, 1996; Cole, 2005; Bernier & Meins, 2008).

A child's attachment style would be of only minor consequence were it not for the fact that the quality of attachment between infants and their mothers has significant consequences for relationships at later stages of life. For example, boys who are securely attached at the age of 1 year show fewer psychological difficulties at older ages than do avoidant or ambivalent children. Similarly, children who are securely attached as infants tend to be more socially and emotionally competent later, and others view them more positively. Adult romantic relationships are associated with the kind of attachment style developed during infancy (Simpson et al., 2007; MacDonald et al., 2008; Bergman, Blom, & Polyak, 2012).

At the same time, we cannot say that children who do not have a secure attachment style during infancy invariably experience difficulties later in life, nor can we say that those with a secure attachment at age 1 always have good adjustment later on. In fact, some evidence suggests that children with avoidant and ambivalent attachment—as measured by the Strange Situation—do quite well (Fraley & Spieker, 2003; Alhusen, Hayat, & Gross, 2013; Smith-Nielsen et al., 2016).

In cases in which the development of attachment has been severely disrupted, children may suffer from *reactive attachment disorder*, a psychological problem characterized by extreme difficulty in forming attachments to others. In young children, this disorder can be displayed as feeding difficulties, unresponsiveness to social overtures from others, and a general failure

**avoidant attachment pattern** A style of attachment in which children do not seek proximity to the mother; after the mother has left, they seem to avoid her when she returns as if they are angered by her behavior

**ambivalent attachment pattern** A style of attachment in which children display a combination of positive and negative reactions to their mothers; they show great distress when the mother leaves, but upon her return they may simultaneously seek close contact but also hit and kick her

**disorganized-disoriented attachment pattern** A style of attachment in which children show inconsistent, often contradictory behavior, such as approaching the mother when she returns but not looking at her; they may be the least securely attached children of all to thrive. Reactive attachment disorder is rare and is typically the result of abuse or neglect (Hornor, 2008; Schechter & Willheim, 2009; Puckering et al., 2011).

## Producing Attachment: The Roles of the Mother and Father

**LO 7.8  Explain the roles of mothers and fathers in an infant's development of attachment.**

*As 5-month-old Annie cries passionately, her mother comes into the room and gently lifts her from her crib. After just a few moments, as her mother rocks Annie and speaks softly, Annie's cries cease, and she cuddles in her mother's arms. But the moment her mother places her back in the crib, Annie begins to wail, leading her mother to pick her up once again.*

The pattern is familiar to most parents: The infant cries, the parent reacts, and the child responds in turn. Such seemingly insignificant sequences as these, repeatedly occurring in the lives of infants and parents, help pave the way for the development of relationships between children, their parents, and the rest of the social world. We'll consider how each of the major caregivers and the infant play a role in the development of attachment.

**MOTHERS AND ATTACHMENT.**   Sensitivity to their infants' needs and desires is the hallmark of mothers of securely attached infants. Such a mother tends to be aware of her child's moods, and she takes into account her child's feelings as they interact. She is also responsive during face-to-face interactions, provides feeding "on demand," and is warm and affectionate to her infant (McElwain & Booth-LaForce, 2006; Priddis & Howieson, 2009; Evans, Whittingham, & Boyd, 2012).

It is not only a matter of responding in *any* fashion to their infants' signals that separates mothers of securely attached and insecurely attached children. Mothers of secure infants tend to provide the appropriate level of response. Research has shown that overly responsive mothers are just as likely to have insecurely attached children as under-responsive mothers. In contrast, mothers whose communication involves *interactional synchrony*, in which caregivers respond to infants appropriately and both caregiver and child match emotional states, are more likely to produce secure attachment (Hane, Feldstein, & Dernetz, 2003; Ambrose & Menna, 2013).

The research showing the correspondence between mothers' sensitivity to their infants and the security of the infants' attachment is consistent with Ainsworth's arguments that attachment depends on how mothers react to their infants' emotional cues. Ainsworth suggests that mothers of securely attached infants respond rapidly and positively to their infants. For example, Annie's mother responds quickly to her cries by cuddling and comforting her. In contrast, the way for mothers to produce insecurely attached infants, according to Ainsworth, is to ignore their behavioral cues, to behave inconsistently with them, and to ignore or reject their social efforts. For example, picture a child who repeatedly and unsuccessfully tries to gain her mother's attention by calling or turning and gesturing from her stroller while her mother, engaged in conversation, ignores her. This baby is likely to be less securely attached than a child whose mother acknowledges her child more quickly and consistently (Higley & Dozier, 2009).

But how do mothers learn how to respond to their infants? One way is from their own mothers. Mothers typically respond to their infants based on their own attachment styles. As a result, there is substantial similarity in attachment patterns from one generation to the next (Peck, 2003).

It is important to realize that a mother's (and others') behavior toward infants is at least in part a reaction to the child's ability to provide effective cues. A mother may not be able to respond effectively to a child whose own behavior is unrevealing, misleading, or ambiguous. For instance, children who clearly display their anger or fear or unhappiness will be easier to read—and respond effectively to—than children whose behavior is ambiguous. Consequently, the kind of signals an infant sends may in part determine how successful the mother will be in responding.

**FATHERS AND ATTACHMENT.**   Up to now, we've barely touched upon one of the key players involved in the upbringing of a child: the father. In fact, if you looked at the early theorizing and research on attachment, you'd find little mention of the father and his potential contributions to the life of the infant (Tamis-LeMonda & Cabrera, 1999).

There are at least two reasons for this absence. First, John Bowlby, who provided the initial theory of attachment, suggested that there was something unique about the mother–child relationship. He believed the mother was uniquely equipped, biologically, to provide sustenance for the child, and he concluded that this capability led to the development of a special relationship between mothers and children. Second, the early work on attachment was influenced by the traditional social views of the time, which considered it "natural" for the mother to be the primary caregiver, while the father's role was to work outside the home to provide a living for his family.

Several factors led to the demise of this view. One was that societal norms changed, and fathers began to take a more active role in childrearing activities. More important, it became increasingly clear from research findings that—despite societal norms that relegated fathers to secondary childrearing roles—some infants formed their primary initial relationship with their fathers (Brown et al., 2007; Diener et al., 2008; Music, 2011; McFarland-Piazza et al., 2012).

In addition, a growing body of research has shown that fathers' expressions of nurturance, warmth, affection, support, and concern are extremely important to their children's emotional and social well-being. Certain kinds of psychological disorders, such as substance abuse and depression, have been found to be related more to fathers' than mothers' behavior (Roelofs et al., 2006; Condon et al., 2013; Braungart-Rieker et al., 2015).

Infants' social bonds extend beyond their parents, especially as they grow older. For example, one study found that although most infants formed their first primary relationship with one person, around one-third had multiple relationships, and it was difficult to determine which attachment was primary. Furthermore, by the time the infants were 18 months old, most had formed multiple relationships. In sum, infants may develop attachments not only to their mothers, but to a variety of others as well (Booth, Kelly, & Spieker, 2003; Seibert & Kerns, 2009).

**ARE THERE DIFFERENCES IN ATTACHMENT TO MOTHERS AND FATHERS?** Although infants are fully capable of forming attachments to both mothers and fathers—as well as to other individuals—the nature of attachment between infants and mothers on the one hand and infants and fathers on the other hand is not identical. For example, when they are in unusually stressful circumstances, most infants prefer to be soothed by their mothers rather than by their fathers (Schoppe-Sullivan et al., 2006; Yu et al., 2012; Dumont & Paquette, 2013).

One reason for qualitative differences in attachment involves the differences in what fathers and mothers do with their children. Mothers spend a greater proportion of their time feeding and directly nurturing their children. In contrast, fathers spend more time, proportionally, playing with infants. Almost all fathers do contribute to child care: Surveys show that 95 percent say they do some child care chores every day. But on average they still do less than mothers. For instance, 30 percent of fathers with wives who work do three or more hours of daily child care. In comparison, 74 percent of employed married mothers spend that amount of time every day in child care activities (Grych & Clark, 1999; Kazura, 2000; Whelan & Lally, 2002).

Furthermore, the nature of fathers' play with their babies is often quite different from that of mothers. Fathers engage in more physical, rough-and-tumble activities with their children. In contrast, mothers play traditional games such as peek-a-boo and games with more verbal elements (Paquette, Carbonneau, & Dubeau, 2003).

These differences in the ways that fathers and mothers play with their children occur even in the minority of families in the United States in which the father is the primary caregiver. Moreover, the differences occur in very diverse cultures: Fathers in Australia, Israel, India, Japan, Mexico, and even in the Aka Pygmy tribe in central Africa all engage more in play than in caregiving, although the amount of time they spend with their infants varies widely. For instance, Aka fathers spend more time caring for their infants than members of any other known culture, holding and cuddling their babies at a rate some five times higher than anywhere else in the world (Roopnarine, 1992; Bronstein, 1999; Hewlett & Lamb, 2002).

These similarities and differences in childrearing practices across different societies raise an important question: How does culture affect attachment?

# Infant Interactions: Developing a Working Relationship

**LO 7.9**   **Compare the roles other people play in infants' social development.**

Research on attachment is clear in showing that infants may develop multiple attachment relationships and that over the course of time the specific individuals with whom the infant is primarily attached may change. These variations in attachment emphasize that the development of relationships is an ongoing process, not only during infancy, but throughout our lifetimes.

The differences in the ways that fathers and mothers play with their children occur even in families in which the father is the primary caregiver. Based on this observation, how does culture affect attachment?

**PARENTAL INTERACTION.** Which processes underlie the development of relationships during infancy? One answer comes from studies that examine how parents interact with their children. For one thing, parents, and in fact all adults, appear to be genetically preprogrammed to be sensitive to infants. Brain scanning techniques have found that the facial features of infants (but not adults) activate a specialized structure in the brain called the *fusiform gyrus* within a seventh of a second. Such reactions may help elicit nurturing behavior and trigger social interaction (Kringelbach et al., 2008; Zebrowitz et al., 2009; Kassuba et al., 2011).

In addition, studies have found that across almost all cultures, mothers behave in typical ways with their infants. They tend to exaggerate their facial and vocal expressions—the nonverbal equivalent of the infant-directed speech that they use when they speak to infants (as we discussed in Chapter 6). Similarly, they often imitate their infants' behavior, responding to distinctive sounds and movements by repeating them. There are even types of games, such as peek-a-boo, itsy-bitsy spider, and pat-a-cake, that are nearly universal (Harrist & Waugh, 2002; Kochanska, 1997, 2002).

Furthermore, according to the **mutual regulation model**, it is through these sorts of interactions that infants and parents learn to communicate emotional states to one another and to respond appropriately. For instance, in pat-a-cake, both infant and parent act jointly to regulate turn-taking behavior, with one individual waiting until the other completes a behavioral act before starting another. Consequently, at the age of 3 months, infants and their mothers have about the same influence on each other's behavior. Interestingly, by the age of 6 months, infants have more control over turn taking, although by the age of 9 months both partners once again become roughly equivalent in terms of mutual influence (Tronick, 2003; Salley et al., 2016).

One of the ways infants and parents signal each other when they interact is through facial expressions. As we saw earlier in this chapter, even quite young infants are able to read, or decode, the facial expressions of their caregivers, and they react to those expressions.

For example, an infant whose mother, during an experiment, displays a stony, immobile facial expression reacts by making a variety of sounds, gestures, and facial expressions of her own in response to such a puzzling situation—and possibly to elicit some new response from her mother. Infants also show more happiness themselves when their mothers appear happy, and they look at their mothers longer. By contrast, infants are apt to respond with sad looks and to turn away when their mothers display unhappy expressions (Crockenberg & Leerkes, 2003; Reissland & Shepherd, 2006; Yato et al., 2008).

**From a social worker's perspective:** Imagine you are a social worker visiting a foster home. It is 11 A.M. You find the breakfast dishes in the sink and books and toys all over the floor. The infant you have placed in the home is happily pounding on pots and pans while his foster mother claps along. The kitchen floor is sticky under the baby's high chair. What is your assessment?

In short, the development of attachment in infants does not merely represent a reaction to the behavior of the people around them. Instead, there is a process

**mutual regulation model** The model in which infants and parents learn to communicate emotional states to one another and to respond appropriately

# DEVELOPMENTAL DIVERSITY AND YOUR LIFE
## Does Attachment Differ Across Cultures?

John Bowlby's observations of the biologically motivated efforts of the young of other species to seek safety and security were the basis for his views on attachment and his reason for suggesting that seeking attachment was a biological universal, one that we should find not only in other species, but among humans of all cultures as well.

Research has shown, however, that human attachment is not as culturally universal as Bowlby predicted. Certain attachment patterns seem more likely among infants of particular cultures. For example, one study of German infants showed that most fell into the avoidant category. Other studies, conducted in Israel and Japan, have found a smaller proportion of infants who were securely attached than in the United States. Finally, comparisons of Chinese and Canadian children show that Chinese children are more inhibited than Canadians in the Ainsworth Strange Situation (Grossmann et al., 1982; Takahashi, 1986; Chen et al., 1998; Rothbaum et al., 2000; Kieffer, 2012).

Do such findings suggest that we should abandon the notion that attachment is a universal biological tendency? Not necessarily. While it is possible that Bowlby's claim that the desire for attachment is universal was too strongly stated, most of the data on attachment have been obtained by using the Ainsworth Strange Situation, which may not be the most appropriate measure in non-Western cultures. For example, Japanese parents seek to avoid separation and stress during infancy, and they don't strive to foster independence to the same degree as parents in many Western societies. Because of their relative lack of prior experience in separation, then, infants placed in the Strange Situation may experience unusual stress—producing the appearance of less secure attachment in Japanese children. If a different measure of attachment were used, one that might be administered later in infancy, more Japanese infants could likely be classified as secure (Vereijken et al., 1997; Dennis et al., 2002; Mesman et al., 2016).

Attachment is now viewed as susceptible to cultural norms and expectations. Cross-cultural and within-cultural differences in attachment reflect the nature of the measure employed and the expectations of various cultures. Keller (2013) points out that the primacy of mother-infant bond for attachment may only be the norm

Japanese parents seek to avoid separation and stress during infancy and do not foster independence. As a result, Japanese children often have the appearance of being less securely attached according to the Strange Situation, but using other measurement techniques, they may well score higher in attachment.

in Western middle-class families. Keller observed that the assumptions of monotropy, the conception of stranger anxiety as well as the definition of attachment in mainstream attachment research are in line with the conception of psychological autonomy, adaptive for Western middle-class, but it deviated from the cultural values of many non-Western and mainly rural eco-social environments. In most cultures and socioeconomic groups like existing in India, as a cultural practice or due to limited resources and daily survival needs, caregiving is distributed across a network of relatives, including aunts, uncles, grandparents, and siblings.

Some developmental specialists suggest that attachment should be viewed as a general tendency, but one that varies in the way it is expressed according to how actively caregivers in a society seek to instill independence in their children. Secure attachment, as defined by the Western-oriented Strange Situation, may be seen earliest in cultures that promote independence, but may be delayed in societies in which independence is a less important cultural value (Rothbaum et al., 2000; Rothbaum, Rosen, & Ujiie, 2002; Hong et al., 2013).

of **reciprocal socialization**, in which infants' behaviors invite further responses from parents and other caregivers. In turn, the caregivers' behaviors bring about a reaction from the child, continuing the cycle. Recall, for instance, Annie, the baby who kept crying to be picked up when her mother put her in her crib. Ultimately, the actions and reactions of parents and child lead to an increase in attachment, forging and strengthening bonds between infants and caregivers as they communicate their needs and responses to each other. Figure 7.4 summarizes the sequence of infant–caregiver interaction (Kochanska & Aksan, 2004; Spinrad & Stifter, 2006).

**INFANT–INFANT INTERACTION.** Although they do not form "friendships" in the traditional sense, babies do react positively to the presence of peers from early in life, and they engage in rudimentary forms of social interaction.

Infants' sociability is expressed in several ways. From the earliest months of life, they smile, laugh, and vocalize while looking at their peers. They show more interest in peers than in inanimate objects, and they pay greater attention to other infants than they do to a mirror image of themselves. They also begin to show preferences for peers with whom they are familiar compared with those they do not know. For example, studies of identical twins show that twins exhibit a higher level of social behavior toward each other than toward an unfamiliar infant (Eid et al., 2003; Legerstee, 2014).

Infants' level of sociability generally rises with age; 9- to 12-month-olds mutually present and accept toys,

> **reciprocal socialization** A process in which infants' behaviors invite further responses from parents and other caregivers, which in turn bring about further responses from the infants

---

## Figure 7.4 Sequence of Infant–Caregiver Interaction

The actions and reactions of caregivers and infants influence each other in complex ways. Do you think a similar pattern shows up in adult–adult interactions?

**SOURCE:** Adapted from Bell, S. M., & Ainsworth, M. D. S. (1972). Infant crying and maternal responsiveness. Child Development, 43, 1171–1190; Tomlinson-Keasey, C. (1985). Child development: Psychological, sociological, and biological factors. Homewood, IL: Dorsey.

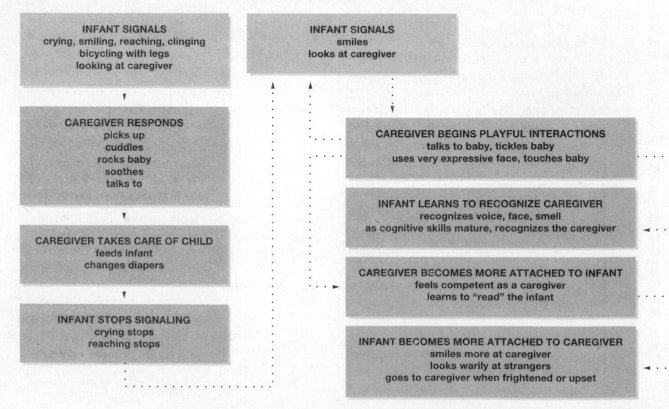

particularly if they know each other. They also play social games, such as peek-a-boo or crawl-and-chase. Such behavior is important, as it serves as a foundation for future social exchanges in which children will try to elicit responses from others and then offer reactions to those responses. These kinds of exchanges are important to learn, because they continue even into adulthood. For example, someone who says, "Hi, what's up?" may be trying to elicit a response to which he or she can then reply (Endo, 1992; Eckerman & Peterman, 2001).

Finally, as infants age, they begin to imitate one another. For instance, 14-month-old infants who are familiar with one another sometimes reproduce each other's behavior. Such imitation serves a social function and can also be a powerful teaching tool (Ray & Heyes, 2011; Brownell, 2016).

According to Andrew Meltzoff, a developmental psychologist at the University of Washington, infants learn a considerable amount from other babies. Specifically, what Meltzoff calls "expert" babies are able to teach skills and information to other infants, and the material learned from the "experts" is retained and later used to a remarkable degree. Learning by exposure starts early in life. Recent evidence shows that even 7-week-old infants can perform delayed imitation of a novel stimulus to which they have earlier been exposed, such as an adult sticking the tongue out of the side of the mouth (Meltzoff & Moore, 1999; Meltzoff, 2002; Meltzoff, Waismeyer, & Gopnik, 2012).

To some developmentalists, the capacity of young children to engage in imitation suggests that imitation may be inborn. In support of this view, research has identified a class of neurons in the brain that seems to be related to an innate ability to imitate. *Mirror neurons* are neurons that fire not only when an individual carries out a particular behavior but also when the individual simply observes *another* organism carrying out the same behavior. For instance, when you throw a ball, certain neurons in the brain fire. If you see someone else throwing a ball, some of the same neurons fire—and these are known as mirror neurons (Falck-Ytter et al., 2006; Lepage & Théret, 2007).

More specifically, research on brain functioning shows activation of the inferior frontal gyrus both when an individual carries out a particular task and when observing another individual carrying out the same task. Mirror neurons may help infants understand others' actions and to develop a theory of mind. Dysfunction of mirror neurons may be related to the development of disorders involving children's theory of mind as well as autism spectrum disorder, a psychological problem involving significant emotional and linguistic difficulties (Martineau et al., 2008; Welsh et al., 2009; Yang et al., 2013).

The idea that through exposure to other children, infants learn new behaviors, skills, and abilities has several implications. For one thing, it suggests that interactions between infants provide more than social benefits; they may have an impact on children's future cognitive development as well. Even more important, these findings illustrate that infants may benefit from participation in child care centers (which we consider later in this chapter). Although we don't know for sure, the opportunity to learn from their peers may prove to be a lasting advantage for infants in group child care settings.

# Differences Among Infants

*Lincoln was a difficult baby, his parents both agreed. For one thing, it seemed like they could never get him to sleep at night. He cried at the slightest noise, a problem because his crib was near the windows facing a busy street. Worse yet, once he started crying, it seemed to take forever to calm him down again. One day his mother, Aisha, was telling her mother-in-law, Mary, about the challenges of being Lincoln's mom. Mary recalled that her own son, Lincoln's father, Malcolm, had been much the same way. "He was my first child, and I thought this was how all babies acted. So, we just kept trying different ways until we found out how he worked. I remember we put his crib all over the apartment until we finally found out where he could sleep, and it ended up being in the hallway for a long time. Then his sister, Maleah, came along, and she was so quiet and easy, I didn't know what to do with my extra time!"*

As the story of Lincoln's family shows, babies are not all alike, and neither are their families. As we'll see, some of the differences among people seem to be present from the moment they are born. The differences among infants include overall personality and temperament and differences in the lives they lead—differences based on their gender, the nature of their families, and the ways in which they are cared for.

# Personality Development: The Characteristics That Make Infants Unique

### LO 7.10  Explain how infants develop unique personalities.

The origins of **personality**, the sum total of the enduring characteristics that differentiate one individual from another, stem from infancy. From birth onward, infants begin to show unique, stable traits and behaviors that ultimately lead to their development as distinct, special individuals (Caspi, 2000; Kagan, 2000; Shiner, Masten, & Roberts, 2003).

According to psychologist Erik Erikson, whose approach to personality development we first discussed in Chapter 1, infants' early experiences are responsible for shaping one of the key aspects of their personalities: whether they will be basically trusting or mistrustful.

**Erikson's theory of psychosocial development** considers how individuals come to understand themselves and the meaning of others'—and their own—behavior (Erikson, 1963). The theory suggests that developmental change occurs throughout people's lives in eight distinct stages, the first of which occurs in infancy.

According to Erikson, during the first 18 months of life, we pass through the **trust-versus-mistrust stage**. During this period, infants develop a sense of trust or mistrust, largely depending on how well their needs are met by their caregivers. In the previous example, Mary's attention to Malcolm's needs probably helped him develop a basic sense of trust in the world. Erikson suggests that if, on the one hand, infants are able to develop trust, they experience a sense of hope, which permits them to feel as if they can fulfill their needs successfully. On the other hand, feelings of mistrust lead infants to see the world as harsh and unfriendly, and they may have later difficulties in forming close bonds with others.

During the end of infancy, children enter the **autonomy-versus-shame-and-doubt stage**, which lasts from around 18 months to 3 years. During this period, children develop independence and autonomy if parents encourage exploration and freedom within safe boundaries. If children are restricted and overly protected, however, they feel shame, self-doubt, and unhappiness.

Erikson argues that personality is primarily shaped by infants' experiences. But as we discuss next, other developmentalists concentrate on consistencies of behavior that are present at birth, even before the experiences of infancy. These consistencies are viewed as largely genetically determined and as providing the raw material of personality.

# Temperament: Stabilities in Infant Behavior

### LO 7.11  Define temperament in infants and explain its origins.

*Sarah's parents thought there must be something wrong. Unlike her older brother Josh, who had been so active as an infant that he seemed never to be still, Sarah was much more placid. She took long naps and was easily soothed on those relatively rare occasions when she became agitated. What could be producing her extreme calmness?*

The most likely answer: The difference between Sàrah and Josh reflected differences in temperament. As we first discussed in Chapter 3, **temperament** encompasses patterns of arousal and emotionality that are consistent and enduring characteristics of an individual (Kochanska & Aksan, 2004; Rothbart, 2007).

Temperament refers to *how* children behave, as opposed to *what* they do or *why* they do it. Infants show temperamental differences in general disposition

---

**personality**  The sum total of the enduring characteristics that differentiate one individual from another

**Erikson's theory of psychosocial development**  The theory that considers how individuals come to understand themselves and the meaning of others'—and their own—behavior

**trust-versus-mistrust stage**  According to Erik Erikson, the period during which infants develop a sense of trust or mistrust, largely depending on how well their needs are met by their caregivers

**autonomy-versus-shame-and-doubt stage**  The period during which, according to Erik Erikson, toddlers (age 18 months to 3 years) develop independence and autonomy if they are allowed the freedom to explore, or shame and self-doubt if they are restricted and overprotected

**temperament**  Patterns of arousal and emotionality that are consistent and enduring characteristics of an individual

According to Erikson, children from 18 months to 3 years develop independence and autonomy if parents encourage exploration and freedom, within safe boundaries. What does Erikson theorize if children are restricted and overly protected at this stage?

**Table 7.2** Dimensions of Temperament

| Dimension | Definition |
|---|---|
| Activity level | Proportion of active time periods to inactive time periods |
| Approach–withdrawal | The response to a new person or object, based on whether the child accepts the new situation or withdraws from it |
| Adaptability | How easily the child is able to adapt to changes in his or her environment |
| Quality of mood | The contrast of the amount of friendly, joyful, and pleasant behavior with unpleasant, unfriendly behavior |
| Attention span and persistence | The amount of time the child devotes to an activity and the effect of distraction on that activity |
| Distractibility | The degree to which stimuli in the environment alter behavior |
| Rhythmicity (regularity) | The regularity of basic functions such as hunger, excretion, sleep, and wakefulness |
| Intensity of reaction | The energy level or reaction of the child's response |
| Threshold of responsiveness | The intensity of stimulation needed to elicit a response |

**SOURCE:** Thomas, Chess, and Birch (1968).

from the time of birth, largely due at first to genetic factors, as you'll learn next, and temperament tends to be fairly stable well into adolescence. However, temperament is not fixed and unchangeable: Childrearing practices can modify temperament significantly. In fact, some children show little consistency in temperament from one age to another (Rothbart & Derryberry, 2002; Werner et al., 2007; de Lauzon-Guillain et al., 2012).

Temperament is reflected in several dimensions of behavior. One central dimension is *activity level*, which reflects the degree of overall movement. Some babies (like Sarah and Maleah, in the earlier examples) are relatively placid, and their movements are slow and almost leisurely. In contrast, the activity level of other infants (like Josh) is quite high, with strong, restless movements of the arms and legs.

Another important dimension of temperament is the nature and quality of an infant's mood, and in particular a child's *irritability*. Like Lincoln, who was described in the example at the beginning of this section, some infants are easily disturbed and cry easily, while others are relatively easygoing. Irritable infants fuss a great deal, and they are easily upset. They are also difficult to soothe when they do begin to cry. Such irritability is relatively stable: Infants who are irritable at birth remain irritable at the age of 1, and even at age 2 they are still more easily upset than infants who were not irritable just after birth (Worobey & Bajda, 1989). (Other aspects of temperament are listed in Table 7.2.)

**THE BIOLOGICAL BASIS OF TEMPERAMENT.** Recent approaches to temperament grow out of the framework of behavioral genetics that we discussed in Chapter 3. From this perspective, temperamental characteristics are seen as inherited traits that are fairly stable during childhood and across the entire life span. These traits are viewed as making up the core of personality and playing a substantial role in future development (Sheese et al., 2009; Goodnight et al., 2016).

Consider, for example, the trait of physiological reactivity, characterized by a high degree of motor and muscle activity in response to novel stimuli. This high reactivity, which has been termed *inhibition to the unfamiliar*, is exhibited as shyness.

A clear biological basis underlies inhibition to the unfamiliar, in which any novel stimulus produces a rapid increase in heartbeat, blood pressure, and pupil dilation, as well as high excitability of the brain's limbic system. For example, people categorized as inhibited at 2 years of age show high reactivity in their brain's amygdala in adulthood when viewing unfamiliar faces. The shyness associated with this physiological pattern seems to continue through childhood and even into adulthood (Arcus, 2001; Schwartz et al., 2003; Propper & Moore, 2006; Kagan et al., 2007; Anzman-Frasca et al., 2013b).

High reactivity to unfamiliar situations in infants has also been linked to greater susceptibility to depression and anxiety disorders in adulthood. Furthermore, when they reach adulthood, infants who are highly reactive develop an anterior prefrontal cortex that is thicker compared with those who are less reactive. Because the prefrontal cortex is closely linked to the amygdala (which controls emotional responses) and the hippocampus (which controls fear responses), the difference in prefrontal cortex may help explain the higher rates of depression and anxiety disorders (Schwartz & Rauch, 2004; Schwartz, 2008).

**CATEGORIZING TEMPERAMENT: EASY, DIFFICULT, AND SLOW-TO-WARM BABIES.** Because temperament can be viewed along so many dimensions, some researchers have asked whether broader categories can be used to describe children's overall behavior. According to Alexander Thomas and Stella Chess, who carried out a large-scale study of a group of infants that has come to be known as the *New York Longitudinal Study* (Thomas & Chess, 1980), babies can be described according to one of several profiles:

- *Easy babies.* **Easy babies** have a positive disposition. Their body functions operate regularly, and they are adaptable. They show curiosity about new situations, and their emotions are moderate or low in intensity. This category applies to about 40 percent (the largest number) of infants.

- *Difficult babies.* **Difficult babies** have more negative moods and are slow to adapt to new situations. When confronted with a new situation, they tend to withdraw. About 10 percent of infants belong in this category.

- *Slow-to-warm babies.* **Slow-to-warm babies** are inactive, showing relatively calm reactions to their environment. Their moods are generally negative, and they withdraw from new situations, adapting slowly. Approximately 15 percent of infants are slow-to-warm.

As for the remaining 35 percent, they cannot be consistently categorized. These children show a variety of combinations of characteristics. For instance, one infant may have relatively sunny moods, but react negatively to new situations, or another may show little stability of any sort in terms of general temperament.

**DOES TEMPERAMENT MATTER?** One obvious question to emerge from the findings of the relative stability of temperament is whether a particular kind of temperament is beneficial. The answer seems to

be that no single type of temperament is invariably good or bad. Instead, children's long-term adjustment depends on the **goodness-of-fit** of their particular temperament and the nature and demands of the environment in which they find themselves. For instance, children with a low activity level and low irritability may do particularly well in an environment in which they are left to explore on their own and are allowed largely to direct their own behavior. In contrast, high-activity-level, highly irritable children may do best with greater direction, which permits them to channel their energy in particular directions (Thomas & Chess, 1980; Strelau, 1998; Schoppe-Sullivan et al., 2007).

Certain temperaments are, in general, more adaptive than others. For instance, difficult children, in general, are more likely to show behavior problems by school age than those classified in infancy as easy children. But not all difficult children experience problems. The key determinant seems to be the way parents react to their infants' difficult behavior. If they react by showing anger and inconsistency—responses that their child's difficult, demanding behavior readily evokes—then the child is ultimately more likely to experience behavior problems. In contrast, parents who display more warmth and consistency in their responses are more likely to have children who avoid later problems (Pauli-Pott, Mertesacker, & Bade, 2003; Canals, Hernández-Martínez, & Fernández-Ballart, 2011; Salley, Miller, & Bell, 2013).

Furthermore, temperament seems to be at least weakly related to infants' attachment to their adult caregivers. For example, infants vary considerably in how much emotion they display nonverbally. Some are "poker-faced," showing little expressivity,

---

**easy babies** Babies who have a positive disposition; their body functions operate regularly, and they are adaptable

**difficult babies** Babies who have negative moods and are slow to adapt to new situations; when confronted with a new situation, they tend to withdraw

**slow-to-warm babies** Babies who are inactive, showing relatively calm reactions to their environment; their moods are generally negative, and they withdraw from new situations, adapting slowly

**goodness-of-fit** The notion that development is dependent on the degree of match between children's temperament and the nature and demands of the environment in which they are being raised

while others' reactions tend to be much more easily decoded. More expressive infants may provide more easily discernible cues to others, thereby easing the way for caregivers to be more successful in responding to their needs and facilitating attachment (Feldman & Rimé, 1991; Laible, Panfile, & Makariev, 2008; Sayal et al., 2014).

Cultural differences also have a major influence on the consequences of a particular temperament. For instance, children who would be described as "difficult" in Western cultures actually seem to have an advantage in the East African Maasai culture. The reason? Mothers offer their breast to their infants only when they fuss and cry; therefore, the irritable, more difficult infants are apt to receive more nourishment than are the more placid, easy infants. Particularly when environmental conditions are bad, such as during a drought, difficult babies may have an advantage (deVries, 1984; Gaias, et al., 2012; Farkas & Vallotton, 2016).

## Gender: Why Do Boys Wear Blue and Girls Wear Pink?

**LO 7.12** Explain the causes and consequences of gender differentiation.

"It's a boy." "It's a girl." One of these two statements is probably the first announcement made after the birth of a child. From that moment on, girls and boys are treated differently. Their parents send out different kinds of birth announcements. They are dressed in different clothes and wrapped in different-colored blankets. They are given different toys (Coltrane & Adams, 1997; Serbin, Poulin-Dubois, & Colburne, 2001).

Parents play with boy and girl babies differently, too: Fathers tend to interact more with sons than with daughters, while mothers interact more with daughters than with sons. As we noted earlier in the chapter, because mothers and fathers play in different ways (with fathers typically engaging in more physical, rough-and-tumble activities and mothers in traditional games such as peek-a-boo), male and female infants are clearly exposed to different styles of activity and interaction from their parents (Laflamme, Pomerleau, & Malcuit, 2002; Clearfield & Nelson, 2006; Parke, 2007).

The behavior exhibited by girls and boys is interpreted in very different ways by adults. For instance, when researchers showed adults a video of an infant

Parents of girls who play with toys related to activities typically associated with boys are apt to be less concerned than parents of boys who play with toys typically associated with girls.

whose name was given as either "John" or "Mary," adults perceived "John" as adventurous and inquisitive, while "Mary" was considered fearful and anxious, although it was the same baby performing a single set of behaviors (Condry & Condry, 1976). Clearly, adults view the behavior of children through the lens of gender. **Gender** refers to our sense of being male or female. The term "gender" is often used to mean the same thing as "sex," but they are not actually the same. *Sex* typically refers to sexual anatomy and sexual behavior, while *gender* refers to the social perceptions of maleness or femaleness. All cultures prescribe *gender roles* for males and females, but these roles differ greatly between one culture to another.

**GENDER DIFFERENCES.** There is a considerable amount of disagreement over both the extent and causes of such gender differences, even though most agree that boys and girls do experience at least partially different worlds based on gender. Some gender differences are fairly clear from the time of birth. For example, male infants tend to be more active and fussier than female infants. Boys' sleep tends to be more disturbed than that of girls. Boys grimace more, although no gender difference exists in the overall amount of crying. There is also some evidence that male newborns are more irritable than female newborns, although the findings are inconsistent (Eaton & Enns, 1986; Guinsburg et al., 2000; Losonczy-Marshall, 2008).

Differences between male and female infants, however, are generally minor. In most ways infants seem so

**gender** The sense of being male or female

similar that usually adults cannot discern whether a baby is a boy or girl, as the "John" and "Mary" video research shows. Furthermore, it is important to remember that there are much larger differences among individual boys and among individual girls than there are, on average, between boys and girls (Crawford & Unger, 2004).

**GENDER ROLES.** Gender differences emerge more clearly as children age—and become increasingly influenced by the gender roles that society sets out for them. For instance, by age 1, infants are able to distinguish between males and females. Girls at this age prefer to play with dolls or stuffed animals, while boys seek out blocks and trucks. Often, of course, these are the only options available to them, owing to the choices their parents and other adults have made in the toys they provide (Cherney, Kelly-Vance, & Glover, 2003; Alexander, Wilcox, & Woods, 2009).

Children's preferences for certain kinds of toys are reinforced by their parents. In general, however, parents of boys are more apt to be concerned about their child's choices than are parents of girls. Boys receive more reinforcement for playing with toys that society deems appropriate for boys, and this reinforcement increases with age. A girl playing with a truck is viewed with considerably less concern than a boy playing with a doll might be. Girls who play with toys seen by society as "masculine" are less discouraged for their behavior than are boys who play with toys seen as "feminine" (Schmalz & Kerstetter, 2006; Hill & Flom, 2007).

By the time they reach age 2, boys behave more independently and less compliantly than girls. Much of this behavior can be traced to parental reactions to earlier behavior. For instance, when a child takes his or her first steps, parents tend to react differently, depending on the child's gender: Boys are encouraged more to go off and explore the world, while girls are hugged and kept close. It is hardly surprising, then, that by age 2, girls tend to show less independence and greater compliance (Poulin-Dubois, Serbin, & Eichstedt, 2002; Laemmle, 2013).

Societal encouragement and reinforcement do not, however, completely explain differences in behavior between boys and girls. For example, as we'll discuss further in Chapter 10, one study examined girls who were exposed before birth to abnormally high levels of *androgen*, a male hormone, because their mothers unwittingly took a drug containing the hormone while pregnant. Later, these girls were more likely to play with toys stereotypically preferred by boys (such as cars) and less likely to play with toys stereotypically associated with girls (such as dolls). Although there are many alternative explanations for these results—you can probably think of several yourself—one possibility is that exposure to male hormones affected the brain development of the girls, leading them to favor toys that involve certain kinds of preferred skills (Mealey, 2000; Servin et al., 2003).

In sum, differences in behavior between boys and girls begin in infancy, and—as we will see in future chapters— continue throughout childhood (and beyond). Although gender differences have complex causes, representing some combination of innate, biologically related and environmental factors, they play a profound role in the social and emotional development of infants.

# Family Life in the 21st Century

**LO 7.13  Describe how the definition of "family" has changed in recent years.**

A look back at television shows from several decades ago finds a world of families portrayed in a way that today seems oddly old-fashioned and quaint: mothers and fathers, married for years, and their good-looking children making their way in a world that appears to have few, if any, serious problems.

Over the years, the family structure, the nature of relationship among members, and the roles of family members have been changing with the advent of modernization, industrialization, and migration, and also with the impact of western culture. The number of joint families is diminishing, and the nature of care for the children is changing with the mothers joining the workforce. At the same time, society is adapting to the new realities of family life in the 21st century. Several kinds of social support exist for the parents of infants, and society is evolving new institutions to help in their care. One example is the growing array of child care arrangements available to help working parents, as we discuss next.

> **From a social worker's perspective:** What might a social worker seeking to find a good home for a foster child look for when evaluating potential foster parents?

# How Does Infant Child Care Affect Later Development?

**LO 7.14 Describe the impact of nonparental child care on infants.**

*Because I work at home, I decided to put my daughter into day care from age 2 until preschool. But she seemed sad every time I dropped her off, and I never got over feeling guilty. Was I hurting her emotionally? Was I depriving her of something essential? Would she be damaged because of my selfishness?*

Every day, parents ask themselves questions like these. The issue of how infant child care affects later development is a pressing one for many parents, who, because of economic, family, or career demands, leave their children to the care of others for a portion of the day. What effects do such arrangements have on later development?

First, the good news. According to most of the evidence, high-quality child care outside the home produces only minor differences from home care in most respects. For example, research finds little or no difference in the strength or nature of parental attachment bonds of infants who have been in high-quality child care compared with infants raised solely by their parents (NICHD Early Child Care Research Network, 2001b; Vandell et al., 2005; Sosinsky & Kim, 2013; Ruzek et al., 2014).

In addition to the direct benefits from involvement in child care outside the home, such as having the opportunity to interact with a wide array of peers, there are indirect benefits. For example, children in lower-income households and those whose mothers are single may benefit from the educational and social experiences in child care, as well as from the higher income produced by parental employment (Love et al., 2003; Dearing, McCartney, & Taylor, 2009).

Furthermore, children who participate in Head Start—a program that serves at-risk infants and toddlers in high-quality child care centers—can solve problems better, pay greater attention to others, and use language more effectively than poor children who do not participate in the program. In addition, their parents (who are also involved in the program) benefit from their participation. They talk and read more to their children, and they are less likely to spank them. Likewise, children who receive good, responsive child care were more likely to play well with other children (Maccoby & Lewis, 2003; Loeb et al., 2004; Fuhs & Day, 2011).

However, some of the findings on participation in child care outside the home are less positive. Infants may be somewhat less secure when they are placed in low-quality child care, if they are placed in multiple child care arrangements, or if their mothers are relatively insensitive and unresponsive. Also, children who spend long hours in outside-the-home child care situations have a lower ability to work independently and have less effective time management skills (Vandell et al., 2005).

The newest research, which focuses on preschoolers, finds that children who spend 10 or more hours a week in group child care for a year or more are more likely to be disruptive in class and that the effect continues through the sixth grade. Although the increased likelihood of disruptive activity is not substantial—every year spent in a child care center resulted in a 1 percent higher score on a standardized measure of problem behavior completed by teachers—the results were quite reliable (Belsky et al., 2007).

High-quality infant child care seems to produce only minor differences from home care in most respects, and some aspects of development may even be enhanced. What aspects of development might be enhanced by participation in infant child care outside the home?

# BECOMING AN INFORMED CONSUMER OF CHILD DEVELOPMENT

## Choosing the Right Infant Child Care Provider

One finding that emerges with absolute clarity from research conducted on the consequences of infant child care programs is that the benefits of child care—peer learning, greater social skills, greater independence—occur only when child care is of high quality. But what distinguishes high-quality child care from low-caliber programs? The American Psychological Association suggests that parents consider these questions in choosing a program (Committee on Children, Youth and Families, 1994; Zigler & Styfco, 2004; Love et al., 2003; de Schipper et al., 2006):

- *Are there enough providers?* A desirable ratio is one adult for every three infants, although one to four can be adequate.
- *Are group sizes manageable?* Even with several providers, a group of infants should not be larger than eight.
- *Has the center complied with all governmental regulations, and is it licensed?*
- *Do the people providing the care seem to like what they are doing?* What is their motivation? Is child care just a temporary job, or is it a career? Are they experienced? Do they seem happy in the job, or is offering child care just a way to earn money?
- *What do the caregivers do during the day?* Do they spend their time playing with, listening and talking to, and paying attention to the children? Do they seem genuinely interested in the children, rather than merely going through the motions of caring for them? Is there a television constantly on?
- *Are the children safe and clean?* Does the environment allow infants to move around safely? Are the equipment and furniture in good repair? Do the providers adhere to the highest levels of cleanliness? After changing a baby's diaper, do providers wash their hands?
- *What training do the providers have in caring for children?* Do they demonstrate a knowledge of the basics of infant development and an understanding of how normal children develop? Do they seem alert to signs that development may depart from normal patterns?
- *Finally, is the environment happy and cheerful?* Child care is not just a babysitting service. For the time an infant is there, it is the child's whole world. You should feel fully comfortable and confident that the child care center is a place where your infant will be treated as an individual.

In addition to following these guidelines, you may contact the National Association for the Education of Young Children, from which you can get the name of a resource and referral agency in your area. Go to their Web site at http://www.naeyc.org or call (800) 424-2460.

In sum, the ballooning body of research finds that the effects of participation in group child care are neither unambiguously positive nor unambiguously negative. What is clear, however, is that the *quality* of child care is critical. Ultimately, more research is needed on just who makes use of child care and how members of different segments of society use it to fully understand its consequences (NICHD Early Child Care Research Network, 2005; de Schipper et al., 2006; Belsky, 2006, 2009).

# The Case of …
## The Different Temperaments

Anita Sharma and Luma were neighbors and friends. Since both worked at home, they would meet frequently over coffee to swap news and ideas. When they both had babies within a few weeks of each other, childrearing seemed another thing to share. They not only exchanged childrearing ideas (it turned out that Anita was a disciplinarian, while Luma was more easygoing), they also began to swap child care hours, with one of them taking care of both children while the other went off on her own.

Anita considered Luma's son Tiku a wonderfully placid, quiet boy—completely unlike her daughter Mita. While Mita would crawl all around the house, endlessly trying to climb chairs and tables and incessantly curious about cell phones, kitchen drawers, and closed doors, Tiku would lie on the floor or sit at the table with crayons and paper, drawing for hours. When the weather turned mild enough for outdoor play, Anita had to watch Mita carefully every minute, but wherever she put Tiku—the porch, under the tree—that's where he'd be when she looked for him.

A bit frustrated, Anita found herself envying easy-going Luma. How had she managed to produce such a well-behaved child without constantly disciplining and controlling him?

Finally, she screwed up her courage and shared her feelings with Luma. "How do you do it? I wish I could get Mita to be as calm as Tiku. What's your secret?" Luma only stared at her. "That's funny," she said. "I was going to ask how you managed to get Mita to be so active, so curious. I'd love it if Teo would show the energy and spark of Mita."

1. How much of Mita's high activity level is likely to have genetic roots, and how much might be due to her environment?

2. Is it surprising that Anita the disciplinarian would have an active child? That easygoing Luma would have a placid child? Could their children have turned out the opposite of how they actually are?

3. Suppose both mothers have another child. What are the chances that the same pattern will repeat itself? Could Anita's second child be more placid and Luma's more active? Explain.

4. How would you advise both mothers about their tendency to compare the personal characteristics of their children with those of other children? What may change when the children attend school, and there is a larger pool of children for comparison?

5. If the two children continue to play together, do you think they will engage in social referencing? Do you think the characteristics of each child will begin to influence the behaviors of the other?

## Epilogue

The road infants travel as they develop as social individuals is a long and winding one. We saw in this chapter that infants begin decoding and encoding emotions early, using social referencing and eventually developing a theory of mind. We also considered how the attachment patterns that infants display can have long-term effects, influencing even what kind of parent the child eventually becomes. In addition to examining Erik Erikson's theory of psychosocial development, we discussed temperament and explored the nature and causes of gender differences. We concluded with a discussion of infant child care options.

Return to the prologue of this chapter, which describes Chantelle Evans, the 10-month-old girl who sobbed for 2 hours when her mother left her with a neighbor, and answer the following questions.

1. Do you think Chantelle is experiencing stranger anxiety, separation anxiety, or both? How would you explain to her mother that this indicates a positive, healthy development?

2. How might Chantelle's lack of self-awareness be related to her anxiety over her mother's absence?

3. Are Chantelle's red face and tears indications that she is experiencing emotions—genuine feelings of distress and grief? Explain your thinking.

4. Using what you know about social referencing in infants of Chantelle's age, what advice could you give to Michelle that might help her ease her daughter's transition to the neighbor's care?

## Looking Back

**LO 7.1  Describe the way infants experience and decode emotions.**

- Infants display a variety of facial expressions, which are similar across cultures and appear to reflect basic emotional states.

- Most researchers agree that infants are born with an array of emotional expressions, which they expand, modify, and learn to control as they age.

- The smiles of infants proceed from virtually meaningless expressions to social smiling, which grows increasingly more targeted and controlled between 6 weeks and 18 months.

- Early in life, infants develop the capability of nonverbal decoding: determining the emotional states of others based on their facial and vocal expressions.

**LO 7.2  Explain how infants develop a sense of who they are.**

- Infants begin to develop self-awareness at about the age of 12 months.

- By the age of 18 to 24 months, infants have developed an awareness of their own physical characteristics and capabilities, and they understand that their appearance is stable over time.

**LO 7.3  Provide examples of how infants use others' emotions to interpret social situations.**

- Through social referencing, infants from the age of 8 or 9 months use the expressions of others to clarify ambiguous situations and learn appropriate reactions to them.

**LO 7.4  Describe the mental lives of infants.**

- At a surprisingly early age, infants begin to develop a theory of mind: knowledge and beliefs about how they and others think.

- By age 2, children begin to demonstrate empathy, an emotional response to the feelings of others.

**LO 7.5  Explain the causes of stranger and separation anxiety in infants.**

- By the end of the first year, infants often develop both stranger anxiety, wariness around an unknown person, and separation anxiety, distress displayed when a customary care provider departs.

- Both stranger anxiety and separation anxiety are important aspects of social development, reflecting cognitive advances and growing bonds between infants and caregivers.

**LO 7.6  Define attachment in infancy.**

- Attachment, a strong, positive emotional bond that forms between an infant and one or more significant persons, is a crucial factor in enabling individuals to develop social relationships.

**LO 7.7  Summarize how attachment affects an individual's future social competence.**

- Infants display one of four major attachment patterns: securely attached, avoidant, ambivalent, and disorganized-disoriented. Research suggests an association between an infant's attachment pattern and his or her adult social and emotional competence.

**LO 7.8  Explain the roles of mothers and fathers in an infant's development of attachment.**

- Mothers who are sensitive to their infants' needs, desires, and feelings and respond to them appropriately seem most likely to produce securely attached infants.

- As men have taken a more active role in childrearing, infants have shown the ability to form attachments to their fathers as well as their mothers. In fact, some infants form their primary initial relationship with their father.

- Although infants are fully capable of forming attachments to both mother and father—as well as to other individuals—the nature of attachment between infants and mothers, on the one hand, and infants and fathers, on the other hand, is not identical. For example, when they are in unusually stressful circumstances, most infants prefer to be soothed by their mothers rather than by their fathers.

**LO 7.9  Compare the roles other people play in infants' social development.**

- Mothers' interactions with their babies are particularly important for social development. Mothers who respond effectively to their babies' social overtures appear to contribute to the babies' ability to become securely attached.

- Through a process of reciprocal socialization, infants and caregivers interact and affect one another's behavior, which strengthens their mutual relationship.

- From the earliest months of life, infants smile, laugh, and vocalize while looking at their peers.

- Infants also show more interest in peers than in inanimate objects and pay greater attention to other infants than they do to a mirror image of themselves.

## LO 7.10 Explain how infants develop unique personalities.

- The origins of personality, the sum total of the enduring characteristics that differentiate one individual from another, arise during infancy.

- Erik Erikson theorized that babies' early experiences shape their personalities as they pass through different stages of development during their infancy.

## LO 7.11 Define temperament in infants and explain its origins.

- Temperament encompasses enduring levels of arousal and emotionality that are characteristic of an individual. It is reflected in central and stable dimensions of behavior, including activity level and irritability.

- Recent approaches regard temperamental characteristics as inherited traits that are surprisingly stable across not only childhood, but the entire life span.

- Temperamental differences underlie the broad classification of infants into easy, difficult, and slow-to-warm categories.

- While no one type of temperament is invariably good or bad, children's long-term adjustment depends on the goodness-of-fit between their temperament and their environment. Temperament also seems to be related to infants' attachment to caregivers.

## LO 7.12 Explain the causes and consequences of gender differentiation.

- As infants age, gender differences become more pronounced, mostly due to environmental influences. Differences are accentuated by parental expectations and behavior.

- Gender differences are not neutral phenomena; they lead to differences in gender roles, children's actual behavior and preferences, and societal expectations.

## LO 7.13 Describe how the definition of "family" has changed in recent years.

- Families have changed since in the middle of the 20th century, as the so-called "nuclear family" began to decline.

- Since that time, the number of single-parent families has increased, the average family size has shrunk, mothers increasingly work outside the home, the incidence of teenage births has risen, and more families with children are classified as low-income households.

## LO 7.14 Describe the impact of nonparental child care on infants.

- Child care, a societal response to the changing nature of the family, can be beneficial to the social development of children, fostering social interaction and cooperation, if it is of high quality.

# Key Terms and Concepts

social smile (p. 173)
self-awareness (p. 175)
social referencing (p. 176)
theory of mind (p. 176)
empathy (p. 177)
stranger anxiety (p. 1780)
separation anxiety (p. 178)
attachment (p. 179)
Ainsworth Strange Situation
(p. 180)
secure attachment pattern (p. 180)

avoidant attachment pattern
(p. 181)
ambivalent attachment pattern
(p. 181)
disorganized-disoriented
attachment pattern (p. 181)
mutual regulation model (p. 184)
reciprocal socialization (p. 186)
personality (p. 188)
Erikson's theory of psychosocial
development (p. 188)

trust-versus-mistrust stage
(p. 188)
autonomy-versus-shame-
and-doubt stage (p. 188)
temperament (p. 188)
easy babies (p. 190)
difficult babies (p. 190)
slow-to-warm babies (p. 190)
goodness-of-fit (p. 190)
gender (p. 191)

# Putting It All Together

## Infancy

### Physical, Cognitive, and Social and Personality Development in Infancy

*Four-month-old Alex was a model infant in almost every respect. There was one aspect of his behavior, however, that posed a dilemma: how to respond when he woke up in the middle of the night and cried despondently. It usually was not a matter of being hungry, because typically he had been fed recently. And it was not caused by his diaper being soiled, because usually that had been changed recently. Instead, it seemed that Alex just wanted to be held and entertained, and when he wasn't, he cried and shrieked dramatically until someone came to him.*

### Physical Development

- Alex develops various rhythms (repetitive, cyclical patterns). Part of Alex's temperament is that he is irritable. Irritable infants fuss a great deal and are easily upset; they are also difficult to soothe when they do begin to cry (p. 121).

- Since irritability is relatively stable, Alex will continue to display this temperament at age 1 and even age 2 (p. 122).

- Alex will sleep in spurts of around 2 hours, followed by periods of wakefulness until about 16 weeks, when he will begin to sleep as much as 6 continuous hours (p. 123).

- Since sense of touch is one of his most highly developed senses (and one of the earliest developed), he will respond to gentle touches, such as a soothing caress, which can calm a crying, fussy infant (p. 138).

### Cognitive Development

- Alex will learn that his behavior (crying) can produce a desired effect (someone holding and entertaining him) (p. 145).

- As Alex's brain develops, he is able to separate people he knows from people he doesn't; this is why he responds so positively when someone he is familiar with comes to comfort him during the night (p. 151).

### Social and Personality Development

- Alex has developed attachment (the positive emotional bond between him and particular individuals) to those who care for him (p. 178).

- In order to feel secure, Alex needs to know that his caregivers will provide an appropriate response to the signals he is sending (p. 183).

### From a PARENT'S perspective:

- What strategies would you use in dealing with Alex? Would you go to him every time he cried? Or would you try to wait him out, perhaps setting a time limit before going to him?

  HINT: **Review pages 187–189.**

### From a NURSE'S perspective:

- How would you recommend that Alex's caregivers deal with the situation? Are there any dangers the caregivers should be aware of?

  HINT: **Review pages 187–189.**

### From an EDUCATOR'S perspective:

- Suppose Alex spends a few hours every weekday afternoon in day care. If you were a child care provider, how would you deal with Alex if he wakes up from naps soon after falling asleep?

  HINT: **Review pages 121–123.**

### From YOUR perspective:

- How would you deal with Alex? What factors would affect your decision? Based on your reading, how do you think Alex will respond?

  HINT: **Review pages 138–141.**

# Chapter 8
# Physical Development in Preschoolers

## Learning Objectives

**LO 8.1** Describe the bodily changes children experience in the preschool years.

**LO 8.2** Summarize how children's brains change during the preschool years.

**LO 8.3** Explain how brain growth affects cognitive and sensory development.

**LO 8.4** Describe preschoolers' sleep patterns.

**LO 8.5** Outline the nutritional needs of preschool children, and explain what causes obesity.

**LO 8.6** Identify the illnesses preschool children experience.

**LO 8.7** Explain why injuries pose the greatest threat to wellness in preschool children.

**LO 8.8** Explain the types of child abuse and psychological maltreatment and what causes their occurrence.

**LO 8.9** List the personal traits that contribute to a child's resilience.

**LO 8.10** Explain the development of children's gross and fine motor skills during the preschool years.

**LO 8.11** Identify the factors that determine when a child is ready for toilet training.

**LO 8.12** Explain how handedness and artistic expression develop during the preschool years.

# Prologue: Depressed in Preschool

"I don't think I would have caught it on my own," says Parul, a preschool teacher in Delhi. "Like any teacher, I'm alert for issues that our children may have, but Dev was an *easy* 4-year-old, always seeking to please, always empathizing with other kids when they cried. Still, when his parents mentioned *their* concerns, I looked more closely.

"I noticed that Dev never seemed 'fun-loving'—never running around or climbing the slide or swinging on the swings. When I asked him about this, he told me matter-of-factly, 'Those things aren't fun. They're boring.' One time he threw a LEGO block against the wall. When I approached, he said 'I'm no good at LEGOs. I'll never be good at them. I shouldn't play with them.'

"I began to notice that Dev quickly turned learning frustrations into personal sources of guilt. For instance, he would never even try to say the days of the week in Circle Time until he was sure he would get them right. In fact, he never tried anything—the alphabet, counting

to 10—until he was certain he had mastered it. When I noticed Dev sometimes staring off into space, generally a normal behavior, I began to wonder if he wasn't just distracted but truly bothered by something.

"I talked to our principal, and we met with Dev's parents. They decided to take him to a child psychologist, who eventually determined that Dev had childhood depression."

# Looking Ahead

By the time they enter preschool, children who could barely lift their heads a few years earlier now move with confidence—running, jumping, and building things with blocks. These advances in mobility are challenging to parents, who must rise to a whole new level of vigilance in order to prevent injuries.

But the physical development that children undergo at this age results in more than leaping and climbing. It also brings new issues, such as the mental complexity that enabled Dev at one and the same time to try to build things, to feel inadequate about his efforts, and to express his feeling of shame to his teacher.

The preschool period is an exciting time in children's lives. In one sense, it marks a time of preparation: a period spent anticipating and getting ready for the start of a child's formal education, through which society will begin the process of passing on its intellectual tools to a new generation.

But it is a mistake to take the label "preschool" too literally. The years between 3 and 6 are hardly a mere way station in life, an interval spent waiting for the next, more important period to start. Instead, the preschool years are a time of tremendous change and growth, where physical, intellectual, and social development proceeds at a rapid pace.

In this chapter, we focus on the physical changes that occur during the preschool years. We begin by considering the nature of growth during those years. We discuss the rapid changes in the body's weight and height, as well as developmental changes in the brain and its neural byways. We also consider some intriguing findings relating to the ways the brain functions in terms of gender and culture.

Next, we examine health and wellness in the preschool years. After discussing the nutritional needs of preschoolers, we study the risk of illness and injury that they face. We also look at the grimmer side of some children's lives: child abuse and psychological maltreatment.

The chapter ends with a discussion of the development of gross and fine motor skills. We consider the significant changes that occur during the preschool period in motor performance and what these changes allow children to accomplish. We also look at the impact of being right- or left-handed and discuss how artistic abilities develop during the preschool years.

# Physical Growth

*It is an unseasonably warm spring day at the Cushman Hill Preschool, one of the first nice days after a long winter. The children in Mary Scott's class have happily left their winter coats in the classroom, and they are excitedly playing outside. Jessie plays a game of catch with Germaine, and Sarah and Molly are climbing up the slide. Craig and Marta chase one another, while Jesse and Bernstein try, with gales of giggles, to play leapfrog. Virginia and Ollie sit across from each other on the teeter-totter, successively bumping it so hard into the ground that they both are in danger of being knocked off. Erik, Jim, Scott, and Paul race around the perimeter of the playground, running for the sheer joy of it.*

These same children, now so active and mobile, were unable even to crawl or walk just a few years earlier. Just how far they have developed is apparent when we look at the specific changes they have undergone in their size, shape, and abilities.

## The Growing Body

### LO 8.1  Describe the bodily changes children experience in the preschool years.

Two years after birth, the average child in the United States weighs 25 to 30 pounds and is close to 36 inches tall—around half the height of the average adult. Children grow steadily during the preschool period, and by the time they are 6 years old, they weigh, on average, about 46 pounds and stand 46 inches tall.

**INDIVIDUAL DIFFERENCES IN HEIGHT AND WEIGHT.** These averages mask great individual differences in height and weight. For instance, 10 percent of 6-year-olds weigh 55 pounds or more, and 10 percent weigh 36 pounds or less. Furthermore, average differences in height and weight between boys and girls increase during the preschool years. Although at age 2 the differences are relatively small, during the preschool years, boys start becoming taller and heavier, on average, than girls.

Global economics also affect these averages. Profound differences in height and weight exist among children in economically developed countries and those in developing countries. The better nutrition and health care received by children in developed countries translates into significant differences in growth. For instance, the average Swedish 4-year-old is as tall as the average 6-year-old in Bangladesh (Leathers & Foster, 2004; Chakravarty & Pati, 2013; Mendoza et al., 2017).

Differences in height and weight reflect economic factors within the United States as well. For instance, children in families whose incomes are below the poverty level are far more likely to be unusually short than children raised in more affluent homes (Barrett & Frank, 1987; Ogden et al., 2002).

From a health care worker's perspective: How might biology and environment combine to affect the physical growth of a child adopted as an infant from a developing country and reared in a more industrialized one?

**CHANGES IN BODY SHAPE AND STRUCTURE.** If we compare the bodies of a 2-year-old and a 6-year-old, we find that the bodies vary not only in height and weight, but also in shape. During the preschool years, boys and girls become less chubby and roundish and more slender. They begin to burn off some of the fat they have carried from their infancy, and they no longer have a potbellied appearance. Moreover, their arms and legs lengthen, and the size relationship between the head and the rest of the body becomes more adult-like. In fact, by the time children reach 6 years of age, their proportions are quite similar to those of adults.

The changes in size, weight, and appearance we see during the preschool years are only the tip of the iceberg. Internally, other physical changes are occurring. Children grow stronger as their muscle size increases and their bones become sturdier. The sense organs continue their development. For instance, the *eustachian tube* in the ear, which carries sounds from the external to the internal part of the ear, moves from a position that is almost parallel to the ground at birth to a more angular position. This change sometimes leads to an increase in the frequency of earaches during the preschool years.

# The Growing Brain

**LO 8.2   Summarize how children's brains change during the preschool years.**

The brain grows at a faster rate than does any other part of the body. Two-year-olds who have received proper nutrients have brains that are about three-fourths the size and weight of an adult brain. By age 5, children's brains weigh 90 percent of the average adult's brain weight. In comparison, the average 5-year-old's total body weight is just 30 percent of the average adult's body weight (Nihart, 1993; House, 2007).

**GROWTH FACTORS.** Why does the brain grow so rapidly? One reason is an increase in the number of interconnections among cells, as we saw in Chapter 5. These interconnections allow for more complex communication between neurons, and they permit the rapid growth of cognitive skills that we discuss later in the chapter. In addition, the amount of myelin—the protective insulation that surrounds parts of neurons—increases, which speeds the transmission of electrical impulses along brain cells but also adds to brain weight. This rapid brain growth not only allows for increased cognitive abilities, but also helps in the development of more sophisticated fine and gross motor skills (Dalton & Bergenn, 2007; Klingberg & Betteridge, 2013; Dean et al., 2014).

By the end of the preschool period, some parts of the brain have undergone particularly significant growth. For example, the *corpus callosum*, a bundle of nerve fibers that connect the two hemispheres of the brain, becomes considerably thicker, developing as many as 800 million individual fibers that help coordinate brain functioning between the two hemispheres.

In contrast, children who are malnourished show delays in brain development. For example, severely malnourished children develop less myelination protecting their neurons (Hazin, Alves, & Rodrigues Falbo, 2007).

**BRAIN LATERALIZATION.** The two halves of the brain also begin to become increasingly differentiated and specialized. **Lateralization**, the process by which certain functions are located more in one hemisphere than in the other, becomes more pronounced during the preschool years.

For most people, the left hemisphere is involved primarily with tasks that necessitate verbal competence, such as speaking, reading, thinking, and reasoning. The right hemisphere develops its own strengths, especially in nonverbal areas such as comprehension of spatial relationships, recognition of patterns and drawings, music, and emotional expression (Pollak, Holt, & Wismer Fries, 2004; Watling & Bourne, 2007; Dundas, Plaut & Behrmann, 2013; see Figure 8.1).

Each of the two hemispheres also begins to process information in a slightly different manner. Whereas the left hemisphere considers information sequentially, one piece of data at a time, the right hemisphere processes information in a more global manner, reflecting on it as a whole (Ansaldo, Arguin, & Roch-Locours, 2002; Holowaka & Petitto, 2002; Barber et al., 2012).

---

**lateralization** The process whereby certain functions are located more in one hemisphere of the brain than in the other

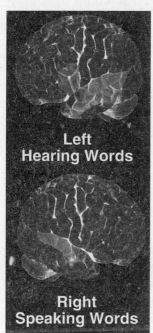

**Figure 8.1** Brain Activity

This set of PET scans of the brain shows that activity in the right or left hemisphere differs according to the task in which a person is engaged. How might educators use this finding in their approach to teaching?

Although there is some specialization of the hemispheres, in most respects the two hemispheres act in tandem. They are interdependent, and the differences between the two are minor. Even the hemispheric specialization in certain tasks is not absolute. In fact, each hemisphere can perform most of the tasks of the other. For example, the right hemisphere does some language processing and plays an important role in language comprehension (Hall, Neal, & Dean, 2008; Rowland & Noble, 2011; Hodgson, Hirst, & Hudson, 2016).

Furthermore, the brain has remarkable resiliency. In another example of human plasticity, if the hemisphere that specializes in a particular type of information is damaged, the other hemisphere can take up the slack. For instance, when young children suffer brain damage to the left side of the brain (which specializes in verbal processing) and initially lose language capabilities, the linguistic deficits are often not permanent. In such cases, the right side of the brain pitches in and may be able to compensate substantially for the damage to the left hemisphere (Kolb & Gibb, 2006; Elkana et al., 2011).

There are also individual differences in lateralization. For example, many of the 10 percent of people who are left-handed or ambidextrous (able to use both hands interchangeably) have language centered in their right hemispheres or have no specific language center (Isaacs et al., 2006; Szaflarski et al., 2012; Porac,

2016). Even more intriguing are differences in lateralization related to gender and culture, as we consider in the *Developmental Diversity and Your Life* box.

## The Links Between Brain Growth and Cognitive and Sensory Development

**LO 8.3** Explain how brain growth affects cognitive and sensory development.

Neuroscientists are just beginning to understand the ways in which brain development is related to cognitive and sensory development.

**COGNITIVE DEVELOPMENT.** It appears that there are periods during childhood in which the brain shows unusual growth spurts, and these periods are linked to advances in cognitive abilities. One study that measured electrical activity in the brain across the life span found unusual spurts between 1½ and 2 years, a time when language abilities increase rapidly. Other spurts occurred around other ages when cognitive advances are particularly intense (see Figure 8.2; Mabbott et al., 2006; Westermann et al., 2007).

**Figure 8.2** Brain Growth Spurt

According to one study, electrical activity in the brain has been linked to advances in cognitive abilities at various stages of life. In this graph, activity increases dramatically between 18 and 24 months, a period during which language rapidly develops.

**SOURCE:** Fischer and Rose (1995).

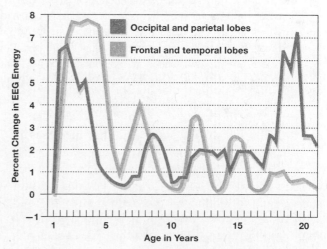

# DEVELOPMENTAL DIVERSITY AND YOUR LIFE
## Are Gender and Culture Related to the Brain's Structure?

Among the most controversial findings relating to the specialization of the hemispheres of the brain is evidence that lateralization is related to gender and culture. For instance, starting during the first year of life and continuing in the preschool years, boys and girls show some hemispheric differences associated with lower body reflexes and the processing of auditory information. Boys also clearly tend to show greater specialization of language in the left hemisphere; among girls, language is more evenly divided between the two hemispheres. Such differences may help explain why—as we'll see later in the chapter—girls' language development proceeds at a more rapid pace during the preschool years than does boys' language development (Grattan et al., 1992; Bourne & Todd, 2004; Huster, Westerhausen, & Herrmann, 2011).

According to psychologist Simon Baron-Cohen, the differences between male and female brains may help explain the puzzling riddle of *autism spectrum disorder*, the profound developmental disability that often produces language deficits and great difficulty in interacting with others. Baron-Cohen argues that children with autism spectrum disorder (who are predominately male) have what he calls an "extreme male brain." The extreme male brain, though relatively good at systematically sorting out the world, is poor at understanding the emotions of others and experiencing empathy for others' feelings. To Baron-Cohen, individuals with an extreme male brain have traits associated with the normal male brain, but display the traits to such an extent that their behavior is viewed as autistic (Stauder, Cornet, & Ponds, 2011; Auyeung & Baron-Cohen, 2012; Lau et al., 2013).

Although Baron-Cohen's theory is quite controversial, it is clear that some kind of gender differences exist in lateralization. But we still don't know the extent of the differences, and why they occur. One explanation is genetic: Female brains and male brains are predisposed to function in slightly different ways. Such a view is supported by data suggesting that there are minor structural differences between males' and females' brains. For instance, a section of the corpus callosum is proportionally larger in women than in men. Furthermore, studies conducted among other species, such as primates, rats, and hamsters, have found size and structural differences in the brains of males and females (Matsumoto, 1999; Király et al., 2016).

Before we accept a genetic explanation for the differences between female and male brains, we need to consider an equally plausible alternative: It may be that verbal abilities emerge earlier in girls because girls receive greater encouragement for verbal skills than boys do. For instance, even as infants, girls are spoken to more than boys. Such higher levels of verbal stimulation may produce growth in particular areas of the brain that does not occur in boys. Consequently, environmental factors rather than genetic ones may lead to the gender differences we find in brain lateralization (Beal, 1994; Rosenberg, 2013).

Is the culture in which one is raised related to brain lateralization? Some research suggests it is. For instance, native speakers of Japanese process information related to vowel sounds primarily in the left hemisphere of the brain. In comparison, North and South Americans and Europeans—as well as people of Japanese ancestry who learn Japanese as a second language—process vowel sounds primarily in the brain's right hemisphere.

The explanation for this cultural difference in processing of vowels seems to rest on the nature of the Japanese language. Specifically, the Japanese language allows for the expression of complex concepts using only vowel sounds. Consequently, a specific type of brain lateralization may develop while learning and using Japanese at a relatively early age (Tsunoda, 1985; Hiser & Kobayashi, 2003).

This explanation, which is speculative, does not rule out the possibility that some type of subtle genetic difference may also be at work in determining the difference in lateralization. Once again, then, we find that teasing out the relative impact of heredity and environment is a challenging task.

Other research has suggested that increases in **myelin**, the protective insulation that surrounds parts of neurons, may be related to preschoolers' growing cognitive capabilities. For example, myelination of the reticular formation, an area of the brain associated with attention and concentration, is completed by the time children are about 5. This may be associated with children's growing attention spans as they approach school age. The improvement in memory that occurs may also be associated with myelination: During the preschool years, myelination is completed

**myelin** Protective insulation that surrounds parts of neurons

in the hippocampus, an area associated with memory (Rolls, 2000).

We do not yet know the direction of causality. (Does brain development produce cognitive advances, or do cognitive accomplishments fuel brain development?) It is clear, however, that increases in our understanding of the physiological aspects of the brain will eventually have important implications for parents and teachers.

**SENSORY DEVELOPMENT.** The increasing development of the brain permits improvements in the senses during the preschool period. For instance, brain maturation leads to better control of eye movements and focusing. Still, preschoolers' eyes are not as capable as they will be in later stages of development. Specifically, preschool children are unable to easily and precisely scan groupings of small letters, as is required when reading small print. Consequently, preschoolers who start to read often focus on just the initial letter of a word and guess at the rest—leading, as you might expect, to relatively frequent errors. It is not until they are approximately 6 years of age that children can effectively focus and scan. Even at this point, however, they still don't have the capabilities of adults (Willows, Kruk, & Corcos, 1993).

Preschool children also begin a gradual shift in the way they view objects made up of multiple parts. For instance, consider the rather unusual vegetable-fruit-bird combination shown in Figure 8.3. Rather than identifying it as a bird, as most adults do, preschool children see the figure in terms of the parts that make it up ("carrots" and "cherries" and "a pear"). Not until they reach middle childhood, about age 7 or 8, do they begin to look at the figure in terms of both its overall organization and its parts ("a bird made of fruit").

Preschoolers' judgments of objects may reflect the way in which their eyes move when perceiving figures (Zaporozhets, 1965). Until age 3 or 4, preschoolers devote most of their looking to the insides of two-dimensional objects they are scanning, concentrating on the internal details and largely ignoring the perimeter of the figure. In contrast, 4- and 5-year-olds begin to look more at the surrounding boundaries of the figure, and at ages 6 and 7, they look at the outside systematically, with far less scanning of the inside. The result is a greater awareness of the overall organization of the figure. (For more on changes in visual perception, see the *From Research to Practice* box.)

**Figure 8.3** Sensory Development

Preschool children who view this odd vegetable-fruit-bird combination focus on the components that make it up. Not until they reach middle childhood do they begin to look at the figure as a whole in addition to its parts.

**SOURCE:** Elkind (1978).

Of course, vision is not the only sense that improves during the preschool period. *Auditory acuity*, or the sharpness of hearing, improves as well. Because hearing is more fully developed at the start of the preschool period, the improvement is not as significant as that seen with vision.

One area in which preschoolers' auditory acuity does show some deficits is in their ability to isolate specific sounds when many sounds are heard simultaneously (Moores & Meadow-Orlans, 1990). This deficiency may account for why some preschoolers are easily distracted by competing sounds in group situations such as classrooms.

## Sleep

### LO 8.4 Describe preschoolers' sleep patterns.

No matter how tired they may be, some active preschoolers find it difficult to make the transition from the excitement of the day to settling down for a night's rest. This may lead to friction between caregivers and preschoolers over bedtime. Children may object to being told to sleep, and it may take them some time before they are able to fall asleep.

Although most children settle down fairly easily and drift off into sleep, for some, sleep presents a real

# FROM RESEARCH TO PRACTICE
## Preschoolers Notice What Adults Miss

If you're like most people, you've seen the classic film *The Wizard of Oz* at least once—and also like most people, whether you've seen the film once or a hundred times, you probably never noticed its frequent continuity errors, such as the many times that Dorothy's hair length and style inexplicably change from shot to shot. And if you've ever struggled to find the five small specific differences between two otherwise identical drawings in a children's puzzle book, you understand just how fiendishly difficult it can be to detect changes in a visual stimulus. This difficulty in detecting changes in visual stimuli is known as *change blindness* (Bergmann et al., 2016).

Change blindness may seem like a failure to pay attention to a stimulus properly. But it's more accurate to call it the result of *success* in attention. When adults fail to see changes in the visual field, it's usually because their attention is narrowly focused on task-relevant features; simply put, we get very good at tuning out unimportant information. But this is a skill that develops with age, and young children just don't yet have the cognitive capacity to operate this kind of attentional filter (Posner & Rothbart, 2007). This raises the question of whether young children are therefore less susceptible to change blindness than adults are.

To test this hypothesis, researchers used a change detection task. They showed children ages 4–5 and college-age adults a series of images in which two outline shapes, one red and one green, were overlapped. For example, a red outline of a five-pointed star shape might be drawn on top of a green outline of a heart shape. On each trial an image was shown for 1 second, masked for half a second, and then shown for 1 second again, and participants were asked to indicate whether the second showing was different from the first. The red shape always changed for the first five trials, focusing participants' attention on the red shapes. Then on subsequent trials, sometimes the red shape changed, sometimes the green shape did, and sometimes there was no change (Plebanek & Sloutsky, in press).

As you might expect, the adults outperformed the 4- and 5-year-olds on accurately detecting when the attention-focused shape (the red shape) changed. But the children outperformed the adults on detecting when the non-attention-focused shape (the green shape) changed. Whereas adults were cued to focus on the red shape and filter out the green, children distributed their attention more equally to the two kinds of shapes, thereby giving them the advantage of noticing what the adults were missing.

As the researchers pointed out, reduced susceptibility to change blindness in young children is probably a good thing. It means that they remain open to noticing and exploring a broader base of information rather than tuning out what may be important learning opportunities. By promoting exploration and novelty seeking, young children's deficient attentional focus may therefore play a crucial role in their cognitive development (Deng & Sloutsky, 2015; Plebanek & Sloutsky, in press).

- **How might a preschool teacher apply these research findings in the classroom?**
- **What benefits do young children derive from their reduced susceptibility to change blindness? What might be some costs?**

---

problem. As many as 20 to 30 percent of preschoolers experience difficulties lasting more than an hour in getting to sleep. Furthermore, they may wake in the night and call to their parents for comfort. Having a consistent bedtime routine and eliminating media exposure close to bedtime can help reduce sleep disturbances (Morgenthaler et al., 2006).

Once they do get to sleep, most preschoolers sleep fairly soundly through the night; however, between 10 and 50 percent of children ages 3 to 5 experience nightmares, with the frequency higher in boys than in girls. **Nightmares** are vivid bad dreams, usually occurring toward morning. Although an occasional nightmare is no cause for concern, when they occur repeatedly and cause a child anxiety during waking hours, they may be indicative of a problem (Pagel, 2000; Zisenwine et al., 2013; Floress et al., 2016).

**Night terrors** produce intense physiological arousal and cause a child to wake up in a deep state of panic. After waking from a night terror, children are not easily comforted, and they cannot say why they are so disturbed and cannot recall having a bad dream. The following morning, they cannot remember anything about the incident. Night terrors are much less frequent than

---

**nightmare** A vivid bad dream, usually occurring toward morning

**night terror** An intense physiological arousal that causes a child to awaken in a state of panic

nightmares, occurring in just 1 to 5 percent of children (Bootzin et al., 1993).

# Health and Wellness

*Nina Mishra worries that her 3-year-old son, Kanu, is not getting enough food. "He used to eat everything on his plate, and now he barely touches anything," she says. "I'm concerned he won't grow properly." Nina also worries that the constant mealtime "wars" are affecting her relationship with her son. "If I could just be sure he is getting the nutrition he needs, I could relax," she says. "But I can't believe anyone could survive on so little."*

## Nutrition: Eating the Right Foods

**LO 8.5   Outline the nutritional needs of preschool children, and explain what causes obesity.**

Because the rate of growth during the preschool period is slower than the rate of growth during infancy, preschoolers need less food to maintain their growth. The change in food consumption may be so noticeable that parents sometimes worry that their preschooler is not eating enough. Fortunately, children tend to be quite adept at maintaining an appropriate intake of food, if they are provided with nutritious meals. In fact, anxiously encouraging children to eat more than they seem to want naturally may lead them to increase their food intake beyond an appropriate level.

Ultimately, some children's food consumption can become so high that they become *overweight*, defined as *a body mass index (BMI)* between the 85th and 95th percentiles of children of the same weight and height. (BMI is calculated by dividing a child's weight in kilograms by the square of their height in meters). If the BMI is even greater, then children are considered obese. **Obesity** is defined as a BMI at or above the 95th percentile for children of the same age and sex.

The prevalence of obesity among older preschoolers increased significantly through the 1980s and 1990s. However, research released in 2014 found that the incidence of obesity declined over the prior 10 years from nearly 14 percent to just over 8 percent—a significant breakthrough in children's health (Robertson et al., 2012; Tavernise, 2014; Ogden et al., 2016).

How do parents ensure that their children have good nutrition without turning mealtimes into a tense,

adversarial situation? In most cases, the best strategy is to make sure that a variety of foods, low in fat and high in nutritional content, is available. Foods that have a relatively high iron content are particularly important: Iron deficiency anemia, which causes chronic fatigue, is one of the prevalent nutritional problems not only in developing countries but also in developed countries like United States. High-iron foods include dark green vegetables (such as broccoli), whole grains, and some kinds of meat, such as lean ground beef. It is also important to avoid foods with high sodium content and to include foods with low fat content (Grant et al., 2007; Akhtar-Danesh et al., 2011; Jalonick, 2011).

Because preschool children, like adults, will not find all foods equally appealing, children should be given the opportunity to develop their own natural preferences. As long as their overall diet is adequate, no single food is indispensable. Exposing children to wide variety of foods by encouraging them to take just one bite of new foods is often a relatively low-stress way of expanding children's diets (Busick et al., 2008; Struempler et al., 2014).

In behavior called the *just-right phenomenon*, some preschool children develop strong rituals and routines about the kinds of foods they will eat. They may only eat certain foods that are prepared in a particular way and presented to them in a particular manner on a plate. In adults, such rigidity would be a sign of a psychological disorder, but it is normal in young children. Almost all preschoolers eventually outgrow it (Evans et al., 1997).

## Illness in the Preschool Years

**LO 8.6   Identify the illnesses preschool children experience.**

In India, the major causes of childhood illness are malnutrition, diarrhea, and respiratory diseases. According to the 2005–06 National Family Health Survey (NFHS-3), 60 percent of the children were brought to hospitals with diarrhea, 69 percent with acute respiratory infection, and 71 percent having high fever. Despite being easily preventable, diarrhea is one of the major killer for children under the age of 5. In addition, in recent days, environmental hazards are of serious concern for children's health.

---

**obesity** A BMI at or above the 95th percentile for children of the same age and sex

WHO (2017) stated that more than 1 in 4 deaths could be prevented by cleaning the environment. To quote WHO facts, "Environmental risks that children are particularly vulnerable to include air pollution, inadequate water, sanitation and hygiene, hazardous chemicals and wastes, radiation, climate change as well as emerging threats like e-waste."

**MINOR ILLNESSES.**  The average preschooler has seven to 10 minor colds and other minor respiratory illnesses in each of the years from age 3 to 5. Although the sniffles and coughs that are the symptoms of such illnesses are certainly distressing to children, the unpleasantness is usually not too severe, and the illnesses usually last only a few days (Kalb, 1997).

Actually, such minor illnesses may offer some unexpected benefits: Not only may they help children build up immunity to more severe illnesses to which they may be exposed in the future, but they also may provide some emotional benefits. Specifically, some researchers argue that minor illness helps children to understand their bodies better. It also may permit them to learn coping skills that will help them deal more effectively with future, more severe diseases. Furthermore, it gives them the ability to understand better what others who are sick are going through. This ability to put oneself in another's shoes, known as empathy, may teach children to be more sympathetic and better caretakers (Notaro, Gelman, & Zimmerman, 2002; Raman & Winer, 2002; Williams & Binnie, 2002).

**MAJOR ILLNESSES.**  The preschool years were not always a period of relatively good health. Before the discovery of vaccines and the routine immunization of children, the preschool period was a dangerous time. Even today, this period is risky in many parts of the world, as well as in certain lower socioeconomic segments of the U.S. population (Ripple & Zigler, 2003).

Why does the United States, the richest nation in the world, provide less than ideal health care for its children? Culture provides a major part of the answer. The U.S. cultural tradition is that children are the complete responsibility of their parents, not of the government or of other individuals. What this means is that socioeconomic factors prevent some children from getting good health care and that members of minority groups, which tend to have less disposable income, suffer from inferior care.

In other cultures, however, childrearing is regarded as a shared, collective responsibility. Until the United States gives greater priority to the health of its children, the country will continue to lag behind in the effectiveness of its child care (Ren, Pritzker, & Leung, 2016).

The most frequent major illness to strike preschoolers is cancer, particularly in the form of leukemia. Leukemia causes the bone marrow to produce an excessive amount of white blood cells, inducing severe anemia and, potentially, death. Although just two decades ago a diagnosis of leukemia was the equivalent of a death sentence, today the story is quite different. Due to advances in treatment, more than 70 percent of victims of childhood leukemia survive (Ford & Martinez-Ramirez, 2006; Brown et al., 2008; Krull & Brinkman, 2013).

One childhood disease that presents a more discouraging picture is AIDS, or acquired immune deficiency syndrome. Children with this disease face many difficulties. For instance, even though there is virtually no risk of spreading the disease through everyday contact, children with AIDS may be shunned by others. Furthermore, because their parents may suffer from the disease themselves—children with AIDS typically have contracted the disease prenatally from their mothers—there are often severe disruptions in the family due to a parent's death. However, treatment options are expanding, and the number of cases of AIDS in children is declining due to increasing use of drugs that reduce prenatal transmission from mothers to children (Plowfield, 2007).

**REACTIONS TO HOSPITALIZATION.**  For ill preschoolers who must spend time in the hospital, the experience is quite difficult. The most frequent reaction of 2- to 4-year-olds is anxiety, most typically brought about by the separation from their parents. At slightly older ages, preschoolers may become upset because they interpret their hospitalization, on some level, as desertion or rejection by their family. Their anxiety may result in the development of new fears, such as fear of the dark or of hospital staff (Taylor, 1991).

One of the ways that hospitals deal with the anxieties of young patients is to allow a parent to stay for lengthy periods of time with the child or even, in some cases, permitting parents to spend the night on a cot in the child's room. But it does not have to be a parent who can alleviate a child's fears: Assigning children a "substitute mother," a nurse or other care provider who is supportive and nurturing, can go a long way toward reducing children's concerns. In addition, providing older children with the opportunity to participate in decisions about their care leads to anxiety reduction (Branstetter, 1969; Runeson, Martenson, & Enskar, 2007).

**PSYCHOLOGICAL DISORDERS.** Although physical illness is typically a minor problem during the preschool years, an increasing number of children are being treated with drugs for psychological disorders such as depression, formally known as *depressive disorders*. For example, it is now believed that depression affects around 4 percent of preschoolers in the United States, and the rate of diagnosis has increased significantly. Other problems include phobias, anxiety disorders, and behavioral disorders. In addition, the use of drugs such as antidepressants and stimulants has grown significantly (Bufferd et al., 2012; Muller, 2013; Black, Jukes & Willoughby, 2017).

However, it is not clear why the increase in diagnosis and treatment of psychological disorders has occurred. In fact, some experts believe that psychological disorders are over-diagnosed and instead simply represent normal developmental patterns of behavior. In some cases, parents and preschool teachers may be seeking in drug treatments a quick fix for behavior problems that may, in fact, represent normal difficulties (Zito et al., 2000; Colino, 2002; Zito, 2002; Mitchell et al., 2008).

## Injuries: Playing It Safe

**LO 8.7    Explain why injuries pose the greatest threat to wellness in preschool children.**

The greatest risk that preschoolers face comes from neither illness nor nutritional problems but from accidents. Before age 10, children have twice the likelihood of dying from an injury as from an illness. Children in the United States have a 1 in 3 chance every year of receiving an injury that requires medical attention. Globally, a child dies from a preventable injury every 30 seconds (Field & Behrman, 2003; National Safety Council, 2013).

The danger of injuries during the preschool years is in part a result of children's high levels of physical activity. A 3-year-old might think that it is perfectly reasonable to climb on an unsteady chair to get something that is out of reach, and a 4-year-old might enjoy holding on to a low tree branch and swinging her legs up and down. It is this physical activity, in combination with the curiosity and lack of judgment that also

characterize this age group, that make preschoolers so accident-prone (MacInnes & Stone, 2008).

Furthermore, some children are more apt to take risks, and such preschoolers are more likely to be injured than are their more cautious peers. Boys, who are more active than girls and tend to take more risks, have a higher rate of injuries. Ethnic differences, probably due to variances in cultural norms about how closely children need to be supervised, can also be seen in accident rates. Asian American children in the United States, who tend to be supervised with particular strictness by their parents, have one of the lowest accident rates for children. Economic factors also play a role. Children raised under conditions of poverty in urban areas, whose inner-city neighborhoods may contain more hazards than more affluent areas, are two times more likely to die of injuries than children living in affluence (Morrongiello & Hogg, 2004; Morrongiello, Klemencic, & Corbett, 2008; Steinbach et al., 2016).

The range of dangers that preschoolers face is wide. Injuries come from falls, burns from stoves and fires, drowning in bathtubs indoors and standing water outdoors, and suffocation in places such as abandoned refrigerators. Auto accidents also account for a large number of injuries. Finally, children face injuries from poisonous substances, such as household cleaners.

Preschoolers' high level of physical activity and their curiosity increase the risk of injury.

**LEAD POISONING RISK.** Parents and teachers also need to be aware of the dangers from long-term hazards, such as lead poisoning (Morrongiello, Corbett, & Bellissimo, 2008; Morrongiello et al., 2009; Sengoelge et al., 2014). Some 14 million children are at risk for lead poisoning resulting from exposure to lead, according to the Centers for Disease Control and Prevention. Despite stringent legal restrictions on the amount of lead in paint and gasoline, lead is still found on painted walls and window frames—particularly in older homes—and in ceramics, lead-soldered pipes, automobile and truck exhaust, and even dust and water (Fiedler, 2012; Dozor & Amler, 2013; Herendeen & MacDonald, 2014).

Even tiny amounts of lead in the water drunk by children can lead to permanent health and developmental problems. This point was made apparent, tragically, in the case of Flint, Michigan, where the city water supply became contaminated with lead when water was rerouted through water pipes that allowed lead to leak into the water supply starting in 2014. Residents had to use bottled water until the situation could be remedied (Goodnough & Atkinson, 2016).

Because even tiny amounts of lead can permanently harm children, the U.S. Department of Health and Human Services has called lead poisoning the most severe health threat to children younger than age 6. Exposure to lead has been linked to lower intelligence, problems in verbal and auditory processing, and hyperactivity and distractibility. High lead levels have also been linked to higher levels of antisocial behavior, including aggression and delinquency in school-age children (see Figure 8.4). At yet higher levels of exposure, lead poisoning results in illness and death (Brown, 2008; Zhang et al., 2013; Earl et al., 2016).

Poor children are particularly susceptible to lead poisoning, and the results of poisoning tend to be worse for them than for children from more affluent families. Children living in poverty are more apt to reside in housing that contains peeling and chipping lead paint or to live near heavily trafficked urban areas with high levels of air pollution. At the same time, many families living in poverty may be less stable and unable to provide consistent opportunities for intellectual stimulation that might serve to offset some of the cognitive problems caused by the poisoning (Dilworth-Bart & Moore, 2006; Polivka, 2006).

**REDUCING THE RISKS.** Although we can never completely prevent exposure to dangerous substances

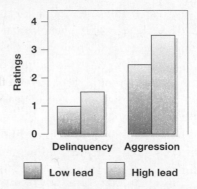

**Figure 8.4** The Consequences of Lead Poisoning

High levels of lead have been linked to higher levels of antisocial behavior, including aggression and delinquency in school-age children. What roles can social workers and health care workers play in preventing lead poisoning among children?

**SOURCE:** Needleman et al. (1996).

such as lead, accidents, and injuries, the risks can be reduced. Poisons, medicines, household cleaners, and other potentially dangerous substances can be removed from the house or kept under lock and key, and parents can strap their children into car seats whenever they take them along for a ride. Because drowning can occur in just a few inches of water and in a short time, young children should never be left unattended in the bathtub. Finally, children can be taught basic safety rules from the earliest age. Ultimately, adults need to concentrate on "injury control" rather than focus on preventing "accidents," which implies a random act in which no one is at fault (Schwebel & Gaines, 2007).

## Child Abuse and Psychological Maltreatment: The Grim Side of Family Life

**LO 8.8** Explain the types of child abuse and psychological maltreatment and what causes their occurrence.

The figures are gloomy and disheartening: **Child abuse** or maltreatment constitutes all forms of physical and/or emotional ill-treatment; sexual abuse; and neglect/negligent treatment/commercial or other exploitation, which result in actual or potential harm to the child's health, survival, and development (WHO, 1999).

**child abuse** The physical or psychological maltreatment or neglect of children

In 2007, the Ministry of Women and Child Development in India conducted a survey covering 13 states. The survey reported that about 21 percent of the participants were exposed to extreme forms of sexual abuse. Among the participants who reported being abused, 57.3 percent were boys and 42.7 percent were girls, and about 40 percent of the participants were 5–12 years of age. As reported by CHILDLINE (2014), which is a project of Ministry of Women and Child Development, India has the world's largest number of child sexual abuse cases. As per their report, for every 155th minute, a child less than 16 years of age is raped; for every 13th hour, a child under the age of 10 is sexually abused; and one in every 10 children is sexually abused at any point of time. It is important to note that many more cases go unreported due to social stigma, fear, and threat.

In India, child sexual abuse laws have been enacted as part of the nation's child protection policies. The Parliament of India passed the Protection of Children against Sexual Offences Bill, 2018.

**PHYSICAL ABUSE.** Child abuse can occur in any household, regardless of economic well-being or the social status of the parents. It is most frequent in families living in stressful environments. Poverty, single-parenthood, and higher-than-average levels of marital conflict help create such environments. Stepfathers are more likely to commit abuse against stepchildren than genetic fathers are against their own offspring. Child abuse is also more likely when there is a history of violence between spouses (Osofsky, 2003; Evans, 2004; Herrenkohl et al., 2008; Ezzo & Young, 2012). (Table 8.1 lists some of the warning signs of abuse.)

Abused children are more likely to be fussy, resistant to control, and not readily adaptable to new situations. They have more headaches and stomachaches, experience more bedwetting, are generally more anxious, and may show developmental delays (Haugaard, 2000; Pandey, 2011; Carmody et al., 2014).

As you consider this information about the characteristics of abused children, keep in mind that

---

**Figure 8.5** Child Abuse and Neglect Fatalities

Although neglect is the most frequent form of abuse, other types of abuse are also prevalent. How can caregivers and educators, as well as health care and social workers, take the lead in identifying child abuse before it becomes serious?

**SOURCE:** Child Welfare Information Gateway, 2014.

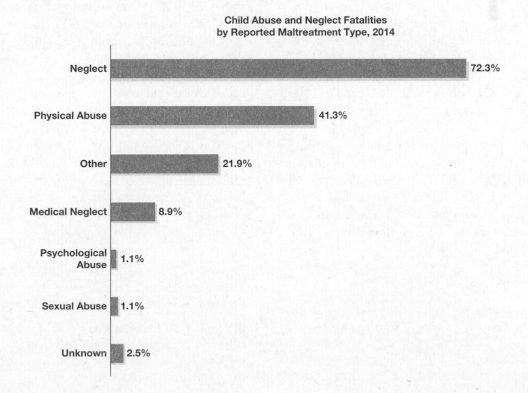

**Child Abuse and Neglect Fatalities by Reported Maltreatment Type, 2014**

| | |
|---|---|
| Neglect | 72.3% |
| Physical Abuse | 41.3% |
| Other | 21.9% |
| Medical Neglect | 8.9% |
| Psychological Abuse | 1.1% |
| Sexual Abuse | 1.1% |
| Unknown | 2.5% |

## Table 8.1 What Are the Warning Signs of Child Abuse?

Because child abuse is typically a secret crime, identifying the victims of abuse is particularly difficult. Still, there are several signs in a child that indicate that he or she is the victim of violence

- Visible, serious injuries that have no reasonable explanation
- Bite or choke marks
- Burns from cigarettes or immersion in hot water
- Extreme watchfulness, as if getting ready for something bad to happen
- Fear of adults or care providers
- Sudden, unexplained changes in behavior or school performance
- Inappropriate attire in warm weather (long sleeves, long pants, high-necked garments)—possibly to conceal injuries to the neck, arms, and legs
- Extreme behavior—highly aggressive, extremely passive, extremely withdrawn
- Fear of physical contact

If you suspect a child is a victim of abuse, it is your responsibility to act. Call your local police or the department of social services in your city or state, or call Childhelp at 1-800-422-4453. Talk to a teacher or a member of the clergy. Remember, by acting decisively, you can literally save someone's life.

**SOURCE:** Child Welfare Information Gateway, 2013.

labeling children as being at higher risk for receiving abuse does not make them responsible for their abuse; the family members who carry out the abuse are at fault. Statistical findings simply suggest that children with such characteristics are more at risk of being the recipients of family violence.

Why does physical abuse occur? Most parents certainly do not intend to hurt their children. Indeed, most parents who abuse their children later express bewilderment and regret about their own behavior.

One reason for child abuse is the vague demarcation between permissible and impermissible forms of physical punishment. The line between "spanking" and "beating" is not clear, and spankings begun in anger can escalate easily into abuse.

Another factor that leads to high rates of abuse is the privacy in which child care is conducted in Western societies. In many other cultures, childrearing is seen as the joint responsibility of several people and even society as a whole. In most Western cultures—and particularly the United States—children are raised in private, isolated households. Because child care is seen as the sole responsibility of the parent, other people are typically not available to help out when a parent's patience is tested (Chaffin, 2006; Elliott & Urquiza, 2006).

Sometimes abuse is the result of an adult's unrealistically high expectations regarding children's abilities to be quiet and compliant at a particular age. Children's failure to meet these unrealistic expectations may provoke abuse (Peterson, 1994).

**From a social worker's perspective:** If a society's emphasis on family privacy contributes to the prevalence of child abuse, what sorts of social policies regarding privacy do you think are appropriate? Why?

Many times, those who abuse children were themselves abused as children. According to the **cycle-of-violence hypothesis**, the abuse and neglect that children suffer predispose them as adults to abuse and neglect their own children (Widom, 2000; Heyman & Slep, 2002).

The hypothesis states that victims of abuse have learned from their childhood experiences that violence is an appropriate and acceptable form of discipline. Violence may be perpetuated from one generation to another, as each generation learns to behave abusively (and fails to learn the skills needed to solve problems and instill discipline without resorting to physical violence) through its participation in an abusive, violent family (Blumenthal, 2000; Craig & Sprang, 2007; Ehrensaft et al., 2015).

Being abused as a child does not inevitably lead to abuse of one's own children. In fact, statistics show that only about one-third of people who were abused or neglected as children abuse their own children; the remaining two-thirds of people abused as children do not turn out to be child abusers. Clearly, suffering abuse as a child is not the full explanation for child abuse in adults (Ethier, Couture, & Lacharite, 2004; Noll, Reader, & Bensman, 2017).

**PSYCHOLOGICAL MALTREATMENT.** Children may also be the victims of more subtle forms of mistreatment. **Psychological maltreatment** occurs when

**cycle-of-violence hypothesis** The theory that abuse and neglect that children suffer predispose them as adults to abuse and neglect their own children

**psychological maltreatment** Harm to children's behavioral, cognitive, emotional, or physical functioning caused by parents or other caregivers verbally, through their actions, or through neglect

parents or other caregivers harm children's behavioral, cognitive, emotional, or physical functioning. It may occur through either overt behavior or neglect (Higgins & McCabe, 2003; Arias, 2004; Garbarino, 2013).

For example, abusive parents may frighten, belittle, or humiliate their children, thereby intimidating and harassing them. Children may be made to feel like disappointments or failures, or they may be constantly reminded that they are a burden to their parents. Parents may tell their children that they wish they had never had children and specifically that they wish that their children had never been born. Children may be threatened with abandonment or even death. In other instances, older children may be exploited. They may be forced to seek employment and then to give their earnings to their parents.

In other cases of psychological maltreatment, the abuse takes the form of neglect. In **child neglect**, parents ignore their children or are emotionally unresponsive to them. In such cases, children may be given unrealistic responsibilities or may be left to fend for themselves.

No one is certain how much psychological maltreatment occurs each year because figures separating psychological maltreatment from other types of abuse are not routinely gathered. Most maltreatment occurs in the privacy of people's homes. Furthermore, psychological maltreatment typically causes no physical damage, such as bruises or broken bones, to alert physicians, teachers, and other authorities. Consequently, many cases of psychological maltreatment probably are not identified. It is clear, however, that profound neglect that involves children who are unsupervised or uncared for is the most frequent form of psychological maltreatment (Hewitt, 1997).

What are the consequences of psychological maltreatment? Some children are sufficiently resilient to survive the abuse and grow into psychologically healthy adults. In many cases, unfortunately, lasting damage results. For example, psychological maltreatment has been associated with low self-esteem, lying, misbehavior, and underachievement in school. In extreme cases, it can produce criminal behavior, aggression, and murder. In other instances, children who have been psychologically maltreated become depressed and even commit suicide (Koenig, Cicchetti, & Rogosch, 2004; Allen, 2008; Tarber et al., 2016).

One reason that psychological maltreatment—as well as physical abuse—produces so many negative

### Figure 8.6 Abuse Alters the Brain

The limbic system, comprising the hippocampus and amygdala, can be permanently altered as a result of childhood abuse.

**SOURCE:** *Scientific American*, March 2002, p. 71.

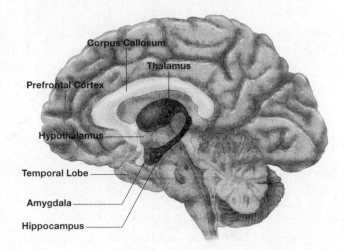

consequences is that the brains of victims undergo permanent changes due to the abuse (see Figure 8.6). For example, childhood maltreatment can lead to reductions in the size of the amygdala and hippocampus in adulthood. The fear and terror produced by abuse may also lead to permanent changes in the brain due to overexcitation of the limbic system, which is involved in the regulation of memory and emotion, leading to antisocial behavior during adulthood (Rick & Douglas, 2007; Twardosz & Lutzker, 2009; Thielen et al., 2016).

## Resilience: Overcoming the Odds

**LO 8.9 List the personal traits that contribute to a child's resilience.**

For many children, childhood is a difficult time. According to the United Nations Children's Fund, more than a billion children—one out of every two of the world's children—experience intense deprivation due to war, HIV and AIDS, or poverty. More than 640 million children live in homes with mud floors or extremely overcrowded conditions. Close to 30,000 children die every day, often from preventable causes. Two million children, most of them girls, are involved in commercial sex industries (United Nations Children's Fund, 2004).

---

**child neglect** Ignoring one's children or being emotionally unresponsive to them

Yet not all children succumb to the adversity that life dishes out to them. In fact, some do surprisingly well, considering the types of problems they have encountered. What enables some children to overcome stress and trauma that may scar others for life?

The answer appears to be a quality that psychologists have termed resilience. **Resilience** is the ability to overcome circumstances that place a child at high risk for psychological or physical damage, such as extremes of poverty, prenatal stress, or homes that are racked with violence or other forms of social disorder. Several factors seem to reduce—and, in certain cases, eliminate—some children's reactions to difficult circumstances that produce profoundly negative consequences in others (Trickett, Kurtz, & Pizzigati, 2004; Bonanno & Mancini, 2007; Monahan, Beeber & Harden, 2012).

According to developmental psychologist Emmy Werner, resilient children tend to have temperaments that evoke positive responses from a wide variety of caregivers. They tend to be affectionate, easygoing, and good-natured. They are easily soothed as infants, and they are able to elicit care from the most nurturing people in any environment in which they find themselves. In a sense, then, resilient children are successful in making their own environments by drawing out behavior in others that is necessary for their own development (Werner & Smith, 2002; Martinez-Torteya et al., 2009; Newland, 2014).

**resilience** The ability to overcome circumstances that place a child at high risk for psychological or physical damage

# BECOMING AN INFORMED CONSUMER OF CHILD DEVELOPMENT

## Keeping Preschoolers Healthy

There's no way around it: Even the healthiest preschooler occasionally gets sick. Social interactions with others ensure that illnesses are going to be passed from one child to another. Some diseases are preventable, however, and others can be minimized if these simple precautions are taken:

- *Preschoolers should eat a well-balanced diet containing the proper nutrients, particularly foods with sufficient protein.* The recommended energy intake for children ages 2 to 4 is about 1,300 calories a day; for those ages 4 to 6, it is around 1,700 calories a day. Because preschoolers' stomachs are small, they may need to eat as often as five to seven times a day.
- *Preschoolers should be encouraged to exercise.* Children who exercise are less likely to become obese than those who are sedentary.
- *Children should get as much sleep as they wish.* Being run-down from lack of either nutrition or sleep makes children more susceptible to illness.
- *Children should avoid contact with others who are ill.* Parents should make sure that children wash their hands after playing with other kids who are obviously sick (as well as emphasizing the importance of hand-washing generally).
- *Children should be placed on an appropriate schedule of immunizations.* As illustrated in Table 8.2, current

recommendations state that a child should have received nine different vaccines and other preventive medicines in five to seven separate visits to the doctor.

The importance of vaccinations cannot be overstated. Despite the beliefs of some parents, based in part on what they hear in popular culture from some misguided celebrities such as Jenny McCarthy, there is absolutely no scientific basis for believing that common vaccinations should be avoided because they increase the risk of a child showing symptoms of autism spectrum disorder. In fact, parents who don't vaccinate their children put their children at considerable risk for contracting a wide variety of diseases. Moreover, they put others at risk by passing on illnesses to those who can't be immunized, such as infants under the age of 6 months and people with depressed immune systems due to cancer and other illnesses (Sifferlin, 2013; Turville & Golden, 2015).

In short, *children should receive all recommended vaccinations*, according to the American Academy of Pediatrics and the U.S. Centers for Disease Control and Prevention, unless otherwise told not to by a reputable medical professional.

- **Finally, if a child does get ill, remember that minor illnesses during childhood sometimes provide immunity to more serious illnesses later on.**

## Table 8.2

| Vaccine | Birth | 1 mo | 2 mos | 4 mos | 6 mos | 9 mos | 12 mos | 15 mos | 18 mos | 19-23 mos | 2-3 yrs | 4-6 yrs | 7-10 yrs | 11-12 yrs | 13-15 yrs | 16 yrs | 17-18 yrs |
|---|---|---|---|---|---|---|---|---|---|---|---|---|---|---|---|---|---|
| Hepatitis B (HepB) | 1st dose | ←--- 2nd dose ---→ | | | ←------------------ 3rd dose ------------------→ | | | | | | | | | | | | |
| Rotavirus (RV) RV1 (2-dose series); RV5 (3-dose series) | | | 1st dose | 2nd dose | | | | | | | | | | | | | |
| Diphtheria, tetanus, & acellular pertussis (DTaP: <7 yrs) | | | 1st dose | 2nd dose | 3rd dose | | ←------ 4th dose ------→ | | | | | 5th dose | | | | | |
| *Haemophilus influenzae* type b (Hib) | | | 1st dose | 2nd dose | | | ←--- 3rd 4th dose ---→ | | | | | | | | | | |
| Pneumococcal conjugate (PCV13) | | | 1st dose | 2nd dose | 3rd dose | | ←------ 4th dose ------→ | | | | | | | | | | |
| Inactivated poliovirus (IPV: <18 yrs) | | | 1st dose | 2nd dose | ←------------------ 3rd dose ------------------→ | | | | | | | 4th dose | | | | | |
| Influenza (IIV) | | | | | Annual vaccination (IIV) 1 or 2 doses | | | | | | | | Annual vaccination (IIV) 1 dose only | | | | |
| Measles, mumps, rubella (MMR) | | | | | | | ←----- 1st dose -----→ | | | | | 2nd dose | | | | | |
| Varicella (VAR) | | | | | | | ←----- 1st dose -----→ | | | | | 2nd dose | | | | | |
| Hepatitis A (HepA) | | | | | | | ←------- 2-dose series -------→ | | | | | | | | | | |
| Meningococcal (Hib-MenCY ≥6 weeks; MenACWY-D ≥9 mos; MenACWY-CRM ≥2 mos) | | | | | | | | | | | | | | 1st dose | | 2nd dose | |
| Tetanus, diphtheria, & acellular pertussis (Tdap: ≥7 yrs) | | | | | | | | | | | | | | Tdap | | | |
| Human papillomavirus (HPV) | | | | | | | | | | | | | | | | | |
| Meningococcal B | | | | | | | | | | | | | | | | | |
| Pneumococcal polysaccharide (PPSV23) | | | | | | | | | | | | | | | | | |

| | Range of recommended ages for all children | | Range of recommended ages for catch-up immunization | | Range of recommended ages for certain high-risk groups | | Range of recommended ages for non-high-risk groups that may receive vaccine, subject to individual clinical decision making | | No recommendation |
|---|---|---|---|---|---|---|---|---|---|

**SOURCE:** Centers for Disease Control and Prevention. (2017). *Recommended immunization schedule for children and adolescents aged 18 years or younger, United States, 2017.* Washington, DC: Centers for Disease Control and Prevention.

Similar traits are associated with resilience in older children. The most resilient school-age children are those who are socially pleasant, outgoing, and have good communication skills. They tend to be relatively intelligent, and they are independent, feeling that they can shape their own fate, and are not dependent on others or luck (Curtis & Cicchetti, 2003; Kim & Cicchetti, 2003; Mathiesen & Prior, 2006).

The characteristics of resilient children suggest ways to improve the prospects of children who are at risk from a variety of developmental threats. For instance, in addition to decreasing their exposure to factors that put them at risk in the first place, we need to increase their competence by teaching them ways to deal with their situation. Programs that have been successful in helping especially vulnerable children have a common thread: They provide competent and caring adult models who can teach the children problem-solving skills and help them to communicate their needs to those who are in a position to help them (Ortega, Beauchemin, & Kaniskan, 2008; Goldstein & Brooks, 2013; Hills, Meyer-Weitz, & Asante, 2016).

# Motor Development

*Anya sat in the sandbox at the park, chatting with the other parents and playing with her two children, 5-year-old Nicholai and 13-month-old Sofia. While she talked, she kept a close eye on Sofia, who would sometimes still put sand in her mouth if she wasn't stopped. Today, however, Sofia seemed content to run the sand through her hands and try to put it into a bucket. Nicholai, meanwhile, was busy with two other boys, rapidly filling and emptying the other sand buckets to build an elaborate sand city, which they would then destroy with toy trucks.*

When children of different ages gather at a playground, it's easy to see that preschoolers have come a long way in their motor development since infancy. Both their gross and their fine motor skills have become increasingly fine-tuned. Sofia, for example, is still mastering putting sand into a bucket, while her brother, Nicholai, uses that skill easily as part of his larger goal of building a sand city.

## Gross and Fine Motor Skills

**LO 8.10** **Explain the development of children's gross and fine motor skills during the preschool years.**

How do major changes in motor skills develop so quickly? What underlying advances support the rapid development of the motor skills? Is the pace of change uniform among children? Let's examine these questions by taking a look at the processes involved in the development of the motor skills in preschoolers.

**GROSS MOTOR SKILLS.** In general, by the time they are 3 years old, children have mastered a variety of skills: jumping, hopping on one foot, skipping, and running. By ages 4 and 5, their skills have become more refined as they have gained greater control over their muscles. For instance, at age 4 they can throw a ball with enough accuracy that a friend can catch it, and by age 5 they can toss a ring and have it land on a peg 5 feet away. Five-year-olds can learn to ride bikes, climb ladders, and ski downhill—activities that all require considerable coordination. Table 8.3 summarizes major gross motor skills that emerge during the preschool years.

The advances in gross motor skills are related to brain development and myelination of neurons in areas of the brain related to balance and coordination. Another reason motor skills develop at such a rapid clip during the preschool years is that children spend a great deal of time practicing them. During this period, the general level of activity is extraordinarily high: Preschoolers seem to be perpetually in motion. In fact, the activity level is higher at age 3 than at any other point in the entire life span. In addition, as they age, preschoolers increase in general physical agility (Planinsec, 2001).

Despite generally high activity levels, there are also significant variations among children. Some differences are related to inherited temperament—children who are unusually active during infancy tend to continue in this way during the preschool years, whereas those who are relatively docile during infancy generally remain fairly docile during those years. Furthermore, monozygotic (identical) twins tend to show more similar activity levels than do dizygotic twins, a fact that suggests the importance of genetics in determining activity level (Wood et al., 2007).

Of course, genetics is not the sole determinant of preschoolers' activity levels. Environmental factors, such as a parent's style of discipline and, more broadly, a particular culture's view of what is appropriate and inappropriate behavior, also play a role. Some cultures are fairly lenient in allowing preschoolers to play vigorously, whereas others are considerably more restrictive.

Ultimately, a combination of genetic and environmental factors determines just how active a child will be. But the preschool period generally represents the most active time of the child's entire life.

> **From an educator's perspective:** How might culture influence activity level in children? What might the long-term effects be on children influenced in this way?

Girls and boys differ in several aspects of gross motor coordination. In part, this difference is

**Table 8.3** Significant Gross Motor Skills in Early Childhood

| 3-Year-Olds | 4-Year-Olds | 5-Year-Olds |
|---|---|---|
| Cannot turn or stop suddenly or quickly | Have more effective control of stopping, starting, and turning | Start, turn, and stop effectively in games |
| Jump a distance of 15 to 24 inches | Jump a distance of 24 to 33 inches | Make a running jump of 28 to 36 inches |
| Ascend a stairway unaided, alternating the feet | Descend a long stairway alternating the feet, if supported | Descend a long stairway alternating the feet |
| Can hop, using an irregular series of jumps with some variations added | Hop 4 to 6 steps on one foot | Easily hop a distance of 16 feet |

**SOURCE:** C. Corbin (1973).

produced by variations in muscle strength, which is somewhat greater in boys than in girls. For instance, boys can typically throw a ball better and jump higher. Furthermore, boys' overall activity levels are generally higher than those of girls (Pelligrini & Smith, 1998; Spessato et al., 2013).

Although they are not as strong as boys and have lower overall activity levels, girls generally surpass boys in tasks that involve the coordination of their arms and legs. For instance, at age 5, girls are better than boys at performing jumping jacks and balancing on one foot (Cratty, 1979).

The differences among preschoolers on some tasks involving gross motor skills are due to a number of factors. In addition to genetically determined differences in strength and activity levels, social factors likely play a role. As we will discuss further in Chapter 10, gender increasingly determines the sorts of activities that are seen by society as appropriate for girls and appropriate for boys. For instance, if the games that are considered acceptable for preschool boys tend to involve gross motor skills more than the games deemed appropriate for girls, boys will have more practice than girls in gross motor activities and will ultimately be more proficient in them (Yee & Brown, 1994; Shala & Bahtiri, 2011).

Regardless of their gender, however, children typically show significant improvement in their gross motor skills during the preschool years. Such improvement permits them, by the time they are 5, to climb ladders, play follow-the-leader, and snowboard with relative ease.

**FINE MOTOR SKILLS.** At the same time that gross motor skills are developing, children are progressing

**Table 8.4** Fine Motor Skills in Early Childhood

| 3-Year-Olds | 4-Year-Olds | 5-Year-Olds |
| --- | --- | --- |
| Cuts paper | Folds paper into triangles | Folds paper into halves and quarters |
| Pastes using finger | Prints name | Draws triangle, rectangle, circle |
| Builds bridge with three blocks | Strings beads | Uses crayons effectively |
| Draws 0 and 1 | Copies X | Creates clay objects |
| Draws doll | Builds bridge with five blocks | Copies letters |
| Pours liquid from pitcher without spilling | Pours from various containers | Copies two short words |
| Completes simple jigsaw puzzle | Opens and positions clothespins | |

in their ability to use fine motor skills, which involve smaller, more delicate body movements. Fine motor skills encompass such varied activities as using a fork and spoon, cutting with scissors, tying one's shoelaces, and playing the piano.

The skills involved in fine motor movements require a good deal of practice, as anyone knows who has watched a 4-year-old struggling painstakingly to copy letters of the alphabet. Yet fine motor skills show clear developmental patterns (see Table 8.4). At age 3, children can undo their clothes when they go to the bathroom, they can put a simple jigsaw puzzle together, and they can fit blocks of different shapes into matching holes. They do not, however, show much polish in accomplishing such tasks; for instance, they may try to force puzzle pieces into place.

During the preschool years, children grow in both gross and fine motor skills.

By age 4, children's fine motor skills are considerably better. For example, they can fold paper into triangular designs and print their name with a crayon. And by the time they are 5, most children are able to hold and manipulate a thin pencil properly.

Another aspect of muscular skills—one that parents of toddlers often find most problematic—is bowel and bladder control. As we see next, the timing and nature of toilet training is a controversial issue.

## Potty Wars: When—and How— Should Children Be Toilet Trained?

**LO 8.11  Identify the factors that determine when a child is ready for toilet training.**

Few child care issues raise so much concern among parents as toilet training. And on few issues are there so many opposing opinions from experts and laypersons. Often the various viewpoints are played out in the media and even take on political overtones. On the one hand, for instance, the well-known pediatrician T. Berry Brazelton suggests a flexible approach to toilet training, advocating that it be put off until the child shows signs of readiness. On the other hand, psychologist John Rosemond, known primarily for his media advocacy of a conservative, traditional stance to childrearing, argues for a more rigid approach, saying that toilet training should be done early and quickly (Brazelton & Sparrow, 2006).

What is clear is that the age at which toilet training takes place has been rising over the past few decades. For example, in 1957, fully 92 percent of children were toilet trained by the age of 18 months. In 1999, only 25 percent were toilet trained at that age, and just 60 percent at 36 months. Two percent were still not toilet trained at age 4 (Goode, 1999).

The current guidelines of the American Academy of Pediatrics support Brazelton's position, suggesting that there is no single time to begin toilet training and that training should begin only when children show that they are ready. Children have no bladder or bowel control until the age of 12 months and only slight control for 6 months after that. Although some children show signs of readiness for toilet training between 18 and 24 months, some are not ready until 30 months or older (Fritz & Rockney, 2004; Connell-Carrick, 2006; Greer, Neidert, & Dozier, 2016).

The signs of readiness include staying dry at least 2 hours at a time during the day or waking up dry after

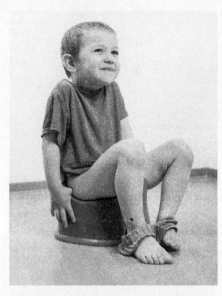

Among the signs that a child is ready to give up diapers is evidence that he or she is able to follow directions and can get to the bathroom and undress on his or her own.

naps; having regular and predictable bowel movements; giving an indication, through facial expressions or words, that urination or a bowel movement is about to occur; having the ability to follow simple directions; having the ability to get to the bathroom and undress alone; expressing discomfort with soiled diapers; asking to use the toilet or potty chair; and having the desire to wear underwear. Furthermore, children must be ready not only physically but also emotionally, and if they show strong signs of resistance to toilet training, it should be put off.

Even after children are toilet trained during the day, it often takes months or years before they are able to achieve control at night. Around three-quarters of boys and most girls are able to stay dry after age 5.

Complete toilet training eventually occurs in almost all children as they mature and attain greater control over their muscles; however, delayed toilet training can be a cause for concern if a child is upset about it or if it makes the child a target of ridicule from siblings or peers. In such cases, several types of treatments have proved effective. In particular, treatments in which children are rewarded for staying dry or are awakened by a battery-powered device that senses when they have wet the bed are often effective (Houts, 2003; Vermandel et al., 2008; Millei & Gallagher, 2012).

## Handedness and Expression

**LO 8.12  Explain how handedness and artistic expression develop during the preschool years.**

How do preschoolers decide which hand to hold the pencil in as they work on their copying and other fine motor skills? And what role does art play in their development?

**SEPARATING RIGHTIES FROM LEFTIES.** By the end of the preschool years, most children show a clear preference for the use of one hand over the other—the development of **handedness**. Actually, some signals of future handedness are seen early in infancy, when infants may show a preference for one side of the body over the other. By the age of 7 months, some infants seem to favor one hand by grabbing more with it than with the other. Many children, however, show no preference until the end of the preschool years, and a few remain ambidextrous, using both hands with equal ease (Segalowitz & Rapin, 2003; Marschik et al. 2008; Bryden, Mayer & Roy, 2011).

By age 5, most children display a clear tendency to use one hand over the other, with 90 percent being right-handed and 10 percent left-handed. More boys than girls are left-handed.

Much speculation has been devoted to the meaning of handedness, fueled in part by long-standing myths about the sinister nature of left-handedness. (The word *sinister* itself is derived from a Latin word meaning "on the left.") In Islamic cultures, for instance, the left hand is generally used when going to the toilet, and it is considered uncivilized to serve food with that hand. In Christian art, portrayals of the devil often show him as left-handed.

There is no scientific basis for myths that suggest that there is something wrong with being left-handed. In fact, some evidence exists that left-handedness may be associated with certain advantages. For example, a study of 100,000 students who took the Scholastic Assessment Test (SAT) showed that 20 percent in the highest-scoring category were left-handed—double the proportion of left-handed people in the general population. Such gifted individuals as Michelangelo, Leonardo da Vinci, Benjamin Franklin, and Pablo Picasso were left-handed (Bower, 1985).

Although some educators of the past tried to force left-handed children to use the right hand, particularly when learning to write, thinking has changed. Most teachers now encourage children to use whichever hand they prefer. Still, most left-handed people will agree that the design of desks, scissors, and most other everyday objects favors the right-handed. In fact, the world is so "right biased" that it may prove to be a dangerous place for lefties: Left-handed people have more accidents and are at greater risk of dying younger than right-handed people (Ellis & Engh, 2000; Bhushan & Khan, 2006; Dutta & Mandal, 2006).

Much speculation has been devoted to the meaning of handedness, but there are few conclusions. Some research finds that left-handedness is related to higher achievements, other research shows no advantage for being left-handed, and some findings suggest that children who are ambidextrous perform less well on academic tasks. Clearly, the jury is out on the consequences of handedness (Corballis, Hattie, & Fletcher, 2008; Casasanto & Henetz, 2012; Nelson, Campbell & Michel, 2013).

**ART: THE PICTURE OF DEVELOPMENT.** It is a basic feature of many kitchens: the refrigerator covered with recent art created by the children of the house. Yet the art that children create is far more important than mere kitchen decoration. Developmentalists suggest that art plays an important role in honing fine motor skills, as well as in several other aspects of development.

At the most basic level, the production of art involves practice with tools such as paintbrushes, crayons, pencils, and markers. As preschoolers learn to manipulate these tools, they gain motor control skills that will help them as they learn to write.

But art also teaches several important lessons. For example, children learn the importance of planning, restraint, and self-correction. When 3-year-olds pick up a brush, they tend to swish it across the page, with little thought of the ultimate product. By the time they are 5, however, children spend more time thinking about and planning the final product. They are more likely to have a goal in mind when they start out, and when they are finished, they examine their creation to see how successful they have been. Older children will also produce the same artwork over and over, seeking to overcome their previous errors and improve the final product.

According to developmental psychologist Howard Gardner, the rough, unformed art of preschoolers represents the equivalent of linguistic babbling in infants. He argues that the random marks that young preschoolers make contain all the building blocks of more sophisticated creations that will be produced later (Gardner & Perkins, 1989; Golomb, 2002).

---

**handedness** A clear preference for the use of one hand over the other

**Figure 8.7** Art of Development

As preschoolers enter the pictorial stage between ages 4 and 5, their drawings begin to approximate recognizable objects.

Other researchers suggest that children's art proceeds through a series of stages during the preschool years. The first is the *scribbling* stage, in which the end product appears to be random scrawls across a paper. But this is not the case: Instead, scribbles can be categorized, consisting of 20 distinct types, such as horizontal lines and zigzags.

The *shape* stage, which is reached around age 3, is marked by the appearance of shapes such as squares and circles. In this stage, children draw shapes of various sorts, as well as X's and plus signs. After reaching this stage, they soon move into the *design* stage, which is characterized by the ability to combine more than one simple shape into a more complex one.

Finally, children enter the *pictorial* stage between ages 4 and 5. At this point, drawings begin to approximate recognizable objects (see Figure 8.7).

The depiction of recognizable real-world objects, known as representational art, may appear to be a substantial advance over previous art, and adults often strongly encourage its creation. In some respects, this change to representational art is regrettable, for it marks a shift in focus away from an interest in form and design. Because form and design are important and in some ways essential, a focus on representation may ultimately have disadvantages. As the great artist Pablo Picasso once remarked, "It has taken me a whole lifetime to learn to draw like children" (Winner, 1989).

# The Case of ...
## Frustrated Desires

At age 4, Eva Dale had one desire: to keep up with her big brother, Ricky. Ricky, a lively 8-year-old, could ride a skateboard. He played soccer. He read chapter books and drew elaborate pictures of dragons. Eva was determined to do everything he did. She was tired of being "the baby."

Eva's parents were pleased she wanted to learn to read. They purchased a set of early reader books that made use of rhyming words. They also bought a box of colored pencils "just for Eva." They were less pleased about Eva's interest in skateboards. "You're too little for that," her mother told her. "You'll get hurt," her father cautioned.

Eva didn't need her parents' worries to frustrate her. She felt plenty frustrated already. The letters on the pages of her early readers kept getting away from her somehow. It was often impossible to make them into words. She had more success with drawing, but she still struggled to make the colored pencils copy the images she saw in her mind. "Stay with it," her father said, giving her a pat on the back. "The more you draw, the better you'll get."

The day Eva turned 5, her mother said, "Let's get in the car. I have a big surprise for you." Eva was so excited. She was sure her mom was taking her for soccer sign-up. You could play on a soccer team at age 5. Instead, Eva's mom drove her to the local dance school, where Eva was given a pink leotard and her first ballet lesson. Eva was so disappointed that she refused to follow the teacher's instructions. "Don't worry," the teacher told Eva's mom. "In a few weeks, she'll be a little dancing princess."

1. Eva's parents worry that she'll get hurt on a skateboard. What could you tell them about gross motor development in girls versus boys at this age that might change their mind? How might they support Eva in learning to use a skateboard safely?

2. What do you know about sensory development that could help explain why Eva is finding it difficult to master her early readers? How is this likely to change in the next 2 years?

3. Researchers have defined stages in children's production of art. What stage do you think Eva has reached? What evidence is there in the story for your answer?

4. Eva's parents were delighted to encourage her interest in reading and drawing, but not so eager to discourage her attraction to skateboards and soccer. Would you describe Eva's mom and dad as supportive parents? Why or why not? How might their various responses to Eva's interests affect her development?

5. The ballet teacher assured Eva's mother that "she'd be a little dancing princess" in no time. If the teacher's prediction comes true, do you think this would be a good thing for Eva? Why or why not?

## Epilogue

We saw in this chapter the enormous physical changes, including changes in the brain, that accompany the progression from infancy to the preschool years. Beginning with the growth of their bodies, both in weight and height, preschoolers make enormous physical strides. As their brains develop, the way is also paved for cognitive development and psychological complexity. Although preschoolers face threats to their health from sickness and accidental injury, for the most part they are healthy, energetic, inquisitive, and mastering an impressive list of physical accomplishments during the preschool years.

Before we move on to a discussion of children's cognitive development, turn back to this chapter's prologue, which describes Dev, a preschooler who was diagnosed with childhood depression, and consider these questions:

1. Were the activities, toys, and games available in Dev's preschool a good match developmentally for the children? Explain your answer in terms of motor, sensory, and brain development.

2. Why was it difficult for Dev's teacher to notice his depression? When she says that she was "alert for issues" in her students, what do you think she is referring to? What issues may she have dismissed because of Dev's observed behaviors?

3. Explain the changes in Dev's brain that enabled him to feel frustration with manipulating LEGOs and to experience fear about displaying inability in naming the days of the week or reciting the alphabet. Do you think such feelings may interfere with his further learning and cognitive development?

4. What sorts of things do you think the psychologist may recommend for Dev's teachers and parents to help him overcome his feelings of depression? Are any changes in the classroom environment needed to help him and other children feel safe to make mistakes while learning?

## Looking Back

**LO 8.1 Describe the bodily changes children experience in the preschool years.**

- Children's physical growth during the preschool period proceeds steadily. Differences in height and weight reflect individual differences, gender, and economic status.

- In addition to gaining height and weight, the body of the preschooler undergoes changes in shape and structure. Children grow more slender, and their bones and muscles strengthen.

### LO 8.2 Summarize how children's brains change during the preschool years.

- Brain growth is particularly rapid during the preschool years, with the number of interconnections among cells and the amount of myelin around neurons increasing greatly. Through the process of lateralization, the two halves of the brain begin to specialize in somewhat different functions. Despite lateralization, however, the two hemispheres function as a unit and in fact differ only slightly.

- There is some evidence that the structure of the brain differs by gender and culture. For instance, boys and girls show some hemispheric differences in lower body reflexes, the processing of auditory information, and language. Furthermore, some studies suggest that such structural features as the processing of vowel sounds may show cultural differences.

### LO 8.3 Explain how brain growth affects cognitive and sensory development.

- Some research suggests that increases in myelin during the preschool years may be related to growth in cognitive abilities, an increase in attention span, and better memory. One study also found spurts in electrical activity in the brain that coincided with a rapid increase in language abilities in preschoolers.

- Brain development permits improvements in sensory processing during the preschool years, including better control of eye movements and focusing and improved visual perception and auditory acuity. Still, preschoolers' eyes are not as capable as they will be in later stages of development.

### LO 8.4 Describe preschoolers' sleep patterns.

- Sleep presents real difficulties for some. Sleep-related problems include nightmares and night terrors.

- Most preschool children sleep well at night.

### LO 8.5 Outline the nutritional needs of preschool children, and explain what causes obesity.

- Preschoolers need less food than they did in the early years. Primarily, they require balanced nutrition. If parents and caregivers provide a good variety of healthful foods, children will generally achieve an appropriate intake of nutrients.

- Obesity is caused by both genetic and environmental factors. One strong environmental influence appears to be parents and caregivers, who may substitute their own interpretations of their children's food needs for the children's internal tendencies and controls.

### LO 8.6 Identify the illnesses preschool children experience.

- Children in the preschool years generally experience only minor illnesses, but they are susceptible to some dangerous diseases, including childhood leukemia and AIDS.

- In the economically developed world, immunization programs have largely controlled most life-threatening diseases during these years. This is not the case, however, in economically disadvantaged sectors of the world.

### LO 8.7 Explain why injuries pose the greatest threat to wellness in preschool children.

- Preschool children are at greater risk from accidents than from illness or nutritional problems. The danger is due partly to children's high activity levels and partly to environmental hazards, such as lead poisoning.

### LO 8.8 Explain the types of child abuse and psychological maltreatment and what causes their occurrence.

- Child abuse may be physical in nature, but it may also be more subtle. Psychological maltreatment may involve neglect of parental responsibilities, emotional negligence, intimidation or humiliation, unrealistic demands and expectations, or exploitation of children.

- Child abuse occurs with alarming frequency in the United States and other countries, especially in stressful home environments. Firmly held notions regarding family privacy and norms that support the use of physical punishment in childrearing contribute to the high rate of abuse.

- The cycle-of-violence hypothesis points to the likelihood that persons who were abused as children may turn into abusers as adults.

**LO 8.9** **List the personal traits that contribute to a child's resilience.**

- Resilience is a personal characteristic that permits some children at risk for abuse to overcome their dangerous situations. Resilient children tend to be affectionate and easygoing, able to elicit a nurturing response from people in their environment.

**LO 8.10** **Explain the development of children's gross and fine motor skills during the preschool years.**

- Gross motor skills advance rapidly during the preschool years, a time when the activity levels of children are at their peak. Genetic and cultural factors determine how active a given child will be.

- During these years, gender differences in gross motor skill levels begin to emerge clearly, with boys displaying greater strength and activity levels and girls showing greater coordination of arms and legs. Both genetic and social factors probably play a role in determining these differences.

- Fine motor skills also develop during the preschool years, with increasingly delicate movements being mastered through extensive practice.

**LO 8.11** **Identify the factors that determine when a child is ready for toilet training.**

- Children 18 months and younger have little or no bladder or bowel control.

- The American Academy of Pediatrics stresses that there is no one right time to begin toilet training. The child must be ready both physically and emotionally. Signs of readiness include: staying dry at least 2 consecutive hours during the day or waking up dry after naps; having regular, predictable bowel movements; asking to use the potty; expressing discomfort with soiled diapers; being able to follow simple directions.

**LO 8.12** **Explain how handedness and artistic expression develop during the preschool years.**

- Handedness asserts itself, with the great majority of children showing a clear preference for the right hand, by the end of the preschool years.

- The meaning of handedness is unclear, but the right-handed have certain practical advantages because of the "right bias" of the world.

- The development of artistic expression progresses during the preschool years through the scribbling, shape, design, and pictorial stages. Artistic expression entails the development of important related skills, including planning, restraint, and self-correction.

# Key Terms and Concepts

lateralization (p. 204)
myelin (p. 206)
nightmare (p. 208)
night terror (p. 208)

obesity (p. 209)
child abuse (p. 212)
cycle-of-violence hypothesis
  (p. 214)

psychological maltreatment (p. 214)
child neglect (p. 215)
resilience (p. 216)
handedness (p. 221)

# Chapter 9
# Cognitive Development in the Preschool Years

 **Learning Objectives**

**LO 9.1** Discuss Piaget's theory of cognitive development during the preschool years.

**LO 9.2** Summarize the information-processing approaches to cognitive development in the preschool years.

**LO 9.3** Explain Vygotsky's approach to cognitive development.

**LO 9.4** Describe how children's language abilities develop in the preschool years.

**LO 9.5** Explain the effect of poverty on language development.

**LO 9.6** Describe the ways in which preschool children are educated.

**LO 9.7** Discuss some of the consequences of child care outside the home.

**LO 9.8** Describe the effectiveness of Head Start and similar preschool readiness programs.

**LO 9.9** Describe the evidence for the importance of reading to children.

**LO 9.10** Identify the effects of television and digital media on preschoolers.

# Prologue: Cognitive Apprentices

Ava and Natalia, preschool classmates, are putting together a floor puzzle. "You need to find the piece that fits *exactly* with this piece, like this." Ava demonstrates. "Or the puzzle doesn't work." Natalia watches Ava put together three more pieces before testing her own skill at puzzle-solving. It's not easy to find just the right piece, but after several tries Natalia's choice fits. "Good job!" Ava says, mimicking the preschool teacher.

Later, at home, Natalia's mother overhears her daughter talking to herself. "Find the piece that fits *exactly* with this one. *Exactly.*" She peeks into the living room to see Natalia assembling a dog puzzle that used to belong to her older brother Carlos. The 3-year-old claps her hands when she finds the right piece.

# Looking Ahead

For preschool children like Ava and Natalia, play is learning, and peers may often prove effective teachers. As we shall see, the experience of attending school for the first time marks the start of an intellectual—as well as a social—journey that will continue for many years and shape the development of children in significant ways.

In this chapter, we focus on the cognitive and linguistic growth that occurs during the preschool years. We begin by examining the major approaches to cognitive development, including Piaget's theory, information-processing approaches, and the increasingly influential view of Russian developmental psychologist Lev Vygotsky, which takes culture into account.

We then turn to the important advances in language development that occur during the preschool years. We consider several different explanations for the rapid increase in language abilities that characterizes the preschool period and consider the effects that poverty has on language development.

Finally, we discuss two of the major factors that influence cognitive development during the preschool years: schooling and the media. We consider the different types of child care and preschool programs, and we end with a discussion of how exposure to television and computers affects preschool viewers.

# Intellectual Development

*Three-year-old Sam was talking to himself. As his parents listened with amusement from another room, they could hear him using two very different voices. "Find your shoes," he said in a low voice. "Not today. I'm not going. I hate the shoes,"* *he said in a higher-pitched voice. The lower voice answered, "You are a bad boy. Find the shoes, bad boy." The higher-voiced response was "No, no, no."*

*Sam's parents realized that he was playing a game with his imaginary friend, Gill. Gill was a bad boy who often disobeyed his mother, at least in Sam's imagination. In fact, according to Sam's musings, Gill often was guilty of the very same misdeeds for which his parents blamed Sam.*

In some ways, the intellectual sophistication of 3-year-olds is astounding. Their creativity and imagination leap to new heights, their language is increasingly complex, and they reason and think about the world in ways that would have been impossible even a few months earlier. But what underlies the dramatic advances in intellectual development that start in the preschool years and continue throughout that period? We can consider several approaches, starting with a look at Piaget's findings on the cognitive changes that occur during the preschool years.

## Piaget's Stage of Preoperational Thinking

**LO 9.1 Discuss Piaget's theory of cognitive development during the preschool years.**

Swiss psychologist Jean Piaget, whose stage approach to cognitive development we discussed in Chapter 6, saw the preschool years as a time of both stability and great change. He suggested that the preschool years fit entirely into a single stage of cognitive development—the preoperational stage—which lasts from the age of 2 years until around 7 years.

During the **preoperational stage**, children's use of symbolic thinking grows, mental reasoning emerges, and the use of concepts increases. Seeing Mom's car keys may prompt a question, "Go to store?" as the child comes to see the keys as a symbol of a car ride. In this way, children become better at representing events internally, and they grow less dependent on the use of direct sensorimotor activity to understand the world around them. Yet they are still not capable of **operations**: organized, formal, logical mental processes. It is only at the end of the preoperational stage that the ability to carry out operations comes into play.

According to Piaget, a key aspect of preoperational thought is **symbolic function**, the ability to use a mental symbol, a word, or an object to stand for or represent something that is not physically present. For example, during this stage, preschoolers can use a mental symbol for a car (the word *car*), and they likewise understand that a small toy car is representative of the real thing. Because of their ability to use symbolic function, children have no need to get behind the wheel of an actual car to understand its basic purpose and use.

**THE RELATIONSHIP BETWEEN LANGUAGE AND THOUGHT.** Symbolic function is at the heart of one of the major advances that occurs in the preoperational period: the increasingly sophisticated use of language. As we discuss later in this chapter, children make substantial progress in language skills during the preschool period.

Piaget suggests that language and thinking are tightly interconnected and that the advances in language that occur during the preschool years reflect several improvements over the type of thinking that is possible during the earlier sensorimotor period. For instance, thinking embedded in sensorimotor activities is relatively slow, since it depends on actual movements of the body that are bound by human physical limitations. In contrast, the use of symbolic thought, such as the development of an imaginary friend, allows preschoolers to represent actions symbolically, permitting much greater speed.

Even more important, the use of language allows children to think beyond the present to the future. Consequently, rather than being grounded in the here and now, preschoolers can imagine future possibilities through language in the form of sometimes elaborate fantasies and daydreams.

Do the improved language abilities of preschoolers lead to improvements in thinking, or is it the other way around, with the improvements in thinking during the preoperational period leading to enhancements in language ability? This question—whether thought determines language or language determines thought—is one of the enduring and most controversial questions within the field of psychology. Piaget's answer is that language grows out of cognitive advances, rather than the other way around. He argues that improvements during the earlier sensorimotor period are necessary

---

**preoperational stage** According to Piaget, the stage that lasts from ages 2 to 7 during which children's use of symbolic thinking grows, mental reasoning emerges, and the use of concepts increases

**operations** Organized, formal, logical mental processes

**symbolic function** According to Piaget, the ability to use a mental symbol, a word, or an object to represent something that is not physically present

**Figure 9.1** Which Row Contains More Buttons?

When preschoolers are shown these two rows and asked which row has more buttons, they usually respond that the lower row of buttons contains more, because it looks longer. They answer in this way even though they know quite well that 10 is greater than 8. Do you think an educator could teach preschoolers to answer correctly?

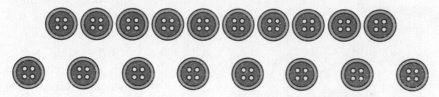

for language development and that continuing growth in cognitive ability during the preoperational period provides the foundation for language ability.

**CENTRATION: WHAT YOU SEE IS WHAT YOU THINK.** Place a dog mask on a cat, and what do you get? According to 3- and 4-year-old preschoolers, you get a dog. To them, a cat with a dog mask ought to bark like a dog, wag its tail like a dog, and eat dog food. In every respect, the cat has been transformed into a dog (deVries, 1969).

To Piaget, the root of this belief is centration, a key element, and limitation, of the thinking of children in the preoperational period. **Centration** is the process of concentrating on one limited aspect of a stimulus and ignoring other aspects.

Preschoolers are unable to consider all available information about a stimulus. Instead, they focus on superficial, obvious elements that are within their sight. These external elements come to dominate preschoolers' thinking, leading to inaccuracy in thought.

Consider what happens when preschoolers are shown two rows of buttons, one row of 10 buttons spaced closely together and another row of 8 buttons spread farther apart to form a longer row (see Figure 9.1). If asked which of the rows contains more buttons, children who are 4 or 5 usually choose the row that looks longer, rather than the one that actually contains more buttons. This occurs in spite of the fact that children this age know quite well that 10 is more than 8.

The cause of the children's mistake is that the visual image of the longer row dominates their thinking. Rather than taking into account their understanding of quantity, they focus on appearance. To a preschooler, appearance is everything. Preschoolers' focus on appearances might be related to another aspect of preoperational thought: the lack of conservation.

**CONSERVATION: LEARNING THAT APPEARANCES ARE DECEIVING.** Consider the following scenario:

*Four-year-old Jaime is shown two drinking glasses of different shapes. One is short and broad; the other is tall and thin. A teacher half-fills the short, broad glass with apple juice. The teacher then pours the same amount of apple juice into the tall, thin glass. The juice fills the tall glass almost to the brim. The teacher asks Jaime a question: Is there more juice in the second glass than there was in the first?*

If you view this as an easy question, so do children like Jaime. They have no trouble answering; however, they almost always get the answer wrong.

Most 4-year-olds respond that there is more apple juice in the tall, thin glass than there is in the short, broad one. If the juice is poured back into the shorter glass, they are quick to say that there is now less juice than there was in the taller glass (see Figure 9.2).

The reason for the error in judgment is that children of this age have not mastered conservation. **Conservation** is the knowledge that quantity is unrelated to the arrangement and physical appearance of objects. Because they are unable to conserve, preschoolers can't understand that changes in one dimension (such as a change in appearance) do not necessarily mean that other dimensions (such as quantity) change. For example, children who do not yet understand the principle of conservation feel quite comfortable in asserting that the amount of liquid changes as it is

---

**centration** The process of concentrating on one limited aspect of a stimulus and ignoring other aspects

**conservation** The knowledge that quantity is unrelated to the arrangement and physical appearance of objects

## Figure 9.2 Which Glass Contains More?

Most 4-year-olds believe that the amount of liquid in these two glasses differs because of the differences in the containers' shapes, even though they may have seen equal amounts of liquid being poured into each.

poured between glasses of different sizes. They simply are unable to realize that the transformation in appearance does not imply a transformation in quantity.

The lack of conservation also manifests itself in children's understanding of area, as illustrated by Piaget's cow-in-the-field problem (Piaget, Inhelder, & Szeminska, 1960). In the problem, two sheets of green paper, equal in size, are shown to a child, and a toy cow is placed in each field. Next, a toy barn is placed in each field, and children are asked which cow has more grass to eat. The typical—and, so far, correct—response is that the cows have the same amount.

In the next step, a second toy barn is placed in each field. But in one field, the barns are placed adjacent to one another, while in the second field, they are separated from one another. Children who have not mastered conservation usually say that the cow in the field with the adjacent barns has more grass to eat than the cow in the field with the separated barns. In contrast, children who can conserve answer, correctly, that the amount available is identical. (Some other conservation tasks are shown in Figure 9.3).

Why do children in the preoperational stage make errors on tasks that require conservation? Piaget suggests that the main reason is that their tendency toward centration prevents them from focusing on the relevant features of the situation. Furthermore, they cannot follow the sequence of transformations that accompanies changes in the appearance of a situation.

**INCOMPLETE UNDERSTANDING OF TRANSFORMATION.** A preoperational preschool child who sees several worms during a walk in the woods may believe that they are all the same worm. The reason: She views each sighting in isolation and is unable to form an idea about the transformation it would take for the worm to move quickly from one sighting to the next. She cannot yet realize that worms can't transform themselves into creatures that can do that.

As Piaget used the term, **transformation** is the process by which one state is changed into another. For instance, adults know that if a pencil that is held upright is allowed to fall down, it passes through a series of successive stages until it reaches its final, horizontal resting spot (see Figure 9.4). In contrast, children in the preoperational period are unable to envision or recall the successive transformations that the pencil followed in moving from the upright to the horizontal position. If asked to reproduce the sequence in a drawing, they draw the pencil upright and lying down, with nothing in between. Basically, they ignore the intermediate steps.

**EGOCENTRISM: THE INABILITY TO TAKE OTHERS' PERSPECTIVES.** Another hallmark of the preoperational period is egocentric thinking. **Egocentric thought** is thinking that does not take into account the viewpoints of others. Preschoolers do not understand that others have different perspectives from their own. Egocentric thought takes two forms: the lack of awareness that others see things from a different physical perspective and the failure to realize that others may hold thoughts, feelings, and points of view that differ from theirs. (Note what egocentric thought does *not* imply: that preoperational children intentionally think in a selfish or inconsiderate manner.)

Egocentric thinking is what is behind children's lack of concern over their nonverbal behavior and the impact it has on others. For instance, a 4-year-old who is given an unwanted gift of socks when he was expecting something more desirable may frown and scowl as he opens the package, unaware that his face can be seen by others and may reveal his true feelings about the gift (Cohen, 2013).

---

**transformation** The process whereby one state is changed into another

**egocentric thought** Thinking that does not take the viewpoints of others into account

**Figure 9.3** Common Tests of Children's Understanding of the Principle of Conservation

From the perspective of an educator, why would knowledge of a child's level of understanding of conservation be important?

| Type of Conservation | Modality | Change in Physical Appearance | Average Age Invariance Is Grasped |
|---|---|---|---|
| Number | Number of elements in a collection  | Rearranging or dislocating elements  | 6–7 years |
| Substance (mass) | Amount of a malleable substance (e.g., clay or liquid) 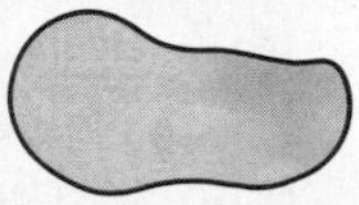 | Altering shape 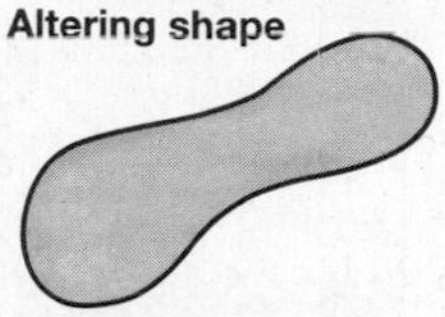 | 7–8 years |
| Length | Length of a line or object  | Altering shape or configuration 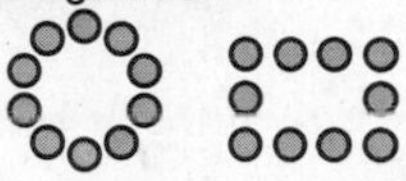 | 7–8 years |
| Area | Amount of surface covered by a set of plane figures 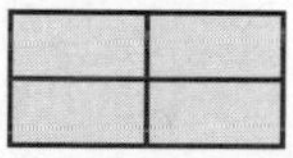 | Rearranging the figures 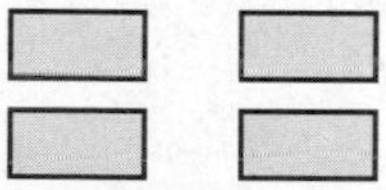 | 8–9 years |
| Weight | Weight of an object  | Altering shape  | 9–10 years |
| Volume | Volume of an object (in terms of water displacement) 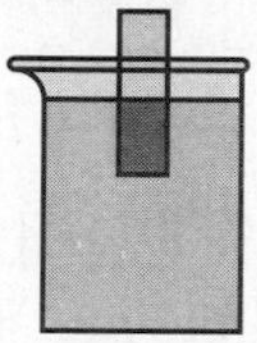 | Altering shape  | 14–15 years |

Egocentrism lies at the heart of several types of behavior during the preoperational period. For example, preschoolers may talk to themselves, even in the presence of others, and at times they simply ignore what others are telling them. Rather than being a sign of eccentricity, such behavior illustrates the egocentric nature of preoperational children's thinking: the lack of awareness that their behavior acts as a trigger to others' reactions and responses. Consequently, a considerable amount of verbal behavior on the part of preschoolers has no social motivation behind it but is meant for the preschoolers' own consumption.

Similarly, egocentrism can be seen in hiding games with children during the preoperational stage. In a game of hide-and-seek, 3-year-olds may attempt to hide by covering their faces with a pillow—even though they remain in plain view. Their reasoning: If they cannot see others, others cannot see them. They assume that others share their view.

**Figure 9.4** The Falling Pencil

Children in Piaget's preoperational stage do not understand that as a pencil falls from the upright to the horizontal position, it moves through a series of intermediary steps. Instead, they think that there are no intermediate steps in the change from the upright to horizontal position.

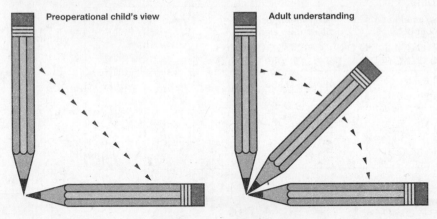

Preoperational child's view          Adult understanding

**THE EMERGENCE OF INTUITIVE THOUGHT.** Because Piaget labeled the preschool years as the "*preoperational period*," it is easy to assume that this is a period of marking time, waiting for the more formal emergence of operations. As if to support this view, many of the characteristics of the preoperational period highlight deficiencies—cognitive skills that the preschooler has yet to master. The preoperational period is far from idle, however. Cognitive development proceeds steadily, and in fact, several new types of ability emerge. A case in point: the development of intuitive thought.

**Intuitive thought** refers to preschoolers' use of primitive reasoning and their avid acquisition of knowledge about the world. From about ages 4 through 7, children's curiosity blossoms. They constantly seek out the answers to a wide variety of questions, asking, "Why?" about nearly everything. At the same time, children may act as if they are authorities on particular topics, feeling certain that they have the correct—and final—word on an issue. If pressed, they are unable to explain how they know what they know. In other words, their intuitive thought leads them to believe that they know answers to all kinds of questions, but there is little or no logical basis for this confidence in their understanding of the way the world operates. This may lead a preschooler to state authoritatively that airplanes can fly because they move their wings up and down like a bird, even if the child has never seen an airplane's wings moving in that way.

In the late stages of the preoperational period, children's intuitive thinking does have certain qualities that prepare them for more sophisticated forms of reasoning. For instance, preschoolers come to understand that pushing harder on the pedals makes a bicycle move faster or that pressing a button on a remote control makes the television change channels. By the end of the preoperational stage, preschoolers begin to understand the notion of *functionality*, the idea that actions, events, and outcomes are related to one another in fixed patterns. Children also begin to show an awareness of the concept of identity in the later stages of the preoperational period. *Identity* is the understanding that certain things stay the same, regardless of changes in shape, size, and appearance.

For instance, knowledge of identity allows one to understand that a lump of clay contains the same amount of clay regardless of whether it is clumped into a ball or stretched out like a snake. Comprehension of identity is necessary for children to develop an understanding of conservation, the ability to understand that quantity is not related to physical appearances, as we discussed earlier. Piaget regarded children's development of conservation as a skill that marks the transition from the preoperational period to the next stage, concrete operations, which we will discuss in Chapter 12.

**EVALUATING PIAGET'S APPROACH TO COGNITIVE DEVELOPMENT.** Piaget, a masterful observer of children's behavior, provided a detailed portrait of preschoolers' cognitive abilities. The broad outlines of his approach have given us a useful way of thinking about the progressive advances in cognitive ability that occur during the preschool years (Siegal, 1997).

It is important, however, to consider Piaget's approach to cognitive development within the appropriate historical context and in light of more recent research findings. As we discussed in Chapter 6, his

**intuitive thought** Thinking that reflects preschoolers' use of primitive reasoning and their avid acquisition of knowledge about the world

theory is based on extensive observations of relatively few children. Despite Piaget's insightful and groundbreaking observations, recent experimental investigations suggest that in certain regards, he underestimated children's capabilities.

Take, for instance, Piaget's views of how children in the preoperational period understand numbers. Piaget contended that preschoolers' thinking is seriously handicapped, as evidenced by their performance on tasks involving conservation and reversibility, the understanding that a transformation can be reversed to return something to its original state. Yet more recent experimental work suggests otherwise. Developmental psychologist Rochel Gelman has found that children as young as 3 can easily tell the difference between rows of two and three toy animals, regardless of the animals' spacing. Older children are able to note differences in number, performing tasks such as identifying which of two numbers is larger and indicating that they understand some rudiments of addition and subtraction problems (McNeil et al., 2011; Brandone et al., 2012; Dietrich et al., 2016).

Based on such evidence, Gelman concludes that children have an innate ability to count, one akin to the ability to use language that some theorists see as universal and genetically determined. Such a conclusion is clearly at odds with Piagetian notions, which suggest that children's numerical abilities do not blossom until after the preoperational period.

Some developmentalists (particularly those who favor the information-processing approach, as we'll see later in the chapter) also believe that cognitive skills develop in a more continuous manner than Piaget's stage theory implies. They believe that rather than thought changing in quality, as Piaget argues, developmental changes are more quantitative in nature, improving gradually. Such critics regard the underlying processes that produce cognitive skill as undergoing only minor changes with age.

There are further difficulties with Piaget's view of cognitive development. His contention that conservation does not emerge until the end of the preoperational period, and in some cases even later, has not stood up to careful experimental scrutiny. Children can be taught to answer correctly on conservation tasks following certain training and experiences. The fact that one can improve children's performance on these tasks argues against the Piagetian view that children in the preoperational period have not reached a level of

cognitive maturity that would permit them to understand conservation (Ping & Goldin-Meadow, 2008).

Clearly, children are more capable at an earlier age than Piaget's account would lead us to believe. Why did Piaget underestimate children's cognitive abilities? One answer is that his questioning of children used language that was too difficult to allow children to answer in a way that would provide a true picture of their skills. In addition, as we've seen, Piaget tended to concentrate on preschoolers' *deficiencies* in thinking, focusing his observations on children's lack of logical thought. By focusing more on children's competence, recent theorists have found increasing evidence for a surprising degree of capability in preschoolers.

# Information-Processing Approaches to Cognitive Development

**LO 9.2** **Summarize the information-processing approaches to cognitive development in the preschool years.**

*Even as an adult, Piku has clear recollections of his first trip to a farm, which he took when he was 3 years old. He was visiting his grandfather, who lived in Ranchi, when the two of them went to a nearby farm. Piku recounts seeing what seemed like hundreds of chickens, and he clearly recalls his fear of the pigs, who seemed huge, smelly, and frightening. Most of all, he recalls the thrill of riding on a horse with his grandfather.*

The fact that Piku has a clear memory of his farm trip is not surprising: Most people have unambiguous, and seemingly accurate, memories dating as far back as age 3. But are the processes used to form memories during the preschool years similar to those that operate later in life? More broadly, what general changes in the processing of information occur during the preschool years?

Information-processing approaches focus on changes in the kinds of "mental programs" that children use when approaching problems. They view the changes that occur in children's cognitive abilities during the preschool years as analogous to the way a computer program becomes more sophisticated as a programmer modifies it on the basis of experience. For many child developmentalists, information-processing approaches represent the dominant, most comprehensive, and ultimately the most accurate explanation of how children develop cognitively (Lacerda, von Hofsten, & Heimann, 2001).

In the next section, we'll focus on two areas that highlight the approach taken by information-processing theorists: understanding of numbers and memory development during the preschool years.

**PRESCHOOLERS' UNDERSTANDING OF NUMBERS.** As we saw earlier, one of the flaws critics have noticed in Piaget's theory is that preschoolers have a greater understanding of numbers than Piaget thought. Researchers using information-processing approaches to cognitive development have found increasing evidence that preschoolers have a sophisticated understanding of numbers. The average preschooler is able not only to count, but to do so in a fairly systematic, consistent manner (Siegler, 1998).

For instance, preschoolers follow a number of principles in their counting. When shown a group of several items, they know they should assign just one number to each item and that each item should be counted only once. Moreover, even when they get the *names* of numbers wrong, they are consistent in their usage. For example, a 4-year-old who counts three items as "1, 3, 7" will say "1, 3, 7" when counting another group of different items. And if asked how many there are, she will probably answer that there are seven items in the group (Le Corre & Carey, 2007; Slusser, Ditta, & Sarnecka, 2013; Xu & LeFevre, 2016).

In short, preschoolers may demonstrate a surprisingly sophisticated understanding of numbers, although their understanding is not totally precise. Still, by age 4, most are able to carry out simple addition and subtraction problems by counting, and they are able to compare different quantities quite successfully (Gilmore & Spelke, 2008).

**MEMORY: RECALLING THE PAST.** Think back to your earliest memory. If you are like Paco, described earlier, and most other people too, it probably is of an event that occurred after age 3. **Autobiographical memory**, memory of particular events from one's own life, achieves little accuracy until after 3 years of age. Accuracy then increases gradually and slowly throughout the preschool years (Reese & Newcombe, 2007; Wang, 2008; Bohn & Berntsen, 2011).

Preschool children's recollections of events that happened to them are sometimes, but not always, accurate. For instance, 3-year-olds can remember central features of routine occurrences, such as the sequence of events involved in eating at a restaurant, fairly well. In addition, preschoolers are typically accurate in their responses to open-ended questions, such as "What rides did you like best at the amusement park?" (Pathman et al., 2013; Valentino et al., 2014; McDonnell et al., 2016).

The accuracy of preschoolers' memories is partly determined by how soon the memories are accessed. Unless an event is particularly vivid or meaningful, it is not likely to be remembered at all. Moreover, not all autobiographical memories last into later life. For instance, a child may remember the first day of kindergarten 6 months or a year later, but later in life might not remember that day at all.

Memories are also affected by cultural factors. For example, Chinese college students' memories of early childhood are more likely to be unemotional and reflect activities involving social roles, such as working in their family's store, whereas U.S. college students' earliest memories are more emotionally elaborate and focus on specific events such as the birth of a sibling (Peterson, Wang, & Hou, 2009; Stevenson, Heiser, & Resing, 2016).

Preschoolers' autobiographical memories not only fade, but what is remembered may not be wholly accurate. For example, if an event happens often, such as a trip to a grocery store, it may be hard to remember one specific time it happened. Preschoolers' memories of familiar events are often organized in terms of **scripts**, broad representations in memory of events and the order in which they occur.

For example, a young preschooler might represent eating in a restaurant in terms of a few steps: talking to a waitress, getting the food, and eating. With age, the scripts become more elaborate: getting in the car, being seated at the restaurant, choosing food, ordering, waiting for the meal to come, eating, ordering dessert, and paying for the food. Because events that are frequently repeated tend to be melded into scripts, particular instances of a scripted event are recalled with less accuracy than those that are unscripted in memory (Fivush, Kuebli, & Clubb, 1992; Sutherland, Pipe, & Schick, 2003).

---

**autobiographical memory** Memory of particular events from one's own life

**scripts** Broad representations in memory of events and the order in which they occur

There are other reasons why preschoolers may not have entirely accurate autobiographical memories. Because they have difficulty describing certain kinds of information, such as complex causal relationships, they may oversimplify recollections. For example, a child who has witnessed an argument between his grandparents may only remember that Grandma took the cake away from Grandpa, not the discussion of his weight and cholesterol that led up to the action. And, as we consider next, preschoolers' memories are also susceptible to the suggestions of others. This is a special concern when children are called upon to testify in legal situations, such as when abuse is suspected.

## FORENSIC DEVELOPMENTAL PSYCHOLOGY: BRINGING CHILD DEVELOPMENT TO THE COURTROOM.

*I was looking and then I didn't see what I was doing and it got in there somehow.... The mouse-trap was in our house because there's a mouse in our house.... The mousetrap is down in the base-ment, next to the firewood.... I was playing a game called Operation and then I went downstairs and said to Dad, "I want to eat lunch," and then it got stuck in the mousetrap.... My daddy was down in the basement collecting firewood.... [My brother] pushed me [into the mousetrap].... It happened yesterday. The mouse was in my house yesterday. I caught my finger in it yesterday. I went to the hospital yesterday. (Ceci & Bruck, 1993, p. A23).*

Despite the detailed account by this 4-year-old boy of his encounter with a mousetrap and subsequent trip to the hospital, there's a problem: The incident never happened, and the memory is entirely false.

The 4-year-old's explicit recounting of a mousetrap incident that had not actually occurred was the product of a study on children's memory. Each week for 11 weeks, the 4-year-old boy was told, "You went to the hospital because your finger got caught in a mouse-trap. Did this ever happen to you?"

The first week, the child quite accurately said, "No. I've never been to the hospital." But by the second week, the answer changed to, "Yes, I cried." In the third week, the boy said, "Yes. My mom went to the hospital with me." By the eleventh week, the answer had expanded to the quote above (Bruck & Ceci, 2004; Powell, Wright, & Hughes-Scholes, 2011).

The research study that elicited the child's false memories is part of a new and rapidly growing field within child development: forensic developmental psychology. *Forensic developmental psychology* focuses on the reliability of children's autobiographical memories in the context of the legal system. It considers children's abilities to recall events in their lives and the reliability of children's courtroom accounts where they are witnesses or victims (Bruck & Ceci, 2004; Goodman, 2006; McAuliff & Kovera, 2012).

The embellishment of a completely false incident is characteristic of the fragility, impressionability, and inaccuracy of memory in young children. Young children may recall things quite mistakenly, but with great conviction, contending that events occurred that never really happened and forgetting events that did occur.

Children's memories are susceptible to the suggestions of adults asking them questions. This is particularly true of preschoolers, who are considerably more vulnerable to suggestion than either adults or school-age children. Preschoolers are also more prone to make inaccurate inferences about the reasons behind others' behavior and are less able to draw appropriate conclusions based on their knowledge of a situation (e.g., "He was crying because he didn't like the sandwich.") (Goodman & Melinder, 2007; Havard & Memon, 2013; Otgaar, Howe, & Muris, 2017.)

Of course, preschoolers recall many things accurately; as we discussed earlier in the chapter, children as young as 3 remember some events in their lives without distortion. Not all recollections are accurate, however, and some events that are recalled with seeming accuracy never actually occurred.

The conviction of preschool teacher Kelly Michaels for sexually molesting several preschool children may have been the result of leading questions posed to the children.

The error rate for children is heightened when the same question is asked repeatedly. False memories—of the type reported by the 4-year-old who "remembered" going to the hospital after his finger was caught in a mousetrap—may actually be more persistent than actual memories. In addition, when questions are highly suggestive (i.e., when questioners attempt to lead a person to particular conclusions), children are more apt to make mistakes in recall (Loftus & Bernstein, 2005; Goodman & Quas, 2008; Boseovski, 2012).

How can children be questioned to produce the most accurate recollections? One way is to question them as soon as possible after an event has occurred. The longer the time between the actual event and the questioning, the less firm are children's recollections. Additionally, specific questions (e.g., "Did you go downstairs with Brian?") are answered more accurately than general ones. Asking the questions outside of a courtroom is also preferable, as the courtroom setting can be intimidating and frightening (Ceci & Bruck, 2007; Hanna et al., 2013; also see Table 9.1).

**INFORMATION-PROCESSING THEORIES IN PERSP- ECTIVE.** According to information-processing approaches, cognitive development consists of gradual improvements in the ways people perceive, understand, and remember information. With age and practice, preschoolers process information more efficiently and with greater sophistication, and they are able to handle increasingly complex problems. In the eyes of proponents of information-processing approaches, it is these quantitative advances in information processing—and not the qualitative changes suggested by Piaget—that constitute cognitive development (Zhe & Siegler, 2000; Rose, Feldman, & Jankowski, 2009).

For supporters of information-processing approaches, the reliance on well-defined processes that can be tested, with relative precision, by research is one of the perspective's most important features. Rather than relying on concepts that are somewhat vague, such as Piaget's notions of assimilation and accommodation, information-processing approaches provide a comprehensive, logical set of concepts.

For instance, as preschoolers grow older, they have longer attention spans, can monitor and plan what they are attending to more effectively, and become increasingly aware of their cognitive limitations. As we discussed earlier in this chapter, these advances may be due to brain development. Such increasing attention spans place some of Piaget's findings in a different light. For instance, increased attention span allows older children to attend to both the height *and* the width of tall and short glasses into which liquid is poured. This permits them to understand that the amount of liquid in the glasses stays the same when it is poured back and forth. Preschoolers, in contrast, are unable to attend to both dimensions simultaneously, and thus are less able to conserve (Hudson, Sosa, & Shapiro, 1997).

Proponents of information-processing theory have also been successful in focusing on important cognitive processes to which alternative approaches traditionally have paid little attention, such as the contribution of mental skills like memory and attention to children's thinking. They suggest that information processing provides a clear, logical, and full account of cognitive development.

Yet information-processing approaches have their detractors, who raise significant points. For one thing, the focus on a series of single, individual cognitive processes leaves out of consideration some important factors that appear to influence cognition. For instance, information-processing theorists pay relatively little attention to social and cultural factors—a deficiency that the approach we'll consider next attempts to remedy.

An even more important criticism is that information-processing approaches "lose sight of the forest for the trees." In other words, information-processing approaches pay so much attention to the detailed,

**Table 9.1** Eliciting Accurate Recollections From Children

| Recommended Practice |
| --- |
| **Play Dumb.**<br>INTERVIEWER: *Now that I know you a little better, tell me why you are here today.* |
| **Ask Follow-up Questions.**<br>CHILD: Bob touched my private area. INTERVIEWER: *Tell me everything about that.* |
| **Encourage Children to Describe Events.**<br>INTERVIEWER: *Tell me everything that happened at Bob's house from the beginning to the end.* |
| **Avoid Suggesting That Interviewers Expect Descriptions of Particular Kinds of Events.** |
| **Avoid Offering Rewards or Expressing Disapproval.** |

SOURCE: Poole, D. A., & Lamb, M. E. (1998). Investigative interviews of children: A guide for helping professionals. Washington, DC: American Psychological Association.

individual sequence of processes that compose cognitive processing and development that they never adequately paint a whole, comprehensive picture of cognitive development—which Piaget clearly did quite well.

Developmentalists using information-processing approaches respond to such criticisms by saying that their model of cognitive development has the advantage of being precisely stated and capable of leading to testable hypotheses. They also argue that there is far more research supporting their approach than there is for alternative theories of cognitive development. In short, they suggest that their approach provides a more accurate account than any other.

Information-processing approaches have been highly influential over the past several decades. They have inspired a tremendous amount of research that has helped us gain some insights into how children develop cognitively.

## Vygotsky's View of Cognitive Development: Taking Culture Into Account

**LO 9.3** **Explain Vygotsky's approach to cognitive development.**

*With her daughter watching, a Chilcotin woman takes a square of bark and begins the process of making a traditional birch basket. After several minutes, her daughter asks about a detail in the process of stitching the bark around the rim. In reply, the mother takes another piece of bark and starts the process again. In the Chilcotin view, children can truly learn a procedure only by comprehending the entire process, not by learning its individual components.*

The Chilcotin view of how children learn about the world contrasts with the prevalent view of Western society, which assumes that only by mastering the separate parts of a problem can one fully comprehend it. Do differences in the ways particular cultures and societies approach problems influence cognitive development? According to Russian developmental psychologist Lev Vygotsky (1896–1934), the answer is a clear "yes."

Vygotsky viewed cognitive development as a result of social interactions in which children learn through guided participation, working with mentors to solve problems. Instead of concentrating on individual performance, as Piaget and many alternative approaches do, Vygotsky's increasingly influential view focuses on the social aspects of development and learning.

Vygotsky saw children as apprentices, learning cognitive strategies and other skills from adult and peer mentors who not only present new ways of doing things, but also provide assistance, instruction, and motivation. Consequently, he focused on the child's social and cultural world as the source of cognitive development. According to Vygotsky, children gradually grow intellectually and begin to function on their own because of the assistance that adult and peer partners provide (Vygotsky, 1926/1997; Tudge & Scrimsher, 2003).

Vygotsky contends that the nature of the partnership between developing children and adults and peers is determined largely by cultural and societal factors. For instance, culture and society establish the institutions, such as preschools and play groups, that promote development by providing opportunities for cognitive growth. Furthermore, by emphasizing particular tasks, culture and society shape the nature of specific cognitive advances. Unless we look at what is important and meaningful to members of a given society, we may seriously underestimate the nature and level of cognitive abilities that ultimately will be attained (Balakrishnan & Claiborne, 2012; Nagahashi, 2013; Veraksa et al., 2016).

> **From an educator's perspective:** If children's cognitive development is dependent on interactions with others, what obligations does society have regarding such social settings as preschools and neighborhoods?

For example, children's toys reflect what is important and meaningful in a particular society. In Western society, preschoolers commonly play with toy wagons, automobiles, and other vehicles, in part reflecting the mobile nature of the culture.

Societal expectations about gender also play a role in how children come to understand the world. For instance, one study conducted at a science museum found that parents provided more detailed scientific explanations to boys than to girls at museum displays. Such differences in level of explanation may lead to more sophisticated understanding of science in boys and ultimately may produce later gender differences in science learning (Crowley et al., 2001).

Russian developmentalist Lev Vygotsky proposed that the focus of cognitive development should be on a child's social and cultural world, as opposed to the Piagetian approach, which concentrates on individual performance.

Vygotsky's approach is therefore quite different from that of Piaget. Where Piaget looked at developing children and saw junior scientists, working by themselves to develop an independent understanding of the world, Vygotsky saw cognitive apprentices, learning from master teachers the skills that are important in the child's culture. Where Piaget saw preschoolers who were egocentric, looking at the world from their own, limited vantage point, Vygotsky saw preschoolers as using others to gain an understanding of the world.

In Vygotsky's view, then, children's cognitive development is dependent on interaction with others. Vygotsky argued that it is only through partnership with other people—peers, parents, teachers, and other adults—that children can fully develop their knowledge, thinking processes, beliefs, and values (Fernyhough, 1997; Edwards, 2004).

**THE ZONE OF PROXIMAL DEVELOPMENT AND SCAFFOLDING: FOUNDATIONS OF COGNITIVE DEVELOPMENT.** Vygotsky proposed that children's cognitive abilities increase through exposure to information that is new enough to be intriguing, but not too difficult for the child to contend with. He called this the **zone of proximal development (ZPD)**, the level at which a child can *almost*, but not fully,

perform a task independently, but can do so with the assistance of someone more competent. When appropriate instruction is offered within the ZPD, children are able to increase their understanding and master new tasks. In order for cognitive development to occur, then, new information must be presented—by parents, teachers, or more skilled peers—within the ZPD. For example, a preschooler might not be able to figure out by herself how to successfully attach a handle on the clay pot she's making, but she could do it with some advice from her child care teacher (Zuckerman & Shenfield, 2007; Norton & D'Ambrosio, 2008; Warford, 2011).

The concept of the zone of proximal development suggests that even though two children might be able to achieve the same amount without help, if one child receives aid, he or she may improve substantially more than the other. The greater the improvement that comes with help, the larger the ZPD.

The assistance or structuring provided by others has been termed scaffolding. **Scaffolding** is the support for learning and problem solving that encourages independence and growth (Puntambekar & Hübscher, 2005; Blewitt et al., 2009; Jadallah et al., 2011).

To Vygotsky, the process of scaffolding not only helps children solve specific problems, but also aids in the development of their overall cognitive abilities. Scaffolding takes its name from the scaffolds that are put up to aid in the construction of a building and removed once the building is complete. In education, scaffolding involves, first of all, helping children think about and frame a task in an appropriate manner. In addition, a parent or teacher is likely to provide clues to task completion that are appropriate to the child's level of development and to model behavior that can lead to completion of the task. As in construction, the scaffolding that more competent people provide, which facilitates the completion of identified tasks, is removed once children are able to solve a problem on their own (Taumoepeau & Ruffman, 2008; Eitel et al., 2013; Leonard & Higson, 2014; Muhonen et al., 2016).

**zone of proximal development (ZPD)** According to Vygotsky, the level at which a child can almost, but not fully, comprehend or perform a task without assistance

**scaffolding** The support for learning and problem solving that encourages independence and growth

To illustrate how scaffolding operates, consider the following conversation between mother and son:

MOTHER: Do you remember how you helped me make the biscuits before?

CHILD: No.

MOTHER: We made the dough and put it in the oven. Do you remember that?

CHILD: When *Dadi* (grandmother) came?

MOTHER: Yes, that's right. Would you help me shape the dough into biscuits?

CHILD: OK.

MOTHER: Can you remember how big we made the biscuits when Dadi was here?

CHILD: Big.

MOTHER: Right. Can you show me how big?

CHILD: We used the big wooden spoon.

MOTHER: That's right! Good job remembering. We used the wooden spoon, and we made big biscuits. But let's try something different today by using the ice cream scoop to form the biscuits.

Although this conversation isn't particularly sophisticated, it illustrates the practice of scaffolding. The mother is supporting her son's efforts, and she gets him to respond conversationally. In the process, she not only expands her son's abilities by using a different tool (the scoop instead of the spoon) but she also models how conversations proceed.

In some societies, parental support for learning differs by gender. In one study, Mexican mothers were found to provide more scaffolding than fathers. A possible explanation is that mothers may be more aware of their children's cognitive abilities than are fathers (Tenenbaum & Leaper, 1998; Tamis-LeMonda & Cabrera, 2002).

One key aspect of the aid that more accomplished individuals provide to learners comes in the form of cultural tools. *Cultural tools* are actual, physical items (e.g., pencils, paper, calculators, computers, and so forth), as well as an intellectual and conceptual framework for solving problems. The intellectual and conceptual framework available to learners includes the language that is used within a culture, its alphabetical and numbering schemas, its mathematical and scientific systems, and even its religious systems. These cultural tools provide a structure that can be used to help children define and solve specific problems, as well as an intellectual point of view that encourages cognitive development.

For example, consider the cultural differences in how people talk about distance. In cities, distance is usually measured in blocks ("the store is about 15 blocks away"). To a child from a rural background, such a unit of measurement is meaningless, and more meaningful distance-related terms may be used, such as yards, miles; such practical rules of thumb as "a stone's throw"; or references to known distances and landmarks ("about half the distance to town"). To make matters more complicated, "how far" questions are sometimes answered in terms not of distance, but of time ("it's about 15 minutes to the store"), which will be understood variously to refer to walking or riding time, depending on context—and, if riding time, to different forms of riding. For some children, the ride to the store will be conceived of as being by oxcart, for others, by bicycle, bus, canoe, or automobile, again depending on cultural context. The nature of the tools available to children to solve problems and perform tasks is highly dependent on the culture in which they live.

**EVALUATING VYGOTSKY'S CONTRIBUTIONS.** Vygotsky's view—that the specific nature of cognitive development can be understood only by taking into account cultural and social context—has become increasingly influential in the past decade. In some ways, this is surprising, in light of the fact that Vygotsky died more than eight decades ago at the young age of 37 (Winsler, 2003; Gredler & Shields, 2008).

Several factors explain Vygotsky's growing influence. One is that until fairly recently, he was largely unknown to developmentalists. His writings are only now widely disseminated in the United States due to the growing availability of good English translations. In fact, for most of the 20th century, Vygotsky was not widely known even within his native land. His work was banned for some time due to his reliance on Western theorists, and it was not until the 1991 breakup of the Soviet Union that it became freely available in the formerly Soviet countries. Thus, Vygotsky, long hidden from his fellow developmentalists, only emerged onto the scene long after his death (Wertsch, 2008).

Even more important, though, is the quality of Vygotsky's ideas. They represent a consistent theoretical system and help explain a growing body of research attesting to the importance of social interaction in promoting cognitive development. The idea that children's comprehension of the world is an outcome of their interactions with their parents, peers, and other members of society is both appealing and well supported by research findings. It is also consistent with a growing body of multicultural and cross-cultural research, which finds evidence that cognitive development is shaped, in part, by cultural factors (Hedegaard & Fleer, 2013; Friedrich, 2014; Yasnitsky, 2016).

Of course, not every aspect of Vygotsky's theorizing has been supported, and his conceptualization of cognitive growth can be criticized for its lack of precision. For instance, such broad concepts as the zone of proximal development are not terribly precise, and they do not always lend themselves to experimental tests (Wertsch, 1999; Daniels, 2006).

Furthermore, Vygotsky was largely silent on how basic cognitive processes such as attention and memory develop and how children's natural cognitive capabilities unfold. Because of his emphasis on broad cultural influences, he did not focus on how individual bits of information are processed and synthesized. These processes, which must be taken into account if we are to have a complete understanding of cognitive development, are more directly addressed by information-processing theories.

Still, Vygotsky's melding of the cognitive and social worlds of children has been an important advance in our understanding of cognitive development. We can only imagine what his impact would have been if he had lived a longer life. (See Table 9.2 for a comparison of Piaget's theory, information-processing theories, and the Vygotskian approach.)

# The Growth of Language

*The truck is really red and I like it.*

*Rinku got the truck in the mud and it got all dirty.*

*Papa came and picked me up when I fell over.*

*I didn't know dogs went in water and floated and moved.*

*Where did you put my big green blanket?*

*Mama kept the biscuits in a big box on a shelf.*

*Give it to me and I will keep it until I have to go in.*

*Bring your own car if you want to play "traffic road" with me.*

*When I grow up I'll have a big truck to drive.*

Listen to Rinku, at age 3. In addition to recognizing most letters of the alphabet, printing the first letter of his name, and writing the word "HI," he is readily capable of producing the complex sentences quoted above.

During the preschool years, children's language skills reach new heights of sophistication. Children begin the period with reasonable linguistic capabilities, although with significant gaps in both comprehension and production. In fact, no one would mistake the language used by a 3-year-old for that of an adult. By the end of the preschool years, however, children can hold their own with adults, both comprehending and producing language that has many of the qualities of adults' language. How does this transformation occur?

## Language Development During the Preschool Years

**LO 9.4  Describe how children's language abilities develop in the preschool years.**

Language blooms so rapidly between the late twos and the mid-threes that researchers have yet to

**Table 9.2** Comparison of Piaget's Theory, Information-Processing Theories, and Vygotsky's Approach to Cognitive Development

|  | Piaget | Information Processing | Vygotsky |
|---|---|---|---|
| **Key concepts** | Stages of cognitive development; qualitative growth from one stage to another | Gradual, quantitative improvements in attention, perception, understanding, and memory | Culture and social context drive cognitive development |
| **Role of stages** | Heavy emphasis | No specific stages | No specific stages |
| **Importance of social factors** | Low | Low | High |
| **Educational perspective** | Children must have reached a given stage of development for specific types of educational interventions to be effective. | Education is reflected in gradual increments in skills. | Education is very influential in promoting cognitive growth; teachers serve as facilitators. |

understand the exact pattern. What is clear is that sentence length increases at a steady pace, and the ways in which children at this age combine words and phrases to form sentences—known as **syntax**—doubles each month. By the time a preschooler is 3, the various combinations reach into the thousands (Pinker, 2005; Rowland & Noble, 2011).

In addition to the increasing complexity of sentences, there are enormous leaps in the number of words children use. By age 6, the average child has a vocabulary of around 14,000 words. To reach this number, preschoolers acquire vocabulary at a rate of nearly one new word every 2 hours, 24 hours a day. They manage this feat through a process known as **fast mapping**, in which new words are associated with their meaning after only a brief encounter (Kan & Kohnert, 2009; Marinellie & Kneile, 2012; Venker, Kover, & Weismer, 2016).

By age 3, preschoolers routinely use plurals and possessive forms of nouns (such as *boys* and *boy's*), employ the past tense (adding *-ed* at the end of words), and use articles (*the* and *a*). They can ask, and answer, complex questions ("Where did you say my book is?" and "Those are trucks, aren't they?")

Preschoolers' skills extend to the appropriate formation of words that they have never before encountered. For example, in one classic experiment, preschool children were shown cards with drawings of a cartoon-like bird, such as those shown in Figure 9.5

### Figure 9.5 Appropriate Formation of Words

Even though preschoolers—like the rest of us—are unlikely to have ever before encountered a "wug," they are able to produce the appropriate word to fill in the blank (which, for the record, is "wugs").

**SOURCE:** Adapted from Berko, J. (1958). The child's learning of English morphology. Word, vol. 14, 150–177.

**This is a wug.**

**Now there is another one.
There are two of them.
There are two _____ .**

(Berko, 1958). The experimenter told the children that the figure was a "wug," and then showed them a card with two of the cartoon figures. "Now there are two of them," the children were told, and they were then asked to supply the missing word in the sentence, "There are two" (the answer to which, as *you* no doubt know, is "wugs").

Not only did children show that they knew rules about the plural forms of nouns, but they understood possessive forms of nouns and the third-person singular and past-tense forms of verbs—all for words that they never had previously encountered because they were nonsense words with no real meaning (O'Grady & Aitchison, 2005).

Preschoolers also learn what *cannot* be said as they acquire the principles of grammar. **Grammar** is the system of rules in a given language that determine how our thoughts can be expressed. (Grammar is a broad, general term that encompasses syntax and other linguistic rules.) For instance, preschoolers come to learn that "I am sitting" is correct, while the similarly structured "I am knowing [that]" is incorrect. Although they still make frequent mistakes of one sort or another, 3-year-olds follow the principles of grammar most of the time. Some errors are very noticeable—such as the use of *mens* and *catched*—but these errors are actually quite rare, occurring between one-tenth of a percent and 8 percent of the time. Put another way, young preschoolers are correct in their grammatical constructions more than 90 percent of the time (Pinker, 1994; Guasti, 2002).

Some developmentalists suggest that **private speech**, speech by children that is spoken and directed to themselves, performs an important function. It's a common behavior: In even a short visit to a preschool, you're likely to notice some children talking to themselves during play periods. A child might be reminding a doll that the two of them are going to the grocery

**syntax** The way in which words and phrases are combined to form meaningful sentences

**fast mapping** The process in which new words are associated with their meaning after only a brief encounter

**grammar** The system of rules in a given language that determine how thoughts can be expressed

**private speech** Spoken language that is not intended for others and is commonly used by children during the preschool years

store later, or another child, while playing with a toy racing car, might speak of an upcoming race. In some cases, the talk is sustained, as when a child, working on a puzzle (as was the case with Natalia in the prologue), says things like, "This piece goes here.... Uh-oh, this one doesn't fit.... Where can I put this piece?...This can't be right."

Vygotsky suggested that private speech is used as a guide to behavior and thought. By communicating with themselves through private speech, children are able to try out ideas, acting as their own sounding boards. In this way, private speech facilitates children's thinking and helps them control their behavior. (Have you ever said to yourself, "Take it easy" or "Calm down" when trying to control your anger over some situation?) In Vygotsky's view, then, private speech ultimately serves an important social function, allowing children to solve problems and reflect upon difficulties they encounter. He also suggested that private speech is a forerunner to the internal dialogues that we use when we reason with ourselves during thinking (Al-Namlah, Meins, & Fernyhough, 2012; McGonigle-Chalmers, Slater, & Smith, 2014).

In addition, private speech may be a way for children to practice the practical skills required in conversation, also known as pragmatics. **Pragmatics** is the aspect of language relating to communicating effectively and appropriately with others. The development of pragmatic abilities permits children to understand the basics of conversations—turn-taking, sticking to a topic, and what should and should not be said according to the conventions of society. When children are taught that the appropriate response to receiving a gift is to say "thank you" or that they should use different language in various settings (on the playground with their friends versus in the classroom with their teacher), they are learning the pragmatics of language.

The preschool years also mark the growth of social speech. **Social speech** is speech directed toward another person and meant to be understood by that person. Before age 3, children may seem to be speaking only for their own entertainment, apparently unconcerned about whether anyone else can understand. During the preschool years, however, children begin to direct their speech to others, wanting others to listen and becoming frustrated when they cannot make themselves understood. As a result, they begin to adapt their speech to others through pragmatics, as discussed earlier. Recall that Piaget contended that

most speech during the preoperational period was egocentric: Preschoolers were seen as taking little account of the effect their speech was having on others. More recent experimental evidence, however, suggests that children are somewhat more adept in taking others into account than Piaget initially suggested. (Also see the *From Research to Practice* box.)

## How Living in Poverty Affects Language Development

**LO 9.5 Explain the effect of poverty on language development.**

The language that preschoolers hear at home has profound implications for future cognitive success, according to results of a landmark series of studies by psychologists Betty Hart and Todd Risley (Hart & Risley, 1995; Hart, 2000, 2004). The researchers studied the language used over a 2-year period by a group of parents of varying levels of affluence as they interacted with their children. Their examination of some 1,300 hours of everyday interactions between parents and children produced several major findings:

- The greater the affluence of the parents, the more they spoke to their children. The rate at which language was addressed to children varied significantly according to the economic level of the family.

- In a typical hour, parents classified as professionals spent almost twice as much time interacting with their children as parents who received welfare assistance.

- By age 4, children in families that received welfare assistance were likely to have been exposed to some 13 million fewer words than those in families classified as professionals.

- The kind of language used in the home differed among the various types of families. Children in families that received welfare assistance were apt to hear prohibitions ("no" or "stop," for example) twice as frequently as those in families classified as professionals.

---

**pragmatics** The aspect of language relating to communicating effectively and appropriately with others

**social speech** Speech directed toward another person and meant to be understood by that person

# FROM RESEARCH TO PRACTICE
## How Writing by Hand Stimulates Brain Development

Are you the type of student who carries around a laptop or other mobile device and types everything, including your class notes? Or perhaps you prefer to take notes by hand because you feel that you just learn better that way? Our increasingly digital society puts pressure on schools to start children learning keyboard skills at ever younger ages, even to the point where learning to write by hand is getting pushed aside. But this would be a mistake, as research suggests that learning to write by hand plays an important role in children's cognitive development.

In a recent study, 5-year-old children who had not yet learned to read or write were shown a letter and asked to reproduce it. Some of the children were instructed to write the letter by hand on a blank piece of paper. Others were instructed to trace the letter over a dotted outline of it. Finally, a third group was instructed to type the letter on a keyboard. Then all of the children were again shown an image of the letter that they had just reproduced, but this time while they were undergoing a functional MRI (a scan that shows what regions of the brain are currently active).

The functional MRI revealed telling differences between the children based on how they originally reproduced the letter. The children who wrote the letter freehand showed increased activation in three regions of the brain that are associated with reading and writing in adults. The children who typed the letter on a keyboard and the children who traced an outline of the letter did not show the same activation of these brain regions. These results show that freehand writing produces changes in the brain that mere typing (or tracing) does not. The researchers theorize that the process of trying to duplicate letter shapes without assistance engages the brain in important ways—it requires careful attention to the form of

the letter and planning of the steps and movements needed to recreate it (James & Engelhardt, 2012).

Perhaps most importantly, it requires tolerance of variability in the appearance of the letters. After all, your *g* differs from your best friend's *g*, and it's likely that neither one of them bear much resemblance at all to a keyboard-generated *g*. Struggling to write your own letters, and often getting them not quite right, is likely to help you recognize letters accurately even though different sources write them differently. Merely learning to recognize letter shapes that never vary because they are printed on a keyboard isn't as likely to help with that.

Other research shows that printing, cursive writing, and typing are associated with different patterns of brain activity in young children. When the children in this study wrote their thoughts by hand, they wrote more and expressed a greater richness of ideas than children who composed their thoughts on a keyboard. When they were thinking about writing topics during a functional MRI, children who had better hand writing skills showed greater brain activity in areas associated with memory and reading and writing. Again, learning to write by hand seems to train children's brains to think better about writing (Berninger et al., 2006).

- **What might be a reason why tracing a dotted-line outline of a letter doesn't produce the same kind of learning as writing the letter freehand?**

- **If you were a parent or a teacher of young children, how might you apply these research findings to help your children learn to read and write better?**

Ultimately, the study found that the type of language to which children were exposed was associated with their performance on tests of intelligence. The greater the number and variety of words children heard, for instance, the better was their performance at age 3 on a variety of measures of intellectual achievement.

**From a social worker's perspective:** What do you think are the underlying reasons for differences between poor and more affluent households in the use of language, and how do such language differences affect a family's social interactions?

Although the findings are correlational, and thus cannot be interpreted in terms of cause and effect, they clearly suggest the importance of early exposure to language, in terms of both quantity and variety. They also suggest that intervention programs that teach parents to speak to their children more often and use more varied language may be useful in alleviating some of the potentially damaging consequences of poverty.

The research is also consistent with an increasing body of evidence that family income and poverty have powerful consequences for children's general cognitive development and behavior. By age 5, children raised in poverty tend to have lower IQ scores and perform less well on other measures of cognitive development than children raised in affluence. Furthermore, the longer children live in poverty, the more severe are the consequences. Poverty not only reduces the educational resources available to children, but it also has such negative effects on *parents* that it limits the psychological support they can provide their families. In short, the consequences of poverty are severe, and they linger (Barone, 2011; Leffel & Suskind, 2013; Sharkins, Leger, & Ernest, 2016).

# Schooling and Society

*In the Roseland Ballroom, hundreds of young actors are in a line stretching around the corner of Broadway and 52nd Street. It's the first-ever open casting call for* Sesame Street, *which is looking for a new neighbor for its 44th season. The role is for a Hispanic character, in keeping with an emphasis on diversity that has been part of the show's culture since the 1970s.*

*"Sesame Street is how I learned English," says one of the hopefuls in the line. Another aspiring actor adds, "I was an extra on the show when I was 5. I was shocked to discover that there were people operating the Muppets. But I got over it, and now I want to be one of them." (Based on McCue, 2012.)*

Ask almost any preschooler, and she or he will be able to identify Elmo, as well as Big Bird, Bert, Ernie, and a host of other characters as the members of the cast of *Sesame Street*, the most successful television show in history targeted at preschoolers, with a daily audience in the millions.

Preschoolers do more than watch TV, however. Many spend a good portion of their day involved in some form of child care setting outside their own homes, designed, in part, to enhance their cognitive development. What are the consequences of these activities? We turn now to a consideration of how early childhood education and television and other media are related to preschool development.

## Early Childhood Education: Taking the "Pre-" out of the Preschool Period

**LO 9.6 Describe the ways in which preschool children are educated.**

The term "preschool period" is something of a misnomer, because many children engage in some form of educational experiences during this stage. Almost three-quarters of children in the United States are enrolled in some type of care outside the home, much of which is designed either explicitly or implicitly to teach skills that will enhance intellectual as well as social abilities. One important reason for this increase is the rise in the number of families in which both parents work outside the home. For instance, a high proportion of fathers work outside the home, and close to 60 percent of women with children under 6 are employed, most of them full time (Borden, 1998; Tamis-LeMonda & Cabrera, 2002).

There is another cause for the increase in preschool enrollment, one less tied to the practical considerations of child care: developmentalists have found increasing evidence that children can benefit substantially from involvement in some form of educational activity before they enroll in formal schooling, which typically takes place at age 5 or 6 in the United States. When compared to children who stay at home and have no formal educational involvement, those children enrolled in *good* preschools experience clear cognitive and social benefits (Campbell, Ramey, & Pungello, 2002; Friedman, 2004; National Association for the Education of Young Children, 2005).

The variety of early education alternatives is vast. Some outside-the-home care for children is little more than babysitting, whereas other options are designed to promote intellectual and social advances. Among the major choices of the latter type are the following:

- *Child care centers* typically provide care for children all day, while their parents are at work. (Child care centers were previously referred to as *day care centers*; however, because a significant number of parents work nonstandard schedules and therefore require care for their children at times other than the day, the preferred label has changed to *child care centers*.) Although many child care centers were first established as safe, warm environments where children could be cared for and could interact with other children, today their purpose tends to be broader, aimed at providing some form of intellectual stimulation. Still, their primary purpose tends to be more social and emotional than cognitive.

- Some child care is provided in *family child care centers*, small operations run in private homes. Because centers in some areas are unlicensed, the quality of care can be uneven, and parents should consider whether a family child care center is licensed before enrolling their children. In contrast, providers of center-based care, which is offered in institutions such as school classrooms, community centers, and churches and synagogues, are typically licensed and regulated by governmental authorities. Because teachers in such programs are more often trained professionals than those who provide family child care, the quality of care is often higher.

- *Preschools* are explicitly designed to provide intellectual and social experiences for children. They tend to be more limited in their schedules than family care centers, typically providing care for only 3 to 5 hours per day. Because of this limitation, preschools mainly serve children from middle and higher socioeconomic levels, in cases where parents don't need to work full time.

Like child care centers, preschools vary enormously in the activities they provide. Some emphasize social skills, while others focus on intellectual development. Some do both.

For instance, Montessori preschools, which use a method developed by Italian educator Maria Montessori, employ a carefully designed set of materials to create an environment that fosters sensory, motor, and language development through play. Children are provided with a variety of activities to choose from, with the option of moving from one to another (Gutek, 2003; Greenberg, 2011).

Similarly, in the Reggio Emilia preschool approach—another Italian import—children participate in what is called a "negotiated curriculum" that emphasizes the joint participation of children and teachers. The curriculum builds on the interests of children, promoting their cognitive development through the integration of the arts and participation in weeklong projects (Rankin, 2004; Paolella, 2013; Mages, 2016).

- *School child care* is provided by some local school systems in the United States. Almost half the states in the United States fund prekindergarten programs for 4-year-olds, often aimed at disadvantaged children. Because they typically are staffed by better-trained teachers than less-regulated child care centers, school child care programs are often of higher quality than other early education alternatives.

# The Effectiveness of Child Care

**LO 9.7  Discuss some of the consequences of child care outside the home.**

How effective are child care programs? Most research suggests that preschoolers enrolled in child care centers show intellectual development that at least matches that of children at home, and often is better. For instance, some studies find that preschoolers in child care are more verbally fluent, show memory and comprehension advantages, and even achieve higher IQ scores than at-home children. Other studies find that early and long-term participation in child care is particularly helpful for children from impoverished home environments or who are otherwise at risk. Some research even shows that child care programs can have positive consequences 25 years later (Clarke-Stewart & Allhusen, 2002; Vandell, 2004; Mervis, 2011a; Reynolds et al., 2011).

Similar advantages are found for social development. Children in high-quality programs tend to be more self-confident, independent, and knowledgeable about the social world in which they live than those who do not participate. However, not all the outcomes of outside-the-home care are positive: Children in child care have been found to be less polite, less compliant, less respectful of adults, and sometimes more competitive and aggressive than their peers. Furthermore, children who spend more than 10 hours a week in preschools have a slightly higher likelihood of being disruptive in class, extending through the sixth grade (NICHD Early Child Care Research Network, 2003a; Belsky et al., 2007; Douglass & Klerman, 2012; Vivanti et al., 2014).

Another way to consider the effectiveness of child care is to take an economic approach. For instance, one study of prekindergarten education in Texas found that every $1 invested in high-quality preschool programs produced $3.50 in benefits. Benefits included increased graduation rates, higher earnings, reduction in juvenile crime, and reductions in child welfare costs (Aguirre et al., 2006).

It is important to keep in mind that not all early childhood care programs are equally effective. As we observed of infant child care in Chapter 7, one key factor is program *quality*: high-quality care provides intellectual and social benefits, while low-quality care not only is unlikely to furnish benefits, but may harm children as well (Votruba-Drzal, Coley, & Chase-Lansdale, 2004; NICHD Early Child Care Research Network, 2006b; Dearing, McCartney, & Taylor, 2009).

How can we define "high quality"? Several characteristics are important; they include the following (Vandell, Shumow, & Posner, 2005; Layzer & Goodson, 2006; Leach et al., 2008; Rudd, Cain, & Saxon, 2008; Lloyd, 2012; also see the *Developmental Diversity and Your Life* box):

- The care providers are well trained, preferably with bachelor's degrees.
- The child care center has an appropriate overall size and ratio of care providers to children. Single groups should not have many more than 14 to 20 children, and there should be no more than five to ten 3-year-olds per caregiver, or seven to ten 4- or 5-year-olds per caregiver.
- The child–teacher ratio should be 10:1 or better.
- The curriculum of a child care facility is not left to chance, but is carefully planned out and coordinated among the teachers.
- The language environment is rich, with a great deal of conversation.
- The caregivers are sensitive to children's emotional and social needs, and they know when and when not to intervene.
- Materials and activities are age-appropriate.
- Basic health and safety standards are followed.
- Children should be screened for vision, hearing, and health problems.
- At least one meal a day should be served.
- The facility should provide at least one family support service.

# DEVELOPMENTAL DIVERSITY AND YOUR LIFE

## Preschools Around the World: The Case of Early Childhood Education in India

Culture and history of development of a country plays an important role on the belief and need for preschool education. Preschools differ significantly from one country to another; it depends on views that different societies hold of the purpose of early childhood education (Lamb et al., 1992). For instance, in a cross-country comparison of preschools in China, Japan, and the United States, researchers found that parents in these three countries view the purpose of preschools very differently. While parents in China tended to see preschools primarily as a way of giving children a good start academically, Japanese parents viewed them primarily as a way of giving children the opportunity to be members of a group. In the United States, in comparison, parents regarded the primary purpose of preschools as making children more independent and self-reliant, although obtaining a good academic start and having group experience were also deemed important (Huntsinger et al., 1997; Johnson et al., 2003; Land, Lamb, & Zheng, 2011).

A look at the history of family care for children indicates that much of the early care and education was informal within the families largely through grandmother's caring practices involving lullabies, storytelling, traditional infant games, etc. Over the years, due to the change in family structure, parent's occupations, and modernization led to gradual diminution of the traditional child care practices at home. One of the reasons for the inception of early childhood care and education was this change in social structure. In addition, research all over the world strongly asserts the early childhood as the most crucial stage of development in terms of brain and physical growth, cognitive and language development, and socio-emotional and personality growth of the child. This leads to another reason for the need for ECCE (Early Childhood Care and Education) drive in India. The National Policy of Education (1986) has given a great deal of importance to this aspect and views it as a crucial input in the strategy of human resource development as a feeder and support program for primary education (EFA Report, 2007). Further, the initiative of the Government of India to increase literacy among the citizens requires strengthening the potential of a child to continue schooling and thus reduce school dropouts. Therefore, preschool programs aim at developing school readiness in children.

In many places in the world, early childhood care and education has been treated as a right of the citizens. In France and Belgium, access to preschool is a legal right. In Sweden and Finland, the governments provide childcare to preschoolers whose parents work. Russia has an extensive system of state-run *yasli-sads*, nursery schools, and kindergartens attended by 75 percent of children ages 3 to 7 in urban areas.

In India, the Article 45 of the Constitution states that the State shall endeavor to provide ECCE for all children until they complete the age of six years. The Right of Children to Free and Compulsory Education Act, 2009, states that with a view to prepare children above the age of three years for elementary education and to provide ECCE for all children until they complete the age of six years, the appropriate government may make necessary arrangement for providing free preprimary education for such children. One of the world's unique and largest outreach program which functions through the Anganwadi centers is the Integrated Child Development Services (ICDS) that is being satisfactorily operated for more than three decades of its existence. Apart from the government-initiated early childhood care and education, there are also many private preschools for children in India. While the public-sponsored ICDS caters to children from disadvantaged communities, private initiatives are targeted towards children of socio-economically better off families. These impart preschool education through nurseries, kindergarten, and pre-primary classes in private schools.

# Preparing Preschoolers for Academic Pursuits

**LO 9.8  Describe the effectiveness of Anganwadi and similar preschool readiness programs.**

Although many programs designed for preschoolers focus primarily on social and emotional factors, some are geared primarily toward promoting cognitive gains and preparing preschoolers for the more formal instruction they will experience when they start kindergarten. In India, the best-known program designed to promote future academic success is Anganwadi under the ICDS program. This project was designed to serve the "whole child," including children's physical health, self-confidence, social responsibility, and social and emotional development.

In addition to Anganwadi, other types of preschool readiness programs also provide advantages throughout the school years. Studies show that those who participate in and graduate from such preschool programs are less likely to repeat grades, and they complete school more frequently than those who are not in the programs.

The most recent comprehensive evaluation of early intervention programs suggests that, taken as a group, they can provide significant benefits and that government funds invested early in life may ultimately lead to a reduction in future costs.

An early evaluation by the National Institute of Public Cooperation and Child Development or NIPCCD (1985; 1987;1994) indicated a positive impact of participation in the ICDS program in language and cognitive development, primary school enrollment, school adjustment, and readiness of children. Kaul (1999) continuously followed up a cohort of children from the ECE stage through five grades of primary education; it also indicated significant and continuous gains from a quality ECE program on mathematics learning in the primary grades. Studies conducted across India to evaluate the ICDS and National Crèche Fund and Crèche services for children (NCAER 2001; NIPCCD, 2003, 1995; & NCERT, 2003) concluded that ECCE, across different programs, is perceived by all stakeholders to have benefited not only the younger children but also the older siblings, particularly girls who are freed from sibling care responsibility and are able to join regular schools.

Not everyone agrees that programs that seek to enhance academic skills during the preschool years are a good thing. According to developmental psychologist David Elkind, U.S. society tends to push children so rapidly that they begin to feel stress and pressure at a young age (Elkind, 1994).

Elkind argues that academic success is largely dependent on factors out of parents' control, such as inherited abilities and a child's rate of maturation. Consequently, children of a particular age cannot be expected to master educational material without taking into account their current level of cognitive development. In short, children require **developmentally appropriate educational practice**, which is education based on both typical development and the unique characteristics of a given child (Robinson & Stark, 2005).

Rather than arbitrarily expecting children to master material at a particular age, Elkind suggests that a

---

**developmentally appropriate educational practice**
Education based on both typical development and the unique characteristics of a given child

better strategy is to provide an environment in which learning is encouraged, but not pushed. By creating an atmosphere in which learning is facilitated—for instance, by reading to preschoolers—parents will allow children to proceed at their own pace rather than at one that pushes them beyond their limits (van Kleeck & Stahl, 2003).

Although Elkind's suggestions are appealing—it is certainly hard to disagree that increases in children's anxiety levels and stress should be avoided—they are not without their detractors. For instance, some educators have argued that pushing children is largely a phenomenon of the middle and higher socioeconomic levels, possible only if parents are relatively affluent. For poorer children, whose parents may not have substantial resources available to push their children, nor the easy ability to create an environment that promotes learning, the benefits of formal programs that promote learning are likely to outweigh their drawbacks. Furthermore, developmental researchers have found that there are ways for parents to prepare their children for future educational success, such as reading to them, as we discuss next.

> **From an educator's perspective:** Should the United States develop a more encouraging and more supportive preschool policy? If so, what sort of policy? If not, why not?

## The Importance of Reading to Young Children

### LO 9.9 Describe the evidence for the importance of reading to children.

Everyone has heard that it's a good idea for parents to spend time reading to young children. Story-time hours and bedtime stories are certainly enjoyable activities for parents and children alike, and the quiet interaction contributes to a healthy parent–child relationship. But do children also benefit intellectually when parents read to them?

Yes, they do. At least that's the finding of a large-scale meta-analysis (a way of statistically summarizing the results of multiple experiments) of nearly 100 studies. Establishing a routine of reading with children before age 2 seems to lay the groundwork for enhanced language development. It sets up a self-reinforcing relationship between reading and language, in which the early exposure to print media helps to develop children's vocabulary and ability with syntax, which in turn facilitates future interest in books and reading (Collins, 2010; Mol & Bus, 2011).

The meta-analysis also found that children with better comprehension and literacy skills tended to read more, and reading more tended to further their comprehension and literacy. Reading to young children also makes it more likely that they will continue to engage in leisure-time reading as they grow. This increased exposure to print media is related to a number of beneficial literacy outcomes, including comprehension, technical reading skills, spelling, and oral language skills. This relationship exists throughout childhood and adolescence and even extends into the college years.

Even low-ability readers benefited from more leisure-time exposure to print media. In fact, the benefits were greatest for low-ability readers, although their initial greater difficulty with reading makes parental encouragement and support all the more important. The researchers concluded that reading books to young children in the home is an effective way of encouraging children's language, reading, and spelling abilities throughout their preschool and childhood years and beyond (Mol & Bus, 2011).

## Learning From the Media: Television and Digital Exposure

### LO 9.10 Identify the effects of television and digital media on preschoolers.

Television, computers, and handheld devices play a central role in many U.S. households. How does this affect preschoolers, in particular? We are just beginning to understand the ways. We do know that prior to age 2, they are not learning much, if anything, from their media use. In fact, even if they do seem to learn from digital media use, it's typically because parents work with them and re-teach the material they've seen online to their preschoolers. However, shows like *Sesame Street* have some educational value, and video-chat platforms such as Skype and FaceTime do seem to encourage conversations and interaction (DeLoache et al., 2010).

**MEDIA CONSUMPTION.** The average preschooler is exposed to over 4 hours per day of screen time, which includes watching TV and using computers. Furthermore, more than a third of households with children 2 to 7 years of age say that the television is on "most of the

## Figure 9.6 Television Time

Television is a nearly universal technology in the United States, whereas only about two-thirds of families with children age 11 or younger have computers. On a typical day, more than 80 percent of toddlers and preschoolers in the United States watch TV, and it remains the most frequently used medium by children from 0 to 11 years of age (Gutnick et al., 2010).

**SOURCE:** Gutnick, A. L., Robb, M., Takeuchi, L., & Kotler, J. (2010). Always connected: The new digital media habits of young children. New York: The Joan Ganz Cooney Center at Sesame Workshop. p. 15.

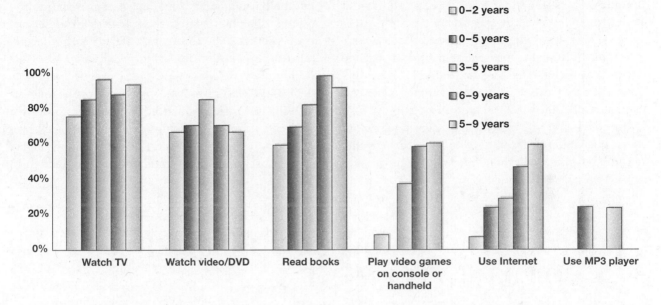

time" in their homes (see Figure 9.6; Bryant & Bryant, 2003; Gutnick et al., 2010; Tandon et al., 2011).

One concern about preschoolers' use of media relates to the inactivity it produces. Preschoolers who

Technology has become an influential part of the lives of preschoolers.

watch more than 2 hours per day of television and videos or who use computers for significant amounts of time have a higher risk of obesity than those who watch less (Jordan & Robinson, 2008; Strasburger, 2009; Cox et al., 2012).

It is also unclear what, exactly, children are learning from media exposure. When they do watch television or online videos, preschool children often do not fully understand the plots of the stories they are viewing, particularly in longer programs. They are unable to recall significant story details after viewing a program, and the inferences they make about the motivations of characters are limited and often erroneous. Moreover, preschool children may have difficulty separating fantasy from reality in programming, with some believing, for example, that there is a real Big Bird living on *Sesame Street* (Wright et al., 1994).

Preschool-age children exposed to advertising are not able to critically understand and evaluate the messages to which they are exposed. Consequently, they are likely to fully accept advertisers' claims about their products. The likelihood of children believing advertising messages is so high that the American

Psychological Association has recommended that television advertising targeting children under the age of 8 be restricted (Pine, Wilson, & Nash, 2007; Nash, Pine, & Messer, 2009; Nicklas et al., 2011).

In addition, the American Academy of Pediatrics recommended in 2016 that children younger than 18 months be discouraged from using screen media other than video chats. For preschoolers older than 2 years of age, they suggest limiting media to 1 hour or less of high-quality programming per day. They also recommend that no screens should be used during meals and for 1 hour before bedtime (American Academy of Pediatrics, 2016).

In short, the world to which preschoolers are exposed is imperfectly understood and unrealistic. As they get older and their information-processing capabilities improve, preschoolers' understanding of the material they see on television and on the computer improves. They remember things more accurately, and they become better able to focus on the central message of what they're watching. This improvement suggests that the powers of media may be harnessed to bring about cognitive gains—exactly what the producers of *Sesame Street* set out to do (Berry, 2003; Uchikoshi, 2006; Njoroge et al., 2016).

*SESAME STREET.* *Sesame Street* is one of the longest-running and most popular educational programs for children in the United States. Almost half of all preschoolers in the United States watch the show, and it is broadcast in almost 100 different countries and in 13

# BECOMING AN INFORMED CONSUMER OF CHILD DEVELOPMENT

## Promoting Cognitive Development in Preschoolers: From Theory to the Classroom

We have considered the notion that one focus of the preschool period should be on promoting future academic success, and we have also discussed the alternative view that pushing children too hard academically may be hazardous to their well-being.

There is, however, a middle ground. Drawing on research conducted by developmental psychologists who examine cognitive development during the preschool years (Reese & Cox, 1999), we can make several suggestions for parents and preschool teachers who wish to improve the academic readiness of children without creating undue stress. Among them are the following:

- *Parents and teachers should be aware of the stage of cognitive development, with its capabilities and limitations, that each individual child has reached.* Unless they are aware of a child's current level of development, it will be impossible to provide appropriate materials and experiences.
- *Instruction should be at a level just slightly higher than each student's current level of cognitive development.* With too little novelty, children will be bored; with too much, they will be confused.
- *Instruction should be individualized as much as possible.* Because children of the same age may be at different levels of cognitive development, curriculum materials that are prepared individually stand a better chance of success.
- *Opportunities for social interaction—both with other students and with adults—should be provided.* By receiving feedback from others and observing how others react in given situations, preschoolers learn new approaches and new ways of thinking about the world.
- *Let students make mistakes.* Cognitive growth often flows from confronting and correcting errors.
- *Do not push preschoolers too far ahead of their current state of cognitive development.* Cognitive development can only occur when children have achieved the appropriate level of maturation.
- *Read to children.* Children learn from hearing stories read to them, and it can motivate them to learn to read themselves.

foreign languages. As noted, characters like Big Bird and Elmo have become familiar throughout the world to both adults and preschoolers (Bickham, Wright, & Huston, 2000; Cole, Arafat, & Tidhar, 2003; Moran, 2006).

*Sesame Street* was devised with the express purpose of providing an educational experience for preschoolers. Its specific goals include teaching letters and numbers, increasing vocabulary, and teaching preliteracy skills. Has *Sesame Street* achieved its goals? Most evidence suggests that it has.

For example, preschoolers living in lower-income households who watch the show are better prepared for school, and they perform significantly higher on several measures of verbal and mathematics ability at ages 6 and 7 than those who do not watch it. Furthermore, viewers of *Sesame Street* spend more time reading than nonviewers. And by the time they are 6 and 7, viewers of *Sesame Street* and other educational programs tend to be better readers and judged more positively by their teachers. The findings for *Sesame Street* are mirrored for other educationally oriented shows such as *Dora the Explorer* and *Blue's Clues* (Augustyn, 2003; Linebarger & Walker, 2005).

More recent evaluations show even more positive findings. In a 2015 study, viewing *Sesame Street* was found to be as valuable as attending preschool. In fact, viewing the show was associated with increases in the likelihood of remaining at appropriate grade level by several percentage points. The effect was especially strong for boys, African Americans, and children who grow up in disadvantaged areas (Kearney & Levine, 2015).

However, *Sesame Street* has not been without its critics. For instance, some educators claim that the frenzied pace at which different scenes are shown makes viewers less receptive to the traditional forms of teaching they will experience when they begin school. Careful evaluations of the program, however, find no evidence that viewing *Sesame Street* leads to declines in enjoyment of traditional schooling. Overall, then, the most recent findings demonstrate quite positive outcomes for viewers of *Sesame Street* and other educational shows similar to it (Fisch, 2004; Zimmerman & Christakis, 2007; Penuel et al., 2012).

# The Case of …
## The Secret Reader

Deepika Mohan had handled the situation badly. As an assistant teacher in an urban preschool, she had been concerned that one of her students, Anant Sehgal, showed little interest in books and story time. She wanted to encourage the mother to try harder to help Anant value reading.

The next time she chatted with Mrs. Sehgal, she mentioned how important it was for Anant to take an active interest in academics, to be exposed to books in the home, and to develop an enjoyment of books and learning. When Mrs. Sehgal asked what she meant, she explained that Anant never joined reading circle and never picked a book to look through, choosing instead to play with LEGOs and trucks and other physical toys.

Deepika noticed that Mrs. Sehgal paused before answering. "Thank you for your concern, Ms. Mohan, but Anant probably doesn't sit in reading circle because he is a shy boy who likes to be by himself most of the time. And he may not choose your books because he's read most of them already. I take him to the library every Wednesday evening and Saturday morning, no matter how tired I am, and I read to him and let him read to me. He's been through nearly every book in the preschool section. He may want to play with LEGOs because we don't have any of those at home."

Deepika didn't know what to say.

1. Had Deepika interpreted Anant's classroom decisions accurately? Why had she made the interpretation that she had?
2. Is it plausible for a preschooler like Anant to have a "secret reading life"? Could he really have the language skills to read books at his age?
3. Should Deepika still be concerned about Anant's reading? Should she quietly test his abilities one-on-one?
4. Is it possible for an academically able student to emerge from circumstances like Anant's? Why or why not? What factors might affect his academic achievement?

# Epilogue

In this chapter, we looked at children in the preschool years. We discussed cognitive development from the Piagetian perspective, with its description of the characteristics of thought in the preoperational stage, and from the perspective of information-processing theorists and Lev Vygotsky. We then discussed the burst in linguistic ability that occurs during the preschool years. We concluded with a discussion of preschool education and the influence of television and computers on preschoolers' development.

Return to the prologue, which describes preschooler Ava teaching her classmate Natalia how to put together a floor puzzle, and answer these questions.

1. How does the interaction between Ava and Natalia reflect Vygotsky's view of children as apprentices?
2. What function does private speech serve for Natalia as she attempts to assemble a puzzle on her own at home?
3. Reflecting on what you have learned about language development in the preschool years, do you think Ava would have been capable of explaining to Natalia how to assemble a puzzle a year earlier, when the children were just 2 years old?
4. What changes take place in language development between ages 2 and 3?

# Looking Back

### LO 9.1  Discuss Piaget's theory of cognitive development during the preschool years.

- During Piaget's preoperational stage, children cannot yet engage in organized, formal, logical thinking. But their development of symbolic function permits quicker and more effective thinking than during the sensorimotor stage.

- Children in the preoperational stage engage in intuitive thought for the first time, actively applying rudimentary reasoning skills to the acquisition of world knowledge.

- Symbolic function is at the heart of the increasingly sophisticated use of language that characterizes the preoperational stage.

- According to Piaget, preschoolers have trouble with centration, conservation, and transformation. Centration is focusing on one aspect of a stimulus and ignoring other aspects. Conservation is the understanding that objects do not necessarily change in quantity when they change their appearance. And transformation involves grasping the concept that things may appear in different states and forms.

- Egocentrism, or egocentric thought, is thinking that does not take account of the viewpoints of others. It can lead preschoolers to think and act without reference to the thoughts or feelings of others.

- Children's knowledge and reasoning are under development from the moment of birth. In the preoperational stage, children engage in intuitive thought for the first time, actively applying rudimentary reasoning skills to the acquisition of world knowledge.

### LO 9.2  Summarize the information-processing approaches to cognitive development in the preschool years.

- A different approach to cognitive development is taken by proponents of information-processing theories, who focus on preschoolers' storage and recall of information and on quantitative changes in information-processing abilities (such as attention).

- Information-processing theorists have focused on areas such as memory, especially the development of autobiographical memory during a child's early years. They have found that autobiographical memories, no matter how vivid and convincing, may not be entirely accurate.

- Memory during the preschool years can be unreliable. It is possible for false memories to be implanted by others, whether willfully or unintentionally. For young children's memories to be useful in a court of law, questioning should take place as soon after an event as possible, and it should be done by questioners trained to be neutral and to ask specific rather than general questions.

- Information-processing approaches remind us of the value of well-defined questions and a focus on processes that can be tested and measured quantitatively.

## LO 9.3 Explain Vygotsky's approach to cognitive development.

- Lev Vygotsky proposed that the nature and progress of children's cognitive development are dependent on the children's social and cultural context.

- Vygotsky proposed that children's comprehension of the world is an outcome of their interactions with their parents, peers, and other members of society. It is also consistent with a growing body of multicultural and cross-cultural research, which finds evidence that cognitive development is shaped, in part, by cultural factors.

- Vygotsky suggested that an increase in children's cognitive abilities can be fostered by exposing them to information that is almost, but not quite, within their grasp. He dubbed the realm of such just-over-the-horizon knowledge the *zone of proximal development* (ZPD).

- A consequence of the ZPD is that children need others in their society to help them move further into the ZPD and thereby increase the knowledge that they acquire. This process is called scaffolding.

## LO 9.4 Describe how children's language abilities develop in the preschool years.

- Children rapidly progress from two-word utterances to longer, more sophisticated expressions that reflect their growing vocabularies and emerging grasp of grammar.

- The process of fast mapping enables children to expand their vocabularies very rapidly.

- Private speech is the speech that children direct to themselves, while social speech is the speech they direct to others.

- Private speech facilitates thinking, controls behavior, and provides practice in pragmatics, the practical conventions of communicating with others.

## LO 9.5 Explain the effect of poverty on language development.

- The development of linguistic abilities is affected by socioeconomic status. The result can be lowered linguistic—and ultimately academic—performance by poorer children.

## LO 9.6 Describe the ways in which preschool children are educated.

- Preschool educational programs are conducted in child care centers, family child care centers, preschools, and school child care.

## LO 9.7 Discuss some of the consequences of child care outside the home.

- Most research suggests that preschoolers enrolled in child care centers show intellectual development that at least matches that of children at home, and often is better.

- Some studies find that preschoolers in child care are more verbally fluent, show memory and comprehension advantages, and even achieve higher IQ scores than at-home children.

## LO 9.8 Describe the effectiveness of Head Start and similar preschool readiness programs.

- Programs like Head Start are largely successful in preparing young children for formal education. Head Start graduates have better school adjustment than non–Head Start peers and are less likely to be enrolled later in special education classes.

- Studies show that children who have completed preschool readiness programs are less likely to repeat grades and more likely to complete high school.

- Some researchers have expressed concerns that focusing too early on academic success can cause stress and pressure in children. Other researchers point out that the benefits of formal programs outweigh their potential drawbacks, especially for poorer children.

## LO 9.9 Describe the evidence for the importance of reading to children.

- Research shows that reading to children produces several types of cognitive benefits.

- Early exposure to print media helps to develop children's vocabulary and ability with syntax, which in turn encourages future interest in books and reading.

**LO 9.10 Identify the effects of television and digital media on preschoolers.**

- The effects of exposure to television and other media sources, such as computers, are mixed. Some programs can be educationally beneficial, but only if preschoolers' exposure to such media is controlled and limited.

- Although preschoolers' constant exposure to situations that are not representative of the real world have raised concerns, they can attain cognitive advances from programs such as *Sesame Street*.

---

## Key Terms and Concepts

preoperational stage (p. 228)
operations (p. 228)
symbolic function (p. 228)
centration (p. 229)
conservation (p. 229)
transformation (p. 230)
egocentric thought (p. 230)

intuitive thought (p. 232)
autobiographical memory (p. 234)
scripts (p. 234)
zone of proximal development (ZPD) (p. 238)
scaffolding (p. 238)
syntax (p. 241)

fast mapping (p. 241)
grammar (p. 241)
private speech (p. 241)
pragmatics (p. 242)
social speech (p. 242)
developmentally appropriate educational practice (p. 247)

# Chapter 10
# Social and Personality Development in the Preschool Years

## ⌄ Learning Objectives

**LO 10.1** Explain how preschool-age children develop a concept of who they are.

**LO 10.2** Compare the different perspectives on the ways children develop their sense of gender.

**LO 10.3** Describe the social relationships and play in which preschool-age children engage.

**LO 10.4** Discuss how preschoolers develop a theory of mind.

**LO 10.5** Describe the types of disciplinary styles parents employ and the effects they have on their children.

**LO 10.6** Compare cultural differences in childrearing practices.

**LO 10.7** Compare the different approaches to moral development in children.

**LO 10.8** Explain how aggression develops in preschool-age children.

**LO 10.9** Describe how social learning and cognitive approaches explain aggression.

**LO 10.10** Explain the kinds of effects violent TV programs and video games can have on preschool-age children.

## Prologue: A Helping Hand

Four-year-old Lara Sinha watches her mother prepare lunch to take to a neighbor who has just returned from the hospital. When Lara asks why her mom is bringing food to the lady across the street, her mother explains that when people are having a hard time, it's nice to help them out by making meals or running their errands.

An hour later, Lara's friend Rita comes over to play. Rita is unusually quiet and solemn. Lara asks if she is sad, and Rita says her grandma is dying. Lara thinks for a minute, then suggests singing. "I'm a great singer," she tells Rita, "but I sing even better with a friend." Lara's mom puts on some music, and soon the girls are singing, dancing, and laughing. When Rita leaves, Lara says, "I knew music would help Rita. Music makes everyone happy."

## Looking Ahead

Lara's effort to cheer up her friend is an example of the growing ability of preschool-age children to understand the emotions of others. In this chapter, we address social and personality development during the preschool period, a time of enormous growth and change.

We begin by examining how preschool-age children continue to form a sense of self, focusing on how they develop their self-concepts. We especially consider issues of self relating to gender, a central aspect of children's views of themselves and others.

Preschoolers' social lives are the focus of the next part of the chapter. We look at how children play with one another, examining the various types of play. We consider how parents and other authority figures use discipline to shape children's behavior.

Finally, we discuss two key aspects of preschool-age children's social behavior: moral development and aggression. We consider how children develop a notion of right and wrong and how that development can lead them to be helpful to others. We also look at the other side of the coin—aggression—and examine the factors that lead preschool-age children to behave in a way that hurts others. We end on an optimistic note: considering how we may help preschool-age children to be more moral and less aggressive individuals.

## Forming a Sense of Self

Although the question "Who am I?" is not explicitly posed by most preschool-age children, it underlies a considerable amount of development during the preschool years. During this period, children wonder about the nature of the self, and the way they answer the "Who am I?" question may affect them for the rest of their lives.

## Psychosocial Development and Self-Concept

**LO 10.1** Explain how preschool-age children develop a concept of who they are.

*Saranya's preschool teacher raised her eyebrows slightly when the 4-year-old took off her coat. Saranya, usually dressed in well-matched play suits, was a medley of prints. She had on a pair of flowered pants, along with a completely clashing plaid top. The outfit was accessorized with a striped headband, socks in an animal print, and Saranya's polka-dot rain boots. Saranya's mom gave a slightly embarrassed shrug. "Saranya got dressed all by herself this morning," she explained as she handed over a bag containing spare shoes, just in case the rain boots became uncomfortable during the day.*

Psychoanalyst Erik Erikson may well have praised Saranya's mother for helping Saranya develop a sense of initiative (if not of fashion). The reason: Erikson suggested that, during the preschool years, children face a key conflict relating to psychosocial development that involves the development of initiative. At the same time, they begin to develop a self-concept.

**RESOLVING CONFLICTS.** As we discussed in Chapter 7, **psychosocial development** encompasses changes in individuals' understanding of both their own and others' behavior. According to Erikson, society and culture present the developing person with particular challenges, which shift as people age. Erikson believed that people pass through eight distinct stages, each characterized by a crisis or conflict which the person must resolve. Our experiences as we try to resolve these conflicts lead us to develop ideas about ourselves that can last for the rest of our lives.

In the early part of the preschool period, children are ending the autonomy-versus-shame-and-doubt stage, which lasts from around 18 months to 3 years. In this period, children either become more independent and autonomous if their parents encourage exploration and freedom, or they experience shame and self-doubt if they are restricted and overprotected.

The preschool years largely encompass what Erikson called the **initiative-versus-guilt stage**, which lasts from around age 3 to age 6. During this period, children's views of themselves change as preschool-age children face conflicts between, on the one hand, the desire to act independently of their parents and do things on their own, and, on the other hand, the guilt that comes from failure when they don't succeed. They are eager to do things on their own ("Let *me* do it" is a popular refrain among preschoolers), but they feel guilt if their efforts fail. They come to see themselves as persons in their own right, and they begin to make decisions on their own. Parents who react positively to

this transformation toward independence (as Saranya's mother did) can help their children resolve the opposing feelings that are characteristic of this period. By providing their children with opportunities to act self-reliantly, while still giving them direction and guidance, parents can support and encourage their children's initiative. By contrast, parents who discourage their children's efforts to seek independence may contribute to a sense of guilt that persists throughout their lives as well as affects their self-concept, which begins to develop during this period.

> **From a child care provider's perspective:** How would you relate Erikson's stages of trust-versus-mistrust, autonomy-versus-shame-and-doubt, and initiative-versus-guilt to the issue of secure attachment discussed in an earlier chapter?

**THINKING ABOUT THE SELF.** If you ask preschool-age children to specify what makes them different from other kids, they readily respond with answers like, "I'm a good runner" or "I like to color" or "I'm a big girl." Such answers relate to **self-concept**—their identity, or their set of beliefs about what they are like as individuals (Tessor, Felson, & Suls, 2000; Marsh, Ellis, & Craven, 2002; Bhargava, 2014).

The statements that describe children's self-concepts are not necessarily accurate. In fact, preschool children typically overestimate their skills and knowledge across all domains of expertise. Consequently, their view of the future is quite rosy: They expect to win the next game they play, to beat all opponents in an upcoming race, or to write great stories when they grow up. Even when they have just experienced failure at a task, they are likely to expect to do well in the future. This optimistic view is held, in part, because they have not yet started to compare themselves and

---

**psychosocial development** The approach to the study of development that encompasses changes in the understanding individuals have of their interactions with others, of others' behavior, and of themselves as members of society

**initiative-versus-guilt stage** According to Erik Erikson, the period during which children age 3 to 6 years experience conflict between independence of action and the sometimes negative results of that action

**self-concept** A person's identity or set of beliefs about what one is like as an individual

their performance against others. Their inaccuracy is helpful, freeing them to take chances and try new activities (Verschueren, Doumen, & Buyse, 2012; Ehm, Lindberg, & Hasselhorn, 2013; Jia et al., 2016).

Preschool-age children's view of themselves also reflects the way their particular culture considers the self. For example, many Asian societies tend to have a **collectivistic orientation**, promoting the notion of interdependence. People in such cultures tend to regard themselves as parts of a larger social network in which they are interconnected with and responsible to others. In contrast, children in Western cultures are more likely to develop a view of the self reflecting an **individualistic orientation** that emphasizes personal identity and the uniqueness of the individual. They are more apt to see themselves as self-contained and autonomous, in competition with others for scarce resources. Consequently, children in Western cultures are more likely to focus on what sets them apart from others—what makes them special.

Such views pervade a culture, sometimes in subtle ways. For instance, one well-known saying in Western cultures states that "the squeaky wheel gets the grease." Preschoolers who are exposed to this perspective are encouraged to gain the attention of others by standing out and making their needs known. In contrast, children in Asian cultures are exposed to a different perspective; they are told that "the nail that stands out gets pounded down." This perspective suggests to preschoolers that they should attempt to blend in and refrain from making themselves distinctive (Lehman, Chiu, & Schaller, 2004; Wang, 2006; Aykil, et al., 2016).

Preschoolers' developing self-concepts can also be affected by their culture's attitudes toward various racial and ethnic groups. As described in the *Developmental Diversity and Your Life* box, preschoolers' awareness of their ethnic or racial identity develops slowly, and is subtly influenced by the attitudes of the people, schools, and other cultural institutions with which they come into contact in their community.

## Gender Identity: Developing Femaleness and Maleness

**LO 10.2  Compare the different perspectives on the ways children develop their sense of gender.**

> *Boys' awards: Very Best Thinker, Most Eager Learner, Most Imaginative, Most Enthusiastic, Most Scientific, Best Friend, Mr. Personality, Hardest Worker, Best Sense of Humor.*
>
> *Girls' awards: All-Around Sweetheart, Sweetest Personality, Cutest Personality, Best Sharer, Best Artist, Biggest Heart, Best Manners, Best Helper, Most Creative.*

What's wrong with this picture of a kindergarten graduation ceremony? To the parents of a daughter receiving one of the girls' awards, maybe quite a bit (Deveny, 1994). While the girls are getting pats on the back for their pleasing personalities, the boys are receiving awards for their intellectual and analytical skills.

Such a situation is not rare: Girls and boys often live in very different worlds. Differences in the ways males and females are treated begin at birth, continue during the preschool years, and, as we'll see later, extend into adolescence and beyond (Martin & Ruble, 2004; Bornstein et al., 2008; Eklund, 2011; Brinkman et al., 2014).

The view of the self that preschoolers develop depends in part on the culture in which they grow up.

---

**collectivistic orientation** A philosophy that promotes the notion of interdependence

**individualistic orientation** A philosophy that emphasizes personal identity and the uniqueness of the individual

# DEVELOPMENTAL DIVERSITY AND YOUR LIFE
## Developing Cultural and Ethnic Awareness

The preschool years mark an important turning point for children. Their answer to the question of who they are begins to take into account their racial and ethnic identity. For most preschool-age children, racial awareness comes relatively early. Certainly, even infants are able to distinguish different skin colors; their perceptual abilities allow for such color distinctions quite early in life. It is only later that children begin to attribute meaning to different racial and ethnic characteristics. The socio-cultural context of India is more complicated as there are variations in terms of religion, language, and regional/local cultures of the states. Thus, the cultural practice varies among families belonging to different religion and region (East, West, South, and North). Even in places like New Delhi, where because of migration people from all over the country live together and share their culture, there are subtle variations in cultural practices. These variations are not so obvious for preschoolers and, therefore, it would be too early for them to realize that they belong to a Bengali or a Punjabi family. However, language probably is one of the sensitive indicator of cultural differences perceived by children. Preschoolers who were bilingual, speaking both Spanish and English, were most apt to be aware of their ethnic identity. Ultimately, both race and ethnicity play a significant role in the development of children's overall identities (Quintana et al., 2006; Mesinas & Perez, 2016).

Although early in the preschool years, they do not realize that ethnicity and race are enduring features of who they are, later they progressively begin to develop an understanding of the significance that society gives to ethnic and racial membership (Quintana et al., 2008; McMillian-Robinson, Frierson, & Campbell, 2011). Research in the West has shown that preschoolers have mixed feelings about their racial and ethnic identity. Some experience **race dissonance**, the phenomenon in which minority children indicate preferences for majority values or people. For instance, some studies find that as many as 90 percent of African-American children, when asked about their reactions to drawings of Black and White children, react more negatively to the drawings of Black children than to those of White children. However, these negative reactions did not translate into lower self-esteem for the African American subjects. Instead, their preferences appear to be a result of the powerful influence of the dominant White culture, rather than a disparagement of their own racial characteristics (Holland, 1994; Quintana, 2007; Copping et al., 2013). Ethnic identity emerges somewhat later than racial identity, because it is usually less conspicuous than race. For instance, in one study of Mexican American ethnic awareness, preschoolers displayed only a limited knowledge of their ethnic identity; however, as they became older, they grew more aware of the significance of their ethnicity.

---

Gender, the sense of being male or female, is well established by the time children reach the preschool years. (As we first noted in Chapter 7, "gender" and "sex" do not mean the same thing. *Sex* typically refers to sexual anatomy and sexual behavior, whereas *gender* refers to the perception of maleness or femaleness related to membership in a given society.) By age 2, children consistently label themselves and those around them as male or female (Raag, 2003; Campbell, Shirley, & Candy, 2004).

One way gender shows up is in play. Preschool boys spend more time than girls do in rough-and-tumble play, while preschool girls spend more time than boys do in organized games and role-playing. Rough-and-tumble play is important because it promotes the development of the prefrontal cortex and helps teach preschoolers to regulate their emotions (Kestly, 2014).

During the preschool years, boys begin to play more with boys, and girls play more with girls, a trend that increases during middle childhood. Girls begin to prefer same-sex playmates a little earlier than boys do. They first have a clear preference for interacting with other girls at age 2, while boys don't show much preference for same-sex playmates until age 3 (Martin & Fabes, 2001; Raag, 2003).

Such same-sex preferences appear in many cultures. For instance, studies of kindergartners in mainland China show no examples of mixed-gender play. Similarly, gender "outweighs" ethnic variables when it comes to play: For example, a Hispanic boy would

---

**race dissonance** The phenomenon in which minority children indicate preferences for majority values or people

rather play with a White boy than with a Hispanic girl (Whiting & Edwards, 1988; Aydt & Corsaro, 2003).

Preschool-age children often have very strict ideas about how boys and girls are supposed to act. Their expectations about gender-appropriate behavior are even more gender-stereotyped than those of adults and may be less flexible during the preschool years than at any other point in the life span. Beliefs in gender stereotypes become increasingly pronounced up to age 5, and although they become somewhat less rigid by age 7, they do not disappear (Halim, Ruble & Tamis-LeMonda, 2013; Halim et al., 2014; Emilson, Folkesson, & Lindberg, 2016).

And what is the nature of preschoolers' gender expectations? Like adults, preschoolers expect that males are more apt to have traits involving competence, independence, forcefulness, and competitiveness. In contrast, females are viewed as more likely to have traits such as warmth, expressiveness, nurturance, and submissiveness. Although these are *expectations*, and they say nothing about the way that men and women actually behave, such expectations provide the lens through which preschool-age children view the world and affect preschoolers' behavior as well as the way they interact with peers and adults (Blakemore, 2003; Gelman, Taylor, & Nguyen, 2004; Martin & Dinella, 2012).

The prevalence and strength of preschoolers' gender expectations, and the differences in behavior between boys and girls, have proven puzzling. Why should gender play such a powerful role during the preschool years (as well as during the rest of the life span)? Developmentalists have proposed several explanations, including the biological and psychoanalytic perspectives.

**BIOLOGICAL PERSPECTIVES ON GENDER DIFFERENCES.** Since gender relates to the sense of being male or female, and sex refers to the physical characteristics that differentiate males and females, it would hardly be surprising to find that the biological characteristics associated with sex might themselves lead to gender differences. This has been shown to be true.

Hormones are one sex-related biological characteristic that have been found to affect gender-based behaviors. Girls exposed to unusually high levels of *androgens* (male hormones) prenatally are more likely to display behaviors associated with male stereotypes than are their sisters who were not exposed to androgens (Knickmeyer & Baron-Cohen, 2006; Burton et al., 2009; Mathews et al., 2009).

Androgen-exposed girls preferred boys as playmates and spent more time than other girls playing with toys associated with the male role, such as cars and trucks. Similarly, boys exposed prenatally to atypically high levels of female hormones are apt to display more behaviors that are stereotypically female than is usual (Servin et al., 2003; Knickmeyer & Baron-Cohen, 2006).

Moreover, biological differences exist in the structure of female and male brains. For instance, part of the *corpus callosum*, the bundle of nerves that connects the hemispheres of the brain, is proportionally larger in women than in men. To some theoreticians, evidence such as this suggests that gender differences may be produced by biological factors like hormones (Westerhausen, et al., 2004).

Before accepting such contentions, however, it is important to note that alternative explanations abound. For example, it may be that the *corpus callosum* is proportionally larger in women as a result of certain kinds of experiences that influence brain growth in particular ways. We know, as discussed in Chapter 6, that girls are spoken to more than boys as infants, which might produce certain kinds of brain development. If this is true, environmental experience produces biological change—and not the other way around.

Other developmentalists see gender differences as serving the biological goal of survival of the species through reproduction. Basing their work on an evolutionary approach, these theorists suggest that our male ancestors who showed more stereotypically masculine qualities, such as forcefulness and competitiveness, may have been able to attract women who were able to provide them with hardy offspring. Women who excelled at stereotypically feminine tasks, such as nurturing, may have been valuable partners because they could increase the likelihood that children would survive the dangers of childhood (Browne, 2006; Ellis, 2006; McMillian-Robinson, Frierson, & Campbell, 2011).

As in other domains that involve the interaction of inherited biological characteristics and environmental influences, it is difficult to attribute behavioral characteristics unambiguously to biological factors. Because of this problem, we must consider other explanations for gender differences.

**PSYCHOANALYTIC PERSPECTIVES ON GENDER DIFFERENCES.** You may recall from Chapter 1 that Freud's psychoanalytic theory suggests that we move through a series of stages related to biological urges. To Freud, the preschool years encompass the *phallic stage,* in which the focus of a child's pleasure relates to genital sexuality.

Freud argued that the end of the phallic stage is marked by an important turning point in development: the Oedipal conflict. According to Freud, the *Oedipal conflict* occurs at around the age of 5, when the anatomical differences between males and females become particularly evident. Boys begin to develop sexual interests in their mothers, viewing their fathers as rivals.

As a consequence, boys conceive a desire to kill their fathers—just as Oedipus did in the ancient Greek tragedy. But because they view their fathers as all-powerful, boys develop a fear of retaliation, which takes the form of *castration anxiety.* In order to overcome this fear, boys repress their desires for their mothers and instead begin to identify with their fathers, attempting to be as similar to them as possible. **Identification** is the process in which children attempt to be similar to their same-sex parent, incorporating the parent's attitudes and values.

Girls, according to Freud, go through a different process. They begin to feel sexual attraction toward their fathers and experience *penis envy*—a view that not unexpectedly has led to accusations that Freud viewed women as inferior to men. In order to resolve their penis envy, girls ultimately identify with their mothers, attempting to be as similar to them as possible.

In the cases of both boys and girls, the ultimate result of identifying with the same-sex parent is that the children adopt their parents' gender attitudes and values. In this way, says Freud, society's expectations about the ways females and males "ought" to behave are perpetuated into new generations.

You may find it difficult to accept Freud's elaborate explanation of gender differences. So do most developmentalists, who believe that gender development is best explained by other mechanisms. In part, they base their criticisms of Freud on the lack of scientific support for his theories.

For example, children learn gender stereotypes much earlier than age 5. This learning occurs even in single-parent households. Some aspects of psychoanalytic theory have been supported, however, such as

findings indicating that preschool-age children whose same-sex parents support sex-stereotyped behavior tend to demonstrate that behavior also. Still, far simpler processes can account for this phenomenon, and many developmentalists have searched for explanations of gender differences other than Freud's (Martin & Ruble, 2004; Chen & Rao, 2011).

**SOCIAL LEARNING APPROACHES TO GENDER DIFFERENCES.** As their name implies, social learning approaches see children as learning gender-related behavior and expectations by observing others. Children watch the behavior of their parents, teachers, siblings, and even peers. A little boy sees the glory of a Major League Baseball player and becomes interested in sports. A little girl watches her high-school neighbor practicing cheerleading moves and begins to try them herself. The observation of the rewards that these others attain for acting in a gender-appropriate manner leads the child to conform to such behavior themselves (Rust et al., 2000).

Books and the media, and in particular television and video games, also play a role in perpetuating traditional views of gender-related behavior from which preschoolers may learn. Analyses of the most popular television shows, for example, find that male characters outnumber female characters by 2 to 1. Furthermore, females are more apt to appear with males, whereas female–female relationships are relatively uncommon (Calvert, Kotler, & Zehnder, 2003; Chapman, 2016).

Television also presents men and women in traditional gender roles. Television shows typically define female characters in terms of their relationships with men. Women are more likely to appear as victims than are men. They are less likely to be presented as productive or as decision makers, and more likely to be portrayed as characters interested in romance, their homes, and their families. Such models, according to social learning theory, are apt to have a powerful influence on preschoolers' definitions of appropriate behavior (Nassif & Gunter, 2008; Prieler et al., 2011; Matthes, Prieler & Adam, 2016).

In some cases, learning of social roles does not involve models, but occurs more directly. For example, many of us may have heard preschool-age children being told by their parents to act like a "little lady" or a

---

**identification** The process in which children attempt to be similar to their parent of the same sex, incorporating the parent's attitudes and values

According to social learning approaches, children observe the behavior of adults of the same sex as themselves and come to imitate it.

"man." What this generally means is that girls should behave politely and courteously, or that boys should be tough and stoic—traits associated with society's traditional stereotypes of men and women. Such direct training sends a clear message about the behavior expected of a preschool-age child (Leaper, 2002).

**COGNITIVE APPROACHES TO GENDER DIFFERENCES.** In the view of some theorists, one aspect of preschoolers' desire to form a clear sense of identity is the wish to establish a **gender identity**, a perception of themselves as male or female. To do this, they develop a **gender schema**, a cognitive framework that organizes information relevant to gender (Martin & Ruble, 2004; Signorella & Frieze, 2008; Halim et al., 2014).

Gender schemas are developed early in life and serve as a lens through which preschoolers view the world. For instance, preschoolers use their increasing cognitive abilities to develop "rules" about what is right and what is inappropriate for males and females. Thus, some girls decide that wearing pants is inappropriate for a female and apply the rule so rigidly that they refuse to wear anything but dresses. Or a preschool boy may reason that since makeup is typically worn by females, it is inappropriate for him to wear makeup even when he is in a preschool play and all the other boys and girls are wearing it (Frawley, 2008).

According to *cognitive-developmental theory*, proposed by Lawrence Kohlberg, this rigidity is in part a reflection of preschoolers' understanding of gender (Kohlberg, 1966). Rigid gender schemas are influenced by the preschooler's erroneous beliefs about sex differences. Specifically, young preschoolers believe that sex differences are based not on biological factors but on differences in appearance or behavior. Employing this view of the world, a girl may reason that she can be a father when she grows up, or a boy may think he could turn into a girl if he put on a dress and tied his hair in a ponytail. By the time they reach the age of 4 or 5, children develop an understanding of **gender constancy**, the fact that people are permanently males or females, depending on fixed, unchangeable biological factors.

Interestingly, research on children's growing understanding of gender constancy during the preschool period indicates that it has no particular effect on gender-related behavior. In fact, the appearance of gender schemas occurs well before children understand gender constancy. Even young preschool-age children assume that certain behaviors are appropriate—and others are not—on the basis of stereotypic views of gender (Martin & Ruble, 2004; Ruble et al., 2007; Karniol, 2009).

Like the other approaches to gender development (summarized in Table 10.1), the cognitive perspective does not imply that differences between the two sexes are in any way improper or inappropriate. Instead, it suggests that preschoolers should be taught to treat others as individuals. Furthermore, preschoolers need to learn the importance of fulfilling their own talents, acting as individuals and not as representatives of a particular gender.

# Friends and Family: Preschoolers' Social Lives

*When Ronu was 3, he met his first best friend, Mannu. Ronu and Mannu, who lived in the same apartment building in Noida, were soon inseparable. They played incessantly with toy cars, racing them*

---

**gender identity** The perception of oneself as male or female

**gender schema** A cognitive framework that organizes information relevant to gender

**gender constancy** The fact that people are permanently males or females, depending on fixed, unchangeable biological factors

**Table 10.1** Four Approaches to Gender Development

| Perspective | Key Concepts | Applying the Concepts to Preschool Children |
|---|---|---|
| **Biological** | Our ancestors who behaved in ways that are now stereotypically feminine or masculine may have been more successful in reproducing. Brain differences may lead to gender differences. | Girls may be genetically "programmed" by evolution to be more expressive and nurturing, whereas boys are "programmed" to be more competitive and forceful. Hormone exposure before birth has been linked to both boys and girls behaving in ways typically expected of the other gender. |
| **Psychoanalytic** | Gender development is the result of identification with the same-sex parent, achieved by moving through a series of stages related to biological urges. | Girls and boys whose parents of the same sex behave in stereotypically masculine of feminine ways are likely to do so, too, perhaps because they identify with those parents. |
| **Social learning** | Children learn gender-related behavior and expectations from their observation of others' behavior. | Children notice that other children and adults are rewarded for behaving in ways that conform to standard gender stereotypes, and that they are sometimes punished for violating those stereotypes. |
| **Cognitive** | Through the use of gender schemas developed early in life, preschoolers form a lens through which they view the world. They use their increasing cognitive abilities to develop "rules" about what is appropriate for males and females. | Preschoolers are more rigid in their rules about proper gender behavior than are people at other ages, perhaps because they have just developed gender schemas that don't yet permit much variation from stereotypical expectations. |

*up and down the apartment hallways until some of the neighbors began to complain about the noise. They pretended to read to one another, and sometimes they slept over at each other's home—a big step for 3-year-olds. Neither boy seemed more joyful than when he was with his "best friend"—the term each used for the other.*

An infant's family can provide nearly all the social contact he or she needs. As preschoolers, however, many children, like Ronu and Mannu, begin to discover the joys of friendship with their peers. Although they may expand their social circles considerably, parents and family nevertheless remain very influential. Let's take a look at both sides of preschoolers' social development: friends and family.

# The Development of Friendships and Play

**LO 10.3** **Describe the social relationships and play in which preschool-age children engage.**

Before age 3, most social activity involves simply being in the same place at the same time, without real social interaction. At around age 3, however, children begin to develop real friendships like Ronu and Mannu's as peers come to be seen as individuals who hold some special qualities and rewards. While preschoolers' relations with adults reflect children's needs for care, protection, and direction, their relations with peers are based more on their desire for companionship, play, and fun.

As preschoolers age, their ideas about friendship gradually evolve. They come to view friendship as a continuing state, a stable relationship that not only takes place in the immediate moment but also offers the promise of future activity (Sebanc et al., 2007; Proulx & Poulin, 2013; Paulus, 2016).

The quality and kinds of interactions children have with friends change during the preschool period. For 3-year-olds, the focus of friendship is the enjoyment of carrying out shared activities—doing things together and playing jointly, as when Ronu and Mannu played with their toy cars in the hallway. Older preschoolers, however, pay more attention to abstract concepts such as trust, support, and shared interests. Throughout the preschool years, playing together remains an important part of all friendships. Like friendship itself, these play patterns change over time (Park, Lay, & Ramsay, 1993; Kawabata & Crick, 2011).

Preschoolers' friendships are not color-blind. Children begin to make distinctions on the basis of race as young as the age of 1 year, and friendships often reflect racial similarity. However, many children develop cross-racial friendships during the preschool years (McDonald et al., 2013; Markant, Oakes, & Amso, 2016)

Play is more than what children of preschool age do to pass the time. Instead, play helps preschoolers develop in important ways. In fact, the American Academy of Pediatrics states that play is essential for the cognitive, physical, social, and emotional well-being of children and youth. The United Nations High

As preschoolers get older, their conception of friendship evolves, and the quality of their interactions changes.

In parallel play, children play with similar toys, in a similar manner, but don't necessarily interact with one another.

Commission for Human Rights maintains that play is a basic right of every child (Whitebread et al., 2009; McGinnis, 2012; Holmes & Romeo, 2013).

At the beginning of the preschool years, children engage in **functional play**—simple, repetitive activities typical of 3-year-olds. Functional play may include objects such as dolls or cars, or repetitive muscular movements like skipping, jumping, or rolling and unrolling a piece of clay. Functional play involves doing something for the sake of being active rather than with the aim of creating an end product (Bober, Humphry, & Carswell, 2001; Kantrowitz & Evans, 2004).

As children get older, functional play declines. By the time they are 4, they become involved in a more sophisticated form of play. In **constructive play**, children manipulate objects to produce or build something. A child who builds a house out of LEGOs or puts a puzzle together is involved in constructive play: He or she has an ultimate goal—to produce something. Such play is not necessarily aimed at creating something novel, since children may repeatedly build a house of blocks, let it fall into disarray, and then rebuild it.

Constructive play gives children a chance to test their developing physical and cognitive skills and to practice their fine muscle movements. They gain experience in solving problems about the ways and the sequences in which things fit together. They also learn to cooperate with others—a development we observe as the social nature of play shifts during the preschool period. Consequently, it's important for adults who care for preschoolers to provide a variety of toys that allow for both functional and constructive play (Edwards,

2000; Shi, 2003; Love & Burns, 2006; Oostermeijer, Boonen, & Jolles, 2014).

If two preschoolers are sitting at a table side by side, each putting a different puzzle together, are they engaged jointly in play?

According to pioneering work done by Mildred Parten (1932), the answer is yes. She suggests that these preschoolers are engaged in **parallel play**, in which children play with similar toys, in a similar manner, but do not interact with each other. Parallel play is typical for children during the early preschool years. Preschoolers also engage in another form of play, a highly passive one: onlooker play. In **onlooker play**, children simply watch others at play, but do not actually participate themselves. They may look on silently, or they may make comments of encouragement or advice.

As they get older, however, preschool-age children engage in more sophisticated forms of social play that involve a greater degree of interaction. In **associative play**, two or more children actually interact with one

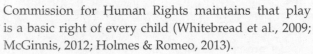

**functional play** Play that involves simple, repetitive activities typical of 3-year-olds

**constructive play** Play in which children manipulate objects to produce or build something

**parallel play** Play in which children play with similar toys, in a similar manner, but do not interact with each other

**onlooker play** Play in which children simply watch others at play but do not actually participate themselves

**associative play** Play in which two or more children interact by sharing or borrowing toys or materials, although they do not do the same thing

## Table 10.2 Preschoolers Play

| Type of Play | Description | Examples |
|---|---|---|
| **General Categories** | | |
| Functional play | Simple, repetitive activities typical of 3-year-olds. May involve objects or repetitive muscular movements. | Moving dolls or cars repetitively. Skipping, jumping, rolling or unrolling a piece of clay. |
| Constructive play | More sophisticated play in which children manipulate objects to produce or build something. Developed by age 4, constructive play lets children test physical and cognitive skills and practice fine muscle movements. | Building a dollhouse or car garage out of LEGOs, putting together a puzzle, making an animal out of clay. |
| **Social Aspects of Play (Parten's Categories)** | | |
| Parallel play | Play in which children play with similar toys, in a similar manner, but do not interact with each other. | Jake plays with a toy car next to Amos, who is also playing with a car, but they don't engage in any joint activity. |
| Onlooker play | Play in which children simply watch others at play but do not actually participate themselves. | Jenna watches Dan and Maura playing with each other, but Jenna doesn't do more than watch them. |
| Associative play | Play in which two or more children interact by sharing or borrowing toys or materials, although they do not do the same thing. | Joachim shares one of his trucks with Max, but they play with the trucks separately. |
| Cooperative play | Play in which children genuinely interact with one another, taking turns, playing games, or devising contests. | Miles and Alex play a game of racing cars with one another, seeing who can push his car the furthest. |

another by sharing or borrowing toys or materials, although they do not do the same thing. In **cooperative play**, children genuinely play with one another, taking turns, playing games, or devising contests. (The various types of play are summarized in Table 10.2.)

Associative and cooperative play do not typically become common until children reach the end of the preschool years. But children who have had substantial preschool experience are more apt to engage in more social forms of behavior, such as associative and cooperative play, fairly early in the preschool years than those with less experience (Brownell, Ramani, & Zerwas, 2006; Dyer & Moneta, 2006; Trawick-Smith & Dziurgot, 2011).

Solitary and onlooker play continue in the later stages of the preschool period. There are simply times when children prefer to play by themselves. And when newcomers join a group, one strategy for becoming part of the group—often successful—is to engage in onlooker play, waiting for an opportunity to join the play more actively (Lindsey & Colwell, 2003).

**From an educator's perspective:** How might a nursery school teacher encourage a shy child to join a group of preschoolers who are playing?

The nature of pretend, or make-believe, play also changes during the preschool period. In some ways, pretend play becomes increasingly *un*realistic—and even more imaginative—as preschoolers change from using only realistic objects to using less concrete ones. Thus, at the start of the preschool period, children may pretend to listen to a radio only if they actually have a plastic radio that looks realistic. Later, however, they are more likely to use an entirely different object, such as a large cardboard box, as a pretend radio (Parsons & Howe, 2013; Thibodeau et al., 2016).

Russian developmentalist Lev Vygotsky, whom we discussed in Chapter 9, argued that pretend play, particularly if it involves social play, is an important means for expanding preschool-age children's cognitive skills. Through make-believe play, children are able to "practice" activities (like pretending to use a computer or read a book) that are a part of their particular culture and broaden their understanding of the way the world functions.

Furthermore, play helps the brain to develop and become more sophisticated. Based on experiments with nonhumans, neuroscientist Sergio Pellis has found not only that certain sorts of damage to the brain leads to abnormal sorts of play, but that depriving animals of the ability to play affects the course of brain development (Pellis & Pellis, 2007; Bell, Pellis, & Kolb, 2010).

**cooperative play** Play in which children genuinely interact with one another, taking turns, playing games, or devising contests

**Figure 10.1** Comparing Play Complexity

An examination of Korean American and Anglo-American preschoolers' play complexity finds clear differences in patterns of play. How would a child care provider explain this conclusion?

**SOURCE:** Adapted from Farver, J. M., Kim, Y. K., & Lee-Shin, Y. (1995). "Cultural differences in Korean- and Anglo-American preschoolers' social interaction and play behaviors." Child Development, vol. 66, pp. 1088–1099.

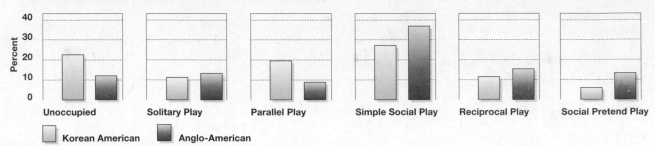

For instance, in one experiment, Pellis and his colleagues observed rats under two different conditions. In the control condition, a juvenile target rat was housed with three other young females, allowing them the opportunity to engage in the equivalent of rat play. In the experimental condition, the young target rats were housed with three adult females. Although young rats caged with adults don't have the opportunity to play, they do encounter social experiences with the adults, who will groom and touch them. When Pellis examined the brains of the rats, he found that the play-deprived rats showed deficiencies in the development of their prefrontal cortex (Henig, 2008; Bell, Pellis, & Kolb, 2009; Pellis & Burghardt, 2017).

Although it's a big leap from rat play to toddler play, the results of the study do suggest the significance of play in promoting brain and cognitive development. Ultimately, play may be one of the engines that fuels the intellectual development of preschoolers.

Finally, culture also affects children's styles of play. For example, Korean American children engage in a higher proportion of parallel play than their Anglo-American counterparts, while Anglo-American preschoolers are involved in more pretend play (see Figure 10.1; Farver, Kim, & Lee-Shin, 1995; Farver & Lee-Shin, 2000; Bai, 2005; Pellegrini, 2009).

## Preschoolers' Theory of Mind: Understanding What Others Are Thinking

**LO 10.4** Discuss how preschoolers develop a theory of mind.

One reason behind the changes in children's play is the continuing development of preschoolers' theory of mind. As we first discussed in Chapter 7, *theory of mind* refers to knowledge and beliefs about how the mind operates. Using their theory of mind, preschool children are able to come up with explanations for how *others* think and reasons for why they behave the way they do. In other words, children increasingly can see the world from others' perspectives. Even children as young as 2 are able to understand that others have emotions.

By age 3 or 4, preschoolers can distinguish between something in their minds and physical actuality. For instance, 3-year-olds know that they can imagine something that is not physically present, such as a zebra, and that others can do the same. They can also pretend that something has happened and react as if it really had occurred, a skill that becomes part of their imaginative play. And they know that others have the same capability (Cadinu & Kiesner, 2000; Mauritzson & Saeljoe, 2001; Andrews, Halford, & Bunch, 2003; Wellman, 2012; Wu & Su, 2014).

Preschool-age children also become more insightful regarding the motives and reasons behind people's behavior. They begin to understand that their mother is angry because she was late for an appointment, even if they themselves haven't seen the event occur. Furthermore, by age 4, preschool-age children's understanding that people can be fooled by or mistaken about physical reality (such as magic tricks involving sleight of hand) becomes surprisingly sophisticated. This increase in understanding helps children become more socially skilled as they gain insight into what others are thinking (Eisbach, 2004; Petrashek & Friedman, 2011; Fernández, 2013).

There are limits, however, to 3-year-olds' theory of mind. Although they understand the concept of "pretend" by the age of 3, their understanding of "belief" is still not complete. The difficulty experienced by 3-year-olds in comprehending "belief" is illustrated by their performance on the *false belief* task. In the false belief task, preschoolers are shown a doll named Maxi who places chocolate in a cabinet and then leaves. After Maxi is gone, though, his mother moves the chocolate somewhere else.

After viewing these events, a preschooler is asked where Maxi will look for the chocolate when he returns. Three-year-olds answer (erroneously) that Maxi will look for it in the new location. In contrast, 4-year-olds correctly realize that Maxi has the false belief that the chocolate is still in the cabinet, and that's where he will look for it (Amsterlaw & Wellman, 2006; Brown & Bull, 2007; Lecce et al., 2014; Ornaghi, Pepe, & Grazzani, 2016).

By the end of the preschool years, most children easily solve false belief problems. One group, however, has considerable difficulties throughout their lifetimes: children with autism spectrum disorder. *Autism spectrum disorder* is a psychological disorder that produces significant language and emotional difficulties. Children with autism spectrum disorder find it particularly difficult to relate to others, in part because they find it difficult to understand what others are thinking. According to the Centers for Disease Control and Prevention, about 1 in 68 children (primarily males) have autism spectrum disorder, which is characterized by a lack of connection to other people, even parents, and an avoidance of interpersonal situations. Individuals with autism spectrum disorder are bewildered by false belief problems no matter how old they are (Carey, 2012; Miller, 2012; Peterson, 2014).

What factors are involved in the emergence of theory of mind? Certainly, brain maturation is an important factor. As myelination within the frontal lobes becomes more pronounced, preschoolers develop more emotional capacity involving self-awareness. In addition, hormonal changes seem to be related to emotions that are more evaluative in nature (Davidson, 2003; Schore, 2003; Sabbagh et al., 2009).

Developing language skills are also related to the increasing sophistication of children's theory of mind. In particular, the ability to understand the meaning of words such as "think" and "know" is important in helping preschool-age children understand the mental lives of others (Astington & Baird, 2005; Farrant, Fletcher, & Maybery, 2006; Farrar et al., 2009; Babu, 2008).

As much as the child's developing theory of mind promotes more engaged social interactions and play, the process is reciprocal: Opportunities for social interaction and make-believe play are also critical in promoting the development of theory of mind. For example, preschool-age children with siblings (who provide high levels of social interaction and scope for pretend play) have more sophisticated theories of mind than those without siblings (Das & Babu, 2004). In addition, abused children show delays in their ability to correctly answer the false belief task, in part due to reduced experience with normal social interaction (McAlister & Peterson, 2006; Nelson, Adamson, & Bakeman, 2008; Müller et al., 2011).

Cultural factors also play an important role in the development of theory of mind and the interpretations that children bring to bear on others' actions. For example, children in more industrialized Western cultures may be more likely to see others' behavior as due to the kind of people they are—a function of the person's personal traits and characteristics ("She won the race because she is really fast"). In contrast, children in non-Western cultures may see others' behavior as produced by forces that are less under their personal control ("She won the race because she was lucky") (Tardif, Wellman, & Cheung, 2004; Wellman et al., 2006; Liu et al., 2008). (Also see the *From Research to Practice* box.)

## Preschoolers' Family Lives

**LO 10.5 Describe the types of disciplinary styles parents employ and the effects they have on their children.**

> *Four-year-old Babu was watching TV while his mom cleaned up after dinner. After a while, he wandered in and grabbed a towel, saying, "Maa, let me help you do the dishes." Surprised by this unprecedented behavior, she asked him, "Where did you learn to do dishes?"*
>
> *"I saw it on TV," he replied.*

For an increasing number of preschool-age children, life does not mirror what we see in reruns of old sitcoms. Many face the realities of an increasingly complicated world. For instance, as we noted in Chapter 7 and will discuss in greater detail in Chapter 13, children are increasingly likely to live with only one parent. In 1960, less than 10 percent of all children under the age of 18 lived with one parent. Three decades later, a single parent heads a quarter of all families. There are also large racial disparities: Nearly half of all African American children and a quarter of Hispanic children live with a

# FROM RESEARCH TO PRACTICE
## How Children Learn to Become Better Liars

Preschool-age children learn that it's better to admit the truth than to lie about their misbehavior at around age 3. But knowing that lying is wrong and refraining from lying are different things. Young children do lie, but to lie successfully, they must do two things: They must understand the social norms that make lying more or less acceptable, and they must have established some theory of mind (Feldman, 2010; Lee, 2013).

Understanding social norms is important because some social circumstances permit lying—and even expect it. Politeness, for example, dictates expressing gratitude for a gift, even if you don't like it; at other times white lies protect others from embarrassment or unnecessary hurt feelings. In one study, children between the ages of 3 and 7 were asked to take a photograph of a model who had a large and distinctly visible mark on his or her nose. Before the photograph was taken, the model asked the child if he or she looked okay. Most of the children said that yes he or she did, but later confirmed to the experimenter that they didn't actually think the model looked okay.

In another study, children in the same age group received a gift from the experimenter, which turned out to be an undesirable bar of soap. Many said that they liked it, even though their facial expressions upon opening it indicated otherwise (Talwar & Lee, 2002a; Talwar, Murphy, & Lee, 2007).

When the children who said they liked the soap were immediately asked by the experimenter why they liked it, the older children told even more elaborate lies, such as that they ran out of soap at home or that they actually collect soap bars. This behavior requires a theory of mind, which enables effective deception by maintaining a plausible charade. In another study, children are told not to peek at a hidden toy while the experimenter leaves the room. But most of the children did peek, and they lied about peeking. When asked what they thought it might be, most 2- and 3-year-olds blurted out the identity of the toy, unwittingly revealing their lie. But older children knew to feign complete unawareness—once they advanced one false premise (not having peeked at the toy), they knew they had to construct other false premises (that they were clueless about the toy's identity) to maintain congruence from the listener's perspective.

Verbal deception, then, entails both knowing when to lie and remembering to keep subsequent words and behaviors consistent with the lie—skills that develop quickly during the preschool years (Talwar & Lee, 2002b, 2008; Lee, 2013).

- Why do you think children learn at a young age to lie to protect others' feelings?
- Why does effective lying depend heavily on theory of mind?

single parent, compared with 22 percent of White children (Grall, 2009).

Still, for most children, the preschool years are not a time of upheaval and turmoil. Instead, the period encompasses a growing interaction with the world at large. For instance, as we've seen, preschoolers begin to develop genuine friendships with other children, in which close ties emerge. One central factor leading preschoolers to develop friendships comes when parents provide a warm, supportive home environment. Strong, positive relationships between parents and children encourage children's relationships with others (Howes, Galinsky, & Kontos, 1998). How do parents nurture that relationship? Consider the following:

*While she thinks no one is looking, Maria goes into her brother Alejandro's bedroom, where he has been saving his Halloween candy. Just as she takes his last Reese's Peanut Butter Cup, the children's mother walks into the room and immediately takes in the situation.*

If you were Maria's mother, which of the following reactions seems most reasonable?

1. Tell Maria that she must go to her room and stay there for the rest of the day and that she is going to lose access to her favorite blanket, the one she sleeps with every night and during naps.

2. Mildly tell Maria that what she did was not such a good idea and that she shouldn't do it in the future.

3. Explain why Alejandro will be upset and tell her that she must go to her room for an hour as punishment.

4. Forget about it and let the children sort it out themselves.

## Table 10.3  Parenting Styles

| How Demanding Parents Are of Children | Demanding | Undemanding |
|---|---|---|
| **How Responsive Parents Are to a Child** | **Authoritative** | **Permissive** |
| **Highly Responsive** | **Characteristics:** firm, setting clear and consistent limits<br>**Relationship With Children:** Although they tend to be relatively strict, like authoritarian parents, they are loving and emotionally supportive and encourage their children to be independent. They also try to reason with their children, giving explanations for why they should behave in a particular way, and communicate the rationale for any punishment they may impose. | **Characteristics:** lax and inconsistent feedback<br>**Relationship With Children:** They require little of their children, and they don't see themselves as holding much responsibility for how their children turn out. They place few or no limits or controls on their children's behavior. |
| | **Authoritarian** | **Uninvolved** |
| **Low Responsive** | **Characteristics:** controlling, punitive, rigid, cold<br>**Relationship With Children:** Their word is law, and they value strict, unquestioning obedience from their children. They also do not tolerate expressions of disagreement. | **Characteristics:** displaying indifferent, rejecting behavior<br>**Relationship With Children:** They are detached emotionally and see their role as only providing food, clothing, and shelter. In its extreme form, this parenting style results in neglect, a form of child abuse. |

**SOURCE:** Based on Baumrind, D. (1971). ""Current patterns of parental authority."" Developmental Psychology Monographs, vol. 4, no. 1, pt. 2.; Maccoby, E. E., & Martin, J. A. (1983). ""Socialization in the context of the family: Parent–child interaction."" In P. H. Mussen (Ed.) & E. M. Hetherington (Vol. Ed.), Handbook of child psychology: Vol. 4. Socialization, personality, and social development (4th ed.). New York: Wiley.

Each of these four alternative responses represents one of the major parenting styles identified by Diana Baumrind and later updated by Eleanor Maccoby and colleagues (Maccoby & Martin, 1983; Baumrind, 1980, 2005).

**Authoritarian parents** respond as in the first alternative. They are controlling, punitive, rigid, and cold. Their word is law, and they value strict, unquestioning obedience from their children. They also do not tolerate expressions of disagreement.

**Permissive parents**, in contrast, provide lax and inconsistent feedback, as in the second alternative. They require little of their children, and they don't see themselves as holding much responsibility for how their children turn out. Although they place few or no limits or controls on their children's behavior, permissive parents are warm and nurturing.

**Authoritative parents** are firm, setting clear and consistent limits. Although they tend to be relatively strict, like authoritarian parents, they are loving, warm, and emotionally supportive. They also try to reason with their children, giving explanations for why they should behave in a particular way ("Alejandro will be upset") and communicate the rationale for any punishment they may impose. Authoritative parents encourage their children to be independent.

Finally, **uninvolved parents** show virtually little or no interest in their children, displaying indifferent, rejecting behavior. They are detached emotionally and see their role as no more than feeding, clothing, and providing shelter for their child. In its most extreme form, uninvolved parenting results in *neglect*, a form of child abuse. (The four patterns are summarized in Table 10.3.)

Does the particular style of discipline that parents use result in differences in children's behavior? The answer is very much yes—although, as you might expect, there are many exceptions (Jia & Schoppe-Sullivan, 2011; Lin, Chiu, & Yeh, 2012; Flouri & Midouhas, 2017):

- Children of authoritarian parents tend to be withdrawn, showing relatively little sociability. They are not very friendly, often behaving uneasily

**authoritarian parents** Parents who are controlling, punitive, rigid, and cold and whose word is law; they value strict, unquestioning obedience from their children and do not tolerate expressions of disagreement

**permissive parents** Parents who provide lax and inconsistent feedback and require little of their children

**authoritative parents** Parents who are firm, setting clear and consistent limits, but try to reason with their children, explaining why they should behave in a particular way

**uninvolved parents** Parents who show virtually no interest in their children, displaying indifferent, rejecting behavior

around their peers. Girls raised by authoritarian parents are especially dependent on their parents, whereas boys are unusually hostile.

- Permissive parents have children who, in many ways, share the undesirable characteristics of children of authoritarian parents. Children with permissive parents tend to be dependent and moody, and they are low in social skills and self-control.

- Children of authoritative parents fare best. They generally are independent, friendly with their peers, self-assertive, and cooperative. They have strong motivation to achieve, and they are typically successful and likable. They regulate their own behavior effectively, both in terms of their relationships with others and emotional self-regulation.

Some authoritative parents also display several characteristics that have come to be called *supportive parenting*, including parental warmth, proactive teaching, calm discussion during disciplinary episodes, and interest and involvement in children's peer activities. Children whose parents engage in such supportive parenting show better adjustment and are better protected from the consequences of later adversity they may encounter (Pettit, Bates, & Dodge, 1997; Belluck, 2000; Kaufmann et al., 2000).

- Children whose parents show uninvolved parenting styles are the worst off. Their parents' lack of involvement disrupts their emotional development considerably, leading them to feel unloved and emotionally detached, and it impedes their physical and cognitive development as well.

Although such classification systems are useful ways of categorizing and describing parents' behavior, they are not a recipe for success. Parenting and growing up are more complicated than that! For instance, in a significant number of cases the children of authoritarian and permissive parents develop quite successfully.

Furthermore, most parents are not entirely consistent. Although the authoritarian, permissive, authoritative, and uninvolved patterns describe general styles, sometimes parents switch from their dominant mode to one of the others. For instance, when a child darts into the street, even the most laid-back and permissive parent is likely to react in a harsh, authoritarian manner, laying down strict demands about safety. In such cases, authoritarian styles may be most effective (Eisenberg & Valiente, 2002; Gershoff, 2002).

# Cultural Differences in Childrearing Practices

**LO 10.6 Compare cultural differences in childrearing practices.**

It's important to keep in mind that the findings regarding childrearing styles we have been discussing are chiefly applicable to Western societies. The style of parenting that is most successful may depend quite heavily on the norms of a particular culture—and what parents in a particular culture are taught regarding appropriate childrearing practices (Nagabhushan, 2011; Calzada et al., 2012; Dotti Sani & Treas, 2016).

For example, the Chinese concept of *chiao shun* suggests that parents should be strict, firm, and in tight control of their children's behavior. Parents are seen to have a duty to train their children to adhere to socially and culturally desirable standards of behavior, particularly those manifested in good school performance. Children's acceptance of such an approach to discipline is seen as a sign of parental respect (Ng, Pomerantz, & Lam, 2007; Lui & Rollock, 2013; Frewen et al., 2015).

Typically, parents in China and India are highly directive with their children, pushing them to excel and controlling their behavior to a considerably higher degree than parents do in Western countries. And it works: Children of Asian parents tend to be quite successful, particularly academically (Steinberg, Dornbusch, & Brown, 1992; Nelson et al., 2006).

In contrast, U.S. parents are generally advised to use authoritative methods and explicitly to avoid authoritarian measures. Interestingly, it wasn't always this way. Until World War II, the point of view that dominated the advice literature was authoritarian, apparently founded on Puritan religious influences that suggested that children had "original sin" or that they needed to have their wills broken (Smuts & Hagen, 1985).

For Hispanic parents, one central value relates to the concept of respect. Hispanic parents believe that children should listen to rules and should be obedient to authority figures (O'Connor et al., 2013).

In short, the childrearing practices that parents are urged to follow reflect cultural perspectives about the nature of children as well as about the appropriate role of parents and their support system. No single parenting pattern or style, then, is likely to be universally

# BECOMING AN INFORMED CONSUMER OF CHILD DEVELOPMENT

## Disciplining Children

The question of how best to discipline children has been raised for generations. Answers from developmentalists today include the following advice (Brazelton & Sparrow, 2003; Flouri, 2005; Mulvaney & Mebert, 2007):

- *For most children in Western cultures, authoritative parenting works best.* Parents should be firm and consistent, providing clear direction for desirable behavior. Authoritative disciplinarians provide rules, but they explain why those rules make sense, using language that children can understand.
- *Spanking is never an appropriate discipline technique*, according to the American Academy of Pediatrics. Not only is spanking less effective than other techniques in curbing undesirable behavior, but it leads to additional, unwanted outcomes, such as the potential for more aggressive behavior. Even though most Americans were spanked as children, the research is

clear in demonstrating that spanking is inappropriate (Bell & Romano, 2012; American Academy of Pediatrics, 2012).

- *Use time-out for punishment*, in which children are removed from a situation in which they have misbehaved and not permitted to engage in enjoyable activities for a set period of time.
- *Tailor parental discipline to the characteristics of the child and the situation.* Try to keep the child's particular personality in mind, and adapt discipline to it.
- *Use routines (such as a bath routine or a bedtime routine) to avoid conflict.* For instance, bedtime can be the source of a nightly struggle between a resistant child and an insistent parent. Parental strategies for gaining compliance that involve making the situation predictably enjoyable—such as routinely reading a bedtime story or engaging in a nightly "wrestling" match with the child—can defuse potential battles.

---

appropriate or invariably to produce successful children (Chang, Pettit, & Katsurada, 2006; Wang, Pomerantz, & Chen, 2007; Pomerantz et al., 2011).

# Moral Development and Aggression

> *Bubbly arrived late to preschool and began playing with the only remaining item in the play box, an old yellow school bus. Next to her, her friend Kriti had sole possession of a set of big LEGOs. As Kriti played happily with her LEGOs, Bubbly looked at her school bus and began to cry. After a few seconds, Kriti responded to Bubbly's disappointment by offering her some LEGOs. Bubbly took them, and soon the two were playing together. Kriti had put herself in Bubbly's place, understanding what she was feeling and thinking, and had then shown compassion.*

In this short scenario we see many of the key elements of morality, as it is played out among preschool-age children. Changes in children's views of what is ethically

right and what is the right way to behave are an important element of growth during the preschool years.

At the same time, the kind of aggression displayed by preschoolers is also changing. We can consider the development of morality and aggression as two sides of the coin of human conduct, and both involve a growing awareness of others.

## Developing Morality: Following Society's Rights and Wrongs

**LO 10.7  Compare the different approaches to moral development in children.**

**Moral development** refers to changes in people's sense of justice and of what is right and wrong, and in their behavior related to moral issues. Developmentalists have considered moral development in terms of children's reasoning about morality, their attitudes toward

---

**moral development** The maturation of people's sense of justice, of what is right and wrong, and their behavior in connection with such issues

moral lapses, and their behavior when faced with moral issues. In the process of studying moral development, psychologists have evolved several approaches. We will discuss Piaget's theory first.

**PIAGET'S VIEW OF MORAL DEVELOPMENT.**   Child psychologist Jean Piaget (1896–1980) was one of the first to study questions of moral development. He suggested that moral development, like cognitive development, proceeds in stages (Piaget, 1932). The earliest stage is a broad form of moral thinking he called *heteronomous morality*, in which rules are seen as invariant and unchangeable. During this stage, which lasts from about age 4 through age 7, children play games rigidly, assuming that there is one—and only one—way to play, and that every other way is wrong. At the same time, though, preschool-age children may not even fully grasp game rules. Consequently, a group of children may be playing together, with each child playing according to a slightly different set of rules. Nevertheless, they enjoy playing with others. Piaget suggests that every child may "win" such a game, because winning is equated with having a good time, as opposed to truly competing with others.

This rigid heteronomous morality is ultimately replaced by two later stages of morality: incipient cooperation and autonomous cooperation. As its name implies, in the *incipient cooperation stage*, which lasts from around age 7 to age 10, children's games become more clearly social. Children learn the actual formal rules of games, and they play according to this shared knowledge. Consequently, rules are still seen as largely unchangeable. There is a "right" way to play the game, and preschool children play according to these formal rules.

It is not until the *autonomous cooperation stage*, which begins at about age 10, that children become fully aware that formal game rules can be modified if the people who play them agree. The later transition into more sophisticated forms of moral development—which we will consider in Chapter 15 when we discuss Lawrence Kohlberg and Carol Gilligan, two influential researchers— also is reflected in school-age children's understanding that rules of law are created by people and are subject to change according to the will of people.

Until these later stages are reached, however, children's reasoning about rules and issues of justice is bounded in the concrete. Furthermore, children in the

Piaget believed that at the heteronomous morality stage, this child would feel that the degree to which she had done the wrong thing is directly related to the number of items broken.

heteronomous morality stage do not take *intention* into account.

Children in the heteronomous stage of moral development also believe in immanent justice. *Immanent justice* is the notion that rules that are broken earn immediate punishment. Preschool children believe that if they do something wrong, they will be punished instantly—even if no one sees them carrying out their misdeeds. In contrast, older children understand that punishments for misdeeds are determined and meted out by people. Children who have moved beyond the heteronomous morality stage have come to understand that one must make judgments about the severity of a transgression based on whether the person intended to do something wrong.

**EVALUATING PIAGET'S APPROACH TO MORAL DEVELOPMENT.**   Recent research suggests that although Piaget was on the right track in his description of how moral development proceeds, his approach suffers from the same problem we encountered in his theory of cognitive development. Specifically, Piaget underestimated the age at which children's moral skills are honed.

It is now clear that preschool-age children understand the notion of intentionality by about age 3, and this allows them to make judgments based on intent at an earlier age than Piaget supposed. Specifically, when provided with moral questions that emphasize intent, preschool children judge someone who is intentionally bad as more "naughty" than someone who is unintentionally bad, but who creates more objective damage. Moreover, by age 4, they judge intentional lying as being wrong (Yuill & Perner, 1988; Bussey, 1992; LoBue et al., 2011).

**SOCIAL LEARNING APPROACHES TO MORALITY.** Social learning approaches to moral development stand in stark contrast to Piaget's approach. While Piaget emphasized how limitations in preschoolers' cognitive development lead to particular forms of moral *reasoning*, social learning approaches focus more on how the environment in which preschoolers operate produces **prosocial behavior**, helping behavior that benefits others (Caputi et al., 2012; Schulz et al., 2013; Buon, Habib, & Frey, 2017).

Social learning approaches build upon the established behavioral approaches that we first discussed in Chapter 1. They acknowledge that some instances of children's prosocial behavior stem from situations in which they have received positive reinforcement for acting in a morally appropriate way. For instance, when Claire's mother tells her she has been a "good girl" for sharing a box of candy with her brother Dan, Claire's behavior has been reinforced. As a consequence, she is more likely to engage in sharing behavior in the future (Ramaswamy & Bergin, 2009).

Social learning approaches go a step further, however, arguing that not all prosocial behavior has to be directly performed and subsequently reinforced for learning to occur. According to social learning approaches, children also learn moral behavior more indirectly by observing the behavior of others, called *models* (Bandura, 1977). Children imitate models who receive reinforcement for their behavior, and ultimately they learn to perform the behavior themselves. For example, when Claire's friend Jake watches Claire share her candy with her brother, and Claire is praised for her behavior, Jake is more likely to engage in sharing behavior himself at some later point.

Quite a few studies illustrate the power of models and of social learning more generally in producing prosocial behavior in preschool-age children. For example, experiments have shown that children who view someone behaving generously or unselfishly are apt to follow the model's example, subsequently behaving in a generous or unselfish manner themselves when put in a similar situation. The opposite also holds true: If a model behaves selfishly, children who observe such behavior tend to behave more selfishly themselves (Hastings et al., 2007).

Not all models are equally effective in producing prosocial responses. For instance, preschoolers are more apt to model the behavior of warm, responsive adults than of adults who appear colder. Furthermore, models viewed as highly competent or high in prestige are more effective than others.

Children do more than simply mimic unthinkingly behavior that they see rewarded in others. By observing moral conduct, they are reminded of society's norms about the importance of moral behavior as conveyed by parents, teachers, and other powerful authority figures. They notice the connections between particular situations and certain kinds of behavior. This increases the likelihood that similar situations will elicit similar behavior in the observer.

Consequently, modeling paves the way for the development of more general rules and principles in a process called **abstract modeling**. Rather than always modeling the particular behavior of others, older preschoolers begin to develop generalized principles that underlie the behavior that they observe. After observing repeated instances in which a model is rewarded for acting in a morally desirable way, children begin the process of inferring and learning the general principles of moral conduct (Bandura, 1991).

Cultural psychologists like Shweder and Haidt (2001, 2007, & 2009) endorsed the importance of culture in shaping moral conceptualizations. In a study conducted by Saxena and Babu (2015) in an urban Indian context, it was observed how family discourses revolve around moral values that probably influence morality development of preschoolers. They found four predominant moral values that emerged from parent-child discourses: respecting elders, sharing, caring, and reference to God. In this study, the participant children were between 3 and 5 years of age. In accordance to the Piaget's stages of cognitive development, the children were at the pre-operational level, wherein the ability to understand the abstract concepts is limited.

---

**prosocial behavior** Helping behavior that benefits others

**abstract modeling** The process in which modeling paves the way for the development of more general rules and principles

The parents, thus, socialize children to the above-mentioned values in a concrete manner, by emphasizing on certain behavioral markers, or giving clear deontic reasoning. For example, parents emphasized on greeting elders (*namaste*), touching feet, not addressing them by name, and using words like *didi* or *bhaiya* to address an elder girl or boy as indicators of respect. The discourses provided an insightful understanding of 'sharing', as a value that involves parting away with something precious to one's self rather than simply giving away an excessive resource. The families involved in the study were Hindu families, and Hinduism has a rich mythology which is communicated to children in the form of animated cartoons. Parents often drew reference to God in their everyday conversations with their children, in order to impart moral values or to discipline them. Reference to Lord Shiva's third eye to imply the wrath of God if someone upsets Him or reference to Lord Hanuman's strength to make a child finish food are some examples.

**GENETIC APPROACHES TO MORALITY: BORN TO BE GOOD?**  The newest—and highly controversial—approach to morality suggests that particular genes may underlie some aspects of moral behavior. According to this view, preschoolers have a genetic predisposition to behave generously or selfishly.

In one study designed to illustrate this approach, researchers gave preschoolers the opportunity to behave generously by sharing stickers. Those who were more selfish and less generous were more likely to have a variation in a gene called AVPR1A, which regulates a hormone in the brain that is related to social behavior (Avinum et al., 2011).

It is unlikely that the gene mutation fully accounts for the preschoolers' lack of generosity. The environment in which the children were raised also is likely to play a significant, and perhaps predominant, role in determining moral behavior. Still, the findings are provocative in showing that generosity may have genetic roots.

**EMPATHY AND MORAL BEHAVIOR.**  **Empathy** is an emotional response that corresponds to the feelings of another person. Put simply, empathy is an understanding of what another individual feels. According to some developmentalists, empathy lies at the heart of moral behavior.

The roots of empathy grow early. One-year-old infants cry when they hear other infants crying. By ages 2 and 3, toddlers will offer gifts and spontaneously share toys with other children and adults, even if they are strangers (Zahn-Waxler & Radke-Yarrow, 1990).

During the preschool years, empathy continues to grow. Some theorists believe that increasing empathy—as well as other positive emotions, such as sympathy and admiration—leads children to behave in a more moral fashion. In addition, some negative emotions—such as anger at an unfair situation or shame over previous transgressions—also may promote moral behavior (Vinik, Almas, & Grusec, 2011; Bischof-Köhler, 2012; Eisenberg, Spinrad, & Morris, 2014).

The notion that negative emotions may promote moral development is one that Freud first suggested in his theory of psychoanalytic personality development. Recall from Chapter 2 that Freud argued that a child's *superego*, the part of the personality that represents societal do's and don'ts, is developed through resolution of the *Oedipal conflict*. Children come to identify with their same-sex parent, incorporating that parent's standards of morality in order to avoid unconscious guilt raised by the Oedipal conflict.

Whether or not we accept Freud's account of the Oedipal conflict and the guilt it produces, his theory is consistent with more recent findings. These suggest that preschoolers' attempts to avoid experiencing negative emotions sometimes lead them to act in more moral, helpful ways. For instance, one reason children help others is to avoid the feelings of personal distress that they experience when they are confronted with another person's unhappiness or misfortune (Valiente, Eisenberg, & Fabes, 2004; Eisenberg, Valiente, & Champion, 2004; Cushman et al., 2013).

# Aggression and Violence in Preschoolers

**LO 10.8  Explain how aggression develops in preschool-age children.**

*Four-year-old Dev could not contain his anger and frustration anymore. Although he usually was mild-mannered, when Ishaan began to tease him about the split in his pants and kept it up for several minutes, Dev finally snapped. Rushing*

---

**empathy** An emotional response that corresponds to the feelings of another person

*over to Ishaan, Dev pushed him to the ground and began to hit him with his small, closed fists. Because he was so distraught, Dev's punches were not terribly effective, but they were severe enough to hurt Ishaan and bring him to tears before the preschool teachers could intervene.*

Aggression among preschoolers is quite common, though attacks such as this one are not. The potential for verbal hostility, shoving matches, kicking, and other forms of aggression is present throughout the preschool period, but the degree to which aggression is acted out changes as children become older.

Ishaan's taunting was also a form of aggression. **Aggression** is intentional injury or harm to another person. Infants don't act aggressively; it is hard to contend that their behavior is *intended* to hurt others, even if they inadvertently manage to do so. In contrast, by the time they reach preschool age, children demonstrate true aggression.

During the early preschool years, some of the aggression is addressed at attaining a desired goal, such as getting a toy away from another person or using a particular space occupied by another person. Consequently, in some ways the aggression is inadvertent, and minor scuffles may in fact be a typical part of early preschool life. It is the rare child who does not demonstrate at least an occasional act of aggression.

However, extreme and sustained aggression is a cause of concern. In most children, the amount of aggression declines as they move through the preschool years, as do the frequency and average length of episodes of aggressive behavior (Persson, 2005; Olson et al., 2011).

The child's personality and social development contribute to this decline in aggression. Throughout the preschool years, children become better at controlling the emotions that they are experiencing. **Emotional self-regulation** is the capability to adjust emotions to a desired state and level of intensity. Starting at age 2, children are able to talk about their feelings, and they engage in strategies to regulate them. As they get older, they develop more effective strategies, learning to better cope with negative emotions. In addition to their increasing self-control, children are also, as we've seen, developing sophisticated social skills. Most learn to use language to express their wishes, and they become increasingly able to negotiate with others (Philippot & Feldman, 2005; Helmsen, Koglin, & Petermann, 2012; Rose et al., 2016).

Despite these typical declines in aggression, some children remain aggressive throughout the preschool period. Furthermore, aggression is a relatively stable characteristic: The most aggressive preschoolers tend to be the most aggressive children during the school-age years, and the least aggressive preschoolers tend to be the least aggressive school-age children (Tremblay, 2001; Schaeffer, Petras, & Ialongo, 2003; Davenport & Bourgeois, 2008).

Boys typically show higher levels of physical, instrumental aggression than do girls. **Instrumental aggression** is aggression motivated by the desire to obtain a concrete goal, such as playing with a toy that another child is playing with.

Although girls show lower levels of instrumental aggression, they may be just as aggressive as boys, but in different ways. Girls are more likely to practice **relational aggression**, which is nonphysical aggression that is intended to hurt another person's feelings. Such aggression may be demonstrated through name-calling, withholding friendship, or simply saying mean, hurtful things that make the recipient feel bad (Werner & Crick, 2004; Murray-Close, Ostrov, & Crick, 2007; Valles & Knutson, 2008).

How can we explain the aggression of preschoolers? Some theoreticians suggest that to behave aggressively is an instinct, part and parcel of the human condition. For instance, Freud's psychoanalytic theory suggests that we all are motivated by sexual and aggressive instincts (Freud, 1920). According to ethologist Konrad Lorenz, an expert in animal behavior, animals—including humans—share a fighting instinct that stems from primitive urges to preserve territory, maintain a steady supply of food, and weed out weaker animals (Lorenz, 1974).

Similar arguments are made by evolutionary psychologists, scientists who consider the biological roots of social behavior. They argue that aggression leads to increased opportunities to mate, improving

---

**aggression** Intentional injury or harm to another person

**emotional self-regulation** The capability to adjust one's emotions to a desired state and level of intensity

**instrumental aggression** Aggression motivated by the desire to obtain a concrete goal

**relational aggression** Nonphysical aggression that is intended to hurt another person's psychological well-being

the likelihood that one's genes will be passed on to future generations. In addition, aggression may help to strengthen the species and its gene pool as a whole, because the strongest survive. Ultimately, then, aggressive instincts promote the survival of one's genes to pass on to future generations (Archer, 2009; Farbiash et al., 2013).

Although instinctual explanations of aggression are logical, most developmentalists believe they are not the whole story. Not only do instinctual explanations fail to take into account the increasingly sophisticated cognitive abilities that humans develop as they get older, but they also have relatively little experimental support. Moreover, they provide little guidance in determining when and how children, as well as adults, will behave aggressively, other than noting that aggression is an inevitable part of the human condition. Consequently, developmentalists have turned to other approaches to explain aggression and violence.

## Social Learning and Cognitive Approaches to Aggression

**LO 10.9 Describe how social learning and cognitive approaches explain aggression.**

*The day after Dev lashed out at Ishaan, Lita, who had watched the entire scene, got into an argument with Lita. They verbally bickered for a while, and suddenly Lita balled her hand into a fist and tried to punch Lila. The preschool teachers were stunned: It was rare for Lita to get upset, and she had never displayed aggression before.*

Is there a connection between the two events? Most of us would answer yes, particularly if we subscribed to the view, suggested by social learning approaches, that aggression is largely a learned behavior.

**SOCIAL LEARNING APPROACHES TO AGGRESSION.** Social learning approaches to aggression contend that aggression is based on observation and prior learning. To understand the causes of aggressive behavior, then, we should look at the system of rewards and punishments that exists in a child's environment.

Social learning approaches to aggression emphasize how social and environmental conditions teach individuals to be aggressive. These ideas grow out of behavioral perspectives, which suggest that aggressive behavior is learned through direct reinforcement.

For instance, preschool-age children may learn that they can continue to play with the most desirable toys by aggressively refusing their classmates' requests for sharing. In the parlance of traditional learning theory, they have been reinforced for acting aggressively (by continued use of the toy), and they are more likely to behave aggressively in the future.

But social learning approaches suggest that reinforcement also comes in less direct ways. A good deal of research contends that exposure to aggressive models leads to increased aggression, particularly if the observers are themselves angered, insulted, or frustrated. For example, Albert Bandura and his colleagues illustrated the power of models in a classic study of preschool-age children (Bandura, Ross, & Ross, 1962). One group of children watched a film of an adult playing aggressively and violently with a Bobo doll (a large, inflated plastic clown designed as a punching bag for children, which always returns to an upright position after being pushed down). In comparison, children in another group watched a film of an adult playing sedately with a set of Tinkertoys (see Figure 10.2). Later, the preschool-age children were allowed to play with a number of toys, which included both the Bobo doll and the Tinkertoys. But first the children were led to feel frustration by being refused the opportunity to play with a favorite toy.

As predicted by social learning approaches, the preschool-age children modeled the behavior of the adult. Those who had seen the aggressive model playing with the Bobo doll were considerably more aggressive than those who had watched the calm, unaggressive model playing with the Tinkertoys.

Later research has supported this early study, and it is clear that exposure to aggressive models increases the likelihood that aggression on the part of observers will follow. These findings have profound consequences, particularly for children who live in communities in which violence is prevalent. For instance, one-third of the children in some urban neighborhoods have seen a homicide, and two-thirds have seen a serious assault. Such frequent exposure to violence increases the probability that observers will behave aggressively themselves (Farver et al., 1997; Evans, 2004; Huesmann et al., 2016).

**COGNITIVE APPROACHES TO AGGRESSION: THE THOUGHTS BEHIND VIOLENCE.** Two children, waiting for their turn in a game of kickball,

## Figure 10.2 Modeling Aggression

This series of photos is from Albert Bandura's classic Bobo doll experiment, designed to illustrate social learning of aggression. The photos clearly show how the adult model's aggressive behavior (in the first row) is imitated by children who had viewed the aggressive behavior (second and third rows).

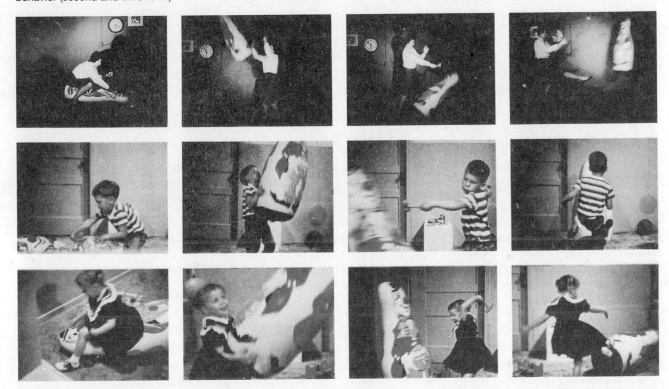

inadvertently knock into one another. One child's reaction is to apologize; the other's is to shove, saying angrily, "Cut it out."

Despite the fact that each child bears the same responsibility for the minor event, very different reactions result. The first child interprets the event as an accident, while the second sees it as a provocation and reacts with aggression.

The cognitive approach to aggression suggests that the key to understanding moral development is to examine preschoolers' interpretations of others' behavior and of the environmental context in which a behavior occurs. According to developmental psychologist Kenneth Dodge and his colleagues, some children are more prone than others to assume that actions are aggressively motivated. They are unable to pay attention to the appropriate cues in a situation and unable to interpret the behaviors in a given situation accurately. Instead, they assume—often erroneously—that what is happening is related to others' hostility. Subsequently, in deciding how to respond, they base their behavior on their inaccurate interpretation of

behavior. In sum, they may behave aggressively in response to a situation that never in fact existed (Pettit & Dodge, 2003).

For example, consider Nathan, who is drawing at a table with Gary. Nathan reaches over and takes a red crayon that Gary had just decided he was going to use next. Gary is instantly certain that the Nathan "knew" that he was going to use the red crayon, and that is taking it just to be mean. With this interpretation in mind, Gary hits Nathan for "stealing" his crayon.

Although the cognitive approach to aggression provides a description of the process that leads some children to behave aggressively, it is less successful in explaining how certain children come to be inaccurate perceivers of situations in the first place. Furthermore, it fails to explain why such inaccurate perceivers so readily respond with aggression, and why they assume that aggression is an appropriate and even desirable response.

However, cognitive approaches to aggression are useful in pointing out a means to reduce aggression: By teaching preschool-age children to be more accurate

# BECOMING AN INFORMED CONSUMER OF CHILD DEVELOPMENT

## Increasing Moral Behavior and Reducing Aggression in Preschool-Age Children

The numerous points of view on the cause of aggression in preschool children are useful for the various methods for encouraging preschoolers' moral conduct and reducing the incidence of aggression they suggest. Here are some of the most practical and readily accomplished strategies (Bor & Bor, 2004; Larson & Lochman, 2011; Eisenberg, 2012):

- *Provide opportunities for preschool-age children to observe others acting in a cooperative, helpful, prosocial manner.* Encourage them to interact with peers in joint activities in which they share a common goal. Such cooperative activities can teach the importance and desirability of working with—and helping—others. Further, encourage children to engage in activities that benefit others, such as sharing. But don't directly reward them for doing it with concrete reinforcements such as candy or money. Verbal praise is fine. In addition, talk to preschoolers about how others must feel in difficult situations, thereby fostering empathy.

- *Do not ignore aggressive behavior.* Parents and teachers should intervene when they see aggression in preschoolers and send a clear message that aggression is an unacceptable means to resolve conflicts.

- *Help preschoolers devise alternative explanations for others' behavior.* This is particularly important for

children who are prone to aggression and who may be apt to view others' conduct as more hostile than it actually is. Parents and teachers should help such children see that the behavior of their peers has several possible interpretations.

- *Monitor preschoolers' television viewing, particularly the violence that they see.* There is good evidence that observation of televised aggression results in subsequent increases in children's levels of aggression. At the same time, encourage preschoolers to watch particular shows that are designed, in part, to increase the level of moral conduct, such as *Sesame Street, Dora the Explorer,* or *SpongeBob SquarePants.*

- *Help preschoolers understand their feelings.* When children become angry—and all children do—they need to learn how to deal with their feelings in a constructive manner. Tell them *specific* things they can do to improve the situation ("I see you're really angry with Liam for not giving you a turn. Don't hit him, but tell him you want a chance to play with the game.")

- *Explicitly teach reasoning and self-control.* Preschoolers can understand the rudiments of moral reasoning, and they should be reminded why certain behaviors are desirable. For instance, explicitly saying, "If you take all the cookies, others will have no dessert" is preferable to saying, "Good children don't eat all the cookies."

---

interpreters of a situation, we can induce them to be less prone to view others' behavior as being motivated by hostility, and consequently less likely to respond with aggression themselves. The guidelines in *Becoming an Informed Consumer of Child Development* are based on the various theoretical perspectives on aggression and morality that we've discussed in this chapter.

## Violent TV Programs and Video Games: Are They Harmful?

**LO 10.10** Explain the kinds of effects violent TV programs and video games can have on preschool-age children.

Even the majority of preschool-age children who are not witnesses to real-life violence are typically exposed to aggression via the medium of television. Children's television programs actually contain higher levels of violence (69 percent) than other types of programs (57 percent). In an average hour, children's programs contain more than twice as many violent incidents than other types of programs (Wilson et al., 2002).

This high level of televised violence and Bandura and others' research findings on modeling violence raise a significant question: Does viewing aggression increase the likelihood that children (and later, adults) will enact actual—and ultimately deadly—aggression? It is hard to answer the question definitively, primarily because scientists are unable to conduct true experiments outside of laboratory settings.

Although it is clear that laboratory observation of aggression on television leads to higher levels of aggression, evidence showing that real-world viewing of aggression is associated with subsequent aggressive behavior is correlational. (Think, for a moment, of what would be required to conduct a true experiment involving children's viewing habits. It would require that we control children's viewing of television in their homes for extended periods, exposing some to a steady diet of violent shows and others to nonviolent ones—something that most parents would not agree to.)

Despite the fact, then, that the results are primarily correlational, the overwhelming weight of research evidence is clear in suggesting that observation of televised aggression does lead to subsequent aggression. Longitudinal studies have found that children's preferences for violent television shows at age 8 are related to the seriousness of criminal convictions by age 30. Other evidence supports the notion that observation of media violence can lead to bullying, a greater readiness to act aggressively, and an insensitivity to the suffering of victims of violence (Christakis & Zimmerman, 2007; Kirsh, 2012; Merritt et al., 2016).

Television is not the only source of media violence. Many video games contain a significant amount of aggressive behavior, and children are playing such games at high rates. For example, 14 percent of children 3 and younger and around 50 percent of those 4 to 6 play video games. Because research conducted with adults shows that playing violent video games is associated with behaving aggressively, children who play video games containing violence may be at higher risk for behaving aggressively (Barlett, Harris, & Baldassaro, 2007; Polman, de Castro, & van Aken, 2008; Bushman, Gollwitzer, & Cruz, 2014).

For instance, one of the leading researchers in this area, psychologist Craig Anderson, and his colleagues have conducted a meta-analysis in which he concludes that playing violent video games is a risk factor for increased aggressiveness (Anderson et al., 2010; Bastian, Jetten, & Radke, 2012).

The researchers examined more than 130 published studies on the effects of violent video game play using a total of more than 130,000 participants. The outcome variables they focused on were aggressive thoughts, aggressive behaviors, aggressive feelings, physiological arousal, empathy/desensitization, and helping behavior. Their analysis included longitudinal studies of all of these variables (except arousal, which is a short-term phenomenon) and looked for cross-cultural and gender differences as well.

The results of the meta-analysis were quite clear: Increased levels of violent video game play were associated with more aggressive thoughts, feelings, and behaviors, and these findings applied equally well to studies using cross-sectional, longitudinal, or experimental research methods, and they did not differ between Western and Eastern cultures. Violent video game play was also associated with desensitization to violence, lack of empathy, and lack of helping behavior. All of these effects applied to females and to males (Anderson et al., 2010).

Anderson and his team were careful to point out that in addition to being theoretically important, the results they found also have real-world practical significance. In the case of violent video game play, the effects are cumulative over time, they are being applied to a large percentage of the population (everyone who plays these games), and they can interact with other variables to produce serious consequences.

The researchers note that the contribution of violent video game play to aggressiveness found by this analysis is equivalent to the contributions of such other risk factors as substance abuse, abusive parents, and poverty. They argue that the discussion of violent video games should shift from whether they have harmful effects—clearly they do—to what parents, schools, and society in general can do about it (Anderson et al., 2010).

Fortunately, social learning principles that lead preschoolers to learn aggression from television and

Social learning explanations of aggression suggest that playing violent video games prompts children to act aggressively.

video games suggest ways to reduce the negative influence of the medium. For instance, children can be explicitly taught to view violence with a more skeptical, critical eye. Being taught that violence is not representative of the real world, that the viewing of violence can affect them negatively, and that they should refrain from imitating the behavior they have seen on television and in video games can help children interpret the violent programs differently and be less influenced by them (Persson & Musher-Eizenman, 2003; Donnerstein, 2005).

> **From an educator's perspective:** How might a preschool teacher or parent help children notice the violence in the programs they watch and protect them from its effects?

Furthermore, just as exposure to aggressive models leads to aggression, observation of *non*aggressive models can *reduce* aggression. Preschoolers don't learn from others only how to be aggressive; they can also learn how to avoid confrontation and to control their aggression.

# The Case of …
## The Wrong Role Models?

Vinod Chabra has been watching his son Jeet carefully. Because Vinod runs a business 90 minutes from home, his wife, Trupti, who works right in the neighborhood, has had primary responsibility for raising Jeet, and Vinod has been growing steadily more worried over the four years of Jeet's life.

First, it was Jeet's soft voice and shy, gentle mannerisms. Then it was his quiet insistence on getting a doll for his birthday at age 3, which Vinod felt he had at least managed to sabotage by picking a G.I. Joe. Of course, Vinod's anxiety mounted when Jeet spent more time dressing Joe in different outfits than making him run around and blow things up. Then it was Jeet's love of drawing and making clay models instead of playing with the neat toy guns and sports gear that Vinod brought home for him.

Vinod has long believed that his big mistake was letting Trupti place Jeet in a local day care where all the other kids are girls. Vinod is convinced that this environment has influenced Jeet's choices and made him more feminine. He is hoping that next year Jeet's kindergarten class will have more boys in it so his son can escape from the undue pressure to conform to a girl's lifestyle.

1. Given what you know about gender differences in preschoolers, are Vinod's worries about Jeet's mannerisms and habits justified? Why or why not?
2. Vinod attributes Jeet's behaviors to environmental influences. Could genetics also be a factor? Can the relative influences of nature and nurture be determined accurately?
3. If Jeet attended an all-boys day care, would his behavior and preferences necessarily be different? Why or why not?
4. Which perspective—biological, psychoanalytic, social learning, or cognitive—provides the most satisfying explanation for Jeet's behavior? Why?
5. Do you think Vinod is right that exposure to boys in kindergarten will change Jeet's behavior? If so, how might this work?

# Epilogue

This chapter examined the social and personality development of preschool-age children, including their development of self-concept. The changing social relationships of preschool-age children can be seen in the shifting nature of play. We considered typical styles of parental discipline and their effects later in life, and we examined how parenting styles vary across cultures. We discussed the development of a moral sense from several developmental perspectives, and we concluded with a discussion of aggression.

Before moving on to the next chapter, take a moment to reread the prologue about Lara Sinha, the 4-year-old girl who understood that her friend was sad and made an effort to cheer her up. Then answer the following questions:

1. In what ways do Lara's actions indicate that she is developing a theory of mind?
2. How would social learning theorists explain Lara's behavior toward Rita?

**3.** What clues to Lara's self-concept do you see in the story? How do you think Lara would answer the question, *Who am I?*

**4.** Based on the story, how would you characterize the quality and kinds of interactions Lara has with her friends? What type(s) of play would you expect Lara to engage in?

# Looking Back

**LO 10.1 Explain how preschool-age children develop a concept of who they are.**

- According to Erik Erikson, preschool-age children initially are in the autonomy-versus-shame-and-doubt stage (18 months to 3 years) in which they develop independence and mastery over their physical and social worlds or feel shame, self-doubt, and unhappiness. Later, in the initiative-versus-guilt stage (ages 3 to 6), preschool-age children face conflicts between the desire to act independently and the guilt that comes from the unintended consequences of their actions.

- Preschoolers' self-concepts are formed partly from their own perceptions and estimations of their characteristics, partly from their parents' behavior toward them, and partly from cultural influences.

**LO 10.2 Compare the different perspectives on the ways children develop their sense of gender.**

- Gender differences emerge early in the preschool years as children form expectations—which generally conform to social stereotypes—about what is appropriate and inappropriate for each sex.

- The strong gender expectations held by preschoolers are explained in different ways by different theorists.

- The biological perspective points to genetic factors such as sex-related hormones and sex-related differences in brain structure as evidence for a biological explanation of gender differences. However, because children experience a wide variety of environmental influences after birth, it is difficult to claim that behavioral characteristics are solely attributable to biological factors.

- Freud's psychoanalytic theory stressed that when anatomical differences between males and females become evident to children (at about age 5), they repress their desires toward the parent of the opposite sex and seek to identify with the parent of the same sex. This process of identification, Freud believed, perpetuates the parents' attitudes and values. Girls imitate their mothers, and boys copy their fathers.

- Freud's explanation of the development of gender differences has largely been discredited, in part because of the lack of scientific support for his theory.

- Social learning theorists focus on environmental influences. They believe children learn gender-related behavior and expectation by observing others, including parents, teachers, peers, and the media, while cognitive theorists propose that children form gender schemas, cognitive frameworks that organize information that the children gather about gender.

**LO 10.3 Describe the social relationships and play in which preschool-age children engage.**

- For preschool-age children, social relationships with peers are at first based on a desire for companionship and fun, but as preschoolers mature, friendships deepen and are likely to involve trust and shared interests. Children come to understand that friendship is a stable, continuing relationship.

- Early in the preschool years, children engage mostly in functional play. As they mature, preschool-age children more often engage in constructive play where the aim is to create some kind of end product through building or the manipulation of objects. They also engage in more associative and cooperative play than younger preschoolers, who do more parallel and onlooker play.

- Pretend play becomes more imaginative as preschoolers move from using realistic objects in their games to using objects that are less concrete. Lev Vygotsky suggested that pretend play can expand a child's cognitive skills because it involves "practicing" activities that are part of a child's culture, thus increasing the child's understanding of how the world functions.

**LO 10.4 Discuss how preschoolers develop a theory of mind.**

- Preschool-age children can increasingly see the world from other people's point of view. They are able to develop explanations for how other people think and reasons for others' behavior.

- A child's developing theory of mind is enhanced by more engaged social interactions, which, in their turn, promote a more sophisticated theory of mind. Cultural factors also contribute to this development.

**LO 10.5 List the types of disciplinary styles parents employ and the effects they have on their children.**

- Disciplinary styles differ both individually and culturally. In the United States and other Western societies, parents' styles tend to be mostly authoritarian, permissive, uninvolved, or authoritative, with the last regarded as the most effective.

- Children of authoritarian and permissive parents may develop dependency, hostility, and low self-control, while children of uninvolved parents may feel unloved and emotionally detached. Children of authoritative parents tend to be more independent, friendly, self-assertive, and cooperative.

**LO 10.6 Compare cultural differences in childrearing practices.**

- The style of parenting that is most successful depends on the norms of a particular culture and what parents are taught regarding appropriate childrearing practices.

- Typically, parents in China are more directive with their children than parents in Western countries.

**LO 10.7 Compare the different approaches to moral development in children.**

- Jean Piaget believed that preschool-age children are in the heteronomous morality stage of moral development, characterized by a belief in external, unchangeable rules of conduct and sure, immediate punishment for all misdeeds.

- Social learning approaches to morality emphasize interactions between environment and behavior in moral development in which models of behavior play an important role in development.

- In contrast, genetic approaches to moral development suggest that specific genes may affect some aspects of moral behavior, such as generosity and selfishness.

- Some developmentalists believe that moral behavior is rooted in a child's development of empathy. Other emotions, including the negative emotions of anger and shame, may also promote moral behavior.

**LO 10.8 Explain how aggression develops in preschool-age children.**

- Aggression, which involves intentional harm to another person, begins to emerge in the preschool years. As children age and improve their language skills, acts of aggression typically decline in frequency and duration.

- Some ethologists, such as Konrad Lorenz, believe that aggression is simply a biological fact of human life—a belief held also by many sociobiologists, who focus on competition within species to pass genes on to the next generation.

**LO 10.9 Describe how social learning and cognitive approaches explain aggression.**

- Social learning theorists focus on the role of the environment, including the influence of models and social reinforcement, as factors influencing aggressive behavior.

- The cognitive approach to aggression emphasizes the role of interpretations of the behaviors of others in determining aggressive or nonaggressive responses.

**LO 10.10 Explain the kinds of effects violent TV programs and video games can have on preschool-age children.**

- Lab observations suggest that frequent exposure to violent TV shows leads to higher levels of aggression in children, including bullying. Longitudinal studies have linked a preference for violent TV shows at age 8 to serious criminal convictions in adulthood.

- Through social learning principles, children can learn to control the aggressive feelings brought on by exposure to violent media. They can be explicitly taught to view violence with a critical eye, and exposed to models of *non*aggression.

# Key Terms and Concepts

psychosocial development (p. 257)

initiative-versus-guilt stage (p. 257)

self-concept (p. 257)

collectivistic orientation (p. 258)

individualistic orientation (p. 258)

race dissonance (p. 259)

identification (p. 261)

gender identity (p. 262)

gender schema (p. 262)

gender constancy (p. 262)

functional play (p. 264)

constructive play (p. 264)

parallel play (p. 264)

onlooker play (p. 264)

associative play (p. 264)

cooperative play (p. 265)

authoritarian parents (p. 269)

permissive parents (p. 269)

authoritative parents (p. 269)

uninvolved parents (p. 269)

moral development (p. 271)

prosocial behavior (p. 273)

abstract modeling (p. 273)

empathy (p. 274)

aggression (p. 275)

emotional self-
regulation (p. 275)

instrumental
aggression (p. 275)

relational aggression (p. 275)

# Putting It All Together

## The Preschool Years

### Physical, Cognitive, and Social and Personality Development in the Preschool Years

*At the beginning of the preschool years, some children may initially be shy and passive in social situations with peers. They do not always understand the dynamics of social interaction with other children, and they may not yet have the skills to stand up for themselves or solve problems that arise. As preschoolers become older, however, they improve their ability to navigate the complex social dynamics of peer interaction. Older preschoolers can use their newfound moral sense, together with their evolving language skills, to successfully participate in more complex interactions, and to solve problems that arise in a social context.*

### Physical Development

- Preschoolers grow bigger, heavier, and stronger during these years **(p. 196)**.

- Their brains grow, along with their cognitive abilities, including the ability to plan and to use language as a tool **(p. 197)**.

- Preschoolers learn to use and control their gross and fine motor skills **(p. 210)**.

### Cognitive Development

- During the preschool years, a child's memory capabilities increase **(p. 224)**.

- Preschoolers watch others and learn from peers and from adults how to handle different situations **(p. 227)**.

- Preschoolers use their growing language skills to function more effectively **(p. 230)**.

### Social and Personality Development

- Preschool-age children use play as a way to grow socially, cognitively, and physically **(p. 252)**.

- Preschoolers learn the rules of play, such as turn-taking and playing fairly **(p. 259–60)**.

- They also develop theories of mind that help them to understand what others are thinking **(p. 254)**.

- They develop the beginnings of a sense of justice and moral behavior **(p. 259–260)**.

- They are eventually able to adjust their emotions to a desired intensity level and can use language to express their wishes and deal with others **(p. 262)**.

## From a PARENT'S perspective:

- How would you help a shy preschooler become more assertive, both at home and at school? How would you help him prepare to deal with bullies in preschool and older siblings at home?

  **HINT: Review pages 251–253.**

## From a SOCIAL WORKER'S perspective:

- How would you help the parents of a preschooler provide appropriate kinds of discipline? How would you help them to optimize their home environment to promote physical, cognitive, and social development for their children?

  **HINT: Review pages 255–257.**

## From an EDUCATOR'S perspective:

- What strategies would you use to promote cognitive and social development? How would you deal with instances of bullying in your preschool classroom, both in terms of children who were victimized as well as dealing with the bully?

  **HINT: Review pages 261–265.**

## From YOUR perspective:

- What would you do to promote a preschooler's development? What specific advice would you give to parents and teachers on how to help a preschooler overcome his shyness and to interact more effectively with other children?

  **HINT: Review pages 251–253.**

# Chapter 11
# Physical Development in Middle Childhood

 ## Learning Objectives

**LO 11.1** Describe the ways in which children grow during the school years and the factors that influence their growth.

**LO 11.2** Explain the nutritional needs of school-age children and the consequences of improper nutrition.

**LO 11.3** List the causes and effects of childhood obesity and explain how can it be treated.

**LO 11.4** Summarize the health threats faced by school-age children.

**LO 11.5** Describe the psychological disorders that affect school-age children.

LO 11.6 Explain how motor development evolves during middle childhood.

LO 11.7 Discuss the safety threats that affect school-age children and what can be done about them.

LO 11.8 Explain the effects of visual, auditory, and speech problems on school-age children.

LO 11.9 Describe attention-deficit/hyperactivity disorder and the methods that are used to treat it.

# Prologue: A Heads-Up Play

It was nine-year-old Mira Singh's first basketball game. She had encouraging parents who supported her playing basketball. Buoyed by parental encouragement, Mira had tried out for her class team and now she is playing for the school team. In a match, she was given a chance to shoot the ball, but she missed. The second player took over, started dribbling, and passed it again to Mira; though Mira was focusing, she missed it again. Though she was disappointed, Mira remained alert. Her coach had always said, "Basketball is more than jumping and catching. You need to use your head." Now, it was her last chance to shoot the ball. She could see her partner throwing the ball to her; and this time, Mira could catch, dribble, and with appropriate aim throw the ball into the basket. Her school won the match.

# Looking Ahead

Middle childhood is characterized by a procession of moments such as these, as children's physical, cognitive, and social skills ascend to new heights. In this chapter, we focus on the physical aspects of middle childhood, both in typical children and in children with special needs. Beginning at age 6 and continuing to the start of adolescence at around age 12, middle childhood is often referred to as the "school years" because it marks the beginning of formal education for most children. Sometimes the physical and cognitive growth that occurs during middle childhood is gradual, other times it is sudden, but always it is remarkable.

We begin our consideration of middle childhood by examining physical and motor development. We discuss how children's bodies change and the twin problems of malnutrition and—the other side of the coin—childhood obesity. Subsequently, we turn to motor development. We examine the growth of gross and fine motor skills and the role that physical competence plays in children's lives. We also discuss threats to children's safety, including a new one that enters the home through the personal computer.

Finally, the chapter ends with a discussion of some of the special needs that affect the sensory and physical abilities of exceptional children. It concludes by focusing on the question of how children with special needs should be integrated into society.

# The Growing Body

*Cinderella, dressed in yella,*
*Went upstairs to kiss her fellah.*
*But she made a mistake and kissed a snake.*
*How many doctors did it take?*
*One, two, …*

While the other girls chanted the classic jump-rope rhyme, Kat proudly displayed her newly developed ability to jump backward. In second grade, Kat was starting to get quite good at jumping rope. In first grade, she had not been able to master it. But over the summer, she had spent many hours practicing, and now that practice seemed to be paying off.

As Kat is gleefully experiencing, middle childhood is the time when children make great physical strides, mastering all kinds of new skills as they grow bigger and stronger. How does this progress occur?

## Physical Development

**LO 11.1  Describe the ways in which children grow during the school years and the factors that influence their growth.**

If three words could characterize the nature of growth during middle childhood, they would be *slow but steady*. Especially when compared to the swift growth during the first 5 years of life and the remarkable growth spurt characteristic of adolescence, middle childhood is relatively tranquil. But the body has not shifted into neutral. Physical growth continues, although at a slower pace than it did during the preschool years.

While they are in elementary school, children in the United States grow, on average, 2 to 3 inches a year. By age 11, the average height for girls is 4 feet, 10 inches, and the average height for boys is slightly shorter at 4 feet, 9 1/2 inches. This is the only time during the life span when girls are, on average, taller than boys. This height difference reflects the slightly more rapid physical development of girls, who start their adolescent growth spurt around age 10.

Weight gain follows a similar pattern. During middle childhood, both boys and girls gain around 5 to 7 pounds a year. Weight is also redistributed. As the rounded look of "baby fat" disappears, children's bodies become more muscular.

These average height and weight increases disguise significant individual differences, as anyone who has seen a line of fourth graders walking down a school corridor has doubtless noticed. It is not unusual to see children of the same age who are 6 or 7 inches apart in height.

Middle childhood is also characterized by increased strength. During this period, children double their strength, with boys typically stronger than girls due to their greater number of muscle cells. In addition, children's bones become harder, a process called *ossification*.

Significant tooth development occurs during middle childhood. Around age 6, primary teeth start falling out and are replaced by permanent teeth. Permanent teeth replace primary teeth at the rate of about four per year starting at age 6.

## Nutrition: Links to Overall Functioning

**LO 11.2  Explain the nutritional needs of school-age children and the consequences of improper nutrition.**

The level of nutrition children experience during their lives significantly affects many aspects of their behavior. For instance, research conducted over many years in Guatemalan villages shows that children's nutritional backgrounds are related to several dimensions of social and emotional functioning at school age. Children who received more nutrients were more involved with their peers, showed more positive emotion, had less anxiety, and had more moderate activity levels than their peers who had received less adequate nutrition (Barrett & Frank, 1987; Stutts et al., 2011; Nyaradi et al., 2013).

Nutrition is also linked to cognitive performance. For instance, in one study, children in Kenya who were well nourished performed better on a test of verbal abilities and on other cognitive measures than those who had mild to moderate undernutrition. Other research suggests that malnutrition may influence cognitive development by dampening children's curiosity, responsiveness, and motivation to learn (Wachs, 2002; Grigorenko, 2003; Drewett, 2007; Kessels et al., 2011; Jackson, 2015; Tooley, Makhoul, & Fisher, 2016).

**CULTURAL PATTERNS OF GROWTH.**  Most children in North America receive sufficient nutrients to grow to their full potential. In other parts of the world, however, inadequate nutrition and disease take their toll, producing children who are shorter and weigh less than they would if they had sufficient nutrients.

Children in poorer areas of cities, such as these youngsters in Kolkata, are shorter and weigh less than those who were raised in more affluent places.

The discrepancies can be dramatic: Children in poorer areas of cities such as Kolkata, Hong Kong, and Rio de Janeiro are smaller than their counterparts in affluent areas of the same cities.

In the United States, most variations in height and weight are the result of different people's unique genetic inheritance, including genetic factors relating to racial and ethnic background. For instance, children from Asian and Oceanic Pacific backgrounds tend to be shorter, on average, than those with northern and central European heritages. In addition, the rate of growth during childhood is generally more rapid for Blacks than for Whites (Deurenberg, Deurenberg-Yap, & Guricci, 2002; Deurenberg et al., 2003).

Of course, even within particular racial and ethnic groups, there is significant variation between individuals. Moreover, we cannot attribute racial and ethnic differences solely to genetic factors because dietary customs as well as possible variations in levels of affluence also may contribute to the differences. Further, severe stress—brought on by factors such as parental conflict or alcoholism—can affect the functioning of the pituitary gland, thereby affecting growth (Koska et al., 2002).

**PROMOTING GROWTH WITH HORMONES: SHOULD SHORT CHILDREN BE MADE TO GROW?** Being tall is considered an advantage by most of U.S. society. Because of this cultural preference, parents frequently worry about their children's growth if their children are short. Some parents react by giving their children artificial human growth hormones that can make short children grow taller than

they naturally would (Sandberg & Voss, 2002; Lagrou et al., 2008; Pinquart, 2013).

Should children be given such drugs? The question is a relatively new one: Artificial hormones to promote growth have become available only in the past two decades. Although tens of thousands of children who have insufficient natural growth hormone are taking such drugs, some observers question whether shortness is a serious enough problem to warrant the use of the drug. Certainly, one can function well in society without being tall. Furthermore, the drug is costly and has potentially dangerous side effects. In some cases, the drug may lead to the premature onset of puberty, which may—ironically—restrict later growth.

However, there is no denying that artificial growth hormones are effective in increasing children's height, in some cases adding well over a foot in height to extremely short children, placing them within normal height ranges. Ultimately, until long-term studies of the safety of such treatments are completed, parents and medical personnel must carefully weigh the pros and cons before administering the drug to their children (Heyman et al., 2003; Ogilvy-Stuart & Gleeson, 2004; Wang et al., 2011; Webb et al., 2012; Dykens, Roof, & Hunt-Hawkins, 2016).

> **From a health care provider's perspective:** Under what circumstances would you recommend the use of a growth hormone? Is shortness primarily a physical or a cultural problem?

## Childhood Obesity

**LO 11.3** List causes and effects of childhood obesity and explain how can it be treated.

*When her mother asks Ruby if she would like butter on her roti with her meal, Ruby replies that she had better not—she thinks that she may be getting fat. Ruby, who is of normal weight and height, is 6 years old.*

Although height can be of concern to both children and parents during middle childhood, maintaining the appropriate weight is an even greater worry for some. Concern about weight can border on obsession, particularly among girls. For instance, many 6-year-old girls worry about becoming fat, and some 40 percent of 9- and 10-year-olds are trying to lose weight. Why?

In spite of this widely held view that thinness is a virtue, increasing numbers of children are obese in middle childhood. *Obesity* is defined as a BMI (body mass index) at or above the 95th percentile for children of the same age and sex.

There are very few research or survey available on obesity among children in India. A research done among children in South India found that there has been an increase from 4.94 percent in 2003 to 6.75 percent in 2005 in the total number of students affected by obesity thus suggesting its rapid growth as an epidemic (Raj, Paul, Deepa, & Kumar, 2007). In North India, childhood obesity prevalence of 5.59 percent in the higher socio-economic strata compared to 0.42 percent in the lower socio-economic strata has been reported (Marwaha, Tandon, Singh, et al., 2006).

Various agencies have reported different prevalence rates for overweight and obesity in 8- and 18-year-old children, respectively: International Obesity Task Force (IOTF) cutoffs 14.4 percent and 2.8 percent, Center for Disease Control (CDC) cutoffs 14.5 percent and 4.8 percent, and World Health Organization (WHO) cutoffs 18.5 percent and 5.3 percent (Misra et al., 2011). Based on these data, it was projected that 3.16 million urban boys and 5.39 million urban girls in India would have abdominal obesity. Epidemiological studies have showed a substantial burden of abdominal obesity among children in India. Obesity is an important determinant of Type-II diabetes (Ehtisham, Barrett, et al., 2002).

Praveen and Tandon (2016) have suggested the need for a life-course approach in the prevention and control of childhood obesity. A comprehensive multilevel, multicomponent obesity-prevention strategy addressing a wide range of issues, starting from maternal and childhood undernutrition, and including sociodemographic and environmental factors, is a necessity in India.

The costs of childhood obesity last a lifetime. Children who are obese are more likely to be overweight as adults, as well as having a greater risk of heart disease, diabetes, and other diseases. Some scientists believe that an epidemic of obesity may be leading to a decline in life span in the United States. (Krishnamoorthy, Hart, & Jelalian, 2006; Park, 2008; Mehlenbeck, Farmer, & Ward, 2014).

**CAUSES OF OBESITY.** Obesity is caused by a combination of genetic and environmental factors. Particular inherited genes are related to obesity and predispose certain children to be overweight. For example, adopted children tend to have weights that are more similar to those of their birth parents than to those of their adoptive parents (Whitaker et al., 1997; Bray, 2008; Skledar et al., 2012; Maggi et al., 2015).

But it is not just a matter of a genetic predisposition that leads to weight problems. Poor diet also contributes to obesity. Despite their knowledge that certain foods are necessary for a balanced, nutritious diet, many parents provide their children with too few fruits and vegetables and more fats and sweets than recommended. School lunch programs have sometimes contributed to the problem by failing to provide nutritious options (Johnston, Delva, & O'Malley, 2007; Story, Nanney, & Schwartz, 2009).

Another major factor in childhood obesity is a lack of exercise. School-age children, by and large, tend to engage in relatively little exercise and are not particularly fit. For instance, around 40 percent of boys ages 6 to 12 are unable to do more than one pull-up, and a quarter can't do any. Furthermore, school fitness surveys reveal that children in the United States have shown little or no improvement in the amount of exercise they get, despite national efforts to increase the level of fitness of school-age children. From ages 6 to 18, boys decrease their physical activity by 24 percent and girls by 36 percent (Moore, Gao, & Bradlee, 2003; Stork & Sanders, 2008; Ige, DeLeon, & Nabors, 2017).

Why, when our visions of childhood include children running happily on school playgrounds, playing sports, and chasing one another in games of tag, is the actual level of exercise relatively low? One answer is that many kids are inside their homes, watching television and computer screens. Such sedentary activities not only keep children from exercising, but often also encourage them to snack while viewing TV, playing video games, or surfing the Web (Davis et al., 2011; Goldfield, 2012; Cale & Harris, 2013; Lambrick et al., 2016).

Furthermore, many children return from school to homes without adult supervision because their parents are at work. In such situations, parents may prohibit their children from leaving the home for safety reasons, meaning that children are unable to engage in exercise even if they wanted to (Murphy & Polivka, 2007; Speroni, Earley, & Atherton, 2007).

**TREATING OBESITY.** Regardless of what causes a child to become obese, treatment is tricky, because creating too strong a concern about food and dieting

# BECOMING AN INFORMED CONSUMER OF CHILD DEVELOPMENT

## Keeping Children Fit

*From Monday to Friday, Terry sits at a desk all day. He gets no physical exercise, not even on weekends. He eats high-fat, low-nutrition meals both at home and at fast-food restaurants. He spends evenings on the sofa staring at the tube, munching on potato chips and guzzling sodas.*

Although this sketch could apply to many adult men and women, Terry is actually a 6-year-old. He is one of many school-age children in the United States who get little or no regular exercise and who are consequently physically unfit and at risk for obesity and other health problems.

Several things can be done to encourage children to become more physically active (Tyre & Scelfo, 2003; Okie, 2005):

- *Make exercise fun.* In order for children to build the habit of exercising, they need to find it enjoyable. Activities that keep children on the sidelines or that are overly competitive may give children with inferior skills a lifelong distaste for exercise.
- *Be an exercise role model.* Children who see that exercise is a regular part of the lives of their parents, teachers, or adult friends may come to think of fitness as a regular part of their lives, too.
- *Gear activities to the child's physical level and motor skills.* For instance, use child-size equipment that can make participants feel successful.

- *Encourage the child to find a partner.* It could be a friend, a sibling, or a parent. Exercising can involve a variety of activities, such as roller-skating or hiking, but almost all activities are carried out more readily if someone else is doing them, too.
- *Start slowly.* Sedentary children—those who aren't used to regular physical activity—should start off gradually. For instance, they could start with 5 minutes of exercise a day, 7 days a week. Over 10 weeks, they could move toward a goal of 30 minutes of exercise 3 to 5 days a week.
- *Urge participation in organized sports activities, but do not push too hard.* Not every child is athletically inclined, and pushing too hard for involvement in organized sports may backfire. Make participation and enjoyment—not winning—the goals of such activities.
- *Don't make physical activity, such as jumping jacks or push-ups, a punishment for unwanted behavior.* Instead, schools and parents should encourage children to participate in organized programs that seek to involve children in ways that are enjoyable.
- *Provide a healthy diet.* Children who eat a healthy diet will have more energy to engage in physical activity than those who have a diet heavy in soda and snack foods.

must be avoided. Children need to learn to control their eating themselves. Parents who are particularly controlling and directive regarding their children's eating may produce children who lack internal controls to regulate their own food intake (Wardle, Guthrie, & Sanderson, 2001; Okie, 2005; Doub, Small & Brich, 2016).

One strategy is to monitor the food that is available in the home. By stuffing the cupboards and refrigerator with healthy foods—and keeping high-calorie, highly processed foods out of the house—children are essentially forced to eat a healthy diet. Furthermore, avoiding fast foods, which are high in calories and fats, is important (Campbell, Crawford,

& Ball, 2006; Lindsay et al., 2006; Hoerr, Murashima, & Keast, 2008).

Another strategy is to increase the amount of exercise through programs conducted during school recess. When children are engaged in planned recess activities, obesity declines. In fact, simply increasing the amount of recess times is associated with weight loss (Fernandes & Sturm, 2010; Ickes, Erwin & Beighle, 2013).

In most cases, the goal of treatment for obesity is to temporarily maintain a child's current weight through an improved diet and increased exercise, rather than actually seeking to lose weight. In time, obese children's normal growth in height will result in their weight becoming more normal.

# Health During Middle Childhood

**LO 11.4** Summarize the health threats faced by school-age children.

*Imani was miserable. Her nose was running, her lips were chapped, and her throat was sore. Although she had been able to stay home from school and spend the day watching old reruns on TV, she still felt that she was suffering mightily.*

Despite her misery, Imani's situation is not so bad. She'll get over the cold in a few days and be no worse for having experienced it. In fact, she may be a little *better* off, for she is now immune to the specific cold germs that made her ill in the first place.

Imani's cold may end up being the most serious illness that she gets during middle childhood. For most children, this is a period of robust health, and most of the ailments they do contract tend to be mild and brief. Routine immunizations during childhood have produced a considerably lower incidence of the life-threatening illnesses that 50 years ago claimed the lives of a significant number of children.

Illness is not uncommon, however. For instance, more than 90 percent of children are likely to have at least one serious medical condition over the 6-year period of middle childhood, according to the results of one large survey. And although most children have short-term illnesses, about one in nine has a chronic, persistent condition, such as repeated migraine headaches. And some illnesses are actually becoming more prevalent (Dey & Bloom, 2005).

Asthma is among the diseases that have shown a significant increase in prevalence in recent decades. **Asthma** is a chronic condition characterized by periodic attacks of wheezing, coughing, and shortness of breath. More than 7 million U.S. children suffer from this disorder, and worldwide, the number is more than 150 million. Racial and ethnic minorities are particularly at risk for the disease (Akinbami, 2011; Celano, Holsey & Kobrynski, 2012; Bowen, 2013; Gandhi et al., 2016).

Asthma occurs when the airways leading to the lungs constrict, partially blocking the passage of air. Because the airways are obstructed, more effort is needed to push air through them, making breathing more difficult. As air is forced through the obstructed airways, it makes the whistling sound called wheezing.

Not surprisingly, children are often exceedingly frightened by asthma attacks, and the anxiety and

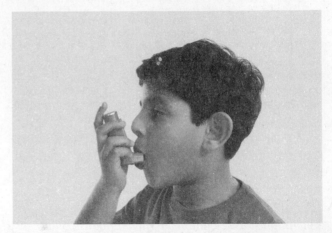

The incidence of asthma, a chronic respiratory condition, has increased dramatically over the past several decades.

agitation produced by their breathing difficulties may actually make the attack worse. In some cases, breathing becomes so difficult that further physical symptoms develop, including sweating, an increased heart rate, and—in the most severe cases—blueness in the face and lips due to a lack of oxygen.

Asthma attacks are triggered by a variety of factors. Among the most common are respiratory infections (such as colds or flu), allergic reactions to airborne irritants (such as pollution, cigarette smoke, dust mites, and animal dander and excretions), stress, and exercise. Sometimes even a sudden change in air temperature or humidity is enough to bring on an attack (Tibosch, Verhaak, & Merkus, 2011; Ross et al., 2012; Sicouri et al., 2017).

Although asthma can be serious, treatment is increasingly effective for those who suffer from the disorder. Some children who experience frequent asthma attacks use a small aerosol container with a special mouthpiece to spray drugs into the lungs. Other patients take tablets or receive injections (Israel, 2005).

One of the most puzzling questions about asthma is why more and more children are suffering from it. Some researchers suggest that increasing air pollution has led to the rise; others believe that cases of asthma that might have been missed in the past are being identified more accurately. Still others have suggested that exposure to "asthma triggers," such as dust, may be increasing because new buildings are more weatherproof—and therefore less drafty—than old ones, and consequently the flow of air within them is more restricted.

---

**asthma** A chronic condition characterized by periodic attacks of wheezing, coughing, and shortness of breath

Finally, poverty may play an indirect role. Children living in poverty have a higher incidence of asthma than other children, probably due to poorer medical care and less sanitary living conditions. For instance, poor youngsters are more likely than more affluent ones to be exposed to triggering factors that are associated with asthma, such as dust mites, cockroach feces and body parts, and rodent feces and urine (Johnson, 2003; Caron, Gjelsvik, & Buechner, 2005; Coutinho, McQuaid & Koinis-Mitchell, 2013).

## Psychological Disorders

**LO 11.5  Describe the psychological disorders that affect school-age children.**

*At just under 4 ½ feet tall, 7-year-old Ron Turner is striking, with curly brown hair and deep brown eyes. He is charming one minute and angry, suspicious, and hostile the next. He can move from uproarious laughter to deep depression in the blink of an eye. He has little sense of danger, running headlong through the woods, bouncing off trees, and tumbling head over heels down hills. Ron has bipolar disorder, a serious illness, which leaves his parents distraught and Ron himself frightened and unhappy.*

Bipolar disorder such as Ron's is diagnosed when a person cycles back and forth between two emotional states: unrealistically high spirits and energy at one extreme, and depression on the other. For years, most people neglected the symptoms of such psychological disorders in children, and even today parents and teachers may overlook their presence.

Yet psychological disorders are not uncommon: Between 13 percent and 20 percent of children living in the United States experience a mental disorder in a given year. For example, about 5 percent of preteens suffer from childhood major depressive disorder, and 13 percent of children between ages 9 and 17 experience an anxiety disorder. The estimated cost of treatment of children's psychological disorders is $250 billion (Tolan & Dodge, 2005; Cicchetti & Cohen, 2006; Kluger, 2010; Holly et al., 2015).

Furthermore, the prevalence of psychological conditions has increased over the past several decades. Although there is no clear explanation for the increase—it may simply be due to an increase in the use of diagnostic labels, rather than an actual rise in the incidence of disorder—it is clear that psychological disorders affect many children.

Part of the difficulty in diagnosing psychological disorders occurs because children's symptoms are not entirely consistent with the ways adults express similar disorders. Moreover, even when childhood psychological disorders are diagnosed, the correct treatment is not always apparent. For example, antidepressant drugs have become a popular treatment for a variety of childhood psychological disorders, including major depressive disorder and anxiety. More than 10 million prescriptions are written for children under age 18. Surprisingly, though, antidepressant drugs have never been approved by governmental regulators for use with children. Still, because the drugs have received approval for adult use, it is perfectly legal for physicians to write prescriptions for children (Goode, 2004).

Advocates for the increased use of antidepressants such as Prozac, Zoloft, Paxil, and Wellbutrin for children suggest that depression and other psychological disorders can be treated quite successfully using drug therapies. In many cases, more traditional nondrug therapies that largely employ traditional psychotherapy simply are ineffective. In such cases, drugs can provide the only form of relief. Furthermore, at least one clinical test has shown that the drugs are effective in children (Vela et al., 2011; Hirschtritt et al., 2012; Lawrence et al., 2017).

Critics, however, contend that there is little evidence for the long-term effectiveness of antidepressants in children. Even worse, no one knows the consequences of the use of antidepressants on children's developing brains, nor the long-term consequences more generally. Little is known about the correct dosages for children of given ages or sizes. Furthermore, some observers suggest that the use of special children's versions of the drugs, in orange- or mint-flavored syrups, might lead to overdoses or perhaps eventually encourage the use of illegal drugs (Cheung, Emslie, & Mayes, 2006; Rothenberger & Rothenberger, 2013; Seedat, 2014).

Finally, there is some evidence linking the use of antidepressant medication with an increased risk of suicide. Although the link has not been firmly established, the U.S. Food and Drug Administration issued a warning about the use of a class of antidepressants known as SSRIs in 2004. Some experts have urged a complete ban on the use of these antidepressants in children and adolescents (Bostwick, 2006; Gören, 2008; Sammons, 2009).

Although the use of antidepressant drugs to treat children is controversial, it is clear that childhood depression and other psychological disorders remain a significant problem for many children. Childhood psychological disorders must not be ignored. Not only are the disorders disruptive during childhood, but those who suffer from psychological problems as children are at risk for future disorders during adulthood (Vedantam, 2004; Bostwick, 2006; Sapyla & March, 2012).

As we'll see later in the chapter, adults also need to pay attention to other, ongoing special needs that affect many school-age children.

# Motor Development and Safety

*Pratham Gupta was different from the other kids in fourth grade. He hated kickball but loved books. He didn't play video games but adored checkers and Monopoly. And he liked schoolwork, even for math and history.*

*Pratham's parents encouraged him to try sports, but no matter what he tried—football, cricket, basketball—he came to the same conclusion: "This isn't for me."*

*Then one day he saw an Olympic gymnastics competition on TV and, out of the blue, said to his mother, "That's it. That's what I'd like to do. Can Dad teach me that?"*

*Dad couldn't, but a local gymnastics center could. Pratham enrolled and was hooked. Now he takes classes three times a week and is working toward his first competition in the spring.*

*According to his mother, he's changed in more ways than just the physical. "Pratham is happier, he talks more, and he's got more friends. It's like he's had a new engine installed."*

During middle childhood, children's athletic abilities play an important role in determining how they see themselves, as well as how they are viewed by others. This is also a time when such physical proficiencies develop substantially.

## Motor Skills: Continuing Improvement

**LO 11.6  Explain how motor development evolves during middle childhood.**

Watching a schoolyard softball player pitch a ball past a batter to the catcher or a third-grade runner reach the finish line in a race, it is hard not to be struck by the huge strides that children have made since the more awkward days of preschool. Both gross and fine motor skills improve significantly during the middle childhood years.

**GROSS MOTOR SKILLS.**  One important improvement in gross motor skills is in the realm of muscle coordination. For instance, most school-age children can readily learn to ride a bike, ice skate, swim, and jump rope, skills that earlier they could not perform well (see Figure 11.1).

Do boys and girls differ in their motor skills? Years ago, developmentalists contended that gender differences in gross motor skills become increasingly pronounced during these years, with boys outperforming girls (Espenschade, 1960). More recent research, however, casts some doubt on this claim. When comparisons are made between boys and girls who regularly take part in similar activities such as softball, gender variations in gross motor skills are found to be minimal (Jurimae & Saar, 2003).

What accounts for the discrepancy in earlier observations? Performance differences were probably found because of differences in motivation and expectations. Society told girls that they would do worse than boys in sports, and the girls' performance reflected that message.

Today, however, society's message has changed, at least officially. For instance, the American Academy of Pediatrics suggests that boys and girls should engage in the same sports and games and that they can do so together in mixed-gender groups. There

During middle childhood, children master many types of skills that earlier they could not perform well, such as riding a bike, ice skating, swimming, and skipping rope.

## Figure 11.1    Gross Motor Skills Developed Between the Ages of 6 and 12 Years

Why would it be important that a social worker be aware of this period of development?

**SOURCE:** Adapted from Cratty, Bryant J. (1979). Perceptual and Motor Development in Infants and Children. Second Edition. New Jersey: Prentice Hall.

| 6 Years | 7 Years | 8 Years | 9 Years | 10 Years | 11 Years | 12 Years |
|---|---|---|---|---|---|---|
| Girls superior in accuracy of movement; boys superior in more forceful, less complex acts.<br><br>Can throw with the proper weight shift and step.<br><br>Acquire the ability to skip. | Can balance on one foot with eyes closed.<br><br>Can walk on a 2-inch-wide balance beam without falling off.<br><br>Can hop and jump accurately into small squares (hopscotch).<br><br>Can correctly execute a jumping-jack exercise. | Can grip objects with 12 pounds of pressure.<br><br>Can engage in alternate rhythmical hopping in a 2-2, 2-3, or 3-3 pattern.<br><br>Girls can throw a small ball 33 feet; boys can throw a small ball 59 feet.<br><br>The number of games participated in by both sexes is the greatest at this age. | Girls can jump vertically 8.5 inches over their standing height plus reach; boys can jump vertically 10 inches.<br><br>Boys can run 16.6 feet per second and throw a small ball 41 feet; girls can run 16 feet per second and throw a small ball 41 feet. | Can judge and intercept directions of small balls thrown from a distance.<br><br>Both girls and boys can run 17 feet per second. | Boys can achieve standing broad jump of 5 feet; girls can achieve standing broad jump of 4.5 feet. | Can achieve high jump of 3 feet. |

is no reason to separate the sexes in physical exercise and sports until puberty, when the smaller size of females begins to make them more susceptible to injury in contact sports (American Academy of Pediatrics, 2004; Kanters et al., 2013; Deaner, Balish, & Lombardo, 2016).

**FINE MOTOR SKILLS.**   Typing at a computer keyboard, writing in cursive with pen or pencil, drawing detailed

Fine motor skills, such as typing on a keyboard, improve during early and middle childhood.

pictures—these are just some of the accomplishments that depend on improvements in fine motor coordination that occur during early and middle childhood. Children 6 and 7 years old are able to tie their shoes and fasten buttons; by age 8, they can use each hand independently; and by 11 and 12, they can manipulate objects with almost as much dexterity as they will have in adulthood.

One reason for advances in fine motor skills is that the amount of myelin in the brain increases significantly between the ages of 6 and 8. *Myelin* provides protective insulation around parts of nerve cells. Because increased levels of myelin raise the speed at which electrical impulses travel between neurons, messages can reach muscles more rapidly and control them better.

**THE SOCIAL BENEFITS OF PHYSICAL COMPETENCE.** Is Matt, a fifth grader who is a clear standout on his Saturday morning soccer team, more popular as a result of his physical talents?

He may well be. According to a long history of research on the topic, school-age children who perform well physically are often more accepted and better liked by their peers than those who perform less well (Pintney, Forlands, & Freedman, 1937; Branta, Lerner, & Taylor, 1997).

The link between physical competence and popularity, however, is considerably stronger for boys than it is for girls. The reason for this sex difference most likely relates to differing societal standards for appropriate male and female behavior. Despite the increasing evidence that girls and boys do not differ substantially in athletic performance, a lingering "physical toughness" standard still exists for males but not for females. Regardless of age, males who are bigger, stronger, and more physically competent are seen as more desirable than those who are smaller, weaker, and less physically competent. In contrast, standards for females are less supportive of physical success. In fact, women receive less admiration for physical prowess than men do throughout the life span. These societal standards may be changing, with women's participation in sports activities becoming more frequent and valued; however, gender biases remain (Bowker, Gadbois, & Cornock, 2003).

Although the social desirability of athletically proficient boys increases throughout elementary school and continues into secondary school, at some point the positive consequences of motor ability begin to diminish. Presumably, other traits become increasingly important in determining social attractiveness—some of which we'll discuss in Chapter 13.

Furthermore, it is difficult to sort out the extent to which advantages from exceptional physical performance are due to actual athletic competence, as opposed to being a result of earlier maturation. Boys who physically mature at a more rapid pace than their peers or who happen to be taller, heavier, and stronger tend to perform better at athletic activities due to their relative size advantage. Consequently, it may be that early physical maturity is ultimately of greater consequence than physical skills per se.

Still, it is clear that athletic competence and motor skills in general play a notable role in school-age children's lives; however, it is important to help children avoid overemphasizing the significance of physical ability. Participation in sports should be fun, not something that separates one child from another or raises children's and parents' anxiety levels. Consequently, it is important to match the sport to a child's level of development. When the skills required by participation in a sport go beyond children's physical and mental capabilities, they

The goals of participation in sports and other physical activities should be to maintain physical fitness, learn physical skills, and have fun in the process.

may feel inadequate and frustrated (American Academy of Pediatrics, 2001).

In fact, some forms of organized sports, such as Little League baseball, are sometimes criticized for the emphasis they may place on winning at any cost. When children feel that success in sports is the sole goal, the pleasure of playing the game is diminished, particularly for children who are not naturally athletic and do not excel (Weber, 2005).

In sum, the goals of participation in sports and other physical activities should be to maintain physical fitness, to learn physical skills, and to become comfortable with one's body—and children should have fun in the process.

## Threats to Children's Safety, Offline and Online

**LO 11.7 Discuss the safety threats that affect school-age children and what can be done about them.**

The increasing independence and mobility of school-age children give rise to new safety issues. In fact, the rate of injury for children increases between the ages of 5 and 14. Boys are more apt to be injured than girls, probably because their overall level of physical activity is greater. Some ethnic and racial groups are at greater risk than others:

**ACCIDENTS.** The increased mobility of school-age children is a source of several kinds of accidents. For instance, children who regularly walk to school on their own, many traveling such a distance alone for the first time in their lives, face the risk of being hit by a car or a truck. Because of their lack of experience, they may misjudge distances when calculating just how far they are from an oncoming vehicle. Furthermore, bicycle accidents pose an increasing risk, particularly as children more frequently venture out onto busy roads (Schnitzer, 2006; Green, Muir, & Maher, 2011).

The most frequent source of injury to children is automobile accidents.

Two ways to reduce auto and bicycle injuries are to use seat belts consistently inside the car and to wear appropriate protective gear outside. Bicycle helmets have significantly reduced head injuries, and in many localities their use is mandatory. Similar protection is available for other activities; for example, knee and elbow pads have proven to be important sources of injury reduction for rollerblading and skateboarding (Lee, Schofer, & Koppelman, 2005; Blake et al., 2008; Lachapelle, Noland & Von Hagen, 2013).

**CRIME AGAINST CHILDREN.** The offences committed against children or the crimes in which children are the victims, are considered as **Crime Against Children**. During 2016, the major crimes under crimes against children in India were kidnapping and abduction (52.3%) and cases under the Protection of Children from Sexual Offences Act, 2012 (34.4%) including child rape. The maximum number of cases under crime against children were reported in the states of Uttar Pradesh, Maharashtra, and Madhya Pradesh with figures of 15.3 percent, 13.6 percent, and 13.1 percent, respectively.

A total of 1,11,569 children (41,175 males and 70,394 females) were reported missing in which the maximum children missing were reported from West Bengal (16,881 children—4,595 males and 12,286 females) followed by Delhi (14,661 children—6,125 males and 8,536 females), and Madhya Pradesh (12,068 children—3,446 males and 8,622 females) during 2016 (National Crime Record Bureau).

**SAFETY IN CYBERSPACE.** One contemporary threat to the safety of school-age children comes from the Internet. Cyberspace makes available material that many parents find objectionable.

There are more than 400 million people who have access to the Internet either through smartphones or computers. Though the users in urban areas outnumbered that of rural areas, children in general are susceptible to cyber crimes. Due to the lack of comprehensive surveys, there are no reliable figures on the extent, patterns, and trends of child online abuse and exploitation in India. The following is a summary of the report prepared by UNICEF (2016) on cybercrime in children:

- In terms of children's Internet usage, the Internet and Mobile Association of India (IAMAI) survey undertaken in 35 Indian cities indicated that about 28 million out of a total of 400 million Internet users were school-going children.

- Children's digital literacy is an emerging challenge in India. In 2012, Telenor India did a study on child online safety in 12 countries and found that children in India are in the highest risk category due to a combination of increased access enabled by affordable Internet and smartphones, low resilience with parents, and children lacking the knowledge of how to safeguard themselves against different cyber threats.

- A study commissioned by Microsoft in 2012 ranked India third for high online bullying rates (after China and Singapore) among 25 countries that were surveyed. The study noted, half of the Indian children aged 8–17 years who responded to the survey said that they had been subjected to a range of online activities that some may consider to be online bullying or to have adverse effects. About 22 percent reported being subjected to mean or unfriendly treatment, 29 percent had been made fun of or teased, and 25 percent had been called mean names. The findings of recent research indicate similar or higher rates of cyberbullying in India with a significant number of children reporting having witnessed some acts of cyberbullying. The 2014 report of the Parliamentary Committee on Information Technology recognized that online bullying of children by their peers was probably far more common than other offences.

- In January 2016, six youths and two minors were arrested for their alleged involvement in two different rape cases at a homestay in Fort Kochi in Kerala. The same person allegedly recorded the sexual assaults on his mobile phone to blackmail the victims in both the incidents. After the sexual offenders were arrested, the police recovered images of another assault from their mobile phone. The other incident had taken place earlier in the month and also involved two minors (*The Indian Express*, 25 January 2016).

- In March 2016, the arrest of a college dropout in a blackmail and rape case in Bahadurpura in Hyderabad revealed shocking details of sexual exploitation, extortion, and criminal intimidation of a teenage girl over a period of three years. The youth had shot some videos of intimate moments during a brief relationship with the victim's sister and used these to blackmail and rape the 17-year-old victim in 2012 (*Deccan Chronicle*, 22 March 2016).

Although certain programs can be used to automatically block known sites that are dangerous to children or that contain objectionable material, most experts feel that the most reliable safeguard is close supervision by parents. According to the National Center for Missing and Exploited Children, a nonprofit organization that works with the U.S. Department of Justice, parents should warn their children never to provide personal information, such as home addresses or telephone numbers, to people on public computer "bulletin boards" or in chat rooms. In addition, children should not be allowed to hold face-to-face meetings with people they meet via computer, at least not without a parent present.

> **From an educator's perspective:** Do you think using blocking software or computer chips to screen potentially offensive content on the Internet is a practical idea? A good idea? Are such controls the best way to keep children safe in cyberspace?

There are no reliable statistics that provide a true sense of the risk presented by exposure to cyberspace. But certainly a potential hazard exists, and parents must offer their children guidance. It is wrong to assume that just because children are in the supposed safety of their own bedrooms, logged on to home computers, they are truly safe (Mitchell et al., 2011a; Reio & Ortega, 2016).

# Children With Special Needs

*Sumit Sen, 8, couldn't read. Going to school was misery, and his parents watched his frustration mounting.*

*"We didn't know what to do," said his mother. "Sumit would pretend to be sick so he could stay home. He was falling behind in all his subjects."*

Children with special needs present major challenges for both care providers and teachers.

*Finally, she insisted that the school administer diagnostic tests. It turned out that Sumit had brain processing deficits: He couldn't read because his mind had trouble untangling letters and sounds. Sumit, now officially labeled "learning disabled," had a legal right to help.*

Sumit joined millions of other children who are classified as having a *specific learning disorder*, one of several types of special needs that children can have. Although every child has different specific capabilities, children with *special needs* differ significantly from typical children in terms of physical attributes or learning abilities. Their needs present major challenges for both care providers and teachers.

We turn now to the most prevalent exceptionalities that affect children of average intelligence: sensory difficulties, specific learning disorders, and attention-deficit disorders. (We will consider the special needs of children who are significantly below and above average in Chapter 12.)

## Sensory Difficulties: Visual, Auditory, and Speech Problems

**LO 11.8  Explain the effects of visual, auditory, and speech problems on school-age children.**

Anyone who has temporarily lost his or her eyeglasses or a contact lens has had a glimpse of how difficult even rudimentary everyday tasks must be for those with sensory impairments. To function with less than typical vision, hearing, or speech can be a tremendous challenge.

**Visual impairment** can be considered in both a legal and an educational sense. The definition of legal impairment is quite straightforward: *Blindness* is visual acuity of less than 20/200 after correction (meaning the inability to see even at 20 feet what a typical person can see at 200 feet), whereas *partial sightedness* is visual acuity of less than 20/70 after correction.

Even if individuals are not so severely impaired as to be legally blind, their visual problems may still seriously affect their schoolwork. For one thing, the legal criterion pertains solely to distance vision, while most educational tasks require close-up vision. In addition, the legal definition does not consider abilities in the perception of color, depth, and light—all of which might influence a student's educational success. About 1 student in 1,000 requires special education services relating to a visual impairment.

Most severe visual problems are identified fairly early, but it sometimes happens that an impairment goes undetected. Visual problems can also emerge gradually as children develop physiologically and changes occur in the apparatus of the eye. Parents and teachers need to be aware of the signals of visual problems in children. Frequent eye irritation (redness, sties, or infection), continual blinking and facial contortions when reading, holding reading material unusually close to the face, difficulty in writing, and frequent headaches, dizziness, or burning eyes are some of the signs of visual problems.

**Auditory impairments** can also cause academic problems, and they can produce social difficulties as well, since considerable peer interaction takes place through informal conversation. Hearing loss, which affects 1 to 2 percent of the school-age population, is not simply a matter of not hearing enough. Rather, auditory problems can vary along a number of dimensions (Smith, Bale, & White, 2005; Martin-Prudent et al., 2016).

In some cases of hearing loss, the child's hearing is impaired at only a limited range of frequencies, or pitches. For example, the loss may be great at pitches in the normal speech range yet quite minor in other frequencies, such as those of very high or low sounds. A child with this kind of loss may require different levels of amplification at different frequencies; a hearing aid that indiscriminately amplifies all frequencies equally may be ineffective because it will amplify the sounds the person can hear to an uncomfortable degree.

How a child adapts to this impairment depends on the age at which the hearing loss begins. If the loss of hearing occurs in infancy, the effects will probably be much more severe than if it occurs after the age of 3. Children who have had little or no exposure to the sound of language are unable to understand or produce oral language themselves. Conversely, loss of hearing after a child has learned language will have consequences that are not as serious in terms of subsequent linguistic development. Severe and early loss of hearing is also associated with difficulties in abstract thinking. Because hearing-impaired children may have limited exposure to language, they may have more trouble mastering abstract concepts that can be understood fully only with language than with concrete concepts that can be illustrated visually. For example, it is difficult to explain the concept of "freedom" or "soul" without use of language (Butler & Silliman, 2003; Marschark, Spencer, & Newsom, 2003; Meinzen-Derr et al., 2014).

Auditory difficulties are sometimes accompanied by speech impairments, one of the most public types of exceptionality: Every time the child speaks aloud, the impairment is obvious to listeners. The definition of **speech impairment** suggests that speech is impaired when it deviates so much from the speech of others that it calls attention to itself, interferes with communication, or produces maladjustment in the speaker. In other words, if a child's speech sounds impaired, it probably is. Speech impairments are present in around 3 to 5 percent of the school-age population (Bishop & Leonard, 2001).

**Childhood-onset fluency disorder**, or *stuttering*, involves a substantial disruption in the rhythm and fluency of speech and is the most common speech impairment. Despite a great deal of research, no specific cause of stuttering has been identified. Occasional stuttering is not unusual in young children—and it occasionally occurs in normal adults—but chronic stuttering can be a severe problem. Not only does stuttering hinder

---

**visual impairment** Difficulties in seeing that may include blindness or partial sightedness

**auditory impairment** A special need that involves the loss of hearing or some aspect of hearing

**speech impairment** Speech that deviates so much from the speech of others that it calls attention to itself, interferes with communication, or produces maladjustment in the speaker

**childhood-onset fluency disorder (stuttering)** Substantial disruption in the rhythm and fluency of speech; the most common speech impairment

communication, but it can produce embarrassment and stress in children, who may become inhibited from conversing with others and speaking aloud in class (Whaley & Parker, 2000; Altholz & Golensky, 2004; Logan et al., 2011; Sasisekaran, 2014).

Parents and teachers can adopt several strategies for dealing with stuttering. For starters, attention should not be drawn to the stuttering, and children should be given sufficient time to finish what they begin to say, no matter how protracted the statement becomes. It does not help stutterers to finish their sentences for them or otherwise correct their speech (Ryan, 2001; Beilby, Byrnes & Young, 2012).

Some 1 in 10 school-age children are labeled as having specific learning disorders. **Specific learning disorders** are characterized by difficulties in the ability to learn or use specific academic skills such as reading, writing, or arithmetic. A somewhat ill-defined, grab-bag category, specific learning disorders are diagnosed when there is a discrepancy between children's actual academic performance and their apparent potential to learn (Lerner, 2002; Bos & Vaughn, 2005; Bonifacci et al., 2016).

Such a broad definition encompasses a wide and extremely varied range of difficulties. For instance, some children suffer from *dyslexia*, a reading disability that can result in the misperception of letters during reading and writing, unusual difficulty in sounding out letters, confusion between left and right, and difficulties in spelling. Although dyslexia is not fully understood, one likely explanation for the disorder is a problem in the part of the brain responsible for breaking words into the sound elements that make up language (Paulesu et al., 2001; McGough, 2003; Lachmann et al., 2005).

The causes of specific learning disorders in general are not well understood. Although they are generally attributed to some form of brain dysfunction, probably due to genetic factors, some experts suggest that they are produced by such environmental causes as poor early nutrition or allergies (Shaywitz, 2004).

# Attention-Deficit/Hyperactivity Disorder

**LO 11.9 Describe attention-deficit/hyperactivity disorder and the methods that are used to treat it.**

*Charlie Marner's parents take turns dealing with him. While his father, Ray, shaves and showers,*

*Charlie's mother, Cerise, prepares breakfast. Seven-year-old Charlie is in the kitchen with her, running at full tilt around the table. The cereal box goes flying and its contents cover the floor. While Cerise sweeps them up, Charlie pulls the milk out of the refrigerator but loses control and adds a pool of milk to the mess on the floor.*

*Not a moment too soon, Ray enters and swoops up Charlie, but Charlie is in no mood to be held. He kicks and slaps at Ray who, though accustomed to such outbursts, receives a kick in the stomach and loses his eyeglasses. Cerise finishes cleaning the floor, and Ray manages to seat Charlie at the table with some toast and a spill-proof cup of milk.*

*After taking a few mouthfuls, Charlie jumps from his chair to chase the cat. He knocks over a lamp and then drags his blanket through the house, causing more damage. Next, he spots an unfinished jigsaw puzzle on the table and scatters the pieces.*

*Cerise takes over, trying to engage Charlie in a story while Ray gets ready for work.*

*So begins another day in the Marner household.*

Seven-year-old Charlie Marner's high energy and low attention span are caused by attention-deficit/hyperactivity disorder, which occurs in 3 to 5 percent of the school-age population.

**Attention-deficit/hyperactivity disorder** (ADHD), is marked by inattention, impulsiveness, a low tolerance for frustration, and generally a great deal of inappropriate activity. All children show such traits some of the time, but for those diagnosed with ADHD, such behavior is common and interferes with their home and school functioning (Nigg, 2001; Whalen et al., 2002; Van Neste et al., 2015).

It is often difficult to distinguish between children who simply have a high level of activity and those with ADHD. Some of the most common symptoms of ADHD include:

- Persistent difficulty in finishing tasks, following instructions, and organizing work
- Inability to watch an entire television program

**specific learning disorder** Difficulties in the ability to learn or use specific academic skills such as reading, writing, or arithmetic

**attention-deficit/hyperactivity disorder (ADHD)** A learning disorder marked by inattention, impulsiveness, a low tolerance for frustration, and a great deal of inappropriate activity

- Frequent interruption of others or excessive talking
- A tendency to jump into a task before hearing all the instructions
- Difficulty in waiting or remaining seated
- Fidgeting, squirming

Because there is no simple test to identify whether a child has ADHD, it is hard to know for sure how many children have the disorder. The Centers for Disease Control and Prevention puts the proportion of children 3 to 17 years of age with ADHD at 9 percent, with boys being twice as likely to be diagnosed with the disorder as girls. Other estimates are lower. Only a trained clinician can make an accurate diagnosis following an extensive evaluation of the child and interviews with parents and teachers (Sax & Kautz, 2003).

The treatment of children with ADHD has been a source of considerable controversy. Because it has been found that doses of Ritalin or Dexedrine (which,

paradoxically, are stimulants) reduce activity levels in hyperactive children, many physicians routinely prescribe drug treatment (List & Barzman, 2011; Weissman et al., 2012; Pelham et al., 2016).

Although in many cases such drugs are effective in increasing attention span and compliance, in some cases the side effects (such as irritability, reduced appetite, and depression) are considerable, and the long-term health consequences of this treatment are unclear. It is also true that though the drugs often help scholastic performance in the short run, the long-term evidence for continuing improvement is mixed, as we discuss in the *From Research to Practice* box. In any case, the drugs are being prescribed with increasing frequency (Graham et al., 2011; Prasad et al., 2014; Thapar & Cooper, 2016).

In addition to the use of drugs for treating ADHD, behavior therapy is often employed. With behavior therapy, parents and teachers are trained in techniques

# FROM RESEARCH TO PRACTICE
## Do ADHD Drugs Produce Long-Term Benefits?

At least 3.5 million children in the United States are taking medication to treat attention-deficit/hyperactivity disorder (ADHD) to improve their performance in school. Stimulant drugs such as Ritalin and Adderall have been shown to improve short-term cognitive functioning in children with ADHD. Specifically, these medications produce increases in attention and concentration, allowing children diagnosed with ADHD to keep their thoughts focused on the task at hand for a longer time. Some evidence even shows that stimulant drugs can improve memory for children diagnosed with ADHD, bringing their performance in line with children without the disorder (Bidwell, McClernon, & Kollins, 2011; Maul & Advokat, 2013; Visser et al., 2014).

But the evidence that these drugs actually help improve the long-term academic performance of children with ADHD is surprisingly lacking. A multiyear governmental study known as the Multimodal Treatment Study of Children with ADHD (MTA) assigned hundreds of children with ADHD to one of four treatment conditions: medication, therapy, both, or a control group that received no new treatment. After the 14-month treatment period, only the group receiving both medication and therapy outperformed the control group in measures of academic achievement. After 3 years, even that difference disappeared, and there were no significant differences between the four groups in measures of academic achievement—grades, test scores, and social adjustment

all looked alike. The same was true after 8 years: Medication produced no measurable improvement in long-term academic achievement (Parker et al., 2013; Sharpe, 2014).

What could explain this discrepancy between short- and long-term effectiveness of ADHD drugs? One possibility is that adherence to the drug regimen drops off over time. Children also may develop a tolerance to the drug, or their dosage may not keep up with their increasing size, or they may stop taking the drug due to side effects or changing priorities. Other explanations, though, speak more to the complex relationship between short-term behavioral changes and long-term performance improvements. For instance, it may be the case that students who take ADHD drugs become so much more calm and manageable in the classroom that their teachers no longer give them the attention and help that they still need to succeed (Currie, Stabile, & Jones, 2013; Sharpe, 2014).

Another possibility is that the improvements that ADHD drugs produce are just a small part of what goes into long-term academic achievement. Better focus and calmer behavior help, but they don't overcome differences in intelligence, academic aptitude, study skills, time-management skills, family support, socioeconomic status, parental education, and other important factors. Analysis of the MTA data shows that initially these other factors were better predictors of long-term academic success than the assigned treatment condition. It may also be the case that continuing treatment beyond 14 months would produce changes that continue over the long term. But even if not, it's still the case that short-term benefits have their place—after all, before you can work on your college applications, you do have to manage to get through second grade (Parker et al., 2013; Sharpe, 2014)!

- Should stimulant drugs still be used to treat the symptoms of ADHD in children even if the evidence for long-term benefits is lacking? Why or why not?

- How would you explain the findings of this research to a friend whose young child was recently diagnosed with ADHD?

for improving behavior, primarily by using rewards (such as verbal praise) for desired behavior. Moreover, teachers can increase the structure of classroom activities and use other class management techniques to help children with ADHD, who have great difficulty with unstructured tasks. (Chronis, Jones, & Raggi, 2006; DuPaul & Weyandt, 2006). (Parents and teachers can receive support from the Children and Adults With Attention-Deficit/Hyperactivity Disorder organization at www.chadd.org.)

This educational approach to special education, designed to end the segregation of exceptional students as much as possible, has come to be called mainstreaming. In **mainstreaming**, exceptional children are integrated as much as possible into the traditional educational system and are provided with a broad range of educational alternatives.

Mainstreaming was meant to provide a mechanism to equalize the opportunities available to all children. The ultimate objective of mainstreaming was to ensure that all persons, regardless of ability or disability, had—to the greatest extent possible—opportunities to choose their goals on the basis of a full education, enabling them to obtain a fair share of life's rewards (Burns, 2003).

> **mainstreaming** An educational approach in which exceptional children are integrated as much as possible into the traditional educational system and are provided with a broad range of educational alternatives

# DEVELOPMENTAL DIVERSITY AND YOUR LIFE
## Mainstreaming and Full Inclusion of Children With Special Needs

Are exceptional children best served by providing specialized services that separate them from their peers who do not have special needs, or do they benefit more from being integrated with their peers to the fullest extent? If you had asked these questions three decades ago, the answer would have been simple: Exceptional children were assumed to do best when removed from their regular classes and placed in a class taught by a special-needs teacher. Such classes often accommodated a hodgepodge of afflictions (emotional difficulties, severe reading problems, and physical disabilities like multiple sclerosis). In addition, they kept students segregated from the regular educational process.

Recommendations to send children with special needs to mainstream schools were first made in the Sargent Report in 1944 and again in 1964 by the Kothari Commission (Julka, 2005). In 1987, the UNICEF and the government-funded National Council of Educational Research and Training (NCERT) launched the Project on Integrated Education for Disabled (PIED) in few districts and villages, which focused on teacher training in order to encourage integration. PIED was later extended to 27 states (Julka, 2005). While enrolment of differently-abled children in the mainstream increased and retention was high (Julka, 2005), coverage remained "miniscule" with only 2-3 percent of children with special needs integrated in mainstream institutions (Julka, 2005). Again in 1995, the Persons with Disability Act (PDA) was introduced that stated, differently-abled children should be educated in integrated settings wherever possible. Although the Government of India has attempted to create policies that are inclusive for people with special needs, their implementation efforts have not resulted in an inclusive system of education. It could be because of the absence of accountability mechanisms, which results in poor policy implementation. In order to ensure implementation of 1995's Persons with Disabilities Act, some kind of legal enforcement mechanism needs to be created (Alur, 2002).

Mainstreaming of exceptional children into traditional educational systems has provided opportunities that were previously denied.

To some extent, the benefits extolled by proponents of mainstreaming have been realized; however, classroom teachers must receive substantial support in order for mainstreaming to be effective. It is not easy to teach a class in which students' abilities vary greatly. Furthermore, providing the necessary support for children with special needs is expensive, and sometimes budgetary tensions exist that pit parents of children with special needs against parents of nonexceptional children (Jones, 2004; Waite, Bromfield, & McShane, 2005; Lindsay et al., 2013).

The benefits of mainstreaming have led some professionals to promote an alternative educational model known as full inclusion. **Full inclusion** is the integration of all students, even those with the most severe disabilities, into regular classes. In such a system, separate special education programs would cease to operate. Full inclusion is controversial, and it remains to be seen how widespread the practice will become (Begeny & Martens, 2007; Magyar, 2011; Greenstein, 2016).

> **From an educator's perspective:** What are the advantages of mainstreaming and full inclusion? What challenges do they present? Are there situations in which you would not support mainstreaming and full inclusion?

# The Case of ...
## Taking a Breather

"Sickly." Ever since he could remember, 10-year-old Ishaan Dubey had been "sickly." Everybody said so, especially his mother. She made sure he was always "bundled up," and she warned him constantly against "exerting himself." And she was even more vigilant since he had developed asthma.

He was taking medicine, of course, but he still lost his breath and often had to sit down, gasping, until he could pull out his inhaler and bring some relief to his lungs. His mother insisted that he stay away from sports, so he found himself on the sidelines, always.

Today he was watching a game of Ultimate Frisbee. The players were running, leaping high, making astounding catches, and in one smooth motion, sending the Frisbee sailing downfield. One of his classmates, Ricky Chandra, was particularly impressive in the height of his jumps and the strength of his throws.

When the game ended, Ishaan's eyes nearly popped out of his head as he saw Ricky take an inhaler out of his sports bag and draw on it greedily. He found himself walking up to Ricky—a boy he had never even spoken to before, even though they lived in the same neighborhood.

"What's up, Ishaan?" said Ricky.

"Uh, Ricky, you, you have *asthma?*" Ishaan said.

Ricky laughed. "Yeah. Since I was, like, 6. It sucks, but what can you do? How long have you had yours?"

Ishaan was surprised that Ricky knew. "But you play sports," he said. "You run and everything. Don't you get overexerted?"

"Overexerted? Don't know about that, but I have my inhaler, and I take my pills, and I don't let it bother me." Ricky's next words surprised Ishaan. "You should try it. Maybe I could help you out. You know, we could practice together, or whatever."

Ishaan nodded happily, resolving to go home and have a long talk with his mother. He was done with the sidelines.

1. What do you think is motivating Ishaan's mother in forbidding him to play sports? Is she justified in her concerns?

2. How would you advise Ishaan's to discuss with his mother his desire to begin participating in sports? What resources might he enlist to help him, either at school or in his community?

3. What effects might Ishaan's not taking part in sports have on his motor development and physical

**full inclusion** The integration of all students, even those with the most severe disabilities, into regular classes and all other aspects of school and community life

health? What precautions should he take when he begins to participate?

4. Is Ishaan's decision to take up a sport likely to have any effects on his social development? Explain.

5. Are Ishaan's nutritional needs likely to change once he begins taking part in sports? Will he be less likely to become obese? To be overweight in later life?

# Epilogue

In this chapter, we have focused on physical development during middle childhood. We began with a look at how children's height and weight increase during this period and then examined gross and fine motor development, considering the importance of physical competence. Finally, we discussed children with special needs in the areas of sensory and physical abilities.

Look back to the prologue, about Mira Singh's game-winning double play, and answer the following questions:

1. What kinds of physical abilities permit Mira to play basketball? How did these abilities change as she moved from preschool into middle childhood?

2. What physical abilities does Mira probably still lack, given her developmental stage? How will these deficits affect her physical abilities?

3. What evidence in Mira's story shows that she has achieved what Piaget calls concrete operational thinking?

4. If Mira had special needs that reduced her physical abilities, should she be encouraged to participate in sports with other children? If so, under what circumstances should such participation occur?

# Looking Back

**LO 11.1** **Describe the ways in which children grow during the school years and the factors that influence their growth.**

- The middle childhood years are characterized by slow and steady growth, with children gaining, on average, about 5 to 7 pounds per year and 2 to 3 inches in height. Weight is redistributed as baby fat disappears.

- In part, growth is genetically determined, but societal factors such as affluence, dietary habits, nutrition, and disease also contribute significantly.

**LO 11.2** **Explain the nutritional needs of school-age children and the consequences of improper nutrition.**

- Adequate nutrition is important because of its contributions to growth, health, social and emotional functioning, and cognitive performance.

- Dietary customs and variations in levels of affluence contribute to differences in levels of nutrition.

Stress can also contribute to malnutrition, as in the case of parental conflict or alcoholism.

**LO 11.3** **List the causes and effects of childhood obesity and explain how can it be treated.**

- Obesity is partially influenced by genetic factors but is also associated with children's lack of internal controls, overeating, overindulgence in sedentary activities such as television viewing, and avoidance of physical exercise.

- Childhood obesity can have lifelong effects. Children who are obese tend to be overweight as adults and to have greater risk of heart disease, diabetes, and other diseases. Obesity also leads to a lack of exercise, which can cause additional health problems later in life.

- Treating childhood obesity is difficult, but excessive concern about weight carries its own dangers. Children have to be helped to learn how to control their eating themselves. Making healthy foods available—and high-calorie or highly processed foods scarce—can help children learn to eat properly.

## LO 11.4 Summarize the health threats faced by school-age children.

- The health of children in the school years is generally good, and few health problems arise; however, the incidence of some diseases that affect children, such as asthma, is on the rise.

## LO 11.5 Describe the psychological disorders that affect school-age children.

- School-age children can suffer from psychological disorders, including childhood depression. Because childhood depression can lead to adult mood disorders or even to suicide, it should be taken seriously.

## LO 11.6 Explain how motor development evolves during middle childhood.

- During the middle-childhood years, great improvements occur in gross motor skills. Cultural expectations probably underlie most gross motor skill differences between boys and girls. Fine motor skills also develop rapidly.

- Physical competence is important for a number of reasons, some of which relate to self-esteem and confidence. Physical competence also brings social benefits during this period, especially for boys.

## LO 11.7 Discuss the safety threats that affect school-age children and what can be done about them.

- Threats to safety in middle childhood relate mainly to children's increasing independence and mobility. Accidents, especially those related to automobiles, other vehicles (such as bicycles and skateboards), and sports, account for most injuries. In most cases, the use of proper protective gear can greatly reduce injuries.

- An emerging area of potential danger for children is cyberspace. Unsupervised access to the Internet may permit children to explore offensive areas and come into contact with people who might take advantage of them.

## LO 11.8 Explain the effects of visual, auditory, and speech problems on school-age children.

- Visual impairments include difficulties with close-up vision and the perception of color, depth, and light. Deficits in these areas can lead to academic and social problems and must be handled with sensitivity and appropriate assistance.

- Auditory impairments can interfere with classroom learning and social interactions, depriving students of the full school experience. Remedies are available in some cases, but these are rarely completely effective.

- Speech impairments are particularly noticeable in classroom and social settings, and they can cause self-consciousness and lead to awkwardness and isolation. Speech problems can often be treated with time and effort.

- Specific learning disorders, characterized by difficulties in the ability to learn or use specific academic skills such as reading, writing, or arithmetic, affect a small proportion of the population. Although the causes of specific learning disorders are not well understood, some form of brain dysfunction seems to be involved.

## LO 11.9 Describe attention-deficit/hyperactivity disorder and the methods that are used to treat it.

- Children with attention-deficit/hyperactivity disorder exhibit another form of special need. ADHD is characterized by inattention, impulsiveness, failure to complete tasks, lack of organization, and excessive amounts of uncontrollable activity.

- Treatment of ADHD with drugs is controversial. The drugs Ritalin and Dexedrine have been used extensively, but they have potentially serious side effects and may lack long-term benefits.

- Behavior therapy is also used, with a focus on helping children control their impulses and achieve positive goals.

- Children with exceptionalities are generally placed in the least restrictive environment, typically the regular classroom. Mainstreaming and full inclusion can benefit exceptional students by permitting them to focus on strengths and gain useful skills of social interaction.

# Key Terms and Concepts

asthma (p. 292)

visual impairment (p. 299)

auditory impairment (p. 299)

speech impairment (p. 299)

childhood-onset fluency disorder (stuttering) (p. 299)

specific learning disorder (p. 300)

attention-deficit/hyperactivity disorder (ADHD) (p. 300)

mainstreaming (p. 302)

full inclusion (p. 303)

# Chapter 12
# Cognitive Development in Middle Childhood

 ## Learning Objectives

**LO 12.1** Summarize Piaget's theoretical approaches to cognitive development in middle childhood.

**LO 12.2** Explain the development of memory according to information-processing approaches.

**LO 12.3** Describe the classroom practices that Vygotsky recommends to advance children's cognitive development.

**LO 12.4** Explain how language develops during middle childhood.

**LO 12.5** Describe the consequences of bilingualism.

**LO 12.6** Define the trends affecting schooling worldwide and in the India.

**LO 12.7** List the factors that contribute to positive academic outcomes for children.

**LO 12.8** Discuss the outcomes of multicultural education.

**LO 12.9** Describe the ways in which intelligence can be measured.

LO 12.10 Explain how bias may occur in traditional intelligence testing.

LO 12.11 Compare and contrast alternative conceptions of intelligence with traditional definitions.

LO 12.12 Describe how children who fall outside the normal range of intelligence are classified.

# Prologue: Seeding a Garden

In her Class III math class, Dipti Rawat is introducing her students to word problems. After they work through some problems together, Dipti asks, "How would *you* write a word problem?"

Silence. Finally one student ventures, "Well, they're about normal things, like the size of a rug or something." Then the class takes off.

"Yeah, or painting a wall or dividing up a pizza."

"But you have to tell people what to do and it has to have math."

"Let's make it about pizza."

"How about a garden?"

"Yeah, like how many bags of seeds you need to cover it."

Eventually a plausible word problem emerges.

"Word problems are scary," Dipti says later, "so I make students think about how they're made—a form of metacognition. Writing a problem cooperatively

reveals the main features of such problems, and those are the keys to solving them. After writing some problems, students approach solving them in a much more mindful way."

# Looking Ahead

Middle childhood is characterized by a procession of moments like this, in which children's cognitive skills ascend to new heights. In this chapter, we consider the cognitive advances made by children during middle childhood. After beginning with Piaget's explanation for intellectual development, we turn to information-processing approaches. We discuss the development of memory and how memory can be improved.

Next, we turn to the important strides that occur in language development during the middle childhood years. We focus on increases in linguistic skill and examine the consequences of bilingualism, the

use of more than one language to communicate. We then discuss schooling and the ways in which society transmits knowledge, beliefs, values, and wisdom to a new generation. We consider such topics as how children explain their academic performance and how teachers' expectations can affect student achievement.

Finally, the chapter ends by focusing on intelligence. It highlights what developmentalists mean when they speak of intelligence, how intelligence is related to school success, and the ways in which children differ from one another in terms of intelligence.

# Cognitive and Language Development

*Javed's parents were delighted when he came home from kindergarten one day and explained that he had learned why the sky was blue. He talked about Earth's atmosphere—although he didn't pronounce the word correctly—and how tiny bits of moisture in the air reflect the sunlight. Although his explanation had rough edges (he couldn't quite grasp what the atmosphere was), he still had the general idea, and that, his parents felt, was quite an achievement for their 5-year-old.*

Fast-forward 6 years. Javed, now age 11, had already spent an hour laboring over his evening's homework. After completing a two-page worksheet on multiplying and dividing fractions, he had begun work on his Indian Constitution project. He was taking notes for his report, which would explain what political factions had been involved in the writing of the document and how the Constitution had been amended since its creation.

Javed is not alone in having made vast intellectual advances during middle childhood. During this period, children's cognitive abilities broaden, and they become increasingly able to understand and master complex skills. At the same time, though, their thinking is still not fully adult.

What are the advances—and the limitations—in thinking during childhood? Several perspectives explain what goes on cognitively during middle childhood.

## Piagetian Approaches to Cognitive Development

**LO 12.1** **Summarize Piaget's theoretical approaches to cognitive development in middle childhood.**

Let's return for a moment to Jean Piaget's view of the preschooler, which we considered in Chapter 9. According to the Piagetian perspective, the preschooler thinks *preoperationally*. This type of thinking is largely egocentric. Preoperational children lack the ability to use *operations*—organized, formal, and logical mental processes.

**THE RISE OF CONCRETE OPERATIONAL THOUGHT.** All this changes, according to Piaget, during the concrete operational period, which coincides with the school years. The **concrete operational stage**, which

occurs between 7 and 12 years of age, is characterized by the active and appropriate use of logic.

Concrete operational thought involves applying *logical thinking* to concrete problems. For instance, when children in the concrete operational stage are confronted with a conservation problem (such as determining whether a constant amount of liquid poured from one container to another container of a different shape stays the same), they use cognitive and logical processes to answer, and are no longer influenced solely by appearance. They are able to reason correctly that because none of the liquid has been lost, the amount stays the same. Because they are less egocentric, they can take multiple aspects of a situation into account, an ability known as **decentering**. Javed, the sixth grader described earlier, was using his decentering skills to consider the views of the different factions involved in creating the U.S. Constitution.

The shift from preoperational thought to concrete operational thought does not happen overnight, of course. During the 2 years before children move firmly into the concrete operational period, they shift back and forth between preoperational and concrete operational thinking. For instance, they typically pass through a period when they can answer conservation problems correctly but can't articulate why they did so. When asked to explain the reasoning behind their answers, they may respond with an unenlightening, "Because."

Once concrete operational thinking is fully engaged, however, children show several cognitive advances representative of their logical thinking. For instance, they attain the concept of *reversibility*, which is the notion that processes transforming a stimulus can be reversed, returning the stimulus to its original form. Grasping reversibility permits children to understand that a ball of clay that has been squeezed into a long, snakelike rope can be returned to its original state. More abstractly, it allows school-age children to understand that if 3 plus 5 equals 8, then 5 plus 3 also equals 8—and later during the period, that 8 minus 3 equals 5.

Concrete operational thinking also permits children to understand such concepts as the relationship between time, speed, and distance—comprehending,

---

**concrete operational stage** The period of cognitive development between 7 and 12 years of age, characterized by the active and appropriate use of logic

**decentering** The ability to take multiple aspects of a situation into account

**Figure 12.1** Sample Problem in Concrete Operational Thinking

After being told that the two cars traveling Routes 1 and 2 start and end their journeys in the same amount of time, children who are just entering the concrete operational period still reason that the cars are traveling at identical rates of speed. Later, however, they reach the correct conclusion that the car traveling the longer route must be moving at a higher speed if it starts and ends its journey at the same time as the car traveling the shorter route.

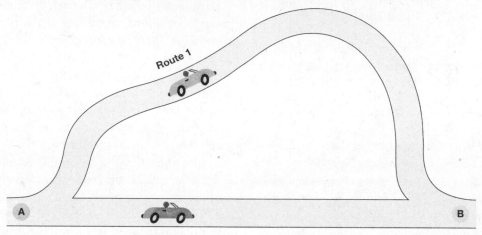

for example, that an increase in speed can compensate for greater distance in a journey. For instance, consider the problem shown in Figure 12.1, in which two cars start and finish at the same points in the same amount of time but travel different routes. Children who are just entering the concrete operational period reason that the cars are traveling at the same speed. Between the ages of 8 and 10, however, children begin to draw the right conclusion: that the car traveling the longer route must be moving faster if it arrives at the finish point at the same time as the car traveling the shorter route.

Despite the advances that occur during the concrete operational stage, children still experience one critical limitation in their thinking. They remain tied to concrete, physical reality; they are unable to understand truly abstract or hypothetical questions or ones that involve formal logic.

**PIAGET IN PERSPECTIVE: PIAGET WAS RIGHT, PIAGET WAS WRONG.** As we learned in our prior consideration of Piaget's views in Chapters 6 and 9, researchers following in Piaget's footsteps have found much to cheer about, as well as much to criticize.

Piaget was a virtuoso observer of children, and his many books contain pages of brilliant, careful observations of children at work and play. His theories have powerful educational implications, and many schools

employ principles derived from his views to guide the nature and presentation of instructional materials (Siegler & Ellis, 1996; Brainerd, 2003).

In some ways, Piaget's approach was quite successful in describing cognitive development. At the same time, though, critics have voiced justifiable objections. As we have noted before, many researchers argue that Piaget underestimated children's capabilities, in part because of the limited nature of the mini-experiments he conducted. When a broader array of experimental tasks is used, children show less consistency within stages than Piaget would predict (Bjorklund, 1997; Bibace, 2013; Siegler, 2016).

Furthermore, Piaget seems to have misjudged the age at which children's cognitive abilities emerge. As might be expected from our earlier discussions of Piaget's stages, increasing evidence suggests that children's capabilities develop earlier than Piaget envisioned. Some children show evidence of a form of concrete operational thinking before the age of 7, the time at which Piaget proposed these abilities first appear.

Still, we cannot dismiss the Piagetian approach, although some early cross-cultural research seemed to imply that children in certain cultures never left the preoperational stage and failed to master conservation and to develop concrete operations. For example, pioneering work by Patricia Greenfield (1966) found that among the

Wolof children in Senegal, a West African country, only half of children ages 10 to 13 understood conservation of liquid. Studies in other non-Western areas, such as the jungles of New Guinea and Brazil and remote villages in Australia, confirmed her findings. When a broad sample of children are studied—children who have had very different experiences from the western European children on whom Piaget based his theory—not everyone reaches the concrete operational stage (Dasen, 1977). It appears, then, that Piaget's claims that his stages provided a universal description of cognitive development were exaggerated.

For instance, with proper training in conservation, children in non-Western cultures who do not conserve can readily learn to do so. In one study, urban Australian children—who develop concrete operations on the same timetable as Piaget suggested—were compared to rural Aborigine children, who typically do not demonstrate an understanding of conservation at the age of 14 (Dasen, Ngini, & Lavallée, 1979). When the rural Aborigine children were given training, they showed conservation skills similar to those of their urban counterparts, although with a time lag of around 3 years.

Dash and Das (1984) examined the influence of age and schooling on the development of concrete and operational thought as well as information processing. As predicted, performance on Piagetian tasks increased as a function of age only, and schooling has an insignificant role. In a similar study, Mishra and Padhee (1987) studied the effects of parents' formal schooling and SES on volume conservation ability of 7–11 years old unschooled and schooled children drawn from low and high SES background. Their result also confirmed that the development of conservation ability was age-dependent; schooling and SES had no significant effect on the development of conservation ability (demonstrated in volume conservation task) which was age-dependent. Pattnaik and Mohanty (1984) had reported similar results in an earlier study carried out with monolingual and bilingual children of 6, 8, and 10 years of age, confirming again that bilingualism does not enhance cognitive abilities as measured by Piagetian conservation tasks. At large, Indian researchers had shown little interest in Piagetian theory (Anandalakshmy, 1980), which has diminished in India during the last decade. Mishra (2014) highlighted three reasons for the same:

- A general lack of interest for research on child development with more focus on problems of adolescence and aging;

- Researchers, who study cognitive development, followed information processing approach over Piagetian tasks; and

- A fascination for physiological methods which do not match with the clinical method of Piaget.

He further stated that child development is still a marginalized field of research in the departments of psychology at Indian universities (Mishra, 2014).

Furthermore, when children are interviewed by researchers from their own culture, who know the language and customs of the culture well and who use reasoning tasks that are related to domains important to the culture, the children are considerably more likely to display concrete operational thinking (Nyiti, 1982; Jahoda, 1983). Ultimately, such research suggests that Piaget was right when he argued that concrete operations were universally achieved during middle childhood. Although school-age children in some cultures may differ from Westerners in the demonstration of certain cognitive skills, the most probable explanation of the difference is that the non-Western children have had different sorts of experiences from those that permit children in Western societies to perform well on Piagetian measures of conservation and concrete operations. The progress of cognitive development, then, cannot be understood without looking at the nature of a child's culture (Maynard, 2008; Crisp & Turner, 2011; Wang et al., 2016).

# Information Processing in Middle Childhood

### LO 12.2 Explain the development of memory according to information-processing approaches.

It is a significant achievement for first graders to learn basic math tasks, such as addition and subtraction of single-digit numbers, as well as the spelling of simple words such as *dog* and *run*. But by the time they reach sixth grade, children are able to work with fractions and decimals, like the fractions worksheet that Javed, the boy in the example at the start of this section, completed for his sixth-grade homework. They can also spell such words as *exhibit* and *residence*.

According to *information-processing approaches*, children become increasingly sophisticated in their handling of information. Like computers, they can process more data as the size of their memory increases and the "programs" they use to process information become increasingly sophisticated (Kail, 2003; Zelazo et al., 2003).

**MEMORY.** As we saw in Chapter 6, in the information-processing model, **memory** is the ability to encode, store, and retrieve information. For a child to remember a piece of information, the three processes must all function properly. Through *encoding*, the child initially records the information in a form usable to memory. Children who were never taught that 5 plus 6 equals 11, or who didn't pay attention when they were exposed to this fact, will not be able to recall it. They never encoded the information in the first place.

But mere exposure to a fact is not enough; the information also has to be *stored*. In our example, the information that 5 plus 6 equals 11 must be placed and maintained in the memory system. Finally, proper functioning of memory requires that material that is stored in memory must be *retrieved*. Through retrieval, material in memory storage is located, brought into awareness, and used.

According to the *three-system approach to memory* that has dominated our understanding of memory, there are three different memory storage systems or stages that describe how information is processed in order for it to be recalled (Atkinson & Shiffrin, 1971). *Sensory memory* refers to the initial, momentary storage of information that lasts only an instant. Sensory memory records an exact replica of the stimulus. In the second stage, *short-term memory* (also known as *working memory*), information is stored for 15 to 25 seconds according to its meaning. Finally, the third type of storage system is *long-term memory*, in which information is stored relatively permanently, although it may be difficult to retrieve.

During middle childhood, short-term memory capacity improves significantly. For instance, children are increasingly able to hear a string of digits ("1-5-6-3-4") and then repeat the string in reverse order ("4-3-6-5-1"). At the start of the preschool period, they can remember and reverse only about two digits; by the beginning of adolescence, they can perform the task with as many as six digits (Jack, Simcock & Hayne, 2012; Jarrold & Hall, 2013; Resing et al., 2017).

Memory capacity may shed light on another issue in cognitive development. Some developmental psychologists suggest that the difficulty children experience in solving conservation problems during the preschool period may stem from memory limitations

(Siegler & Richards, 1982). They argue that young children simply may not be able to recall all the necessary pieces of information that enter into the correct solution of conservation problems.

**Metamemory**, an understanding about the processes that underlie memory, also emerges and improves during middle childhood. By the time they enter first grade and their theory of mind becomes more sophisticated, children have a general notion of what memory is, and they are able to understand that some people have better memories than others (Ghetti et al., 2008; Jaswal & Dodson, 2009; Grammer et al., 2011).

School-age children's understanding of memory becomes more sophisticated as they grow older and increasingly engage in *control strategies*—conscious, intentionally used tactics to improve cognitive processing. For instance, school-age children are aware that rehearsal, the repetition of information, is a useful strategy for improving memory, and they increasingly employ it over the course of middle childhood. Similarly, they progressively make more effort to organize material into coherent patterns, a strategy that permits them to recall it better. When faced with remembering a list that includes cups, knives, forks, and plates, for example, older school-age children are more likely to group the items into coherent patterns—cups and plates, forks, and knives—than are children just entering the school-age years (Sang, Miao, & Deng, 2002; Dionne & Cadoret, 2013).

Similarly, children in middle childhood increasingly use *mnemonics* (pronounced *neh-MON-ix*), which are formal techniques for organizing information in a way that makes it more likely to be remembered. For instance, they may learn that the spaces on the music staff spell the word *face* or learn the rhyme "Thirty days hath September, April, June, and November …" to try to recall the number of days in each month (Bellezza, 2000; Carney & Levin, 2003; Sprenger, 2007). (Also see the *From Research to Practice* box.)

**IMPROVING MEMORY.** Can children be trained to be more effective in the use of control strategies? Definitely. School-age children can be taught to use

---

**memory** The process by which information is recorded, stored, and retrieved

**metamemory** An understanding about the processes that underlie memory that emerges and improves during middle childhood

# FROM RESEARCH TO PRACTICE
## The Key to Better Math Skills Is at Children's Fingertips

When you learned to do simple arithmetic, did you start by learning to count on your fingers? And did your parents or teachers at some point actively discourage you from doing that? Perhaps even today you still mentally count up or down to do addition and subtraction (and maybe even feel an occasional twinge of guilt about it)? If so, fear not—what you're doing is common and natural, and research suggests that it's just part of how we learn to think about numbers as young children.

Counting objects—whether they are beads, coins, fingers, or something else—is an important tactic for giving children a concrete understanding of simple mathematical operations. Educators emphasize that it's perfectly appropriate for children to use this strategy and to continue using it until they develop the ability to mentally manipulate numbers and no longer need the crutch (Berteletti & Booth, 2016).

Recent research confirms the importance of finger counting to the development of math skill. Children ages 8 to 13 were subjected to fMRI scans while they mentally solved simple arithmetic problems involving subtraction and multiplication. Regions of the brain associated with the fingers lit up when the children were doing subtraction—one in the somatosensory cortex and one in the motor cortex—as if the children were counting on their fingers, although none of

them were. Solving multiplication problems did not activate these finger-associated regions of the brain, suggesting that multiplication and subtraction involve different neural networks in the brain. This makes sense given that multiplication is usually learned by rote memorization rather than by counting (Berteletti & Booth, 2015).

Moreover, children who are more skilled at finger perception—that is, who are better able to accurately detect which finger is being touched without looking—tend to be more skilled at math. Indeed, finger perception is a good predictor of future math success, and training in finger perception improves math performance. While researchers can't say for sure whether this association means that the development of math skill definitely depends on finger perception, it is consistent with the observation that visualization facilitates understanding of mathematical concepts. It seems that while most of us outgrow counting on our fingers, our brains never really do (Berteletti & Booth, 2016).

- **How might a parent or a teacher apply this research to help children develop stronger math skills?**
- **Why do you think some parents and teachers discourage children from counting on their fingers? How would you explain this research to them?**

particular mnemonic strategies, although such teaching is not a simple matter. For instance, children need to know not only how to use a memory strategy but also when and where to use it most effectively.

Take, for example, an innovative technique called the keyword strategy, which can help students learn the vocabulary of a foreign language, the capitals of the states, or other information in which two sets of words or labels are paired. In the *keyword strategy*, one word is paired with another that sounds like it (Wyra, Lawson, & Hungi, 2007).

For instance, in learning foreign-language vocabulary, a foreign word is paired with a common English word that has a similar sound. The English word is the keyword. Thus, to learn the Spanish word for duck (*pato*, pronounced *pot-o*), the keyword might be "pot"; for the Spanish word for horse (*caballo*, pronounced *cob-eye-yo*), the keyword might be "eye." Once the

keyword is chosen, children then form a mental image of the two words interacting with one another. For example, a student might use an image of a duck taking a bath in a pot to remember the word *pato*, or a horse with bulging eyes to remember the word *caballo*.

Other memory strategies include *rehearsal*, consistent repetition of information that children wish to remember; *organization*, which is placing material into categories (such as coastal states or types of food); and *cognitive elaboration*, in which mental images are linked with information that someone wants to recall. For example, in trying to remember where Cape Cod is on a map of Massachusetts, an 8-year-old might think of a muscle-bound Pilgrim to link the image of the shape of Cape Cod (which looks something like a flexing, curved arm) with its location. Whatever memory strategies children use, they use such strategies more often and more effectively as they get older.

# Vygotsky's Approach to Cognitive Development and Classroom Instruction

**LO 12.3** Describe the classroom practices that Vygotsky recommends to advance children's cognitive development.

Recall from Chapter 9 that Russian developmentalist Lev Vygotsky proposed that cognitive advances occur through exposure to information within a child's *zone of proximal development (ZPD)*. The ZPD is the level at which a child can almost, but not quite, understand or perform a task.

Vygotsky's approach has been particularly influential in the development of several classroom practices based on the proposition that children should actively participate in their educational experiences. In this approach, classrooms are seen as places where children should have the opportunity to experiment and try out new activities (Vygotsky, 1926/1997; Gredler & Shields, 2008; Gredler, 2012).

According to Vygotsky, education should focus on activities that involve interaction with others. Both child–adult and child–child interactions can provide the potential for cognitive growth. The nature of the interactions must be carefully structured to fall within each individual child's ZPD.

Several current and noteworthy educational innovations have borrowed heavily from Vygotsky's work. For example, *cooperative learning*, in which children work together in groups to achieve a common goal, incorporates several aspects of Vygotsky's theory. Students working in cooperative groups benefit from the insights of others, and if they go off on the wrong track, they may be brought back to the correct course by others in their group. Of course, not every peer is equally helpful to members of a cooperative learning group: As Vygotsky's approach would imply, children benefit most when at least some of the other members of the group are more competent at the task and can act as experts (DeLisi, 2006; Law, 2008; Slavin, 2013; Gillies, 2014).

Reciprocal teaching is another educational practice that reflects Vygotsky's approach to cognitive development. *Reciprocal teaching* is a technique to teach reading comprehension strategies. Students are taught to skim the content of a passage, raise questions about its central point, summarize the passage, and finally predict what will happen next. A key to this technique is its reciprocal nature, its emphasis on giving students a chance to take on the role of teacher. In the beginning, teachers lead students through the comprehension strategies. Gradually, students progress through their ZPDs, taking more and more control over use of the strategies, until they are able to take on a teaching role. The method has shown impressive success in raising reading comprehension levels, particularly for students experiencing reading difficulties (Spörer, Brunstein, & Kieschke, 2009; Lundberg & Reichenberg, 2013; Davis & Voirin, 2016).

> **From an educator's perspective:** How might a teacher use Vygotsky's approach to teach 10-year-olds about colonial America?

# Language Development: What Words Mean

**LO 12.4** Explain how language develops during middle childhood.

If you listen to what school-age children say to one another, their speech, at least at first hearing, sounds not too different from that of adults; however, the apparent similarity is deceiving. The linguistic sophistication of children, particularly at the start of the school-age period—still requires refinement to reach adult levels of expertise.

**MASTERING THE MECHANICS OF LANGUAGE.** Vocabulary continues to increase during the school years at a fairly rapid clip. For instance, the average 6-year-old has a vocabulary of 8,000 to 14,000 words, whereas the vocabulary grows by another 5,000 words between the ages of 9 and 11.

School-age children's mastery of grammar also improves. For example, the use of the passive voice is rare during the early school-age years (as in "The dog was walked by Jon," compared with the active-voice "Jon walked the dog"). Most 6- and 7-year-olds only infrequently use conditional sentences, such as "If Sarah will set the table, I will wash the dishes." Over the course of middle childhood, however, the use of both passive voice and conditional sentences increases. In addition, children's understanding of *syntax*, the rules that indicate how words and phrases can be combined to form sentences, grows during middle childhood.

By the time they reach first grade, most children pronounce words quite accurately, although certain *phonemes*—units of sound—remain troublesome. For instance, the ability to pronounce *j, v, th,* and *zh* sounds develops later than the ability to pronounce other phonemes.

School-age children also may have difficulty decoding sentences when the meaning depends on *intonation,* or tone of voice. For example, consider the sentence, "George gave a book to David, and he gave one to Bill." If the word "he" is emphasized, the meaning is "George gave a book to David, and David gave a different book to Bill." But if the intonation emphasizes the word "and," then the meaning changes to "George gave a book to David and George also gave a book to Bill." School-age children cannot easily sort out subtleties such as these (Wells, Peppé, & Goulandris, 2004; Bosco et al., 2013).

In addition to language skills, conversational skills develop during middle childhood. Children become more competent in their use of *pragmatics,* the rules governing the use of language to communicate in a given social setting.

For example, although children are aware of the rules of conversational turn-taking at the start of the early childhood period, their use of these rules is sometimes primitive. Consider the following conversation between 6-year-olds Yonnie and Max:

YONNIE: My dad drives a FedEx truck.

MAX: My sister's name is Molly.

YONNIE: He gets up really early in the morning.

MAX: She wet her bed last night.

Later, however, conversations show more give-and-take, with the second child actually responding to the comments of the first. For instance, this conversation between 11-year-olds Mia and Josh reflects a more sophisticated mastery of pragmatics:

MIA: I don't know what to get Claire for her birthday.

JOSH: I'm getting her earrings.

MIA: She already has a lot of jewelry.

JOSH: I don't think she has that much.

**METALINGUISTIC AWARENESS.** One of the most significant developments in middle childhood is children's increasing understanding of their own use of language or **metalinguistic awareness.** By the time children are 5 or 6, they understand that language is governed by a set of rules. Whereas in the early years they learn and comprehend these rules implicitly,

The increase in metalinguistic skills during middle childhood allows children to enter into the give-and-take of conversation more successfully.

during middle childhood, children come to understand them more explicitly (Benelli et al., 2006; Saiegh-Haddad, 2007).

Metalinguistic awareness helps children achieve comprehension when information is fuzzy or incomplete. For instance, when preschoolers are given ambiguous or unclear information, such as directions for how to play a complicated game, they rarely ask for clarification, and they tend to blame themselves if they do not understand. By the time they reach 7 or 8, children realize that miscommunication may be due to factors attributable not only to themselves but also to the person communicating with them. Consequently, school-age children are more likely to ask for clarification of information that is unclear to them (Apperly & Robinson, 2002). Vasanta, Sastry, and Maruth (1995) found that metalinguistic ability in Telgu speaking children improved between 4–5 years and 8.5 years of age. Prakash and Mohanty (2004) noted a significant relationship between metalinguistic awareness and reading achievement across Oriya speaking children studying in Class 1 to 5.

**HOW LANGUAGE PROMOTES SELF-CONTROL.** The growing sophistication of their language helps school-age children control their behavior. For instance, in one experiment, children were told that they could have one marshmallow treat if they chose to eat one immediately but two treats if they waited.

**metalinguistic awareness** An understanding of one's own use of language

Most of the children, who ranged in age from 4 to 8, chose to wait, but the strategies they used while waiting differed significantly.

The 4-year-olds often chose to look at the marshmallows while waiting, a strategy that was not terribly effective. In contrast, 6- and 8-year-olds used language to help them overcome temptation, although in different ways. The 6-year-olds spoke and sang to themselves, reminding themselves that if they waited, they would get more treats in the end. The 8-year-olds focused on aspects of the marshmallows that were not related to taste, such as their appearance, which helped them to wait.

In short, children used "self-talk" to help regulate their own behavior. Furthermore, the effectiveness of their self-control grew as their linguistic capabilities increased.

# Bilingualism: Speaking in Many Tongues

## LO 12.5 Describe the consequences of bilingualism.

From the smallest towns to the biggest cities, the voices with which children speak are changing. In most of the cities in India, the voices with which children speak are changing. A large number of children speak a language other than mother tongue. **Bilingualism**—the proficient use of two languages—is becoming increasingly common (Shin & Bruno, 2003; Graddol, 2004; Hoff & Core, 2013; see Figure 12.2).

In Indian schools, the medium of instruction is either the regional language (the official language of

---

**bilingualism** The ability to proficiently use two languages

**Figure 12.2** Language Diversity in India

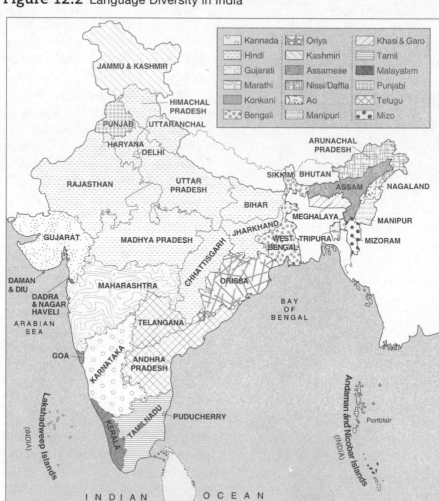

the state, for instance, Oriya, Bengali, Marathi, etc.), Hindi (the national language), or English. At present, most Indian schools teach three languages up to the primary grade level. Other than schools, there are various other reasons for people to get exposed to multiple languages. Because of migration from different states of the country and across nations, children are often exposed to many languages. For example, a child in India may be exposed to Tamil (because the father speaks Tamil), Bengali (because the mother speaks Bengali), Hindi (because the maid speaks Hindi), and English (because he attends an English medium school).

With a wide range of linguistic possibilities to choose from in assessing a situation, speakers of two languages have greater cognitive flexibility. Multilingualism is perceived as a "resource" for linguistic, social, and cognitive development. They often have greater metalinguistic awareness, and they understand the rules of language explicitly. They can solve problems with greater creativity and versatility.

Mohanty (2000, 2001, 2003c) suggests a model to explain psycholinguistic processes such as early language development and the use of language for literacy and education in the multilingual and multicultural context of India. He has shown how language socialization in India has encouraged the development of competent multilinguals. He has identified three stages of the development of language socialization in the multilingual setup in India: the period of language differentiation (roughly 4 years), the period of awareness of languages (roughly 4 to 5 years), and the period of multilingual functioning.

When children enter school, they have little proficiency in the language of instruction if it's not same as their native language. For instance, children getting admission in English medium schools in general or a child from Tamil Nadu entering a Hindi medium school in India. In this context, it is important to introduce bilingual education, in which children are initially taught in their native language, while, at the same time, they are learning English. With bilingual instruction, students are able to develop a strong foundation in the basic subject areas using their native language. Research in India (Mohanty, 1994b, 1998; Patra and Babu, 1999) indicates the need for mother-tongue medium of instruction at the pre-primary level and subsequent introduction of second and third languages at later levels.

A number of research suggests that knowing more than one language offers several cognitive advantages. Because they have a wider range of linguistic possibilities to choose from as they assess a situation, speakers of two languages show greater cognitive flexibility. They can solve problems with greater creativity and versatility. Furthermore, learning in one's native tongue is associated with higher self-esteem in minority students (Bialystok & Viswanathan, 2009; Hermanto, Moreno & Bialystok, 2012; Hsin & Snow, 2017).

Finally, because many linguists contend that universal processes underlie language acquisition, instruction in a native language may enhance instruction in a second language. In fact, many educators believe that second-language learning should be a regular part of elementary schooling for *all* children (McCardle & Hoff, 2006; Pollard-Durodola, Cárdenas-Hagan, & Tong, 2014; Kuhl et al., 2016).

# Schooling: The Three Rs (and More) of Middle Childhood

*As the eyes of the six other children in his reading group turned to him, Gagan shifted uneasily in his chair. Reading had never come easily to him, and he always felt anxious when it was his turn to read aloud. But as his teacher nodded in encouragement, he plunged in, hesitantly at first, then gaining momentum as he read the story about a mother's first day on a new job. He found that he could read the passage quite nicely, and he felt a surge of happiness and pride at his accomplishment. When he was done, he broke into a broad smile as his teacher said simply, "Well done, Gagan."*

Small moments such as these, repeated over and over, make—or break—a child's educational experience. Schooling marks a time when society formally attempts to transfer to new generations its accumulated body of knowledge, beliefs, values, and wisdom. The success with which this transfer is managed determines, in a very real sense, the future fortunes of the world.

## Schooling Around the World: Who Gets Educated?

**LO 12.6** **Define the trends affecting schooling worldwide and in India.**

In India, as in most developed countries, a primary school education is both a universal right and a legal

**Figure 12.3** Plague of Illiteracy

Illiteracy remains a significant problem worldwide, particularly for women. Across the world, nearly 800 million people—two-thirds of them women—are illiterate throughout their lives. (Although data are not included in this chart for North America, Europe, and Australia, the rate of illiteracy in these areas is extremely low relative to other parts of the world.)

**SOURCE:** UNESCO Institute for Statistics, September 2015.

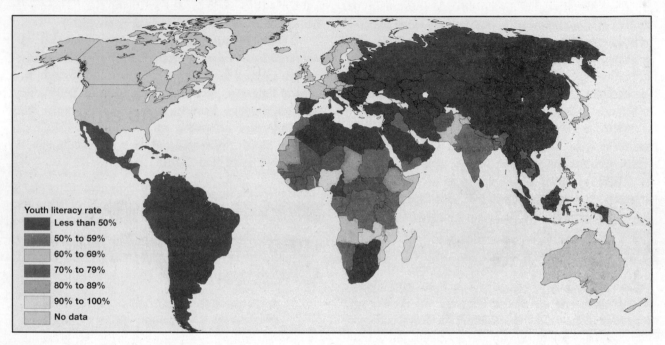

Youth literacy rate
- Less than 50%
- 50% to 59%
- 60% to 69%
- 70% to 79%
- 80% to 89%
- 90% to 100%
- No data

requirement. Virtually, all children are provided with a free education through the 12th grade. In India, 71.2 percent of the population above 15 years can read and write (The World Factbook, 2015).

More than 160 million of the world's children do not have access to even a primary school education. An additional 100 million children do not progress beyond a level comparable to the elementary education in developed countries, and nearly 800 million adults (two-thirds of them women) are illiterate throughout their lives (International Literacy Institute, 2001; see Figure 12.3).

In almost all developing countries, fewer females than males receive formal education, a discrepancy found at every level of schooling. Even in developed countries, women lag behind men in their exposure to science and technology. These differences reflect widespread and deeply held cultural and parental biases that favor males over females. Despite all attempts to reduce gender disparity in India, it is still evident in the context of school education.

**EDUCATIONAL TRENDS: BEYOND THE THREE RS.**
Schooling in the 21st century has changed significantly, with schools shifting from the traditional three Rs

(reading, writing, and arithmetic) to focus on children's overall socio-emotional and physical development. Children are given credit for their involvement in co-curricular activities. These days elementary schools also stress individual accountability. Teachers may be held responsible for their students' learning, and both students and teachers may be required to take state or national tests to assess their competence.

**CULTURAL ASSIMILATION OR PLURALISTIC SOCIETY?** Multicultural education, in part, is a response to a cultural assimilation model in which the goal was to assimilate individual cultural identities into a unified whole.

In India, the educational system is considered a means of diminishing discrimination by religion, caste, class, and gender. The Indian constitution provides for a right of admission to educational institutions regardless of religion, race, caste, or language. Efforts have been made by the government of India to achieve unity amidst diversity in the educational setting. Government-initiated programs like Universal Elementary Education and Education for All attempt to reduce disparities based on gender, caste, or religion in schools. But in so doing, they neglect the culture-specific value systems of children from various backgrounds. Such initiatives presuppose equality without addressing equity (Chakravarty, 2001). Implementation of standard curricula, textbooks, and pedagogy in all schools across India is believed to minimize disparity and bring a uniform level of achievement for all. Under such conditions, however, children may remain ignorant about important aspects of their own background and culture. Aware of this problem and aiming to respect diversity while working for unity, the government of India has made provisions for mother-tongue medium of instruction up to at least the primary school level. Attempts have also been made to educate tribal and disadvantaged children in their own cultural contexts. Towards this end, textbooks are now being developed in tribal and regional languages.

This is comparable to multicultural education in the US, where people from all over the world cater to the needs of children from India, Iran, China, Mexico, Japan, and so on. In recent years, educators have argued that students from diverse cultures enrich and broaden the education of all students. Pupils and teachers exposed to other cultures better understand the world and become sensitive to the values and practices of others.

**MULTICULTURAL EDUCATION** Classrooms in India have always been populated with students with diverse backgrounds and experiences. Only recently, though, variations in student backgrounds have been viewed as a major challenge—and opportunity—that educators face. In fact, this diversity in the classroom relates to a fundamental objective of education, which is to transmit the information a society deems important. As the famous anthropologist Margaret Mead (1942) once said, "In its broadest sense, education is the cultural process, the way in which each newborn human infant, born with a potentiality for learning greater than that of any other mammal, is transformed into a full member of a specific human society, sharing with the other members of a specific human culture" (p. 633). Culture, then, can be seen as a set of behaviors, beliefs, values, and expectations shared by the members of a society. But culture is not simply "Western culture" or "Asian culture." It is also made up of subcultural groups. Membership in a cultural or subcultural group might be of minor concern to educators if it didn't substantially impact the way students experience school.

**SHOULD SCHOOLS TEACH EMOTIONAL INTELLIGENCE?** In many elementary schools, the hottest topic in the curriculum has little to do with the traditional three *R*s. Instead, a significant trend for educators throughout the United States is the use of techniques to increase students' **emotional intelligence**, the set of skills that underlie the accurate assessment, evaluation, expression, and regulation of emotions (Mayer, 2001; Hastings, 2004; Fogarty, 2008; Abdolrezapour, 2016).

Psychologist Daniel Goleman (2005) argues that emotional literacy should be a standard part of the school curriculum. He points to several programs that succeed in teaching students to manage their emotions more effectively. For instance, in one program, children are provided with lessons in empathy, self-awareness, and social skills. In another, children are taught about caring and friendship as early as first grade through exposure to stories (Fasano & Pellitteri, 2006).

Programs meant to increase emotional intelligence have not been met with universal acceptance. Critics suggest that the nurturance of emotional intelligence is best left to students' families and that schools ought to concentrate on more traditional curriculum matters. Others contend that adding emotional intelligence to an already crowded curriculum may reduce time spent on academics. Finally, some critics argue that there is no well-specified set of criteria for what constitutes emotional intelligence, and consequently it is difficult to develop appropriate, effective curriculum materials (Roberts, Zeidner, & Matthews, 2001).

Still, most people consider emotional intelligence worthy of nurturance. It is clear that emotional intelligence is quite different from the traditional conceptions of intelligence that we consider in the next section of the chapter. The goal of emotional intelligence training is to produce people who are not only cognitively sophisticated but also able to manage their emotions effectively (Brackett & Katulak, 2007; Ulutas & Ömeroglu, 2007; Malik & Shujja, 2013).

## School Readiness, Reading, and Success

**LO 12.7 List the factors that contribute to positive academic outcomes for children.**

Many parents have a hard time deciding exactly when to enroll their children in school for the first time. One

---

**emotional intelligence** The set of skills that underlie the accurate assessment, evaluation, expression, and regulation of emotions

of the key questions involves a child's readiness for reading, a fundamental for school success. Teachers' expectations also profoundly influence their students' academic performance.

## WHAT MAKES CHILDREN READY FOR SCHOOL?

Do children who are younger than most of the other children in their grade suffer as a result of the age difference? According to traditional wisdom, the answer is yes. Because younger children are assumed to be slightly less advanced developmentally than their peers, it has been assumed that such children would be at a competitive disadvantage. In some cases, teachers recommended that students delay entry into kindergarten in order to cope better academically and emotionally (Noel & Newman, 2008).

But a massive study conducted by developmental psychologist Frederick Morrison contradicts the traditional view. He found that children who are among the youngest in first grade progress at the same rate as the oldest. Although they were slightly behind older first graders in reading, the difference was negligible. It was also clear that parents who chose to hold their children back in kindergarten, thereby ensuring that they would be among the oldest in first grade and after, were not doing their children a favor. These older children did no better than their younger classmates (Morrison, Smith, & Dow-Ehrensberger, 1995; Morrison, Bachman, & Connor, 2005; Skibbe et al., 2011).

Other research even has identified some later negative reaction to delayed entry. For example, one longitudinal study examined adolescents whose entrance into kindergarten was delayed by a year. Even though many seemed to show no ill effects from the delay during elementary school, during adolescence a surprising number of these children had emotional and behavioral problems (Byrd, Weitzman, & Auinger, 1997; Stipek, 2002).

In short, delaying children's entry into school does not necessarily provide an advantage and in some cases may actually be harmful. Ultimately, age, per se, is not a critical indicator of when children should begin school. Instead, the start of formal schooling is more reasonably tied to overall developmental readiness, the product of a complex combination of several factors.

**READING STAGES.** Reading involves a significant number of skills, from low-level cognitive skills (the identification of single letters and associating letters with sounds) to higher-level skills (matching written

**Table 12.1** Development of Reading Skills

| Stage | Age | Key Characteristics |
|-------|-----|---------------------|
| 0 | Birth to start of first grade | Learns prerequisites for reading, such as identification of the letters |
| 1 | First and second grades | Learns phonological recoding skills; starts reading |
| 2 | Second and third grades | Reads aloud fluently, but without much meaning |
| 3 | Fourth to eighth grades | Uses reading as a means for learning |
| 4 | Eighth grade and beyond | Understands reading in terms of reflecting multiple points of view |

**SOURCE:** Based on Chall, J. S. (1979). "The great debate: Ten years later, with a modest proposal for reading stages." In L. B. Resnick & P. A. Weaver (Eds.), Theory and practice of early reading. Hillsdale, NJ: Erlbaum.

words with meanings located in long-term memory and using context and background knowledge to determine the meaning of a sentence).

The development of reading skills generally occurs in several broad and frequently overlapping stages (Chall, 1992; see Table 12.1). In *Stage 0*, which lasts from birth to the start of first grade, children learn the essential prerequisites for reading, including identification of the letters in the alphabet, sometimes writing their names, and reading a few very familiar words (such as their own names or *stop* on a stop sign).

*Stage 1* brings the first real type of reading, but it largely involves *phonological recoding* skills. At this stage, which usually encompasses the first and second grades, children can sound out words by blending the letters together. Children also complete the job of learning the names of letters and the sounds that go with them.

In *Stage 2*, typically around second and third grades, children learn to read aloud with fluency. They do not attach much meaning to the words, however, because the effort involved in simply sounding out words is usually so great that relatively few cognitive resources are left over to process the meaning of the words.

The next period, *Stage 3*, extends from fourth to eighth grades. Reading becomes a means to an end—in particular, a way to learn. Whereas earlier reading was an accomplishment in and of itself, by this point children use reading to learn about the world. Even at this age, understanding gained from reading is not complete. For instance, one limitation children have at this stage is that they are able to comprehend information only when it is presented from a single perspective.

# BECOMING AN INFORMED CONSUMER OF CHILD DEVELOPMENT

## Creating an Atmosphere That Promotes School Success

What makes children succeed in school? Although there are many factors, some of which we discuss in the next chapter, there are several practical steps that can be taken to maximize children's chances of success. Among them are these:

- *Promote a "literacy environment."* Parents should read to their children and familiarize them with books and reading. Adults should provide reading models so that children see that reading is an important activity in the lives of the adults with whom they interact.

- *Talk to children.* Discuss events in the news, talk about their friends, and share hobbies. Getting children to think about and discuss the world around them is one of the best preparations for school.
- *Provide a place for children to work.* This can be a desk, a corner of a table, or an area of a room. What's important is that it be a separate, designated area.
- *Encourage children's problem-solving skills.* To solve a problem, they should learn to identify their goal, what they know, and what they don't know; to design and carry out a strategy; and finally to evaluate their result.

---

In the final period, *Stage 4*, children are able to read and process information that reflects multiple points of view. This ability, which begins during the transition into high school, permits children to develop a far more sophisticated understanding of material. This explains why great works of literature are not read at an earlier stage of education. It is not so much that younger children do not have the vocabulary to understand such works (although this is partially true); it is that they lack the ability to understand the multiple points of view that sophisticated literature invariably presents.

**HOW SHOULD WE TEACH READING?** Educators have long been engaged in an ongoing debate regarding the most effective means of teaching reading. At the heart of this debate is a disagreement about the nature of the mechanisms by which information is processed during reading. According to proponents of *code-based approaches to reading*, reading should be taught by presenting the basic skills that underlie reading. Code-based approaches emphasize the components of reading, such as the sounds of letters and their combinations—phonics—and how letters and sounds are combined to make words. They suggest that reading consists of processing the individual components of words, combining them into words, and then using the words to derive the meaning of written sentences and passages (Gray et al., 2007; Hagan-Burke et al., 2013; Cohen et al., 2016).

In contrast, some educators argue that reading is taught most successfully by using a whole-language approach. In *whole-language approaches to reading*, reading is viewed as a natural process, similar to the acquisition of oral language. According to this view, children should learn to read through exposure to complete writing—sentences, stories, poems, lists, charts, and other examples of actual uses of writing. Instead of being taught to sound out words, children are encouraged to make guesses about the meaning of words based on the context in which they appear. Through such a trial-and-error approach, children come to learn whole words and phrases at a time, gradually becoming proficient readers (Shaw, 2003; Sousa, 2005; Donat, 2006).

A growing body of data, based on careful research, suggests that code-based approaches to reading instruction are superior to whole-language approaches. For example, one study found that a group of children tutored in phonics for a year not only improved substantially in their reading, compared to a group of good readers, but that the neural pathways involved in reading became closer to those of good readers (Shaywitz et al., 2004; Shapiro & Solity, 2016).

Whatever approach is used to teach it, reading produces significant changes in the wiring of the brain. It boosts the organization of the visual cortex of the brain, and it improves the processing of spoken language.

**HOW TEACHERS' EXPECTATIONS INFLUENCE THEIR STUDENTS.** Suppose you were an elementary school teacher and were told that certain children in your class were expected to bloom intellectually in the coming year. Would you treat them differently from the children who were not so designated?

You probably would treat them differently, according to the results of a classic but controversial study. Teachers do, in fact, treat children for whom they have expectations of improvement differently from those for whom they have no such expectations (Rosenthal & Jacobson, 1968). In the experiment, elementary school teachers were told at the beginning of a new school year that based on test results, five children in their classes would be likely to "bloom" in the upcoming year. In reality, however, the information was bogus: The names of the children had been picked at random, although the teachers didn't know that. At the end of the year, the children completed an intelligence test that was identical to one taken a year earlier. The results showed that clear differences existed in the intellectual growth of the so-called bloomers, compared with that of the other members of their classes. Those randomly designated as likely to make significant gains did, in fact, improve more than the other children.

When the findings of the experiment, reported in a book titled *Pygmalion in the Classroom*, were published, they caused an immediate stir among educators—and among the public at large. The reason for this furor was the implication of the results: If merely holding high expectations is sufficient to bring about gains in achievement, wouldn't holding low expectations lead to slowed achievement? And because teachers may sometimes hold low expectations for children from lower socioeconomic and minority backgrounds, did this mean that children from such backgrounds were destined to show low achievement throughout their educational careers?

Although the original experiment has been criticized on methodological and statistical grounds (Wineburg, 1987), enough subsequent evidence has been amassed to make it clear that the expectations of teachers are communicated to their students and can in fact bring about the expected performance. The phenomenon has come to be called the **teacher expectancy effect**—the cycle of behavior in which a teacher transmits an expectation about a child and thereby actually brings about the expected behavior (Rosenthal, 2002; Anderson-Clark, Green, & Henley, 2008; Sciarra & Ambrosino, 2011; see Figure 12.4).

**Figure 12.4** Teacher Expectations and Student Performance

Teachers' expectations about their students—positive or negative—can actually bring about positive or negative performance from their students. How does this relate to what we know about self-esteem?

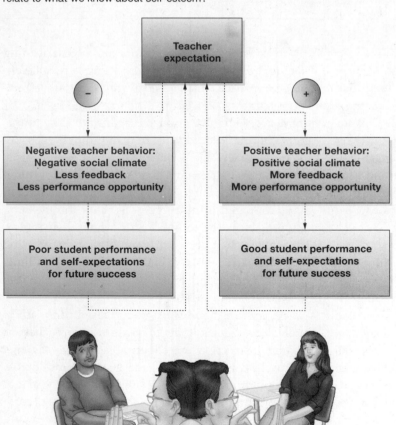

**teacher expectancy effect** The phenomenon whereby an educator's expectations for a given child actually bring about the expected behavior

The teacher expectancy effect can be viewed as a special case of a broader concept known as a *self-fulfilling prophecy*, in which a person's expectation is capable of bringing about an outcome. For instance, physicians have long known that providing patients with placebos (pills with no active ingredients) can sometimes "cure" them simply because the patients expect the medicine to work.

In the case of teacher expectancy effects, the basic explanation seems to be that teachers, after forming an initial expectation about a child's ability—often inappropriately based on such factors as previous school records, physical appearance, gender, or even race—transmit their expectation to the child through a complex series of verbal and nonverbal cues. These communicated expectations in turn indicate to the child what behavior is appropriate, and the child behaves accordingly (Carpenter, Flowers, & Mertens, 2004; Gewertz, 2005; Trouilloud et al., 2006; McKown & Weinstein, 2008).

## Multicultural Education

### LO 12.8 Discuss the outcomes of multicultural education.

It has always been the case that schools in India have been populated by individuals from a broad range of backgrounds and experiences. Yet it is only relatively recently that variations in student backgrounds have been viewed as one of the major challenges—and opportunities—that educators face.

The diversity of background and experience in the classroom relates to a fundamental objective of education, which is to provide a formal mechanism to transmit the information a society deems important. As the famous anthropologist Margaret Mead (1942, p. 633) once said, "In its broadest sense, education is the cultural process, the way in which each newborn human infant, born with a potentiality for learning greater than that of any other mammal, is transformed into a full member of a specific human society, sharing with the other members of a specific human culture."

*Culture*, then, can be thought of as a set of behaviors, beliefs, values, and expectations shared by members of a particular society. But although culture is often thought of in a relatively broad context (as in "Western culture" or "Asian culture"), it is also possible to focus on particular *subcultural* groups within a larger, more encompassing culture. For example, we can consider particular racial, ethnic, religious, socioeconomic, or even gender groups in India as manifesting characteristics of a subculture.

Membership in a cultural or subcultural group might be of only passing interest to educators were it not for the fact that students' cultural backgrounds have a substantial impact on the way that they—and their peers—are educated. In fact, in recent years, a considerable amount of thought has gone into establishing **multicultural education**, in which the goal is to help minority students develop competence in the culture of the majority group while maintaining positive group identities that build on their original cultures (Nieto, 2005; Brandhorst, 2011).

**MULTICULTURAL CLASSROOMS IN INDIA** India is a multicultural country with the coexistence of diverse groups in terms of caste, language, and regional social practices such as clothing, literary activities, cuisines, and festivities. Though the states are demarcated by strict geographical boundaries, there has been migration across borders for better opportunities over the past few decades. It has led to the multicultural existence of people in India, particularly in the larger cities. Multiculturalism has always been discussed by historians and philosophers in India. The Indian constitution had made provision for recognizing the country's diversity in education and employment. Since the Kothari Commission Report (1966), there has been substantial attention to cultural pluralism and social equality in education. Further in 2005, the National Curriculum Framework (NCF) published by the NCERT lays down certain points with special reference to multicultural education such as: strengthening national system of education in a pluralistic society based on curricular practices that respects social justice, equality, and secularism, and the core values of the Indian constitution. Further, it states that the multilingual character of Indian society should be seen as a resource for the enrichment of school life and effort should be made to implement the three-language formula emphasizing the recognition of children's home language or mother tongue as the best medium of instruction. Diversity in Indian schools is both an opportunity as well as a challenge. It's an opportunity as it fosters development of children who are better able to understand diversity and gradually become sensitive to the realities of a diverse culture in India. It's a challenge in terms of

---

**multicultural education** Education in which the goal is to help students from minority cultures develop competence in the culture of the majority group while maintaining positive group identities that build on their original cultures

developing curriculum, textbooks, and trained teachers. Nowadays, the classrooms in India are enriched with cultural, language, ethnic, and socio-cultural diversity, which is evident in terms of the prescribed textbooks, curriculum, and classroom instruction.

In the United States, multicultural education developed in part as a reaction to a **cultural assimilation model**, in which the goal of education is to assimilate individual cultural identities into a unique, unified American culture. In the early 1970s, however, educators and members of minority groups began to suggest that the cultural assimilation model ought to be replaced by a **pluralistic society model**. According to this conception, American society is made up of diverse, coequal cultural groups that should preserve their individual cultural features. The pluralistic society model grew in part from the belief that teachers, by emphasizing the dominant culture and discouraging students who were non-native speakers from using their native tongues, had the effect of devaluing minority subcultural heritages and lowering those students' self-esteem. Instructional materials, such as readers and history lessons, inevitably feature culture-specific events and understandings; children who never saw examples

representing their own cultural heritage might never be exposed to important aspects of their backgrounds. For example, English-language texts rarely present some of the great themes that appear throughout Spanish literature and history (such as the search for the Fountain of Youth and the Don Juan legend). Hispanic students immersed in such texts might never come to understand important components of their own heritage. Ultimately, educators began to argue that the presence of students representing diverse cultures enriched and broadened the educational experience of all students. Pupils and teachers exposed to people from different backgrounds could better understand the world and gain greater sensitivity to the values and needs

**cultural assimilation model** The view of American society as a "melting pot" in which all cultures are amalgamated into a unique, unified American culture

**pluralistic society model** The concept that American society is made up of diverse, coequal cultures that should preserve their individual features

**bicultural identity** The maintenance of one's original cultural identity while becoming integrated into the majority culture

# DEVELOPMENTAL DIVERSITY AND YOUR LIFE
## Fostering Multicultural Classroom

Bourdieu (1986) wrote about how cultural capital from family and society determine academic success and later, social activities. The impact of this orientation is seen in the attention paid to recognizing diversity among students in relation to their social-cultural and economic backgrounds. The teachers are required to be sensitive to the cultural diversity of their classrooms and implement a culturally sensitive curriculum in the schools of India.

Multicultural classroom is one of the major challenges for the educators in India in current days as the students are from diverse backgrounds: migrants, cultural minorities, and those from disadvantaged communities. Therefore, it becomes important to maintain an inclusive curriculum that is respectful of differences. A culturally-sensitive curriculum would encourage teachers to understand and recognize student's cultural life and background. It helps students from a minority background develop a sense of identity as individuals. In recent years, all over the world, there is a move toward pedagogy of diversity. This covers many aspects, such

as gender, a student's cultural and socio-economic background, educational and curricular strategies, and so on. In this pedagogy, the aim is to combine social and educational approaches to assist socially excluded families and children. One of the pedagogical approach could be to encourage the students to research and share information about different cultural groups (their own as well as their classmate's) as well as analyze and celebrate differences in traditions and beliefs. It would foster cultural sensitivity and ultimately a trusting relationship with fellow classmates.

In many places in the world, currently, school systems urge children to maintain their original cultural identity while they integrate themselves into the dominant culture. This view emphasizes on **bicultural identity** (in the context of India, we need to talk about multicultural identity) which suggests that an individual can live as a member of two cultures, with two cultural identities, without having to choose one over the other (Lu, 2001; Oyserman et al., 2003; Vyas, 2004; Marks, Patton, & Coll, 2011; Collins, 2012).

of others (Levin et al., 2012; Thijs & Verkuyten, 2013; Theodosiou-Zipiti & Lamprianou, 2016).

> **From an educator's perspective:**  Should one goal of instruction be to foster cultural assimilation and maintain multicultural education for children from other cultures? Why, or why not?

# Intelligence: Determining Individual Strengths

*"Why should you tell the truth?" "How far is Los Angeles from New York?" "A table is made of wood; a window of _____."*

*As 10-year-old Hyacinth sat hunched over her desk, trying to answer a long series of questions like these, she tried to guess the point of the test she was taking in her fifth-grade classroom. Clearly, the test didn't cover material that her teacher, Ms. White-Johnston, had talked about in class.*

*"What number comes next in this series: 1, 3, 7, 15, 31, _____?"*

*As Hyacinth continued to work her way through the questions, she gave up trying to guess the rationale for the test. She'd leave that to her teacher, she sighed to herself. Rather than attempt to figure out what it all meant, she simply tried to do her best on the individual test items.*

Hyacinth was taking an intelligence test. She might be surprised to learn that she was not alone in questioning the meaning and import of the items on the test. Intelligence test items are painstakingly prepared, and intelligence tests show a strong relationship to success in school (for reasons we will soon discuss). Many developmentalists, however, would admit to harboring their own doubts as to whether questions such as those on Hyacinth's test are entirely appropriate to the task of assessing intelligence.

Understanding just what is meant by the concept of intelligence has proven to be a major challenge for researchers interested in delineating what separates intelligent from unintelligent behavior. Although nonexperts have their own conceptions of intelligence (one survey found, for instance, that laypersons believe that intelligence consists of three components: problem-solving ability, verbal ability, and social competence), it has been more difficult for

experts to concur (Sternberg et al., 1981; Howe, 1997). Still, a general definition of intelligence is possible: **Intelligence** is the capacity to understand the world, think with rationality, and use resources effectively when faced with challenges (Wechsler, 1975).

Part of the difficulty in defining intelligence stems from the many—and sometimes unsatisfactory—paths that have been followed over the years in the quest to distinguish more intelligent people from less intelligent ones. To understand how researchers have approached the task of assessing intelligence by devising *intelligence tests*, we need to consider some of the historical milestones in the area of intelligence.

## Intelligence Benchmarks: Differentiating the Intelligent From the Unintelligent

**LO 12.10  Describe the ways in which intelligence can be measured.**

The Paris school system was faced with a problem at the turn of the 20th century: A significant number of children were not benefiting from regular instruction. Unfortunately, these children—many of whom we would now call intellectually disabled—were generally not identified early enough to shift them to special classes. The French minister of instruction approached psychologist Alfred Binet (1857–1911) with this problem and asked Binet to devise a technique for the early identification of students who might benefit from instruction outside the regular classroom.

**BINET'S TEST.**  Binet tackled his task in a thoroughly practical manner. His years of observing school-age children suggested to him that previous efforts to distinguish intelligent from unintelligent students—some of which were based on reaction time or keenness of sight—were off the mark. Instead, he launched a trial-and-error process in which items and tasks were administered to students who had been previously identified by teachers as being either "bright" or "dull." Tasks that the bright students completed correctly and the dull students failed to complete correctly were retained for the test. Tasks that did not

---

**intelligence** The capacity to understand the world, think rationally, and use resources effectively when faced with challenges

discriminate between the two groups were discarded. The result of this process was a test that reliably distinguished students who had previously been identified as fast or slow learners.

Binet's pioneering efforts in intelligence testing left several important legacies. The first was his pragmatic approach to the construction of intelligence tests. Binet did not have theoretical preconceptions about what intelligence was. Instead, he used a trial-and-error approach to psychological measurement that continues to serve as the predominant approach to test construction today. His definition of intelligence as *that which his test measured* has been adopted by many modern researchers, and it is particularly popular among test developers, who respect the widespread utility of intelligence tests but wish to avoid arguments about the underlying nature of intelligence.

Binet's legacy extends to his linking intelligence and school success. His procedure for constructing an intelligence test ensured that intelligence—defined as performance on the test—and school success would be virtually one and the same. Thus, Binet's intelligence test, and today's tests that follow in its footsteps, have become reasonable indicators of the degree to which students possess attributes that contribute to successful school performance. However, they do not provide useful information regarding a vast number of other attributes that are largely unrelated to academic proficiency, such as social skills or personality characteristics.

Finally, Binet developed a procedure of linking each intelligence test score with a **mental age**, the age of the children taking the test who, on average, achieved that score. For example, if a 6-year-old girl received a score of 30 on the test, and this was the average score received by 10-year-olds, her mental age would be considered 10 years. Similarly, a 15-year-old boy who scored a 90 on the test—thereby matching the mean score for 15-year-olds—would be assigned a mental age of 15 years (Wasserman & Tulsky, 2005).

Although assigning a mental age to students provides an indication of whether they are performing at the same level as their peers, it does not permit adequate comparisons among students who each have a different **chronological (physical) age**. By using mental age alone, for instance, it would be assumed that a 15-year-old responding with a mental age of 17 years would be as bright as a 6-year-old responding with a mental age of 8 years, when actually the 6-year-old would be showing a much greater *relative* degree of brightness.

French educator Alfred Binet originated the intelligence test.

A solution to this problem comes in the form of the **intelligence quotient (IQ)**, a score that takes into account a student's mental *and* chronological age. The traditional method of calculating an IQ score uses the following formula, in which MA stands for mental age and CA stands for chronological age:

$$\text{IQ score} = \frac{\text{MA}}{\text{CA}} \times 100$$

As a bit of trial and error with this formula demonstrates, people whose mental age (MA) is equal to their chronological age (CA) will always have an IQ of 100. Furthermore, if the chronological age exceeds the mental age—implying below-average intelligence—the score will be below 100; if the chronological age is lower than the mental age—suggesting above-average intelligence—the score will be above 100.

Using this formula, we can return to our earlier example of a 15-year-old who scores at a 17-year-old mental age. This student's IQ is $17/15 \times 100$, or 113. In comparison, the IQ of a 6-year-old scoring at a mental age of 8 is $8/6 \times 100$, or 133—a higher IQ score than the 15-year-old's.

IQ scores today are calculated in a more mathematically sophisticated manner and are known as *deviation IQ scores*. The average deviation IQ score remains set at 100, but tests are now devised so that

**mental age** The typical intelligence level found for people of a given chronological age

**chronological (physical) age** A person's age according to the calendar

**intelligence quotient (IQ)** A score that expresses the ratio between a person's mental and chronological ages

the degree of deviation from this score permits the calculation of the proportion of people who have similar scores. For instance, approximately two-thirds of all people fall within 15 points of the average score of 100, achieving scores between 85 and 115. As scores rise or fall beyond this range, the percentage of people in the same score category drops significantly (see Figure 12.5).

**PRESENT-DAY APPROACHES TO INTELLIGENCE.** Since the time of Binet, tests of intelligence have become increasingly accurate measures of IQ. Most of them can still trace their roots to his original work in one way or another. For example, one of the most widely used tests, the **Stanford-Binet Intelligence Scale**, Fifth Edition (SB5)—began as an American revision of Binet's original test. The test consists of a series of items that vary according to the age of the person being tested. For instance, young children are asked to answer questions about everyday activities or to copy complex figures. Older people are asked to explain proverbs, solve analogies, and describe similarities between groups of words. The test is administered orally, and test-takers are given progressively more difficult problems until they are unable to proceed.

The **Wechsler Intelligence Scale for Children, Fourth Edition (WISC-IV)** is another widely used intelligence test. The test (which stems from its adult counterpart, the *Wechsler Adult Intelligence Scale*) provides separate measures of verbal and performance (or nonverbal) skills, as well as a total score. As you can see from the sample items in Figure 12.6, the verbal tasks are traditional word problems that test skills such as understanding a passage, whereas typical nonverbal tasks include copying a complex design, arranging pictures in a logical order, and assembling objects. The separate portions of the test allow for easier identification of any specific problems a test-taker may have. For example, significantly higher scores on the performance part of the test than on the verbal part may indicate difficulties in linguistic development (Zhu & Weiss, 2005).

The **Kaufman Assessment Battery for Children, Second Edition (KABC-II)** takes a different approach

### Figure 12.5 IQ Scores

The most common and average IQ score is 100, with 68.3 percent of all people falling within 15 points of 100. About 95 percent of the population has scores that are within 30 points above or below 100; fewer than 3 percent score below 55 or above 145.

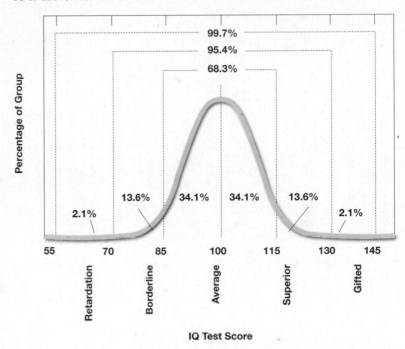

from the SB5 and WISC-IV. In it, children are tested on their ability to integrate different kinds of stimuli simultaneously and to use step-by-step thinking. A special virtue of the KABC-II is its flexibility. It allows the person giving the test to use alternative wording or gestures, or even to pose questions in a different language, in order to maximize a test-taker's performance. This capability of the KABC-II makes testing more valid and equitable for children to whom English is a second language (Kaufman et al., 2005; McGill & Spurgin, 2016).

**Stanford-Binet Intelligence Scale** A test that consists of a series of items that vary according to the age of the person being tested

**Wechsler Intelligence Scale for Children, Fourth Edition (WISC-IV)** A test for children that provides separate measures of verbal and performance (nonverbal) skills, as well as a total score

**Kaufman Assessment Battery for Children, Second Edition (KABC—II)** An intelligence test that measures children's ability to integrate different stimuli simultaneously and use step-by-step thinking

## Figure 12.6 Measuring Intelligence

The Wechsler Intelligence Scale for Children (WISC-IV) includes items such as these. What do such items cover? What do they miss?

| Name | Goal of Item | Example |
|---|---|---|
| **Verbal Scale** | | |
| Information | Assess general information | How many nickels make a dime? |
| Comprehension | Assess understanding and evaluation of social norms and past experience | What is the advantage of keeping money in the bank? |
| Arithmetic | Assess math reasoning through verbal problems | If two buttons cost 15 cents, what will be the cost of a dozen buttons? |
| Similarities | Test understanding of how objects or concepts are alike, tapping abstract reasoning | In what way are an hour and a week alike? |
| **Performance Scale** | | |
| Digit symbol | Assess speed of learning | Match symbols to numbers using key. 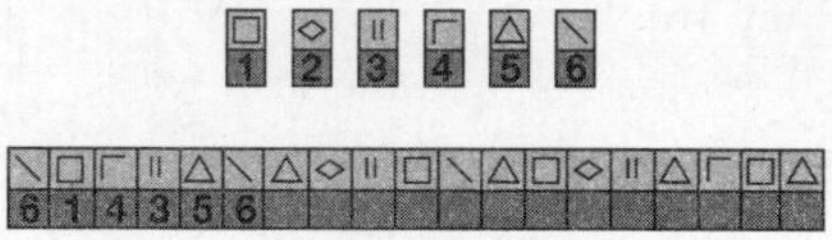 |
| Picture completion | Visual memory and attention | Identify what is missing.  |
| Object assembly | Test understanding of relationship of parts to wholes | Put pieces together to form a whole.  |

What do the IQ scores derived from IQ tests mean? For most children, IQ scores are reasonably good predictors of their school performance. That's not surprising, given that the initial impetus for the development of intelligence tests was to identify children who were having difficulties in school (Sternberg & Grigorenko, 2002).

But when it comes to performance outside of academic spheres, the story is different. For instance, although people with higher IQ scores are apt to finish more years of schooling, once this is statistically controlled for, IQ scores are not closely related to income and later success in life. Furthermore, IQ scores are frequently inaccurate when it comes to predicting a particular individual's future success. For example, two people with different IQ scores may finish their bachelor's degrees at the same college, and the person with a lower IQ might end up with a higher income and a more successful career. Because of these difficulties with traditional IQ scores, researchers have turned to alternative approaches to measuring intelligence (McClelland, 1993).

## Group Differences in IQ

**LO 12.11  Explain how bias may occur in traditional intelligence testing.**

A jontry is an example of a

a. rulpow
b. flink
c. spudge
d. bakwoc

If you were to find an item composed of nonsense words such as this on an intelligence test, your immediate—and quite legitimate—reaction would likely be to complain. How could a test that purports to measure intelligence include test items that incorporate meaningless terminology?

Yet for some people, the items actually used on traditional intelligence tests might appear equally nonsensical. To take a hypothetical example, suppose children living in rural areas were asked details about subways, while those living in urban areas were asked about the mating practices of sheep. In both cases, we would expect that the previous experiences of test-takers would have a substantial effect on their ability to answer the questions. And if questions about such matters were included on an IQ test, the test could rightly be viewed as a measure of prior experience rather than of intelligence.

Although the questions on traditional IQ tests are not so obviously dependent on test-takers' prior experiences, our examples, cultural background, and experience do have the potential to affect intelligence test scores. Many educators suggest that traditional measures of intelligence are subtly biased in favor of

White, upper- and middle-class students, and against groups with different cultural experiences (Ortiz & Dynda, 2005).

**EXPLAINING RACIAL DIFFERENCES IN IQ.**  The issue of how cultural background and experience influence IQ test performance has led to considerable debate among researchers. The debate has been fueled by the finding that IQ scores of certain racial groups are consistently lower, on average, than the IQ scores of other groups. For example, the mean score of African Americans tends to be about 15 IQ points lower than the mean score of Whites—although the measured difference varies a great deal depending on the particular IQ test employed (Fish, 2001; Maller, 2003).

The question that emerges from such differences, of course, is whether they reflect actual differences in intelligence or, instead, are caused by bias in the intelligence tests themselves in favor of majority groups and against minorities. For example, if Whites perform better on an IQ test than African Americans because of their greater familiarity with the language used in the test items, the test hardly can be said to provide a fair measure of the intelligence of African Americans. Similarly, an intelligence test that solely used African American vernacular English could not be considered an impartial measure of intelligence for Whites.

The question of how to interpret differences among intelligence scores of different cultural groups lies at the heart of one of the major controversies in child development: To what degree is an individual's intelligence determined by heredity and to what degree by environment? The issue is important because of its social implications. For instance, if intelligence is primarily determined by heredity and is therefore largely fixed at birth, attempts to alter cognitive abilities later in life, such as schooling, will meet with limited success. However, if intelligence is largely environmentally determined, modifying social and educational conditions is a more promising strategy for bringing about increases in cognitive functioning (Weiss, 2003; Nisbett et al., 2012).

*THE BELL CURVE* **CONTROVERSY.**  Although investigations into the relative contributions of heredity and environment to intelligence have been conducted for decades, the smoldering debate became a raging fire with the publication of a book by Richard J. Herrnstein and Charles Murray (1994) titled *The Bell Curve*. In the book, Herrnstein and Murray argue that the average 15-point IQ difference between Whites and African

Americans is due primarily to heredity rather than to environment. Furthermore, they argue that this IQ difference accounts for the higher rates of poverty, lower employment, and higher use of welfare among minority groups as compared with majority groups.

The conclusions reached by Herrnstein and Murray (1994) raised a storm of protest, and many researchers who examined the data reported in the book came to conclusions that were quite different. Most developmentalists and psychologists responded by arguing that the racial differences in measured IQ can be explained by environmental differences between the races. In fact, when a variety of indicators of economic and social factors are statistically taken into account simultaneously, mean IQ scores of Black and White children turn out to be actually quite similar. For instance, children from similar middle-class backgrounds, whether African American or White, tend to have similar IQ scores (Brooks-Gunn, Klebanov, & Duncan, 1996; Alderfer, 2003).

Furthermore, critics maintained that there is little evidence to suggest that IQ is a cause of poverty and other social ills. Some critics suggested, as mentioned earlier in this discussion, that IQ scores were unrelated in meaningful ways to later success in life (e.g., Nisbett, 1994; Reifman, 2000; Sternberg, 2005).

Finally, members of cultural and social minority groups may score lower than members of the majority group due to the nature of the intelligence tests themselves. It is clear that traditional intelligence tests may discriminate against minority groups who have not been exposed to the same type of environment that majority group members have experienced (Fagan & Holland, 2007; Razani et al., 2007).

Most traditional intelligence tests are constructed using White, English-speaking, middle-class populations as their test subjects. As a result, children from different cultural backgrounds may perform poorly on the tests—not because they are less intelligent, but because the tests use questions that are culturally biased in favor of majority group members. And these abstract test performances come with real consequences: A classic study found that in one California school district, Mexican American students were 10 times more likely than Whites to be placed in special-education classes (Mercer, 1973; Hatton, 2002).

More recent findings show that nationally, twice as many African American students as White students are classified as mildly intellectually disabled, a difference that experts attribute primarily to cultural bias and

poverty. Although certain IQ tests (such as the *System of Multicultural Pluralistic Assessment* [SOMPA]) have been designed to be equally valid regardless of the cultural background of test-takers, no test can be completely without bias (Sandoval et al., 1998; Hatton, 2002; Ford, 2011).

In short, most experts in the area of IQ were not convinced by *The Bell Curve*'s contention that differences in group IQ scores are largely determined by genetic factors. Still, we cannot put the issue to rest, largely because it is impossible to design a definitive experiment that can determine the cause of differences in IQ scores among members of different groups. (Thinking about how such an experiment might be designed shows the futility of the enterprise: One cannot ethically assign children to different living conditions to find the effects of environment, nor would one wish to genetically control or alter intelligence levels in unborn children.)

Today, IQ is seen as the product of *both* nature and nurture interacting with one another in a complex manner. Rather than seeing intelligence as being produced by either genes or experience, genes are considered to affect experiences, and experiences are viewed as influencing the expression of genes. For instance, psychologist Eric Turkheimer has found evidence that although environmental factors play a larger role in influencing the IQ of poor children, genes are more influential in the IQ of affluent children (Turkheimer et al., 2003; Harden, Turkheimer, & Loehlin, 2007).

Ultimately, it may be less important to know the absolute degree to which intelligence is determined by genetic and environmental factors than it is to learn how to improve children's living conditions and educational experiences. By enriching the quality of children's environments, we will be in a better position to permit all children to reach their full potential and to maximize their contributions to society, whatever their individual levels of intelligence (Posthuma & de Geus, 2006).

# What IQ Tests Don't Tell: Alternative Conceptions of Intelligence

**LO 12.12  Compare and contrast alternative conceptions of intelligence with traditional definitions.**

The intelligence tests used most frequently in school settings today are based on the idea that intelligence is a single factor, a unitary mental ability. This one main attribute has commonly been called *g* (Spearman, 1927; Lubinski, 2004). The *g* factor is assumed to underlie performance on every aspect of intelligence, and it is the *g* factor that intelligence tests presumably measure.

Many theorists, however, dispute the notion that intelligence is one-dimensional. Some developmentalists suggest that, in fact, two kinds of intelligence exist: fluid intelligence and crystallized intelligence. **Fluid intelligence** reflects information-processing capabilities, reasoning, and memory. For example, a student asked to group a series of letters according to some criterion or to remember a set of numbers would be using fluid intelligence (Shangguan & Shi, 2009; Ziegler et al., 2012; Kenett et al., 2016).

In contrast, **crystallized intelligence** is the accumulation of information, skills, and strategies that people have learned through experience and that they can apply in problem-solving situations. A student would likely be relying on crystallized intelligence to solve a puzzle or deduce the solution to a mystery, in which it was necessary to draw on past experience (Alfonso, Flanagan, & Radwan, 2005; McGrew, 2005; Hill et al., 2013; Thorsen, Gustafsson, & Cliffordson, 2014).

Other theorists divide intelligence into an even greater number of parts. For example, psychologist Howard Gardner suggests that we have eight distinct types of intelligence, each relatively independent (see Figure 12.7). Gardner states that these separate types of intelligence operate not in isolation, but together, depending on the type of activity in which we are engaged (Chen & Gardner, 2005; Gardner & Moran, 2006; Roberts & Lipnevich, 2012).

Russian psychologist Lev Vygotsky, whose approach to cognitive development we first discussed in Chapter 2, had a very different take on intelligence. He suggested that to assess intelligence, we should look not only at those cognitive processes that are fully developed but also at those that are currently being developed. To do this, Vygotsky contended that assessment tasks should involve cooperative interaction between the individual who is being assessed and the person who is doing the assessment—a process called *dynamic assessment*. In short, intelligence is seen as being reflected not only in how children can perform on their own but also in terms of how well they perform when helped by adults (Vygotsky, 1927/1976; Lohman, 2005).

Vygotsky also argued that intelligence needed to be looked at through the lens of culture. Consequently, what would be considered intelligent behavior would be demonstrated in different ways depending on the culture in which a person lived.

Support for the importance of culture in considering intelligence and its measurement comes from a classic cross-cultural study that highlights the challenges in conceptualizing and measuring intelligence. In the study, researchers examined 6- to 15-year-old children living on the streets of Brazil who made a living by selling candy, fruit, and other products. Although they lacked much in the way of formal schooling, they were quite proficient in the math needed to sell effectively. For instance, they would change prices as a function in the inflation rate, and they could figure discounts for large purchases. In fact, their math skills often exceeded those of children who had been exposed to considerable math in school (Saxe & de Kirby, 2014; Saxe, 2015).

Taking yet another approach, psychologist Robert Sternberg (1990, 2003a) suggests that intelligence is best thought of in terms of information processing. In this view, the way in which people store material in memory and later use it to solve intellectual tasks provides the most precise conception of intelligence. Rather than focus on the various subcomponents that make up the *structure* of intelligence, information-processing approaches examine the *processes* that underlie intelligent behavior (Floyd, 2005).

Studies of the nature and speed of problem-solving processes show that people with higher intelligence levels differ from others not only in the number of problems they ultimately are able to solve but also in their method of solving the problems. People with high IQ scores spend more time on the initial stages of problem solving, retrieving relevant information from memory. In contrast, those who score lower on traditional IQ tests tend to spend less time on the initial stages, instead skipping ahead and making less informed guesses. The processes used in solving problems, then, may reflect important differences in intelligence (Sternberg, 2005).

Sternberg's work on information-processing approaches to intelligence has led him to develop the

---

**fluid intelligence** Intelligence that reflects information-processing capabilities, reasoning, and memory

**crystallized intelligence** The accumulation of information, skills, and strategies that people have learned through experience and that they can apply in problem-solving situations

## Figure 12.7 Gardner's Eight Intelligences

Howard Gardner has theorized that there are eight distinct types of intelligence, each relatively independent of one another. How do you fit into this categorization?

**SOURCE:** Based on Walters, E., & Gardner, H. (1986). "The theory of multiple intelligences: Some issues and answers." In R. J. Sternberg & R. K. Wagner (Eds.), Practical intelligence. New York: Cambridge University Press.

*Musical intelligence* (skills in tasks involving music). Case example: When he was 3, Yehudi Menuhin was smuggled into the San Francisco Orchestra concerts by his parents. The sound of Louis Persinger's violin so entranced the youngster that he insisted on a violin for his birthday and Louis Persinger as his teacher. He got both. By the time he was 10 years old, Menuhin was an international performer.

*Naturalist intelligence* (ability to identify and classify patterns in nature). Case example: In prehistoric periods, hunter-gatherers required naturalist intelligence in order to identify what types of plants were edible.

*Bodily kinesthetic intelligence* (skills in using the whole body or various portions of it in the solution of problems or in the construction of products or displays, exemplified by dancers, athletes, actors, and surgeons). Case example: Fifteen-year-old Babe Ruth played third base. During one game, his team's pitcher was doing poorly and Babe loudly criticized him from third base. Brother Mathias, the coach, called out, "Ruth, if you know so much about it, *you* pitch!" Babe was surprised and embarrassed because he had never pitched before, but Brother Mathias insisted. Ruth said later that at the very moment he took the pitcher's mound, he *knew* he was supposed to be a pitcher.

*Intrapersonal intelligence* (knowledge of the internal aspects of oneself; access to one's own feelings and emotions). Case example: In her essay "A Sketch of the Past," Virginia Woolf displays deep insight into her own inner life through these lines, describing her reaction to several specific memories from her childhood that still, in adulthood, shock her: "Though I still have the peculiarity that I receive these sudden shocks, they are now always welcome; after the first surprise, I always feel instantly that they are particularly valuable. And so I go on to suppose that the shock-receiving capacity is what makes me a writer."

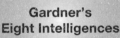

**Gardner's Eight Intelligences**

*Logical mathematical intelligence* (skills in problem solving and scientific thinking). Case example: Barbara McClintock won the Nobel Prize in medicine for her work in microbiology. She describes one of her breakthroughs, which came after thinking about a problem for half an hour...: "Suddenly I jumped and ran back to the [corn] field. At the top of the field [the others were still at the bottom] I shouted, 'Eureka, I have it!'"

*Interpersonal intelligence* (skills in interacting with others, such as sensitivity to the moods, temperaments, motivations, and intentions of others). Case example: When Anne Sullivan began instructing the deaf and blind Helen Keller, her task was one that had eluded others for years. Yet, just 2 weeks after beginning her work with Keller, Sullivan achieved a great success. In her words, "My heart is singing with joy this morning. A miracle has happened! The wild little creature of 2 weeks ago has been transformed into a gentle child."

*Linguistic intelligence* (skills involved in the production and use of language). Case example: At the age of 10, T.S. Elliot created a magazine called *Fireside*, to which he was the sole contributor. In a 3-day period during his winter vacation, he created eight complete issues.

*Spatial intelligence* (skills involving spatial configurations, such as those used by artists and architects). Case example: Navigation around the Caroline Islands... is accomplished without instruments.... During the actual trip, the navigator must envision mentally a reference island as it passes under a particular star and from that he computes the number of segments completed, the proportion of the trip remaining, and any corrections in heading.

---

**triarchic theory of intelligence**. According to this model, intelligence consists of three aspects of information processing: the componential element, the experiential element, and the contextual element. The *componential* aspect of intelligence reflects how efficiently people can process and analyze information. Efficiency in these areas allows people to infer relationships among different parts of a problem, solve the problem, and then evaluate their solution. People who are strong on the componential element score highest on traditional tests of intelligence (Sternberg, 2005; Gardner, 2011; Sternberg, 2016).

The *experiential* element is the insightful component of intelligence. People who have a strong experiential element can easily compare new material with

**triarchic theory of intelligence** The belief that intelligence consists of three aspects of information processing: the componential element, the experiential element, and the contextual element

what they already know and can combine and relate facts that they already know in novel and creative ways. Finally, the *contextual* element of intelligence concerns practical intelligence, or ways of dealing with the demands of the everyday environment.

In Sternberg's view, people vary in the degree to which each of these three elements is present. Our level of success at any given task reflects the match between the task and our own specific pattern of strength on the three components of intelligence (Sternberg, 2003b, 2008).

## Falling Below and Above Intelligence Norms

**LO 12.13** **Describe how children who fall outside the normal range of intelligence are classified.**

*Although Connie kept pace with her classmates in kindergarten, by the time she reached first grade, she was academically the slowest in almost every subject. It was not that she didn't try, but rather that it took her longer than other students to catch on to new material, and she regularly required special attention to keep up with the rest of the class.*

*Yet in some areas she excelled: When asked to draw or produce something with her hands, she not only matched her classmates' performance but exceeded it, producing beautiful work that was much admired by her classmates. Although the other students in the class felt that there was something different about Connie, they were hard-pressed to identify the source of the difference, and in fact they didn't spend much time pondering the issue.*

Connie's parents and teacher, though, knew what made her special. Extensive testing in kindergarten had shown that Connie's intelligence was well below normal, and she was officially classified as a special-needs student.

**BELOW THE NORM: INTELLECTUAL DISABILITY (MENTAL RETARDATION).** Approximately 1 to 3 percent of the school-age population is considered to be intellectually disabled. Estimates vary so widely because the most commonly accepted definition of intellectual disability—which was previously referred to professionally as mental retardation (a term that is still used frequently)—is one that leaves a great deal of room for interpretation. According to the American Association on Intellectual and Developmental Disabilities, **intellectual disability** is a disability characterized by significant limitations both in intellectual functioning and in adaptive behavior, which covers many everyday social and practical skills. (American Association on Intellectual and Developmental Disabilities, 2012).

Most cases of intellectual disability are classified as *familial intellectual disability* (or *familial retardation*), in which no cause is apparent, but there is a history of intellectual disability in the family. In other cases, there is a clear biological cause. The most common biological causes are *fetal alcohol syndrome*, which is caused by a mother's use of alcohol while pregnant, and *Down syndrome*, which results from the presence of an extra chromosome. Birth complications, such as a temporary lack of oxygen, may also produce retardation (Plomin, 2005; West & Blake, 2005; Manning & Hoyme, 2007).

Although limitations in intellectual functioning can be measured in a relatively straightforward manner—using standard IQ tests—it is more difficult to determine how to gauge limitations in other areas. Ultimately, this imprecision leads to a lack of uniformity in the ways experts apply the labels "intellectual disability" and "mental retardation." Furthermore, it has resulted in significant variation in the abilities of people who are categorized as experiencing intellectual disability. Accordingly, intellectually disabled people range from those who can be taught to work and function with little special attention to those who are virtually untrainable and who never develop speech or such basic motor skills as crawling or walking.

The vast majority of the intellectually disabled—some 90 percent—have relatively minor levels of deficits. Classified with **mild intellectual disability**, they score in the range of 50 or 55 to 70 on IQ tests. Typically, their retardation is not even identified before they reach school, although their early development is often slower than average. Once they enter elementary school, their retardation and their need for special attention usually become apparent, as it did with Connie, the first grader profiled at the beginning of this discussion. With appropriate training, these students can ultimately reach a third- to sixth-grade educational level, and although they cannot carry out complex intellectual tasks, they are able to hold jobs and function independently and successfully.

---

**intellectual disability** A significantly subaverage level of intellectual functioning that occurs with related limitations in two or more skill areas

**mild intellectual disability** Intellectual disability with IQ scores in the range of 50 or 55 to 70

Children with intellectual disability are often educated in classes with typical children and perform well.

Intellectual and adaptive limitations become more apparent, however, at more extreme levels of mental retardation. People whose IQ scores range from around 35 or 40 to 50 or 55 are classified with **moderate intellectual disability**. Accounting for 5 to 10 percent of those classified as intellectually disabled, the moderately retarded display distinctive behavior early in their lives. They are slow to develop language skills, and their motor development is also affected. Regular schooling is usually not effective in training people with moderate retardation to acquire academic skills because generally they are unable to progress beyond the second-grade level. Still, they are capable of learning occupational and social skills, and they can learn to travel independently to familiar places. Typically, they require moderate levels of supervision.

At the most significant levels of retardation—in individuals with **severe intellectual disability** (IQs ranging from around 20 or 25 to 35 or 40) and **profound intellectual disability** (IQs below 20 or 25)—the ability to function is severely limited. Usually, such people produce little or no speech, have poor motor control, and may need 24-hour nursing care. At the same time, though, some people with severe intellectual disability are capable of learning basic self-care skills, such as dressing and eating, and they may even develop the potential to become partially independent as adults. Still, the need for relatively high levels of care continues throughout the life span, and most individuals with severe and profound intellectual disabilities are institutionalized for most of their lives.

## ABOVE THE NORM: THE GIFTED AND TALENTED.

*Before her second birthday, Audry Walker recognized sequences of five colors. When she was 6, her* *father, Michael, overheard her telling a little boy, "No, no, no, Hunter, you don't understand. What you were seeing was a flashback."*

*At school, Audry quickly grew bored as the teacher drilled letters and syllables until her classmates caught on. She flourished, instead, in a once-a-week class for gifted and talented children, where she could learn as fast as her nimble brain could take her. (Schemo, 2004, p. A18)*

It sometimes strikes people as curious that the gifted and talented are considered to have a form of exceptionality. Yet the 3 to 5 percent of school-age children who are gifted and talented present special challenges of their own.

Which students are considered to be **gifted and talented?** Little agreement exists among researchers on a single definition of this rather broad category of students. The federal government considers the term *gifted* to include "children who give evidence of high-performance capability in areas such as intellectual, creative, artistic, leadership capacity, or specific academic fields, and who require services or activities not ordinarily provided by the school in order to fully develop such capabilities" (Sec. 582, P.L. 97–35). Intellectual capabilities, then, represent only one type of exceptionality; unusual potential in areas outside the academic realm is also included in the concept. Gifted and talented children have so much potential that they, no less than students with low IQs, warrant special concern—although special school programs for them are often the first to be dropped when school systems face budgetary problems (Schemo, 2004; Mendoza, 2006; Olszewski-Kubilius & Thomson, 2013).

Despite the stereotypic description of the gifted—particularly those with exceptionally high intelligence—as "unsociable," "poorly adjusted," and "neurotic," most research suggests that highly intelligent people tend to be outgoing, well adjusted, and popular

**moderate intellectual disability** Intellectual disability with IQ scores from around 35 or 40 to 50 or 55

**severe intellectual disability** Intellectual disability with IQ scores that range from around 20 or 25 to 35 or 40

**profound intellectual disability** Intellectual disability with IQ scores below 20 or 25

**gifted and talented** Showing evidence of high-performance capability in intellectual, creative, or artistic areas, in leadership capacity, or in specific academic fields

(Bracken & Brown, 2006; Shaunessy et al., 2006; Cross et al., 2008).

For instance, one landmark long-term study of 1,500 gifted students, which began in the 1920s, found that not only were the gifted smarter than average, but also they were healthier, better coordinated, and psychologically better adjusted than their less intelligent classmates. Furthermore, their lives played out in ways that most people would envy. The subjects received more awards and distinctions, earned more money, and made many more contributions in art and literature than the average person. For instance, by the time they had reached age 40, they had collectively produced more than 90 books, 375 plays and short stories, and 2,000 articles, and they had registered more than 200 patents. Perhaps not surprisingly, they reported greater satisfaction with their lives than did the nongifted (Sears, 1977; Shurkin, 1992; Reis & Renzulli, 2004).

Yet being gifted and talented is no guarantee of success in school, as we can see if we consider the particular components of the category. For example, the verbal abilities that allow the eloquent expression of ideas and feelings can equally permit the expression of glib and persuasive statements that happen to be inaccurate. Furthermore, teachers may sometimes misinterpret the humor, novelty, and creativity of unusually gifted children, and see their intellectual fervor as disruptive or inappropriate. And peers are not always sympathetic: Some very bright children try to hide their intelligence in an effort to fit in better with other students (Swiatek, 2002).

Educators have devised two approaches to teaching the gifted and talented: acceleration and enrichment. **Acceleration** allows gifted students to move ahead at their own pace, even if this means skipping to higher grade levels. The materials that students receive under acceleration programs are not necessarily different from what other students receive; they simply are provided at a faster pace than they would be for the average student (Smutny, Walker, & Meckstroth, 2007; Wells, Lohman, & Marron, 2009; Steenbergen-Hu & Moon, 2011; Lee, Olszewski-Kubilius & Thomson, 2013).

An alternative approach is **enrichment**, through which students are kept at grade level but are enrolled in special programs and given individual activities to allow greater depth of study on a given topic. In enrichment, the material provided to gifted students differs not only in the timing of its presentation but also in its sophistication. Thus, enrichment materials are designed to provide an intellectual challenge to the gifted student, encouraging higher-order thinking (Worrell, Szarko, & Gabelko, 2001; Rotigel, 2003).

Acceleration programs can be remarkably effective. Most studies have shown that gifted students who begin school even considerably earlier than their age-mates do as well as or better than those who begin at the traditional age. One of the best illustrations of the benefits of acceleration is the "Study of Mathematically Precocious Youth," an ongoing program at Vanderbilt University. In this program, seventh and eighth graders who have unusual abilities in mathematics participate in a variety of special classes and workshops. The results have been nothing short of sensational, with students successfully completing college courses and sometimes even enrolling in college early. Some students have even graduated from college before the age of 18 (Lubinski & Benbow, 2001, 2006; Webb, Lubinski, & Benbow, 2002).

# The Case of …
## Ignacio: The great engineer

Nine-year-old Ignacio Gomez lives for the weekend. Weekends are when along with his father he fixes stuff around in their home, or talk about cricket, or maybe even watch sports channel on the TV. Ignacio prides himself on knowing the players of every national and international team and all their stats. Ignacio has also learned to fix leaking faucets and clanking radiators. He knows all the tools in his father's toolbox and has developed an instinctive feel for the right size drill bit for any repair. "You're a smart one, Ignacio," his father says. "You're going to be a big engineer someday." Ignacio loves these words because he is not at all recognized in his third-grade classroom. At school,

---

**acceleration** The provision of special programs that allow gifted students to move ahead at their own pace, even if this means skipping to higher grade levels

**enrichment** Approach in which gifted students are kept at grade level but are enrolled in special programs and given individual activities to allow greater depth of study on a given topic

Ignacio is a "slow learner" and a "poor reader," according to his teacher. The other kids call him a "dummy." In the last examination, Ignacio tried his best but the questions were hard to read—there was nothing on the test about cricket or fixing things—and the time went fast. Later, he overheard his teacher tell another teacher that he had the IQ of a rock. Ignacio was smart enough to know rocks don't have any intelligence. Rocks are dumber than dumb.

1. Do you think Ignacio has an intellectual disability? Why or why not?

2. What are some reasons Ignacio might have done poorly on the IQ test? Do you think a written test could be constructed that Ignacio might perform better on? What would the test look like?

3. Why does Ignacio's father say, "You're going to be a big engineer someday. What do you think his father understands about Ignacio's cognitive abilities that his teacher and the IQ test don't recognize?

4. What role might teacher expectancy effect play in the relationship between Ignacio and his teacher? What suggestions would you make to Ignacio's teacher to guide her in becoming a more effective teacher for him?

5. How do you think Vygotsky might approach working with a student like Ignacio?

## Epilogue

In this chapter, we discussed children's cognitive growth during the middle childhood years, tracing its development through the different lenses provided by Piaget, information-processing approaches, and Vygotsky. We noted the increased capabilities that children develop during middle childhood in the areas of memory and language, both of which facilitate and support gains in many other areas.

We then looked at some aspects of schooling worldwide. We touched on such trends as the reemphasis on the academic basics, the great debate on reading instruction, and the changing picture for multicultural education and diversity.

Finally, we concluded the chapter with an examination of the controversial issue of intelligence: how it is defined, how it is tested, how IQ test differences are interpreted, and how children who fall significantly below or above the intellectual norm are educated and treated.

Look back to the prologue about Dipti Rawat teaching his third-grade class to solve math word problems by having them write one, and answer the following questions:

1. Dipti calls his approach to word problems an example of "metacognition." What does he mean by this? How would metacognition help his third graders learn to solve such problems?

2. Relate Dipti's method of teaching word problems to the developmental theories of Piaget, information processing, and Vygotsky's theory of development. Which approach do you think most clearly describes what Dipti is doing in this lesson?

3. Some teachers might consider Dipti's approach to teaching word problems ambitious, and yet his students seem to "get it." How does this result relate to the concept of teacher expectancy?

4. In solving word problems in this way, do you think Dipti's students are relying more on fluid or crystallized intelligence? Why?

## Looking Back

**LO 12.1 Summarize Piaget's theoretical approaches to cognitive development in middle childhood.**

• School-age children enter the concrete operational period and for the first time become capable of applying logical thought processes to concrete problems.

• Although Piaget was a virtuoso observer of children, and his theories have been widely employed in education, subsequent research, using a broader array of experimental tasks, suggests that Piaget underestimated children's capabilities and misjudged the age at which their cognitive abilities emerge.

- Piaget's stages of cognitive development may be less universal and more culture-specific than he supposed. However, when non-Western children are given tasks related to important domains in their culture and are interviewed by researchers familiar with the language and customs of their culture, they are more likely to display concrete operational thinking.

**LO 12.2** **Explain the development of memory according to information-processing approaches.**

- According to information-processing approaches, children's intellectual development in the school years can be attributed to substantial increases in memory capacity and the sophistication of the "programs" children can handle.

- Metamemory, an understanding of what memory is and its underlying processes, emerges and improves during middle childhood.

- School-age children consciously employ control strategies to improve their cognitive processing. Examples of control strategies include rehearsal and repetition, organizing materials into coherent patterns for easier recall, and the use of mnemonics. Children can be taught when and where to use the various control strategies most effectively.

**LO 12.3** **Describe the classroom practices that Vygotsky recommends to advance children's cognitive development.**

- Vygotsky recommends that students focus on active learning through child–adult and child–child interactions that fall within each child's zone of proximal development.

**LO 12.4** **Explain how language develops during middle childhood.**

- The language development of children in the school years is substantial, with improvements in vocabulary, syntax, and pragmatics.

- Children learn to control their behavior through linguistic strategies, and they learn more effectively by seeking clarification when they need it.

**LO 12.5** **Describe the consequences of bilingualism.**

- Bilingualism can be beneficial in the school years.

- Children who are taught all subjects in their first language with simultaneous instruction in English appear to experience several linguistic and cognitive advantages.

**LO 12.6** **Define the trends affecting schooling worldwide and in the United States.**

- Schooling, which is available to nearly all children in most developed countries, is not as accessible to children, especially girls, in many less developed countries.

- After a period of emphasis on social well-being and allowing students more choice in their studies, U.S. schools are returning to a set curriculum emphasizing the fundamentals with a stress on individual accountability for both teacher and student.

- Emotional intelligence is the set of skills that permit people to manage their emotions effectively.

**LO 12.7** **List the factors that contribute to positive academic outcomes for children.**

- Contrary to widely held beliefs, researchers have found that children who are younger than most of their classmates do not suffer a disadvantage and tend to progress at the same rate as their slightly older peers. Indeed, some studies suggest that delaying a child's entrance into kindergarten may have negative effects in the adolescent years.

- The development of reading skills, which are fundamental to schooling, generally occurs in several stages. Research suggests that code-based (phonics) approaches are superior to whole-language approaches.

- The expectations of others, particularly teachers, can produce outcomes that conform to those expectations by leading students to modify their behavior.

**LO 12.8** **Discuss the outcomes of multicultural education.**

- Multicultural education was established to help minority students achieve competence in the culture of the majority group while recognizing their original cultures and supporting a positive group identity built upon those cultures.

- Multiculturalism and diversity are significant issues in U.S. schools, where the melting-pot society, in which minority cultures were assimilated to the majority culture, is being replaced by the pluralistic society, in which individual cultures maintain their own identity while participating in the definition of a larger culture.

**LO 12.9** **Describe the ways in which intelligence can be measured.**

- Intelligence testing has traditionally focused on factors that differentiate successful academic performers from unsuccessful ones. The intelligence quotient (IQ) reflects the ratio of a person's mental age to his or her chronological age. Other conceptualizations of intelligence focus on different types of intelligence or on different aspects of information processing.

**LO 12.10** **Explain how bias may occur in traditional intelligence testing.**

- Most traditional IQ measures have been constructed using White, middle-class English speakers as test subjects. Children from different class or cultural backgrounds may perform poorly because the test questions are biased in favor of majority group members.

- The question of whether there are racial differences in IQ, and how to explain those differences, is highly controversial and has been extensively debated among researchers.

**LO 12.11** **Compare and contrast alternative conceptions of intelligence with traditional definitions.**

- Traditional measures have defined intelligence as a unitary mental ability, a single factor that is presumed to affect performance on every aspect of intelligence.

- Alternative conceptions stress that intelligence is multidimensional.

**LO 12.12** **Describe how children who fall outside the normal range of intelligence are classified.**

- Children who are both above and below the norm benefit from special educational programs.

- Acceleration and enrichment are used to educate children who are gifted and talented.

## Key Terms and Concepts

concrete operational stage (p. 309)
decentering (p. 309)
memory (p. 312)
metamemory (p. 312)
metalinguistic awareness (p. 315)
bilingualism (p. 316)
emotional intelligence (p. 319)
teacher expectancy effect (p. 322)
multicultural education (p. 323)
cultural assimilation model (p. 324)
pluralistic society model (p. 324)
bicultural identity (p. 324)
intelligence (p. 325)
mental age (p. 326)

chronological (physical) age (p. 326)
intelligence quotient (or IQ score) (p. 326)
Stanford-Binet Intelligence Scale (p. 327)
Wechsler Intelligence Scale for Children, Fourth Edition (WISC-IV) (p. 327)
Kaufman Assessment Battery for Children, Second Edition (KABC-II) (p. 327)
fluid intelligence (p. 331)
crystallized intelligence (p. 331)

triarchic theory of intelligence (p. 332)
intellectual disability (p. 333)
mild intellectual disability (p. 333)
moderate intellectual disability (p. 334)
severe intellectual disability (p. 334)
profound intellectual disability (p. 334)
gifted and talented (p. 334)
acceleration (p. 335)
enrichment (p. 335)

# Chapter 13
# Social and Personality Development in Middle Childhood

## ∨ Learning Objectives

**LO 13.1** Explain how children's views of themselves change during middle childhood.

**LO 13.2** Describe the importance of self-esteem during the middle childhood years.

**LO 13.3** List the types of relationships and friendships that are typical of middle childhood.

**LO 13.4** Define social competence, and explain which personal characteristics lead to popularity.

**LO 13.5** Explain how gender affects friendships.

**LO 13.6** Describe how race affects friendships.

**LO 13.7** Explain the causes of bullying and how it can be prevented.

**LO 13.8** Describe today's changing home environment.

**LO 13.9** Summarize the effects on children when caregivers work outside the home.

**LO 13.10** List some examples of how today's diverse family arrangements affect children.

**LO 13.11** Describe the influence of race and poverty on children's family life.

**LO 13.12** Describe the nature of group care in the 21st century.

# Prologue: Who Is This Kid?

Ask five different people about Rudra Prasad and you might get five different descriptions of this 10-year-old. "Rudra is awesome!" says his best friend, Pradeep. "He's really good at math and is a genius," Rudra's teacher agrees that he has above-average abilities. "But he's a bit lazy," she says. "Homework comes in late. Careless spelling errors." The captain of the fourth-grade basketball team thinks that Rudra is sort of a nerd. "He's not much into sports, but he's funny, so that's okay." A classmate who's in the school band with Rudra says, "He's really into music. He plays the drums, and when he lets go, he's amazing." His mother affectionately calls him Big Brother. "Rudra is the eldest child," she explains. "He's so good with his younger siblings, always inventing games to play with them."

And how does Rudra view himself? "I kind of like to go my own way," he says. "My mind is always thinking up new projects or a way to do something better. I've got a couple of friends. I really don't need more."

# Looking Ahead

As children grow into middle childhood, they experience significant transformations in the way they relate to others and the way they think of themselves. Rudra's story shows that personality development becomes multifaceted and complex in these years, and it has profound implications for social relationships with both peers and adults.

In this chapter, we focus on social and personality development during middle childhood. We start our consideration of personality and social development by examining the changes that occur in the ways children see themselves. We discuss how they view their personal characteristics, and we examine the complex issue of self-esteem.

Next, the chapter turns to relationships during middle childhood. We discuss the stages of friendship and the ways gender and ethnicity affect how and with whom children interact. We also examine how to improve children's social competence.

The last part of the chapter explores the central societal institution in children's lives: the family. We consider the consequences of divorce, self-care children, and the phenomenon of group care.

# The Developing Self

*Kavita Dubey is nine years old, and she has just entered Class 5. In the summer vacation, she started making her doll house. During the weekend, her father helped her in designing the house and cutting cardboard into pieces. The reset of the days, she was completely engaged in making the house on her own. Her vacation will be over in a few days; she was almost nearing completion of her doll house with little bit of finishing touches like painting, putting window curtains, etc. By this time, she has developed a clear sense of pride that her dolls have a house of their own, and she can play along with her friends in the doll house.*

According to Erik Erikson, middle childhood encompasses the industry-versus-inferiority stage, characterized by a focus on meeting the challenges presented by the world.

Trey's growing sense of competence is reflected in the passage above, as he describes how he and his mother built his treehouse. Conveying what psychologist Erik Erikson calls "industriousness," Trey's pride in his accomplishment illustrates one of the ways in which children's views of themselves evolve.

## Psychosocial Development and Self-Understanding in Middle Childhood

**LO 13.1 Explain how children's views of themselves change during middle childhood.**

According to Erik Erikson, whose approach to psychosocial development we discussed in Chapter 10, middle childhood is very much about competence. Lasting from roughly age 6 to age 12—the period in which children are in elementary school—the **industry-versus-inferiority stage** is characterized by a focus on efforts to meet the challenges presented by parents, peers, school, and the other complexities of the modern world.

As children move through middle childhood, school presents enormous challenges. Children must direct their energies not only to mastering what they are presented, which encompasses an enormous body of information, but also to making a place for themselves in their social worlds. They increasingly work with others in group activities and must navigate among different social groups and roles, including relationships involving teachers, friends, and families.

Success in the industry-versus-inferiority stage brings with it feelings of mastery and proficiency and a growing sense of competence, like those expressed by Trey when he talks about his building experience. By contrast, difficulties in this stage lead to feelings of failure and inadequacy. As a result, children may withdraw both from academic pursuits, showing less interest and motivation to excel, and from interactions with peers.

Children such as Trey may find that attaining a sense of industry during the middle childhood years has lasting consequences. For example, one classic study examined how childhood industriousness and hard work were related to adult behavior by following a group of 450 men over a 35-year period, starting in early childhood (Vaillant & Vaillant, 1981). The men who were most industrious and hardworking during childhood were most successful as adults, both in occupational attainment and in their personal lives. In fact, childhood industriousness was more closely associated with adult success than intelligence or family background.

> **From an educator's perspective:** If industriousness is a more accurate predictor of future success than IQ, how might an individual's industriousness be improved? Should this be a focus of schooling?

During middle childhood, children continue their efforts to answer the question "Who am I?" as they seek to understand the nature of the self. Although the question does not yet have the urgency it will assume in adolescence, elementary school–age children still seek to pin down their place in the world.

**THE SHIFT IN SELF-UNDERSTANDING FROM THE PHYSICAL TO THE PSYCHOLOGICAL.** Children are on a quest for self-understanding during middle childhood. Helped by the cognitive advances that we discussed in the previous chapter, such as an increased understanding of theory of mind and increased information-processing capabilities, they begin to view themselves less in terms of external

---

**industry-versus-inferiority stage** According to Erik Erikson, the period from ages 6 to 12 that is characterized by a focus on efforts to attain competence in meeting the challenges presented by parents, peers, school, and the other complexities of the modern world

As children become older, they begin to characterize themselves in terms of their psychological attributes (such as being a responsible and nurturing individual) as well as by their physical achievements.

physical attributes and more in terms of psychological traits (Lerner, Theokas, & Jelicic, 2005; Eggum et al., 2011; Bosacki, 2013; Aronson & Bialostok, 2016).

For instance, 6-year-old Carey describes herself as "a fast runner and good at drawing"—both characteristics that are highly dependent on motor skills. In contrast, 11-year-old Meiping characterizes herself as "pretty smart, friendly, and helpful to my friends." Meiping's view of herself is based on psychological characteristics, inner traits that are more abstract than the younger child's descriptions. The use of inner traits to determine self-concept results from the child's increasing cognitive skills, a development that we discussed in Chapter 12.

In addition to shifting focus from external characteristics to internal psychological traits, children's views of who they are became less simplistic and have greater complexity. In Erikson's view, children are seeking endeavors where they can be successfully industrious. As they get older, children discover that they may be good at some things and not so good at others. Ten-year-old Ginny, for instance, comes to understand that she is good at arithmetic but not very good at spelling; 11-year-old Alberto determines that he is good at softball but doesn't have the stamina to play soccer very well.

Children's self-concepts also become divided into personal and academic spheres. As can be seen in Figure 13.1, children evaluate themselves in four major areas, and each of these areas can be broken down even further. For instance, the nonacademic self-concept includes the components of physical appearance, peer relations, and physical ability. The academic self-concept is similarly divided. Research on students' self-concepts in English, mathematics, and nonacademic realms has found that the separate self-concepts are not always correlated, although there is overlap among them. For example, a child who sees herself as a star math student is not necessarily going to feel she is great at English (Ehm, Lindberg & Hasselhorn, 2013; Lohbeck, Tietjens, & Bund, 2016).

**SOCIAL COMPARISON.** If someone asked you how good you are at math, how would you respond? Most of us would compare our performance to that of others who are roughly of the same age and educational level. It is unlikely that we'd answer the question by comparing ourselves either to Albert Einstein or to a kindergartner just learning about numbers.

Elementary school–age children begin to follow the same sort of reasoning when they seek to understand their own abilities. When they were younger, they tended to consider their abilities in terms of some hypothetical standard, making a judgment that they are good or bad in an absolute sense. In middle childhood, they begin to use social comparison processes, comparing themselves to others to determine their levels of accomplishment.

**Social comparison** is the desire to evaluate one's own behavior, abilities, expertise, and opinions by comparing them to those of others. According to a theory first suggested by psychologist Leon Festinger (1954), when concrete, objective measures of ability are lacking, people turn to *social reality* to evaluate themselves. Social reality refers to understanding that is derived from how others act, think, feel, and view the world.

But who provides the most adequate comparison? When they cannot objectively evaluate their ability, children during middle childhood increasingly look to others who are similar to themselves. In addition, children may use *upward social comparison,* in which they evaluate their abilities against those who appear to be more proficient and successful than they are. While using upward social comparison may provide aspirational models, it can sometimes make individuals feel worse about themselves because they fear they can never

**social comparison** The desire to evaluate one's own behavior, abilities, expertise, and opinions by comparing them to those of others

**Figure 13.1** Looking Inward: The Development of Self

As children get older, their views of themselves become more differentiated, composed of several personal and academic spheres. What cognitive changes make this possible?

**SOURCE:** Adapted from Shavelson, R., Hubner, J. J., & Stanton, J. C. (1976). "Self-concept: Validation of construct interpretations." Review of Educational Research, vol. 46, 407–441.

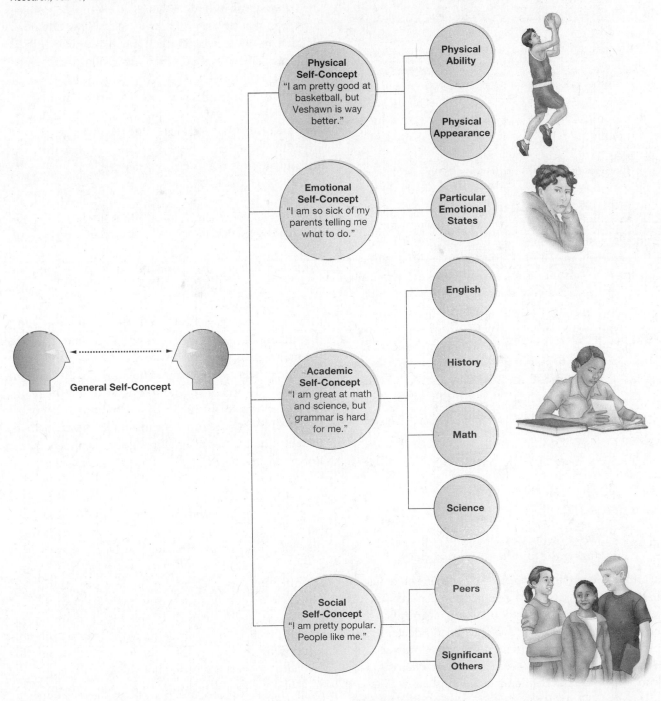

be as good as their more successful peers (Summers, Schallert, & Ritter, 2003; Boissicat et al., 2012).

**DOWNWARD SOCIAL COMPARISON.** Although children typically compare themselves to similar others, in some cases—particularly when their self-esteem is at stake—they choose to make *downward social comparisons* with those who are obviously less competent or successful (Vohs & Heatherton, 2004; Hui et al., 2006; Hosogi et al., 2012).

Downward social comparison protects children's self-esteem. By comparing themselves to those who are less able, children ensure that they will come out on top and thereby preserve an image of themselves as successful.

Downward social comparison helps explain why some students in elementary schools with generally low achievement levels are found to have stronger academic self-esteem than very capable students in schools with high achievement levels. The reason is that students in the low-achievement schools observe others who are not doing terribly well academically, and they feel relatively good by comparison. In contrast, students in the high-achievement schools may find themselves competing with a more academically proficient group of students, and their perception of their performance may suffer in comparison. At least in terms of self-esteem, then, it is better to be a big fish in a small pond than a small fish in a big one (Marsh et al., 2008; Visconti, Kochenderfer-Ladd, & Clifford, 2013).

## Self-Esteem: Developing a Positive—or Negative—View of Oneself

**LO 13.2** Describe the importance of self-esteem during the middle childhood years.

Children don't dispassionately view themselves just in terms of an itemization of physical and psychological characteristics. Instead, they make judgments about themselves as being good or bad in particular ways. **Self-esteem** is an individual's overall and specific positive and negative self-evaluation. Whereas self-concept reflects beliefs and cognitions about the self (*I am good at trumpet; I am not so good at social studies*), self-esteem is more emotionally oriented (*Everybody thinks I'm a nerd*) (Davis-Kean & Sandler, 2001; Bracken & Lamprecht, 2003; Mruk, 2013).

Self-esteem develops in important ways during middle childhood. As we noted previously, children increasingly compare themselves to others, and as they do, they assess how well they measure up to society's standards. In addition, they increasingly develop their own internal standards of success, and they can see how well they compare to those. One of the advances that occurs during middle childhood is that, like self-concept, self-esteem becomes increasingly differentiated. At age 7, most children have self-esteem that reflects a global, fairly simple view of themselves. If their overall self-esteem is positive, they believe that they are relatively good at all things. Conversely, if their overall self-esteem is negative, they feel that they are inadequate at most things (Harter, 2006; Hoersting & Jenkins, 2011; Coelho, Marchante, & Jimerson, 2016).

As children progress into the middle childhood years, however, their self-esteem is higher in some areas and lower in others. For example, a boy's overall self-esteem may be positive as it relates to his artistic ability and negative as it relates to his athletic skills.

**CHANGE AND STABILITY IN SELF-ESTEEM.** Generally, overall self-esteem increases during middle childhood, with a brief decline around age 12. Although there are probably several reasons for the decline, the main one appears to be the school transition that typically occurs around this age: Students leaving elementary school and entering either middle school or junior high school show a decline in self-esteem, which then gradually rises again (Twenge & Campbell, 2001; Robins & Trzesniewski, 2005; Poorthuis et al., 2014).

In contrast, some children have chronically low self-esteem. Children with low self-esteem face a tough road, in part because their self-esteem becomes enmeshed in a cycle of failure that grows increasingly difficult to break. Assume, for instance, that Harry, a student with chronically low self-esteem, is facing an important test. Because of his low self-esteem, he expects to do poorly. As a consequence, he is quite anxious—so anxious that he is unable to concentrate well and study effectively. Furthermore, he may decide not to study much, because he figures that if he's going to do badly anyway, he needn't bother studying.

Ultimately, of course, Harry's high anxiety and lack of effort bring about the result he expected: He

---

**self-esteem** An individual's overall and specific positive and negative self-evaluation

**Figure 13.2** Cycles of Self-Esteem

Because children with low self-esteem may expect to do poorly on a test, they may experience high anxiety and not work as hard as those with higher self-esteem. As a result, they actually do perform badly on the test, which in turn confirms their negative view of themselves. In contrast, those with high self-esteem have more positive expectations, which lead to lower anxiety and higher motivation. As a consequence, they perform better, reinforcing their positive self-image. How would a teacher help students with low self-esteem break out of a negative cycle?

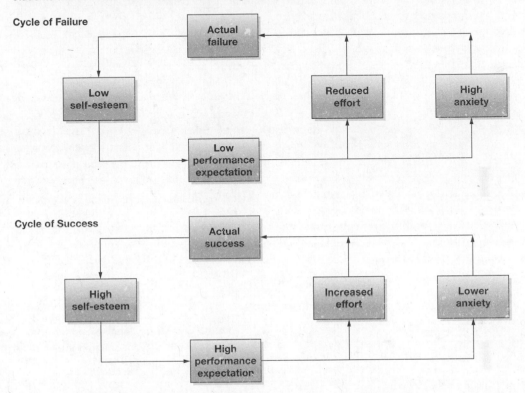

does poorly on the test. This failure, which confirms Harry's expectation, reinforces his low self-esteem, and the cycle of failure continues (see Figure 13.2).

In contrast, students with high self-esteem travel a more positive path, falling into a cycle of success. Having higher expectations leads to increased effort and lower anxiety, increasing the probability of success. In turn, this helps affirm the higher self-esteem that began the cycle.

Parents can help break the cycle of failure by promoting their child's self-esteem. The best way to do this is through the use of the *authoritative* childrearing style that we discussed in Chapter 10. Authoritative parents are warm and emotionally supportive, while still setting clear limits for their children's behavior. In contrast, other parenting styles have less positive effects on self-esteem. Parents who are highly punitive and controlling send a message to their children

that they are untrustworthy and unable to make good decisions—a message that can undermine children's sense of adequacy. Highly indulgent parents, who indiscriminately praise and reinforce their children regardless of their actual performance, can create a false sense of self-esteem in their children, which ultimately may be just as damaging to children (Raboteg-Saric & Sakic, 2013; Harris et al., 2015; Orth, 2017; also see the *From Research to Practice* box).

**RACE AND SELF-ESTEEM.** If you were part of a racial group whose members routinely experienced prejudice and discrimination, it seems reasonable to predict that your self-esteem would be affected. Early research confirmed that hypothesis and found that African Americans had lower self-esteem than Whites. For example, a set of pioneering studies several generations ago found that African American children shown Black and

# FROM RESEARCH TO PRACTICE
## The Danger of Inflated Praise

If you knew that a child was having some self-esteem problems, what do you think might be some helpful things to say to that child? If you guessed that lavish praise would encourage the child to feel better about himself or herself, you're not alone. Most adults believe that children need praise in order to feel good about themselves, and parenting advice in popular media often reinforces this notion (Brummelman, Thomaes, de Castro, et al., 2014; Brummelman, Thomaes, Overbeek, et al., 2014).

But how do children actually respond to praise? Research has shown that praise isn't always the beneficial thing we presume it to be. For example, praising children's native ability ("How smart you are!") rather than their effort ("You studied really hard!") has been shown to cause children to avoid challenges. It's easier to risk failure when all it means is that you didn't try hard enough rather than that you aren't good enough. So how would low-self-esteem children respond to well-intentioned, inflated praise?

Not well, it turns out. In a recent study, children between 8 and 12 were shown a work of art and asked to draw a copy of it. Most of them then received written feedback on their drawings from a purported famous artist, who randomly told some children that they had made a beautiful drawing and told other children that they had made an incredibly beautiful drawing. Then the children were offered a choice of other works of art to attempt to copy—some were simple and easy, whereas others were complex and difficult. It was emphasized to the children that they would learn more by trying the complex works, but they would make fewer mistakes by trying the simple ones (Brummelman et al., 2014).

Among the children who received restrained praise ("you made a beautiful drawing"), those with lower self-esteem tended to choose more challenging drawings to attempt next. But the pattern reversed for children who received inflated praise ("you made an *incredibly* beautiful drawing"), such that those with lower self-esteem tended to choose more simple drawings for their next attempt. The researchers concluded that inflated praise tends to trigger low-self-esteem children to want to avoid revealing their presumed deficiencies, but tends to trigger high-self-esteem children to want to show off the extent of their abilities. When it comes to using praise to boost children's self-esteem, the adage that less is more seems particularly apt (Brummelman et al., 2014).

- **Why might it be the case that non-inflated praise has a greater tendency to induce challenge-seeking for low-self-esteem children than it does for high-self-esteem children?**

White dolls preferred the White dolls over the Black ones (Clark & Clark, 1947). The interpretation that was drawn from the study: The self-esteem of the African American children was low.

More recent research, however, has shown these early assumptions to be overstated. The picture is more complex regarding relative levels of self-esteem among members of different racial and ethnic groups. For example, although White children initially show higher self-esteem than Black children, Black children begin to show slightly higher self-esteem than White children around age 11. This shift occurs as African American children become more closely identified with their racial group and increasingly view the positive aspects of their group membership (Dulin-Keita et al., 2011; Sprecher, Brooks, & Avogo, 2013; Davis et al., 2017).

Hispanic children also show an increase in self-esteem toward the end of middle childhood, although

In pioneering research conducted in the 1940s, African American girls' preference for White dolls was viewed as an indication of low self-esteem. More recent evidence, however, suggests that White and African American children show little difference in self-esteem.

even in adolescence Their self-esteem still trails that of Whites. In contrast, Asian American children show the opposite pattern: Their self-esteem in elementary school is higher than that of Whites and Blacks, but by the end of childhood, their self-esteem is lower than that of Whites (Umana-Taylor, Diveri, & Fine, 2002; Tropp & Wright, 2003; Verkuyten, 2008).

One explanation for the complex relationship between self-esteem and minority group status comes from *social identity theory*. According to the theory, members of a minority group are likely to accept the negative views held by a majority group only if they perceive that there is little realistic possibility of changing the power and status differences between the groups. If minority group members feel that prejudice and discrimination can be reduced, and they blame society, and not themselves, for the prejudice, self-esteem should not differ between majority and minority groups (Tajfel & Turner, 2004; Thompson, Briggs-King, & LaTouche-Howard, 2012).

As group pride and ethnic awareness among minority group members has grown, differences in self-esteem among members of different ethnic groups have narrowed. This trend has been supported by an increased sensitivity to the importance of multiculturalism (Negy, Shreve, & Jensen, 2003; Lee, 2005; Tatum, 2007).

# DEVELOPMENTAL DIVERSITY AND YOUR LIFE
## Are the Children of Immigrant Families Well Adjusted?

Immigrant children tend to fare quite well in the United States, partly because many come from societies that emphasize collectivism and consequently may feel more obligation and duty to their family to succeed. What are some other cultural differences that can support the success of immigrant children?

Immigration to the United States has risen significantly in the past 30 years. Children in immigrant families account for almost 25 percent of children in the population; they are the fastest-growing segment of children in the country (Hernandez, Denton, & McCartney, 2008).

In many ways, children of immigrants fare quite well. On the one hand, they are better off than their nonimmigrant peers. For example, they tend to have equal or better grades in school than children whose parents were born in the United States. Psychologically, they also do quite well, showing similar levels of self-esteem to nonimmigrant children, although they do report feeling less popular and less in control of their lives (Kao, 2000; Driscoll, Russell, & Crockett, 2008; Jung & Zhang, 2016).

On the other hand, many children of immigrants face challenges. Their parents often have limited education, and they work at jobs that pay poorly. Unemployment rates are often higher for immigrants than for the general population. In addition, parental English proficiency may be lower, and many children of immigrants lack good health insurance, and their access to health care may be limited (Hernandez, Denton, & McCartney, 2008; Turney & Kao, 2009).

Even the immigrant children who are not financially well off, however, are often more highly motivated to succeed and place greater value on education than children in nonimmigrant families. Moreover, many immigrant children come from societies that emphasize collectivism, and consequently they may feel they have a greater obligation and duty to their family to succeed. Finally, their country of origin may give some immigrant children a strong enough cultural identity to prevent them from adopting undesirable "American" behaviors—such as materialism or selfishness (Fuligni & Yoshikawa, 2003; Suárez-Orozco, Suárez-Orozco, & Todorova, 2008).

During the middle childhood years, it thus appears that children in immigrant families typically do quite well in the United States. The story is less clear, however, when immigrant children reach adolescence and adulthood. For instance, some research shows higher rates of obesity (a key indicator of physical health) in adolescents. Research is just beginning to clarify how effectively immigrants cope over the course of the life span (Perreira & Ornelas, 2011; Fuligni, 2012).

# Relationships: Building Friendships in Middle Childhood

*The schoolyard is as tense as a Wild West town before a gunfight. Randa and her classmates are wary as they eye each other skeptically. Boys look at but don't approach the girls, and vice versa. Everyone wants to find someone to play with, but so far no one has broken the ice.*

*The schoolyard is fraught with potential missteps and disasters. The kids have no guides, no protectors. They can lose face just like that. They can do something that starts a fight, or show themselves to be fools or weaklings in an instant.*

*It's a jungle, the schoolyard. You are either predator or prey, and you need allies. The children are looking for them.*

As Randa and her classmates demonstrate, friendship comes to play an increasingly important role during middle childhood. Children grow progressively more sensitive to the importance of friends, and building and maintaining friendships becomes a large part of their social lives.

Friends influence children's development in several ways. For instance, friendships provide children with information about the world and other people, as well as about themselves. Friends provide emotional support that allows children to respond more effectively to stress. Having friends makes a child less likely to be the target of aggression, and it can teach children how to manage and control their emotions and help them interpret their own emotional experiences (Berndt, 2002; Lundby, 2013).

Friendships in middle childhood also provide a training ground for communicating and interacting with others. In addition, they can foster intellectual growth by increasing children's range of experiences (Nangle & Erdley, 2001; Gifford-Smith & Brownell, 2003; Majors, 2012).

Although friends and other peers become increasingly influential throughout middle childhood, they are not more important than parents and other family members. Most developmentalists believe that children's psychological functioning and their development in general are the product of a combination of factors, including peers and parents (Vandell, 2000;

Parke, Simpkins, & McDowell, 2002; Altermatt, 2011; Laghi et al., 2014). For that reason, we talk more about the influence of family later in this chapter.

## Stages of Friendship: Changing Views of Friends

**LO 13.3** **List the types of relationships and friendships that are typical of middle childhood.**

During middle childhood, a child's conception of the nature of friendship undergoes some profound changes. According to developmental psychologist William Damon, a child's view of friendship passes through three distinct stages (Damon & Hart, 1988).

**STAGE 1: BASING FRIENDSHIP ON OTHERS' BEHAVIORS.** In the first stage, which ranges from around 4 to 7 years of age, children see friends as others who like them and with whom they share toys and other activities. They view the children with whom they spend the most time as their friends. For instance, a kindergartner who was asked, "How do you know that someone is your best friend?" responded in this way:

*He lets me play sailors and pirates with his friends. I go to his house sometimes. Last time, he showed me his push car and let me drive for a while. He likes me.*

What children in this first stage don't do much of, however, is take others' personal qualities into consideration. For instance, they don't see their friendship as being based on their peers' unique positive personal traits. Instead, they use a very concrete approach to deciding who is a friend, primarily dependent upon others' behavior. They like those who share and with whom they can share, while they don't like those who don't share, who hit, or who don't play with them. In sum, in the first stage, friends are viewed largely in terms of presenting opportunities for pleasant interactions.

**STAGE 2: BASING FRIENDSHIP ON TRUST.** In the next stage, however, children's view of friendship becomes more complicated. Lasting from around age 8 to age 10, this stage covers a period in which children take others' personal qualities and traits, as well as the rewards they provide, into consideration. But the centerpiece of friendship in this second stage is mutual trust. Friends are seen as those who can be

Mutual trust is considered the centerpiece of friendship during middle childhood.

**Table 13.1** Most-Liked and Least-Liked Behaviors That Children Note in Their Friends, in Order of Importance

| Most-Liked Behaviors | Least-Liked Behaviors |
| --- | --- |
| Having a sense of humor | Verbal aggression |
| Being nice or friendly | Expressions of anger |
| Being helpful | Dishonesty |
| Being complimentary | Being critical or criticizing |
| Inviting one to participate in games, etc. | Being greedy or bossy |
| Sharing | Physical aggression |
| Avoiding unpleasant behavior | Being annoying or bothersome |
| Giving one permission or control | Teasing |
| Providing instructions | Interfering with achievements |
| Loyalty | Unfaithfulness |
| Performing admirably | Violating rules |
| Facilitating achievements | Ignoring others |

**SOURCE:** Adapted from Zarbatany, L., Hartmann, D. P., & Rankin, D. B. (1990). The psychological functions of preadolescent peer activities. Child Development, vol. 61, pp. 1067–1080.

counted on to help out when they are needed. This means that violations of trust are taken very seriously, and friends cannot make amends for such violations just by engaging in positive play, as they might at earlier ages. Instead, the expectation is that formal explanations and formal apologies must be provided before a friendship can be reestablished.

**STAGE 3: BASING FRIENDSHIP ON PSYCHOLOGICAL CLOSENESS.** The third stage of friendship begins toward the end of middle childhood, from 11 to 15 years of age. During this period, children begin to develop the view of friendship that they hold during adolescence. Although we discuss this perspective in detail in Chapter 16, the main criteria for friendship shift toward intimacy and loyalty. Friendship at this stage is characterized by feelings of closeness, usually brought on by sharing personal thoughts and feelings through mutual disclosure. Friendships are also somewhat exclusive. By the time they reach the end of middle childhood, children seek out friends who will be loyal, and they come to view friendship not so much in terms of shared activities but in terms of the psychological benefits that friendship brings.

Children also develop clear ideas about which behaviors they seek in their friends—and which they dislike. As can be seen in Table 13.1, fifth and sixth graders most enjoy others who invite them to participate in activities and who are helpful, both physically and psychologically. In contrast, displays of physical or verbal aggression, among other behaviors, are disliked.

## Individual Differences in Friendship: What Makes a Child Popular?

**LO 13.4** **Define social competence, and explain which personal characteristics lead to popularity.**

Children's friendships typically sort themselves out according to popularity. More popular children tend to form friendships with more popular individuals, while less popular children are more likely to have friends who are less popular. Popularity is also related to the number of friends a child has: More popular children are more apt to have a greater number of friends than those with lower popularity. In addition, more popular children are more likely to form *cliques*, groups that are viewed as exclusive and desirable, and they tend to interact with a greater number of other children.

Why is it that some children are the schoolyard equivalent of the life of the party, while others are social isolates whose overtures toward their peers are dismissed or disdained? To answer this question, developmentalists have considered the personal characteristics of popular children.

Popular children are usually helpful, cooperating with others on joint projects. They are also funny, tending to have good senses of humor and to appreciate others' attempts at humor. Compared with children who are less popular, they are better able to read others' nonverbal behavior and understand others' emotional experiences. They also can control their nonverbal behavior more effectively, thereby presenting themselves well. In short, popular children are high in **social competence**, the collection of individual social skills that permit individuals to perform successfully in social settings (Feldman, Tomasian, & Coats, 1999; McQuade et al., 2016).

Although generally popular children are friendly, open, and cooperative, one subset of popular boys displays an array of negative behaviors, including being aggressive, being disruptive, and causing trouble. Despite these behaviors, they may be viewed as cool and tough by their peers, and they are often remarkably popular. This popularity may occur in part because they are seen as boldly breaking rules that others feel constrained to follow (Meisinger et al., 2007; Woods, 2009; Schonert-Reichl et al., 2012; Scharf, 2014).

**SOCIAL PROBLEM-SOLVING ABILITIES.** Another factor that relates to children's popularity is their skill at social problem-solving. **Social problem-solving** refers to the use of strategies for solving social conflicts in ways that are satisfactory both to oneself and to others. Because social conflicts among school-age children are not an infrequent occurrence—even among the best of friends—successful strategies for dealing with them are an important element of social success (Rose & Asher, 1999; Murphy & Eisenberg, 2002; Dereli-İman, 2013).

According to developmental psychologist Kenneth Dodge, successful social problem-solving proceeds through a series of steps that correspond to children's information-processing strategies (see Figure 13.3). Dodge argues that the manner in which children solve social problems is a consequence of the decisions that they make at each point in the sequence (Dodge, Lansford, & Burks, 2003; Lansford et al., 2006).

By carefully delineating each of the stages, Dodge provides a means by which interventions can

be targeted toward a specific child's deficits. For instance, some children routinely misinterpret the meaning of other children's behavior (Step 2), and then respond according to their misinterpretation.

Suppose Max, a fourth grader, is playing a game with Will. While playing the game, Will begins to get angry because he is losing, and he complains about the rules. If Max is not able to understand that much of Will's anger is frustration at not winning, he is likely to react in an angry way himself, defending the rules, criticizing Will, and making the situation worse. If Max interprets the source of Will's anger more accurately, Max may be able to behave in a more effective manner, perhaps by reminding Will, "Hey, you beat me at Connect Four," thereby defusing the situation.

Generally, children who are popular are better at interpreting the meaning of others' behavior accurately. Furthermore, they possess a wider inventory of techniques for dealing with social problems. In contrast, less popular children tend to be less effective at understanding the causes of others' behavior and, as a result, their reactions to others may be inappropriate. In addition, their strategies for dealing with social problems are more limited; they sometimes simply don't know how to apologize or help someone who is unhappy feel better (Rose & Asher, 1999; Rinaldi, 2002; Lahat et al., 2014).

Unpopular children may become victims of a phenomenon known as *learned helplessness*. Because they don't understand the root causes of their unpopularity, children may feel that they have little or no ability to improve their situation. As a result, they may simply give up and not even try to become more involved with their peers. In turn, their learned helplessness becomes a self-fulfilling prophecy, reducing the chances that they will become more popular in the future (Seligman, 2007; Aujoulat, Luminet, & Deccache, 2007).

**TEACHING SOCIAL COMPETENCE.** Can anything be done to help unpopular children learn social competence? Happily, the answer appears to be yes. Several

---

**social competence** The collection of social skills that permit individuals to perform successfully in social settings

**social problem-solving** The use of strategies for solving social conflicts in ways that are satisfactory both to oneself and to others

## Figure 13.3 Problem-Solving Steps

Children's problem solving proceeds through several steps involving different information-processing strategies. In what ways might an educator use children's problem-solving skills as a learning tool?

**SOURCE:** Adapted from Dodge, K. A. (1985). "A social information processing model of social competence in children." In M. Perlmutter (Ed.), Minnesota Symposia on Child Psychology, vol. 18, 77–126.

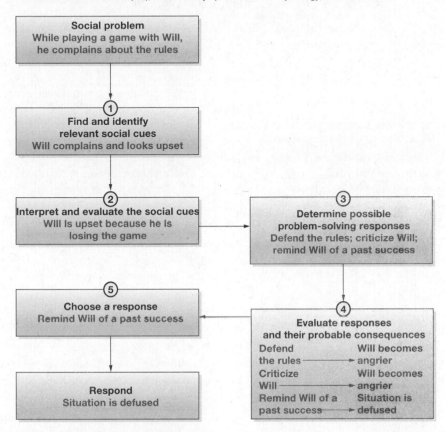

A variety of factors lead some children to be unpopular and socially isolated from their peers.

programs have been developed to teach children a set of social skills that seem to underlie general social competence. For example, in one experimental program, a group of unpopular fifth and sixth graders was taught how to hold a conversation with friends. They were taught ways to disclose material about themselves, to learn about others by asking questions, and to offer help and suggestions to others in a nonthreatening way.

Compared with a group of children who did not receive such training, the children who were in the experiment interacted more with their peers, held more conversations, developed higher self-esteem, and—most critically—were more accepted by their peers than before training (Bierman, 2004; Fransson et al., 2016).

# BECOMING AN INFORMED CONSUMER OF CHILD DEVELOPMENT

## Increasing Children's Social Competence

Building and maintaining friendships is critical in children's lives. Is there anything that parents and teachers can do to increase children's social competence?

The answer is a clear yes. Among the strategies that can work are the following:

- *Encourage social interaction.* Teachers can devise ways in which children are led to take part in group activities, and parents can encourage membership in such groups as Brownies and Cub Scouts or participation in team sports.
- *Teach listening skills to children.* Show them how to listen carefully and respond to the underlying meaning of a communication as well as to its overt content.

- *Make children aware that people display emotions and moods nonverbally* and that consequently they should pay attention to others' nonverbal behavior, not only to what they are saying on a verbal level.
- *Teach conversational skills,* including the importance of asking questions and self-disclosure. Encourage students to use "I" statements in which they clarify their own feelings or opinions, and to avoid making generalizations about others.
- *Don't ask children to choose teams or groups publicly.* Instead, assign children randomly: It works just as well in ensuring a distribution of abilities across groups and avoids the public embarrassment of a situation in which some children are chosen last.

## Gender and Friendships: The Sex Segregation of Middle Childhood

**LO 13.5  Explain how gender affects friendships.**

> *Girls rule; boys drool.*
> *Boys are idiots. Girls have cooties.*
> *Boys go to college to get more knowledge; girls go to Jupiter to get more stupider.*

Those are some of the views of boys and girls regarding members of the opposite sex during the elementary school years. Avoidance of the opposite sex becomes quite pronounced at this time, to the degree that the social networks of most boys and girls consist almost entirely of same-sex groupings (Mehta & Strough, 2009; Rancourt et al., 2012; Zosuls et al., 2014; Braun & Davidson, 2016).

Interestingly, the segregation of friendships according to gender occurs in almost all societies. In nonindustrialized societies, same-gender segregation may be the result of the types of activities that children engage in. For instance, in many cultures, boys are assigned one type of chore and girls another (Whiting & Edwards, 1988). But participation in different activities may not provide the whole explanation for sex segregation; even children in more developed countries,

who attend the same schools and participate in many of the same activities, still tend to avoid members of the other gender.

When boys and girls make occasional forays into the other gender's territory, the action often has romantic overtones. For instance, girls may threaten to kiss a boy, or boys might try to lure girls into chasing them. Such behavior, termed "border work," helps emphasize the clear boundaries that exist between the two sexes. In addition, it may pave the way for future interactions that do involve romantic or sexual interests, when school-age children reach adolescence and cross-sex interactions become more socially endorsed (Beal, 1994).

The lack of cross-gender interaction in the middle childhood years means that boys' and girls' friendships are restricted to members of their own sex. Furthermore, the nature of friendships within these two groups is quite different (Lansford & Parker, 1999; Rose, 2002; Lee & Troop-Gordon, 2011).

Boys typically have larger networks of friends than girls, and they tend to play in groups, rather than pair off. Differences in status within the group are usually quite pronounced, with an acknowledged leader and members falling into particular levels of status. Because of the fairly rigid rankings that represent the relative social power of those in the group, known as the **dominance hierarchy**, members of higher status can safely question and oppose children lower in the hierarchy (Beal, 1994; Pedersen et al., 2007).

Boys tend to be concerned with their place in the dominance hierarchy, and they attempt to maintain their status and improve on it. This makes for a style of play known as restrictive. In *restrictive play*, interactions are interrupted when a child feels that his status is challenged. Thus, a boy who feels that he is unjustly challenged by a peer of lower status may attempt to end the interaction by scuffling over a toy or otherwise behaving assertively. Consequently, boys' play tends to come in bursts, rather than in more extended, tranquil episodes (Estell et al., 2008; Cheng et al., 2016).

The language of friendship used among boys reflects their concern over status and challenge. For instance, consider this conversation between two boys who were good friends:

ROHIT:   You better get off that swing.

TUSHAR:  How you gonna make me get off?

ROHIT:   You don't wanna make me show you how.

TUSHAR:  You won't make me cuz you can't. Go play on the slide.

ROHIT:   *You* go play on the slide.

TUSHAR:  I don't want to play on the slide. Don't make me hurt you.

ROHIT:   Don't make *me* hurt *you.*

Friendship patterns among girls are quite different. Rather than having a wide network of friends, school-age girls focus on one or two "best friends" who are of relatively equal status. In contrast to boys, who seek out status differences, girls profess to avoid differences in status, preferring to maintain friendships at equal-status levels.

Conflicts among school-age girls are usually solved through compromise, by ignoring the situation, or by giving in, rather than by seeking to make one's own point of view prevail. In sum, the goal is to smooth over disagreements, making social interaction easy and nonconfrontational (Goodwin, 1990; Noakes & Rinaldi, 2006).

The motivation of girls to solve social conflict indirectly does not stem from a lack of self-confidence or from apprehension over the use of more direct approaches. In fact, when school-age girls interact with other girls who are not considered friends or with boys, they can be quite confrontational. Among friends, however, their goal is to maintain equal-status

relationships—relationships lacking a dominance hierarchy (Beal, 1994; Zahn-Waxler, Shirtcliff, & Marceau, 2008).

The language used by girls tends to reflect their view of relationships. Rather than blatant demands ("Give me the pencil"), girls are more apt to use language that is less confrontational and directive. Girls tend to use indirect forms of verbs, such as "Let's go to the movies" or "Would you want to trade books with me?" rather than "I want to go to the movies" or "Let me have these books" (Goodwin, 1990; Besag, 2006).

## Cross-Race Friendships: Integration In and Out of the Classroom

### LO 13.6   Describe how race affects friendships.

Are friendships color-blind? For the most part, the answer is no. Children's closest friendships tend largely to be with others of the same race. As they age, there is a decline in the number and depth of friendships outside their own racial group. By the time they are 11 or 12 years old, African American children become particularly aware of and sensitive to the prejudice and discrimination directed toward members of their race. At that point, they are more likely to make distinctions between members of ingroups (groups to which people feel they belong) and members of outgroups (groups to which people do not perceive membership) (Aboud & Sankar, 2007; Rowley et al., 2008; McDonald et al., 2013; Bagci et al., 2014).

For instance, when third graders from one long-integrated school were asked to name a best friend, around one-fourth of White children and two-thirds of African American children chose a child of the other race. In contrast, by the time they reached tenth grade, fewer than 10 percent of Whites and 5 percent of African Americans named a different-race best friend. Moreover, cross-race friendships are related to the degree of diversity in the setting, with some research showing that greater diversity leads to *fewer* cross-race friendships (Chan & Birman, 2009; Rodkin & Ryan, 2012; Munniksma et al., 2017).

Still, although they may not choose each other as best friends, Whites and African Americans—as well as

---

**dominance hierarchy** Rankings that represent the relative social power of those in a group members of other minority groups—can show a high degree of mutual acceptance. This pattern is particularly true in schools with ongoing integration efforts. This makes sense: A good deal of research supports the notion that contact between majority and minority group members can reduce prejudice and discrimination (Hewstone, 2003; Quintana et al., 2008).

> **From a social worker's perspective:** How might it be possible to decrease the segregation of friendships along racial lines? What factors would have to change in individuals or in society?

# Schoolyard—and Cyber-Yard—Bullies

**LO 13.7 Explain the causes of bullying and how it can be prevented.**

> *Tushar was slightly built but funny and popular with the other boys. He was happy enough at school until a group of girls started making fun of how short and skinny he was.*
>
> *Soon, the taunting spread to his private life. The girls texted and messaged him and posted notes on Facebook about what a weakling he was. They kept taunting him to do daring things that were beyond his abilities. They wouldn't stop.*
>
> *Tushar chatted with his friends online and let slip that he was thinking about ending it all. One of them told his mother, who alerted Tushar's mother.*
>
> *"Those girls were basically daring him to do something self-destructive," she says. "They were pushing him toward suicide like it was a game."*

Tushar is not alone in facing the torment of bullying, whether it comes at school or online. A large number of students experience harassment in terms of name calling, hitting, teasing, etc. Others encounter bullying on the Web, which may be even more painful because often the bullying is done anonymously or may involve public postings (Mishna, Saini, & Solomon, 2009; van Goethem, Scholte, & Wiers, 2010; Juvonen, Wang, & Espinoza, 2011).

There are four general types of bullying. In *verbal bullying*, victims are called names, threatened, or made fun of because of physical or other attributes. *Physical bullying* represents actual aggression, in which children may be hit, pushed, or touched inappropriately. *Relational bullying* may be more subtle; it occurs when children are socially attacked, by deliberately excluding them from social activities. Finally, *cyberbullying* occurs when victims are attacked online or by the spreading of malicious lies meant to damage their reputation (Espelage & Colbert, 2016; Osanloo, Reed, & Schwartz, 2017).

Those children who experience frequent bullying are often loners who are fairly passive. They tend to cry easily, and they often lack the social skills that might otherwise defuse a bullying situation. For example, they are unable to think of humorous comebacks to bullies' taunts. But though children such as these are more likely to be bullied, even children without these characteristics occasionally are bullied during their school careers: Some 90 percent of middle-school students report being bullied at some point in their time at school, beginning as early as the preschool years (Li, 2007; Katzer, Fetchenhauer, & Belschak, 2009; Jansen et al., 2016).

About 10 percent to 15 percent of students bully others at one time or another. About half of all bullies come from abusive homes—meaning, of course, that half don't. They tend to watch more television containing violence, and they misbehave more at home and at school than nonbullies. When their bullying gets them into trouble, they may try to lie their way out of the situation, and they show little remorse for their victimization of others. Furthermore, bullies, compared with their peers, are more likely to break the law as adults. Although bullies are sometimes popular among their peers, some ironically become victims of bullying themselves (Haynie et al., 2001; Ireland & Archer, 2004; Barboza et al., 2009).

One of the most effective ways to reduce the incidence of bullying is through school programs that enlist and involve students and seek to change the overall school climate. For example, schools can train students to intervene when they see an instance of bullying, rather than watching passively. Empowering students to stand up for victims also has been shown to reduce bullying significantly. But we also know what has *not* been shown to be effective in reducing bullying, including instituting zero-tolerance policies for fighting and putting troubled students together in therapy groups or classrooms (Monks & Coyne, 2011; Munsey, 2012; Juvonen et al., 2016).

How can children in middle childhood deal with bullying? Among the strategies experts suggest are refusing to engage when provocations occur, speaking up against bullying (saying something such as "stop it"), and talking with parents, teachers, and other trusted adults to get their help. Ultimately, children need to recognize that one has the right *not* to be bullied (Saarento, Boulton, & Salmivalli, 2014).

Mittal and Babu (2017) studied the underlying process of bullying using interview narratives of six participants (four males and two females with a mean age of 12.34 years) in a school context. The narratives indicated the reasons for occurrence of bullying and the consequences of bullying behavior of the participants.

A combination of various factors and conditions like impulsivity, restlessness, impatience, being naughty and/or mischievous, high confidence level, being clever, low frustration tolerance, and a general indifference towards feelings of others (a sign of low empathy) were identified. In addition, some of the situational characteristics like provocation, abuse, and humiliation sometimes trigger bullying behavior. The consequences of the bullying behavior have been sub-divided on three levels—cognitive, emotional, and behavioral. The cognitive consequences include positive view of self, high confidence, increase in social status, power and control over others, sense of achievement as well as relief. The emotions experienced by the students after engaging in bullying behaviors are calm (after hitting), reduction in anger, pleasure, and also sometimes feeling of sadness. In terms of behavioral consequences, there is variety of behaviors such as lack of interest in studies and distraction. Most of the consequences described here serve as positive reinforcers, and hence, also serve as the maintaining conditions whereby the chances of repeated engagement in similar behaviors by the students are multiplied. The findings of this research support the theoretical work by Postigo, Gonzalez, Montoya, and Ordonez (2013).

# The Family

*Tamara's mother, Brenda, waited outside the door of her second-grade classroom for the end of the school day. Tamara came over to greet her mother as soon as she spotted her.*

*"Mom, can Anna come over to play today?" Tamara demanded. Brenda had been looking forward to spending some time alone with Tamara, who had been at her dad's house for the last three days. But, Brenda reflected, Tamara hardly ever got to ask kids over after school, so she agreed to the request.*

*Unfortunately, it turned out today wouldn't work for Anna's family, so they tried to find an alternate date. "How about Thursday?" Anna's mother suggested. Before Tamara could reply, her mother reminded her, "You'll have to ask your dad. You're at his house that night." Tamara's expectant face fell. "OK," she mumbled.*

How will Tamara's adjustment be affected by dividing her time between the two homes where she lives with her divorced parents? What about the adjustment of her friend, Anna, who lives with both her parents, both of whom work outside the home? These are just a few of the questions we need to consider as we look at the ways that home life affects middle childhood.

# The Changing Home Environment

**LO 13.8 Describe today's changing home environment.**

*Ms Malini's students in Class 1 are making family trees to honor the diversity in their families. And what diversity there is! Mitali has mother, father, one brother, grandparents, uncles and aunts, her cousin sisters; Rohan has his parents, sister, and brother-in-law (his sister's husband); Sneha only has her mother and one sister as her father died last year; Meena has no siblings and lives with her parents; Mohan lives with his adopted parents.*

We've already noted in earlier chapters the changes that have occurred in the structure of the family over the past few decades. With an increase in the number of parents who both work outside of the home, a soaring divorce rate, and a rise in single-parent families, the environment faced by children passing through middle childhood in the 21st century is very different from that faced by prior generations.

One of the biggest challenges facing children and their parents is the increasing independence that characterizes children's behavior during middle childhood. During this period, children move from being almost completely controlled by their parents to increasingly controlling their own destinies—or at least their everyday conduct. Middle childhood, then, is a period of **coregulation**, in which children and parents jointly control behavior. Increasingly, parents provide broad, general guidelines for conduct, whereas children have

---

**coregulation** A period in which parents and children jointly control children's behavior

control over their everyday behavior. For instance, parents may urge their daughter to buy a balanced, nutritious school lunch each day, but their daughter's decision to regularly buy pizza and two desserts is very much her own.

During the middle years of childhood, children spend significantly less time with their parents than in earlier years. Still, parents remain the major influence in their children's lives, and they are seen as providing essential assistance, advice, and direction (Parke, 2004).

Siblings also have an important influence—for good and bad—on children during middle childhood. Although brothers and sisters can provide support, companionship, and a sense of security, they can also be a source of strife.

*Sibling rivalry* can occur, with siblings competing or quarreling with one another. Such rivalry can be most intense when siblings are similar in age and of the same sex. Parents may intensify sibling rivalry by being perceived as favoring one child over another. Such perceptions may or may not be accurate. For example, older siblings may be permitted more freedom, which the younger sibling may interpret as favoritism. In some cases, perceived favoritism not only leads to sibling rivalry, but may damage the self-esteem of the younger sibling. Of course, sibling rivalry is not inevitable, and many siblings get along with each other quite well (Caspi, 2012; Edward, 2013; Skrzypek, Maciejewska-Sobczak, & Stadnicka-Dmitriew, 2014).

Cultural differences are linked to sibling experiences. For example, in Mexican American families, which have particularly strong values regarding the importance of family, siblings are less likely to respond negatively when younger siblings receive preferential treatment (McHale et al., 2005; McGuire & Shanahan, 2010).

What about children who have no siblings? Although only children have no opportunity to develop sibling rivalry, they also miss out on the benefits that siblings can bring. Generally, despite the stereotype that only children are spoiled and self-centered, the reality is that they are as well adjusted as children with brothers and sisters. In some ways, only children are better-adjusted, often having higher self-esteem and stronger motivation to achieve. This is particularly good news for parents in China, where a strict, government-imposed one-child policy had been in effect for decades until it was phased out in 2015. Studies there show that Chinese only-children often academically outperform children with siblings (Miao & Wang, 2003).

Sibling rivalry occurs when brothers and sisters compete or fight with one another.

## When Both Parents Work Outside the Home: How Do Children Fare?

**LO 13.9  Summarize the effects on children when caregivers work outside the home.**

*When 10-year-old Jasmine Seth comes home after finishing a day at school, the first thing she does is grab a few cookies and turn on the computer. She takes a quick look at her Facebook, and then goes over to the television and typically spends the next hour watching. During commercials, she takes a look at her homework.*

*But she doesn't chat with her parents—because neither of them are there. She's home alone.*

Jasmine is a **self-care child**, the term for children who let themselves into their homes after school and wait alone until their parents return from work.

In the past, concern about self-care children centered on their lack of supervision and the emotional costs of being alone. Such children were previously called *latchkey children*, evoking images of sad, pathetic, and neglected children. But a new view of self-care children is emerging. According to sociologist Sandra Hofferth, given the hectic schedule of many children's lives, a few hours alone may provide a helpful period of decompression. Furthermore, it may give children the opportunity to develop a greater sense of autonomy (Hofferth & Sandberg, 2001).

Research has identified few differences between self-care children and children who return to homes with

**self-care children** Children who let themselves into their homes after school and wait alone until their caretakers return from work; previously known as *latchkey children*

parents. Although some children report negative experiences while at home by themselves (such as loneliness), they do not seem emotionally damaged by the experience. In addition, if they stay at home by themselves rather than "hang out" unsupervised with friends, they may avoid involvement in activities that can lead to difficulties (Belle, 1999; Goyette-Ewing, 2000).

However, there can be negative consequences of being left alone at too early an age or for too long. For example, self-care has been associated with higher levels of lying, stealing, bullying, and aggressive behavior (Atherton et al., 2016).

In sum, although some negative consequences of being a self-care child have been found, generally the consequences of being a self-care child are not necessarily harmful. In fact, children may develop an enhanced sense of independence and competence. Furthermore, the time spent alone provides an opportunity to work uninterrupted on homework and school or personal projects. Children with employed parents may have higher self-esteem because they feel they are contributing to the household in significant ways (Goyette-Ewing, 2000).

Of course, not every child with working parents is a self-care child. Some working parents make alternative arrangements for caring for their children after school, such as by hiring someone to look after them or arranging for them to go to a neighbor's or relative's house. How do these children fare?

In many cases, children whose parents both work full time outside the home fare quite well. Children whose parents are loving, are sensitive to their children's needs, and provide appropriate substitute care typically develop no differently from children in families in which one of the parents does not work (Harvey, 1999; Goyette-Ewing, 2000).

The good adjustment of children whose mothers and fathers both work relates to the psychological adjustment of the parents, especially mothers. In general, women who are satisfied with their lives tend to be more nurturing with their children. When work provides a high level of satisfaction, then mothers who work outside of the home may be more psychologically supportive of their children. Thus, it is not so much a question of whether a mother chooses to work full time, to stay at home, or to arrange some combination of the two. What matters is how satisfied she is with the choices she has made (Gilbert, 1994; Haddock & Rattenborg, 2003).

Although we might expect that children whose parents both work would spend comparatively less time with their parents than children with one parent at home full time, research suggests otherwise. Children with mothers and fathers who work full time spend essentially the same amount of time with family, with friends in class, and alone as children in families where one parent stays at home (Gottfried, Gottfried, & Bathurst, 2002).

## Diverse Family Arrangements

**LO 13.10  List some examples of how today's diverse family arrangements affect children.**

Having divorced parents, like Tamara, the second grader who was described earlier, is no longer very distinctive. Only around half the children in the United States spend their entire childhood living in the same household with both their parents. The rest will live in single-parent homes or with stepparents, grandparents, or other nonparental relatives, and some will end up in foster care (Harvey & Fine, 2004; Nicholson et al., 2014).

**DIVORCED FAMILIES.** How do children react to divorce? The answer depends on how soon you ask the question following a divorce, as well as how old the children are at the time of the divorce. Immediately after a divorce, both children and parents may show several types of psychological maladjustment for a period that may last from 6 months to 2 years. For instance, children may be anxious, experience depression, or show sleep disturbances and phobias. Even though children most often live with their mothers following a divorce, the quality of the mother–child relationship declines in the majority of cases, often because children see themselves caught in the middle between their mothers and fathers (Juby et al., 2007; Lansford, 2009; Maes, De Mol, & Buysse, 2012; Weaver & Schofield, 2015).

During the early stage of middle childhood, children whose parents are divorcing often blame themselves for the breakup. By age 10, children feel pressure to choose sides, taking the position of either the mother or the father. As a result, they experience some degree of divided loyalty (Shaw, Winslow, & Flanagan, 1999).

Although researchers agree that the short-term effects of divorce can be quite difficult, the longer-term consequences are less clear. Some studies have found that 18 months to 2 years later, most children begin to return to their pre-divorce state of psychological adjustment. For many children, there are minimal long-term consequences (Hetherington & Kelly, 2002; Guttmann & Rosenberg, 2003; Harvey & Fine, 2004).

Other evidence, however, suggests that the fall-out from divorce lingers. For example, twice as many children of divorced parents enter psychological counseling as do children from intact families (although sometimes a judge will mandate counseling as part of the divorce). In addition, people who have experienced parental divorce are more at risk for experiencing divorce themselves later in life (Huurre, Junkkari, & Aro, 2006; South, 2013; Schaan & Vögele, 2016).

How children react to divorce depends on several factors. One is the economic standing of the family the child is living with. In many cases, divorce brings a decline in both parents' standards of living. When this occurs, children may be thrown into poverty (Ozawa & Yoon, 2003; Fischer, 2007).

In other cases, the negative consequences of divorce are less severe because the divorce reduces the hostility and anger in the home. If the household before the divorce was overwhelmed by parental strife—as is the case in around 30 percent of divorces—the greater calm of a post-divorce household may be beneficial to children. This is particularly true for children who maintain a close, positive relationship with the parent with whom they do not live (Davies et al., 2002; Vélez et al., 2011).

For some children, then, divorce is an improvement over living with parents who have an intact but unhappy marriage that is high in conflict. But in about 70 percent of divorces, the pre-divorce level of conflict is not high, and children in these households may have a more difficult time adjusting to divorce (Amato & Booth, 1997).

> **From a health care worker's perspective:** How might the development of self-esteem in middle childhood be affected by a divorce? Can constant hostility and tension between parents lead to a child's health problems?

**SINGLE-PARENT FAMILIES.** Many children in India are raised by single parent due to either divorce or death of a parent. Further, though it is rare, in recent times, people are opting to have children without having a spouse. In the vast majority of cases, the single parent who is present is the mother.

What consequences are there for children living in homes with just one parent? This is a difficult question to answer. Much depends on whether a second parent was present earlier and the nature of the parents' relationship at that time. Furthermore, the economic status of the single-parent family plays a role in determining the consequences for children. Single-parent families are often less well-off financially than two-parent families, and living in relative poverty has a negative impact on children (Davis, 2003; Harvey & Fine, 2004; Sarsour et al., 2011; Nicholson et al., 2014).

In sum, the impact of living in a single-parent family is not, by itself, invariably negative or positive. Given the large number of single-parent households, the stigma that was once attached to such families has largely declined. The ultimate consequences for children depend on a variety of factors that accompany single parenthood, such as the economic status of the family, the amount of time that the parent is able to spend with the child, and the degree of stress in the household.

**GRANDPARENTS AS PARENTS.** In many households, grandparents are the primary caretakers of their grandchildren. While there are clear benefits of having a grandparent step in and care for their grandchild if the parents are incapacitated or absent, grandparents' health and stamina may be compromised by their age. Even younger grandparents may feel considerable stress from raising their grandchildren as they are involved in multiple roles (Luo et al., 2012).

Demographically, grandparents with lower income and less education are more likely to serve as caregivers for their grandchildren. In addition, grandparents belonging to minority groups are statistically more likely to serve as primary caregivers (Nanthamongkolchai, Munsawaengsub, & Nanthamongkolchai, 2011; Yancura, 2013).

**MULTIGENERATIONAL FAMILIES.** Some households consist of several generations, in which children, parents, and grandparents live together. The presence of multiple generations in the same house can make for a rich living experience for children, who experience the influence of both their parents and their grandparents. At the same time, multigenerational families also have the potential for conflict, with several adults acting as disciplinarians without coordinating what they do. The prevalence of three-generation families is on the decline in India. Most such instances are there in rural and suburban cultures.

**BLENDED FAMILIES.** For many children, the aftermath of divorce includes the subsequent remarriage of one or both parents.

Living in a **blended family** is challenging for the children involved. Often there is a fair amount of *role*

---

**blended family** A remarried couple that has at least one stepchild living with them *ambiguity*, in which roles and expectations are unclear. Children may be uncertain about their responsibilities, how to behave toward stepparents and stepsiblings, and how to make a host of decisions that have wide-ranging implications for their role in the family. For instance, a child in a blended family may have to choose which parent to spend each vacation and holiday with, or to decide between the conflicting advice coming from a biological parent and a stepparent (Sabatino & Mayer, 2011; Guadalupe & Welkley, 2012; Mundy & Wofsy, 2017).

In many cases, however, school-age children in blended families often do surprisingly well. In comparison to adolescents, who have more difficulties, school-age children adjust with relative ease to blended arrangements, for several reasons. For one thing, the family's financial situation often improves after a parent remarries. In addition, in a blended family there are more people to share the burden of household chores. Finally, the simple fact that the family contains more individuals increases the opportunities for social interaction (Hetherington & Elmore, 2003; Purswell & Dillman Taylor, 2013).

Not all children, of course, adjust well to life in a blended family. Some find the disruption of routine and of established networks of family relationships difficult. For instance, a child who is used to having her mother's complete attention may find it difficult to observe her mother showing interest and affection to a stepchild. The most successful blending of families occurs when the parents create an environment that supports children's self-esteem and permits all family members to feel a sense of togetherness. Generally, the younger the children, the easier the transition is within a blended family (Jeynes, 2007; Kirby, 2006).

**CHILDREN WITH GAY AND LESBIAN PARENTS.** How do children in lesbian and gay households fare? A growing body of research on the effects of same-sex parenting on children shows that children develop similarly to the children of heterosexual families. Their sexual orientation is unrelated to that of their parents, their behavior is no more or less gender-typed, and they seem equally well adjusted (Patterson, 2002, 2003, 2009).

One large-scale analysis that examined 19 studies of children raised by gay and lesbian parents conducted over a 25-year period, encompassing well over 1,000 gay, lesbian, and heterosexual families, confirmed these findings. The analysis found no significant differences between children raised by heterosexual parents and children raised by gay or lesbian parents on measures of

children's gender role, gender identity, cognitive development, sexual orientation, and social and emotional development. The one significant difference that did emerge was the quality of the relationship between parent and child; interestingly, the gay and lesbian parents reported having *better* relationships with their children than heterosexual parents (Crowl, Ahn, & Baker, 2008).

Other research shows that children of lesbian and gay parents have similar relationships with their peers as children of heterosexual parents. They also relate to adults—both those who are gay and those who are straight—no differently from children whose parents are heterosexual. And when they reach adolescence, their romantic relationships and sexual behavior are no different from those of adolescents living with opposite-sex parents (Patterson, 1995, 2009; Golombok et al., 2003; Wainwright, Russell, & Patterson, 2004).

In short, research shows that there is little developmental difference between children whose parents are gay and lesbian and those who have heterosexual parents. What is clearly different for children with same-sex parents is the possibility of discrimination and prejudice because of their parents' sexual orientation, although U.S. society has become considerably more tolerant of same-sex unions. In fact, the 2015 Supreme Court ruling legalizing same-sex marriages should accelerate the trend of acceptance of such unions (Davis, Saltzburg, & Locke, 2009; Kantor, 2015; Miller, Kors, & Macfie, 2017).

# Race, Poverty, and Family Life

### LO 13.11 Describe the influence of race and poverty on children's family life.

Although there are as many types of families as there are individuals, research does find some consistencies related to the association among race, poverty, and family life (Parke, 2004). And regardless of race, children living in families that are economically disadvantaged face significant hardships.

**RACE.** African American families often have a particularly strong sense of family. Members of African American families are frequently willing to welcome and offer support to extended family members in their homes. Because there is a relatively high level of female-headed households among African Americans, the social and economic support of extended family often is critical. In addition, there is a relatively high proportion of families headed by older adults, such as grandparents, and some studies find that children in grandmother-headed households are particularly well adjusted (McLoyd et al., 2000; Smith & Drew, 2002; Taylor, 2002).

Hispanic families also often stress the importance of family life, as well as community and religious organizations. Children are taught to value their ties to their families, and they come to see themselves as a central part of an extended family.

Although relatively little research has been conducted on Asian American families, emerging findings suggest that fathers are more apt to be powerful figures, maintaining discipline. In keeping with the more collectivist orientation of Asian cultures, children tend to believe that family needs have a higher priority than personal needs, and male children, in particular, are expected to care for their parents throughout their lifetimes (Ishi-Kuntz, 2000).

**POVERTY.** Poor families have fewer basic everyday resources, and there are more disruptions in children's lives. For example, parents may be forced to look for less expensive housing or may move the entire household in order to find work. The result frequently is family environments in which parents are less responsive to their children's needs and provide less social support (Evans, 2004).

The stress of difficult family environments, along with other stresses in the lives of poor children—such as living in unsafe neighborhoods with high rates of violence and attending inferior schools—ultimately takes its toll. Economically disadvantaged children are at risk for poorer academic performance, higher rates of aggression, and conduct problems. In addition, declines in economic well-being have been linked to mental health problems (Sapolsky, 2005; Morales & Guerra, 2006; Tracy et al., 2008).

## Group Care: Orphanages in the 21st Century

**LO 13.12** **Describe the nature of group care in the 21st century.**

The term *orphanage* evokes images of pitiful youngsters clothed in rags, eating porridge out of tin cups, and housed in huge, prisonlike institutions. The reality today is different. Even the term *orphanage* is rarely used, having been replaced by *group home* or *residential treatment center*. Typically housing a relatively small number of children, group homes are used for children whose parents are no longer able to care for them adequately. They are usually funded by a combination of federal, state, and local aid.

# The Case of …
## Too Rich for Me

When 12-year-old Aditi Banerjee moved from Kolkata after her father was transferred to a different office in Delhi. She got admission in a new school. She knew absolutely no one in her new school. On her first day, Aditi had to stand in front of her new classmates and "tell a little bit about herself." Their reactions ranged from boredom to outright suspicion—until she mentioned that she had been to California, United States, to participate in an International Quiz contest. Suddenly, she saw a spark of interest, especially among a group of girls seated in the front of the class. At lunch, one of them approached her and invited her to sit with them, and she quickly found herself part of their set. She was delighted to have made new friends so fast, and when she figured out that her friends were the top circle in seventh grade, she was even happier. Aditi was accepted. Her delight lasted nearly a semester. But then she saw that she was expected to dress a certain way (expensively), enjoy certain things (like shopping that she detested), and hang out with people who weren't into what she enjoyed (like reading). Aditi didn't know what to do. She couldn't keep up with these girls, and she didn't even enjoy them. She felt like a total fraud. But how could she break ties with such an influential group? She would become an outcast and move from the top of the heap to the bottom. She would be alone.

What should she do?

1. How does Aditi's experience in her new school reflect typical social and personality development issues in middle childhood?
2. What do you think motivated Aditi's new friends to accept her so quickly into their set? What appears to be the basis of their offer of friendship?
3. What stage of friendship is Aditi in, and how is it likely to affect her decision to stay within her new circle or to leave it?
4. What social advantages does Aditi receive from joining her new set? What are the disadvantages? How does the issue of popularity relate to her joining this particular group of girls?

# Epilogue

In this chapter, we considered social and personality development in the middle-childhood years and examined self-esteem. During middle childhood, children rely on deeper relationships and friendships, and we looked at the ways gender and race can affect friendships. We saw that the changing nature of family arrangements can also affect social and personality development.

Return to the prologue—about the different views of Rudra Prasad—and answer the following questions.

1. How would you describe Rudra's social status among his peers? What clues does the story provide?

2. Do you think Rudra's statement that he likes to go his own way implies that he makes little use of social comparison? Cite examples from the story to support your answer.

3. Taking into account all the different views of Rudra, including his own, how would you say Rudra is managing what Erik Erikson calls the industry-versus-inferiority stage?

4. How is Rudra's self-concept an example of the changes that typically occur from the preschool age to the middle-grade years? What would you estimate Rudra's self-esteem to be?

# Looking Back

**LO 13.1 Explain how children's views of themselves change during middle childhood.**

- According to Erik Erikson, children in the middle childhood years are in the industry-versus-inferiority stage, focusing on achieving competence and responding to a wide range of personal challenges.

- Children in these years are engaged in making a place for themselves in their social world by working increasingly with others and navigating different social groups and roles.

- Children in the middle childhood years begin to view themselves in terms of psychological characteristics and to differentiate their self-concepts into separate areas. They use social comparison to evaluate their behavior, abilities, expertise, and opinions.

**LO 13.2 Describe the importance of self-esteem during the middle childhood years.**

- Children in these years are developing self-esteem; those with chronically low self-esteem can become trapped in a cycle of failure in which low self-esteem feeds on itself by producing low expectations and poor performance.

**LO 13.3 List the types of relationships and friendships that are typical of middle childhood.**

- Children's understanding of friendship passes through stages, from a focus on mutual liking and time spent together through the consideration of personal traits and the rewards that friendship provides to an appreciation of intimacy and loyalty.

**LO 13.4 Define social competence, and explain which personal characteristics lead to popularity.**

- Popular children generally are helpful to others, have a good sense of humor, are able to understand the emotions of others, and can control their nonverbal behavior.

- Popularity in children is related to traits that underlie social competence. Because of the importance of social interactions and friendships, developmental researchers have engaged in efforts to improve social problem-solving skills and the processing of social information.

**LO 13.5 Explain how gender affect friendships.**

- Boys and girls in middle childhood increasingly prefer same-gender friendships. Male friendships are characterized by groups, clear dominance hierarchies, and restrictive play. Female friendships tend to involve one or two close relationships, equal status, and a reliance on cooperation.

**LO 13.6 Describe how race affects friendships.**

- Cross-race friendships diminish in frequency as children age. Equal-status interactions among members of different racial groups can lead to improved understanding, mutual respect and acceptance, and a decreased tendency to stereotype.

**LO 13.7 Explain the causes of bullying and how it can be prevented.**

- Bullying is associated with a history of watching violent television shows, misbehavior at home, and an abusive family life.

- School-based programs focus on training students to intervene when they witness bullying, rather than standing by and watching. Potential victims of bullying are advised to refuse to engage the bully, speak up against bullying, and talk to parents, teachers, and other adults.

**LO 13.8 Describe today's changing home environment.**

- The home environment has changed significantly over the past few decades. Today, children have to deal with working parents, single parents, and divorce to a greater extent than in previous generations.

- In this challenging and changing environment, children and parents have to achieve coregulation—jointly controlled behavior—as a way to accommodate children's need for increased independence.

**LO 13.9 Summarize the effects on children when caregivers work outside the home.**

- Children in families in which caregivers work outside the home generally fare well. Self-care children who fend for themselves after school may develop independence and a sense of competence and contribution.

**LO 13.10 List some examples of how today's diverse family arrangements affect children.**

- Immediately after a divorce, the effects on children in the middle childhood years can be serious, depending on the financial condition of the family and the hostility level between spouses before the divorce.

- The consequences of living in a single-parent family depend on the financial condition of the family and, if there had been two parents, the level of hostility that existed between them.

- Multigenerational families in which children, parents, and grandparents live together can make for a rich living environment, but are also prone to conflict if parents and grandparents have different disciplinary styles.

- Blended families present challenges to the child but can also offer opportunities for increased social interaction.

**LO 13.11 Describe the influence of race and poverty on children's family life.**

- African Americans have a strong sense of family, and families are often extended. Many African American families are headed by mothers or grandmothers.

- Hispanic families also have a strong sense of family and rely on community and religious organizations. Hispanic families tend to be large and extended.

- Asian American families appear to have strong father figures at the helm to maintain discipline. Asian children are taught to place family needs before personal needs.

- Regardless of race, children living in economically disadvantaged families face challenges such as the lack of basic resources, frequent disruptions in living arrangements, unsafe houses and neighborhoods, and parents too busy and tired to respond to their children's needs as they might wish.

**LO 13.12 Describe the nature of group care in the 21st century.**

- Children in group care often have been victims of neglect and abuse. About 25 percent of them will spend their childhood years in group care.

- Experts believe that group care is inherently neither good nor bad. Instead, the consequences of living away from one's family may be positive or negative, depending on the particular characteristics of the staff of the group home and whether child- and youth-care workers are able to develop an effective, stable, and strong emotional bond with a child.

# Key Terms and Concepts

industry-versus-inferiority stage (p. 341)
social comparison (p. 342)

self-esteem (p. 344)
social competence (p. 350)
social problem-solving (p. 350)

dominance hierarchy (p. 353)
coregulation (p. 355)
self-care children (p. 357)
blended family (p. 358)

# Putting It All Together

## Middle Childhood

**Physical, Cognitive, and Social and Personality Development in Middle Childhood**

*Children entering middle childhood are poised to make great strides in every area of their development. Their gross and fine motor skills improve dramatically, and their cognitive development enables them to apply their new skills to the pursuit of more complex tasks, such as reading and sports. Sensory difficulties and deficits in cognitive and physical capabilities, however, can interfere with reading and writing. Being singled out can lead to children being ignored, and even bullied, by some of their peers. With proper treatment, though, children's physical and social skills can advance to match their cognitive abilities. This can help them become more engaged in their schoolwork and more open to friendships.*

### Physical Development

- Steady growth and increased abilities characterize children's physical development in these years **(p. 274)**.

- Gross and fine motor skills develop as muscle coordination improves and new skills are practiced **(p. 280)**.

- Sensory problems can interfere with schoolwork and create social difficulties **(p. 284)**.

### Cognitive Development

- Intellectual abilities such as language and memory became more developed in middle childhood **(p. 298)**.

- One of the key academic tasks for children during middle childhood is to read fluently and with appropriate comprehension **(p. 303)**.

- There are many components and types of intelligence that are displayed, and the development of intellectual skills is aided by social interactions **(p. 309)**.

### Social and Personality Development

- In this period, children master many of the challenges presented by school and peers, which take on central importance in their lives **(p. 324)**.

- The development of self-esteem is particularly crucial; when children feel they are inadequate, their self-esteem may suffer **(p. 327)**.

- Children's friendships help provide emotional support and foster intellectual growth **(p. 331)**.

## From a PARENT'S perspective:

- What strategies would you use to help a child overcome difficulties and function effectively? How would you bolster the child's self-esteem?

  **HINT: Review pages 327–329.**

## From an EDUCATOR'S perspective:

- How would you deal with a child's difficulties in reading and writing? What would you do to help integrate a child into a class and help him or her make friends with classmates? What would you recommend in terms of educational specialists to deal with these problems?

  **HINT: Review pages 303–306.**

## From a HEALTH CARE PROVIDER'S perspective:

- How might you respond to a child's vision and motor problems? What if his or her parents refuse to believe that there was anything physically wrong? How would you convince them to get treatment for their child?

  **HINT: Review pages 284–285, 286–288.**

## From YOUR perspective:

- How would you deal with a situation in which your child had physical disabilities that would prevent him or her from progressing in school? How would you encourage your child? How would you deal with your child's frustration at falling behind in school?

  **HINT: Review pages 286–288.**

# Chapter 14
# Physical Development in Adolescence

## ⌄ Learning Objectives

**LO 14.1** Describe the physical changes adolescents experience.

**LO 14.2** Explain how puberty affects adolescents.

**LO 14.3** Summarize the nutritional needs of adolescents.

**LO 14.4** Describe the causes and effects of eating disorders among adolescents.

**LO 14.5** Explain how brain development contributes to cognitive growth in adolescence.

**LO 14.6** List the causes and consequences of stress.

**LO 14.7** Describe how adolescents can cope with stress.

**LO 14.8** Describe how prevalent illegal drug use is among adolescents and the dangers it poses.

**LO 14.9** Describe the incidence of alcohol use among adolescents.

**LO 14.10** Explain why adolescents smoke and the prevalence of smoking.

**LO 14.11** Describe the dangers and consequences of adolescent sexual practices.

# Prologue: A Jury of Their Peers

Best friends Juhi and Maya, 14, take several selfies after getting their hair cut and styled. In a trendy clothing store, they snap another dozen pics of themselves modeling the lacy tees they just bought. From the shop, the girls go to Maya's house, where they dress up and put on lots of makeup. After taking loads of selfies, they each choose their best shot and post it in a beauty contest on Instagram. They also post the pics on Facebook and Tumblr.

The feedback starts pouring in. Juhi gets some "likes," but Maya gets three times as many. While Maya is garnering comments like "hot" and "eye candy," Juhi's photo elicits only "cute" or a smiley face.

Juhi stares at herself in the mirror. The makeup covers most of her acne but not all. Her brown eyes are bright but too small for her round face. And she's not exactly a size 0. *I'm hopeless,* Juhi thinks.

# Looking Ahead

Many adolescents struggle to meet society's—and their own—demands as they traverse the challenges of the teenage years. These challenges extend far beyond managing an overstuffed schedule. With bodies that are conspicuously changing; temptations of sex, alcohol, and other drugs; cognitive advances that make the world seem increasingly complex; social networks that are in constant flux; and careening emotions, adolescents find themselves in a period of life that evokes excitement, anxiety, glee, and despair, sometimes in equal measure.

**Adolescence** is the developmental stage that lies between childhood and adulthood. It is generally viewed as starting just before the teenage years and ending just after them. In this transitional stage, adolescents are no longer considered children, but they are not yet adults either. It is a time of considerable physical and psychological growth and change.

This chapter focuses on physical growth during adolescence. We begin by considering the extraordinary physical maturation that occurs during adolescence, triggered by the onset of puberty. We then discuss the consequences of early and late maturation and how they differ for males and females. We also consider nutrition during adolescence. After discussing the causes—and consequences—of obesity, we study eating disorders, which are surprisingly common during this period.

We then turn to stress and coping. We examine the causes of stress during adolescence, as well as the short- and long-term consequences of stress. We also discuss the ways in which people can cope with it.

The chapter concludes with a discussion of several of the major threats to adolescents' well-being. We focus on drug, alcohol, and tobacco use, as well as on sexually transmitted diseases.

---

**adolescence** The developmental stage between childhood and adulthood

# Physical Maturation

*For the male members of the Awa tribe, the beginning of adolescence is signaled by an elaborate and—to Western eyes—gruesome ceremony marking the transition from childhood to adulthood. The boys are whipped for two or three days with sticks and prickly branches. Through the whipping, they atone for their previous infractions and honor tribesmen who were killed in warfare. But that's just for starters; the ritual continues for days more.*

Most of us probably feel gratitude that we did not have to endure such physical trials when we entered adolescence. But members of Western cultures do have their own—admittedly less fearsome—rites of passage into adolescence, such as bar mitzvahs and bat mitzvahs at age 13 for Jewish boys and girls, and confirmation ceremonies in many Christian denominations (Dunham, Kidwell, & Wilson, 1986; Eccles, Templeton, & Barber, 2003; Hoffman, 2003).

Regardless of the nature of the ceremonies celebrated by various cultures, their underlying purpose tends to be similar from one culture to the next: symbolically celebrating the onset of the physical changes that turn a child's body into an adult body capable of reproduction. With these changes, the child exits childhood and arrives at the doorstep of adulthood.

## Growth During Adolescence: The Rapid Pace of Physical and Sexual Maturation

**LO 14.1  Describe the physical changes adolescents experience.**

In only a few months, adolescents can grow several inches and require a whole new wardrobe as they are transformed, at least in physical appearance, from children to young adults. During the **adolescent growth spurt**, a period of very rapid growth in height and weight, on average, boys grow 4.1 inches a year, and girls 3.5 inches a year. Some adolescents grow as much as 5 inches in a single year (Tanner, 1972; Caino et al., 2004).

Boys' and girls' adolescent growth spurts begin at different times. As you can see in Figure 14.1, girls begin their spurts around age 10, while boys start at about age 12. During the 2-year period starting at age 11, girls tend to be taller than boys. But by age 13, boys, on average, are taller than girls—a state of affairs that persists for the remainder of the life span.

**Puberty**, the period during which the sexual organs mature, begins when the pituitary gland in the brain signals other glands in children's bodies to begin producing the sex hormones, *androgens* (male hormones) or *estrogens* (female hormones), at adult levels. (Males and females produce both types of sex hormones, but males have a higher concentration of androgens, and females have a higher concentration of estrogens.) The pituitary gland also signals the body to increase production of growth hormones that interact with the sex hormones to cause the growth spurt and puberty. In addition, the hormone leptin appears to play a role in the start of puberty.

The brain's hypothalamus, pituitary gland, and the gonads (ovaries in women, testicles in men) operate in a feedback loop that produces and maintains the level of androgens and estrogens. The interaction between the hypothalamus, pituitary gland, and gonads is known as the *HPG axis*. The HPG axis operates when the hypothalamus calls for the pituitary gland to release a larger or smaller amount of hormones. In turn, the pituitary gland instructs the gonads to actually release the hormones. Then, when the optimal level of hormones is reached, the hypothalamus tells the pituitary gland to cease increasing the level of hormones.

Hormonal releases are significant for several reasons. First, they organize the way the brain physically develops during adolescence, as well as at other points in life. Second, they activate and drive certain behaviors that are central to human existence, including sexual drives, hunger, and thirst.

Like the growth spurt, puberty begins earlier for girls than for boys. Girls start puberty at around 11 or 12 years of age, and boys begin at around 13 or 14 years of age. There are wide variations among individuals, however. For example, some girls begin puberty as early as 7 or 8 or as late as 16.

**PUBERTY IN GIRLS.** It is not clear why puberty begins at a particular time. What is clear is that environmental and cultural factors play a role. For example,

---

**adolescent growth spurt** A period of very rapid growth in height and weight during adolescence

**puberty** The period during which the sexual organs mature

## Figure 14.1 Growth Patterns

Patterns of growth are depicted in two ways. The figure on the left shows height at a given age, whereas the figure on the right shows the height increase that occurs from birth through the end of adolescence. Notice that girls begin their growth spurt around age 10; boys start about 2 years later. By age 13, however, boys tend to be taller than girls. Why is it important that educators be aware of the social consequences of being taller or shorter than average for boys and girls?

SOURCE: Adapted from Cratty, B. (1986). Perceptual and motor development in infants and children (3rd ed.). Englewood Cliffs, NJ: Prentice-Hall.

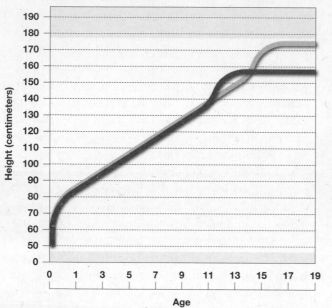

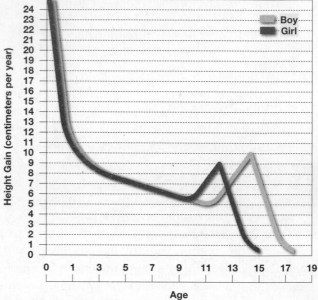

**menarche**, the onset of menstruation and probably the most obvious signal of puberty in girls, varies greatly in different parts of the world. In poorer, developing countries, menstruation begins later than it does in more economically advantaged countries. Even within wealthier countries, girls in more affluent groups begin to menstruate earlier than those in less affluent groups (see Figure 14.2).

Consequently, it appears that girls who are better nourished and healthier are more apt to start menstruation at an earlier age than those who suffer from malnutrition or chronic disease. In fact, some studies have suggested that weight or the proportion of fat to muscle in the body plays a critical role in the timing of menarche. For example, in the United States, athletes with a low percentage of body fat may start menstruating later than less active girls. Conversely, obesity—which results in an increase in the secretion of leptin, a hormone associated with the onset of menstruation—leads to earlier puberty (Woelfle, Harz, &

**menarche** The onset of menstruation

## Figure 14.2 Onset of Menstruation

The onset of menstruation occurs earlier in more economically advantaged countries than in poorer nations. But even in wealthier countries, girls living in more affluent circumstances begin to menstruate earlier than those living in less affluent situations.

SOURCE: Adapted from Eveleth, P., & Tanner, J. (1976). Worldwide variation in human growth. New York: Cambridge University Press.

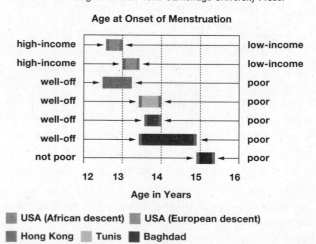

Roth, 2007; Sanchez-Garrido & Tena-Sempere, 2013; Shen et al., 2016).

Other factors can affect the timing of menarche. For instance, environmental stress due to parental divorce or high levels of family conflict can bring about an early onset (Kaltiala-Heino, Kosunen, & Rimpela, 2003; Ellis, 2004; Belsky et al., 2007).

Over the past 100 years or so, girls in the United States and other cultures have been experiencing puberty at earlier ages. Near the end of the 19th century, menstruation began, on average, around age 14 or 15, compared with today's age 11 or 12. Other indicators of puberty, such as the age at which adult height and sexual maturity are reached, have also appeared at earlier ages, probably due to reduced disease and improved nutrition (McDowell, Brody, & Hughes, 2007; Harris, Prior, & Koehoorn, 2008; James et al., 2012).

The earlier start of puberty is an example of a significant **secular trend**, a pattern of change occurring over several generations. Secular trends occur when a physical characteristic changes over the course of several generations, such as earlier onset of menstruation or increased height that has occurred as a result of better nutrition over the centuries.

Menstruation is just one of several changes in puberty that are related to the development of primary and secondary sex characteristics. **Primary sex characteristics** are associated with the development of the organs and structures of the body that directly relate to reproduction. In contrast, **secondary sex characteristics** are the visible signs of sexual maturity that do not involve the sex organs directly.

In girls, the development of primary sex characteristics involves changes in the vagina and uterus. Secondary sex characteristics include the development of breasts and pubic hair. Breasts begin to grow at about age 10, and pubic hair begins to appear at about age 11. Underarm hair appears about 2 years later.

For some girls, indications of puberty start unusually early. One of seven Caucasian girls develops breasts or pubic hair by age 8. Even more surprisingly,

**Figure 14.3** The Changes of Sexual Maturation During Adolescence

Changes in sexual maturation occur for both males and females primarily during early adolescence.

SOURCE: Adapted from Tanner J. M. (1978). Education and Physical Growth (2nd ed.), New York: International Universities Press.

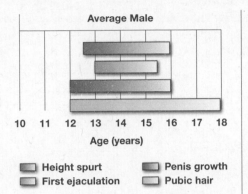

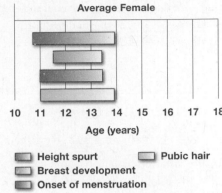

the figure is one out of two for African American girls. The reasons for this earlier onset of puberty are unclear, and the demarcation between normal and abnormal onset of puberty is a point of controversy among specialists (Ritzen, 2003; Mensah et al., 2013).

**PUBERTY IN BOYS.** Boys' sexual maturation follows a somewhat different course. The penis and scrotum begin to grow at an accelerated rate at around age 12, and they reach adult size about 3 or 4 years later. As boys' penises enlarge, other primary sex characteristics are developing, with enlargement of the prostate gland and seminal vesicles, which produce semen (the fluid that carries sperm). A boy's first ejaculation, known as *spermarche*, usually occurs around age 13, more than a year after the body has begun producing sperm. At first, the semen contains relatively few sperm, but the amount of sperm increases significantly with age.

Secondary sex characteristics are also developing. Pubic hair begins to grow at around age 12, followed by the growth of underarm and facial hair. Finally, boys' voices deepen as the vocal cords become longer and the larynx becomes larger. (Figure 14.3 summarizes the changes that occur in sexual maturation during early adolescence.)

**secular trend** A statistical tendency observed over several generations

**primary sex characteristics** Characteristics associated with the development of the organs and structures of the body that directly relate to reproduction

**secondary sex characteristics** The visible signs of sexual maturity that do not involve the sex organs directly

The surge in production of hormones that triggers the start of adolescence also may lead to rapid swings in mood. For example, boys may have feelings of anger and annoyance that are associated with higher hormone levels. In girls, the emotions produced by hormone production are somewhat different: Higher levels of hormones are associated with anger and depression (Fujisawa & Shinohara, 2011; Sun et al., 2016).

## Body Image: Reactions to Physical Changes in Adolescence

**LO 14.2 Explain how puberty affects adolescents.**

Unlike infants, who also undergo extraordinarily rapid growth, adolescents are well aware of what is happening to their bodies, and they may react with horror or joy, spending long periods in front of mirrors. Few, though, are neutral about the changes they are witnessing.

Some of the changes of adolescence carry psychological weight. In the past, girls tended to react to menarche with anxiety because Western society emphasized the more negative aspects of menstruation, such as the potential of cramps and messiness. Today, however, society's view of menstruation is more positive, in part because menstruation has been demystified and discussed more openly (for instance, television commercials for tampons are commonplace). As a consequence, menarche is typically accompanied by an increase in self-esteem, a rise in status, and greater self-awareness, as adolescent girls see themselves as becoming adults (Johnson, Roberts, & Worell, 1999; Matlin, 2003; Wilkosz et al., 2011; Yuan, 2012; Chakraborty & De, 2014).

A boy's first ejaculation is roughly equivalent to menarche in a girl; however, although girls generally tell their mothers about the onset of menstruation, boys rarely mention their first ejaculation to their parents or even to their friends (Stein & Reiser, 1994). Why? One reason is that girls require tampons or sanitary napkins, and mothers provide them. It also may be that boys see the first ejaculation as an indication of their budding sexuality, an area about which they are quite uncertain and therefore reluctant to discuss with others.

Menstruation and ejaculations occur privately, but changes in body shape and size are quite public. Consequently, teenagers entering puberty frequently are embarrassed by the changes that are occurring.

Girls, in particular, are often unhappy with their new bodies. Ideals of beauty in many Western countries call for an unrealistic thinness that is quite different from the actual shape of most women. Puberty brings a considerable increase in the amount of fatty tissue, as well as enlargement of the hips and buttocks—a far cry from the slenderness that society seems to demand (McCabe & Ricciardelli, 2006; Cotrufo et al., 2007; Kretsch et al., 2016).

> **From an educator's perspective:** Why do you think the passage to adolescence is regarded in many cultures as a significant transition that calls for unique ceremonies?

How children react to the onset of puberty depends in part on when it happens. Girls and boys who mature either much earlier or later than most of their peers are especially affected by the timing of puberty.

**EARLY MATURATION.** For boys, early maturation is largely a plus. Early maturing boys tend to be more successful at athletics, presumably because of their larger size. They also tend to be more popular and to have a more positive self-concept.

Early maturation in boys does have a downside, however. Boys who mature early are more apt to have difficulties in school, and they are more likely to

Boys who mature early tend to be more successful in athletics and have a more positive self-concept. Why might there be a downside to early maturation?

become involved in delinquency and substance abuse. The reason: Their larger size makes it more likely that they will seek out the company of older boys who may involve them in activities that are inappropriate for their age. Overall, though, the pluses seem to outweigh the minuses for early maturing boys (Taga, Markey, & Friedman, 2006; Costello et al., 2007; Lynne et al., 2007; Beltz et al., 2014).

The story is a bit different for early maturing girls. For them, the obvious changes in their bodies—such as the development of breasts—may lead them to feel uncomfortable and different from their peers. Moreover, because girls, in general, mature earlier than boys, early maturation tends to come at a very young age. Early maturing girls may have to endure ridicule from their less mature classmates (Olivardia & Pope, 2002; Mendle, Turkheimer, & Emery, 2007; Hubley & Arim, 2012; Skoog & Özdemir, 2016).

Early maturation is not a completely negative experience for girls. Girls who mature earlier tend to be sought after more as potential dates, and their popularity may enhance their self-concepts. But this attention has a price; they may not be socially ready to participate in the kind of one-on-one dating situations that most girls deal with at a later age, and such situations may be psychologically challenging for them. Moreover, the conspicuousness of their deviance from their later-maturing classmates may have a negative effect, producing anxiety, unhappiness, and depression (Kaltiala-Heino, Kosunen, & Rimpela, 2003; Galvao et al., 2013).

Cultural norms and standards regarding how women should look play a big role in how girls experience early maturation. For instance, in the United States, the notion of female sexuality is looked on with a degree of ambivalence, being promoted in the media yet frowned on socially. Girls who appear "sexy" attract both positive and negative attention.

Consequently, unless a young girl who has developed secondary sex characteristics early can handle the disapproval she may encounter when she conspicuously displays her growing sexuality, the outcome of early maturation may be negative. In countries in which attitudes about sexuality are more liberal, the results of early maturation may be more positive. For example, in cultures that have a more open view of sex, early maturing girls have higher self-esteem than such girls in the United States. Furthermore, the consequences of early maturation vary even within the United States, depending on the views of girls' peer groups and on prevailing community standards regarding sex (Petersen, 2000; Güre, Uçanok, & Sayil, 2006).

**LATE MATURATION.** As with early maturation, the situation with late maturation is mixed, although in this case boys fare worse than girls. For instance, boys who are smaller and lighter than their more physically mature peers tend to be viewed as less attractive. Because of their smaller size, they are at a disadvantage when it comes to sports activities. Furthermore, boys are expected to be bigger than their dates, so the social lives of late-maturing boys may suffer.

Ultimately, if the difficulties in adolescence lead to a decline in self-concept, the disadvantages of late maturation for boys could extend well into adulthood. However, coping with the challenges of late maturation may actually help boys in some ways. For example, late-maturing boys grow up to have several positive qualities such as assertiveness and insightfulness (Kaltiala-Heino, Kosunen, & Rimpela, 2003; Benoit, Lacourse, & Claes, 2014).

The picture for late-maturing girls is actually quite positive. In the short term, girls who mature later may be overlooked in dating and other mixed-sex activities during junior high school and middle school, and they may have relatively low social status. But by the time they are in the 10th grade and have begun to mature visibly, late-maturing girls' satisfaction with themselves and their bodies may be greater than that of early maturers. In fact, late-maturing girls may end up with fewer emotional problems. The reason? Late-maturing girls are more apt to fit the societal ideal of a slender, "leggy" body type than early maturers, who tend to look heavier in comparison (Kaminaga, 2007; Leen-Feldner, Reardon, & Hayward, 2008).

In sum, the reactions to early and late maturation present a complex picture. As we have seen repeatedly, we need to take into consideration the complete constellation of factors affecting individuals in order to understand their development. Some developmentalists suggest that other factors, such as changes in peer groups, family dynamics, and particularly schools and other societal institutions, may be more pertinent in determining an adolescent's behavior than early and later maturation, and the effects of puberty in general (Stice, 2003; Mendle, Turkheimer, & Emery, 2007; Hubley & Arim, 2012).

# Nutrition and Food: Fueling the Growth of Adolescence

### LO 14.3 Summarize the nutritional needs of adolescents.

*Neet Mohan felt hungry all the time. He skipped breakfast but munched on cookies between classes. At lunch, he ate several sandwiches. After school, it was pizza or burgers with friends, and then dinner with the family. While doing homework or surfing the Internet, he was never without a large bag of chips. By the end of 10th class, Neet was 8 Kgs heavier than when he started high school. Some of that was due to normal adolescent growth, but most of it was the result of too much junk food—too much food, period. His doctor said he was obese.*

The rapid physical growth of adolescence is fueled by an increase in food consumption. During the teenage years, the average girl requires some 2,200 calories a day, and the average boy 2,800.

Of course, not just any calories help nourish adolescents' growth. Several key nutrients are essential, including, in particular, calcium and iron. The calcium provided by milk helps bone growth, which may prevent the development of osteoporosis—the thinning of bones—that affects 25 percent of women later in their lives. Similarly, iron is necessary to prevent iron-deficiency anemia, an ailment that is not uncommon among teenagers.

For most adolescents, the major nutritional issue is ensuring the consumption of a sufficient balance of appropriate foods. Two extremes of nutrition can be a major concern for a substantial minority and can create a real threat to health. Among the most prevalent problems: obesity and eating disorders. (We'll discuss the latter in the next section.)

One in five adolescents is overweight, and 1 in 20 can be formally classified, as Neet Mohan was, as obese (body weight that is more than 20 percent heavier than average). Moreover, the proportion of female adolescents who are classified as obese increases over the course of adolescence (Kimm et al., 2002; Critser, 2003; Mikulovic et al., 2011).

Although adolescents are obese for the same reasons as younger children, the psychological consequences may be particularly severe during a time of life when body image is of special concern. Furthermore, the potential health consequences of obesity during adolescence are problematic. For instance, obesity taxes

Obesity has become the most common nutritional concern during adolescence. In addition to issues of health, what are some psychological concerns about obesity in adolescence?

the circulatory system, increasing the likelihood of high blood pressure and diabetes. Finally, obese adolescents stand an 80 percent chance of becoming obese adults (Wang et al., 2008; Patton et al., 2011; Morrison et al., 2015; Gowey et al., 2016).

Lack of exercise is one of the main culprits. One survey found that by the end of the teenage years, most girls get virtually no exercise outside of physical education classes in school. In fact, the older they are, the less exercise female adolescents engage in. The problem is particularly pronounced for older Black female adolescents, more than half of whom report *no* physical exercise outside of school, compared with about one-third of White adolescents who report no exercise (see Figure 14.4; Reichert et al., 2009; Nicholson & Browning, 2012; Puterman et al., 2016).

Why do adolescent women get so little exercise? It may reflect a lack of organized sports or good athletic

## Figure 14.4 Decline in Physical Activity

Physical activity among both White and Black adolescent females declines substantially over the course of adolescence. What might be the reasons for this decline?

**SOURCE:** Kimm, S. Y., et al. (2002). "Decline in physical activity in black girls and white girls during adolescence." New England Journal of Medicine, vol. 347, pp. 709–715.

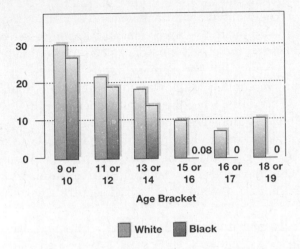

**Age Bracket**

White   Black

facilities for women. It may even be the result of lingering cultural norms suggesting that athletic participation is more the realm of boys than of girls.

There are additional reasons for the high rate of obesity during adolescence. One is the availability of fast foods, which deliver large portions of high-calorie, high-fat cuisine at prices adolescents can afford. In addition, many adolescents spend a significant proportion of their leisure time inside their homes watching television, playing video games, and surfing the Web. Such sedentary activities not only keep adolescents from exercising, but they often are accompanied by snacks of junk foods (Bray, 2008; Thivel et al., 2011; Laska et al., 2012).

## Eating Disorders: Anorexia Nervosa and Bulimia

**LO 14.4  Describe the causes and effects of eating disorders among adolescents.**

*Jenna Tamlin, 18, subsisted on a small bowl of dry cereal in the morning and a pear or an apple for dinner. Terrified at the prospect of becoming fat (like all the women in her family, she said), Jenna had put herself on a strict diet when she entered college in Chicago. But when she returned home to*

*Seattle for summer vacation, her mother's look of shock was unmistakable.*

*"You could trace her bones right through her blouse," Jenna's mother said. When Jenna's older sister, whom Jenna idolized, came home from college later that week, she took one look at her sister and burst into tears.*

*"That pretty much did it," said Jenna. "When I saw Claire's reaction, I had to take a hard look at myself." At 5'8" tall, Jenna weighed only 86 pounds—20 pounds less than a year before. "I still had a tough time believing it," Jenna said. "I thought the scale was wrong. What I saw in the mirror was a blimp, a whale. I couldn't get it into my head that I was as thin as a ghost."*

As we have seen, the cultural ideal of slim and fit favors late-developing girls. But when those developments do occur, how do girls, and increasingly, boys, cope when the image in the mirror deviates from the ideal presented in popular media?

The fear of being fat and the desire to avoid obesity sometimes becomes so strong that it turns into a problem. For instance, Jenna Tamlin suffered from **anorexia nervosa**, a severe eating disorder in which individuals refuse to eat. Their troubled body image leads them to deny that their behavior and their appearance, which may become skeletal, are out of the ordinary.

Anorexia is a dangerous psychological disorder; some 15 percent to 20 percent of its victims literally starve themselves to death. It primarily afflicts women between the ages of 12 and 40; those most susceptible are intelligent, successful, and attractive White adolescent girls from affluent homes. Anorexia is also becoming a problem for more boys. About 5 percent to 15 percent of victims are male, a percentage that is increasing and is associated with the use of steroids (Ricciardelli & McCabe, 2004; Crisp et al., 2006; Schecklmann et al., 2012).

Even though they eat little, people with anorexia are often focused on food. They may go shopping often, collect cookbooks, talk about food, or cook huge meals for others. Although they may be incredibly thin, their body image is so distorted that they see their reflections in mirrors as disgustingly fat and try to lose more and more weight. Even when they look like skeletons, they are unable to see what they have become.

**anorexia nervosa** A severe and potentially life-threatening eating disorder in which individuals refuse to eat, while denying that their behavior or skeletal appearance is out of the ordinary

**Bulimia**, another eating disorder, is characterized by *bingeing*, eating large quantities of food, followed by *purging* of the food through vomiting or the use of laxatives. Bulimics may eat an entire gallon of ice cream or a whole package of tortilla chips. But after such a binge, sufferers experience powerful feelings of guilt and depression, and they intentionally rid themselves of the food.

Although the weight of a person with bulimia remains fairly normal, the disorder is quite hazardous. The constant vomiting and diarrhea of the binge-and-purge cycles may produce a chemical imbalance that can lead to heart failure.

Finally, some adolescents suffer from binge-eating disorder. **Binge-eating disorder** is a severe eating disorder in which individuals eat large quantities of food, often very quickly and often to the point of discomfort, and experience a loss of control and shame. Unlike bulimia, there is no purging following a binge, and victims may become quite obese.

Binge eating disorder often starts in late adolescence, although it afflicts both younger and older individuals. About 40 percent of those with the disorder are male.

The exact reasons for the occurrence of eating disorders are not clear, although several factors appear to be implicated. Dieting often precedes the development of eating disorders, as even normal-weight individuals are spurred on by societal standards of slenderness to seek to lower their weight. The feelings of control and success may encourage them to lose more and more weight. Furthermore, girls who mature earlier than their peers and who have a higher level of body fat are more susceptible to eating disorders during later adolescence as they try to bring their maturing bodies back into line with the cultural standard of a thin, boyish physique. Adolescents who are clinically depressed are also more likely to develop eating disorders later (Bodell et al., 2011; Wade & Watson, 2012; Schvey, Eddy, & Tanofsky-Kraff, 2016).

Some experts suggest that a biological cause lies at the root of eating disorders. Twin studies indicate that there are genetic components to the disorders. In addition, hormonal imbalances sometimes occur in sufferers (Wade et al., 2008; Baker et al., 2009; Xu et al., 2017).

Other attempts to explain the eating disorders emphasize psychological and social factors. For example, some experts suggest that the disorders are a result of perfectionistic, over-demanding parents or by-products of other family difficulties. Culture also plays a role. Anorexia nervosa, for instance, is found only in cultures that idealize slender female bodies. Because in most places such a standard does not hold, anorexia is not prevalent outside the United States (Harrison & Hefner, 2006; Bennett, 2008; Bodell, Joiner, & Ialongo, 2012).

For example, anorexia is nonexistent in all of Asia, with two interesting exceptions: the upper classes of Japan and those of Hong Kong, where Western influence is greatest. Furthermore, anorexia nervosa is a fairly recent disorder. It was not seen in the 17th and 18th centuries, when the ideal of the female body was a plump corpulence. The increasing number of boys with anorexia in the United States may be related to a growing emphasis on a muscular male physique that features little body fat (Mangweth, Hausmann, & Walch, 2004; Makino et al., 2006; Greenberg, Cwikel, & Mirsky, 2007).

Mammen et al. (2007) stated that the prevalence of eating disorders (ED) in India is lower than that of Western countries but appears to be increasing. They further stated that the overall prevalence of eating disorders was lower than the Western data that has focused on anorexia and bulimia nervosa, but was comparable with most of the non-Western literature. The six-year period prevalence of eating disorder was 1.25 percent in their study population. The predominant ED among the study sample was psychogenic vomiting (85.4 percent); only six cases (14.6 percent) of anorexia nervosa were noted. Upadhyah et al. (2014) noted the prevalence of eating disorder symptoms and disordered eating attitudes and behaviors in a sample of 120 adolescent girls came out to be 26.67 percent. Kumar et al. (2016) in their study found that girls have more risk of eating disorder than the boys.

Because eating disorders are products of both biological and environmental causes, treatment typically involves a mix of approaches. For instance, both psychological therapy and dietary modifications are likely to be needed for successful treatment. In

---

**bulimia** An eating disorder that primarily afflicts adolescent girls and young women, characterized by binges on large quantities of food followed by purges of the food through vomiting or the use of laxatives

**binge-eating disorder** an eating disorder in which individuals eat large quantities of food, often very quickly and often to the point of discomfort, and experience a loss of control and shame

more extreme cases, hospitalization may be necessary (Wilson, Grilo, & Vitousek, 2007; Keel & Haedt, 2008; Stein, Latzer, & Merick, 2009).

# Brain Development and Thought: Paving the Way for Cognitive Growth

**LO 14.5** **Explain how brain development contributes to cognitive growth in adolescence.**

Adolescence brings greater independence as teenagers begin to assert themselves more and more. This independence is, in part, the result of changes in the brain that pave the way for the significant advances that occur in cognitive abilities during adolescence, as we consider in the next part of the chapter. As the number of neurons (the cells of the nervous system) continues to grow, and their interconnections become richer and more complex, adolescent thinking also becomes more sophisticated (Petanjek et al., 2008; Blakemore, 2012; Konrad, Firk, & Uhlhaas, 2013).

The brain produces an oversupply of gray matter during adolescence, which is later pruned back at the rate of 1 percent to 2 percent per year. Myelinization—the process in which nerve cells are insulated by a covering of fat cells—increases and continues to make the transmission of neural messages more efficient. Both the pruning process and increased myelinization contribute to the growing cognitive abilities of adolescents (Sowell et al., 2001; Sowell et al., 2003; Mychasiuk & Metz, 2016).

One specific area of the brain that undergoes considerable development throughout adolescence is the prefrontal cortex, which is not fully developed until the early 20s. The *prefrontal cortex* is the part of the brain that allows people to think, evaluate, and make complex judgments in a uniquely human way. It underlies the increasingly complex intellectual achievements that are possible during adolescence.

During adolescence, the prefrontal cortex becomes increasingly efficient in communicating with other parts of the brain. This helps build a communication system within the brain that is more distributed and sophisticated, permitting the different areas of the brain to process information more effectively (Scherf, Sweeney, & Luna, 2006; Hare et al., 2008; Wiggins et al., 2014).

The prefrontal cortex also provides for impulse control. Rather than simply reacting to emotions such as anger or rage, an individual with a fully developed prefrontal cortex is able to inhibit the desire for action that stems from such emotions.

Because during adolescence the prefrontal cortex is biologically immature, the ability to inhibit impulses is not fully developed. This brain immaturity may lead to some of the risky and impulsive behaviors that are characteristic of adolescence. Furthermore, some researchers theorize that not only do adolescents underestimate the dangers of risky behavior, but they overestimate the rewards that will come from the behavior. Regardless of the causes of risk-taking in adolescents, these findings have led to a heated discussion of whether the death penalty should be applied to adolescents, as we discuss next (Steinberg & Scott, 2003; Shad et al., 2011; Casey, Jones, & Somerville, 2011; Gopnik, 2012).

The immaturity of the prefrontal cortex also may lead to positive behaviors. For example, adolescents may show emotional intensity that leads to the passionate embrace of ideals, and it may result in increased creativity.

Adolescent brain development also produces changes in regions involving dopamine sensitivity and production. As a result of these alterations, adolescents may become less susceptible to the effects of alcohol, and it requires more drinks for adolescents to experience its reinforcing qualities—leading to higher alcohol intake. In addition, alterations in dopamine sensitivity may make adolescents more sensitive to stress, leading to further alcohol use (Spear, 2002).

## THE IMMATURE BRAIN ARGUMENT: TOO YOUNG FOR THE DEATH PENALTY?

*The case was shocking: Christopher Simmons, 17, and Charles Benjamin, 15, intent on burglary, broke into the house of Shirley Crook, 46, tied her up, covered her eyes and mouth with tape, and tossed her off a bridge to her death. Simmons and Benjamin were apprehended and confessed to the crime, detailing its planning and execution and even reenacting the murder for the police. The jury, considering the nature of the crime and the clear premeditation that was involved, returned a guilty verdict and recommended the death penalty.*

Benjamin was sentenced to life in prison, and Simmons was given the death penalty. But Simmons's lawyers appealed, and ultimately the U.S. Supreme Court ruled that he—and anyone else under the age of 18—could not be executed because of their youth.

Among the facts that the Supreme Court weighed in its decision was evidence from neuroscientists and child developmentalists that the brains of adolescents are still developing in important ways and that they therefore lack judgment because of this brain immaturity. According to this reasoning, adolescents are not fully capable of making reasonable decisions because their brains are not yet wired like those of adults.

The argument that adolescents may not be as responsible for their crimes as adults stems from research showing that the brain continues to grow and mature during the teenage years, and sometimes beyond. For example, neurons that make up unnecessary gray matter of the brain begin to disappear during adolescence. In their place, the volume of white matter of the brain begins to increase. The decline in gray matter and the increase in white matter permit more sophisticated, thoughtful cognitive processing (Beckman, 2004; Ferguson, 2013; Luna & Wright, 2016).

For instance, when the frontal lobes of the brain contain more white matter, they are better at restraining impulsivity. As neuroscientist Ruben Gur puts it, "If you've been insulted, your emotional brain says, 'Kill,' but your frontal lobe says you're in the middle of a cocktail party, 'so let's respond with a cutting remark'" (Beckman, 2004, p. 597).

In adolescents, that censoring process may not occur as efficiently. As a result, teenagers may act impulsively, responding with emotion rather than reason. Furthermore, adolescents' ability to foresee the consequences of their actions may also be hindered as a result of their less mature brains.

Are the brains of adolescents so immature that teenage offenders should receive less harsh punishment for their crimes than those with older, and therefore more mature, brains? It is not a simple question, and the answer probably will come more from those studying morality than from scientists (Aronson, 2007).

**SLEEP DEPRIVATION.** With increasing academic and social demands placed on them, adolescents go to bed later and get up earlier. As a result, they often lead their lives in something of a sleep-deprived daze.

The sleep deprivation comes at a time when adolescents' internal clocks shift. Older adolescents in particular experience the need to go to bed later and to sleep later in the morning, and they require 9 hours of sleep each night to feel rested. Because they typically have early morning classes but don't feel sleepy until late at night, they end up getting far less sleep than their bodies crave (Wolfson, & Richards, 2011; Dagys et al., 2012; Cohen-Zion et al., 2016).

Sleep deprivation takes its toll. Sleepy teens have lower grades, are more depressed, and have greater difficulty controlling their moods. In addition, they are at great risk for car accidents (Roberts, Roberts, & Duong, 2009; Roberts, Roberts, & Xing, 2011).

# Stress and Coping

*It was only 10:34 A.M., and already Jennifer Jackson had put in what seemed like a full day. After getting up at 6:30 A.M., she studied a bit for an American history exam scheduled later in the afternoon. She gulped down breakfast, and then headed off to the campus bookstore, where she worked part time.*

*Her car was in the shop with some undiagnosed ailment, so she had to take the bus. The bus was late, so Jennifer didn't have time to stop off at the library before work to pick up the reserved book she needed. Making a mental note to try to get the book at lunchtime (although she thought it probably wouldn't be available by then), she sprinted from the bus to the store, arriving a few minutes late. Her supervisor didn't say anything, but she looked irritated as Jennifer explained why she was late. Feeling that she needed to make amends, Jennifer volunteered to sort invoices—a task that she, and everyone else, hated. As she sorted the invoices, she also answered the phone and jumped up to serve a steady stream of customers who were placing special orders. When the phone rang at 10:34 A.M., it was her mechanic telling her that the car repair would cost several hundred dollars—a sum she did not have.*

If you were to monitor Jennifer Jackson's heart rate and blood pressure, you wouldn't be shocked to find that both were higher than normal. You also wouldn't be surprised if she reported experiencing stress.

Few of us need much of an introduction to **stress**, the response to events that threaten or challenge us. Stress is a part of nearly everyone's existence, and most

---

**stress** The physical response to events that threaten or challenge us

people's lives are crowded with events and circumstances, known as *stressors*, that produce threats to our well-being. Stressors need not be unpleasant events: Even the happiest events, such as obtaining admission to a sought-after college or graduating from high school, can produce stress for adolescents.

Stress brings about several outcomes. The most immediate is typically a biological reaction, as certain hormones, secreted by the adrenal glands, cause a rise in heart rate, blood pressure, respiration rate, and sweating. In some situations, these immediate effects may be beneficial because they produce an "emergency reaction" in the sympathetic nervous system that prepares people to defend themselves from a sudden, threatening situation. A person challenged by a snarling, ferocious dog, for instance, would want all the bodily preparedness possible to deal with the emergency situation.

Long-term, continuous exposure to stressors, however, may result in a reduction of the body's ability to deal with stress. As stress-related hormones are constantly secreted, the heart, blood vessels, and other body tissues may deteriorate. As a consequence, people become more susceptible to diseases as their ability to fight off germs declines. In short, both *acute stressors* (sudden, one-time events) and *chronic stressors* (long-term, continuing events or circumstances) have the potential to produce significant physiological consequences (Graham, Christian, & Kiecolt-Glaser, 2006; Brugnera et al., 2017).

## Origins of Stress: Reacting to Life's Challenges

### LO 14.6  List the causes and consequences of stress.

Although stress is experienced long before adolescence, it becomes particularly wearing during the teenage years, and it can produce formidable costs. Over the long run, the constant wear and tear caused by the physiological arousal that occurs as the body tries to fight off stress produces negative effects. For instance, headaches, backaches, skin rashes, indigestion, chronic fatigue, sleep disturbances, and even the common cold are stress-related illnesses (Cohen et al., 1993; Reid et al., 2002; Grant et al., 2011).

Stress may also lead to **psychosomatic disorders**, medical problems caused by the interaction of psychological, emotional, and physical difficulties. For instance,

**Table 14.1**  How Stressed Are You?

The following statements will help you determine your level of stress. Mark the appropriate number in each box; then add up those numbers to find your score. Your answers should reflect your experiences in the past month only. To help you rate the extent of your stress, use the key at the bottom.

1. I become upset when something happens unexpectedly.
   0 = never, 1 = almost never, 2 = sometimes, 3 = fairly often, 4 = very often

2. I feel I'm unable to control the things that are most important in my life.
   0 = never, 1 = almost never, 2 = sometimes, 3 = fairly often, 4 = very often

3. I feel nervous and "stressed."
   0 = never, 1 = almost never, 2 = sometimes, 3 = fairly often, 4 = very often

4. I feel confident about my ability to handle my personal problems.
   4 = never, 3 = almost never, 2 = sometimes, 1 = fairly often, 0 = very often

5. In general, I feel things are going my way.
   4 = never, 3 = almost never, 2 = sometimes, 1 = fairly often, 0 = very often

6. I'm able to control irritations in my life.
   4 = never, 3 = almost never, 2 = sometimes, 1 = fairly often, 0 = very often

7. I feel I cannot cope with all the things I need to do.
   0 = never, 1 = almost never, 2 = sometimes, 3 = fairly often, 4 = very often

8. Generally, I feel on top of things.
   4 = never, 3 = almost never, 2 = sometimes, 1 = fairly often, 0 = very often

9. I get angry at things that are beyond my control.
   0 = never, 1 = almost never, 2 = sometimes, 3 = fairly often, 4 = very often

10. I feel problems pile up to such an extent that I cannot overcome them.
   0 = never, 1 = almost never, 2 = sometimes, 3 = fairly often, 4 = very often

**How Do You Measure Up?**

**Stress levels vary from person to person, but you can compare your total score to the following averages:**

| Age | Gender | Marital Status |
|---|---|---|
| 18–29… 14.2 | Men…12.1 | Widowed…12.6 |
| 30–44…13.0 | Women…13.7 | Married or living with…12.4 |
| 45–54…2.6 | | Single or never wed…14.1 |
| 55–64… 11.9 | | Divorced…14.7 |
| 65 & over…12.0 | | Separated…16.6 |

ulcers, asthma, arthritis, and high blood pressure may—although not invariably—be produced or worsened by stress (Siegel & Davis, 2008; Marin et al., 2009).

Stress may even cause more serious, even life-threatening illnesses. According to some research, the greater the number of stressful events a person experiences over the course of a year, the more likely he or she is to have a major illness (see Table 14.1; Holmes & Rahe, 1967; Alverdy, Zaborina, & Wu, 2005).

Before you start calculating whether you are overdue for a major illness, however, keep in mind some important limitations to the research. Not everyone who experiences high stress becomes ill, and the weights

---

**psychosomatic disorders** Medical problems caused by the interaction of psychological, emotional, and physical difficulties

given to particular stressors probably vary from one person to the next. Furthermore, there is a kind of circularity to such enumerations of stressors: Because the research is correlational, it is possible that someone who has a major illness to begin with is more likely to experience some of the stressors on the list. For example, a person may have lost a job because of the effects of an illness, rather than develop an illness because of the loss of a job. Still, the list of stressors does provide a way to consider how most people react to various potentially stressful events in their lives.

## Meeting the Challenge of Stress

**LO 14.7 Describe how adolescents can cope with stress.**

Some adolescents are better than others at **coping**, making efforts to control, reduce, or tolerate the threats and challenges that lead to stress. What is the key to successful coping?

Some individuals use *problem-focused coping*, in which they attempt to manage a stressful problem or situation by directly changing the situation to make it less stressful. For example, a high school student who is having academic difficulties may speak to his teachers and ask that they extend the deadlines for assignments, or a worker who is dissatisfied with her job assignment can ask that she be assigned other tasks.

Other adolescents employ *emotion-focused coping*, which involves the conscious regulation of emotion. For instance, a teenager who is having problems getting along with her boss in her after-school job may tell herself that she should look at the bright side: at least she has a job in a difficult economy (Vingerhoets, Nyklicek, & Denollet, 2008; Master et al., 2009; Khalid & Ijaz, 2013).

Coping is also aided by the presence of *social support*, assistance and comfort supplied by others. Turning to others in the face of stress can provide both emotional support (in the form of a shoulder to cry on) and practical, tangible support (such as an advance on one's allowance) (Boehmer, Linde, & Freund, 2005; Schwarzer & Knoll, 2007).

In addition, others—in person or online—can provide information, offering specific advice on how to deal with stressful situations. The ability to learn from others' experiences is one of the reasons that people use the Web (Green, DeCourville, & Sadava, 2012; Schroder et al., 2017).

---

**coping** Efforts to control, reduce, or tolerate the threats and challenges that lead to stress

---

# BECOMING AN INFORMED CONSUMER OF CHILD DEVELOPMENT

## Coping With Stress

Although no single formula can cover all cases of stress, some general guidelines can help everyone cope with the stress that is part of life:

- **Seek control over the situation producing the stress.** Putting yourself in charge of a situation that is producing stress can take you a long way toward coping with it.
- **Redefine the "threat" as a "challenge."** Changing the definition of a situation can make it seem less threatening. "Look for the silver lining" isn't bad advice.
- **Get social support.** Almost any difficulty can be faced more easily with the help of others. Friends, family members, and even telephone hotlines staffed by trained counselors can provide significant support. (For help in identifying appropriate hotlines, the U.S. Public Health Service maintains a master toll-free number that can provide phone numbers and addresses of many national groups. Call 800-336-4794.)
- **Use relaxation techniques.** Procedures that reduce the physiological arousal brought about by stress can be particularly effective. A variety of techniques produce relaxation, including transcendental meditation, Zen, yoga, progressive muscle relaxation, and even hypnosis; these have been shown to be effective in reducing stress. One that works particularly well, devised by physician Herbert Benson (1993), is illustrated in Table 14.2.
- **Exercise!** Vigorous exercise not only leads to greater fitness and health but also helps cope with stress and can lead to a sense of psychological well-being.
- **If all else fails, keep in mind that a life without any stress at all would be a dull one.** Stress is a natural part of life, and successfully coping with it can be a gratifying experience.

**Table 14.2** How to Produce the Relaxation Response

Some general advice on regular practice of the relaxation response:
- Try to find 10 to 20 minutes in your daily routine; before breakfast is a good time.
- Sit comfortably.
- For the period you will practice, try to arrange your schedule so you won't have distractions. Allow calls to go to voicemail, and ask someone else to watch the kids.
- Time yourself by glancing periodically at a clock or watch (but don't set an alarm). Commit yourself to a specific length of practice, and try to stick to it.

There are several approaches to eliciting the relaxation response. Here is one standard set of instructions:
Step 1.
Pick a focus word or short phrase that's firmly rooted in your personal belief system. For example, a nonreligious individual might choose a neutral word like *one* or *peace* or *love*. A Christian person desiring to use a prayer could pick the opening words of Psalm 23, *The Lord is my shepherd*; a Jewish person could choose *Shalom*.
Step 2.
Sit quietly in a comfortable position.
Step 3.
Close your eyes.
Step 4.
Relax your muscles.
Step 5.
Breathe slowly and naturally, repeating your focus word or phrase silently as you exhale.
Step 6.
Throughout, assume a passive attitude. Don't worry about how well you're doing. When other thoughts come to mind, simply say to yourself, "Oh, well," and gently return to the repetition.
Step 7.
Continue for 10 to 20 minutes. You may open your eyes to check the time, but do not use an alarm. When you finish, sit quietly for a minute or so, at first with your eyes closed and later with your eyes open. Then do not stand for 1 or 2 minutes.
Step 8.
Practice the technique once or twice a day.

**SOURCE:** Benson, H. (1993). "The relaxation response." In D. Goleman & J. Guerin (Eds.), Mind–body medicine: How to use your mind for better health. Yonkers, NY: Consumer Reports Publications.

Finally, even if adolescents don't consciously cope with stress, some psychologists suggest that they may unconsciously use defensive coping mechanisms that aid in stress reduction. *Defensive coping* involves the unconscious use of strategies that distort or deny the true nature of a situation. For instance, a person may deny the seriousness of a threat, trivialize a life-threatening illness, or tell himself that academic failure on a series of tests is unimportant. The problem with such defensive coping is that it does not deal with the reality of the situation but merely avoids or ignores the problem.

> **From a health care provider's perspective:** Are there periods of life that are relatively stress-free, or do people of all ages experience stress? Do stressors differ from age to age?

# Threats to Adolescents' Well-Being

*Mike probably started to change in middle school, but I didn't notice it. Call me oblivious and naïve,*
*but the thought of drugs never even crossed my mind. I was convinced that drugs came with high school or even college.*

*Now I'm wiser. I've learned that it's not unusual for kids to start using drugs as young as 11. If I'd known, maybe I'd have picked up on the clues that he left all over the place. In sixth grade his school work started to suffer, he began hanging out with kids I could sense were a little shaky, and one day he stole an expensive bat from a sports store. I caught him, gave him a stern lecture, and made him return it—and I congratulated myself on nipping his "youthful rebellion" in the bud.*

*But that was only the beginning. His moods began to swing from morose to apathetic to wildly ecstatic. He started sneaking out of the house at night. Truth was that high school was like Club Marijuana to him. We finally found out when his grades hit rock bottom that his typical school day involved sneaking out of school at 9:05 and smoking pot at a friend's house until it was time to come home.*

Mike's parents learned that marijuana was not the only drug he was using. As his friends later admitted, Mike was what they called a "garbage head." He would try anything. Despite efforts to curb his use of drugs, he never succeeded in stopping. He died at age 16, hit by a passing car after wandering into the street while high.

Few cases of adolescent drug use produce such extreme results, but the use of drugs, as well as other kinds of substance use and abuse, is one of several kinds of threats to health during adolescence, usually one of the healthiest periods of life. Although the extent of risky behavior is difficult to gauge, preventable problems such as drug, alcohol, and tobacco use, as well as sexually transmitted diseases, represent serious threats to adolescents' health and well-being.

## Illegal Drugs

### LO 14.8 Describe how prevalent illegal drug use is among adolescents and the dangers it poses.

How common is illegal drug use during adolescence? Nowadays, it has become very common for children to experiment with drugs quite early in life (Qadri et al., 2013). Alcohol and other substance use are on the rise among the youth across the globe. Ahmad et al. (2007) found that substance abuse was negligible among 10–13 year olds, but a bit marked among 14–15 year olds and maximum in the age group of 16–19. In India, the choice of substance among the young varied from tobacco products, alcohol, opioids, and heroin to prescribed medications (Kapil et al., 2005; Saluja et al., 2007; and Srivastava et al., 2004). Among the users, the gender differences were significant with regard to the magnitude of substance abuse, but not the choice of substances (Kapil et al., 2005). A study by Saluja et al. (2007) on adolescents at Postgraduate Institute of Medical Education and Research in Chandigarh showed that there was a consistent rise in adolescents registered in de-addiction OPD – 27 in the first 20 years (1978–1997), 31 in over the next four years (1998-2001), and 27 over the final two years (2002–2003). A study in Jaipur by Singh et al. (2006) on students of classes 9–12, aged between 13–18 years reported that 2.1 percent boys and 1.7 percent girls were tobacco users. The habit of smoking cigarettes was present in 72.8 percent boys and 50 percent girls with drug abuse. Smoking and tobacco usage was reported higher in adolescents who have families using tobacco and smoke (86.4 percent in boys and 68.8 percent in case of girls). In another study by Juyal et al. (2008) on substance abuse

among inter-college students showed that 58.7 percent students were ever users, while 31.3 percent were regular user of any drug. It was found that the regular drug abuse was higher in urban students as compared to rural ones (Urban—37.9 percent and Rural—24.4 percent).The study also stated that the drug abuse was more prevalent among male students than female students.

The World Health Organization (WHO) estimated that globally, 25–90 percent of street children indulge in substance abuse (Kar, Debroy, Sharma, & Islam, 2014). As per the UNDP report (1997), substance abuse has increased among children in sizeable proportions in many Indian states, e.g., Punjab, Haryana, Rajasthan, Gujarat, Hyderabad, and Andhra Pradesh. There are different forms of drugs that are used by children, and the most common among them are nicotine in the form of cigarettes or *bidis* and *gutkha* and inhalant/volatile substance used in the form of sniffing of adhesive glue, petrol, and gasoline (Rao, 2010).

A study by Tsering, Pal, and Dasgupta (2010) among 416 high schools of West Bengal, from class 8, 9, and 10 indicated the incidence and reason for drug use. Out of the total sample, 52 (12.5 percent) used or abused any one of the substances. More than two-thirds (73.07 percent) of the respondents expressed a desire to quit substance use and 57.69 percent had tried to stop. 'Easy availability' and 'relief from tension' were the most frequent reasons for continuation of substance use. It was interesting to note that inspite of being aware of the harmful effects of substance use, adolescents take up this habit.

These children are also at a higher risk of contracting blood-borne and sexually-transmitted infections such as HIV/AIDS and STD.

Adolescents have a variety of reasons for using drugs. Some use them for the pleasurable experience they supposedly provide. Others try to escape from the pressures of everyday life, however, temporarily. Some adolescents try drugs simply for the thrill of doing something illegal.

It was found that most of the users had initiated substance abuse during 15–18 years of age, with peer influence, curiosity, and a sense of growing being the major reasons for the same (Gopiram & Kishore, 2014). 'Feel good' and socialization were the main reasons for maintenance.

It is also understood that the initial reasons for substance abuse among the adolescents was peer pressure, but it was duly attributed to many reasons such as sources of enjoyment (e.g., partying, celebrating festivals, etc.) as well as to escape stress related to love failures, parental pressure (particularly from fathers), family problems, etc. Both peer and family played a vital role in the initiation and continuation of substance abuse (Kangule, Darbastwar, & Kokiwar, 2011). Peer influence was consistently identified as a source of encouragement for initiation as well as maintenance of substance use (Chowdhury & Sen, 1992).

Dube et al. (2003) have measured correlations between the number of adverse childhood experiences (ACEs) and future substance abuse behavior. Adverse childhood events included abuse (physical, emotional, or sexual), neglect (physical or emotional), growing up with household substance abuse, criminality of household members, mental illness among household members, parental discord, and illicit drug use. The study specifically compared the number of ACEs resulting in a greater likelihood of drug use initiation under 14 years of age and also compared the number of ACEs associated with increased risk of developing addiction. The research also demonstrated that each additional ACE increased the likelihood for drug use under 14 years of age by two to fourfold and raised the risk of later addiction by five times.

One of the newest reasons for using drugs is to enhance academic performance. A growing number of high school students are using drugs such as Adderall, an amphetamine prescribed for attention-deficit/hyperactivity disorder. When used illegally, Adderall is assumed to increase focus and the ability to study for many hours (Schwarz et al., 2013; Munro et al., 2017).

The alleged drug use of celebrities like Drew Barrymore and athletes like Michael Phelps also contributes to drug use. Finally, peer pressure plays a role: Adolescents, as we'll discuss in greater detail in Chapter 16, are particularly susceptible to the perceived standards of their peer groups (Urberg, Luo, & Pilgrim, 2003; Nation & Heflinger, 2006; Young et al., 2006).

The use of illegal drugs is dangerous in several respects. For instance, some drugs are addictive. **Addictive drugs** are drugs that produce a biological or psychological dependence in users, leading to increasingly powerful cravings for them.

When drugs produce a biological addiction, their presence in the body becomes so common that the body is unable to function in their absence. Furthermore, addiction causes actual physical—and potentially

lingering—changes in the nervous system. In such cases, drug intake no longer may provide a "high," but may be necessary simply to maintain the perception of everyday normalcy (Cami & Farré, 2003; Munzar, Cami, & Farré, 2003).

In addition to physical addiction, drugs also can produce psychological addiction. In such cases, people grow to depend on drugs to cope with the everyday stress of life. If drugs are used as an escape, they may prevent adolescents from confronting—and potentially solving—the problems that led them to drug use in the first place. Finally, drugs may be dangerous because even casual users of less hazardous drugs can escalate to more dangerous forms of substance abuse (Toch, 1995; Segal & Stewart, 1996).

## Alcohol: Use and Abuse

### LO 14.9 Describe the incidence of alcohol use among adolescents.

Three-fourths of college students have something in common: They've consumed at least one alcoholic drink during the past 30 days. More than 40 percent say they've had five or more drinks within the past 2 weeks, and some 16 percent drink 16 or more drinks per week. High-school students, too, are drinkers: Nearly three-quarters of high-school seniors report having had consumed alcohol by the end of high school, and about two-fifths have done so by eighth grade. More than half of 12th graders and nearly one-fifth of eighth graders say that they have been drunk at least once in their lives (Ford, 2007; Johnston et al., 2009).

Concern around potentially increasing alcohol use among young people has been growing in the research forum in India with an estimate that 75 million people are alcohol users (Srivastava, Pal, Dwivedi, & Pandey, 2002). A study on Andaman school students by Sinha et al. (2006) showed that the onset of regular use of alcohol in early adolescence is associated with the highest rate of alcohol consumption in adult life as compared to later onset of drinking. In a National Household Survey carried out by Ray et al. (2004) on a representative male sample of 40,697 between the age group of 12–60 years, 21.8 percent (n = 8,587) between 12 and 18 years were found to be using alcohol and drug.

---

**addictive drugs** Drugs that produce a biological or psychological dependence in users, leading to increasingly powerful cravings for them

Alcohol is found to be the choice among youth, which result in consequences of drinking too much, at too early an age and leads to public health problem due to underage drinking. There is an increase in the social acceptance of alcohol even for frequent self-induced intoxication and easier access is now responsible for driving adolescents toward substance use and a trend is being noted toward lower ages of onset of alcohol use (Saddichha, Manjunath & Khess, 2010). In many parts of India, including the Northeast, alcoholic drinks are prepared in households taking rice as the main ingredient or other available ingredients by fermentation, while some people use these alcoholic drinks in religious and social functions. Further, homemade alcoholic drinks (HADs) are used in front of parents and elders in social functions without inhibition. As such, in most cases, adolescent boys and girls get the taste of alcoholic drinks in the early part of life. They continue in tolerable doses; later, some of them shift to commercially available alcoholic drinks (CADs), and gradually, they become habitual drinker or addicts. Early use of alcohol adversely impacts sexual-risk behavior, substance use, criminal and violent behaviors, academic underachievement, mood disorders, and injury.

Binge drinking is a particular problem on college campuses. It is defined for men as drinking five or more drinks in one sitting; for women, who tend to weigh less and whose bodies absorb alcohol less efficiently, binge drinking is defined as four drinks in one sitting. Surveys find that almost half of male college students and over 40 percent of female college students say they participated in binge drinking during the previous two weeks (Harrell & Karim, 2008; Beets et al., 2009).

Drinking, even moderately, has potential negative consequences. Alcohol slows the functioning of the cerebral cortex, and the frontal lobes—responsible for planning, decision-making, and self-control—are less adept at making good choices and exerting impulse control. In the long run, alcohol can permanently damage nerve tissue in the brains of heavy drinkers, impeding girls' ability to understand visual information and boys' attention span. In addition, the thickness of the cortex is affected by alcohol use (Brumback et al., 2016; Jacobus et al., 2016; Meruelo et al., 2017).

Binge drinking affects even those who don't drink or who drink very little. Two-thirds of lighter drinkers reported that they had been disturbed by drunken students while sleeping or studying. Around a third had been insulted or humiliated by a drunken student, and 25 percent of women said they had been the target of an unwanted sexual advance by a drunk classmate. Furthermore, brain scans show damaged tissue in teenage binge drinkers compared to non–binge drinkers (Wechsler et al., 2002; Weitzman, Nelson, & Wechsler, 2003; McQueeny, 2009; Squeglia et al., 2012; Spear, 2013).

Adolescents start to drink for many reasons. For some—especially male athletes, whose rate of drinking tends to be higher than that of the general adolescent population—drinking is seen as a way of proving they can drink as much as anybody. Others drink for the same reason that some use drugs: It releases inhibitions and tension and reduces stress. Many begin because the conspicuous examples of drunkenness around campus cause them to assume that everyone is drinking heavily, something known as the *false consensus effect* (Weitzman, Nelson, & Wechsler, 2003; Dunn et al., 2012; Drane, Modecki, & Barber, 2017).

For some adolescents, alcohol use becomes a habit that cannot be controlled. **Alcoholics**, those with alcohol problems, learn to depend on alcohol and are unable to control their drinking. They also become increasingly able to tolerate alcohol, and therefore need to drink ever-larger amounts of liquor in order to bring about the positive effects they crave. Some drink throughout the day, whereas others go on binges in which they consume huge quantities of alcohol.

The reasons that some adolescents—or anyone—become alcoholics are not fully known. Genetics plays a role: Alcoholism runs in families. For those adolescents, alcoholism may be triggered by efforts to deal with the stress that having an alcoholic parent or family member can cause. At the same time, not all alcoholics have family members with alcohol problems (Clarke et al., 2008; Mares et al., 2011; Edwards & Kendler, 2013).

The origins of an adolescent's problems with alcohol or drugs are less important than getting help. Parents, teachers, and friends can provide the help a teen needs to address the problem—if they realize there is a problem. How can concerned friends and family members tell if an adolescent they know is having difficulties with alcohol or drugs? Some of the tell-tale signs are described next.

---

**alcoholics** People who have learned to depend on alcohol and are unable to control their drinking

# BECOMING AN INFORMED CONSUMER OF CHILD DEVELOPMENT

## Hooked on Drugs or Alcohol?

Although it is not always easy to determine whether an adolescent has a drug or alcohol abuse problem, there are some signals. Among them are the following:

### Identification with the drug culture

- Drug-related magazines or slogans on clothing
- Conversation and jokes that are preoccupied with drugs
- Hostility when discussing drugs
- Collection of beer cans

### Signs of physical deterioration

- Memory lapses, short attention span, difficulty concentrating
- Poor physical coordination; slurred or incoherent speech
- Unhealthy appearance; indifference to hygiene and grooming
- Bloodshot eyes, dilated pupils

### Dramatic changes in school performance

- Marked downturn in grades—not just from Cs to Fs, but from As to Bs and Cs; assignments not completed

- Increased absenteeism or tardiness

### Changes in behavior

- Chronic dishonesty (lying, stealing, cheating); trouble with the police
- Changes in friends; evasiveness in talking about new ones
- Possession of large amounts of money
- Increasing and inappropriate anger, hostility, irritability, secretiveness
- Reduced motivation, energy, self-discipline, self-esteem
- Diminished interest in extracurricular activities and hobbies

**SOURCE:** Adapted from Franck, I., & Brownstone, D. (1991). The parent's desk reference. New York: Prentice-Hall., pp. 593–594.

If an adolescent—or anyone else, for that matter—fits any of these descriptors, help is probably needed. A good place to start is a national hotline run by the National Institute on Drug Abuse at 800-662-4357 or its Web site at www.nida.nih.gov. In addition, those who need advice can find a local listing for Alcoholics Anonymous online.

# Tobacco: The Dangers of Smoking

**LO 14.10** **Explain why adolescents smoke and the prevalence of smoking.**

Most adolescents are well aware of the dangers of smoking, but many still indulge in it. Recent figures show that, overall, a smaller proportion of adolescents smoke than did in prior decades, but the numbers remain substantial; within certain groups the numbers are increasing. Tobacco is the most common substance of abuse among adolescents in India. The WHO considers smoking along with substance abuse as one of the most dangerous risk behavior affecting health. A majority of young people who start smoking as teenagers will become heavy smokers as adults and will continue smoking for at least 16–20 years. Cultural, social, and familial environment is known to influence such behaviors. More specifically, tobacco use among adolescents is related to the number of one's friends who smoke (Srivastava et al., 2004). Most of the Indian researches on drug abuse are based on tobacco abuse as compared to other substances. India is the third largest consumer and producer of tobacco in the world. A college based study by Bhojani et al. (2009) in Bangalore reported that 5.3 percent of the sample studied were tobacco users. Their mean age for initiation of tobacco consumption was 14.7 years. Tobacco is mostly smoked in the forms of bidi and cigarettes or using devices such as chillum and hooka. A survey by the National Sample Survey Organization of the Indian government showed that about 20 million children in the age range of 10–14 years were estimated to be tobacco addicted. To this shocking figure, about 5,500 new users are added every year (Chadda and Sengupta, 2002). As per the Global Youth Survey (GYTS), 3.8 percent children were smokers, while 11.9 percent were using smokeless tobacco (Sinha et al., 2006).

Smoking is becoming a habit that is hard to maintain. There are growing social sanctions against it. It's becoming more difficult to find a comfortable place to smoke: More places, including schools and places of business, have become "smoke-free." Even so, a good number of adolescents still smoke, despite knowing the dangers of smoking and of secondhand smoke. Why, then, do adolescents begin to smoke and maintain the habit?

One reason is that for some adolescents, smoking is seen as a rite of passage, a sign of growing up. In addition, seeing influential models, such as film stars, parents, and peers, smoking increases the chances that an adolescent will take up the habit. Cigarettes are also very addictive. Nicotine, the active chemical ingredient of cigarettes, can lead to biological and psychological dependency very quickly. Although one or two cigarettes generally do not usually produce a lifetime smoker, it takes only a little more to start the habit. People who smoke as few as 10 cigarettes early in their lives stand an 80 percent chance of becoming habitual smokers (Tucker et al., 2008; Wills et al., 2008; Holliday & Gould, 2016).

One of the newest trends in smoking is the use of e-cigarettes. *E-cigarettes* are battery-powered cigarette-shaped devices that deliver nicotine that is vaporized to form a mist. E-cigarettes offer an experience not unlike actual tobacco, and they appear to be less harmful than traditional cigarettes. However, as we consider in the *From Research to Practice* box, their health effects are unclear, and the U.S. government has sought to regulate their sale (Tavernise, 2014; Lanza, Russell, & Braymiller, 2017).

## Sexually Transmitted Infections

**LO 14.11 Describe the dangers and consequences of adolescent sexual practices.**

*Jeremy Constant of Portland, Oregon, finally got a clean bill of health. After he had been suffering from AIDS-related illnesses for three years, his virus finally dropped to undetectable levels. The key was the addition of a third drug to the two-drug cocktail that he had been taking.*

*"It was like night and day," Jeremy says. "My health came way up and my levels went way down. I'm feeling much healthier. I also just plain feel like a human again."*

*The cost of Jeremy's turnaround isn't low: he has to spend about $1,500 per year for his three-drug mix, but at least he can now think about a future.*

*Acquired immunodeficiency syndrome (AIDS)* is one of the leading causes of death among young people across the globe. AIDS has no cure. Although it can be treatable with a "cocktail" of powerful drugs, the worldwide death toll from the disease is significant.

Because AIDS is spread primarily through sexual contact, it is classified as a **sexually transmitted infection (STI)**. Although it began as a problem that primarily affected gays, it has spread to other populations, including heterosexuals and intravenous drug users. Minorities have been particularly hard hit: African Americans and Hispanics account for 70 percent of new AIDS cases, and African American males have almost eight times the prevalence of AIDS as White males.

Already, over 35 million people have died from AIDS, and people living with the virus that causes AIDS number 70 million worldwide. However, there is also good news about the AIDS epidemic: new infections are declining, and there are fewer deaths due to AIDS (World Health Organization, 2017).

**AIDS AND ADOLESCENT BEHAVIOR.** It is no secret how AIDS is transmitted—through the exchange of bodily fluids, including semen and blood. However, in recent years, the use of condoms during sexual intercourse has increased, and people are less likely to engage in casual sex with new acquaintances (Everett et al., 2000; Hoppe et al., 2004).

But the temptation to think, "It can't hurt this one time," is always there. The use of safer sex practices is far from universal. As we discussed earlier in the chapter, teens are prone to feeling invulnerable and are therefore more likely to engage in risky behavior, believing their chances of contracting AIDS are minimal. This is particularly true when adolescents perceive that their partner is "safe"—someone they know well and with whom they are involved in a relatively long-term relationship (Tinsley, Lees, & Sumartojo, 2004; Haley & Vasquez, 2008; Widman et al., 2014).

---

**sexually transmitted infection (STI)** A disease that is spread through sexual contact

## Table 14.3 Safer Sex Practices

The only foolproof method of avoiding a sexually transmitted infection (STI) is abstinence. However, by following the "safer sex" practices listed here, one can significantly reduce the risk of contracting an STI:

- *Know your sexual partner—well.* Before having sex with someone, learn about his or her sexual history.

- *Use condoms.* For those in sexual relationships, condoms are the most reliable means of preventing transmission of STIs.

- *Avoid the exchange of bodily fluids, particularly semen.* In particular, avoid anal intercourse. The AIDS virus in particular can spread through small tears in the rectum, making anal intercourse without condoms particularly dangerous. Oral sex, once thought relatively safe, is now viewed as potentially dangerous for contracting the AIDS virus.

- *Stay sober.* Using alcohol and drugs impairs judgment and can lead to poor decisions—and it makes using a condom correctly more difficult.

- *Consider the benefits of monogamy.* People in long-term monogamous relationships with partners who have been faithful are at a lower risk of contracting STIs.

Unfortunately, unless an individual knows the complete sexual history and HIV status of a partner, unprotected sex remains risky business. And learning a partner's complete sexual history is difficult. Not only is it embarrassing to ask, but also partners may not be accurate reporters, whether from ignorance of their own exposure, embarrassment, a sense of privacy, or simply forgetfulness.

Short of abstinence, there is no certain way to avoid AIDS. There are things you can do to make sex safer; these are listed in Table 14.3.

**OTHER SEXUALLY TRANSMITTED INFECTIONS.** AIDS is the deadliest sexually transmitted infection, but other STIs are far more common. One in four adolescents contracts an STI before graduating from high school. Overall, around 2.5 million teenagers contract an STI, such as the ones listed here, each year (Weinstock, Berman, & Cates, 2004).

The most common STI is *human papilloma virus (HPV).* HPV can be transmitted through genital contact without intercourse. Most infections do not have symptoms, but HPV can produce genital warts and in some cases lead to cervical cancer. A vaccine that protects against some kinds of HPV is now available.

Another common STI is *trichomoniasis*, an infection in the vagina or penis that is caused by a parasite. Initially without symptoms, it can eventually cause a painful discharge. *Chlamydia*, a bacterial infection, initially has few symptoms, but later it causes burning urination and a discharge from the penis or vagina. It can lead to pelvic inflammation and even to sterility. Chlamydial infections can be treated successfully with antibiotics (Nockels & Oakeshott, 1999; Fayers et al., 2003).

*Genital herpes* is a virus not unlike the cold sores that sometimes appear around the mouth. The first symptoms of herpes are often small blisters or sores around the genitals, which may break open and become quite painful. Although the sores may heal after a few weeks, the infection often recurs after an interval, and the cycle repeats itself. When the sores reappear, the infection, for which there is no cure, is contagious.

*Gonorrhea* and *syphilis* are the STIs that have been recognized for the longest time; cases were recorded by ancient historians. Until the advent of antibiotics, both infections were deadly; however, today both can be treated quite effectively.

Contracting an STI is not only an immediate problem during adolescence, but could become a problem later in life, too, since some infections increase the chances of future infertility and cancer.

The incidence of sexually transmitted disease (STD) among children in India is on the rise, which is primarily causing an increase in child sexual abuse. Dhawan, Gupta, and Kumar (2010) in their article cited a number of survey reports and indicated the prevalence of child sexual abuse in the country and its link with STD in children. The Indian government's Ministry of Women and Child Development has conducted the largest national level survey among 17,220 children and adolescents in the age range of 5–18 years to estimate the burden of sexual abuse, and the results were shocking. It was found that every second child in the country was sexually abused. Among them, 52.94 percent were boys and 47.06 percent were girls, mostly in the age group of 12 to 15 years. Assam reported the highest percentage of sexual abuse (57.27 percent) followed by Delhi (41 percent), Andhra Pradesh (33.87 percent), and Bihar (33.27 percent) (reported by Dhawan, Gupta & Kumar, 2010).

Jain, Agarwal, and Jain (2009) in their study has shown the prevalence of pediatric STD to 1.02 percent from Rohtak, North India, while Burzin, Parmar, and Bilmoria has reported a prevalence of 1.98 percent between 2002 and 2005 in Ahmedabad (Western India). In children with sexually transmitted infections (STIs), boys usually outnumber the girls with proportion of boys ranging from 52–78 percent.

> **From a health care provider's perspective:** Why do adolescents' increased cognitive abilities, including the ability to reason and to think experimentally, fail to deter them from irrational behavior such as drug and alcohol abuse, tobacco use, and unsafe sex practices? How might you use these abilities to design a program to help prevent these problems?

# The Case of …
## Moving Too Fast

Viva was used to being the best at whatever she did. Best grades in her class. The lead in the annual school play. A champion swimmer. She started dating before she was 12, and she often went out with three different boys in a single weekend. Being the "hottest" girl in her class was great. Or was it?

Many of the boys who asked her out were 3 or 4 years older than Viva. They put a lot of pressure on her to engage in sexual activities. Viva eventually had sex with several of the ones she liked most. She also began drinking and smoking at 13. It seemed to go with the glamorous image others had of her. But Viva began to have a hard time keeping it all together. First, her grades took a serious nosedive. Then, disaster struck. Viva was diagnosed with an STI, chlamydia, 2 weeks before her fifteenth birthday.

1. How do Viva's experiences with early physical maturation differ from what an early maturing boy might experience?
2. What psychological challenges might Viva have faced if she had physically matured later than most of her peers?
3. Why do you think Viva felt the need to begin drinking and smoking? How else might she have managed her feelings?
4. What mixed messages might Viva be getting from society and the media to cause her further confusion about her new mature body?
5. How would you advise Viva to deal with sexual pressure from the boys she dates?

# Epilogue

To call adolescence a period of great change in people's lives is an understatement. This chapter looked at the significant physical and psychological changes that adolescents undergo and at some of the consequences of entering and living through adolescence.

Before turning to the next chapter, return for the moment to the opening prologue, about Juhi and Maya, two girls seeking approval for their appearance from their peers online. In light of what you now know about adolescence, consider the following questions about Juhi and Maya.

1. Juhi worries that she's not a size 0. What health problems does Juhi risk if she becomes fixated on dropping a lot of weight? What suggestions would you make to help her focus on maintaining a healthy body instead of worrying about her dress size?
2. Cyber beauty pageants place a lot of stress on teen girls to look and dress hot. What messages does this give to young girls about their self-worth? How would you counter these messages?
3. Social media is a fact of life for all teens. What suggestions could you make to Juhi to bolster her self-esteem while still being able to interact with friends online?
4. Fourteen-year-old Maya is a very attractive girl. She receives positive feedback from friends and strangers whenever she posts her picture on social media sites. Do you think there may be a negative side to Maya's online popularity? Explain your answer.

# Looking Back

## LO 14.1 Describe the physical changes adolescents experience.

- The adolescent years are marked by a physical growth spurt that mirrors the rapid growth rate of infancy. Girls' growth spurts begin around age 10, about 2 years earlier than boys' growth spurts.

- The most significant event during adolescence is the onset of puberty, which begins for most girls at around age 11 and for most boys at around age 13. As puberty commences, the body begins to produce male or female hormones at adult levels, the sex organs develop and change, menstruation and ejaculation begin, and other body changes occur.

- The timing of puberty is linked to cultural and environmental factors, as well as to biological ones. Compared with the past, girls in the United States today experience menarche—the onset of menstruation—at the significantly younger age of 11 or 12, most likely because of better nutrition and overall health.

## LO 14.2 Explain how puberty affects adolescents.

- The physical changes that accompany puberty, which adolescents usually experience with keen interest, often have psychological effects, which may involve an increase in self-esteem and self-awareness, as well as some confusion and uncertainty about sexuality.

- Adolescents who mature either early or late may experience a variety of consequences. For boys, early maturation can lead to increased athleticism, greater popularity, and a more positive self-concept. Although early maturation can lead to increased popularity and an enhanced social life, girls may also experience embarrassment over the changes in their bodies that differentiate them from their peers. Furthermore, early physical maturation can lead both boys and girls into activities and situations for which they are not adequately prepared.

- Late maturers, who tend to be smaller for a longer period during adolescence, may be at a distinct physical and social disadvantage, which can affect self-concept and have lasting negative consequences. Girls who mature late may suffer neglect by their peers of both sexes, but ultimately they appear to suffer no lasting ill effects and may even benefit from late maturation.

## LO 14.3 Summarize the nutritional needs of adolescents.

- Even though most adolescents have no greater nutritional worries than fueling their growth with appropriate foods, some are obese or overweight and may suffer psychological and physical consequences. For example, obesity stresses the circulatory system, increasing the risk of high blood pressure and diabetes.

## LO 14.4 Describe the causes and effects of eating disorders among adolescents.

- The major eating disorders that affect adolescents are anorexia nervosa (a refusal to eat because of a perception of being overweight), bulimia (a cycle of binge eating followed by purges via self-induced vomiting or use of laxatives), and binge eating disorder (binge eating without purges). Both biological and environmental factors, including an extreme fear of obesity, appear to contribute to these disorders. Treatment typically involves psychological therapy and dietary changes.

## LO 14.5 Explain how brain development contributes to cognitive growth in adolescence.

- In adolescence, thinking becomes more sophisticated as the number of neurons increases and their interconnections become more complex.

- Myelinization also increases, making the transmission of neural messages more efficient. At the same time, the brain overproduces gray matter, which is later pruned back. The two processes—myelinization growth and gray-matter pruning—contribute to cognitive growth in adolescence.

- The prefrontal cortex, a part of the brain that allows people to evaluate situations and make complex judgments, undergoes tremendous growth in adolescence. However, because the prefrontal cortex is not yet fully mature, adolescents still struggle with impulse control.

## LO 14.6  List the causes and consequences of stress.

- Stressors are events or circumstances that produce threats to one's well-being. Acute stressors are sudden, one-time events, while chronic stressors are long-term, continuous events or circumstances that produce stress.

- Even pleasant events can be stressful.

- Moderate, occasional stress is biologically healthy, producing physical reactions that facilitate the body's defense against threats, but long exposure to stressors produces damaging physical and psychosomatic effects.

- Stress has been linked to many common ailments, including headaches, back pain, rashes, indigestion, and even the common cold. It has also been linked to psychosomatic disorders, such as ulcers, asthma, arthritis, and high blood pressure, and to more serious and even life-threatening illnesses.

## LO 14.7  Describe how adolescents can cope with stress.

- People cope with stress in a number of ways, including problem-focused coping, by which they attempt to modify the stressful situation, and emotion-focused coping, by which they attempt to regulate the emotional response to stress.

- Coping is aided by social support from others. Defensive coping, which is the unconscious resort to a strategy of denial, is less successful because it represents a failure to deal with the reality of the situation.

## LO 14.8  Describe how prevalent illegal drug use is among adolescents and the dangers it poses.

- The use of illicit drugs is alarmingly prevalent among adolescents, who are motivated by pleasure seeking, pressure avoidance, the desire to flout authority, or the imitation of role models.

- Drug use is dangerous not only because it can escalate and lead to addiction but also because adolescents' avoidance of underlying problems can have serious effects.

## LO 14.9  Describe the incidence of alcohol use among adolescents.

- Alcohol use is prevalent among adolescents, who may view drinking as a way to lower inhibitions or to manifest adult behavior.

- Binge drinking, defined as consuming five or more drinks in one sitting for men (four drinks for women), has become a serious problem on college campuses. Nearly half of all students report participating in binge drinking, with the numbers only slightly less for women than men. Not only is binge drinking unhealthy, it can also lead to obnoxious, even violent, behavior.

- Among the warning signs that an adolescent may have a problem with drugs or alcohol are identification with the drug culture, evidence of physical deterioration, dramatic declines in school performance, and significant changes in behavior.

## LO 14.10  Explain why adolescents smoke and the prevalence of smoking.

- Even though the dangers of smoking are well known and accepted by adolescents, tobacco use continues. Despite a reduction in smoking among adolescents in general, smoking within some groups has actually increased. Adolescents who smoke appear to be motivated by a desire to appear adult and "cool."

- The use of e-cigarettes is a growing concern to health experts.

## LO 14.11  Describe the dangers and consequences of adolescent sexual practices.

- AIDS is one of the leading causes of death among young people, affecting minority populations with particular severity. Adolescent behavior patterns and attitudes, such as not inquiring about a partner's HIV or AIDS status and a belief in personal invulnerability, work against the use of safer sex practices that can prevent the disease.

- Other sexually transmitted diseases, including chlamydia, genital herpes, trichomoniasis, gonorrhea, and syphilis, occur frequently among the adolescent population and can also be prevented by adopting safer sex practices or abstinence.

# Key Terms and Concepts

adolescence (p. 366)
adolescent growth spurt (p. 367)
puberty (p. 367)
menarche (p. 368)
secular trend (p. 369)
primary sex characteristics
    (p. 369)

secondary sex characteristics
    (p. 369)
anorexia nervosa (p. 373)
bulimia (p. 374)
binge eating disorder
    (p. 374)
stress (p. 376)

psychosomatic disorders
    (p. 377)
coping (p. 378)
addictive drugs (p. 381)
alcoholics (p. 382)
sexually transmitted infection
    (STI) (p. 384)

# Chapter 15
# Cognitive Development in Adolescence

 ## Learning Objectives

**LO 15.1** Explain how adolescents develop abstract thinking, and explore the consequences of this development.

**LO 15.2** Describe the information-processing perspective on cognitive development.

**LO 15.3** Summarize the aspects of cognitive development that cause difficulties for adolescents.

**LO 15.4** Describe the stages of moral development through which adolescents progress.

**LO 15.5** Summarize the gender differences in moral development.

**LO 15.6** Analyze the factors that affect adolescent school performance during the elementary school to middle school transition.

**LO 15.7** Explain how socioeconomic status and ethnic and racial differences affect school performance.

**LO 15.8** Evaluate the advantages and disadvantages of working during high school.

**LO 15.9** Describe the demographic characteristics of college students.

**LO 15.10** Identify how career choices are made.

**LO 15.11** Describe the relationship between gender and career development.

# Prologue: Not a Child Anymore

Govind Saxena is locked in an argument with his dad. Though it's not their first battle, it's the biggest one to date. Fifteen-year-old Govind is set on traveling to Kashmir next month at the end of the school year to create an awareness campaign for school children. His father is equally set against the idea. "Grandpa was a freedom fighter," Govind argues. "And you fought the 1972 war."

"Grandpa was 18 when he went for his struggle for freedom," Govind's father reminds him, "and I was 20 when I fought for Indo-Pak war in 1972."

"But I'm almost 16," Govind cries, his voice cracking. "Besides, kids grow up a lot faster today."

Govind's dad looks at his son, who now towers several inches above him, and sees a boy just one year out of high school asking to travel far from home on his own. Govind looks at his father and sees a jailer bent on limiting his life and treating him like a child. The argument is once again in stalemate, but Govind is determined. He falls asleep that night, imagining himself talking to the young Kashmiris: helping people to build a new and better life, maybe even saving lives. In Kashmir, he thinks, people will appreciate him, look up to him.

# Looking Ahead

Like Govind, many adolescents crave independence and feel that their parents fail to see how much they've matured. They are keenly aware of their changing bodies and their increasingly complex cognitive abilities. Daily, they deal with careening emotions, social networks that are in constant flux, and the temptations of sex, alcohol, and drugs. In this period of life that evokes excitement, anxiety, glee, and despair, they—like Govind—are eager to prove they can handle whatever challenges come their way.

In this chapter, we explore cognitive development during adolescence. Our study begins with an examination of several theories that seek to explain cognitive development. We first consider the Piagetian approach, discussing the way in which adolescents use what Jean Piaget calls formal operations to solve problems.

We then turn to the increasingly influential information-processing perspectives, which provide a different point of view. We consider the growth of metacognitive capabilities, through which adolescents become increasingly aware of their own thinking processes.

The chapter then discusses the development of moral reasoning and behavior. We consider two major approaches, both of which seek to explain the ways adolescents differ from one another in their moral judgments.

The chapter ends with an examination of school performance and career choices. After discussing the profound impact that socioeconomic status has on school achievement, we consider school performance and ethnicity. We close with a discussion of the ways in which adolescents make career choices.

# Intellectual Development

*Ms. Mejia smiled as she read a particularly creative paper. As part of her eighth-grade American Government class every year, she asked students to write about what their lives would be like if America had not won its war for independence from Britain. She had tried something similar with her sixth graders, but many of them seemed unable to imagine anything different from what they already knew. By eighth grade, however, they were able to come up with some very interesting scenarios. One boy imagined that he would be known as Lord Lucas; a girl imagined that she would be a servant to a rich landowner; another, that she would be helping to plot an overthrow of the government.*

What is it that sets adolescents' thinking apart from that of younger children? One of the major changes is the ability to think beyond the concrete, current situation to what *might* or *could* be. Adolescents are able to keep a variety of abstract possibilities in their heads, and they can see issues in relative, as opposed to absolute, terms. Instead of viewing problems as having black-and-white solutions, they are capable of perceiving shades of gray.

Once again, we can use several approaches to explain adolescents' cognitive development. We begin by returning to Piaget's theory, which has had a significant influence on how developmentalists think about thinking during adolescence.

## Piaget's Formal Operational Stage and Adolescent Cognitive Development

**LO 15.1  Explain how adolescents develop abstract thinking, and explore the consequences of this development.**

*Fourteen-year-old Leigh is asked to solve a problem that anyone who has seen a grandfather clock may have pondered: What determines the speed at which a pendulum moves back and forth? In the version of the problem that she is asked to solve, Leigh is given a weight hanging from a string. She is told that she can vary several things: the length of the string, the weight of the object at the end of the string, the amount of force used to push the string, and the height to which the weight is raised in an arc before it is released.*

Leigh doesn't remember, but she was asked to solve the same problem when she was 8 years old, as part of a longitudinal research study. At that time, she was in the concrete operational period, and her efforts to solve the problem were not successful. She approached the problem haphazardly, with no systematic plan of action. For instance, she simultaneously tried to push the pendulum harder *and* shorten the length of the string *and* increase the weight on the string. Because she was varying so many factors at once, when the speed of the pendulum changed, she had no way of knowing which factor or factors made a difference.

Now, however, Leigh is much more systematic. Rather than immediately beginning to push and pull at the pendulum, she stops a moment and thinks about what factors to take into account. She considers how she might test each one, forming a hypothesis about which is most important. Then, just like a scientist conducting an experiment, she varies only one factor at a time. By examining each variable separately and systematically, she is able to come to the correct solution: The length of the string determines the speed of the pendulum.

**USING FORMAL OPERATIONS TO SOLVE PROBLEMS.** Leigh's approach to the pendulum question, a problem devised by Piaget, illustrates that she has moved into the formal operational period of cognitive development (Piaget & Inhelder, 1958). The **formal operational stage** is the stage at which people develop the ability to think abstractly. Piaget suggested that people reach this stage at the start of adolescence, around age 12. Leigh was able to think about the various aspects of the pendulum problem in an abstract manner and to understand how to test out the hypotheses that she had formed.

By bringing formal principles of logic to bear on problems they encounter, adolescents are able to consider problems in the abstract rather than only in concrete terms. They are able to test their understanding by systematically carrying out rudimentary experiments on problems and situations and observing what their experimental "interventions" bring about.

Adolescents in the formal operational stage use *hypothetico-deductive* reasoning, in which they start with a general theory about what produces a particular outcome and then deduce explanations for specific

---

**formal operational stage** The stage at which people develop the ability to think abstractly

Like scientists who form hypotheses, adolescents in the formal operational stage use hypothetico-deductive reasoning. They start with a general theory about what produces a particular outcome and then deduce explanations for specific situations in which they see that particular outcome.

situations in which they see that particular outcome. Like scientists who form hypotheses, they can then test their theories. What distinguishes this kind of thinking from earlier cognitive stages is the ability to start with abstract possibilities and move to the concrete; in previous stages, children are tied to the concrete here and now. For example, at age 8, Leigh just started moving things around to see what would happen in the pendulum problem, a concrete approach. At age 12, however, she started with the abstract idea that each variable—the string, the size of the weight, and so forth—should be tested separately.

Adolescents are also able to employ propositional thought during the formal operational stage. *Propositional thought* is reasoning that uses abstract logic in the absence of concrete examples. For example, propositional thinking allows adolescents to understand that if certain premises are valid, then a conclusion must also be valid. For example, consider the following:

| | |
|---|---|
| All men are mortal. | [*premise*] |
| Socrates is a man. | [*premise*] |
| Therefore, Socrates is mortal. | [*conclusion*] |

Not only can adolescents understand that if both premises are valid, then so is the conclusion, but also they are capable of using similar reasoning when premises and conclusions are stated more abstractly, as follows:

| | |
|---|---|
| All A's are B. | [*premise*] |
| C is an A. | [*premise*] |
| Therefore, C is a B. | [*conclusion*] |

Although Piaget proposed that children enter the formal operational stage at the beginning of adolescence, you may recall that he also hypothesized that—as with all the stages of cognitive development—full capabilities do not emerge suddenly, in one stroke. Instead, they gradually unfold through a combination of physical maturation and environmental experiences. According to Piaget, it is not until adolescents are around 15 years old that they are fully settled in the formal operational stage.

Some evidence suggests that a sizable proportion of people hone their formal operational skills at a later age and in some cases never fully employ formal operational thinking at all. For instance, most studies show that only 40 percent to 60 percent of college students and adults achieve formal operational thinking completely, and some estimates run as low as 25 percent. But many of those adults who do not show formal operational thought in every domain are fully competent in *some* aspects of formal operations (Keating, 1990, 2004).

Why are there inconsistencies in the use of formal operations? Why don't older adolescents consistently use formal operational thinking? One reason is that all of us are often cognitively lazy, relying on intuition and mental shortcuts rather than on formal reasoning. In addition, we are more apt to think abstractly and use formal operational thought on tasks on which we have considerable experience; in unfamiliar situations, we find it more difficult to think using formal operations. An English major finds it easy to identify the themes of a Faulkner play, while a biology major may struggle. Of course, the biology major may find the concepts of cell division simple, while the English major may find the concept bedeviling (Klaczynski, 2004).

Furthermore, adolescents differ in their use of formal operations because of the culture in which they were raised. People who live in isolated, scientifically unsophisticated societies and who have little formal education are less likely to perform at the formal operational level than formally educated persons living in more technologically sophisticated societies (Segall et al., 1990; Asadi, Amiri, & Molvadi, 2014).

Does this mean that adolescents (and adults) from cultures in which formal operations tend not to emerge are incapable of attaining them? Not at all. A more probable conclusion is that the scientific reasoning that characterizes formal operations is not equally valued in all societies. If everyday life does not require or promote a certain type of reasoning, it is unreasonable to expect people to employ that type of reasoning when confronted with a problem.

**THE EFFECTS OF FORMAL OPERATIONS ON ADOLESCENTS' THINKING.** Adolescents' ability to reason abstractly, embodied in their use of formal operations, leads to a change in their everyday behavior. Whereas earlier they may have unquestioningly accepted rules and explanations set out for them, their increased abstract reasoning abilities may lead them to question their parents and other authority figures far more strenuously. Advances in abstract thinking also lead to greater idealism, which may make adolescents impatient with imperfections in institutions such as schools and the government.

Because of their newfound cognitive skills, many adolescents become more argumentative. They enjoy using abstract reasoning to poke holes in others' explanations, and their increased ability to think critically makes them acutely sensitive to parents' and teachers' perceived shortcomings. For instance, they may note the inconsistency in their parents' arguments against using drugs, even though they know that their parents used them when they were adolescents and nothing much came of it. At the same time, adolescents can be indecisive, as they are able to see the merits of multiple sides to issues (Alberts, Elkind, & Ginsberg, 2007; Klaczynski, 2011; Knoll et al., 2016).

Coping with the increased critical abilities of adolescents can be challenging for parents, teachers, and other adults who deal with adolescents. But it also makes adolescents more interesting, as they actively seek to understand the values and justifications that they encounter in their lives. (Also see the *From Research to Practice* box.)

**EVALUATING PIAGET'S APPROACH.** Each time we've considered Piaget's theory in previous chapters, several concerns have cropped up. Let's summarize the issues here:

- Piaget suggests that cognitive development proceeds in universal advances that occur at particular stages. Yet we find significant differences

# FROM RESEARCH TO PRACTICE
## Do Video Games Improve Cognitive Ability?

Although considerable research suggests that there are harmful effects due to playing violent video games, there are many kinds of effects that video games can have. In fact, some researchers believe that the focus on aggressive behaviors has obscured the possibility that playing video games can have beneficial consequences as well. More recent research holds out promise that this indeed may be the case (Granic, Lobel, & Engels, 2014).

Far from the mind-numbing activity that some people label it, playing video games is in fact cognitively stimulating. This is true even of the violent type of action or "shooter" video games. When participants who are not game players were randomly assigned to play either a shooter or non-shooter video game, those who played the shooter game showed improvements in attention, visual processing, and mental rotation abilities. A comprehensive meta-analysis showed that these kinds of games produce improvements in spatial skills that are comparable to formal spatial-skill training and are furthermore quickly acquired, relatively long-lasting, and transferrable to other kinds of tasks. These kinds of skills predict future achievement in science, technology, engineering, and math careers, and ironically, they are not enhanced by playing puzzle-solving or other types of non-shooter games. It seems that the fast-paced, split-second decision making and immersive three-dimensional environments of shooter games play a pivotal role in the cognitive enhancement effect (Green et al., 2012; Uttal et al., 2013).

Other kinds of cognitive enhancements can come from video game play as well. Most games involve problem solving of some kind, so it's not much of a leap to hypothesize that they may enhance problem-solving skills. The research so far is very limited, but promising: One study has shown that playing strategic games produced improved self-reported problem-solving skills the following year. While more research needs to be done, it's clear that video games may have as much potential to be helpful to children as they do to be harmful (Adachi & Willoughby, 2013).

- **Do you think that the benefits of playing shooter-type video games justify the problems of exposing adolescents to their violent content? Why or why not?**

in cognitive abilities from one person to the next, especially when we compare individuals from different cultures. Furthermore, we find inconsistencies even within the same individual; people may be able to accomplish some tasks that indicate they have reached a certain level of thinking, but not other tasks. If Piaget were correct, a person ought to perform uniformly well once she or he reaches a given stage (Siegler, 2016).

- The notion of stages proposed by Piaget suggests that cognitive abilities do not grow gradually or smoothly. Instead, the stage point of view implies that cognitive growth is typified by relatively rapid shifts from one stage to the next. In contrast, many developmentalists argue that cognitive development proceeds in a more continuous fashion, increasing not so much in qualitative leaps forward as in quantitative accumulations. They also contend that Piaget's theory is better at *describing* behavior at a given stage than at *explaining* why the shift from one stage to the next occurs (Anisfeld, 2005).

- Because of the nature of the tasks Piaget employed to measure cognitive abilities, critics suggest that he underestimated the age at which certain capabilities emerge. It is now widely accepted that infants and children are more sophisticated at an earlier age than Piaget asserted (Bornstein & Lamb, 2005; Kenny, 2013).

- Piaget had a relatively narrow view of what is meant by *thinking* and *knowing*. To Piaget, knowledge consists primarily of the kind of understanding displayed in the pendulum problem; however, as we discussed in Chapter 12, developmentalists such as Howard Gardner suggest that we have many kinds of intelligence, separate from and independent of one another (Gardner, 2000, 2006).

- Finally, some developmentalists argue that formal operations do not represent the epitome of thinking and that more sophisticated forms of thinking do not actually emerge until early adulthood. For instance, developmental psychologist Giesela Labouvie-Vief argues that the complexity of society requires thought that is not necessarily based on pure logic. Instead, a kind of thinking is required that is flexible, allows for interpretive processes, and reflects the fact that reasons behind events in the real world are subtle—something that Labouvie-Vief calls *postformal thinking* (Labouvie-Vief & Diehl, 2000; Hamer & Van Rossum, 2016).

On the one hand, these criticisms and concerns regarding Piaget's approach to cognitive development have considerable merit. On the other hand, Piaget's theory has been the impetus for an enormous number of studies on the development of thinking capacities and processes, and it also spurred a good deal of classroom reform. Finally, his bold statements about the nature of cognitive development provided a fertile soil from which many opposing positions on cognitive development have bloomed, including the information-processing perspective, to which we turn next (Taylor & Rosenbach, 2005; Kuhn, 2008; Bibace, 2013).

## Information-Processing Perspectives: Gradual Transformations in Abilities

**LO 15.2 Describe the information-processing perspective on cognitive development.**

Unlike Piaget's view that the increasing cognitive sophistication of the adolescent is a reflection of stage-like spurts, from the perspective of proponents of **information-processing approaches** to cognitive development, adolescents' mental abilities to take in, use, and store information grow gradually and continuously. A number of progressive changes occur in the ways people organize their thinking about the world, develop strategies for dealing with new situations, sort facts, and achieve advances in memory capacity and perceptual abilities (Pressley & Schneider, 1997; Wyer, 2004).

Adolescents' general intelligence—as measured by traditional IQ tests—remains stable, but there are dramatic improvements in the specific mental abilities that underlie intelligence. Verbal, mathematical, and spatial abilities increase, making many adolescents quicker with a comeback, impressive sources of information, and accomplished athletes. Memory capacity grows, and adolescents become more adept at effectively dividing their attention across more than one stimulus at a time—such as simultaneously studying for a biology test and listening to music.

---

**information-processing approaches** Approaches to the study of cognitive development that seek to identify the ways individuals take in, use, and store information

Furthermore, as Piaget noted, adolescents grow increasingly sophisticated in their understanding of problems, their ability to grasp abstract concepts and to think hypothetically, and their comprehension of the possibilities inherent in situations. This permits them, for instance, to endlessly dissect the course that their relationship might hypothetically take.

Adolescents know more about the world, too. Their store of knowledge increases as the amount of material to which they are exposed grows. Taken as a whole, the mental abilities that underlie intelligence show a marked improvement during adolescence (Kail, 2004; Kail & Miller, 2006; Atkins et al., 2012).

According to information-processing explanations of cognitive development during adolescence, one of the most important reasons for advances in mental abilities is the growth of metacognition. **Metacognition** is the knowledge that people have about their own thinking processes and their ability to monitor their cognition. Although school-age children can use some metacognitive strategies, adolescents are much more adept at understanding their own mental processes.

For example, as adolescents improve their understanding of their memory capacity, they get better at gauging how long they need to study a particular kind of material to memorize it for a test. Furthermore, they can judge when they have fully memorized the material with considerably more accuracy than they could when they were younger. These improvements in metacognitive abilities permit adolescents to comprehend and master school material more effectively (Dimmit & McCormick, 2012; Martins et al., 2013; Thielsch, Andor, & Ehring, 2015; Rahko et al., 2016; Zakrzewski, Johnson, & Smith, 2017).

These new abilities also can make adolescents particularly introspective and self-conscious—two hallmarks of the period that, as we see next, may produce a high degree of egocentrism.

## Egocentrism in Thinking: Adolescents' Self-Absorption

**LO 15.3 Summarize the aspects of cognitive development that cause difficulties for adolescents.**

*Amit thinks of his parents as "control freaks." He cannot figure out why they insist that, when he borrows their car, he call home and let them know where he is. Juhi is thrilled that Milli bought*

*earrings just like hers, thinking it is the ultimate compliment, even though it's not clear that Milli even knew that Juhi had a similar pair when she bought them. Leena is upset with his biology teacher, Mrs. Mehta, for giving a long, difficult midterm exam on which he didn't do well.*

Adolescents' newly sophisticated metacognitive abilities enable them to readily imagine that others are thinking about them, and they may construct elaborate scenarios about others' thoughts. **Adolescent egocentrism**, a state of self-absorption in which the world is viewed as focused on oneself, may also dominate adolescents' thinking. This egocentrism makes adolescents highly critical of authority figures such as parents and teachers, unwilling to accept criticism, and quick to find fault with others' behavior (Alberts, Elkind, & Ginsberg, 2007; Schwartz, Maynard, & Uzelac, 2008; Inagaki, 2013; Lin, 2016).

The kind of egocentrism we see in adolescence helps explain why adolescents sometimes perceive that they are the focus of everyone else's attention. Adolescents may develop what has been called an **imaginary audience**, fictitious observers who pay as much attention to the adolescents' behavior as adolescents do themselves.

The imaginary audience is usually perceived as focusing on the one thing that adolescents think most about: themselves. Unfortunately, these scenarios may suffer from the same kind of egocentrism as the rest of their thinking. For instance, a student sitting in a class may be sure a teacher is focusing on her, and a teenager at a basketball game is likely to be convinced that everyone around is focusing on the pimple on his chin.

Egocentrism leads to a second distortion in thinking: the notion that one's experiences are unique. Adolescents develop **personal fables**, the view that what happens to them is unique, exceptional, and shared by no one else. For instance, teenagers whose

---

**metacognition** The knowledge that people have about their own thinking processes and their ability to monitor their cognition

**adolescent egocentrism** A state of self-absorption in which the world is viewed from one's own point of view

**imaginary audience** Fictitious observers who pay as much attention to adolescents' behavior as they do themselves

**personal fables** The view held by some adolescents that what happens to them is unique, exceptional, and shared by no one else

romantic relationships have ended may feel that no one has ever experienced the hurt they feel, that no one has ever been treated so badly, that no one can understand what they are going through (Alberts, Elkind, & Ginsberg, 2007; Hill & Lapsley, 2011; Rai et al., 2016).

Personal fables also may make adolescents construct an *invincibility fable,* in which they feel invulnerable to the risks that threaten others. Much of adolescents' risk-taking may well be traced to the invincibility fables they create. For example, they may think that there is no need to use condoms during sex because, in the invincibility fable they construct, pregnancy and sexually transmitted infections such as AIDS only happen to other kinds of people, not to them. They may drive after drinking because their invincibility fable paints them as careful drivers, always in control (Greene et al., 2000; Vartanian, 2000; Aalsma, Lapsley, & Flannery, 2006).

Adolescent egocentrism also may lead to feelings of stupidity when an adolescent misses the answer to an obvious, simple question because he or she adds unnecessary complexity in thinking about it. This phenomenon, known as *pseudostupidity,* occurs not because adolescents are "stupid" but because they lack experience with their newly attained ability to think about multiple possibilities at the same time.

---

**From a social worker's perspective:** In what ways does adolescent egocentrism complicate adolescents' social and family relationships? Do adults entirely outgrow egocentrism and personal fables?

---

# Moral Development

*Your wife is near death from an unusual kind of cancer. One drug exists that the physicians think might save her—a form of radium that a scientist in a nearby city has recently developed. The drug, however, is expensive to manufacture, and the scientist is charging 10 times what the drug costs him to make. He pays $1,000 for the radium but charges $10,000 for a small dose. You have gone to everyone you know to borrow money, but you can get together only $2,500—one quarter of what you need. You've told the scientist that your wife is dying and asked him to sell it more cheaply or let you pay later. But the scientist has said, "No, I discovered the drug, and I'm going to make money from it." In desperation, you consider breaking into the scientist's laboratory to steal the drug for your wife. Should you do it?*

According to developmental psychologist Lawrence Kohlberg and his colleagues, the answer that adolescents give to this question reveals central aspects of their sense of morality and justice. He suggests that people's responses to moral dilemmas such as this one reveal the stage of moral development they have attained—as well as yield information about their general level of cognitive development (Kohlberg, 1984; Colby & Kohlberg, 1987).

## Kohlberg's Approach to Moral Development

**LO 15.4   Describe the stages of moral development through which adolescents progress.**

Kohlberg contends that people pass through a series of stages as their sense of justice evolves and in the kind of reasoning they use to make moral judgments. Primarily due to cognitive characteristics that we discussed earlier, younger school-age children tend to think either in terms of concrete, unvarying rules ("It is always wrong to steal" or "I'll be punished if I steal") or in terms of the rules of society ("Good people don't steal" or "What if everyone stole?").

By the time they reach adolescence, however, individuals are able to reason on a higher plane, typically having reached Piaget's stage of formal operations. They are capable of comprehending abstract, formal principles of morality, and they consider cases such as the one presented previously in terms of broader issues of morality and of right and wrong ("stealing may be acceptable if you are following your own conscience and doing the right thing").

Kohlberg suggests that moral development emerges in a three-level sequence, which is further subdivided into six stages (see Table 15.1). At the lowest level, *preconventional morality* (Stages 1 and 2), people follow rigid rules based on punishments or rewards. For example, a student at the preconventional level might evaluate the moral dilemma posed in the story by saying that it was not worth stealing the drug because if you were caught, you would go to jail.

In the next level, that of *conventional morality* (Stages 3 and 4), people approach moral problems in terms of their own position as good, responsible

## Table 15.1 Kohlberg's Sequence of Moral Reasoning

| Sample Moral Reasoning | | | |
|---|---|---|---|
| Level | Stage | In Favor of Stealing | Against Stealing |
| **LEVEL 1** | **STAGE 1** | | |
| Preconventional morality: The main considerations are the avoidance of punishment and the desire for rewards. | Obedience and punishment orientation: People obey rules to avoid being punished. Obedience is its own reward. | "You shouldn't just let your wife die. People will blame you for not doing enough, and they'll blame the scientist for not selling you the drug for less money." | "You can't steal the drug because you'll be arrested and go to jail. Even if you aren't caught, you'll feel guilty, and you'll always worry that the police may figure out what you did." |
| | **STAGE 2** | | |
| | Reward orientation: People obey rules in order to earn rewards for their own benefit. | "Even if you get caught, the jury will understand and give you a short sentence. Meanwhile, your wife is alive. And if you're stopped before you get the drug to your wife, you could probably just return the drug without penalty." | "You shouldn't steal the drug because you're not responsible for your wife's cancer. If you get caught, your wife will still die, and you'll be in jail." |
| **LEVEL 2** | **STAGE 3** | | |
| Conventional morality: Membership in society becomes important. People behave in ways that will win the approval of others. | "Good boy" morality: People want to be respected by others and try to do what they're supposed to do. | "Who will blame you if you steal a lifesaving drug? But if you just let your wife die, you won't be able to hold your head up in front of your family or your neighbors." | "If you steal the drug, everyone will treat you like a criminal. They will wonder why you couldn't have found some other way to save your wife." |
| | **STAGE 4** | | |
| | Authority and social-order-maintaining morality: People believe that only society, not individuals, can determine what is right. Obeying society's rules is right in itself. | "A husband has certain responsibilities toward his wife. If you want to live an honorable life, you can't let fear of the consequences get in the way of saving her. If you ever want to sleep again, you have to save her." | "You shouldn't let your concern for your wife cloud your judgment. Stealing the drug may feel right at the moment, but you'll live to regret breaking the law." |
| **LEVEL 3** | **STAGE 5** | | |
| Postconventional morality: People accept that there are certain ideals and principles of morality that must govern our actions. These ideals are more important than any particular society's rules. | Morality of contract, individual rights, and democratically accepted law: People rightly feel obligated to follow the agreed rules of society. But as societies develop over time, rules have to be updated to make societal changes reflect underlying social principles. | "If you simply follow the law, you will violate the underlying principle of saving your wife's life. If you do take the drug, society will understand your actions and respect them. You can't let an outdated law prevent you from doing the right thing." | "Rules represent society's thinking on the morality of actions. You can't let your short-term emotions interfere with the more permanent rules of society. If you do, society will judge you negatively, and in the end you will lose self-respect." |
| | **STAGE 6** | | |
| | Morality of individual principles and conscience: People accept that laws are attempts to write down specific applications of universal moral principles. Individuals must test these laws against their conscience, which tends to express an inborn sense of those principles. | "If you allow your wife to die, you will have obeyed the letter of the law, but you will have violated the universal principle of life preservation that resides within your conscience. You will blame yourself forever if your wife dies because you obeyed an imperfect law." | "If you become a thief, your conscience will blame you for putting your own interpretation of moral issues above the legitimate rule of law. You will have betrayed your own standards of morality." |

**SOURCE:** Based on Kohlberg, L. (1969). "Stage and sequence: The cognitive-developmental approach to socialization." In D. Goslin (Ed.), Handbook of socialization theory and research. Chicago: Rand McNally.

members of society. Some at this level would decide *against* stealing the drug because they think they would feel guilty or dishonest for violating social norms. Others would decide *in favor* of stealing the drug because if they did nothing in this situation, they would be unable to face others. All of these people would be reasoning at the conventional level of morality.

Finally, individuals using *postconventional morality* (Level 3; Stages 5 and 6) invoke universal moral principles that are considered broader than the rules of the particular society in which they live. People who feel that they would condemn themselves if they did not steal the drug because they would not be living up to their own moral principles would be reasoning at the postconventional level.

Kohlberg's theory proposes that people move through the periods of moral development in a fixed order and that they are unable to reach the highest stage until adolescence, due to deficits in cognitive development that are not overcome until then. Not everyone, however, is presumed to reach the highest stages; Kohlberg found that postconventional reasoning is relatively rare (Hedgepeth, 2005).

Although Kohlberg's theory provides a good account of the development of moral *judgments*, the links with moral *behavior* are less strong. Still, students at higher levels of moral reasoning are less likely to engage in antisocial behavior at school (such as breaking school rules) and in the community (engaging in juvenile delinquency) (Carpendale, 2000; Paciello et al., 2013).

Furthermore, one experiment found that 15 percent of students who reasoned at the postconventional level of morality—the highest category—cheated when given the opportunity, although they were not as likely to cheat as those at lower levels, where more than half of the students cheated. Clearly, though, knowing what is morally right does not always mean acting that way (Hart, Burock, & London, 2003; Semerci, 2006; Krettenauer, Jia, & Mosleh, 2011; Wagnsson et al., 2016).

Kohlberg's theory has also been criticized because it is based solely on observations of members of Western cultures. In fact, cross-cultural research finds that members of more industrialized, technologically advanced cultures move through the stages more rapidly than members of nonindustrialized countries. Why? One explanation is that Kohlberg's higher stages are based on moral reasoning involving governmental and societal institutions like the police and court system. In less industrialized areas, morality may be based more on relationships among people in a particular village. In short, the nature of morality may differ in diverse cultures, and Kohlberg's theory is more suited for Western cultures (Fu et al., 2007).

**From an educator's perspective:** Should moral development be taught in public schools?

An aspect of Kohlberg's theory that has proved even more problematic is the difficulty it has explaining *girls'* moral judgments. Because the theory initially was based largely on data from male subjects, some researchers have argued that it does a better job describing boys' moral development than girls' moral development. This would explain the surprising finding that women typically score at a lower level than men do on tests of moral judgments using Kohlberg's stage sequence. This result has led to an alternative account of moral development for girls.

## Gilligan's Approach to Moral Development: Gender and Morality

**LO 15.5 Summarize the gender differences in moral development.**

Psychologist Carol Gilligan (1987, 1996) has suggested that differences in the ways boys and girls are raised in our society lead to basic distinctions in how men and women view moral behavior. According to Gilligan, boys view morality primarily in terms of broad principles such as justice or fairness, whereas girls see it in terms of responsibility toward individuals and willingness to sacrifice themselves to help specific individuals within the context of particular relationships. Compassion for individuals, then, is a more prominent factor in moral behavior for women than it is for men (Gilligan, Lyons, & Hammer, 1990; Gump, Baker, & Roll, 2000).

Carol Gilligan argues that boys and girls view morality differently, with boys seeing it primarily in terms of broad principles and girls considering it in terms of personal relationships and responsibility toward individuals.

**Table 15.2** Gilligan's Three Stages of Moral Development in Women

| Stage | Characteristics | Example |
|---|---|---|
| **STAGE 1** | | |
| Orientation toward individual survival | Initial concentration is on what is practical and best for self. Gradual transition from selfishness to responsibility, which includes thinking about what would be best for others. | A first grader may insist on playing only games of her own choosing when playing with a friend. |
| **STAGE 2** | | |
| Goodness as self-sacrifice | Initial view is that a woman must sacrifice her own wishes to what other people want. Gradual transition from "goodness" to "truth," which takes into account needs of both self and others. | Now older, the same girl may believe that to be a good friend, she must play the games her friend chooses, even if she herself doesn't like them. |
| **STAGE 3** | | |
| Morality of nonviolence | A moral equivalence is established between self and others. Hurting anyone—including oneself—is seen as immoral. This is the most sophisticated form of reasoning, according to Gilligan. | The same girl may realize that both friends must enjoy their time together and look for activities that both she and her friend can enjoy. |

**SOURCE:** Based on Kohlberg, L. (1969). "Stage and sequence: The cognitive-developmental approach to socialization." In D. Goslin (Ed.), Handbook of socialization theory and research. Chicago: Rand McNally.

Gilligan views morality as developing among girls in a three-stage process (summarized in Table 15.2). In the first stage, called "orientation toward individual survival," girls first concentrate on what is practical and best for them, gradually making a transition from selfishness to responsibility, in which they think about what would be best for others. In the second stage, termed "goodness as self-sacrifice," girls begin to think that they must sacrifice their own wishes in favor of what other people want.

Ideally, women make a transition from "goodness" to "truth," in which they take into account their own needs plus those of others. This transition leads to the third stage, "morality of nonviolence," in which women come to see that hurting anyone—including themselves—is immoral. This realization establishes a moral equivalence between themselves and others and represents, according to Gilligan, the most sophisticated level of moral reasoning.

These students exemplify Gilligan's stage of moral development in which violence against others (as well as oneself) is viewed as immoral.

It is obvious that Gilligan's sequence of stages is quite different from Kohlberg's, and some developmentalists have suggested that her rejection of Kohlberg's work is too sweeping and that gender differences are not as pronounced as first thought (Colby & Damon, 1987). For instance, some researchers argue that both men and women use similar "justice" and "care" orientations in making moral judgments. Clearly, the question of how boys and girls differ in their moral orientations, as well as the nature of moral development in general, is far from settled (Weisz & Black, 2002; Jorgensen, 2006; Tappan, 2006; Donleavy, 2008; Fragkaki, Cima, & Meesters, 2016).

# Schooling and Cognitive Development

*I LOVE MIDDLE SCHOOL!!!!!!! none of my old friends are really in my classes though (ok I have some in gym and Steph in get the facs but that's only like 1 class per person) but Joe just happened to be in 4 of my classes so I spend 5 periods of every day with him, sitting by him in 3 of them. he's gotten nicer though, kinda. anyway I LOVE MIDDLE SCHOOL!!!!! it's the greatest. and plus there's Vivi who is sick right now but I have my last 3 periods with her and Morgan… I love Latin too it's so much fun and I love my teacher Mrs. Whittaker. She's the best.*

\*\*\*

*From 4th grade till the summer before 6th grade I was depressed. it was in 6th grade that I decided*

*that I needed to live. I figured that since I was moving to middle school I might be able to sort of start over. however that was not the case. my brothers had by this point stopped messing with me for the most part. but school was horrible I was the kid that everyone picked on. that lasted for 2 years until I realized that if I stopped reacting to being made fun of people stopped making fun of me. so throughout middle school I was a loner. I had a lot of people who would claim to be my friends but they would still make fun of me so I became a loner.*

If nothing else, middle school evokes strong feelings on the part of adolescents, as these two reactions illustrate. That's hardly surprising, given that the transition from elementary school to middle school comes at a time when students are changing radically along a variety of dimensions.

We'll now turn to the consequences of this educational transition on adolescents. We'll see how schools promote both academic progress and adolescent development.

# The Transition From Elementary School to Middle School

**LO 15.6 Analyze the factors that affect adolescent school performance during the elementary school to middle school transition.**

Do the advances in meta cognition, reasoning, and other cognitive abilities lead to improved school performance? If we use grade as the measure of performance, the answer is yes. The grades of high school students have risen in recent times. The Central Board of Secondary Education (CBSE) witnessed rapid growth and expansion at the level of secondary education, which resulted in improved quality and standard of education in institutions. The passing percentage for the CBSE Class 12 results in 2017 stood at 82.02 percent, which is a 1.5 percent drop from previous year's 83.05 percent. However, we are yet to achieve the millennium goal of the United Nations Educational Scientific and Cultural Organization (UNESCO) and the ultimate goal of Sarva Shiksha Abhiyan program of the Government of India.

In India, more than half of all grade five students' reading ability stands at grade two level (ASER, 2015). In their research, Shasidhar, Rao, and Hedge (2009) found 13.5 percent of adolescents were low

achievers in India, and the causes of their scholastic underachievement are many and complex. There are many factors that contribute to student's achievement in schools; over and above the individual factors, socio demography, family, school system, curriculum and pedagogy are some of them. Studies have found that home environment, parent's education, quality of maternal care, and relationship between parents play a significant role in a child's academic achievement (Nair, 2003; Dev, 2016). It was also observed that classroom climate, positive student-teacher relationship, and regular attendance boosted scholastic performance of students. In terms of student-teacher relationship, students' perception of an encouraging and impartial teacher plays an important role in motivating them to attend school.

UNESCO (2014) has reported that 250 million children are functionally illiterate and innumerate despite 50 percent of them having spent at least four years in school. Teacher qualifications and attendance is equally problematic with less than 75 percent of primary school teachers in developing countries being trained according to national standards (UNESCO, 2014).

There has been an attempt by international and Indian policy-making bodies (such as the WHO and the UNESCO and the Ministry of Human Resource Development, the NITI Aayog, NCERT, and CBSE, respectively) to bring about reformation in education. In 1990, a major shift in policy formulation was ushered in by the World Declaration on 'Education for All', which was adopted by the UNESCO and more recently by the current formulation of the Millennium Development Goals (MDGs) where access to education represents a cornerstone for expanding human competence (UNESCO, 2007).

Masino and Niño-Zarazúa (2016) conducted a systematic review of policy intervention to improve quality of education in developing countries, which in turn were expected to lead to enhanced productivity, economic growth, and development. The review clearly indicated that poor quality of education remains endemic in developing countries. Quality education was recognized to have the highest economic returns in developing countries (Psacharopoulos, 1981, 1985; Psacharopoulos et al., 1986; Petrakis and Stamatakis, 2002; Psacharopoulos and Patrinos, 2004; Asiedu and Nandwa, 2007). Hanushek and Kimko (2000) and Barro (2001), for example, found that test scores were better predictors of real per capita GDP growth than years of schooling attainment. Hanushek and Woessmann (2008 and 2012), Hanushek et al. (2010), Jamison et al. (2007), Laurini and Andrade (2012), and UNESCO (2011), among others, have shown that cognitive skills were more strongly associated with increases in earnings and development outcomes than schooling attainment.

# Socioeconomic Status, Race, Ethnicity, and School Performance

**LO 15.7 Explain how socioeconomic status and ethnic and racial differences affect school performance.**

All students are entitled to the same opportunity in the classroom, but it is very clear that certain groups have more educational advantages than others. One of the most telling indicators of this reality is the relationship between educational achievement and socioeconomic status (SES).

**SOCIOECONOMIC STATUS.** Middle- and high-SES students, on average, earn higher grades, score higher on standardized tests of achievement, and complete more years of schooling than students from lower-SES homes. Of course, this disparity does not start in adolescence; the same findings hold for children in lower grades. By the time students are in high school, however, the effects of SES become even more pronounced (Frederickson & Petrides, 2008; Shernoff & Schmidt, 2008; Tucker-Drob & Harden, 2012: Roy & Raver, 2014).

Why do students from middle- and high-SES homes show greater academic success? There are several reasons. For one thing, children living in poverty lack many of the advantages enjoyed by other children. Their nutrition and health may be less adequate. Often living in crowded conditions and attending inadequate schools, they may have few places to do homework. Their homes may lack the books and computers commonplace in more economically advantaged households (Prater, 2002; Chiu & McBride-Chang, 2006).

For these reasons, students from impoverished backgrounds may be at a disadvantage from the day they begin their schooling. As they grow older, their school performance may continue to lag, and their disadvantage may snowball. Because later school success builds heavily on basic skills presumably learned early

in school, children who experience early problems may find themselves falling increasingly behind the academic eight ball as adolescents (Biddle, 2001; Hoff, 2012; Duncan, Magnuson, & Votruba-Drzal, 2017).

**ETHNIC AND RACIAL DIFFERENCES IN SCHOOL ACHIEVEMENT.** Achievement differences between ethnic and racial groups are significant, and they paint a troubling picture of American education.

What is the source of such ethnic and racial differences in academic achievement? Clearly, much of the difference is due to socioeconomic factors: Because a higher proportion of African American and Hispanic families live in poverty than the proportion of Whites living in poverty, their economic disadvantage may be reflected in their school performance. When we take socioeconomic levels into account by comparing different ethnic and racial groups at the same socioeconomic level, achievement differences diminish, but they do not vanish (Cokley, 2003; Guerrero et al., 2006; Kurtz-Costes, Swinton, & Skinner, 2014).

Anthropologist John Ogbu (1992) argues that members of certain minority groups may perceive school success as relatively unimportant. They may believe that societal prejudice in the workplace will dictate that they will not succeed, no matter how much effort they expend. Their conclusion is that hard work in school will have no eventual payoff.

Ogbu suggests that members of minority groups who enter a new culture voluntarily are more likely to be successful in school than those who are brought into a new culture against their will. For instance, he notes that Korean children who are the sons and daughters of voluntary immigrants to the United States tend to be, on average, quite successful in school. But Korean children in Japan, whose parents were forced to immigrate during World War II and work as forced laborers, tend to do relatively poorly in school. The reason for the disparity? The process of involuntary immigration apparently leaves lasting scars, reducing the motivation to succeed in subsequent generations. Ogbu suggests that in the United States, the involuntary immigration—through the slave trade—of the ancestors of many African American students might be related to their motivation to succeed (Ogbu, 1992; Gallagher, 1994).

**DROPPING OUT OF SCHOOL.** Numerous studies found that adolescents who leave school do so for a variety of reasons. Some drop out because of their poor score, they could not get a seat for further study; others leave because of poverty and lack of skills. Poverty plays a large role in determining if a student could complete high school. Students from lower-income households are three times more likely to drop out than those from middle- and upper-income households. As economic success is quite dependent on education, dropping out often perpetuates a cycle of poverty.

> **From an educator's perspective:** Why might descendants of people who were forced to immigrate to a country be less successful academically than those who came voluntarily? What approaches might be used to overcome this obstacle?

## Part-Time Work: Students on the Job

### LO 15.8 Evaluate the advantages and disadvantages of working during high school.

Working offers several advantages. In addition to providing funds for recreational activities and sometimes necessities, it helps students learn responsibility, gives them practice with handling money, and can help teach them workplace skills. Students can also develop good work habits that may help them do better academically. Finally, participation in jobs and internships can help students understand the nature of work in specific employment settings.

But there are also significant drawbacks to work. Many jobs available to high school students are high on drudgery and low on transferable skills. Employment also may prevent students from participating in extracurricular activities such as sports.

The most troubling consequence of high school employment is that school performance is negatively related to the number of hours a student works: Generally, the more hours on the job, the lower a student's grades. One reason for this relationship is that there are only 24 hours in each day, and with more hours at work, students are unable to devote enough time to their studies. But it is also possible that students who work a greater number of hours are more psychologically invested in their work than in high school—an explanation called the *primary orientation model*. Consequently, their motivation to do well

academically is lower (Warren, 2002; Warren, Lee, & Cataldi, 2004).

A premature focus on work also may cause some adolescents to experience a phenomenon known as pseudomaturity. *Pseudomaturity* involves an unusually early entry into adult roles before an adolescent is developmentally ready to assume them. Some adolescents, particularly those who do not have strong ties to school or their peers, may see early entry into adulthood as a desirable escape from their current roles, and this may provide them with great satisfaction. In such cases, working many hours at a job may be a way for such adolescents to escape from current sources of stress. In other situations, however, socioeconomic pressures force adolescents into pseudomaturity (Staff, Mortimer, & Uggen, 2004).

In short, the consequences of working during high school are mixed. For some students, particularly those who work a limited number of hours each work, the advantages of working can be substantial. But for those who work long hours, employment is likely to hinder academic performance.

As per the Right to Education Act, education is free and compulsory for Indian children up to primary school. There has been other action plans and policies to promote education and reduce school dropout so that each and every child should complete his or her education without any financial hurdle. As per the Child Labor (Prohibition and Regulation) Act, 1986, amended in 2016, Indian children up to the age of 14 are prohibited from employment of any form. Children between the age of 14 and 18 are adolescents and are allowed to be employed except in the listed hazardous occupation and processes, which include mining, inflammable substance and explosives-related work, etc.

## College: Pursuing Higher Education

### LO 15.9 Describe the demographic characteristics of college students.

*For Enrico Vasquez, there was never any doubt: He was headed for college. Enrico, the son of a wealthy Cuban immigrant who had made a fortune in the medical supply business after fleeing Cuba 5 years before Enrico's birth, had had the importance of education constantly drummed into him by his family. In fact, the question was never whether he would go to college, but what college he would be able to get into. As a consequence, Enrico found high school to be a pressure cooker: Every grade and extracurricular activity was evaluated in terms of its helping or hindering his chances of admission to a good college.*

*Armando Williams's letter of admission to Dallas County Community College is framed on the wall of his mother's apartment. To her, the letter represents nothing short of a miracle, an answer to her prayers. Growing up in a neighborhood infamous for its drugs and drive-by shootings, Armando had always been a hard worker and a "good boy," in his mother's view. But when he was growing up, she never even entertained the possibility of his making it to college. To see him reach this stage in his education fills her with joy.*

Whether a student's enrollment seems almost inevitable or signifies a triumph over the odds, attending college is a significant accomplishment. Although students already enrolled may feel that college attendance is nearly universal, this is not the case at all: Nationwide, only a fraction of high school graduates enter college.

## WHAT TYPE OF STUDENTS ENTER COLLEGE?

Higher education is an important way for people to improve their economic well-being. In India, higher education has witnessed a dramatic growth in the last few years in terms of establishment of central universities, state universities, technical institutions like the IITs and IIMs, institutions for medical education, etc. But considering the population of youth, this increase is miniscule. Still there is high competition to get entry into technical and professional education like engineering, medicine, etc. Many aspirant graduates are waiting for their admissions into higher education for years. To consider, the type of students entering higher education in India, one should keep in mind that there is a reservation policy for students coming from scheduled caste, scheduled tribe, and other backward classes so that all socio-economic strata and castes are well represented in higher education.

## THE GENDER GAP IN COLLEGE ATTENDANCE

Women constitute around 48 percent of the total population of India. Equity in education, especially gender equity, was one of the major issues in the country, and there has been a tremendous growth in women

enrolling for higher education since independence, thus reducing the gender gap in higher education. Many women have enrolled in professional courses in recent times.

The Indian government continues to encourage higher education for women through programs like Indira Gandhi scholarship for single girl child for pursuing higher education by constructing women hostels in institutions.

## GENDER AND COLLEGE.

*I still remember the frustration and humiliation I felt the first time I raised my hand in a freshman Principles of Physics course in college. The professor, a man really only a few years older than I, ignored me. A few minutes later, when my hand was the only one up, he had to call on me, but he did it while rolling his eyes and remarking, "Let's see what the little lady has to add to the discussion." I reddened and got so flustered I could barely speak.*

*A year later, I saw that professor in the cafeteria and decided to confront him. "Hi, Professor," I said, "Do you remember embarrassing me by calling me a 'little lady' in your physics class last year?"*

*He paused and looked at me. "Were you in my class? What were you doing there?"*

*Unbelievably, he had managed to make my humiliation even worse.*

Although such incidents of blatant sexism are less likely to occur today, prejudice and discrimination directed at women are still a fact of college life. For example, the next time you are in class, consider the gender of your classmates and the subject matter of the class. Although men and women attend college in roughly equal numbers, there is significant variation in the classes they take. Classes in education and the social sciences, for instance, typically have a larger proportion of women than men; classes in engineering, the physical sciences, and mathematics tend to have more men than women.

The gender gap is also apparent when we look at college instructors. Although the number of female faculty members has increased, there is still evidence of discrimination. For example, the more prestigious the institution, the smaller the proportion of women who have attained the highest rank. The situation is even more pronounced in the fields of math, science, and engineering, where women are significantly underrepresented (Wilson, 2004; Carbonaro, Ellison, & Covay, 2011).

The persistent differences in gender distribution across subject areas likely reflect the powerful influence of gender stereotypes that operate throughout the world of education and beyond. For instance, when women in their first year of college are asked to name a likely career choice, they are much less apt to choose careers that have traditionally been dominated by men, such as engineering or computer programming, and more likely to choose professions that have traditionally been populated by women, such as nursing and social work (White & White, 2006; DiDonato & Strough, 2013).

Male and female college students also have different expectations regarding their areas of competence. For instance, one survey asked first-year college students whether they were above or below average on a variety of traits and abilities. As can be seen in Figure 15.1, men were more likely than women to think of themselves as above average in overall academic and mathematical ability, competitiveness, and emotional health.

Both male and female college professors treat men and women differently in their classes, even though the different treatment is largely unintentional, and often the professors are unaware of their actions. For instance, professors may call on men in class more frequently than on women. Furthermore, male students are more likely than female students to receive extra help from their professors (Sadker & Sadker, 2005; Simon, Wagner, & Killion, 2017).

The different treatment of men and women in the classroom has led some educators to argue in favor of single-sex education for women. They point to evidence that the rate of participation and

ultimately the success of women in the sciences is greater for graduates of women's colleges than for graduates of coeducational institutions. Furthermore, some research suggests that women who attend single-sex colleges may show higher self-esteem than those attending coeducational colleges, although the evidence is not entirely consistent on this count (Sax, 2005).

Why might women do better in single-sex environments? One reason is that they receive more attention than they would in coeducational settings, where professors are affected, however inadvertently, by societal biases, as noted. In addition, women's colleges tend to have more female professors than coeducational institutions do, and they thereby provide more role models for women. Finally, women attending women's colleges may receive more encouragement for participation in nontraditional subjects such as mathematics and science than those in coeducational colleges (Robinson & Gillibrand, 2004; Kinzie et al., 2007; Pahlke & Hyde, 2016).

**Figure 15.1** Self-Assessments in Various Categories by Male and Female College Students

During their first year of college, men are more likely than women to view themselves as above average in areas relevant to academic success. How can educators be made more aware of this problem, and how might it be addressed?

**SOURCE:** From Astin, A. W., Korn, W. S., & Berz, E. R. (2004). The American freshman: National norms for fall 2004. Los Angeles, CA: Higher Education Research Institute, Graduate School of Education, UCLA © 2008 The Regents of the University of California. All Rights Reserved.

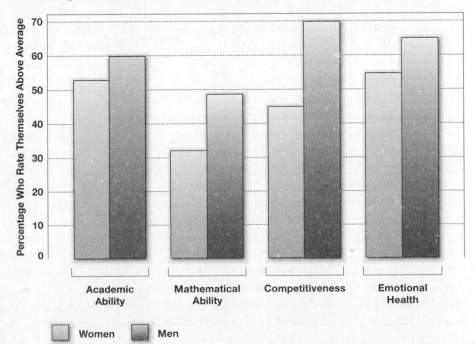

## ACADEMIC PERFORMANCE AND STEREOTYPE THREAT.

Consider this fact: When women take college classes in math, science, and engineering, they are more likely to do poorly than are men who enter college with the same level of preparation and identical SAT scores. Strangely, however, this phenomenon does not hold true for other areas of the curriculum, where men and women perform at similar levels.

According to psychologist Claude Steele, the reason behind women's declining levels of performance is *academic disidentification*, a lack of personal identification with an academic domain. For women, disidentification is specific to math and science. Negative societal stereotypes produce a state of *stereotype threat* in which members of the group fear that their behavior will indeed confirm the stereotype (Carr & Steele, 2009).

For instance, women seeking to achieve in nontraditional fields that rely on math and science may be hindered as they become distracted by worries about the failure that society predicts for them. In some cases, a woman may decide that failure in a male-dominated field, because it would confirm societal stereotypes, presents such great risks that, paradoxically, the struggle to succeed is not worth the effort. In that instance, the woman may not even try very hard (Inzlicht & Ben-Zeev, 2000).

But there is a bright side to Steele's analysis: If women can be convinced that societal stereotypes regarding achievement are invalid, their performance might well improve. And in fact, this is just what Steele found in a series of experiments he conducted at the University of Michigan and Stanford University (Steele, 1997).

In one study, male and female college students were told they would be taking two math tests: one in which there were gender differences—men supposedly performed better than women—and a second in which there were no gender differences. In reality, the tests were entirely similar, drawn from the same pool of difficult items. The reasoning behind the experimental manipulation was that women would be vulnerable to societal stereotypes on a test that they thought supported those stereotypes but would not be vulnerable on a test supposedly lacking gender differences.

The results fully supported Steele's reasoning. When the women were told there were gender differences in the test, they greatly underperformed the men. But when they were told there were no gender differences, they performed virtually the same as the men.

Women choosing traditionally male fields such as math and science can overcome even long-standing societal stereotypes if they are convinced that other women have been successful.

In short, the evidence from this study and others clearly suggests that women are vulnerable to expectations regarding their future success, whether the expectations come from societal stereotypes or from information about the prior performance of women on similar tasks. More encouraging, the evidence suggests that if women can be convinced that others have been successful in given domains, they may overcome even long-standing societal stereotypes (Croizet et al., 2004; Davies, Spencer, & Steele, 2005; Good, Aronson, & Harder, 2008).

We should also keep in mind that women are not the only group susceptible to society's stereotyping. Members of minority groups, such as African Americans and Hispanic Americans, are also vulnerable to stereotypes about academic success. In fact, Steele suggests that African Americans may work under the pressure of feeling that they must disconfirm the negative stereotype regarding their academic performance. The pressure can be anxiety-provoking and threatening, and can reduce their performance below their true ability level. Ironically, stereotype threat may be most severe for better, more confident students, who have not internalized the negative stereotype to the extent of questioning their own abilities (Carr & Steele, 2009; McClain & Cokley, 2017). In addition, African Americans may "disidentify" with

# DEVELOPMENTAL DIVERSITY AND YOUR LIFE
## Overcoming Gender and Racial Barriers to Achievement

*Luisa Mauro handed out a whiteboard and marker to each student in her 10th-grade math class. She then projected a complicated problem from her computer to a screen in the room.*

*"Hold up your board when you finish answering the question," she said. The students diligently wrote on their boards and, one by one, held them up.*

*This basic change in procedure eliminated the competitive hand waving and shouting that used to prevail in her class and leveled the playing field for a group of students who were routinely outshouted and outwaved—girls.*

This simple innovation is part of a large-scale, and ultimately successful, effort to improve the teaching of math in English schools. Although meant to benefit all children, it has had an unintended result: erasing a gender gap that favored boys over girls in math performance.

As Illustrated In Figure 15.2, the introduction of the new math curriculum in the late 1980s brought about a rise in overall math exam scores. But the rise was more pronounced for girls, and today girls outperform boys on some standardized math tests.

What changes in the curriculum led to the improvement in performance? Teachers were taught to be on the alert for gender stereotyping in their courses, and they were encouraged to include girls in discussions more vigorously. In addition, gender stereotypes were removed from textbooks.

**Figure 15.2** The New Math

After the introduction of a new math curriculum and exams in England, girls' and boys' performance began to converge.

**SOURCE:** Department for Education and Skills, England (2004).

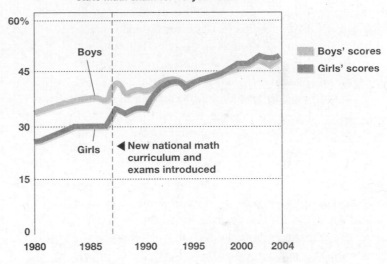

Percentage of English boys and girls earning passing grades of A through C on the state math exam for 18-year-olds

Classrooms were made "safer" for girls by discouraging students from shouting out answers and by encouraging girls more directly to participate. Tests were changed, too, to give partial credit when students write out their thinking—something that benefited girls, who tend to be more methodical when working on test items.

academic success by putting forth less effort on academic tasks and generally downgrading the importance of academic achievement. Ultimately, such disidentification may act as a self-fulfilling prophecy, increasing the chances of academic failure (Davis, Aronson, & Salinas, 2006; Kellow & Jones, 2008; Kronberger & Horwath, 2013).

> **From an educator's perspective:** Some people advocate single-sex (and even single-ethnicity) high schools and colleges as a way to combat the disadvantages of discrimination. Why might this be effective? What drawbacks do you see?

# Choosing an Occupation

Some people know from childhood that they want to be physicians or actors or go into business, and they follow direct paths toward that goal. For others, the choice of a career is very much a matter of chance, of searching through a career website and seeing what's available.

Regardless of how a career is chosen, it is unlikely to be the only career that people will have during the course of their lifetime. As technology alters the nature of work at a rapid pace, changing careers at least once, and sometimes several times, is likely to be the norm in the 21st century.

# Choosing a Career

**LO 15.10  Identify how career choices are made.**

Researchers have proposed a variety of approaches to understanding how adolescents choose an initial career to pursue. In the following section, we focus on two of these, one based on developmental periods in people's lives and the other on personality types.

**GINZBERG'S THREE PERIODS.** According to Eli Ginzberg (1972), people generally move through several stages in choosing a career. In the **fantasy period**, which lasts until around age 11, career choices are made—and discarded—without regard to skills, abilities, or available job opportunities. Instead, choices are made solely on the basis of what sounds appealing. Thus, a child may decide that she wants to be a veterinarian, despite the fact that she is allergic to dogs and cats.

People begin to take practical considerations into account during the tentative period, which spans adolescence. During the **tentative period**, people begin to think in pragmatic terms about the requirements of various jobs and how their own abilities might fit with those requirements. They also consider their personal values and goals, exploring how well a particular occupation might satisfy them. Finally, in early adulthood, people enter the **realistic period**, in which they explore specific career options either through actual experience on the job or through training for a profession. They begin to narrow their choices to a few alternative careers and eventually make a commitment to a particular one.

**HOLLAND'S SIX PERSONALITY TYPES.** Although the three stages make intuitive sense, the stage approach oversimplifies the process of choosing a career. Consequently, some researchers suggest that it is more fruitful to examine the match between job-seekers' personality types and career requirements. For example, according to researcher John Holland, certain personality types match particularly well with certain careers. Specifically, he suggests that six personality types are important in career choice (Gottfredson & Holland, 1990; Donohue, 2007; Nauta, 2010):

- *Realistic:* Realistic people are down-to-earth, practical problem-solvers who are physically strong, but their social skills are mediocre. They make good farmers, laborers, and truck drivers.

- *Intellectual:* Intellectual types are oriented toward the theoretical and the abstract. Although not particularly good with people, they are well suited to careers in math and science.

- *Social:* The traits associated with the social personality type are related to verbal skills and interpersonal relations. Social types are good at working with people and consequently make good salespersons, teachers, and counselors.

- *Conventional:* Conventional individuals prefer highly structured tasks. They make good clerks, secretaries, and bank tellers.

- *Enterprising:* These individuals are risk-takers and take-charge types. They are good leaders and may be particularly effective as managers or politicians.

- *Artistic:* Artistic types use art to express themselves, and they often prefer the world of art to interactions with people. They are best suited to occupations involving art.

Of course, not everyone fits neatly into one particular personality type. Furthermore, there are certainly exceptions to the typology, with jobs being held successfully by people who don't have the predicted personality. Still, the theory forms the foundation of several instruments designed to assess the occupational options for which a given person is particularly suited (Randahl, 1991).

# Gender and Career Choices: Women's Work

**LO 15.11  Describe the relationship between gender and career development.**

*HELP WANTED: Family firm seeks full-time worker for financial management, bookkeeping, child care, cooking, cleaning, laundering, mending, gardening, and shopping.*

---

**fantasy period** According to Eli Ginzberg, the period of life when career choices are made—and discarded—without regard to skills, abilities, or available job opportunities

**tentative period** The second stage of Eli Ginzberg's theory, which spans adolescence, in which people begin to think in pragmatic terms about the requirements of various jobs and how their own abilities might fit with those requirements

**realistic period** The stage in late adolescence and early adulthood during which people explore career options through job experience or training, narrow their choices, and eventually make a commitment to a career

*HOURS: Typical workweek 60 hours, with possibility of extra duty up to 24 hours per day, 7 days per week.*

*SALARY AND BENEFITS: No cash remuneration, but generous benefits package includes meals, clothing, and shelter, plus small personal shopping allowance. Vacation and retirement at will of employer. Job security at will of employer. No opportunity for promotion.*

*QUALIFICATIONS: Previous experience not necessary. Driver's license and health care experience a plus. Only women need apply.*

Only three or four decades ago, many women entering early adulthood assumed that this admittedly exaggerated job description matched the work for which they were best suited and to which they aspired: housewife. Even those women who sought work outside the home were relegated to certain professions. For instance, until the 1960s, employment ads in newspapers throughout the United States were almost always divided into two sections: "Help Wanted: Male" and "Help Wanted: Female." The men's job listings encompassed such professions as police officer, construction worker, and legal counsel; the women's listings were for secretaries, teachers, cashiers, and librarians.

The breakdown of jobs deemed appropriate for men and women reflected society's traditional view of what the two genders were best suited for. Traditionally, women were considered most appropriate for **communal professions**, occupations associated with relationships. In contrast, men were perceived as best suited for **agentic professions**. Agentic professions are associated with getting things accomplished. It is probably no coincidence that communal professions typically have lower status and lower salaries than agentic professions do (Trapnell & Paulhus, 2012; Li Kusterer, Lindholm, & Montgomery, 2013; Sinclair, Carlsson, & Björklund, 2016).

Although discrimination based on gender is far less blatant today than it was several decades ago—it is now illegal, for instance, to advertise a position specifically for a man or a woman, as was once common—remnants of traditional gender-role prejudice persist. One reflection of this is illustrated by the discrepancy between women's and men's salaries. Women's annual earnings are less than men's, and have been for decades. On average, women earn 80 cents for every dollar that men earn. Moreover, women who are members of minority groups earn even less. Although progress has been made in decreasing the gap, it is not

Discrimination based on gender is less blatant than it once was, but it remains a potent force. However, strides have been made in many professions.

until 2059 that the pay gap is expected to disappear, according to projections (U.S. Bureau of the Census, 2011; AAUW, 2017).

Despite this gap, more women are working outside the home than ever before. Women today make up nearly half the labor force. Almost all women expect to earn a living, and almost all do at some point in their lives. Furthermore, in households in which both partners work, 29 percent of women earn more than their husbands (Chalabi, 2015; Bureau of Labor Statistics, 2016).

In addition, opportunities for women are considerably greater than they were in earlier years. Women are more likely to be physicians, lawyers, insurance agents, and bus drivers than they were in the past; however, as noted earlier, within specific job categories, there are still notable gender differences. For example, female bus drivers are more apt to have lower-paid, part-time school bus routes, while men hold better-paying full-time routes in cities. Similarly, female pharmacists are more likely to work in lower-paying jobs in hospitals, while men work in higher-paying jobs in retail stores (Unger & Crawford, 2003).

Women and minorities in high-status, visible professional roles still often hit what has come to be called the *glass ceiling*. The *glass ceiling* is an invisible barrier in an organization that prevents individuals from being promoted beyond a certain level because

---

**communal professions** Occupations associated with relationships

**agentic professions** Occupations associated with getting things accomplished

# BECOMING AN INFORMED CONSUMER OF CHILD DEVELOPMENT

## Choosing a Career

One of the greatest challenges people face in late adolescence will have lifelong implications: choosing a career. Although there is no single correct choice—most people can be happy in any of several different jobs—the options can be daunting. Here are some guidelines for starting to come to grips with the question of what occupational path to follow:

- *Systematically evaluate a variety of choices.* Libraries and the Internet contain a wealth of information about potential paths, and most colleges and universities have career centers that can provide occupational data and guidance.
- *Know yourself.* Evaluate your strengths and weaknesses, perhaps by completing a questionnaire at a college career center that can provide insight into your interests, skills, and values.
- *Create a "balance sheet"* listing the potential gains and losses that you will incur from a particular profession. First, list the gains and losses that you will experience directly, and then list the gains and losses for others. Next, write down the projected social approval or disapproval you are likely to receive from others. By systematically evaluating a set of potential careers

according to each of these criteria, you will be in a better position to compare different possibilities.

- *"Try out" different careers* through paid or unpaid internships. By experiencing a job firsthand, interns are able to get a better sense of what an occupation is truly like.
- *Remember that if you make a mistake, you can change careers.* In fact, people today increasingly change careers in early adulthood or even beyond. No one should feel locked into a decision made earlier in life.
- *It is reasonable to expect* that shifting values, interests, abilities, and life circumstances might make a different career more appropriate later in life than the one chosen during early adulthood.

As we've seen throughout this book, people develop substantially as they age, and this development continues beyond adolescence through the entire life span. It is reasonable to expect that shifting values, interests, abilities, and life circumstances might make a different career more appropriate later in life than the one chosen in late adolescence.

---

of discrimination. It operates subtly, and the people responsible for keeping the glass ceiling in place may not even be aware of how their actions perpetuate discrimination against women and minorities. For instance, a male supervisor in the oil exploration business may conclude that a particular task is "too dangerous" for a female employee. As a consequence of his decision, he may be preventing female candidates for the job from obtaining the experience they need to get promoted (Stroh, Langlands, & Simpson, 2004; Zeng, 2011; Auster & Prasad, 2016).

# The Case of ...

## The Clueless Dreamer

Ashutosh Jha, a high school student, dreamed of being a math teacher, but he knew that fulfilling his dream

would be a challenge. He liked math and was good at it, but he knew that to be a teacher, he'd have to get a college degree.

No one in Ashutosh's family had gone to college. His father was an auto mechanic, and his mother was a factory worker. Ashutosh, the eldest of six children, worked after school at a fast-food restaurant to help make ends meet. How was *he* going to get a college degree?

Ashutosh asked one of his college-bound friends about college. His friend talked about scoring above 90 percent in the Board examination is very much required. Ashutosh still had no idea what the first step should be, what colleges were available, how to pay for courses, and whether he could hold down a job while attending college. He was on the verge of forgetting the whole thing.

Then one day Ashutosh came home to a surprise. His father announced that he had asked his customers for information about college. One of them, a teacher at the local college, offered to help. In fact, she was coming by after dinner to answer Ashutosh's questions about college.

Ashutosh was shocked. He didn't even know his father believed in his dreams, but here he was doing what he could to make them come true.

1. Given his background, what disadvantages does Ashutosh have in pursuing a college degree? What advantages does he have?
2. Where might Ashutosh's dreams have come from? What distinguishes his dreams from the unrealistic egocentrism of adolescence?

3. How is Ashutosh demonstrating metacognition in his assessment of his chances of becoming a math teacher? Do his self-assessment and ambition appear to be realistic?
4. Do you think Ashutosh's choice to seek information about college from a fellow student was his best course? What other sources of information might he have tapped into?
5. What are some advantages and disadvantages of Ashutosh having a part-time job in college?

# Epilogue

This chapter focused on the cognitive advances that occur during adolescence. We began by considering Piagetian and information-processing approaches to cognitive development and then saw how adolescents' self-absorption occurs in part because of the state of their cognitive abilities. We then turned to moral development, focusing on moral reasoning and men's and women's different conceptions of morality. Finally, we looked at school performance and its relationship to cognitive development.

Before turning to the next chapter, return for a moment to the prologue, about Govind, the boy who wants to travel on his own to Kashmir. In light of what you now know about adolescence, consider the following questions:

1. How are Govind's dreams of Kashmir typical of the egocentrism of adolescence?
2. What worries might Govind's dad have about allowing his 15-year-old son to go to Kashmir on his own? From what you have learned about adolescent development, which of these concerns might be justified?
3. How do Govind's arguments exemplify the cognitive changes and abilities of adolescence?
4. Do you think Govind is right about kids growing up a lot faster these days? Explain your answer in terms of both physical and cognitive development.

# Looking Back

**LO 15.1  Explain how adolescents develop abstract thinking, and explore the consequences of this development.**

• Cognitive growth during adolescence is rapid, with gains in abstract thinking, reasoning, and the ability to view possibilities in relative rather than in absolute terms.

• Adolescence coincides with Piaget's formal operations period of development, when people begin to engage in abstract thought and experimental reasoning.

• Adolescents' heightened critical abilities can lead them to become argumentative, question authority, grow more idealistic, and become indecisive as they weigh pros and cons.

• Dealing with adolescents' critical abilities can cause conflict with parents, teachers, and other adults.

**LO 15.2  Describe the information-processing perspective on cognitive development.**

• According to information-processing approaches, cognitive growth during adolescence is gradual and quantitative, involving improvements in memory capacity, mental strategies, and other aspects of cognitive functioning.

- Another major area of cognitive development is the growth of metacognition, which permits adolescents to monitor their thought processes and accurately assess their cognitive capabilities.

**LO 15.3 Summarize the aspects of cognitive development that cause difficulties for adolescents.**

- Hand in hand with the development of metacognition is the growth of adolescent egocentrism, a self-absorption that makes it hard for adolescents to accept criticism and tolerate authority figures.
- Adolescents may play to an imaginary audience of critical observers, and they may develop personal fables, which emphasize the uniqueness of their experiences and supposed invulnerability to risks.

**LO 15.4 Describe the stages of moral development through which adolescents progress.**

- According to Lawrence Kohlberg, people pass through three major levels and six stages of moral development as their sense of justice and their moral reasoning evolve.
- The levels of moral development encompass preconventional morality (motivated by rewards and punishments), conventional morality (motivated by social reference), and postconventional morality (motivated by a sense of universal moral principles)—a level that may be reached during adolescence but that many people never attain.
- Although Kohlberg's theory provides a good account of moral judgments, it is less adequate in predicting moral behavior.

**LO 15.5 Summarize the gender differences in moral development.**

- There appear to be gender differences in moral development not reflected in Kohlberg's work. Carol Gilligan has sketched out an alternative progression for girls, from an orientation toward individual survival through goodness as self-sacrifice to the morality of nonviolence.

**LO 15.6 Analyze the factors that affect adolescent school performance during the elementary school to middle school transition.**

- The transition from elementary to middle and high school can be challenging because of the physical, intellectual, and social changes that adolescents are experiencing at this time.
- Middle school students are often entering puberty and experiencing significant bodily changes as they change schools, at the same time as their relationships with family, friends, and teachers are growing complicated.
- Middle school students must typically deal with a different educational structure, a greater number and variety of teachers, and a group of fellow students who may be more diverse than their elementary school classmates. They must manage this transition from a position of social weakness, since they are generally the youngest, smallest, and least experienced students in the building.

**LO 15.7 Explain how socioeconomic status and ethnic and racial differences affect school performance.**

- The academic achievement of students from different racial and ethnic groups varies in ways that are related to socioeconomic status.
- Members of some groups may perceive that societal prejudice will inevitably make their academic efforts unsuccessful, no matter how hard they try.
- Socioeconomic factors play a large role in determining whether students drop out of high school or complete their education. Students from lower-income households are far more likely to drop out than students from higher-income households.

**LO 15.8 Evaluate the advantages and disadvantages of working during high school.**

- Having a part-time job has the advantage of providing more money, instilling a sense of responsibility, offering practice in money management, and teaching workplace skills and good work habits.
- However, work can decrease the time that students can spend on their studies, negatively affect their grades, and interfere with extracurricular activities, which also teach valuable skills.

- A premature focus on work may lead to pseudo-maturity, the assumption of adult roles before adolescents are ready for them.

### LO 15.9 Describe the demographic characteristics of college students.

- Despite recent changes, the U.S. college population is still largely White and middle class. The proportion of White high school graduates that enter and complete college is larger than that of African American or Hispanic high school graduates.

- However, minority students make up an increasingly larger proportion of the U.S. college population each year, and in some major colleges, Whites are now in the minority.

- The college experience differs for men and women in the courses and majors that they choose and the expectations they have for financial success upon graduation. The differences appear to be attributable to gender stereotypes.

### LO 15.10 Identify how career choices are made.

- According to Eli Ginzberg, people proceed through stages as they consider careers, from the fantasy period, in which dream choices are made without regard to practical factors; through the tentative period, which spans adolescence and involves pragmatic thought about job requirements and personal abilities and goals; and to the realistic period of early adulthood, in which career options are explored through actual experience and training.

- Other theories of career choice, such as John Holland's, link personality characteristics and career options.

### LO 15.11 Describe the relationship between gender and career development.

- Career choice and attitudes and behaviors on the job are influenced by gender. Traditionally, women have been associated with communal professions, which tend to be lower paid, and men with agentic professions, which pay better.

- Women and minorities in professional roles may find themselves hitting the *glass ceiling*, an invisible barrier in an organization that prevents career advancement beyond a certain level because of conscious or unconscious discrimination.

## Key Terms and Concepts

formal operational stage (p. 392)
information-processing
    approaches (p. 395)
metacognition (p. 396)
adolescent egocentrism (p. 396)

imaginary audience (p. 396)
personal fables (p. 396)
fantasy period (p. 408)
tentative period (p. 408)

realistic period (p. 408)
communal professions (p. 409)
agentic professions (p. 409)

# Chapter 16
# Social and Personality Development in Adolescence

 **Learning Objectives**

**LO 16.1** Explain how the development of self-concept and self-esteem proceeds during adolescence.

**LO 16.2** Describe how Erikson's theory of identity formation proceeds through adolescence.

**LO 16.3** Explain the categories of adolescent identity according to Marcia.

**LO 16.4** Describe the roles that religion and spirituality play in identity formation.

**LO 16.5** Illustrate the challenges that ethnic and minority groups face in establishing identities.

**LO 16.6** Identify the factors that contribute to psychological difficulties.

**LO 16.7** Explain how family relationships change during adolescence.

**LO 16.8** Describe how peer relationships change during adolescence.

**LO 16.9** Describe popularity and responses to peer pressure.

**LO 16.10** Explain how some adolescents become involved in criminal activity.

**LO 16.11** Summarize the functions and characteristics of dating during adolescence.

**LO 16.12** List the types of sexual activity in which adolescents engage.

**LO 16.13** Explain the types of sexual orientation and how sexual orientation develops.

**LO 16.14** Describe the challenges of teen pregnancy and prevention programs.

## Prologue: Keeping Up Appearances

Ruhi Bajaj, 16, spends all the cash from her part-time job (taking tuitions for small children in her colony) on makeup, hair products, and clothes. "It's hard to keep up with the other girls," she says. "There are a lot of rich kids at my school, but I'm not one of them." Still, Ruhi always manages to surround herself with a circle of friends.

She admits that there isn't much carryover in these friendships from year to year. "People change."

She shrugs. "*I* change." The important thing, she insists, is to be part of a clique. "No one wants to be seen as a loser." Through it all, Ruhi's grades have remained good—mostly *B*s sprinkled with *A*s. She says she could do better but "it doesn't pay to be labelled a nerd." Lately, however, she's begun to struggle to get the *B*s. "I get tired just thinking about school."

## Looking Ahead

The issues of identity and self-esteem Ruhi is grappling with are ones that virtually every adolescent experiences. As painful and confusing as these questions are, most teenagers pass through the period without major turmoil. Although they may "try on" different roles and flirt with activities that their parents find objectionable, the majority of teenagers find adolescence an exciting time during which friendships grow, intimate relationships develop, and their sense of themselves deepens.

This is not to say that the transitions adolescents pass through are not challenging. As we shall see in this chapter, in which we discuss social and personality development, adolescence brings about major changes in how individuals must deal with the world.

We begin by considering how adolescents form their views of themselves. We look at self-concept,

self-esteem, and identity development. We also examine two major psychological difficulties: depression and suicide.

Next, we discuss relationships during adolescence. We consider how adolescents reposition themselves within the family and how the influence of family members declines in some spheres as peers take on new importance. We also examine the ways in which adolescents interact with their friends and the ways in which popularity is determined.

Finally, the chapter considers dating and sexual behavior. We look at the role of dating and close relationships in adolescents' lives, and we consider sexual behavior and the standards that govern adolescents' sex lives. We conclude by looking at teenage pregnancy and at programs that seek to prevent unwanted pregnancy.

# Identity: Asking "Who Am I?"

*Thirteen? Thirteen is all about cool. It's not about funny or strong or smart anymore. Just cool. You have to like the right music, wear the right shoes. Your shirts have to be just this way, and your pants can't be too high or too low on your middle, know what I mean? Sure, there are drugs everywhere, and you just try to stay away 'cause your parents want you to be good, but at the same time, you can't be all holy-holy about it.*

The thoughts of 13-year-old Lennie Ortega demonstrate a clear awareness—and self-consciousness—regarding his newly forming place in society and life. During adolescence, questions like "Who am I?" and "Where do I belong in the world?" begin to take a front seat.

# Self-Concept and Self-Esteem

**LO 16.1  Explain how the development of self-concept and self-esteem proceeds during adolescence.**

Why should issues of identity become so important during adolescence? One reason is that adolescents' intellectual capacities become more like those of adults. They are able to see how they stack up against others and become aware that they are individuals, apart not just from their parents, but from all others. The dramatic physical changes during puberty make adolescents acutely aware of their own bodies and that others are reacting to them in ways to which they are unaccustomed. Whatever the cause, adolescence often brings substantial changes in teenagers' self-concept and self-esteem—in sum, their notions of their own identity.

**WHAT AM I LIKE?**  Ask Valerie to describe herself, and she says, "Others look at me as laid-back, relaxed, and not worrying too much. But really, I'm often nervous and emotional."

The fact that Valerie distinguishes others' views of her from her own perceptions represents a developmental advance of adolescence. In childhood, Valerie would have characterized herself according to a list of traits that would not differentiate her view of herself and others' perspectives. Adolescents, however, are able to make the distinction, and when they try to describe who they are, they take both their own and others' views into account (Chen et al., 2012; Preckel et al., 2013; McLean & Syed, 2015).

This broader view of themselves is one aspect of adolescents' increasing understanding of who they are. They can see various aspects of the self simultaneously, and this view of the self becomes more organized and coherent. They look at the self from a psychological perspective, viewing traits not as concrete entities but as abstractions (Adams, Montemayor, & Gullotta, 1996). For example, teenagers are more likely than younger children to describe themselves in terms of their ideology (saying something like, "I'm an environmentalist") than in terms of physical characteristics (such as, "I'm the fastest runner in my class").

In some ways, this broader, more multifaceted self-concept is a mixed blessing, especially during the earlier years of adolescence. At that time, adolescents may be troubled by the multiple aspects of their personalities. During the beginning of adolescence, for instance, teenagers may want to view themselves in a certain way ("I'm a sociable person and love to be with people"), and they may become concerned when their behavior is inconsistent with that view ("Even though I want to be sociable, sometimes I can't stand being around my friends, and I just want to be alone"). By the end of adolescence, however, teenagers find it easier to accept that different situations elicit different behaviors and feelings (Trzesniewski, Donnellan, & Robins, 2003; Hitlin, Brown, & Elder, 2006).

**HOW DO I LIKE MYSELF?**  *Knowing* who you are and *liking* who you are two different things. Although adolescents become increasingly accurate in understanding who they are (their self-concept), this knowledge does not guarantee that they like themselves (their self-esteem) any better. In fact, their increasing accuracy in understanding themselves permits them to see themselves fully—warts and all. It's what they do with these perceptions that leads them to develop a sense of their self-esteem.

The same cognitive sophistication that allows adolescents to differentiate various aspects of the self also leads them to evaluate those aspects in different ways (Chan, 1997; Cohen, 1999). For instance, an adolescent may have high self-esteem in terms of academic performance, but lower self-esteem in terms of relationships with others. Or it may be just the opposite, as articulated by this adolescent:

> *Do I like myself? What a question! Well, let's see. I like some of what I am, like I'm a good listener and a good friend, but I don't like other things, like my jealous side. I'm no genius at schoolwork—my parents would like me to do better—but if you're too smart, you don't have a lot of friends. I'm pretty good at sports, especially swimming. But the best thing about me is that I'm a good friend, you know, loyal. I'm pretty well known for that, and pretty popular.*

What determines an adolescent's self-esteem? Several factors make a difference. One is gender: Particularly during early adolescence, girls' self-esteem tends to be lower and more vulnerable than boys' (McLean & Breen, 2009; Mäkinen et al., 2012; Jenkins & Demaray, 2015).

One reason is that, compared to boys, girls tend to be more concerned about physical appearance and social success—in addition to academic achievement. Although boys are also concerned about these things, their attitudes are often more casual. In addition, societal messages suggesting that female academic achievement is a roadblock to social success can put girls in a difficult bind: If they do well academically, they jeopardize their social success. No wonder that the self-esteem of adolescent girls is more fragile than that of boys (Ricciardelli & McCabe, 2003; Ata, Ludden, & Lally, 2007; Ayres & Leaper, 2013).

Although generally self-esteem is higher in adolescent boys than in girls, boys do have vulnerabilities of their own. For example, society's stereotypical gender expectations may lead boys to feel that they should be confident, tough, and fearless all the time. Boys facing difficulties, such as not making a sports team or being rejected by a girl they want to go out with, are likely to feel not only miserable about the defeat they face but also incompetent because they don't measure up to the stereotype (Pollack, Shuster, & Trelease, 2001; Witt, Donnellan, & Trzesniewski, 2011; Levant et al., 2016).

The research by Jain and Dixit (2014) has revealed that among many causes, the most common cause for reduction in self-esteem has been the inability to meet academic expectations of self, parents, and teachers. As a result, it could be seen that expectations and pressure posed by the society to be the best in academics, is a matter of concern for the Indian youth today.

Socioeconomic status (SES) and race also influence self-esteem. Adolescents of higher SES generally have higher self-esteem than those of lower SES, particularly during middle and later adolescence. It may be that the social status factors that especially enhance one's standing and self-esteem—such as having more expensive clothes or a car—become more conspicuous in the later periods of adolescence (Dai et al., 2012; Cuperman, Robinson, & Ickes, 2014).

Race and ethnicity also play a role in self-esteem, but their impact has lessened as prejudicial treatment of minorities has eased. Early studies argued that minority status would lead to lower self-esteem, and this was initially supported by research. African Americans and Hispanics, researchers explained, had lower self-esteem than Caucasians because prejudicial attitudes in society made them feel disliked and rejected, and this feeling was incorporated into their self-concepts. More recent research paints a different picture. Most findings suggest that African American adolescents differ little from Whites in their levels of self-esteem (Harter, 1990). Why should this be? One explanation is that social movements within the African American community that bolster racial pride help support African American adolescents. Research finds that a stronger sense of racial identity is related to a higher level of self-esteem in African Americans and Hispanics (Phinney, 2008; Smith & Silva, 2011; Kogan et al., 2014).

Another reason for overall similarity in self-esteem levels between adolescents of different racial groups is that teenagers in general focus their preferences and priorities on those aspects of their lives at which they excel. Consequently, African American youths may concentrate on the things that they find most satisfying and gain self-esteem from being successful at them (Gray-Little & Hafdahl, 2000; Yang & Blodgett, 2000; Phinney, 2005).

Finally, self-esteem may be influenced not by race alone but by a complex combination of factors. For instance, some developmentalists have considered race and gender simultaneously, coining the term *ethgender* to refer to the joint influence of race and gender. One study that simultaneously took both race and gender into account found that African American and Hispanic male adolescents had the highest levels of self-esteem, while Asian and Native American female adolescents had the lowest levels (Saunders, Davis, & Williams, 2004; Biro et al., 2006; Park et al., 2012).

# Identity Formation: Change or Crisis?

**LO 16.2    Describe how Erikson's theory of identity formation proceeds through adolescence.**

According to psychologist Erik Erikson, whose theory we last discussed in Chapter 13, the search for identity inevitably leads some adolescents into substantial psychological turmoil as they encounter the adolescent identity crisis (Erikson, 1963). Erikson's theory regarding this stage, which is summarized with his other stages in Table 16.1, suggests that teenagers try to figure out what is unique and distinctive about themselves—something they are able to do with increasing sophistication because of the cognitive gains that occur during adolescence.

**Table 16.1** A Summary of Erikson's Stages

| Stage | Approximate Age | Positive Outcomes | Negative Outcomes |
|---|---|---|---|
| 1. Trust-versus-mistrust | Birth–1.5 years | Feelings of trust based on support from parents, others | Fear and concern regarding others |
| 2. Autonomy-versus-shame-and-doubt | 1.5–3 years | Self-sufficiency if exploration is encouraged | Self-doubt, lack of independence |
| 3. Initiative-versus-guilt | 3–6 years | Discovery of ways to act on the world | Guilt from actions and thoughts |
| 4. Industry-versus-inferiority | 6–12 years | Development of sense of competence | Feelings of inferiority, no sense of mastery |
| 5. Identity-versus-identity-confusion | Adolescence | Awareness that the self is unique, knowledge of roles to be followed | Inability to identify appropriate roles in life |
| 6. Intimacy-versus-isolation | Early adulthood | Development of close friendships and loving, sexual relationships | Fear of relationships with others |
| 7. Generativity-versus-stagnation | Middle adulthood | Sense of contribution to continuity of life | Trivialization of one's activities |
| 8. Ego-integrity-versus-despair | Late adulthood | Sense of unity in life's accomplishments | Regret over lost opportunities of life |

SOURCE: Based on Erikson, E. H. (1963). Childhood and society. New York: Norton.

Erikson argues that adolescents strive to discover their particular strengths and weaknesses and the roles they can best play in their future lives. This discovery process often involves "trying on" different roles or choices to see if they fit an adolescent's capabilities and views about himself or herself. Through this process, adolescents seek to understand who they are by narrowing and making choices about their personal, occupational, sexual, and political commitments. Erikson calls this the **identity-versus-identity-confusion stage**.

In Erikson's view, adolescents who stumble in their efforts to find a suitable identity may go off course in several ways. On the one hand, they may adopt socially unacceptable roles as a way of expressing what they do *not* want to be, or they may have difficulty forming and maintaining long-lasting close personal relationships. In general, their sense of self becomes "diffuse," failing to organize around a central, unified core identity.

On the other hand, those who are successful in forging an appropriate identity set a course that provides a foundation for future psychosocial development. They learn their unique capabilities and believe in them, and they develop an accurate sense of who they are. They are prepared to set out on a path that takes full advantage of whatever their unique strengths permit them to do (Allison & Schultz, 2001).

**SOCIETAL PRESSURES AND RELIANCE ON FRIENDS AND PEERS.** As if teenagers' self-generated identity issues were not difficult enough, societal pressures are also high during the identity-versus-identity-confusion stage, as any student knows who has been repeatedly asked by parents and friends, "What's your major?" and "What are you going to do when you graduate?" Adolescents feel pressure to decide whether their post–high school plans include work or college and, if they choose work, which occupational track to follow. Up to this point in their development, their educational lives have been pretty much programmed by U.S. society, which lays out a universal educational track. But the track ends at high school, and consequently, adolescents face difficult choices about which of several possible future paths they will follow.

During this period, adolescents increasingly rely on their friends and peers as sources of information. At the same time, their dependence on adults declines. As we discuss later in the chapter, this increasing dependence on the peer group enables adolescents to forge close relationships. Comparing themselves to others helps them clarify their own identity.

This reliance on peers to help adolescents define their identity and learn to form relationships is the link between this stage of psychosocial development and the next stage Erikson proposed, known as *intimacy versus isolation*. It also relates to the subject of gender differences in identity formation. When Erikson developed

**Identity-versus-identity-confusion stage** The period during which teenagers seek to determine what is unique and distinctive about themselves

his theory, he suggested that men and women move through the identity-versus-identity-confusion period differently. He argued that men are more likely to proceed through the social development stages in the order shown in Table 16.1, developing a stable identity before committing to an intimate relationship with another person. In contrast, he suggested that women reverse the order, seeking intimate relationships and then defining their identities through these relationships. These ideas largely reflect the social conditions at the time he was writing, when women were less likely to go to college or establish their own careers and instead often married early. Today, however, the experiences of boys and girls seem relatively similar during the identity-versus-identity-confusion period.

**PSYCHOLOGICAL MORATORIUM.** Because of the pressures of the identity-versus-identity-confusion period, Erikson suggested that many adolescents pursue a "psychological moratorium." The *psychological moratorium* is a period during which adolescents take time off from the upcoming responsibilities of adulthood and explore various roles and possibilities. For example, many college students take a semester or year off to travel, work, or find some other way to examine their priorities.

Of course, many adolescents cannot, for practical reasons, pursue a psychological moratorium involving a relatively leisurely exploration of various identities. Some adolescents, for economic reasons, must work part time after school and then take jobs immediately after graduation from high school. As a result, they have little time to experiment with identities and engage in a psychological moratorium. Does this mean such adolescents will be psychologically damaged in some way? Probably not. The satisfaction that can come from successfully holding a part-time job while attending school may be a sufficient psychological reward to outweigh the inability to try out various roles.

**LIMITATIONS OF ERIKSON'S THEORY.** One criticism that has been raised regarding Erikson's theory is that he uses male identity development as the standard against which to compare female identity. In particular, he saw men as developing intimacy only after they have achieved a stable identity, which is viewed as the normative pattern. To critics, Erikson's view is based on male-oriented concepts of individuality and competitiveness. In an alternative conception, psychologist Carol Gilligan has suggested that women develop

identity through the establishment of relationships. In this view, a key component of a woman's identity is the building of caring networks between herself and others (Gilligan, 2004; Kroger, 2006).

## Marcia's Approach to Identity Development: Updating Erikson

**LO 16.3** Explain the categories of adolescent identity according to Marcia.

Using Erikson's theory as a springboard, psychologist James Marcia suggests that identity can be seen in terms of which of two characteristics—crisis and commitment—is present or absent. *Crisis* is a period of identity development in which an adolescent consciously chooses between various alternatives and makes decisions. *Commitment* is a psychological investment in a course of action or an ideology. We can see the differences between an adolescent who careens from one activity to another, with nothing lasting more than a few weeks, compared with one who becomes totally absorbed in volunteer work at a homeless shelter (Peterson, Marcia, & Carpendale, 2004; Marcia, 2007; Crocetti, 2017).

After conducting lengthy interviews with adolescents, Marcia proposed four categories of adolescent identity (see Table 16.2):

1. **Identity achievement.** Teenagers within this identity status have successfully explored and thought through who they are and what they

**Table 16.2** Marcia's Four Categories of Adolescent Development

| | | Commitment | |
|---|---|---|---|
| | | **Present** | **Absent** |
| CRISIS/EXPLORATION | PRESENT | Identity achievement | Moratorium |
| | | "I love animals; I'm going to become a vet." | "I'm going to work at the mall while I figure out what to do next." |
| | ABSENT | Identity foreclosure | Identity diffusion |
| | | "I'm going into law, just like Mom." | "I don't have a clue." |

**SOURCE:** Marcia, J. E. (1980). "Identity in adolescence." In J. Adelson (Ed.), Handbook of adolescent psychology. New York: Wiley.

**identity achievement** The status of adolescents who commit to a particular identity following a period of crisis during which they consider various alternatives

want to do. Following a period of crisis during which they considered various alternatives, these adolescents have committed to a particular identity. Teens who have reached this identity status tend to be the most psychologically healthy, higher in achievement motivation and moral reasoning than adolescents of any other status.

2. **Identity foreclosure**. These are adolescents who have committed to an identity, but rather than struggling to find their own identity, they have accepted others' decisions about what is best for them. Typical adolescents in this category are a son who enters the family business because it is expected of him, or a daughter who decides to become a physician simply because her mother is one. Although foreclosers are not necessarily unhappy, they tend to have what can be called "rigid strength": happy and self-satisfied; they also have a high need for social approval and tend to be authoritarian.

3. **Moratorium**. Although adolescents in the moratorium category have explored various alternatives to some degree, they have not yet committed themselves to a particular path. As a consequence, Marcia suggests, they show relatively high anxiety and experience psychological conflict. However, they are often lively and appealing, seeking intimacy with others. Adolescents of this status typically settle on an identity, but only after something of a struggle.

4. **Identity diffusion**. Adolescents in this category neither explore nor commit to consider various alternatives. They tend to be inconsistent and impulsive, shifting from one thing to the next. Moreover, their lack of commitment impairs their ability to form close relationships, and they are often socially withdrawn.

It is important to note that adolescents are not necessarily stuck in one of the four categories. Some move back and forth between moratorium and identity achievement in what has been called a "MAMA" cycle (**m**oratorium—identity **a**chievement—**m**oratorium—identity **a**chievement). For instance, even though a forecloser may have settled on a career path during early adolescence with little active decision making, he or she may reassess the choice later and move into another category. For some individuals, then, identity formation may take place beyond the period of adolescence; however,

identity jells in the late teens and early 20s for most people (Al-Owidha, Green, & Kroger, 2009; Duriez et al., 2012; Mrazek, Harada, & Chiao, 2015).

In some ways, Marcia's identity status perspective foreshadows what other researchers have called emerging adulthood. *Emerging adulthood* is the period beginning in the late teenage years and extending into the mid-20s. It is a transitional stage between adolescence and adulthood that spans the third decade of life. It is typically a period of uncertainty, in which post-adolescents are working to determine who they are and their path forward (Arnett, 2016).

The pattern of identity development amongst adolescents living in the urban and rural areas of West Bengal was studied by Basak and Gosh (2008). The researchers observed that the ego-identity status of students differed with respect to gender and rural-urban location. Female students, even from rural areas, were observed to have identity crisis with respect to occupation, ideological beliefs, and interpersonal relationships. Adolescents with identity achievement status have higher self-esteem, whereas identity moratorium, identity foreclosure, and identity diffused adolescents have lower self-esteem.

> **From a guidance counselor's perspective:**  Are there stages in Marcia's theory of development that may be more difficult to achieve for adolescents who live in poverty? Why?

# Religion and Spirituality

**LO 16.4  Describe the roles that religion and spirituality play in identity formation.**

> *Ever wonder why God made mosquitos? How about why God gave Adam and Eve the ability to rebel if He knew how much of mess it would cause? Can someone be saved and later lose their salvation? Do pets go to heaven?*

**identity foreclosure** The status of adolescents who prematurely commit to an identity without adequately exploring alternatives

**moratorium** The status of adolescents who may have explored various identity alternatives to some degree, but have not yet committed themselves

**identity diffusion** The status of adolescents who consider various identity alternatives, but never commit to one or never even consider identity options in any conscious way

As exemplified in this blog post, questions of religion and spirituality begin to be asked during adolescence. Religion is important to many people because it offers a formal means of satisfying spirituality needs. *Spirituality* is a sense of attachment to some higher power such as God, nature, or something sacred. Although spirituality needs are typically tied to religious beliefs, they may be independent. Many people who consider themselves to be spiritual individuals do not participate in formal religious practices or are not affiliated with any particular religion (Harris, 2015).

Because their cognitive abilities increase during adolescence, teenagers are able to think more abstractly about religious matters. Furthermore, as they grapple with general questions of identity, they may question their religious identity. After having accepted their religious identity in an unquestioning manner during childhood, adolescents may view religion more critically and seek to distance themselves from formal religion. In other cases, they may be drawn more closely to their religious affiliation because it offers answers to such abstract questions as "Why am I here on this earth?" and "What is the meaning of life?" Religion provides a way of viewing the world and universe as having intentional design—a place that was created by something or someone (Levenson, Aldwin, & Igarashi, 2013; Longo, Bray, & Kim-Spoon, 2017).

According to James Fowler, our understanding and practice of faith and spirituality proceeds through a series of stages that extend throughout the lifetime. During childhood, individuals hold a fairly literal view of God and biblical figures. For example, children may think of God as living at the top of the earth and being able to see what everyone is doing (Fowler & Dell, 2006; Boyatzis, 2013).

In adolescence, the view of spirituality becomes more abstract. As they build their identity, adolescents typically develop a core set of beliefs and values. However, in many cases, adolescents do not consider their views either in depth or systematically, and it is not until later that they become more reflective.

As they leave adolescence, people typically move into the *individuative-reflective stage* of faith in which they reflect on their beliefs and values. They understand that their view is one of many, and that multiple views of God are possible. Ultimately, the final stage of faith development is the *conjunctive stage*, in which individuals develop a broad, inclusive view of religion and all humanity. They see humanity as a whole, and they may work to promote a common good. In this stage, they may move beyond formal religion and hold a unified view of people across the globe.

## Identity, Race, and Ethnicity

**LO 16.5** **Illustrate the challenges that ethnic and minority groups face in establishing identities.**

Although the path to forming an identity is often difficult for adolescents, it presents a particular challenge for members of racial and ethnic groups that have traditionally been discriminated against. Society's contradictory values are one part of the problem. On the one hand, adolescents are told that society should be color-blind, that race and ethnic background should not matter in terms of opportunities and achievement, and that if they do achieve, society will accept them. Based on a traditional *cultural assimilation model*, this view holds that individual cultural identities should be assimilated into a unified culture in the United States—the proverbial "melting pot" model.

The *pluralistic society model* suggests that U.S. society is made up of diverse, coequal cultural groups that should preserve their individual cultural features. The pluralistic society model grew in part from the belief that the cultural assimilation model denigrates the cultural heritage of minorities and lowers their self-esteem.

The pluralistic society model suggests that India is made up of diverse, coequal cultural groups that should preserve their individual cultural features. The pluralistic society model grew in part from the belief that the cultural assimilation model denigrates the cultural heritage of minorities and lowers their self-esteem. According to this view, adolescents' identity and are not submerged in an attempt to assimilate into the majority culture. From this perspective, identity development includes development of minority group identity—that is, the sense of membership in a minority group and the feelings that are associated with that membership. It includes a sense of commitment and ties with a particular group. There is a middle ground. Minority group members can form a bicultural identity in which they draw from their own cultural identity while integrating themselves into the dominant culture. This view suggests that an individual can live as a member of two cultures, with two cultural identities, without having to choose one over the other (LaFromboise, Coleman, & Gerton, 1993; Shi & Lu, 2007).

The process of identity formation is not simple for anyone and may be doubly difficult for minority group members. Racial and ethnic identity takes time to form, and for some individuals, it may occur over a prolonged period. Still, the ultimate result can be the formation of a rich, multifaceted identity (Quintana, 2007; Jensen, 2008; Klimstra et al., 2012).

The process of identity formation is not simple for anyone and may be doubly difficult for minority group members. Racial and ethnic identity takes time to form, and for some individuals it may occur over a prolonged period. Still, the ultimate result can be the formation of a rich, multifaceted identity (Jensen, 2008; Klimstra et al., 2012; Yoon et al., 2017).

## Psychological Difficulties in Adolescence

**LO 16.6  Identify the factors that contribute to psychological difficulties.**

*"You don't have to be poor to feel hopeless," says 14-year-old Deepika Rathore. "We lived in a big house in Gurugram. My parents loved me. We had everything, but still I felt buried under a ton of despair."*

*Her despair followed her everywhere: school, friends' houses, movies, basketball games. "I was trapped. I couldn't escape it. I couldn't make myself feel anything, certainly not happy."*

*Deepika began experimenting with drugs and stopped doing homework. When her mother found out she had quit basketball, they shared an evening of anger, tears, and heartache.*

*Before going to bed, Deepika swallowed every pill in the medicine cabinet. Luckily her mother found her and rushed her to the hospital.*

Although the vast majority of teenagers weather the search for identity—as well as the other challenges presented by the period—without major psychological difficulties, some find adolescence particularly stressful. Some, in fact, develop severe psychological problems. Two of the most serious are adolescent depression and suicide.

**ADOLESCENT DEPRESSION.**  No one is immune to periods of sadness, unhappiness, and feeling emotionally upset—and adolescents are no exception. The end of a relationship, failure at an important task, the death of a loved one—all may produce profound feelings of sadness, loss, and grief. In situations such as these, depression is a fairly typical reaction.

How common are feelings of depression in adolescence? More than one-fourth of adolescents report feeling so sad or hopeless for 2 or more weeks in a row that they stopped doing their normal activities. Almost two-thirds of teenagers say they have experienced such feelings at one time or another. However, only a small minority of adolescents—some 3 percent—experience *major depressive disorder*, a full-blown psychological disorder in which depression is severe and lingers for long periods (Grunbaum, Lowry, & Kann, 2001; Galambos, Leadbeater, & Barker, 2004).

Gender, ethnic, and racial differences also are found in depression rates. As is the case among adults, adolescent girls, on average, experience major depressive disorder more often than boys. Some studies have found that African American adolescents have

Between 25 percent and 40 percent of girls and 20 percent to 35 percent of boys experience occasional episodes of depression during adolescence, although the incidence of major depression is far lower.

higher rates of depression than White adolescents, although not all research supports this conclusion. Native Americans, too, have higher rates of depression (Sanchez, Lambert, & Ialongo, 2012; English, Lambert & Ialongo, 2014; Blom et al., 2016).

In cases of severe, long-term major depressive disorder, biological factors are often involved. Although some adolescents seem to be genetically predisposed to experience depression, environmental and social factors relating to the extraordinary changes in the social lives of adolescents are also important influences. An adolescent who experiences the death of a loved one, for example, or one who grows up with an alcoholic or a depressed parent, is at higher risk of depression. In addition, being unpopular, having few close friends, and experiencing rejection are associated with adolescent depression (Eley, Liang, & Plomin, 2004; Zalsman et al., 2006; Herberman Mash et al., 2014).

In India, adolescent depression is an under researched area. Psychiatric morbidity among school samples of adolescents was found in about 29 percent of girls and 23 percent of boys with depression being the most common disorder. Jayanthi and Thirunavukarasu (2015) have also shown a high level of depression (25 percent) in a school sample of adolescents in South India. Nair et al. (2004) have assessed the prevalence of depression, and they found it to be 3 percent among 13–19 year old school going adolescents. Trivedi et al. (2017) found that 22.45 percent students were depressed. They found students reported borderline depression (6.9 percent), with moderate depression (8.9 percent), severe depression (4.1 percent), extreme depression (2.6 percent), and mood disturbances (18.1 percent). Depression was detected among a significant number of older adolescents (ages 14 and 15 years), and girls were significantly more depressed. Students who were comfortable with friends and those who received moral support from their families were significantly less depressed. Moderately and severely depressed students displayed abnormal eating habits, and those whose families did not spend enough time with them were more susceptible to depression.

India is home to an estimated 57 million people (18 percent of the global estimate) affected by depression. With India witnessing significant changes (including globalization, urbanization, migration, and modernization) that is coupled with rapid sociodemographic transition, depression is likely to increase in the coming years (WHO, 2017).

As per NMHS (2015–16) in India, one in 20 (5.25 percent) people over 18 years of age have ever suffered (that is, at least once in their lifetime) from depression, which amounted to a total of over 45 million people with depression in 2015. The overall prevalence rates of childhood depression in India vary anywhere between 0.3 percent and about 1.2 percent. The NMHS (2015–16) reported a prevalence rate of 0.8 percent (0.3–1.4) for depression among 13–17 year-old children. Traumatic experiences in early childhood, frequent migration, negative life events, educational setbacks, early relationship problems, family history of mental illness as well as stress at school and in the family are linked in varying degrees to depression among children and adolescent.

The National Mental Health Policy, 2014 (http://www.mohfw.nic.in/), recognizes the various factors and circumstances that lead to depression and emphasizes the role of different sectors like education and workplace in mental health promotion and prevention of depression. Highlighting the relationship between poverty and depression, the policy has stressed the need for reducing poverty and income disparity in the country to improve mental health outcomes. Under the ambit of mental illness, depression is considered a disabling condition in the Rights of Persons with Disabilities Act, 2016, benefitting the persons affected with depression. The Mental Health Action Plan 365 provides a framework of actions for realizing the objectives of mental health policy, which also includes provision of counselling services for children with mental distress in schools and colleges. However, in view of the significant burden of depression and with relatively greater proportional morbidity among those with mental disorders, there is need for a policy level focus on depression.

One of the most puzzling questions about depressive disorders is why their incidence is higher among girls than boys. There is little evidence that these disorders are linked to hormone differences or a particular gene. Instead, some psychologists speculate that stress is more pronounced for girls than for boys in adolescence due to the many, sometimes conflicting, demands of the traditional female gender role. Recall, for instance, the situation of the adolescent girl who was quoted in our discussion of self-esteem. She worries not only about doing well in school but also about being popular. If she feels that academic success undermines her popularity, she is placed in a bind that can leave her feeling helpless. Added to this is the fact that traditional gender roles still result in higher status being given to men than women (Hyde, Mezulis, & Abramson, 2008; Chaplin, Gillham, & Seligman, 2009; Castelao & Kröner-Herwig, 2013).

Girls' generally higher levels of depressive disorders during adolescence may reflect gender differences in ways of coping with stress, rather than gender differences in mood. In comparison to boys, girls are more likely to react to stress by turning inward, thereby experiencing a sense of helplessness and hopelessness. In contrast, boys more often react by externalizing the stress and acting more impulsively or aggressively, or by turning to drugs and alcohol (Wu et al., 2007; Brown et al., 2012; Anyan & Hjemdal, 2016).

**ADOLESCENT SUICIDE.** India's National Crime Records Bureau collects data on suicides from police recorded suicides cases. It has been observed that youth in the age range of 18 and above years and below 30 years are one of the most vulnerable groups resorting to suicides, and it had 33 percent share of the total suicides. "Family problems" and "illness" were the major causes of suicides in 2015, which accounted for 28 percent and 16 percent of total suicides, respectively. Out of the overall suicide victims, 68.5 percent were males and 31.5 percent were females.

In the US, it has been observed that in adolescence, the rate of suicide is higher for boys than for girls, although girls *attempt* suicide more frequently. Suicide attempts among boys are more likely to result in death because of the methods they use: Boys tend to use more violent means, such as guns, while girls are more apt to choose a drug overdose. Some estimates suggest that there are as many as 200 attempted suicides by both sexes for every successful one (Dervic et al., 2006; Pompili et al., 2009; Payá-González et al., 2015).

The reasons behind the increase in adolescent suicide are unclear. The most obvious explanation is that the stress experienced by teenagers has increased, leading those who are most vulnerable to be more likely to commit suicide. But why should stress have increased only for adolescents, given that the suicide rate for other segments of the population has remained fairly stable over the same time period?

Although we are not yet sure why adolescent suicide has increased, it is clear that certain factors heighten the risk of suicide. One factor is depression. Depressed teenagers who are experiencing a profound sense of hopelessness are at greater risk of committing suicide (although most depressed individuals do not commit suicide). Moreover, social inhibition, perfectionism, and a high level of stress and anxiety are related to a greater risk of suicide. The easy availability of guns—which are more prevalent in the United States than in other industrialized nations—also contributes to the suicide rate (Zalsman, Levy, & Shoval, 2008; Wright, Wintemute, & Claire, 2008; Hetrick et al., 2012).

In addition to depression, some cases of suicide are associated with family conflicts and relationship or school difficulties. Others stem from a history of abuse and neglect. The rate of suicide among drug and alcohol abusers is also relatively high. Finally, certain demographics are related to suicide. For instance, lesbians, gays, and transsexuals are at higher risk for suicide.

Some suicides appear to be caused by exposure to the suicide of others. In *cluster suicide*, one suicide leads to attempts by others to kill themselves. For instance, some high schools have experienced a series of suicides following a well-publicized case. As a result, many schools have established crisis intervention

Contrary to popular belief, talking about suicide does not encourage it. In fact, it actually combats suicide by providing supportive feedback and breaking down the sense of isolation many suicidal people have.

teams to counsel students when one student commits suicide (Daniel & Goldston, 2009; Pompili et al., 2011; Abrutyn & Mueller, 2014).

Several warning signs should sound an alarm regarding the possibility of suicide, including the following:

- Direct or indirect talk about suicide, such as "I wish I were dead" or "You won't have me to worry about any longer"

- School difficulties, such as missed classes or a decline in grades

- Making arrangements as if preparing for a long trip, such as giving away prized possessions or arranging for the care of a pet

- Writing a will

- Loss of appetite or excessive eating

- General depression, including a change in sleeping patterns, slowness and lethargy, and uncommunicativeness

- Dramatic changes in behavior, such as a shy person suddenly acting outgoing

- Preoccupation with death in music, art, or literature

# Relationships: Family and Friends

*When 13-year-old Mina tells her father about her friend Nina's upcoming birthday party followed by dance and music, he says that he will pick her up at 12:00 at night. Mina goes ballistic. "12!", "Dad, it's a sleep over! Every body's is getting picked up at noon the next day." Her father asks, "And when will the boys be going home?" Mina looks at him, "Noon the next day, same as everyone."*

*Her father sighs. "There is no way you are going to sleep over anywhere there are boys." Mina's disbelief is palpable. "But Dad," she explains impatiently,*

# BECOMING AN INFORMED CONSUMER OF CHILD DEVELOPMENT

## Adolescent Suicide: How to Help

If you suspect that an adolescent—or anyone else, for that matter—is contemplating suicide, don't stand idly by. Act! Here are several suggestions:

- *Talk to the person*, listen without judging, and give the person an understanding forum in which to try to talk things through.

- *Talk specifically about suicidal thoughts*, asking such questions as: Does the person have a plan? Has he or she bought a gun? Where is it? Has he or she stockpiled pills? Where are they? The Public Health Service notes that "contrary to popular belief, such candor will not give a person dangerous ideas or encourage a suicidal act."

- *Evaluate the situation*, trying to distinguish between general upset and more serious danger, as when suicide plans *have* been made. If the crisis is acute, *do not leave the person alone*.

- *Be supportive*, let the person know you care, and try to break down his or her feelings of isolation.

- *Take charge of finding help,* without concern about invading the person's privacy. Do not try to handle the problem alone; get professional help immediately.

- *Make the environment safe*, removing from the premises (not just hiding) guns, razors, scissors, medication, and other potentially dangerous household items.

- *Do not keep suicide talk or threats secret*; these are calls for help and require immediate action.

- *Do not challenge, dare, or use verbal shock treatment* on the person in an effort to make them realize the errors in their thinking. These can have tragic effects.

- *Make a contract with the person*, getting a promise or commitment, preferably in writing, not to make any suicidal attempt until you have talked further.

- *Don't be overly reassured by a sudden improvement of mood.* Such seemingly quick recoveries sometimes reflect the relief of finally deciding to commit suicide or the temporary release of talking to someone, but most likely the underlying problems have not been resolved.

For immediate help with a suicide-related problem, call (800) 784-2433 National Suicide Prevention Lifeline or (800) 621-4000, National Runaway Switchboard, national hotlines staffed with trained counselors.

*"Mina's mother will be there. Nothing is going to happen. Nobody is going to sleep anyway."*

*Speechless, Mina's father signals time out, resolving to talk to other parents about this strange new world he has somehow landed in.*

The social world of adolescents is considerably wider than that of younger children. As adolescents' relationships with people outside the home grow increasingly important, their interactions with their families evolve and take on a new, and sometimes difficult, character (Collins, Gleason, & Sesma, 1997; Collins & Andrew, 2004).

## Family Ties: Changing Relationships

**LO 16.7  Explain how family relationships change during adolescence.**

*When Narayan Rao entered secondary school, his relationship with his parents changed drastically. What had been a good relationship had become tense by the middle of seventh grade. Narayan felt his parents always seemed to be "on his case." Instead of giving him more freedom, which he felt he deserved at age 13, they actually seemed to be becoming more restrictive.*

Narayan's parents would probably see things differently. They would likely suggest that they were not the source of the tension in the household—Narayan was. From their point of view, Narayan, with whom they'd established what seemed to be a close, stable, loving relationship throughout much of his childhood, suddenly seemed transformed. They felt he was shutting them out of his life, and when he did speak with them, it was merely to criticize their politics, their dress, and their preferences in TV shows. To his parents, Narayan's behavior was upsetting and bewildering.

**THE QUEST FOR AUTONOMY.**  Parents are sometimes angered, and even more frequently puzzled, by adolescents' conduct. Children who have previously accepted their parents' judgments, declarations, and guidelines begin to question—and sometimes rebel against—their parents' views of the world.

These clashes are caused in part by the shifting roles that both children and parents must deal with during adolescence. Adolescents increasingly seek **autonomy**— independence and a sense of control over their lives. Most parents intellectually realize that this shift is a normal part of adolescence, representing one of the primary developmental tasks of the period, and in many ways they welcome it as a sign of their children's growth; however, in many cases, the day-to-day realities of adolescents' increasing autonomy may prove difficult for them to handle (Smetana, 1995). But understanding this growing independence intellectually and agreeing to allow a teen to attend a party when no parents will be present are two different things. To the adolescent, her parents' refusal indicates a lack of trust or confidence. To the parent, it's simple good sense: "I trust you," they may say. "It's everyone else who will be there that I worry about."

In most families, teenagers' autonomy grows gradually over the course of adolescence. For instance, one study of changes in adolescents' views of their parents found that increasing autonomy led them to perceive parents less in idealized terms and more as persons in their own right. Rather than seeing their parents as authoritarian disciplinarians reminding them to do their homework, they may come to see their parents' emphasis on excelling in school as evidence of parental regrets about their own lack of education and a wish to see their children have more options in life. At the same time, adolescents come to depend more on themselves and to feel more like separate individuals.

The increase in adolescent autonomy changes the relationship between parents and teenagers. At the start of adolescence, the relationship tends to be asymmetrical: Parents hold most of the power and influence over the relationship. By the end of adolescence, however, power and influence have become more balanced, and parents and children end up in a more symmetrical, or egalitarian, relationship. Power and influence are shared, although parents typically retain the upper hand (Goede, Branje, & Meeus, 2009; Inguglia et al., 2015).

**CULTURE AND AUTONOMY.**  The degree of autonomy that is eventually achieved varies from one family and one child to the next. Cultural factors play an important role. In Western societies, which tend to value individualism, adolescents seek autonomy at a relatively early stage of adolescence. In contrast, Asian

---

**autonomy** Having independence and a sense of control over one's life

## Figure 16.1 Family Obligations

Adolescents from Asian and Latin American groups feel a greater sense of respect and obligation toward their families than adolescents with European backgrounds.

**SOURCE:** Fuligni, A. J., Tseng, V., & Lam, M. (1999). "Attitudes toward family obligations among American adolescents with Asian, Latin American, and European backgrounds." Child Development, vol. 70, pp. 1030–1044.

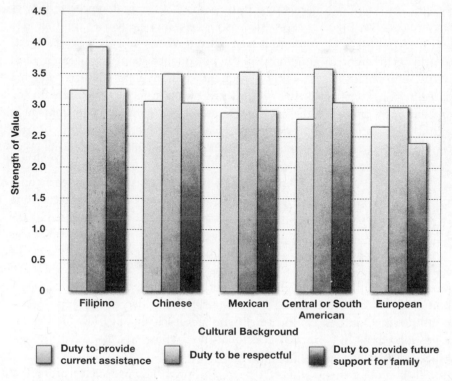

- Duty to provide current assistance
- Duty to be respectful
- Duty to provide future support for family

**Cultural Background**

societies are collectivistic; they promote the idea that the well-being of the group is more important than that of the individual. In such societies, adolescents' aspirations to achieve autonomy are less pronounced (Raeff, 2004; Supple et al., 2009; Perez-Brena, Updegraff, & Umaña-Taylor, 2012).

Adolescents from different cultural backgrounds also vary in their feelings of obligation to their family. Those in more collectivistic cultures tend to feel greater obligation to their families, in terms of fulfilling their expectations about their duty to provide assistance, show respect, and support their families in the future, than those from more individualistic societies. In collectivistic societies, the push for autonomy is less strong, and the timetable during which autonomy is expected to develop is slower (see Figure 16.1; Leung, Pe-Pua, & Karnilowicz, 2006; Chan & Chan, 2013; Hou, Kim, & Wang, 2016).

For example, when asked at what age an adolescent would be expected to carry out certain behaviors (such

as going to a concert with friends), adolescents and parents provide different answers depending on their cultural background. In comparison to Asian adolescents and parents, Caucasian adolescents and parents indicate an earlier timetable, anticipating greater autonomy at an earlier age (Feldman & Wood, 1994).

Does the extended timetable for the development of autonomy in more collectivistic cultures have negative consequences for adolescents in those cultures? Apparently not. The more important factor is the degree of match between cultural expectations and developmental patterns. What probably matters most is how well the development of autonomy matches societal expectations, not the specific timetable of autonomy (Rothbaum et al., 2000; Updegraff et al., 2006).

In addition to cultural factors affecting autonomy, gender plays a role. In general, male adolescents are permitted more autonomy at an earlier age than female adolescents. The encouragement of male autonomy is consistent with more general traditional male stereotypes, in which boys are perceived as more independent and

In collectivistic societies, the well-being of the group is promoted as more important than individual autonomy.

girls, conversely, are seen as more dependent on others. The more parents hold traditional stereotypical views of gender, the less likely they are to encourage their daughters' autonomy (Bumpus, Crouter, & McHale, 2001).

**THE MYTH OF THE GENERATION GAP.** Teen movies often depict adolescents and their parents with totally opposing points of view about the world. For example, the parent of an environmentalist teen might turn out to own a polluting factory. These exaggerations are often funny because we assume there is a kernel of truth in them, in that parents and teenagers often don't see things the same way. According to this argument, there is a **generation gap**, a deep divide between parents and children in attitudes, values, aspirations, and worldviews.

The reality, however, is quite different. The generation gap, when it exists, is really quite narrow. Adolescents and their parents tend to see eye to eye in a variety of domains. Republican parents generally have Republican children; members of evangelical Christian churches have children who espouse similar views; parents who advocate for abortion rights have children who are pro-choice. On social, political, and religious issues, parents and adolescents tend to be in sync, and children's worries mirror those of their parents. Adolescents' concerns about society's problems are those with which most adults would probably agree (Knafo & Schwartz, 2003; Smetana, 2005; Grønhøj & Thøgersen, 2012).

As we have stated, most adolescents and their parents get along quite well. Despite their quest for autonomy and independence, most adolescents have deep love, affection, and respect for their parents—and parents feel the same way about their children. Although some parent–adolescent relationships are seriously troubled, the majority of relationships are more positive than negative and help adolescents avoid the kind of peer pressure we discuss later in the chapter (Black, 2002).

Even though adolescents spend decreasing amounts of time with their families in general, the amount of time they spend alone with each parent remains remarkably stable across adolescence. In short, there is no evidence suggesting that family problems are worse during adolescence than at any other stage of development (Larson et al., 1996; Granic, Hollenstein, & Dishion, 2003).

**CONFLICTS WITH PARENTS.** Of course, if most adolescents get along with their parents most of the time, that means some of the time they don't; relationships aren't always sweetness and light. Parents and teens may hold similar attitudes about social and political issues, but they often hold different views on matters of personal taste, such as music preferences and styles of dress. Also, as we've seen, parents and children may run into disagreements when children seek to achieve autonomy and independence sooner than parents feel is right. Consequently, parent-child conflicts are more likely to occur during adolescence, particularly during the early stages, although it's important to remember that not every family is affected to the same degree (Smetana, Daddis, & Chuang, 2003; García-Ruiz et al., 2013).

Why should conflict be greater during early adolescence than at later stages of the period? According to developmental psychologist Judith Smetana, the reason involves differing definitions of, and rationales for, appropriate and inappropriate conduct. On the one hand, parents may feel, for instance, that getting one's ear pierced in three places is inappropriate because society traditionally deems it inappropriate. On the other hand, adolescents may view the issue in terms of personal choice (Smetana, 2005, 2006; Rote et al., 2012).

Furthermore, the newly sophisticated reasoning of adolescents (discussed in the previous chapter) leads teenagers to think about parental rules in more complex ways. Arguments that might be convincing to a school-age child ("Do it because I tell you to do it") are less compelling to an adolescent.

The argumentativeness and assertiveness of early adolescence at first may lead to an increase in conflict, but in many ways these qualities play an important role in the evolution of parent-child relationships. Although parents may initially react defensively to the challenges that their children present and may grow inflexible and rigid, in most cases they eventually come to realize that their children *are* growing up and that they want to support them in that process.

As parents come to see that their adolescent children's arguments are often compelling and not so unreasonable, and that their daughters and sons can

---

**generation gap** A divide between parents and adolescents in attitudes, values, aspirations, and worldviews

in fact be trusted with more freedom, they become more yielding, allowing and eventually perhaps even encouraging independence. As this process occurs during the middle stages of adolescence, the combativeness of early adolescence declines.

This pattern does not apply for all adolescents. Although the majority of teenagers maintain stable relations with their parents throughout adolescence, as many as 20 percent pass through a fairly rough time (Dmitrieva, Chen, & Greenberg, 2004).

> **From a social worker's perspective:** In what ways do you think parents with different styles—authoritarian, authoritative, permissive, and uninvolved—react to attempts to establish autonomy during adolescence? Are the styles of parenting different for a single parent? Are there cultural differences?

**CULTURAL DIFFERENCES IN PARENT-CHILD CONFLICTS DURING ADOLESCENCE.** Although parent-child conflicts are found in every culture, there does seem to be less conflict between parents and their teenage children in "traditional" preindustrial cultures. Teens in such traditional cultures also experience fewer mood swings and instances of risky behavior than teens in industrialized countries (Wu & Chao, 2011; Jensen & Dost-Gözkan, 2014; Shah et al., 2016).

Why? The answer may relate to the degree of independence that adolescents expect and adults permit. In more industrialized societies, in which the value of individualism is typically high, independence is an expected component of adolescence. Consequently, adolescents and their parents must negotiate the amount and timing of the adolescent's increasing independence—a process that often leads to strife.

In contrast, in more traditional societies, individualism is not valued as highly, and therefore adolescents are less inclined to seek out independence. With diminished independence seeking on the part of adolescents, the result is less parent-child conflict (Dasen & Mishra, 2002).

# Relationships With Peers: The Importance of Belonging

**LO 16.8 Describe how peer relationships change during adolescence.**

In the eyes of many parents, the most fitting symbols of adolescence are the cellphone, or perhaps the computer, on which incessant text messaging occurs. For many of their sons and daughters, communicating with friends is experienced as an indispensable lifeline, sustaining ties to individuals with whom they may have already spent many hours earlier in the day.

The seemingly compulsive need to communicate with friends demonstrates the role that peers play in adolescence. Continuing the trend that began in middle childhood, adolescents spend increasing amounts of time with their peers, and the importance of peer relationships grows as well. In fact, there is probably no period of life in which peer relationships are as important as they are in adolescence.

**SOCIAL COMPARISON.** Peers become more important in adolescence for a number of reasons. For one thing, they provide each other with the opportunity to compare and evaluate opinions, abilities, and even physical changes—a process called *social comparison*. Because the physical and cognitive changes of adolescence are so unique to this age group and so pronounced, especially during the early stages of puberty, adolescents turn increasingly to others who share, and consequently can shed light on, their own experiences (Rankin, Lane, & Gibbons, 2004; Li & Wright, 2013; Schaefer & Salafia, 2014).

Parents are unable to provide social comparison. Not only are they well beyond the changes that adolescents undergo, but also adolescents' questioning of adult authority and their motivation to become more autonomous make parents, other family members, and adults in general inadequate and invalid sources of knowledge. Who is left to provide such information? Peers.

**REFERENCE GROUPS.** As we have said, adolescence is a time of experimentation, of trying out new identities, roles, and conduct. Peers provide information about what roles and behavior are most acceptable by serving as a reference group. **Reference groups** are groups of people with whom one compares oneself. Just as a professional ballplayer is likely to compare his performance against that of other professional players, so do teenagers compare themselves to those who are similar to them.

Reference groups present a set of *norms*, or standards, against which adolescents can judge their

---

**reference groups** Groups of people with whom one compares oneself

abilities and social success. An adolescent need not even belong to a group for it to serve as a reference group. For instance, unpopular adolescents may find themselves belittled and rejected by members of a popular group, yet use that more popular group as a reference group (Berndt, 1999).

**CLIQUES AND CROWDS: BELONGING TO A GROUP.** One of the consequences of the increasing cognitive sophistication of adolescents is the ability to group others in more discriminating ways. Consequently, even if they do not belong to the group they use for reference purposes, adolescents typically are part of some identifiable group. Rather than defining people in concrete terms relating to what they do ("football players" or "musicians") as a younger school-age child might, adolescents use more abstract terms packed with greater subtleties ("jocks" or "skaters" or "stoners") (Brown & Klute, 2003).

Adolescents tend to belong to two types of groups: cliques and crowds. **Cliques** are groups of from 2 to 12 people whose members have frequent social interactions with one another. In contrast, **crowds** are larger, comprising individuals who share particular characteristics but who may not interact with one another. For instance, "jocks" and "nerds" are representative of crowds found in many high schools.

Membership in particular cliques and crowds is often determined by the degree of similarity with members of the group. One of the most important dimensions of similarity relates to substance use; adolescents tend to choose friends who use alcohol and other drugs to the same extent that they do. Their friends are also often similar in terms of their academic success, although this is not always true. For instance, during early adolescence, attraction to peers who are particularly well behaved seems to decrease, whereas, at the same time, those who behave more aggressively become more attractive (Kupersmidt & Dodge, 2004; Hutchinson & Rapee, 2007; Kiuru et al., 2009).

The emergence of distinct cliques and crowds during adolescence reflects in part the increased cognitive capabilities of adolescents. Group labels are abstractions, requiring teens to make judgments of people with whom they may interact only rarely and of whom they have little direct knowledge. It is not until mid-adolescence that teenagers are sufficiently sophisticated cognitively to make the subtle judgments that underlie distinctions between different cliques and crowds (Burgess & Rubin, 2000; Brown & Klute, 2003).

**GENDER RELATIONS.** As children enter adolescence from middle childhood, their groups of friends are composed almost universally of same-sex individuals. Boys hang out with boys; girls hang out with girls. Technically, this sex segregation is called the **sex cleavage**.

This situation changes as members of both sexes enter puberty. Boys and girls experience the hormonal surge that marks puberty and causes the maturation of the sex organs (see Chapter 14). At the same time, societal pressures suggest that the time is appropriate for romantic involvement. These developments lead to a change in the ways adolescents view the opposite sex. Whereas a 10-year-old is likely to see every member of the other sex as "annoying" and "a pain," heterosexual teenage boys and girls begin to regard each other with greater interest in terms of both personality and sexuality. (For gays and lesbians, pairing off holds its own complexities, as we discuss later when we consider adolescent dating.)

As they move into puberty, boys' and girls' cliques, which previously had moved along parallel but separate tracks, begin to converge. Adolescents begin to attend boy–girl dances or parties, although most of the time the boys still spend their time with boys, and the girls spend their time with girls (Richards et al., 1998).

A little later, however, adolescents increasingly spend time with members of the other sex. New cliques emerge, composed of both boys and girls. Not everyone participates initially: Early on, the teenagers who are leaders of the same-sex cliques and who have the highest status lead the way. Eventually, however, most adolescents find themselves in cliques that include boys and girls.

Cliques and crowds undergo yet another transformation at the end of adolescence: They become less influential and may dissolve as a result of the increased pairing off that occurs.

---

**cliques** Groups of from 2 to 12 people whose members have frequent social interactions with one another

**crowds** Groups larger than cliques, composed of individuals who share particular characteristics but who may not interact with one another

**sex cleavage** Sex segregation in which boys interact primarily with boys and girls primarily with girls

**Figure 16.2** The Social World of Adolescents

An adolescent's popularity can fall into one of four categories, depending on the opinions of his or her peers. Popularity is related to differences in status, behavior, and adjustment.

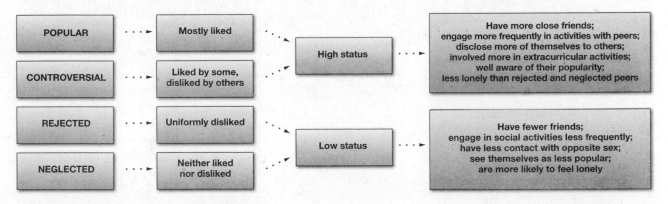

## Popularity and Peer Pressure in Adolescence

### LO 16.9 Describe popularity and responses to peer pressure.

Most adolescents have well-tuned antennae when it comes to determining who is popular and who is not. For some teenagers, concerns over popularity—or lack of it—may be a central focus of their lives.

**POPULARITY AND REJECTION.** Actually, the social world of adolescents is not divided solely into popular and unpopular individuals; the differentiations are more complex (see Figure 16.2). For instance, some adolescents are controversial; in contrast to *popular* adolescents, who are mostly liked, **controversial adolescents** are liked by some and disliked by others. For example, a controversial adolescent may be highly popular within a particular group, such as the string orchestra, but not popular among other classmates. Furthermore, there are **rejected adolescents**, who are uniformly disliked, and **neglected adolescents**, who are neither liked nor disliked. Neglected adolescents are the forgotten students—the ones whose status is so low that they are overlooked by almost everyone.

In most cases, popular and controversial adolescents tend to be similar in that their overall status is higher, whereas rejected and neglected adolescents share a generally lower status. Popular and controversial adolescents have more close friends, engage more frequently in activities with their peers, and disclose more about themselves to others than less popular students. They are also more involved in extracurricular school activities. In addition, they are well aware of their popularity, and they are less lonely than their less popular classmates (Becker & Luthar, 2007; Closson, 2009; Estévez, et al., 2014).

In contrast, the social world of rejected and neglected adolescents is considerably less pleasant. They have fewer friends, engage in social activities less

Unpopular adolescents fall into several categories. Controversial adolescents are liked by some and disliked by others, rejected adolescents are uniformly disliked, and neglected adolescents are neither liked nor disliked.

---

**controversial adolescents** Children who are liked by some peers and disliked by others

**rejected adolescents** Children who are uniformly disliked

**neglected adolescents** Children who receive relatively little attention from their peers in the form of either positive or negative interactions

# DEVELOPMENTAL DIVERSITY AND YOUR LIFE

## Adolescent Peer Relationship: Data Based on Interview with Adolescents in Delhi

*Bakaya (2012) identified three subtypes of popular peers in her study among adolescents in Delhi. The interview data was analyzed as follows:*

- *High Academic Achievers.* This group was reported to involve adolescents who had exceptionally good academic records and were considered intelligent by their peers. These adolescents were often referred to as "studious" and *"kitaabi keedas"* (bookworms). They were perceived as engaging in academic related discussions with their peers and being disinterested in fashion or the latest trends. They were seen to prefer small peer circles consisting of those who were academically at par with them.

  An early adolescent girl said, *"They always......talk about studies. They mostly discuss their homework... even in recess. Some are kitaabi keedas......are always reading books.....even in arrangement. I think they can't live without books. They are......always scoring high.......out of 50, they will get 47 or 48......we are like...how can they get so many marks?"*

  Further, high academic achievers were mostly seen as obedient, respectful to teachers, and helpful. Past research supports the relationship between academic competence and popularity (Vaillancourt & Hymel, 2006). However, the participants also pointed out that there were some high academic achievers who were unhelpful to peers or were arrogant and thus were not popular.

- *Stylish/fashionable/cool.* Adolescents belonging to this peer group were seen to lay great stress on physical appearance and fashion. This emphasis on appearance was reported to involve wearing the school uniform somewhat untidily (for instance, not tucking in their shirts, not straightening their ties, etc.) in order to look trendy. Some of the adolescents in this group were also perceived to be arrogant and self-focused. A 17-year-old girl said, *"Their way of talking is very different...... they talk more about themselves....... don't give much chance to the other person to speak. They show off to each other. They also don't like to study much......but... uhhh.... some of them are also good in studies. They look good and fashionable. People try to copy them. They are popular because of the way they dress."* It has been found that some popular adolescents lay great

emphasis on their appearance, adhering to strict norms with respect to fashion, makeup, hairstyles, and accessories (Vaillancourt & Hymel, 2006). De Bruyn and Van den Boom (2005) found that consensual popularity is highly related to fashion, style, and being perceived as not boring. Cillessen and Borch (2006) found that popular kids were found arrogant and show-offs.

- *Bullies.* Adolescents belonging to this peer group were seen to have a strong physique that they used to command others. They were referred to by many names such as "Mess Makers" and "Badmaash." They were also referred to as "Gundas," a commonly used term in Hindi for highly aggressive individuals engaged in antisocial activities. Participants stated that bullies made fun of others and ridiculed them for their own entertainment. They broke rules, played pranks in class, spoke derisively with peers, and used abusive language. A 11-year-old said, *"They hold someone......take in toilet and put water on them...or they will hold someone...put them on floor...and then all of them will jump on him... will pull out someone's shirt...pull pants....abuse them... physically they are stronger so......they make a separate group, they trouble others, they fight."* Most were seen as associated with individuals or gangs outside schools. Peers were reported to readily agree to the demands of bullies out of fear. *"They do pranks on others. They also have 'backing' ... so others are scared of complaining against them because then they will beat them outside school,"* as reported by a 17-year-old boy. Despite engaging in socially disapproved activities, bullies were popular among peers. Another 17-year-old girl said, *"Everyone likes to break rules and regulations and ...those who have the guts to break rules are admired by others. Bullies...want everyone to come to them and they think it's very good to be famous."* Recent studies (Pronk & Zimmer-Gembeck, 2010) show that aggressive children are popular among their peers because aggression is associated with power and status. In 1993, Moffitt's developmental taxonomy predicts that, during adolescence, antisocial behavior comes to be viewed as desirable because it represents adult status and access to adult opportunities.

- *Rejected Peers.* This group involved adolescents who were not accepted by their peers. Participants reported that peers were rejected for various reasons such as being a bully (not each and every bully was popular), having poor academic performance, physical appearance such as those who were fat and/or applied hair oil, and displayed inappropriate/clingy behavior.

The following passage reported by an early adolescent boy, highlights the behavior of a *chep* or clingy peer.

"There is a boy (named) Abhishek who is not good in studies and irritates others. He tries to get very close to others and hugs them. He washes his hands in class.......eats ice in science period. Everybody says he is mad. He twirls his eyelids and scares everyone..... so no one likes him." Results revealed that some peers were rejected simply on the basis of their physical appearance. Asher and Coie (1990) found that multiple factors cause peer rejection including, names, physical appearances, ethnic bias, and stereotyping. These lines by a 17-year-old girl highlight the role of good looks in peer relationships. "There is a girl Jaanvi who is fat and uses hair oil that stinks and so no one wants to be with her." Asher and Coie (1990) found that multiple factors cause peer rejection including, names, physical appearances, ethnic bias, and stereotyping. In the event of a peer being weak academically he or she was considered unintelligent and thus was rejected. Patterson, Capaldi, and Bank (1991) contend that academic failure can lead to peer rejection. The following lines stated by an early adolescent boy and girl, respectively, highlight this.

"If someone is not intelligent then he or she may not have any friend. I have seen one girl in another section. She is a failure and has no friend."

"There is a girl Tanya Chaddha. She failed and has no friend. She is poor in academics and failed. She is *nalayak* in studies and is always scolded by teachers." Another category of peers who were rejected are those who are mentally challenged. A 17-year-old girl said, "There is a mentally-challenged girl. She always sits alone and stays involved in herself. Nobody talks much to her." Similar views were expressed by a 17-year-old boy, "There's a girl. No one likes her because she is a special case. Even when we talk to her she gets very childish and disturbs us in studying." A possible reason for the rejection of those who were mentally challenged could be their lack of "fit" with other peers. Perhaps adolescents could not relate to such peers and therefore experienced rejection. It has been found that adolescents with impairments are at times rejected by normal children (Farmer and Rodkin, 1996; Nabasoku and Smith, 1993).

- *Neglected Peers.* Adolescents belonging to this peer group were seen to be introverts, remaining very quiet, engaging in little communication with others and rarely initiating interaction (Ollendick and Schroeder, 2003). They engage in minimum communication with others and rarely ever initiate interaction (Coie, Dodge, and Coppotelli, 1982). The following statement by a late adolescent girl highlights this:

*"There is a boy in class who is alone. He doesn't talk much to anyone and always sits alone. Boys tease him but he never says anything to anyone. He is very docile. After coming to this class, he has not made any new friends."*

- A 11-year-old boy said:

*"Raghav has no friend. He is repeating the class. He sits quietly and alone. He absents a lot. He comes to school, does what teacher tells him to do, studies, and goes home. He is not interested in anything else. He doesn't talk much to others.......and all his friends are in the other class now. He feels shy to talk to his old friends and gets irritated very quickly."*

In a study by Ollendick and Schroeder (2003), it was found that as a result of their introvert nature, neglected peers go unnoticed many times.

---

frequently, and have less contact with the opposite sex. They see themselves—accurately, it turns out—as less popular, and they are more likely to feel lonely. They may find themselves in conflicts with others, some of which escalate into full-blown fights that require mediation (McElhaney, Antonishak, & Allen, 2008; Woodhouse, Dykas, & Cassidy, 2012).

What is it that determines status in high school? Men and women have different perceptions. For example, college men suggest that physical attractiveness is the most important factor in determining high school girls' status, whereas college women believe it is a high school girl's grades and intelligence (Suitor et al., 2001).

**CONFORMITY.** Whenever Aldos Henry said he wanted to buy a particular brand of sneakers or a certain style of shirt, his parents complained that he was just giving in to peer pressure and told him to make up his own mind about things.

In arguing with Aldos, his parents were subscribing to a view of adolescence that is quite prevalent in U.S. society: that teenagers are highly susceptible to **peer pressure**, the influence of one's peers to conform to their behavior and attitudes. Were his parents correct in saying that he was a victim of peer pressure?

The research suggests that in some cases, adolescents *are* highly susceptible to the influence of their peers. For instance, when considering what to wear, whom to date, and what movies to see, adolescents are apt to follow the lead of their peers. Wearing the right clothes, down to the correct brand of the right clothes, sometimes can be a ticket to membership in a popular group. It shows you know what's what. However, when it comes to many nonsocial matters, such as choosing a career path or trying to solve a problem, adolescents are more likely to turn to an experienced adult (Phelan, Yu, & Davidson, 1994).

In short, particularly in middle and late adolescence, teenagers turn to those they see as experts on a given dimension. If they have social concerns, they turn to the people most likely to be experts—their peers. If the problem is one about which parents or other adults are most likely to have expertise, teenagers tend to turn to them for advice and are most susceptible to their opinions (Young & Ferguson, 1979; Perrine & Aloise-Young, 2004).

Overall, then, it does not appear that susceptibility to peer pressure suddenly soars during adolescence. Instead, adolescence brings about a change in the people to whom an individual conforms. Whereas children conform fairly consistently to their parents during childhood, in adolescence, conformity shifts to the peer group, in part because pressures to conform to peers increase as adolescents seek to establish their identity apart from their parents.

Ultimately, however, adolescents conform less to both peers *and* adults as they develop increasing autonomy in their lives. As they grow in confidence and in the ability to make their own decisions, adolescents are more apt to remain independent and to reject pressures from others, no matter who those others are. Before they learn to resist the urge to conform to their peers, however, teenagers may get into trouble, often along with their friends (Cook, Buehler, & Henson, 2009; Monahan, Steinberg, & Cauffman, 2009; Meldrum, Miller, & Flexon, 2013).

# Juvenile Delinquency: The Crimes of Adolescence

**LO 16.10 Explain how some adolescents become involved in criminal activity.**

Adolescents, along with young adults, are more likely to commit crimes than any other age group. This is a misleading statistic in some respects: Because certain behaviors (such as drinking) are illegal for adolescents but not for older individuals, it is rather easy for adolescents to break the law by doing something that, were they a few years older, would be legal. But even when such crimes are disregarded, adolescents are disproportionately involved in violent crimes, such as murder, assault, and rape, as well as in property crimes involving theft, robbery, and arson.

Adolescents and youth involvement in serious offences like murder, attempt to murder, kidnapping, and abduction is of major concern all over India. As per National Crime Records Bureau (NCRB), there is an increase in the number of cases registered against juveniles in conflict with law from 18,939 (in 2005) to 31,396 (in 2015) (Aggarwal, 2018). As per Juvenile Justice Act of 2000, if a boy or a girl below 18 years of age commits an offence, they shall be considered as juvenile in conflict with law, that is, juvenile offender.

The Nirbhaya case brought about change in the Juvenile Justice Act in India. Here is a synopsis of the ghastly act which shook the nation and the world.

> On 16 December 2012 in Munirka, a South Delhi neighborhood, a 23-year-old female (who came to be known as Nirbhaya, meaning fearless, later) was gangraped and her friend was assaulted by six people in a bus. One of the offenders was a juvenile. Mohammad Afro,z according to some reports, was declared as 17 years and six months old on the day of the crime by the Juvenile Justice Board (JJB), which relied on his birth certificate and school documents. On 28 January 2013, the JJB determined that he would not be tried as an adult. On 31 August 2013, he was convicted of rape and murder under the Juvenile Justice Act and given the maximum sentence of three years' imprisonment in a reform facility. He was released on 20 December 2015. Following the verdict for the juvenile and his release there was protest all over India, which ultimately brought about a change in the Juvenile Justice Act.

**peer pressure** The influence of one's peers to conform to their behavior and attitudes

On 22 December 2015, Rajya Sabha passed the Juvenile Justice Bill, which proposed that the accused who are above 16 years of age will be treated as an adult in the court of law for heinous crimes like rape. In such cases, the JJBs—comprising a metropolitan magistrate or a judicial magistrate and two social workers—will have the discretion to decide whether the offender should be tried by courts of law like adults, or whether the offender should be tried as a juvenile. The Juvenile Justice Act of 2016 can be seen as a very progressive step of the Indian government towards keeping pace with changing trends in juvenile crimes (Aggarwal, 2018).

Why do adolescents become involved in criminal activity? Some offenders, known as **undersocialized delinquents**, are adolescents who were raised with little discipline or with harsh, uncaring parental supervision. Although they are influenced by their peers, these children have not been socialized appropriately by their parents and were not taught standards of conduct to regulate their own behavior. Undersocialized delinquents typically begin criminal activities at an early age, well before the onset of adolescence (Hoeve et al., 2008).

Undersocialized delinquents share several characteristics. They tend to be relatively aggressive and violent fairly early in life—characteristics that lead to rejection by peers and to academic failure. They also are more likely to be less intelligent than average (Rutter, 2003; Peach & Gaultney, 2013).

Undersocialized delinquents often suffer from psychological difficulties, and as adults they fit a psychological pattern called *antisocial personality disorder*. They are relatively unlikely to be successfully rehabilitated, and many undersocialized delinquents live on the margins of society throughout their lives (Rönkä & Pulkkinen, 1995; Lynam, 1996; Frick et al., 2003).

A larger group of adolescent offenders are socialized delinquents. **Socialized delinquents** know and subscribe to the norms of society; they are fairly normal psychologically. For them, transgressions committed during adolescence do not lead to a life of crime. Instead, most socialized delinquents pass through a period during adolescence when they engage in some petty crimes (such as shoplifting), but they do not continue lawbreaking into adulthood.

Typically, socialized delinquents are highly influenced by their peers, and their delinquency often occurs in groups. In addition, some research suggests that parents of socialized delinquents supervise their children's behavior less closely than other parents. But like other aspects of adolescent behavior, these minor delinquencies are often a result of giving in to group pressure or seeking to establish one's identity as an adult (Fletcher et al., 1995; Thornberry & Krohn, 1997; Goldweber et al., 2011).

How can we prevent delinquency? One approach is *positive youth development,* a model in which adolescents are proactively engaged in community activities, school events, organizations, and with their peer groups. Such programs, especially those that involve early intervention, have been shown to be effective (Smith, Faulk, & Sizer, 2016).

# Dating, Sexual Behavior, and Teenage Pregnancy

*It took him almost a month, but Sylvester Chiu finally got up the courage to ask Jackie Durbin to go to the movies. It was hardly a surprise to Jackie, though. Sylvester had first told his friend Erik about his resolve to ask her out, and Erik had told Jackie's friend Cynthia about Sylvester's plans. Cynthia, in turn, had told Jackie, who was primed to say "yes" when Sylvester finally did call.*

Welcome to the complex world of dating, an important and changing ritual of adolescence. We consider dating, as well as several other aspects of adolescents' relationships with one another, in the remainder of the chapter.

## Dating: Close Relationships in the 21st Century

**LO 16.11 Summarize the functions and characteristics of dating during adolescence.**

When and how adolescents begin to date is determined by cultural factors that change from one generation to another. Until fairly recently, exclusively dating a single individual was seen as something of a cultural

---

**undersocialized delinquents** Adolescent delinquents who are raised with little discipline or with harsh, uncaring parental supervision

**socialized delinquents** Adolescent delinquents who know and subscribe to the norms of society and who are fairly normal psychologically

ideal, viewed in the context of romance. Society often encouraged dating in adolescence, in part as a way for adolescents to explore relationships that might eventually lead to marriage. Today, some adolescents believe that the concept of dating is outmoded and limiting, and in some places the practice of "hooking up"—a vague term that covers everything from kissing to sexual intercourse—is viewed as more appropriate. Despite changing cultural norms, dating remains the dominant form of social interaction that leads to intimacy among adolescents (Denizet-Lewis, 2004; Manning, Giordano, & Longmore, 2006; Bogle, 2008).

**THE FUNCTIONS OF DATING.** Although on the surface dating is part of a pattern of courtship that can potentially lead to marriage, it serves other functions as well, especially early on. Dating is a way to learn how to establish intimacy with another individual. It can provide entertainment and, depending on the status of the person one is dating, prestige. It even can be used to develop a sense of one's own identity (Adams & Williams, 2011; Paludi, 2012; Kreager et al., 2016).

Just how well dating serves such functions, particularly the development of psychological intimacy, is an open question. What specialists in adolescence do know, however, is surprising: Dating in early and middle adolescence is not terribly successful at facilitating intimacy. On the contrary, dating is often a superficial activity in which the participants so rarely let down their guards that they never become truly close and never expose themselves emotionally to each other. Psychological intimacy may be lacking even when sexual activity is part of the relationship (Collins, 2003; Furman & Shaffer, 2003; Tuggle, Kerpelman, & Pittman, 2014).

True intimacy becomes more common during later adolescence. At that point, the dating relationship may be taken more seriously by both participants, and it may be seen as a way to select a mate and as a potential prelude to marriage.

For gay and lesbian adolescents, dating presents special challenges. In some cases, blatant homophobic prejudice expressed by classmates may lead gays and lesbians to date members of the other sex in an effort to fit in. If they do seek relationships with other gays and lesbians, they may find it difficult to find partners who are comfortable openly expressing their sexual orientation. Homosexual couples who do openly date face possible harassment, making the development of a relationship all the more difficult (Savin-Williams, 2003).

**DATING, RACE, AND ETHNICITY.** Culture influences dating patterns among adolescents of different racial and ethnic groups, particularly those whose parents have immigrated to the United States from other countries. Parents may try to control their children's dating behavior in an effort to preserve their culture's traditional values or to ensure that their child dates within his or her racial or ethnic group.

For example, Asian parents may be especially conservative in their attitudes and values, in part because they themselves may have had no experience of dating. (In many cases, the parents' marriage was arranged by others, and the entire concept of dating is unfamiliar.) They may insist that dating be conducted with chaperones, or not at all. As a consequence, they may find themselves involved in substantial conflict with their children (Hoelterk, Axinn, & Ghimire, 2004; Lau et al., 2009).

**TEEN DATING VIOLENCE.** Violence is part of a surprising number of adolescent dating relationships. Surveys show that 10 percent of high school students reported physical victimization and 10 percent reported sexual victimization from a dating partner in the previous 10 months (Vagi et al., 2015).

There are many causes of violence. Among the risk factors is the belief that violence is acceptable, involvement in early sexual activity, depression and anxiety, and other symptoms of trauma. In some cases, adolescents believe that teasing or name calling are simply normal parts of relationships (Vagi et al., 2013).

Dating violence produces both short- and long-term negative consequences. Experiencing dating violence can cause depression, anxiety, and increased use of drugs, tobacco, and alcohol. It can also lead to involvement in antisocial behaviors and suicidal thoughts (CDC, 2016).

# Sexual Relationships

**LO 16.12 List the types of sexual activities in which adolescents engage.**

The hormonal changes of puberty bring the maturation of the sexual organs and a new range of feelings and possibilities in relations with others: sexuality. Sexual behavior and thoughts are among the central concerns of adolescents. Almost all adolescents think about sex, and many think about it a good deal of the time (Kelly, 2001; Ponton, 2001).

**MASTURBATION.** The first type of sex in which adolescents engage is often solitary sexual self-stimulation or **masturbation**. By age 15, some 80 percent of teenage boys and 20 percent of teenage girls report that they have masturbated. Masturbation in boys occurs more frequently in the early teens and then begins to decline, whereas in girls, the frequency is lower initially and increases throughout adolescence. In addition, patterns of masturbation frequency show differences according to race. For example, African American men and women masturbate less than Whites do (Schwartz, 1999; Hyde & DeLamater, 2004).

Although masturbation is widespread, it still may produce feelings of shame and guilt. There are several reasons for this. One is that adolescents may believe that masturbation signifies the inability to find a sexual partner—an erroneous assumption, because statistics show that three-fourths of married men and 68 percent of married women report masturbating between 10 and 24 times a year (Davidson, Darling, & Norton, 1995; Das, 2007; Gerressu et al., 2008).

For some, the sense of shame about masturbation is the result of a lingering legacy of misguided views of masturbation. For instance, 19th-century physicians and laypersons warned of the supposed horrible effects of masturbation, including "dyspepsia, spinal disease, headache, epilepsy, various kinds of fits … impaired eyesight, palpitation of the heart, pain in the side and bleeding at the lungs, spasm of the heart, and sometimes sudden death" (Gregory, 1856). Suggested remedies included bandaging the genitals, covering them with a cage, tying the hands, male circumcision without anesthesia (so that it might better be remembered), and for girls, the administration of carbolic acid to the clitoris. One physician, J. W. Kellogg, believed that certain grains would be less likely to provoke sexual excitation—a belief that led to his invention of corn flakes (Hunt, 1974; Michael et al., 1994).

The reality of masturbation is different. Today, experts on sexual behavior view it as a normal, healthy, and harmless activity. Some suggest that it provides a useful way to learn about one's own sexuality (Levin, 2007; Hyde & DeLamater, 2010).

**SEXUAL INTERCOURSE.** Although it may be preceded by many different types of sexual intimacy, including deep kissing, massaging, petting, and oral sex, sexual intercourse remains a major milestone in the perceptions of most adolescents. Consequently, the main focus of researchers investigating sexual behavior has been on the act of heterosexual intercourse.

The average age at which adolescents first have sexual intercourse has been steadily declining over the past 50 years, and about 13 percent of adolescents have had sex before age 15. Overall, the average age of first sexual intercourse is 17, and around 70 percent of adolescents have had sex before age 20. At the same time, though, many teenagers are postponing sex, and the number of adolescents who say they have never had sexual intercourse increased by 13 percent from 1991 to 2007 (MMWR, 2008; Guttmacher Institute, 2012).

There also are racial and ethnic differences in the timing of initial sexual intercourse: African Americans generally have sex for the first time earlier than Puerto Ricans, who have sex earlier than Whites. These racial and ethnic differences likely reflect differences in socioeconomic conditions, cultural values, and family structure (Singh & Darroch, 2000; Hyde, Mezulis, & Abramson, 2008).

It is impossible to consider sexual activities without also looking at the societal norms governing sexual conduct. The prevailing norm several decades ago was the *double standard* in which premarital sex was considered permissible for men but not for women. Women were told by society that "nice girls don't," whereas men heard that premarital sex was permissible—although they should be sure to marry virgins.

Today, the double standard has begun to give way to a new norm, called *permissiveness with affection*. According to this standard, premarital intercourse is viewed as permissible for both men and women if it occurs in the context of a long-term, committed, or loving relationship (Hyde & DeLamater, 2004; Earle et al., 2007).

The demise of the double standard is far from complete; attitudes toward sexual conduct are still typically more lenient for men than for women, even in relatively socially liberal cultures. And in some cultures, the standards for men and women are quite distinct. For example, in North Africa, the Middle East, and the majority of Asian countries, most women conform to societal norms suggesting that they abstain from sexual intercourse until they are married. In Mexico, where there are strict standards against premarital sex, men are also considerably more likely than women to have premarital sex. In contrast, in sub-Saharan Africa,

**masturbation** Sexual self-stimulation

women are more likely to have sexual intercourse prior to marriage, and intercourse is common among unmarried teenage women (Johnson et al., 1992; Peltzer & Pengpid, 2006; Wellings et al., 2006; Ghule, Balaiah, & Joshi, 2007).

## Sexual Orientation: Heterosexual, Homosexual, Bisexual, and Transsexual

**LO 16.13** Explain the types of sexual orientation and how sexual orientation develops.

When we consider adolescents' sexual development, the most frequent pattern is *heterosexuality*, sexual attraction and behavior directed to the other sex. Yet some teenagers are *homosexual*— attracted to members of their own sex. (Most male homosexuals prefer the term *gay* and female homosexuals the label *lesbian*, because they refer to a broader array of attitudes and lifestyles than the term *homosexual*, which focuses on the sexual act.) Other people find they are *bisexual*— sexually attracted to people of both sexes.

Many teens experiment with homosexuality. At one time or another, around 20 percent to 25 percent of adolescent boys and 10 percent of adolescent girls have at least one same-sex sexual encounter. In fact, homosexuality and heterosexuality are not completely distinct sexual orientations. Alfred Kinsey, a pioneer sex researcher, argued that sexual orientation should be viewed as a continuum in which "exclusively homosexual" is at one end and "exclusively heterosexual" is at the other (Kinsey, Pomeroy, & Martin, 1948). In between are people who show both homosexual and heterosexual behavior. Although accurate figures are difficult to obtain, most experts believe that between 4 percent and 10 percent of both men and women are exclusively homosexual during extended periods of their lives (Michael et al., 1994; Diamond, 2003a, 2003b; Russell & Consolacion, 2003; Pearson & Wilkinson, 2013).

The determination of sexual orientation is further complicated by distinctions between sexual orientation and gender identity. While sexual orientation relates to the object of one's sexual interests, *gender identity* is the gender a person believes he or she is psychologically. Sexual orientation and gender identity are not necessarily related to one another: A man who has a strong masculine gender identity may be attracted to other men. Consequently, the extent to which men and women enact traditional "masculine" or "feminine" behavior is not necessarily related to their sexual orientation or gender identity (Hunter & Mallon, 2000; Greydanus & Pratt, 2016).

Some individuals identify as transsexuals. *Transsexuals* feel that they are trapped in the body of the other gender. Transsexualism represents a gender issue involving one's sexual identity.

Transsexuals may seek sex-change operations, in which their genitals are surgically removed and the genitals of the desired sex are created. It is a difficult path, one involving counseling, hormone injections, and living as a member of the desired sex for several years prior to surgery. Ultimately, though, the outcome can be very positive.

Transsexuals are different from individuals who are called *intersex* or the older term *hermaphrodite*. An intersex person is born with an atypical combination of sexual organs or chromosomal or gene patterns. For instance, they may be born with both male and female sex organs, or ambiguous organs. Only 1 in 4,500 births are intersex infants (Diamond, 2003b).

The factors that induce people to develop as heterosexual, homosexual, bisexual, or transsexual are not well understood. Evidence suggests that genetic and biological factors may play an important role. Studies of twins show that identical twins are more likely to both be homosexual than pairs of siblings who don't share their genetic makeup. Other research finds that various structures of the brain are different in homosexuals and heterosexuals, and that hormone production also seems to be linked to sexual orientation (Ellis et al., 2008; Fitzgerald, 2008; Santilla et al., 2008).

Still other researchers have suggested that family or peer environmental factors play a role. For example, Sigmund Freud argued that homosexuality was the result of inappropriate identification with the opposite-sex parent (Freud, 1922/1959). The difficulty with Freud's theoretical perspective and other, similar perspectives that followed is that there simply is no evidence to suggest that any particular family dynamic or childrearing practice is consistently related to sexual orientation. Similarly, explanations based on learning theory, which suggest that homosexuality arises because of rewarding, pleasant homosexual experiences and unsatisfying heterosexual ones, do not appear to be the complete answer (Isay, 1990; Golombok & Taker, 1996).

In short, there is no fully accepted explanation of why adolescents develop a particular sexual orientation. Most experts believe that sexual orientation evolves out of a complex interplay of genetic, physiological, and environmental factors (LeVay & Valente, 2003).

What is clear is that adolescents with a nontraditional sexual orientation may face a more difficult time than other teens. U.S. society still harbors ignorance and prejudice regarding homosexuality and transsexuality, persisting in the belief that people have a choice in the matter. Gay, lesbian, and transsexual teens may be rejected by their family or peers, or even harassed and assaulted if they are open about their orientation. The result is that gay, lesbian, and transsexual adolescents are at greater risk for depression, and suicide rates are significantly higher for homosexual adolescents than for heterosexual adolescents. Gays, lesbians, and transsexuals who do not conform to gender stereotypes are particularly susceptible to victimization, and they may have lower rates of adjustment (Toomey et al., 2010; Madsen & Green, 2012; Mitchell, Ybarra, & Korchmaros, 2014).

Ultimately, however, most people are able to come to grips with their sexual orientation and become comfortable with it. Although lesbians, gays, and bisexuals may experience mental health difficulties as a result of the stress, prejudice, and discrimination they face, homosexuality is not considered a psychological disorder by any major psychological or medical associations. All of them endorse efforts to reduce discrimination against homosexuals. Furthermore, society's attitudes toward homosexuality are changing, particularly among younger individuals. For example, a majority of U.S. citizens support gay marriage, which became legal in the United States in 2015 (Baker & Sussman, 2012; Farr & Patterson, 2013; Hu, Xu & Tornello, 2016).

## Teenage Pregnancies

**LO 16.14** **Describe the challenges of teen pregnancy and prevention programs.**

*It was a one-night stand that changed 17-year-old Malti, who eloped with her boyfriend and stayed in a rented house in Shastri Vihar. Everything went well and after one month, Malti realized that she had not taken either birth control pills or any other prevention and now she is pregnant. They were going through a lot of hardship as both of them were studying and had not taken up any employment. Malti had to quit school and take care of her baby. It's hard for her and her boyfriend to take so much of responsibility.*

Often the terms "teenage pregnancy" and "adolescent pregnancy" are used as synonyms. World Health Organization (2006) defines teenage pregnancy as "any pregnancy from a girl who is 10–19 years of age," the age being defined as her age at the time the baby is born (WHO, 2004). According to UNICEF (2001), worldwide every fifth child is born to teenage mother. Globally, 13 million births each year is reported by girls younger than 19 years. The incidence of teenage pregnancies varies from country to country.

Teenage pregnancies are considered problematic because complications from pregnancy and childbirth are the leading causes of death in teenage girls aging between 15 and 19 years in developing countries. It is estimated that 70,000 female teenagers die each year because they are pregnant before they are physically mature enough for successful motherhood (Mayor, 2004).

In the developing countries, adolescent marriage and adolescent fertility rates are disturbingly high. Unlike in most other countries, adolescent fertility in India occurs mainly within the context of marriage. As a result of early marriage, about half of all young women are sexually active by the time they are 18 years; and almost one in five by the time they are 15 (Jejeebhoy, 1998, p.1286).

Women married as minors are more likely than those married as adults to report early, frequent, and unplanned pregnancies (typically as a consequence of non-contraceptive use), which have been consistently linked to increased risk for maternal and infant morbidity and mortality (UNICEF, 2007,2008; UNFPA 2005). India is one of the 10 countries with the greatest numbers (11,875,182) of women aged 20—24 who give birth by age of 18 (UNFPA, 2013).

India, being the largest and most prosperous nation within South Asia, has maintained laws against child marriage since 1929, although at that time, the legal age of marriage was set at 12 years. Though, the legal age for marriage was increased to 18 years for girls in 1978, till date, marriage of adolescent girls below their legal age is still prevalent in the country (Raj et al., 2009, p.2).

Several factors explain the drop in teenage pregnancies:

- New initiatives have raised awareness among teenagers of the risks of unprotected sex. For example, about two-thirds of high schools in the

United States have established comprehensive sex education programs (Villarosa, 2003; Corcoran & Pillai, 2007).

- The rates of sexual intercourse among teenagers have declined. The percentage of teenage girls who have ever had sexual intercourse dropped from 51 percent in 1988 to 43 percent in 2006–2010 (Martinez, Copen, & Abma, 2011).

- The use of condoms and other forms of contraception has increased. For example, virtually all sexually experienced girls age 15 to 19 have used some method of contraception (Martinez, Copen, & Abma, 2011).

- Substitutes for sexual intercourse are more prevalent. For example, oral sex, which many teenagers do not even consider "sex," is increasingly viewed as an alternative to sexual intercourse (Bernstein, 2004; Chandra et al., 2011).

**THE CHALLENGES OF TEENAGE PREGNANCY.** Even with the decline in the birth rate for U.S. teenagers, the rate of teenage pregnancy in the United States is 2 to 10 times higher than that of other industrialized countries. For example, teenagers in the United States are two times more likely to become pregnant than Canadian teenagers, four times more likely than French teenagers, and six times more likely than Swedish teenagers (Singh & Darroch, 2000).

The results of an unintended pregnancy can be devastating to both mother and child. In comparison to earlier times, teenage mothers today are much less likely to be married. In a high percentage of cases, mothers care for their children without the help of the father. Without financial or emotional support, a mother may have to abandon her own education, and consequently she may be relegated to unskilled, poorly paying jobs for the rest of her life. In other cases, she may develop long-term dependency on welfare. An adolescent mother's physical and mental health may suffer as she faces unrelenting stress due to continual demands on her time (Manlove et al., 2004; Lall, 2007; Kelly, 2013).

These difficulties also affect the children of teenage mothers. They are more likely to suffer from poor health and to show poorer school performance when compared to children of older mothers. Later, they are more likely to become teenage parents themselves, participating in a cycle of pregnancy and poverty from which it is very difficult to extricate themselves (Spencer, 2001; East, Reyes, & Horn, 2007).

**VIRGINITY PLEDGES.** One thing that apparently *hasn't* led to a reduction in teenage pregnancies is asking adolescents to take a virginity pledge. Public pledges to refrain from premarital sex—a centerpiece of some forms of sex education—have a mixed record. Initial studies of virginity pledges were promising, showing that adolescents who took a pledge to defer sexual intercourse until marriage delayed sex about 18 months longer than those who had never taken such a pledge (Bearman & Bruckner, 2004).

But even this early research called virginity pledges into question. For example, the effectiveness of pledging depended on a student's age. For older adolescents (18 years old and above), taking a pledge had no effect. Pledges were effective only for 16- and 17-year-olds. Furthermore, the pledges worked only when a minority of people in a school took such a pledge. When more than 30 percent took such a pledge, the effectiveness of the pledge diminished substantially.

The reason for this surprising finding relates to why virginity pledges might work: They offer adolescents a sense of identity, similar to the way joining a club does. When a minority of students take a virginity pledge, they feel part of a special group, and they are more likely to adhere to the norms of that group—in this case, remaining a virgin. In contrast, if a majority of students take a pledge of virginity, the pledge becomes less unique, and adherence is less likely.

Most recent research finds that virginity pledges are ineffective. For example, in one study of 12,000 teenagers, 88 percent reported eventually having sexual intercourse, although taking a pledge did delay the start of sex (Bearman & Bruckner, 2004).

Because abstinence programs have not been successful, some researchers have called for more comprehensive education programs to replace ones that focus on abstinence as the only option. Most parents and teachers agree that abstinence education should be emphasized, but that information on contraception and safer sex practices should be included as well. Research supports these beliefs: While abstinence-only programs and programs that include contraception education do not clearly differ in their effects on adolescents' sexual activity, the addition of contraception education does improve adolescents' understanding and use of birth-control strategies (Dailard, 2001; Manlove et al., 2002; Bennett & Assefi, 2005; Giami et al., 2006; Santelli et al., 2006).

*Safer Choices*, a 2-year program for adolescents in high school, is one such program that combines encouragement of abstinence with education on contraceptive use. Its goals are to reduce the number of students who are sexually active while in high school and to increase condom usage in students who do have sex by addressing adolescent sexual activity on multiple fronts. The program attempts to modify students' attitudes and norms about sexual behavior, abstinence, and condom use (including adolescents' perceived barriers to condom use). It also addresses students' confidence in their ability to refuse sex, to discuss safer sex with their partners, and to use a condom, and it teaches students about sexually transmitted infections (STIs) and their risks of infection. Finally, the program seeks to improve students' communication with their parents about sex (Advocates for Youth, 2003; Kirby et al., 2004).

# The Case of …
## Too Much of a Good Thing

Bala Pandit was the eldest child in a close-knit family of five. He parents took pride in the fact that the family spent all their weekends together, hiking, gardening, or going to the movies. They assumed this would always be true, and Bala himself was happy to bask in so much familial love—until the year he turned 13. That was the year he entered middle school and his whole world changed.

Bala discovered he had lots of interests. He joined the drama at his school and painted scenery for student productions. On weekends, he went to the mall and the movies with friends.

"We never see you anymore," his parents complained. At first, Bala shrugged it off, but when his parents began to criticize everything from the clothes he wore to the music he preferred, he got annoyed. When they began scrutinizing his friends and calling his cellphone every hour to see whom he was with and where he was, he became enraged. "You just won't let me have a life!" he shouted when they demanded he cancel plans with friends to spend weekend time with the family. Deep down, Bala knew his parents loved him, and he still loved them, but increasingly he felt a strong need to escape their complaints and restraints.

1. How do the changes in Bala reflect normal social development in adolescence?
2. What specific advice would you give Bala's parents to help ease the conflict with their daughter?
3. Do you feel Bala is exercising an appropriate level of autonomy and independence for his age? Why or why not?
4. Given what we know about social and personality development in adolescence, what changes would you expect to occur in Bala's relationship with his parents over the next 5 years?
5. Do you think Bala and his parents are experiencing a true generation gap? Why or why not?

# Epilogue

We continued our consideration of adolescence in this chapter, looking at social and personality issues. Self-concept, self-esteem, and identity develop during adolescence, which can be a period of self-discovery. We looked at adolescents' relationships with family and peers, and at gender, race, and ethnic relations during adolescence. Our discussion concluded with a look at dating, sexuality, and sexual orientation.

Recall the prologue about Ruhi Bajaj and the confusion she was experiencing over her identity. Consider the following questions.

1. What gender pressures does Ruhi face? How might her experience be different if she were a boy?
2. What do you think Ruhi's self-esteem has been based on in adolescence? How do you see this changing in her current assessment of her life?
3. Ruhi seems to be experiencing identity confusion. What risks does she face if she cannot resolve the question of who she is?
4. Ruhi has always made certain she is part of a clique. What price do you think she has paid for her need to belong?

# Looking Back

**LO 16.1 Explain how the development of self-concept and self-esteem proceeds during adolescence.**

- During adolescence, self-concept differentiates to encompass others' views as well as one's own and to include multiple aspects simultaneously. Differentiation of self-concept can cause confusion, as behaviors reflect a complex definition of the self.

- Adolescents also differentiate their self-esteem, evaluating particular aspects of themselves differently.

- Issues of identity become increasingly important during adolescence because adolescent intellectual capacities become more like those of adults.

- Adolescents are better able to see how they compare to others and become aware that they are individuals, separate from their parents, peers, and others.

**LO 16.2 Describe how Erikson's theory of identity formation proceeds through adolescence.**

- According to Erik Erikson, adolescents are in the identity-versus-identity-confusion stage, seeking to discover their individuality and identity. They may become confused and exhibit dysfunctional reactions, and they may rely on friends and peers for help and information more than on adults.

- One criticism of Erikson's theory is that it employs male identity development, which stresses competitiveness and individuality, as the standard for both men and women. Carol Gilligan suggests that women develop identity in the context of building and maintaining relationships.

**LO 16.3 Explain the categories of adolescent identity according to Marcia.**

- James Marcia identifies four identity statuses that individuals may experience in adolescence and in later life: identity achievement, identity foreclosure, identity diffusion, and moratorium.

- An adolescent's identity status is related to the absence or presence of two characteristics, crisis and commitment. An adolescent may move between statuses even into adulthood.

**LO 16.4 Describe the roles that religion and spirituality play in identity formation.**

- Increased cognitive abilities allow teenagers to think more abstractly about religious matters. They may draw more closely to their religious affiliation if they have one, change their religious affiliation, or reject formal religion entirely. Many adolescents who consider themselves to be spiritual individuals are not affiliated with any particular religion.

**LO 16.5 Illustrate the challenges that ethnic and minority groups face in establishing identities.**

- The traditional cultural assimilation model holds that individual cultural identities must be assimilated into a unified culture, while the pluralistic society model stresses that diverse cultural groups are coequal and their individual cultural features must be preserved. A third increasingly popular model allows minority group members to form a bicultural identity, drawing on their own cultural identity while integrating themselves into the dominant culture.

**LO 16.6 Identify the factors that contribute to psychological difficulties.**

- Many adolescents have feelings of sadness and hopelessness, and some experience major depression. Biological, environmental, and social factors contribute to depression, and there are gender, ethnic, and racial differences in its occurrence.

- The rate of adolescent suicide is rising, with suicide now the second most common cause of death in the 15- to 24-year-old age bracket.

- Risk factors for suicide among teens include depression, perfectionism, social inhibition, and high levels of stress and anxiety. The easy availability of guns in the United States also contributes to the suicide rate.

**LO 16.7 Explain how family relationships change during adolescence.**

- Adolescents' quest for autonomy often brings confusion and tension to their relationships with their parents, but the actual "generation gap" between parents' and teenagers' attitudes is usually small.

**LO 16.8  Describe how peer relationships change during adolescence.**

- Peers are important during adolescence because they provide social comparison and reference groups against which to judge social success. Relationships among adolescents are characterized by the need to belong.

- During adolescence, boys and girls begin to spend time together in groups and pair off toward the end of adolescence.

**LO 16.9  Describe popularity and responses to peer pressure.**

- Degrees of popularity during adolescence include popular and controversial adolescents (on the high end of popularity) and neglected and rejected adolescents (on the low end).

- Peer pressure is not a simple phenomenon. Adolescents conform to their peers in areas in which they feel their peers are expert and to adults in areas of adult expertise. As adolescents grow in confidence, their conformity to both peers and adults declines.

**LO 16.10  Explain how some adolescents become involved in criminal activity.**

- Although most adolescents do not commit crimes, they are disproportionately involved in criminal activities.

- Undersocialized delinquents were raised with little discipline or harsh parenting and were not taught standards of conduct. Socialized delinquents understand and generally follow the rules of society. The transgressions they commit during adolescence tend to be petty and do not continue into adulthood.

**LO 16.11  Summarize the functions and characteristics of dating during adolescence.**

- During adolescence, dating provides intimacy, entertainment, and prestige. Achieving psychological intimacy, though difficult at first, becomes easier as adolescents mature, gain confidence, and take relationships more seriously.

**LO 16.12  List the types of sexual activities in which adolescents engage.**

- For most adolescents, masturbation is often the first step into sexuality. The age of first intercourse, which is now in the teens, has declined as the double standard has faded and the norm of permissiveness with affection has gained ground; in addition, the overall rate of sexual intercourse has declined.

**LO 16.13  Explain the types of sexual orientation and how sexual orientation develops.**

- Sexual orientation develops out of a complex interplay of genetic, physiological, and environmental factors.

**LO 16.14  Describe the challenges of teen pregnancy and prevention programs.**

- Teenage mothers are likely to raise their child without emotional or financial help from the father. Many have to abandon their education, which may lead to a lifetime of unskilled, poorly paid jobs.

- Virginity pledges and other abstinence-only programs have not proven effective. By contrast, programs that emphasize the dangers of unprotected sex and give teens information on contraceptive use—while they do not prevent adolescent sexual activity—do improve teens' use of birth-control strategies.

# Key Terms and Concepts

identity-versus-identity-confusion stage (p. 418)
identity achievement (p. 419)
identity foreclosure (p. 420)
moratorium (p. 420)
identity diffusion (p. 420)
autonomy (p. 426)
generation gap (p. 428)
reference groups (p. 429)
cliques (p. 430)
crowds (p. 430)
sex cleavage (p. 430)
controversial adolescents (p. 431)
rejected adolescents (p. 431)
neglected adolescents (p. 431)
peer pressure (p. 434)
undersocialized delinquents (p. 435)
socialized delinquents (p. 435)
masturbation (p. 437)

# Putting It All Together

## Adolescence

**Physical, Cognitive, and Social and Personality Development in Adolescence**

*An adolescent can change from a seemingly "together" teenager to a troubled youth and then to an increasingly confident and independent person. Early in adolescence, the struggle to define oneself can lead to some decidedly unwise choices. An adolescent may dabble with drugs and alcohol. Depression and suicide are also high risks for this age group. Adolescents seeking help for their difficulties may kick their bad habits, begin to work on their self-concept, and enter into positive relationships with family and friends.*

### Physical Development

- Adolescents have many physical issues to deal with (p. 350).
- Some adolescents resort to drugs as a strategy for coping with the stresses of the period (p. 363).
- Adolescent brain development permits adolescents to engage in complex thinking, which can sometimes lead to confusion (p. 358).
- Many adolescents display a lack of impulse control, which is typical of a not yet fully developed prefrontal cortex (p. 359).

### Cognitive Development

- Adolescents' personal fables include a sense of invulnerability, which contributes to their impulsive decisions (p. 379).
- Depression may stem from the adolescent tendency toward introspection and self-consciousness (p. 379).
- A declining interest in school and academics may be attributable to depression (p. 384).
- It is not unusual for an adolescent to have school difficulties (p. 383).

### Social and Personality Development

- Adolescents' struggles with identity represent the characteristic internal conflict of adolescence (p. 400).
- In balancing friendships with the desire to be alone, adolescents struggle to accommodate an increasingly complex personality (p. 402).
- A more accurate self-concept may in fact lower an adolescent's self-esteem (p. 400).
- In relying on peers, adolescents often define their identity in terms of a questionable reference group (p. 412).
- There is a higher incidence of depression among adolescent girls (p. 406).
- Most adolescents are eventually successful at establishing a more mature connection with their parents and begin to assume true independence (p. 409).

### From a PARENT'S perspective:

- What warning signs should parents watch for to protect their adolescent from depression and suicide? Is there anything they can do?

    HINT: Review pages 406–408.

### From a SOCIAL WORKER'S perspective:

- When an adolescent shows a definite decline in academic performance, are the symptoms likely to be interpreted differently depending on whether the adolescent comes from an affluent or impoverished background? How can a professional care provider prevent different interpretation and treatment?

    HINT: Review pages 385–387.

### From an EDUCATOR'S perspective:

- What signals might a teacher observe in a student's classroom performance to suggest that he or she is having a drug problem? What steps might the teacher take?

    HINT: Review pages 363–366.

### From YOUR perspective:

- If your friend was depressed and possibly suicidal, what advice and support would you give her to prevent a suicide attempt? What advice and support would you provide during her recovery from depression or an attempted suicide?

    HINT: Review pages 406–408.

# Glossary

**Abstract modeling**   The process in which modeling paves the way for the development of more general rules and principles

**Acceleration**   The provision of special programs that allow gifted students to move ahead at their own pace, even if this means skipping to higher grade levels

**Accommodation**   Changes in existing ways of thinking that occur in response to encounters with new stimuli or events

**Addictive drugs**   Drugs that produce a biological or psychological dependence in users, leading to increasingly powerful cravings for them

**Adolescence**   The developmental stage between childhood and adulthood

**Adolescent egocentrism**   A state of self-absorption in which the world is viewed from one's own point of view

**Adolescent growth spurt**   A period of very rapid growth in height and weight during adolescence

**Affordances**   The action possibilities that a given situation or stimulus provides

**Agentic professions**   Occupations associated with getting things accomplished

**Aggression**   Intentional injury or harm to another person

**Ainsworth Strange Situation**   A sequence of staged episodes that illustrates the strength of attachment between a child and (typically) his or her mother

**Alcoholics**   People who have learned to depend on alcohol and are unable to control their drinking

**Ambivalent attachment pattern**   A style of attachment in which children display a combination of positive and negative reactions to their mothers; they show great distress when the mother leaves, but upon her return they may simultaneously seek close contact but also hit and kick her

**Amniocentesis**   The process of identifying genetic defects by examining a small sample of fetal cells drawn by a needle inserted into the amniotic fluid surrounding the unborn fetus

**Anorexia nervosa**   A severe and potentially life-threatening eating disorder in which individuals refuse to eat, while denying that their behavior or skeletal appearance is out of the ordinary

**Anoxia**   A restriction of oxygen to the baby, lasting a few minutes during the birth process, which can produce brain damage

**Apgar scale**   A standard measurement system that looks for a variety of indications of good health in newborns

**Applied research**   Research meant to provide practical solutions to immediate problems

**Artificial insemination**   A process of fertilization in which a man's sperm is placed directly into a woman's vagina by a physician

**Assimilation**   The process in which people understand an experience in terms of their current stage of cognitive development and way of thinking

**Associative play**   Play in which two or more children interact by sharing or borrowing toys or materials, although they do not do the same thing

**Asthma**   A chronic condition characterized by periodic attacks of wheezing, coughing, and shortness of breath

**Attachment**   The positive emotional bond that develops between a child and a particular individual

**Attention-deficit/hyperactivity disorder (ADHD)**   A learning disorder marked by inattention, impulsiveness, a low tolerance for frustration, and a great deal of inappropriate activity

**Auditory impairment**   A special need that involves the loss of hearing or some aspect of hearing

**Authoritarian parents**   Parents who are controlling, punitive, rigid, and cold and whose word is law; they value strict, unquestioning obedience from their children and do not tolerate expressions of disagreement

**Authoritative parents**   Parents who are firm, setting clear and consistent limits, but try to reason with their children, explaining why they should behave in a particular way

**Autobiographical memory**   Memory of particular events from one's own life

**Autonomy**   Having independence and a sense of control over one's life

**Autonomy-versus-shame-and-doubt stage**   The period during which, according to Erik Erikson, toddlers (age 18 months to 3 years) develop independence and autonomy if they are allowed the freedom to explore, or shame and self-doubt if they are restricted and overprotected

**Avoidant attachment pattern**   A style of attachment in which children do not seek proximity to the mother; after the mother has left, they seem to avoid her when she returns as if they are angered by her behavior

**Babbling**   Making speechlike but meaningless sounds

**Bayley Scales of Infant Development**   A measure that evaluates an infant's development from 2 to 42 months

**Behavior modification**   A formal technique for promoting the frequency of desirable behaviors and decreasing the incidence of unwanted ones

**Behavioral genetics**   The study of the effects of heredity on behavior

**Behavioral perspective**   The approach to the study of development that suggests that the keys to understanding development are observable behavior and outside stimuli in the environment

**Bicultural identity**   The maintenance of one's original cultural identity while becoming integrated into the majority culture

**Bilingualism**   The ability to speak two languages

**Binge eating disorder** An eating disorder in which individuals eat large quantities of food, often very quickly and often to the point of discomfort, and experience a loss of control and shame

**Bioecological approach** The perspective that suggests that different levels of the environment simultaneously influence every biological organism

**Blended family** A remarried couple that has at least one stepchild living with them

**Bonding** Close physical and emotional contact between parent and child during the period immediately following birth, argued by some to affect later relationship strength

**Brazelton Neonatal Behavioral Assessment Scale (NBAS)** A measure designed to determine infants' neurological and behavioral responses to their environment

**Bulimia** An eating disorder that primarily afflicts adolescent girls and young women, characterized by binges on large quantities of food followed by purges of the food through vomiting or the use of laxatives

**Case studies** Extensive, in-depth interviews with a particular individual or small group of individuals

**Centration** The process of concentrating on one limited aspect of a stimulus and ignoring other aspects

**Cephalocaudal principle** The principle that growth follows a pattern that begins with the head and upper body parts and then proceeds down to the rest of the body

**Cerebral cortex** The upper layer of the brain

**Cesarean delivery** A birth in which the baby is surgically removed from the uterus, rather than traveling through the birth canal

**Child abuse** The physical or psychological maltreatment or neglect of children

**Child development** The field that involves the scientific study of the patterns of growth, change, and stability that occur from conception through adolescence

**Child neglect** Ignoring one's children or being emotionally unresponsive to them

**Childhood-onset fluency disorder (stuttering)** Substantial disruption in the rhythm and fluency of speech; the most common speech impairment

**Chorionic villus sampling (CVS)** A test used to find genetic defects; involves taking samples of hair-like material that surrounds the embryo

**Chromosomes** Rod-shaped portions of DNA that are organized in 23 pairs

**Chronological (physical) age** A person's age according to the calendar

**Classical conditioning** A type of learning in which an organism responds in a particular way to a neutral stimulus that normally does not bring about that type of response

**Cliques** Groups of from 2 to 12 people whose members have frequent social interactions with one another

**Cognitive development** Development involving the ways that growth and change in intellectual capabilities influence a person's behavior

**Cognitive neuroscience approaches** Approaches to the study of cognitive development that focus on how brain processes are related to cognitive activity

**Cognitive perspective** The approach to the study of development that focuses on the processes that allow people to know, understand, and think about the world

**Cohort** A group of people born at around the same time in the same place

**Collectivistic orientation** A philosophy that promotes the notion of interdependence

**Communal professions** Occupations associated with relationships

**Concrete operational stage** The period of cognitive development between 7 and 12 years of age, characterized by the active and appropriate use of logic

**Conservation** The knowledge that quantity is unrelated to the arrangement and physical appearance of objects

**Constructive play** Play in which children manipulate objects to produce or build something

**Contextual perspective** The perspective that considers the relationship between individuals and their physical, cognitive, personality, social, and physical worlds

**Continuous change** Gradual development in which achievements at one level build on those of previous levels

**Control group** The group in an experiment that receives either no treatment or an alternative treatment

**Controversial adolescents** Children who are liked by some peers and disliked by others

**Cooperative play** Play in which children genuinely interact with one another, taking turns, playing games, or devising contests

**Coping** Efforts to control, reduce, or tolerate the threats and challenges that lead to stress

**Coregulation** A period in which parents and children jointly control children's behavior

**Correlational research** Research that seeks to identify whether an association or relationship between two factors exists

**Critical period** A specific time during development when a particular event has its greatest consequences

**Cross-sectional research** Research in which people of different ages are compared at the same point in time

**Crowds** Groups larger than cliques, composed of individuals who share particular characteristics but who may not interact with one another

**Crystallized intelligence** The accumulation of information, skills, and strategies that people have learned through experience and that they can apply in problem-solving situations

**Cultural assimilation model** The view of American society as a "melting pot" in which all cultures are amalgamated into a unique, unified American culture

**Cycle-of-violence hypothesis** The theory that abuse and neglect that children suffer predispose them as adults to abuse and neglect their own children

**Decentering** The ability to take multiple aspects of a situation into account

**Deferred imitation** An act in which a person who is no longer present is imitated by children who have witnessed a similar act

**Dependent variable** The variable in an experiment measured and expected to change as a result of the experimental manipulation

**Developmental quotient** An overall developmental score that relates to performance in four domains: motor skills, language use, adaptive behavior, and personal-social

**Developmentally appropriate educational practice** Education based on both typical development and the unique characteristics of a given child

**Difficult babies** Babies who have negative moods and are slow to adapt to new situations; when confronted with a new situation, they tend to withdraw

**Discontinuous change** Development that occurs in distinct steps or stages, with each stage bringing about behavior assumed to be qualitatively different from behavior at earlier stages

**Disorganized-disoriented attachment pattern** A style of attachment in which children show inconsistent, often contradictory behavior, such as approaching the mother when she returns but not looking at her; they may be the least securely attached children of all

**Dizygotic twins** Twins who are produced when two separate ova are fertilized by two separate sperm at roughly the same time

**DNA (deoxyribonucleic acid) molecules** The substance that genes are composed of that determines the nature of every cell in the body and how it will function

**Dominance hierarchy** Rankings that represent the relative social power of those in a group

**Dominant trait** The one trait expressed when two competing traits are present

**Down syndrome** A disorder produced by the presence of an extra chromosome on the 21st pair; once referred to as *mongolism*

**Dynamic systems theory** A theory of how motor skills develop and are coordinated

**Easy babies** Babies who have a positive disposition; their body functions operate regularly, and they are adaptable

**Egocentric thought** Thinking that does not take the viewpoints of others into account

**Embryonic stage** The period from 2 to 8 weeks following fertilization during which significant growth occurs in the major organs and body systems

**Emotional intelligence** The set of skills that underlie the accurate assessment, evaluation, expression, and regulation of emotions.

**Emotional self-regulation** The capability to adjust one's emotions to a desired state and level of intensity

**Empathy** An emotional response that corresponds to the feelings of another person

**Enrichment** Approach in which gifted students are kept at grade level but are enrolled in special programs and given individual activities to allow greater depth of study on a given topic

**Episiotomy** An incision sometimes made to increase the size of the opening of the vagina to allow the baby to pass

**Erikson's theory of psychosocial development** The theory that considers how individuals come to understand themselves and the meaning of others'—and their own—behavior

**Evolutionary perspective** The theory that seeks to identify behavior that is the result of our genetic inheritance from our ancestors

**Experiment** A process in which an investigator, called an experimenter, devises two different experiences for subjects or participants

**Experimental research** Research designed to discover causal relationships between various factors

**Expressive style** A style of language use in which language is used primarily to express feelings and needs about oneself and others

**Fantasy period** According to Eli Ginzberg, the period of life when career choices are made—and discarded—without regard to skills, abilities, or available job opportunities

**Fast mapping** The process in which new words are associated with their meaning after only a brief encounter

**Fertilization** The process by which a sperm and an ovum—the male and female gametes, respectively—join to form a single new cell

**Fetal alcohol effects (FAE)** A condition in which children display some, although not all, of the problems of fetal alcohol spectrum disorder due to the mother's consumption of alcohol during pregnancy

**Fetal alcohol spectrum disorder (FASD)** Cognitive disorder caused by the pregnant mother consuming substantial quantities of alcohol during pregnancy, potentially resulting in intellectual disability and delayed growth in the child

**Fetal monitor** A device that measures the baby's heartbeat during labor

**Fetal stage** The stage that begins at about 8 weeks after conception and continues until birth

**Fetus** A developing child, from 8 weeks after conception until birth

**Field study** A research investigation carried out in a naturally occurring setting

**Fluid intelligence** Intelligence that reflects information-processing capabilities, reasoning, and memory

**Formal operational stage** The stage at which people develop the ability to think abstractly

**Fragile X syndrome** A disorder produced by injury to a gene on the X chromosome, producing mild to moderate intellectual disability

**Full inclusion** The integration of all students, even those with the most severe disabilities, into regular classes and all other aspects of school and community life

**Functional play**   Play that involves simple, repetitive activities typical of 3-year-olds

**Gametes**   The sex cells from the mother and father that form a new cell at conception

**Gender constancy**   The fact that people are permanently males or females, depending on fixed, unchangeable biological factors

**Gender identity**   The perception of oneself as male or female

**Gender schema**   A cognitive framework that organizes information relevant to gender

**Gender**   The sense of being male or female

**Generation gap**   A divide between parents and adolescents in attitudes, values, aspirations, and worldviews

**Genes**   The basic units of genetic information

**Genetic counseling**   The discipline that focuses on helping people deal with issues relating to inherited disorders

**Genotype**   The underlying combination of genetic material present (but not outwardly visible) in an organism

**Germinal stage**   The first—and shortest—stage of the prenatal period, which takes place during the first 2 weeks following conception

**Gifted and talented**   Showing evidence of high-performance capability in intellectual, creative, or artistic areas, in leadership capacity, or in specific academic fields

**Goal-directed behavior**   Behavior in which several schemas are combined and coordinated to generate a single act to solve a problem

**Goodness-of-fit**   The notion that development is dependent on the degree of match between children's temperament and the nature and demands of the environment in which they are being raised

**Grammar**   The system of rules that determine how thoughts can be expressed

**Habituation**   The decrease in the response to a stimulus that occurs after repeated presentations of the same stimulus

**Handedness**   A clear preference for the use of one hand over the other

**Heterozygous**   Inheriting from parents different forms of a gene for a given trait

**Holophrases**   One-word utterances that stand for a whole phrase, whose meaning depends on the particular context in which they are used

**Homozygous**   Inheriting from parents similar genes for a given trait

**Hypothesis**   A prediction stated in a way that permits it to be tested

**Identification**   The process in which children attempt to be similar to their parent of the same sex, incorporating the parent's attitudes and values

**Identity achievement**   The status of adolescents who commit to a particular identity following a period of crisis during which they consider various alternatives

**Identity diffusion**   The status of adolescents who consider various identity alternatives, but never commit to one or never even consider identity options in any conscious way

**Identity foreclosure**   The status of adolescents who prematurely commit to an identity without adequately exploring alternatives

**Identity-versus-identity-confusion stage**   According to Erik Erikson, the period during which teenagers seek to determine what is unique and distinctive about themselves

**Imaginary audience**   Fictitious observers who pay as much attention to adolescents' behavior as they do themselves

**In vitro fertilization (IVF)**   A procedure in which a woman's ova are removed from her ovaries, and a man's sperm are used to fertilize the ova in a laboratory

**Independent variable**   The variable in an experiment manipulated by researchers

**Individualistic orientation**   A philosophy that emphasizes personal identity and the uniqueness of the individual

**Industry-versus-inferiority stage**   According to Erik Erikson, the period from ages 6 to 12 characterized by a focus on efforts to attain competence in meeting the challenges presented by parents, peers, school, and the other complexities of the modern world

**Infant mortality**   Death within the first year of life

**Infant-directed speech**   A type of speech directed toward infants, characterized by short, simple sentences

**Infantile amnesia**   The lack of memory for experiences that occurred prior to 3 years of age

**Infertility**   The inability to conceive after 12 to 18 months of trying to become pregnant

**Information-processing approaches**   Approaches to the study of cognitive development that seek to identify the ways individuals take in, use, and store information

**Initiative-versus-guilt stage**   According to Erik Erikson, the period during which children age 3 to 6 years experience conflict between independence of action and the sometimes negative results of that action

**Instrumental aggression**   Aggression motivated by the desire to obtain a concrete goal

**Intellectual disability**   A significantly subaverage level of intellectual functioning that occurs with related limitations in two or more skill areas

**Intelligence quotient (IQ)**   A score that expresses the ratio between a person's mental and chronological ages

**Intelligence**   The capacity to understand the world, think rationally, and use resources effectively when faced with challenges

**Intuitive thought**   Thinking that reflects preschoolers' use of primitive reasoning and their avid acquisition of knowledge about the world

**Kaufman Assessment Battery for Children, Second Edition (KABC-II)**   An intelligence test that measures children's ability to integrate different stimuli simultaneously and use step-by-step thinking

**Klinefelter's syndrome**   A disorder resulting from the presence of an extra X chromosome that produces underdeveloped genitals, extreme height, and enlarged breasts

**Laboratory study** A research investigation conducted in a controlled setting explicitly designed to hold events constant

**Language** The systematic, meaningful arrangement of symbols, which provides the basis for communication

**Language-acquisition device (LAD)** A neural system of the brain hypothesized to permit understanding of language

**Lateralization** The process whereby certain functions are located more in one hemisphere of the brain than in the other

**Learning theory approach** The theory that language acquisition follows the basic laws of reinforcement and conditioning

**Least restrictive environment** The setting most similar to that of children without special needs

**Longitudinal research** Research in which the behavior of one or more individuals is measured as the subjects age

**Low-birthweight infants** Infants who weigh less than 2,500 grams (around 5½ pounds) at birth

**Mainstreaming** An educational approach in which exceptional children are integrated as much as possible into the traditional educational system and are provided with a broad range of educational alternatives

**Masturbation** Sexual self-stimulation

**Maturation** The process of the predetermined unfolding of genetic information

**Memory** The process by which information is initially recorded, stored, and retrieved

**Menarche** The onset of menstruation

**Mental age** The typical intelligence level found for people of a given chronological age

**Mental representation** An internal image of a past event or object

**Metacognition** The knowledge that people have about their own thinking processes and their ability to monitor their cognition

**Metalinguistic awareness** An understanding of one's own use of language

**Metamemory** An understanding about the processes that underlie memory that emerges and improves during middle childhood

**Mild intellectual disability** Intellectual disability with IQ scores in the range of 50 or 55 to 70

**Moderate intellectual disability** Intellectual disability with IQ scores from around 35 or 40 to 50 or 55

**Monozygotic twins** Twins who are genetically identical

**Moral development** The maturation of people's sense of justice, of what is right and wrong, and their behavior in connection with such issues

**Moratorium** The status of adolescents who may have explored various identity alternatives to some degree, but have not yet committed themselves

**Multicultural education** Education in which the goal is to help students from minority cultures develop competence in the culture of the majority group while maintaining positive group identities that build on their original cultures

**Multifactorial transmission** The determination of traits by a combination of both genetic and environmental factors in which a genotype provides a range within which a phenotype may be expressed

**Multimodal approach to perception** The approach that considers how information collected by various individual sensory systems is integrated and coordinated

**Mutual regulation model** The model in which infants and parents learn to communicate emotional states to one another and to respond appropriately

**Myelin** A fatty substance that helps insulate neurons and speeds the transmission of nerve impulses

**Nativist approach** The theory that a genetically determined, innate mechanism directs language development

**Naturalistic observation** Studies in which researchers observe some naturally occurring behavior without intervening or making changes in the situation

**Neglected adolescents** Children who receive relatively little attention from their peers in the form of either positive or negative interactions

**Neonate** The term used for newborns

**Neuron** The basic nerve cell of the nervous system

**Night terror** An intense physiological arousal that causes a child to awaken in a state of panic

**Nightmare** A vivid bad dream, usually occurring toward morning

**Nonorganic failure to thrive** A disorder in which infants stop growing due to a lack of stimulation and attention as the result of inadequate parenting

**Norms** The average performance of a large sample of children of a given age

**Obesity** A body weight more than 20 percent higher than the average weight for a person of a given age and height

**Object permanence** The concept that people and objects exist even when they cannot be seen

**Onlooker play** Action in which children simply watch others at play but do not actually participate themselves

**Operant conditioning** A form of learning in which a voluntary response is strengthened or weakened, depending on its association with positive or negative consequences

**Operations** Organized, formal, logical mental processes

**Overextension** The overly broad use of words, overgeneralizing their meaning

**Parallel play** Action in which children play with similar toys, in a similar manner, but do not interact with each other

**Peer pressure** The influence of one's peers to conform to their behavior and attitudes

**Perception** The sorting out, interpretation, analysis, and integration of stimuli involving the sense organs and the brain

**Permissive parents** Parents who provide lax and inconsistent feedback and require little of their children

**Personal fables** The view held by some adolescents that what happens to them is unique, exceptional, and shared by no one else

**Personality**   The sum total of the enduring characteristics that differentiate one individual from another

**Personality development**   Development involving the ways that the enduring characteristics that differentiate one person from another change over the life span

**Phenotype**   An observable trait; the trait that actually is seen

**Physical development**   Development involving the body's physical makeup, including the brain, nervous system, muscles, and senses, as well as the need for food, drink, and sleep

**Placenta**   A conduit between the mother and fetus, providing nourishment and oxygen via the umbilical cord

**Plasticity**   The degree to which a developing behavior or physical structure is modifiable

**Pluralistic society model**   The concept that American society is made up of diverse, coequal cultures that should preserve their individual features

**Polygenic inheritance**   Inheritance in which a combination of multiple gene pairs is responsible for the production of a particular trait

**Postmature infants**   Infants still unborn 2 weeks after the mother's due date

**Pragmatics**   The aspect of language relating to communicating effectively and appropriately with others

**Preoperational stage**   According to Jean Piaget, the stage that lasts from ages 2 to 7 during which children's use of symbolic thinking grows, mental reasoning emerges, and the use of concepts increases

**Preterm infants**   Infants who are born prior to 38 weeks after conception (also known as *premature infants*)

**Primary sex characteristics**   Characteristics associated with the development of the organs and structures of the body that directly relate to reproduction

**Principle of hierarchical integration**   The principle that simple skills typically develop separately and independently but are later integrated into more complex skills

**Principle of the independence of systems**   The principle that different body systems grow at different rates

**Private speech**   Spoken language not intended for others and is commonly used by children during the preschool years

**Profound intellectual disability**   Intellectual disability with IQ scores below 20 or 25

**Prosocial behavior**   Helping behavior that benefits others

**Proximodistal principle**   The principle that development proceeds from the center of the body outward

**Psychoanalytic theory**   The theory proposed by Sigmund Freud that suggests that unconscious forces act to determine personality and behavior

**Psychodynamic perspective**   The approach to the study of development that states behavior is motivated by inner forces, memories, and conflicts of which a person has little awareness or control

**Psychological maltreatment**   Harm to children's behavioral, cognitive, emotional, or physical functioning caused by parents or other caregivers verbally, through their actions, or through neglect

**Psychophysiological methods**   A research approach that focuses on the relationship between physiological processes and behavior

**Psychosexual development**   According to Sigmund Freud, a series of stages that children pass through in which pleasure, or gratification, is focused on a particular biological function and body part

**Psychosocial development**   The approach to the study of development that encompasses changes in the understanding individuals have of their interactions with others, of others' behavior, and of themselves as members of society

**Psychosomatic disorders**   Medical problems caused by the interaction of psychological, emotional, and physical difficulties

**Puberty**   The period during which the sexual organs mature

**Race dissonance**   The phenomenon in which minority children indicate preferences for majority values or people

**Rapid eye movement (REM) sleep**   The period of sleep found in older children and adults and associated with dreaming

**Realistic period**   The stage in late adolescence and early adulthood during which people explore career options through job experience or training, narrow their choices, and eventually make a commitment to a career

**Recessive trait**   A trait within an organism that is present but not expressed

**Reciprocal socialization**   A process in which infants' behaviors invite further responses from parents and other caregivers, which in turn bring about further responses from the infants

**Reference groups**   Groups of people with whom one compares oneself

**Referential style**   A style of language use in which language is used primarily to label objects

**Reflexes**   Unlearned, organized, involuntary responses that occur automatically in the presence of certain stimuli

**Rejected adolescents**   Children who are uniformly disliked

**Relational aggression**   Nonphysical aggression intended to hurt another person's psychological well-being

**Resilience**   The ability to overcome circumstances that place a child at high risk for psychological or physical damage

**Rhythms**   Repetitive, cyclical patterns of behavior

**Sample**   A group of participants chosen for an experiment

**Scaffolding**   The support for learning and problem solving that encourages independence and growth

**Schema**   Organized mental structure and patterns

**Scientific method**   The process of posing and answering questions using careful, controlled techniques that include systematic, orderly observation and the collection of data

**Scripts**   Broad representations in memory of events and the order in which they occur

**Secondary sex characteristics**   The visible signs of sexual maturity that do not involve the sex organs directly

**Secular trend**   A statistical tendency observed over several generations

**Secure attachment pattern**   A style of attachment in which children use the mother as a kind of home base and are at ease when she is present; when she leaves, they become upset and go to her as soon as she returns

**Self-awareness**   Knowledge of oneself

**Self-care children**   Children who let themselves into their homes after school and wait alone until their caretakers return from work; previously known as *latchkey children*

**Self-concept**   A person's identity or set of beliefs about what one is like as an individual

**Self-esteem**   An individual's overall and specific positive and negative self-evaluation

**Sensation**   The physical stimulation of the sense organs

**Sensitive period**   A specific time when organisms are particularly susceptible to certain kinds of stimuli in their environment

**Sensorimotor stage (of cognitive development)**   Jean Piaget's initial major stage of cognitive development, which can be broken down into six substages

**Separation anxiety**   The distress displayed by infants when a customary care provider departs

**Sequential studies**   Studies in which researchers examine members of a number of different age groups at several points in time

**Severe intellectual disability**   Intellectual disability with IQ scores that range from around 20 or 25 to 35 or 40

**Sex cleavage**   Sex segregation in which boys interact primarily with boys and girls primarily with girls

**Sexually transmitted infection (STI)**   A disease spread through sexual contact

**Sickle-cell anemia**   A blood disorder that gets its name from the shape of the red blood cells in those who have it

**Slow-to-warm babies**   Babies who are inactive, showing relatively calm reactions to their environment; their moods are generally negative, and they withdraw from new situations, adapting slowly

**Small-for-gestational-age infants**   Infants who, because of delayed fetal growth, weigh 90 percent (or less) of the average weight of infants of the same gestational age

**Social comparison**   The desire to evaluate one's own behavior, abilities, expertise, and opinions by comparing them to those of others

**Social competence**   The collection of social skills that permit individuals to perform successfully in social settings

**Social development**   The way in which individuals' interactions with others and their social relationships grow, change, and remain stable over the course of life

**Social problem-solving**   The use of strategies for solving social conflicts in ways that are satisfactory both to oneself and to others

**Social referencing**   The intentional search for information about others' feelings to help explain the meaning of uncertain circumstances and events

**Social smile**   Smiling in response to other individuals

**Social speech**   Speech directed toward another person and meant to be understood by that person

**Social-cognitive learning theory**   An approach to the study of development that emphasizes learning by observing the behavior of another person, called a model

**Socialized delinquents**   Adolescent delinquents who know and subscribe to the norms of society and who are fairly normal psychologically

**Sociocultural theory**   An approach that emphasizes how cognitive development proceeds as a result of social interactions between members of a culture

**Specific learning disorder**   Difficulties in the acquisition and use of listening, speaking, reading, writing, reasoning, or mathematical abilities

**Speech impairment**   Speech that deviates so much from the speech of others that it calls attention to itself, interferes with communication, or produces maladjustment in the speaker

**Stanford-Binet Intelligence Scale**   A test that consists of a series of items that vary according to the age of the person being tested

**State**   The degree of awareness an infant displays to both internal and external stimulation

**States of arousal**   Different degrees of sleep and wakefulness, ranging from deep sleep to great agitation

**Stillbirth**   The delivery of a child who is not alive, occurring in fewer than 1 delivery in 100

**Stranger anxiety**   The caution and wariness displayed by infants when encountering an unfamiliar person

**Stress**   The physical response to events that threaten or challenge us

**Sudden infant death syndrome (SIDS)**   The unexplained death of a seemingly healthy baby

**Sudden unexpected infant death (SUID)**   The death of an infant less than 1 year old and that has no immediately obvious cause

**Survey research**   Research in which a group of people chosen to represent some larger population are asked questions about their attitudes, behavior, or thinking on a given topic

**Symbolic function**   According to Jean Piaget, the ability to use a mental symbol, a word, or an object to represent something not physically present

**Synapse**   The gap at the connection between neurons, through which neurons chemically communicate with one another

**Syntax**   The combining of words and phrases to form meaningful sentences

**Tay–Sachs disease**   A disorder that produces blindness and muscle degeneration prior to death; there is no treatment

**Teacher expectancy effect**   The phenomenon whereby an educator's expectations for a given child actually bring about the expected behavior

**Telegraphic speech**   Speech in which words not critical to the message are left out

**Temperament**   Patterns of arousal and emotionality that are consistent and enduring characteristics of an individual

**Tentative period** The second stage of Eli Ginzberg's theory, which spans adolescence, in which people begin to think in pragmatic terms about the requirements of various jobs and how their own abilities might fit with those requirements

**Teratogen** A factor that produces a birth defect

**Theoretical research** Research designed specifically to test some developmental explanation and expand scientific knowledge

**Theories** Explanations and predictions concerning phenomena of interest, providing a framework for understanding the relationships among an organized set of facts or principles

**Theory of mind** Knowledge and beliefs about how the mind works and how it affects behavior

**Transformation** The process whereby one state is changed into another

**Treatment** A procedure applied by an experimental investigator based on two different experiences devised for subjects or participants

**Treatment group** The group in an experiment that receives the treatment

**Triarchic theory of intelligence** The belief that intelligence consists of three aspects of information processing: the componential element, the experiential element, and the contextual element

**Trust-versus-mistrust stage** According to Erik Erikson, the period during which infants develop a sense of trust or mistrust, largely depending on how well their needs are met by their caregivers

**Ultrasound sonography** A process in which high-frequency sound waves scan the mother's womb to produce an image of the unborn baby, whose size and shape can then be assessed

**Underextension** The overly restrictive use of words, common among children just mastering spoken language

**Undersocialized delinquents** Adolescent delinquents who are raised with little discipline or with harsh, uncaring parental supervision

**Uninvolved parents** Parents who show virtually no interest in their children, displaying indifferent, rejecting behavior

**Universal grammar** Noam Chomsky's theory that all the world's languages share a similar underlying structure

**Very-low-birthweight infants** Infants who weigh less than 1,250 grams (around 2¼ pounds) or, regardless of weight, have been in the womb fewer than 30 weeks

**Visual impairment** Difficulties in seeing that may include blindness or partial sightedness

**Wechsler Intelligence Scale for Children, Fourth Edition (WISC-IV)** A test for children that provides separate measures of verbal and performance (nonverbal) skills, as well as a total score

**X-linked genes** Genes that are considered recessive and are located only on the X chromosome

**Zone of proximal development (ZPD)** According to Lev Vygotsky, the level at which a child can almost, but not fully, comprehend or perform a task without assistance

**Zygote** The new cell formed by the process of fertilization

# References

Aalsma, M., Lapsley, D., & Flannery, D. (2006, April). Personal fables, narcissism, and adolescent adjustment. *Psychology in the Schools, 43*(4), 481–491.

AAUW. (2017). *The simple truth about the gender pay gap (Spring 2017)*. Washington, DC: American Association of University Women.

Abdolrezapour, P. (2016). Improving learners' oral fluency through computer-mediated emotional intelligence activities. *Recall: Journal of Eurocall, 29*, 80–98.

Aboud, F., & Sankar, J. (2007, September). Friendship and identity in a language-integrated school. *International Journal of Behavioral Development, 31*(5), 445–453.

Abrutyn, S., & Mueller, A. S. (2014). Are suicidal behaviors contagious in adolescence? Using longitudinal data to examine suicide suggestion. *American Sociological Review, 79*, 211–227.

Achenbach, T. A. (1992). Developmental psychopathology. In M. H. Bornstein & M. E. Lamb (Eds.), *Developmental psychology: An advanced textbook*. Hillsdale, NJ: Erlbaum.

Acheva, A., Ghita, M., Patel, G., Prise, K. M., & Schettino, G. (2014). Mechanisms of DNA damage response to targeted irradiation in organotypic 3D skin cultures. *PLoS One*. Retrieved February 8, 2014, from http://www.plosone.org/article/info%3Adoi%2F10.1371%2Fjournal.pone.0086092.

Ackerman, B. P., & Izard, C. E. (2004). Emotion cognition in children and adolescents: Introduction to the special issue. *Journal of Experimental Child Psychology, 89* [Special issue: Emotional cognition in children], 271–275.

Acocella, J. (August 18 & 25, 2003). Little people. *The New Yorker*, 138–143.

ACOG. (2002). *Guidelines for perinatal care*. Elk Grove, IN: American Congress of Obstetricians and Gynecologists.

Adachi, P. C., & Willoughby, T. (2013). Do video games promote positive youth development?. *Journal Of Adolescent Research, 28*, 155–165.

Adams, G. R., Montemayor, R., & Gullotta, T. P. (Eds.). (1996). *Psychosocial development during adolescence*. Thousand Oaks, CA: Sage Publications.

Adams, H. L., & Williams, L. (2011). Advice from teens to teens about dating: Implications for healthy relationships. *Children and Youth Services Review, 33*, 254–264.

Adamson, L., & Frick, J. (2003). The still face: A history of a shared experimental paradigm. *Infancy, 4*, 451–473.

Addy, S., Engelhardt, W., & Skinner, C. (2013). *Basic facts about low-income children*. New York: National Center for Children in Poverty.

Adorno, M., Sikandar, S., Mitra, S. S., et al. (2013). Usp16 contributes to somatic stem-cell defects in Down's syndrome. *Nature, 501*, 380–384.

Advocates for Youth. (2003) *Science and success. Sex educations and other programs that work to prevent teen pregnancy*. Washington, DC. Retrieved March 4, 2006, from http://www.advocatesforyouth.org/publications/ScienceSuccess.pdf.

Agarwal, D. (2018). Juvenile Delinquency in India – Latest Trends and Entailing Amendments in Juvenile Justice Act. *People: International Journal of Social Sciences, 3*(3), 1365-1383.

Agarwal, M., Nischal, A., Agarwal, A., Verma, J., & Dhanasekaran, S. (2013). Substance abuse in children and adolescents in India. *The Journal of Indian Association for Child and Adolescent Mental Health, 9*(3), 62-79 [2].

Aguirre, E., Gleeson, T., McCutchen, A., et al. (2006). *A cost-benefit analysis of universally accessible pre-kindergarten education in Texas*. Bush School of Government & Public Service: Texas A&M University.

Ahmad, A., Khalique, N., Khan, Z., & Amir, A. (2007). Prevalence of psychosocial problems among school going male adolescents. *Indian Journal of Community Medicine*. 32:219–21.

Ahn, W., Gelman, S., & Amsterlaw, J. (2000). Causal status effect in children's categorization. *Cognition, 76*, B35–B43.

Ainsworth, M. D. S., Blehar, M. C., Waters, E., & Wall, S. (1978). *Patterns of attachment: A psychological study of the strange situation*. Hillsdale, NJ: Erlbaum.

Aitken, R. J. (1995, July 7). The complexities of conception. *Science, 269*, 39–40.

Akers, K. G., Martinez-Canabal, A., Restivo, L., Yiu, A. P., De Cristofaro, A., Hsiang, H. (., & … Frankland, P. W. (2014). Hippocampal neurogenesis regulates forgetting during adulthood and infancy. *Science, 344*, 598–602.

Akhtar-Danesh, N., Dehghan, M., Morrison, K. M., & Fonseka, S. (2011). Parents' perceptions and attitudes on childhood obesity: A Q-methodology study. *Journal of the American Academy of Nurse Practitioners, 23*, 67–75.

Akinbami, L. J. (2011, January 12). Asthma prevalence, health care use, and mortality: United States, 2005–2009. *National Health Statistics Reports, 32*, 1–15.

Akmajian, A., Demers, R. A., & Harnish, R. M. (1984). *Linguistics*. Cambridge, MA: MIT Press.

Akyil, Y., Prouty, A., Blanchard, A., & Lyness, K. (2016). Experiences of families transmitting values in a rapidly changing society: Implications for family therapists. *Family Process, 55*, 368–381.

Alan Guttmacher Institute (2000). Risks and realities of early childbearing. Alan Guttmacher Institute.

Alberts, A., Elkind, D., & Ginsberg, S. (2007). The personal fable and risk-taking in early adolescence. *Journal of Youth and Adolescence, 36*, 71–76.

Alderfer, C. (2003). The science and nonscience of psychologists' responses to *The Bell Curve. Professional Psychology: Research & Practice, 34*, 287–293.

Alexander, B., Turnbull, D., & Cyna, A. (2009). The effect of pregnancy on hypnotizability. *American Journal of Clinical Hypnosis, 52*, 13–22.

Alexander, G., Wilcox, T., & Woods, R. (2009). Sex differences in infants' visual interest in toys. *Archives of Sexual Behavior, 38*, 427–433.

Alexander, G. M., & Hines, M. (2002). Sex differences in response to children's toys in nonhuman primates. *Evolution and Human Behavior, 23*, 467–479.

Alfonso, V. C., Flanagan, D. P., & Radwan, S. (2005). The impact of the Cattell-Horn-Carroll theory on test development and interpretation of cognitive and academic abilities. In D. P. Flanagan & P. L. Harrison (Eds.), *Contemporary intellectual assessment: Theories, tests, and issues*. New York: Guilford Press.

Alfred, M. V., & Chlup, D. T. (2010). Making the invisible, visible: Race matters in human resource development. *Advances In Developing Human Resources, 12*, 332–351.

Alhusen, J. L., Hayat, M. J., & Gross, D. (2013). A longitudinal study of maternal attachment and infant developmental outcomes. *Archives of Women's Mental Health, 16*, 521–529.

Alibali, M., Phillips, K., & Fischer, A. (2009). Learning new problem-solving strategies leads to changes in problem representation. *Cognitive Development, 24*, 89–101.

Allam, M., Marlier, L., & Schaal, B. (2006). Learning at the breast: Preference formation for an artificial scent and its attraction against the odor of maternal milk. *Infant Behavior & Development, 29*, 308–321.

Allen, A., & Gawlik, M. (2012). Charter schools: Meeting the democratic mission of public education. In E. Murakami-Ramalho & A. Pankake (Eds.). *Educational leaders encouraging the intellectual and professional capacity of others: A social justice agenda*. Charlotte, NC: IAP Information Age Publishing.

Allen, B. (2008). An analysis of the impact of diverse forms of childhood psychological maltreatment on emotional adjustment in early adulthood. *Child Maltreatment, 13*, 307–312.

Allen, M., & Bissell, M. (2004). Safety and stability for foster children: The policy context. *The Future of Children, 14*, 49 74.

Allison, A. C. (1954). Protection afforded by sickle cell trait against subtertian malarial infection. *British Medical Journal, 1*, 290–294.

Allison, B., & Schultz, J. (2001). Interpersonal identity formation during early adolescence. *Adolescence, 36*, 509–523.

Allison, M. (2013). Genomic testing reaches into the womb. *Nature Biotechnology, 31*, 595–601.

Al-Namlah, A. S., Meins, E., & Fernyhough, C. (2012). Self-regulatory private speech relates to children's recall and organization of autobiographical memories. *Early Childhood Research Quarterly*. Retrieved July 18, 2012, from http://www.sciencedirect.com/science/article/pii/S0885200612000300.

Al-Owidha, A., Green, K., & Kroger, J. (2009). On the question of an identity status category order: Rasch model step and scale statistics used to identify category order. *International Journal of Behavioral Development, 33*, 88–96.

Altermatt, E. (2011). Capitalizing on academic success: Students' interactions with friends as predictors of school adjustment. *The Journal of Early Adolescence, 31*, 174–203.

Altholz, S., & Golensky, M. (2004). Counseling, support, and advocacy for clients who stutter. *Health & Social Work, 29*, 197–205.

Alur, M. (2002). Introduction in Hegarty, S. & Alur, M. (eds) (2002). Education and children with special needs: from segregation to inclusion, New Delhi: Sage Publications.

Alverdy, J., Zaborina, O., & Wu, L. (2005). The impact of stress and nutrition on bacterial–host interactions at the intestinal epithelial surface. *Current Opinion in Clinical Nutrition and Metabolic Care, 8*, 205–209.

Amato, P., & Booth, A. (1997). *A generation at risk*. Cambridge, MA: Harvard University Press.

Ambrose, H. N., & Menna, R. (2013). Physical and relational aggression in young children: The role of mother–child interactional synchrony. *Early Child Development and Care, 183*(2), 207–222.

American Academy of Pediatrics. (1997, April 16). Breast feeding and the use of human milk. *Pediatrics, 101*, 45–51.

American Academy of Pediatrics. (1999, August). Media education. *Pediatrics, 104*, 341–343.

American Academy of Pediatrics. (2000). Clinical practice guideline: Diagnosis and evaluation of the child with attention-deficit/hyperactivity disorder. Retrieved August 5, 2017, from http://www.pediatrics.org/cgi/content/full/105/5/1158.

American Academy of Pediatrics. (2001). Organized sports for children and preadolescents. *Pediatrics, 107*, 1459–1462.

American Academy of Pediatrics. (2004, June 3). *Sports programs*. Available online at http://www.medem.com/medlb/article_detaillb_for_printer.cfm?article_ID=ZZZD2QD5M7C&sub_cat=405.

American Academy of Pediatrics. (2005, May 12). *AAP endorses newborn screening report from the American College of Medical Genetics*. Press release.

American Academy of Pediatrics. (2012, March 5). Discipline and Your Child. Retrieved July 23, 2012, from http://www.healthychildren.org/english/family-life/family-dynamics/communication-discipline/pages/disciplining-your-child.

American Academy of Pediatrics (2016). American Academy of Pediarics announces new recommendations for children's media use. Retrieved online 11/23/17; https://www.aap.org/en-us/about-the-aap/aap-press-room/pages/american-academy-of-pediatrics-announces-new-recommendations-for-childrens-media-use.aspx.

American Academy of Pediatrics Committee on Fetus and Newborn. (2004). Hospital stay for healthy term newborns. *Pediatrics, 113*, 1434–2436.

American Association on Intellectual and Developmental Disabilities (2012). *Definition of intellectual disability*. Retrieved July 23, 2012, from www.aamr.org.

American College of Medical Genetics. (2006). *Genetics in Medicine, 8*(5), Supplement.

American Psychological Association. (2002). *Ethical principles of psychologists and code of conduct. Updated*. Washington, DC: Author.

Amitai, Y., Haringman, M., Meiraz, H., Baram, N., & Leventhal, A. (2004). Increased awareness, knowledge and utilization of preconceptional folic acid in Israel following a national campaign. *Preventive Medicine: An International Journal Devoted to Practice and Theory, 39*, 731–737.

Amsterlaw, J., & Wellman, H. (2006). Theories of mind in transition: A microgenetic study of the development of false belief understanding. *Journal of Cognition and Development, 7*, 139–172.

Anandalakshmy, S. (1980). Developmental processes. In U. Pareek (Ed.), A survey of research in psychology, 1971–76, Part I (pp. 168–207). New Delhi: Indian Council of Social Science Research.

Anand, K. J. S., & Hickey, P. R. (1992). Halothane-morphine compared with high-dose sufentanil for anesthesia and postoperative analgesia in neonatal cardiac surgery. *New England Journal of Medicine, 326*(1), 1–9.

Anders, T. F., & Taylor, T. (1994). Babies and their sleep environment. *Children's Environments, 11*, 123–134.

Anderson, M. (2007). *Tall tales about the mind & brain: Separating fact from fiction*. S. Della Sala (Ed.). New York: Oxford University Press.

Anderson, C. A., Bushman, B. J., Donnerstein, E., Hummer, T. A., & Warburton, W. (2015). SPSSI research summary on media violence. *Analyses of Social Issues and Public Policy (ASAP), 15*(1), 4–19.

Anderson C. A., Shibuya A., Ihori N., et al. (2010). Violent video game effects on aggression, empathy, and prosocial behavior in eastern and western countries: A meta-analytic review. *Psychological Bulleting, 136,* 151–73.

Anderson-Clark, T., Green, R., & Henley, T. (2008, March). The relationship between first names and teacher expectations for achievement motivation. *Journal of Language and Social Psychology, 27*(1), 94–99.

Andersson, P., Juth, N., Petersén, Å., Graff, C., & Edberg, A. (2013). Ethical aspects of undergoing a predictive genetic testing for Huntington's disease. *Nursing Ethics, 20,* 189–199.

Andrews, G., Halford, G., & Bunch, K. (2003). Theory of mind and relational complexity. *Child Development, 74,* 1476–1499.

Anisfeld, M. (1996). Only tongue protrusion modeling is matched by neonates. *Developmental Review, 16,* 149–161.

Anisfeld, M. (2005). No compelling evidence to dispute Piaget's timetable of the development of representational imitation in infancy. In S. Hurley & N. Chater (Eds.), *Perspectives on imitation: From neuroscience to social science: Vol. 2: Imitation, human development, and culture* (pp. 107–131). Cambridge, MA: MIT Press.

Ansaldo, A. I., Arguin, M., & Roch-Locours, L. A. (2002). The contribution of the right cerebral hemisphere to the recovery from aphasia: A single longitudinal case study. *Brain Languages, 82,* 206–222.

Anyan, F., & Hjemdal, O. (2016). Adolescent stress and symptoms of anxiety and depression: Resilience explains and differentiates the relationships. *Journal of Affective Disorders, 203,* 213–220.

Anzman-Frasca, S., Liu, S., Gates, K. M., Paul, I. M., Rovine, M. J., & Birch, L. L. (2013). Infants' transitions out of a fussing/crying state are modifiable and are related to weight status. *Infancy, 18,* 662–686.

Anzman-Frasca, S., Stifter, C. A., Paul, I. M., & Birch, L. L. (2013b). Infant temperament and maternal parenting self-efficacy predict child weight outcomes. *Infant Behavior & Development, 36,* 494–497.

APA Reproductive Choice Working Group. (2000). *Reproductive choice and abortion: A resource packet.* Washington, DC: American Psychological Association.

Apgar, V. (1953). A proposal for a new method of evaluation in the newborn infant. *Current Research in Anesthesia and Analgesia, 32,* 260.

Apperly, I., & Robinson, E. (2002). Five-year-olds' handling of reference and description in the domains of language and mental representation. *Journal of Experimental Child Psychology, 83,* 53–75.

Aram, D., Meidan, I. C., & Deitcher, D. B. (2016). A comparison between homeschooled and formally schooled kindergartners: Children's early literacy, mothers' beliefs, and writing mediation. *Reading Psychology, 37,* 995–1024.

Archer, J. (2009). The nature of human aggression. *International Journal of Law and Psychiatry, 32,* 202–208.

Arcus, D. (2001). Inhibited and uninhibited children: Biology in the social context. In T. D. Wachs & G. A. Kohnstamm (Eds.), *Temperament in context.* Mahwah, NJ: Lawrence Erlbaum Associates.

Arias, I. (2004). The legacy of child maltreatment: Long-term health consequences for women. *Journal of Women's Health, 13,* 468–473.

Ariès, P. (1962). *Centuries of childhood.* New York: Knopf.

Armstrong, J., Hutchinson, I., Laing, D., & Jinks, A. (2007). Facial electromyography: Responses of children to odor and taste stimuli. *Chemical Senses, 32,* 611–621.

Arnett, J. (2011). Emerging adulthood(s): The cultural psychology of a new life stage. In L. Jensen & L. Jensen (Eds.), *Bridging cultural and developmental approaches to psychology: New syntheses in theory, research, and policy.* New York: Oxford University Press.

Arnett, J. J. (2016). *The Oxford handbook of emerging adulthood.* New York: Oxford University Press.

Arnon, I., & Ramscar, M. (2012). Granularity and the acquisition of grammatical gender: How order-of-acquisition affects what gets learned. *Cognition, 122,* 292–305.

Aronson, J. D. (2007). Brain imaging, culpability and the juvenile death penalty. *Psychology, Public Policy, and Law, 13,* 115–142.

Aronson, M., & Bialostok, S. (2016). 'Do some wondering': Children and their self-understanding selves in early elementary classrooms. *Symbolic Interaction, 39,* 229–251.

Arseneault, L., Moffitt, T. E., & Caspi, A. (2003). Strong genetic effects on cross-situational antisocial behavior among 5-year-old children according to mothers, teachers, examiner-observers, and twins' self-reports. *Journal of Child Psychology and Psychiatry and Allied Disciplines, 44,* 832–848.

Asadi, S., Amiri, S., & Molavi, H. (2014). Development of post-formal thinking from adolescence through adulthood. *Journal of Iranian Psychologists, 10,* 161–174.

Asendorpf, J. (2002). Self-awareness, other-awareness, and secondary representation. In A. Meltzoffa & W. Prinz (Eds.), *The imitative mind: Development, evolution, and brain bases.* New York: Cambridge University Press.

Asiedu, E. & Nandwa, B. (2007). On the impact of foreign aid in education on growth: how relevant is the heterogeneity of aid flows and the heterogeneity of aid recipients? *Review of World Economics, 143* (4), 631–649.

Asendorpf, J. B., Warkentin, V., & Baudonniere, P. (1996). Self-awareness and other-awareness II: Mirror self-recognition, social contingency awareness, and synchronic imitation. *Developmental Psychology, 32,* 313–321.

Astin, A., Korn, W., & Berg, E. (2004). The American Freshman: National norms for Fall, 2004. Los Angeles: University of California, Los Angeles, American Council on Education.

Astington, J., & Baird, J. (2005). *Why language matters for theory of mind.* New York: Oxford University Press.

Ata, R., Ludden, A., & Lally, M. (2007, November). The effects of gender and family, friend, and media influences on eating behaviors and body image during adolescence. *Journal of Youth and Adolescence, 36*(8), 1024–1037.

Athanasiu, L., Giddaluru, S., Fernandes, C., et al. (2017). A genetic association study of CSMD1 and CSMD2 with cognitive function. *Brain, Behavior, and Immunity, 61,* 209–216.

Athanasopoulou, E., & Fox, J. E. (2014). Effects of kangaroo mother care on maternal mood and interaction patterns between parents and their preterm, low birth weight infants: A systematic review. *Infant Mental Health Journal, 35,* 245–262.

Atherton, O. E., Schofield, T. J., Sitka, A., Conger, R. D., & Robins, R. W. (2016). Unsupervised self-care predicts conduct problems: The moderating roles of hostile aggression and gender. *Journal of Adolescence, 48,* 1–10.

Atkins, S. M., Bunting, M. F., Bolger, D. J., & Dougherty, M. R. (2012). Training the adolescent brain: Neural plasticity and the acquisition of cognitive abilities. In V. F. Reyna, S. B. Chapman, M. R. Dougherty, & J. Confrey (Eds.), *The adolescent brain: Learning, reasoning, and decision making.* Washington, DC: American Psychological Association.

Atkinson, R.C., & Shiffrin, R. M. (1971). The control of short-term memory. *Scientific American, 225,* 82–90.

Auestad, N., Scott, D. T., Janowsky, J. S., et al. (2003). Visual cognitive and language assessments at 39 months: A follow-up study of children fed formulas containing long-chain polyunsaturated fatty acids to 1 year of age. *Pediatrics, 112*, e177–e183.

Augustyn, M. (2003). "G" is for growing. Thirty years of research on children and *Sesame Street. Journal of Developmental and Behavioral Pediatrics, 24*, 451.

Aujoulat, I., Luminet, O., & Deccache, A. (2007). The perspective of patients on their experience of powerlessness. *Qualitative Health Research, 17*, 772–785.

Auster, E. R., & Prasad, A. (2016). Why do women still not make it to the top? Dominant organizational ideologies and biases by promotion committees limit opportunities to destination positions. *Sex Roles, 75*, 177–196.

Austin, J. (2016). 2020 vision: Genetic counselors as acknowledged leaders in integrating genetics and genomics into healthcare. *Journal of Genetic Counseling, 25*, 1–5.

Auyeung, B., & Baron-Cohen, S. (2012). Fetal testosterone in mind: Human sex differences and autism. In F. M. de Waal & P. Ferrari (Eds.), *The primate mind: Built to connect with other minds*. Cambridge, MA: Harvard University Press.

Avinum, R., Israel, S., Shalev, I., et al. (2011). AVPRIA variant associated with preschoolers' lower altruistic behavior. *PLoS One, 6*(9), Retrieved July 5, 2014, from http://www.sprouton-line.com/kindnesscounts/dr-nancy-eisenberg/eight-tips-for-developing-caring-kids.

Axelson, H. W., Winkler, T., Flygt, J., Djupsjö, A., Hånell, A., & Marklund, N. (2013). Plasticity of the contralateral motor cortex following focal traumatic brain injury in the rat. *Restorative Neurology and Neuroscience, 31*, 73–85.

Axia, G., Bonichini, S., & Denini, F. (1995). Pain in infancy: Individual differences. *Perceptual and Motor Skills, 81*, 142.

Aydt, H., & Corsaro, W. (2003). Differences in children's construction of gender across culture: An interpretive approach. *American Behavioral Scientist, 46*, 1306–1325.

Aylward, G. P., & Verhulst, S. J. (2000). Predictive utility of the Bayley Infant Neurodevelopmental Screener (BINS) risk status classifications: Clinical interpretation and application. *Developmental Medicine & Child Neurology, 42*, 25–31.

Ayoub, N. C. (2005, February 25). A pleasing birth: Midwives and maternity care in the Netherlands. *Chronicle of Higher Education*, 9.

Ayres, M. M., & Leaper, C. (2013). Adolescent girls' experiences of discrimination: An examination of coping strategies, social support, and self-esteem. *Journal of Adolescent Research, 28*, 479–508.

Aznar, A., & Tenenbaum, H. R. (2016). Parent–child positive touch: Gender, age, and task differences. *Journal of Nonverbal Behavior, 40*, 317–333.

Bakaya, S. (2012). Conceptualization of Peer Relationship among Adolescents, Unpublished Ph.D Dissertation, University of Delhi.

Bacchus, L., Mezey, G., & Bewley, S. (2006). A qualitative exploration of the nature of domestic violence in pregnancy. *Violence Against Women, 12*, 588–604.

Bachevalier, J., Nemanic, S., & Alvarado, M. C. (2015). The influence of context on recognition memory in monkeys: Effects of hippocampal, parahippocampal and perirhinal lesions. *Behavioural Brain Research, 285*, 89–98.

Badenhorst, W., Riches, S., Turton, P., & Hughes, P. (2006). The psychological effects of stillbirth and neonatal death on fathers: Systematic review. *Journal of Psychosomatic Obstetrics & Gynecology, 27*, 245–256.

Bader, A. P. (1995). Engrossment revisited: Fathers are still falling in love with their newborn babies. In J. L. Shapiro, M. J. Diamond, & M. Grenberg (Eds.), *Becoming a father*. New York: Springer.

Baer, J. S., Sampson, P. D., & Barr, H. M. (2003). A 21-year longitudinal analysis of the effects of prenatal alcohol exposure on young adult drinking. *Archives of General Psychiatry, 60*, 377–385.

Bagci, S. C., Kumashiro, M., Smith, P. K., Blumberg, H., & Rutland, A. (2014). Cross-ethnic friendships: Are they really rare? Evidence from secondary schools around London. *International Journal of Intercultural Relations, 41*, 125–137.

Bahrick, L. E., Todd, J. T., Castellanos, I., & Sorondo, B. M. (2016). Enhanced attention to speaking faces versus other event types emerges gradually across infancy. *Developmental Psychology, 52*, 1705–1720.

Bai, L. (2005). Children at play: A childhood beyond the Confucian shadow. *Childhood: A Global Journal of Child Research, 12*, 9–32.

Baillargeon, R. (2004). Infants' physical world. *Current Directions in Psychological Science, 13*, 89–94.

Baillargeon, R. (2008). Innate ideas revisited: For a principle of persistence in infants' physical reasoning. *Perspectives on Psychological Science, 3*, 2–13.

Baillargeon, R., Scott, R. M., He, Z., et al. (2015). Psychological and sociomoral reasoning in infancy. In M. Mikulincer, P. R. Shaver, E. Borgida, et al. (Eds.), *APA handbook of personality and social psychology, Volume 1: Attitudes and social cognition*. Washington, DC: American Psychological Association.

Baker, J., Maes, H., Lissner, L., Aggen, S., Lichtenstein, P., & Kendler, K. (2009). Genetic risk factors for disordered eating in adolescent males and females. *Journal of Abnormal Psychology, 118*, 576–586.

Baker, P., & Sussman, D. (2012, May 15). Obama's switch on same-sex marriage stirs skepticism. *The New York Times*, p. A17.

Baker, T., Brandon, T., & Chassin, L. (2004). Motivational influences on cigarette smoking. *Annual Review of Psychology, 55*, 463–491.

Balaban, M. T., Snidman, N., & Kagan, J. (1997). Attention, emotion, and reactivity in infancy and early childhood. In P. J. Lang, R. F. Simons, & M. T. Balaban (Eds.), *Attention and orienting: Sensory and motivational processes* (pp. 369–391). Mahwah, NJ: Erlbaum.

Balakrishnan, V., & Claiborne, L. (2012). Vygotsky from ZPD to ZCD in moral education: Reshaping Western theory and practices in local context. *Journal of Moral Education, 41*, 225–243.

Ball, H. L., & Volpe, L. E. (2013). Sudden Infant Death Syndrome (SIDS) risk reduction and infant sleep location—Moving the discussion forward. *Social Science & Medicine, 79*, 84–91.

Balsam, R. (2013). Freud, females, childbirth, and dissidence: Margarete Hilferding, Karen Horney, and Otto Rank. *Psychoanalytic Review, 100*, 695–716.

Bandura, A. (1977). *Social learning theory*. Englewood Cliffs, NJ: Prentice-Hall.

Bandura, A. (1991). Social cognitive theory of moral thought and action. In W. M. Kurtines & J. L. Gewirtz (Eds.), *Handbook of moral behavior and development*. Hillsdale, NJ: Erlbaum.

Bandura, A. (1994). Social cognitive theory of mass communication. In J. Bryant & D. Zillmann (Eds.), *Media effects: Advances in theory and research. LEA's communication series*. Hillsdale, NJ: Erlbaum.

Bandura, A. (2002). Social cognitive theory in cultural context. *Applied Psychology: An International Review, 51* [Special Issue], 269–290.

Bandura, A., Grusec, J. E., & Menlove, F. L. (1967). Vicarious extinction of avoidance behavior. *Journal of Personality and Social Psychology, 5,* 16–23.

Bandura, A., Ross, D., & Ross, S. (1962). Vicarious extinction of avoidance behavior. *Journal of Personality and Social Psychology, 67,* 601–607.

Baptista, T., Aldana, E., Angeles, F., & Beaulieu, S. (2008). Evolution theory: An overview of its applications in psychiatry. *Psychopathology, 41,* 17–27.

Barbaro, N., Boutwell, B. B., Barnes, J. C., & Shackelford, T. K. (2017). Rethinking the transmission gap: What behavioral genetics and evolutionary psychology mean for attachment theory: A comment on Verhage et al. *Psychological Bulletin, 143,* 107–113.

Barber, A. D., Srinivasan, P., Joel, S. E., Caffo, B. S., Pekar, J. J., & Mostofsky, S. H. (2012). Motor "dexterity"?: Evidence that left hemisphere lateralization of motor circuit connectivity is associated with better motor performance in children. *Cerebral Cortex, 22,* 51–59.

Barber, S., & Gertler, P. (2009). Empowering women to obtain high quality care: Evidence from an evaluation of Mexico's conditional cash transfer programme. *Health Policy and Planning, 24,* 18–25.

Barboza, G., Schiamberg, L., Oehmke, J., Korzeniewski, S., Post, L., & Heraux, C. (2009). Individual characteristics and the multiple contexts of adolescent bullying: An ecological perspective. *Journal of Youth and Adolescence, 38,* 101–121.

Bard, K. A., Todd, B. K., Bernier, C., Love, J., & Leavens, D. A. (2006). Self-Awareness in Human and Chimpanzee Infants: What is Measured and What is Meant by the Mark and Mirror Test? *Infancy, 9,* 191–219.

Barlett, C., Chamberlin, K., & Witkower, Z. (2017). Predicting cyberbullying perpetration in emerging adults: A theoretical test of the Barlett Gentile Cyberbullying Model. *Aggressive Behavior, 43*(2), 147–154.

Barlett, C., Harris, R., & Baldassaro, R. (2007). Longer you play, the more hostile you feel: Examination of first person shooter video games and aggression during video game play. *Aggressive Behavior, 33,* 486–497.

Barnard, W. (2007). Publicly funded programs and their benefits for children. *Evidence-based practices and programs for early childhood care and education* (pp. 67–87). Thousand Oaks, CA: Corwin Press.

Barnes, J. C., & Boutwell, B. B. (2012). On the relationship of past to future involvement in crime and delinquency: A behavior genetic analysis. *Journal of Criminal Justice, 40*(1), 94–102.

Barone, D. (2011). Welcoming families: A parent literacy project in a linguistically rich, high-poverty school. *Early Childhood Education Journal, 38,* 377–384.

Barr, R. G. (2011). Mother and child: Preparing for a life. In D. P. Keating & D. P. Keating (Eds.), *Nature and nurture in early child development.* New York: Cambridge University Press.

Barrett, D. E., & Frank, D. A. (1987). *The effects of undernutrition on children's behavior.* New York: Gordon & Breach.

Barrett, D. E., & Radke-Yarrow, M. R. (1985). Effects of nutritional supplementation on children's responses to novel, frustrating, and competitive situations. *American Journal of Clinical Nutrition, 42,* 102–120.

Barrett, T., & Needham, A. (2008). Developmental differences in infants' use of an object's shape to grasp it securely. *Developmental Psychobiology, 50,* 97–106.

Barro, R. (1991). Economic growth in a cross section of countries. Quarterly Journal of Economics, CVI, 363–394.

Basak, R. & Ghosh, A. (2008). Ego-identity status and its relationship with self-esteem in a group of late adolescents. *Journal of the Indian Academy of Applied Psychology, 34*(2), 337-344.

Bask, M., & Salmela-Aro, K. (2013). Burned out to drop out: Exploring the relationship between school burnout and school dropout. *European Journal of Psychology of Education, 28,* 511–528.

Bastian, B., Jetten, J., & Radke, H. M. (2012). Cyber-dehumanization: Violent video game play diminishes our humanity. *Journal of Experimental Social Psychology, 48,* 486–491.

Bates, J. E., Marvinney, D., Kelly, T., Dodge, K. A., Bennett, D. S., & Pettit, G. S. (1994). Child-care history and kindergarten adjustment. *Developmental Psychology, 30,* 690–700.

Bauer, P. J. (2007). Recall in infancy: A neurodevelopmental account. *Current Directions in Psychological Science, 16,* 142–146.

Bauer, P. J., Wenner, J. A., Dropik, P. L., & Wewerka, S. S. (2000). Parameters of remembering and forgetting in the transition from infancy to early childhood. With commentary by Mark L. Howe. *Monographs of the Society for Research in Child Development, 65,* 4.

Baumrind, D. (1971). Current patterns of parental authority. *Developmental Psychology Monographs, 4* (1, pt. 2).

Baumrind, D. (1980). New directions in socialization research. *Psychological Bulletin, 35,* 639–652.

Baumrind, D. (2005). Patterns of parental authority. *New Directions in Child Adolescent Development, 108,* 61–69.

Bayley, N. (1993). Manual for the Bayley Scales of Infant Development. New York: Psychological Corporation.

Beal, C. R. (1994). *Boys and girls: The development of gender roles.* New York: McGraw-Hill.

Bearman, P., & Bruckner, H. (2004). Study on teenage virginity pledge. Paper presented at meeting of the National STD Prevention Conference, Philadelphia, PA.

Becker, B., & Luthar, S. (2007, March). Peer-perceived admiration and social preference: Contextual correlates of positive peer regard among suburban and urban adolescents. *Journal of Research on Adolescence, 17,* 117–144.

Beckman, M. (2004, July 30). Neuroscience: Crime, culpability, and the adolescent brain. *Science, 305,* 596–599.

Beets, M., Flay, B., Vuchinich, S., Li, K., Acock, A., & Snyder, F. (2009). Longitudinal patterns of binge drinking among first year college students with a history of tobacco use. *Drug and Alcohol Dependence, 103,* 1–8.

Begeny, J., & Martens, B. (2007). Inclusionary education in Italy: A literature review and call for more empirical research. *Remedial and Special Education, 28,* 80–94.

Begley, S. (1995, July 10). Deliver, then depart. *Newsweek,* 62.

Behm, I., Kabir, Z., Connolly, G. N., & Alpert, H. R. (2012). Increasing prevalence of smoke-free homes and decreasing rates of sudden infant death syndrome in the United States: An ecological association study. *Tobacco Control: An International Journal, 21*(1), 6–11.

Beilby, J. M., Byrnes, M. L., & Young, K. N. (2012). The experiences of living with a sibling who stutters: A preliminary study. *Journal of Fluency Disorders, 37,* 135–148.

Bell, H., Pellis, S., & Kolb, B. (2010). Juvenile peer play experience and the development of the orbitofrontal and medial prefrontal cortices. *Behavioural Brain Research, 207*(1),7–13.

Bell, M. (2012). A psychobiological perspective on working memory performance at 8 months of age. *Child Development*, *83*, 251–265.

Bell, S. M., & Ainsworth, M. D. S. (1972). Infant crying and maternal responsiveness. *Child Development, 43*, 1171–1190.

Bell, T., & Romano, E. (2012). Opinions about child corporal punishment and influencing factors. *Journal of Interpersonal Violence, 27*, 2208–2229.

Belle, D. (1999). *The after-school lives of children: Alone and with others while parents work*. Mahwah, NJ: Erlbaum.

Bellezza, F. S. (2000). Mnemonic devices. In A. E. Kazdin (Ed.), *Encyclopedia of psychology* (vol. 5, pp. 286–287). Washington, DC: American Psychological Association.

Belluck, P. (2000, October 18). New advice for parents: Saying 'that's great!' may not be. *The New York Times*, A14.

Belsky, J. (2006). Early child care and early child development: Major findings from the NICHD Study of Early Child Care. *European Journal of Developmental Psychology, 3*, 95–110.

Belsky, J. (2009). Classroom composition, childcare history and social development: Are childcare effects disappearing or spreading? *Social Development, 18*, 230–238.

Belsky, J., Vandell, D. L., Burchinal, M., Clarke-Stewart, A. K., McCartney, K., & Owen, M. T. (2007). Are there long-term effects of early child care? *Child Development, 78*, 188–193.

Beltz, A. M., Corley, R. P., Bricker, J. B., Wadsworth, S. J., & Berenbaum, S. A. (2014). Modeling pubertal timing and tempo and examining links to behavior problems. *Developmental Psychology, 50*, 2715–2726.

Benelli, B., Belacchi, C., Gini, G., & Lucangeli, D. (2006, February). "To define means to say what you know about things": The development of definitional skills as metalinguistic acquisition. *Journal of Child Language, 33*, 71–97.

Benegal, V., Bhushan, K., Seshadri, S., & Karott, M. (2016). Drug abuse among street children in Bangalore (Monograph funded by CRY-1998), accessed from: http://www.nimhans.kar.nic.in/.

Bengtson, V. L., Acock, A. C., Allen, K. R., & Dilworth-Anderson, P. (Eds.). (2004). *Sourcebook of family theory and research*. Thousand Oaks, CA: Sage Publications.

Bennet, S., & Assefi, N. (2005). School-based teenage pregnancy prevention programs: A systematic review of randomized controlled trials. *Journal of Adolescent Health, 36*, 72–81.

Berger, L. M., Hill, J., & Waldfogel, J. (2005). Maternity leave, early maternal employment and child health and development in the US. *Economic Journal, 115*(501), F29–F47.

Berninger, V. W., Abbott, R. D., Jones, J., et al. (2006). Early development of language by hand: Composing, reading, listening, and speaking connections; three letter-writing modes; and fast mapping in spelling. *Developmental Neuropsychology, 29*, 61–92.

Bennett, J. (2008, September 15). It's not just white girls. *Newsweek*, 96.

Bennett, S.E. and Assefi, N.P. (2005) School-based teenage pregnancy prevention programs: A systematic review of randomized controlled trials. Journal of Adolescent Health, 36, 72-81.

Benoit, A., Lacourse, E., & Claes, M. (2014). Pubertal timing and depressive symptoms in late adolescence: The moderating role of individual, peer, and parental factors. *Development and Psychopathology, 25*, 455–471.

Benson, E. (2003, March). "Goo, gaa, grr?" *Monitor on Psychology*, 50–51.

Benson, H. (1993). The relaxation response. In D. Goleman & J. Guerin (Eds.), *Mind–body medicine: How to use your mind for better health*. Yonkers, NY: Consumer Reports Publications.

Bergelson, E., & Swingley, D. (2012). At 6–9 months, human infants know the meanings of many common nouns. *PNAS Proceedings of the National Academy of Science of the United States of America,, 109*, 3253–3258.

Bergen, H., Martin, G., & Richardson, A. (2003). Sexual abuse and suicidal behavior: A model constructed from a large community sample of adolescents. *Journal of the American Academy of Child & Adolescent Psychiatry, 42*, 1301–1309.

Berger, L. (2000, April 11). What children do when home and alone. *The New York Times*, p. F8.

Bergman, A., Blom, I., & Polyak, D. (2012). Attachment and separation-individuation: Two ways of looking at the mother/infant relationship. In S. Akhtar (Ed.), *The mother and her child: Clinical aspects of attachment, separation, and loss*. Lanham, MD: Jason Aronson.

Bergman, A., Blom, I., Polyak, D., & Mayers, L. (2015). Attachment and separation–individuation: Two ways of looking at the mother–infant relationship. *International Forum of Psychoanalysis, 24*, 16–21.

Bergmann, K., Schubert, A., Hagemann, D., & Schankin, A. (2016). Age-related differences in the P3 amplitude in change blindness. *Psychological Research, 80*(4), 660–676.

Bergmann, R. L., Bergman, K. E., & Dudenhausen, J. W. (2008). Undernutrition and growth restriction in pregnancy. *Nestle Nutritional Workshop Series; Pediatrics Program, 61*, 1030–121.

Berko, J. (1958). The child's learning of English morphology. *Word, 14*, 150–177.

Berndt, T. J. (1999). Friends' influence on students' adjustment to school. *Educational Psychologist, 34*, 15–28.

Berndt, T. J. (2002). Friendship quality and social development. *Current Directions in Psychological Science, 11*, 7–10.

Bernier, A., & Meins, E. (2008). A threshold approach to understanding the origins of attachment disorganization. *Developmental Psychology, 44*, 969–982.

Bernstein, N. (2004, March 7). Behind fall in pregnancy, a new teenage culture of restraint. *The New York Times*, pp. 1, 20.

Berry, G. L. (2003). Developing children and multicultural attitudes: The systemic psychosocial influences of television portrayals in a multimedia society. *Cultural Diversity and Ethnic Minority Psychology, 9*, 360–366.

Berteletti, I., & Booth, J. R. (2015). Perceiving fingers in single-digit arithmetic problems. *Frontiers in Psychology, 6*.

Berteletti, I., & Booth, J. R. (2016). Finger representation and finger-based strategies in the acquisition of number meaning and arithmetic. In D. B. Berch, D. C. Geary, & K. Mann Koepke (Eds.), *Development of mathematical cognition: Neural substrates and genetic influences* (pp. 109–139). San Diego, CA: Elsevier Academic Press.

Bertin, E., & Striano, T. (2006, April). The still-face response in newborn, 1.5-, and 3-month-old infants. *Infant Behavior & Development, 29*, 294–297.

Besag, V. E. (2006). *Understanding girls' friendships, fights and feuds: A practical approach to girls' bullying*. Maidenhead, Berkshire: Open University Press/McGraw-Hill Education.

Bhagabati, D., Das, B. & Das, S. (2013). Pattern of alcohol consumption in underage population in an Indian city. *Dysphrenia*. 4. 36-41. Accessed from https://www.researchgate.net/ on Jun 18, 2017.

Bhagat, N., Laskar, A., & Sharma, N. (2012). Women's perception about sex selection in an urban slum in Delhi. *Journal of Reproductive and Infant Psychology, 30*, 92–104.

Bhargava, P. (2014). 'I have a family, therefore I am': Children's understanding of self and others. In N. Chaudhary, S. Anandalakshmy, & J. Valsiner (Eds.), *Cultural realities of being: Abstract ideas within everyday lives*. New York: Routledge/Taylor & Francis Group.

Bhat, C.S., Ragan, M.A., Selvaraj, P.R. et al. (2017). *Internal Journal of Advancement Counselling* (2017), 39: 112. https://doi.org/10.1007/s10447-017-9286-y.

Bhogal, C.S., Chauhan, S., & Baruah, M.C. (2002). Pattern of childhood STDs in a major hospital of East Delhi. *Indian Journal of Dermatology, Venereology, and Leprology*, 68, 210-212.

Bhojani, U. M., Chander, S.J., & Devadasan, N. (2009). Tobacco use and related factors among pre-university students in a college in Bangalore, India. *National Medical Journal of India*, 22(6), 2009 [4].

Bhushan, B., & Khan, S. (2006, September). Laterality and accident proneness: A study of locomotive drivers. *Laterality: Asymmetries of Body, Brain and Cognition*, 11(5), 395–404.

Bialystok, E., & Viswanathan, M. (2009). Components of executive control with advantages for bilingual children in two cultures. *Cognition*, 112, 494–500.

Bibace, R. (2013). Challenges in Piaget's legacy. *Integrative Psychological & Behavioral Science*, 47, 167–175.

Bickham, D. S., Wright, J. C., & Huston, A. C. (2000). Attention, comprehension and the educational influences of television. In D. G. Singer & J. L. Singer (Eds.), *Handbook of children and the media*. Thousand Oaks, CA: Sage.

Biddle, B. J. (2001). *Social class, poverty, and education*. London: Falmer Press.

Bidwell, L. C., McClernon, F. J., & Kollins, S. H. (2011). Cognitive enhancers for the treatment of ADHD. *Pharmacology, Biochemistry and Behavior*, 99, 262–274.

Bierman, K. L. (2004). *Peer rejection: Developmental processes and intervention strategies*. New York: Guilford Press.

Bierman, K., Torres, M., Domitrovich, C., Welsh, J., & Gest, S. (2009). Behavioral and cognitive readiness for school: Cross-domain associations for children attending Head Start. *Social Development*, 18, 305–323.

Biesecker, B., & Peay, H. (2013). Genomic sequencing for psychiatric disorders: Promise and challenge. *International Journal of Neuropsychopharmacology*, 16, 1667–1672.

Bigelow, A. E., & Power, M. (2012). The effect of mother–infant skin-to-skin contact on infants' response to the Still Face Task from newborn to three months of age. *Infant Behavior & Development*, 35, 240–251.

Bijeljac-Babic, R., Bertoncini, J., & Mehler, J. (1993). How do 4-day-old infants categorize multisyllabic utterances? *Developmental Psychology*, 29, 711–721.

Birch, E. E., Garfield, S., Hoffman, D. R., Uauy, R., & Birch, D. G. (2000). A randomized controlled trial of early dietary supply of long-chain polyunsaturated fatty acids and mental development in term infants. *Developmental Medicine and Child Neurology*, 42, 174–181.

Biro, F., Striegel-Moore, R., Franko, D., Padgett, J., & Bean, J. (2006, October). Self-esteem in adolescent females. *Journal of Adolescent Health*, 39, 501–507.

Bischof-Köhler, D. (2012). Empathy and self-recognition in phylogenetic and ontogenetic perspective. *Emotion Review*, 4, 40–48.

Bishop, D. V. M., & Leonard, L. B. (Eds.). (2001). *Speech and language impairments in children: Causes, characteristics, intervention and outcome*. Philadelphia, PA: Psychology Press.

Bjorklund, D. (2006). Mother knows best: Epigenetic inheritance, maternal effects, and the evolution of human intelligence. *Developmental Review*, 26(2), 213–242.

Bjorklund, D. F. (1997). The role of immaturity in human development. *Psychological Bulletin*, 122(2), 153–169.

Bjorklund, D. F., & Ellis, B. (2005). Evolutionary psychology and child development: An emerging synthesis. In B. J. Ellis (Ed.), *Origins of the social mind: Evolutionary psychology and child development*. New York: Guilford Press.

Black, K. (2002). Associations between adolescent–mother and adolescent–best friend interactions. *Adolescence*, 37, 235–253.

Black, M. M., Jukes, M. H., & Willoughby, M. T. (2017). Behavioural and emotional problems in preschool children. *The Lancet Psychiatry*, 4, 89–90.

Blair, P., Sidebotham, P., Berry, P., Evans, M., & Fleming, P. (2006). Major epidemiological changes in sudden infant death syndrome: A 20-year population-based study in the UK. *Lancet*, 367, 314–319.

Blake, G., Velikonja, D., Pepper, V., Jilderda, I., & Georgiou, G. (2008). Evaluating an in-school injury prevention programme's effect on children's helmet wearing habits. *Brain Injury*, 22, 501–507.

Blake, J., & de Boysson-Bardies, B. (1992). Patterns in babbling: A cross-linguistic study. *Journal of Child Language*, 19, 51–74.

Blakemore, J. (2003). Children's beliefs about violating gender norms: Boys shouldn't look like girls, and girls shouldn't act like boys. *Sex Roles*, 48, 411–419.

Blakemore, S. (2012). Imaging brain development: The adolescent brain. *Neuroimage*, 61, 397–406.

Blass, E. M., & Camp, C. A. (2001). The ontogeny of face recognition: Eye contact and sweet taste induce face preference in 9- and 12-week-old human infants. *Developmental Psychology*, 37(6), 762–774.

Blatt, B. Tagalog in California, Cherokee in Arkansas. What language does your state speak? Slate, May 23, 2014. Retrieved August 5, 2017, from http://www.slate.com/articles/arts/culturebox/2014/05/language_map_what_s_the_most_popular_language_in_your_state.html.

Blewitt, P., Rump, K., Shealy, S., & Cook, S. (2009). Shared book reading: When and how questions affect young children's word learning. *Journal of Educational Psychology*, 101, 294–304.

Block, J. S., Weinstein, J., & Seitz, M. (2005). School and parent partnerships in the preschool years. In D. Zager (Ed.), *Autism spectrum disorders: Identification, education, and treatment* (3rd ed.). Mahwah, NJ: Erlbaum.

Blom, E. H., Ho, T. C., Connolly, C. G., et al. (2016). The neuroscience and context of adolescent depression. *Acta Paediatrica*, 105, 358–365.

Blomberg, J., & Karasti, H. (2013). Reflections on 25 years of ethnography in CSCW. *Computer Supported Cooperative Work (CSCW)*, 22(4–6), 373–423.

Bloss, C. S., Schork, N, J., & Topol E. J. (2011) Effect of direct-to-consumer genomewide profiling to assess disease risk. *The New England Journal of Medicine*, 364, 524–534.

Blount, B. G. (1982). Culture and the language of socialization: Parental speech. In D. A. Wagner & H. W. Stevenson (Eds.), *Cultural perspectives on child development*. San Francisco: Freeman.

Blue, S. N., Kazama, A. M., & Bachevalier, J. (2013). Development of memory for spatial locations and object/place associations in infant rhesus macaques with and without neonatal hippocampal lesions. *Journal of the International Neuropsychological Society*, 19(10), 1053–1064.

Blum, D. (2002). *Love at Goon Park: Harry Harlow and the science of affection*. New York: Perseus Publishing.

Blumenshine, P. M., Egerter, S. A., Libet, M. L., & Braveman, P. A. (2011). Father's education: An independent marker of risk for preterm birth. *Maternal and Child Health Journal, 15*, 60–67.

Blumenthal, S. (2000). Developmental aspects of violence and the institutional response. *Criminal Behaviour & Mental Health, 10*, 185–198.

Boatella-Costa, E., Costas-Moragas, C., Botet-Mussons, F., Fornieles-Deu, A., & De Cáceres-Zurita, M. (2007). Behavioral gender differences in the neonatal period according to the Brazelton scale. *Early Human Development, 83*, 91–97.

Bober, S., Humphry, R., & Carswell, H. (2001). Toddlers' persistence in the emerging occupations of functional play and self-feeding. *American Journal of Occupational Therapy, 55*, 369–376.

Bodell, L. P., Joiner, T. E., & Ialongo, N. S. (2012). Longitudinal association between childhood impulsivity and bulimic symptoms in African American adolescent girls. *Journal of Consulting and Clinical Psychology, 80*, 313–316.

Bodell, L. P., Smith, A. R., Holm-Denoma, J. M., Gordon, K. H., & Joiner, T. E. (2011). The impact of perceived social support and negative life events on bulimic symptoms. *Eating Behaviors, 12*, 44–48.

Boehmer, U., Linde, R., & Freund, K. M. (2005). Sexual minority women's coping and psychological adjustment after a diagnosis of breast cancer. *Journal of Women's Health, 14*, 213–224.

Bogle, K. A. (2008). 'Hooking Up': What educators need to know. *The Chronicle of Higher Education, 54*, A32.

Bohn, A., & Berntsen, D. (2011). The reminiscence bump reconsidered: Children's prospective life stories show a bump in young adulthood. *Psychological Science, 22*, 197–202.

Boissicat, N., Pansu, P., Bouffard, T., & Cottin, F. (2012). Relation between perceived scholastic competence and social comparison mechanisms among elementary school children. *Social Psychology of Education, 15*(4), 603–614.

Bonanno, G., & Mancini, A. (2007, February). The human capacity to thrive in the face of potential trauma. *Pediatrics, 121*(2), 369–375.

Bonifacci, P., Storti, M., Tobia, V., & Suardi, A. (2016). Specific learning disorders: A look inside children's and parents' psychological well-being and relationships. *Journal of Learning Disabilities, 49*, 532–545.

Bonke, B., Tibben, A., Lindhout, D., Clarke, A. J., & Stijnen, T. (2005). Genetic risk estimation by healthcare professionals. *Medical Journal of Autism, 182*, 116–118.

Bonnicksen, A. (2007). Oversight of assisted reproductive technologies: The last twenty years. *Reprogenetics: Law, policy, and ethical issues.* Baltimore, MD: Johns Hopkins University Press.

Bookstein, F. L., Sampson, P. D., Streissguth, A. P., & Barr, H. M. (1996). Exploiting redundant measurement of dose and developmental outcome: New methods from the behavioral teratology of alcohol. *Developmental Psychology, 32*, 404–415.

Booth, C., Kelly, J., & Spieker, S. (2003). Toddlers' attachment security to child-care providers: The Safe and Secure Scale. *Early Education & Development, 14*, 83–100.

Bootzin, R. R., Manber, R., Perlis, M. L., Salvio, M., & Wyatt, J. K. (1993). Sleep disorders. In P. B. Sutker & H. E. Adams (Eds.), *Comprehensive handbook of psychopathology* (2nd ed.). New York: Plenum.

Bor, W., & Bor, W. (2004). Prevention and treatment of childhood and adolescent aggression and antisocial behaviour: A selective review. *Australian & New Zealand Journal of Psychiatry, 38*, 373–380.

Borden, M. E. (1998). *Smart start: The parents' complete guide to preschool education.* New York: Facts on File.

Bornstein, M. H. (2000). Infant into conversant: Language and nonlanguage processes in developing early communication. In N. Budwig & I. C. Uzgiris (Eds.), *Communication: An arena of development.* Westport, CT: Ablex Publishing.

Bornstein, M. H., Cote, L., & Maital, S. (2004). Cross-linguistic analysis of vocabulary in young children: Spanish, Dutch, French, Hebrew, Italian, Korean, and American English. *Child Development, 75*, 1115–1139.

Bornstein, M. H., & Lamb, M. E. (1992). Development in infancy: An introduction. New York: McGraw-Hill.

Bornstein, M. H., & Lamb, M. E. (Eds.). (2005). *Developmental science.* Mahwah, NJ: Lawrence Erlbaum Associates.

Bornstein, M. H., & Lansford, J. E. (2013). Assessing early childhood development. In P. Britto, P. L. Engle, C. M. Super (Eds.), *Handbook of early childhood development research and its impact on global policy.* New York: Oxford University Press.

Bornstein, M. H., Putnick, D. L., Heslington, et al. (2008, May). Mother-child emotional availability in ecological perspective: Three countries, two regions, two genders. *Developmental Psychology, 44*(3), 666–680.

Bornstein, M. H., Putnick, D. L., Suwalsky, T. D., & Gini, M. (2006). Maternal chronological age, prenatal and perinatal history, social support, and parenting of infants. *Child Development, 77*, 875–892.

Bornstein, M. H., Suwalsky, J. T. D., & Breakstone, D. A. (2012). Emotional relationships between mothers and infants: Knowns, unknowns, and unknown unknowns. *Development and Psychopathology, 24*, 113–123.

Borse, N. N., Gilchrist, J., Dellinger. A. M., Rudd, R. A., Ballesteros, M. F., & Sleet, D. A. (2008). *CDC childhood injury report: Patterns of unintentional injuries among 0–19-year-olds in the United States, 2000–2006.* Atlanta, GA: Centers for Disease Control and Prevention, National Center for Injury Prevention and Control.

Bos, A. F. (2013). Bayley-II or Bayley-III: What do the scores tell us? *Developmental Medicine & Child Neurology, 55*, 978–979.

Bos, C. S., & Vaughn, S. S. (2005). *Strategies for teaching students with learning and behavior problems* (6th ed.). Boston: Allyn & Bacon.

Bos, H. W., Knox, J. R., van Rijn-van Gelderen, L., & Gartrell, N. K. (2016). Same-sex and different-sex parent households and child health outcomes: Findings from the National Survey of Children's Health. *Journal of Developmental and Behavioral Pediatrics, 37*(3), 179–187.

Bosacki, S. (2013). Theory of mind understanding and conversational patterns in middle childhood. *The Journal of Genetic Psychology: Research and Theory on Human Development, 174*, 170–191.

Bosco, F. M., Angeleri, R., Colle, L., Sacco, K., & Bara, B. G. (2013). Communicative abilities in children: An assessment through different phenomena and expressive means. *Journal of Child Language, 40*, 741–778.

Boseley, S. (2008, July 24). Gates joins campaign to curb smoking in developing world: Foundation adds $125m to Bloomberg's $375m fund: Initiative to show health risks and push for bans. *The Guardian,* p. 21.

Boseovski, J. J. (2012). Trust in testimony about strangers: Young children prefer reliable informants who make positive attributions. *Journal of Experimental Child Psychology, 111*, 543–551.

Bostwick, J. (2006, February). Do SSRIs cause suicide in children? The evidence is underwhelming. *Journal of Clinical Psychology, 62*(2), 235–241.

Bouchard, T. J., Jr. (1997, September/October). Whenever the twain shall meet. *The Sciences*, 52–57.

Bouchard, T. J., Jr. (2004). Genetic influence on human psychological traits: A survey. *Current Directions in Psychological Science*, *13*, 148–153.

Bouchard, T. J., Jr., Lykken, D. T., McGue, M., Segal, N. L., & Tellegen, A. (1990, October 12). Sources of human psychological differences: The Minnesota Study of twins reared apart. *Science*, *250*, 223–228.

Bouchard, T. J., & McGue, M. (1981). Familial studies of intelligence: A review. *Science*, *212*, 1055–1059.

Bourdieu, P. (1986). The forms of capital. In Richardson, J., *Handbook of Theory and Research for the Sociology of Education*, Westport, CT: Greenwood, 241–58.

Bourne, V., & Todd, B. (2004). When left means right: An explanation of the left cradling bias in terms of right hemisphere specializations. *Developmental Science*, *7*, 19–24.

Bowen, F. (2013). Asthma education and health outcomes of children aged 8 to 12 years. *Clinical Nursing Research*, *22*, 172–185.

Bower, B. (1985). The left hand of math and verbal talent. *Science News*, *127*, 263.

Bower, T. G. R. (1977). *A primer of infant development*. San Francisco: Freeman.

Bowker, A., Gadbois, S., & Cornock, B. (2003). Sports participation and self-esteem: Variations as a function of gender and gender role orientation. *Sex Roles*, *49*, 47–58.

Bowlby, J. (1951). Maternal care and mental health. *Bulletin of the World Health Organization*, *3*, 355–534.

Bowlby, R. (2007). Babies and toddlers in non-parental daycare can avoid stress and anxiety if they develop a lasting secondary attachment bond with one carer who is consistently accessible to them. *Attachment & Human Development*, *9* [Special issue: The Life and Work of John Bowlby: A Tribute to His Centenary], 307–319.

Boyatzis, C. J. (2013). The nature and functions of religion and spirituality in children. In K. I. Pargament, J. J. Exline, & J. W. Jones (Eds.), *APA handbook of psychology, religion, and spirituality (Vol 1): Context, theory, and research*. Washington, DC: American Psychological Association.

Bracey, J., Bamaca, M., & Umana-Taylor, A. (2004). Examining ethnic identity and self-esteem among biracial and monoracial adolescents. *Journal of Youth & Adolescence*, *33*, 123–132.

Bracken, B., & Brown, E. (2006, June). Behavioral identification and assessment of gifted and talented students. *Journal of Psychoeducational Assessment*, *24*, 112–122.

Bracken, B., & Lamprecht, M. (2003). Positive self-concept: An equal opportunity construct. *School Psychology Quarterly*, *18*, 103–121.

Brackett, M., & Katulak, N. (2007). Emotional intelligence in the classroom: Skill-based training for teachers and students. *Applying emotional intelligence: A practitioner's guide* (pp. 1–27). New York, NY: Psychology Press.

Bradshaw, M., & Ellison, C. (2008). Do genetic factors influence religious life? Findings from a behavior genetic analysis of twin siblings. *Journal for the Scientific Study of Religion*, *47*, 529–544.

Brady, S. A. (2011). Efficacy of phonics teaching for reading outcomes: Indications from post-NRP research. In S. A. Brady, D. Braze, & C. A. Fowler (Eds.), *Explaining individual differences in reading: Theory and evidence*. New York: Psychology Press.

Brainerd, C. (2003). Jean Piaget, learning research, and American education. In B. Zimmerman (Ed.), *Educational psychology: A century of contributions*. Mahwah, NJ: Lawrence Erlbaum Associates.

Brandhorst, A. R. (2011). Multicultural education reform movement. In S. Totten & J. E. Pedersen (Eds.), *Teaching and studying social issues: Major programs and approaches*. Greenwich, CT: IAP Information Age Publishing.

Brandone, A. C., Cimpian, A., Leslie, S., & Gelman, S. A. (2012). Do lions have manes? For children, generics are about kinds rather than quantities. *Child Development*, *83*, 423–433.

Branstetter, E. (1969). The young child's response to hospitalization: Separation anxiety or lack of mothering care? *American Journal of Public Health*, *59*, 92–97.

Branta, C. F., Lerner, J. V., & Taylor, C. S. (Eds.). (1997). *Physical activity and youth sports: Social and moral issues*. Mahwah, NJ: Erlbaum.

Branum, A. (2006). Teen maternal age and very preterm birth of twins. *Maternal & Child Health Journal*, *10*, 229–233.

Braun, S. S., & Davidson, A. J. (2016). Gender (non)conformity in middle childhood: A mixed methods approach to understanding gender-typed behavior, friendship, and peer preference. *Sex Roles*. Accessed online, 8-9-17; https://link.springer.com/article/10.1007/s11199-016-0693-z

Braungart-Rieker, J. M., Zentall, S., Lickenbrock, D. M., Ekas, N. V., Oshio, T., & Planalp, E. (2015). Attachment in the making: Mother and father sensitivity and infants' responses during the still-face paradigm. *Journal of Experimental Child Psychology*, *125*, 63–84.

Bray, G. (2008). Causes of childhood obesity. *Obesity in childhood and adolescence, Vol 1: Medical, biological, and social issues* (pp. 25–57). Westport, CT: Praeger Publishers/Greenwood Publishing Group.

Brazelton, T. B. (1990). Saving the bathwater. *Child Development*, *61*, 1661–1671.

Brazelton, T. B., & Sparrow, J. D. (2003). *Discipline: The Brazelton way*. New York: Perseus.

Brazelton, T. B. & Sparrow, J. D. (2006). *Touchpoints—Birth to three*. New York: Da Capo Press.

Bremner, G., & Fogel, A. (Eds.). (2004). *Blackwell handbook of infant development*. Malden, MA: Blackwell Publishers.

Bremner, J. G., Slater, A. M., & Johnson, S. P. (2015). Perception of object persistence: The origins of object permanence in infancy. *Child Development Perspectives*, *9*, 7–13.

Bridgett, D., Gartstein, M., Putnam, S., et al. (2009). Maternal and contextual influences and the effect of temperament development during infancy on parenting in toddlerhood. *Infant Behavior & Development*, *32*, 103–116.

Briley, D. A., & Tucker-Drob, E. M. (2017). Comparing the developmental genetics of cognition and personality over the life span. *Journal of Personality*, *85*, 51–64.

Brinkman, B. G., Rabenstein, K. L., Rosén, L. A., & Zimmerman, T. S. (2014). Children's gender identity development: The dynamic negotiation process between conformity and authenticity. *Youth & Society*, *46*, 835–852.

Brock, C., Lapp, D., Flood, J., Fisher, D., & Han, K. (2007, July). Does homework matter? An investigation of teacher perceptions about homework practices for children from nondominant backgrounds. *Urban Education*, *42*(4), 349–372.

Broesch, T. L., & Bryant, G. A. (2015). Prosody in infant-directed speech is similar across Western and traditional cultures. *Journal of Cognition and Development*, *16*, 31–43.

Bornstein, M.H., Tal, J., Rahn, C., Galperin, C., et al. (1992). Functional analysis of the contents of maternal speech to infants of 5 and 13 months in four cultures: Argentina, France, Japan, and the United States. *Developmental Psychology*. 28(4):593–603.

Bronstein, P. (1999). Differences in mothers' and fathers' behaviors toward children: A cross-cultural comparison. In L. A. Peplau, R. C. Venigas, & P. L. Taylor (Eds.), *Gender, culture, and ethnicity: Current research about women and men.* Mountain View, CA: Mayfield Publishing.

Bronfenbrenner, U. (1989). Ecological systems theory. In R. Vasta (Ed.), *Six theories of child development.* Greenwich, CT: JAI Press.

Bronfenbrenner, U. (2000). Ecological systems theory. In A. E. Kazdin, A. E. Kazdin (Eds.), *Encyclopedia of Psychology, Vol. 3.* Washington, DC, US; New York: American Psychological Association.

Bronfenbrenner, U. (2002). Preparing a world for the infant in the twenty-first century: The research challenge. In J. Gomes-Pedro, J. K. Nugent, J. G. Young, T. B. Brazelton, J. Gomes-Pedro, J. K. Nugent, … T. B. Brazelton (Eds.), *The infant and family in the twenty-first century.* New York: Brunner-Routledge.

Bronfenbrenner, U., & Morris, P. (1998). The ecology of developmental processes. In W. Damon (Ed.), *Handbook of child psychology* (Vol. 1, 5th ed.). New York: Wiley.

Brooks-Gunn, J. (2003). Do you believe in magic? What we can expect from early childhood intervention programs. *Social Policy Report, 17,* 1–16.

Brooks-Gunn, J., Klebanov, P. K., & Duncan, G. J. (1996). Ethnic differences in children's intelligence test scores: Role of economic deprivation, home environment, and maternal characteristics. *Child Development, 67,* 396–408.

Brown, A. (2009). The influence of tobacco marketing on adolescent smoking intentions via normative beliefs. *Health Education Research, 24,* 721–733.

Brown, B. B., & Klute, C. (2003). Friendships, cliques, and crowds. In G. R. Adams, & M. D. Berzonsky (Eds.), *Blackwell handbook of adolescence.* Malden, MA: Blackwell Publishing.

Brown, C., Pikler, V., Lavish, L., Keune, K., & Hutto, C. (2008, January). Surviving childhood leukemia: Career, family, and future expectations. *Qualitative Health Research, 18*(1), 19–30.

Brown, D. L., Jewell, J. D., Stevens, A. L., Crawford, J. D., & Thompson, R. (2012). Suicidal risk in adolescent residential treatment: Being female is more important than a depression diagnosis. *Journal of Child and Family Studies, 21,* 359–367.

Brown, E. L., & Bull, R. (2007). Can task modifications influence children's performance on false belief tasks? *European Journal of Developmental Psychology, 4,* 274–292.

Brown, J. V., Bakeman, R., Coles, C. D., Platzman, K. A., & Lynch, M. E. (2004). Prenatal cocaine exposure: A comparison of 2-year-old children in prenatal and non-parental care. *Child Development, 75,* 1282–1295.

Brown, G., McBride, B., Shin, N., & Bost, K. (2007). Parenting predictors of father-child attachment security: Interactive effects of father involvement and fathering quality. *Fathering, 5,* 197–219.

Brown, M. J. (2008). Childhood lead poisoning prevention: getting the job done by 2010. *Journal of Environmental Health.* 7056–7057.

Brown, R., & Fraser, C. (1963). The acquisition of syntax. In C. N. Cofer & B. Musgrave (Eds.), *Verbal behavior and learning: Problems and processes.* New York: McGraw-Hill.

Brown, S. A. (2004). Measuring youth outcomes from alcohol and drug treatment. *Addiction, 99,* 38–46.

Brown, W. M., Hines, M., & Fane, B. A. (2002). Masculinized finger length patterns in human males and females with congenital adrenal hyperplasia. *Hormones and Behavior, 42,* 380–386.

Browne, K. (2006, March). Evolved sex differences and occupational segregation. *Journal of Organizational Behavior, 27,* 143–162.

Brownell, C. A. (2016). Prosocial behavior in infancy: The role of socialization. *Child Development Perspectives, 10,* 222–227.

Brownell, C. A., Ramani, G. B., & Zerwas, S. (2006). Becoming a social partner with peers: Cooperation and social understanding in one- and two-year-olds. *Child Development, 77,* 803–821.

Bruck, M., & Ceci, S. (2004). Forensic developmental psychology: Unveiling four common misconceptions. *Current Directions in Psychological Science, 13,* 229–232.

Brugnera, A., Zarbo, C., Adorni, R., et al. (2017). Cortical and cardiovascular responses to acute stressors and their relations with psychological distress. *International Journal of Psychophysiology, 114,* 38–46.

Brumback, T. Y., Worley, M., Nguyen-Louie, T. T., Squeglia, L. M., Jacobus, J., & Tapert, S. F. (2016). Neural predictors of alcohol use and psychopathology symptoms in adolescents. *Development and Psychopathology, 28*(4), 1209–1216.

Brummelman, E., Thomaes, S., de Castro, B. O., Overbeek, G., & Bushman, B. J. (2014). 'That's not just beautiful—that's incredibly beautiful!': The adverse impact of inflated praise on children with low self esteem. *Psychological Science, 25,* 728–735.

Brummelman, E., Thomaes, S., Overbeek, G., Orobio de Castro, B., van den Hout, M. A., & Bushman, B. J. (2014). On feeding those hungry for praise: Person praise backfires in children with low self-esteem. *Journal Of Experimental Psychology: General, 143,* 9–14.

Brune, C., & Woodward, A. (2007). Social cognition and social responsiveness in 10-month-old infants. *Journal of Cognition and Development, 8,* 133–158.

Bryant, J., & Bryant, J. (2003). Effects of entertainment televisual media on children. In E. Palmer & B. Young (Eds.), *The faces of televisual media: Teaching, violence, selling to children.* Mahwah, NJ: Lawrence Erlbaum Associates.

Bryden, P. J., Mayer, M. M., & Roy, E. A. (2011). Influences of task complexity, object location, and object type on hand selection in reaching in left- and right-handed children and adults. *Developmental Psychobiology, 53,* 47–58.

Bufferd, S. J., Dougherty, L. R., Carlson, G. A., Rose, S., & Klein, D. N. (2012). Psychiatric disorders in preschoolers: Continuity from ages 3 to 6. *Journal of American Psychiatry, 169,* 1157–1164.

Bullinger, A. (1997). Sensorimotor function and its evolution. In J. Guimon (Ed.), *The body in psychotherapy* (pp. 25–29). Basil, Switzerland: Karger.

Bumpus, M. F., Crouter, A. C., & McHale, S. M. (2001). Parental autonomy granting during adolescence: Exploring gender differences in context. *Developmental Psychology, 37,* 163–173.

Buon, M., Habib, M., & Frey, D. (2017). Moral development: Conflicts and compromises. In J. A. Sommerville & J. Decety (Eds.), *Social cognition: Development across the life span.* New York: Routledge/Taylor & Francis Group.

Burakevych, N., Mckinlay, C. D., Alsweiler, J. M., Wouldes, T. A., & Harding, J. E. (2017). Bayley-III motor scale and neurological examination at 2 years do not predict motor skills at 4.5 years. *Developmental Medicine & Child Neurology, 59,* 216–223.

Burbach, J., & van der Zwaag, B. (2009). Contact in the genetics of autism and schizophrenia. *Trends in Neurosciences, 32,* 69–72.

Burd, L., Cotsonas-Hassler, T. M., Martsolf, J. T., & Kerbeshian, J. (2003). Recognition and management of fetal alcohol syndrome. *Neurotoxicological Teratology, 25,* 681–688.

Burdjalov, V. F., Baumgart, S., & Spitzer, A. R. (2003). Cerebral function monitoring: A new scoring system for the evaluation of brain maturation in neonates. *Pediatrics, 112*, 855–861.

Bureau of Labor Statistics, U.S. Department of Labor. (2017). *Occupational outlook handbook, 2016–17 edition*, Childcare Workers. Retrieved March 3, 2017, from https://www.bls.gov/ooh/personal-care-and-service/childcare-workers.htm.

Bureau of Labor Statistics (2016). ____Table 3: Employment Status of the Civilian Noninstitutional Population by Age, Sex, and Race, Current Population Survey (2016). Retrieved August 5, 2017, from https://www.bls.gov/cps/cpsaat03.pdf.

Burgess, K. B., & Rubin, K. H. (2000). Middle childhood: Social and emotional development. In A. E. Kazdin (Ed.), *Encyclopedia of psychology* (Vol. 5). Washington, DC: American Psychological Association.

Burnham, M., Goodlin-Jones, B., & Gaylor, E. (2002). Nighttime sleep–wake patterns and self-soothing from birth to one year of age: A longitudinal intervention study. *Journal of Child Psychology & Psychiatry & Allied Disciplines, 43*, 713–725.

Burns, E. (2003). *A handbook for supplementary aids and services: A best practice and IDEA guide to enable children with disabilities to be educated with nondisabled children to the maximum extent appropriate.* Springfield, IL: Charles C. Thomas.

Burton, L., Henninger, D., Hafetz, J., & Cofer, J. (2009). Aggression, gender-typical childhood play, and a prenatal hormonal index. *Social Behavior and Personality, 37*, 105–116.

Burzin, K.K., Parmar, K.S., Rao, M.V., & Bilimoria, F.E. (2007). Profile of sexually transmitted diseases in pediatric patients. *Indian Journal of Sexually Transmitted Diseases, 28*, 76-78.

Bushman, B. J., Gollwitzer, M., & Cruz, C. (2014). There is broad consensus: Media researchers agree that violent media increase aggression in children, and pediatricians and parents concur. *Psychology of Popular Media Culture.* Retrieved March 20, 2015, from http://psycnet.apa.org/psycinfo/2014-41977-001/.

Busick, D., Brooks, J., Pernecky, S., Dawson, R., & Petzoldt, J. (2008). Parent food purchases as a measure of exposure and preschool-aged children's willingness to identify and taste fruit and vegetables. *Appetite, 51*, 468–473.

Buss, A. H. (2012). *Pathways to individuality: Evolution and development of personality traits.* Washington, DC: American Psychological Association.

Buss, K. A., & Kiel, E. J. (2004). Comparison of sadness, anger, and fear facial expressions when toddlers look at their mothers. *Child Development, 75*, 1761–1773.

Bussey, K. (1992). Lying and truthfulness: Children's definition, standards, and evaluative reactions. *Child Development, 63*, 1236–1250.

Butler, K. G., & Silliman, E. R. (Eds.). (2003). *Speaking, reading, and writing in children with language learning disabilities: New paradigms in research and practice.* Mahwah, NJ: Lawrence Erlbaum.

Butler, R. J., Wilson, B. L., & Johnson, W. G. (2012). A modified measure of health care disparities applied to birth weight disparities and subsequent mortality. *Health Economics, 21*, 113–126.

Butterworth, G. (1994). Infant intelligence. In J. Khalfa (Ed.), *What is intelligence? The Darwin College lecture series* (pp. 49–71). Cambridge, England: Cambridge University Press.

Byrd, D., Katcher, M., Peppard, P., Durkin, M., & Remington, P. (2007). Infant mortality: Explaining black/white disparities in Wisconsin. *Maternal and Child Health Journal, 11*, 319–326.

Byrd, R. S., Weitzman, M., & Auinger, P. (1997). Increased behavior problems associated with delayed school entry and delayed school progress. *Pediatrics, 100*, 654–661.

Byun, S., & Hyunjoon, P. (2012). The academic success of East Asian American youth: The role of shadow education. In R. Arum & M. Velez (Eds.), *Improving learning environments: School discipline and student achievement in comparative perspective.* Palo Alto, CA: Stanford University Press.

Cabera, N. J. (2013). Positive development of minority children. *SRCD Social Policy Report, 27*, 1–22.

Cabrera, N., Shannon, J., & Tamis-LeMonda, C. (2007). Fathers' influence on their children's cognitive and emotional development: From toddlers to pre-K. *Applied Developmental Science, 11*, 208–213.

Cacciatore, J., & Bushfield, S. (2007). Stillbirth: The mother's experience and implications for improving care. *Journal of Social Work in End-of-Life & Palliative Care, 3*, 59–79.

Cadinu, M. R., & Kiesner, J. (2000). Children's development of a theory of mind. *European Journal of Psychology of Education, 15*, 93–111.

Caino, S., Kelmansky, D., Lejarraga, H., & Adamo, P. (2004). Short-term growth at adolescence in healthy girls. *Annals of Human Biology, 31*, 182–195.

Cale, L., & Harris, J. (2013). 'Every child (of every size) matters' in physical education! Physical education's role in childhood obesity. *Sport, Education And Society, 18*, 433–452.

Calhoun, F., & Warren, K. (2007). Fetal alcohol syndrome: Historical perspectives. *Neuroscience & Biobehavioral Reviews, 31*, 168–171.

Callaghan, B.L., Li, S., & Richardson, R. (2014). The elusive engram: What can infantile amnesia tell us about memory? *Trends in Neurosciences, 37*, 47–53.

Callister, L. C., Khalaf, I., Semenic, S., Kartchner, R., & Vehvilainen-Julkunen, K. (2003). The pain of childbirth: Perceptions of culturally diverse women. *Pain Management Nursing, 4*, 145–154.

Calvert, S. L., Kotler, J. A., Zehnder, S., & Shockey, E. (2003). Gender stereotyping in children's reports about educational and informational television programs. *Media Psychology, 5*, 139–162.

Calzada, E. J., Huang, K., Anicama, C., Fernandez, Y., & Brotman, L. (2012). Test of a cultural framework of parenting with Latino families of young children. *Cultural Diversity and Ethnic Minority Psychology, 18*, 285–296.

Cami, J., & Farré, M. (2003). Drug addiction. *New England Journal of Medicine, 349*, 975–986.

Campbell, A., Shirley, L., & Candy, J. (2004). A longitudinal study of gender-related cognition and behaviour. *Developmental Science, 7*, 1–9.

Campbell, D., Scott, K., Klaus, M., & Falk, M. (2007). Female relatives or friends trained as labor doulas: Outcomes at 6 to 8 weeks postpartum. *Birth: Issues in Perinatal Care, 34*, 220–227.

Campbell, F., Ramey, C., & Pungello, E. (2002). Early childhood education: Young adult outcomes from the Abecedarian Project. *Applied Developmental Science, 6*, 42–57.

Campbell, K., Crawford, D., & Ball, K. (2006, August). Family food environment and dietary behaviors likely to promote fatness in 5–6-year-old children. *International Journal of Obesity, 30*(8), 1272–1280.

Campos, J. J., Langer, A., & Krowitz, A. (1970). Cardiac responses on the visual cliff in prelocomotor human infants. *Science, 170*, 196–197.

Camras, L., Oster, H., Bakeman, R., Meng, Z., Ujiie, T., & Campos, J. (2007). Do infants show distinct negative facial expressions for fear and anger? Emotional expression in 11-month-old European American, Chinese, and Japanese Infants. *Infancy, 11,* 131–155.

Canals, J., Fernandez-Ballart, J., & Esparo, G. (2003). Evolution of Neonatal Behavior Assessment Scale scores in the first month of life. *Infant Behavior & Development, 26,* 227–237.

Canals, J., Hernández-Martínez, C., & Fernández-Ballart, J. D. (2011). Relationships between early behavioural characteristics and temperament at 6 years. *Infant Behavior & Development, 34,* 152–160.

Caplan, L. J., & Barr, R. A. (1989). On the relationship between category intensions and extensions in children. *Journal of Experimental Child Psychology, 47,* 413–429.

Caputi, M., Lecce, S., Pagnin, A., & Banerjee, R. (2012). Longitudinal effects of theory of mind on later peer relations: The role of prosocial behavior. *Developmental Psychology, 48,* 257–270.

Carbonaro, W., Ellison, B. J., & Covay, E. (2011). Gender inequalities in the college pipeline. *Social Science Research, 40,* 120–135.

Carey, B. (2012, March 29). Diagnoses of autism on the rise, report says. *New York Times,* p. A20.

Carmody, K., Haskett, M. E., Loehman, J., & Rose, R. A. (2014). Physically abused children's adjustment at the transition to school: Child, parent, and family factors. *Journal of Child and Family Studies.* Retrieved February 13, 2014, from http://link.springer.com/article/10.1007%2Fs10826-014-9906-7#page-1.

Carnell, S., Benson, L., Pryor, K., & Driggin, E. (2013). Appetitive traits from infancy to adolescence: Using behavioral and neural measures to investigate obesity risk. *Physiology & Behavior.* Retrieved February 11, 2014, from http://europepmc.org/abstract/MED/23458627/reload=0;jsessionid=7zatjr4EShvPiUnmQKcu.2.

Carney, R. N., & Levin, J. R. (2003) Promoting higher-order learning benefits by building lower-order mnemonic connections. *Applied Cognitive Psychology, 17,* 563–575.

Caron, A. (2009). Comprehension of the representational mind in infancy. *Developmental Review, 29,* 69–95.

Caron, C., Gjelsvik, A., & Buechner, J. S. (2005). The impact of poverty on prevention practices and health status among persons with asthma. *Medicine Health Rhode Island, 88,* 60–62.

Carpendale, J. I. M. (2000). Kohlberg and Piaget on stages and moral reasoning. *Developmental Review, 20,* 181–205.

Carpenter, D. M. H., Flowers, N., & Mertens, S. B. (2004). High expectations for every student. *Middle School Journal, 35,* 64.

Carr, P. B., & Steele, C. M. (2009). Stereotype threat and inflexible perseverance in problem solving. *Journal of Experimental Social Psychology, 45,* 853–859.

Carson, A., Chabot, C., Greyson, D., Shannon, K., Duff, P., & Shoveller, J. (2016). A narrative analysis of the birth stories of early-age mothers. *Sociology Of Health & Illness.* Retrieved March 3, 2017, from http://onlinelibrary.wiley.com/doi/10.1111/1467-9566.12518/abstract.

Casalin, S., Luyten, P., Vliegen, N., & Meurs, P. (2012). The structure and stability of temperament from infancy to toddlerhood: A one-year prospective study. *Infant Behavior & Development, 35,* 94–108.

Casasanto, D., & Henetz, T. (2012). Handedness shapes children's abstract concepts. *Cognitive Science, 36,* 359–372.

Case, R., Demetriou, A., & Platsidou, M. (2001). Integrating concepts and tests of intelligence from the differential and developmental traditions. *Intelligence, 29,* 307–336.

Caselli, M., Rinaldi, P., Stefanini, S., & Volterra, V. (2012). Early action and gesture "vocabulary" and its relation with word comprehension and production. *Child Development, 83,* 526–542.

Casey, B. J., Jones, R. M., & Somerville, L. H. (2011). Braking and accelerating of the adolescent brain. *Journal of Research on Adolescence, 21,* 21–33.

Caskey, R., Lindau, S., & Caleb Alexander, G. (2009). Knowledge and early adoption of the HPV vaccine among girls and young women: Results of a national survey. *Journal of Adolescent Health, 45,* 453–462.

Caspi, A. (2000). The child is father of the man: Personality continuities from childhood to adulthood. *Journal of Personality and Social Psychology, 78,* 158–172.

Caspi, J. (2012). *Sibling aggression: Assessment and treatment.* New York: Springer Publishing Co.

Cassidy, J., & Berlin, L. J. (1994). The insecure/ambivalent pattern of attachment: Theory and research. *Child Development, 65,* 971–991.

Castelao, C., & Kröner-Herwig, B. (2013). Different trajectories of depressive symptoms in children and adolescents: Predictors and differences in girls and boys. *Journal of Youth and Adolescence, 42,* 1169–1182.

Cataldi, E. F., Laird, J., KewalRamani, A., & Chapman, C. (2009). *High school dropout and completion rates in the United States: 2007.* Washington, DC: U.S. Department of Education.

Catalini, M. (2017, March 11). Forget cribs. A cardboard box may be the safest place for your baby to sleep. *Boston Globe.* Retrieved March 14, 2017, from https://www.bostonglobe.com/lifestyle/2017/03/11/forget-cribs-carboard-box-may-safest-place-for-your-baby-sleep/wwEakqRSAHh10ZZturXBHL/story.html.

Catherine, S. (1999). MPH, National Drug and Alcohol Research Center, University of South Wales, Sydney 2052, Australia, [5].

Cauce, A. (2008). Parenting, culture, and context: Reflections on excavating culture. *Applied Developmental Science, 12,* 227–229.

Cauce, A., & Domenech-Rodriguez, M. (2002). Latino families: myths and realities. In J. M. Contreras, J. K. A., Kerns, & A. M. Neal-Barnett (Eds.), *Latino children and families in the United States.* Westport, CT: Praeger.

Cavallini, A., Fazzi, E., & Viviani, V. (2002). Visual acuity in the first two years of life in healthy term newborns: An experience with the Teller Acuity Cards. *Functional Neurology: New Trends in Adaptive & Behavioral Disorders, 17,* 87–92.

CDC (2016). *Understanding teen dating violence: Fact sheet.* National Center for Injury Prevention and Control, Division of Violence Prevention. Washington, DC: Centers for Disease Control.

CDC (2016a). *Reduced disparities in birth rates among teens aged 15–19 years—United States, 2006–2007 and 2013–2014.* MMWR 2016. Retrieved August 5, 2017, from https://www.cdc.gov/mmwr/volumes/65/wr/mm6516a1.htm.

CDC/National Center for Health Statistics (2017). *Compressed mortality file.* Atlanta, GA: Centers for Disease Control.

Ceci, S. J., & Bruck, M. (1993). The suggestibility of the child witness: A historical review and synthesis. *Psychological Bulletin, 113,* 403–439.

Ceci, S., & Bruck, M. (2007). Loftus's lineage in developmental forensic research: Six scientific misconceptions about children's suggestibility. In *Do justice and let the sky fall: Elizabeth Loftus and her contributions to science, law, and academic freedom* (pp. 65–77). Mahwah, NJ, US: Lawrence Erlbaum Associates Publishers.

Celano, M. P., Holsey, C., & Kobrynski, L. J. (2012). Home-based family intervention for low-income children with asthma: A randomized controlled pilot study. *Journal of Family Psychology, 26,* 171–178.

Centers for Disease Control and Prevention. (2016). *Understanding bullying: Fact sheet.* Washington, DC: National Center for Injury Prevention and Control, Division of Violence Prevention, Centers for Disease Control and Prevention.

Centers for Disease Control and Prevention. (2016). Tobacco use among middle and high school students—United States, 2011–2015. *Morbidity and Mortality Weekly Report, 65(14),* 361–367.

Centers for Disease Control and Prevention. (2017). *Recommended immunization schedule for children and adolescents aged 18 years or younger, United States, 2017.* Washington, DC: Centers for Disease Control.

Centers for Disease Control and Prevention/National Center for Health Statistics. (2012). *National Vital Statistics Report.* Hyattsville, MD: Centers for Disease Control.

Central Intelligence Agency (2016). *The World Factbook.* Washington, DC: Central Intelligence Agency.

Central Statistics Office Ministry of Statistics and Programme Implementation Government of India (Social Statistics Division) (2017). Youth in India 2017 http://mospi.nic.in/sites/default/files/publication_reports/Youth_in_India-2017.pdf

Chadda, R. K. & Sengupta, S. N. (2002). Tobacco use by Indian adolescents. *Tobacco Induced Diseases,* 1: 111, doi: 10.1186/1617-9625-1-2-111. [6].

Chaffin, M. (2006). The changing focus of child maltreatment research and practice within psychology. *Journal of Social Issues, 62,* 663–684.

Chakraborty, R., & De, S. (2014). Body image and its relation with the concept of physical self among adolescents and young adults. *Psychological Studies, 59,* 419–426.

Chakravarty, N., & Pati, S. (2013). Do inequalities in child health get wider as countries develop? *International Journal of Child Health and Human Development, 6,* 275–280.

Chalabi, M. (2015, February 5.) How many women earn more than their husbands? *FiveThirtyEight.* Retrieved May 5, 2017, from https://fivethirtyeight.com/datalab/how-many-women-earn-more-than-their-husbands/.

Chall, J. (1992). The new reading debates: Evidence from science, art, and ideology. *Teachers College Record, 94,* 315–328.

Chall, J. S. (1979). The great debate: Ten years later, with a modest proposal for reading stages. In L. B. Resnick & P. A. Weaver (Eds.), Theory and practice of early reading. Hillsdale, NJ: Lawrence Erlbaum.

Chamberlain, P., Price, J., Reid, J., Landsverk, J., Fisher, P., & Stoolmiller, M. (2006, April). Who disrupts from placement in foster and kinship care? *Child Abuse & Neglect, 30,* 409–424.

Chan, D. W. (1997). Self-concept and global self-worth among Chinese adolescents in Hong Kong. *Personality & Individual Differences, 22,* 511–520.

Chan, S., & Chan, K. (2013). Adolescents' susceptibility to peer pressure: Relations to parent–adolescent relationship and adolescents' emotional autonomy from parents. *Youth & Society, 45,* 286–302.

Chan, W. Y., & Birman, D. (2009). Cross- and same-race friendships of Vietnamese immigrant adolescents: A focus on acculturation and school diversity. *International Journal of Intercultural Relations, 33,* 313–324.

Chandra, A., Mosher, W. D., Copen. C., & Sionean, C. (2011). Sexual behavior, sexual attraction, and sexual identity in the United States: Data from the 2006–2008 National Survey of Family Growth. *National health statistics reports; no 36.* Hyattsville, MD: National Center for Health Statistics.

Chang, I., Pettit, R., & Katsurada, E. (2006, May). Where and when to spank: A comparison between U.S. and Japanese college students. *Journal of Family Violence, 21(4),* 281–286.

Chaplin, T., Gillham, J., & Seligman, M. (2009). Gender, anxiety, and depressive symptoms: A longitudinal study of early adolescents. *Journal of Early Adolescence, 29,* 307–327.

Chapman, R. (2016). A case study of gendered play in preschools: How early childhood educators' perceptions of gender influence children's play. *Early Child Development and Care, 186,* 1271–1284.

Chaudhary, N., & Sharma, N. (2012). India. In J. Arnett (Ed.), *Adolescent psychology around the world.* New York: Psychology Press.

Chen, J., Chen, T., & Zheng, X. (2012). Parenting styles and practices among Chinese immigrant mothers with young children. *Early Child Development and Care, 182,* 1–21.

Chen, S., Hwang, F., Yeh, Y., & Lin, S. J. (2012). Cognitive ability, academic achievement and academic self-concept: Extending the internal/external frame of reference model. *British Journal of Educational Psychology, 82,* 308–326.

Chen, E., & Rao, N. (2011). Gender socialization in Chinese kindergartens: Teachers' contributions. *Sex Roles, 64(1–2),* 103–116.

Chen, J., & Gardner, H. (2005). Assessment based on multiple-intelligences theory. In D. P. Flanagan & P. L. Harrison (Eds.), *Contemporary intellectual assessment: Theories, tests, and issues.* New York, Guilford Press.

Chen, X., Hastings, P. D., Rubin, K. H., Chen, H., Cen, G., & Stewart, S. L. (1998). Child-rearing attitudes and behavioral inhibition in Chinese and Canadian toddlers: A cross-cultural study. *Developmental Psychology, 34,* 677–686.

Cheng, J. T., Tracy, J. L., Ho, S., & Henrich, J. (2016). Listen, follow me: Dynamic vocal signals of dominance predict emergent social rank in humans. *Journal of Experimental Psychology: General, 145,* 536–547.

Cherney, I., Kelly-Vance, L., & Glover, K. (2003). The effects of stereotyped toys and gender on play assessment in children aged 18–47 months. *Educational Psychology, 23,* 95–105.

Chertok, I., Luo, J., & Anderson, R. H. (2011). Association between changes in smoking habits in subsequent pregnancy and infant birth weight in West Virginia. *Maternal and Child Health Journal, 15,* 249–254.

Cheung, A., Emslie, G., & Mayes, T. (2006, January). The use of antidepressants to treat depression in children and adolescents. *Canadian Medical Association Journal, 174(2),* 193–200

Cheung, W., Maio, G. R., Rees, K. J., Kamble, S., & Mane, S. (2016). Cultural differences in values as self-guides. *Personality and Social Psychology Bulletin, 42,* 769–781.

Chien, S., Bronson-Castain, K., Palmer, J., & Teller, D. (2006). Lightness constancy in 4-month-old infants. *Vision Research, 46,* 2139–2148.

Child Health USA. (2003). *The health and well-being of children.* Rockville, MD: Health Resources and Services Administration.

Childline India. Childline 1098 service. [Last cited on 2014 Aug 20]. Available from: http://www.childlineindia.org.in/.

ChildStats.gov. (2009). America's children 2009. Washington, DC: National Maternal and Child Health Clearinghouse.

Child Welfare Information Gateway. (2013). *What is child abuse and neglect? Recognizing the signs and symptoms*. Washington, DC: U.S. Department of Health and Human Services, Children's Bureau.

Child Welfare Information Gateway. (2016). *Child abuse and neglect fatalities 2014: Statistics and interventions*. Washington, DC: U.S. Department of Health and Human Services, Children's Bureau.

Child Welfare Information Gateway. (2017). *Foster care statistics 2015*. Washington, DC: U.S. Department of Health and Human Services, Children's Bureau.

Chiodo, L. M., Bailey, B. A., Sokol, R. J., Janisse, J., Delaney-Black, V., & Hannigan, J. H. (2012). Recognized spontaneous abortion in mid-pregnancy and patterns of pregnancy alcohol use. *Alcohol, 46*, 261–267.

Chiu, M., & McBride-Chang, C. (2006). Gender, context, and reading: A comparison of students in 43 countries. *Scientific Studies of Reading, 10*(4), 331–362.

Chomsky, N. (1968). *Language and mind*. New York: Harcourt Brace Jovanovich.

Chomsky, N. (1978). On the biological basis of language capacities. In G. A. Miller & E. Lennenberg (Eds.), *Psychology and biology of language and thought* (pp. 199–220). New York: Academic Press.

Chomsky, N. (1991). Linguistics and cognitive science: Problems and mysteries. In A. Kasher (Ed.), *The Chomskyan turn*. Cambridge, MA: Blackwell.

Chomsky, N. (1999). On the nature, use, and acquisition of language. In W. C. Ritchie & T. J. Bhatia (Eds.), *Handbook of child language acquisition*. San Diego: Academic Press.

Chomsky, N. (2005). Editorial: Universals of human nature. *Psychotherapy and Psychosomatics [serial online], 74*, 263–268.

Chonchaiya, W., Tardif, T., Mai, X., et al. (2013). Developmental trends in auditory processing can provide early predictions of language acquisition in young infants. *Developmental Science, 16*, 159–172.

Chowdhury, A.N., & Sen, P. (1992). Initiation of heroin abuse: the role of peers. *Indian Journal of Pediatrics, 34*: 34–5.

Choy, C. M., Yeung, Q. S., Briton-Jones, C. M., Cheung, C. K., Lam, C. W., & Haines, C. J. (2002). Relationship between semen parameters and mercury concentrations in blood and in seminal fluid from subfertile males in Hong Kong. *Fertility and Sterility, 78*, 426–428.

Christakis, D., & Zimmerman, F. (2007). Violent television viewing during preschool is associated with antisocial behavior during school age. *Pediatrics, 120*, 993–999.

Christoff, K., Cosmelli, D., Legrand, D., & Thompson, E. (2011). Specifying the self for cognitive neuroscience. *Trends in Cognitive Sciences, 15*, 104–112.

Chronis, A., Jones, H., & Raggi, V. (2006, June). Evidence-based psychosocial treatments for children and adolescents with attention-deficit/hyperactivity disorder. *Clinical Psychology Review, 26*, 486–502.

Cicchetti, D., & Cohen, D. J. (2006). *Developmental psychopathology, Vol. 1: Theory and method* (2nd Ed.). Hoboken, NJ: John Wiley & Sons.

Cina, V., & Fellmann, F. (2006). Implications of predictive testing in neurodegenerative disorders. *Schweizer Archiv für Neurologie und Psychiatrie, 157*, 359–365.

Cirulli, F., Berry, A., & Alleva, E. (2003). Early disruption of the mother–infant relationship: Effects on brain plasticity and implications for psychopathology. *Neuroscience & Biobehavioral Reviews, 27*, 73–82.

Clark, K. B., & Clark, M. P. (1947). Racial identification and preference in Negro children. In T. M. Newcomb & E. L. Hartley (Eds.), *Readings in social psychology*. New York: Holt, Rinehart & Winston.

Clark, M. A., Gleason, P. M., Tuttle, C. C., & Silverberg, M. K. (2015). Do charter schools improve student achievement? *Educational Evaluation and Policy Analysis, 37*(4).

Clarke, T-K., Treutlein, J., Zimmermann, U. S., et al. (2008). HPA-axis activity in alcoholism: Examples for a gene-environment interaction. *Addiction Biology, 13*, 1–14.

Clarke-Stewart, K., & Allhusen, V. (2002). Nonparental caregiving. (2002). In M. Bornstein (Ed.), *Handbook of parenting: Vol. 3: Being and becoming a parent* (2nd ed.). Mahwah, NJ: Lawrence Erlbaum Associates.

Clayton, H. B., Li, R., Perrine, C. G., & Scanlon, K. S. (2013). Prevalence and reasons for introducing infants early to solid foods: Variations by milk feeding type. *Pediatrics*. Retrieved September 5, 2014, from http://pediatrics.aappublications. org/content/131/4/e1108.

Clearfield, M., & Nelson, N. (2006, January). Sex differences in mothers' speech and play behavior with 6-, 9-, and 14-month-old infants. *Sex Roles, 54*, 127–137.

Clifton, R. (1992). The development of spatial hearing in human infants. In L. A. Werner & E. W. Rubel (Eds.), *Developmental psychoacoustics* (pp. 135–157). Washington, DC: American Psychological Association.

Cline, K. D., & Edwards, C. P. (2017). Parent–child book-reading styles, emotional quality, and changes in early head start children's cognitive scores. *Early Education and Development, 28*(1), 41–58.

Close, F. T., Suther, S., Foster, A., El-Amin, S., & Battle, A. M. (2013). Community perceptions of Black infant mortality: A qualitative inquiry. *Journal of Health Care for the Poor and Underserved, 24*, 1089–1101.

Closson, L. (2009). Status and gender differences in early adolescents' descriptions of popularity. *Social Development, 18*, 412–426.

Coates, S. W. (2016). Can babies remember trauma? Symbolic forms of representation in traumatized infants. *Journal of the American Psychoanalytic Association, 64*, 751–776.

Cockrill, K., & Gould H. (2012). Letter to the editor: Response to "What women want from abortion counseling in the United States: A qualitative study of abortion patients in 2008." *Social Work in Health Care, 51*, 191–194.

Coelho, V. A., Marchante, M., & Jimerson, S. R. (2017). Promoting a positive middle school transition: A randomized-controlled treatment study examining self-concept and self-esteem. *Journal of Youth and Adolescence*. Retrieved June 13, 2016, from http://www.ncbi.nlm.nih.gov/pubmed/27230119.

Cogan, L. W., Josberger, R. E., Gesten, F. C., & Roohan, P. J. (2012). Can prenatal care impact future well-child visits? The experience of a low-income population in New York State Medicaid managed care. *Maternal and Child Health Journal, 16*, 92–99.

Cohen, D. (2013). *How the child's mind develops* (2nd ed.). New York: Routledge/Taylor & Francis Group.

Cohen, J. (1999, March 19). Nurture helps mold able minds. *Science, 283*, 1832–1833.

Cohen, L. B., & Cashon, C. H. (2003). Infant perception and cognition. In R. M. Lerner & M. A. Easterbrooks (Eds.), *Handbook of psychology: Developmental psychology* (Vol. 6). New York: John Wiley & Sons.

Cohen, R. A., Mather, N., Schneider, D. A., & White, J. M. (2016). A comparison of schools: Teacher knowledge of explicit code-based reading instruction. *Reading and Writing.* Retrieved March 16, 2017, from http://link.springer.com/article/10.1007/s11145-016-9694-0.

Cohen, S., Tyrell, D. A., & Smith, A. P. (1993). Negative life events, perceived stress, negative affect, and susceptibility of the common cold. *Journal of Personality and Social Psychology, 64*, 131–140.

Cohen-Zion, M., Shabi, A., Levy, S., Glasner, L., & Wiener, A. (2016). Effects of partial sleep deprivation on information processing speed in adolescence. *Journal of the International Neuropsychological Society, 22*, 388–398.

Cokley, K. (2003). What do we know about the motivation of African American students? Challenging the "anti-intellectual" myth. *Harvard Educational Review, 73*, 524–558.

Colby, A., & Damon, W. (1987). Listening to a different voice: A review of Gilligan's *In a different voice.* In M. R. Walsh (Ed.), *The psychology of women.* New Haven, CT: Yale University Press.

Colby, A., & Kohlberg, L. (1987). *The measurement of moral adjudgment* (Vols. 1–2). New York: Cambridge University Press.

Cole, C. F., Arafat, C., & Tidhar, C. (2003). The educational impact of Rechov Sumsum/Shara'a Simsim: A *Sesame Street* television series to promote respect and understanding among children living in Israel, the West Bank and Gaza. *International Journal of Behavioral Development, 27*, 409–422.

Cole, M. (1992). Culture in development. In M. H. Bornstein & M. E. Lamb (Eds.), *Developmental psychology: An advanced textbook* (3rd ed.). Hillsdale, NJ: Erlbaum.

Cole, P. M., & Moore, G. A. (2015). About face! Infant facial expression of emotion. *Emotion Review, 7*(2), 116–120.

Cole, S. A. (2005). Infants in foster care: Relational and environmental factors affecting attachment. *Journal of Reproductive & Infant Psychology, 23*, 43–61.

Colino, S. (2002, February 26). Problem kid or label? *The Washington Post,* p. HE01.

Collins, M. F. (2010). ELL preschoolers' English vocabulary acquisition from storybook reading. *Early Childhood Research Quarterly, 25*, 84–97.

Collins, J. (2012). Growing up bicultural in the United States: The case of Japanese-Americans. In R. Josselson & M. Harway (Eds.), *Navigating multiple identities: Race, gender, culture, nationality, and roles.* New York: Oxford University Press.

Collins, W. (2003). More than myth: The developmental significance of romantic relationships during adolescence. *Journal of Research on Adolescence, 13*, 1–24.

Collins, W., & Andrew, L. (2004). Changing relationships, changing youth: Interpersonal contexts of adolescent development. *Journal of Early Adolescence, 24*, 55–62.

Collins, W. A., Gleason, T., & Sesma, A. (1997). Internalization, autonomy, and relationships: Development during adolescence. In J. E. Grusec & L. Kuczynski (Eds.), *Parenting and children's internalization of values: A handbook of contemporary theory* (pp. 78–99). New York: Wiley.

Colom, R., Lluis-Font, J. M., & Andrés-Pueyo, A. (2005). The generational intelligence gains are caused by decreasing variance in the lower half of the distribution: Supporting evidence for the nutrition hypothesis. *Intelligence, 33*, 83–91.

Colombo, J., & Mitchell, D. (2009). Infant visual habituation. *Neurobiology of Learning and Memory, 92*, 225–234.

Colpin, H., & Soenen, S. (2004). Bonding. Through an adoptive mother's eyes. *Midwifery Today, 70*, 30–31.

Coltrane, S., & Adams, M. (1997). Children and gender. In T. Arendell (Ed.), *Contemporary parenting: Challenges and issues. Understanding Families* (Vol. 9, pp. 219–253). Thousand Oaks, CA: Sage.

Committee on Children, Youth and Families. (1994). *When you need child day care.* Washington, DC: American Psychological Association.

Committee to Study the Prevention of Low Birthweight. (1985). *Preventing low birthweight.* Washington, DC: National Academy Press.

Condon, J., Corkindale, C., Boyce, P., & Gamble, E. (2013). A longitudinal study of father-to-infant attachment: Antecedents and correlates. *Journal of Reproductive and Infant Psychology, 31*, 15–30.

Condry, J., & Condry, S. (1976). Sex differences: A study of the eye of the beholder. *Child Development, 47*, 812–819.

Conel, J. L. (1930/1963). *Postnatal development of the human cortex* (Vols. 1–6). Cambridge, MA: Harvard University Press.

Conley, D., & Rauscher, E. (2013). Genetic interactions with prenatal social environment: Effects on academic and behavioral outcomes. *Journal of Health and Social Behavior, 54*, 109–127.

Connell-Carrick, K. (2006). Early child care and early child development: Major findings of the NICHD Study of Early Child Care. *Child Welfare Journal, 85*, 819–836.

Conner, K., & Goldston, D. (2007, March). Rates of suicide among males increase steadily from age 11 to 21: Developmental framework and outline for prevention. *Aggression and Violent Behavior, 12*(2), 193–207.

Cook, E., Buehler, C., & Henson, R. (2009). Parents and peers as social influences to deter antisocial behavior. *Journal of Youth and Adolescence, 38*, 1240–1252.

Copping, K. E., Kurtz-Costes, B., Rowley, S. J., & Wood, D. (2013). Age and race differences in racial stereotype awareness and endorsement. *Journal of Applied Social Psychology, 43*, 971–980.

Corballis, M. C., Hattie, J., & Fletcher, R. (2008). Handedness and intellectual achievement: an even-handed look. *Neuropsychologia, 46*, 374–8.

Corbetta, D., & Snapp-Childs, W. (2009). Seeing and touching: The role of sensory-motor experience on the development of infant reaching. *Infant Behavior & Development, 32*, 44–58.

Corbett, C., & Callister, L.C. (2012). Giving birth: the voices of women in Tamil Nadu, childbearing beliefs and practices among women in Australia. Midwifery 16, 22–34.

Corbin, C. (1973). *A textbook of motor development.* Dubuque, IA: Brown.

Corcoran, J., & Pillai, V. (2007, January). Effectiveness of secondary pregnancy prevention programs: A meta-analysis. *Research on Social Work Practice, 17*, 5–18.

Cordón, I. M., Pipe, M., Sayfan, L., Melinder, A., & Goodman, G. S. (2004). Memory for traumatic experiences in early childhood. *Developmental Review, 24*, 101–132.

Cornwell, T., & McAlister, A. R. (2011). Alternative thinking about starting points of obesity. Development of child taste preferences. *Appetite, 56*, 428–439.

Corrow, S., Granrud, C. E., Mathison, J., & Yonas, A. (2012). Infants and adults use line junction information to perceive 3D shape. *Journal of Vision, 12*, 22–29.

Costello, E., Compton, S., & Keeler, G. (2003). Relationships between poverty and psychopathology: A natural experiment. *Journal of the American Medical Association, 290*, 2023–2029.

Costello, E., Sung, M., Worthman, C., & Angold, A. (2007, April). Pubertal maturation and the development of alcohol use and abuse. *Drug and Alcohol Dependence, 88*, S50–S59.

Cotrufo, P., Cella, S., Cremato, F., & Labella, A. (2007, December). Eating disorder attitude and abnormal eating behaviours in a sample of 11–13 year-old school children: The role of pubertal body transformation. *Eating and Weight Disorders, 12*(4), 154–160.

Couperus, J., & Nelson, C. (2006). Early brain development and plasticity. *Blackwell handbook of early childhood development*. New York: Blackwell Publishing.

Coutinho, M., McQuaid, E. L., & Koinis-Mitchell, D. (2013). Contextual and cultural risks and their association with family asthma management in urban children. *Journal of Child Health Care, 17*, 138–152.

Couzin, J. (2002, June 21). Quirks of fetal environment felt decades later. *Science, 296*, 2167–2169.

Cox, R., Skouteris, H., Rutherford, L., Fuller-Tyszkiewicz, M., Dell' Aquila, D., & Hardy, L. L. (2012). Television viewing, television content, food intake, physical activity and body mass index: a cross-sectional study of preschool children aged 2-6 years. *Health Promotion Journal of Australia, 23*, 58–62.

Coyne, S. M. (2016). Effects of viewing relational aggression on television on aggressive behavior in adolescents: A three-year longitudinal study. *Developmental Psychology, 52*, 284–295.

Craig, C., & Sprang, G. (2007, April). Trauma exposure and child abuse potential: Investigating the cycle of violence. *American Journal of Orthopsychiatry, 77*(2), 296–305.

Cramer, M., Chen, L., Roberts, S., & Clute, D. (2007). Evaluating the social and economic impact of community-based prenatal care. *Public Health Nursing, 24*, 329–336.

Cratty, B. (1979). *Perceptual and motor development in infants and children* (2nd ed.). Englewood Cliffs, NJ: Prentice-Hall.

Cratty, B. (1986). *Perceptual and motor development in infants and children* (3rd ed.). Englewood Cliffs, NJ: Prentice-Hall.

Crawford, M., & Unger, R. (2004). *Women and gender: A feminist psychology* (4th ed.). New York: McGraw-Hill.

Crisp, A., Gowers, S., Joughin, N., et al. (2006, May). Anorexia nervosa in males: Similarities and differences to anorexia nervosa in females. *European Eating Disorders Review, 14*, 163–167.

Crisp, R. J., & Turner, R. N. (2011). Cognitive adaptation to the experience of social and cultural diversity. *Psychological Bulletin, 137*, 242–266.

Critser, G. (2003). *Fat land: How Americans became the fattest people in the world*. Boston: Houghton Mifflin.

Crocetti, E. (2017). Identity formation in adolescence: The dynamic of forming and consolidating identity commitments. *Child Development Perspectives*. Retrieved March 22, 2017, from http://onlinelibrary.wiley.com/doi/10.1111/cdep.12226/abstract.

Crockenberg, S., & Leerkes, E. (2003). Infant negative emotionality, caregiving, and family relationships. In A. Crouter & A. Booth (Eds.), *Children's influence on family dynamics: The neglected side of family relationships* (pp. 57–78). Mahwah, NJ: Lawrence Erlbaum Associates.

Cross, T., Cassady, J., Dixon, F., & Adams, C. (2008). The psychology of gifted adolescents as measured by the MMPI-A. *Gifted Child Quarterly, 52*, 326–339.

Croizet, J., Després, G., Gauzins, M., Huguet, P., Leyens, J., & Méot, A. (2004). Stereotype threat undermines intellectual performance by triggering a disruptive mental load. *Personality and Social Psychology Bulletin, 30*, 721–731.

Crowl, A., Ahn, S., & Baker, J. (2008). A meta-analysis of developmental outcomes for children of same-sex and heterosexual parents. *Journal of GLBT Family Studies, 4*, 385–407.

Crowley, K., Callaman, M. A., Tenenbaum, H. R., & Allen, E. (2001). Parents explain more often to boys than to girls during shared scientific thinking. *Psychological Science, 12*, 258–261.

Curl, M. N., Davies, R., Lothian, S., Pascali-Bonaro, D., Scaer, R. M., & Walsh, A. (2004). Childbirth educators, doulas, nurses, and women respond to the six care practices for normal birth. *Journal of Perinatal Education, 13*, 42–50.

Cuperman, R., Robinson, R. L., & Ickes, W. (2014). On the malleability of self-image in individuals with a weak sense of self. *Self And Identity, 13*, 1–23.

Curley, J. P., Jensen, C. L., Mashoodh, R. R., & Champagne, F. A. (2011). Social influences on neurobiology and behavior: Epigenetic effects during development. *Psychoneuroendocrinology, 36*, 352–371.

Currie, J., Stabile, M., Jones, L. (2014). Do stimulant medications improve educational and behavioral outcomes for children with ADHD? *Journal of Health Economics, 37*, 58–69.

Curtis, W. J., & Cicchetti, D. (2003). Moving research on resilience into the 21st century: Theoretical and methodological considerations in examining the biological contributors to resilience. *Development and Psychopathology, 15*, 126–131.

Cushman, F., Sheketoff, R., Wharton, S., & Carey, S. (2013). The development of intent-based moral judgment. *Cognition, 127*, 6–21.

Dagys, N., McGlinchey, E. L., Talbot, L. S., Kaplan, K. A., Dahl, R. E., & Harvey, A. G. (2012). Double trouble? The effects of sleep deprivation and chronotype on adolescent affect. *Journal of Child Psychology and Psychiatry, 53*, 660–667.

Dahl, A., Satlof-Bedrick, E. S., Hammond, S. I., Drummond, J. K., Waugh, W. E., & Brownell, C. A. (2017). Explicit scaffolding increases simple helping in younger infants. *Developmental Psychology, 53*, 407–416.

Dahl, A., Sherlock, B. R., Campos, J. J., & Theunissen, F. E. (2014). Mothers' tone of voice depends on the nature of infants' transgressions. *Emotion, 14*, 651–665.

Dai, D., Tan, X., Marathe, D., Valtcheva, A., Pruzek, R. M., & Shen, J. (2012). Influences of social and educational environments on creativity during adolescence: Does SES matter? *Creativity Research Journal, 24*, 191–199.

Dailard, C. (2001). Sex education: Politicians, parents, teachers and teens. *The Guttmacher Report on Public Policy (Alan Guttmacher Institute), 4*, 1–4. Retrieved March 4, 2006, from http://www.guttmacher.org/pubs/tgr/04/1/gr040109.pdf.

Daley, B. (2014, December 14). Oversold prenatal tests spur some to choose abortions. *Boston Globe*, M1.

Daley, K. C. (2004). Update on sudden infant death syndrome. *Current Opinion in Pediatrics, 16*, 227–232.

Dallas, D., Guerrero, A., Khaldi, N., Borghese, R., Bhandari, A., Underwood, M., Lebrilla, C., German, J., & Barile, D. (2014). A peptidomic analysis of human milk digestion in the infant stomach reveals protein-specific degradation patterns. *Journal of Nutrition, 144*, 815–820.

Dalton, T. C., & Bergenn, V. W. (2007). *Early experience, the brain, and consciousness: An historical and interdisciplinary synthesis*. Mahwah, NJ: Lawrence Erlbaum Associates Publishers.

Damon, W., & Hart, D. (1988). *Self-understanding in childhood and adolescence*. New York: Cambridge University Press.

Daniel, S., & Goldston, D. (2009). Interventions for suicidal youth: A review of the literature and developmental considerations. *Suicide and Life-Threatening Behavior, 39*, 252–268.

Daniels, H. (2006, February). The 'Social' in post-Vygotskian theory. *Theory & Psychology, 16*, 37–49.

Danish, S. J., Taylor, T. E., & Fazio, R. J. (2006). Enhancing adolescent development through sports and leisure. In G. R. Adams & M. D. Berzonsky (Eds.), *Blackwell handbook of adolescence*. Malden, MA: Blackwell Publishing.

Dare, W. N., Noronha, C. C., Kusemiju, O. T., & Okanlawon, O. A. (2002). The effect of ethanol on spermatogenesis and fertility in male Sprague-Dawley rats pretreated with acetylsalicylic acid. *Nigeria Postgraduate Medical Journal, 9*, 194–198.

Das, A. (2007). Masturbation in the United States. *Journal of Sex & Marital Therapy, 33*, 301–317.

Dasen, P., Inhelder, B., Lavallee, M., & Retschitzki, J. (1978). *Naissance de l'intelligence chez l'enfant Baoule de Cote d'Ivorie*. Berne: Hans Huber.

Dasen, P., Ngini, L., & Lavallee, M. (1979). Cross-cultural training studies of concrete operations. In L. H. Eckenberger, W. J. Lonner, & Y. H. Poortinga (Eds.), *Cross-cultural contributions to psychology*. Amsterdam: Swets & Zeilinger.

Dasen, P. R. (1977). Are cognitive processes universal? A contribution to cross-cultural Piagetian psychology. In N. Warren (Ed.), *Studies in cross-cultural psychology* (Vol. 1). New York: Academic Press.

Dasen, P. R., & Mishra, R. C. (2002). Cross-cultural views on human development in the third millennium. In W. W. Hartup & R. K. Silbereisen, *Growing points in developmental science: An introduction*. Philadelphia, PA: Psychology Press.

Dash, J., & Dash, A. S. (1983). Developmental levels of cognitive representation. *Psychological Studies, 28*, 41–43.

Dash, U. N., & Das, J. P. (1984). Development of concrete operational thought and information coding in schooled and unschooled children. *British Journal of Developmental Psychology, 2*, 63–72.

Daum, M. M., Prinz, W., & Aschersleben, G. (2011). Perception and production of object-related grasping in 6-month-olds. *Journal of Experimental Child Psychology, 108*, 810–818.

Davenport, B., & Bourgeois, N. (2008). Play, aggression, the preschool child, and the family: A review of literature to guide empirically informed play therapy with aggressive preschool children. *International Journal of Play Therapy, 17*, 2–23.

Davidson, J. K., Darling, C. A., & Norton, L. (1995). Religiosity and the sexuality of women: Sexual behavior and sexual satisfaction revisited. *Journal of Sex Research, 32*, 235–243.

Davidson, R. J. (2003). Affective neuroscience: A case for interdisciplinary research. In F. Kessel & P. L. Rosenfield (Eds.), *Expanding the boundaries of health and social science: Case studies in interdisciplinary innovation*. London: Oxford University Press.

Davies, K., Tropp, L. R., Aron, A. P., Thomas, F., & Wright, S. C. (2011). Cross-group friendships and intergroup attitudes: A meta-analytic review. *Personality and Social Psychology Review, 15*, 332–351.

Davies, P. G., Spencer, S. J., & Steele, C. M. (2005). Clearing the air: Identity safety moderates the effects of stereotype threat on women's leadership aspirations. *Journal of Personality & Social Psychology, 88*, 276–287.

Davies, P. T., Harold, G. T., Goeke-Morey, M. C., & Cummings, E. M. (2002). Child emotional security and interparental conflict. *Monographs of the Society for Research in Child Development, 67*.

Davis, A. (2003). *Your divorce, your dollars: Financial planning before, during, and after divorce*. Bellingham, WA: Self-Counsel Press.

Davis, A. (2008). Children with Down syndrome: Implications for assessment and intervention in the school. *School Psychology Quarterly, 23*, 271–281.

Davis, B. L., Smith-Bynum, M. A., Saleem, F. T., Francois, T., & Lambert, S. F. (2017). Racial socialization, private regard, and behavior problems in African American youth: Global self-esteem as a mediator. *Journal of Child and Family Studies, 26*, 709–720.

Davis, C., Aronson, J., & Salinas, M. (2006, November). Shades of threat: Racial identity as a moderator of stereotype threat. *Journal of Black Psychology, 32*(4), 399–417.

Davis, C. L., Tomporowski, P. D., McDowell, J. E., et al. (2011). Exercise improves executive function and achievement and alters brain activation in overweight children: A randomized, controlled trial. *Health Psychology, 30*, 91–98.

Davis, M., & Emory, E. (1995). Sex differences in neonatal stress reactivity. *Child Development, 66*, 14–27.

Davis, N. L., & Voirin, J. (2016). Reciprocal writing as a creative technique. *Journal of Creativity in Mental Health, 11*, 66–77.

Davis, R. R., & Hofferth, S. L. (2012). The association between inadequate gestational weight gain and infant mortality among U.S. infants born in 2002. *Maternal and Child Health Journal, 16*, 119–124.

Davis, T. S., Saltzburg, S., & Locke, C. R. (2009). Supporting the emotional and psychological well being of sexual minority youth: Youth ideas for action. *Children and Youth Services Review, 31*, 1030–1041.

Davis-Kean, P. E., & Sandler, H. M. (2001). A meta-analysis of measures of self-esteem for young children: A framework for future measures. *Child Development, 72*, 887–906.

De C. Williams, A. C., Morris, J. J., Stevens, K. K., Gessler, S. S., Cella, M. M., & Baxter, J. J. (2013). What influences midwives in estimating labour pain? *European Journal of Pain, 17*, 86–93.

De Dios, A. (2012). United States of America. In J. Arnett (Ed.), *Adolescent psychology around the world*. New York: Psychology Press.

De Gelder, B. (2000). Recognizing emotions by ear and by eye. In R. D. Lane & L. Nadel (Eds.), *Cognitive neuroscience of emotion. Series in affective science*. New York: Oxford University Press.

De Graag, J. A., Cox, R. A., Hasselman, F., Jansen, J., & de Weerth, C. (2012). Functioning within a relationship: Mother–infant synchrony and infant sleep. *Infant Behavior & Development, 35*, 252–263.

De Jesus-Zayas, S. R., Buigas, R., & Denney, R. L. (2012). Evaluation of culturally diverse populations. In D. Faust (Ed.), *Coping with psychiatric and psychological testimony: Based on the original work by Jay Ziskin* (6th ed.). New York: Oxford University Press.

De Lauzon-Guillain, B., Wijndaele, K., Clark, M., et al. (2012). Breastfeeding and infant temperament at age three months. *Plos ONE, 7*, 182–190.

De Onis, M., Garza, C., Onyango, A. W., & Borghi, E. (2007). Comparison of the WHO child growth standards and the CDC 2000 growth charts. *Journal of Nutrition, 137*, 144–148.

De Pauw, S. W., & Mervielde, I. (2011). The role of temperament and personality in problem behaviors of children with ADHD. *Journal of Abnormal Child Psychology: An Official Publication of the International Society for Research in Child and Adolescent Psychopathology, 39*, 277–291.

de Schipper, E. J., Riksen-Walraven, J. M., & Geurts, S. A. E. (2006). Effects of child–caregiver ratio on the interactions between caregivers and children in child-care centers: An experimental study. *Child Development, 77*, 861–874.

De St. Aubin, E., McAdams, D. P., & Kim, T. C. (Eds.). (2004). *The generative society: Caring for future generations*. Washington, DC: American Psychological Association.

Dean, D. I., O'Muircheartaigh, J., Dirks, H., et al. (2014). Modeling healthy male white matter and myelin development: 3 through 60 months of age. *NeuroImage, 81*, 742–752.

Deaner, R. O., Balish, S. M., & Lombardo, M. P. (2016). Sex differences in sports interest and motivation: An evolutionary perspective. *Evolutionary Behavioral Sciences, 10*, 73–97.

Dearing, E., McCartney, K., & Taylor, B. (2009). Does higher quality early child care promote low-income children's math and reading achievement in middle childhood? *Child Development, 80*, 1329–1349.

Deater-Deckard, K., & Cahill, K. (2007). Nature and nurture in early childhood. *Blackwell handbook of early childhood development* (pp. 3–21). New York: Blackwell Publishing.

Decarrie, T. G. (1969). A study of the mental and emotional development of the thalidomide child. In B. M. Foss (Ed.), *Determinants of infant behavior* (Vol. 4). London: Methuen.

DeCasper, A. J., & Fifer, W. P. (1980). Of human bonding: Newborns prefer their mothers' voices. *Science, 208*, 1174–1176.

DeCasper, A. J., & Prescott, P. (1984). Human newborns' perception of male voices: Preference, discrimination, and reinforcing value. *Developmental Psychobiology, 17*, 481–491.

DeCasper, A. J., & Spence, M. J. (1986). Prenatal material speech influences newborns' perception of speech sounds. *Infant Behavior and Development, 9*, 133 150.

DeFrancisco, B., & Rovee-Collier, C. (2008). The specificity of priming effects over the first year of life. *Developmental Psychobiology, 50*, 486–501.

Degroot, A., Wolff, M. C., & Nomikos, G. G. (2005). Acute exposure to a novel object during consolidation enhances cognition. *Neuroreport, 16*, 63–67.

Dehaene-Lambertz, G., Hertz-Pannier, L., & Dubois, J. (2006). Nature and nurture in language acquisition: Anatomical and functional brain-imaging studies in infants. *Neurosciences, 29*, Special issue: *Nature and Nurture in Brain Development and Neurological Disorders*, 367–373.

Dehaene-Lambertz, G. (2017). The human infant brain: A neural architecture able to learn language. *Psychonomic Bulletin & Review, 24*, 48–55.

DeLisi, M. (2006). Zeroing in on early arrest onset: Results from a population of extreme career criminals. *Journal of Criminal Justice, 34*, 17–26.

DeLoache, J. S., Chiong, C., Sherman, K., Islam, N., Vanderborght, M., Troseth, G. L., & O'Doherty, K. (2010). Do babies learn from baby media? *Psychological Science, 21*, 1570–1574.

Deng, W., & Sloutsky, V. M. (2015). Linguistic labels, dynamic visual features, and attention in infant category learning. *Journal of Experimental Child Psychology, 134*, 62–77.

Denizet-Lewis, B. (2004, May 30). Friends, friends with benefits and the benefits of the local mall. *New York Times Magazine*, pp. 30–35, 54–58.

Denmark, F. L., & Fernandez, L. C. (1993). Historical development of the psychology of women. In F. L. Denmark & M. A. Paludi (Eds.), *Psychology of women: A handbook of issues and theories*. Westport, CT: Greenwood Press.

Dennehy, T. C., Smith, J. S., Moore, C., & Dasgupta, N. (In press). Stereotype threat and stereotype inoculation: barriers that prevent and interventions that promote the success of underrepresented students in the first year of college. In R. S. Feldman (ed.), *The first year of college: Research, theory, and practice on improving the student experience and increasing retention*. Cambridge, England: Cambridge University Press.

Dennis, J. G. (2004). *Homeschooling high school: Planning ahead for college admission*. Cambridge, MA: Emerald Press.

Dennis, T. A., Cole, P. M., Zahn-Wexler, C., & Mizuta, I. (2002). Self in context: Autonomy and relatedness in Japanese and U.S. mother–preschooler dyads. *Child Development, 73*, 1803–1817.

DePaolis, R., Vihman, M. M., & Nakai, S. (2013). The influence of babbling patterns on the processing of speech. *Infant Behavior and Development, 36*, 642–649.

Department for Education and Skills (England). (2004). *Five year strategy for children and learners*. Presented to Parliament by the secretary of state for Education and Skills, July 2004. London: DfES.

Dereli-İman, E. (2013). Adaptation of social problem solving for children questionnaire in 6 age groups and its relationships with preschool behavior problems. *Kuram Ve Uygulamada Eğitim Bilimleri, 13*, 491–498.

Dervic, K., Friedrich, E., Oquendo, M., Voracek, M., Friedrich, M., & Sonneck, G. (2006, October). Suicide in Austrian children and young adolescents aged 14 and younger. *European Child & Adolescent Psychiatry, 15*, 427–434.

Desilver, D. (2017). U.S. students' academic achievement still lags that of their peers in many other countries. Retrieved May 5, 2017, from http://www.pewresearch.org/fact-tank/2017/02/15/u-s-students-internationally-math-science/.

Deurenberg, P., Deurenberg-Yap, M., Foo, L. F., Schmidt, G., & Wang, J. (2003). Differences in body composition between Singapore Chinese, Beijing Chinese and Dutch children. *European Journal of Clinical Nutrition, 57*, 405–409.

Deurenberg, P., Deurenberg-Yap, M., & Guricci, S. (2002). Asians are different from Caucasians and from each other in their body mass index/body fat percent relationship. *Obesity Review, 3*, 141–146.

DeVader, S. R., Neeley, N. L., Myles, T. D., & Leet, T. L. (2007). Evaluation of gestational weight gain guidelines for women with normal prepregnancy body mass index. *Obstetrics and Gynecology, 110*, 745–751.

Deveny, K. (1994, December 5). Chart of kindergarten awards. *The Wall Street Journal*, p. B1.

Devlin, B., Daniels, M., & Roeder, K. (1997). The heritability of IQ. *Nature, 388*, 468–471.

deVries, M. W. (1984). Temperament and infant mortality among the Masai of East Africa. *American Journal of Psychiatry, 141*, 1189–1194.

deVries, R. (1969). Constancy of generic identity in the years 3 to 6. *Monographs of the Society for Research in Child Development, 34* (3, Serial No. 127).

DeVries, R. (2005). *A pleasing birth*. Philadelphia, PA: Temple University Press.

DeWall, C. N., Anderson, C. A., & Bushman, B. J. (2013). Aggression and violence. In *Handbook of psychology, Vol. 5: Personality and social psychology* (2nd ed.). H. Tennen, J. Suls, & I. B. Weiner (Eds.). Hoboken, NJ: John Wiley & Sons.

Dey, A. N., & Bloom, B. (2005). Summary health statistics for U.S. children: National Health Interview Survey, 2003. *Vital Health Statistics 10 (223)*, 1–78.

Dhawan, J., Gupta, S., & Kumar, B. (2010). Sexually transmitted diseases in children in India. *Indian Journal of Dermatology*, Sep-Oct, 76(5), 489-93. doi: 10.4103/0378-6323.69056.

Diambra, L., & Menna-Barretio, L. (2004). Infradian rhythmicity in sleep/wake ratio in developing infants. *Chronobiology International, 21*, 217–227.

Diamond, L. (2003a). Love matters: Romantic relationships among sexual-minority adolescents. In P. Florsheim (Ed.), *Adolescent romantic relations and sexual behavior: Theory, research, and practical implications*. Mahwah, NJ: Lawrence Erlbaum Associates.

Diamond, L. (2003b). Was it a phase? Young women's relinquishment of lesbian/bisexual identities over a 5-year period. *Journal of Personality & Social Psychology, 84*, 352–364.

Diamond, M. (2013c). Transsexuality among twins: Identity concordance, transition, rearing, and orientation. *International Journal of Transgenderism, 14*, 24–38.

Dick, D., Rose, R., & Kaprio, J. (2006). The next challenge for psychiatric genetics: Characterizing the risk associated with identified genes. *Annals of Clinical Psychiatry, 18*, 223–231.

DiCorcia, J. A., Snidman, N., Sravish, A. V., & Tronick, E. (2016). Evaluating the nature of the Still-Face effect in the double Face-to-Face Still-Face paradigm using different comparison groups. *Infancy, 21(3)*, 332–352.

DiDonato, L., & Strough, J. (2013). Do college students' gender-typed attitudes about occupations predict their real-world decisions? *Sex Roles, 68*, 536–549.

Diego, M., Field, T., & Hernandez-Reif, M. (2009). Procedural pain heart rate responses in massaged preterm infants. *Infant Behavior & Development, 32*, 226–229.

Diego, M., Field, T., Hernandez-Reif, M., Vera, Y., Gil, K., & Gonzalez-Garcia, A. (2007). Caffeine use affects pregnancy outcome. *Journal of Child & Adolescent Substance Abuse, 17*, 41–49.

Diener, M., Isabella, R., Behunin, M., & Wong, M. (2008). Attachment to mothers and fathers during middle childhood: Associations with child gender, grade, and competence. *Social Development, 17*, 84–101.

Dietrich, J. F., Huber, S., Dackermann, T., Moeller, K., & Fischer, U. (2016). Place-value understanding in number line estimation predicts future arithmetic performance. *British Journal of Developmental Psychology, 34*, 502–517.

Dietz, W. H., & Stern, L. (Eds.). (1999). *American Academy of Pediatrics guide to your child's nutrition: Making peace at the table and building healthy eating habits for life*. New York: Villard.

Dildy, G. A., Jackson, G. M., Fowers, G. K., Oshiro, B. T., Varner, M. W., & Clark, S. L. (1996). Very advanced maternal age: Pregnancy after 45. *American Journal of Obstetrics and Gynecology, 175*, 668–674.

Dilworth-Bart, J., & Moore, C. (2006, March). Mercy mercy me: Social injustice and the prevention of environmental pollutant exposures among ethnic minority and poor children. *Child Development, 77*, 247–265.

Dimmitt, C., & McCormick, C. B. (2012). Metacognition in education. In K. R. Harris, S. Graham, T. Urdan, C. B. McCormick, G. M. Sinatra, J. Sweller (Eds.), *APA educational psychology handbook, Vol. 1: Theories, constructs, and critical issues*. Washington, DC: American Psychological Association.

DiNallo, J. M., Downs, D., & Le Masurier, G. (2012). Objectively assessing treadmill walking during the second and third pregnancy trimesters. *Journal of Physical Activity & Health, 9*, 21–28.

Dionne, J., & Cadoret, G. (2013). Development of active controlled retrieval during middle childhood. *Developmental Psychobiology, 55*, 443–449.

DiPietro, J. A., Bornstein, M. H., & Costigan, K. A. (2002). What does fetal movement predict about behavior during the first two years of life? *Developmental Psychobiology, 40*, 358–371.

DiPietro, J. A., Costigan, K. A., & Gurewitsch, E. D. (2005). Maternal psychophysiological change during the second half of gestation. *Biological Psychology, 69*, 23–39.

Dittman, M. (2005). Generational differences at work. *Monitor on Psychology, 36*, 54–55.

Dixon, R. A., & Lerner, R. M. (1999). History and systems in developmental psychology. In M. H. Bornstein & M. E. Lamb (Eds.), *Developmental psychology: An advanced textbook*. Mahwah, NJ: Erlbaum.

Dixon, W. E. Jr. (2004). There's a long, long way to go. *PsycCRITIQUES*.

Dmitrieva, J., Chen, C., & Greenberg, E. (2004). Family relationships and adolescent psychosocial outcomes: Converging findings from Eastern and Western cultures. *Journal of Research on Adolescence, 14*, 425–447.

Dobson, V. (2000). The developing visual brain. *Perception, 29*, 1501–1503.

DocuTicker. (2010). *Domestic violence and the child welfare system*. Retrieved August 23, 2014, from http://web.docuticker.com/go/docubase/34851.

Dodge, K. A. (1985). A social information processing model of social competence in children. In M. Perlmutter (Ed.), *Minnesota Symposia on Child Psychology, 18*, 77–126.

Dodge, K. A., Lansford, J. E., & Burks, V. S. (2003). Peer rejection and social information-processing factors in the development of aggressive behavior problems in children. *Child Development, 74*, 374–393.

Doman, G., & Doman, J. (2002). *How to teach your baby to read*. Gentle Revolution Press.

Dominguez, H. D., Lopez, M. F., & Molina, J. C. (1999). Interactions between perinatal and neonatal associative learning defined by contiguous olfactory and tactile stimulation. *Neurobiology of Learning and Memory, 71*, 272–288.

Domsch, H., Lohaus, A., & Thomas, H. (2009). Prediction of childhood cognitive abilities from a set of early indicators of information processing capabilities. *Infant Behavior & Development, 32*, 91–102.

Donat, D. (2006, October). Reading their way: A balanced approach that increases achievement. *Reading & Writing Quarterly: Overcoming Learning Difficulties, 22*, 305–323.

Dondi, M., Simion, F., & Caltran, G. (1999). Can newborns discriminate between their own cry and the cry of another newborn infant? *Developmental Psychology, 35*, 418–426.

Donleavy, G. (2008). No man's land: Exploring the space between Gilligan and Kohlberg. *Journal of Business Ethics, 80*, 807–822.

Donnerstein, E. (2005, January). *Media violence and children: What do we know, what do we do?* Paper presented at the annual National Teaching of Psychology meeting, St. Petersburg Beach, FL.

Donohue, R. (2007, April). Examining career persistence and career change intent using the career attitudes and strategies inventory. *Journal of Vocational Behavior, 70(2)*, 259–276.

Dotti Sani, G. M., & Treas, J. (2016). Educational gradients in parents' child-care time across countries, 1965–2012. *Journal of Marriage and Family, 78*, 1083–1096.

Doub, A. E., Small, M., & Birch, L. L. (2016). A call for research exploring social media influences on mothers' child feeding practices and childhood obesity risk. *Appetite, 99*, 298–305.

Douglass, A., & Klerman, L. (2012). The strengthening families initiative and child care quality improvement: How strengthening families influenced change in child care programs in one state. *Early Education and Development, 23*, 373–392.

Douglass, R., & McGadney-Douglass, B. (2008). The role of grandmothers and older women in the survival of children with kwashiorkor in urban Accra, Ghana. *Research in Human Development, 5*, 26–43.

Doussard-Roosevelt, J. A., Porges, S. W., Scanlon, J. W., Alemi, B., & Scanlon, K. B. (1997). Vagal regulation of heart rate in the prediction of developmental outcome for very low birth weight preterm infants. *Child Development, 68*, 173–186.

Doyle, R. (2004, April). By the numbers: A surplus of women. *Scientific American, 290*, 33.

Dozor, A. J., & Amler, R. W. (2013). Children's environmental health. *The Journal Of Pediatrics, 162*, 6–7.

Drane, C. F., Modecki, K. L., & Barber, B. L. (2017). Disentangling development of sensation seeking, risky peer affiliation, and binge drinking in adolescent sport. *Addictive Behaviors, 66*, 60–65.

Drewett, R. (2007). *The nutritional psychology of childhood*. New York, NY: Cambridge University Press.

Driscoll, A. K., Russell, S. T., Crockett, L. J. (2008). Parenting styles and youth well-being across immigrant generations. *Journal of Family Issues, 29*, 185–209.

Dromi, E. (1987). *Early lexical development*. Cambridge, England: Cambridge University Press.

Dube, S.R., Felitti, V.J., Dong, M., Chapman, D.P., Giles, W.H., & Anda, R.F. (2003). Childhood abuse, neglect, and household dysfunction and the risk of illicit drug use: the adverse childhood experience study. *Pediatrics, 111*: 564–72.

DuBois, D. L., & Hirsch, B. J. (1990). School and neighborhood friendship patterns of blacks and whites in early adolescence. *Child Development, 61*, 524–536.

Dubow, E. F., Huesmann, L. R., Boxer, P., & Smith, C. (2016). Childhood and adolescent risk and protective factors for violence in adulthood. *Journal Of Criminal Justice, 45*, 26–31.

DuBreuil, S. C., Garry, M., & Loftus, E. F. (1998). Tales from the crib: Age regression and the creation of unlikely memories. In S. J. Lynn & K. M. McConkey (Eds.), *Truth in memory*. New York: The Guilford Press.

Dudding, T. C., Vaizey, C. J., & Kamm, M. A. (2008). Obstetric anal sphincter injury: incidence, risk factors, and management. *Annals of Surgery, 247*, 224–237.

Duenwald, M. (2003, July 15). After 25 years, new ideas in the prenatal test tube. *The New York Times*, p. D5.

Duenwald, M. (2004, May 11). For couples, stress without a promise of success. *The New York Times*, p. D3.

Duijts, L, Jaddoe, V. W. V., Hofman, A., & Moll, H. A. (2010, June 21). Prolonged and exclusive breastfeeding reduces the risk of infectious diseases in infancy. *Pediatrics*; 2008-3256.

Dulin-Keita, A., Hannon, L., Fernandez, J. R., & Cockerham, W. C. (2011). The defining moment: Children's conceptualization of race and experiences with racial discrimination. *Ethnic and Racial Studies, 34*, 662–682.

Dumka, L., Gonzales, N., Bonds, D., & Millsap, R. (2009). Academic success of Mexican origin adolescent boys and girls: The role of mothers' and fathers' parenting and cultural orientation. *Sex Roles, 60*, 588–599.

Dumont, C., & Paquette, D. (2013). What about the child's tie to the father? A new insight into fathering, father–child attachment, children's socio-emotional development and the activation relationship theory. *Early Child Development And Care, 183*, 430–446.

Duncan, G. J., Magnuson, K., & Votruba-Drzal, E. (2017). Moving beyond correlations in assessing the consequences of poverty. *Annual Review of Psychology, 68*, 413–434.

Dundas, E. M., Plaut, D. C., & Behrmann, M. (2013). The joint development of hemispheric lateralization for words and faces. *Journal of Experimental Psychology: General, 142*, 348–358.

Duncan, G. J., & Brooks-Gunn, J. (2000). Family poverty, welfare reform, and child development. *Child Development, 71*, 188–196.

Dunfield, K. A., & Kuhlmeier, V. A. (2010). Intention-mediated selective helping in infancy. *Psychological Science, 21*, 523–527.

Dunham, R. M., Kidwell, J. S., & Wilson, S. M. (1986). Rites of passage at adolescence: A ritual process paradigm. *Journal of Adolescent Research, 1*, 139–153.

Dunkel, C. S., Kim, J. K., & Papini, D. R. (2012). The general factor of psychosocial development and its relation to the general factor of personality and life history strategy. *Personality and Individual Differences, 52*, 202–206.

Dunn, M., Thomas, J. O., Swift, W., & Burns, L. (2012). Elite athletes' estimates of the prevalence of illicit drug use: Evidence for the false consensus effect. *Drug and Alcohol Review, 31*, 27–32.

DuPaul, G., & Weyandt, L. (2006, June). School-based intervention for children with attention deficit hyperactivity disorder: Effects on academic, social, and behavioural functioning. *International Journal of Disability, Development and Education, 53*, 161–176.

Duriez, B., Luyckx, K., Soenens, B., & Berzonsky, M. (2012). A process-content approach to adolescent identity formation: Examining longitudinal associations between identity styles and goal pursuits. *Journal of Personality, 80*, 135–161.

Dutta, T., & Mandal, M. (2006, July). Hand preference and accidents in India. *Laterality: Asymmetries of Body, Brain and Cognition, 11*(4), 368–372.

Dyer, S., & Moneta, G. (2006). Frequency of parallel, associative, and co-operative play in British children of different socioeconomic status. *Social Behavior and Personality, 34*, 587–592.

Dykens, E. M., Roof, E., & Hunt-Hawkins, H. (2016). Cognitive and adaptive advantages of growth hormone treatment in children with Prader-Willi syndrome. *Journal of Child Psychology and Psychiatry*. Retrieved March 14, 2017, from http://onlinelibrary.wiley.com/doi/10.1111/jcpp.12601/abstract.

Dyson, A. H. (2003). "Welcome to the jam": Popular culture, school literacy and making of childhoods. *Harvard Educational Review, 73*, 328–361.

Earl, R., Burns, N., Nettelbeck, T., & Baghurst, P. (2016). Low-level environmental lead exposure still negatively associated with children's cognitive abilities. *Australian Journal of Psychology, 68*, 98–106.

Earle, J., Perricone, P., Davidson, J., Moore, N., Harris, C., & Cotten, S. (2007, March). Premarital sexual attitudes and behavior at a religiously-affiliated university: Two decades of change. *Sexuality & Culture: An Interdisciplinary Quarterly, 11*(2), 39–61.

East, P., Reyes, B., & Horn, E. (2007, June). Association between adolescent pregnancy and a family history of teenage births. *Perspectives on Sexual and Reproductive Health, 39*(2), 108–115.

Easterbrooks, M., Bartlett, J., Beeghly, M., & Thompson, R. A. (2013). Social and emotional development in infancy. In R. M. Lerner, M. Easterbrooks, J. Mistry, I. B. Weiner (Eds.), *Handbook of psychology, Vol. 6: Developmental psychology* (2nd ed.). Hoboken, NJ: John Wiley & Sons Inc.

Eastman, Q. (2003, June 20). Crib death exoneration in new gene tests. *Science, 300*, 1858.

Easton, J., Schipper, L., & Shackelford, T. (2007). Morbid jealousy from an evolutionary psychological perspective. *Evolution and Human Behavior, 28*, 399–402.

Eaton, W. O., & Enns, L. R. (1986). Sex differences in human motor activity level. *Psychological Bulletin, 100*, 19–28.

Eaves, B. J., Feldman, N. H., Griffiths, T. L., & Shafto, P. (2016). Infant-directed speech is consistent with teaching. *Psychological Review, 123*, 758–771.

Eccles, J., Templeton, J., & Barber, B. (2003). Adolescence and emerging adulthood: The critical passageways to adulthood. In M. Bornstein & L. Davidson (Eds.), *Well-being: Positive development across the life course*. Mahwah, NJ: Lawrence Erlbaum Associates.

Ecenbarger, W. (1993, April 1). America's new merchants of death. *The Reader's Digest, 50*.

Eckerman, C. O., & Oehler, J. M. (1992). Very-low-birthweight newborns and parents as early social partners. In S. L. Friedman & M. D. Sigman (Eds.), *The psychological development of low-birthweight children*. Norwood, NJ: Ablex.

Eckerman, C., & Peterman, K. (2001). Peers and infant social/communicative development. In G. Bremner & A. Fogel (Eds.), *Blackwell handbook of infant development* (pp. 326–350). Malden, MA: Blackwell Publishers.

Edgerley, L., El-Sayed, Y., Druzin, M., Kiernan, M., & Daniels, K. (2007). Use of a community mobile health van to increase early access to prenatal care. *Maternal & Child Health Journal, 11*, 235–239.

Editorial Board (2018). 47 million Indian youth drop out by Class 10. Accessed from https://scroll.in/ on 19 November 2018.

Edwards, A. C., & Kendler, K. S. (2013). Alcohol consumption in men is influenced by qualitatively different genetic factors in adolescence and adulthood. *Psychological Medicine, 43*, 1857–1868.

Edwards, C. P. (2000). Children's play in cross-cultural perspective: A new look at the Six Cultures study. *Cross-Cultural Research: The Journal of Comparative Social Science, 34*, 318–338.

Edward, J. (2013). Sibling discord: A force for growth and conflict. *Clinical Social Work Journal, 41*, 77–83.

Edwards, L. A., Wagner, J. B., Simon, C. E., & Hyde, D. C. (2016). Functional brain organization for number processing in preverbal infants. *Developmental Science, 19*, 757–769.

Edwards, S. (2004). Constructivism does not only happen in the individual: Sociocultural theory and early childhood education. *Child Development & Care, 175*, 37–47.

Eggum, N. D., Eisenberg, N., Kao, K., Spinrad, T. L., Bolnick, R., Hofer, C., & Fabricius, W. V. (2011). Emotion understanding, theory of mind, and prosocial orientation: Relations over time in early childhood. *Journal of Positive Psychology, 6*, 4–16.

Ehm, J., Lindberg, S., & Hasselhorn, M. (2013). Reading, writing, and math self-concept in elementary school children: Influence of dimensional comparison processes. *European Journal of Psychology of Education*. Retrieved February 18, 2014, from http://link.springer.com/article/10.1007%2Fs10212-013-0198-x#page-1.

Ehrensaft, M. K., Knous-Westfall, H. M., Cohen, P., & Chen, H. (2015). How does child abuse history influence parenting of the next generation? *Psychology of Violence, 5*, 16–25.

Ehtisham, S., Barrett, T.G., & Shaw, N.J. (2000). Type 2 diabetes mellitus in UK children – an emerging problem. *Diabetic Medicine*. 17 (12), 867–71; accessed from doi:dme 409 [pii].

Eid, M., Riemann, R., Angleitner, A., & Borkenau, P. (2003). Sociability and positive emotionality: genetic and environmental contributions to the covariation between different facets of extraversion. *Journal of Personality, 71*, 319–346.

Eiden, R., Foote, A., & Schuetze, P. (2007). Maternal cocaine use and caregiving status: Group differences in caregiver and infant risk variables. *Addictive Behaviors, 32*, 465–476.

Eimas, P. D., Sigueland, E. R., Jusczyk, P., & Vigorito, J. (1971). Speech perception in infants. *Science, 171*, 303–306.

Eisbach, A. O. (2004). Children's developing awareness of diversity in people's trains of thought. *Child Development, 75*, 1694–1707.

Eisenberg, N. (2012). *Eight tips to developing caring kids*. Retrieved July 15, 2012, from, http://youngreaders.ca/downloads/Eight_Tips_Eisenberg.pdf.

Eisenberg, N., Spinrad, T. L., & Morris, A. (2014). Empathy-related responding in children. In M. Killen, J. G. Smetana, M. Killen, & J. G. Smetana (Eds.), *Handbook of moral development* (2nd ed.). New York: Psychology Press.

Eisenberg, N., & Valiente, C. (2002). Parenting and children's prosocial and moral development. In M. Bornstein (Ed.), *Handbook of parenting: Vol. 5: Practical issues in parenting*. Mahwah, NJ: Lawrence Erlbaum Associates.

Eisenberg, N., Valiente, C., & Champion, C. (2004). Empathy-related responding: Moral, social, and socialization correlates. In A. G. Miller (Ed.), *Social psychology of good and evil*. New York: Guilford Press.

Eitel, A., Scheiter, K., Schüler, A., Nyström, M., & Holmqvist, K. (2013). How a picture facilitates the process of learning from text: Evidence for scaffolding. *Learning and Instruction, 28*, 48–63.

Eklund, L. (2011). 'Good citizens prefer daughters': Gender, rurality and the Care for Girls Campaign. In T. Jacka, S. Sargeson (Eds.), *Women, gender and rural development in China*. Northampton, MA: Edward Elgar Publishing.

El Ayoubi, M., Patkai, J., Bordarier, C., et al. (2016). Impact of fetal growth restriction on neurodevelopmental outcome at 2 years for extremely preterm infants: A single institution study. *Developmental Medicine & Child Neurology, 58*(12), 1249–1256.

Eley, T., Liang, H., & Plomin, R. (2004). Parental familial vulnerability, family environment, and their interactions as predictors of depressive symptoms in adolescents. *Child & Adolescent Social Work Journal, 21*, 298–306.

Elkana, O., Frost, R., Kramer, U., et al. (2011). Cerebral reorganization as a function of linguistic recovery in children: An fMRI study. *Cortex: A Journal Devoted to the Study of the Nervous System and Behavior, 47*, 202–216.

Elkind, D. (1978). The children's reality: Three developmental themes. In S. Coren & L. M. Ward (Eds.), *Sensation and perception*. Hillsdale, NJ: Erlbaum.

Elkind, D. (1994). *Ties that stress: The new family imbalance*. Cambridge, MA: Harvard University Press.

Elliott, K., & Urquiza, A. (2006). Ethnicity, culture, and child maltreatment. *Journal of Social Issues, 62*, 787–809.

Ellis, B. J. (2004). Timing of pubertal maturation in girls: An integrated life history approach. *Psychological Bulletin, 130*, 920–958.

Ellis, L. (2006, July). Gender differences in smiling: An evolutionary neuroandrogenic theory. *Physiology & Behavior, 88*, 303–308.

Ellis, L., & Engh, T. (2000). Handedness and age of death: New evidence on a puzzling relationship. *Journal of Health Psychology, 5*, 561–565.

Ellis, L., Ficek, C., Burke, D., & Das, S. (2008, February). Eye color, hair color, blood type, and the rhesus factor: Exploring possible genetic links to sexual orientation. *Archives of Sexual Behavior, 37*(1), 145–149.

Emilson, A., Folkesson, A., & Lindberg, I. M. (2016). Gender beliefs and embedded gendered values in preschool. *International Journal of Early Childhood, 48*, 225–240.

Endo, S. (1992). Infant–infant play from 7 to 12 months of age: An analysis of games in infant–peer triads. *Japanese Journal of Child and Adolescent Psychiatry, 33,* 145–162.

Engineer, N., Darwin, L., Nishigandh, D., Ngianga-Bakwin, K., Smith, S. C., & Grammatopoulos, D. K. (2013). Association of glucocorticoid and type 1 corticotropin-releasing hormone receptors gene variants and risk for depression during pregnancy and post-partum. *Journal of Psychiatric Research, 47,* 1166–1173.

England, L., Bunnell, R., Pechacek, T., Tong, V., & McAfee, T. (2015). Nicotine and the developing human. *American Journal of Preventive Medicine, 49,* 286–293.

English, D., Lambert, S. F., & Ialongo, N. S. (2014). Longitudinal associations between experienced racial discrimination and depressive symptoms in African American adolescents. *Developmental Psychology, 50,* 1190–1196.

Ennett, S. T., & Bauman, K. E. (1996). Adolescent social networks: School, demographic, and longitudinal considerations. *Journal of Adolescent Research, 11,* 194–215.

Erikson, E. H. (1963). *Childhood and society.* New York: Norton.

Espelage, D. L., & Colbert, C. L. (2016). School-based bullying: Definition, prevalence, etiology, outcomes, and preventive strategies. In M. K. Holt, A. E. Grills, M. K. Holt, & A. E. Grills (Eds.), *Critical issues in school-based mental health: Evidence-based research, practice, and interventions* (pp. 132–144). New York: Routledge/Taylor & Francis Group

Espenschade, A. (1960). Motor development. In W. R. Johnson (Ed.), *Science and medicine of exercise and sports.* New York: Harper & Row.

Estell, D. B., Jones, M. H., Pearl, R., Van Acker, R., Farmer, T. W., & Rodkin, P. C. (2008). Peer groups, popularity, and social preference: Trajectories of social functioning among students with and without learning disabilities. *Journal of Learning Disabilities, 41,* 5–14.

Estévez, E., Emler, N. P., Cava, M. J., & Inglés, C. J. (2014). Psychosocial adjustment in aggressive popular and aggressive rejected adolescents at school. *Psychosocial Intervention, 23,* 57–67.

Ethier, L., Couture, G., & Lacharite, C. (2004). Risk factors associated with the chronicity of high potential for child abuse and neglect. *Journal of Family Violence, 19,* 13–24.

Evans, D. W., Leckman, J. F., Carter A., et al. (1997). Ritual, habit, and perfectionism: The prevalence and development of compulsive-like behavior in normal young children. *Child Development, 68*(1), 58–68.

Evans, G. W. (2004). The environment of childhood poverty. *American Psychologist, 59,* 77–92.

Evans, T., Whittingham, K., & Boyd, R. (2012). What helps the mother of a preterm infant become securely attached, responsive and well-adjusted? *Infant Behavior & Development, 35,* 1–11.

Eveleth, P., & Tanner, J. (1976). *Worldwide variation in human growth.* New York: Cambridge University Press.

Evenson, K. R. (2011). Towards an understanding of change in physical activity from pregnancy through postpartum. *Psychology of Sport and Exercise, 12,* 36–45.

Everett, S. A., Malarcher, A. M., Sharp, D. J., Husten, C. G., & Giovino, G. A. (2000). Relationship between cigarette, smokeless tobacco, and cigar use, and other health risk behaviors among U.S. high school students. *Journal of School Health, 70,* 234–240.

Ewing, C. P. (2014). *Preventing the sexual victimization of children: Psychological, legal, and public policy perspectives.* New York: Oxford University Press

Ezzo, F., & Young, K. (2012). Child Maltreatment Risk Inventory: Pilot data for the Cleveland Child Abuse Potential Scale. *Journal of Family Violence, 27,* 145–155.

Fagan, J., & Holland, C. (2007). Racial equality in intelligence: Predictions from a theory of intelligence as processing. *Intelligence, 35,* 319–334.

Fagan, J., & Ployhart, R. E. (2015). The information processing foundations of human capital resources: Leveraging insights from information processing approaches to intelligence. *Human Resource Management Review, 25,* 4–11.

Fagan, M. (2009). Mean length of utterance before words and grammar: Longitudinal trends and developmental implications of infant vocalizations. *Journal of Child Language, 36,* 495–527.

Faith, M. S., Johnson, S. L., & Allison, D. B. (1997). Putting the behavior into the behavior genetics of obesity. *Behavior Genetics, 27,* 423–439.

Falck-Ytter, T., Gredeback, G., & von Hofsten, C. (2006). Infants predict other people's action goals. *Nature and Neuroscience, 9,* 878–879.

Falco, M. (2012, July 3). Since IVF began, 5 million babies born. *CNN News.* Retrieved July 3, 2012, from http://thechart .blogs.cnn.com/2012/07/02/5-million-babies-born-so-far -thanks-to-ivf/.

Falk, D. (2004). Prelinguistic evolution in early hominins: Whence motherese? *Behavioral and Brain Sciences, 27,* 491–503.

Fanger, S., Frankel, L., & Hazen, N. (2012). Peer exclusion in preschool children's play: Naturalistic observations in a playground setting. *Merrill-Palmer Quarterly, 58,* 224–254.

Fantz, R. (1963). Pattern vision in newborn infants. *Science, 140,* 296–297.

Farbiash, T., Berger, A., Atzaba-Poria, N., & Auerbach, J. G. (2013). Prediction of preschool aggression from drd4 risk, parental ADHD symptoms, and home chaos. *Journal of Abnormal Child Psychology.* Retrieved February 18, 2014, from http://link.springer.com/article/10.1007%2Fs10802-013-9791-3#page-1.

Farhat, R., & Rajab, M. (2011). Length of postnatal hospital stay in healthy newborns and re-hospitalization following early discharge. *North American Journal of Medical Science, 3,* 146–151.

Farkas, C., & Vallotton, C. (2016). Differences in infant temperament between Chile and the US. *Infant Behavior & Development, 44,* 208–218.

Farr, R. H., & Patterson, C. J. (2013). Coparenting among lesbian, gay and heterosexual couples: Associations with adopted children's outcomes. Child Development, 84, 1226-1240.

Farrant, B., Fletcher, J., & Maybery, M. (2006, November). Specific language impairment, theory of mind, and visual perspective taking: Evidence for simulation theory and the developmental role of language. *Child Development, 77,* 1842–1853.

Farrar, M., Johnson, B., Tompkins, V., Easters, M., Zilisi-Medus, A., & Benigno, J. (2009). Language and theory of mind in preschool children with specific language impairment. *Journal of Communication Disorders, 42,* 428–441.

Farroni, T., Menon, E., Rigato, S., & Johnson, M. (2007). The perception of facial expressions in newborns. *European Journal of Developmental Psychology, 4,* 2–13.

Farver, J. M., & Lee-Shin, Y. (2000). Acculturation and Korean-American children's social and play behavior. *Social Development, 9,* 316–336.

Farver, J. M., Kim, Y. K., & Lee-Shin, Y. (1995). Cultural differences in Korean- and Anglo-American preschoolers' social interaction and play behaviors. *Child Development, 66,* 1088–1099.

Farver, J. M., Welles-Nystrom, B., Frosch, D. L., & Wimbarti, S. (1997). Toy stories: Aggression in children's narratives in the United States, Sweden, Germany, and Indonesia. *Journal of Cross-Cultural Psychology, 28,* 393–420.

Fasano, C., & Pellitteri, J. (2006). Infusing emotional learning into the school environment. *Emotionally intelligent school counseling* (pp. 65–79). Mahwah, NJ: Lawrence Erlbaum Associates Publishers.

Fayers, T., Crowley, T., Jenkins, J. M., & Cahill, D. J. (2003). Medical student awareness of sexual health is poor. *International Journal STD/AIDS, 14,* 386–389.

Feldman, R., & Masalha, S. (2007). The role of culture in moderating the links between early ecological risk and young children's adaptation. *Development and Psychopathology, 19,* 1–21.

Feldman, R. S. (2010). *The liar in your life: The way to truthful relationships.* New York: Twelve.

Feldman, R. S., & Rimé, B. (Eds.). (1991). *Fundamentals of nonverbal behavior.* Cambridge, England: Cambridge University Press.

Feldman, R. S., Tomasian, J., & Coats, E. J. (1999). Adolescents' social competence and nonverbal deception abilities: Adolescents with higher social skills are better liars. *Journal of Nonverbal Behavior, 23,* 237–249.

Feldman, S. S., & Wood, D. N. (1994). Parents' expectations for preadolescent sons' behavioral autonomy: A longitudinal study of correlates and outcomes. *Journal of Research on Adolescence, 4,* 45–70.

Fenwick, K. D., & Morrongiello, B. A. (1998). Spatial co-location and infants' learning of auditory-visual associations. *Behavior & Development, 21,* 745–759.

Ferguson, C. J. (2013). *Adolescents, crime, and the media: A critical analysis.* New York: Springer Science + Business Media.

Fergusson, D. M., Horwood, L. J., & Ridder, E. M. (2006). Abortion in young women and subsequent mental health. *Journal of Child Psychology and Psychiatry, 47,* 16–24.

Fergusson, D., Horwood, L., Boden, J., & Jenkin, G. (2007, March). Childhood social disadvantage and smoking in adulthood: Results of a 25-year longitudinal study. *Addiction, 102,* 475–482.

Fernald, A. (2001). Hearing, listening, and understanding: Auditory development in infancy. In G. Bremner & A. Fogel (Eds.), *Blackwell handbook of infant development.* Malden, MA: Blackwell Publishers.

Fernald, A., & Morikawa, H. (1993). Common themes and cultural variations in Japanese and American mothers' speech to infants. *Child Development, 64,* 637–656.

Fernandes, M., & Sturm, R. (2010). Facility provision in elementary schools: Correlates with physical education, recess, and obesity. *Preventive Medicine: An International Journal Devoted to Practice and Theory, 50*(Suppl), S30–S35.

Fernández, C. (2013). Mindful storytellers: Emerging pragmatics and theory of mind development. *First Language, 33,* 20–46.

Fernyhough, C. (1997). Vygotsky's sociocultural approach: Theoretical issues and implications for current research. In S. Hala (Ed.), *The development of social cognition* (pp. 65–92). Hove, England: Psychology Press/Erlbaum, Taylor & Francis.

Ferri, R., Novelli, L., & Bruni, O. (2017). Sleep structure and scoring from infancy to adolescence. In S. Nevšímalová & O. Bruni (Eds.), *Sleep disorders in children.* Cham, Switzerland: Springer International Publishing.

Feshbach, S., & Tangney, J. (2008). Television viewing and aggression: Some alternative perspectives. *Perspectives on Psychological Science, 3,* 387–389.

Festinger, L. (1954). A theory of social comparison processes. *Human Relations, 7,* 117–140.

Field, M. J., & Behrman, R. E. (Eds.) (2002). *When children die.* Washington, DC: National Academies Press.

Field, M. J., & Behrman, R. E. (Eds.). (2003). *When children die.* Washington, DC: National Academies Press.

Field, T. (2001). Massage therapy facilitates weight gain in preterm infants. *Current Directions in Psychological Science, 10,* 51–54.

Field, T., Diego, M., & Hernandez-Reif, M. (2006). Prenatal depression effects on the fetus and newborn: A review. *Infant Behavior & Development, 29,* 445–455.

Field, T., Diego, M., & Hernandez-Reif, M. (2008). Prematurity and potential predictors. *International Journal of Neuroscience, 118,* 277–289.

Field, T., Greenberg, R., Woodson, R., Cohen, D., & Garcia, R. (1984). Facial expression during Brazelton neonatal assessments. *Infant Mental Health Journal, 5,* 61–71.

Field, T., & Walden, T. (1982). Perception and production of facial expression in infancy and early childhood. In H. Reese & L. Lipsitt (Eds.), *Advances in child development and behavior* (Vol. 16). New York: Academic Press.

Field, T. M. (1982). Individual differences in the expressivity of neonates and young infants. In R. S. Feldman (Ed.), *Development of nonverbal behavior in children.* New York: Springer-Verlag.

Fiedler, N. L. (2012). Gender (sex) differences in response to prenatal lead exposure. In M. Lewis & L. Kestler (Eds.), *Gender differences in prenatal substance exposure.* Washington, DC: American Psychological Association.

Fifer, W. (1987). Neonatal preference for mother's voice. In N. A. Kasnegor, E. M. Blass, & M. A. Hofer (Eds.), *Perinatal development: A psychobiological perspective. Behavioral biology* (pp. 111–124). Orlando, FL: Academic Press.

Finer, L. B., & Philbin, J. M. (2013). Sexual initiation, contraceptive use, and pregnancy among young adolescents. *Pediatrics, 131*(5), 886–891.

Finkelstein, D. L., Harper, D. A., & Rosenthal, G. E. (1998). Does length of hospital stay during labor and delivery influence patient satisfaction? Results from a regional study. *American Journal of Managed Care, 4,* 1701–1708.

Fisch, S. M. (2004). *Children's learning from educational television: Sesame Street and beyond.* Mahwah, NJ: Erlbaum.

Fischbach, R. L., Harris, M. J., Ballan, M. S., Fischbach, G. D., & Link, B. G. (2016). Is there concordance in attitudes and beliefs between parents and scientists about autism spectrum disorder? *Autism, 20*(3), 353–363.

Fischer, K. W., & Rose, S. P. (1995). Concurrent cycles in the dynamic development of brain and behavior. *Newsletter of the Society for Research in Child Development,* p. 16.

Fischer, N. (2012). Mother-infant attachment: The demystification of an enigma. In S. Akhtar (Ed.), *The mother and her child: Clinical aspects of attachment, separation, and loss.* Lanham, MD: Jason Aronson.

Fischer, T. (2007). Parental divorce and children's socio-economic success: Conditional effects of parental resources prior to divorce, and gender of the child. *Sociology, 41,* 475–495.

Fish, J. M. (Ed.). (2001). *Race and intelligence: Separating science from myth.* Mahwah, NJ: Erlbaum.

Fisher, C. (2005). Deception research involving children: Ethical practices and paradoxes. *Ethics & Behavior, 15,* 271–287.

Fisher, C. B. (2004). Informed consent and clinical research involving children and adolescents: Implications of the revised APA Ethics Code and HIPAA. *Journal of Clinical Child & Adolescent Psychology, 33,* 832–839.

Fisher, C., Hauck, Y., & Fenwick, J. (2006). How social context impacts on women's fears of childbirth: A Western Australian example. *Social Science & Medicine, 63*, 64–75.

Fisher-Thompson, D. (2017). Contributions of look duration and gaze shift patterns to infants' novelty preferences. *Infancy, 22*, 190–222.

Fitzgerald, H. (2006). Cross cultural research during infancy: Methodological considerations. *Infant Mental Health Journal, 27*, 612–617.

Fitzgerald, P. (2008). A neurotransmitter system theory of sexual orientation. *Journal of Sexual Medicine, 5*, 746–748.

Fivush, R., Kuebli, J., & Clubb, P. A. (1992). The structure of events and event representations: A developmental analysis. *Child Development, 63*, 188–201.

Fletcher, A. C., Darling, N. E., Steinberg, L., & Dornbusch, S. M. (1995). The company they keep: Relation of adolescents' adjustment and behavior to their friends' perceptions of authoritative parenting in the social network. *Developmental Psychology, 31*, 300–310.

Flom, R., & Bahrick, L. (2007). The development of infant discrimination of affect in multimodal and unimodal stimulation: The role of intersensory redundancy. *Developmental Psychology, 43*, 238–252.

Flom, R., & Johnson, S. (2011). The effects of adults' affective expression and direction of visual gaze on 12-month-olds' visual preferences for an object following a 5-minute, 1-day, or 1-month delay. *British Journal of Developmental Psychology, 29*, 64–85.

Floress, M. T., Kuhn, B. R., Bernas, R. S., & Dandurand, M. (2016). Nightmare prevalence, distress, and anxiety among young children. *Dreaming, 26*, 280–292.

Flouri, E. (2005). *Fathering and child outcomes.* New York: Wiley & Sons.

Flouri, E., & Midouhas, E. (2017). Environmental adversity and children's early trajectories of problem behavior: The role of harsh parental discipline. *Journal of Family Psychology, 31*, 234–243.

Floyd, R. G. (2005). Information-processing approaches to interpretation of contemporary intellectual assessment instruments. In D. P. Flanagan, & P. L. Harrison (Eds.), *Contemporary intellectual assessment: Theories, tests, and issues.* New York, Guilford Press.

Fogarty, R. (2008). The intelligence-friendly classroom: It just makes sense. *Teaching for intelligence* (2nd ed.). (pp. 142–148). Thousand Oaks, CA: Corwin Press.

Fok, M. S. M., & Tsang, W. Y. W. (2006). "Development of an instrument measuring Chinese adolescent beliefs and attitudes towards substance use": Response to commentary. *Journal of Clinical Nursing, 15*, 1062–1063.

Ford, A. M., & Martinez-Ramirez, A. (2006). Therapeutic opportunities and targets in childhood leukemia. *Clinical and Translational Oncology, 8*, 560–565.

Ford, D. Y. (2011). *Reversing underachievement among gifted Black students* (2nd ed.). Waco, TX: Prufrock Press.

Ford, J. (2007, August). Alcohol use among college students: A comparison of athletes and nonathletes. *Substance Use & Misuse, 42*(9), 1367–1377.

Foroud, A., & Whishaw, I. Q. (2012). The consummatory origins of visually guided reaching in human infants: A dynamic integration of whole-body and upper-limb movements. *Behavioural Brain Research, 231*, 343–355.

Fowers, B. J., & Davidov, B. J. (2006). The virtue of multiculturalism: Personal transformation, character, and openness to the other. *American Psychologist, 61*, 581–594.

Fowler, J. W., & Dell, M. L. (2006). Stages of faith from infancy through adolescence: Reflections on three decades of faith development theory. In E. C. Roehlkepartain, P. E. King, L. Wagener, & P. L. Benson (Eds.), *The handbook of spiritual development in childhood and adolescence.* Thousand Oaks, CA: Sage Publications.

Fowler, R. C. (2017). Reframing the debate about the relationship between learning and development: An effort to resolve dilemmas and reestablish dialogue in a fractured field. *Early Childhood Education Journal, 45*, 155–162.

Fowler, S. A., Thomas, D. V., Corr, C., & Danner, N. (2015). The interrelated roles of early childhood policy and early childhood research. In O. N. Saracho, O. N. Saracho (Eds.), *Handbook of research methods in early childhood education: Review of research methodologies, Vol. II* (pp. 95–113). Charlotte, NC: Information Age Publishing.

Fragkaki, I., Cima, M., & Meesters, C. (2016). The association between callous–unemotional traits, externalizing problems, and gender in predicting cognitive and affective morality judgments in adolescence. *Journal of Youth and Adolescence, 45*, 1917–1930.

Fraley, R. C., & Spieker, S. J. (2003). Are infant attachment patterns continuously or categorically distributed? A taxometric analysis of Strange Situation behavior. *Developmental Psychology, 39*, 387–404.

Franck, I., & Brownstone, D. (1991). *The parent's desk reference.* New York: Prentice-Hall.

Frankenburg, W. K., Dodds, J., Archer, P., Shapiro, H., & Bresnick, B. (1992). The Denver II: A major revision and restandardization of the Denver Developmental Screening Test. *Pediatrics, 89*, 91–97.

Frankenhuis, W. E., Barrett, H., & Johnson, S. P. (2013). Developmental origins of biological motion perception. In K. L. Johnson & M. Shiffrar (Eds.), *People watching: Social, perceptual, and neurophysiological studies of body perception.* New York: Oxford University Press.

Fransson, M., Granqvist, P., Marciszko, C., Hagekull, B., & Bohlin, G. (2016). Is middle childhood attachment related to social functioning in young adulthood? *Scandinavian Journal of Psychology, 57*, 108–116.

Frawley, T. (2008). Gender schema and prejudicial recall: How children misremember, fabricate, and distort gendered picture book information. *Journal of Research in Childhood Education, 22*, 291–303.

Frazier, L. M., Grainger, D. A., Schieve, L. A., & Toner, J. P. (2004). Follicle-stimulating hormone and estradiol levels independently predict the success of assisted reproductive technology treatment. *Fertility and Sterility, 82*, 834–840.

Frederickson, N., & Petrides, K. (2008). Ethnic, gender, and socioeconomic group differences in academic performance and secondary school selection: A longitudinal analysis. *Learning and Individual Differences, 18*, 144–151.

Freedman, D. G. (1979, January). Ethnic differences in babies. *Human Nature*, 15–20.

Freeman, J. M. (2007). Beware: the misuse of technology and the law of unintended consequences. *Neurotherapeutics, 4*, 549–554.

Freud, S. (1920). *A general introduction to psychoanalysis.* New York: Boni & Liveright.

Freud, S. (1922/1959). *Group psychology and the analysis of the ego.* London: Hogarth.

Frewen, A. R., Chew, E., Carter, M., Chunn, J., & Jotanovic, D. (2015). A cross-cultural exploration of parental involvement and child-rearing beliefs in Asian cultures. *Early Years: An International Journal of Research and Development, 35*, 36–49.

Frick, P. J., Cornell, A. H., Bodin, S. D., Dane, H. A., Barry, C. T., & Loney, B. R. (2003). Callous-unemotional traits and developmental pathways to severe conduct problems. *Developmental Psychology, 39*, 246–260.

Fridlund, A. J., Beck, H. P., Goldie, W. D., & Irons, G. (2012). Little Albert: A neurologically impaired child. *History of Psychology.* Retrieved July 9, 2012, from http://psycnet.apa.org/psycinfo/2012-01974-001/.

Friedman, D. E. (2004). *The new economics of preschool.* Washington, DC: Early Childhood Funders' Collaborative/NAEYC.

Friedman, S., Heneghan, A., & Rosenthal, M. (2009). Characteristics of women who do not seek prenatal care and implications for prevention. *Journal of Obstetric, Gynecologic, & Neonatal Nursing: Clinical Scholarship for the Care of Women, Childbearing Families, & Newborns, 38*, 174–181.

Friedrich, J. (2014). Vygotsky's idea of psychological tools. In A. Yasnitsky, R. van der Veer, & M. Ferrari (Eds.), *The Cambridge handbook of cultural-historical psychology.* New York: Cambridge University Press.

Fritz, G., & Rockney, R. (2004). Summary of the practice parameter for the assessment and treatment of children and adolescents with enuresis. *Work Group on Quality Issues; Journal of the American Academy of Child & Adolescent Psychiatry, 43*, 123–125.

Fu, G., Xu, F., Cameron, C., Heyman, G., & Lee, K. (2007, March). Cross-cultural differences in children's choices, categorizations, and evaluations of truths and lies. *Developmental Psychology, 43*(2), 278–293.

Fuhs, M., & Day, J. D. (2011). Verbal ability and executive functioning development in preschoolers at head start. *Developmental Psychology, 47*, 404–416.

Fujioka, T., Mourad, N., & Trainor, L. J. (2011). Development of auditory-specific brain rhythm in infants. *European Journal of Neuroscience, 33*, 521–529.

Fujisawa, T. X., & Shinohara, K. (2011). Sex differences in the recognition of emotional prosody in late childhood and adolescence. *Journal of Physiological Science, 61*, 429–435.

Fuligni, A. J. (2012). The intersection of aspirations and resources in the development of children from immigrant families. In C. Coll & A. Marks (Eds.), *The immigrant paradox in children and adolescents: Is becoming American a developmental risk?* Washington, DC: American Psychological Association.

Fuligni, A. J., Tseng, V., & Lam, M. (1999). Attitudes toward family obligations among American adolescents with Asian, Latin American, and European backgrounds. *Child Development, 70*, 1030–1044.

Fuligni, A., & Yoshikawa, H. (2003). Socioeconomic resources, parenting, and child development among immigrant families. In M. Bornstein & R. Bradley (Eds.), *Socioeconomic status, parenting, and child development.* Mahwah, NJ: Lawrence Erlbaum Associates.

Furman, W., & Shaffer, L. (2003). The role of romantic relationships in adolescent development. In P. Florsheim (Ed.), *Adolescent romantic relations and sexual behavior: Theory, research, and practical implications.* Mahwah, NJ: Lawrence Erlbaum Associates.

Gagneux, P. (2016). Assisted reproductive technologies: Evolution of human niche construction? Paper presented at the annual meeting of the American Association for the Advancement of Science. Washington, DC.

Gaias, L. M., Räikkönen, K., Komsi, N., Gartstein, M. A., Fisher, P. A., & Putnam, S. P. (2012). Cross-cultural temperamental differences in infants, children, and adults in the United States of America and Finland. *Scandinavian Journal of Psychology, 53*, 119–128.

Galambos, N., Leadbeater, B., & Barker, E. (2004). Gender differences in and risk factors for depression in adolescence: A 4-year longitudinal study. *International Journal of Behavioral Development, 28*, 16–25.

Gallagher, J. J. (1994). Teaching and learning: New models. *Annual Review of Psychology, 45*, 171–195.

Galland, B. C., Taylor, B. J., Elder, D. E., & Herbison, P. (2012). Normal sleep patterns in infants and children: A systematic review of observational studies. *Sleep Medicine Reviews, 16*, 213–222.

Galvao, T. F., Silva, M. T., Zimmermann, I. R., Souza, K. M., Martins, S. S., & Pereira, M. G. (2013). Pubertal timing in girls and depression: A systematic review. *Journal of Affective Disorders.* Retrieved January 28, 2014, from http://www.ncbi.nlm.nih.gov/pubmed/24274962.

Gandhi, P. K., Schwartz, C. E., Reeve, B. B., DeWalt, D. A., Gross, H. E., & Huang, I. (2016). An item-level response shift study on the change of health state with the rating of asthma-specific quality of life: A report from the promis® pediatric asthma study. *Quality of Life Research: An International Journal of Quality of Life Aspects of Treatment, Care & Rehabilitation.* Retrieved June 13, 2016, from http://www.ncbi.nlm.nih.gov/pubmed/27061424.

Garbarino, J. (2013). The emotionally battered child. In R. D. Krugman & J. E. Korbin (Eds.), *C. Henry Kempe: A 50 year legacy to the field of child abuse and neglect.* New York: Springer Science + Business Media.

García-Ruiz, M., Rodrigo, M., Hernández-Cabrera, J. A., & Máiquez, M. (2013). Contribution of parents' adult attachment and separation attitudes to parent-adolescent conflict resolution. *Scandinavian Journal of Psychology, 54*, 459–467.

Gardner, H. (2000). *Intelligence reframed: Multiple intelligences for the 21st century.* New York: Basic Books.

Gardner, H. (2006). Changing minds: The art and science of changing our own and other peo-ple's minds. Cambridge, MA: Harvard Business Press.

Gardner, H., & Perkins, D. (1989). *Art, mind, and education: Research from project zero.* Champaign, IL: University of Illinois Press.

Gardner, H., & Moran, S. (2006). The science of multiple intelligences theory: A response to Lynn Waterhouse. *Educational Psychologist, 41*, 227–232.

Gardner, M. K. (2011). Theories of intelligence. In M. A. Bray, T. J. Kehle, M. A. Bray, & T. J. Kehle (Eds.), *The Oxford handbook of school psychology.* New York: Oxford University Press.

Garlick, D. (2003). Integrating brain science research with intelligence research. *Current Directions in Psychological Science, 12*, 185–189.

Gartrell, N., & Bos, H. (2010). US National Longitudinal Lesbian Family Study: Psychological adjustment of 17-year-old adolescents. *Pediatrics, 126*, 28–36.

Gates, G. J. (2013, February). *LGBT parenting in the United States.* Los Angeles: The Williams Institute.

Gazmararian, J. A., Petersen, R., Spitz, A. M., Goodwin, M. M., Saltzman, L. E., & Marks, J. S. (2000). Violence and reproductive health: Current knowledge and future research directions. *Mat Child Health, 4*, 79–84.

Geary, D. C., & Berch, D. B. (2016). *Evolutionary perspectives on child development and education.* Cham, Switzerland: Springer International Publishing.

Geller, P. A., Nelson, A. R., & Bonacquisti, A. (2013). Women's health psychology. In A. M. Nezu, C. Nezu, P. A. Geller, & I.

B. Weiner (Eds.), *Handbook of psychology, Vol. 9: Health psychology* (2nd ed.). Hoboken, NJ: John Wiley & Sons Inc.

Gelman, S. A., Taylor, M. G., & Nguyen, S. (2004). Mother–child conversations about gender. *Monographs of the Society for Research in Child Development, 69.*

Genovese, J. (2006). Piaget, pedagogy, and evolutionary psychology. *Evolutionary Psychology, 4,* 127–137.

Gentilucci, M., & Corballis, M. (2006). From manual gesture to speech: A gradual transition. *Neuroscience & Biobehavioral Reviews, 30,* 949–960.

Gerard, C. M., Harris, K. A., & Thach, B. T. (2002). Spontaneous arousals in supine infants while swaddled and unswaddled during rapid eye movement and quiet sleep. *Pediatrics, 110,* 70.

Gerressu, M., Mercer, C., Graham, C., Wellings, K., & Johnson, A. (2008). Prevalence of masturbation and associated factors in a British national probability survey. *Archives of Sexual Behavior, 37,* 266–278.

Gerrish, C. J., & Mennella, J. A. (2000). Short-term influence of breastfeeding on the infants' interaction with the environment. *Developmental Psychobiology, 36,* 40–48.

Gershkoff-Stowe, L., & Thelen, E. (2004). U-shaped changes in behavior: A dynamic systems perspective. *Journal of Cognition & Development, 5,* 88–97.

Gershoff, E. T. (2002). Parental corporal punishment and associated child behaviors and experiences: A meta-analytic and theoretical review. *Psychological Bulletin, 128,* 539–579.

Gervain, J., Macagno, F., Cogoi, S., Peña, M., & Mehler, J. (2008). The neonate brain detects speech structure. *PNAS Proceedings of the National Academy of Sciences of the United States of America, 105,* 14222–14227.

Gesell, A. L. (1946). The ontogenesis of infant behavior. In L. Carmichael (Ed.), *Manual of child psychology.* New York: Harper.

Gewertz, C. (2005, April 6). Training focuses on teachers' expectations. *Education Week, 24,* 1–3.

Gfellner, B. M., & Armstrong, H. D. (2013). Racial-ethnic identity and adjustment in Canadian indigenous adolescents. *Journal of Early Adolescence, 33,* 635–662.

Ghetti, S., Lyons, K., Lazzarin, F., & Cornoldi, C. (2008, March). The development of metamemory monitoring during retrieval: The case of memory strength and memory absence. *Journal of Experimental Child Psychology, 99*(3), 157–181.

Ghule, M., Balaiah, D., & Joshi, B. (2007, September). Attitude towards premarital sex among rural college youth in Maharashtra, India. *Sexuality & Culture: An Interdisciplinary Quarterly, 11*(4), 1–17.

Giami, A., Ohlrichs, Y., Quilliam, S., Wellings, K., Pacey, S., & Wylie, K. (2006, November). Sex education in schools is insufficient to support adolescents in the 21st century. *Sexual and Relationship Therapy, 21*(4), 485–490.

Gibbs, N. (2002, April 15). Making time for a baby. *Time,* 48–54.

Gibson, E. J., & Walk, R. D. (1960). The 'visual cliff.' *Scientific American, 202,* 64–71.

Gifford-Smith, M., & Brownell, C. (2003). Childhood peer relationships: Social acceptance, friendships, and peer networks. *Journal of School Psychology, 41,* 235–284.

Gilbert, L. A. (1994). Current perspectives on dual-career families. *Current Directions in Psychological Science, 3,* 101–105.

Gillies, R. M. (2014). Developments in cooperative learning: Review of research. *Anales De Psicología, 30,* 792–801.

Gilligan, C. (1987). Adolescent development reconsidered. In C. E. Irwin (Ed.), *Adolescent social behavior and health.* San Francisco: Jossey-Bass.

Gilligan, C. (1996). The centrality of relationship in human development: A puzzle, some evidence, and a theory. In G. G. Noam & K. W. Fischer (Eds.), *Development and vulnerability in close relationships.* Hillsdale, NJ: Lawrence Erlbaum Associates, Inc.

Gilligan, C. (2004). Recovering psyche: Reflections on life-history and history. *Annual of Psychoanalysis, 32,* 131–147.

Gilligan, C., Lyons, N. P., & Hammer, T. J. (Eds.). (1990). *Making connections.* Cambridge, MA: Harvard University Press.

Gilmore, C. K., & Spelke, E. S. (2008). Children's understanding of the relationship between addition and subtraction. *Cognition, 107,* 932–945.

Ginzberg, E. (1972). Toward a theory of occupational choice: A restatement. *Vocational Guidance Quarterly, 12,* 10–14.

Gitto, E., Aversa, S., Salpietro, C., Barberi, I., Arrigo, T., Trimarchi, G., & Pellegrino, S. (2012). Pain in neonatal intensive care: Role of melatonin as an analgesic antioxidant. *Journal of Pineal Research: Molecular, Biological, Physiological and Clinical Aspects of Melatonin, 52,* 291–295.

Glaser, D. (2012). Effects of child maltreatment on the developing brain. In M. Garralda, J. Raynaud (Eds.), *Brain, mind, and developmental psychopathology in childhood.* Lanham, MD: Jason Aronson.

Glasson, E. J., Jacques, A., Wong, K., Bourke, J., & Leonard, H. (2016). Improved survival in Down syndrome over the last 60 years and the impact of perinatal factors in recent decades. *The Journal of Pediatrics, 169,* 214–220.

Gleason, J., & Ely, R. (2002). Gender differences in language development. In A. McGillicuddy-De Lisi & R. De Lisi (Eds.), *Biology, society, and behavior: The development of sex differences in cognition* (pp. 127–154). Westport, CT: Ablex Publishing.

Gleason, J. B., Perlmann, R. U., Ely, R., & Evans, D. W. (1991). The babytalk register: Parents' use of diminutives. In J. L. Sokolov, & C. E. Snow (Eds.), *Handbook of research in language development using CHILDES.* Hillsdale, NJ: Erlbaum.

Gleason, J. B., Perlmann, R. U., Ely, R., & Evans, D. W. (1994). The babytalk register: Parents' use of diminutives. In J. L. Sokolov & C. E. Snow (Eds.), *Handbook of research in language development using CHILDES.* Mahwah, NJ: Erlbaum.

Gleason, P., Clark, M., Tuttle, C., and Dwoyer, E. (2010). The Evaluation of Charter School Impacts (NCEE 2010-4029). Washington, DC: U.S. Department of Education, Institute of Education Sciences, National Center for Education Evaluation and Regional Assistance.

Gliga, T., Elsabbagh, M., Andravizou, A., & Johnson, M. (2009). Faces attract infants' attention in complex displays. *Infancy, 14,* 550–562.

Glynn, L. M., & Sandman, C. A. (2014). Evaluation of the association between placental corticotrophin-releasing hormone and postpartum depressive symptoms. *Psychosomatic Medicine, 76,* 355–362.

Goddnough, A. & Atkinson, S. (2016, April 30). A potent side effect to the flint water crisis: Mental health problems. *The New York Times,* A16.

Goede, I., Branje, S., & Meeus, W. (2009). Developmental changes in adolescents' perceptions of relationships with their parents. *Journal of Youth and Adolescence, 38,* 75–88.

Goetz, A., & Shackelford, T. (2006). Modern application of evolutionary theory to psychology: Key concepts and clarifications. *American Journal of Psychology, 119,* 567–584.

Gogate, L.J., Bahrick, L.E., Watson, J.D. (2000). A study of multimodal motherese: the role of temporal synchrony between verbal labels and gestures. *Child Development.* 71(4):876–892.

Gogate, L.J., Maganti, M., & Bahrick, L.E. (2015). Cross-cultural evidence for multimodal motherese: Asian-Indian mothers' adaptive use of synchronous words and gestures. *Journal of Experimental Child Psychology.* 129: 110–126. doi:10.1016/j.jecp.2014.09.002.

Gogtay, N., Sporn, A., Clasen, L. S., Nugent, T. I., Greenstein, D., Nicolson, R., & … Rapoport, J. L. (2004). Comparison of Progressive Cortical Gray Matter Loss in Childhood-Onset Schizophrenia With That in Childhood-Onset Atypical Psychoses. *Archives Of General Psychiatry, 61,* 17–22.

Goldberg, A. E. (2004). But do we need universal grammar? Comment on Lidz et al. *Cognition, 94,* 77–84.

Goldfarb, Z. (2005, July 12). Newborn medical screening expands. *Wall Street Journal,* p. D6.

Goldfield, G. S. (2012). Making access to TV contingent on physical activity: Effects on liking and relative reinforcing value of TV and physical activity in overweight and obese children. *Journal of Behavioral Medicine, 35,* 1–7.

Goldschmidt, L., Richardson, G., Willford, J., & Day, N. (2008). Prenatal marijuana exposure and intelligence test performance at age 6. *Journal of the American Academy of Child & Adolescent Psychiatry, 47,* 254–263.

Goldsmith, L. T. (2000). Tracking trajectories of talent: Child prodigies growing up. In R. C. Friedman & B. M. Shore (Eds.), *Talents unfolding: Cognition and development.* Washington, DC: American Psychological Association.

Goldstein, S., & Brooks, R. B. (2013). *Handbook of resilience in children* (2nd ed.). New York: Springer Science + Business Media.

Goldweber, A., Dmitrieva, J., Cauffman, E., Piquero, A. R., & Steinberg, L. (2011). The development of criminal style in adolescence and young adulthood: Separating the lemmings from the loners. *Journal of Youth and Adolescence, 40*(3), 332–346.

Goleman, D. (2005). What makes a leader? In R. L. Taylor & W. E. Rosenbach, *Military leadership: In pursuit of excellence* (5th ed.). Boulder, CO: Westview Press.

Golomb, C. (2002). *Child art in context: A cultural and comparative perspective.* Washington, DC: American Psychological Association.

Golombok, S., Golding, J., Perry, B., et al. (2003). Children with lesbian parents: A community study. *Developmental Psychology, 39,* 20–33.

Golombok, S., & Taker, F. (1996). Do parents influence the sexual orientation of their children? Findings from a longitudinal study of lesbian families. *Developmental Psychology, 32,* 3–11.

Göncü, A., & Gauvain, M. (2012). Sociocultural approaches to educational psychology: Theory, research, and application. In K. R. Harris, S. Graham, T. Urdan, C. B. McCormick, G. M. Sinatra, J. Sweller (Eds.), APA educational psychology handbook, Vol 1: Theories, constructs, and critical issues. Washington, DC: American Psychological Association.

Good, C., Aronson, J., & Harder, J. A. (2008). Problems in the pipeline: Stereotype threat and women's achievement in high-level math courses. *Journal Of Applied Developmental Psychology, 29,* 17–28.

Goode, E. (1999, January 12). Clash over when, and how, to toilet-train. *The New York Times,* pp. A1, A17.

Goode, E. (2004, February 3). Stronger warning is urged on antidepressants for teenagers. *The New York Times,* p. A12.

Goodlin-Jones, B. L., Burnham, M. M., & Anders, T. F. (2000). Sleep and sleep disturbances: Regulatory processes in infancy. In A. J. Sameroff, M. Lewis, & S. M. Miller (Eds.), *Handbook of developmental psychopathology* (2nd ed.). New York: Kluwer Academic/Plenum Publishers.

Goodman, G. S. (2006). Children's eyewitness memory: A modern history and contemporary commentary. *Journal of Social Issues, 62,* 811–832.

Goodman, G., & Melinder, A. (2007, February). Child witness research and forensic interviews of young children: A review. *Legal and Criminological Psychology, 12,* 1–19.

Goodman, G., & Quas, J. (2008). Repeated interviews and children's memory: It's more than just how many. *Current Directions in Psychological Science, 17,* 386–390.

Goodman, S., Broth, M., Hall, C., & Stowe, Z. (2008). Treatment of postpartum depression in mothers: Secondary benefits to the infants. *Infant Mental Health Journal, 29,* 492–513.

Goodnight, J. A., Donahue, K. L., Waldman, I. D., et al. (2016). Genetic and environmental contributions to associations between infant fussy temperament and antisocial behavior in childhood and adolescence. *Behavior Genetics, 46,* 680–692.

Goodnough, A. and Atkinson, S. (April 2016). A Potent Side Effect to the Flint Water Crisis: Mental Health Problems. Retrieved from nytimes.com/2016/05/01/us/flint-michigan-water-crisis-mental-health.html

Goodwin, M. H. (1990). Tactical uses of stories: Participation frameworks within girls' and boys' disputes. *Discourse Processes, 13,* 33–71.

Gopiram, P., & Kishore, M.T. (2014). Psychosocial attributes of substance abuse among adolescents and young adults: a comparative study of users and non-users, *Indian Journal of Psychological Medicine,* Jan-Mar, 36(1): 58–61.

Gopnik, A. (2010, July). How babies think. *Scientific American,* pp. 76–81.

Gopnik, A. (2012, January 28). What's wrong with the teenage mind? *Wall Street Journal,* C1–C2.

Gopnik, A., Meltzoff, A. N., & Kuhl, P. K. (2002). *The scientist in the crib: What early learning tells us about the mind.* New York: HarperCollins.

Gordon, I., Voos, A. C., Bennett, R.H., Bolling, D. Z., Pelphrey, K. A., & Kaiser, M. D. (2013). Brain mechanisms for processing affective touch. *Human Brain Mapping, 34,* 914–922.

Gören, J.L. (2008). Antidepressants use in pediatric populations. *Expert Opinion on Drug Safety, 7,* 223–225.

Gormley, W. T., Jr., Gayer, T., Phillips, D., & Dawson, B. (2005). The effects of universal pre-K on cognitive development. *Developmental Psychology, 41,* 872–884.

Gottesman, I. I. (1991). *Schizophrenia genesis: The origins of madness.* New York: Freeman.

Gottfredson, G. D., & Holland, J. L. (1990). A longitudinal test of the influence of congruence: Job satisfaction, competency utilization, and counterproductive behavior. *Journal of Counseling Psychology, 37,* 389–398.

Gottfried, A., Gottfried, A., & Bathurst, K. (2002). Maternal and dual-earner employment status and parenting. In M. Bornstein (Ed.), *Handbook of parenting: Vol. 2: Biology and ecology of parenting.* Mahwah, NJ: Lawrence Erlbaum Associates.

Gottlieb, G., & Blair, C. (2004). How early experience matters in intellectual development in the case of poverty. *Preventive Science, 5,* 245–252.

Gould, S. J. (1977). *Ontogeny and phylogeny.* Cambridge, MA: Harvard University Press.

Gowey, M. A., Reiter-Purtill, J., Becnel, J., Peugh, J., Mitchell, J. E., & Zeller, M. H. (2016). Weight-related correlates of psychological dysregulation in adolescent and young adult (AYA) females with severe obesity. *Appetite, 99,* 211–218.

Gowin, J. L., Green, C. E., Alcorn, J. L., Swann, A. C., Moeller, F. G., & Lane, S. D. (2013). The role of cortisol and psychopathy in the cycle of violence. *Psychopharmacology, 227,* 661–672.

Goyette-Ewing, M. (2000). Children's after school arrangements: A study of self-care and developmental outcomes. *Journal of Prevention & Intervention in the Community, 20,* 55–67.

Graddol, D. (2004, February 27). The future of language. *Science, 303,* 1329–1331.

Graham, I., Carroli, G., Davies, C., & Medves, J. (2005). Episiotomy rates around the world: An update. *Birth: Issues in Perinatal Care, 32,* 219–223.

Graham, J. E., Christian, L. M., & Kiecolt-Glaser, J. K. (2006). Stress, age, and immune function: toward a lifespan approach. *Journal of Behavioral Medicine, 29,* 389–400.

Graham, J., Banaschewski, T., Buitelaar, J., et al. (2011). European guidelines on managing adverse effects of medication for ADHD. European Guidelines Group; *European Child & Adolescent Psychiatry, 20,* 17–37.

Graham, S. A., Nilsen, E., Mah, J. T., et al. (2014). An examination of communicative interactions of children from Romanian orphanages and their adoptive mothers. *Canadian Journal of Behavioural Science/Revue Canadienne Des Sciences Du Comportement, 46,* 9–19.

Grall, T. S. (2009). Custodial mothers and fathers and their child support: 2007. *Current population reports.* Washington, DC: U.S. Bureau of the Census.

Grammer, J. K., Purtell, K. M., Coffman, J. L., & Ornstein, P. A. (2011). Relations between children's metamemory and strategic performance: Time-varying covariates in early elementary school. *Journal of Experimental Child Psychology, 108,* 139–155.

Granic, I., Hollenstein, T., & Dishion, T. (2003). Longitudinal analysis of flexibility and reorganization in early adolescence: A dynamic systems study of family interactions. *Developmental Psychology, 39,* 606–617.

Granic, I., Lobel, A., & Engels, R. C. M. E. (2014). The benefits of playing video games. American Psychologist, 69(1), 66-78.

Grant, C., Wall, C., Brewster, D., et al. (2007). Policy statement on iron deficiency in preschool-aged children. *Journal of Paediatrics and Child Health, 43,* 513–521.

Grant, K. E., McMahon, S. D., Duffy, S. N., Taylor, J. J., & Compas, B. E. (2011). Stressors and mental health problems in childhood and adolescence. In R. J. Contrada & A. Baum (Eds.), *The handbook of stress science: Biology, psychology, and health.* New York: Springer Publishing Co.

Grant, R. J. (2017). *Play-based intervention for autism spectrum disorder and other developmental disabilities.* New York: Routledge/ Taylor & Francis Group.

Grantham-McGregor, S., Ani, C., & Fernald, L. (2001). The role of nutrition in intellectual development. In R. J. Sternberg & E. L. Grigorenko (Eds.), *Environmental effects on cognitive abilities.* Mahwah, NJ: Erlbaum.

Grantham-McGregor, S., Powell, C., Walker, S., Chang, S., & Fletcher, P. (1994). The long-term follow-up of severely malnourished children who participated in an intervention program. *Child Development, 65,* 428–439.

Grattan, M. P., DeVos, E. S., Levy, J., & McClintock, M. K. (1992). Asymmetric action in the human newborn: Sex differences in patterns of organization. *Child Development, 63,* 273–289.

Gray, C., Ferguson, J., Behan, S., Dunbar, C., Dunn, J., & Mitchell, D. (2007, March). Developing young readers through the linguistic phonics approach. *International Journal of Early Years Education, 15,* 15–33.

Gray-Little, B., & Hafdahl, A. R. (2000). Factors influencing racial comparisons of self-esteem: A quantitative review. *Psychological Bulletin, 126,* 26–54.

Gredebäck, G., Eriksson, M., Schmitow, C., Laeng, B., & Stenberg, G. (2012). Individual differences in face processing: Infants' scanning patterns and pupil dilations are influenced by the distribution of parental leave. *Infancy, 17,* 79–101.

Gredler, M., & Shields, C. (2008). *Vygotsky's legacy: A foundation for research and practice.* New York, NY: Guilford Press.

Gredler, M. E. (2012). Understanding Vygotsky for the classroom: Is it too late? *Educational Psychology Review, 24,* 113–131.

Green, C., Sugarman, M. A., Medford, K., Klobusicky, E., & Bavelier, D. (2012). The effect of action video game experience on task-switching. *Computers In Human Behavior, 28,* 984–994.

Green, J., Muir, H., & Maher, M. (2011). Child pedestrian casualties and deprivation. *Accident Analysis and Prevention, 43,* 714–723.

Green, M., DeCourville, N., & Sadava, S. (2012). Positive affect, negative affect, stress, and social support as mediators of the forgiveness-health relationship. *The Journal of Social Psychology, 152,* 288–307.

Greenberg, J. (2011). The impact of maternal education on children's enrollment in early childhood education and care. *Children and Youth Services Review.*

Greenberg, J. (2012). The impact of maternal education on children's enrollment in early childhood education and care. *Children and Youth Services Review.*

Greenberg, L., Cwikel, J., & Mirsky, J. (2007, January). Cultural correlates of eating attitudes: A comparison between native-born and immigrant university students in Israel. *International Journal of Eating Disorders, 40,* 51–58.

Greene, K., Krcmar, M., Walters, L. H., Rubin, D. L., & Hale, J. L. (2000). Targeting adolescent risk-taking behaviors: The contribution of egocentrism and sensation-seeking. *Journal of Adolescence, 23,* 439–461.

Greene, M. M., Patra, K., Silvestri, J. M., & Nelson, M. N. (2013). Re-evaluating preterm infants with the Bayley-III: Patterns and predictors of change. *Research in Developmental Disabilities, 34,* 2107–2117.

Greenfield, P. M. (1966). On culture and conservation. In J. S. Bruner, R. R. Olver, & P. M. Greenfield (Eds.), *Studies in cognitive growth.* New York: Wiley.

Greenstein, A. (2016). *Radical inclusive education: Disability, teaching and struggles for liberation.* New York, NY, US: Routledge/ Taylor & Francis Group.

Greenwood, D. N., & Pietromonaco, P. R. (2004). The interplay among attachment orientation, idealized media images of women, and body dissatisfaction: A social psychological analysis. In L. J. Shrum (Ed.), *Psychology of entertainment media: Blurring the lines between entertainment and persuasion.* Mahwah, NJ: Lawrence Erlbaum Associates.

Greer, B. D., Neidert, P. L., & Dozier, C. L. (2016). A component analysis of toilet-training procedures recommended for young children. *Journal of Applied Behavior Analysis, 49,* 69–84.

Gregory, K. (2005). Update on nutrition for preterm and full-term infants. *Journal of Obstetrics and Gynecological Neonatal Nursing, 34,* 98–108.

Gregory, S. (1856). *Facts for young women.* Boston.

Greydanus, D. E., & Pratt, H. D. (2016). Human sexuality. *International Journal of Child and Adolescent Health, 9,* 291–312.

Griffith, D. R., Azuma, S. D., & Chasnoff, I. J. (1994). Three-year outcome of children exposed prenatally to drugs. *Journal of the American Academy of Child and Adolescent Psychiatry, 33,* 20–27.

Grigorenko, E. (2003). Intraindividual fluctuations in intellectual functioning: Selected links between nutrition and the mind. In R. Sternberg & J. Lautrey (Eds.), *Models of intelligence: International perspectives*. Washington, DC: American Psychological Association.

Grinkevičiūtė, D., Jankauskaitė, L., Kėvalas, R., & Gurskis, V. (2016). Shaken baby syndrome and consciousness. In G. Leisman & J. Merrick (Eds.), *Considering consciousness clinically*. Hauppauge, NY: Nova Biomedical Books.

Grønhøj, A., & Thøgersen, J. (2012). Action speaks louder than words: The effect of personal attitudes and family norms on adolescents' pro-environmental behaviour. *Journal of Economic Psychology, 33*, 292–302.

Groome, L. J., Swiber, M. J., Atterbury, J. L., Bentz, L. S., & Holland, S. B. (1997). Similarities and differences in behavioral state organization during sleep periods in the perinatal infant before and after birth. *Child Development, 68*, 1–11.

Groome, L. J., Swiber, M. J., Bentz, L. S., Holland, S. B., & Atterbury, J. L. (1995). Maternal anxiety during pregnancy: Effect on fetal behavior at 38 to 40 weeks of gestation. *Developmental and Behavioral Pediatrics, 16*, 391–396.

Groopman, J. (1998 February 8). Decoding destiny. *The New Yorker*, 42–47.

Gross, R. T., Spiker, D., & Haynes, C. W. (Eds.). (1997). *Helping low-birthweight, premature babies: The Infant Health and Development Program*. Stanford, CA: Stanford University Press.

Grossmann, K. E., Grossman, K., Huber, F., & Wartner, U. (1982). German children's behavior towards their mothers at 12 months and their fathers at 18 months in Ainsworth's Strange Situation. *International Journal of Behavioral Development, 4*, 157–181.

Grossmann, T., Striano, T., & Friederici, A. (2006, May). Crossmodal integration of emotional information from face and voice in the infant brain. *Developmental Science, 9*, 309–315.

Grunbaum, J. A., Lowry, R., & Kann, L. (2001). Prevalence of health-related behaviors among alternative high school students as compared with students attending regular high schools. *Journal of Adolescent Health, 29*, 337–343.

Grych, J. H., & Clark, R. (1999). Maternal employment and development of the father–infant relationship in the first year. *Developmental Psychology, 35*, 893–903.

Guinsburg, R., de Araújo Peres, C., Branco de Almeida, M. F., et al. (2000). Differences in pain expression between male and female newborn infants. *Pain, 85*, 127–133.

Guadalupe, K. L., & Welkley, D. L. (2012). *Diversity in family constellations: Implications for practice*. Chicago: Lyceum Books.

Guasti, M. T. (2002). *Language acquisition: The growth of grammar*. Cambridge, MA: MIT Press.

Guerrero, A., Hishinuma, E., Andrade, N., Nishimura, S., & Cunanan, V. (2006, July). Correlations among socioeconomic and family factors and academic, behavioral, and emotional difficulties in Filipino adolescents in Hawaii. *International Journal of Social Psychiatry, 52*, 343–359.

Guerrini, I., Thomson, A., & Gurling, H. (2007). The importance of alcohol misuse, malnutrition and genetic susceptibility on brain growth and plasticity. *Neuroscience & Biobehavioral Reviews, 31*, 212–220.

Guggenmos, M., Rothkirch, M., Obermayer, K., Haynes, J., & Sterzer, P. (2015). A hippocampal signature of perceptual learning in object recognition. *Journal Of Cognitive Neuroscience, 27*(4), 787–797.

Gump, L. S., Baker, R. C., & Roll, S. (2000). Cultural and gender differences in moral judgment: A study of Mexican Americans and Anglo-Americans. *Hispanic Journal of Behavioral Sciences, 22*, 78–93.

Gupta, R., Pascoe, J., Blanchard, T., et al. (2009). Child health in child care: A multistate survey of Head Start and non–Head Start child care directors. *Journal of Pediatric Health Care, 23*, 143–149.

Gura, T. (2014). Nature's first functional food. *Science, 345*, 747–749.

Güre, A., Uçanok, Z., & Sayil, M. (2006) The associations among perceived pubertal timing, parental relations and self-perception in Turkish adolescents. *Journal of Youth and Adolescence, 35*, 541–550.

Gutek, G. L. (2003). Maria Montessori: Contributions to educational psychology. In B. J. Zimmerman (Ed.), *Educational psychology: A century of contributions*. Mahwah, NJ: Lawrence Erlbaum Associates.

Guthrie, W., Swineford, L. B., Nottke, C., & Wetherby, A. M. (2013). Early diagnosis of autism spectrum disorder: Stability and change in clinical diagnosis and symptom presentation. *Journal of Child Psychology and Psychiatry, 54*, 582–590.

Gutnick, A. L., Robb, M., Takeuchi, L., & Kotler, J. (2010). *Always connected: The new digital media habits of young children*. New York: The Joan Ganz Cooney Center at Sesame Workshop.

Guttmacher Institute (2012, February). *Facts on American Teens' Sexual and Reproductive Health*. New York: Guttmacher Institute.

Guttmann, J., & Rosenberg, M. (2003). Emotional intimacy and children's adjustment: A comparison between single-parent divorced and intact families. *Educational Psychology, 23*, 457–472.

Guttmannova, K., Hill, K. G., Bailey, J. A., Hartigan, L. A., Small, C. M., & Hawkins, J. D. (2016). Parental alcohol use, parenting, and child on-time development. *Infant and Child Development*. Retrieved March 3, 2017, from http://onlinelibrary.wiley.com/doi/10.1002/icd.2013/abstract.

Guzzetta, A., Fiori, S., Scelfo, D., Conti, E., & Bancale, A. (2013). Reorganization of visual fields after periventricular haemorrhagic infarction: Potentials and limitations. *Developmental Medicine & Child Neurology, 55*(Suppl 4), 23–26.

Hack, M., Flannery, D. J., Schluchter, M., Cartar, L., Borawski, E., & Klein, N. (2002). Outcomes in young adulthood for very low birth weight infants. *New England Journal of Medicine, 346*, 149–157.

Haddock, S., & Rattenborg, K. (2003). Benefits and challenges of dual-earning: Perspectives of successful couples. *American Journal of Family Therapy, 31*, 325–344.

Hagan-Burke, S., Coyne, M. D., Kwok, O., et al. (2013). The effects and interactions of student, teacher, and setting variables on reading outcomes for kindergarteners receiving supplemental reading intervention. *Journal of Learning Disabilities, 46*, 260–277.

Hagerman, R. J. (2011) Fragile X syndrome and fragile X-associated disorders. In S. Goldstein & C. R. Reynolds (Eds.), *Handbook of neurodevelopmental and genetic disorders in children* (2nd ed.). New York: Guilford Press.

Haith, M. H. (1986). Sensory and perceptual processes in early infancy. *Journal of Pediatrics, 109*(1), 158–171.

Haight, B. K. (1991). Psychological illness in aging. In E. M. Baines (Ed.), *Perspectives on gerontological nursing*. Newbury Park, CA: Sage.

Hakim, D. (2015, July 1). U.S. chamber travels the world, fighting curbs on smoking. *The New York Times*, A1.

Haley, M., Vasquez, J. (2008). A future in jeopardy: Sexuality issues in adolescence. In D. Capuzzi & D. R. Gross (Eds.), *Youth at risk: A prevention resource for counselors, teachers, and parents*. Alexandria, VA: American Counseling Association.

Halgunseth, L. C., Ispa, J. M., & Rudy, D. (2006). Parental control in Latino families: An integrated review of the literature. *Child Development*, 77, 1282–1297.

Halim, M. L., Ruble, D. N., Tamis-LeMonda, C. S., Zosuls, K. M., Lurye, L. E., & Greulich, F. K. (2014). Pink frilly dresses and the avoidance of all things 'girly': Children's appearance rigidity and cognitive theories of gender development. *Developmental Psychology*, 50, 1091–1101.

Hall, G. S. (1916). *Adolescence*. New York: Appleton. (Original work published 1904).

Hall, J., Neal, T., & Dean, R. (2008). Lateralization of cerebral functions. *The neuropsychology handbook* (3rd ed.). New York, NY: Springer Publishing Co.

Hall, R., Huitt, T., Thapa, R., Williams, D., Anand, K., & Garcia-Rill, E. (2008). Long-term deficits of preterm birth: Evidence for arousal and attentional disturbances. *Clinical Neurophysiology*, 119, 1281–1291.

Halpern, L. F., MacLean, W. E., & Baumeister, A. A. (1995). Infant sleep-wake characteristics: Relation to neurological status and the prediction of developmental outcome. *Developmental Review*, 15, 255–291.

Hamer, R., & van Rossum, E. J. (2016). Six languages in education—looking for postformal thinking. *Behavioral Development Bulletin*. Retrieved March 21, 2017, from http://psycnet.apa.org/psycinfo/2016-59293-001/.

Hamilton, B. E., Martin, J. A., Ventura, S. J. (2011). Births: Preliminary data for 2010. *National Vital Statistics Reports*, 60(2).

Hamilton, B. E., Martin, J. A., Osterman, M. J. K., et al. (2015). Births: Final data for 2014. *National Vital Statistics Report*, 64(12):1–64.

Hamilton, B. S., & Ventura, S. J. (2012, April.) Birth rates for U.S. teenagers reach historic lows for all age and ethnic groups. *NCHS Data Brief* (No. 89). Washington, DC: National Center for Health Statistics.

Hamilton, G. (1998). Positively testing. *Families in Society*, 79, 570–576.

Hamlin, J. K., Wynn, K., Bloom, P., & Mahajan, N. (2011). How infants and toddlers react to antisocial others. *Proceedings of the National Academy of Sciences*, 108, 19931–19936.

Handwerk, M. L. (2002). Least restrictive alternative: Challenging assumptions and further implications. *Children's Services: Social Policy, Research, & Practice*, 5, 99–103.

Hane, A., Feldstein, S., & Dernetz, V. (2003). The relation between coordinated interpersonal timing and maternal sensitivity in four-month-old infants. *Journal of Psycholinguistic Research*, 32, 525–539.

Hanna, K., Davies, E., Henderson, E., & Hand, L. (2013). Questioning child witnesses: Exploring the benefits and risks of intermediary models in New Zealand. *Psychiatry, Psychology and Law*, 20, 527–542.

Hanson, D. R., & Gottesman, I. I. (2005). Theories of schizophrenia: A genetic-inflammatory-vascular synthesis. *BMC Medical Genetics*, 6, 7.

Hanson, J. D. (2012). Understanding prenatal health care for American Indian women in a northern plains tribe. *Journal of Transcultural Nursing*, 23, 29–37.

Hanushek, E.A., & Kimko, D.D. (2000). Schooling, labor-force quality, and the growth of nations. *American Economic Review*, 90 (5), 1184–1208.

Hanushek, E.A., Machin, S.J., & Woessmann, L. (2010). *Handbook of the Economics of Education*. Elsevier Science.

Hanushek, E.A., & Woessmann, L. (2008). The role of cognitive skills in economic development. *Journal of Economic Literature*. 46 (3), 607–668.

Hanushek, E., Woessmann, L., 2012. Do better schools lead to more growth? Cognitive skills, economic outcomes, and causation. Journal of Economic Growth, 17 (4), 267–321.

Harden, K., Turkheimer, E., & Loehlin, J. (2007). Genotype by environment interaction in adolescents' cognitive aptitude. *Behavior Genetics*, 37, 273–283.

Hare, T., Tottenham, N., Galvan, A., Voss, H., Glover, G., & Casey, B. (2008, May). Biological substrates of emotional reactivity and regulation in adolescence during an emotional go-nogo task. *Biological Psychiatry*, 63(10), 927–934.

Harlow, H. F., & Zimmerman, R. R. (1959). Affectional responses in the infant monkey. *Science*, 130, 421–432.

Harrell, J. S., Bangdiwala, S. I., Deng, S., Webb, J. P., & Bradley, C. (1998). Smoking initiation in youth: The roles of gender, race, socioeconomics, and developmental status. *Journal of Adolescent Health*, 23, 271–279.

Harrell, Z., & Karim, N. (2008, February). Is gender relevant only for problem alcohol behaviors? An examination of correlates of alcohol use among college students. *Addictive Behaviors*, 33(2), 359–365.

Harris, A., Kelly, S. E., & Wyatt, S. (2013). Counseling customers: Emerging roles for genetic counselors in the direct-to-consumer genetic testing market. *Journal of Genetic Counseling*, 22, 277–288.

Harris, J., Vernon, P., & Jang, K. (2007). Rated personality and measured intelligence in young twin children. *Personality and Individual Differences*, 42, 75–86.

Harris, M., Prior, J., & Koehoorn, M. (2008). Age at menarche in the Canadian population: Secular trends and relationship to adulthood BMI. *Journal of Adolescent Health*, 43, 548–554.

Harris, M. A., Gruenenfelder-Steiger, A. E., Ferrer, E., et al. (2015). Do parents foster self-esteem? Testing the prospective impact of parent closeness on adolescent self-esteem. *Child Development*. Retrieved March 22, 2015, from http://www.ncbi.nlm.nih.gov/pubmed/25703089.

Harris, P. L. (1987). The development of search. In P. Sallapatek & L. Cohen (Eds.), *Handbook of infant perception: From perception to cognition* (Vol. 2, pp. 155–207). Orlando, FL: Academic Press.

Harris, S. (2015). *Waking up: A guide to spirituality without religion*. NY: Simon & Schuster.

Harrison, K., & Hefner, V. (2006, April). Media exposure, current and future body ideals, and disordered eating among preadolescent girls: A longitudinal panel study. *Journal of Youth and Adolescence*, 35, 153–163.

Harrist, A., & Waugh, R. (2002). Dyadic synchrony: Its structure and function in children's development. *Developmental Review*, 22, 555–592.

Hart, B. (2000). A natural history of early language experience. *Topics in Early Childhood Special Education*, 20, 28–32.

Hart, B. (2004). What toddlers talk about. *First Language*, 24, 91–106.

Hart, B., & Risley, T. R. (1995). *Meaningful differences in the everyday experience of young American children*. Baltimore, MD: Paul H Brookes Publishing.

Hart, D., Burock, D., & London, B. (2003). Prosocial tendencies, antisocial behavior, and moral development. In A. Slater & G. Bremner (Eds.), *An introduction to developmental psychology*. Malden, MA: Blackwell Publishers.

Hartley, C. A., & Lee, F. S. (2015). Sensitive periods in affective development: Nonlinear maturation of fear learning. *Neuropsychopharmacology*, 40, 50–60.

Harter, S. (2006). The development of self-esteem. *Self-esteem issues and answers: A sourcebook of current perspectives* (pp. 144–150). New York, NY: Psychology Press.

Harter, S. (1990). Issues in the assessment of self-concept of children and adolescents. In A. LaGreca (Ed.), *Through the eyes of a child*. Boston: Allyn & Bacon.

Hartshorne, J., & Ullman, M. (2006). Why girls say 'holded' more than boys. *Developmental Science, 9*, 21–32.

Harvey, E. (1999). Short-term and long-term effects of early parental employment on children of the National Longitudinal Survey of Youth. *Developmental Psychology, 35*, 445–459.

Harvey, J. H., & Fine, M. A. (2004). *Children of divorce: Stories of loss and growth*. Mahwah, NJ: Lawrence Erlbaum Associates.

Haslam, C., & Lawrence, W. (2004). Health-related behavior and beliefs of pregnant smokers. *Health Psychology, 23*, 486–491.

Hastings, P. D., McShane, K. E., Parker, R., & Ladha, F. (2007). Ready to make nice: Parental socialization of young sons' and daughters' prosocial behaviors with peers. *Journal of Genetic Psychology, 168*, 177–200.

Hastings, S. (2004, October 15). Emotional intelligence. *The Times Educational Supplement, London*, p. F1.

Hatton, C. (2002). People with intellectual disabilities from ethnic minority communities in the United States and the United Kingdom. In L. M. Glidden (Ed.), *International review of research in mental retardation (Vol. 25)*. San Diego, CA: Academic Press.

Haugaard, J. J. (2000). The challenge of defining child sexual abuse. *American Psychologist, 55*, 1036–1039.

Havard, C., & Memon, A. (2013). The mystery man can help reduce false identification for child witnesses: Evidence from video line-ups. *Applied Cognitive Psychology, 27*, 50–59.

Hawkins-Rodgers, Y. (2007). Adolescents adjusting to a group home environment: A residential care model of reorganizing attachment behavior and building resiliency. *Children and Youth Services Review, 29*, 1131–1141.

Hay, D. F., Pawlby, S., & Angold, A. (2003). Pathways to violence in the children of mothers who were depressed postpartum. *Developmental Psychology, 39*, 1083–1094.

Hayashi, A., & Mazuka, R. (2017). Emergence of Japanese infants' prosodic preferences in infant-directed vocabulary. *Developmental Psychology, 53*, 28–37.

Haynie, D. L., Nansel, T., Eitel, P., et al. (2001). Bullies, victims, and bully/victims: Distinct groups of at-risk youth. *Journal of Early Adolescence, 21*, 29–49.

Hazin, A. N., Alves, J. G., & Rodrigues Falbo, A. (2007). The myelination process in severely malnourished children: MRI findings. *International Journal of Neuroscience, 117*, 1209–1214.

Hedegaard, M., & Fleer, M. (2013). *Play, learning, and children's development: Everyday life in families and transition to school*. New York: Cambridge University Press.

Hedgepeth, E. (2005). Different lenses, different vision. *School Administrator, 62*, 36–39.

Heimann, M. (2001). Neonatal imitation—a "fuzzy" phenomenon? In F. Lacerda & C. von Hofsten (Eds.), *Emerging cognitive abilities in early infancy*. Mahwah, NJ: Lawrence Erlbaum Associates.

Heimann, M., Strid, K., Smith, L., Tjus, T., Ulvund, S., & Meltzoff, A. (2006). Exploring the relation between memory, gestural communication, and the emergence of language in infancy: A longitudinal study. *Infant and Child Development, 15*, 233–249.

Helms, J. E., Jernigan, M., & Mascher, J. (2005). The meaning of race in psychology and how to change it: A methodological perspective. *American Psychologist, 60*, 27–36.

Helmsen, J., Koglin, U., & Petermann, F. (2012). Emotion regulation and aggressive behavior in preschoolers: The mediating role of social information processing. *Child Psychiatry and Human Development, 43*, 87–101.

Henig, J. R. (2008). Spin cycle: How research is used in policy debates: The case of charter schools. New York: Russell Sage.

Henry J. Kaiser Family Foundation (2014). *Sexual heath of adolescents and young adults in the United States*. Menlo Park, CA: The Henry J. Kaiser Family Foundation.

Hepach, R. & Westerman, G. (2013). Infants' sensitivity to the congruence of others' emotions and actions. *Journal of Experimental Child Psychology, 115*, 16–29.

Herberman Mash, H. B., Fullerton, C. S., Shear, M. K., & Ursano, R. J. (2014). Complicated grief and depression in young adults: Personality and relationship quality. *Journal of Nervous and Mental Disease, 202*, 539–543.

Herbert, J. S., Eckerman, C. O., Goldstein, R. F., Stanton, M. E. (2004). Contrasts in infant classical eyeblink conditioning as a function of premature birth. *Infancy, 5*, 367–383.

Herendeen, L. A., & MacDonald, A. (2014). Planning for healthy homes. In I. L. Rubin, J. Merrick, I. L. Rubin, J. Merrick (Eds.), *Environmental health: Home, school and community*. Hauppauge, NY: Nova Biomedical Books.

Hermanto, N., Moreno, S., & Bialystok, E. (2012). Linguistic and metalinguistic outcomes of intense immersion education: How bilingual? *International Journal of Bilingual Education and Bilingualism, 15*, 131–145.

Hernandez, D. J., Denton, N. A., McCartney, S. E. (2008). Children in immigrant families: Looking to America's future. *Social Policy Report, 22*, 3–24.

Hernandez-Reif, M., Field, T., Diego, M., Vera, Y., & Pickens, J. (2006, January). Brief report: Happy faces are habituated more slowly by infants of depressed mothers. *Infant Behavior & Development, 29*, 131–135.

Herrenkohl, T., Sousa, C., Tajima, E., Herrenkohl, R., & Moylan, C. (2008, April). Intersection of child abuse and children's exposure to domestic violence. *Trauma, Violence, & Abuse, 9*(2), 84–99.

Herrnstein, R. J., & Murray, C. (1994). *The bell curve: Intelligence and class structure in American life*. New York: Free Press.

Hertenstein, M. J. (2002). Touch: Its communicative functions in infancy. *Human Development, 45*, 70–94.

Hertenstein, M. J., & Campos, J. J. (2004). The retention effects of an adult's emotional displays on infant behavior. *Child Development, 75*, 595–613.

Hespos, S. J., & Baillargeon, R. (2008). Young infants' actions reveal their developing knowledge of support variables: Converging evidence for violation-of-expectation findings. *Cognition, 107*, 304–316.

Hespos, S. J., & vanMarle, K. (2012). Everyday Physics: How infants learn about objects and entities in their environment. Invited manuscript for Wiley Interdisciplinary Reviews, Cognitive Science.

Heterelendy, F. & Zakar, T. (2004). Prostaglandins and the mymetrium and cervix. *Prostaglandins, Leukotrienes and Essential Fatty Acids, 70*, 207–222.

Hetherington, E., & Elmore, A. (2003). Risk and resilience in children coping with their parents' divorce and remarriage. In S. Luthar (Ed.), *Resilience and vulnerability: Adaptation in the context of childhood adversities*. New York: Cambridge University Press.

Hetherington, E. M., & Kelly, J. (2002). *For better or worse: Divorce reconsidered*. New York: Norton.

Hetrick, S. E., Parker, A. G., Robinson, J., Hall, N., & Vance, A. (2012). Predicting suicidal risk in a cohort of depressed children and adolescents. *Crisis: The Journal of Crisis Intervention and Suicide Prevention, 33,* 13–20.

Hewitt, B. (1997, December 15). A day in the life. *People Magazine,* pp. 49–58.

Hewlett, B., & Lamb, M. (2002). Integrating evolution, culture and developmental psychology: Explaining caregiver-infant proximity and responsiveness in central Africa and the USA. In H. Keller & Y. Poortinga (Eds.), *Between culture and biology: Perspectives on ontogenetic development* (pp. 241–269). New York: Cambridge University Press.

Hewstone, M. (2003). Intergroup contact: Panacea for prejudice? *Psychologist, 16,* 352–355.

Heyman, J. D., Breu, G., Simmons, M., & Howard, C. (2003, September 15). Drugs can make short kids grow but is it right to prescribe them? *People Magazine,* 103–104.

Heyman, R., & Slep, A. M. (2002). Do child abuse and interparental violence lead to adulthood family violence? *Journal of Marriage & Family, 64,* 864–870.

Hietala, J., Cannon, T. D., & van Erp, T. G. M. (2003). Regional brain morphology and duration of illness in never-medicated first-episode patients with schizophrenia. *Schizophrenia, 64,* 79–81.

Higgins, D., & McCabe, M. (2003). Maltreatment and family dysfunction in childhood and the subsequent adjustment of children and adults. *Journal of Family Violence, 18,* 107–120.

Higley, E., & Dozier, M. (2009). Nighttime maternal responsiveness and infant attachment at one year. *Attachment & Human Development, 11,* 347–363.

Hill, B. D., Foster, J. D., Elliott, E. M., Shelton, J., McCain, J., & Gouvier, W. (2013). Need for cognition is related to higher general intelligence, fluid intelligence, and crystallized intelligence, but not working memory. *Journal of Research in Personality, 47,* 22–25.

Hill, P. L., & Lapsley, D. K. (2011). Adaptive and maladaptive narcissism in adolescent development. In C. T. Barry, P. K. Kerig, K. K. Stellwagen, & T. D. Barry (Eds.), *Narcissism and Machiavellianism in youth: Implications for the development of adaptive and maladaptive behavior.* Washington, DC: American Psychological Association.

Hill, S., & Flom, R. (2007, February). 18- and 24-month-olds' discrimination of gender-consistent and inconsistent activities. *Infant Behavior & Development, 30,* 168–173.

Hillis, S., Mercy, J., Amobi, A., & Kress, H. (2016). Global prevalence of past-year violence against children: A systematic review and minimum estimates. *Pediatrics, 137*(3), e20154079.

Hills, F., Meyer-Weitz, A., & Asante, K. O. (2016). The lived experiences of street children in Durban, South Africa: Violence, substance use, and resilience. *International Journal of Qualitative Studies on Health and Well-Being, 11,* 88–99.

Hirsch, H. V., & Spinelli, D. N. (1970). Visual experience modifies distribution of horizontally and vertically oriented receptive fields in cats. *Science, 168,* 869–871.

Hirschtritt, M. E., Pagano, M. E., Christian, K. M., McNamara, N. K., Stansbrey, R. J., Lingler, J., & Findling, R. L. (2012). Moderators of fluoxetine treatment response for children and adolescents with comorbid depression and substance use disorders. *Journal of Substance Abuse Treatment, 42,* 366–372.

Hirsh-Pasek, K., & Michnick-Golinkoff, R. (1995). *The origins of grammar: Evidence from early language comprehension.* Cambridge, MA: MIT Press.

Hiser, E., & Kobayashi, J. (2003). Hemisphere lateralization differences: A cross-cultural study of Japanese and American students in Japan. *Journal of Asian Pacific Communication, 13,* 197–229.

Hitchcock, J. (2012). The debate over shaken baby syndrome. *Journal of Neonatal Nursing, 18,* 20–21.

Hitlin, S., Brown, J. S., & Elder, G. H., Jr. (2006). Racial self-categorization in adolescence: Multiracial development and social pathways. *Child Development, 77,* 1298–1308.

Hjelmstedt, A., Widström, A., & Collins, A. (2006). Psychological correlates of prenatal attachment in women who conceived after in vitro fertilization and women who conceived naturally. *Birth: Issues in Perinatal Care, 33,* 303–310.

Hocking, D. R., Kogan, C. S., & Cornish, K. M. (2012). Selective spatial processing deficits in an at-risk subgroup of the fragile X premutation. *Brain and Cognition, 79,* 39–44.

Hodapp, R. M., Burke, M. M., Urbano, R. C. What's age got to do with it? Implications of maternal age on families of offspring with down syndrome. *International Review of Research in Developmental Disabilities, 42,* 109–145.

Hodgson, J. C., Hirst, R. J., & Hudson, J. M. (2016). Hemispheric speech lateralisation in the developing brain is related to motor praxis ability. *Developmental Cognitive Neuroscience, 22,* 9–17.

Hoelterk L. F., Axinn, W. G., & Ghimire, D. J. (2004). Social change, premarital nonfamily experiences, and marital dynamics. *Journal of Marriage & Family, 66,* 1131–1151.

Hoerr, S., Murashima, M., & Keast, D. (2008). Nutrition and obesity. *Obesity in childhood and adolescence, Vol. 1: Medical, biological, and social issues.* Westport, CT: Praeger Publishers/Greenwood Publishing Group.

Hoersting, R. C., & Jenkins, S. (2011). No place to call home: Cultural homelessness, self-esteem and cross-cultural identities. *International Journal of Intercultural Relations, 35,* 17–30.

Hoeve, M., Blokland, A., Dubas, J., Loeber, R., Gerris, J., & van der Laan, P. (2008). Trajectories of delinquency and parenting styles. *Journal of Abnormal Child Psychology: An Official Publication of the International Society for Research in Child and Adolescent Psychopathology, 36,* 223–235.

Hoff, E. (2012). Interpreting the early language trajectories of children from low-SES and language minority homes: Implications for closing achievement. *Developmental Psychology.* Retrieved July 22, 2012, from http://www.ncbi.nlm.nih.gov/pubmed/22329382.

Hoff, E., & Core, C. (2013). Input and language development in bilingually developing children. *Seminars in Speech and Language, 34,* 215–226.

Hofferth, S., & Sandberg, J. F. (2001). How American children spend their time. *Journal of Marriage and the Family, 63,* 295–308.

Hoffman, L. (2003). Why high schools don't change: What students and their yearbooks tell us. *High School Journal, 86,* 22–37.

Holland, J. (2008). Reading aloud with infants: The controversy, the myth, and a case study. *Early Childhood Education Journal, 35,* 383–385.

Hoffman, J. (2011, March 27) A girl's nude photo and altered lives *The Nerw York Times,* A1, A18-A19.

Holland, N. (1994, August). *Race dissonance—Implications for African American children.* Paper presented at the annual meeting of the American Psychological Association, Los Angeles, CA.

Hollich, G. J., Hirsh-Pasek, K., Golinkoff, R. M., et al. (2000). Breaking the language barrier: An emergentist coalition model of the origins of word learning. *Monographs of the Society for Research in Child Development, 65* (3, Serial No. 262).

Holliday, E., & Gould, T. J. (2016). Nicotine, adolescence, and stress: A review of how stress can modulate the negative consequences of adolescent nicotine abuse. *Neuroscience and Biobehavioral Reviews, 65*, 173–184.

Hollingworth, H. L. (1943/1990). *Letta Stetter Hollingworth: A biography*. Boston: Anker.

Holly, L. E., Little, M., Pina, A. A., & Caterino, L. C. (2015). Assessment of anxiety symptoms in school children: A cross-sex and ethnic examination. *Journal of Abnormal Child Psychology, 43*, 297–309.

Holmes, R. M., & Romeo, L. (2013). Gender, play, language, and creativity in preschoolers. *Early Child Development and Care, 183*, 1531–1543.

Holmes, T. H., & Rahe, R. H. (1967). The social readjustment scale. *Journal of Psychosomatic Research, 11*, 251–261.

Holowaka, S., & Petitto, L. A. (2002). Left hemisphere cerebral specialization for babies while babbling. *Science, 287*, 1515.

Homae, F., Watanabe, H., Nakano, T., & Taga, G. (2012). Functional development in the infant brain for auditory pitch processing. *Human Brain Mapping, 33*, 596–608.

Hong, Y., Fang, Y., Yang, Y., & Phua, D. Y. (2013). Cultural attachment: A new theory and method to understand cross-cultural competence. *Journal of Cross-Cultural Psychology, 44*, 1024–1044.

Hooks, B., & Chen, C. (2008). Vision triggers an experience-dependent sensitive period at the retinogeniculate synapse. *Journal of Neuroscience, 28*, 4807–4817.

Hopkins, B., & Westra, T. (1989). Maternal expectations of their infants' development: Some cultural differences. *Developmental Medicine and Child Neurology, 31*, 384–390.

Hopkins, B., & Westra, T. (1990). Motor development, maternal expectation, and the role of handling. *Infant Behavior and Development, 13*, 117–122.

Hoppe, M. J., Graham, L., Wilsdon, A., Wells, E. A., Nahom, D., & Morrison, D. M. (2004). Teens speak out about HIV/AIDS: Focus group discussions about risk and decision-making. *Journal of Adolescent Health, 35*, 27–35.

Horne, R. C. (2017). Sleep disorders in newborns and infants. In S. Nevšímalová & O. Bruni (Eds.), *Sleep disorders in children*. Cham, Switzerland: Springer International Publishing.

Hornor, G. (2008). Reactive attachment disorder. *Journal of Pediatric Health Care, 22*, 234–239.

Horwitz, B. N., Luong, G., & Charles, G. T. (2008). Neuroticism and extraversion share genetic and environmental effects with negative and positive mood spillover in a nationally representative sample. *Personality and Individual Differences, 45*, 636–642.

Hosogi, M., Okada, A., Fuji, C., Noguchi, K., & Watanabe, K. (2012). Importance and usefulness of evaluating self-esteem in children. *Biopsychosocial Medicine, 6*, 80–88.

Hotelling, B. A., & Humenick, S. S. (2005). Advancing normal birth: Organizations, goals, and research. *Journal of Perinatal Education, 14*, 40–48.

Hou, Y., Kim, S. Y., & Wang, Y. (2016). Parental acculturative stressors and adolescent adjustment through interparental and parent–child relationships in Chinese American families. *Journal of Youth and Adolescence, 45*, 1466–1481.

House, S. H. (2007). Nurturing the brain nutritionally and emotionally from before conception to late adolescence, *Nutritional Health, 19*, 143–61.

Houts, A. (2003). Behavioral treatment for enuresis. In A. Kazdin (Ed.), *Evidence-based psychotherapies for children and adolescents* (pp. 389–406). New York: Guilford Press.

Howard, L., Kirkwood, G., & Latinovic, R. (2007). Sudden infant death syndrome and maternal depression. *Journal of Clinical Psychiatry, 68*, 1279–1283.

Howe, M. J. (1997). *IQ in question: The truth about intelligence*. London, England: Sage.

Howe, M. L., Courage, M. L., & Edison, S. C. (2004). When autobiographical memory begins. In S. Algarabel, A. Pitarque, T. Bajo, S. E. Gathercole, & M. A. Conway (Eds.), *Theories of memory: (Vol. 3)*. New York: Psychology Press.

Howes, C., Galinsky, E., & Kontos, S. (1998). Child care caregiver sensitivity and attachment. *Social Development, 7*, 25–36.

Howes, O., & Kapur, S. (2009). The dopamine hypothesis of schizophrenia: Version III—The final common pathway. *Schizophrenia Bulletin, 35*, 549–562.

Hsin, L., & Snow, C. (2017). Social perspective taking: A benefit of bilingualism in academic writing. *Reading and Writing*. Retrieved March 16, 2017, from http://link.springer.com/article/10.1007/s11145-016-9718-9.

Hu, Y., Xu, Y., & Tornello, S. L. (2016). Stability of self-reported same-sex and both-sex attraction from adolescence to young adulthood. *Archives of Sexual Behavior, 45*, 651–659.

Huang, C. T. (2012). Outcome-based observational learning in human infants. *Journal of Comparative Psychology, 126*, 139–149.

Hubel, D. H., & Wiesel, T. N. (1979). Brain mechanisms of vision. *Scientific American, 241*, 150–162.

Hubel, D. H., & Wiesel, T. N. (2004). *Brain and visual perception: The story of a 25-year collaboration*. New York: Oxford University Press.

Hubley, A. M., & Arım, R. G. (2012). Subjective age in early adolescence: Relationships with chronological age, pubertal timing, desired age, and problem behaviors. *Journal of Adolescence, 35*, 357–366.

Hudson, J. A., Sosa, B. B., & Shapiro, L. R. (1997). Scripts and plans: The development of preschool children's event knowledge and event planning. In S. L. Friedman & E. K. Scholnick (Eds.), *The developmental psychology of planning: Why, how and when do we plan?* (pp. 77–102). Mahwah, NJ: Erlbaum.

Huesmann, L. R. (2017). An Integrative theoretical understanding of aggression. In B. J. Bushman (Ed.). Aggression and violence. New York: Routledge.

Hueston, W., Geesey, M., & Diaz, V. (2008). Prenatal care initiation among pregnant teens in the United States: An analysis over 25 years. *Journal of Adolescent Health, 42*, 243–248.

Huh, S. Y., Rifas-Shiman, S. L., Zera, C. A., Rich Edwards, J. W., Oken, E., Weiss, S. T., & Gilmann, M. W. (2012). Delivery by caesarean section and risk of obesity in preschool age children: a prospective cohort study. *Archives of Disable Children, 34*, 66–79.

Hui, A., Lau, S., Li, C., Tong, T., & Zhang, J. (2006). A cross-societal comparative study of Beijing and Hong Kong children's self-concept. *Social Behavior and Personality, 34*(5), 511–524.

Huijbregts, S., Tavecchio, L., Leseman, P., & Hoffenaar, P. (2009). Child rearing in a group setting: Beliefs of Dutch, Caribbean Dutch, and Mediterranean Dutch caregivers in center-based child care. *Journal of Cross-Cultural Psychology, 40*, 797–815.

Huizink, A., Mulder, E., & Buitelaar, J. (2004). Prenatal stress and risk for psychopathology: Specific effects or induction of general susceptibility? *Psychological Bulletin, 130*, 115–142.

Human Genome Project. (2006). Retrieved August 5, 2017, from http://web.ornl.gov/sci/techresources/Human_Genome/index.shtml.

Humphries, M. L., & Korfmacher, J. (2012). The good, the bad, and the ambivalent: Quality of alliance in a support program for young mothers. *Infant Mental Health Journal, 33*, 22–33.

Hunnius, S., de Wit, T. J., Vrins, S., & von Hofsten, C. (2011). Facing threat: Infants' and adults' visual scanning of faces with neutral, happy, sad, angry, and fearful emotional expressions. *Cognition and Emotion, 25*, 193–205.

Hunt, M. (1974). *Sexual behaviors in the 1970s.* New York: Dell.

Hunt, M. (1993). *The story of psychology.* New York: Doubleday.

Hunter, J., & Mallon, G. P. (2000). Lesbian, gay, and bisexual adolescent development: Dancing with your feet tied together. In B. Greene & G. L. Croom (Eds.), *Education, research, and practice in lesbian, gay, bisexual, and transgendered psychology: A resource manual* (Vol. 5). Thousand Oaks, CA: Sage.

Huntsinger, C. S., Jose, P. E., Liaw, F., & Ching, W-D. (1997). Cultural differences in early mathematics learning: A comparison of Euro-American, Chinese-American, and Taiwan-Chinese families. *International Journal of Behavioral Development, 21*, 371–388.

Huotilainen, M. (2013). A new dimension on foetal language learning. *Acta Paediatrica, 102*, 102–103.

Huster, R. J., Westerhausen, R. R., & Herrmann, C. S. (2011). Sex differences in cognitive control are associated with midcingulate and callosal morphology. *Brain Structure & Function, 215*, 225–235.

Hutcheon, J. A., Joseph, K. S., Kinniburgh, B., & Lee, L. (2013). Maternal, care provider, and institutional-level risk factors for early term elective repeat cesarean delivery: A population-based cohort study. *Maternal and Child Health Journal.* Retrieved February 8, 2014, from http://www.perinatalservicesbc.ca/NR/rdonlyres/3D43DD9D-2367-4729-AF6D-602B5F3ABABA/0/MaternalCareProviderInstit_RiskFactors_2014.pdf.

Hutchinson, D., & Rapee, R. (2007). Do friends share similar body image and eating problems? The role of social networks and peer influences in early adolescence. *Behaviour Research and Therapy, 45*, 1557–1577.

Hutton, P. H. (2004). *Phillippe Aries and the politics of French cultural history.* Amherst: University of Massachusetts Press.

Huurre, T., Junkkari, H., & Aro, H. (2006, June). Long-term psychosocial effects of parental divorce: A follow-up study from adolescence to adulthood. *European Archives of Psychiatry and Clinical Neuroscience, 256*, 256–263.

Hyde, J., Mezulis, A., & Abramson, L. (2008, April). The ABCs of depression: Integrating affective, biological, and cognitive models to explain the emergence of the gender difference in depression. *Psychological Review, 115*(2), 291–313.

Hyde, J. S., & DeLamater, J. D. (2004). *Understanding human sexuality* (9th ed.). Boston: McGraw Hill.

Hyde, J. S., & DeLamater, J. D. (2010). *Understanding human sexuality* (11th ed.). New York: McGraw-Hill.

Hyman, S. E. (2011, February 25). The meaning of the human genome project for neuropsychiatric disorders. *Science, 331*, 1026.

Hyssaelae L., Rautava, P., & Helenius, H. (1995). Fathers' smoking and use of alcohol: The viewpoint of maternity health care clinics and well-baby clinics. *Family Practice, 12*, 22–27.

Ickes, M. J., Erwin, H., & Beighle, A. (2013). Systematic review of recess interventions to increase physical activity. *Journal of Physical Activity & Health, 10*(6), 910–926.

Ige, T. J., DeLeon, P., & Nabors, L. (2017). Motivational interviewing in an obesity prevention program for children. *Health Promotion Practice, 18*, 263–274.

Iglesias, J., Eriksson, J., Grize, F., Tomassini, M., & Villa, A. E. (2005). Dynamics of pruning in simulated large-scale spiking neural networks. *Biosystems, 79*, 11–20.

Iles, J., Slade, P., & Spiby, H. (2011). Posttraumatic stress symptoms and postpartum depression in couples after childbirth: The role of partner support and attachment. *Journal of Anxiety Disorders, 25*, 101–109.

Inagaki, M. (2013). Developmental transformation of narcissistic amae in early, middle, and late adolescents: Relation to ego identity. *Japanese Journal of Educational Psychology, 61*, 56–66.

Ingersoll, E. W., & Thoman, E. B. (1999). Sleep/wake states of preterm infants: Stability, developmental change, diurnal variation, and relation with caregiving activity. *Child Development, 70*, 1–10.

Inguglia, C., Ingoglia, S., Liga, F., Lo Coco, A., & Lo Cricchio, M. G. (2015). Autonomy and relatedness in adolescence and emerging adulthood: Relationships with parental support and psychological distress. *Journal of Adult Development, 22*, 1–15.

International Human Genome Sequencing Consortium. (2001). Initial sequencing and analysis of the human genome. *Nature, 409*, 860–921.

International Institute for Population Sciences (IIPS) and Macro International. 2007. National Family Health Survey (NFHS-3), 2005–06: India: Volume I. Mumbai: IIPS.

International Literacy Institute. (2001). Literacy overview. Available online at http://www.literacyonline.org/explorer/.

Inzlicht, M., & Ben Zeev, T. (2000). A threatening intellectual environment: Why females are susceptible to experiencing problem-solving deficits in the presence of males. *Psychological Science, 11*, 365–371.

Ip, W., Tang, C., & Goggins, W. (2009). An educational intervention to improve women's ability to cope with childbirth. *Journal of Clinical Nursing, 18*, 2125–2135.

Ireland, J. L., & Archer, J. (2004). Association between measures of aggression and bullying among juvenile young offenders. *Aggressive Behavior, 30*, 29–42.

Isaacs, K., Barr, W., Nelson, P., & Devinsky, O. (2006, June). Degree of handedness and cerebral dominance. *Neurology, 66*(12), 1855–1858.

Isay, R. A. (1990). *Being homosexual: Gay men and their development.* New York: Avon.

Isenberg, E. (2007). What have we learned about homeschooling? *Peabody Journal of Education, 82*(2), 387–409.

Ishi-Kuntz, M. (2000). Diversity within Asian-American families. In D. H. Demo, K. R. Allen, & M. A. Fine (Eds.), *Handbook of family diversity.* New York: Oxford.

Israel, E. (2005). Introduction: The rise of the age of individualism—variability in the pathobiology, response to treatment, and treatment outcomes in asthma. *Journal of Allergy and Clinical Immunology, 115*, S525.

Izard, C., King, K., Trentacosta, C., et al. (2008, December). Accelerating the development of emotion competence in Head Start children: Effects on adaptive and maladaptive behavior. *Development and Psychopathology, 20*(1), 369–397.

Iyengar, S.D., Iyengar, K., Martines, J.C., Dashora, K., & Deora K.K. (2008). Childbirth practices in rural Rajasthan, India: implications for neonatal health and survival. Journal of Perinatology 28, 23–30. doi:10.1038/jp.2008.174.

Izard, J., Haines, C., Crouch, R., Houston, S., & Neill, N. (2003). Assessing the impact of the teaching of modelling: Some implications. In S. Lamon, W. Parker, & K. Houston (Eds.), *Mathematical modelling: A way of life: ICTMA 11.* Chichester, England: Horwood Publishing.

Jack, F., Simcock, G., & Hayne, H. (2012). Magic memories: Young children's verbal recall after a 6-year delay. *Child Development, 83*, 159–172.

Jackson, M. I. (2015). Early childhood WIC participation, cognitive development and academic achievement. *Social Science & Medicine, 126,*145–153.

Jacobson, C., Batejan, K., Kleinman, M., & Gould, M. (2013). Reasons for attempting suicide among a community sample of adolescents. *Suicide and Life-Threatening Behavior, 43,* 646–662.

Jacobus, J., Castro, N., Squeglia, L. M., et al. (2016). Reprint of 'Adolescent cortical thickness pre- and post-marijuana and alcohol initiation.' *Neurotoxicology and Teratology, 58,* 78–87.

Jadallah, M., Anderson, R. C., Nguyen-Jahiel, K., et al. (2011). Influence of a teacher's scaffolding moves during child-led small-group discussions. *American Educational Research Journal, 48,* 194–230.

Jahoda, G. (1983). European "lag" in the development of an economic concept: A study in Zimbabwe. *British Journal of Developmental Psychology, 1,* 113–120.

Jain, S. & Dixit, P. (2014). Self-esteem: A gender based comparison and the causal factors reducing it among Indian youth, *International Journal of Humanities and Social Science Invention, 3*(4), 09-15.

Jain, V.K., Dayal, S., Aggarwal, K., & Jain, S. (2009). Profile of sexually transmitted diseases in children at Rohtak. *Indian Journal of Sexually Transmitted Diseases, 30,* 53-58.

Jalonick, M. C. (2011, January 13). New guidelines would make school lunches healthier. *The Washington Post.*

James, J., Ellis, B. J., Schlomer, G. L., & Garber, J. (2012). Sex-specific pathways to early puberty, sexual debut, and sexual risk taking: Tests of an integrated evolutionary–developmental model. *Developmental Psychology, 48,* 687–702.

James, K. H. & Engelhardt, L. (2012). The effects of handwriting experience on functional brain development in pre-literate children. *Trends in Neuroscience and Education, 1*(1), 32–42.

James, W. (1890/1950). *The principles of psychology.* New York: Holt.

Jamison, E.A., Jamison, D.T., & Hanushek, E.A. (2007). The effects of education quality on income growth and mortality decline. *Economics of Education Review.* 26 (6), 771–788.

Jansen, P. W., Mieloo, C. L., Dommisse-van Berkel, A., et al. (2016). Bullying and victimization among young elementary school children: The role of child ethnicity and ethnic school composition. *Race and Social Problems, 8,* 271–280.

Jared, D., Cormier, P., Levy, B., & Wade-Woolley, L. (2011). Early predictors of biliteracy development in children in French immersion: A 4-year longitudinal study. *Journal of Educational Psychology, 103,* 119–139.

Jardri, R., Houfflin-Debarge, V., Delion, P., Pruvo, J., Thomas, P., & Pins, D. (2012). Assessing fetal response to maternal speech using a noninvasive functional brain imaging technique. *International Journal of Developmental Neuroscience, 30,* 159–161.

Jarrold, C., & Hall, D. (2013). The development of rehearsal in verbal short-term memory. *Child Development Perspectives, 7,* 182–186.

Jaswal, V., & Dodson, C. (2009). Metamemory development: Understanding the role of similarity in false memories. *Child Development, 80,* 629–635.

Jayanthi, P. & Thirunavukarasu, M. (2015). Prevalence of depression among school going adolescents in South India. *International Journal of Pharmaceutical and Clinical Research, 7*(1): 61-63.

Jejeebhoy, S.J. (1998). Adolescent sexual and reproductive behavior: a review of the evidence from India. *Social Science and Medicine.* 46 (10), 1275-1290.

Jenkins, L. N., & Demaray, M. K. (2015). Indirect effects in the peer victimization-academic achievement relation: The role of academic self-concept and gender. *Psychology in the Schools, 52,* 235–247.

Jensen, A. (2003). Do age-group differences on mental tests imitate racial differences? *Intelligence, 31,* 107–21.

Jensen, G., Ward, R. D., & Balsam, P. D. (2013). Information: Theory, brain, and behavior. *Journal of the Experimental Analysis of Behavior, 100,* 408–431.

Jensen, L. (2008). Coming of age in a multicultural world: Globalization and adolescent cultural identity formation. *Adolescent identities: A collection of readings* (pp. 3–17). New York: Analytic Press/Taylor & Francis Group.

Jensen, L. A., & Dost-Gözkan, A. (2014). Adolescent–parent relations in Asian Indian and Salvadoran immigrant families: A cultural–developmental analysis of autonomy, authority, conflict, and cohesion. *Journal of Research on Adolescence.* Retrieved March 22, 2017, from http://onlinelibrary.wiley.com/doi/10.1111/jora.12116/abstract.

Jeynes, W. (2007). The impact of parental remarriage on children: A meta-analysis. *Marriage & Family Review, 40*(4), 75–102.

Jia, R., & Schoppe-Sullivan, S. J. (2011). Relations between coparenting and father involvement in families with preschool-age children. *Developmental Psychology, 47,* 106–118.

Jia, R., Lang, S. N., & Schoppe-Sullivan, S. J. (2016). A developmental examination of the psychometric properties and predictive utility of a revised psychological self-concept measure for preschool-age children. *Psychological Assessment, 28,* 226–238.

Jobling, M. A., Rasteiro, R., & Wetton, J. H. (2016). In the blood: The myth and reality of genetic markers of identity. *Ethnic and Racial Studies, 39,* 142–161.

Joe, S., & Marcus, S. (2003). Datapoints: Trends by race and gender in suicide attempts among U.S. adolescents, 1991–2001. *Psychiatric Services, 54,* 454.

Johnson, A. M., Wadsworth, J., Wellings, K., & Bradshaw, S. (1992). Sexual lifestyles and HIV risk. *Nature, 360,* 410–412.

Johnson, D. J., Jaeger, E., Randolph, S. M., Cauce, A. M., Ward, J., & National Institute of Child Health and Human Development: Early Child Care Research Network. (2003). Studying the effects of early child care experiences on the development of children of color in the United States: Toward a more inclusive research agenda. *Child Development, 74,* 1227–1244.

Johnson, N. (2003). Psychology and health: Research, practice, and policy. *American Psychologist, 58,* 670–677.

Johnson, N. G., Roberts, M. C., & Worell, J. (Eds.). (1999). *Beyond appearance: A new look at adolescent girls.* Washington, DC: American Psychological Association.

Johnston, L. D., Bachman, J. G., & O'Malley, P. M. (2009). *Monitoring the future study.* Lansing: University of Michigan.

Johnston, L. D., O'Malley, P. M., Miech, R. A, Bachman, J. G., & Schulenberg, J. E. (2016). *Monitoring the future national survey results on drug use: 1975–2016: Overview, key findings on adolescent drug use.* Ann Arbor: Institute for Social Research, University of Michigan.

Johnston, L., Delva, J., & O'Malley, P. (2007). Soft drink availability, contracts, and revenues in American secondary schools. *American Journal of Preventive Medicine, 33,* S209–SS225.

Jolly, J. L., Matthews, M. S., & Nester, J. (2013). Homeschooling the gifted: A parent's perspective. *Gifted Child Quarterly, 57,* 121–134.

Jones, C. (2004). *Supporting inclusion in the early years.* Maidenhead: England: Open University Press.

Jones, D. E., Carson, K. A., Bleich, S. N., & Cooper, L. A. (2012). Patient trust in physicians and adoption of lifestyle behaviors to control high blood pressure. *Patient Education and Counseling*. Retrieved July 22, 2012, from http://www.ncbi.nlm.nih.gov/pubmed/22770676.

Jones, H. E. (2006). Drug addiction during pregnancy: Advances in maternal treatment and understanding child outcomes. *Current Directions in Psychological Science, 15*, 126–132.

Jones, P. R., Kalwarowsky, S., Braddick, O. J., Atkinson, J., & Nardini, M. (2015). Optimizing the rapid measurement of detection thresholds in infants. *Journal of Vision, 15*(11).

Jones, S. (2006). Exploration or imitation? The effect of music on 4-week-old infants' tongue protrusions. *Infant Behavior & Development, 29*, 126–130.

Jones, S. (2007). Imitation in infancy: The development of mimicry. *Psychological Science, 18*, 593–599.

Jones, T. (2013). Through the lens of home-educated children: Engagement in education. *Educational Psychology in Practice, 29*, 107–121.

Jordan, A., & Robinson, T. (2008, January). Children's television viewing, and weight status: Summary and recommendations from an expert panel meeting. *Annals of the American Academy of Political and Social Science, 615*(1), 119–132.

Jordan-Young, R. M. (2012). Hormones, context, and "brain gender": A review of evidence from congenital adrenal hyperplasia. *Social Science & Medicine, 74*, 1738–1744.

Jorgensen, G. (2006, June). Kohlberg and Gilligan: Duet or duel? *Journal of Moral Education, 35*, 179–196.

Juby, H., Billette, J., Laplante, B., & Le Bourdais, C. (2007, September). Nonresident fathers and children: Parents' new unions and frequency of contact. *Journal of Family Issues, 28*(9), 1220–1245.

Julka, A. (2005). Educational provisions and practices for learners with disabilities in India, paper presented at the Inclusive and Supportive Education Congress 2005, University of Strathclyde, Glasgow.

Jung, E., & Zhang, Y. (2016). Parental involvement, children's aspirations, and achievement in new immigrant families. *The Journal of Educational Research, 109*, 333–350.

Jurimae, T., & Saar, M. (2003). Self-perceived and actual indicators of motor abilities in children and adolescents. *Perception and Motor Skills, 97*, 862–866.

Juvonen, J., Schacter, H. L., Sainio, M., & Salmivalli, C. (2016). Can a school-wide bullying prevention program improve the plight of victims? Evidence for risk × intervention effects. *Journal of Consulting and Clinical Psychology, 84*, 334–344.

Juvonen, J., Wang, Y., & Espinoza, G. (2011). Bullying experiences and compromised academic performance across middle school grades. *The Journal of Early Adolescence, 31*, 152–173.

Juyal, R., Bansal, R., Kishore, S., Negi, K.S., Chandra, R., & Semwal, J. (2006). Substance use among intercollege students in District Dehradun. *Indian Journal of Community Medicine, 31*, 252-54 [7].

Kabir, A. A., Pridjian, G., Steinmann, W. C., Herrera, E. A., & Khan, M. M. (2005). Racial differences in cesareans: An analysis of U.S. 2001 national inpatient sample data. *Obstetrics & Gynecology, 105*, 710–718.

Kagan, J. (2000, October). Adult personality and early experience. *Harvard Mental Health Letter*, pp. 4–5.

Kagan, J. (2003a). An unwilling rebel. In R. J. Sternberg (Ed.), *Psychologists defying the crowd: Stories of those who battled the establishment and won*. Washington, DC: American Psychological Association.

Kagan, J. (2008). In defense of qualitative changes in development. *Child Development, 79*.

Kagan, J. (2013). *The human spark: The science of human development*. NY: Basic Books.

Kagan, J., Arcus, D., & Snidman, N. (1993). The idea of temperament: Where do we go from here? In R. Plomin & G. E. McClearn (Eds.), *Nature, nurture, and psychology*. Washington, DC: American Psychological Association.

Kagan, J., Arcus, D., Snidman, N., Feng, W. Y., Hendler, J., & Greene, S. (1994). Reactivity in infants: A cross-national comparison. *Developmental Psychology, 30*, 342–345.

Kagan, J., Snidman, N., Kahn, V., & Towsley, S. (2007). The preservation of two infant temperaments into adolescence. *Monographs of the Society for Research in Child Development, 72*, 1–75.

Kail, R. (2003). Information processing and memory. In M. Bornstein & L. Davidson (Eds.), *Well-being: Positive development across the life course*. Mahwah, NJ: Lawrence Erlbaum Associates.

Kail, R. V. (2004). Cognitive development includes global and domain-specific processes. *Merrill-Palmer Quarterly, 50* [Special issue: 50th anniversary issue: Part II, the maturing of the human development sciences: Appraising past, present, and prospective agendas], 445–455.

Kail, R., & Miller, C. (2006). Developmental change in processing speed: Domain specificity and stability during childhood and adolescence. *Journal of Cognition and Development, 7*(1), 119–137.

Kaiser, L. L., Allen, L., & American Dietetic Association. (2002). Position of the American Dietetic Association: Nutrition and lifestyle for a healthy pregnancy outcome. *Journal of the American Dietetic Association, 102*, 1479–1490.

Kalb, C. (1997, Spring/Summer). The top 10 health worries. *Newsweek Special Issue*, 42–43.

Kalb, C. (2004, January 26). Brave new babies. *Newsweek*, 45–53.

Kalb, C. (2012, February). Fetal armor. *Scientific American*, p. 73.

Kalfoglou, A. L., Kammersell, M., Philpott, S., & Dahl, E. (2013). Ethical arguments for and against sperm sorting for nonmedical sex selection: A review. *Reproductive BioMedicine Online*. Retrieved February 8, 2014, from http://www.ncbi.nlm.nih.gov/pubmed/23337421.

Kaltiala-Heino, R., Kosunen, E., & Rimpela, M. (2003). Pubertal timing, sexual behaviour and self-reported depression in middle adolescence. *Journal of Adolescence, 26*, 531–545.

Kamerman, S. B. (2000a). From maternity to parental leave policies: Women's health employment, and child and family well-being. The Journal of the Women's Medical Association, 55, Table 1.

Kamerman, S. B. (2000b). Parental leave policies: An essential ingredient in early childhood education and care policies. Social Policy Report 14, Table 1.0.

Kaminaga, M. (2007). Pubertal timing and depression in adolescents. *Japanese Journal of Educational Psychology, 55*, 370–381.

Kan, P., & Kohnert, K. (2009). Fast mapping by bilingual preschool children. *Journal of Child Language, 35*, 495–514.

Kandler, C., Bleidorn, W., & Riemann, R. (2012). Left or right? Sources of political orientation: The roles of genetic factors, cultural transmission, assortative mating, and personality. *Journal of Personality and Social Psychology, 102*, 633–645.

Kangule, D., Darbastwar, M., & Kokiwar, P. (2011). A cross sectional study of prevalence of substance use and its determinants among male tribal youths. *Journal of Pharmaceutical and Biomedical Sciences*. 2:61–4. Accessed from http://www.pharmainterscience.com/.

Kanters, M. A., Bocarro, J. N., Edwards, M. B., Casper, J. M., & Floyd, M. F. (2013). School sport participation under two school sport policies: Comparisons by race/ethnicity, gender, and socioeconomic status. *Annals of Behavioral Medicine, 45*(Suppl 1), S113-S121.

Kantor, J. (2015, June 27). Historic Day for Gay Rights, but a Twinge of Loss for Gay Culture. *The New York Times*, A1.

Kantrowitz, E. J., & Evans, G. W. (2004). The relation between the ratio of children per activity area and off-task behavior and type of play in day care centers. *Environment & Behavior, 36*, 541–557.

Kao, G. (2000). Psychological well-being and educational achievement among immigrant youth. In D. J. Hernandez (Ed.), *Children of immigrants: Health, adjustment, and public assistance*. Washington, DC: National Academy Press.

Kapil, U., Goindi, G., Singh, V., Kaur, S., & Singh, P. (2005). Consumption of tobacco, alcohol, and betel leaf amongst school children in Delhi. *Indian Journal of Pediatrics, 72*: 993.

Kaplan, H., & Dove, H. (1987). Infant development among the Ache of Eastern Paraguay. *Developmental Psychology, 23*, 190–198.

Karniol, R. (2009). Israeli kindergarten children's gender constancy for others' counter-stereotypic toy play and appearance: The role of sibling gender and relative age. *Infant and Child Development, 18*, 73–94.

Kar, S., Debroy, A., Sharma, R., & Islam, F. (2014). Substance abuse amongst the street children in Guwahati City, Assam. *Annals of Medical and Health Sciences Research, 4* (9), 233. Accessed from http://dx.doi.org/10.4103/2141-9248.141965.

Kassuba, T., Klinge, C., Hölig, C., et al. (2011). The left fusiform gyrus hosts trisensory representations of manipulable objects. *NeuroImage*. Retrieved August 5, 2017, from http://www.sciencedirect.com/science/journal/10538119.

Kato, K., & Pedersen, N. L. (2005). Personality and coping: A study of twins reared apart and twins reared together. *Behavior Genetics, 35*, 147–158.

Katzer, C., Fetchenhauer, D., & Belschak, F. (2009). Cyberbullying: Who are the victims?: A comparison of victimization in internet chatrooms and victimization in school. *Journal of Media Psychology: Theories, Methods, and Applications, 21*, 25–36.

Kaufmann, D., Gesten, E., Santa Lucia, R. C., Salcedo, O., Rendina-Gobioff, G., & Gadd, R. (2000). The relationship between parenting style and children's adjustment: The parents' perspective. *Journal of Child & Family Studies, 9*, 231–245.

Kaufman, J. C., Kaufman, A. S., Kaufman-Singer, J., & Kaufman, N. L. (2005). The Kaufman Assessment Battery for Children—Second Edition and the Kaufman Adolescent and Adult Intelligence Test. In D. P. Flanagan & P. L. Harrison (Eds.), *Contemporary intellectual assessment: Theories, tests, and issues*. New York, Guilford Press.

Kaul, V. (1999). Early childhood care and education in the context of EFA. Paper Prepared for the Government of India. Education for All: The Year 2000 Assessment Report. New Delhi.

Kawabata, Y., & Crick, N. R. (2011). The antecedents of friendships in moderately diverse classrooms: Social preference, social impact, and social behavior. *International Journal of Behavioral Development, 35*, 48–57.

Kayton, A. (2007). Newborn screening: A literature review. *Neonatal Network, 26*, 85–95.

Kazura, K. (2000). Fathers' qualitative and quantitative involvement: An investigation of attachment, play, and social interactions. *Journal of Men's Studies, 9*, 41–57.

Kearney, M. S. & Levine, P. B. (2015). *Early childhood education by MOOC: Lessons from Sesame Street, Working Paper 21229*. Cambridge, MA: National Bureau of Economic Research.

Keating, D. (1990). Adolescent thinking. In S. S. Feldman & G. R. Elliott (Eds.), *At the threshold*. Cambridge, MA: Harvard University Press.

Keating, D. (Ed.). (2011). *Nature and nurture in early child development*. New York, NY: Cambridge University Press.

Keating, D. P. (2004). Cognitive and brain development. In R. M. Lerner & L. Steinberg (Eds.), *Handbook of adolescent psychology* (2nd ed.). Hoboken, NJ: John Wiley & Sons.

Keel, P., & Haedt, A. (2008). Evidence-based psychosocial treatments for eating problems and eating disorders. *Journal of Clinical Child and Adolescent Psychology, 37*, 39–61.

Kelch-Oliver, K. (2008). African American grandparent caregivers: Stresses and implications for counselors. *The Family Journal, 16*, 43–50.

Keller, H., Voelker, S., & Yovsi, R. D. (2005). Conceptions of parenting in different cultural communities: The case of West African Nso and northern German women. *Social Development, 14*, 158–180.

Keller, H., Yovsi, R., Borke, J., Kärtner, J., Henning, J., & Papaligoura, Z. (2004). Developmental consequences of early parenting experiences: Self-recognition and self-regulation in three cultural communities. *Child Development, 75*, 1745–1760.

Kellman, P., & Arterberry, M. (2006). Infant visual perception. In W. Damon & R. M. Lerner (Eds.), *Handbook of child psychology: Vol. 2, Cognition, perception, and language* (6th ed.). New York: John Wiley & Sons Inc.

Kelly, G. (2001). *Sexuality today: A human perspective*. (7th ed.) New York: McGraw-Hill.

Kelloway, E., & Francis, L. (2013). Longitudinal research and data analysis. In R. R. Sinclair, M. Wang, & L. E. Tetrick (Eds.), *Research methods in occupational health psychology: Measurement, design, and data analysis*. New York: Routledge/Taylor & Francis Group.

Kellow, J., & Jones, B. (2008, February). The effects of stereotypes on the achievement gap: Reexamining the academic performance of African American high school students. *Journal of Black Psychology, 34*(1), 94–120.

Kelly, C. (2013). Review: Teen pregnancy and parenting: A qualitative study into attitudes and behaviours of teenaged long-term Hispanics in New Mexico. *Journal of Research in Nursing, 18*, 233–234.

Kelly-Weeder, S., & Cox, C. (2007). The impact of lifestyle risk factors on female infertility. *Women & Health, 44*, 1–23.

Kenett, Y. N., Beaty, R. E., Silvia, P. J., Anaki, D., & Faust, M. (2016). Structure and flexibility: Investigating the relation between the structure of the mental lexicon, fluid intelligence, and creative achievement. *Psychology of Aesthetics, Creativity, and the Arts, 10*, 377–388.

Kennell, J. H. (2002). On becoming a family: Bonding and the changing patterns in baby and family behavior. In J. Gomes-Pedro & J. K. Nugent (Eds.), *The infant and family in the twenty-first century*. New York: Brunner-Routledge.

Kenny, D. T. (2013). *Bringing up baby: The psychoanalytic infant comes of age*. London: Karnac Books.

Kessels, L. E., Ruiter, R. C., Brug, J., & Jansma, B. M. (2011). The effects of tailored and threatening nutrition information on message attention. Evidence from an event-related potential study. *Appetite, 56*, 32–38.

Kestly, T. A. (2014). *The interpersonal neurobiology of play: Brain-building interventions for emotional well-being*. New York: Norton.

Khalid, A., & Ijaz, T. (2013). Development of coping style scale for school-going adolescents. *Vulnerable Children and Youth Studies, 8*, 237–242.

Kieffer, C. C. (2012). Secure connections, the extended family system, and the socio-cultural construction of attachment theory. In S. Akhtar (Ed.), *The mother and her child: Clinical aspects of attachment, separation, and loss.* Lanham, MD: Jason Aronson.

Killeen, L. A., & Teti, D. M. (2012). Mothers' frontal EEG asymmetry in response to infant emotion states and mother–infant emotional availability, emotional experience, and internalizing symptoms. *Development and Psychopathology, 24,* 9–21.

Kim, B., Chow, S., Bray, B., & Teti, D. M. (2017). Trajectories of mothers' emotional availability: Relations with infant temperament in predicting attachment security. *Attachment & Human Development, 19,* 38–57.

Kim, H., Sherman, D., & Taylor, S. (2008). Culture and social support. *American Psychologist, 63,* 518–526.

Kim, H. I., & Johnson, S. P. (2013). Do young infants prefer an infant-directed face or a happy face? *International Journal of Behavioral Development, 37,* 125–130.

Kim, J., Bushway, S., & Tsao, H. (2016). Identifying classes of explanations for crime drop: Period and cohort effects for New York State. *Journal of Quantitative Criminology, 32,* 357–375.

Kim, J., & Cicchetti, D. (2003). Social self-efficacy and behavior problems in maltreated children. *Journal of Clinical Child & Adolescent Psychology, 32,* 106–117.

Kim, Y., Choi, J. Y., Lee, K. M., et al. (2007). Dose-dependent protective effect of breast-feeding against breast cancer among never-lactated women in Korea. *European Journal of Cancer Prevention, 16,* 124–129.

Kimball, J. W. (1983). *Biology* (5th ed.). Reading, MA: Addison-Wesley.

Kimm, S. Y., Glynn, N. W., Kriska, A. M., et al. (2002). Decline in physical activity in black girls and white girls during adolescence. *New England Journal of Medicine, 347,* 709–715.

Kinney, H. C., Randall, L. L., Sleeper, L. A., et al. (2003). Serotonergic brainstem abnormalities in Northern Plains Indians with the sudden infant death syndrome. *Journal of Neuropathology and Experimental Neurology, 62,* 1178–1191.

Kinsey, A. C., Pomeroy, W. B., & Martin, C. E. (1948). *Sexual behavior in the human male.* Philadelphia: Saunders.

Kinzie, J., Thomas, A., Palmer, M., Umbach, P., & Kuh, G. (2007, March). Women students at coeducational and women's colleges: How do their experiences compare? *Journal of College Student Development, 48*(2), 145–165.

Király, A., Szabó, N., Tóth, E., et al. (2016). Male brain ages faster: The age and gender dependence of subcortical volumes. *Brain Imaging and Behavior, 10,* 901–910.

Kirby, D., Baumler, E., Coyle, K., et al. (2004). The "Safer Choices" intervention: Its impact on the sexual behaviors of different subgroups of high school students. *Journal of Adolescent Health, 35,* 442–452.

Kirby, J. (2006, May). From single-parent families to stepfamilies: Is the transition associated with adolescent alcohol initiation? *Journal of Family Issues, 27,* 685–711.

Kirchengast, S., & Hartmann, B. (2003). Impact of maternal age and maternal-somatic characteristics on newborn size. *American Journal of Human Biology, 15,* 220–228.

Kirsh, S. J. (2012). *Children, adolescents, and media violence: A critical look at the research* (2nd ed.). Thousand Oaks, CA: Sage Publications, Inc.

Kitamura, C., & Lam, C. (2009). Age-specific preferences for infant-directed affective intent. *Infancy, 14,* 77–100.

Kiuru, N., Nurmi, J., Aunola, K., & Salmela-Aro, K. (2009). Peer group homogeneity in adolescents' school adjustment varies according to peer group type and gender. *International Journal of Behavioral Development, 33,* 65–76.

Klaczynski, P. A. (2004). A dual-process model of adolescent development: Implications for decision making, reasoning, and identity. In R. V. Kail (Ed.), *Advances in child development and behavior* (Vol. 32). San Diego, CA: Elsevier Academic Press.

Klaczynski, P. A. (2011). Age differences in understanding precedent-setting decisions and authorities' responses to violations of deontic rules. *Journal of Experimental Child Psychology, 109,* 1–24.

Klier, C. M., Muzik, M., Dervic, K., et al. (2007). The role of estrogen and progesterone in depression after birth. *Journal of Psychiatric Research, 41,* 273–279.

Klimstra, T. A., Luyckx, K., Germeijs, V., Meeus, W. J., & Goossens, L. (2012). Personality traits and educational identity formation in late adolescents: Longitudinal associations and academic progress. *Journal of Youth and Adolescence, 41,* 346–361.

Klingberg, T., & Betteridge, N. (2013). *The learning brain: Memory and brain development in children.* New York: Oxford University Press.

Klitzman, R. L. (2012). *Am I my genes? Confronting fate and family secrets in the age of genetic testing.* New York: Oxford University Press.

Kloep, M., Güney, N., Çok, F., & Simsek, Ö. (2009). Motives for risk-taking in adolescence: A cross-cultural study. *Journal of Adolescence, 32,* 135–151.

Kluger, J. (2010, November 1). Keeping young minds healthy. *Time,* pp. 40–50.

Knafo, A., & Schwartz, S. H. (2003). Parenting and accuracy of perception of parental values by adolescents. *Child Development, 73,* 595–611.

Knickmeyer, R., & Baron-Cohen, S. (2006, December). Fetal testosterone and sex differences. *Early Human Development, 82,* 755–760.

Knifsend, C. A., & Juvonen, J. (2014). Social identity complexity, cross-ethnic friendships, and intergroup attitudes in urban middle schools. *Child Development, 85,* 709–721.

Knight, Z. G. (2017). A proposed model of psychodynamic psychotherapy linked to Erik Erikson's eight stages of psychosocial development. *Clinical Psychology & Psychotherapy.* Retrieved March 2, 2017, from https://www.ncbi.nlm.nih.gov/pubmed/28124459.

Knoll, L. J., Fuhrmann, D., Sakhardande, A. L., Stamp, F., Speekenbrink, M., & Blakemore, S. (2016). A window of opportunity for cognitive training in adolescence. *Psychological Science, 27,* 1620–1631.

Knorth, E., Harder, A., Zandberg, T., & Kendrick, A. (2008, February). Under one roof: A review and selective meta-analysis on the outcomes of residential child and youth care. *Children and Youth Services Review, 30*(2), 123–140.

Kochanska, G. (1997). Mutually responsive orientation between mothers and their young children: Implications for early socialization. *Child Development, 68,* 94–112.

Kochanska, G. (2002). Mutually responsive orientation between mothers and their young children: A context for the early development of conscience. *Current Directions in Psychological Science, 11,* 191–195.

Kochanska, G., & Aksan, N. (2004). Development of mutual responsiveness between parents and their young children. *Child Development, 75,* 1657–1676.

Koenig, A., Cicchetti, D., & Rogosch, F. (2004). Moral development: The association between maltreatment and young children's prosocial behaviors and moral transgressions. *Social Development, 13,* 97–106.

Koenig, M., & Cole, C. (2013). Early word learning. In D. Reisberg (Ed.), *The Oxford handbook of cognitive psychology.* New York: Oxford University Press.

Koenig, L. B., McGue, M., Krueger, R. F., & Bouchard, T. J. Jr. (2005). Genetic and environmental influences on religiousness: Findings for retrospective and current religiousness ratings. *Journal of Personality, 73,* 471–488.

Kogan, S. M., Yu, T., Allen, K. A., & Brody, G. H. (2014). Racial microstressors, racial self-concept, and depressive symptoms among male African Americans during the transition to adulthood. *Journal of Youth and Adolescence, 44,* 898–909.

Kohlberg, L. (1966). A cognitive-developmental analysis of children's sex-role concepts and attitudes. In E. E. Maccoby (Ed.), *The development of sex differences.* Stanford, CA: Stanford University Press.

Kohlberg, L. (1969). Stage and sequence: The cognitive-developmental approach to socialization. In D. Goslin (Ed.), *Handbook of socialization theory and research.* Chicago: Rand McNally.

Kohlberg, L. (1984). *The psychology of moral development: Essays on moral development* (Vol. 2). San Francisco: Harper & Row.

Kohut, S. & Pillai, R. (2008). Does the NFCS discriminate between infants experiencing pain-related and non-pain related distress? Paper presented at the Canadian Pain Society Annual Conference, Victoria, BC, May 2008. *Pain Research and Management, 12,* 120.

Kolata, G. (2004, May 11). The heart's desire. *The New York Times,* p. D1.

Kolb, B., & Gibb, R. (2006). Critical periods for functional recovery after cortical injury during development. *Reprogramming the cerebral cortex: Plasticity following central and peripheral lesions.* New York: Oxford University Press.

Konrad, K., Firk, C., & Uhlhaas, P. J. (2013). Brain development during adolescence. *Deutsches Ärzteblatt International, 110,* 425–431.

Kornides, M., & Kitsantas, P. (2013). Evaluation of breastfeeding promotion, support, and knowledge of benefits on breastfeeding outcomes. *Journal of Child Health Care, 17,* 264–273.

Korotchikova, I., Stevenson, N. J., Livingstone, V., Ryan, C. A., & Boylan, G. B. (2016). Sleep–wake cycle of the healthy term newborn infant in the immediate postnatal period. *Clinical Neurophysiology, 127,* 2095–2101.

Koshmanova, T. (2007). Vygotskian scholars: Visions and implementation of cultural-historical theory. *Journal of Russian & East European Psychology, 45,* 61–95.

Koska, J., Ksinantova, L., Sebokova, E., et al. (2002). Endocrine regulation of subcutaneous fat metabolism during cold exposure in humans. *Annals of the New York Academy of Science, 967,* 500–505.

Kotre, J., & Hall, E. (1990). *Seasons of life.* Boston: Little, Brown.

Kramer, M. S. (2003). Food supplementation during pregnancy and functional outcomes. *Journal of Health, Population and Nutrition, 21,* 81–82.

Kreager, D. A., Molloy, L. E., Moody, J., & Feinberg, M. E. (2016). Friends first? The peer network origins of adolescent dating. *Journal of Research on Adolescence, 26,* 257–269.

Kretch, K. S., & Adolph, K. E. (2013). Cliff or step? Posture-specific learning at the edge of a drop-off. *Child Development, 84,* 226–240.

Kretsch, N., Mendle, J., Cance, J. D., & Harden, K. P. (2016). Peer group similarity in perceptions of pubertal timing. *Journal of Youth and Adolescence, 45,* 1696–1710.

Krettenauer, T., Jia, F., & Mosleh, M. (2011). The role of emotion expectancies in adolescents' moral decision making. *Journal of Experimental Child Psychology, 108,* 358–370.

Kringelbach, M. L., Lehtonen A., Squire S., et al. (2008). A specific and rapid neural signature for parental instinct. *PLoS ONE, 3*(2), e1664.

Krishnamoorthy, J. S., Hart, C., & Jelalian, E, (2006). The epidemic of childhood obesity: Review of research and implications for public policy. *Social Policy Report, 19,* 3–19.

Krishnan-Sarin, S., Morean, M., Kong, G., et al. (2017). E-cigarettes and "dripping" among high-school youth. *Pediatrics, 139*(3), e20163224.

Kroger, J. (2006). *Identity development: Adolescence through adulthood.* Thousand Oaks, CA: Sage Publications.

Kronberger, N., & Horwath, I. (2013). The ironic costs of performing well: Grades differentially predict male and female dropout from engineering. *Basic and Applied Social Psychology, 35*(6), 534–546.

Kronholz, J. (2003, August 19). Trying to close the stubborn learning gap. *The Wall Street Journal,* pp. B1, B5.

Krueger, G. (2006, September). Meaning-making in the aftermath of sudden infant death syndrome. *Nursing Inquiry, 13,* 163–171.

Krull, K. R., & Brinkman, T. (2013). Childhood acute lymphoblastic leukemia: A lifespan perspective. In I. Baron, C. Rey-Casserly (Eds.), *Pediatric neuropsychology: Medical advances and lifespan outcomes.* New York: Oxford University Press.

Kshirsagar, V.V, Agarwal, R., & Bavdekar, S.B. (2007). Bullying in schools: Prevalence and Short Come Impacts, *Indian Pediatrics, 44;* 25-28.

Kuhl, P. K., Andruski, J. E., Chistovich, I. A., et al. (1997, August 1). Cross-language analysis of phonetic units in language addressed to infants. *Science, 277,* 684–686.

Kuhl, P. K., Stevenson, J., Corrigan, N. M., van den Bosch, J. F., Can, D. D., & Richards, T. (2016). Neuroimaging of the bilingual brain: Structural brain correlates of listening and speaking in a second language. *Brain and Language, 162,* 1–9.

Kuhn, D. (2008). Formal operations from a twenty-first century perspective. *Human Development, 51,* 48–55.

Kulkarni, A., Kaushik, J. S., Gupta, P., Sharma, H., & Agrawal, R. K. (2011). Massage and touch therapy in neonates: The current evidence. *Indian Pediatrics, 47,* 771.

Kulkarni, M. & Pattabhi, Y. (1988). The evaluation of effectiveness of ICDS in 7 Anganwadi Centers on the health status of preschool children. *Indian Journal of Community Medicine; 13:*86-91.

Kumar, S. S., Kumar, A., Kaur, M., & Sharma, A. (2016). The prevalence of eating disorder among young girls and boys by using eating attitude test (Eat-26), *International Journal of Physical Education,* Sports and Health, 3(5): 378-381.

Kupersmidt, J. B., & Dodge, K. A. (Eds.). (2004). *Children's peer relations: From development to intervention.* Washington, DC: American Psychological Association.

Kurtz-Costes, B., Swinton, A. D., & Skinner, O. D. (2014). Racial and ethnic gaps in the school performance of Latino, African American, and White students. In F. L. Leong, L. Comas-Díaz, G. C. Nagayama Hall, V. C. McLoyd, &J. E. Trimble (Eds.), *APA handbook of multicultural psychology, Vol. 1: Theory and research.* Washington, DC: American Psychological Association.

Labouvie-Vief, G., & Diehl, M. (2000). Cognitive complexity and cognitive–affective integration: Related or separate domains of adult development? *Psychology & Aging, 15,* 490–504.

Lacerda, F., von Hofsten, C., & Heimann, M. (2001). *Emerging cognitive abilities in early infancy.* Mahwah, NJ: Erlbaum.

Lachapelle, U., Noland, R. B., & Von Hagen, L. (2013). Teaching children about bicycle safety: An evaluation of the New Jersey Bike School program. *Accident Analysis and Prevention*, 52, 237–249.

Lachmann, T., Berti, S., Kujala, T., & Schroger, E. (2005). Diagnostic subgroups of developmental dyslexia have different deficits in neural processing of tones and phonemes. *International Journal of Psychophysiology*, 56, 105–120.

LaCoursiere, D., Hirst, K. P., & Barrett-Connor, E. (2012). Depression and pregnancy stressors affect the association between abuse and postpartum depression. *Maternal and Child Health Journal*, 16, 929–935.

Laemmle, J. (2013). Review of children at play: Learning gender in the early years. *Journal of Youth and Adolescence*, 42, 305–307.

Laflamme, D., Pomerleau, A., & Malcuit, G. (2002). A comparison of fathers' and mothers' involvement in childcare and stimulation behaviors during free-play with their infants at 9 and 15 months. *Sex Roles*, 47, 507–518.

Lafuente, M. J., Grifol, R., Segarra, J., & Soriano, J. (1997). Effects of the Firstart method of prenatal stimulation on psychomotor development: The first six months. *Pre- & PeriNatal Psychology*, 11, 151–162.

Laghi, F., Baiocco, R., Di Norcia, A., Cannoni, E., Baumgartner, E., & Bombi, A. S. (2014). Emotion understanding, pictorial representations of friendship and reciprocity in school-aged children. *Cognition and Emotion*, 28, 1338–1346.

Lagrou, K., Froidecoeur, C., Thomas, M., et al. (2008). Concerns, expectations and perception regarding stature, physical appearance and psychosocial functioning before and during high-dose growth hormone treatment of short pre-pubertal children born small for gestational age. *Hormone Research*, 69, 334–342.

Lahat, A., Walker, O. L., Lamm, C., Degnan, K. A., Henderson, H. A., & Fox, N. A. (2014). Cognitive conflict links behavioural inhibition and social problem solving during social exclusion in childhood. *Infant and Child Development*, 23, 273–282.

Laible, D., Panfile, T., & Makariev, D. (2008). The quality and frequency of mother-toddler conflict: Links with attachment and temperament. *Child Development*, 79, 426–443.

Lall, M. (2007, August). Exclusion from school: Teenage pregnancy and the denial of education. *Sex Education*, 7(3), 219–237.

Lamaze, F. (1979). *Painless childbirth: The Lamaze method*. Chicago: Regnery.

Lamb, M. E., Sternberg, K. J., Hwang, C. P., & Broberg, A. G. (Eds.). (1992). Child care in context: Cross-cultural perspectives. Hillsdale, NJ: Erlbaum.

Lambrick, D., Westrupp, N., Kaufmann, S., Stoner, L., & Faulkner, J. (2016). The effectiveness of a high-intensity games intervention on improving indices of health in young children. *Journal of Sports Sciences*, 34, 190–198.

Lamorey, S., Robinson, B. E., & Rowland, B. H. (1998). *Latchkey kids: Unlocking doors for children and their families*. Newbury Park, CA: Sage.

Land, K. C., Lamb, V. L., & Zheng, H. (2011). How are the kids doing? How do we know? Recent trends in child and youth well-being in the United States and some international comparisons. *Social Indicators Research*, 100, 463–477.

Landgraf, M. N., Nothacker, M., Kopp, I. B., & Heinen, F. (2013). The diagnosis of fetal alcohol syndrome. *Deutsches Ärzteblatt International*, 110, 703–710.

Langford, R., Albanese, P, Prentice, S (Eds.). (2017). *Caring for children: Social movements and public policy in Canada*. Vancouver, BC: UBC Press.

Langfur, S. (2013). The You-I event: On the genesis of self-awareness. *Phenomenology and the Cognitive Sciences*, 12, 769–790.

Langille, D. (2007). Teenage pregnancy: Trends, contributing factors and the physician's role. *Canadian Medical Association Journal*, 176, 1601–1602.

Lansford, J. (2009). Parental divorce and children's adjustment. *Perspectives on Psychological Science*, 4, 140–152.

Lansford, J. E., Malone, P. S., Dodge, K. A., Crozier, J. C., Pettit, G. S., & Bates, J. E. (2006). A 12-year prospective study of patterns of social information processing, problems and externalizing behaviors. *Journal of Abnormal Child Psychology*, 34, 715–724.

Lansford, J. E., & Parker, J. G. (1999). Children's interactions in triads: Behavioral profiles and effects of gender and patterns of friendships among members. *Developmental Psychology*, 35, 80–93.

Lanza, S. T., Russell, M. A., & Braymiller, J. L. (2017). Emergence of electronic cigarette use in US adolescents and the link to traditional cigarette use. *Addictive Behaviors*, 67, 38–43.

Larsen, K. E., O'Hara, M. W., & Brewer, K. K. (2001). A prospective study of self-efficacy expectancies and labor pain. *Journal of Reproductive and Infant Psychology*, 19, 203–214.

Larson, J., & Lochman, J. E. (2011). *Helping schoolchildren cope with anger: A cognitive-behavioral intervention* (2nd ed.). New York: Guilford Press.

Larson, R. W., Richards, M. H., Moneta, G., Holmbeck, G., & Duckett, E. (1996). Changes in adolescents' daily interactions with their families from ages 10 to 18: Disengagement and transformation. *Developmental Psychology*, 32, 744–754.

Laska, M. N., Murray, D. M., Lytle, L. A., & Harnack, L. J. (2012). Longitudinal associations between key dietary behaviors and weight gain over time: Transitions through the adolescent years. *Obesity*, 20, 118–125.

Lau, M., Markham, C., Lin, H., Flores, G., & Chacko, M. (2009). Dating and sexual attitudes in Asian-American adolescents. *Journal of Adolescent Research*, 24, 91–113.

Lau, T.K., Chan, M.K., Salome, Lo P.S., Chan, H.Y. & Chan, W.K. et al. (2012) Non-invasive prenatal screening of fetal sex chromosomal abnormalities: perspective of pregnant women. *Journal of Maternal Fetal Neonatal Medicine*, 25, 2616–2619.

Lau, Y. C., Hinkley, L. N., Bukshpun, P., et al. (2013). Autism traits in individuals with agenesis of the corpus callosum. *Journal of Autism and Developmental Disorders*, 43, 1106–1118.

Lauricella, T. (2001, November). The education of a home schooler. *Smart Money*, pp. 115–121.

Laurini, M.P. & Andrade, de Carvalho E. (2012). New evidence on the role of cognitive skill in economic development. *Economics Letters*. 117 (1), 123–126.

Layzer, J. I., & Goodson, B. D., (2006). The "quality" of early care and education settings: Definitional and measurement issues. *Evaluation Review*, 30, 556–576.

Law, Y. (2008). Effects of cooperative learning on second graders' learning from text. *Educational Psychology*, 28, 567–582.

Lawrence, H. R., Nangle, D. W., Schwartz-Mette, R. A., & Erdley, C. A. (2017). Medication for child and adolescent depression: Questions, answers, clarifications, and caveats. *Practice Innovations*, 2, 39–53.

Leach, P., Barnes, J., Malmberg, L., Sylva, K., & Stein, A. (2008, February). The quality of different types of child care at 10 and 18 months: A comparison between types and factors related to quality. *Early Child Development and Care*, 178(2), 177–209.

Leaper, C. (2002). Parenting girls and boys. In M. Bornstein (Ed.), *Handbook of parenting: Vol. 1: Children and parenting*. Mahwah, NJ: Lawrence Erlbaum Associates.

Leathers, H. D., & Foster, P. (2004). *The world food problem: Tackling causes of undernutrition in the third world*. Boulder, CO: Lynne Rienner Publishers.

Leavitt, L. A., & Goldson, E. (1996). Introduction to special section: Biomedicine and developmental psychology: New areas of common ground. *Developmental Psychology, 32*, 387–389.

Le Corre, M., & Carey, S. (2007). One, two, three, four, nothing more: An investigation of the conceptual sources of the verbal counting principles. *Cognition, 105*, 395–438.

Lecce, S., Bianco, F., Demicheli, P., & Cavallini, E. (2014). Training preschoolers on first-order false belief understanding: Transfer on advanced ToM skills and metamemory. *Child Development, 85*, 2404–2418.

Lee, B. H., Schofer, J. L., & Koppelman, F. S. (2005a). Bicycle safety helmet legislation and bicycle-related non-fatal injuries in California. *Accidental Analysis and Prevention, 37*, 93–102.

Lee, B. R., Bright, C. L., Svoboda, D. V., Fakunmoju, S., & Barth, R. P. (2011). Outcomes of group care for youth: A review of comparative studies. *Research on Social Work Practice, 21*, 177–189.

Lee, E., & Troop-Gordon, W. (2011). Peer processes and gender role development: Changes in gender atypicality related to negative peer treatment and children's friendships. *Sex Roles, 64*, 90–102.

Lee, K. (2013). Little liars: Development of verbal deception in children. *Child Development Perspectives, 7*, 91–96.

Lee, R., Zhai, F., Brooks-Gunn, J., Han, W., & Waldfogel, J. (2014). Head start participation and school readiness: Evidence from the early childhood longitudinal study–birth cohort. *Developmental Psychology, 50*, 202–215.

Lee, R. M. (2005b). Resilience against discrimination: Ethnic identity and other-group orientation as protective factors for Korean Americans. *Journal of Counseling Psychology, 52*, 36–44.

Lee, S., Olszewski-Kubilius, P., & Thomson, D. (2012). Academically gifted students' perceived interpersonal competence and peer relationships. *Gifted Child Quarterly, 56*, 90–104.

Lee, V. E. & Burkam, D. T. (2003). Inequality at the starting gate: Background differences in achievement as children begin school. New York: Economic Policy Institute.

Leen-Feldner, E. W., Reardon, L. E., & Hayward, C. (2008). The relation between puberty and adolescent anxiety: Theory and evidence. In M. J. Zvolensky & J. A. J. Smits (Eds.), *Anxiety in health behaviors and physical illness*. New York: Springer Science + Business Media.

Leffel, K., & Suskind, D. (2013). Parent-directed approaches to enrich the early language environments of children living in poverty. *Seminars in Speech and Language, 34*, 267–278.

Legerstee, M. (2014). The developing social brain: Social connections and social bonds, social loss, and jealousy in infancy. In M. Legerstee, D. W. Haley, M. H. Bornstein (Eds.), *The infant mind: Origins of the social brain*. New York: Guilford Press.

Legerstee, M., Anderson, D., & Schaffer, A. (1998). Five- and eight-month-old infants recognize their faces and voices as familiar and social stimuli. *Child Development, 69*, 37–50.

Legerstee, M., & Markova, G. (2008). Variations in 10-month-old infant imitation of people and things. *Infant Behavior & Development, 31*, 81–91.

Legerstee, M., Haley, D. W., & Bornstein, M. H. (2013). *The infant mind: Origins of the social brain*. New York: Guilford Press.

Lehman, D., Chiu, C., & Schaller, M. (2004). Psychology and culture. *Annual Review of Psychology, 55*, 689–714.

Leis-Newman, E. (2012, June). Miscarriage and loss. *Monitor on Psychology*, 57–59.

Leloux-Opmeer, H., Kuiper, C., Swaab, H., & Scholte, E. (2016). Characteristics of children in foster care, family-style group care, and residential care: A scoping review. *Journal of Child and Family Studies, 25*, 2357–2371.

Leonard, J., & Higson, H. (2014). A strategic activity model of enterprise system implementation and use: Scaffolding fluidity. *Journal of Strategic Information Systems, 23*, 62–86.

Lepage, J. F., & Théret, H. (2007). The mirror neuron system: Grasping others' actions from birth? *Developmental Science, 10*, 513–523.

Lerner, J. W. (2002). *Learning disabilities: Theories, diagnosis, and teaching strategies*. Boston: Houghton Mifflin.

Lerner, R. M., Fisher, C. B., & Weinberg, R. A. (2000). Toward a science for and of the people: Promoting civil society through the application of developmental science. *Child Development, 71*, 11–20.

Lerner, R. M., Theokas, C., & Jelicic, H. (2005). Youth as active agents in their own positive development: A developmental systems perspective. In W. Greve, K. Rothermund & D. Wentura, *Adaptive self: Personal continuity and intentional self-development*. Ashland, OH: Hogrefe & Huber Publishers.

Lessard, A., Butler-Kisber, L., Fortin, L., Marcotte, D., Potvin, P., & Royer, É. (2008, February). Shades of disengagement: High school dropouts speak out. *Social Psychology of Education, 11*(1), 25–42.

Leung, C., Pe-Pua, R., & Karnilowicz, W. (2006, January). Psychological adaptation and autonomy among adolescents in Australia: A comparison of Anglo-Celtic and three Asian groups. *International Journal of Intercultural Relations, 30*, 99–118.

Levant, R. F., McDermott, R. C., Hewitt, A. A., Alto, K. M., & Harris, K. T. (2016). Confirmatory factor analytic investigation of variance composition, gender invariance, and validity of the Male Role Norms Inventory-Adolescent-revised (MRNI-A-r). *Journal of Counseling Psychology, 63*, 543–556.

LeVay, S., & Valente, S. M. (2003). *Human sexuality*. Sunderland, MA: Sinauer Associates.

Levenson, D. (2012). Genomic testing update: Whole genome sequencing may be worth the money. *Annals of Neurology, 71*, A7–A9.

Levenson, M. R., Aldwin, C. M., & Igarashi, H. (2013). Religious development from adolescence to middle adulthood. In R. F. Paloutzian & C. L. Park (Eds.), *Handbook of the psychology of religion and spirituality* (2nd ed.). New York: Guilford Press.

Levin, R. (2007, February). Sexual activity, health and well-being—the beneficial roles of coitus and masturbation. *Sexual and Relationship Therapy, 22*(1), 135–148.

Levin, S., Matthews, M., Guimond, S., et al. (2012). Assimilation, multiculturalism, and colorblindness: Mediated and moderated relationships between social dominance orientation and prejudice. *Journal of Experimental Social Psychology, 48*, 207–212.

Levine, M., & Levine, A. (2014). Charters and foundations: Are we losing control of our public schools? *American Journal of Orthopsychiatry, 84*, 1–6.

Levine, R. (1994). *Child care and culture*. Cambridge: Cambridge University Press.

Lewis, J., & Elman, J. (2008). Growth-related neural reorganization and the autism phenotype: A test of the hypothesis that altered brain growth leads to altered connectivity. *Developmental Science, 11*, 135–155.

Lewis, M., & Carmody, D. (2008). Self-representation and brain development. *Developmental Psychology, 44*, 1329–1334.

Lewis, M., & Ramsay, D. (2004). Development of self-recognition, personal pronoun use, and pretend play during the 2nd year. *Child Development, 75*, 1821–1831.

Lewkowicz, D. (2002). Heterogeneity and heterochrony in the development of intersensory perception. *Cognitive Brain Research, 14*, 41–63.

Leyens, J. P., Camino, L., Parke, R. D., & Berkowitz, L. (1975). Effects of movie violence on aggression in a field setting as a function of group dominance and cohesion. *Journal of Personality and Social Psychology, 32*, 346–360.

Li, Q. (2007, July). New bottle but old wine: A research of cyberbullying in schools. *Computers in Human Behavior, 23*(4), 1777–1791.

Li, J., Laursen, T. M., Precht, D. H., Olsen, J., & Mortensen, P. B. (2005). Hospitalization for mental illness among parents after the death of a child. *New England Journal of Medicine, 352*, 1190–1196.

Li, S. (2003). Biocultural orchestration of developmental plasticity across levels: The interplay of biology and culture in shaping the mind and behavior across the life span. *Psychological Bulletin, 129*, 171–194.

Li, Y., & Wright, M. F. (2013). Adolescents' social status goals: Relationships to social status insecurity, aggression, and prosocial behavior. *Journal of Youth and Adolescence, 43*, 146–160.

Li Kusterer, H., Lindholm, T., & Montgomery, H. (2013). Gender typing in stereotypes and evaluations of actual managers. *Journal of Managerial Psychology, 28*, 561–579.

Lian, C., Wan Muda, W., Hussin, Z., & Thon, C. (2012). Factors associated with undernutrition among children in a rural district of Kelantan, Malaysia. *Asia-Pacific Journal of Public Health, 24*(2), 330–342.

Libertus, K., Joh, A. S., & Needham, A. W. (2016). Motor training at 3 months affects object exploration 12 months later. *Developmental Science, 19*, 1058–1066.

Liew, J., Eisenberg, N., Spinrad, T. L., et al. (2011). Physiological regulation and fearfulness as predictors of young children's empathy-related reactions. *Social Development, 20*, 111–134.

Lilienfeld, S.O., & Arkowtiz, H. (2014, January 1). Why "just say no" doesn't work. *Scientific American Mind*. Retrieved March 3, 2017, from https://www.scientificamerican.com/article/why-just-say-no-doesnt-work/.

Lillard, A.S. (2008). *Montessori: The Science Behind the Genius*. Updated Edition. Oxford, England: Oxford University Press.

Lin, C., Chiu, H., & Yeh, C. (2012). Impact of socio-economic backgrounds, experiences of being disciplined in early childhood, and parenting value on parenting styles of preschool children's parents. *Chinese Journal of Guidance and Counseling, 32*, 123–149.

Lin, P. (2016). Risky behaviors: Integrating adolescent egocentrism with the theory of planned behavior. *Review of General Psychology, 20*, 392–398.

Lindsay, A., Sussner, K., Kim, J., & Gortmaker, S. (2006). The role of parents in preventing childhood obesity. *The Future of Children, 16*, 169–186.

Lindsay, S., Proulx, M., Thomson, N., & Scott, H. (2013). Educators' challenges of including children with autism spectrum disorder in mainstream classrooms. *International Journal of Disability, Development and Education, 60*, 347–362.

Lindsey, E., & Colwell, M. (2003). Preschoolers' emotional competence: Links to pretend and physical play. *Child Study Journal, 33*, 39–52.

Linebarger, D. L., & Walker, D. (2005). Infants' and Toddlers' television viewing and language outcomes. *American Behavioral Scientist, 48*, 624–645.

Lines, P. M. (2001). Homeschooling. *Eric Digest*, EDO-EA-10–08, 1–4

Lippman, J. R., & Campbell, S. W. (2014). Damned if you do, damned if you don't…if you're a girl: Relational and normative contexts of adolescent sexting in the United States. *Journal of Children and Media, 8*(4), 371–386.

Lipsitt, L. (2003). Crib death: A biobehavioral phenomenon? *Current Directions in Psychological Science, 12*, 164–170.

Lipsitt, L. P. (1986). Toward understanding the hedonic nature of infancy. In L. P. Lipsitt & J. H. Cantor (Eds.), *Experimental child psychologist: Essays and experiments in honor of Charles C. Spiker*. Hillsdale, NJ: Erlbaum.

Lipsitt, L. P., & Rovee-Collier, C. (2012). The psychophysics of olfaction in the human newborn: Habituation and cross-adaptation. In G. M. Zucco, R. S. Herz, & B. Schaal (Eds.), *Olfactory cognition: From perception and memory to environmental odours and neuroscience*. Amsterdam, Netherlands: John Benjamins Publishing Company.

List, B. A., & Barzman, D. H. (2011). Evidence-based recommendations for the treatment of aggression in pediatric patients with attention deficit hyperactivity disorder. *Psychiatric Quarterly, 82*, 33–42.

Litovsky, R. Y., & Ashmead, D. H. (1997). Development of binaural and spatial hearing in infants and children. In R. H. Gilkey & T. R. Andersen (Eds.), *Binaural and spatial hearing in real and virtual environments* (pp. 571–592). Mahwah, NJ: Erlbaum.

Liu, D., Wellman, H., Tardif, T., & Sabbagh, M. (2008, March). Theory of mind development in Chinese children: A meta-analysis of false-belief understanding across cultures and languages. *Developmental Psychology, 44*(2), 523–531.

Lloyd, K. K. (2012). Health-related quality of life and children's happiness with their childcare. *Child: Care, Health and Development, 38*, 244–250.

Lobel, M., & DeLuca, R. (2007). Psychosocial sequelae of cesarean delivery: Review and analysis of their causes and implications. *Social Science & Medicine, 64*, 2272–2284.

LoBue, V., Nishida, T., Chiong, C., DeLoache, J. S., & Haidt, J. (2011). When getting something good is bad: Even three-year-olds react to inequality. *Social Development, 20*, 154–170.

Loeb, S., Fuller, B., Kagan, S. L., & Carrol, B. (2004). Child care in poor communities: Early learning effects of type, quality and stability. *Child Development, 75*, 47–65.

Loewen, S. (2006). Exceptional intellectual performance: A neo-Piagetian perspective. *High Ability Studies, 17*, 159–181.

Loftus, E. F., & Bernstein, D. M. (2005). Rich false memories: The royal road to success. In A. F. Healy, *Experimental cognitive psychology and its applications*. Washington, DC: American Psychological Association.

Logan, K. J., Byrd, C. T., Mazzocchi, E. M., & Gillam, R. B. (2011). Speaking rate characteristics of elementary-school-aged children who do and do not stutter. *Journal of Communication Disorders, 44*, 130–147.

Loggins, S., & Andrade, F. D. (2014). Despite an overall decline in U.S. infant mortality rates, the Black/White disparity persists: Recent trends and future projections. *Journal of Community Health: The Publication for Health Promotion and Disease Prevention, 39*, 118–123.

Lohbeck, A., Tietjens, M., & Bund, A. (2016). Physical self-concept and physical activity enjoyment in elementary school children. *Early Child Development and Care, 186*, 1792–1801.

Lohman, D. F. (2005). Reasoning abilities. In R. J. Sternberg & J. E. Pretz (Eds.), *Cognition and intelligence: Identifying the mechanisms of the mind*. New York, NY: Cambridge University Press.

Lois, J. (2006, September). Role strain, emotion management, and burnout: Homeschooling mothers' adjustment to the teacher role. *Symbolic Interaction, 29*(4), 507–530.

Longo, G. S., Bray, B. C., & Kim-Spoon, J. (2017). Profiles of adolescent religiousness using latent profile analysis: Implications for psychopathology. *British Journal of Developmental Psychology, 35*, 91–105.

Lorang, M. R., McNiel, D. E., & Binder, R. L. (2016). Minors and sexting: Legal implications. *Journal of the American Academy of Psychiatry and the Law, 44*(1), 73–81.

Lorenz, K. (1957). Companionship in bird life. In C. Scholler (Ed.), *Instinctive behavior*. New York: International Universities Press.

Lorenz, K. (1974). *Civilized man's eight deadly sins*. New York: Harcourt Brace Jovanovich.

Lorenz, K. Z. (1965). *Evolution and the modification of behavior*. Chicago: University of Chicago Press.

Lósonczy-Marshall, M. (2008). Gender differences in latency and duration of emotional expression in 7- through 13-month-old infants. *Social Behavior and Personality, 36*, 267–274.

Lothian, J. (2005). *The official Lamaze guide: Giving birth with confidence*. Minnetonka, MN: Meadowbrook Press.

Love, A., & Burns, M. (2006, December). 'It's a hurricane! It's a hurricane!': Can music facilitate social constructive and sociodramatic play in a preschool classroom? *Journal of Genetic Psychology, 167*(4), 383–391.

Love, J., Tarullo, L., Raikes, H., & Chazan-Cohen, R. (2006). Head start: What do we know about its effectiveness? What do we need to know? *Blackwell handbook of early childhood development*. Malden, MA: Blackwell Publishing.

Love, J. M., Harrison, L., Sagi-Schwartz, A., et al. (2003). Child care quality matters: How conclusions may vary with context. *Child Development, 74*, 1021–1033.

Low, J., & Perner, J. (2012). Implicit and explicit theory of mind: State of the art. *British Journal of Developmental Psychology, 30*, 1–13.

Lowe, M. R., Doshi, S. D., Katterman, S. N., & Feig, E. H. (2013). Dieting and restrained eating as prospective predictors of weight gain. *Frontiers in Psychology, 4*, 577–586.

Lu, M. C., Prentice, J., Yu, S. M., Inkelas, M., Lange, L. O., & Halfon, N. (2003). Childbirth education classes: Sociodemographic disparities in attendance and the association of attendance with breastfeeding initiation. *Maternal Child Health, 7*, 87–93.

Lu, X. (2001). Bicultural identity development and Chinese community formation: An ethnographic study of Chinese schools in Chicago. *Howard Journal of Communications, 12*, 203–220.

Lubienski, C., Puckett, T., & Brewer, T. (2013). Does homeschooling 'work'? A critique of the empirical claims and agenda of advocacy organizations. *Peabody Journal of Education, 88*, 378–392.

Lubinski, D. (2004). Introduction to the special section on cognitive abilities: 100 years after Spearman's (1904) "'General Intelligence,' objectively determined and measured." *Journal of Personality and Social Psychology, 86*, 96–111.

Lubinski, D., & Benbow, C. P. (2001). Choosing excellence. *American Psychologist, 56*, 76–77.

Lubinski, D., & Benbow, C. P. (2006). Study of mathematically precocious youth after 35 years: Uncovering antecedents for the development of math-science expertise. *Perspectives on Psychological Science, 1*, 316–345.

Lucas, S. R., & Berends, M. (2002). Sociodemographic diversity, correlated achievement, and de facto tracking. *Sociology of Education, 75*, 328–349.

Lucassen, A. (2012). Ethical implications of new genetic technologies. *Developmental Medicine & Child Neurology, 54*, 124–130.

Ludlow, V., Newhook, L., Newhook, J., Bonia, K., Goodridge, J., & Twells, L. (2012). How formula feeding mothers balance risks and define themselves as 'good mothers.' *Health, Risk & Society, 14*, 291–306.

Ludwig, M., & Field, T. (2014). Touch in parent-infant mental health: Arousal, regulation, and relationships. In K. Brandt, B. D. Perry, S. Seligman, et al (Eds.), *Infant and early childhood mental health: Core concepts and clinical practice*. Arlington, VA: American Psychiatric Publishing, Inc.

Luke, B. & Brown, M. B. (2008). Maternal morbidity and infant death in twin vs. triplet and quadruplet pregnancies. *American Journal of Obstetrics and Gynecology, 198*, 1–10.

Lui, P. P. & Rollock, D. (2013). Tiger mother: Popular and psychological scientific perspectives on Asian culture and parenting. *American Journal of Orthopsychiatry, 83*, 450–456.

Luna, B., & Wright, C. (2016). Adolescent brain development: Implications for the juvenile criminal justice system. In K. Heilbrun, D. DeMatteo, & N. S. Goldstein (Eds.), *APA handbook of psychology and juvenile justice*. Washington, DC: American Psychological Association.

Lundberg, I., & Reichenberg, M. (2013). Developing reading comprehension among students with mild intellectual disabilities: An intervention study. *Scandinavian Journal of Educational Research, 57*, 89–100.

Lundby, E. (2013). 'You can't buy friends, but…' Children's perception of consumption and friendship. *Young Consumers, 14*, 360–374.

Luo, Y., Kaufman, L., & Baillargeon R. (2009). Young infants' reasoning about physical events involving inert and self-propelled objects. *Cognitive Psychology, 58*, 441–486

Luo, Y., LaPierre, T. A., Hughes, M. E., & Waite, L. J. (2012). Grandparents providing care to grandchildren: A population-based study of continuity and change. *Journal of Family Issues, 33*(9), 1143–1167.

Luyten, P. (2011). Review of 'Mind to mind: Infant research, neuroscience and psychoanalysis.' *Clinical Social Work Journal, 39*, 116–118.

Lynam, D. R. (1996). Early identification of chronic offenders: Who is the fledgling psychopath? *Psychological Bulletin, 120*, 209–234.

Lynn, R. (2009). What has caused the Flynn effect? Secular increases in the Development Quotients of infants. *Intelligence, 37*, 16–24.

Lynne, S., Graber, J., Nichols, T., Brooks-Gunn, J., & Botvin, G. (2007, February). Links between pubertal timing, peer influences, and externalizing behaviors among urban students followed through middle school. *Journal of Adolescent Health, 40*, 35–44.

Mabbott, D. J., Noseworthy, M., Bouffet, E., Laughlin, S., & Rockel, C. (2006). White matter growth as a mechanism of cognitive development in children. *Neuroimaging, 15*, 936–946.

Macchi C. V., Picozzi, M., Girelli, L., & de Hevia, M. (2012). Increasing magnitude counts more: Asymmetrical processing of ordinality in 4-month-old infants. *Cognition, 124*, 183–193.

Maccoby, E. E., & Lewis, C. C. (2003). Less day care or different day care? *Child Development, 74*, 1069–1075.

Maccoby, E. E., & Màrtin, J. A. (1983). Socialization in the context of the family: Parent–child interaction. In P. H. Mussen (Ed.)

& E. M. Hetherington (Vol. Ed.), *Handbook of child psychology: Vol. 4. Socialization, personality, and social development* (4th ed.). New York: Wiley.

MacDonald, H., Beeghly, M., Grant-Knight, W., et al. (2008). Longitudinal association between infant disorganized attachment and childhood posttraumatic stress symptoms. *Development and Psychopathology, 20,* 493–508.

MacDorman, M., Declercq, E., Menacker, F., & Malloy, M. (2008). Neonatal mortality for primary cesarean and vaginal births to low-risk women: Application of an 'intention-to-treat' model. *Birth: Issues in Perinatal Care, 35,* 3–8.

MacDorman, M. F., & Matthews, T. J. (2009). Behind International Rankings of Infant Mortality: How the United States Compares with Europe. *NCHS Data Brief, # 23.*

MacDorman, M. F., Hoyert, D. L., & Mathews, T. J. (2013). Recent declines in infant mortality in the United States, 2005–2011. *NCHS data brief, no. 120.* Washington DC: U. S. Department of Health and Human Services, Centers for Disease Control and Prevention, National Center for Health Statistics.

MacDorman, M. F., Martin, J. A., Mathews, T. J., Hoyert, D. L., & Ventura, S. J. (2005). Explaining the 2001–02 infant mortality increase: Data from the linked birth/infant death data set. *National Vital Statistics Report, 53,* 1–22.

MacInnes, K., & Stone, D. H. (2008). Stages of development and injury: an epidemiological survey of young children presenting to an emergency department. *BMC Public Health,* 8.

Madison, G., Mosing, M. A., Verweij, K. H., Pedersen, N. L., & Ullén, F. (2016). Common genetic influences on intelligence and auditory simple reaction time in a large Swedish sample. *Intelligence, 59,* 157–162.

Madsen, P. B., & Green, R. (2012). Gay adolescent males' effective coping with discrimination: A qualitative study. *Journal of LGBT Issues in Counseling, 6,* 139–155.

Maes, S. J., De Mol, J., & Buysse, A. (2012). Children's experiences and meaning construction on parental divorce: A focus group study. *Childhood: A Global Journal of Child Research, 19,* 266–279.

Mages, W. K. (2016). Taking inspiration from Reggio Emilia: An analysis of a professional development workshop on fostering authentic art in the early childhood classroom. *Journal of Early Childhood Teacher Education, 37,* 175–185.

Maggi, S., Busetto, L., Noale, M., Limongi, F., & Crepaldi, G. (2015). Obesity: Definition and epidemiology. In A. Lenzi, S. Migliaccio, & L. M. Donini (Eds.), *Multidisciplinary approach to obesity: From assessment to treatment.* Cham, Switzerland: Springer International Publishing.

Magyar, C. I. (2011). *Developing and evaluating educational programs for students with autism.* New York: Springer Science + Business Media.

Majors, K. (2012). Friendships: The power of positive alliance. In S. Roffey (Ed.), *Positive relationships: Evidence based practice across the world.* New York: Springer Science + Business Media.

Makino, M., Hashizume, M., Tsuboi, K., Yasushi, M., & Dennerstein, L. (2006, September). Comparative study of attitudes to eating between male and female students in the People's Republic of China. *Eating and Weight Disorders, 11,* 111–117.

Mäkinen, M., Puukko-Viertomies, L., Lindberg, N., Siimes, M. A., & Aalberg, V. (2012). Body dissatisfaction and body mass in girls and boys transitioning from early to mid-adolescence: Additional role of self-esteem and eating habits. *BMC Psychiatry, 12,* 123–131.

Malik, F., & Shujja, S. (2013). Emotional intelligence and academic achievement: implications for children's performance in schools. *Journal of the Indian Academy of Applied Psychology, 39,* 51–59.

Mallan, K. M., Sullivan, S. E., de Jersey, S. J., & Daniels, L. A. (2016). The relationship between maternal feeding beliefs and practices and perceptions of infant eating behaviours at 4 months. *Appetite, 105,* 1–7.

Maller, S. (2003). Best practices in detecting bias in nonverbal tests. In R. McCallum (Ed.), *Handbook of nonverbal assessment.* New York: Kluwer Academic/Plenum Publishers.

Mameli, M. (2007). Reproductive cloning, genetic engineering and the autonomy of the child: The moral agent and the open future. *Journal of Medical Ethics, 33,* 87–93.

Mammen, P., Russell, S., & Russell, P.S. (2007). Prevalence of eating disorders and psychiatric co-morbidity among children and adolescents, *Indian Pediatrics, 44,* 357-359.

Manaseki-Holland, S., Spier, E., Bavuusuren, B., Bayandorj, T., Sprachman, S., & Marshall, T. (2010). Effects of traditional swaddling on development: A randomized controlled trial. *Pediatrics, 126*(6), e1485–e1492.

Mangweth, B., Hausmann, A., & Walch, T. (2004). Body fat perception in eating-disordered men. *International Journal of Eating Disorders, 35,* 102–108.

Manlove, J., Franzetta, K., McKinney, K., Romano-Papillo, A., & Terry-Humen, E.(2004). *No time to waste: Programs to reduce teen pregnancy among middle school-aged youth.* Washington, DC: National Campaign to Prevent Teen Pregnancy.

Manlove, J., Terry-Humen, E., Romano Papillo, A., Franzetta, K., Williams, S., & Ryan, S. (2002). *Preventing teenage pregnancy, childbearing, and sexually transmitted diseases: What the research shows.* Washington, DC: Child Trends. Retrieved March 4, 2006, from http://www.childtrends.org/Files/K1Brief.pdf.

Manning, M., & Hoyme, H. (2007). Fetal alcohol spectrum disorders: A practical clinical approach to diagnosis. *Neuroscience & Biobehavioral Reviews, 31,* 230–238.

Manning, R. C., Dickson, J. M., Palmier-Claus, J., Cunliffe, A., & Taylor, P. J. (2017). A systematic review of adult attachment and social anxiety. *Journal of Affective Disorders, 211,* 44–59.

Manning, W., Giordano, P., & Longmore, M. (2006, September). Hooking up: The relationship contexts of "nonrelationship" sex. *Journal of Adolescent Research, 21,* 459–483.

Manzanares, S., Cobo, D., Moreno-Martínez, M., Sánchez-Gila, M., & Pineda, A. (2013). Risk of episiotomy and perineal lacerations recurring after first delivery. *Birth: Issues in Perinatal Care, 40,* 307–311.

Mao, A., Burnham, M. M., Goodlin-Jones, B. L., Gaylor, E. E., & Anders, T. F. (2004). A comparison of the sleep-wake patterns of cosleeping and solitary-sleeping infants. *Child Psychiatry and Human Development, 35,* 95–105.

Marcia, J. E. (1980). Identity in adolescence. In J. Adelson (Ed.), *Handbook of adolescent psychology.* New York: Wiley.

Marcia, J. E. (2007). Theory and measure: The identity status interview. In M. Watzlawik & A. Born (Eds.), *Capturing identity: Quantitative and qualitative methods.* Lanham, MD: University Press of America.

Marcovitch, S., Zelazo, P., & Schmuckler, M. (2003). The effect of the number of a trials on performance on the A-not-B task. *Infancy, 3,* 519–529.

Marcus, J., & Le, H. (2013). Interactive effects of levels of individualism–collectivism on cooperation: A meta-analysis. *Journal of Organizational Behavior, 34,* 813–834.

Mares, S. W., van der Vorst, H., Engels, R. E., & Lichtwarck-Aschoff, A. (2011). Parental alcohol use, alcohol-related problems, and alcohol-specific attitudes, alcohol-specific communication, and adolescent excessive alcohol use and alcohol-related problems: An indirect path model. *Addictive Behaviors, 36*, 209–216.

Marin, T., Chen, E., Munch, J., & Miller, G. (2009). Double-exposure to acute stress and chronic family stress is associated with immune changes in children with asthma. *Psychosomatic Medicine, 71*, 378–384.

Marinellie, S. A., & Kneile, L. A. (2012). Acquiring knowledge of derived nominals and derived adjectives in context. *Language, Speech, and Hearing Services in Schools, 43*, 53–65.

Markant, J., Oakes, L. M., & Amso, D. (2016). Visual selective attention biases contribute to the other-race effect among 9-month-old infants. *Developmental Psychobiology, 58*(3), 355–365.

Marks, A. K., Patton, F., & Coll, C. (2011). Being bicultural: A mixed-methods study of adolescents' implicitly and explicitly measured multiethnic identities. *Developmental Psychology, 47*, 270–288.

Marschark, M., Spencer, P. E., & Newsom, C. A. (Eds.). (2003). *Oxford handbook of deaf students, language, and education.* London: Oxford University Press.

Marschik, P., Einspieler, C., Strohmeier, A., Plienegger, J., Garzarolli, B., & Prechtl, H. (2008). From the reaching behavior at 5 months of age to hand preference at preschool age. *Developmental Psychobiology, 50*, 512–518.

Marsh, H., Ellis, L., & Craven, R. (2002). How do preschool children feel about themselves? Unraveling measurement and multidimensional self-concept structure. *Developmental Psychology, 38*, 376–393.

Marsh, H., Seaton, M., Trautwein, U., et al. (2008). The big-fish-little-pond-effect stands up to critical scrutiny: Implications for theory, methodology, and future research. *Educational Psychology Review, 20*, 319–350.

Martin, A., Onishi, K. H., & Vouloumanos, A. (2012). Understanding the abstract role of speech in communication at 12 months. *Cognition, 123*, 50–60.

Martin, C., & Dinella, L. M. (2012). Congruence between gender stereotypes and activity preference in self-identified tomboys and non-tomboys. *Archives of Sexual Behavior, 41*, 599–610.

Martin, C., & Fabes, R. (2001). The stability and consequences of young children's same-sex peer interactions. *Developmental Psychology, 37*, 431–446.

Martin, C. L., & Ruble, D. (2004). Children's search for gender cues: Cognitive perspectives on gender development. *Current Directions in Psychological Science, 13*, 67–70.

Martin, J. A., Hamilton, B. E., Sutton, P. D., Ventura, S. J., Menacker, F., & Munson, M. L. (2005). Births: Final data for 2003. *National Vital Statistics Reports, 54*, Table J, 21.

Martin, L., McNamara, M., Milot, A., Halle, T., & Hair, E. (2007). The effects of father involvement during pregnancy on receipt of prenatal care and maternal smoking. *Maternal and Child Health Journal, 11*, 595–602.

Martin, S., Li, Y., Casanueva, C., Harris-Britt, A., Kupper, L., & Cloutier, S. (2006). Intimate partner violence and women's depression before and during pregnancy. *Violence Against Women, 12*, 221–239.

Martin-Prudent, A., Lartz, M., Borders, C., & Meehan, T. (2016). Early intervention practices for children with hearing loss: Impact of professional development. *Communication Disorders Quarterly, 38*, 13–23.

Martins, I., Lauterbach, M., Luís, H., et al. (2013). Neurological subtle signs and cognitive development: A study in late childhood and adolescence. *Child Neuropsychology, 19*, 466–478.

Martineau, J., Cochin, S., Magne, R., & Barthelemy, C. (2008). Impaired cortical activation in autistic children: Is the mirror neuron system involved? *International Journal of Psychophysiology, 68*, 35–40.

Martinez, G., Copen, C. E., Abma, J. C. (2011). Teenagers in the United States: Sexual activity, contraceptive use, and childbearing, 2006–2010 National Survey of Family Growth. National Center for Health Statistics. *Vital Health Stat, 23*(31).

Martinez-Torteya, C., Bogat, G., von Eye, A., & Levendosky, A. (2009). Resilience among children exposed to domestic violence: The role of risk and protective factors. *Child Development, 80*, 562–577.

Marwaha, R.K., Tandon, N., Singh, Y., Aggarwal, R., Grewal, K., & Mani, K. (2006). A study of growth parameters and prevalence of overweight and obesity in school children from Delhi. *Indian Pediatrics, 43*, 943-52.

Masapollo, M., Polka, L., & Ménard, L. (2015). When infants talk, infants listen: Pre-babbling infants prefer listening to speech with infant vocal properties. *Developmental Science.* Retrieved March 19, 2015, from http://onlinelibrary.wiley.com/doi/10.1111/desc.12298/abstract.

Masataka, N. (1992). Pitch characteristics of Japanese maternal speech to infants. *Journal of Child Language.* 19:213–223 [PubMed: 1527201].

Masataka, N. (1996). Perception of motherese in a signed language by 6-month-old deaf infants. *Developmental Psychology, 32*, 874–879.

Masataka, N. (1998). Perception of motherese in Japanese sign language by 6-month-old hearing infants. *Developmental Psychology, 34*, 241–246.

Masataka, N. (2000). The role of modality and input in the earliest stage of language acquisition: Studies of Japanese sign language. In C. Chamerlain & J. P. Morford (Eds.), *Language acquisition by eye.* Mahwah, NJ: Lawrence Erlbaum Associates.

Masataka, N. (2003). *The onset of language.* Cambridge, England: Cambridge University Press.

Masataka, N. (2006). Preference for consonance over dissonance by hearing newborns of deaf parents and of hearing parents. *Developmental Science, 9*, 46–50.

Mash, C., Bornstein, M. H., & Arterberry, M. E. (2013). Brain dynamics in young infants' recognition of faces: EEG oscillatory activity in response to mother and stranger. *Neuroreport: For Rapid Communication of Neuroscience Research, 24*, 359–363.

Masino, S. & Nin~o-Zarazu, M. (2016). What works to improve the quality of student learning in developing countries? *International Journal of Educational Development, 48*, 53–65.

Masling, J. M., & Bornstein, R. F. (Eds.). (1996). *Psychoanalytic perspectives on developmental psychology.* Washington, DC: American Psychological Association.

Massaro, A., Rothbaum, R., & Aly, H. (2006). Fetal brain development: The role of maternal nutrition, exposures and behaviors. *Journal of Pediatric Neurology, 4*, 1–9.

Master, S., Amodio, D., Stanton, A., Yee, C., Hilmert, C., & Taylor, S. (2009). Neurobiological correlates of coping through emotional approach. *Brain, Behavior, and Immunity, 23*, 27–35.

Mathews, G., Fane, B., Conway, G., Brook, C., & Hines, M. (2009). Personality and congenital adrenal hyperplasia: Possible effects of prenatal androgen exposure. *Hormones and Behavior, 55*, 285–291.

Mathiesen, K., & Prior, M. (2006, December). The impact of temperament factors and family functioning on resilience processes from infancy to school age. *European Journal of Developmental Psychology, 3*(4), 357–387.

Matlin, M. (2003). From menarche to menopause: Misconceptions about women's reproductive lives. *Psychology Science, 45*, 106–122.

Matlung, S. E., Bilo, R. A. C., Kubat, B., & van Rijn, R. R. (2011). Multicystic encephalomalacia as an end-stage finding in abusive head trauma. *Forensic Scientific Medicine and Pathology, 7*, 355–363.

Matsuda, Y., Ueno, K., Waggoner, R., et al. (2011). Processing of infant-directed speech by adults. *NeuroImage, 54*, 611–621.

Matsumoto, A. (1999). *Sexual differentiation of the brain.* Boca Raton, FL: CRC Press.

Matthes, J., Prieler, M., & Adam, K. (2016). Gender-role portrayals in television advertising across the globe. *Sex Roles.* Retrieved May 27, 2016, from http://link.springer.com/article/10.1007/s11199-016-0617-y.

Mattson, S., Calarco, K., & Lang, A. (2006). Focused and shifting attention in children with heavy prenatal alcohol exposure. *Neuropsychology, 20*, 361–369.

Maul, J., & Advokat, C. (2013). Stimulant medications for attention-deficit/hyperactivity disorder (ADHD) improve memory of emotional stimuli in ADHD-diagnosed college students. *Pharmacology, Biochemistry and Behavior, 105*, 58–62.

Mauritzson, U., & Saeljoe, R. (2001). Adult questions and children's responses: Coordination of perspectives in studies of children's theories of other minds. *Scandinavian Journal of Educational Research, 45*, 213–231.

Maxson, S. C. (2013). Behavioral genetics. In R. J. Nelson, S. Y. Mizumori, & I. B. Weiner (Eds.), *Handbook of psychology, Vol. 3: Behavioral neuroscience* (2nd ed.). New York: John Wiley & Sons Ltd.

Mayer, J. D. (2001). Emotion, intelligence, and emotional intelligence. In J. P. Forgas (Ed.), *Handbook of affect and social cognition.* Mahwah, NJ: Erlbaum.

Mayes, L., Snyder, P., Langlois, E., & Hunter, N. (2007). Visuospatial working memory in school-aged children exposed in utero to cocaine. *Child Neuropsychology, 13*, 205–218.

Maynard, A. (2008). What we thought we knew and how we came to know it: Four decades of cross-cultural research from a Piagetian point of view. *Human Development, 51*, 56–65.

Mayor, S. (2004). Pregnancy and childbirth are leading causes of death in teenage girls in developing countries, *BMJ, 328*, 1152.

Mayseless, O. (1996). Attachment patterns and their outcomes. *Human Development, 39*, 206–223.

McAlister, A., & Peterson, C. (2006, November). Mental playmates: Siblings, executive functioning and theory of mind. *British Journal of Developmental Psychology, 24*, 733–751.

McAuliff, B. D., & Kovera, M. (2012). Do jurors get what they expect? Traditional versus alternative forms of children's testimony. *Psychology, Crime & Law, 18*, 27–47.

McBride, D. M., & Cutting, J. C. (2016). *Lab manual for psychological research., Rev. 3rd ed.* Thousand Oaks, CA: Sage Publications, Inc.

McCabe, M., & Ricciardelli, L. (2006, June). A prospective study of extreme weight change behaviors among adolescent boys and girls. *Journal of Youth and Adolescence, 35*(3), 425–434.

McCardle, P., & Hoff, E. (2006). *Childhood bilingualism: Research on infancy through school age.* Clevedon, Avon: Multilingual Matters Ltd.

McClain, S., & Cokley, K. (2017). Academic disidentification in Black college students: The role of teacher trust and gender. *Cultural Diversity and Ethnic Minority Psychology, 23*, 125–133.

McClain, M. R., Hokanson, J. S., Grazel, R., et al. (2017). Critical congenital heart disease newborn screening implementation: Lessons learned. *Maternal and Child Health Journal.*

McClelland, D. C. (1993). Intelligence is not the best predictor of job performance. *Current Directions in Psychological Research, 2*, 5–8.

McCowan, L. M. E., Dekker, G. A., Chan, E., et al. (2009, June 27). Spontaneous preterm birth and small for gestational age infants in women who stop smoking early in pregnancy: Prospective cohort study. *BMJ: British Medical Journal, 338*(7710).

McCrink, K., & Wynn, K. (2007). Ratio abstraction by 6-month-old infants. *Psychological Science, 18*, 740–745.

McCrink, K., & Wynn, K. (2009). Operational momentum in large-number addition and subtraction by 9-month-olds. *Journal of Experimental Child Psychology, 103*, 400–408.

McCue, M. (2012, August 21). In open casting call, *Sesame Street* looks for new neighbor. *The Wall Street Journal.* Retrieved September 21, 2014, from http://online.wsj.com/news/articles/SB10000872396390444443504577603483969328326.

McCullough, M. E., Tsang, J., & Brion, S. (2003). Personality traits in adolescence as predictors of religiousness in early maturity: Findings from the Terman longitudinal study. *Personality & Social Psychology Bulletin, 29*, 980–991.

McCutcheon-Rosegg, S., Ingraham, E., & Bradley, R. A. (1996). *Natural childbirth the Bradley way: Revised edition.* New York: Plume Books.

McDonald, K. L., Dashiell-Aje, E., Menzer, M. M., Rubin, K. H., Oh, W., & Bowker, J. C. (2013). Contributions of racial and sociobehavioral homophily to friendship stability and quality among same-race and cross-race friends. *Journal of Early Adolescence, 33*, 897–919.

McDonnell, C. G., Valentino, K., Comas, M., & Nuttall, A. K. (2016). Mother–child reminiscing at risk: Maternal attachment, elaboration, and child autobiographical memory specificity. *Journal of Experimental Child Psychology, 143*, 65–84.

McDonnell, L. M. (2004). *Politics, persuasion, and educational testing.* Cambridge, MA: Harvard University Press.

McDonough, L. (2002). Basic-level nouns: First learned but misunderstood. *Journal of Child Language, 29*, 357–377.

McDowell, M., Brody, D., & Hughes, J. (2007). Has Age at Menarche Changed? Results from the National Health and Nutrition Examination Survey (NHANES) 1999–2004. *Journal of Adolescent Health, 40*, 227–231.

McElhaney, K., Antonishak, J., & Allen, J. (2008). 'They like me, they like me not': Popularity and adolescents' perceptions of acceptance predicting social functioning over time. *Child Development, 79*, 720–731.

McElwain, N., & Booth-LaForce, C. (2006, June). Maternal sensitivity to infant distress and nondistress as predictors of infant–mother attachment security. *Journal of Family Psychology, 20*, 247–255.

McFarland-Piazza, L., Hazen, N., Jacobvitz, D., & Boyd-Soisson, E. (2012). The development of father–child attachment: Associations between adult attachment representations, recollections of childhood experiences and caregiving. *Early Child Development and Care, 182*, 701–721.

McGill, R. J., & Spurgin, A. R. (2016). Assessing the incremental value of KABC-II Luria model scores in predicting achievement: What do they tell us beyond the MPI? *Psychology in the Schools, 53*, 677–689.

McGinnis, E. (2012). *Skillstreaming in early childhood: A guide for teaching prosocial skills* (3rd ed.). Champaign, IL: Research Press.

McGonigle-Chalmers, M., Slater, H., & Smith, A. (2014). Rethinking private speech in preschoolers: The effects of social presence. *Developmental Psychology, 50*, 829–836.

McGough, R. (2003, May 20). MRIs take a look at reading minds. *The Wall Street Journal*, p. D8.

McGrew, K. S. (2005). The Cattell-Horn-Carroll theory of cognitive abilities: Past, present, and future. In D. P. Flanagan & P. L. Harrison (Eds.), *Contemporary intellectual assessment: Theories, tests, and issues.* New York, Guilford Press.

McGuffin, P., Riley, B., & Plomin, R. (2001, February 16). Toward behavioral genomics. *Science, 291*, 1232–1233.

McGuire, S., & Shanahan, L. (2010). Sibling experiences in diverse family contexts. *Child Development Perspectives, 4*, 72–79.

McHale, S.M., Updegraff, K.A., Shanahna, L., Crouter, A.C., & Killoren, S.E. (2005). Gender, culture, and family dynamics: Diffferential treatment of siblings in Mexican American families. *Journal of Marriage and the Family, 67*, 1259–1274.

McKinney, M., Fitzgerald, H. E., Winn, D., & Babcock, P. (2017). Public policy, child development research and boys at risk: Challenging, enduring and necessary partnership. *Infant Mental Health Journal.* Retrieved March 1, 2017, from http://onlinelibrary.wiley.com/doi/10.1002/imhj.21623/full.

McKown, C., & Weinstein, R. (2008). Teacher expectations, classroom context, and the achievement gap. *Journal of School Psychology, 46*, 235–261.

McLean, K., & Breen, A. (2009). Processes and content of narrative identity development in adolescence: Gender and well-being. *Developmental Psychology, 45*, 702–710.

McLean, K. C. & Syed, M. (2015). *The Oxford handbook of identity development.* New York, NY: Oxford University Press.

McLoyd, V. C. (2006). The legacy of Child Development's 1990 Special Issue on Minority Children: An editorial retrospective. *Child Development, 77*, 1142–1148.

McLoyd, V. C., Cauce, A. M., Takeuchi, D., & Wilson, L. (2000). Marital processes and parental socialization in families of color: A decade review of research. *Journal of Marriage and Family, 62*, 1070–1093.

McMillian-Robinson, M. M., Frierson, H. T., & Campbell, F. A. (2011). Do gender differences exist in the academic identification in African American elementary school-age children? *Journal of Black Psychology, 37*(1), 78–98.

McMurray, B., Aslin, R. N., & Toscano, J. C. (2009). Statistical learning of phonetic categories: insights from a computational approach. *Developmental Science, 12*, 369–378.

McNeil, N. M., Fuhs, M., Keultjes, M., & Gibson, M. H. (2011). Influences of problem format and SES on preschoolers' understanding of approximate addition. *Cognitive Development, 26*, 57–71.

McQuade, J. D., Breaux, R. P., Gómez, A. F., Zakarian, R. J., & Weatherly, J. (2016). Biased self-perceived social competence and engagement in subtypes of aggression: Examination of peer rejection, social dominance goals, and sex of the child as moderators. *Aggressive Behavior.* Retrieved June 13, 2016, from http://onlinelibrary.wiley.com/doi/10.1002/ab.21645/abstract.

McQueeny, T., Schweinsburg, B. C., Schweinsburg, A. D., et al. (2009). Altered white matter integrity in adolescent binge drinkers. *Alcoholism: Clinical and Experimental Research, 33*, 1278–1285.

Mead, M. (1942). *Environment and education, a symposium held in connection with the fiftieth anniversary celebration of the University of Chicago.* Chicago: University of Chicago.

Meade, C., Kershaw, T., & Ickovics, J. (2008). The intergenerational cycle of teenage motherhood: An ecological approach. *Health Psychology, 27*, 419–429.

Mealey, L. (2000). *Sex differences: Developmental and evolutionary strategies.* Orlando, FL: Academic Press.

Mehlenbeck, R. S., Farmer, A. S., & Ward, W. L. (2014). Obesity in children and adolescents. In L. Grossman & S. Walfish (Eds.), *Translating psychological research into practice.* New York: Springer Publishing Co.

Mehta, C. M., & Strough, J. (2009). Sex segregation in friendships and normative contexts across the life span. *Developmental Review, 29*, 201–220.

Meinzen-Derr, J., Wiley, S., Grether, S., et al. (2014). Functional communication of children who are deaf or hard-of-hearing. *Journal of Developmental and Behavioral Pediatrics, 35*, 197–206.

Meisinger, E., Blake, J., Lease, A., Palardy, G., & Olejnik, S. (2007). Variant and invariant predictors of perceived popularity across majority-Black and majority-White classrooms. *Journal of School Psychology, 45*, 21–44.

Meldrum, R. C., Miller, H. V., & Flexon, J. L. (2013). Susceptibility to peer influence, self-control, and delinquency. *Sociological Inquiry, 83*, 106–129.

Meltzoff, A. (2002). Elements of a developmental theory of imitation. In A. Meltzoff & W. Prinz (Eds.), *The imitative mind: Development, evolution, and brain bases* (pp. 19–41). New York: Cambridge University Press.

Meltzoff, A., & Moore, M. (2002). Imitation, memory, and the representation of persons. *Infant Behavior & Development, 25*, 39–61.

Meltzoff, A. N., & Moore, M. K. (1977). Imitation of facial and manual gestures by human neonates. *Science, 198*, 75–78.

Meltzoff, A. N., & Moore, M. K. (1999). Persons and representation: Why infant imitation is important for theories of human development. In J. Nadel & G. Butterworth (Eds.), *Imitation in infancy. Cambridge studies in cognitive perceptual development.* New York: Cambridge University Press.

Meltzoff, A. N., Waismeyer, A., & Gopnik, A. (2012). Learning about causes from people: Observational causal learning in 24-month-old infants. *Developmental Psychology.* Retrieved July 18, 2012, from http://www.alisongopnik.com/Papers_Alison/Observational%20Causal%20Learning.pdf.

Melzer, D., Hurst, A., & Frayling, T. (2007). Genetic variation and human aging: Progress and prospects. *The Journals of Gerontology: Series A: Biological Sciences and Medical Sciences, 62*, 301–307.

Menacker F., & Hamilton, B. E. (2010). Recent trends in cesarean delivery in the United States. *NCHS Data Brief, 35*, 1–8.

Mendle, J., Turkheimer, E., & Emery, R. (2007, June). Detrimental psychological outcomes associated with early pubertal timing in adolescent girls. *Developmental Review, 27*(2), 151–171.

Mendonça, B., Sargent, B., & Fetters, L. (2016). Cross-cultural validity of standardized motor development screening and assessment tools: A systematic review. *Developmental Medicine & Child Neurology, 58*, 1213–1222.

Mendoza, C. (2006, September). Inside today's classrooms: Teacher voices on No Child Left Behind and the education of gifted children. *Roeper Review, 29*, 28–31.

Mendoza, M. M., Dmitrieva, J., Perreira, K. M., Hurwich-Reiss, E., & Watamura, S. E. (2017). The effects of economic and sociocultural stressors on the well-being of children of Latino immigrants living in poverty. *Cultural Diversity and Ethnic Minority Psychology, 23*, 15–26.

Mennella, J. A., & Beauchamp, G. K. (1996). The human infants' response to vanilla flavors in mother's milk and formula. *Infant Behavior & Development, 19,* 13–19.

Mensah, F. K., Bayer, J. K., Wake, M., Carlin, J. B., Allen, N. B., & Patton, G. C. (2013). Early puberty and childhood social and behavioral adjustment. *Journal of Adolescent Health, 53,* 118–124.

Mercado, E. (2009). Cognitive plasticity and cortical modules. *Current Directions in Psychological Science, 18,* 153–158.

Mercer, J. R. (1973). *Labeling the mentally retarded.* Berkeley: University of California Press.

Merlo, L., Bowman, M., & Barnett, D. (2007). Parental nurturance promotes reading acquisition in low socioeconomic status children. *Early Education and Development, 18,* 51–69.

Merritt, A., LaQuea, R., Cromwell, R., & Ferguson, C. J. (2016). Media managing mood: A look at the possible effects of violent media on affect. *Child & Youth Care Forum, 45,* 241–258.

Meruelo, A. D., Castro, N., Cota, C. I., & Tapert, S. F. (2017). Cannabis and alcohol use, and the developing brain. *Behavioural Brain Research, 325*(Part A), 44–50.

Mervis, J. (2004, June 11). Meager evaluations make it hard to find out what works. *Science, 304,* 1583.

Mervis, J. (2011a, 19 August). Past successes shape effort to expand early intervention. *Science, 333,* 952–956.

Mervis, J. (2011b, 19 August). Giving children a head start is possible—but it's not easy. *Science, 333,* 956–957.

Mesinas, M., & Perez, W. (2016). Cultural involvement, indigenous identity, and language: An exploratory study of Zapotec adolescents and their parents. *Hispanic Journal of Behavioral Sciences, 38,* 482–506.

Mesman, J., van Ijzendoorn, M., Behrens, K., et al. (2016). Is the ideal mother a sensitive mother? Beliefs about early childhood parenting in mothers across the globe. *International Journal of Behavioral Development, 40,* 385–397.

Messinger, D. S., Mattson, W. I., Mahoor, M. H., & Cohn, J. F. (2012). The eyes have it: Making positive expressions more positive and negative expressions more negative. *Emotion, 12*(3), 430–436.

Miao, X., & Wang, W. (2003). A century of Chinese developmental psychology. International Journal of Psychology, 38, 258–273.

Michael, R. T., Gagnon, J. H., Laumann, E. O., & Kolata, G. (1994). *Sex in America: A definitive survey.* Boston: Little, Brown.

Mickelson, K. D., Biehle, S. N., Chong, A., & Gordon, A. (2017). Perceived stigma of postpartum depression symptoms in low-risk first-time parents: Gender differences in a dual-pathway model. *Sex Roles, 76,* 306–318.

Miesnik, S., & Reale, B. (2007). A review of issues surrounding medically elective cesarean delivery. *Journal of Obstetric, Gynecologic, & Neonatal Nursing: Clinical Scholarship for the Care of Women, Childbearing Families, & Newborns, 36,* 605–615.

Mikulovic, J., Marcellini, A., Compte, R., et al. (2011). Prevalence of overweight in adolescents with intellectual deficiency. Differences in socio-educative context, physical activity and dietary habits. *Appetite, 56,* 403–407.

Miles, R., Cowan, F., Glover, V., Stevenson, J., & Modi, N. (2006). A controlled trial of skin-to-skin contact in extremely preterm infants. *Early Human Development, 2*(7), 447–455.

Millei, Z., & Gallagher, J. (2012). Opening spaces for dialogue and re-envisioning children's bathroom in a preschool: Practitioner research with children on a sensitive and neglected area of concern. *International Journal of Early Childhood, 44,* 9–29.

Miller, B. G., Kors, S., & Macfie, J. (2017). No differences? Meta-analytic comparisons of psychological adjustment in children of gay fathers and heterosexual parents. *Psychology of Sexual Orientation and Gender Diversity, 4,* 14–22.

Miller, E., Das, M., Tancredi, D. J., et al. (2014). Evaluation of a gender-based violence prevention program for student athletes in Mumbai, India. *Journal of Interpersonal Violence, 29*(4), 758–778.

Miller, E. M. (1998). Evidence from opposite-sex twins for the effects of prenatal sex hormones. In L. Ellis & L. Ebertz (Eds.), *Males, females, and behavior: Toward biological understanding.* Westport, CT: Praeger Publishers/Greenwood Publishing Group.

Miller, J. L., & Eimas, P. D. (1995). Speech perception: From signal to word. *Annual Review of Psychology, 46,* 467–492.

Miller, S. A. (2012). *Theory of mind: Beyond the preschool years.* New York: Psychology Press.

Miltenberger, R. G. (2016). *Behavior modification: Principles and procedures* (6th ed.) Boston: Cengage Learning.

Minagawa-Kawai, Y., van der Lely, H., Ramus, F., Sato, Y., Mazuka, R., & Dupoux, E. (2011). Optical brain imaging reveals general auditory and language-specific processing in early infant development. *Cerebral Cortex, 21,* 254–261.

Ministry of Women and Child development Government of India. (2007). Study on Child Abuse: India 2007. India, [Last cited on 2014 Aug 09]. Available from: wcd.nic.in/childabuse.pdf.

Mireault, G. C., Crockenberg, S. C., Sparrow, J. E., Pettinato, C. A., Woodard, K. C., & Malzac, K. (2014). Social looking, social referencing and humor perception in 6- and 12-month-old infants. *Infant Behavior & Development, 37,* 536–545.

Mirzabagi, E., Deepak, N.N., Koski, A., Tripathi, V. (2013). Uterotonic use during childbirth in Uttar Pradesh: accounts from community members and health providers. *Midwifery 29,* 902–910.

Mishna, F., Saini, M., & Solomon, S. (2009). Ongoing and online: Children and youth's perceptions of cyber bullying. *Children and Youth Services Review, 31,* 1222–1228.

Mishra, C., & Padhee, B. N. (1987). A Piagetian study on schooling and conservation in developmental context. *Social Science International, 3,* 40–51.

Mishra, R.C. (2014). Piagetian studies of cognitive development in India, *Psychological Studies,* DOI 10.1007/s12646-014-0237-y.

Mishra, R.C. (2014). Piagetian studies of cognitive development in India, *Psychological Studies,* DOI 10.1007/s12646-014-0237-y.

Misra, A., Shah, P., Goel, K., Hazra, D.K., Gupta, R., Seth, P., et al. (2011). The high burden of obesity and abdominal obesity in urban Indian schoolchildren: A multicentric study of 38,296 children. *Annals of Nutrition and Metabolism,* 58:203-11; accessed from doi:10.1159/000329431.

Misri, S. (2007). Suffering in silence: The burden of perinatal depression. *The Canadian Journal of Psychiatry/La Revue Canadienne de Psychiatrie, 52,* 477–478.

Mistry, J., & Saraswathi, T. (2003). The cultural context of child development. In R. Lerner & M. Easterbrooks (Eds.), *Handbook of psychology: Developmental psychology* (Vol. 6, pp. 267–291). New York: John Wiley & Sons, Inc.

Mitchell, B., Carleton, B., Smith, A., Prosser, R., Brownell, M., & Kozyrskyj, A. (2008). Trends in psychostimulant and antidepressant use by children in 2 Canadian provinces. *The Canadian Journal of Psychiatry/La Revue canadienne de psychiatrie, 53,* 152–159.

Mitchell, K. J., Finkelhor, D., Wolak, J., Ybarra, M. L., & Turner, H. (2011b). Youth Internet victimization in a broader victimization context. *Journal of Adolescent Health, 48,* 128–134.

Mitchell, K. J., & Porteous, D. J. (2011a). Rethinking the genetic architecture of schizophrenia. *Psychological Medicine: A Journal of Research in Psychiatry and the Allied Sciences, 41*, 19–32.

Mitchell, K. J., Ybarra, M. L., & Korchmaros, J. D. (2014). Sexual harassment among adolescents of different sexual orientations and gender identities. *Child Abuse & Neglect, 38*, 280–295.

Mitchell, S. (2002). *American generations: Who they are, how they live, what they think.* Ithaca, NY: New Strategists Publications.

Mittal, C., & Babu, N. (2017). Explicating bullying in early adolescence. *Indian Journal of Psychology and Education, 7*(1), 53-63.

Mittal, V., Ellman, L., & Cannon, T. (2008). Gene-environment interaction and covariation in schizophrenia: The role of obstetric complications. *Schizophrenia Bulletin, 34*, 1083–1094.

Mizuno, K., & Ueda, A. (2004). Antenatal olfactory learning influences infant feeding. *Early Human Development, 76*, 83–90.

MMWR. (2008, August 1). Trends in HIV- and STD-Related risk behaviors among high school students—United States, 1991–2007. *Morbidity and Mortality Weekly Report, 57*, 817–822.

Mohanty, A. K., & Das, S. P. (1987). Cognitive and metalinguistic ability of unschooled bilingual and unilingual tribal children. *Psychological Studies, 32*, 5–8.

Moher, M., Tuerk, A. S., & Feigenson, L. (2012). Seven-month-old infants chunk items in memory. *Journal of Experimental Child Psychology.* Retrieved July 17, 2012, from http://www.ncbi.nlm.nih.gov/pubmed/22575845.

Mok, A., & Morris, M. W. (2012). Managing two cultural identities: The malleability of bicultural identity integration as a function of induced global or local processing. *Personality and Social Psychology Bulletin, 38*, 233–246.

Mol, S. E., & Bus, A. G. (2011). To read or not to read: A meta-analysis of print exposure from infancy to early adulthood. *Psychological Bulletin, 137*, 267–296.

Moldin, S. O., & Gottesman, I. I. (1997). Genes, experience, and chance in schizophrenia—positioning for the 21st century. *Schizophrenia Bulletin, 23*, 547–561.

Mølgaard-Nielsen, D., Pasternak, B., & Hviid, A. (2013). Use of oral fluconazole during pregnancy and the risk of birth defects. *The New England Journal of Medicine, 369*, 830–839.

Molina, J. C., Spear, N. E., Spear, L. P., Mennella, J. A., & Lewis, M. J. (2007). The International Society for Developmental Psychobiology 39th annual meeting symposium: Alcohol and development: Beyond fetal alcohol syndrome. *Developmental Psychobiology, 49*, 227–242.

Monahan, C. I., Beeber, L. S., & Harden, B. (2012). Finding family strengths in the midst of adversity: Using risk and resilience models to promote mental health. In S. Summers, R. Chazan-Cohen (Eds.), *Understanding early childhood mental health: A practical guide for professionals.* Baltimore: Paul H Brookes Publishing.

Monahan, K., Steinberg, L., & Cauffman, E. (2009). Affiliation with antisocial peers, susceptibility to peer influence, and antisocial behavior during the transition to adulthood. *Developmental Psychology, 45*, 1520–1530.

Monastra, V. (2008). The etiology of ADHD: A neurological perspective. *Unlocking the potential of patients with ADHD: A model for clinical practice.* Washington, DC: American Psychological Association.

Monks, C. P., & Coyne, I. (2011). *Bullying in different contexts.* New York: Cambridge University Press.

Montague, D., & Walker-Andrews, A. (2002). Mothers, fathers, and infants: The role of person familiarity and parental involvement in infants' perception of emotion expressions. *Child Development, 73*, 1339–1352.

Montirosso, R., Borgatti, R., Trojan, S., Zanini, R., & Tronick, E. (2010). A comparison of dyadic interactions and coping with still-face in healthy pre-term and full-term infants. *British Journal of Developmental Psychology, 28*(2), 347–368.

Morgenthaler, T., Owens, J., Alessi, C., et al. (2006, October). Practice parameters for behavioral treatment of bedtime problems and night wakings in infants and young children. *Sleep: Journal of Sleep and Sleep Disorders Research, 29*(10), 1277–1281.

Moon, C. (2002). Learning in early infancy. *Advances in Neonatal Care, 2*, 81–83.

Moore, K. L. (1974). *Before we are born: Basic embryology and birth defects.* Philadelphia: Saunders.

Moore, K. L., & Persaud, T. V. N. (2003). *Before we were born* (6th ed., p. 36). Philadelphia, PA: Saunders.

Moore, L., Gao, D., & Bradlee, M. (2003). Does early physical activity predict body fat change throughout childhood? *Preventive Medicine: An International Journal Devoted to Practice & Theory, 37*, 10–17.

Moore, M. C. & de Costa, C. M. (2006). *Pregnancy and parenting after thirty-five: Mid life, new life.* Baltimore, MD: Johns Hopkins University Press.

Moores, D., & Meadow-Orlans, K. (1990). *Educational and developmental aspects of deafness.* Washington, DC: Gallaudet University Press.

Morales, J. R., & Guerra, N. F. (2006). Effects of multiple context and cumulative stress on urban children's adjustment in elementary school. *Child Development, 77*, 907–923.

Moran, K. C. (2006). The global expansion of children's television: A case study of the adaptation of *Sesame Street* in Spain. *Learning, Media & Technology, 31*, 287–300.

Morrison, F. J., Bachman, H. J., & Connor, C. M. (2005) *Improving literacy in America: Guidelines from research.* New Haven, CT: Yale University Press.

Morrison, F. J., Smith, L., & Dow-Ehrensberger, M. (1995). Education and cognitive development: A natural experiment. *Developmental Psychology, 31*, 789–799.

Morrison, K. M., Shin, S., Tarnopolsky, M., & Taylor, V. H. (2015). Association of depression & health related quality of life with body composition in children and youth with obesity. *Journal of Affective Disorders, 172*, 18–23.

Morrongiello, B., & Hogg, K. (2004). Mothers' reactions to children misbehaving in ways that can lead to injury: Implications for gender differences in children's risk taking and injuries. *Sex Roles, 50*, 103–118.

Morrongiello, B., Corbett, M., & Bellissimo, A. (2008). 'Do as I say, not as I do': Family influences on children's safety and risk behaviors. *Health Psychology, 27*, 498–503.

Morrongiello, B., Klemencic, N., & Corbett, M. (2008). Interactions between child behavior patterns and parent supervision: Implications for children's risk of unintentional injury. *Child Development, 79*, 627–638.

Morrongiello, B., Zdzieborski, D., Sandomierski, M., & Lasenby-Lessard, J. (2009). Video messaging: What works to persuade mothers to supervise young children more closely in order to reduce injury risk? *Social Science & Medicine, 68*, 1030–1037.

Mottl-Santiago, J., Walker, C., Ewan, J., Vragovic, O., Winder, S., & Stubblefield, P. (2008). A hospital-based doula program and childbirth outcomes in an urban, multicultural setting. *Maternal and Child Health Journal, 12*, 372–377.

Moyle, J., Fox, A., Arthur, M., Bynevelt, M., & Burnett, J. (2007). Meta-analysis of neuropsychological symptoms of adolescents and adults with PKU. *Neuropsychology Review, 17*, 91–101.

Mrazek, A. J., Harada, T., & Chiao, J. Y. (2015). Cultural neuroscience of identity development. In K. C. McLean & M. Syed (Eds.), *The Oxford handbook of identity development*. New York, NY: Oxford University Press.

Mruk, J. (2013). Defining self-esteem as a relationship between competence and worthiness: How a two-factor approach integrates the cognitive and affective dimensions of self-esteem. *Polish Psychological Bulletin, 44*, 88–100.

Muenchow, S., & Marsland, K. (2007). Beyond baby steps: Promoting the growth and development of U.S. child-care policy. *Child development and social policy: Knowledge for action*. Washington, DC: American Psychological Association.

Muhonen, H., Rasku-Puttonen, H., Pakarinen, E., Poikkeus, A., & Lerkkanen, M. (2016). Scaffolding through dialogic teaching in early school classrooms. *Teaching and Teacher Education, 55*, 143–154.

Muller, R. T. (2013). Not just a phase: Depression in preschoolers. Recognizing the signs and reducing the risk. *Psychology Today*. Retrieved February 27, 2014, from http://www.psychologytoday.com/blog/talking-about-trauma/201306/not-just-phase-depression-in-preschoolers.

Müller, U., Liebermann-Finestone, D. P., Carpendale, J. M., Hammond, S. I., & Bibok, M. B. (2011). Knowing minds, controlling actions: The developmental relations between theory of mind and executive function from 2 to 4 years of age. *Journal of Experimental Child Psychology, 111*, 331–348.

Müller, U., Ten Eycke, K., & Baker, L. (2015). Piaget's theory of intelligence. In S. Goldstein, D. Princiotta, & J. A. Naglieri (Eds.), *Handbook of intelligence: Evolutionary theory, historical perspective, and current concepts*. New York: Springer Science + Business Media.

Mulvaney, M., & Mebert, C. (2007, September). Parental corporal punishment predicts behavior problems in early childhood. *Journal of Family Psychology, 21*(3), 389–397.

Mundy, B., & Wofsy, M. (2017). Diverse couple and family forms and universal family processes. In S. Kelly (Ed.), *Diversity in couple and family therapy: Ethnicities, sexualities, and socioeconomics*. Santa Barbara, CA: Praeger/ABC-CLIO.

Munniksma, A., Scheepers, P., Stark, T. H., & Tolsma, J. (2017). The impact of adolescents' classroom and neighborhood ethnic diversity on same- and cross-ethnic friendships within classrooms. *Journal of Research on Adolescence, 27*, 20–33.

Munro, B. A., Weyandt, L. L., Marraccini, M. E., & Oster, D. R. (2017). The relationship between nonmedical use of prescription stimulants, executive functioning and academic outcomes. *Addictive Behaviors, 65*, 250–257.

Munsey, C. (2012, February). Anti-bullying efforts ramp up. *Monitor on Psychology*, pp. 54–57.

Munzar, P., Cami, J., & Farré, M. (2003). Mechanisms of drug addiction. *New England Journal of Medicine, 349*, 2365–2365.

Murphy, B., & Eisenberg, N. (2002). An integrative examination of peer conflict: Children's reported goals, emotions, and behaviors. *Social Development, 11*, 534–557.

Murphy, F. A., Lipp, A., & Powles, D. L. (2012, March 14). Follow-up for improving psychological well-being for women after a miscarriage. *Cochrane Database System Reviews, 3*.

Murphy, J. (2014). The social and educational outcomes of homeschooling. *Sociological Spectrum, 34*(3), 244–272.

Murphy, M. (2009). Language and literacy in individuals with Turner syndrome. *Topics in Language Disorders, 29*, 187–194.

Murphy, M., & Mazzocco, M. (2008). Mathematics learning disabilities in girls with fragile X or Turner syndrome during late elementary school. *Journal of Learning Disabilities, 41*, 29–46.

Murphy, M., & Polivka, B. (2007). Parental perceptions of the schools' role in addressing childhood obesity. *The Journal of School Nursing, 23*, 40–6.

Murray, K. E. (2011). Sleep in infants—Sleeping through the night. *Journal of Developmental and Behavioral Pediatrics, 32*, 175–176.

Murray, L., Cooper, P., Creswell, C., Schofield, E., & Sack, C. (2007, January). The effects of maternal social phobia on mother–infant interactions and infant social responsiveness. *Journal of Child Psychology and Psychiatry, 48*, 45–52.

Murray, L., de Rosnay, M., Pearson, J., et al. (2008). Intergenerational transmission of social anxiety: The role of social referencing processes in infancy. *Child Development, 79*, 1049–1064.

Murray-Close, D., Ostrov, J., & Crick, N. (2007, December). A short-term longitudinal study of growth of relational aggression during middle childhood: Associations with gender, friendship intimacy, and internalizing problems. *Development and Psychopathology, 19*, 187–203.

Music, G. (2011). *Nurturing natures: Attachment and children's emotional, sociocultural and brain development*. New York: Psychology Press.

Mychasiuk, R., & Metz, G. S. (2016). Epigenetic and gene expression changes in the adolescent brain: What have we learned from animal models? *Neuroscience and Biobehavioral Reviews, 70*, 189–197.

Myers, R. H. (2004). Huntington's disease genetics. *NeuroRx, 1*, 255–262.

Myklebust, B. M., & Gottlieb, G. L. (1993). Development of the stretch reflex in the newborn: Reciprocal excitation and reflex irradiation. *Child Development, 64*, 1036–1045.

Nagabhushan, P. (2011). Review of 'Asian American parenting and parent-adolescent relationships.' *Journal of Youth and Adolescence, 40*, 245–247.

Nagahashi, S. (2013). Meaning making by preschool children during pretend play and construction of play space. *Japanese Journal of Developmental Psychology, 24*, 88–98.

Nagy, D. (2011). *The practice of qualitative research*. New York: Oxford University Press.

Nagy, E. (2006). From imitation to conversation: The first dialogues with human neonates. *Infant and Child Development, 15*, 223–232.

Nair, M.K.C., Paul, M., & Padmamohan, J. K. (2003). Scholastic performance of adolescents. *Indian Journal of Pediatrics, 70*: 629-631.

Nair, M.K., Paul, M.K., & John, S. (2004). Prevalence of depression among adolescents. *Indian Journal of Pediatrics*. 71: 523-524.

Nakato, E., Otsuka, Y., Kanazawa, S., Yamaguchi, M. K., & Kakigi, R. (2011). Distinct differences in the pattern of hemodynamic response to happy and angry facial expressions in infants—A near-infrared spectroscopic study. *NeuroImage, 54*, 1600–1606.

Nanda, S., & Konnur, N. (2006, October). Adolescent drug & alcohol use in the 21st century. *Psychiatric Annals, 36*, 706–712.

Nangle, D. W., & Erdley, C. A. (Eds.). (2001). *The role of friendship in psychological adjustment*. San Francisco: Jossey-Bass.

Nanthamongkolchai, S., Munsawaengsub, C., & Nanthamongkolchai, C. (2011). Comparison of the health status of children aged between 6 and 12 years reared by grandparents and parents. *Asia-Pacific Journal of Public Health, 23*(5), 766–773.

Narang, S., & Clarke, J. (2014). Abusive head trauma: Past, present, and future. *Journal of Child Neurology, 29*, 1747–1756.

Nash, A., Pine, K., & Messer, D. (2009). Television alcohol advertising: Do children really mean what they say? *British Journal of Developmental Psychology, 27*, 85–104.

Nassif, A., & Gunter, B. (2008). Gender representation in television advertisements in Britain and Saudi Arabia. *Sex Roles, 58*, 752–760.

Nation, M., & Heflinger, C. (2006). Risk factors for serious alcohol and drug use: The role of psychosocial variables in predicting the frequency of substance use among adolescents. *American Journal of Drug and Alcohol Abuse, 32*, 415–433.

National Association for Sport and Physical Education (2006). *Recess for elementary school students*. [Position paper]. Reston, VA: Author.

National Association for the Education of Young Children. (2005). Position statements of the NAEYC. Retrieved August 6, 2017, from http://www.naeyc.org/positionstatements.

National Assessment of Educational Progress (2017). Retrieved May 5, 2017, from https://www.nationsreportcard.gov/reading_math_2015/files/infographic_2015_reading.pdf.

National Center for Children in Poverty (2013). *Poverty and the Achievement Gap*. New York: National Center for Children in Poverty, Columbia University, Mailman School of Public Health.

National Center for Education Statistics. (2002). *Dropout rates in the United States: 2000*. Washington, DC: NCES.

National Center for Education Statistics. (2012). *The condition of education 2011* (NCES 2011-033), Indicator 23.

National Center for Education Statistics (2013). *The condition of education 2012*. Washington, DC: National Center for Education Statistics.

National Center for Education Statistics (2016). *Student reports of bullying: Results from the 2015 School Crime Supplement to the National Crime Victimization Survey (2016)*. Washington, DC: National Center for Education Statistics.

National Center for Health Statistics. (2000). *Health United States, 2000 with adolescent health chartbook*. Hyattsville, MD.

National Center for Missing and Exploited Children. (2017). Retrieved April 28, 2017, from http://www.missingkids.com/publications/ProtectingYourKidsOnline.

National Council of Applied Economic Research (2001). Concurrent Evaluation of ICDS – National Report.

National Council of Educational Research and Training (2003). A study of process and effectiveness of linkages between ECCE and primary education in the context of SSA.

National Council of Educational Research and Training (2000). Early childhood care and education in DPEP –I. an assessment. Mimeo. New Delhi.

National Council of Educational Research and Training (1996). Process based intervention for primary level mathematics – a longitudinal study.

National Council of Educational Research and Training (1993). Impact of ECE on retention in primary grades—a longitudinal study.

National Crime Records Bureau, Ministry of Home Affairs (2016). Crime in India 2016: Statistics. Accessed from http://ncrb.gov.in/StatPublications/CII/CII2016/pdfs/Crime%20Statistics%20-%202016.pdf

National Institute of Public Cooperation and Child Development (1987). An evaluation of non-formal pre-school education component in Mangolpuri ICDS Block. *Technical Bulletin*. No 1.

National Institute of Public Cooperation and Child Development (2003). An evaluation study of creches run under National Creche Fund.

National Institute of Public Cooperation and Child Development (1995). Creche services in India – an evaluation.

National Institute of Public Cooperation and Child Development (1992). National evaluation of ICDS. New Delhi.

National Institute of Public Cooperation and Child Development (1999). National evaluation of the scheme of early childhood care and education.

National Institute of Public Cooperation and Child Development (1985). Pre-school education in ICDS: an impact study.

National Kids Count. (2013). 2013 *Data book: State trends in child well-being*. New York: Annie E. Casey Foundation.

National Longitudinal Study on Adolescent Health (2000). *Teenage Stress*. Chapel Hill, NC: Carolina Population Center.

National Safety Council. (2013). *Accident facts: 2013 edition*. Chicago: National Safety Council.

Nauta, M.M. (2010). The development, evolution, and status of Holland's theory of vocational personalities: Reflections and future directions for counseling psychology. *Journal of Counseling Psychology, 57*, 11–22.

Nazzi, T., & Bertoncini, J. (2003). Before and after the vocabulary spurt: Two modes of word acquisition? *Developmental Science, 6*, 136–142.

NCB (National Children's Bureau) Now. (2011, February 8.) *ABA's anti-bullying tools for schools*. London: England.

NCERT. (2005). National Curriculum Framework 2005. New Delhi: National Council of Educational Research and Training.

Needleman, H. L., Riess, J. A., Tobin, M. J., Biesecker, G. E., & Greenhouse, J. B. (1996, February 7). Bone lead levels and delinquent behavior. *Journal of the American Medical Association, 2755*, 363–369.

Negy, C., Shreve, T., & Jensen, B. (2003). Ethnic identity, self-esteem, and ethnocentrism: A study of social identity versus multicultural theory of development. *Cultural Diversity & Ethnic Minority Psychology, 9*, 333–344.

Neisser, U. (2004). Memory development: New questions and old. *Developmental Review, 24*, 154–158.

Nelson, C. A., & Bosquet, M. (2000). Neurobiology of fetal and infant development: Implications for infant mental health. In C. H. Zeanah Jr. (Ed.), *Handbook of infant mental health* (2nd ed.). New York: Guilford Press.

Nelson, D. A., Hart, C. H., Yang, C., Olsen, J. A., & Jin, S. (2006). Aversive parenting in China: Associations with child physical and relational aggression. *Child Development, 77*, 554–572.

Nelson, E. L., Campbell, J. M., & Michel, G. F. (2013). Early handedness in infancy predicts language ability in toddlers. *Developmental Psychology*. Retrieved February 13, 2014, from http://www.ncbi.nlm.nih.gov/pubmed/23855258.

Nelson, F., & Mann, T. (2011). Opportunities in public policy to support infant and early childhood mental health: The role of psychologists and policymakers. *American Psychologist, 66*, 129–139.

Nelson, K. (1996). *Language in cognitive development: Emergence of the mediated mind*. New York: Cambridge University Press.

Nelson, L. J. (2013). Going it alone: Comparing subtypes of withdrawal on indices of adjustment and maladjustment in emerging adulthood. *Social Development, 22*, 522–538.

Nelson, P., Adamson, L., & Bakeman, R. (2008). Toddlers' joint engagement experience facilitates preschoolers' acquisition of theory of mind. *Developmental Science, 11*, 847–859.

Nesheim, S., Henderson, S., Lindsay, M., et al. (2004). *Prenatal HIV testing and antiretroviral prophylaxis at an urban hospital—Atlanta, Georgia, 1997–2000*. Atlanta, GA: Centers for Disease Control.

Newland, L. A. (2014). Supportive family contexts: Promoting child well-being and resilience. *Early Child Development and Care, 184*(9–10), 1336–1346.

Ng, F., Pomerantz, E., & Lam, S. (2007, September). European American and Chinese parents' responses to children's success and failure: Implications for children's responses. *Developmental Psychology, 43*(5), 1239–1255.

NICHD Early Child Care Research Network. (2001b). Child-care and family predictors of preschool attachment and stability from infancy. *Development psychology, 37,* 847–862.

NICHD Early Child Care Research Network. (2003). Does quality of child care affect child outcomes at age 4? *Developmental Psychology, 39,* 451–469.

NICHD Early Child Care Research Network. (2003a). Does quality of child care affect child outcomes at age 4 1/2? *Developmental Psychology, 39,* 451–469.

NICHD Early Child Care Research Network. (2003b). Families matter—even for kids in child care. *Journal of Developmental and Behavioral Pediatrics, 24,* 58–62.

NICHD Early Child Care Research Network. (2005). *Child care and child development: Results from the NICHD study of early child care and youth development.* New York: Guilford Press.

NICHD Early Child Care Research Network. (2006a). *Child care and child development: Results from the NICHD study of early child care and youth development.* New York: Guilford Press.

NICHD Early Child Care Research Network. (2006b). *The NICHD Study of Early Child Care and Youth Development (SEC-CYD): Findings for children up to age 4 1/2 years.* (Figure 5, p. 20). Washington, DC: National Institute of Child Health and Human Development.

National Institute of Child Health and Human Development Early Child Care Research Network and Duncan, G. J. (2003), Modeling the Impacts of Child Care Quality on Children's Preschool Cognitive Development. Child Development, 74: 1454–1475.

Nicholson, J. M., D'Esposito, F., Lucas, N., & Westrupp, E. M. (2014). Raising children in single-parent families. In A. Abela & J. Walker (Eds.), *Contemporary issues in family studies: Global perspectives on partnerships, parenting and support in a changing world.* New York: Wiley-Blackwell.

Nicholson, L. M., & Browning, C. R. (2012). Racial and ethnic disparities in obesity during the transition to adulthood: The contingent and nonlinear impact of neighborhood disadvantage. *Journal of Youth and Adolescence, 41,* 53–66.

Nicklas, T. A., Goh, E., Goodell, L., et al. (2011). Impact of commercials on food preferences of low-income, minority preschoolers. *Journal of Nutrition Education and Behavior, 43,* 35–41.

Niederhofer, H. (2004). A longitudinal study: Some preliminary results of association of prenatal maternal stress and fetal movements, temperament factors in early childhood and behavior at age 2 years. *Psychological Reports, 95,* 767–770.

Nieto, S. (2005). Public education in the twentieth century and beyond: high hopes, broken promises, and an uncertain future. *Harvard Educational Review, 75,* 43–65.

Nigg, J. T. (2001). Is ADHD a disinhibitory disorder? *Psychological Bulletin, 127,* 571–598.

Nihart, M. A. (1993). Growth and development of the brain. *Journal of Child and Adolescent Psychiatric and Mental Health Nursing, 6,* 39–40.

Nikolas, M., Klump, K. L., & Burt, S. (2012). Youth appraisals of inter-parental conflict and genetic and environmental contributions to attention-deficit hyperactivity disorder: Examination of GxE effects in a twin sample. *Journal of Abnormal Child Psychology, 40,* 543–554.

NIPCID (2009). *Research on ICDS: An Overview.* Vol 2, NIPCID: New Delhi.

Nisbett, R. (1994, October 31). Blue genes. *New Republic, 211,* 15.

Nisbett, R. E., Aronson, J., Blair, C., et al. (2012). Intelligence: New findings and theoretical developments. *American Psychologist, 67,* 130–159.

Njoroge, W. M., Elenbaas, L. M., Myaing, M. T., Garrison, M. M., & Christakis, D. A. (2016). What are young children watching? Disparities in concordant TV viewing. *Howard Journal of Communications, 27,* 203–217.

Noakes, M. A., & Rinaldi, C. M. (2006). Age and gender differences in peer conflict. *Journal of Youth and Adolescence, 35,* 881–891.

Noble, Y., & Boyd, R. (2012). Neonatal assessments for the preterm infant up to 4 months corrected age: A systematic review. *Developmental Medicine & Child Neurology, 54,* 129–139.

Nockels, R., & Oakeshott, P. (1999). Awareness among young women of sexually transmitted chlamydia infection. *Family Practice, 16,* 94.

Noel, A., & Newman, J. (2008). Mothers' plans for children during the kindergarten hold-out year. *Early Child Development and Care, 178*(3), 289–303.

Noll, J. G., Reader, J. M., & Bensman, H. (2017). Environments recreated: The unique struggles of children born to abused mothers. In D. M. Teti (Ed.), *Parenting and family processes in child maltreatment and intervention.* Cham, Switzerland: Springer International Publishing.

Noonan, D. (2003, September 22). When safety is the name of the game. *Newsweek,* 64–66.

Norton, A., & D'Ambrosio, B. (2008). ZPC and ZPD: Zones of teaching and learning. *Journal for Research in Mathematics Education, 39,* 220–246.

Nosarti, C., Reichenberg, A., Murray, R. M., et al. (2012). Preterm birth and psychiatric disorders in young adult life preterm birth and psychiatric disorders. *Archives of General Psychiatry, 155,* 610–617.

Notaro, P., Gelman, S., & Zimmerman, M. (2002). Biases in reasoning about the consequences of psychogenic bodily reactions: Domain boundaries in cognitive development. *Merrill-Palmer Quarterly, 48,* 427–449.

Nugent, J. K., Lester, B. M., & Brazelton, T. B. (Eds.). (1989). *The cultural context of infancy, Vol. 1: Biology, culture, and infant development.* Norwood, NJ: Ablex.

Nyaradi, A., Li, J., Hickling, S., Foster, J., & Oddy, W. H. (2013). The role of nutrition in children's neurocognitive development, from pregnancy through childhood. *Frontiers in Human Neuroscience.* Retrieved February 18, 2014, from http://www.ncbi.nlm.nih.gov/pubmed/23532379.

Nygaard, E., Slinning, K., Moe, V., & Walhovd, K. B. (2017). Cognitive function of youths born to mothers with opioid and poly-substance abuse problems during pregnancy. *Child Neuropsychology, 23,* 159–187.

Nyiti, R. M. (1982). The validity of "culture differences explanations" for cross-cultural variation in the rate of Piagetian cognitive development. In D. Wagner & H. Stevenson (Eds.), *Cultural perspectives on child development.* New York: Freeman.

Nylen, K., Moran, T., Franklin, C., & O'Hara, M. (2006). Maternal depression: A review of relevant treatment approaches for mothers and infants. *Infant Mental Health Journal, 27,* 327–343.

Oakes, L. M., & Kovack-Lesh, K. A. (2013). Infants' visual recognition memory for a series of categorically related items. *Journal of Cognition and Development, 14,* 63–86.

Oberlander, S., Black, M., & Starr, R. (2007, March). African American adolescent mothers and grandmothers: A multigenerational approach to parenting. *American Journal of Community Psychology, 39*(1), 37–46.

O'Connor, M., & Whaley, S. (2006). Health care provider advice and risk factors associated with alcohol consumption following pregnancy recognition. *Journal of Studies on Alcohol, 67*, 22–31.

O'Connor, T. M., Cerin, E., Hughes, S. O., et al. (2013). What Hispanic parents do to encourage and discourage 3–5 year old children to be active: A qualitative study using nominal group technique. *The International Journal of Behavioral Nutrition and Physical Activity, 10.*

O'Doherty, K. (2014). Review of Telling genes: The story of genetic counseling in America. *Journal of the History of the Behavioral Sciences, 50*, 115–117.

O'Grady, W., & Aitchison, J. (2005). *How children learn language.* New York: Cambridge University Press.

O'Neil, J. M., & Denke, R. (2016). An empirical review of gender role conflict research: New conceptual models and research paradigms. In Y. J. Wong & S. R. Wester (Eds.), *APA handbook of men and masculinities.* Washington, DC: American Psychological Association.

OECD. (2014). *PISA 2012 results in focus: What 15-year-olds know and what they can do with what they know.* Paris: Organization for Economic Co-operation and Development (OECD).

OECD (2016.) *PISA 2015 results (Volume I): Excellence and equity in education, PISA,* Paris: OECD Publishing.

Ogbu, J. (1992). Understanding cultural diversity and learning. *Educational Researcher, 21*, 5–14.

Ogden, C. L., Carroll, M. D., Fryar, C. D., & Flegal, K. M. (2015). Prevalence of obesity among adults and youth: United States, 2011–2014. NCHS data brief, no 219. Hyattsville, MD: National Center for Health Statistics.

Ogden, C. L., Kuczmarski, R. J., Flegal, K. M., et al. (2002). Centers for Disease Control and Prevention 2000 growth charts for the United States: Improvements to the 1977 National Center for Health Statistics Version. *Pediatrics, 109*, 45–60.

Ogden, C. L., Carroll, M. D., Lawman, H. G., Fryar, C. D., Kruszon-Moran, D., Kit, B. K., & Flegal, K. M. (2016). Trends in obesity prevalence among children and adolescents in the United States, 1988–1994 through 2013–2014. *JAMA: Journal Of The American Medical Association, 315*, 2292–2299.

Ogilvy-Stuart, A. L., & Gleeson, H. (2004). Cancer risk following growth hormone use in childhood: Implications for current practice. *Drug Safety, 27*, 369–382.

Ohta, H., & Ohgi, S. (2013). Review of 'The Neonatal Behavioral Assessment Scale.' *Brain & Development, 35*, 79–80.

Okie, S. (2005). *Winning the war against childhood obesity.* Washington, DC: Joseph Henry Publications.

Olivardia, R., & Pope, H. (2002). Body image disturbance in childhood and adolescence. In D. Castle & K. Phillips (Eds.), *Disorders of body image.* Petersfield, England: Wrightson Biomedical Publishing.

Oliver, B., & Plomin, R. (2007). Twins' Early Development Study (TEDS): A multivariate, longitudinal genetic investigation of language, cognition and behavior problems from childhood through adolescence. *Twin Research and Human Genetics, 10*, 96–105.

Olness, K. (2003). Effects on brain development leading to cognitive impairment: A worldwide epidemic. *Journal of Developmental & Behavioral Pediatrics, 24*, 120–130.

Olson, E. (2006, April 27). You're in labor, and getting sleeeepy. *New York Times,* p. C2.

Olson, S. L., Lopez-Duran, N., Lunkenheimer, E. S., Chang, H., & Sameroff, A. J. (2011). Individual differences in the development of early peer aggression: Integrating contributions of self-regulation, theory of mind, and parenting. *Development and Psychopathology, 23*, 253–266.

Olszewski-Kubilius, P., & Thomson, D. (2013). Gifted education programs and procedures. In W. M. Reynolds, G. E. Miller, & I. B. Weiner (Eds.), *Handbook of psychology, Vol. 7: Educational psychology* (2nd ed.). Hoboken, NJ: John Wiley & Sons Inc.

Oostermeijer, M., Boonen, A. H., & Jolles, J. (2014). The relation between children's constructive play activities, spatial ability, and mathematical word problem-solving performance: A mediation analysis in sixth-grade students. *Frontiers in Psychology, 5.* Retrieved March 20, 2015, from http://journal.frontiersin.org/article/10.3389/fpsyg.2014.00782/abstract.

Opfer, J. E., & Siegler, R. S. (2007). Representational change and children's numerical estimation. *Cognitive Psychology, 55*, 169–195.

Organization for Economic Cooperation and Development (OECD). (2015). *International infant mortality rates.* Paris: OECD.

Ornaghi, V., Pepe, A., & Grazzani, I. (2016). False-belief understanding and language ability mediate the relationship between emotion comprehension and prosocial orientation in preschoolers. *Frontiers in Psychology, 7*, 212–222.

Ortega, S., Beauchemin, A., & Kaniskan, R. (2008, December). Building resiliency in families with young children exposed to violence: The safe start initiative pilot study. *Best Practices in Mental Health: An International Journal, 4*(1), 48–64.

Oretti, R. G., Harris, B., & Lazarus, J. H. (2003). Is there an association between life events, postnatal depression and thyroid dysfunction in thyroid antibody positive women? *International Journal of Social Psychiatry, 49*, 70–76.

Orth, U. (2017). The family environment in early childhood has a long-term effect on self-esteem: A longitudinal study from birth to age 27 years. *Journal of Personality and Social Psychology.* Retrieved March 17, 2017, from https://www.ncbi.nlm.nih.gov/pubmed/28182449.

Ortiz, S. O., & Dynda, A. M. (2005). Use of intelligence tests with culturally and linguistically diverse populations. In D. P. Flanagan & P. L. Harrison (Eds.), *Contemporary intellectual assessment: Theories, tests, and issues.* New York, Guilford Press.

Osanloo, A. F., Reed, C., & Schwartz, J. P. (2017). *Creating and negotiating collaborative spaces for socially-just anti-bullying interventions for K-12 schools.* Charlotte, NC: Information Age Publishing.

Osofsky, J. (2003). Prevalence of children's exposure to domestic violence and child maltreatment: Implications for prevention and intervention. *Clinical Child & Family Psychology Review, 6*, 161–170.

Otgaar, H., Howe, M. L., & Muris, P. (2017). Maltreatment increases spontaneous false memories but decreases suggestion-induced false memories in children. *British Journal of Developmental Psychology.* Retrieved March 12, 2017, from http://onlinelibrary.wiley.com/doi/10.1111/bjdp.12177/abstract.

Otsuka, Y., Hill, H. H., Kanazawa, S., Yamaguchi, M. K., & Spehar, B. (2012). Perception of Mooney faces by young infants: The role of local feature visibility, contrast polarity, and motion. *Journal of Experimental Child Psychology, 111*, 164–179.

Otsuka, Y., Ichikawa, H., Kanazawa, S., Yamaguchi, M. K., & Spehar, B. (2014). Temporal dynamics of spatial frequency processing in infants. *Journal of Experimental Psychology: Human Perception and Performance, 40*, 995–1008.

Oyserman, D., Kemmelmeier, M., Fryberg, S., Brosh, H., & Hart-Johnson, T. (2003). Racial ethnic self-schemas. *Social Psychology Quarterly, 66*, 333–347.

Ozawa, M., Kanda, K., Hirata, M., Kusakawa, I., & Suzuki, C. (2011). Influence of repeated painful procedures on prefrontal cortical pain responses in newborns. *Acta Paediatrica, 100*, 198–203.

Ozawa, M., & Yoon, H. (2003). Economic impact of marital disruption on children. *Children & Youth Services Review, 25*, 611–632.

Paciello, M., Fida, R., Tramontano, C., Cole, E., & Cerniglia, L. (2013). Moral dilemma in adolescence: The role of values, prosocial moral reasoning and moral disengagement in helping decision making. *European Journal of Developmental Psychology, 10*, 190–205.

Pagel, J. F. (2000). Nightmares and disorders of dreaming. *American Family Physician, 61*, 2037–2042, 2044.

Pahlke, E., & Hyde, J. S. (2016). The debate over single-sex schooling. *Child Development Perspectives, 10*, 81–86.

Paisley, T. S., Joy, E. A., & Price, R. J., Jr. (2003). Exercise during pregnancy: A practical approach. *Current Sports Medicine Reports, 2*, 325–330.

Pajkrt, E., Weisz, B., Firth, H. V., & Chitty, L. S. (2004). Fetal cardiac anomalies and genetic syndromes. *Prenatal Diagnosis, 24*, 1104–1115.

Palermo, L., Geberhiwot, T., MacDonald, A., Limback, E., Hall, S. K., & Romani, C. (2017). Cognitive outcomes in early-treated adults with phenylketonuria (PKU): A comprehensive picture across domains. *Neuropsychology, 31*(3), 255–267.

Palmer, S., Fais, L., Golinkoff, R., & Werker, J. F. (2012). Perceptual narrowing of linguistic sign occurs in the 1st year of life. *Child Development, 83*, 543–553.

Paludi, M. A. (2012). *The psychology of love (Vols. 1–4)*. Santa Barbara, CA: Praeger/ABC-CLIO.

Pandey, S. (2011). Cognitive functioning in children: The role of child abuse, setting and gender. *Journal of the Indian Academy of Applied Psychology, 37*, 98–105.

Paolella, F. (2013). La pedagogia di Loris Malaguzzi. Per una storia del Reggio Emiliaapproach. *Rivista Sperimentale Di Freniatria: La Rivista Della Salute Mentale, 137*, 95–112.

Papousek, H., & Papousek, M. (1991). Innate and cultural guidance of infants' integrative competencies: China, the United States, and Germany. In M. H. Borstein (Ed.), *Cultural approaches to parenting*. Hillsdale, NJ: Erlbaum.

Paquette, D., Carbonneau, R., & Dubeau, D. (2003). Prevalence of father–child rough-and-tumble play and physical aggression in preschool children. *European Journal of Psychology of Education, 18*, 171–189.

Parazzini, F., Cipriani, S., Bianchi, S., Bulfoni, C., Bortolus, R., & Somigliana, E. (2016). Risk of monozygotic twins after assisted reproduction: A population-based approach. *Twin Research and Human Genetics, 19*, 72–76.

Park, A. (2008, June 23). Living large. *Time*, pp. 90–92.

Park, C. L., Riley, K. E., & Snyder, L. B. (2012). Meaning making coping, making sense, and post-traumatic growth following the 9/11 terrorist attacks. *The Journal of Positive Psychology, 7*, 198–207.

Park, K. A., Lay, K., & Ramsay, L. (1993). Individual differences and developmental changes in preschoolers' friendships. *Developmental Psychology, 29*, 264–270.

Park, S., Holloway, S. D., Arendtsz, A., Bempechat, J., & Li, J. (2012). What makes students engaged in learning? A time-use study of within- and between-individual predictors of emotional engagement in low-performing high schools. *Journal of Youth and Adolescence, 41*, 390–401.

Parke, R. D. (2007). Fathers, families, and the future: A plethora of plausible predictions. In G. W. Ladd (Ed.), *Appraising the human developmental sciences: Essays in honor of Merrill-Palmer Quarterly*. Detroit, MI: Wayne State University Press.

Parke, R., Simpkins, S., & McDowell, D. (2002). Relative contributions of families and peers to children's social development. In P. Smith & C. Hart (Eds.), *Blackwell handbook of childhood social development*. Malden, MA: Blackwell Publishers.

Parke, R. D. (2004). Development in the family. *Annual Review of Psychology, 55*, 365–399.

Parker, J., Wales, G., Chalhoub, N., & Harpin, V. (2013). The long-term outcomes of interventions for the management of attention-deficit hyperactivity disorder in children and adolescents: A systematic review of randomized controlled trials. *Psychology Research and Behavior Management, 6*, 87–99.

Parker, S. T. (2005). Piaget's legacy in cognitive constructivism, niche construction, and phenotype development and evolution. In S. T. Parker & J. Langer (Eds.), *Biology and knowledge revisited: From neurogenesis to psychogenesis*. Mahwah, NJ: Lawrence Erlbaum Associates.

Parsons, A., & Howe, N. (2013). 'This is Spiderman's mask.' 'No, it's Green Goblin's': Shared meanings during boys' pretend play with superhero and generic toys. *Journal of Research in Childhood Education, 27*, 190–207.

Parsons, C. E., Young, K. S., Elmholdt, E. J., Stein, A., & Kringelbach, M. L. (2017). Interpreting infant emotional expressions: Parenthood has differential effects on men and women. *The Quarterly Journal of Experimental Psychology, 70*, 554–564.

Parten, M. B. (1932). Social participation among preschool children. *Journal of Abnormal and Social Psychology, 27*, 243–269.

Pascalis, O., de Haan, M., & Nelson, C. A. (2002). Is face processing species-specific during the first year of life? *Science, 296*, 1321–1323.

Paterno, M. T., McElroy, K., & Regan, M. (2016). Electronic fetal monitoring and cesarean birth: A scoping review. *Birth: Issues in Perinatal Care, 43*(4), 277–284.

Pathman, T., Larkina, M., Burch, M. M., & Bauer, P. J. (2013). Young children's memory for the times of personal past events. *Journal of Cognition and Development, 14*, 120–140.

Patterson, C. (2003). Children of lesbian and gay parents. In L. Garnets & D. Kimmel (Eds.), *Psychological perspectives on lesbian, gay, and bisexual experiences* (2nd ed.). New York: Columbia University Press.

Patterson, C. J. (1995). Families of the baby boom: Parents' division of labor and children's adjustment [Special issue: Sexual orientation and human development]. *Developmental Psychology, 31*, 115–123.

Patterson, C. J. (2002). Lesbian and gay parenthood. In M. Bornstein (Ed.), *Handbook of parenting*. Mahwah, NJ: Erlbaum.

Patterson, C. J. (2007). *Handbook of counseling and psychotherapy with lesbian, gay, bisexual, and transgender clients*. (2nd ed.). K. J. Bieschke, R. M. Perez, & K. A. DeBord (Eds.). Washington, DC: American Psychological Association.

Patterson, C. (2009). Children of lesbian and gay parents: Psychology, law, and policy. *American Psychologist, 64*, 727–736.

Patterson, C. J. (2013). Children of lesbian and gay parents: Psychology, law, and policy. *Psychology of Sexual Orientation and Gender Diversity, 1*(S), 27–34.

Patton, G. C., Coffey, C., Carlin, J. B., et al. (2011). Overweight and obesity between adolescence and young adulthood: A

10-year prospective cohort study. *Journal of Adolescent Health, 48*, 275–280.

Paulesu, E., Démonet, J. F., Fazio, F., et al. (2001, March 16). Dyslexia: Cultural diversity and biological unity. *Science, 291*, 2165–2167.

Pauli-Pott, U., Mertesacker, B., & Bade, U. (2003). Parental perceptions and infant temperament development. *Infant Behavior & Development, 26*, 27–48.

Paulus, M. (2016). Friendship trumps neediness: The impact of social relations and others' wealth on preschool children's sharing. *Journal of Experimental Child Psychology, 146*, 106–120.

Pavlov, I. P. (1927). *Conditioned reflexes*. London: Oxford University Press.

Pawluski, J. L., Lonstein, J. S., & Fleming, A. S. (2017). The neurobiology of postpartum anxiety and depression. *Trends in Neurosciences, 40*(2), 106–120.

Payá-González, B., López-Gil, J., Noval-Aldaco, E., & Ruiz-Torres, M. (2015). Gender and first psychotic episodes in adolescence. In M. Sáenz-Herrero (Ed.), *Psychopathology in women: Incorporating gender perspective into descriptive psychopathology*. Cham, Switzerland: Springer International Publishing.

Peach, H. D., & Gaultney, J. F. (2013). Sleep, impulse control, and sensation-seeking predict delinquent behavior in adolescents, emerging adults, and adults. *Journal of Adolescent Health, 53*, 293–299.

Pearson, B. Z. (2007). Social factors in childhood bilingualism in the United States. *Applied Psycholinguistics, 28*, 399–410.

Pearson, J., & Wilkinson, L. (2013). Adolescent sexual experiences. In A. K. Baumle, A. K. Baumle (Eds.), *International handbook on the demography of sexuality*. New York: Springer Science + Business Media.

Pearson, R. M., Lightman, S. L., & Evans, J. J. (2011). The impact of breastfeeding on mothers' attentional sensitivity towards infant distress. *Infant Behavior & Development, 34*, 200–205.

Peck, S. (2003). Measuring sensitivity moment-by-moment: A microanalytic look at the transmission of attachment. *Attachment & Human Development, 5*, 38–63.

Pederson, D. R., Bailey, H. N., Tarabulsy, G. M., Bento, S., & Moran, G. (2014). Understanding sensitivity: Lessons learned from the legacy of Mary Ainsworth. *Attachment & Human Development, 16*, 261–270.

Pedersen, S., Vitaro, F., Barker, E. D., & Borge, A. I. H. (2007). The timing of middle-childhood peer rejection and friendship: Linking early behavior to early-adolescent adjustment. *Child Development, 78*, 1037–1051.

Pejovic, J., & Molnar, M. (2017). The development of spontaneous sound-shape matching in monolingual and bilingual infants during the first year. *Developmental Psychology, 53*, 581–586.

Pelaez, M., Virues-Ortega, J., & Gewirtz, J. L. (2012). Acquisition of social referencing via discrimination training in infants. *Journal of Applied Behavior Analysis, 45*, 23–36.

Pelham, W. J., Fabiano, G. A., Waxmonsky, J. G., et al. (2016). Treatment sequencing for childhood ADHD: A multiple-randomization study of adaptive medication and behavioral interventions. *Journal of Clinical Child and Adolescent Psychology, 45*, 396–415.

Pellegrini, Anthony D. (2009). *The role of play in human development*. New York: Oxford University Press.

Pelligrini, A. D., & Smith, P. K. (1998). Physical activity play: The nature and function of a neglected aspect of play. *Child Development, 69*, 577–598.

Pellis, S. M., & Burghardt, G. M. (2017). Play and exploration. In J. Call, G. M. Burghardt, I. M. Pepperberg, et al. (Eds.), *APA handbook of comparative psychology: Basic concepts, methods, neural substrate, and behavior*. Washington, DC: American Psychological Association.

Pellis, S. M., & Pellis, V. C. (2007). Rough-and-tumble play and the development of the social brain. *Current Directions in Psychological Science, 16*, 95–98.

Peltonen, L., & McKusick, V. A. (2001, February 16). Dissecting the human disease in the postgenomic era. *Science, 291*, 1224–1229.

Peltzer, K., & Pengpid, S. (2006). Sexuality of 16- to 17-year-old South Africans in the context of HIV/AIDS. *Social Behavior and Personality, 34*, 239–256.

Penido, A., de Souza Rezende, G., Abreu, R., et al. (2012). Malnutrition during central nervous system growth and development impairs permanently the subcortical auditory pathway. *Nutritional Neuroscience, 15*, 31–36.

Pennisi, E. (2000, May 19). And the gene number is…? *Science, 288*, 1146–1147.

Penuel, W. R., Bates, L., Gallagher, L. P., et al. (2012). Supplementing literacy instruction with a media-rich intervention: Results of a randomized controlled trial. *Early Childhood Research Quarterly, 27*, 115–127.

Peralta, O., Salsa, A., del Rosario Maita, M., & Mareovich, F. (2013). Scaffolding young children's understanding of symbolic objects. *Early Years: An International Journal of Research and Development, 33*(3), 266–274.

Perez-Brena, N. J., Updegraff, K. A., & Umaña-Taylor, A. J. (2012). Father- and mother-adolescent decision-making in Mexican-origin families. *Journal of Youth and Adolescence, 41*, 460–473.

Perlmann, J., & Waters, M. (Eds.). (2002). *The new race question: How the census counts multiracial individuals*. New York: Russell Sage Foundation.

Perlmann, R. Y., & Gleason, J. B. (1990, July). *Patterns of prohibition in mothers' speech to children*. Paper presented at the Fifth International Congress for the Study of Child Language, Budapest, Hungary.

Perrine, N. E., & Aloise-Young, P. A. (2004). The role of self-monitoring in adolescents' susceptibility to passive peer pressure. *Personality & Individual Differences, 37*, 1701–1716.

Perreira, K. M., & Ornelas, I. J. (2011, Spring). The physical and psychological well-being of immigrant children. *The Future of Children, 21*, 195–218.

Persson, A., & Musher-Eizenman, D. R. (2003). The impact of a prejudice-prevention television program on young children's ideas about race. *Early Childhood Research Quarterly, 18*, 530–546.

Persson, G. E. B. (2005). Developmental perspectives on prosocial and aggressive motives in preschoolers' peer interactions. *International Journal of Behavioral Development, 29*, 80–91.

Petanjek, Z., Judas, M., Kostovic, I., & Uylings, H. B. M. (2008). Lifespan alterations of basal dendritic trees of pyramidal neurons in the human prefrontal cortex: A layer-specific pattern. *Cerebral Cortex, 18*, 915–929.

Peter, C. J., Fischer, L. K., Kundakovic, M., et al. (2016). DNA methylation signatures of early childhood malnutrition associated with impairments in attention and cognition. *Biological Psychiatry, 80*, 765–774.

Petersen, A. (2000). A longitudinal investigation of adolescents' changing perceptions of pubertal timing. *Developmental Psychology, 36*, 37–43.

Peterson, C. (2014). Theory of mind understanding and empathic behavior in children with autism spectrum disorders. *International Journal of Developmental Neuroscience, 39*, 16–21.

Peterson, C., Wang, Q., & Hou, Y. (2009). 'When I was little': Childhood recollections in Chinese and European Canadian grade school children. *Child Development, 80,* 506–518.

Peterson, D. M., Marcia, J. E., & Carpendale, J. I. (2004). Identity: Does thinking make it so? In C. Lightfood, C. Lalonde, & M. Chandler (Eds.), *Changing conceptions of psychological life.* Mahwah, NJ: Lawrence Erlbaum Associates.

Peterson, L. (1994). Child injury and abuse-neglect: Common etiologies, challenges, and courses toward prevention. *Current Directions in Psychological Science, 3,* 116–120.

Peterson, R. A., & Brown, S. P. (2005). On the use of beta coefficients in meta-analysis. *Journal of Applied Psychology, 90,* 175–181.

Petrakis, P.E., & Stamatakis, D. (2002). Growth and educational levels: a comparative analysis. *Economics of Education Review, 21* (5), 513–521.

Petrashek, A. R., & Friedman, O. (2011). The signature of inhibition in theory of mind: Children's predictions of behavior based on avoidance desire. *Psychonomic Bulletin & Review, 18,* 199–203.

Petrou, S. (2006). Preterm birth—What are the relevant economic issues? *Early Human Development, 82*(2), 75–76.

Pettit, G. S., Bates, J. E., & Dodge, K. A. (1997). Supportive parenting, ecological context, and children's adjustment: A seven-year longitudinal study. *Child Development, 68,* 908–923.

Pettit, G., & Dodge, K. A. (2003). Violent children: Bridging development, intervention, and public policy. *Developmental Psychology, Special Issues: Violent Children, 39,* 187–188.

Phelan, P., Yu, H. C., & Davidson, A. L. (1994). Navigating the psychosocial pressures of adolescence: The voices and experiences of high school youth. *American Educational Research Journal, 31,* 415–447.

Philippot, P., & Feldman, R. S. (Eds.). (2005). *The regulation of emotion.* Mahwah, NJ: Lawrence Erlbaum Associates.

Phillips, D., Gormley, W., & Anderson, S. (2016). The effects of Tulsa's CAP Head Start program on middle-school academic outcomes and progress. *Developmental Psychology, 52*(8), 1247–1261.

Phillips-Silver, J., & Trainor, L. J. (2005, June 3). Feeling the beat: Movement influences infant rhythm perception. *Science, 308,* 1430.

Phinney, J. S. (2008). Ethnic identity exploration in emerging adulthood. In D. L. Browning (Ed.), *Adolescent identities: A collection of readings.* New York: The Analytic Press/Taylor & Francis Group.

Phinney, J. S., Ferguson, D. L., & Tate, J. D. (1997). Intergroup attitudes among ethnic minority adolescents: A causal model. *Child Development, 68,* 955–969.

Phinney, J. S. (2005). Ethnic identity in late modern times: A response to Rattansi and Phoenix. *Identity, 5,* 187–194.

Piaget, J. (1932). *The moral judgment of the child.* New York: Harcourt, Brace & World.

Piaget, J. (1952). *The origins of intelligence in children.* New York: International Universities Press.

Piaget, J. (1954). *The construction of reality in the child* (Margaret Cook, Trans.). New York: Basic Books.

Piaget, J. (1962). *Play, dreams and imitation in childhood.* New York: Norton.

Piaget, J. (1983). Piaget's theory. In W. Kessen (Ed.), P. H. Mussen (Series Ed.), *Handbook of child psychology: Vol. 1. History, theory, and methods* (pp. 103–128). New York: Wiley.

Piaget, J., & Inhelder, B. (1958). *The growth of logical thinking from childhood to adolescence* (A. Parsons & S. Seagrin, Trans.). New York: Basic Books.

Piaget, J., Inhelder, B., & Szeminska, A. (1960). *The child's conception of geometry.* New York: Basic Books. (Original work published 1948).

Pianta, R. C., Barnett, W. S., Burchinal, M., & Thornburg, K. R. (2009, August). The effects of preschool education: What we know, how public policy is or is not aligned with the evidence base, and what we need to know. *Psychological Science in the Public Interest, 10,* 49–88.

Picard, A. (2008, February 14). Health study: Tobacco will soon claim one million lives a year. *The Globe and Mail,* p. A15.

Pickles, A., Hill, J., Breen, G., et al. (2013). Evidence for interplay between genes and parenting on infant temperament in the first year of life: Monoamine oxidase a polymorphism moderates effects of maternal sensitivity on infant anger proneness. *Journal of Child Psychology and Psychiatry, 54,* 1308–1317.

Piekarski, D. J., Johnson, C. M., Boivin, J. R., et al. (2017). Does puberty mark a transition in sensitive periods for plasticity in the associative neocortex? *Brain Research, 1654*(Part B), 123–144.

Pine, K., Wilson, P., & Nash, A. (2007, December). The relationship between television advertising, children's viewing and their requests to Father Christmas. *Journal of Developmental & Behavioral Pediatrics, 28*(6), 456–461.

Ping, R., & Goldin-Meadow, S. (2008). Hands in the air: Using ungrounded iconic gestures to teach children conservation of quantity. *Developmental Psychology, 44,* 1277–1287.

Pinker, S. (1994). *The language instinct.* New York: William Morrow.

Pinker, S. (2005). So how does the mind work? *Mind & Language, 20,* 1–24.

Pinquart, M. M. (2013). Body image of children and adolescents with chronic illness: A meta-analytic comparison with healthy peers. *Body Image, 10,* 141–148.

Pintney, R., Forlands, F., & Freedman, H. (1937). Personality and attitudinal similarity among classmates. *Journal of Applied Psychology, 21,* 48–55.

Pisinger, C., & Dossing, M. (2014). A systematic review of health effects of electronic cigarettes. *Preventive Medicine, 69,* 248–260.

Pittman, L., & Boswell, M. (2007). The role of grandmothers in the lives of preschoolers growing up in urban poverty. *Applied Developmental Science, 11*(1), 20–42.

Planalp, E. M., Van Hulle, C., Lemery-Chalfant, K., & Goldsmith, H. H. (2016). Genetic and environmental contributions to the development of positive affect in infancy. Retrieved March 9, 2017, from https://www.ncbi.nlm.nih.gov/pubmed/27797564.

Planinsec, J. (2001). A comparative analysis of the relations between the motor dimensions and cognitive ability of preschool girls and boys. *Kinesiology, 33,* 56–68.

Planning commission (2014) http://planningcommission.nic.in/reports/sereport/index.php?repts=serep

Plante, E., Schmithorst, V., Holland, S., & Byars, A. (2006). Sex differences in the activation of language cortex during childhood. *Neuropsychologia, 44,* 1210–1221.

Plebanek, D. J., & Sloutsky, V. M. (In press). Costs of selective attention: When children notice what adults miss. *Psychological Science.*

Plomin, R. (1994b). Nature, nurture, and social development. *Social Development, 3,* 37–53.

Plomin, R. (2005). Finding genes in child psychology and psychiatry: When are we going to be there? *Journal of Child Psychology and Psychiatry, 46,* 1030–1038.

Plomin, R., DeFries, J. C., Knopik, V. S., & Neiderhiser, J. M. (2016). Top 10 replicated findings from behavioral genetics. *Perspectives on Psychological Science, 11*, 3–23.

Plomin, R., & Rutter, M. (1998). Child development, molecular genetics, and what to do with genes once they are found. *Child Development, 69*, 1223–1242.

Plowfield, L. A. (2007). HIV disease in children 25 years later. *Pediatric Nursing, 33*, 274–8, 273.

Polivka, B. (2006, January). Needs assessment and intervention strategies to reduce lead-poisoning risk among low-income Ohio toddlers. *Public Health Nursing, 23*, 52–58.

Polkinghorne, D. E. (2005). Language and meaning: Data collection in qualitative research. *Journal of Counseling Psychology, 52* [Special issue: Knowledge in context: Qualitative methods in counseling psychology research], 137–145.

Pölkki, T., Korhonen, A., Axelin, A., Saarela, T., & Laukkala, H. (2015). Development and preliminary validation of the Neonatal Infant Acute Pain Assessment Scale (NIAPAS). *International Journal of Nursing Studies, 51*, 1585–1594.

Pollack, W., Shuster, T., & Trelease, J. (2001). *Real boys' voices.* Penguin.

Pollak, S., Holt, L., & Wismer Fries, A. (2004). Hemispheric asymmetries in children's perception of nonlinguistic human affective sounds. *Developmental Science, 7*, 10–18.

Pollard-Durodola, S. D., Cárdenas-Hagan, E., & Tong, F. (2014). Implications of bilingualism for reading assessment. In A. B. Clinton (Ed.), *Assessing bilingual children in context: An integrated approach.* Washington, DC: American Psychological Association.

Polman, H., de Castro, B., & van Aken, M. (2008). Experimental study of the differential effects of playing versus watching violent video games on children's aggressive behavior. *Aggressive Behavior, 34*, 256–264.

Pomares, C. G., Schirrer, J., & Abadie, V. (2002). Analysis of the olfactory capacity of healthy children before language acquisition. *Journal of Developmental Behavior and Pediatrics, 23*, 203–207.

Pomerantz, E. M., Qin, L., Wang, Q., & Chen, H. (2011). Changes in early adolescents' sense of responsibility to their parents in the United States and China: Implications for their academic functioning. *Child Development, 82*, 1136–1151.

Pompili, M., Innamorati, M., Girardi, P., Tatarelli, R., & Lester, D. (2011). Evidence-based interventions for preventing suicide in youths. In M. Pompili & R. Tatarelli (Eds.), *Evidence-based practice in suicidology: A source book.* Cambridge, MA: Hogrefe.

Pompili, M., Masocco, M., Vichi, M., et al. (2009). Suicide among Italian adolescents: 1970–2002. *European Child & Adolescent Psychiatry, 18*, 525–533.

Ponton, L. E. (2001). *The sex lives of teenagers: Revealing the secret world of adolescent boys and girls.* New York: Penguin Putnam.

Poole, D. A., & Lamb, M. E. (1998). *Investigative interviews of children: A guide for helping professionals.* Washington, DC: American Psychological Association.

Poorthuis, A. G., Thomaes, S., Aken, M. G., Denissen, J. A., & de Castro, B. O. (2014). Dashed hopes, dashed selves? A sociometer perspective on self-esteem change across the transition to secondary school. *Social Development, 23*, 770–783.

Porac, C. (2016). *Laterality: Exploring the enigma of left-handedness.* San Diego, CA: Elsevier Academic Press.

Porges, S. W., Lipsitt, R., & Lewis P. (1993). Neonatal responsivity to gustatory stimulation: The gustatory-vagal hypothesis. *Infant Behavior & Development, 16*, 487–494.

Porter, M., van Teijlingen, E., Yip, L., & Bhattacharya, S. (2007). Satisfaction with cesarean section: Qualitative analysis of open-ended questions in a large postal survey. *Birth: Issues in Perinatal Care, 34*, 148–154.

Posner, M. I., & Rothbart, M. K. (2007). Research on attention networks as a model for the integration of psychological science. *Annual Review of Psychology, 58*, 1–23.

Posthuma, D., & de Geus, E. (2006, August). Progress in the molecular-genetic study of intelligence. *Current Directions in Psychological Science, 15*, 151–155.

Poulin-Dubois, D., Serbin, L., & Eichstedt, J. (2002). Men don't put on make-up: Toddlers' knowledge of the gender stereotyping of household activities. *Social Development, 11*, 166–181.

Poulton, R., & Caspi, A. (2005). Commentary: How does socioeconomic disadvantage during childhood damage health in adulthood? Testing psychosocial pathways. *International Journal of Epidemiology, 23*, 51–55.

Powell, M. B., Wright, R., & Hughes-Scholes, C. H. (2011). Contrasting the perceptions of child testimony experts, prosecutors and police officers regarding individual child abuse interviews. *Psychiatry, Psychology and Law, 18*, 33–43.

Prasad, V., Brogan, E., Mulvaney, C., Grainge, M., Stanton, W., & Sayal, K. (2014). How effective are drug treatments for children with ADHD at improving on-task behaviour and academic achievement in the school classroom? A systematic review and meta-analysis. *European Child & Adolescent Psychiatry, 22*, 203–216.

Prater, L. (2002). African American families: Equal partners in general and special education. In F. Obiakor & A. Ford (Eds.), *Creating successful learning environments for African American learners with exceptionalities.* Thousand Oaks, CA: Corwin Press.

Praveen, Pradeep A., & Tandon, N. (2016). *WHO South-East Asia Journal of Public Health, 5* (1).

Preckel, F., Niepel, C., Schneider, M., & Brunner, M. (2013). Self-concept in adolescence: A longitudinal study on reciprocal effects of self-perceptions in academic and social domains. *Journal of Adolescence, 36*, 1165–1175.

Pressley, M., & Schneider, W. (1997). *Introduction to memory development during childhood and adolescence.* Mahwah, NJ: Lawrence Erlbaum.

Price, C. S., Thompson, W. W., Goodson, B., et al. (2010). Prenatal and infant exposure to thimerosal from vaccines and immunoglobulins and risk of autism. *Pediatrics, 126*, 656–664.

Priddis, L., & Howieson, N. (2009). The vicissitudes of mother-infant relationships between birth and six years. *Early Child Development and Care, 179*, 43–53.

Prieler, M., Kohlbacher, F., Hagiwara, S., & Arima, A. (2011). Gender representation of older people in Japanese television advertisements. *Sex Roles, 64*, 405–415.

PRIMEDIA/Roper National Youth Survey. (1999). *Adolescents' view of society's ills.* Storrs, CT: Roper Center for Public Opinion Research.

Prince, C. B., Young, M. B., Sappenfield, W., & Parrish, J. W. (2016). Investigating the decline of fetal and infant mortality rates in Alaska during 2010 and 2011. *Maternal and Child Health Journal.* Retrieved may 21, 2016, from http://www.ncbi.nlm.nih.gov/pubmed/26754348.

Prince, M. (2000, November 13). How technology has changed the way we have babies. *The Wall Street Journal,* pp. R4, R13.

Proctor, C., Barnett, J., & Muilenburg, J. (2012). Investigating race, gender, and access to cigarettes in an adolescent population. *American Journal of Health Behavior, 36*, 513–521.

Propper, C., & Moore, G. (2006, December). The influence of parenting on infant emotionality: A multi-level psychobiological perspective. *Developmental Review, 26*, 427–460.

Proulx, M., & Poulin, F. (2013). Stability and change in kindergartners' friendships: Examination of links with social functioning. *Social Development, 22*, 111–125.

Psacharopoulos, G. (1981). Returns to education: an updated international comparison. Comparative Education Review, 17 (3), 321–341.

Psacharopoulos, G. (1985). Returns to education: a further international update and implications. *Journal of Human Resources,* 20 (4), 583–604.

Psacharopoulos, G. & Patrinos, H.A. (2004). Returns to investment in education: a further update. *Economics of Education Review,* 12 (2), 111–134.

Psacharopoulos, G., Tan, J.P., & Jiminez, E. (1986). Financing education in developing countries: an exploration of policy options. The World Bank, Washington, DC.

Puchalski, M., & Hummel, P. (2002). The reality of neonatal pain. *Advances in Neonatal Care, 2*, 245–247.

Puckering, C., Connolly, B., Werner, C., et al. (2011). Rebuilding relationships: A pilot study of the effectiveness of the Mellow Parenting Programme for children with Reactive Attachment Disorder. *Clinical Child Psychology and Psychiatry, 16*, 73–87.

Pundir, A., Hameed, L., Dikshit, P. C., et al. (2012). Expression of medium and heavy chain neurofilaments in the developing human auditory cortex. *Brain Structure & Function, 217*, 303–321.

Puntambekar, S., & Hübscher, R. (2005). Tools for scaffolding students in a complex learning environment: What have we gained and what have we missed? *Educational Psychologist, 40*, 1–12.

Purswell, K. E., & Dillman Taylor, D. (2013). Creative use of sibling play therapy: An example of a blended family. *Journal of Creativity in Mental Health, 8*, 162–174.

Puterman, E., Prather, A. A., Epel, E. S., et al. (2016). Exercise mitigates cumulative associations between stress and BMI in girls age 10 to 19. *Health Psychology, 35*(2), 191–194.

Qadri, S., Goel, R., Singh, J., Ahluwalia, S., Pathak, R., & Bashir, H. (2013). Prevalence and pattern of substance abuse among school children in northern India: a rapid assessment study. *International Journal of Medical Science and Public Health, 2* (2), 273. Accessed from http://dx.doi.org/10.5455/ijmsph.2013.2.271-280.

Qian, Z., Zhang, D., & Wang, L. (2013). Is aggressive trait responsible for violence? Priming effects of aggressive words and violent movies. *Psychology, 4*, 96–100.

Quinn, M. (1990, January 29). Don't aim that pack at us. *Time*, 60.

Quinn, P. (2008). In defense of core competencies, quantitative change, and continuity. *Child Development, 79*, 1633–1638.

Quinn, P. C., Conforto, A., Lee, K., O'Toole, A. J., Pascalis, O., & Slater, A. M. (2010). Infant preference for individual women's faces extends to girl prototype faces. *Infant Behavior & Development, 33*, 357–360.

Quintana, S. (2007, July). Racial and ethnic identity: Developmental perspectives and research. *Journal of Counseling Psychology, 54*(3), 259–270.

Quintana, S. M., Aboud, F. E., Chao, R. K., et al. (2006). Race, ethnicity, and culture in child. *Child Development, 77*, 1129–1141.

Quintana, S. M., McKown, C., Cross, W. E., & Cross, T. B. (2008). *Handbook of race, racism, and the developing child.* S. M. Quintana & C. McKown (Eds.). Hoboken, NJ: John Wiley & Sons Inc.

Raag, T. (2003). Racism, gender identities and young children: Social relations in a multi-ethnic, inner-city primary school. *Archives of Sexual Behavior, 32*, 392–393.

Rabain-Jamin, J., & Sabeau-Jouannet, E. (1997). Maternal speech to 4-month-old infants in two cultures: Wolof and French. *International Journal of Behavioral Development, 20*, 425–451.

Rabin, R. (2006, June 13). Breast-feed or else. *The New York Times*, p. D1.

Raboteg-Saric, Z., & Sakic, M. (2013). Relations of parenting styles and friendship quality to self-esteem, life satisfaction and happiness in adolescents. *Applied Research in Quality of Life*. Retrieved January 25, 2014, from http://link.springer.com/article/10.1007%2Fs11482-013-9268-0.

Raeff, C. (2004). Within-culture complexities: Multifaceted and interrelated autonomy and connectedness characteristics in late adolescent selves. In M. E. Mascolo & J. Li (Eds.), *Culture and developing selves: Beyond dichotomization.* San Francisco, CA: Jossey-Bass.

Rahko, J. S., Vuontela, V. A., Carlson, S., et al. (2016). Attention and working memory in adolescents with autism spectrum disorder: A functional MRI study. *Child Psychiatry and Human Development, 47*, 503–517.

Rai, R., Mitchell, P., Kadar, T., & Mackenzie, L. (2016). Adolescent egocentrism and the illusion of transparency: Are adolescents as egocentric as we might think? *Current Psychology: A Journal for Diverse Perspectives on Diverse Psychological Issues, 35*, 285–294.

Raj, A., Saggurti, N., Balaiah, D., & Silverman, J.G. (2009). Prevalence of child marriage and its impact on the fertility and fertility control behaviors of young women in India. *Lancet,* 373: 9678: 1883–1889.

Rajhans, P., Jessen, S., Missana, M., & Grossmann, T. (2016). Putting the face in context: Body expressions impact facial emotion processing in human infants. *Developmental Cognitive Neuroscience, 19*, 115–121.

Rakison, D., & Oakes, L. (2003). *Early category and concept development: Making sense of the blooming, buzzing confusion.* London: Oxford University Press.

Rakison, D. H., & Krogh, L. (2012). Does causal action facilitate causal perception in infants younger than 6 months of age? *Developmental Science, 15*, 43–53.

Raman, L., & Winer, G. (2002). Children's and adults' understanding of illness: Evidence in support of a coexistence model. *Genetic, Social, & General Psychology Monographs, 128*, 325–355.

Ramaswamy, V., & Bergin, C. (2009). Do reinforcement and induction increase prosocial behavior? Results of a teacher-based intervention in preschools. *Journal of Research in Childhood Education, 23*, 527–538.

Rancourt, D., Conway, C. C., Burk, W. J., & Prinstein, M. J. (2012). Gender composition of preadolescents' friendship groups moderates peer socialization of body change behaviors. *Health Psychology*. Retrieved July 21, 2012, from http://www.ncbi.nlm.nih.gov/pubmed/22545975.

Randahl, G. J. (1991). A typological analysis of the relations between measured vocational interests and abilities. *Journal of Vocational Behavior, 38*, 333–350.

Ranganath, C., Minzenberg, M., & Ragland, J. (2008). The cognitive neuroscience of memory function and dysfunction in schizophrenia. *Biological Psychiatry, 64*, 18–25.

Rankin, B. (2004). The importance of intentional socialization among children in small groups: A conversation with Loris Malaguzzi. *Early Childhood Education Journal, 32*, 81–85.

Rankin, J., Lane, D., & Gibbons, F. (2004). Adolescent self-consciousness: Longitudinal age changes and gender differences in two cohorts. *Journal of Research on Adolescence, 14,* 1–21.

Ransjö-Arvidson, A. B., Matthiesen, A. S., Lilja, G., Nissen, E., Widström, A. M., & Unväs-Moberg. (2001). Maternal analgesia during labor disturbs newborn behavior: Effects on breastfeeding, temperature, and crying. *Birth, 28,* 5–12.

Rao, A. (2010). India and global history. *History and Technology, 26* (1), 77–84. http://dx.doi.org/10.1080/07341510903545623.

Ratanachu-Ek, S. (2003). Effects of multivitamin and folic acid supplementation in malnourished children. *Journal of the Medical Association of Thailand, 4,* 86–91.

Ray, E., & Heyes, C. (2011). Imitation in infancy: The wealth of the stimulus. *Developmental Science, 14,* 92–105.

Ray, L., Bryan, A., MacKillop, J., McGeary, J., Hesterberg, K., & Hutchison, K. (2009). The dopamine D receptor (4) gene exon III polymorphism, problematic alcohol use and novelty seeking: Direct and mediated genetic effects. *Addiction Biology, 14,* 238–244.

Raj, M., Sundaram, K.R., Paul, M., Deepa, A.S., & Kumar, R.K. (2007). Obesity in Indian children: time trends and relationship with hypertension. *The National Medical Journal of India,* 20, 288-93.

Ray, R. (2004). National survey on extent, pattern, and trends of drug abuse in India. Ministry of Social Justice and Empowerment and United Nations Office on Drug and Crime Regional Office for South Asia, [8].

Rayner, K., Foorman, B. R., Perfetti, C. A., Pesetsky, D., & Seidenberg, M. S. (2002, March). How should reading be taught? *Scientific American,* 85–91.

Razani, J., Murcia, G., Tabares, J., & Wong, J. (2007). The effects of culture on WASI test performance in ethnically diverse individuals. *Clinical Neuropsychologist, 21,* 776–788.

Ready, D., Lee, V,. & Welner, K. G. (2004). Educational equity and school structure: School size, overcrowding, and schools-within-schools. *Teachers College Record,* 106(10), 1989–2014.

Reddy, V. (1999). Prelinguistic communication. In M. Barrett (Ed.), *The development of language* (pp. 25–50). Philadelphia: Psychology Press.

Reddy V, Liebal K, Hicks K, Jonnalgadda S, et al. (2013). The emergent practice of infant compliance: An exploration of two cultures. *Developmental Psychology.* 49(9):1754–1762. [PubMed: 23231690].

Reed, R. K. (2005). *Birthing fathers: The transformation of men in American rites of birth.* New Brunswick, NJ: Rutgers University Press.

Reese, E., & Cox, A. (1999). Quality of adult book reading affects children's emergent literacy. *Developmental Psychology, 35,* 20–28.

Reese, E., & Newcombe, R. (2007). Training mothers in elaborative reminiscing enhances children's autobiographical memory and narrative. *Child Development, 78,* 1153–1170.

Reese, W. J. (2011). *From the common school to "No Child Left Behind."* Baltimore, MD: Johns Hopkins University Press.

Reichert, F., Menezes, A., Wells, J., Dumith, C., & Hallal, P. (2009). Physical activity as a predictor of adolescent body fatness: A systematic review. *Sports Medicine, 39,* 279–294.

Reid, K. J., Zeldow, M., Teplin, L. A., McClelland, G. M., Atom, K. A., & Zee, P. C. (2002). *Steep habits of juvenile detainees in the Chicago area.* Paper presented at the annual meeting of the American Academy of Neurology, Denver.

Reifman, A. (2000). Revisiting *The Bell Curve. Psycoloquy,* 11.

Reiner, W. G., & Gearhart, J. P. (2004). Discordant sexual identity in some genetic males with cloacal exstrophy assigned to female sex at birth. *The New England Journal of Medicine, 350,* 333–341.

Reio, T. J., & Ortega, C. L. (2016). Cyberbullying and its emotional consequences: What we know and what we can do. In S. Y. Tettegah & D. L. Espelage (Eds.), *Emotions, technology, and behaviors.* San Diego, CA: Elsevier Academic Press.

Reis, S., & Renzulli, J. (2004). Current research on the social and emotional development of gifted and talented students: Good news and future possibilities. *Psychology in the Schools, 41,* 119–130.

Reissland, N., & Cohen, D. (2012). *The development of emotional intelligence: A case study.* New York: Routledge/Taylor & Francis Group.

Reissland, N., & Shepherd, J. (2006, March). The effect of maternal depressed mood on infant emotional reaction in a surprise-eliciting situation. *Infant Mental Health Journal, 27,* 173–187.

Rembis, M. (2009). (Re)defining disability in the 'genetic age': Behavioral genetics, 'new' eugenics and the future of impairment. *Disability & Society, 24,* 585–597.

Ren, Y., Pritzker, S., & Leung, P. (2016). Examining children's health equity under the Chinese basic medical insurance system: A comparison between the United States and Mainland China. *International Social Work, 59,* 791–802.

Rentner, T. L., Dixon, L., & Lengel, L. (2012). Critiquing fetal alcohol syndrome health communication campaigns targeted to American Indians. *Journal of Health Communication, 17,* 6–21.

Reproductive Medicine Associates of New Jersey. (2002). *Older women and risks of pregnancy.* Princeton, NJ: American Society for Reproductive Medicine.

Resing, W. M., Bakker, M., Pronk, C. E., & Elliott, J. G. (2017). Progression paths in children's problem solving: The influence of dynamic testing, initial variability, and working memory. *Journal of Experimental Child Psychology, 153,* 83–109.

Reuters Health eLine. (2002, June 26). Baby's injuring points to danger of kids imitating television. *Reuters Health eLine.*

Reynolds, A. J., Temple, J. A., Ou, S. R., Arteaga, I. A., & White, B. A. (2011). School based early childhood education and age 28 well-being: Effects by timing, dosage, and subgroups. *Science, 333,* 360–364.

Rhule, D. (2005). Take care to do no harm: Harmful interventions for youth problem behavior. *Professional Psychology: Research and Practice, 36,* 618–625.

Ricciardelli, L., & McCabe, M. (2003). Sociocultural and individual influences on muscle gain and weight loss strategies among adolescent boys and girls. *Psychology in the Schools, 40,* 209–224.

Ricciardelli, L. A., & McCabe, M. P. (2004). A biopsychosocial model of disordered eating and the pursuit of muscularity in adolescent boys. *Psychological Bulletin, 130,* 179–205.

Rice, W. S., Goldfarb, S. S., Brisendine, A. E., Burrows, S., & Wingate, M. S. (2017). Disparities in infant mortality by race among Hispanic and non-Hispanic infants. *Maternal and Child Health Journal.*

Richards, M. H., Crowe, P. A., Larson, R., & Swarr, A. (1998). Developmental patterns and gender differences in the experience of peer companionship during adolescence. *Child Development, 69,* 154–163.

Richardson, G., Goldschmidt, L., & Willford, J. (2009). Continued effects of prenatal cocaine use: Preschool development. *Neurotoxicology and Teratology, 31,* 325–333.

Richardson, G. A., Larkby, C., Goldschmidt, L., & Day, N. L. (2013). Adolescent initiation of drug use: Effects of prenatal cocaine exposure. *Journal of the American Academy of Child & Adolescent Psychiatry, 52*, 37–46.

Richardson, H., Walker, A., & Horne, R. (2009). Maternal smoking impairs arousal patterns in sleeping infants. *Sleep: Journal of Sleep and Sleep Disorders Research, 32*, 515–521.

Richardson, K. A., Hester, A. K., & McLemore, G. L. (2016). Prenatal cannabis exposure—The 'first hit' to the endocannabinoid system. *Neurotoxicology and Teratology, 58*, 5–14.

Rick, S., & Douglas, D. (2007). Neurobiological effects of childhood abuse. *Journal of Psychosocial Nursing & Mental Health Services, 45*, 47–54.

Rinaldi, C. (2002). Social conflict abilities of children identified as sociable, aggressive, and isolated: Developmental implications for children at-risk for impaired peer relations. *Developmental Disabilities Bulletin, 30*, 77–94.

Ripple, C., & Zigler, E. (2003). Research, policy, and the federal role in prevention initiatives for children. *American Psychologist, 58*, 482–490.

Ritzen, E. M. (2003). Early puberty: What is normal and when is treatment indicated? *Hormone Research, 60*(Suppl. 3), 31–34.

Robb, M., Richert, R., & Wartella, E. (2009). Just a talking book? Word learning from watching baby videos. *British Journal of Developmental Psychology, 27*, 27–45.

Roberts, R., Roberts, C., & Duong, H. (2009). Sleepless in adolescence: Prospective data on sleep deprivation, health and functioning. *Journal of Adolescence, 32*, 1045–1057.

Roberts, R. D., & Lipnevich, A. A. (2012). From general intelligence to multiple intelligences: Meanings, models, and measures. In K. R. Harris, S. Graham, T. Urdan, S. Graham, J. M. Royer, & M. Zeidner (Eds.), *APA educational psychology handbook, Vol. 2: Individual differences and cultural and contextual factors*. Washington, DC: American Psychological Association.

Roberts, R. D., Zeidner, M., & Matthews, G. (2001). Does emotional intelligence meet traditional standards for an intelligence? Some new data and conclusions. *Emotion, 1*, 196–231.

Roberts, R. E., Roberts, C., & Xing, Y. (2011). Restricted sleep among adolescents: Prevalence, incidence, persistence, and associated factors. *Behavioral Sleep Medicine, 9*, 18–30.

Roberts, S. (2007, January 16). 51% of women are now living without spouse. *The New York Times*, p. A1.

Robertson, W. W., Thorogood, M. M., Inglis, N. N., Grainger, C. C., & Stewart-Brown, S. S. (2012). Two-year follow-up of the 'Families for Health' programme for the treatment of childhood obesity. *Child: Care, Health And Development, 38*, 229–236.

Robins, R. W., & Trzesniewski, K. H. (2005). Self-esteem development across the lifespan. *Current Directions in Psychological Science, 14*, 158–162.

Robinson, A. & Stark, D. R. (2005). *Advocates in action*. Washington, DC: National Association for the Education of Young Children.

Robinson, A. J., & Pascalis, O. (2004). Development of flexible visual recognition memory in human infants. *Developmental Science, 7*, 527–533.

Robinson, G. E. (2004, April 16). Beyond nature and nurture. *Science, 304*, 397–399.

Robinson, W. P., & Gillibrand, E. (2004, May 14). Single-sex teaching and achievement in science. *International Journal of Science Education, 26*, 659.

Rocha, N., de Campos, A., dos Santos Silva, F., & Tudella, E. (2013). Adaptive actions of young infants in the task of reaching for objects. *Developmental Psychobiology, 55*, 275–282.

Rocha-Ferreira, E., & Hristova, M. (2016). Plasticity in the neonatal brain following hypoxic-ischaemic injury. *Neural Plasticity, 2016*.

Rochat, P. (Ed.). (1999). *Early social cognition: Understanding others in the first months of life*. Mahwah, NJ: Erlbaum.

Rochat, P. (2004). Emerging co-awareness. In G. Bremner & A. Slater (Eds.), *Theories of infant development*. Malden, MA: Blackwell Publishers.

Rochat, P., Broesch, T., & Jayne, K. (2012). Social awareness and early self-recognition. *Consciousness and Cognition: An International Journal*. Retrieved July 18, 2012, from http://www.sciencedirect.com/science/article/pii/S1053810012001225.

Roche, T. (2000, November 13). The crisis of foster care. *Time*, 74–82.

Rodkey, E. N., & Riddell, R. (2013). The infancy of infant pain research: The experimental origins of infant pain denial. *Journal of Pain, 14*, 338–350.

Rodkin, P. C., & Ryan, A. M. (2012). Child and adolescent peer relations in educational context. In K. R. Harris, S. Graham, T. Urdan, S. Graham, J. M. Royer, M. Zeidner (Eds.), *APA educational psychology handbook, Vol. 2: Individual differences and cultural and contextual factors*. Washington, DC: American Psychological Association.

Rodnitzky, R. L. (2012). Upcoming treatments in Parkinson's disease, including gene therapy. *Parkinsonism & Related Disorders, 18*(Suppl. 1), S37–S40.

Roelofs, J., Meesters, C., Ter Huurne, M., Bamelis, L., & Muris, P. (2006, June). On the links between attachment style, parental rearing behaviors, and internalizing and externalizing problems in non-clinical children. *Journal of Child and Family Studies, 15*, 331–344.

Roffwarg, H. P., Muzio, J. N., & Dement, W. C. (1966). Ontogenic development of the human sleep–dream cycle. *Science, 152*, 604–619.

Rogan, J. (2007). How much curriculum change is appropriate? Defining a zone of feasible innovation. *Science Education, 91*, 439–460.

Rogers, S., & Willams, J. (2006). *Imitation and the social mind: Autism and typical development*. Guilford Press.

Rogers, S. L., & Blissett, J. (2017). Breastfeeding duration and its relation to weight gain, eating behaviours and positive maternal feeding practices in infancy. *Appetite, 108*, 399–406.

Rolls, E. (2000). Memory systems in the brain. *Annual Review of Psychology, 51*, 599–630.

Romero, S. T., Coulson, C. C., & Galvin, S. L. (2012). Cesarean delivery on maternal request: A western North Carolina perspective. *Maternal and Child Health Journal, 16*, 725–734.

Rönkä, A., & Pulkkinen, L. (1995). Accumulation of problems in social functioning in young adulthood: A developmental approach. *Journal of Personality and Social Psychology, 69*, 381–391.

Roopnarine, J. (1992). Father–child play in India. In K. MacDonald (Ed.), *Parent–child play*. Albany: State University of New York Press.

Rose, A. J. (2002). Co-rumination in the friendships of girls and boys. *Child Development, 73*, 1830–1843.

Rose, A. J., & Asher, S. R. (1999). Children's goals and strategies in response to conflicts within a friendship. *Developmental Psychology, 35*, 69–79.

Rose, C. A., Richman, D. M., Fettig, K., Hayner, A., Slavin, C., & Preast, J. L. (2016). Peer reactions to early childhood aggression in a preschool setting: Defenders, encouragers, or neutral bystander. *Developmental Neurorehabilitation, 19*, 246–254.

Rose, R. J., Viken, R. J., Dick, D. M., Bates, J. E., Pulkkinen, L., & Kaprio, J. (2003). It *does* take a village: Nonfamilial environments and children's behavior. *Psychological Science, 14,* 273–278.

Rose, S., Feldman, J., & Jankowski, J. (1999). Visual and auditory temporal processing, cross-modal transfer, and reading. *Journal of Learning Disabilities, 32,* 256–266.

Rose, S., Feldman, J., & Jankowski, J. (2009). Information processing in toddlers: Continuity from infancy and persistence of preterm deficits. *Intelligence, 37,* 311–320.

Rose, S., Jankowski, J., & Feldman, J. (2002). Speed of processing and face recognition at 7 and 12 months. *Infancy, 3,* 435–455.

Rose, S. A., & Feldman, J. F. (1997). Memory and speed: Their role in the relation of infant information processing to later IQ. *Child Development, 68,* 630–641.

Rose, S. A., Feldman, J. F., & Jankowski, J. J. (2004). Dimensions of cognition in infancy. *Intelligence, 32,* 245–262.

Rose, S. A., Feldman, J. F., Jankowski, J. J., & Van Rossem, R. (2011). The structure of memory in infants and toddlers: An SEM study with full-terms and preterms. *Developmental Science, 14,* 83–91.

Rosenberg, T. (2013). The power of talking to your baby. *The New York Times Opinionator Blog.* Retrieved February 27, 2014, from http://opinionator.blogs.nytimes.com/2013/04/10/the-power-of-talking-to-your-baby/?_php=true&_type=blogs&_r=0.

Rosenthal, R. (2002). The Pygmalion effect and its mediating mechanisms. In J. Aronson (Ed.), *Improving academic achievement: Impact of psychological factors on education.* San Diego: Academic Press.

Rosenthal, R., & Jacobson, L. (1968). *Pygmalion in the classroom: Teacher expectation and pupils' intellectual development.* New York: Holt, Rinehart & Winston.

Ross, K. R., Storfer-Isser, A., Hart, M. A., et al. (2012). Sleep-disordered breathing is associated with asthma severity in children. *The Journal of Pediatrics, 160,* 736–742.

Rossetti, A. O., Carrera, E., & Oddo, M. (2012). Early EEG correlates of neuronal injury after brain anoxia. *Neurology, 78,* 796–802.

Rossi, S., Telkemeyer, S., Wartenburger, I., & Obrig, H. (2012). Shedding light on words and sentences: Near-infrared spectroscopy in language research. *Brain and Language, 121,* 152–163.

Rote, W. M., Smetana, J. G., Campione-Barr, N., Villalobos, M., & Tasopoulos-Chan, M. (2012). Associations between observed mother–adolescent interactions and adolescent information management. *Journal of Research on Adolescence, 22,* 206–214.

Roth, M. S. (2016). Psychoanalysis and history. *Psychoanalytic Psychology, 33*(Suppl 1), S19–S33.

Rothbart, M. (2007). Temperament, development, and personality. *Current Directions in Psychological Science, 16,* 207–212.

Rothbart, M., & Derryberry, D. (2002). Temperament in children. In C. von Hofsten & L. Backman (Eds.), *Psychology at the turn of the millennium, Vol. 2: Social, developmental, and clinical perspectives.* Florence, KY: Taylor & Frances/Routledge.

Rothbaum, F., Rosen, K., & Ujiie, T. (2002). Family systems theory, attachment theory and culture. *Family Process, 41,* 328–350.

Rothbaum, F., Weisz, J., Pott, M., Miyake, K., & Morelli, G. (2000). Attachment and culture: Security in the United States and Japan. *American Psychologist, 55,* 1093–1104.

Rothenberger, A., & Rothenberger, L. (2013). Psychopharmacological treatment in children: Always keeping an eye on adherence and ethics. *European Child & Adolescent Psychiatry, 22,* 453–455.

Rotherham, A. J., & Whitmire, R. (2014, March 12). DeBlasio vs. everyone else. *Slate.* Retrieved July 11, 2014, from http://www.slate.com/articles/news_and_politics/education/2014/03/bill_de_blasio_vs_charter_schools_a_feud_in_new_york_city_has_broad_national.html.

Rotigel, J. V. (2003). Understanding the young gifted child: Guidelines for parents, families, and educators. *Early Childhood Education Journal, 30,* 209–214.

Rovee-Collier, C. (1999). The development of infant memory. *Current Directions in Psychological Science, 8,* 80–85.

Rowe, D. C. (1994). *The effects of nurture on individual natures.* New York: Guilford Press.

Rowe-Finkbeiner, K., Martin, R., Abrams, B., Zuccaro, A., & Dardari, Y. (2016). Why paid family and medical leave matters for the future of America's families, businesses and economy. *Maternal and Child Health Journal, 20*(Suppl 1), 8–12.

Rowland, C. F., & Noble, C. L. (2011). The role of syntactic structure in children's sentence comprehension: Evidence from the dative. *Language Learning and Development, 7,* 55–75.

Rowley, S., Burchinal, M., Roberts, J., & Zeisel, S. (2008). Racial identity, social context, and race-related social cognition in African Americans during middle childhood. *Developmental Psychology, 44,* 1537–1546.

Roy, A. L., & Raver, C. C. (2014). Are all risks equal? Early experiences of poverty-related risk and children's functioning. *Journal of Family Psychology, 28,* 391–400.

Ruble, D., Taylor, L., Cyphers, L., Greulich, F., Lurye, L., & Shrout, P. (2007, July). The role of gender constancy in early gender development. *Child Development, 78*(4), 1121–1136.

Ruda, M. A., Ling, Q-D., Hohmann, A. G., Peng, Y. B., & Tachibana, T. (2000, July 28). Altered nociceptive neuronal circuits after neonatal peripheral inflammation. *Science, 289,* 628–630.

Rudd, L., Cain, D., & Saxon, T. (2008). Does improving joint attention in low-quality child-care enhance language development? *Early Child Development and Care, 178*(3), 315–338.

Ruff, H. A. (1989). The infant's use of visual and haptic information in the perception and recognition of objects. *Canadian Journal of Psychology, 43,* 302–319.

Runeson, I., Martenson, E., & Enskar, K. (2007). Children's knowledge and degree of participation in decision making when undergoing a clinical diagnostic procedure. *Pediatric Nursing, 33,* 505–11.

Russell, S., & Consolacion, T. (2003). Adolescent romance and emotional health in the United States: Beyond binaries. *Journal of Clinical Child & Adolescent Psychology, 32,* 499–508.

Rust, J., Golombok, S., Hines, M., Johnston, K., & Golding, J.; ALSPAC Study Team. (2000). The role of brothers and sisters in the gender development of preschool children. *Journal of Experimental Child Psychology, 77,* 292–303.

Rutter, M. (2003). Commentary: Causal processes leading to antisocial behavior. *Developmental Psychology, 39,* 372–378.

Rutter, M. (2006). *Genes and behavior: Nature-nurture interplay explained.* New York: Blackwell.

Ruzek, E., Burchinal, M., Farkas, G., & Duncan, G. J. (2014). The quality of toddler child care and cognitive skills at 24 months: Propensity score analysis results from the ECLS-B. *Early Childhood Research Quarterly, 29,* 12–21.

Ryan, A. M., Shim, S., & Makara, K. A. (2013). Changes in academic adjustment and relational self-worth across the transition to middle school. *Journal of Youth and Adolescence, 42,* 1372–1384.

Ryan, B. P. (2001). Programmed *therapy for stuttering in children and adults* (2nd ed.). Springfield, IL: Charles C. Thomas.

Ryding, E. L., Lukasse, M., Van Parys, A., et al. (2015). Fear of childbirth and risk of cesarean delivery: A cohort study in six European countries. *Birth: Issues in Perinatal Care, 42,* 48–55.

Saarento, S., Boulton, A. J., & Salmivalli, C. (2014). Reducing bullying and victimization: Student- and classroom-level mechanisms of change. *Journal of Abnormal Child Psychology.* Retrieved January 25, 2014, from http://www.ncbi.nlm.nih.gov/pubmed/24390403.

Sabatino, C., & Mayer, L. (2011). Supporting today's blended family. In C. Franklin & R. Fong (Eds.), *The church leader's counseling resource book: A guide to mental health and social problems.* New York: Oxford University Press.

Sabbagh, M., Bowman, L., Evraire, L., & Ito, J. (2009). Neurodevelopmental correlates of theory of mind in preschool children. *Child Development, 80,* 1147–1162.

Saddichha, S., Manjunatha, N., & Khess, C.J. (2010). Clinical course of development of alcohol and opioid dependence: what are the implications in prevention?, *Indian Journal of Community Medicine, 35,* 359-61.

Sadker, D., & Sadker, M. (2005). *Teachers, schools, and society.* New York: McGraw-Hill.

Saiegh-Haddad, E. (2007). Epilinguistic and metalinguistic phonological awareness may be subject to different constraints. Evidence from Hebrew. *First Language, 27,* 385–405.

Salihu, H. M., August, E. M., de la Cruz, C., Mogos, M. F., Weldeselasse, H., & Alio, A. P. (2013). Infant mortality and the risk of small size for gestational age in the subsequent pregnancy: A retrospective cohort study. *Maternal and Child Health Journal, 17,* 1044–1051.

Salley, B., Miller, A., & Bell, M. (2013). Associations between temperament and social responsiveness in young children. *Infant and Child Development, 22,* 270–288.

Salley, B., Sheinkopf, S. J., Neal-Beevers, et al. (2016). Infants' early visual attention and social engagement as developmental precursors to joint attention. *Developmental Psychology, 52*(11), 1721–1731.

Saluja, B.S., Grover, S., Irpati, A.S., Mattoo, S.K., & Basu, D. (2007). Drug dependence in adolescents 1978–2003: A clinical-based observation from North India. *Indian Journal of Pediatrics. 74:* 455-8.

Saluja, B. S., Grover, S., Irpati, A. S., Mattoo, S.K., & Basu, D. (2007). Drug dependence in adolescents 1978–2003: A clinic-based observation from North India. *Indian Journal of Pediatrics, 74,* 455-458. [9].

Samet, J. H., DeMarini, D. M., & Malling, H. V. (2004, May 14). Do airborne particles induce heritable mutations? *Science, 304,* 971.

Sammons, M. (2009). Writing a wrong: Factors influencing the overprescription of antidepressants to youth. *Professional Psychology: Research and Practice, 40,* 327–329.

Sampson, W. A. (2016). *Chicago charter schools: The hype and the reality.* Charlotte, NC: Information Age Publishing.

Sanchez, Y. M., Lambert, S. F., & Ialongo, N. S. (2012). Life events and depressive symptoms in African American adolescents: Do ecological domains and timing of life events matter? *Journal of Youth and Adolescence, 41,* 438–448.

Sanchez-Garrido, M. A., & Tena-Sempere, M. (2013). Metabolic control of puberty: Roles of leptin and kisspeptins. *Hormones and Behavior, 64,* 187–194.

Sandall, J. (2014). The 30th International Confederation of Midwives Triennial Congress: Improving women's health globally. *Birth: Issues in Perinatal Care, 41,* 303–305.

Sandberg, D. E., & Voss, L. D. (2002). The psychosocial consequences of short stature: A review of the evidence. *Best Practice and Research Clinical Endocrinology and Metabolism, 16,* 449–463.

Sandoval, J., Frisby, Cl L., Geisinger, K. F., Scheuneman, J. D., & Grenier, J. R. (Eds.). (1998). *Test interpretation and diversity: Achieving equity in assessment.* Washington, DC: APA Books.

Sang, B., Miao, X., & Deng, C. (2002). The development of gifted and nongifted young children in metamemory knowledge. *Psychological Science (China), 25,* 406–409, 424.

Sankupellay, M., Wilson, S. S., Heussler, H. S., Parsley, C. C., Yuill, M. M., & Dakin, C. C. (2011). Characteristics of sleep EEG power spectra in healthy infants in the first two years of life. *Clinical Neurophysiology, 122,* 236–243.

Santelli, J., Ott, M., Lyon, M., Rogers, J., Summers, D., & Schleifer, R. (2006). Abstinence and abstinence-only education: A review of U.S. policies and programs. *Journal of Adolescent Health, 38,* 72–81.

Santilla, P., Sandnabba, N. K., Harlaar, N., Varjonen, M., Alanko, K., & von der Pahlen, B. (2008). Potential for homosexual response is prevalent and genetic. *Biological Psychology, 77,* 102–105.

Sapolsky, R. (2005, December). Sick of poverty. *Scientific American,* 93–99.

Sapyla, J. J., & March, J. S. (2012). Integrating medical and psychological therapies in child mental health: An evidence-based medicine approach. In M. Garralda, J. Raynaud (Eds.), *Brain, mind, and developmental psychopathology in childhood.* Lanham, MD: Jason Aronson.

Sarsour, K., Sheridan, M., Jutte, D., Nuru-Jeter, A., Hinshaw, S., & Boyce, W. (2011). Family socioeconomic status and child executive functions: The roles of language, home environment, and single parenthood. *Journal of the International Neuropsychological Society, 17,* 120–132.

SART (2012, July 3). 2009 Clinic Summary Report. *Society for Reproductive Medicine.* Retrieved July 14, 2011.

Sasisekaran, J. (2014). Exploring the link between stuttering and phonology: A review and implications for treatment. *Seminars In Speech And Language, 35,* 95–113.

Sato, Y., Fukasawa, T., Hayakawa, M., et al. (2007). A new method of blood sampling reduces pain for newborn infants: A prospective, randomized controlled clinical trial. *Early Human Development, 83,* 389–394.

Saul, S. (2009). The gift of life, and its price. *The New York Times,* p. A1, A26–27.

Saulny, S. (2011, March 24). Census data presents rise in multiracial population of youths. *The New York Times,* p. A3.

Saunders, J., Davis, L., & Williams, T. (2004). Gender differences in self-perceptions and academic outcomes: A study of African American high school students. *Journal of Youth & Adolescence, 33,* 81–90.

Savage-Rumbaugh, E. S., Murphy, J., Sevcik, R. A., Brakke, K. E., Williams, S. L., & Rumbaugh, D. M. (1993). Language and comprehension in ape and child. *Monographs of the Society for Research in Child Development, 58*(3–4, Serial No. 233).

Savin-Williams, R. C. (2003). Are adolescent same-sex romantic relationships on our radar screen? In P. Florsheim (Eds.), *Adolescent romantic relations and sexual behavior: Theory, research, and practical implications.* Mahwah, NJ: Lawrence Erlbaum.

Sawicka, M. (2016). Searching for a narrative of loss. Interactional ordering of ambiguous grief. *Symbolic Interaction.* Retrieved March 3, 2017, from http://onlinelibrary.wiley.com/doi/10.1002/symb.270/full.

Sax, L. (2005, March 2). The promise and peril of single-sex public education. *Education Week, 24*, 48–51.

Sax, L., & Kautz, K. J. (2003). Who first suggests the diagnosis of attention-deficit/hyperactivity disorder? *Annals of Family Medicine, 1*, 171–174.

Saxe, G. B., & de Kirby, K. (2014). Cultural context of cognitive development. *Wires Cognitive Science, 5*(4), 447–461.

Saxe, G. B. (2015). Culture, language, and number. In R. C. Kadosh & A. Dowker, R. C. (Eds.), *The Oxford handbook of numerical cognition* (pp. 367–376). New York: Oxford University Press.

Saxena,V. & Babu, N. (2015). Everyday lessons on sharing. *Journal of Human Values,* 21 (2), 116-126.

Saxena,V. & Babu, N. (2015). Respecting elders as a moral virtue: terminal or instrumental?. *Psychological Studies*. Vol. 60 (2), pp 146–153.

Sayal, K., Heron, J., Maughan, B., Rowe, R., & Ramchandani, P. (2014). Infant temperament and childhood psychiatric disorder: Longitudinal study. *Child: Care, Health and Development, 40*, 292–297.

Scarr, S. (1998). American child care today. *American Psychologist, 53*, 95–108.

Schaan, V. K., & Vögele, C. (2016). Resilience and rejection sensitivity mediate long-term outcomes of parental divorce. *European Child & Adolescent Psychiatry, 25*, 1267–1269.

Schachner, A., & Hannon, E. E. (2011). Infant-directed speech drives social preferences in 5-month-old infants. *Developmental Psychology, 47*, 19–25.

Schachter, E. P. (2005). Erikson meets the postmodern: Can classic identity theory rise to the challenge? *Identity, 5*, 137–160.

Schaeffer, C., Petras, H., & Ialongo, N. (2003). Modeling growth in boys' aggressive behavior across elementary school: Links to later criminal involvement, conduct disorder, and antisocial personality disorder. *Developmental Psychology, 39*, 1020–1035.

Schaefer, M. K., & Salafia, E. B. (2014). The connection of teasing by parents, siblings, and peers with girls' body dissatisfaction and boys' drive for muscularity: The role of social comparison as a mediator. *Eating Behaviors, 15*, 599–608.

Schafer, D. P., & Stevens, B. (2013). Phagocytic glial cells: Sculpting synaptic circuits in the developing nervous system. *Current Opinion in Neurobiology, 23*, 1034–1040.

Scharf, M. (2014). Children's social competence within close friendship: The role of self-perception and attachment orientations. *School Psychology International, 35*, 206–220.

Schechter, D., & Willheim, E. (2009). Disturbances of attachment and parental psychopathology in early childhood. *Child and Adolescent Psychiatric Clinics of North America, 18*, 665–686.

Schecklmann, M., Pfannstiel, C., Fallgatter, A. J., Warnke, A., Gerlach, M., & Romanos, M. (2012). Olfaction in child and adolescent anorexia nervosa. *Journal of Neural Transmission, 119*, 721–728.

Schecter, T., Finkelstein, Y., & Koren, G. (2005). Pregnant "DES daughters" and their offspring. *Canadian Family Physician, 51*, 493–494.

Scheiffelin, B. (1979). Getting it together: An ethnographic approach to the study of the development of communicative competence. In: Ochs, E.; Scheiffelin, B., editors. *Developmental Pragmatics*. New York: Academic Press.

Schemo, D. J. (2003, November 13). Students' scores rise in math, not in reading. *The New York Times*, p. A2.

Schemo, D. J. (2004, March 2). Schools, facing tight budgets, leave gifted programs behind. *The New York Times*, pp. A1, A18.

Schempf, A. H., (2007). Illicit drug use and neonatal outcomes: A critical review. *Obstetrics and Gynecological Surveys, 62*, 745–757.

Scherf, K. S., Sweeney, J. A., & Luna, B. (2006). Brain basis of developmental change in visuospatial working memory. *Journal of Cognitive Neuroscience, 18*, 1045–1058.

Schiller, J. S., & Bernadel, L. (2004). Summary health statistics for the U.S. population: National Health Interview Survey, 2002. *Vital Health Statistics, 10*, 1–110.

Schizophrenia Working Group of the Psychiatric Genomics Consortium (2014). Biological insights from the 108 schizophrenia-associated genetic loci. *Nature, 511*, 421–427.

Schlottmann, A., & Wilkening, F. (2012). Judgment and decision making in young children. In M. K. Dhami, A. Schlottmann & M. R. Waldmann (Eds.), *Judgment and decision making as a skill: Learning, development and evolution*. New York: Cambridge University Press.

Schmalz, D., & Kerstetter, D. (2006). Girlie girls and manly men: Children's stigma consciousness of gender in sports and physical activities. *Journal of Leisure Research, 38*, 536–557.

Schmidt, D., Seehagen, S., Hirschfeld, G., Vocks, S., Schneider, S., & Teismann, T. (2016). Repetitive negative thinking and impaired mother–infant bonding: A longitudinal study. *Cognitive Therapy and Research, 41*(3), 498–507.

Schmidt, M., Pekow, P., Freedson, P., Markenson, G., & Chasan-Taber, L. (2006). Physical activity patterns during pregnancy in a diverse population of women. *Journal of Women's Health, 15*, 909–918.

Schmitow, C., & Stenberg, G. (2013). Social referencing in 10-month-old infants. *European Journal of Developmental Psychology, 10*, 533–545.

Schnitzer, P. G. (2006). Prevention of unintentional childhood injuries. *American Family Physician, 74*, 1864–1869.

Schöner, G., & Thelen, E. (2006). Using Dynamic Field Theory to Rethink Infant Habituation. *Psychological Review, 113*, 273–299.

Schonert-Reichl, K. A., Smith, V., Zaidman-Zait, A., & Hertzman, C. (2012). Promoting children's prosocial behaviors in school: Impact of the 'Roots of Empathy' program on the social and emotional competence of school-aged children. *School Mental Health, 4*, 1–21.

Schoppe-Sullivan, S., Diener, M., Mangelsdorf, S., Brown, G., McHale, J., & Frosch, C. (2006, July). Attachment and sensitivity in family context: The roles of parent and infant gender. *Infant and Child Development, 15*, 367–385.

Schoppe-Sullivan, S., Mangelsdorf, S., Brown, G., & Sokolowski, M. (2007, February). Goodness-of-fit in family context: Infant temperament, marital quality, and early coparenting behavior. *Infant Behavior & Development, 30*, 82–96.

Schore, A. (2003). *Affect regulation and the repair of the self*. New York: W. W. Norton.

Schreiber, G. B., Robins, M., Striegel-Moore, R., Obarzanek, M., Morrison, J. A., & Wright, D. J. (1996). Weight modification efforts reported by black and white preadolescent girls: National Heart, Lung, and Blood Institute Growth and Health Study. *Pediatrics, 98*, 63–70.

Schroder, H. S., Yalch, M. M., Dawood, S., Callahan, C. P., Brent Donnellan, M., & Moser, J. S. (2017). Growth mindset of anxiety buffers the link between stressful life events and psychological distress and coping strategies. *Personality and Individual Differences, 110*, 23–26.

Schuetze, P., Eiden, R., & Coles, C. (2007). Prenatal cocaine and other substance exposure: Effects on infant autonomic regulation at 7 months of age. *Developmental Psychobiology, 49*, 276–289.

Schulz, K., Rudolph, A., Tscharaktschiew, N., & Rudolph, U. (2013). Daniel has fallen into a muddy puddle—Schadenfreude or sympathy? *British Journal of Developmental Psychology, 31*, 363–378.

Schultz, A. H. (1969). *The life of primates*. New York: Universe.

Schutt, R. K. (2001). *Investigating the social world: The process and practice of research*. Thousand Oaks, CA: Sage.

Schvey, N. A., Eddy, K. T., & Tanofsky-Kraff, M. (2016). Diagnosis of feeding and eating disorders in children and adolescents. In B. T. Walsh, E. Attia, D. R. Glasofer, & R. Sysko (Eds.), *Handbook of assessment and treatment of eating disorders*. Arlington, VA: American Psychiatric Publishing, Inc.

Schwartz, C.E., Wright, C.I., Shin, L.M., Kagan, J., Whalen, P.J., McMullin, KG., & Rauch, S.L. Differential amygdalar response to novel versus newly familiar neutral faces: a functional MRI probe developed for studying inhibited temperament. Biological Psychiatry. 2003b;53:854 62.

Schwartz, C. E., & Rauch, S. L. (2004). Temperament and its implications for neuroimaging of anxiety disorders. *CNS Spectrums, 9*, 284–291.

Schwartz, I. M. (1999). Sexual activity prior to coital interaction: A comparison between males and females. *Archives of Sexual Behavior, 28*, 63–69.

Schwartz, P., Maynard, A., & Uzelac, S. (2008). Adolescent egocentrism: A contemporary view. *Adolescence, 43*, 441–448.

Schwarz, A. (2013, May 1). Attention-deficit drugs face new campus rules. New York Times, A10. Accessed from http://www.nytimes.com/2013/05/01/us/colleges-tackleillicit-use-of-adhd-pills.html?ref=us&_r=2&"

Schwarz, T. F., Huang, L., Medina, D., et al. (2012). Four-year follow-up of the immunogenicity and safety of the HPV-16/18 AS04-adjuvanted vaccine when administered to adolescent girls aged 10–14 years. *Journal of Adolescent Health, 50*, 187–194.

Schwarzer, R., & Knoll, N. (2007). Functional roles of social support within the stress and coping process: A theoretical and empirical overview. *International Journal of Psychology, 42*, 243–252.

Schwebel, D. C., & Gaines, J. (2007). Pediatric unintentional injury: behavioral risk factors and implications for prevention. *Journal of Developmental and Behavioral Pediatrics*. 28, 245–254.

Schweinhart, L. J., Barnes, H. V., & Weikart, D. P. (1993). *Significant benefits: The High/Scope Perry Preschool Study through age 27 (Monographs of the High/Scope Educational Research Foundation, No. 10)*. Ypsilanti, MI: High/Scope Press.

Sciarra, D. T., & Ambrosino, K. E. (2011). Post-secondary expectations and educational attainment. *Professional School Counseling, 14*, 231–241.

Scott, J. C., & Henderson, A. E. (2013). Language matters: Thirteen-month-olds understand that the language a speaker uses constrains conventionality. *Developmental Psychology, 49*, 2102–2111.

Scott, R. M., & Baillargeon, R. (2013). Do infants really expect agents to act efficiently? A critical test of the rationality principle. *Psychological Science, 24*, 466–474.

Sears, R. R. (1977). Sources of life satisfaction of the Terman gifted men. *American Psychologist, 32*, 119–129.

Seaton, S. E., King, S., Manktelow, B. N., Draper, E. S., & Field, D. J. (2012). Babies born at the threshold of viability: changes in survival and workload over 20 years. *Archives of Disabled Children and Neonatal Education, 9*, 22–35.

Sebanc, A., Kearns, K., Hernandez, M., & Galvin, K. (2007). Predicting having a best friend in young children: Individual characteristics and friendship features. *Journal of Genetic Psychology, 168*, 81–95.

Sedgh, G., Singh, S., Shah, I. H., Ahman, E., Henshaw, S. K., & Kankole, A. (2012). Induced abortion: Incidence and trends worldwide from 1995 to 2008. *The Lancet, 379*, 625–632.

Seedat, S. (2014). Controversies in the use of antidepressants in children and adolescents: A decade since the storm and where do we stand now? *Journal of Child and Adolescent Mental Health, 26*, iii.

Segal, B. M., & Stewart, J. C. (1996). Substance use and abuse in adolescence: An overview. *Child Psychiatry & Human Development, 26*, 193–210.

Segal, N. L. (1993). Twin, sibling, and adoption methods: Tests of evolutionary hypotheses. *American Psychologist, 48*, 943–956.

Segal, N. L. (2000). Virtual twins: New findings on within-family environmental influences on intelligence. *Journal of Educational Psychology, 92*, 188 194.

Segal, N. L., McGuire, S. A., Graham, J. L., & Stohs, J. (2014). Fullerton virtual twin study: An update. *Twin Research and Human Genetics, 16*, 451–454.

Segall, M. H., Dasen, P. R., Berry, J. W., & Poortinga, Y. H. (1990). *Human behavior in global perspective*. Boston: Allyn & Bacon.

Segalowitz, S. J., & Rapin I. (Eds.). (2003). *Child neuropsychology, Part I*. Amsterdam, Netherlands: Elsevier Science.

Seibert, A., & Kerns, K. (2009). Attachment figures in middle childhood. *International Journal of Behavioral Development, 33*, 347–355.

Seligman, M. E. P. (2007). Coaching and positive psychology. *Australian Psychologist, 42*, 266–267.

Semerci, Ç. (2006). The opinions of medicine faculty students regarding cheating in relation to Kohlberg's moral development concept. *Social Behavior and Personality, 34*, 41–50.

Senghas, A., Kita, S., & Özyürek, A. (2004, September, 17). Children creating core properties of language: Evidence from an emerging sign language in Nicaragua. *Science, 305*, 1779–1782.

Sengoelge, M., Hasselberg, M., Ormandy, D., & Laflamme, L. (2014). Housing, income inequality and child injury mortality in Europe: A cross-sectional study. *Child: Care, Health and Development, 40*(2), 283–291.

Senju, A., Southgate, V., Snape, C., Leonard, M., & Csibra, G. (2011). Do 18 month olds really attribute mental states to others? A critical test. *Science, 331*, 477–480.

Senter, L., Sackoff, J., Landi, K., & Boyd, L. (2011). Studying sudden and unexpected infant deaths in a time of changing death certification and investigation practices: Evaluating sleep-related risk factors for infant death in New York City. *Maternal and Child Health Journal, 15*, 242–248.

Sepehri, A., & Guliani, H. (2017). Regional gradients in institutional cesarean delivery rates: Evidence from five countries in Asia. *Birth: Issues in Perinatal Care, 44*(1), 11–20.

Serbin, L., Poulin-Dubois, D., & Colburne, K. (2001). Gender stereotyping in infancy: Visual preferences for and knowledge of gender-stereotyped toys in the second year. *International Journal of Behavioral Development, 25*, 7–15.

Serbin, L., Poulin-Dubois, D., & Eichstedt, J. (2002). Infants' response to gender-inconsistent events. *Infancy, 3*, 531–542.

Serretti, A., Calati, R., Ferrari, B., & De Ronchi, D. (2007). Personality and genetics. *Current Psychiatry Reviews, 3*, 147–159.

Servin, A., Nordenström, A., Larsson, A., & Bohlin, G. (2003). Prenatal androgens and gender-typed behavior: A study of girls with mild and severe forms of congenital adrenal hyperplasia. *Developmental Psychology, 39*, 440–450.

Sesser, S. (1993, September 13). Opium war redux. *The New Yorker*, pp. 78–89.

Shad, M. U., Bidesi, A. S., Chen, L., Thomas, B. P., Ernst, M., & Rao, U. (2011). Neurobiology of decision-making in adolescents. *Behavioural Brain Research, 217*, 67–76.

Shafto, C. L., Conway, C. M., Field, S. L., & Houston, D. M. (2012). Visual sequence learning in infancy: Domain-general and domain-specific associations with language. *Infancy, 17*, 247–271.

Shah, R., Chauhan, N., Gupta, A. K., & Sen, M. S. (2016). Adolescent-parent conflict in the age of social media: Case reports from India. *Asian Journal of Psychiatry, 23*, 24–26.

Shala, M., & Bahtiri, A. (2011). Differences in gross motor achievements among children of four to five years of age in private and public institutions in Prishtinë, Kosovo. *Early Child Development and Care, 181*, 55–61.

Shangguan, F., & Shi, J. (2009). Puberty timing and fluid intelligence: A study of correlations between testosterone and intelligence in 8- to 12-year-old Chinese boys. *Psychoneuroendocrinology, 34*, 983–988.

Shapiro, L. R., & Solity, J. (2016). Differing effects of two synthetic phonics programmes on early reading development. *British Journal of Educational Psychology, 86*, 182–203.

Sharkins, K. A., Leger, S. E., & Ernest, J. M. (2016). Examining effects of poverty, maternal depression, and children's self-regulation abilities on the development of language and cognition in early childhood: An early head start perspective. *Early Childhood Education Journal*. Retrieved March 12, 2017, from http://link.springer.com/article/10.1007/s10643-016-0787-9.

Sharma, M. (2008). Twenty-first century pink or blue: How sex selection technology facilitates gendercide and what we can do about it. *Family Court Review, 46*, 198–215.

Sharpe, K. (2014, February 13). Medication: The smart-pill oversell. *Nature, 506*, 146–148.

Shashidhar, S., Rao, C., & Hegde, R. (2009). Factors affecting scholastic performances of adolescents, *Indian Journal of Pediatrics, 76* (5): 495-499.

Shaunessy, E., Suldo, S., Hardesty, R., & Shaffer, E. (2006, December). School functioning and psychological well-being of international baccalaureate and general education students: A preliminary examination. *Journal of Secondary Gifted Education, 17*, 76–89.

Shavelson, R., Hubner, J. J., & Stanton, J. C. (1976). Self-concept: Validation of construct interpretations. *Review of Educational Research, 46*, 407–441.

Shavitt, S., Torelli, C. J., & Riemer, H. (2011). Horizontal and vertical individualism and collectivism: Implications for understanding psychological processes. In M. J. Gelfand, C. Chiu, & Y. Hong (Eds.), *Advances in culture and psychology* (Vol. 1). New York: Oxford University Press.

Shaw, D. S., Winslow, E. B., & Flanagan, C. (1999). A prospective study of the effects of marital status and family relations on young children's adjustment among African American and European American families. *Child Development, 70*, 742–755.

Shaw, M. L. (2003). Creativity and whole language. In J. Houtz (Ed.), *The educational psychology of creativity*. Cresskill, NJ: Hampton Press.

Shaywitz, B. A., Shaywitz, S. E., Blachman, B. A., et al. (2004). Development of left occipitotemporal systems for skilled reading in children after a phonologically-based intervention. *Biological Psychiatry, 55*, 926–933.

Shaywitz, S. (2004). *Overcoming dyslexia: A new and complete science-based program for reading problems at any level*. New York: Vintage.

Shea, K. M., Wilcox, A. J., & Little, R. E. (1998). Postterm delivery: A challenge for epidemiologic research. *Epidemiology, 9*, 199–204.

Shealy, C. N. (1995). From Boys Town to Oliver Twist: Separating fact from fiction in welfare reform and out-of-home placement of children and youth. *American Psychologist, 50*, 565–580.

Sheese, B., Voelker, P., Posner, M., & Rothbart, M. (2009). Genetic variation influences on the early development of reactive emotions and their regulation by attention. *Cognitive Neuropsychiatry, 14*, 332–355.

Shelton, A. L., Cornish, K., Clough, M., Gajamange, S., Kolbe, S., & Fielding, J. (2017). Disassociation between brain activation and executive function in Fragile X premutation females. *Human Brain Mapping, 38*, 1056–1067.

Shen, Y., Hu, H., Taylor, B., Kan, H., & Xu, X. (2016). Early menarche and gestational diabetes mellitus at first live birth. *Maternal and Child Health Journal, 21*, 593–598.

Sherlock, J. M., Verweij, K. H., Murphy, S. C., Heath, A. C., Martin, N. G., & Zietsch, B. P. (2017). The role of genes and environment in degree of partner self-similarity. *Behavior Genetics, 47*, 25–35.

Shernoff, D., & Schmidt, J. (2008). Further evidence of an engagement-achievement paradox among U.S. high school students. *Journal of Youth and Adolescence, 37*, 564–580.

Shi, L. (2003). Facilitating constructive parent–child play: Family therapy with young children. *Journal of Family Psychotherapy, 14*, 19–31.

Shi, X., & Lu, X. (2007, October). Bilingual and bicultural development of Chinese American adolescents and young adults: A comparative study. *Howard Journal of Communications, 18*(4), 313–333.

Shin, H. B., & Bruno. R. (2003). *Language use and English speaking ability: 2000*. Washington, DC: U. S. Census Bureau.

Shiner, R., Masten, A., & Roberts, J. (2003). Childhood personality foreshadows adult personality and life outcomes two decades later. *Journal of Personality, 71*, 1145–1170.

Shurkin, J. N. (1992). *Terman's kids: The groundbreaking study of how the gifted grow up*. Boston: Little, Brown.

Sicouri, G., Sharpe, L., Hudson, J. L., et al. (2017). Threat interpretation and parental influences for children with asthma and anxiety. *Behaviour Research and Therapy, 89*, 14–23.

Sidana, A. & Nijhawan, M. (1999). Prevalence of psychiatric morbidity in school going adolescent children and factors related. *Indian Psychiatric Society*. Paper presented at the 51st Annual National Conference of the Indian Psychiatric Society; supplement.

Siegal, M. (1997). *Knowing children: Experiments in conversation and cognition* (2nd ed.). Hove, England: Psychology Press/Erlbaum, Taylor & Francis.

Siegel, L. J., & Davis, L. (2008). Somatic disorders. In R. J. Morris & T. R. Kratochwill (Eds.), *The practice of child therapy* (4th ed.). Mahwah, NJ: Lawrence Erlbaum Associates Publishers.

Siegel, S., Dittrich, R., & Vollmann, J. (2008). Ethical opinions and personal attitudes of young adults conceived by in vitro fertilisation. *Journal of Medical Ethics, 34*, 236–240.

Siegler, R. (2007). Cognitive variability. *Developmental Science, 10*, 104–109.

Siegler, R. S. (1998). *Children's thinking* (3rd ed.). Upper Saddle River, NJ: Prentice Hall.

Siegler, R. S. (2012). From theory to application and back: Following in the giant footsteps of David Klahr. In J. Shrager, S. Carver (Eds.), *The journey from child to scientist: Integrating cognitive development and the education sciences.* Washington, DC: American Psychological Association.

Siegler, R. S. (2016). Continuity and change in the field of cognitive development and in the perspectives of one cognitive developmentalist. *Child Development Perspectives, 10,* 128–133.

Siegler, R. S., & Ellis, S. (1996). Piaget on childhood. *Psychological Science, 7,* 211–215.

Siegler, R. S., & Richards, D. (1982). The development of intelligence. In R. Sternberg (Ed.), *Handbook of human intelligence.* London: Cambridge University Press.

Sifferlin, A. (2013). Parents' not vaccinating kids contributed to whooping cough outbreaks. Retrieved September 30, 2013, from http://healthland.time.com/2013/09/30/parents-not-vaccinating-kids-contributed-to-whooping-cough-outbreaks/#ixzz2uWBlAzuN.

Sigman, M., Cohen, S. E., & Beckwith, L. (1997). Why does infant attention predict adolescent intelligence? *Infant Behavior & Development, 20,* 133–140.

Signorella, M., & Frieze, I. (2008). Interrelations of gender schemas in children and adolescents: Attitudes, preferences, and self-perceptions. *Social Behavior and Personality, 36,* 941–954.

Silventoinen, K., Iacono, W. G., Krueger, R., & McGue, M. (2012). Genetic and environmental contributions to the association between anthropometric measures and IQ: A study of Minnesota twins at age 11 and 17. *Behavior Genetics, 42,* 393–401.

Simcock, G., & Hayne, H. (2002). Breaking the barrier? Children fail to translate their preverbal memories into language. *Psychological Science, 13,* 225–231.

Simkin, P. (2014). Preventing primary cesareans: Implications for laboring women, their partners, nurses, educators, and doulas. *Birth: Issues in Perinatal Care, 41,* 220–222.

Simmons, S. W., Cyna, A. M., Dennis, A. T., & Hughes, D. (2007). Combined spinal-epidural versus epidural analgesia in labour. *Cochrane Database and Systematic Review, 18,* CD003401.

Simon, R. M., Wagner, A., & Killion, B. (2017). Gender and choosing a STEM major in college: Femininity, masculinity, chilly climate, and occupational values. *Journal of Research in Science Teaching, 54,* 299–323.

Simpson, E. (2017, March 3). America's 1st test-tube baby, a Norfolk native, set to meet world's 1st test-tube baby. *Virginian-Pilot.*

Simpson, J., Collins, W., Tran, S., & Haydon, K. (2007, February). Attachment and the experience and expression of emotions in romantic relationships: A developmental perspective. *Journal of Personality and Social Psychology, 92,* 355–367.

Sinclair, S., Carlsson, R., & Björklund, F. (2016). Getting along or ahead: Effects of gender identity threat on communal and agentic self-presentations. *Scandinavian Journal of Psychology, 57,* 427–432.

Singer, L. T., Arendt, R., Minnes, S., Farkas, K., & Salvator, A. (2000). Neurobehavioral outcomes of cocaine-exposed infants. *Neurotoxicology & Teratology, 22,* 653–666.

Singh, S., & Darroch, J. E. (2000). Adolescent pregnancy and childbearing: levels and trends in developed countries. *The Canadian Journal of Human Sexuality, 9,* 67.

Singh, V. & Gupta, R. (2006). Prevalence of tobacco use and awareness of risk among school children in Jaipur. *Journal of Association of Physicians of India,* 54, 2006, 609-12 [10].

Sinha, D. N., Reddy, K. S., Rahman, K., Warren, C. W., Jones, N. R., & Asma, S. (2006). Linking global youth tobacco survey (GYTS) data to the WHO framework convention on tobacco control: The case for India. Indian Journal of Public Health Research & Development, 50, 76-89. Accessed from https://www.drugabuse.gov/ on 08/07/2016. [11].

Skibbe, L. E., Connor, C., Morrison, F. J., & Jewkes, A. M. (2011). Schooling effects on preschoolers' self-regulation, early literacy, and language growth. *Early Childhood Research Quarterly, 26,* 42–49.

Skinner, B. F. (1957). *Verbal behavior.* New York: Appleton-Century-Crofts.

Skinner, J. D., Ziegler, P., Pac, S., & Devaney, B. (2004). Meal and snack patterns of infants and toddlers. *Journal of the American Dietary Association, 104,* S65–S70.

Skledar, M., Nikolac, M., Dodig-Curkovic, K., Curkovic, M., Borovecki, F., & Pivac, N. (2012). Association between brain-derived neurotrophic factor Val66Met and obesity in children and adolescents. *Progress in Neuro-Psychopharmacology & Biological Psychiatry, 36,* 136–140.

Skoog, T., & Özdemir, S. B. (2016). Explaining why early-maturing girls are more exposed to sexual harassment in early adolescence. *The Journal of Early Adolescence, 36,* 490–509.

Skrzypek, K., Maciejewska-Sobczak, B., & Stadnicka-Dmitriew, Z. (2014). *Siblings: Envy and rivalry, coexistence and concern.* London: Karnac Books.

Slaughter, V., & Peterson, C. C. (2012). How conversational input shapes theory of mind development in infancy and early childhood. In M. Siegal, L. Surian (Eds.), *Access to language and cognitive development.* New York: Oxford University Press.

Slavin, R. E. (2013). Cooperative learning and achievement: Theory and research. In W. M. Reynolds, G. E. Miller, I. B. Weiner (Eds.), *Handbook of psychology, Vol. 7: Educational psychology* (2nd ed.). Hoboken, NJ: John Wiley & Sons Inc.

Sloan, S., Gildea, A., Stewart, M., Sneddon, H., & Iwaniec, D. (2008). Early weaning is related to weight and rate of weight gain in infancy. *Child: Care, Health and Development, 34,* 59–64.

Sloane, S., Baillargeon, R., & Premack, D. (2012). Do infants have a sense of fairness? *Psychological Science, 23,* 196–207.

Slusser, E., Ditta, A., & Sarnecka, B. (2013). Connecting numbers to discrete quantification: A step in the child's construction of integer concepts. *Cognition, 129,* 31–41.

Smedley, A., & Smedley, B. D. (2005). Race as biology is fiction, racism as a social problem is real: Anthropological and historical perspectives on the social construction of race. *American Psychologist, 60,* 16–26.

Smetana, J. (2006). Social-cognitive domain theory: Consistencies and variations in children's moral and social judgments. *Handbook of moral development.* Mahwah, NJ: Lawrence Erlbaum Associates.

Smetana, J., Daddis, C., & Chuang, S. (2003). "Clean your room!" A longitudinal investigation of adolescent–parent conflict and conflict resolution in middle-class African American families. *Journal of Adolescent Research, 18,* 631–650.

Smetana, J. G. (1995). Parenting styles and conceptions of parental authority during adolescence. *Child Development, 66,* 299–316.

Smetana, J. G. (2005). Adolescent-parent conflict: Resistance and subversion as developmental process. In L. Nucci (Ed.), *Conflict, contradiction, and contrarian elements in moral development and education.* Mahwah, NJ: Lawrence Erlbaum Associates.

Smiley, P. A., Tan, S. J., Goldstein, A., & Sweda, J. (2016). Mother emotion, child temperament, and young children's helpless responses to failure. *Social Development, 25,* 285–303.

Smith, E. P., Faulk, M., & Sizer, M. A. (2016). Exploring the mesosystem: The roles of community, family, and peers in adolescent delinquency and positive youth development. *Youth & Society, 48*(3), 318–343.

Smith, J. S., Estudillo, A. G., & Kang, H. (2011). Racial differences in eighth grade students' identification with academics. *Education and Urban Society, 43,* 73–90.

Smith, N., & Trainor, L. (2008). Infant-directed speech is modulated by infant feedback. *Infancy, 13,* 410–420.

Smith, P. K., & Drew, L. M. (2002). Grandparenthood. In M. Bornstein (Ed.), *Handbook of parenting.* Mahwah, NJ: Erlbaum.

Smith, R. J., Bale, J. F., Jr., & White, K. R. (2005, March 2). Sensorineural hearing loss in children. *Lancet, 365,* 879–890.

Smith, T. B., & Silva, L. (2011). Ethnic identity and personal well-being of people of color: A meta-analysis. *Journal of Counseling Psychology, 58,* 42–60.

Smith-Nielsen, J., Tharner, A., Steele, H., Cordes, K., Mehlhase, H., & Vaever, M. S. (2016). Postpartum depression and infant-mother attachment security at one year: The impact of co-morbid maternal personality disorders. *Infant Behavior & Development, 44,* 148–158.

Smutny, J., Walker, S., & Meckstroth, E. (2007). *Acceleration for gifted learners, K-5.* Thousand Oaks, CA: Corwin Press.

Smuts, A. B., & Hagen, J. W. (1985). History of the family and of child development: Introduction to Part 1. *Monographs of the Society for Research in Child Development, 50* (4–5, Serial No. 211).

Sneed, A. (2014, August). Why babies forget. *Scientific American, 311,* 28.

Snowdon, C. T., & Burghardt, G. M. (2017). Studying animal behavior: Integration of field and laboratory approaches. In J. Call, G. M. Burghardt, I. M. Pepperberg, et al. (Eds.), *APA handbook of comparative psychology: Basic concepts, methods, neural substrate, and behavior.* Washington, DC: American Psychological Association.

Soderstrom, M. (2007). Beyond babytalk: Re-evaluating the nature and content of speech input to preverbal infants. *Developmental Review, 27,* 501–532.

Soderstrom, M., Blossom, M., Foygel, R., & Morgan, J. (2008). Acoustical cues and grammatical units in speech to two preverbal infants. *Journal of Child Language, 35,* 869–902.

Soderstrom, M., Reimchen, M., Sauter, D., & Morgan, J. L. (2017). Do infants discriminate non-linguistic vocal expressions of positive emotions? *Cognition and Emotion, 31,* 298–311.

Sonne, J. L. (2012). Psychological assessment measures. In *PsycEssentials: A pocket resource for mental health practitioners.* Washington, DC: American Psychological Association.

Sosinsky, L., & Kim, S. (2013). A profile approach to child care quality, quantity, and type of setting: Parent selection of infant child care arrangements. *Applied Developmental Science, 17,* 39–56.

Sousa, D. L. (2005). *How the brain learns to read.* Thousand Oaks, CA: Corwin Press.

South, A. (2013). Perceptions of romantic relationships in adult children of divorce. *Journal of Divorce & Remarriage, 54,* 126–141.

Sowell E. R., Peterson, B. S., Thompson, P. M., Welcome, S. E., Henkenius, A. L., & Toga, A. W. (2003). Mapping cortical change across the human life span. *Nature Neuroscience, 6,* 309–315.

Sowell, E. R., Thompson, P. M., Tessner, K. D., & Toga, A. W. (2001). Mapping continued brain growth and gray matter density reduction in dorsal frontal cortex: Inverse relationships during postadolescent brain maturation. *Journal of Neuroscience, 21,* 8819–8829.

Spear, L. (2013). The teenage brain: Adolescents and alcohol. *Current Directions in Psychological Science, 22*(2), 152–157.

Spear, L. P. (2002). The adolescent brain and the college drinker: Biological basis of propensity to use and misuse alcohol. *Journal of Studies on Alcohol,* [Special issue: College drinking, what it is, and what to do about it: Review of the state of the science], (Suppl. 14), 71–81.

Spearman, C. (1927). *The abilities of man.* London: Macmillan.

Spencer, J. (2001). How to battle school violence. *MSNBC News.* Retrieved from http://www.msnbc.com/news/.

Speroni, K. G., Earley, C., & Atherton, M. (2007). Evaluating the effectiveness of the kids living fit™ program: A comparative study. *Journal of School Nursing, 23,* 329–336.

Spessato, B., Gabbard, C., Valentini, N., & Rudisill, M. (2013). Gender differences in Brazilian children's fundamental movement skill performance. *Early Child Development and Care, 183,* 916–923.

Spinrad, T. L., & Stifter, C. A. (2006). Toddlers' empathy-related responding to distress: predictions from negative emotionality and maternal behavior in infancy. *Infancy, 10,* 97–121.

Spielman, D. A., & Staub, E. (2003). Reducing boys' aggression: Learning to fulfill basic needs constructively. In E. Staub (Ed.), *The psychology of good and evil.* Cambridge, England: Cambridge University Press.

Spörer, N., Brunstein, J., & Kieschke, U. (2009). Improving students' reading comprehension skills: Effects of strategy instruction and reciprocal teaching. *Learning and Instruction, 19,* 272–286.

Sprecher, S., Brooks, J. E., & Avogo, W. (2013). Self-esteem among young adults: Differences and similarities based on gender, race, and cohort (1990–2012). *Sex Roles, 69,* 264–275.

Sprenger, M. (2007). *Memory 101 for educators.* Thousand Oaks, CA: Corwin Press.

Squeglia, L. M., Sorg, S. F. Schweinsburg, A., Dager, W., Reagan, R. & Tapert, S. F. (2012). Binge drinking differentially affects adolescent male and female brain morphometry. *Psychopharmacology, 220,* 529–539.

Srivastava, A., Pal, H., Dwivedi, S.N., Pandey, A. (2002). National household survey of drug abuse in India. Report submitted to the Ministry of Social Justice and Empowerment, Government of India and United Nations Office on Drugs and Crime, Regional Office for South Asia.

Srivastava, A.H., Pal, S.N., Dwivedi, A., & Pandey, J.N. (2004). National Household Survey of Drug and Alcohol Abuse in India, Ministry of Social Justice and Empowerment, Government of India and UN Office for Drug and Crime, Regional Office of South Asia, New Delhi.

Sroufe, L. A. (1996). *Emotional development: The organization of emotional life in the early years.* New York: Oxford University Press.

Staff, J., Mortimer, J. T., & Uggen, C. (2004). Work and leisure in adolescence. In R. M. Lerner & L. Steinberg (Eds.), *Handbook of adolescent psychology* (2nd ed.). New York NY: Wiley.

Starr, A., Libertus, M. E., & Brannon, E. M. (2013). Number sense in infancy predicts mathematical abilities in childhood. *PNAS Proceedings of the National Academy of Sciences of the United States of America, 110,* 18116–18120.

Staub, E. (2011). *Overcoming evil: Genocide, violent conflict and terrorism.* New York: Oxford University Press.

Staub, E. (2013). Building a peaceful society: Origins, prevention, and reconciliation after genocide and other group violence. *American Psychologist, 68,* 576–589.

Stauder, J. A., Cornet, L. M., & Ponds, R. M. (2011). The extreme male brain theory and gender role behaviour in persons with an autism spectrum condition. *Research in Autism Spectrum Disorders, 5,* 1209–1214.

Staunton, H. (2005). Mammalian sleep. *Naturwissenschaften, 35,* 15.

Stecker, M., Wolfe, J., & Stevenson, M. (2013). Neurophysiologic responses of peripheral nerve to repeated episodes of anoxia. *Clinical Neurophysiology, 124,* 792–800.

Steel, A., Adams, J., Sibbritt, D., Broom, A., Frawley, J., & Gallois, C. (2014). The influence of complementary and alternative medicine use in pregnancy on labor pain management choices: Results from a nationally representative sample of 1,835 women. *The Journal of Alternative and Complementary Medicine, 20,* 87–97.

Steele, C. M. (1997). A threat in the air: How stereotypes shape intellectual identity and performance. *American Psychologist, 52,* 613–629.

Steenbergen-Hu, S., & Moon, S. M. (2011). The effects of acceleration on high-ability learners: A meta-analysis. *Gifted Child Quarterly, 55,* 39–53.

Stefanis, N. C., Hatzimanolis, A., Smyrnis, N., et al. (2013). Schizophrenia candidate gene ERBB4: Covert routes of vulnerability to psychosis detected at the population level. *Schizophrenia Bulletin, 39,* 349–357.

Stein, D., Latzer, Y., & Merick, J. (2009). Eating disorders: From etiology to treatment. *International Journal of Child and Adolescent Health, 2,* 139–151.

Stein, J. H., & Reiser, L. W. (1994). A study of white middle-class adolescent boys' responses to "semenarche" (the first ejaculation). *Journal of Youth and Adolescence, 23,* 373–384.

Steinbach, R., Green, J., Kenward, M. G., & Edwards, P. (2016). Is ethnic density associated with risk of child pedestrian injury? A comparison of inter-census changes in ethnic populations and injury rates. *Ethnicity & Health, 21,* 1–19.

Steinberg, L., Dornbusch, S., & Brown, B. B. (1992). Ethnic differences in adolescent achievement: An ecological perspective. *American Psychologist, 47,* 723–729.

Steinberg, L. D., & Scott, S. S. (2003). Less guilty by reason of adolescence: Developmental immaturity, diminished responsibility, and the juvenile death penalty. *American Psychologist, 58,* 1009–1018.

Steiner, J. E. (1979). Human facial expressions in response to taste and smell stimulation. *Advances in Child Development and Behavior, 13,* 257.

Stenberg, G. (2003). Effects of maternal inattentiveness on infant social referencing. *Infant & Child Development, 12,* 399–419.

Stenberg, G. (2009). Selectivity in infant social referencing. *Infancy, 14,* 457–473.

Stephany, C., Frantz, M. G., & McGee, A. W. (2016). Multiple roles for nogo receptor 1 in visual system plasticity. *Neuroscientist, 22,* 653–666.

Steri, A. O., & Spelke, E. S. (1988). Haptic perception of objects in infancy. *Cognitive Psychology, 20,* 1–23.

Sternberg, J. (2005). The triarchic theory of successful intelligence. In D. P. Flanagan & P. L. Harrison (Eds.), *Contemporary Intellectual Assessment: Theories, Tests, and Issues.* New York: Guilford Press.

Sternberg, R. (2003a). A broad view of intelligence: The theory of successful intelligence. *Consulting Psychology Journal: Practice & Research, 55,* 139–154.

Sternberg, R. (2003b). Our research program validating the triarchic theory of successful intelligence: Reply to Gottfredson. *Intelligence, 31,* 399–413.

Sternberg, R. (2008, March). Applying psychological theories to educational practice. *American Educational Research Journal, 45*(1), 150–165.

Sternberg, R. J. (2016). A triangular theory of creativity. *Psychology of Aesthetics, Creativity, and the Arts.* Retrieved March 16, 2017, from http://psycnet.apa.org/index.cfm?fa=buy.optionToBuy&id=2016-60691-001.

Sternberg, R. J. (1990). *Metaphors of mind: Conceptions of the nature of intelligence.* Cambridge, England: Cambridge University Press.

Sternberg, R. J. (2005). The triarchic theory of successful intelligence. In D. P. Flanagan & P. L. Harrison (Eds.), *Contemporary intellectual assessment: Theories, tests, and issues.* New York, Guilford Press.

Sternberg, R. J., Conway, B. E., Ketron, J. L., & Bernstein, M. (1981). Peoples' conceptions of intelligence. *Journal of Personality and Social Psychology, 41,* 37–55.

Sternberg, R. J., & Grigorenko, E. L. (Eds.). (2002). *The general factor of intelligence: How general is it?* Mahwah, NJ: Lawrence Erlbaum.

Stevenson, C. E., Heiser, W. J., & Resing, W. M. (2016). Dynamic testing: Assessing cognitive potential of children with culturally diverse backgrounds. *Learning and Individual Differences, 47,* 27–36.

Stewart, M., Scherer, J., & Lehman, M. (2003). Perceived effects of high frequency hearing loss in a farming population. *Journal of the American Academy of Audiology, 14,* 100–108.

Stice, E. (2003). Puberty and body image. In C. Hayward (Ed.), *Gender differences at puberty.* New York: Cambridge University Press.

Stiles, J. (2012). The effects of injury to dynamic neural networks in the mature and developing brain. *Developmental Psychobiology, 54,* 343–349.

Stipek, D. (2002). At what age should children enter kindergarten? A question for policy makers and parents. *Social Policy Report, 16,* 3–16.

Stolberg, S. G. (1998, April 3). Rise in smoking by young blacks erodes a success story in health. *The New York Times,* p. A1.

Storfer, M. (1990). *Intelligence and giftedness: The contributions of heredity and early environment.* San Francisco: Jossey-Bass.

Stork, S., & Sanders, S. (2008, January). Physical education in early childhood. *The Elementary School Journal, 108*(3), 197–206.

Story, M., Nanney, M., & Schwartz, M. (2009). Schools and obesity prevention: Creating school environments and policies to promote healthy eating and physical activity. *Milbank Quarterly, 87,* 71–100.

Strachan, E., Duncan, G., Horn, E., & Turkheimer, E. (2017). Neighborhood deprivation and depression in adult twins: Genetics and gene × environment interaction. *Psychological Medicine, 47,* 627–638.

Strasburger, V. (2009). Media and children: What needs to happen now? *JAMA: Journal of the American Medical Association, 301,* 2265–2266.

Strassberg, D. S., Cann, D., & Velarde, V. (2017). Sexting by high school students. *Archives Of Sexual Behavior.* Accessed online 8-9-17; https://www.ncbi.nlm.nih.gov/pubmed/28050742

Streissguth, A. (1997). *Fetal alcohol syndrome: A guide for families and communities.* Baltimore: Paul H Brookes Publishing.

Streissguth, A. (2007). Offspring effects of prenatal alcohol exposure from birth to 25 years: The Seattle Prospective Longitudinal Study. *Journal of Clinical Psychology in Medical Settings, 14,* 81–101.

Strelau, J. (1998). *Temperament: A psychological perspective.* New York: Plenum Publishers.

Striano, T., & Vaish, A. (2006, November). Seven- to 9-month-old infants use facial expressions to interpret others' actions. *British Journal of Developmental Psychology, 24,* 753–760.

Stright, A., Gallagher, K., & Kelley, K. (2008). Infant temperament moderates relations between maternal parenting in early childhood and children's adjustment in first grade. *Child Development, 79*(1), 186–200.

Stroh, L., K., Langlands, C. L., & Simpson, P. A. (2004). Shattering the glass ceiling in the new millennium. In M. S. Stockdale & F. J. Crosby (Eds.), *Psychology and management of workplace diversity.* Malden, MA: Blackwell.

Strohmaier, H., Murphy, M., & DeMatteo, D. (2014). Youth sexting: Prevalence rates, driving motivations, and the deterrent effect of legal consequences. *Sexuality Research & Social Policy: A Journal of the NSRC, 11*(3), 245–255.

Stromswold, K. (2006). Why aren't identical twins linguistically identical? Genetic, prenatal and postnatal factors. *Cognition, 101,* 333–384.

Struempler, B. J., Parmer, S. M., Mastropietro, L. M., Arsiwalla, D., & Bubb, R. R. (2014). Changes in fruit and vegetable consumption of third-grade students in body quest: Food of the warrior, a 17-class childhood obesity prevention program. *Journal of Nutrition Education and Behavior, 46,* 286–292.

Stutts, M., Zank, G. M., Smith, K. H., & Williams, S. A. (2011). Nutrition information and children's fast food menu choices. *Journal of Consumer Affairs, 45,* 52–86.

Suárez-Orozco, C., Suárez-Orozco, M., Todorova, I. (2008). *Learning a new land: Immigrant students in American society.* Cambridge, MA: Belknap Press/Harvard University Press.

Subotnik, R. (2006). Longitudinal studies: Answering our most important questions of prediction and effectiveness. *Journal for the Education of the Gifted, 29,* 379–383.

Substance Abuse and Mental Health Services Administration, (2013). *Results from the 2012 National Survey on Drug Use and Health: Summary of National Findings,* NSDUH Series H-46, HHS Publication No. (SMA) 13-4795. Rockville, MD: Substance Abuse and Mental Health Services Administration.

Sudharsanan, N., Behrman, J. R., & Kohler, H. (2016). Limited common origins of multiple adult health-related behaviors: Evidence from U.S. Twins. *Social Science & Medicine, 171,* 67–83.

Sudia-Robinson, T., (2011, March 14). Ethical implications of newborn screening, life-limiting conditions, and palliative care. *MCN, American Journal of Maternal Child Nursing.* Retrieved April 3, 2011, from http://journals.lww.com/mcnjournal/Abstract/publishahead/Ethical_Implications_of_Newborn_Screening,.99982.aspx.

Suitor, J. J., Minyard, S. A., & Carter, R. S. (2001). "Did you see what I saw?" Gender differences in perceptions of avenues to prestige among adolescents. *Sociological Inquiry, 71,* 437–454.

Summers, J., Schallert, D., & Ritter, P. (2003). The role of social comparison in students' perceptions of ability: An enriched view of academic motivation in middle school students. *Contemporary Educational Psychology, 28,* 510–523.

Sun, L. H. (2012, April 25). Infant mortality in the District drops to historic low. *Washington Post.*

Sun, Y., Liu, Y., Yan, S., et al. (2016). Longitudinal pattern of early maturation on morning cortisol and depressive symptoms: Sex-specific effects. *Psychoneuroendocrinology, 71,* 58–63.

Super, C. M. (1976). Environmental effects on motor development: A case of African infant precocity. *Developmental Medicine and Child Neurology, 18,* 561–576.

Super, C. M., & Harkness, S. (1982). The infant's niche in rural Kenya and metropolitan America. In L. Adler (Ed.), *Issues in cross-cultural research.* New York: Academic Press.

Supple, A., Ghazarian, S., Peterson, G., & Bush, K. (2009). Assessing the cross-cultural validity of a parental autonomy granting measure: Comparing adolescents in the United States, China, Mexico, and India. *Journal of Cross-Cultural Psychology, 40,* 816–833.

Sutherland, R., Pipe, M., & Schick, K. (2003). Knowing in advance: The impact of prior event information on memory and event knowledge. *Journal of Experimental Child Psychology, 84,* 244–263.

Suzuki, G. (2013). Grade-level differences in elementary and middle school students' conceptions of learning: Correlation with learning strategy use. *Japanese Journal of Educational Psychology, 61,* 17–31.

Suzuki, K., & Ando, J. (2014). Genetic and environmental structure of individual differences in hand, foot, and ear preferences: A twin study. *Laterality: Asymmetries of Body, Brain and Cognition, 19,* 113–128.

Swain, J. (2004). Is placement in the least restrictive environment a restricted debate? *PsycCRITIQUES,* pp. 23–30.

Swain, J. E., Lorberbaum, J. P., Kose, S., & Strathearn, L. (2007). Brain basis of early parent-infant interactions: Psychology, physiology, and in vivo functional neuroimaging studies. *Journal of Child Psychology and Psychiatry, 48,* 262–287.

Swanson, L. A., Leonard, L. B., & Gandour, J. (1992). Vowel duration in mothers' speech to young children. *Journal of Speech and Hearing Research, 35,* 617–625.

Swiatek, M. (2002). Social coping among gifted elementary school students. *Journal for the Education of the Gifted, 26,* 65–86.

Swingler, M. M., Sweet, M. A., & Carver, L. J. (2007). Relations between mother-child interaction and the neural correlates of face processing in 6-month-olds. *Infancy, 11,* 63–86.

Swingley, D., & Humphrey, C. (2017). Quantitative linguistic predictors of infants' learning of specific English words. *Child Development.* Retrieved March 7, 2017, from https://www.ncbi.nlm.nih.gov/pubmed/28146333.

Szaflarski, J. P., Rajagopal, A., Altaye, M., et al. (2012). Left-handedness and language lateralization in children. *Brain Research, 143,* 85–97.

Taddio, A., Shah, V., & Gilbert-MacLeod, C. (2002). Conditioning and hyperalgesia in newborns exposed to repeated heel lances. *Journal of the American Medical Association, 288,* 857–861.

Taga, K., Markey, C., & Friedman, H. (2006, June). A longitudinal investigation of associations between boys' pubertal timing and adult behavioral health and well-being. *Journal of Youth and Adolescence, 35,* 401–411.

Tajfel, H., & Turner, J. C. (2004). The social identity theory of intergroup behaviour. In J. T. Jost & J. Sidanius (Eds.). *Political psychology: Key readings.* New York: Psychology Press.

Takahashi, K. (1986). Examining the Strange Situation procedure with Japanese mothers and 12-month-old infants. *Developmental Psychology, 22,* 265–270.

Talwar, V., & Lee, K. (2002a). Emergence of white-lie telling in children between 3 and 7 years of age. *Merrill-Palmer Quarterly, 48,* 160–181.

Talwar, V., & Lee, K. (2002b). Development of lying to conceal a transgression: Children's control of expressive behavior during verbal deception. *International Journal of Behavioral Development, 26,* 436–444.

Talwar, V., & Lee, K. (2008). Social and cognitive correlates of children's lying behavior. *Child Development, 79,* 866–881.

Talwar, V., Murphy, S., & Lee, K. (2007). While lie-telling in children for politeness purposes. *International Journal of Behavioral Development, 30,* 1–11.

Tamis-LeMonda, C. S., & Cabrera, N. (1999). Perspectives on father involvement: Research and policy. *Social Policy Report, 13,* 1–31.

Tamis-LeMonda, C. S., & Cabrera, N. (2002). *Handbook of father involvement: Multidisciplinary perspectives.* Mahwah, NJ: Lawrence Erlbaum Associates.

Tamis-LeMonda, C. S., Song, L., Leavell, A., Kahana-Kalman, R., & Yoshikawa, H. (2012). Ethnic differences in mother–infant language and gestural communications are associated with specific skills in infants. *Developmental Science, 15,* 384–397.

Tamis-LeMonda, C., Song, L., Smith, L. A., Kahana-Kalman, R., & Yoshikawa, H. (2012) Ethnic differences in mother–infant language and gestural communications are associated with specific skills in infants. *Developmental Science.* 15(3):384–397 [PubMed: 22490178].

Tan, H., Wen, S. W., Mark, W., Fung, K. F., Demissie, K., & Rhoads, G. G. (2004). The association between fetal sex and preterm birth in twin pregnancies. *Obstetrics and Gynecology, 103,* 327–332.

Tanaka, K., Kon, N., Ohkawa, N., Yoshikawa, N., & Shimizu, T. (2009). Does breastfeeding in the neonatal period influence the cognitive function of very-low-birth-weight infants at 5 years of age? *Brain & Development, 31,* 288–293.

Tandon, P. S., Zhou, C., Lozano, P., & Christakis, D. A. (2011). Preschoolers' total daily screen time at home and by type of child care. *The Journal of Pediatrics, 158*(2), 297–300.

Tang, C., Wu, M., Liu, J., Lin, H., & Hsu, C. (2006). Delayed parenthood and the risk of cesarean delivery—Is paternal age an independent risk factor? *Birth: Issues in Perinatal Care, 33,* 18–26.

Tang, Z., & Orwin, R. (2009). Marijuana initiation among American youth and its risks as dynamic processes: Prospective findings from a national longitudinal study. *Substance Use & Misuse, 44,* 195–211.

Tanner, E., & Finn-Stevenson, M. (2002). Nutrition and brain development: Social policy implications. *American Journal of Orthopsychiatry, 72,* 182–193.

Tanner, J. (1972). Sequence, tempo, and individual variation in growth and development of boys and girls aged twelve to sixteen. In J. Kagan & R. Coles (Eds.), *Twelve to sixteen: Early adolescence.* New York: Norton.

Tanner, J. M. (1978). *Education and physical growth* (2nd ed.). New York: International Universities Press.

Tappan, M. (2006, March). Moral functioning as mediated action. *Journal of Moral Education, 35,* 1–18.

Tarber, D. N., Cohn, T. J., Casazza, S., Hastings, S. L., & Steele, J. (2016). The role of self-compassion in psychological well-being for male survivors of childhood maltreatment. *Mindfulness, 7,* 1193–1202.

Tardif, T. (1996). Nouns are not always learned before verbs: Evidence from Mandarin speakers' early vocabularies. *Developmental Psychology, 32,* 492–504.

Tardif, T., Wellman, H. M., & Cheung, K. M. (2004). False belief understanding in Cantonese-speaking children. *Journal of Child Language, 31,* 779–800.

Tattersall, M., Cordeaux, Y., Charnock-Jones, D., & Smith, G. S. (2012). Expression of gastrin-releasing peptide is increased by prolonged stretch of human myometrium, and antagonists of its receptor inhibit contractility. *The Journal of Physiology, 590,* 2081–2093.

Tatum, B. (2007). *Can we talk about race? And other conversations in an era of school resegregation.* Boston: Beacon Press.

Taumoepeau, M., & Ruffman, T. (2008, March). Stepping stones to others' minds: Maternal talk relates to child mental state language and emotion understanding at 15, 24, and 33 months. *Child Development, 79*(2), 284–302.

Taveras, E. M., Scanlon, K. S., Birch, L., Rifas-Shiman, S. L., Rich-Edwards, J. W., & Gillman, M. W. (2009). Weight status in the first 6 months of life and obesity at 3 years of age. *Pediatrics, 123*(4), 1177–1183.

Tavernise, S. (2014, April 24). New U.S. rules on e-cigarettes to be proposed. *New York Times,* p. A1.

Taylor, D. M. (2002). *The quest for identity: From minority groups to Generation Xers.* Westport, CT: Praeger Publishers/Greenwood Publishing.

Taylor, G., Liu, H., & Herbert, J. S. (2016). The role of verbal labels on flexible memory retrieval at 12 months of age. *Infant Behavior & Development, 45*(Part A), 11–17.

Taylor, H. G., Klein, N., Minich, N. M., & Hack, M. (2000). Middle-school-age outcomes in children with very low birth-weight. *Child Development, 71,* 1495–1511.

Taylor, R. L. & Rosenbach, W. E. (2005). (Eds.), *Military leadership: In pursuit of excellence* (5th ed.). Boulder, CO: Westview Press.

Taylor, S. E. (1991). *Health psychology* (2nd ed.). New York: McGraw-Hill.

Tazopoulou, E., Miljkovitch, R., Truelle, J., et al. (2016). Rehabilitation following cerebral anoxia: An assessment of 27 patients. *Brain Injury, 30,* 95–103.

Tellegen, A., Lykken, D. T., Bouchard, T. J., Jr., Wilcox, K. J., Segal, N. L., & Rich, S. (1988). Personality similarity in twins reared apart and together. *Journal of Personality and Social Psychology, 54,* 1031–1039.

Tenenbaum, H., & Leaper, C. (2003). Parent-child conversations about science: The socialization of gender inequities? *Developmental Psychology, 39,* 34–47.

Tenenbaum, H. R., & Leaper, C. (1998). Gender effects on Mexican-descent parents' questions and scaffolding during toy play: A sequential analysis. *First Language, 18,* 129–147.

Teoli, D. A., Zullig, K. J., & Hendryx, M. S. (2015). Maternal fair/poor self-rated health and adverse infant birth outcomes. *Health Care for Women International, 36,* 108–120.

Terzidou, V. (2007). Preterm labour. Biochemical and endocrinological preparation for parturition. *Best Practices of Research in Clinical Obstetrics and Gynecology, 21,* 729–756.

Tessor, A., Felson, R. B., & Suls, J. M. (Eds.). (2000). *Psychological perspectives on self and identity.* Washington, DC: American Psychological Association.

Thapar, A., & Cooper, M. (2016). Attention deficit hyperactivity disorder. *The Lancet, 387,* 1240–1250.

Thelen, E., & Bates, E. (2003). Connectionism and dynamic systems: Are they really different? *Developmental Science, 6,* 378–391.

Thelen, E., & Smith, L. (2006). *Dynamic systems theories. Handbook of child psychology. Vol. 1: Theoretical models of human development* (6th ed.). New York: John Wiley & Sons Inc.

Theodosiou-Zipiti, G., & Lamprianou, I. (2016). Linguistic and cultural effects on the attainment of ethnic minority students: Some methodological considerations. *British Journal of Sociology of Education, 37,* 1229–1250.

Thibodeau, R. B., Gilpin, A. T., Brown, M. M., & Meyer, B. A. (2016). The effects of fantastical pretend-play on the development of executive functions: An intervention study. *Journal of Experimental Child Psychology, 145*, 120–138.

Thielen, F. W., Have, M., Graaf, R., et al. (2016). Long-term economic consequences of child maltreatment: A population-based study. *European Child & Adolescent Psychiatry*. Retrieved May 27, 2016, from http://www.ncbi.nlm.nih.gov/pubmed/27154047.

Thielsch, C., Andor, T., & Ehring, T. (2015). Metacognitions, intolerance of uncertainty and worry: An investigation in adolescents. *Personality and Individual Differences, 74*, 94–98.

Thijs, J., & Verkuyten, M. (2013). Multiculturalism in the classroom: Ethnic attitudes and classmates' beliefs. *International Journal of Intercultural Relations, 37*, 176–187.

Thivel, D., Isacco, L., Rousset, S., Boirie, Y., Morio, B., & Duché, P. (2011). Intensive exercise: A remedy for childhood obesity? *Physiology & Behavior, 102*, 132–136.

Thoermer, C., Woodward, A., Sodian, B., Perst, H., & Kristen, S. (2013). To get the grasp: Seven-month-olds encode and selectively reproduce goal-directed grasping. *Journal of Experimental Child Psychology, 116*, 499–509.

Thomas, A., & Chess, S. (1980). *The dynamics of psychological development*. New York: Brunner-Mazel.

Thomas, A., Chess, S., & Birch, H. G. (1968). *Temperament and behavior disorders in children*. New York: New York University Press.

Thomas, R. M. (2001). *Recent human development theories*. Thousand Oaks, CA: Sage.

Thomas, T. L., Strickland, O., Diclemente, R., & Higgins, M. (2013). An opportunity for cancer prevention during preadolescence and adolescence: Stopping human papillomavirus (HPV)-related cancer through HPV vaccination. *Journal of Adolescent Health, 52*(Suppl. 5), S60–S68.

Thompson, D. K., Omizzolo, C., Adamson, C., et al. (2014). Longitudinal growth and morphology of the hippocampus through childhood: Impact of prematurity and implications for memory and learning. *Human Brain Mapping, 35*(8), 4129–4139.

Thompson, R., Briggs-King, E. C., & LaTouche-Howard, S. A. (2012). Psychology of African American children: Strengths and challenges. In E. C. Chang, C. A. Downey (Eds.), *Handbook of race and development in mental health*. New York: Springer Science + Business Media.

Thomsen, L., Frankenhus, W. E., Ingold-Smith, M., & Carey, S. (2011). Big and mighty: preverbal infants mentally represent social dominance. *Journal of Physiological Science, 61*, 429–435.

Thöni, A., Mussner K., & Ploner F. (2010). Water birthing: Retrospective review of 2625 water births. Contamination of birth pool water and risk of microbial cross-infection. *Minerva Ginecologia, 62*, 203–211.

Thordstein, M., Löfgren, N., Flisberg, A., Lindecrantz, K., & Kjellmer, I. (2006). Sex differences in electrocortical activity in human neonates. *Neuroreport: For Rapid Communication of Neuroscience Research, 17*, 1165–1168.

Thornberry, T. P., & Krohn, M. D. (1997). Peers, drug use, and delinquency. In D. M. Stoff, J. Breiling, & J. D. Maser (Eds.), *Handbook of antisocial behavior* (pp. 218–233). New York: Wiley.

Thorsen, C., Gustafsson, J., & Cliffordson, C. (2014). The influence of fluid and crystallized intelligence on the development of knowledge and skills. *British Journal of Educational Psychology, 84*, 556–570.

Tibben, A. (2007). Predictive testing for Huntington's disease. *Brain Research Bulletin, 72*, 165–171.

Tibosch, M. M., Verhaak, C. M., & Merkus, P. M. (2011). Psychological characteristics associated with the onset and course of asthma in children and adolescents: A systematic review of longitudinal effects. *Patient Education and Counseling, 82*, 11–19.

Timmermans, S., & Buchbinder, M. (2012). Expanded newborn screening: Articulating the ontology of diseases with bridging work in the clinic. *Sociology of Health & Illness, 34*, 208–220.

Tincoff, R., & Jusczyk, P. W. (1999). Some beginnings of word comprehension in 6-month-olds. *Psychological Science, 10*, 172–175.

Tinsley, B., Lees, N., & Sumartojo, E. (2004). Child and adolescent HIV risk: Familial and cultural perspectives. *Journal of Family Psychology, 18*, 208–224.

Tissaw, M. (2007). Making sense of neonatal imitation. *Theory & Psychology, 17*, 217–242.

Tobin, J. J., Wu, D. Y. H., & Davidson, D. H. (1989). *Preschool in three cultures: Japan, China, and the United States*. New Haven, CT: Yale University Press.

Toch, T. (1995, January 2). Kids and marijuana: The glamour is back. *U.S. News & World Report*, 12.

Todrank, J., Heth, G. & Restrepo, D. (2011). Effects of in utero odorant exposure on neuroanatomical development of the olfactory bulb and odour preferences. *Proceedings of Biological Sciences, 19*, 45–55.

Tolan, P. H., & Dodge, K. A. (2005). Children's mental health as a primary care and concern: A system for comprehensive support and service. *American Psychologist, 60*, 601–614.

Tomasello, M. (2011). Human culture in evolutionary perspective. In M. J. Gelfand, C. Chiu, & Y. Hong (Eds.), *Advances in culture and psychology* (Vol. 1). New York: Oxford University Press.

Tomblin, J. B., Hammer, C. S., & Zhang, X. (1998). The association of prenatal tobacco use and SLI. *International Journal of Language and Communication Disorders, 33*, 357–368.

Toomey, R. B., Ryan, C. D., Rafael, M., Card, N. A., & Russell, S. T. (2010). Gender-nonconforming lesbian, gay, bisexual, and transgender youth: School victimization and young adult psychosocial adjustment. *Developmental Psychology, 46*(6), 1580–1589.

Tomlinson-Keasey, C. (1985). *Child development: Psychological, sociological, and biological factors*. Homewood, IL: Dorsey.

Tongsong, T., Iamthongin, A., Wanapirak, C., et al. (2005). Accuracy of fetal heart-rate variability interpretation by obstetricians using the criteria of the National Institute of Child Health and Human Development compared with computer-aided interpretation. *Journal of Obstetric and Gynaecological Research, 31*, 68–71.

Tooley, U. A., Makhoul, Z., & Fisher, P. A. (2016). Nutritional status of foster children in the U.S.: Implications for cognitive and behavioral development. *Children and Youth Services Review, 70*, 369–374.

Toporek, R. L., Kwan, K., & Williams, R. A. (2012). Ethics and social justice in counseling psychology. In N. A. Fouad, J. A. Carter, & L. M. Subich (Eds.), *APA handbook of counseling psychology, Vol. 2: Practice, interventions, and applications*. Washington, DC: American Psychological Association.

Torvaldsen, S., Roberts, C. L., Simpson, J. M., Thompson, J. F., & Ellwood, D. A. (2006). Intrapartum epidural analgesia and breastfeeding: A prospective cohort study. *International Breastfeeding Journal, 24*, 1–24.

Toson, A. L. (2013). Show me the money: The benefits of for-profit charter schools (aka EMOs). *Education and Urban Society, 45, 658–667.*

Trabulsi, J. C., & Mennella, J. A. (2012). Diet, sensitive periods in flavour learning, and growth. *International Review Of Psychiatry, 24*(3), 219–230.

Trace, S. E., Thornton, L. M., Baker, J. H., et al. (2013). A behavioral-genetic investigation of bulimia nervosa and its relationship with alcohol use disorder. *Psychiatry Research, 208,* 232–237.

Tracy, M., Zimmerman, F., Galea, S., McCauley, E., & Vander Stoep, A. (2008). What explains the relation between family poverty and childhood depressive symptoms? *Journal of Psychiatric Research, 42,* 1163–1175.

Trainor, L., & Desjardins, R. (2002). Pitch characteristics of infant-directed speech affect infants' ability to discriminate vowels. *Psychonomic Bulletin & Review, 9,* 335–340.

Trainor, L. J. (2012). Predictive information processing is a fundamental learning mechanism present in early development: Evidence from infants. *International Journal of Psychophysiology, 83,* 256–258.

Trapnell, P. D., & Paulhus, D. L. (2012). Agentic and communal values: Their scope and measurement. *Journal of Personality Assessment, 94,* 39–52.

Trawick-Smith, J., & Dziurgot, T. (2011). 'Good-fit' teacher–child play interactions and the subsequent autonomous play of preschool children. *Early Childhood Research Quarterly, 26,* 110–123.

Trehub, S., & Hannon, E. (2009). Conventional rhythms enhance infants' and adults' perception of musical patterns. *Cortex, 45,* 110–118.

Trehub, S. E. (2003). The developmental origins of musicality. *Nature Neuroscience, 6,* 669–673.

Trehub, S. E., Schneider, B. A., Morrongiello, B. A., & Thorpe, L. A. (1989). Developmental changes in high-frequency sensitivity. *Audiology, 28,* 241–249.

Tremblay, R. E. (2001). The development of physical aggression during childhood and the prediction of later dangerousness. In G. F. Pinard & L. Pagani (Eds.), *Clinical assessment of dangerousness: Empirical contributions.* New York: Cambridge University Press.

Triche, E. W., & Hossain, N. (2007). Environmental factors implicated in the causation of adverse pregnancy outcome. *Seminars in Perinatology, 31,* 240–242.

Trickett, P. K., Kurtz, D. A., & Pizzigati, K. (2004). Resilient outcomes in abused and neglected children: Bases for strengths-based intervention and prevention policies. In K. I. Maton & C. J. Schellenbach (Eds.), *Investing in children, youth, families and communities: Strength-based research and policy.* Washington, DC: American Psychological Association.

Tripodi, S.J., Bender, K., Litschge, C., Vaughn, M.G. (2010). Interventions for reducing adolescent alcohol abuse: a meta-analytic review. *Archives of Pediatrics & Adolescent Medicine,* 164:85–91.

Trivedi, D., Dhakappa, N., Ghildiyal, P., Deekonda, S., Subramaniam, S., Iyer, J. S., & Kotiyan, M. S. (2016). Depression among adolescent students in South India: How serious is the issue?. *Indian Journal of Pediatrics* [cited 2017 Jun 4], 58, 349-50.

Tronick, E. (2003). Emotions and emotional communication in infants. In J. Raphael-Leff (Ed.), *Parent–infant psychodynamics: Wild things, mirrors and ghosts* (pp. 35–53). London: Whurr Publishers, Ltd.

Tronick, E. Z., Thomas, R. B., & Daltabuit, M. (1994). The Quechua manta pouch: A caretaking practice for buffering the Peruvian infant against the multiple stressors of high altitude. *Child Development, 65,* 1005–1013.

Tropp, L. (2003). The psychological impact of prejudice: Implications for intergroup contact. *Group Processes & Intergroup Relations, 6,* 131–149.

Tropp, L., & Wright, S. (2003). Evaluations and perceptions of self, ingroup, and outgroup: Comparisons between Mexican-American and European-American children. *Self & Identity, 2,* 203–221.

Trouilloud, D., Sarrazin, P., Bressoux, P., & Bois, J. (2006, February). Relation between teachers' early expectations and students' later perceived competence in physical education classes: Autonomy-supportive climate as a moderator. *Journal of Educational Psychology, 98*(1), 75–86.

Trzesniewski, K. H., Donnellan, M. B., & Robins, R. W. (2003). Stability of self-esteem across the life span. *Journal of Personality and Social Psychology, 84,* 205–220.

Tsering, D., Pal, R., & Dasgupta, A. (2010). Substance use among adolescent high school students in India: A survey of knowledge, attitude, and opinion. *Journal of Pharmacy and Bioallied Sciences, 2*(2), 137–140. Accessed from http://doi.org/10.4103/0975-7406.67005.

Tsunoda, T. (1985). *The Japanese brain: Uniqueness and universality.* Tokyo: Taishukan.

Tucker, J., Martínez, J., Ellickson, P., & Edelen, M. (2008, March). Temporal associations of cigarette smoking with social influences, academic performance, and delinquency: A four-wave longitudinal study from ages 13–23. *Psychology of Addictive Behaviors, 22*(1), 1–11.

Tucker-Drob, E. M., & Harden, K. (2012). Intellectual interest mediates gene × socioeconomic status interaction on adolescent academic achievement. *Child Development, 83,* 743–757.

Tudge, J., & Scrimsher, S. (2003). Lev S. Vygotsky on education: A cultural-historical, interpersonal, and individual approach to development. In B. Zimmerman (Ed.), *Educational psychology: A century of contributions.* Mahwah, NJ: Lawrence Erlbaum Associates.

Tuggle, F. J., Kerpelman, J. L., & Pittman, J. F. (2014). Parental support, psychological control, and early adolescents' relationships with friends and dating partners. *Family Relations: An Interdisciplinary Journal of Applied Family Studies, 63,* 496–512.

Turati, C. (2008). Newborns' memory processes: A study on the effects of retroactive interference and repetition priming. *Infancy, 13,* 557–569.

Turkheimer, E., Haley, A., Waldreon, M., D'Onofrio, B., & Gottesman, I. I. (2003). Socioeconomic status modifies heritability of IQ in young children. *Psychological Science, 14,* 623–628.

Turney, K., & Kao, G. (2009). Barriers to school involvement: Are immigrant parents disadvantaged? *Journal of Educational Research, 102,* 257–271.

Turriff, A., Macnamara, E., Levy, H. P., & Biesecker, B. (2016). The impact of living with Klinefelter syndrome: A qualitative exploration of adolescents and adults. *Journal of Genetic Counseling.* Retrieved March 3, 2017, from https://www.ncbi.nlm.nih.gov/pubmed/27832510.

Turton, P., Evans, C., & Hughes, P. (2009). Long-term psychosocial sequelae of stillbirth: Phase II of a nested case-control cohort study. *Archives of Women's Mental Health, 12,* 35–41.

Turville, C., & Golden, I. (2015, October 13). Autism and vaccination: The value of the evidence base of a recent meta-analysis. *Vaccine, 33*(42):5494–5496.

Twardosz, S., & Lutzker, J. (2009). Child maltreatment and the developing brain: A review of neuroscience perspectives. *Aggression and Violent Behavior, 15,* 59–68.

Twenge, J. M., & Campbell, W. K. (2001). Age and birth cohort differences in self-esteem: A cross-temporal meta-analysis. *Personality and Social Psychology Review, 5,* 321–344.

Twenge, J. M., Gentile, B., & Campbell, W. K. (2015). Birth cohort differences in personality. In M. Mikulincer, P. R. Shaver, M. L. Cooper, R. J. Larsen, M. Mikulincer, P. R. Shaver, … R. J. Larsen (Eds.), *APA handbook of personality and social psychology, Volume 4: Personality processes and individual differences.* Washington, DC: American Psychological Association.

Twomey, J. (2006). Issues in genetic testing of children. *MCN: The American Journal of Maternal/Child Nursing, 31,* 156–163.

Tyre, P., & Scelfo, J. (2003, September 22). Helping kids get fit. *Newsweek,* 60–62.

U.S. Bureau of Labor Statistics. (2012). *College enrollment.* Washington: U.S. Department of Labor.

U.S. Bureau of the Census. (2001). *Living arrangements of children.* Washington, DC: U.S. Bureau of the Census.

U.S. Bureau of the Census. (2008). *Statistical abstract of the United States, 2008.* Washington, DC: U.S. Government Printing Office.

U.S. Bureau of the Census. (2010a). *Current population survey.* Washington, DC: U.S. Department of Agriculture, Center for Nutrition Policy and Promotion.

U. S. Bureau of the Census. (2011). Current population survey and annual social and economic supplements. Washington, DC: U.S. Bureau of the Census.

U. S. Bureau of the Census. (2012). *Current population survey and annual social and economic supplements.* Washington, DC: U.S. Bureau of the Census.

U. S. Bureau of the Census. (2013). Current population survey and annual social and economic supplements. Washington, DC: U.S. Bureau of the Census.

U.S. Census Bureau. (2003). *Population reports.* Washington, DC: GPO.

U.S. Census Bureau (2011). *Overview of race and Hispanic origin: 2010–2010 Census briefs.* Washington, DC: U.S. Department of Commerce.

U.S. Census Bureau. (2014). *Projections of the size and composition of the U.S. population: 2014 to 2060.* Washington, DC: U.S. Census Bureau.

U.S. Department of Agriculture, Center for Nutrition Policy and Promotion (2011).

U.S. Department of Commerce, Census Bureau. (2015). Current population survey (CPS), October 1990 through 2014. *Digest of Education Statistics 2015,* table 219.70. Washington, DC: U.S. Department of Commerce.

U.S. Department of Health and Human Services, Health Resources and Services Administration, Maternal and Child Health Bureau. (2009). *Child Health USA 2008–2009.* Rockville, MD: U.S. Department of Health and Human Services.

Uchikoshi, Y. (2006). Early reading in bilingual kindergartners: Can educational television help? *Scientific Studies of Reading, 10,* 89–120.

Ulutas, I., & Ömeroglu, E. (2007). The effects of an emotional intelligence education program on the emotional intelligence of children. *Social Behavior and Personality, 35*(10), 1365–1372.

Umana-Taylor, A., Diveri, M., & Fine, M. (2002). Ethnic identity and self-esteem among Latino adolescents: Distinctions among Latino populations. *Journal of Adolescent Research, 17,* 303–327.

Umaña-Taylor, A. J., Quintana, S. M., Lee, R. M., et al. (2014). Ethnic and racial identity during adolescence and into young adulthood: An integrated conceptualization. *Child Development, 85,* 21–39.

UNDCP World Drug Report. New York; Oxford University press Inc.; 1997.

Underwood, E. (2014). The taste of things to come. *Science, 345,* 750–751.

Underwood, M. (2005). Introduction to the special section: Deception and observation. *Ethics & Behavior, 15,* 233–234.

UNESCO (2007). *EFA Global Monitoring Report 2008 Education for All by 2015 Will We Make it?* United Nations Education, Science and Cultural Organization, Paris.

UNESCO (2011). Education Counts: Towards the Millennium Development Goals. Accessed on 18 November 2013 from http://unesdoc.unesco.org/.

UNESCO (2014). Teaching and Learning: Achieving quality for all. Education for All Global Monitoring Report. UNESCO, Paris.

UNESCO Institute for Statistics (2015). *Adult and youth literacy.* Montreal: UNESCO Institute for Statistics.

UNFPA (2005). State of the world population. Child Marriage Fact Sheet. Available at http://www.unfpa.org/.

UNFPA (2013), Adolescent pregnancy: A review of the evidence, accessed from https://www.unfpa.org/ on 17 December 2018.

Unger, R., & Crawford, M. (2003). *Women and gender: A feminist psychology* (4th ed.). New York: McGraw-Hill.

UNICEF (2001). A league table of teenage births in rich nations. Innocenti Research Centre Florence, Italy.

UNICEF (2008). Progress for children. Protecting against abuse, exploitation, and violence. Child Marriage. Available at: http://www.unicef.org/.

UNICEF (2008). Early Marriage: Child Spouses. *Innocenti Digest,* 7. Available at: http://www.uniceficdc.org/.

UNICEF (2016). Child online protection in India. Accessed from http://www.icmec.org/wp-content/uploads/2016/09/UNICEF-Child-Protection-Online-India-pub_doc115.pdf

UNICEF. (2013). #endviolence against children. Retrieved January 22, 2014, from http://www.unicef.org/endviolence/facts.html.

UNICEF, WHO, World Bank Joint Child Malnutrition Estimates (2016). *Levels and trends in child malnutrition.* Paris: UNICEF, WHO, World Bank.

United Nations Children's Fund. (2004). *Childhood Under Threat.* NY: United Nations.

United Nations Statistics Division. (2012). Statistical Annex Table 2.A Health—*United Nations* Statistics Division.

United Nations World Food Programme (2013). *State of school feeding worldwide, 2013.* Rome: World Food Programme.

University of Akron. (2006). *A longitudinal evaluation of the new curricula for the D.A.R.E. middle (7th grade) and high school (9th grade) programs: Take charge of your life.* Akron, OH: University of Akron.

Upadhyah, A., Misra, R., Parchwani, D., Maheria, P. (2014). Prevalence and Risk Factors for Eating Disorders in Indian Adolescent Females, *National Journal of Physiology, Pharmacy, & Pharmacology,* 4(2), 153–157.

Updegraff, K. A., McHale, S. M., Whiteman, S. D., Thayer, S. M., & Crouter, A. C. (2006). The nature and correlates of Mexican-American adolescents' time with parents and peers. *Child Development, 77,* 1470–1486.

Urberg, K., Luo, Q., & Pilgrim, C. (2003). A two-stage model of peer influence in adolescent substance use: Individual and relationship-specific differences in susceptibility to influence. *Addictive Behaviors, 28,* 1243–1256.

Urso, A. (2007). The reality of neonatal pain and the resulting effects. *Journal of Neonatal Nursing, 13,* 236–238.

Uttal, D. H., Meadow, N. G., Tipton, E., Hand, L. L., Alden, A. R., Warren, C., & Newcombe, N. S. (2013). The malleability of spatial skills: A meta-analysis of training studies. *Psychological Bulletin, 139,* 352–402.

Uylings, H. (2006). Development of the human cortex and the concept of "critical" or "sensitive" periods. *Language Learning, 56,* 59–90.

Vagi, K. J., Rothman, E., Latzman, N. E., Teten Tharp, A., Hall, D. M., & Breiding, M. (2013). Beyond correlates: A review of risk and protective factors for adolescent dating violence perpetration. *Journal of Youth and Adolescence, 42,* 633–649.

Vagi, K. J., Olsen, E. O., Basile, K. C., & Vivolo-Kantor, A. M. (2015). Teen dating violence (physical and sexual) among US high school students: Findings from the 2013 National Youth Risk Behavior Survey. *JAMA Pediatrics, 169,* 474–482.

Vaillant, G. E., & Vaillant, C. O. (1981). Natural history of male psychological health, X: Work as a predictor of positive mental health. *American Journal of Psychiatry, 138,* 1433–1440.

Vaish, A., & Striano, T. (2004). Is visual reference necessary? Contributions of facial versus vocal cues in 12-month-olds' social referencing behavior. *Developmental Science, 7,* 261–269.

Valentino, K., Nuttall, A. K., Comas, M., et al. (2014). *Developmental Psychology, 50,* 1197–1207.

Valiente, C., Eisenberg, N., & Fabes, R. A. (2004). Prediction of children's empathy-related responding from their effortful control and parents' expressivity. *Developmental Psychology, 40,* 911–926.

Valles, N., & Knutson, J. (2008). Contingent responses of mothers and peers to indirect and direct aggression in preschool and school-aged children. *Aggressive Behavior, 34,* 497–510.

Vallotton, C. (2011). Babies open our minds to their minds: How 'listening' to infant signs complements and extends our knowledge of infants and their development. *Infant Mental Health Journal, 32,* 115–133.

Van de Graaff, K. (2000). *Human anatomy* (5th ed.). Boston: McGraw-Hill.

Van der Mark, I., van ijzendoorn, M., & Bakermans-Kranenburg, M. (2002). Development of empathy in girls during the second year of life: Associations with parenting, attachment, and temperament. *Social Development, 11,* 451–468.

van der Veer, R., & Yasnitsky, A. (2016). Vygotsky the published: Who wrote Vygotsky and what Vygotsky actually wrote. In A. Yasnitsky & R. van der Veer (Eds.), *Revisionist revolution in Vygotsky studies.* New York: Routledge/Taylor & Francis Group.

van Ditzhuijzen, J., ten Have, M., de Graaf, R. van Nijnatten, C. H. C. J., & Vollebergh, W. A. M. (2013). Psychiatric history of women who have had an abortion. *Journal of Psychiatric Research, 47,* 1737–1743.

Van Goethem, A. A. J., Scholte, R. H. J., & Wiers, R. W. (2010). Explicit and implicit bullying attitudes in relation to bullying behavior. *Journal of Abnormal Child Psychology: An Official Publication of the International Society for Research in Child and Adolescent Psychopathology, 38,* 829–842.

van Haren, N. M., Rijsdijk, F., Schnack, H. G., et al. (2012). The genetic and environmental determinants of the association between brain abnormalities and schizophrenia: The schizophrenia twins and relatives consortium. *Biological Psychiatry, 71,* 915–921.

Van Kleeck, A., & Stahl, S. (2003). *On reading books to children: Parents and teachers.* Mahwah, NJ: Lawrence Erlbaum Associates.

vanMarle, K., & Wynn, K. (2009). Infants' auditory enumeration: Evidence for analog magnitudes in the small number range. *Cognition, 111,* 302–316.

Van Neste, J., Hayden, A., Lorch, E. P., & Milich, R. (2015). Inference generation and story comprehension among children with ADHD. *Journal of Abnormal Child Psychology, 43,* 259–270.

van Oosten, J. F., & Vandenbosch, L. (2017). Sexy online self-presentation on social network sites and the willingness to engage in sexting: A comparison of gender and age. *Journal of Adolescence, 54,* 42–50.

Van Ouytsel, J., Ponnet, K., Walrave, M. & d'Haenens, L. (2017). Adolescent sexting from a social learning perspective. Telematics and Informatics 34, 287-298

van Reenen, S., & van Rensburg, E. (2013). The influence of an unplanned Caesarean section on initial mother-infant bonding: Mothers' subjective experiences. *Journal of Psychology in Africa, 23,* 269–274.

Vandell, D. L. (2000). Parents, peer groups, and other socializing influences. *Developmental Psychology, 36,* 699–710.

Vandell, D. L. (2004). Early child care: The known and the unknown. *Merrill-Palmer Quarterly, 50* [Special issue: The maturing of human developmental sciences: Appraising past, present, and prospective agendas], 387–414.

Vandell, D. L., Burchinal, M. R., Belsky, J., Owen, M. T., Friedman, S. L., Clarke-Stewart, A., McCartney, K., & Weinraub, M. (2005a). Early child care and children's development in the primary grades: Follow-up results from the NICHD Study of Early Child Care. Paper presented at the biennial meeting of the Society for Research in Child Development, Atlanta, GA.

Vandell, D. L., Shumow, L., & Posner, J. (2005b). After-school programs for low-income children: Differences in program quality. In J. L. Mahoney, R. W. Larson, & J. S. Ecccles, Organized activities as contexts of development: Extracurricular activities, after-school and community programs. Mahwah, NJ: Lawrence Erlbaum.

Vanden Abeele, M., Campbell, S. W., Eggermont, S., & Roe, K. (2014). Sexting, mobile porn use, and peer group dynamics: Boys' and girls' self-perceived popularity, need for popularity, and perceived peer pressure. *Media Psychology, 17*(1), 6–33.

Vanlierde, A., Renier, L. & DeVolder, A. G. (2008). Brain plasticity and multisensory experience in early blind individuals. In J. J. Rieser, D. H. Ashmead, F. F. Ebner, & A. L. Corn (Eds). *Blindness and brain plasticity in navigation and object perception.* Mahwah, NJ: Lawrence Erlbaum Associates.

Vanvuchelen, M., Roeyers, H., & De Weerdt, W. (2011). Development and initial validation of the Preschool Imitation and Praxis Scale (PIPS). *Research in Autism Spectrum Disorders, 5,* 463–473.

Vartanian, L. R. (2000). Revisiting the imaginary audience and personal fable constructs of adolescent egocentrism: A conceptual review. *Adolescence, 35,* 639–646.

Vasanta, D, Sastry, J.V., & Ravi, M.I. (1995). Grammaticality judgement of Telugu speaking elementary school children (pp. 147–160), in Bai, B. L. & Vasanta, D. (Eds). *Language Development and Language Disorders: Perspectives from Indian Languages.* New Delhi: Bahri Publications.

Vaughn, V., McKay, R. J., & Behrman, R. (1979). *Nelson textbook of pediatrics* (11th ed.). Philadelphia: Saunders.

Vedantam, S. (2004, April 23). Antidepressants called unsafe for children: Four medications singled out in analysis of many studies. *The Washington Post,* p. A03.

Vela, R. M., Glod, C. A., Rivinus, T. M., & Johnson, R. (2011). Antidepressant treatment of pediatric depression. In D. A. Ciraulo, R. Shader (Eds.), *Pharmacotherapy of depression* (2nd ed.). New York: Springer Science + Business Media.

Vélez, C. E., Wolchik, S. A., Tein, J., & Sandler, I. (2011). Protecting children from the consequences of divorce: A longitudinal study of the effects of parenting on children's coping processes. *Child Development, 82,* 244–257.

Venker, C. E., Kover, S. T., & Weismer, S. E. (2016). Brief report: Fast mapping predicts differences in concurrent and later language abilities among children with ASD. *Journal of Autism and Developmental Disorders, 46,* 1118–1123.

Veraksa, N., Shiyan, O., Shiyan, I., Pramling, N., & Pramling-Samuelsson, I. (2016). Communication between teacher and child in early child education: Vygotskian theory and educational practice. *Infancia Y Aprendizaje/Journal for the Study of Education and Development, 39,* 221–243.

Verdugo, R. R. (2011). The heavens may fall: School dropouts, the achievement gap, and statistical bias. *Education and Urban Society, 43,* 184–204.

Vereijken, C. M., Riksen-Walraven, J. M., & Kondo-Ikemura, K. (1997). Maternal sensitivity and infant attachment security in Japan: A longitudinal study. *International Journal of Behavioral Development, 21,* 35–49.

Verkuyten, M. (2008). Life satisfaction among ethnic minorities: The role of discrimination and group identification. *Social Indicators Research, 89*(3), 391–404.

Vermandel, A., Weyler, J., De Wachter, S., & Wyndaele, J. (2008). Toilet training of healthy young toddlers: A randomized trial between a daytime wetting alarm and timed potty training. *Journal of Developmental & Behavioral Pediatrics, 29,* 191–196.

Verschueren, K., Doumen, S., & Buyse, E. (2012). Relationships with mother, teacher, and peers: Unique and joint effects on young children's self-concept. *Attachment & Human Development, 14,* 233–248.

Veselka, L., Just, C., Jang, K. L., Johnson, A. M., & Vernon, P. A. (2012). The general factor of personality: A critical test. *Personality and Individual Differences, 52,* 261–264.

Villarosa, L. (2003, December 23). More teenagers say no to sex, and experts are sure why. *The New York Times,* p. D6.

Vingerhoets, A., Nyklicek, I., & Denollet, J. (Eds.). (2008). *Emotion regulation: Conceptual and clinical issues.* New York, NY: Springer Science + Business Media, 2008.

Vinik, J., Almas, A., & Grusec, J. (2011). Mothers' knowledge of what distresses and what comforts their children predicts children's coping, empathy, and prosocial behavior. *Parenting: Science and Practice, 11,* 56–71.

Vinkhuyzen, A. A. E., van der Sluis, S., de Geus, E. J. C., Boomsma, D. I., & Posthuma, D. (2010). Genetic influences on "environmental" factors. *Genes, Brain and Behavior, 9,* 276–287.

Visconti, K., Kochenderfer-Ladd, B., & Clifford, C. A. (2013). Children's attributions for peer victimization: A social comparison approach. *Journal of Applied Developmental Psychology, 34,* 277–287.

Visser, S. N., Danielson, M. L., Bitsko, R. H., et al. (2014). Trends in the parent-report of health care provider diagnosed and medicated ADHD: United States, 2003—2011. *Journal of the American Academy of Child and Adolescent Psychiatry, 53*(1), 34–46.

Vivanti, G., Paynter, J., Duncan, E., Fothergill, H., Dissanayake, C., & Rogers, S. J. (2014). Effectiveness and feasibility of the Early Start Denver Model implemented in a group-based community childcare setting. *Journal of Autism and Developmental Disorders, 44,* 3140–3153.

Vohs, K. D., & Heatherton, T. (2004). Ego threats elicits different social comparison process among high and low self-esteem people: Implications for interpersonal perceptions. *Social Cognition, 22,* 168–191.

Volker, S. (2007). Infants' vocal engagement oriented towards mother versus stranger at 3 months and avoidant attachment behavior at 12 months. *International Journal of Behavioral Development, 31,* 88–95.

Votruba-Drzal, E., Coley, R. L., & Chase-Lansdale, L. (2004). Child care and low-income children's development: Direct and moderated effects. *Child Development, 75,* 396–312.

Vreeswijk, C. M., Maas, A. M., Rijk, C. M., & van Bakel, H. A. (2013). Fathers' experiences during pregnancy: Paternal prenatal attachment and representations of the fetus. *Psychology of Men & Masculinity,* Retrieved February 8, 2014, from http://psycnet.apa.org/psycinfo/2013-27681-001/.

Vyas, S. (2004). Exploring bicultural identities of Asian high school students through the analytic window of a literature club. *Journal of Adolescent & Adult Literacy, 48,* 12–18.

Vygotsky, L. S. (1926/1997). *Educational psychology.* Delray Beach, FL: St. Lucie Press.

Vygotsky, L. S. (1979). *Mind in society: The development of higher mental processes.* Cambridge, MA: Harvard University Press. (Original works published 1930, 1933, and 1935).

Wachs, T. (2002). Nutritional deficiencies as a biological context for development. In W. Hartup, W. Silbereisen, & K. Rainer (Eds.), *Growing points in developmental science: An introduction.* Philadelphia, PA: Psychology Press.

Wachs, T. D. (1992). *The nature of nurture.* Newbury Park, CA: Sage.

Wachs, T. D. (1993). The nature–nurture gap: What we have here is a failure to collaborate. In R. Plomin & G. E. McClearn (Eds.), *Nature, nurture, and psychology.* Washington, DC: American Psychological Association.

Wachs, T. D. (1996). Known and potential processes underlying developmental trajectories in childhood and adolescence. *Developmental Psychology, 32,* 796–801.

Wada, A., Kunii, Y., Ikemoto, K., et al. (2012). Increased ratio of calcineurin immunoreactive neurons in the caudate nucleus of patients with schizophrenia. *Progress in Neuro-Psychopharmacology & Biological Psychiatry, 37,* 8–14.

Wade, N. (2001, October 4). Researchers say gene is linked to language. *The New York Times,* p. A1.

Wade, T., Tiggemann, M., Bulik, C., Fairburn, C., Wray, N., & Martin, N. (2008, February). Shared temperament risk factors for anorexia nervosa: A twin study. *Psychosomatic Medicine, 70*(2), 239–244.

Wade, T. D., & Watson, H. J. (2012). Psychotherapies in eating disorders. In J. Alexander, J. Treasure (Eds.), *A collaborative approach to eating disorders.* New York: Routledge/Taylor & Francis Group.

Wagnsson, S., Stenling, A., Gustafsson, H., & Augustsson, C. (2016). Swedish youth football players' attitudes towards moral decision in sport as predicted by the parent-initiated motivational climate. *Psychology of Sport and Exercise, 25,* 110–114.

Wahlin, T. (2007). To know or not to know: A review of behaviour and suicidal ideation in preclinical Huntington's disease. *Patient Education and Counseling, 65,* 279–287.

Wakschlag, L. S., Leventhal, B. L., Pine, D. S., Pickett, K. E., & Carter, A. S. (2006). Elucidating early mechanisms of developmental psychopathology: The case of prenatal smoking and disruptive behavior. *Child Development, 77*(4), 893–906.

Wainwright, J. L., Russell, S. T., & Patterson, C. J. (2004). Psychosocial adjustment, school outcomes, and romantic relationships of adolescents with same-sex parents. *Child Development, 75*, 1886–1898.

Waite, S. J., Bromfield, C., & McShane, S. (2005). Successful for whom? A methodology to evaluate and inform inclusive activity in schools. *European Journal of Special Needs Education, 20*, 71–88.

Waldman, S. (2010, July 12). In plain English, he wants it to be official. *The Times-Union (Albany, NY)*, A1.

Walker, W. A., & Humphries, C. (2007, September 17). Starting the good life in the womb. *Newsweek*, pp. 56–57.

Walker, W. A., & Humphries, C. (2005). *The Harvard Medical School guide to healthy eating during pregnancy.* New York: McGraw-Hill.

Wallis, C. (2005, January 9). The new science of happiness. *Time*, 12–15.

Walters, E., & Gardner, H. (1986). The theory of multiple intelligences: Some issues and answers. In R. J. Sternberg & R. K. Wagner (Eds.), *Practical intelligence.* New York: Cambridge University Press.

Wang, C., He, Y., Liang, L., et al. (2011). Effects of short - and long-acting recombinant human growth hormone (PEG-rhGH) on left ventricular function in children with growth hormone deficiency. *Acta Paediatrica, 100*, 140–142.

Wang, L., Chyen, D., Lee, S., & Lowry, R. (2008, May). The association between body mass index in adolescence and obesity in adulthood. *Journal of Adolescent Health, 42*(5), 512–518.

Wang, Q. (2006). Culture and the development of self-knowledge. *Current Directions in Psychological Science, 15*, 182–187.

Wang, Q. (2008). Emotion knowledge and autobiographical memory across the preschool years: A cross-cultural longitudinal investigation. *Cognition, 108*, 117–135.

Wang, Q., Pomerantz, E., & Chen, H. (2007). The role of parents' control in early adolescents' psychological functioning: A longitudinal investigation in the United States and China. *Child Development, 78*, 1592–1610.

Wang, Z., Deater-Deckard, K., Cutting, L., Thompson, L. A., & Petrill, S. A. (2012). Working memory and parent-rated components of attention in middle childhood: A behavioral genetic study. *Behavior Genetics, 42*, 199–208.

Wang, Z., Devine, R. T., Wong, K. K., & Hughes, C. (2016). Theory of mind and executive function during middle childhood across cultures. *Journal of Experimental Child Psychology, 149*, 6–22.

Ward, R., Niñonuevo, M., Mills, D., Lebrilla, C., & German, J. (2007). In vitro fermentability of human milk oligosaccharides by several strains of bifidobacteria. *Molecular Nutrition & Food Research, 51*, 1398–1405.

Wardle, F. (2007). Multiracial children in child development textbooks. *Early Childhood Education Journal, 35*, 253–259.

Wardle, J., Guthrie, C., & Sanderson, S. (2001). Food and activity preferences in children of lean and obese parents. *International Journal of Obesity & Related Metabolic Disorders, 25*, 971–977.

Warford, M. K. (2011). The zone of proximal teacher development. *Teaching and Teacher Education, 27*, 252–258.

Warne, R. T., & Liu, J. K. (2017). Income differences among grade skippers and non-grade skippers across genders in the Terman sample, 1936–1976. *Learning and Instruction, 47*, 1–12.

Warren J. R. (2002). Reconsidering the relationship between student employment and academic outcomes: A new theory and better data. *Youth & Society, 33*, 366–370.

Warren, J. R., Lee, J. C., & Cataldi, E. F. (2004). Teenage employment and high school completion. In D. Conley & K. Albright (Eds.), *After the bell—family background, public policy, and educational success.* London: Routledge.

Wasserman, J. D., & Tulsky, D. S. (2005). The history of intelligence assessment. In D. P. Flanagan & P. L. Harrison (Eds.), *Contemporary intellectual assessment: Theories, tests, and issues.* New York, Guilford Press.

Waterhouse, J. M., & DeCoursey, P. J. (2004). Human circadian organization. In J. C. Dunlap & J. J. Loros (Eds.), *Chronobiology: Biological timekeeping.* Sunderland, MA: Sinauer Associates.

Waterland, R. A., & Jirtle, R. L. (2004). Early nutrition, epigenetic changes at transposons and imprinted genes, and enhanced susceptibility to adult chronic diseases. *Nutrition, 63*–68.

Watling, D., & Bourne, V. (2007, September). Linking children's neuropsychological processing of emotion with their knowledge of emotion expression regulation. *Laterality: Asymmetries of Body, Brain and Cognition, 12*(5), 381–396.

Watson-Gegeo, K.; Gegeo, D. (1986). Calling-out and repeating routines in Kwara'ae children's language socialization. In: Scheiffelin, B.; Ochs, E., editors. Language socialization across cultures. New York: Cambridge University Press; p. 17-50.

Watson, J. B. (1925). *Behaviorism.* New York: Norton.

Watson, J. B., & Rayner, R. (1920). Conditioned, emotional reactions. *Journal of Experimental Psychology, 3*, 1–14.

Weaver, J. (2013). How brain waves help us make sense of speech. *Plos Biology, 11*, 18–29.

Weaver, J. M., & Schofield, T. J. (2015). Mediation and moderation of divorce effects on children's behavior problems. *Journal of Family Psychology, 29*, 39–48.

Webb, E. A., O'Reilly, M. A., Clayden, J. D., et al. (2012). Effect of growth hormone deficiency on brain structure, motor function and cognition. *Brain: A Journal of Neurology, 135.*

Webb, R. M., Lubinski, D., & Benbow, C. P. (2002). Mathematically facile adolescents with math/science aspirations: New perspectives on their educational and vocational development. *Journal of Educational Psychology, 94*, 785–794.

Weber, B. (2005, February 25.) From sidelines or in the rink, goalies are targets, even at 8. *New York Times*, p. B1, B8.

Weber, K. (Ed.). (2010). *Waiting for Superman.* New York, NY: Public Affairs.

Wechsler, D. (1975). Intelligence defined and undefined. *American Psychologist, 30*, 135–139.

Wechsler, H., Lee, J. E., Kuo, M., Seibring, M., Nelson, T. F., & Lee, H. (2002). Trends in college binge drinking during a period of increased prevention efforts: Findings from 4 Harvard School of Public Health college alcohol study surveys, 1993–2001.

Weinstock, H., Berman, S., & Cates, W., Jr. (2004). Sexually transmitted diseases among American youth: Incidence and prevalence estimates, 2000. *Perspectives on Sexual and Reproductive Health, 36*, 182–191.

Weisleder, A., & Fernald, A. (2013). Talking to children matters: Early language experience strengthens processing and builds vocabulary. *Psychological Science, 24*(11), 2143–2152.

Weiss, R. (2003, September 2). Genes' sway over IQ may vary with class. *The Washington Post*, p. A1.

Weissman, A. S., Chu, B. C., Reddy, L. A., & Mohlman, J. (2012). Attention mechanisms in children with anxiety disorders and in children with attention deficit hyperactivity disorder: Implications for research and practice. *Journal of Clinical Child and Adolescent Psychology, 41*, 117–126.

Weisz, A., & Black, B. (2002). Gender and moral reasoning: African American youth respond to dating dilemmas. *Journal of Human Behavior in the Social Environment, 5*, 35–52.

Weitzman, E., Nelson, T., & Wechsler, H. (2003). Taking up binge drinking in college: The influences of person, social group, and environment. *Journal of Adolescent Health, 32*, 26–35.

Welch, M. G. (2016). Calming cycle theory: The role of visceral/autonomic learning in early mother and infant/child behaviour and development. *Acta Paediatrica, 105*(11), 1266–1274.

Wellings, K., Collumbien, M., Slaymaker, E., et al. (2006, November). Sexual behaviour in context: A global perspective. *Lancet, 368*(9548), 1706–1738.

Wellman, H., Fang, F., Liu, D., Zhu, L., & Liu, G. (2006, December). Scaling of theory-of-mind understandings in Chinese children. *Psychological Science, 17*, 1075–1081.

Wellman, H., Lopez-Duran, S., LaBounty, J., & Hamilton, B. (2008). Infant attention to intentional action predicts preschool theory of mind. *Developmental Psychology, 44*, 618–623.

Wellman, H. M. (2012). Theory of mind: Better methods, clearer findings, more development. *European Journal of Developmental Psychology, 9*, 313–330.

Wells, B., Peppé, S., Goulandris, N. (2004). Intonation development from five to thirteen. *Journal of Child Language, 31*, 749–778.

Wells, R., Lohman, D., & Marron, M. (2009). What factors are associated with grade acceleration? An analysis and comparison of two U.S. databases. *Journal of Advanced Academics, 20*, 248–273.

Welsh, T., Ray, M., Weeks, D., Dewey, D., & Elliott, D. (2009). Does Joe influence Fred's action? Not if Fred has autism spectrum disorder. *Brain Research, 1248*, 141–148.

Werker, J. F., Pons, F., Dietrich, C., Kajikawa, S., Fais, L., & Amano, S. (2007). Infant-directed speech supports phonetic category learning in English and Japanese. *Cognition, 103*, 147–162.

Werner, E., Myers, M., Fifer, W., et al. (2007). Prenatal predictors of infant temperament. *Developmental Psychobiology, 49*, 474–484.

Werner, E. E., & Smith, R. S. (2002). Journeys from childhood to midlife: Risk, resilience and recovery. *Journal of Developmental and Behavioral Pediatrics, 23*, 456.

Werner, L. A., & Marean, G. C. (1996). *Human auditory development.* Boulder, CO: Westview Press.

Werner, N. E., & Crick, N. R. (2004). Maladaptive peer relationships and the development of relational and physical aggression during middle childhood. *Social Development, 13*, 495–514.

Wertsch, J. (2008). From social interaction to higher psychological processes: A clarification and application of Vygotsky's theory. *Human Development, 51*, 66–79.

Wertsch, J. V. (1999). The zone of proximal development: Some conceptual issues. In P. Lloyd & C. Fernyhough (Eds.), *Lev Vygotsky: Critical assessments, Vol. 3: The zone of proximal development.* New York: Routledge.

West, J. R., & Blake, C. A. (2005). Fetal alcohol syndrome: An assessment of the field. *Experimental Biology and Medicine, 230*, 354–356.

Westerhausen, R., Kreuder, F., Sequeira Sdos, S., et al. (2004). Effects of handedness and gender on macro- and microstructure of the corpus callosum and its subregions: A combined high-resolution and diffusion-tensor MRI study. *Brain Research and Cognitive Brain Research, 21*, 418–426.

Westermann, G., Mareschal, D., Johnson, M. H., Sirois, S., Spratling, M. W., & Thomas, M. S. (2007). Neuroconstructivism. *Developmental Science, 10*, 75–83.

Wexler, B. (2006). *Brain and culture: Neurobiology, ideology, and social change.* Cambridge, MA: MIT Press.

Whalen, C. K., Jamner, L. D., Henker, B., Delfino, R. J., & Lozano, J. M. (2002). The ADHD spectrum and everyday life: Experience sampling of adolescent moods, activities, smoking, and drinking. *Child Development, 73*, 209–227.

Whalen, D., Levitt, A., & Goldstein, L. (2007). VOT in the babbling of French- and English-learning infants. *Journal of Phonetics, 35*, 341–352.

Whaley, B. B., & Parker, R. G. (2000). Expressing the experience of communicative disability: Metaphors of persons who stutter. *Communication Reports, 13*, 115–125.

Whelan, T., & Lally, C. (2002). Paternal commitment and father's quality of life. *Journal of Family Studies, 8*, 181–196.

Whitaker, R. C., Wright, J. A., Pepe, M. S., Seidel, K. D., & Dietz, W. H. (1997, September 25). Predicting obesity in young adulthood from childhood and parental obesity. *The New England Journal of Medicine, 337*, 869–873.

White, K. (2007). Hypnobirthing: The Mongan method. *Australian Journal of Clinical Hypnotherapy and Hypnosis, 28*, 12–24.

White, M., & White, G. (2006, August). Implicit and explicit occupational gender stereotypes. *Sex Roles, 55*(3), 259–266.

White House Initiative on Native American and Alaska Native Education (2017). Tribal colleges and universities. Retrieved May 5, 2017, from https://sites.ed.gov/whiaiane/tribes-tcus/tribal-colleges-and-universities/.

Whitebread, D., Coltman, P., Jameson, H., & Lander, R. (2009). Play, cognition and self-regulation: What exactly are children learning when they learn through play? *Educational and Child Psychology, 26*, 40–52.

Whiting, B. B., & Edwards, C. P. (1988). *Children of different worlds: The formation of social behavior.* Cambridge, MA: Harvard University Press.

Widaman, K. (2009). Phenylketonuria in children and mothers: Genes, environments, behavior. *Current Directions in Psychological Science, 18*, 48–52.

Widman, L., Nesi, J., Choukas-Bradley, S., & Prinstein, M. J. (2014). Safe sext: Adolescents' use of technology to communicate about sexual health with dating partners. *Journal of Adolescent Health, 54*, 612–614.

Widom, C. S. (2000). Motivation and mechanisms in the "cycle of violence" In D. J. Hansen (Ed.), *Nebraska Symposium on Motivation, Vol. 46, 1998: Motivation and child maltreatment* (Current theory and research in motivation series). Lincoln, NE: University of Nebraska Press.

Widom, C. S., & Czaja, S. J. (2012). Childhood trauma, psychopathology, and violence: Disentangling causes, consequences, and correlates. In C. S. Widom, (Ed.), *Trauma, psychopathology, and violence: Causes, consequences, or correlates?* (pp. 291–317). New York: Oxford University Press.

Wigfield, A. & Eccles J. (2002). (Eds.). *Development of achievement motivation.* San Diego: Academic Press.

Wiggins, J. L., Bedoyan, J. K., Carrasco, M., Swartz, J. R., Martin, D. M., & Monk, C. S. (2014). Age-related effect of serotonin transporter genotype on amygdala and prefrontal cortex function in adolescence. *Human Brain Mapping, 35*, 646–658.

Wilcox, A., Skjaerven, R., Buekens, P., & Kiely, J. (1995, March 1). Birth weight and perinatal mortality: A comparison of the United States and Norway. *Journal of the American Medical Association, 273*, 709–711.

Wilcox, H. C., Conner, K. R., & Caine, E. D. (2004). Association of alcohol and drug use disorders and completed suicide: An empirical review of cohort studies. *Drug & Alcohol Dependence, 76* [Special issue: Drug abuse and suicidal behavior], S11–S19.

Wilcox, T., Woods, R., Chapa, C., & McCurry, S. (2007). Multisensory exploration and object individuation in infancy. *Developmental Psychology, 43*, 479–495.

Wildberger, S. (2003, August). So you're having a baby. *Washingtonian, 85–86*, 88–90.

Wilfond, B., & Ross, L. (2009). From genetics to genomics: Ethics, policy, and parental decision-making. *Journal of Pediatric Psychology, 34*, 639–647.

Wilkes, S., Chinn, D., Murdoch, A., & Rubin, G. (2009). Epidemiology and management of infertility: A population-based study in UK primary care. *Family Practice, 26,* 269–274.

Wilkosz, M., Chen, J., Kennedy, C., & Rankin, S. (2011). Body dissatisfaction in California adolescents. *Journal of the American Academy of Nurse Practitioners, 23,* 101–109.

Willford, J. A., Richardson, G. A., & Day, N. L. (2012). Sex-specific effects of prenatal marijuana exposure on neurodevelopment and behavior. In M. Lewis, L. Kestler (Eds.), *Gender differences in prenatal substance exposure.* Washington, DC: American Psychological Association.

Williams, J., & Binnie, L. (2002). Children's concept of illness: An intervention to improve knowledge. *British Journal of Health Psychology, 7,* 129–148.

Willows, D. M., Kruk, R. S., & Corcos, E. (Eds.). (1993). *Visual processes in reading and reading disabilities.* Hillsdale, NJ: Erlbaum.

Wills, T., Sargent, J., Stoolmiller, M., Gibbons, F., & Gerrard, M. (2008). Movie smoking exposure and smoking onset: A longitudinal study of mediation processes in a representative sample of U.S. adolescents. *Psychology of Addictive Behaviors, 22,* 269–277.

Wilson, B. J., Smith, S. L., Potter, W. J., et al. (2002). Violence in children's television programming: Assessing the risks. *Journal of Communication, 52,* 5–35.

Wilson, G., Grilo, C., & Vitousek, K. (2007, April). Psychological treatment of eating disorders. *American Psychologist, 62*(3), 199–216.

Wilson, R. (2004, December 3). Where the elite teach, it's still a man's world. *Chronicle of Higher Education, 51,* A8.

Wilson, S., Schalet, B. D., Hicks, B. M., & Zucker, R. A. (2013). Identifying early childhood personality dimensions using the California child Q-Set and prospective associations with behavioral and psychosocial development. *Journal of Research in Personality, 47,* 339–350.

Wilson, T. S. (2016). Contesting the public school: Reconsidering charter schools as counterpublics. *American Educational Research Journal, 53*(4), 919–952.

Wilsona, C. L., & Simpson, J. A. (2016). Childbirth pain, attachment orientations, and romantic partner support during labor and delivery. *Personal Relationships, 23*(4), 622–644.

Wineburg, S. S. (1987). The self-fulfillment of the self-fulfilling prophecy. *Educational Researcher, 16,* 28–37.

Winger, G., & Woods, J. H. (2004). *A handbook on drug and alcohol abuse: The biomedical aspects.* Oxford, England: Oxford University Press.

Winner, E. (1989). Development in the visual arts. In W. Damon (Ed.), *Child development today and tomorrow.* San Francisco: Jossey-Bass.

Winsler, A. (2003). Introduction to special issue: Vygotskian perspectives in early childhood education. *Early Education and Development, 14* [Special Issue], 253–269.

Wisborg, K., Kesmodel, U., Bech, B. H., Hedegaard, M., & Henriksen, T. B. (2003). Maternal consumption of coffee during pregnancy and stillbirth and infant death in first year of life: Prospective study. *British Medical Journal, 326,* 420.

Withers, M., Kharazmi, N., & Lim, E. (2018). Traditional beliefs and practices in pregnancy, childbirth and postpartum: A review of the evidence from Asian countries. Midwifery 56, 158–170; accessed from www.elsevier.com.

Witt, E. A., Donnellan, M., & Trzesniewski, K. H. (2011). Self-esteem, narcissism, and Machiavellianism: Implications for understanding antisocial behavior in adolescents and young adults. In C. T. Barry, P. K. Kerig, K. K. Stellwagen, & T. D. Barry (Eds.), *Narcissism and Machiavellianism in youth: Implications for the development of adaptive and maladaptive behavior.* Washington, DC: American Psychological Association.

Woelfle, J. F., Harz, K., & Roth, C. (2007). Modulation of circulating IGF-I and IGFBP-3 levels by hormonal regulators of energy homeostasis in obese children. *Experimental and Clinical Endocrinology Diabetes, 115,* 17–23.

Wolfson, A. R., & Richards, M. (2011). Young adolescents: Struggles with insufficient sleep. In M. El-Sheikh & M. El-Sheikh (Eds.), *Sleep and development: Familial and socio-cultural considerations.* New York: Oxford University Press.

Wolitzky, D. L. (2011). Psychoanalytic theories of psychotherapy. In J. C. Norcross, G. R. VandenBos, D. K. Freedheim (Eds.), *History of psychotherapy: Continuity and change* (2nd ed.). Washington, DC: American Psychological Association.

Wonnacott, E. (2013). Learning: Statistical mechanisms in language acquisition. In P. M. Binder, K. Smith (Eds.), *The language phenomenon: Human communication from milliseconds to millennia.* New York: Springer-Verlag Publishing.

Wood, A. C., Saudino, K. J., Rogers, H., Asherson, P., & Kuntsi, J. (2007). Genetic influences on mechanically assessed activity level in children. *Journal of Child Psychology and Psychiatry, 48,* 695–702.

Wood, J. N., & Wood, S. M. (2016). Measuring the speed of newborn object recognition in controlled visual worlds. *Developmental Science.*

Wood, R. (1997). Trends in multiple births, 1938–1995. *Population Trends, 87,* 29–35.

Woodhouse, S. S., Dykas, M. J., & Cassidy, J. (2012). Loneliness and peer relations in adolescence. *Social Development, 21,* 273–293.

Woods, R. (2009). The use of aggression in primary school boys' decisions about inclusion in and exclusion from playground football games. *British Journal of Educational Psychology, 79,* 223–238.

Worobey, J., & Bajda, V. M. (1989). Temperament ratings at 2 weeks, 2 months, and 1 year: Differential stability of activity and emotionality. *Developmental Psychology, 25,* 257–263.

World Food Programme. (2106). *Hunger statistics.* Rome: World Food Programme. Retrieved May 21, 2016, from https://www.wfp.org/hunger/stats.

World Health Organization (1999). Report of the consultation on child abuse prevention; Geneva, accessed from http://www.who.int/.

WHO (2002). Revised global burden of disease (GBD) estimates, World Health Organization, Geneva, accessed from www.medicineNet.com.

WHO (2004). Adolescent pregnancy—Issues in adolescent health and development, WHO discussion papers on adolescence, p. 86.

WHO (2013). United Nations Population Fund: Married adolescents: no place of safety. Geneva: WHO-UNFPA; 2006.

World Health Organization (2017). 10 facts on children's environmental health. Accessed from http://www.who.int/ on Dec 7, 2018.

WHO (2017). Depression in India – Let's Talk. Accessed from http://www.searo.who.int/india/depression_in_india.pdf.

World Health Organization (2017). Global health observatory data. Retrieved May 2, 2017, from http://www.who.int/gho/hiv/en/.

Wörmann, V., Holodynski, M., Kärtner, J., & Keller, H. (2014). The emergence of social smiling: The interplay of maternal and infant imitation during the first three months in cross-cultural comparison. *Journal of Cross-Cultural Psychology, 45,* 339–361.

Worrell, F., Szarko, J., & Gabelko, N. (2001). Multi-year persistence of nontraditional students in an academic talent development program. *Journal of Secondary Gifted Education, 12,* 80–89.

Wright, E.M., & Fagan, A. A. (2013). The cycle of violence in context: Exploring the moderating roles of neighborhood disadvantage and cultural norms. *Criminology: An Interdisciplinary Journal, 51,* 217–249.

Wright, J. C., Huston, A. C., Reitz, A. L., & Piemyat, S. (1994). Young children's perceptions of television reality: Determinants and developmental differences. *Developmental Psychology*, 30, 229–239.

Wright, M., Wintemute, G., & Claire, B. (2008). Gun suicide by young people in California: Descriptive epidemiology and gun ownership. *Journal of Adolescent Health*, 43, 619–622.

Wu, C., & Chao, R. K. (2011). Intergenerational cultural dissonance in parent–adolescent relationships among Chinese and European Americans. *Developmental Psychology*, 47, 493–508.

Wu, P., Hoven, C., Okezie, N., Fuller, C., & Cohen, P. (2007). Alcohol abuse and depression in children and adolescents. *Journal of Child & Adolescent Substance Abuse*, 17(2), 51–69.

Wu, T., Treiber, F. A., & Snieder, H. (2013). Genetic influence on blood pressure and underlying hemodynamics measured at rest and during stress. *Psychosomatic Medicine*, 75, 404–412.

Wu, Y., Tsou, K., Hsu, C., Fang, L., Yao, G., & Jeng, S. (2008). Brief report: Taiwanese infants' mental and motor development–6–24 months. *Journal of Pediatric Psychology*, 33, 102–108.

Wu, Z., & Su, Y. (2014). How do preschoolers' sharing behaviors relate to their theory of mind understanding? *Journal of Experimental Child Psychology*, 120, 73–86.

Wupperman, P., Marlatt, G. A., Cunningham, A., et al. (2012). Mindfulness and modification therapy for behavioral dysregulation: Results from a pilot study targeting alcohol use and aggression in women. *Journal of Clinical Psychology*, 68, 50–66.

Wyer, R. (2004). The cognitive organization and use of general knowledge. In J. Jost & M. Banaji (Eds.), *Perspectivism in social psychology: The yin and yang of scientific progress*. Washington, DC: American Psychological Association.

Wynn, K. (1995). Infants possess a system of numerical knowledge. *Current Directions in Psychological Science*, 4, 172–177.

Wynn, K. (2000). Findings of addition and subtraction in infants are robust and consistent: Reply to Wakeley, Rivera, and Langer. *Child Development*, 71, 1535–1536.

Wyra, M., Lawson, M. J., Hungi, N. (2007). The mnemonic keyword method: The effects of bidirectional retrieval training and of ability to image on foreign language vocabulary recall. *Learning and Instruction*, 17, 360–371.

Xiao, R., Qi, X., Patino, A., et al. (2017). Characterization of infant mu rhythm immediately before crawling: A high-resolution EEG study. *Neuroimage*, 146, 47–57.

Xirasagar, S., Fu, J., Liu, J., Probst, J. C., & Lin, D. (2011). Neonatal outcomes for immigrant vs. native-born mothers in Taiwan: An epidemiological paradox. *Maternal and Child Health Journal*, 15, 269–279.

Xu, C., & LeFevre, J. (2016). Training young children on sequential relations among numbers and spatial decomposition: Differential transfer to number line and mental transformation tasks. *Developmental Psychology*, 52, 854–866.

Xu, J., Harper, J. A., Van Enkevort, E. A., Latimer, K., Kelley, U., & McAdams, C. J. (2017). Neural activations are related to body-shape, anxiety, and outcomes in adolescent anorexia nervosa. *Journal of Psychiatric Research*, 87, 1–7.

Xu, J., Saether, L., & Sommerville, J. A. (2016). Experience facilitates the emergence of sharing behavior among 7.5-month-old infants. *Developmental Psychology*, 52, 1732–1743.

Yamada, J., Stinson, J., Lamba, J., Dickson, A., McGrath, P., & Stevens, B. (2008). A review of systematic reviews on pain interventions in hospitalized infants. *Pain Research & Management*, 13, 413–420.

Yan, Z., & Fischer, K. (2002). Always under construction: Dynamic variations in adult cognitive microdevelopment. *Human Development*, 45, 141–160.

Yang, C., Crain, S., Berwick, R. C., Chomsky, N., & Bolhuis, J. J. (2017). The growth of language: Universal grammar, experience, and principles of computation. *Neuroscience and Biobehavioral Reviews*. Retrieved March 8, 2017, from http://www.sciencedirect.com/science/article/pii/S0149763416305656.

Yang, C. D. (2006). *The infinite gift: How children learn and unlearn the languages of the world*. New York: Scribner.

Yang, D., Bushnell, E. W., Buchanan, D. W., & Sobel, D. M. (2013). Infants' use of contextual cues in the generalization of effective actions from imitation. *Journal of Experimental Child Psychology*, 116, 510–531.

Yang, R., & Blodgett, B. (2000). Effects of race and adolescent decision-making on status attainment and self-esteem. *Journal of Ethnic & Cultural Diversity in Social Work*, 9, 135–153.

Yancura, L. A. (2013). Service use and unmet service needs in grandparents raising grandchildren. *Journal of Gerontological Social Work*, 56(6), 473–486.

Yardley, J. (2001, July 2). Child-death case in Texas raises penalty questions. *The New York Times*, p. A1.

Yarrow, L. (1992, November). Giving birth: 72,000 moms tell all. *Parents*, pp. 148–159.

Yasnitsky, A., & van der Veer, R. (2016). *Revisionist revolution in Vygotsky studies*. New York: Routledge/Taylor & Francis Group.

Yato, Y., Kawai, M., Negayama, K., Sogon, S., Tomiwa, K., & Yamamoto, H. (2008). Infant responses to maternal still-face at 4 and 9 months. *Infant Behavior & Development*, 31, 570–577.

Ybarra M. L., Mitchell K. J. (2014). "Sexting" and its relation to sexual activity and sexual risk behavior in a national survey of adolescents. *Journal of Adolescent Health*. 55(6), 757–764.

Yecke, C. P. (2005). *Mayhem in the middle*. Washington, DC: Thomas B. Fordham Institute.

Yee, M., & Brown, R. (1994). The development of gender differentiation in young children. *British Journal of Social Psychology*, 33, 183–196.

Yim, I., Glynn, L., Schetter, C., Hobel, C., Chicz-DeMet, A., & Sandman, C. (2009). Risk of postpartum depressive symptoms with elevated corticotropin-releasing hormone in human pregnancy. *Archives of General Psychiatry*, 66, 162–169.

Yinger, J. (Ed.). (2004). *Helping children left behind: State aid and the pursuit of educational equity*. Cambridge, MA: MIT Press.

Yoon, E., Adams, K., Clawson, A., Chang, H., Surya, S., & Jérémie-Brink, G. (2017). East Asian adolescents' ethnic identity development and cultural integration: A qualitative investigation. *Journal of Counseling Psychology*, 64, 65–79.

Yott, J., & Poulin-Dubois, D. (2016). Are infants' theory-of-mind abilities well integrated? Implicit understanding of intentions, desires, and beliefs. *Journal of Cognition and Development*, 17, 683–698.

Young, H., & Ferguson, L. (1979). Developmental changes through adolescence in the spontaneous nomination of reference groups as a function of decision context. *Journal of Youth and Adolescence*, 8, 239–252.

Young, S., Rhee, S., Stallings, M., Corley, R., & Hewitt, J. (2006, July). Genetic and environmental vulnerabilities underlying adolescent substance use and problem use: General or specific? *Behavior Genetics*, 36, 603–615.

Yu, C., Hung, C., Chan, T., Yeh, C., & Lai, C. (2012). Prenatal predictors for father-infant attachment after childbirth. *Journal of Clinical Nursing*, 21, 1577–1583.

Yuan, A. (2012). Perceived breast development and adolescent girls' psychological well-being. *Sex Roles*, 66, 790–806.

Yuill, N., & Perner, J. (1988). Intentionality and knowledge in children's judgments of actor's responsibility and recipient's emotional reaction. *Developmental Psychology*, 24, 358–365.

Zafeiriou, D. I. (2004). Primitive reflexes and postural reactions in the neurodevelopmental examination. *Pediatric Neurology, 31*, 1–8.

Zahn-Waxler, C., & Radke-Yarrow, M. (1990). The origins of empathic concern. *Motivation and Emotion, 14*, 107–130.

Zahn-Waxler, C., Shirtcliff, E., & Marceau, K. (2008). Disorders of childhood and adolescence: Gender and psychopathology. *Annual Review of Clinical Psychology, 4*, 275–303.

Zakrzewski, A. C., Johnson, J. M., & Smith, J. D. (2017). The comparative psychology of metacognition. In J. Call, G. M. Burghardt, I. M. Pepperberg, et al. (Eds.), *APA handbook of comparative psychology: Perception, learning, and cognition.* Washington, DC: American Psychological Association.

Zalsman, G., Levy, T., Shoval, G. (2008). Interaction of child and family psychopathology leading to suicidal behavior. *Psychiatric Clinics of North America, 31*, 237–246.

Zalsman, G., Oquendo, M., Greenhill, L., et al. (2006, October). Neurobiology of depression in children and adolescents. *Child and Adolescent Psychiatric Clinics of North America, 15*, 843–868.

Zampi, C., Fagioli, I., & Salzarulo, P. (2002). Time course of EEG background activity level before spontaneous awakening in infants. *Journal of Sleep Research, 11*, 283–287.

Zanardo, V., Nicolussi, S., Giacomin, C., Faggian, D., Favaro, F., & Plebani, M. (2001). Labor pain effects on colostral milk beta-endorphin concentrations of lactating mothers. *Biology of the Neonate, 79*(2), 87–90.

Zaporozhets, A. V. (1965). The development of perception in the preschool child. *Monographs of the Society for Research in Child Development, 30*, 82–101.

Zarbatany, L., Hartmann, D. P., & Rankin, D. B. (1990). The psychological functions of preadolescent peer activities. *Child Development, 61*, 1067–1080.

Zauszniewski, J. A., & Martin, M. H. (1999). Developmental task achievement and learned resourcefulness in healthy older adults. *Archives of Psychiatric Nursing, 13*, 41–47.

Zeanah, C. (2009). The importance of early experiences: Clinical, research and policy perspectives. *Journal of Loss and Trauma, 14*, 266–279.

Zebrowitz, L., Luevano, V., Bronstad, P., & Aharon, I. (2009). Neural activation to babyfaced men matches activation to babies. *Social Neuroscience, 4*, 1–10.

Zeedyk, M., & Heimann, M. (2006). Imitation and socio-emotional processes: Implications for communicative development and interventions. *Infant and Child Development, 15*, 219–222.

Zelazo, N., Zelazo, P. R., Cohen, K., & Zelazo, P. D. (1993). Specificity of practice effects on elementary neuromotor patterns. *Developmental Psychology, 29*, 686–691.

Zelazo, P. D., Muller, U., Frye, D., & Marcovitch, S. (2003). The development of executive function in early childhood. *Monographs of the Society for Research in Child Development, 68*, 103–122.

Zelazo, P. R. (1998). McGraw and the development of unaided walking. *Developmental Review, 18*, 449–471.

Zemach, I., Chang, S., & Teller, D. (2007). Infant color vision: Prediction of infants' spontaneous color preferences. *Vision Research, 47*, 1368–1381.

Zeng, Z. (2011). The myth of the glass ceiling: Evidence from a stock-flow analysis of authority attainment. *Social Science Research, 40*, 312–325.

Zhai, F., Raver, C., & Jones, S. M. (2012). Academic performance of subsequent schools and impacts of early interventions: Evidence from a randomized controlled trial in Head Start settings. *Children and Youth Services Review, 34*, 946–954.

Zhang, N., Baker, H. W., Tufts, M., Raymond, R. E., Salihu, H., & Elliott, M. R. (2013). Early childhood lead exposure and academic achievement: Evidence from Detroit public schools, 2008–2010. *American Journal of Public Health, 103*, e72–e77.

Zhe, C., & Siegler, R. S. (2000). Across the great divide: Bridging the gap between understanding of toddlers' and older children's thinking. *Monographs of the Society for Research in Child Development, 65*, (2, Serial No. 261).

Zhu, J., & Weiss, L. (2005). The Wechsler Scales. In D. P. Flanagan & P. L. Harrison (Eds.), *Contemporary intellectual assessment: Theories, tests, and issues.* New York: Guilford Press.

Zigler, E., & Styfco, S. J. (2004). Moving Head Start to the states: One experiment too many. *Applied Developmental Science, 8*, 51–55.

Zigler, E. F., & Finn-Stevenson, M. (1995). The child care crisis: Implications for the growth and development of the nation's children. *Journal of Social Issues, 51*, 215–231.

Ziegler, M., Danay, E., Heene, M., Asendorpf, J., & Bühner, M. (2012). Openness, fluid intelligence, and crystallized intelligence: Toward an integrative model. *Journal of Research in Personality, 46*(2), 173–183.

Zimmerman, F., & Christakis, D. (2007). Associations between content types of early media exposure and subsequent attentional problems. *Pediatrics, 120*, 986–992.

Zisenwine, T., Kaplan, M., Kushnir, J., & Sadeh, A. (2013). Nighttime fears and fantasy–reality differentiation in preschool children. *Child Psychiatry and Human Development, 44*(1), 186–199.

Zito, J. (2002). Five burning questions. *Journal of Developmental & Behavioral Pediatrics, 23*, S23–S30.

Zito, J. M., Safer, D. J., dosReis, S., Gardner, J. F., Boles, M., & Lynch, F. (2000). Trends in prescribing of psychotropic medications to preschoolers. *Journal of the American Medical Association, 283*, 1025–1030.

Zmiri, P., Rubin, L., Akons, H., Zion, N., & Shaoul, R. (2011). The effect of day care attendance on infant and toddlers' growth. *Acta Paediatrica, 100*, 266–270.

Zosh, J. M., Halberda, J., & Feigenson, L. (2011). Memory for multiple visual ensembles in infancy. *Journal of Experimental Psychology: General, 140*.

Zosuls, K. M., Field, R. D., Martin, C. L., Andrews, N. Z., & England, D. E. (2014). Gender-based relationship efficacy: Children's self-perceptions in intergroup contexts. *Child Development, 85*, 1663–1676.

Zuccarini, M., Sansavini, A., Iverson, J. M., et al. (2016). Object engagement and manipulation in extremely preterm and full term infants at 6 months of age. *Research in Developmental Disabilities, 55*, 173–184.

Zucker, J. & Alexander-Tanner, R. (2017, March 14). Grieving a miscarriage. *New York Times*, p. D4.

Zuckerman, G., & Shenfield, S. (2007, May). Child-adult interaction that creates a zone of proximal development. *Journal of Russian & East European Psychology, 45*(3), 43–69.

Zwelling, E. (2006). A challenging time in the history of Lamaze international: An interview with Francine Nichols. *Journal of Perinatal Education, 15*(4), 10–17.

Zyphur, M. J., Zhang, Z., Barsky, A. P., & Li, W. (2013). An ACE in the hole: Twin family models for applied behavioral genetics research. *The Leadership Quarterly, 24*, 572–594.

# Credits

## Photo Credits

**Front Matter**  p. xv: Robert S. Feldman.

**Chapter 1**  p. 1: Rehan Qureshi/Shutterstock; p. 2: adrian arbib/Alamy Stock Photo; p. 2: Julia Malakie/AP Photo; p. 5: Dinodia Photos/Alamy Stock Photo; p. 7: iofoto/Fotolia; p. 7: BCFC/Shutterstock; p. 7: OJO Images Ltd/Alamy Stock Photo; p. 7: Brian Summers/Getty Images; p. 8: Everett Collection Inc/Alamy Stock Photo; p. 9: Scala/Art Resource: NY.

**Chapter 2**  p. 18: wavebreakmediamicro/123rf.com; p. 19: Marlon Lopez MMG1 Design/Shutterstock; p. 21: Library of Congress Prints and Photographs Division; p. 21: Jon Erikson/Science Source; p. 24: Hulton Archive/Getty Images; p. 24: Associated Press; p. 28: Evan Vucci/Associated Press; p. 28: Du Cane Medical Imaging Ltd/Science Source; p. 31: Jules Selmes/Pearson Education Ltd; p. 32: Nina Leen/The LIFE Picture Collection/Getty Images; p. 36: Picture Partners/Alamy Stock Photo; p. 38: Tudor Photography/ Pearson Education Ltd; p. 39: Simon Fraser/Science Source; p. 43: JackF/Getty Images; p. 43: Billy Hustace/The Image Bank/Getty Images; p. 43: Ariel Skelley/Blend Images/Alamy Stock Photo; p. 47: Dmitriy Shironosov/123RF.

**Chapter 3**  p. 52: David M. Phillips/Science Source; p. 53: Dmitry Kalinovsky/Shutterstock; p. 55: photobank. ch. Shutterstock; p. 56: Alfred Pasieka/Science Source; p. 57: Pictorial Press Ltd/Alamy Stock Photo; p. 63: Saturn Stills/Science Source; p. 68: Loisjoy Thurstun/Alamy Stock Photo.

**Chapter 4**  p. 87: Steve Hix/Somos Images/Corbis/Glow Images; p. 88: shutterstock.India Picture; p. 89: William J. Mahnken/Shutterstock; p. 89: Ross Marks Photography/Alamy Stock Photo; p. 96: Chuck Nacke/Alamy Stock Photo; p. 101: Brocreative/Shutterstock; p. 103: Igor Stepovik/Shutterstock; p. 106: Dr. Tiffany Field; p. 110: Creativa Images/Shutterstock; p. 110: VGstockstudio/Shutterstock; p. 111: Andy Dean Photography/Shutterstock; p. 111: Lisa F. Young/Shutterstock; p. 111: Lisa Payne Photography/Pearson Education Ltd; p. 111: Asia Images Group/Getty Images.

**Chapter 5**  p. 112: shutterstock/Wallenrock; p. 113: Christin Lola/Shutterstock; p. 116: Jon Wilson/Science Source; p. 117: Living Art Enterprises/LLC/Science Source; p. 118: Qingqing/Shutterstock; p. 118: Intellistudies/Fotolia; p. 119: Judith Haeusler/Cultura/Getty Images; p. 121: Milla Kontkanen/Alamy Stock Photo; p. 123: Elizabeth Crews/The Image Works; p. 123: Picture Partners/Alamy Stock Photo; p. 123: Michaela Begsteiger/Getty Images; p. 129: Ingrid Balabanova/Shutter; p. 132: Mark Richard/PhotoEdit; p. 132: Karan Kapoor/The Image Bank/Getty Images; p. 132: Karan Kapoor/The Image Bank/Getty Images; p. 132: Karan Kapoor/The Image Bank/Getty Images; p. 133: From: Science: Vol. 296 (17 May 2002): p.1321–1322: "Is Face Processing Species-Specific During the First Year of Life?" by Olivier Pascalis: Michelle de Haan: Charles A. Nelson. Reprinted with permission from AAAS.; p. 135: Focus Pocus LTD/Fotolia; p. 135: mims/Shutterstock.

**Chapter 6**  p. 141: Russell Kord/Alamy Stock Photo; p. 142: kroomjai. Shutterstock; p. 143: Patrick Grehan/Getty Images; p. 146: Ami Parikh. Shutterstock; p. 148: Sandro Di Carlo Darsa/Alamy; p. 152: OpenRangeStock/Shutterstock; p. 154: Vasiliy Koval/Shutterstock; p. 155: Jupiterimages/Creatas/Thinkstock/Getty Images; p. 159: leolintang/Shutterstock; p. 160: Krantz: S.G. (1999). Conformal mappings. American Scientist: 87: 147.; p. 161: Ami Parikh/Shutterstock; p. 164: Karel Lorier/Alamy Stock Photo; p. 166: Lisa Payne Photography/Pearson Education Ltd.

**Chapter 7**  p. 170: szeyuen/Fotolia; p. 171: Dayna More/Shutterstock; p. 174: Andy Dean Photography. Shutterstock; p. 175: Barbara Stitzer/PhotoEdit; p. 178: 123rf.com; p. 179: Photo Researchers: Inc.; p. 180: Dr. Robert Marvin; p. 181: William Hamilton/Johns Hopkins University/Robert Marvin; p. 181: William Hamilton/Johns Hopkins University/Robert Marvin; p. 181: William Hamilton/Johns Hopkins University/Robert Marvin; p. 184: michaeljung. Shutterstock; p. 185: paylessimages/Fotolia; p. 189: Fernando Cortes/Shutterstock; p. 191: Pavel L Photo and Video/Shutterstock; p. 193: lostinbids/Getty Images; p. 199: Serhiy Kobyakov/Shutterstock; 200: Andy Dean Photography/Shutterstock; p. 200: Lisa F. Young/Shutterstock; p. 200: Lisa Payne Photography/Pearson Education Ltd; p. 200: Asia Images Group/Getty Images.

**Chapter 8**  p. 201: shutterstock/NIKS ADS; p. 202: saisnaps/Shutterstock; p. 205: ZEPHYR/Getty Images; p. 211: Jules Selmes. Pearson Education Ltd; p. 219: Gladskikh Tatiana/Shutterstock; p. 219: Jay Reilly/Getty Images; p. 220: Ilya Andriyanov/Shutterstock; p. 222: vvoe/Shutterstock; p. 222: Ferenc Szelepcsenyi/Shutterstock.

**Chapter 9**  p. 226: Monkey Business Images/Fotolia; p. 227: Monkey Business Images/Shutterstock; p. 230: Lew Merrim/Science Source; p. 235: Mike Derer/AP Photo; p. 238: SPUTNIK/Alamy Stock Photo; p. 249: julaszka/Fotolia.

**Chapter 10** p. 255: Nancy Sheehan/PhotoEdit; p. 258: espies. Shutterstock; p. 262: Tony Freeman/PhotoEdit; p. 264: Hurst Photo/Shutterstock; p. 264: Ami Parikh/Shutterstock; p. 272: Michelle D. Bridwell/PhotoEdit; p. 277: Courtesy of Albert Bandura; p. 279: Purestock/Alamy Stock Photo; p. 284: Andrey Kiselev/123RF; p. 285: Andy Dean Photography/Shutterstock; p. 285: Jim Esposito Photography L.L.C./Photodisc/Getty Images; p. 285: Lisa Payne Photography/Pearson Education Ltd; p. 285: Asia Images Group/Getty Images.

**Chapter 11** p. 286: shutterstock/Snehal Jeevan Pailkar; p. 287: Shutterstock/Rudra Narayan Mitra; p. 289: Pawel Bienkowski/Alamy Stock Photo; p. 292: India Picture/Shutterstock; p. 294: Lisa Payne Photography. Pearson Education Ltd; p. 295: Asia Images Group. Shutterstock; p. 296: Fotokostic/Shutterstock; p. 298: Looker_Studio/Shutterstock; p. 303: E.D. Torial/Alamy Stock Photo.

**Chapter 12** p. 307: Shutterstock/India Picture; p. 308: michaeljung. Shutterstock; p. 315: Golden Pixels LLC/Shutterstock; p. 318: David Grossman/Alamy Stock Photo; p. 326: Albert Harlingue/Roger-Viollet/The Image Works; p. 334: moodboard/Vetta/Getty Images.

**Chapter 13** p. 339: Jules Selmes/Pearson Education Ltd; p. 340: AJP/Shutterstock; p. 341: Arvind Balaraman/Shutterstock; p. 342: Sergey Novikov/Shutterstock; p. 346: knape/Getty Images; p. 347: Eduardo Jose Bernardino/Getty images; p. 349: saurabhpbhoyar/Shutterstock; p. 351: Digital Vision/Photodisc/Thinkstock/Getty Images; p. 356: Ami Parikh/Shutterstock; p. 363: Rubberball/Mike Kemp/Getty Images; p. 364: Andy Dean Photography/Shutterstock; p. 364: Lisa F. Young/Shutterstock; p. 364: Lisa Payne Photography/Pearson Education Ltd; p. 364: Asia Images Group/Getty Images.

**Chapter 14** p. 365: Monkey Business Images/Shutterstock; p. 366: wavebreakmedia/Shutterstock; p. 370: Mark Edward Atkinson/Alamy Stock Photo; p. 372: Gordana Sermek/Shutterstock;

**Chapter 15** p. 390: wavebreakmedia/Shutterstock; p. 393: Kevin Radford/Superstock; p. 399: Jim West/Alamy Stock Photo; p. 400: Paul Hawthorne/Getty Images; p. 409: Omer N Raja/Shutterstock.

**Chapter 16** p. 414: Tony Freeman/PhotoEdit; p. 422: zea_lenanet/Fotolia; p. 424: alexsokolov/Fotolia; p. 427: Digital Vision/Photodisc/Thinkstock/Getty Images; p. 431: Mandy Godbehear/Shutterstock; p. 444: vnlit/Getty Images; p. 445: Andy Dean Photography/Shutterstock; p. 445: Mel Yates/Cultura/Getty Images; p. 445: Lisa Payne Photography/Pearson Education Ltd; p. 445: Asia Images Group/Getty Images.

## Text Credits

**Chapter 2** EXCERPTS p. 24 (left): Watson, J. B. (1925). Behaviorism. New York: Norton. Copyright © 1925 (p. 14);

031: Source: Morton Hunt (1993). The Story of Psychology, New York: Anchor Books; **FIGURES** p. 29: Source: Adapted from Bronfenbrenner & Morris, "The Ecology of Developmental Processes," in W. Damon, ed., Handbook of Child Psychology, Vol I, TTL, 5th ed. Copyright © 1998 John Wiley & Sons, Inc.; p. 41: Based on Leyens, J.-P., et al. (1975). Effects of movie violence on aggression in a field setting as a function of group dominance and cohesion. Journal of Personality and Social Psychology, 32(2), 346–360.

**Chapter 3** p. 59: Adapted from Kimball, John W. (1983). Biology, 5th ed. Reprinted and Electronically reproduced by permission Education, Inc., Upper Saddle River, New Jersey; p. 60: Source: From Macmillan Publishers Ltd.: "International Human Genome Sequencing Consortium, Initial Sequencing and Analysis of the Human Genome," Nature. Copyright © 2001; p. 60: Source: Based on McGuffin, Riley, & Plomin, 2001; Schizophrenia Working Group of the Psychiatric Genomics Consortium, 2014; U.S. National Library of Medicine, 2016; p. 63: Source: Human Genome Project, 2006, http://www.oml.gov/scl/techresources/Human_Genome/medicine/genetest.shtml; p. 70: Source: Adapted from Tellegen, Auke; Lykken, David T.; Bouchard, Thomas J.; Wilcox, Kimerly J.; Segal, Nancy L.; and Rich, Stephen, "Personality similarity in twins reared apart and together," Journal of Personality and Social Psychology, Vol 54, No. 6, 1031–1039 (Jun 1988); p. 71: Source: Gottesman, Irving I. (1991). Schizophrenia Genesis: The Origins of Madness. New York: Henry Holt and Company; p.76: Source: Reproductive Medicine Associates of New Jersey (2002) Older women and risks of pregnancy. Princeton, NJ: American Society for Reproductive Medicine; p. 79: Source: Moore, K.L. (1974). Before we are born: Basic embryology and birth defects. Philadelphia: Saunders.

**Chapter 4** FIGURES p. 91: Source: "A Proposal for a New Method of Evaluation in the Newborn Infant," V. Apgar, Current Research in Anesthesia and Analgesia, 32, 1953, p. 260; p. 98: Source: Adapted from "Committee to Study the Prevention of Low Birthweight," Preventing Low Birthweight, 1985, National Academy Press from Preventing Low Birthweight by the National Academy Press; p. 107: Source: C.O. Eckerman, J.M. Oehler, "Very Low Birthweight Newborns and Parents as Early Social Partners," in S.L. Friedman & M.B. Sigman eds., The Psychological Development of Low-Birthweight Children, NL: Ablex, 1992.

**Chapter 5** FIGURES p. 114: Source: Cratty, Bryant J. (1979), Perceptual and Motor Development in Infants and Children. Second Edition. New Jersey: Prentice Hall; p. 116 Source: Colonel, J. LeRoy. 1939. The Postnatal Development of The Human Cerebral Cortex, Vols. I-VIII. Cambridge, MA: Harvard University Press; p. 120: Source: Based on Roffwarg, Howard P., Muzio, Joseph N., and Dement, William C. "Ontogenetic development of the human sleep-dream cycle," Science, vol. 152, no. 3722, pp. 604–619. (1966); p. 125: Source: Data from Frankenburg, W. K., Dodds, J., Archer, P., Shapiro, H., & Bresnick, B. (1992). The Denver II: A major revision and restandardization of the Denver Developmental Screening Test. Pediatrics, Vol. 89, 91–97; p. 130, Source: UNICEF, WHO, World Bank Joint Child Malnutrition dataset, September 2016 update; p. 131: Source: William James (1918) "The principles of psychology" New York: H. Holt; p. 133: Source: Based on Robert L. Fantz, "Pattern Vision in Newborn Infants," Science, New Series, vol. 140, no. 3564, pp. 296–297 (1961); 144, 06, Source: Jean Piaget (1952), "The Origins of Intelligence in Children" Trans. By Margaret Cook, New York: International Universities Press.

**Chapter 6  EXCERPTS** p. 147: Source: Piaget, J. (1954). The construction of reality in the child (Margaret Cook, Trans.). New York: Basic Books. (p. 296); p. 154: Source: Annie Sneed, "Why Can't You Remember Being a Baby?" Scientific American. July 15, 2014; p. 165: Source: B.G. Blount, "Culture and the Language of Socialization: Parental Speech" in D.A. Wagner & W. W. Stevenson eds., Cultural Perspectives on Child Development. San Francisco: Freeman and Co. **FIGURES** p. 156: Source: Based on Bayley, N. 7 1993. Bayley scales of infant development [BSID-II] 2nd ed., San Antonio, IX: The Psychological Corporation; p. 159: Source: Adapted from Bornstein & Lamb. (1992). Development in Infancy: An Introduction, McGraw-Hill; p. 180: Source: From E. Waters, "The Reliability and Stability of Individual Differences in Infant-Mother Attachment," Child Development, vol. 49, 1978. The Society for Research in Child Development, Inc. pp. 480–494; p. 186: Source: Adapted from Bell, S. M., & Ainsworth, M. D. S. (1972). Infant crying and maternal responsiveness. Child Development, 43, 1171–1190; Tomlinson-Keasey, C. (1985). Child development: Psychological, sociological, and biological factors. Homewood, IL: Dorsey.

**Chapter 7  FIGURES** p. 189, TBL07-02, 07, Source: A. Thomas, S. Chess, & H.G. Birch, "Temperament and Behavior Disorders in Children," New York University Press, 1968.

**Chapter 8  EXCERPTS** p. 222: Source: Winner, E. (1989). Development in the visual arts. In W. Damon (Ed.), Child development today and tomorrow. San Francisco: Jossey-Bass. **FIGURES** p. 205: Source: Fischer & Rose, "Concurrent Cycles in Dynamic Development of Brain and Behavior," Newsletter of the Society of Research in Child Development (1995); p. 207: Source: Elkind, D. (1978). "The children's reality: Three developmental themes." In S. Coren & L. M. Ward (Eds.), Sensation and perception. Hoboken, NJ: Wiley. Used with permission; p. 212: Source: Needleman, H.L., et. al. (1996, February 7). "Bone lead levels and delinquent behavior." JAMA: The Journal of the American Medical Association, vol. 2755, pp. 363–369; p. 213: Child Welfare Information Gateway.

(2016). Child abuse and neglect fatalities 2014: Statistics and interventions. Washington, DC: U.S. Department of Health and Human Services, Children's Bureau. p. 214: Source: Child Welfare Information Gateway, 2013; p. 215: Source: Scientific American, March 2002, p. 71. Used with permission of Carol Donner; p. 217: SOURCE: Centers for Disease Control and Prevention. (2017). Recommended immunization schedule for children and adolescents aged 18 years or Younger, United States, 2017. Washington, DC: Centers for Disease Control; p. 218: Source: C. Corbin, 1973, A Textbook of Motor Development, Dubuque, IA: Wm. C. Brown Publishers.

**Chapter 9  EXCERPTS** p. 235: Source: Ceci, S. J., & Bruck, M. (1993). "The suggestibility of the child witness: A historical review and synthesis." Psychological Bulletin, vol. 113, 403–439. p. A23; p. 244: Source: Based on Matt McCue, "Searching for a New Neighbor on 'Sesame Street'," The Wall Street Journal. Aug 21, 2012. **FIGURES** p. 236: Source: Poole, D. A., & Lamb, M. E. (1998). Investigative interviews of children: A guide for helping professionals. Washington, DC: American Psychological Association; p. 241: Source: Adapted Berko, J. (1958). The child's learning of English morphology. Word, vol. 14, 150–177; p. 249: Source: Gutnick, A. L., et al. (2010). Always connected: The new digital media habits of young children. New York: The Joan Ganz Cooney Center at Sesame Workshop. P. 15.

**Chapter 10  FIGURES** p. 266: Source: Adapted from Farver, J. M., Kim, Y. K., & Lee-Shin, Y. (1995). "Cultural differences in Korean- and Anglo-American preschoolers' social interaction and play behaviors." Child Development, vol. 66, pp. 1088–1099; p. 269: Source: Based on Baumrind, D. (1971). "Current patterns of parental authority." Developmental Psychology Monographs, vol. 4, no. 1, pt. 2.; Maccoby, E. E., & Martin, J. A. (1983). "Socialization in the context of the family: Parent–child interaction." In P. H. Mussen (Ed.) & E. M. Hetherington (Vol. Ed.), Handbook of child psychology: Vol. 4. Socialization, personality, and social development (4th ed.). New York: Wiley.

**Chapter 11** p. 295: Source: Adapted from Cratty, Bryant J. (1979). Perceptual and Motor Development in Infants and Children. Second Edition. New Jersey: Prentice Hall.

**Chapter 12  EXCERPTS** p. 334: Source: Schemo, D. J. (2004, March 2). Schools, facing tight budgets, leave gifted programs behind. The New York Times, pp. A1, A18; p. 334: Source: Sec. 582, P.L. 97–35. p. 318: Source: UNESCO Institute for Statistics, September 2015; p. 320: Source: Based on Chall, J. S. (1979). "The great debate: Ten years later, with a modest proposal for reading stages." In L. B. Resnick & P. A. Weaver (Eds.), Theory and practice of early reading. Hillsdale, NJ: Erlbaum; p. 323: Source: Mead, M. (1942). Environment and education, a symposium held in connection with the fiftieth anniversary celebration of the University of Chicago. Chicago: University of Chicago.

p. 633; p. 332: Source: Based on Walters, E., & Gardner, H. (1986). "The theory of multiple intelligences: Some issues and answers." In R. J. Sternberg & R. K. Wagner (Eds.), Practical intelligence. New York: Cambridge University Press.

**Chapter 13   EXCERPTS** p. 349: Source: Adapted from Zarbatany, L., Hartmann, D. P., & Rankin, D. B. (1990). The psychological functions of preadolescent peer activities. Child Development, vol. 61, pp. 1067–1080. **FIGURES** p. 343: Source: Adapted from Shavelson, R., Hubner, J. J., & Stanton, J. C. (1976). "Self-concept: Validation of construct interpretations." Review of Educational Research, vol. 46, 407–441; p. 351: Source: Adapted from Dodge, K. A. (1985). "A social information processing model of social competence in children." In M. Perlmutter (Ed.), Minnesota Symposia on Child Psychology, vol. 18, 77–126.

**Chapter 14   EXCERPTS** p. 376: Source: Beckman, M. (2004, July 30). Neuroscience: Crime, culpability, and the adolescent brain. Science, 305, 596–599. p. 597. **FIGURES** p. 368: Source: Adapted from Cratty, B. (1986). Perceptual and motor development in infants and children (3rd ed.). Englewood Cliffs, NJ: Prentice-Hall; p. 368: Source: Adapted from Eveleth, P., & Tanner, J. (1976). Worldwide variation in human growth. New York: Cambridge University Press; p. 369: Source: Adapted from Tanner J. M. (1978). Education and Physical Growth (2nd ed.), New York: International Universities Press; p. 373, Fig14-04, 14, Source: Kimm, S. Y., et al. (2002). "Decline in physical activity in black girls and white girls during adolescence." New England Journal of Medicine, vol. 347, pp. 709–715; p. 379: Source: Benson, H. (1993). "The relaxation response." In D. Goleman & J. Guerin (Eds.), Mind–body medicine: How to use your mind for better health. Yonkers, NY: Consumer Reports Publications; p. 383: Source: Adapted from Franck, I., & Brownstone, D. (1991). The parent's desk reference. New York: Prentice-Hall., pp. 593–594.

**Chapter 15   FIGURES** p. 398: Source: Based on Kohlberg, L. (1969). "Stage and sequence: The cognitive-developmental approach to socialization." In D. Goslin (Ed.), Handbook of socialization theory and research. Chicago: Rand McNally; p. 400: Source: Based on Kohlberg, L. (1969). "Stage and sequence: The cognitive-developmental approach to socialization." In D. Goslin (Ed.), Handbook of socialization theory and research. Chicago: Rand McNally; p. 405: Source: From Astin, A. W., Korn, W. S., & Berz, E. R. (2004). The American freshman: National norms for fall 2004. Los Angeles, CA: Higher Education Research Institute, Graduate School of Education, UCLA © 2008 The Regents of the University of California. All Rights Reserved; p. 407: Source: Department for Education and Skills, England 2004.

**Chapter 16** p. 437: Source: Gregory, S. (1856). Facts for young women. Boston. **FIGURES** p. 418: Source: Based on Erikson, E. H. (1963). Childhood and society. New York: Norton; p. 419: Source: Marcia, J. E. (1980). "Identity in adolescence." In J. Adelson (Ed.), Handbook of adolescent psychology. New York: Wiley; p. 427: Source: Fuligni, A. J., Tseng, V., & Lam, M. (1999). "Attitudes toward family obligations among American adolescents with Asian, Latin American, and European backgrounds." Child Development, vol. 70, pp. 1030–1044.

# Name Index

*Note:* Page numbers in *italics* indicate tables and illustrations.

# Subject Index